DATE DUE

			PRINTED IN U.S.A.

THE ENCYCLOPEDIA OF
Hollywood

THE ENCYCLOPEDIA OF
Hollywood

Scott Siegel and Barbara Siegel

Facts On File
New York • Oxford • Sydney

The Encyclopedia of Hollywood

Facts On File, Inc.
460 Park Avenue South
New York, New York 10016

Facts On File Limited
Collins Street
Oxford OX4 1XJ
United Kingdom

Facts On File Pty Ltd
Talavera & Khartoum Rds
North Ryde NSW 2113
Australia

Library of Congress Cataloging-in-Publication Data

Siegel, Scott.
    The encyclopedia of Hollywood / Scott Siegel and Barbara Siegel.
        p.   cm.
    Bibliography: p.
    Includes index.
    ISBN 0-8160-1792-1
    1. Motion picture industry—United States—Dictionaries.
    I. Siegel, Barbara.   II. Title.
PN1993.5.U6S494   1990
384'.8'0979494—dc20   89-11799

British and Australian CIP data available on request from Facts On File.

Facts On File books are available at special discounts when purchased in bulk quantities for businesses, associations, institutions, or sales promotion. Please contact the Special Sales Department at 212/683-2244.
(Dial 800-322-8755, except in NY, AK, HI)

Composition and Manufacturing by Maple-Vail Book Manufacturing Group

10 9 8 7 6 5 4 3 2 1

This book is printed on acid-free paper.

Contents

Acknowledgments

Just as filmmaking is a collaborative process, so is writing a book. Of all those whom we hasten to thank, however, first and foremost is Kate Kelly, whose editorial stewardship, enthusiasm, and unflagging support proved her to be a writer's ideal. In addition, Neal Maillet's efficient and thoughtful efforts made a long and complicated process both pleasant and worry-free; it was a pleasure to work with him. And we certainly must thank Michael Laraque for his heroic job of copyediting this substantial volume.

Special thanks go to Albert J. LaValley, an inspirational professor (and friend) who instilled in Scott an interest in a writing career and respect for movies as an art form. In that same vein, heartfelt thanks are also offered to two hugely influential people: Roger Greenspun and Leslie Clark.

We wish we had the space to detail the reasons why we're thanking the friends listed below, but suffice it to say that they were our movie partners, the people who shared that special time with us between the coming attractions and the final credits: Gary Bordzuk, Steve Bornstein, Doug Byrne, Heda and Steve *(Chan Is Missing)* Chazen, Rowena Coplan, Mimi, Karen and Laurie Dubin, Gene Grady, Lena Halpert, Claire *(Hester Street)* Katz, Steve Kleinman, Rhoda Koenig, Allen *(Burden of Dreams)* Kupfer, Cliff *(Attack of the Star Creatures)* Lacy, Maura Lerner, David Leverenz, David *(The Road Warrior)* Luhn, Matt *(Star Trek—The Motion Picture)* Meis, Eric and Claudia Mink, Marna *(The Way We Were)* Mintzer, Jeff *(The Thin Man)* Pollack, Jerry and Pat Preising, Nancy Prestia, Stewart *(Duck Soup)* Scharfman, Carmine *(The Godfather)* Sessa, Howie *(High Sierra)* Singer, and Terri Wall.

Mimi Dubin's generous help in the area of costuming will be treasured as the very fiber of true friendship; we tip an antique hat to her.

This book was greatly enhanced by the participation of scores of celebrated actors, screenwriters, directors, producers, and composers; their cooperation is gratefully acknowledged.

Finally, we owe a debt of gratitude to Shirley and Samuel Siegel, Clare and Samson Teich, Lillian and Jack Goldberg, and Stephanie Tranen who took us to the movies when we were too young to take ourselves. They were the first to introduce us to the images of light and shadow that would so strongly shape our lives.

Introduction

Hollywood. The name conjures up images of dancing pianos, shootouts at high noon, alien spaceships, and just about any romantic, fantastic, or emotionally wrenching sequence that could possibly be committed to film. The Japanese might make better VCRs, the Germans might make better beer, and the French might make better lovers, but nobody makes better movies than Hollywood, U.S.A. This book is both a celebration of that excellence and a unique history of the American film industry in encylopedic form.

In the pages that follow you will find tens of thousands of facts, figures, and fabulous stories, organized in such fashion that you can easily find what you might like to know, such as the derivation of the term "gaffer," how Ava Gardner was discovered, and the genesis of the monster movie. Be forewarned, this is not a book of lists that endeavors to include every actor, director, etc. who ever appeared on film. Instead, we atempted to strike a balance between the desire to create an abundance of short entries and the more practical and helpful impulse to write fewer entries in greater depth.

There were other decisions that had to be made. For instance, while many film books center around personalities, we chose to widen our focus to also include an examination of film genres, important events, the studios, explanations of jargon and job titles, plus an historical perspective on selected films. And given that the movies are essentially a visual medium, we thought it would be downright criminal if we didn't also pepper the manuscript with a diverse selection of photos (of which you will find more than 150).

The actors, directors, producers, screenwriters, editors, cinematographers, composers, choreographers, studio histories, events, films, genres, job descriptions, term definitions, etc. that you will find in this book were chosen because they seemed to best form a representative collage of the American film industry from Thomas Edison to the present. Most, if not all, of Hollywood's movers and shakers have been included within these pages. If there is a bias in this book, however, it can be found in the predisposition to include a tad more of the old-timers than the new kids on the block. Our reasoning, quite simply, is that hot stars, directors, etc. can come and go rather quickly. Someone who appears to be the next Cary Grant may fall into obscurity two years hence. Time is the ultimate test of the art of the film.

A word of advice. If you look up a person or a film and discover there is no corresponding entry, check the index. A great deal of information is folded into larger categories. For instance, we elected to discuss a number of people within the context of general thematic entries rather than in individual biographies (e.g., The Ritz Brothers can be found under Comedy Teams and Thomas Mitchell under Character Actors). In short, the index is the most valuable tool in this book and you ought to consult it freely.

The research and writing of this volume took a great deal of time, but we enjoyed every moment of it. Whether reliving the pleasure of a favorite old movie or discovering startling facts about a new one, we approached all of our work with the same sense of wonder that we felt when the house lights suddenly dimmed and the magic began. It is our deepest wish that *The Encyclopedia of Hollywood* will touch that same emotion in you.

"A" MOVIE   During the heyday of the studio system (*q.v.*) a film designated as an "A" movie featured one or more of a company's biggest stars, was handled by one of its best directors, and was given a great deal of promotion and publicity. Examples of "A" movies are *Queen Christina* (1933), starring Greta Garbo, directed by Rouben Mamoulian, and *Mr. Smith Goes to Washington* (1939), starring Jimmy Stewart, directed by Frank Capra.

"A" movies were the highlight of double bills, while "B" movies, generally made on a much smaller budget with actors who had a more modest appeal, were often thrown in as fillers.

Since the demise of the studio system, most first-run films are considered "A" movies.
See also: "B" movies

ABBOTT & COSTELLO (Bud Abbott: 1895–1974, Lou Costello: 1906–1959)   One of the most popular comedy teams of the sound era, Abbott & Costello enjoyed enormous success in the 1940s and early 1950s before their brand of inspired childish humor was supplanted by that of the Dean Martin and Jerry Lewis team. Slender, streetwise Bud Abbott was the straight man; the laugh maker was short, round, and innocent Lou Costello. Their humor was hardly sophisticated, yet it was decidedly verbal. Unlike such comedy teams as the Marx Brothers, Laurel & Hardy and even The Three Stooges (*qq.v.*), Abbott and Costello had virtually no visual style—even their physical comedy consisted of little more than Costello's fumbling with his hat. But the team's clever vaudeville-type routines, with the pair bantering back and forth and completely misunderstanding each other, have become legendary.

William A. "Bud" Abbott's parents worked as circus performers, and they inspired their son to pursue a show business career of his own. It was a long time in coming, however. When Abbott was fifteen, he was shanghaied and forced to work as a sailor on a boat heading for Europe. Throughout his twenties and most of his thirties he tried to make a career of entertainment but without success. He had all but given up and was working as a cashier at a Brooklyn vaudeville house in 1931 when a young comic named Lou Costello reported that his partner was sick. Abbott filled in as Costello's straight man that night, and a new comedy team was born.

Louis Francis Cristillo, later known simply as Lou Costello, had an odd assortment of early jobs that included selling newspapers, soda jerking, and working in a hat shop. At one time, he was a rather unlikely prizefighter. Determined to make it in show business, he quit the ring in the late 1920s and made his way to Hollywood. The best he could do, though, was to become a stuntman, at one point assuming the extraordinary responsibility of doubling for Delores del Rio.

After joining up with Bud Abbott, the team honed their routines on the vaudeville and burlesque circuits until they got their big break in 1938, appearing on Kate Smith's popular radio show. They quickly became radio favorites, which led to their appearance in the Broadway revue, *Streets of Paris,* with Carmen Miranada (*q.v.*)

Hollywood beckoned and Abbott and Costello were hired by Universal Pictures (*q.v.*) as comic relief in an innocuous musical called *One Night in the Tropics* (1940). Audiences roared at the antics of the two comedians and Universal promptly signed the team to a long-term contract. They were the stars of their next film, *Buck Privates* (1941).

Buck Privates, a service comedy, was a huge hit and was followed quickly by comic romps in two other branches of the military in *In the Navy* (1941) and *Keep 'em Flying* (1941). The pair made a total of five films in

1

Abbott & Costello was the hottest comedy team of the early 1940s. They are seen here in a public performance of their famous Who's on First routine, which was immortalized on film in *The Naughty Nineties* (1945). Photo courtesy of Movie Star News.

1941 and their combined success put Abbott and Costello among Hollywood's top ten box office draws. Except for the years 1945–47, they would sustain that level of popularity until 1951.

The comedy of Abbott and Costello was silly and escapist, and, therefore, particularly well-suited to help balance the urgency of the war years. The team's early 1940s films, such as *Who Done It?* (1942), *Hit the Ice* (1943), *Lost in a Harem* (1944), and *The Naughty Nineties* (1945), were pleasant, simple comedies. Bud and Lou were usually supported by good-looking contract players involved in an insipid love story, a setup similar to that of the later Marx Brothers movies. Their films only came to life when the team launched into one of their famous dialogues, such as the immortal "Who's on First?" routine.

In the mid-1940s, after the war, Abbott and Costello's popularity took a nose-dive. Films like *Little Giant* (1946) and *The Wistful Widow of Wagon Gap* (1947) suggested that America's love affair with Bud and Lou was over. The team tried to recapture past glory by making films such as *The Time of Their Lives,* a comic horror story reminiscent of their 1941 hit, *Hold That*

Ghost. They even resorted to making *Buck Privates Come Home* (1947) in the hope of reminding audiences of their first big hit. It was all to no avail.

Except for the occasional loanout to other studios, most of Abbott and Costello's films had been made at Universal Pictures, a studio whose main strength had always been its horror films. In the hope of reviving the popularity of their premiere comedy team, Universal decided to combine its two biggest assets in one film, *Abbott & Costello Meet Frankenstein* (1948). The movie boasted supporting performances by Boris Karloff as Frankenstein, Bela Lugosi as Dracula, and Lon Chaney, Jr. as the Wolf Man. The result of Universal's experiment was arguably Abbott and Costello's best, most consistently funny film. It was also, as Universal had hoped, a big success at the box office.

The unfortunate consequence of *Abbott & Costello Meet Frankenstein*'s success, however, was that it spawned a formula that seemed as if it would no sooner die than Dracula himself. With numbing regularity, the team starred in weak movies with repetitious titles: *Abbott & Costello Meet the Killer* (1949), *Abbott & Costello Meet the Invisible Man* (1950), *Abbott & Costello Meet Captain Kidd* (1952), *Abbott & Costello Meet Dr. Jekyll and Mr. Hyde* (1953), *Abbott & Costello Meet the Keystone Kops* (1955), and *Abbott & Costello Meet the Mummy* (1955).

The pair made other films during these years, but their comedy was as uninspired as their horror/comedy formula movies. In the early 1950s, though, the team starred in a TV series, "The Abbott and Costello Show," that reprised many of their best vaudeville routines. A new generation was being weaned on the syndicated reruns of their TV series, which led to the later rediscovery of their movies on television.

Abbott and Costello's last film together was *Dance With Me Henry* (1956). They produced the movie themselves and witnessed it painfully flop at the box office. Abbott soon thereafter announced his retirement, but Costello went on to make one solo film, *The Thirty-Foot Bride of Candy Rock* (1959). He died of a heart attack, however, before the movie was released to poor reviews and even worse receipts.

Both Bud Abbott and Lou Costello had tax trouble with the government and found themselves in financial difficulties at the end of their lives. Bud Abbott suffered still more, however, when he was crippled by a series of strokes, beginning in 1964. He died in a retirement home ten years later.

See also: comedy teams; Martin & Lewis

ABOVE THE LINE The budget of a movie is divided into two major parts: "above-the-line" and "below-the-line" (*q.v.*) expenses. Above-the-line costs are all those that must either be paid or negotiated before the film goes into production. These generally consist of the cost of acquiring rights to the property to be filmed (the novel, play, concept, etc.), the cost of the stars who are hired for the entire shooting schedule, plus the fees for the producer, director, and screenwriter(s). Above-the-line costs tend to be the largest individual items in a film's budget.

Below-the-line expenses are all those that are incurred during production as well as during postproduction.

ACADEMY AWARDS Known by their nickname, "Oscar," the awards are presented early each spring by the Academy of Motion Picture Arts and Sciences, an organization formed on May 4, 1927 to "improve the artistic quality of the film medium." The Academy has done so, in part, by drawing public attention to what its members consider the film community's finest work, bestowing Academy Awards upon its brightest lights.

Academy members are grouped into thirteen specialized categories. The members of each group nominate up to five individuals whom they feel have demonstrated excellence in their respective areas of expertise. For instance, actors nominate actors, screenwriters nominate screenwriters, directors nominate directors, etc. The entire Academy—approximately 3,000 members—then votes on the nominees in order to establish a winner.

The Academy Awards were originally an industry celebration of itself without benefit of media coverage. The first Awards dinner was held on May 16, 1929, honoring the films of 1927–8, and the winners were *Wings* (Best Picture), Emil Jannings (Best Actor for *The Way of all Flesh* and *The Last Command*), Janet Gaynor (Best Actress for performances in *Seventh Heaven, Street Angel,* and *Sunrise*), Frank Borzage (Best Director for *Seventh Heaven*). Curiously, in that first ceremony, an award was given for Best Comedy Director—to Lewis Milestone for *Two Arabian Knights.* The award was given only that year.

The award—which consists of a rather stiff looking fellow grasping a sword while standing upon a reel of film—was designed by the famous art director Cedric Gibbons and sculpted by George Stanley. The gold-plated bronze figure stands thirteen-and-a-half-inches tall and weighs slightly over eight pounds. ·

The statuette was originally known simply as the Academy Award. It had no other name until 1931, when, according to legend, Margaret Herrick, then a secretary for the Academy, spotted the figure and loudly proclaimed, "Why, he looks like my Uncle Oscar!" A reporter heard her comment and printed it, and the name caught on.

It is generally acknowledged that today a Best Picture Oscar is worth an extra $10 million at the box office to the winner. And actors, directors, producers, editors, screenwriters, etc. are almost always able to demand higher salaries after receiving an Academy Award.

The Awards ceremonies—as well as the awards, themselves—have changed over the years. In the early days, an actor might be nominated for several films (see the winners of 1927–28 above). In 1936 the new categories of Best Supporting Actor and Actress were added, and in 1947 foreign-language films were given separate awards.

The Awards ceremonies were first broadcast on radio as early as 1930 and then, finally, on television beginning in 1953. They have, over the decades, been recognized as the granddaddy of all awards shows and regularly receive extremely high viewer ratings.
See also: Gibbons, Cedric

ACTOR-DIRECTORS When Hollywood's studio system *(q.v.)* was at its height of power, movies were turned out quickly and efficiently. For the creative assembly line to work, everyone had his or her task, and there was little room for overlap. Producers produced, directors directed, and actors acted.

Interestingly, writers were the first group to win the opportunity to take on new roles when many were allowed to direct their own scripts in the 1940s. As for actors, when stars were being rushed into four, five or six films per year, giving them the extra time to direct a movie would have cost the studio too much in potential revenue. It is no wonder, then, that there was a dearth of actor-directors through the 1930s and most of the 1940s. (Exceptions included most notably Lionel Barrymore and Orson Wells *[q.v.].*)

Even in the area of comedy, where there was a long-standing tradition of actor-directors from the silent era (e.g., such legends as Charlie Chaplin and Buster Keaton *[qq.v.],* comic films during the '30s and '40s were not directed by their stars. W. C. Fields, Mae West, and the Marx Brothers *(qq.v.)* did not even fully control their own material.

Not until the late 1940s, when the studio system began breaking down, did a small cadre of actors begin working on both sides of the camera. Ida Lupino, Dick Powell, and Robert Montgomery *(qq.v.)* were some of the more interesting early actor-directors of this era, often directing films in which they themselves did not appear. Others followed suit, most of them, however, choosing not to continue their double careers. James Cagney, Burt Lancaster, and Mickey Rooney *(qq.v.)* are among those who tried their hand at directing and then gave it up.

Ever since the 1960s, the number of actors who have tried directing has gone from a trickle to a stream to a flood. And an ever larger number of actors wanting greater control of their own films has resulted not only in successful dual careers but in successful movies as well. Clint Eastwood *(q.v.)* is perhaps the best example of today's premier actor-director. But others have done well, also, such as Paul Newman, John Cassavetes, and Warren Beatty *(qq.v.).*

In the comedy arena, the actor-director mantle has been passed to (among others) Jerry Lewis, Woody Allen, and Mel Brooks *(qq.v.)*. Most comedy actor-directors are also writers, creating and controlling their own comic visions with a totality envied by directors of other genres.

See also: writer-directors

ADAPTATIONS Films based on a work of art from another medium, usually a play or a novel, have been a Hollywood mainstay since 1912 when Adolph Zukor introduced his Famous Players Company *(q.v.)*. Well-known works of art, whether from the stage or the world of letters, served two important functions for the early movie makers: they provided instant, proven plots for an industry that was voracious for new stories and they provided name recognition that would attract paying customers into the theaters. For those two reasons novels, plays, songs, etc. continue to be adapted into movies today.

While virtually every literary classic from *Pride and Prejudice* to *War and Peace* has been adapted into a movie, the overall quality of such adaptations has not been good. The fact is, the better the novel, the less likely it is to be made into a great movie. The unique elements of the novel—the descriptions of internal thoughts and feelings—do not translate well to film. Master directors like John Huston can sometimes accomplish wonders in this area (such as in *The Red Badge of Courage,* 1951), but the film medium seems better suited to capturing the vividly described physical action of pulpier novels such as *Jaws* and *The Godfather*. It should come as no surprise, therefore, that Alfred Hitchcock made many of his greatest films from trashy, mediocre novels.

Given their dependence on language, plays were a surprisingly hot commodity for the movies even before the arrival of the talkies, but there was a virtual stampede to adapt plays to the screen during the first decade after the sound revolution. Though plays are closer to the film medium than novels, at least in regard to their structure and length, "opening up" and turning them into visual stories has often proved difficult. Even such well-known and enjoyable adaptations as *The Petrified Forest* (1936) and *The Philadelphia Story* (1940) tend to be static. In the hands of visually acute and creative directors, however, plays can be turned into great films such as *Amadeus* (1984). And yet there are more than a few absolutely dreadful adaptations of the ilk of *Man of La Mancha* (1972), perhaps one of the worst adaptations in the history of the cinema.

While songs have occasionally been adapted into movies (e.g., *Ode to Billy Joe,* 1976) short stories have proven to be a particularly good source of fine films, probably because the story line must be expanded rather than forcibly cut. Some famous films based on short stories include John Ford's *(q.v.)* classic *Stagecoach* (1939)

and Roger Corman's *(q.v.)* films based on Edgar Allen Poe tales starring Vincent Price *(q.v.)*.

The importance of adaptations to the industry grew during the 1950s and 1960s. Hollywood sought to distinguish its product from that of television, and it did so, in part, by paying hefty sums of money to buy best-sellers and hit plays, turning them into big-budget, big-screen spectaculars. For instance, adaptations such as *From Here to Eternity* (1953), *The Bridge on the River Kwai* (1957), *My Fair Lady* (1964), *The Sound of Music* (1965), and *The Exorcist* (1973) were gargantuan successes.

In more recent years, as the movies have become a recognized art form, there has been a rise in the percentage of movies made from original scripts, and producers have a growing confidence in the salability of movies that haven't already been hits in other media. The widespread use of original material began in earnest with the success of *Easy Rider* (1969), but has fully come into its own thanks to such gigantic hit films based on original screenplays as *Star Wars* (1977), *Raiders of the Lost Ark* (1981), *E.T. The Extra-Terrestrial* (1982), *Back to the Future* (1985), and *Moonstruck* (1987).

AGEE, JAMES (1909–1955) A multi-talented author, Agee numbers among the few American film critics to have made the switch from writing about movies to creating them. Only two other well-known American film critics have successfully made that transition: Frank S. Nugent and Peter Bogdanovich *(qq.v.)*.

James Agee grew up in Tennessee, was graduated from Harvard, and eventually went to work for *Time* magazine, where his passion for the popular arts blossomed. In 1941, he became the regular *Time* magazine film critic. In 1942, while still writing for *Time,* he also wrote a regular column on film for *The Nation*.

Long before the *auteur (q.v.)* theory became fashionable in intellectual film circles of the 1960s, Agee treated movies as an art form. He wrote his film criticism for both publications until 1948, when he decided to try his hand in the industry that he had been commenting on for the past seven years.

He wrote a number of screenplays, including a taut thriller titled *The Night of the Hunter* (1955), which was directed by Charles Laughton *(q.v.)*. But Agee's claim to fame as a screenwriter is the script for *The African Queen* (1951). This John Huston–directed comedy/adventure starring Humphrey Bogart and Katharine Hepburn was a tremendous hit and remains a much-loved film all these years later.

In addition to his screenwriting, Agee also wrote several books: *Let Us Now Praise Famous Men, The Morning Watch,* and *A Death in the Family*. The latter novel was published in 1957, two years after Agee's death from a heart attack, and won the Pulitzer Prize in 1958. Considering Agee's passion for cinema, it is

only fitting that his final novel was made into a first-rate film, *All the Way Home* (1963).
See also: critics

AGENTS Long ignored as a group, agents have had a powerful effect on the motion picture business, shaping its economics and often discovering its stars. They are the middlemen who find work for film artists and negotiate their contracts, usually in exchange for ten percent of the artist's income.

Among the earliest and eventually the most powerful of talent agents in film were William Morris and Jules C. Stein. Morris built his agency by representing theater and vaudeville stars, eventually selling their services to the movies for far more than they were paid for their live performances. Jules Stein was an eye doctor who failed in his chosen profession but built the largest talent agency in the world, calling his company the Music Corporation of America (MCA). His company's original growth came from representing an array of famous musicians and big bands.

Despite the restrictions of the studio system *(q.v.)*, agencies and lone agents began to wield considerable power during the 1930s, especially if they represented popular stars. The keys to an agent's success and desirability to upwardly mobile film actors, directors, and writers were his strong connections in the industry. Myron Selznick, for instance, David O. Selznick's *(q.v.)* brother, became an enormously powerful agent who could turn ruthless when he negotiated with the studio bigwigs, many of whom he blamed for his father Lewis J. Selznick's downfall during the silent era. Another well-connected agent was Zeppo Marx, formerly of the Marx Brothers, the not-so-funny brother was actually the wealthiest of all his siblings, representing a wide array of talent beginning in the mid-1930s. He represented the Marx Brothers only once, however, obtaining $200,000 for them to star in *Room Service* (1938). It was the most money they ever received on any one picture, but Zeppo refused to work with his brothers again—they were too much trouble.

Paul Irving "Swifty" Lazar is one of the last of the old breed of movie agents, wheeling and dealing and keeping everything in his head. According to Whitney Stine, in his book *Stars & Star Handlers,* Lazar received his nickname rather late in his career, earning it in the 1950s when Humphrey Bogart wagered that his agent couldn't get him five deals in one day. Bogart lost. "Swifty" Lazar was born.

Other important agents included Leland Hayward, Louis Shurr, and Henry Wilson. Most agents gained their reputation by handling a large stable of well-known stars. Others gained fame by creating stars. Sue Carol, for example, discovered Alan Ladd *(q.v.)* (whom she later married) and Johnny Hyde helped to create the Marilyn Monroe *(q.v.)* phenomenon.

Since the end of the studio system, agents have become even more powerful than many producers, and are often in the best position to pull all the parties together in order to make a movie deal. One agent or agency may represent all of the principal people in a package: the star, the director, and the screenwriter. MCA, in fact, was so involved in deal making that it finally behooved the agency to go into filmmaking, instead. Lew Wasserman, the longtime head of MCA after Jules Stein retired, bought Universal Pictures *(q.v.)* and sold off their agency contracts. As a result, MCA went from the world's largest talent agency to (eventually) among the most successful of all the major film studios.

The biggest agencies occasionally grow too large. Some entertainers often feel lost or overlooked in such massive companies. In fact, during the much publicized search for the kidnapped Patty Hearst in the early 1970s, the joke going around Hollywood was that Miss Hearst couldn't be found because she was signed with William Morris.

Among the most powerful agencies today are Creative Artists Agency, International Creative Management (ICM), and the William Morris Agency. But there are very successful smaller agencies in abundance all over Los Angeles.

AIRPLANE MOVIES The combination of flying machines and moving pictures came about quite early in the history of the cinema; both were new, exciting technological achievements that were on the cutting edge of our modern society. One-reelers and newsreels captured many of the breakthroughs (and crackups) in aviation's early development. Yet not until they proved their worth in World War I did airplanes begin showing up in a multitude of action films. Inevitably, the greater number of Hollywood airplane movies also happen to be war movies.

The first major aerial combat movie was *Wings* (1927), a film that boasted spectacular flying sequences. It was a huge hit and won the first Best Picture Academy Award. It also began a rash of airplane movies that continued throughout the late 1920s and well into the 1930s. The genre's most famous example is Howard Hughes' *(q.v.)* *Hell's Angels* (1930), an airplane movie made on such a grand scale that, at the time of its making, Hughes actually possessed one of the largest air forces in the world. *Hell's Angels'* flying sequences were so spectacular that portions of them were used many times over in subsequent films.

There were several subgenres in aviation films during the 1930s. The main one celebrated the romantic image of gallant and noble fliers of the World War I era in films such as *The Dawn Patrol* (1930) and its remake in 1938. But flying, itself, was such a daring endeavor that other kinds of airplane movies were also successful,

From *Wings* (1927) to *Top Gun* (1986), movies concerning the wild blue yonder have fascinated filmmakers and filmgoers alike. The romance of flying was very much in evidence in George Roy Hill's nostalgic aviation movie, *The Great Waldo Pepper* (1975), starring Robert Redford. Photo courtesy of Movie Star News.

such as the stunt pilot film *Lucky Devils* (1932) and the classic air mail film *Only Angels Have Wings* (1939).

The advent of World War II brought a spate of patriotic air combat movies that were much less romantic than their World War I counterparts. Movies such as *Dive Bomber* (1941), *Captains of the Clouds* (1942), *Air Force* (1943), *Thirty Seconds Over Tokyo* (1944), and many others were ideal war films because they allowed for the realistic in-depth portrayal of a small group of men in dramatic circumstances.

In the decade after the war came films that examined every aspect of America's aerial preparedness, from the lessons of the past taught by *The Court Martial of Billy Mitchell* (1955) to the cold war future in *Strategic Air Command* (1955). Also in the war's aftermath came a flood of biopics *(q.v.)* about famous combat pilots such as Spig Wead, the hero of *The Wings of Eagles* (1957). Not all of these films were about aces, however; other famous fliers received their due during the late 1940s and 1950s, among them Charles Lindbergh in *The Spirit of St. Louis* (1957).

There was considerable interest in test pilots during the early 1950s when jets replaced propeller-driven aircraft. Movies such as *Chained Lightning* (1950) and *Jet Pilot* (filmed in 1950 but released in 1957) appeared in theaters, introducing audiences to the next phase of the aviation revolution.

Movies that centered around aerial combat went into a modest decline in the 1960s and 1970s as the focus on the importance of nuclear missiles seemed to make dogfights somewhat passé. Most flying movies during those years tended to be nostalgic recreations of a simpler time. Films such as *The Blue Max* (1966) and *The Great Waldo Pepper* (1975) kept the genre alive, while disaster movies such as *Airport* (1970) and its many sequels concerning planes in distress filled the slack.

Finally, in the 1980s, there was a return to the breathtaking aerial spectacular with *Top Gun,* the biggest grossing movie of 1986. Supersonic jet fighters streamed across movie screens with mindboggling technical proficiency, and the classic aviation movie was reborn.

ALDRICH, ROBERT (1918–1983)   A director who produced many of his own films, he was especially well known for making actions movies with strong social and political points of view, and many of his best films depict rebellion against authority. Aldrich was very much an independent filmmaker with a reputation as an iconoclast. He remains an undervalued director, in large part because of his commercial failures during the last fifteen years of his career. In total, Aldrich directed thirty films, with his greatest commercial and critical successes coming in streaks during the late 1950s and 1960s.

Born to one of the most influential and powerful families in Rhode Island, Aldrich was a cousin of the Rockefellers and the progeny of a clan that could trace its lineage back to the Mayflower. Twenty-one years old and not having bothered to graduate from college, he used his connections to land his first job at RKO as a gopher in 1941. He went on to gain his training as an assistant director for some of cinema's most illustrious directors, such as Charlie Chaplin, Jean Renoir, Lewis Milestone, Max Ophuls, William Wellman, and Joseph Losey. He also became the studio manager at Enterprise Studios, a short-lived company that produced such films as *Body and Soul* (1947) and *Force of Evil* (1948).

Ironically, after an apprenticeship of more than a decade in Hollywood, he received his first chance to direct for television in New York, shooting seventeen episodes of "The Doctor" in 1952 and 1953. Finally, he got his chance to direct his first theatrical film, *The Big Leaguer* (1953), a "B" movie *(q.v.)* starring Edward G. Robinson. Then, after coproducing and directing an interesting flop, *World For Ransom* (1954), Aldrich hit the big time when he was hired to direct Burt Lancaster in *Apache* (1954).

Over the next dozen years Aldrich made a number of Hollywood's bellwether films in terms of content and point of view, though not all of them were influential or successful at the time of their release. For instance, his version of Mickey Spillane's *Kiss Me Deadly* (1955) was the apotheosis of the *film noir (q.v.;)* there wasn't a darker, more cynical movie made during the 1950s. In addition, Aldrich made a memorably vicious "inside-story" film about Hollywood called *The Big Knife* (1955), as well as the visceral war movie *Attack!* (1956), a film with a striking combination of violence and morality.

Aldrich is perhaps best remembered as the director of three films, the macabre and campy *What Ever Happened to Baby Jane?* (1962) with Bette Davis and Joan Crawford, *Hush . . . Hush, Sweet Charlotte* (1964), with Bette Davis and Olivia de Havilland, and the rousing war story *The Dirty Dozen* (1967) with Lee Marvin.

The Dirty Dozen was such a huge hit that it allowed Aldrich to buy his own studio in 1968. Unfortunately, he had precious few commercial successes in the years to follow. He did, however, make a number of excellent movies, and among them were *Ulzana's Raid* (1972), which was one of the last great Westerns ever made by Hollywood and a film that many consider the director's best. He also made *The Longest Yard* (1974), starring Burt Reynolds, which was Aldrich's last major box office triumph. His later films included *Twilight's Last Gleaming* (1977) and *The Frisco Kid* (1979), a comedy with Harrison Ford and Gene Wilder. Aldrich's last film was *. . . All the Marbles* (1981).

Though Aldrich had never been nominated for an Oscar, his peers thought enough of him to elect him twice as president of the Directors Guild of America during the 1970s.

In late 1983 Aldrich suffered kidney failure. He chose to die at home rather than accept continued medical intervention.

ALL-STAR MOVIES Films boasting a large cast of well-known stars have long been a Hollywood tradition. While virtually unheard of during the silent movie era, they arrived in full force with the talkies. *The Hollywood Revue of 1929, King of Jazz* (1930), and *Paramount on Parade* (1930) were among the first vehicles the movie studios used to showcase their contract players.

Soon thereafter, a more sophisticated form of all-star movie developed. The class acts of this peculiar genre are films such as *Grand Hotel* (1932), which boasted the luminous cast of Greta Garbo, John and Lionel Barrymore, Joan Crawford, and Wallace Berry *(qq.v.)*, and *Dinner at Eight* (1933), which starred Marie Dressler, John and Lionel Barrymore, Jean Harlow, Wallace Berry *(qq.v.)*, Billie Burke, and Edmund Lowe. *If I Had A Million* (1932), starring Gary Cooper, George Raft, W. C. Fields, Charles Laughton, and Jack Oakie *(qq.v.)* was also a worthy effort. Perhaps the most ambitious all-star movie of the 1930s was Max Reinhardt's version of Shakespeare's *A Midsummer Night's Dream* (1935),

which starred James Cagney, Dick Powell, Olivia de Havilland, Mickey Rooney, *(qq.v.)* and Joe E. Brown.

The 1930s also ushered in the musical all-star film, with a series of *Big Broadcast* movies that proved successful both artistically and commercially. These films usually starred a host of comic radio personalities who later became film stars, such as Burns & Allen, Bob Hope, Jack Benny *(qq.v.)*, and so on. Perhaps the greatest all-star musical film is *Ziegfeld Follies* (1944), which showcased Fred Astaire *(q.v.)* in a series of dazzling numbers, as well as Judy Garland, Gene Kelly, Lena Horne, and others, and included several classic comedy bits from the likes of Red Skelton and Fanny Brice.

During World War II, the quality of the all-star movie took a plunge from which it has never really recovered. Movies such as *Star Spangled Rhythm* (1942) and *Stage Door Canteen* (1943) offered stars galore and plenty of patriotism, but little quality moviemaking.

In the 1950s and 1960s, as the studio system *(q.v.)* broke down and stars were no longer under long-term contract, the all-star movie experienced a modest decline. When they were made, they were almost always big-budget vehicles that featured cameo appearances by expensive stars in the hope of drawing a larger audience. Films such as *Around the World in Eighty Days* (1956), *The Longest Day* (1962), and *Casino Royale* (1967) are examples in this category.

The 1970s brought an entirely new form of all-star film: the disaster movie. It began with *Airport* (1970), and several all-star sequels followed. But there were all-star disasters on land and sea, as well. For instance, *The Poseidon Adventure* (1972) and *The Towering Inferno* (1974) both made their marks on the decade with mammoth casts, budgets, and box office receipts.

The all-star movie of the 1980s has generally been of a new and heartening variety: the serious ensemble film. The best examples of this are *The Big Chill* (1983) and *Crimes of the Heart* (1986), both featuring casts of well-known and/or up-and-coming stars rather than the older established movie and TV actors who had appeared in the all-star film of the 1970s.

It's safe to say that the all-star movie will always exist in one form or another because the most precious commodity in Hollywood is fame. Guest appearances by a truckload of famous actors will have more clout at the box office than expensive special effects or a clever advertising campaign. The continued success of the all-star movie is unfailing evidence that Hollywood knows that when it comes to celebrities, "more is better."

ALLEN, DEDE (1924–)   An editor *(q.v.)*, her creative cutting since the late 1950s has made her stand out as an exceptional talent in a field where few names are known, let alone remembered. One reason that Allen has come to the forefront is that she has rarely been an "invisible" editor. One is often acutely aware of her work; it draws attention to itself, but also tends to add an intellectual and emotional charge that is intrinsic to the story she is helping to tell. Her expressive editing has been greatly influenced by the French New Wave films of Truffaut and Goddard.

Born Corothea Carothers Allen, she began her movie career as a messenger at Columbia Pictures. Fascinated by the technical means by which films were constructed, she eventually landed jobs in the editing department, slowly moving up the ladder from sound cutter to assistant editor (working on such films as the 1948 *Because of Eve*) and finally to editor in 1959 when she spliced together *Odds Against Tomorrow* for director Robert Wise *(q.v.)*, who had once been an editor himself.

Allen went on to edit the films of a small coterie of directors who found her style eminently compatible with their own. She has worked most consistently with Arthur Penn *(q.v.)*, for whom she dazzled audiences with her much-admired editing of *Bonnie and Clyde* (1967), as well as *Alice's Restaurant* (1969), *Little Big Man* (1970), *Night Moves* (1975), and others. She also worked for, among others, Sidney Lumet *(q.v.)*, editing two of his best films, *Serpico* (1973) and *Dog Day Afternoon* (1975), Robert Rossen (*The Hustler* [1961]), Elia Kazan (*America, America* [1963]), and George Roy Hill (*Slaughterhouse Five* [1972] and *Slap Shot* [1977]).

Actors who have benefited from her editing also come back to Dede Allen—especially when they become actor-directors. For instance, Warren Beatty and Paul Newman *(qq.v.)* both starred in a number of Dede Allen-edited films, and she was first on their hiring list when they made their respective films, *Reds* (1981) and *Harry and Son* (1984). It's instructive that Allen was also called in to try and save the virtually uneditable Debra Winger film, *Mike's Murder* (1984); she achieved a higher level of success than most people thought possible, although the movie was still a stinker. Most recently she edited the Richard Dreyfuss *(q.v.)* comedy *Let It Ride* (1989).

ALLEN, WOODY (1935–) The foremost American filmmaker of the 1970s and 1980s, Woody Allen has written, directed, and starred in an impressive body of work, exhibiting an extraordinary ability to grow and change as a filmmaker.

Woody Allen was born Allen Stewart Konigsberg in Brooklyn, N.Y. and lived a life not terribly unlike his young protagonist's in his autobiographical film, *Radio Days* (1987). While still in high school, Allen was selling jokes that appeared in Earl Wilson's syndicated newspaper column. After flunking out of New York University (he failed Motion Picture Production), he joined the NBC Writer's Program and, at the ripe age of

eighteen, began writing for television, eventually teaming up with such writers for the classic 1950s TV series "Your Show of Shows" as Neil Simon, Mel Brooks, and Carl Reiner *(qq.v.)*.

Woody Allen first came to national attention during the early 1960s when, instead of writing for others, he told his own jokes as a stand-up comic. His comic persona, developed during those nightclub years, was a truly modern creation—the neurotic everyman.

In 1964, he was paid $35,000 to rewrite the screenplay of *What's New Pussycat?* The film became the most successful comedy of its time, earning $17 million. Though unhappy with the changes made in his work, Allen was suddenly a recognized screenwriter and actor (he had a small part in the movie).

His next film project was *What's Up Tiger Lily?* (1966). This unique comedy was created by redubbing a Japanese spy thriller and giving it an entirely new comic sound track. With a Japanese superspy named Phil Moscowitz in search of the stolen recipe for the world's greatest egg salad, this James Bond spoof became a cult classic.

It wasn't until 1969, however, that Allen was given a $1.6 million budget to write, direct, and star in his own film. The result was *Take the Money and Run*. It was followed by *Bananas* (1971), a film many fans consider his funniest. Both films were hits, and these two back-to-back moneymakers gave Allen the freedom to continue making his own kind of films without studio interference.

Considering that Allen writes, directs, and stars in the majority of his movies, his output throughout the last two decades has been remarkable. Not counting *Tiger Lily,* he has written and directed more than eighteen high quality films. His 1977 film *Annie Hall* was a landmark comedy. It won Academy Awards for Best Picture, Best Actress (Diane Keaton), Best Screenplay (with Marshall Brickman), and Best Director. Though he didn't win, Allen was also nominated for Best Actor. It was the biggest sweep of top nominations since Orson Welles' *Citizen Kane* (1941, *qq.v.*). And it was the first comedy since the 1930s to be honored as Best Picture. But then *Annie Hall* was more than a comedy. Allen had juxtaposed comic human foibles with the sadness of a relationship gone awry, and created a hysterical yet sweet love story.

It seemed as if Woody Allen had reached the pinnacle of his creative and commercial powers. He could have gone on to make *Annie Hall* clones, but instead he chose a new direction, writing and directing *Interiors* (1978), a Bergmanesque film that was purposefully lacking in humor; Allen refused to do the expected.

Interiors is an example of Woody Allen's constant experimentation to find a new voice. A notable aspect of this filmic searching is how often he has managed to create successful movies without seriously repeating himself. *Manhattan* (1979), *Zelig* (1983), *Broadway Danny Rose* (1984), *The Purple Rose of Cairo* (1985), *Hannah and Her Sisters* (1986), *Another Woman* (1988), and *Crimes and Misdemeanors* (1989) have all established Woody Allen as an independent-minded *auteur (q.v.)* who has been able to create a vision of the world that is distinctly his own. And while not all of his films have been hits, all of them have been provocative and compelling.

Woody Allen's comic antecedents are many. His New York Jewish humor is in the great tradition of Groucho Marx. His impeccable comic timing came from studying Bob Hope movies. But both as a filmmaker and as a comic personality, Woody Allen is closest to Charlie Chaplin. Like Chaplin, he created a character of the little man who triumphs (after a fashion) against all odds. And, like Chaplin, he has allowed his meek character to grow and change with his increasingly sophisticated artistic vision.

ALLIED ARTISTS   The current name of a film production and distribution company with a history dating back to 1924. Allied Artists can trace its roots back to Rayart Pictures, founded by producers W. Ray Johnston and Trem Carr, who changed the name of the initially successful company to Monogram in 1929. Makers of "B" movies *(q.v.)*, particularly westerns, Monogram continued to grow in the early 1930s but the company fell on hard times during the Depression, due to huge debts to Herbert J. Yates' film processing company, which took over Monogram (and several other film companies) and formed Republic Pictures.

Meanwhile, Johnston and Carr didn't give up. They started a new Monogram in 1936, which became successful as the national economy began to improve. Producing the same sorts of low-budget movies as in its old incarnation, Monogram turned out horse operas starring the likes of Tex Ritter, Rex Bell, and Tim McCoy. John Wayne also made films for the company. Besides its westerns, Monogram is best remembered today for having produced the Charlie Chan and Mysterious Mr. Wong series, as well as the Bowery Boys films, movies that were all made cheaply and meant for the second half of double bills.

In 1946, Monogram created a subsidiary called Allied Artists Productions, and under that new name they released their prestige pictures. With the demise of the "B" movie in the early 1950s, Monogram phased out its low-budget product and wisely changed its name and image in 1953 to that of its subsidiary, calling itself Allied Artists Pictures Corporation. New management took over at that point, and directors such as William Wyler and Billy Wilder *(qq.v.)* were hired to create "A" movies *(q.v.)* for the company. Among some of the company's successes were *Love in the Afternoon* (1957) with Gary Cooper and Audrey Hepburn and *Al Capone* (1959) with Rod Steiger.

In the last two decades Allied Artists has concentrated on distribution and television production. They have made the occasional film, such as *Cabaret* (1972), but in recent years Allied Artists has had little direct impact on America's movie screens.

ALLYSON, JUNE (1917–)   A perky actress with a husky voice, June Allyson might have been another Jean Arthur *(q.v.)* but for her endless series of saccharine roles. Hardly another actress in Hollywood during the late 1940s and early 1950s consistently played characters so abysmally sweet as did June Allyson. Consequently, she has been forever stamped as the perfect understanding wife or girlfriend who gives everything to her man and asks for nothing in return—not an appropriate role model for the modern era.

Born Ella Geisman, the young actress worked as a chorus girl on Broadway during the 1930s. During that time she appeared in a few two-reel shorts, but her big break came when she starred in the 1941 Broadway musical *Best Foot Forward* and then traveled with the play to MGM where she repeated her stage success on film in 1943.

Allyson projected a wholesome image and that was exactly what MGM was looking for. The studio signed her up and she appeared with Mickey Rooney and Judy Garland *(qq.v.)* in *Girl Crazy* (1943), as well as several other musicals, with modest distinction. Her reputation as a goody-two-shoes, however, began to firmly take hold in biopics *(q.v.)* of famous men, with Allyson playing the loving wife in films such as *The Stratton Story* (1949), *The Glenn Miller Story* (1954), and *The McConnell Story* (1955). But her syrupy roles didn't end there. Most of her 1950s movies used her in the same way; even an otherwise tough Humphrey Bogart in *Battle Circus* (1953) had to contend with her goo. The one notable exception to her typical 1950s roles came in *The Shrike* (1955), in which she played a she-devil and performed wonderfully.

Allyson, who had been married to Dick Powell *(q.v.)* from 1945 until his death in 1963, had her own TV series from 1959 to 1961 ("The June Allyson Show") and then went into semiretirement, appearing in movies and TV films only rarely since then.

ALTMAN, ROBERT (1925–)   A director/producer whose work arouses deep passions among filmgoers, Robert Altman stirs his audiences to either love or hate his films. Those who love Altman's work perceive a courageous individualist who disdains the usual requirements of form and structure and, instead, makes movies that meander meaningfully toward a striking intellectual honesty. Those who abhor Altman's films see him as a self-indulgent moviemaker who has rarely been able to tell a story with a discernable beginning, middle, and end. And even his best works, his critics would contend, often lack any emotional punch.

Whatever might be said of Altman, though, it is clear that he is very much an actor's director. His loyal performers tend to appear regularly in his movies, and a great many stars such as Paul Newman *(q.v.)* and Carol Burnett have actively pursued the opportunity to work with him because of his improvisational approach to performing, allowing actors an uncommon freedom to interpret their roles. This willingness to improvise causes overlapping dialogue in Altman's films (because actor's don't know when someone has finished with their lines), and the result is a naturalism that is a fresh, if sometimes disconcerting, addition to modern Hollywood movies.

Like many directors', Altman's background was technical; he studied engineering and was a pilot during World War II. His entrance into the movie business came via work on industrial films in the 1950s. By 1957, he ventured into commercial moviemaking with a teenage exploitation film he wrote, directed, and produced called *The Delinquents,* starring the future Billy Jack, Tom Laughlin. After making a documentary on James Dean *(q.v.)* that same year, Altman drifted into television work which enabled him to hone his craft. A decade later, in 1968, he left TV to make the feature film *Countdown,* a highly regarded movie about astronauts that resulted in Altman receiving more directional assignments. But it wasn't until 1970 that he made his big breakthrough with *M*A*S*H,* a movie that excited the critics and public alike.

Over the next eight years, Altman made a series of films that constitute the bulk of his best work. It was a period when generally he was both critically and commercially viable. Not all of his films were hits during this time but his successes far outweighed his failures. Among his better efforts were *McCabe and Mrs. Miller* (1971), *California Split* (1974), *Nashville* (1975), *3 Women* (1978), and *A Wedding* (1978).

1978 was a watershed year for Altman during which he was involved in an astounding five films either as a producer or as a producer/writer/director. Rightly or wrongly, there was a sense among critics that his work couldn't be that good if he could generate it so prolifically. But the film that crippled his career was *Popeye* (1980), a big-budget musical based on the comic strip character starring Robin Williams as the title character and Shelley Duvall as Olive Oyl. It was a perfectly cast movie and by all rights it should have been a major hit. But it wasn't, and Altman received the blame for the rambling, uninvolving box office disappointment.

Soon thereafter Altman found it difficult to find financial backing for his projects and he retreated to the Broadway stage, directing *Come Back to the Five and Dime, Jimmy Dean, Jimmy Dean.* The play received good

reviews and he then brought it to the screen in 1982 (giving Cher her first big acting break both on the stage and in the movies). During the rest of the 1980s, he gained a modest reputation for filming stage plays, most notably *Streamers* (1983), but none of these films have had much commercial success. He received particularly poor reviews and box office response to his film version of Christopher Durang's play *Beyond Therapy* (1985).

Altman continues to direct primarily for television.

AMECHE, DON (1908–) Don Ameche was a busy actor at the star-starved Twentieth Century-Fox of the latter 1930s and early 1940s. An amiable leading man in light comedies and musicals, Ameche occasionally showed his stuff in dramas as well, most memorably in the biopic *(q.v.)* *The Story of Alexander Graham Bell* (1939). The movie was so successful and the actor became so identified by the public with his role as the inventor of the telephone that a phrase of the day was "I'll call you on the Ameche." In later years he disappeared from the big screen only to make a triumphant return in *Cocoon* (1985), in a role turned down by both Red Buttons and Buddy Ebsen and for which he won a Best Supporting Actor Academy Award.

Born Dominic Felix Amici in Kenosha, Wisconsin, his life's goal was to become a lawyer. While in law school, he was asked to fill in for a no-show leading player in a stock production of *Excess Baggage.* He took the role, abandoned law school, and eventually went on to several other acting roles before serving a long stint on radio.

He had his first screen test in 1935 at MGM, but the studio didn't think he had any future in the movies, and they passed on him. The following year, Twentieth Century-Fox retested him and Darryl F. Zanuck *(q.v.),* Fox's president, immediately put the actor to work in *Sins of Man* (1936).

Ameche was handed lead roles in a number of romances, many of them triangles where he ultimately lost the girl to Fox's other male star, Tyrone Power. The studio's only major female star was Alice Faye, and Ameche was often teamed with her. Ultimately, the pair were the leads of many of Fox's cheery musicals of the late 1930s and early 1940s, among them: *You Can't Have Everything* (1937), *In Old Chicago* (1938), *Alexander's Ragtime Band* (1938), *Hollywood Calvacade* (1939), *Lillian Russell* (1940), and *That Night in Rio* (1941).

Overworked and overexposed by Fox in movies far too similar, Ameche's popularity began to sag. Fortunately, however, Fox loaned him to other studios, for which he made several good movies that breathed new life into his ragged career. Films such as *Kiss the Boys Goodbye* (1941), *The Magnificent Dope* (1942), and Ernst Lubitsch's *(q.v.)* *Heaven Can Wait* (1943)—in which he had his best role of all—briefly rekindled his star power.

It didn't last very long. He was unable to survive a series of mediocre movies such as *Greenwich Village* (1944), *Guest Wife* (1945), and *That's My Man* (1947). By the end of the 1940s his Hollywood career appeared to be over.

Ameche has proven to be enormously resilient. He surfaced on TV in the 1950s and resumed his Broadway career, starring in such hits as the original staged musical production of *Silk Stockings* in 1955 (later filmed with Fred Astaire in his role), and *Goldilocks* in 1958. In his later years he returned to the big screen in low-budget movies such as *Picture Mommy Dead* (1966).

Persistence has a way of propelling nearly forgotten Hollywood actors back toward the top. Long after solid performances given in *Suppose They Gave a War and Nobody Came* (1970) and *The Boatniks* (1970), Ameche suddenly aroused a great deal of positive comment for the ease and professional aplomb he brought to his role as the right-wing, racist businessman in the Eddie Murphy *(q.v.)* smash *Trading Places* (1983). The previously mentioned *Cocoon* followed a few years later, and that film's success led Ameche to reprise his role in *Cocoon II* (1988) and a much admired star performance in David Mamets *Things Change* (1988). A vocal believer in health food and vitamins, Ameche has continued to work well into his eighties.

AMERICAN GRAFFITI This 1973 movie about a handful of high school seniors on the verge of adulthood firmly established George Lucas (in only his second feature film) as a director with considerable commercial savvy. That the movie was made at all, however, is due to the fact that Lucas' close friend, Francis Ford Coppola (*[q.v.]*, director of the smash hit *The Godfather* in 1972), agreed to act as producer.

American Graffiti is notable for several reasons. The script (based on Lucas' concept) was written by Willard Huyck and Gloria Katz. It was this very successful screenwriting team's first film. The movie also made a star of Richard Dreyfuss *(q.v.)* and it either introduced or featured a host of actors who went on to achieve greater success, including Ron Howard *(q.v.)*, Charles Martin Smith, Paul Le Mat, Cindy Williams, Candy Clark, Harrison Ford *(q.v.)*, Mackenzie Phillips, Bo Hopkins, Kathy Quinlan, and Suzanne Somers. In addition, the film's success ultimately led to one of television's most popular shows of the mid to late 1970s, "Happy Days" which in turn spun off "Laverne & Shirley."

In yet another way, this small, seemingly unambitious, film had a significant effect on movies that came later; it created a whole new genre of films: music-driven dramas whose rock 'n' roll sound track albums were potentionally worth more than actual ticket sales.

A nostalgic movie, it was advertised with the slogan "Where were you in '62?" *American Graffiti* had a mu-sical sound track like no other previous film. Forty-one rock 'n' roll hits of the past were crammed into it, evoking a veritable flood of memories. The songs were such an integral part of the script that Lucas spent $80,000 (more than ten percent of his total budget) to acquire the music rights.

On the basis of its $750,000 production cost, *American Graffiti* became the best movie investment of its decade, grossing roughly $50,000,000. Thanks to that huge commercial success, Lucas was given an $11 million budget to make a science fiction film at a time when the genre was considered box office poison. That movies was *Star Wars (q.v.)*.
See also: Lucas, George

AMERICAN INTERNATIONAL PICTURES While the big movie studios worried in the 1950s about the effect of TV on their traditional audience, they ignored the powerful and energetic creativity of a whole new generation of actors and filmmakers who came of age working at American International Pictures.

A.I.P. was founded in 1955 by Samuel Z. Arkoff and James H. Nicholson. Their intention, which was fully realized, was to make low-budget movies for the drive-in movie circuits and cater specifically to teenagers. With unashamedly trashy films like *Reform School Girls* (1957), which featured sixteen-year-old Sally Kellerman, and *Naked Paradise* (1957), directed by the soon-to-become-legendary Roger Corman *(q.v.)*, the studio became increasingly successful. During A.I.P.'s existence, future stars such as Charles Bronson *(q.v.)*, Peter Fonda, and Bruce Dern *(q.v.)*, and writer-director Peter Bogdanovich *(q.v.)* all received early training and experience.

It was Corman, however, who was the creative force at A.I.P., directing a highly regarded hit film series based on Edgar Allen Poe's short stories (starring Vincent Price *[q.v.]*), and the original *The Little Shop of Horrors* (1960) featuring Jack Nicholson *(q.v.)*, a film shot in two days!

Apart from Corman, A.I.P. may be best remembered, though, for *Beach Party* (1963), starring Frankie Avalon and Annette Funicello. This film launched a series of "beach" movies *(q.v.)* remarkable for both their absurdity and good-natured innocence.

ANDERSON, G. (GILBERT) M. "BRONCHO BILLY" (1882–1971) He was Hollywood's first western star, as well as a director and a powerful producer. Though he played a number of other roles, "Broncho Billy" Anderson is best remembered for helping to shape the Western genre in a staggering output of nearly 400 "Broncho Billy" one- and two-reelers between 1907 and 1915, virtually all of which he also directed.

Born Max Aronson, the young man was intent on having a show business career, but he failed to make

G. M. Anderson, better known to millions as "Broncho Billy," was the first Hollywood cowboy star. Photo courtesy of The Siegel Collection.

the grade on the New York stage. He made ends meet as a model before he was offered his first movie role in *The Messenger Boy's Mistake* (1902), directed by Edwin S. Porter. Anderson made his first breakthrough, though, in another, more memorable, Porter film, *The Great Train Robbery* (1903). Though he didn't know how to ride a horse, Anderson played a number of characters in this seminal western.

During the following few years, he worked steadily, moving from one company to the next, starring in westerns and occasionally directing. Sensing the growth of the movie industry, Anderson wisely joined George K. Spoor in forming a new film company, Essanay (the name coming from the first letter of each of their last names "S" and "A"). In the same year, Anderson gave himself the lead in a new western called *The Bandit Makes Good*. The lead character's name was Broncho Billy (later, the spelling was changed to "Bronco"). Virtually every week there was a new "Broncho Billy" film released by Essanay and starring Anderson. Later, in 1912, there were also "Alkali Ike" westerns with Anderson playing the title role in all of them as well.

His films were simple dramas with names such as *The Heart of a Cowboy* (1909), *Broncho Billy's Redemption*

(1910), and *The Border Ranger* (1911). The tenor of many future westerns was established with his hero who possessed a pure soul and who would never shoot first. Unfortunately, Anderson's westerns were also extremely unrealistic, which eventually led to the rise of a grittier, more authentic, form of horse opera with genuine westerners such as William S. Hart.

From about 1915, however, Anderson's film company had become prosperous enough to be able to afford Charlie Chaplin's *(q.v.)* immense salary and produced a number of his wonderful shorts. But by the time Chaplin left Essanay in 1916, Anderson's westerns were in decline and the star decided to quit the film business, selling out to his partner. Fancying himself a theatrical producer rather than an actor, he went east to Broadway, his original destination. He failed miserably on the Great White Way and returned to Hollywood a few years later as both an actor and director, although he had little impact. He retired in the early 1920s.

Anderson was a fading memory to the millions of Broncho Billy fans who adored him when the movies were young. In 1957, though, he was rightfully awarded a special Oscar "for his contributions to the development of motion pictures as entertainment." He again slipped into obscurity until he made a cameo appearance along with a number of other former western stars, including Johnny Mack Brown, Bob Steele, and Fuzzy Knight, in *The Bounty Killer* (1965). It was the last time he ever appeared before a movie camera.
See also: westerns

ANDREWS, DANA (1909–   )   An actor who worked steadily in motion pictures, Dana Andrews never really attained genuine stardom. Playing mostly villains in early screen appearances, he quickly became a tough-guy hero in the middle of the 1940s, when his career peaked. Success lasted only a few short years. As a serviceable leading man, however, Andrews continued acting for several more decades, evolving into a dependable workhorse in increasingly minor movies. In the 1950s, he was joined in Hollywood by his kid brother, Steve Forrest, an actor who also had a burst of popularity early in his career.

Born Carver Dana Andrews, the young man grew up to become a bookkeeper for the Gulf Oil Corporation. But handsome and trim, and with a solid baritone speaking voice, he decided that he'd do better in the movies than in the oil patch. He thumbed his way to Hollywood only to end up in the oil business yet again, this time pumping gas while waiting for his big break.

It was at Twentieth Century-Fox, a studio well known for its paucity of stars, that Andrews was given his chance. After a series of small roles—usually heavies—in minor films such as *Sailor's Lady* (1940), and important vehicles such as *The Westerner* (1940), *Tobacco Road*

(1941), and *Ball of fire* (1942), Andrews began to emerge as a potential star.

His breakthrough came in *The Ox-Bow Incident* (1943), when he was singled out by critics for his strong performance as the cowboy set to be lynched by a blood-thirsty mob. As a result, Andrews was given leading roles in such war films as *The Purple Heart* (1944) and *Wing and a Prayer* (1944) before he made his fleeting bid for stardom as the tough, but vulnerable, police detective who fell in love with *Laura* (1944). The film was a major hit and Andrews was swept into other major Fox films, including the highly regarded war movie *A Walk in the Sun* (1945) and the equally classic postwar film *The Best Years of Our Lives* (1946). It's worth noting, however, that most of his best movies were ensemble pieces and he rarely carried a motion picture on his own. One of the rare times he held center stage was in Elia Kazan's *Boomerang* (1947), a well-done suspense film that marked the beginning of the end of Andrews' peak period.

His films during the 1950s were of varying quality. The best of an increasingly bad lot were suspense yarns such as *While the City Sleeps* (1956), *Zero Hour* (1957), and *The Fearmakers* (1958). His career slowed down in the early 1960s, until he appeared in a rash of 1965 films playing supporting roles, many of them big-budget affairs, including *The Satan Bug, In Harm's Way,* and *Battle of the Bulge.* Unfortunately, roles in films of that caliber didn't continue and the aging actor was soon starring in low-budget cheapies such as *Hot Rods to Hell* (1967) and a bizarre Nazi movie, *The Frozen Dead* (1967).

Toward the end of his career, Andrews worked in daytime TV as a recurring character in the soap opera *Bright Promise* (1969–1972) but was later happily enlisted in one of the ever-popular all-star disaster movies, *Airport 1975* (1974). Other roles followed in a variety of movies, the most noteworthy being Elia Kazan's sentimental casting of Andrews in a small role in *The Last Tycoon* (1976). The actor continued to work until the end of the 1970s when he finally retired from the big screen.

ANDREWS, JULIE (1935–) A multitalented actress/singer who has had outstanding, if erratic, success in movies, TV, theater, and recording. Her prim and wholesome image, once an asset in the 1960s, has dogged her throughout her career, and she has spent much of her adult life trying to break the stereotype with only limited success. With her good looks and enchanting English accent, she may forever be remembered as the eternal Mary Poppins, her first film role, which also garnered her an Oscar for Best Actress.

Born Julia Elizabeth Welles to a theatrical family, she grew up in Walton-on-Thames, a small town just west of London. Entertaining her neighbors in air-raid shel-

Julie Andrews was one of the most popular movie stars of the mid-1960s, particularly after her performance in *The Sound of Music* (1965). Married to director Blake Edwards in 1970, she has since acted primarily in her husband's films. Photo by Zoë Dominic, courtesy of Julie Andrews.

ters during World War II, her splendid singing voice was apparent from an early age. While still a child, a throat specialist discovered she already had a full-grown larynx.

At the age of twelve, Andrews made her professional debut in a musical review on the London stage, and she continued to perform in England until she was brought to the United States at the age of nineteen to star in the American version of the British theatrical hit *The Boy Friend.* She followed that stage hit with *My Fair Lady* in both London and New York. There was a hue and cry when the movie version of the play was made and she was passed over for the role of Eliza Doolittle (Audrey Hepburn won the part), but Walt Disney offered her the title role in *Mary Poppins* (1964), and she had a sweet revenge when she won her Oscar.

Andrews' first dramatic film was *The Americanization of Emily* (1964), but she became a musical star of the first magnitude when she played Maria Von Trapp in *The Sound of Music* (1965), which became, at the time, the highest grossing film in movie history. Andrews was nominated for a second Oscar and her career soon reached new heights when she was voted "Star of the Year" (1966 and 1967) by the Theatre Owners of America.

Her films during the latter 1960s, however, were of mixed quality. *Hawaii* (1966) was a poor movie and a box office flop; *Torn Curtain* (1966) was a middling Hitchcock effort, but *Thoroughly Modern Millie* (1967) was a pleasant film and a modest success. *Star!* (1968), however, was a major box office disaster.

Andrews married her second husband, director Blake Edwards, in 1969 (her first husband was set designer Tony Walton), and he subsequently directed her in almost all of her later films, the first of which was *Darling Lili* (1970).

She appeared in only two films during the rest of the 1970s, but both were excellent efforts by Edwards: *The Tamarind Seed* (1974) and *10* (1979). Andrews had a supporting role in the latter film, a smash hit and received fine reviews. The director and star teamed again in 1981 to make a scathing comedy about Hollywood, *S.O.B.*, a controversial film that received mixed reviews and poor ticket sales. The film was the subject of much comment at the time, in any case, as Miss Andrews appeared topless in the film, doing her level best to create a sexier image.

Victor/Victoria (1982) was the film that really helped change the actress' image and it helped show off her flair for comedy. In the process she gained her third Best Actress Oscar nomination for her portrayal of a down-on-her-luck singer in 1935 Paris who pretends to be a man, pretending to be a woman, in order to make a living. The film, again directed by her husband, was a surprise critical and commercial success. Her movies since then have been less successful. *The Man Who Loved Women* (1983) passed virtually unnoticed; *That's Life* (1986) was another box office disappointment; and *Duet for One* (1987) was a critical success but a commercial failure, though it was notable for being the first film Andrews starred in with a director other than her husband since *Star!*.

In addition to her film career, Andrews has had much success on television, as a recording artist, and even as a children's book author (writing as Julie Andrews Edwards). Regardless of who directs her, one suspects that she will develop into a very successful character actress in her later years.
See also: Edwards, Blake

ANIMALS IN FILM Very early in the development of the commercial cinema, Hollywood discovered that audiences loved to see animals perform on film. Mack Sennett *(q.v.)*, for instance, used a cat (Pepper), a horse (Butterfly), and a dog (Teddy) in his stable of animal actors during the early silent era in support of his comic stars. For the most part, animals have traditionally played supporting roles to human actors, but a number of assorted animals have managed to ascend to a star status of their own.

Animals, of course, don't really act but are merely taught tricks that can be photographed in short takes and made to appear as if the animal knows what he or she is doing. Yet an animal that becomes a star for any length of time is almost always an amazing creature capable of responding to an enormous number of commands. In addition, such animals, just like their human counterparts, have an undefinable star quality—that certain something that the camera can pick up and that the mass audience can fully appreciate.

The lion may be king of the jungle, but the dog has been king of the animal movies. The first animal that had star billing was the German shepherd Strongheart (his real name was Etzel von Oeringen), who took America by storm in *The Silent Call* (1921). Strongheart's appeal, however, was short-lived as he was overtaken by the adventures of yet another German shepherd, Rin Tin Tin (his real name), who made his first appearance in *The Man From Hell's River* (1922). Not only was "Rinty" a star, he was Warner Bros'. greatest asset during the silent era, keeping the studio financially afloat until it introduced talkies in 1927.

Rin Tin Tin (Rinty II, actually) was still making movies when MGM made the words collie and Lassie almost synonymous. The film was *Lassie Come Home* (1943) and a new dog star was born. Lassie, whose real name was Pal and who wasn't a she but a he, made a number of films throughout the 1940s. When the dog's films lost their appeal on the big screen, he, like Rin

When animal actors are said to be "chewing the scenery," it's usually meant quite literally. Here, Rin-Tin-Tin hams it up with a lunchbox in his mouth. Photo courtesy of The Siegel Collection.

Tin Tin, began a new life on TV. In the 1970s, an attempt was made to resurrect Lassie's career in *The Magic of Lassie* (1978), a film in which he co-starred opposite Jimmy Stewart. This descendant of the original Pal received good reviews, but the movie was, well, a dog.

In more recent years, a new canine star has emerged. As only a supporting player by the name of Higgins for seven years on the TV series *Petticoat Junction,* the cute little mutt had his name changed to Benji and starred in the movie of the same name in 1974. His offspring have continued making the occasional successful film.

While dogs have enjoyed the lion's share of animal starring roles, they haven't had a monopoly. One of the most notable animal stars of the early 1950s was Francis the Talking Mule, who was introduced to movie audiences in *Francis* (1950). Of course, Francis didn't perform any tricks except move his lips, and Chill Wills supplied the voice, but there were plenty of Hollywood actors who didn't do very much more to earn their keep than Francis.

First cousin to Francis were the equine stars, such as Fury, Flicka, and the Black Stallion. But they, like other animal stars such as Flipper (a dolphin), Rhubarb (a cat), Clarence the Cross-Eyed Lion (in a 1965 film of the same name), and other dog stars such as Old Yeller, had short-lived movie careers.

Let us not forget, however, that in addition to the actual stars there was a whole menagerie of animals who became well-known supporting players. These animals are often as well remembered today as the human actors who were the stars of the films in which they appeared. For instance, there was Cheetah (the chimp) in the *Tarzan* movies, Clyde the orangutan in two of Clint Eastwood's films, *Every Which Way But Loose* (1978) and *Any Which Way You Can* (1980), Asta (the dog) in the *Thin Man* series, Pete (yet another dog) in the *Our Gang* comedies, Ben (a rat) in *Willard* (1971) and *Ben* (1972), and Bozo (not the clown, the bear), who co-starred in *The Life and Times of Grizzly Adams* (1974).

In westerns of the silent era and up into the 1950s, the hero's horse was also an important supporting player. For instance, how far would Ken Maynard *(q.v.)* have travelled without his horse, Tarzan? Or what would have become of Tom Mix without Tony? Gene Autry could sing, but he was just another yodeler without Champion. And Trigger was so important to Roy Rogers *(q.v.)* that rather than forget him, Rogers had him stuffed when he died.

It is an old superstition among performers that there is nothing worse than acting with either a child or an animal—the adult actor is invariably upstaged. It's no wonder, then, that humans will never give an animal a Best Actor Oscar. That's why the Patsy Awards were

established in 1951 to honor the best animal actors each year.
See also: Lassie; Patsy Award; Rin-Tin-Tin

ANIMATION The art of giving the illusion of motion to static drawings, objects, and puppets by photographing them in successive positions. In modern live-action motion pictures, twenty-four frames of film are exposed for each second of the action unfolding in front of the camera. But when making animated movies, filmmakers expose just one frame of film at a time, whereupon the drawing, object, or puppet it records is slightly changed for the next frame. While many kinds of animated films have been made, the technique has most often been centered on drawings.

Successful attempts to bring drawings to life were made during the 19th century, the most well known being the Zoetrope—a wheel with drawings that moved when the wheel was spun. But these were not animated films in the modern sense of the word. The first truly animated movie was made in 1906 by J. Stuart Blackton. It was a one-reeler called *Humorous Phases of Funny Faces,* and it immediately established the cartoon as a vehicle for comedy.

The first major American cartoon character to emerge out of the primitive beginnings of animation was, appropriately, a dinosaur. Winsor McCay created *Gertie the Dinosaur* in 1909 and went on to make the very first feature length animated film in the history of the movies in 1918, *The Sinking of the Lusitania.*

The 1920s was a popular era for animated short subjects. They were regularly shown between features in movie theaters all over the country and, as popular characters were created and sustained from one animated short to the next, more and more were devised in the hope of coming up with the next Coco the Clown, Felix the Cat, or Krazy Kat.

Such was the impetus behind the young Walt Disney, who arrived in Hollywood in 1923. He created a combination live-action and animated series called *Alice in Cartoonland,* then tried another character in *Oswald the Rabbit.* It wasn't until 1928 that Disney finally broke out of the pack with his new creation, Mickey Mouse. But even Mickey didn't fully catch on until Disney broke through the sound barrier in 1928 with *Steamboat Willie,* synchronizing the visuals with a bouncy musical soundtrack.

The combination of sound, music, and animation proved to be electric. Disney's *Silly Symphonies* capitalized on this discovery and virtually every other animation house belatedly tried to copy his success, the most notable example being the Warner Bros.' *Merrie Melodies* and *Looney Tunes.* While others such as Max Fleischer (creator of Popeye) made successful cartoons, in most respects, Disney essentially left his competition in the dust, moving forward with innovation after innovation, bringing three-color Technicolor to his animated shorts as early as 1933, inventing the multiplane camera for greater clarity, depth, and detail, and pushing forward to make ambitious, critically and commercially successful animated features as early as 1938 with the release of *Snow White and the Seven Dwarfs,* followed by *Pinnochio* (1940) and his belatedly appreciated masterpiece, *Fantasia* (1940), among many others.

Disney's success was nearly his undoing. The result of a bitter strike against his thriving company sent a brigade of top-flight animators loose who set up shop in competition with their old employer in 1943. The new firm, UPA (United Productions of America), went on to create characters such as Gerald McBoing Boing and Mr. Magoo. Because of limited resources, they developed a far more economical visual style that was exceedingly spare, but they made up for that with a more sophisticated, wittier content than the increasingly saccharine Disney product.

The rise of television, particularly Saturday morning television, sounded the death knell for animated short subjects. Cartoons were available in great quantities on TV and had necessarily less appeal to theater owners looking to fill their bills. Animated movies, however, made solely by Disney, held their own during the 1950s and 1960s but they became fewer and farther between.

Animation, at least for theatrical distribution, seemed like a dying art form until the Beatles made *Yellow Submarine* (1968), indicating for the first time that a feature-length animated movie need not be geared strictly to very young children. That lesson was taught yet again with a vengeance by Ralph Bakshi, who made the first X-rated animated feature, *Fritz the Cat* (1971). The film caused a storm of controversy but it's iconoclastic style, energy, and undeniable creativity made it a hit. Bakshi continued to make often angry, idiosyncratic animated features throughout the 1970s and early 1980s but even they became less popular over time with mass audiences. And once again, the animated feature seemed to slip into decline.

It was resurrected yet again, and with enormous box office success, during the mid- to late 1980s. After the modest success of producer Steven Spielberg's *An American Tale* (1986) Spielberg and Disney studios collaborated on *Who Framed Roger Rabbit?* (1988). This combined live-action and animated feature, made with the latest advances in computer animation, was a colossal hit both with critics and audiences. There has been a resurgence of interest in animated features, which has continued at a vertible breakneck pace with Disney's return to wholly animated films with *Oliver & Company* (1988), and with the Lucas/Spielberg production of the *The Land Before Time* (1988), a film about baby dinosaurs—a fitting reminder of *Gertie the Dinosaur* and animation's early days.
See also: Bakshi, Ralph; Disney, Walt; Warner Bros. cartoons

ANSWER PRINT Also known as a grading print or an approval print, it is the first complete print of a movie (usually including the sound mix) that is sent from the lab to the filmmaker for assessment of the printing results (i.e., the color values, the relative lightness or darkness of the images, etc.). It is then up to the filmmaker to "answer" the lab's assumed question of whether or not the print is ready to be duplicated or if corrections must be made. If changes are necessary, the lab will produce a second answer print. This process can sometimes generate up to four or five answer prints until the filmmaker is satisfied with the results, at which point the answer print is finally duplicated and the new copies become known as the release prints.

When the answer print is deemed acceptable, it is the standard of quality by which all future prints of the movie are judged.

ANTIHEROES Characters who in the process of fighting the bad guys are less than fully noble themselves, antiheroes share many of the characteristics of villains. They may be violent, break laws, treat women badly, etc., but they generally follow a code of conduct that leaves them on the side of the angels by the final fadeout. Despite (or perhaps, because of) the fact that the antihero is usually a cynical loner, there is something romantic about this movie figure; he's a seemingly hardened man, but while the villains and even the heroine cannot always see his vulnerability, the audience always does—and it takes him to its heart.

The antihero came into being at the very beginning of the *film noir* (*q.v.*) era in the early 1940s, and he was (and remains) best personified by Humphrey Bogart (*q.v.*). There were tough-guy heroes during the 1930s, but they weren't antiheroes. James Cagney, Clark Gable, etc. played their share of hard-edged protagonists, but it wasn't until Bogart played Sam Spade in *The Maltese Falcon* (1941) that the antihero was born.

Bogart continued playing antiheroes in films such as *Casablanca* (1942) and *To Have and Have Not* (1944), but as the 1940s progressed and the *film noir* became a movie staple, actors such as John Garfield and Alan Ladd (*qq.v.*) joined the antihero ranks.

The rise of the western in the 1950s slowed the antihero movement, but it didn't stop it. In fact, westerns were a breeding ground for future antiheroes, as several of the most interesting actor/villains of the 1950s became antihero stars in the 1960s and early 1970s, including Lee Marvin, James Coburn, and Charles Bronson. A great many antihero stars began their careers playing bad guys, but not all of them. Clint Eastwood, for instance, became a star as an antihero in Sergio Leone's spaghetti westerns and in the original *Dirty Harry* (1971), but he has since developed into a more conventional heroic star in the tradition of John Wayne.

The dividing line between heroes and antiheroes has

become blurred in recent years as the viewing public has grown more accepting of violent and lawless behavior on the big screen. As a consequence, stars such as Sylvester Stallone and Arnold Schwarzenegger *(qq.v.)* have some of the elements of the antihero, but they rarely elicit the vulnerability that is part and parcel of the antihero's makeup.

ANTIWAR FILMS It comes as no surprise that there are far more films glorifying war than there are films condemning it. The big surprise, though, is that most antiwar films have been extremely successful at the box office.

In 1925, director King Vidor *(q.v.)* made *The Big Parade,* a shocking new kind of film: the realistic war drama. For the first time in Hollywood history, audiences were presented a fairly authentic view of men at war. For American audiences, an ocean away from World War I's bloody trenches, the movie was a revelation. The film's tenor was decidedly antiwar; it highlighted the terrible pain, agony, and waste of "the war to end all wars." But rather than being repelled by the subject matter, audiences flocked to see the film. *The Big Parade* played in a first-run Broadway movie theater for ninety-six consecutive weeks, a record that remained unbroken for nearly twenty-five years. The film took in roughly $15 million and assured MGM's financial stability.

Several other popular antiwar films followed, including Raoul Walsh's *(q.v.) What Price Glory?* (1926). But there wasn't another film to match the impact of *The Big Parade* until Lewis Milestone *(q.v.)* made the film version of Erich Maria Remarque's novel, *All Quiet on the Western Front* (1930). The graphic battle scenes are so striking that even today, one is compelled to turn away from the screen in horror. The film was both an indictment of war and a box office success.

The antiwar movie virtually disappeared during the later 1930s as Hitler's Germany became an increasing threat to freedom. And when America finally entered World War II in 1941, the antiwar film was a genre of the distant past.

It was only after the conflagration ended that Hollywood took stock of the human cost of war. William Wyler's *(q.v.)* Academy Award winning 1946 film, *The Best Years of Our Lives,* was a thoughtful, realistic story of three veterans who return home exhausted, confused, and in one case, crippled. There are no battles in the movie, except for those fought in the souls of the survivors as they readjust to a changed world. The movie is about people, not politics, and is powerful and somber.

World War II had been a popular, justifiable war and in the cold war with Russia that quickly developed in the later 1940s, antiwar attitudes were equated with being "soft" on communism. The only way to make an antiwar film in that charged atmosphere was to set it in the past. And that's exactly what director Stanley Kubrick *(q.v.)* did. In the only significant antiwar film of its time, Kubrick's *Paths of Glory* (1957) reached back to World War I in order to expose the insanity of warfare.

Thirty years later, Kubrick created yet another antiwar masterpiece, *Full Metal Jacket* (1987). But he was neither alone nor first in using the Vietnam War as a backdrop for his themes. *Coming Home* (1978), *Apocalypse Now* (1979), and *Platoon* (1986) successfully tackled the Vietnam experience—and all of them were commercial hits.

The popularity of many antiwar films, however, has always been subject to criticism. It is often said that antiwar films that make their point through action and adventure also tend to glorify war and ennoble it; the violence inherent in battle scenes may be what draws large audiences, not the underlying antiwar message. But it's worth noting that what draws a moviegoer to the theater may not necessarily be the same element that he or she remembers when the film is over.
See also: war films

ARBUCKLE, ROSCOE "FATTY" (1887–1933) This genial, overweight clown rose to fame during the golden era of Mack Sennett's Keystone Studios (1912–15), and his popularity remained constant until his career and life were shattered by the famous Virginia Rappe rape case in 1921.

Arbuckle was more than simply a fat man mugging for the camera. He was a seasoned vaudevillian with remarkable physical dexterity. He had tremendous running speed (he reportedly outran a matador in Tijuana) and the toughness of a bull (he was famous for taking extraordinary falls for the sake of a gag). The contrast between his immense size and his nimbleness, coupled with his baby face, elicited laughter from his silent film audience.

Arbuckle was originally one of the Keystone Kops, but he emerged out of anonymity to become one of Mack Sennett's biggest stars along with Mabel Normand, Ford Sterling, and (later) Charlie Chaplin *(qq.v.)*.

There was nothing sophisticated about Arbuckle's films. He was satisfied to churn out crude, low-budget two-reelers. And this remained true even after he left Sennett to form his own company, Comique Studios, in 1917. It wasn't until 1920 that he began making feature-length comedies.

He never had the opportunity to grow any further as a comedian and filmmaker. At a Labor Day party, a young woman named Virginia Rappe took ill and died. Arbuckle was accused of rape and manslaughter. The scandal rocked Hollywood and destroyed Arbuckle's career, despite the fact that (after three trials) Arbuckle was acquitted of all charges.

The audience could no longer envision Fatty Arbuckle as a jovial, simple man. Despite his innocence, the

Comic star Roscoe "Fatty" Arbuckle was one of the tragic figures of the silent era. Though cleared of criminal wrong-doing in a famous rape/murder trial, his image was so tarnished that he could no longer find work in Hollywood. Photo courtesy of Movie Star News.

rape case followed him everywhere. His films were pulled from theaters, and many were subsequently lost. He tried a comeback on Broadway but it failed. Later, under the name of William B. Goodrich (a pun—"Will B. Good"), he directed several films of no special note.

Whatever the relative merits of his own films Arbuckle made some valuable contributions to movie comedy. His pants were borrowed by Charlie Chaplin to help create the legendary character of the tramp. And it was Arbuckle who gave Buster Keaton his start in films in 1917. Not least among his accomplishments, Fatty Arbuckle was the very first person on film to be struck in the face with a custard pie. Mabel Normand tossed it in *A Noise From the Deep* (1913).

See also: comedy teams; custard pie; Keaton, Buster; Sennett, Mack

ARKIN, ALAN (1934–   ) Essentially a character actor *(q.v.)* who is cast in lead roles, Arkin generally gets the type of thankless parts that an average star would shirk for being far too uncommercial. As a result, Arkin's roles have often been meaty and complicated, although not always terribly career-boosting.

Born in Brooklyn, New York, Arkin had to go to Chicago to break into show business, gaining attention as a member of the celebrated improvisational revue, Second City. Not long after, he went to Broadway in the stage version of Carl Reiner's *(q.v.)* Enter Laughing, winning a Tony Award for his work.

In his film debut, he joined Carl Reiner on screen in *The Russians Are Coming, The Russians Are Coming* (1966), playing a confused Soviet submariner. His performance brought him the first of his two Oscar nominations. He was nominated again for his dramatic portrayal of a deaf mute in *The Heart Is a Lonely Hunter* (1968), and this time he won the Oscar.

Dark, short, with expressive eyes, Arkin has been cast in a wide variety of roles that have taken advantage of both his malleable physiognimy and his actor's versatility. For instance, he was chilling as the villain in *Wait Until Dark* (1967), warm and vulnerable as the Latin father in *Popi* (1969), wonderfully paranoid as Yossarian in *Catch 22* (1970), comically pathetic in *The Last of the Red Hot Lovers* (1972), loud and bombastic in *Freebie and the Bean* (1974), comically manic in *Th*

Alan Arkin is a gifted actor capable of playing a wide range of roles. Equally adept at comedy or drama, he is also a musician of note. Photo courtesy of Rick Ingersoll.

In-Laws (1979), and believably graspy and ambitious in *Joshua Then and Now* (1985).

Arkin's directorial talent is less well known than his obvious acting skills. He began directing on Off-Broadway with *Eh?,* which introduced Dustin Hoffman *(q.v.).* Among other stage productions, he directed Neil Simon's *The Sunshine Boys* and won an Obie for Jules Feiffer's *Little Murders,* also directing and starring in the latter when it was turned into a movie in 1971. Other film director credits include *Fire Sale* (1977), a truly dark black comedy that he starred in as well, and two shorts that he also wrote, *T.G.I.F.* and *People Soup,* the latter receiving an Oscar nomination for Best Short Subject.

A multitalented individual, Arkin is also an author, a songwriter, and has been a musical performer with a folk group, The Tarriers. He plays the guitar and flute, not to mention the nose whistle.

In recent years, Arkin has been appearing more often in television movies, most notably in "Escape from Sobibor" (1987), for which he was nominated for an Emmy.

ARLEN, HAROLD (1905–) A longtime composer of film scores, Arlen has written the music (and sometimes the lyrics) for a great many memorable Hollywood hits. Best known for his evocative ballads as well as a number of up-tempo tunes, Arlen's music has clearly been influenced by the blues.

Born Hyman Arluck in Buffalo, New York, he was the son of a cantor; and like the Al Jolson *(q.v.)* character in the *Jazz Singer,* he was drawn to popular music. Arlen hit the road as a pianist in a small band when he was just fifteen, but he didn't get his big break until many years later when he wrote "Get Happy," which was performed in the 1928 *9:15 Revue* on Broadway.

Arlen continued to write nightclub revues and music for Broadway shows, but with the coming of sound and the rise of the Hollywood musical, composers were much in demand on the West Coast—and off he went. Among the popular songs Arlen first introduced in the movies were "Let's Fall in Love," "That Old Black Magic," "One For My Baby," "Accentuate the Positive," and "Lydia, the Tattooed Lady." He also wrote "Stormy Weather," and "It's Only a Paper Moon."

His songs were sometimes more memorable than the films in which they appeared, but not always. His music was featured in *Star Spangled Rhythm* (1942), *Cabin in the Sky* (1943), and *A Star is Born* (1954). But his most famous score of all was for *The Wizard of Oz* (1939), for which he won a Best Song Oscar for "Over the Rainbow."

He worked steadily right through to the mid-1960s with scores for films such as *Gay Purr-ee* (1962), *I Could Go on Singing* (1963), and his last movie, *The Swinger* (1966).

ARLISS, GEORGE (1868–1946) A film actor of stature if not skill, Arliss was known in the early 1930s as "The First Gentleman of the Screen." Already well into middle-age when he suddenly and unexpectedly became a movie star, Arliss specialized in playing historical figures, most of whom he had already portrayed on the stage, where he originally established his reputation.

Born George Augustus Andrews in London, the young man worked for his father in a printing shop before embarking on a career in the theater. He achieved some minor success on the English stage but blossomed in America after his arrival there in 1901. He would ultimately stay in the United States for the better part of thirty-five years.

His first starring role on Broadway was in *The Devil* in 1908, but he really made his mark playing the great English prime minister in *Disraeli* in 1911. He flourished on the stage during the next fifteen years and eventually he agreed to recreate his theater triumphs in silent films. He made *The Devil* (1921), *Disraeli* (1921), and *The Green Goddess* (1923), then went on to make several original silent films such as *The Man Who Played God* (1922) and *Twenty Dollars a Week* (1924). His silent films, however, were not major successes.

It wasn't until Warner Bros. *(q.v.)* broke the sound barrier that Arliss shot to the top of the movie business. He was signed, in fact, by Warners to once again recreate his stage success in a sound film version of *Disraeli* (1929). The movie was a huge critical and box office hit, winning Arliss a Best Actor Oscar and a reputation as one of Hollywood's class actors. He followed *Disraeli* with *Alexander Hamilton* (1931) and *Voltaire* (1933), establishing Warners' first cycle of movie biographies. Eventually, Arliss gave way to Paul Muni *(q.v.),* who continued the biopic *(q.v.)* cycle in the mid-to-late 1930s.

Both his early biographical films and other movies were consistent moneymakers, which accounted for Arliss' whopping salary of $10,000 per week, making him one of the highest paid actors in Hollywood. But Arliss, who was a balding, thin-faced, severe looking man with a commanding presence, continued to play famous historical figures even after the critics and the public had begun to catch on to his relentlessly similar portrayals of various characters. He played two roles in *The House of Rothschild* (1934) and he was the title character in *Cardinal Richelieu* (1935), but by this time his stiff, overblown theater acting style seemed hopelessly old-fashioned compared to the work of so many other actors who were quickly learning how to use the film medium to their best advantage. Arliss' career had begun its inevitable slide.

Over the next few years he made several unsuccessful films in England. His last movie was *Dr. Syn* (1937). He retired from the screen when his wife, actress Florence Montgomery (who had appeared in a few of his films), became blind.

ART DIRECTOR The individual responsible for the physical look of the film is known as the art director, although the title "production designer" has come into vogue more recently. Regardless of the title, the job continues to call for someone with an aesthetic sense who is a master of many areas, including architecture, design, and clothing.

After reading the script, the art director must create the right atmosphere for each individual scene (whether shot indoors or out). And having conceived a "look" for each set of each scene, he will call upon the set designer to turn his vision into a physical reality. When the sets are built, the art director will then oversee the work of the set decorator, who dresses the set with appropriate furnishings. The art director oversees the costume designer's work, as well.

An art director's work is usually more apparent in period pieces where sets and costumes tend to stand out. Nonetheless, his or her work is essential to the integrity of any film.

Numbered among Hollywood's most famous art directors are Cedric Gibbons, *(q.v.)* principally of MGM, who won eleven Academy Awards in a career that spanned forty-five years, and William Cameron Menzies, *(q.v.)* who created (among many others) the look of the 1924 Douglas Fairbanks epic, *The Thief of Baghdad,* and the futuristic world of *Things to Come* (1936). *See also:* costume designer; set decorator; set designer

ARTHUR, JEAN (1905–   ) She was a husky-voiced actress who came into her own as a comedienne, playing tough, yet vulnerable, middle-class working girls. Never a great beauty by Hollywood standards, Miss Arthur was uncommonly likeable, and sexy in an unthreatening way. Even more uncommon, however, was her slow rise to stardom. Actresses generally catch on rather quickly if they're going to be stars at all but, like Myrna Loy *(q.v.)*, Jean Arthur was one of those rare exceptions who knocked around Hollywood for a dozen years before lightning finally struck.

Born Gladys Georgianna Greene to a New York photographer, the young and attractive teenager had no trouble finding work as a photographer's model. When one of her pictures was seen by a Fox representative, she found herself at the age of eighteen with a one-year contract and a chance at stardom. Despite her total lack of acting experience, she was handed an important supporting role in John Ford's *Cameo Kirby* (1923). The movie did well, but Arthur didn't. She played out the rest of her contract in minor roles in even more minor movies.

Much like the resilient, resourceful character she would play in the latter 1930s and early 1940s, Miss Arthur didn't give up. She continued acting throughout the silent era in poverty row studio films, rarely attaining leading roles. But when she did have an important part in *The Poor Nut* (1927), Paramount saw something in her and signed her to a contract.

Unfortunately, Paramount didn't have much success with her either. While her husky voice worked well in talkies, no one knew quite how to use her to best effect. She played ingenues in films like *Warming Up* (1928) and killers in movies such as *The Greene Murder Case* (1929); she was just plain decorative in movies such as *Paramount on Parade* (1930). Arthur did appear in a few comedies during this period but a combination of poor material and a lack of acting skill kept her from breaking through.

After a heavy workload that took her through 1931, Miss Arthur left Hollywood. Eight years of performing for the camera had taught her very little about her craft; she decided it was time to learn how to act. She spent almost three years working on Broadway and in stock companies, getting the experience she so sorely needed.

Her return to Hollywood in *Get That Venus* (1933), another low-budget production, might have discouraged another actress but Arthur kept on trying. An important break came in 1934 when she gave a solid supporting performance in a hit Columbia film called *Whirlpool*. Harry Cohn *(q.v.)* signed her to a long-term contract and promptly put her in two stinkers. Finally, after appearing in a total of fifty-four films over a twelve-year period, she found herself again working for John Ford, who promptly turned her into a star in his popular Columbia comedy *The Whole Town's Talking* (1935).

The most significant thing about her breakthrough film was that it firmly established her persona as a wisecracking, cynical woman who would usually start out taking advantage of an idealist, eventually fall in love with him, and then use her worldly knowledge to help him beat the bad guys by the end of the picture. She reached the height of her career in that kind of role, starring in films such as Frank Capra's two classics, *Mr. Deeds Goes to Town* (1936) and *Mr. Smith Goes to Washington* (1939). But these were hardly her only standouts in the second half of the 1930s. She was outstanding in movies such as *Public Hero Number One* (1935), *Diamond Jim* (1935), and *The Ex-Mrs. Bradford* (1936).

Like so many actors, Jean Arthur attained her everlasting star status by working with some of Hollywood's best directors. For instance, she starred in Frank Borzage's *History Is Made at Night* (1937), the Mitchell Leisen–directed and Preston Sturges–*(q.v.)* scripted comedy, *Easy Living* (1937) and Frank Capra's 1938 Oscar-winning Best Picture of the Year, *You Can't Take It With You*. She topped off the decade with an affecting performance in Howard Hawks' *(q.v.)* classic, *Only Angels Have Wings* (1939).

A good many of her best films, except for the Capra

vehicles, were made when she was on loan from Columbia. The studio simply had trouble finding good projects for her; her typical Columbia films were mediocre, at best.

Nonetheless, Arthur's career steamed ahead into the early 1940s with her portrayals of working class comic heroines. She added George Stevens *(q.v.)* to her list of first-class directors with whom she had worked when she starred in two of his finer efforts, *The Talk of the Town* (1942) and *The More the Merrier* (1943), for which she received a Best Actress Oscar nomination for the first and last time.

Arthur had feuded with Harry Cohn over her poor Columbia material throughout the length of her contract. And when she was finally free of Columbia in 1944, she walked away from her film career even though she was still big box office. She had often talked about retirement and it appeared as if she really meant it.

She made only two more movies, both of them hits. Miss Arthur starred in Billy Wilder's *A Foreign Affair* (1948) and then came back to Hollywood one last time to work with her old friend George Stevens in perhaps his greatest film, *Shane* (1953).

After a major success on Broadway as *Peter Pan* in 1950, she was little heard from. There were a few flings with the theater in later years, and then an unexpected guest-starring role on an episode of TV's "Gunsmoke." The experience led her to sign on to star in a short-lived TV series, "The Jean Arthur Show" (1966), in which she played a lawyer.

Though generally she has been out of the limelight since the early 1950s, Miss Arthur hasn't been entirely silent. She has spent a good deal of her retirement years as a teacher, sharing her acting knowledge with students at several colleges.

ARZNER, DOROTHY (1900–1979)   Arzner served her apprenticeship in Hollywood during the silent era as a film editor. Soon after the talkies arrived, Arzner gave up her job as an editor and took the plunge into directing, ultimately becoming the only female director in Hollywood during the 1930s.

Her first feature film, *The Wild Party,* was released in 1929. Before she retired from directing in 1943, Arzner had made a total of thirteen films. Among her more well-known movies were *Christopher Strong* (1933), *Nana* (1934), and, perhaps her most highly regarded film, *Craig's Wife* (1936).

After Arzner, there were no other female directors in Hollywood until actress Ida Lupino *(q.v.)* went behind the camera in 1949. Though she was no longer a director herself, Dorothy Arzner continued to have considerable influence on the future of Hollywood films. She taught directing at UCLA and, in the early 1960s, took a young student named Francis Ford Coppola

(q.v.) under her wing, encouraging his directorial ambitions.

See also: women directors

ASHBY, HAL (1936–1988)   A former editor turned director, Ashby shot to prominence in the 1970s only to fall swiftly out of favor both commercially and critically in the 1980s. In the earlier decade he distinguished himself as a director of sharp satires who was able to express his comedy in human terms. His dramatic films displayed a profound understanding and acceptance of the flaws in ordinary (and extraordinary) people. By contrast, his 1980s films seemed almost as if they were made by another director; the comedies generally skimmed the surface of their subjects, either offering sentimentality or a hard-edged humor that failed to amuse. His dramas were flat and uninspired.

Ashby came up quickly through the Hollywood editing ranks during the 1960s, first as an assistant editor and later as the editor of such films as *The Russians Are Coming, The Russians Are Coming* (1966) and *In the Heat of the Night* (1967), for which he won a Best Editing Oscar. Anxious to get out of the editing room, he used his Academy Award as a springboard to become an associate producer, working for Norman Jewison in the late 1960s, most notably on *The Thomas Crown Affair* (1968).

Ashby's first two directorial opportunities were low-budget comedies, *The Landlord* (1970) and *Harold and Maude* (1971), that both gained cult followings. His next film, *The Last Detail* (1973), had a name star in Jack Nicholson *(q.v.)*. It received a great deal of attention due to its salty language, and it was generally well received by critics.

His subsequent direction of Warren Beatty *(q.v.)* in the rollicking comedy/satire *Shampoo* (1975) brought Ashby his first major blockbuster hit. It was followed by the much admired, if little seen, biopic *(q.v.)* of Woody Guthrie, *Bound for Glory* (1976). His next two films brought Ashby to the peak of his career. He won an Oscar nomination for his direction of the antiwar movie, *Coming Home* (1978), and then made *Being There* (1979), the devastatingly incisive satire with Peter Sellers.

It was all downhill after that. He had shot a film called *The Hampster of Happiness* in the late 1970s that was so bad that it was held up two years before its eventual release as *Second Hand Hearts* (1981). Another disaster, *Lookin' To Get Out* (1982) followed; it was also delayed two years before its eventual release date. He made a concert documentary of the Rolling Stones called *Let's Spend the Night Together* (1983) but it was only a detour before he made two more flops, one of the relatively few Neil Simon strikeouts, *The Slugger's Wife* (1985), and a dead-tired thriller, *Eight Million Ways to Die* (1986).

ASSISTANT DIRECTOR   This job is also known as first assistant director, usually referred to as first A.D. The bigger the production, the more likely there will be a second A.D.

The assistant director's job is not to direct the film in the director's absence, nor to direct minor scenes or second unit action. Instead, the first A.D. performs the script breakdown *(q.v.)* before shooting begins to determine the order in which the individual scenes of the movie will be shot. Usually, the first A.D. also determines how many extras will be needed and handles their hiring.

Once the film is in production, the first A.D. works closely with the director, keeping the set organized so that people and machinery move smoothly from scene to scene. It's fair to say that the first A.D.'s job is more managerial than creative.

ASSOCIATE PRODUCER   Many films list an associate producer among their credits, but the actual job often varies widely from film to film. Most often, the associate producer works as the producer's *(q.v.)* assistant. If the producer isn't on the set while the film is shooting, the production manager will usually fulfill many of the producer's business functions and, therefore, is sometimes given the title of associate producer.

In recent years, with the fragmentation of the movie business into many small, independent production companies, the title of associate producer is often given to an individual who helped bankroll the film, or sometimes to the person who had an option on the script or book on which the movie is based.

ASTAIRE, FRED (1899–1987)   The peerless dancer, singer, actor who was the epitome of grace and style in many of the greatest movie musicals to ever come out of Hollywood.

Born Frederick Austerlitz, Fred Astaire and his sister, Adele, became a Broadway dancing team sensation in the 1920s, starring in such hit shows as *Funny Face* and *The Band Wagon* (both of them serving loosely as the basis of later Astaire movies). After Adele left the act in the early 1930s to marry a titled Englishman, Lord Charles Cavendish, Fred was on his own.

He starred in one more Broadway show, *The Gay Divorce* (also later adapted into a movie), and then decided to try his luck in Hollywood. He made a screen test, and the resulting comment made by an anonymous Goldwyn studio executive has been oft-repeated: "Can't act, can't sing, can dance a little."

History, of course, has proven that Astaire could act with an effortless charm. As a singer, he introduced more hit songs than any other movie star in history. And as for his dancing, he is the only Hollywood entertainer to have become a legend within the first five years of his film career.

Fred Astaire, seen here in a tribute to Bill "Bojangles" Robinson, was the classiest dancer in Hollywood history. Graceful and sophisticated, yet eminently warm, Astaire danced with his entire body, not just his feet. Photo courtesy of Movie Star News.

Goldwyn signed Astaire but let him go after just a few months. RKO, in deep financial trouble, took a chance and signed him up, hoping that his Broadway reputation would bring people into theaters in what was the worst year (1933) of the Great Depression. They planned to make him the second male lead in *Flying Down to Rio,* teaming him with Ginger Rogers *(q.v.)*. But before that film was ready to be shot, they loaned him to MGM, where he played himself in a Joan Crawford *(q.v.)* movie, *Dancing Lady* (1933). Both films did well, especially *Flying Down to Rio* (1933), and RKO teamed Astaire with Rogers again in *The Gay Divorcee* (1934). And this time they were the leads. The film was based on Astaire's last Broadway show, the title subtly changed because RKO studio executives thought the original title too suggestive.

The team of Astaire and Rogers played together for a total of ten films over a period of seventeen years. It was one of the most successful pairings in show business history. While Ginger Rogers wasn't as talented a dancer as Astaire, their chemistry was undeniable; as Katharine Hepburn *(q.v.)* once said, she gave him sex appeal, and he gave her class. All of their movies together are a delight, but the two best are certainly *Top Hat* (1935) and *Swing Time* (1936).

At the height of their popularity, both Astaire and Rogers were earning $150,000 per picture. It was money well spent by RKO, and the Astaire-Rogers films saved the studio from bankruptcy.

In the early 1940s, Astaire left RKO and made a series of musicals, the best of which were *You'll Never Get Rich* (1941) and *You Were Never Lovelier* (1942), both with Rita Hayworth *(q.v.)*. He also made *Holiday Inn* (1942) with Bing Crosby *(q.v.)*. All of these films were critically and commercially successful. But after *The Sky's the Limit* (1943) bombed, Astaire suddenly found himself without any offers of work. There were whispers that Astaire, forty-four years old, was getting a bit long in the tooth for a dancer.

Arthur Freed *(q.v.)*, the great movie musical impressario at MGM, believed in Astaire and showcased him in Vincente Minnelli's *(q.v.)* *Ziegfeld Follies* (1944), in which Astaire performed four magnificent numbers, including a comic dance with Gene Kelly *(q.v.)*. (Whenever asked who his favorite dancing partner had been throughout his long, illustrious career, rather than embarrassing any of his female costars, Astaire would always pick Kelly.)

Astaire's career picked up, especially when he joined with Bing Crosby again in *Blue Skies* (1946). After this hit movie, he announced his retirement; he wanted to quit while he was still on top.

His retirement lasted two years, until Gene Kelly broke his ankle just before filming was to begin on *Easter Parade* (1948). MGM asked Astaire to step in, and Astaire was delighted to help out, thoroughly enjoying the chance to work with Judy Garland *(q.v.)*. The movie was a huge success, and he and Garland were scheduled to follow it up together in *The Barkley's of Broadway* (1949). This time, it was Garland who fell ill, and a replacement was needed. The delightful surprise choice was Ginger Rogers. The reteaming of this famous pair (in what would be the last movie they would make together) helped turn the movie into a major hit.

In 1949, Astaire was honored with a special Oscar for "raising the standard" of movie musicals. Strangely, he had never won—nor even been nominated for—an Academy Award during the 1930s and 1940s.

In the early 1950s, Astaire made two classic musicals, *Royal Wedding* (1951), in which he performed the famous dancing on the ceiling number, and *The Band Wagon* (1953), along with Gene Kelly's *Singin' in the Rain* (1952), among the greatest musicals ever made.

Daddy Long Legs (1955), *Funny Face* (1956), and *Silk Stockings* (1957), the last a musical version of *Ninotchka*, brought Astaire to the seeming end of his dancing career. The word in Hollywood was that the musical was out of fashion.

Astaire kept on working, taking dramatic parts—always in supporting roles—in films such as *On the Beach* (1959) and *The Midas Run* (1969). He was nominated for a Best Supporting Actor Oscar for his performance in *The Towering Inferno* (1974). During these years, he also appeared in comedies, such as *The Pleasure of His Company* (1961) and *The Notorious Landlady* (1962).

But Astaire was fated to dance again. He was cast in the movie musical version of *Finian's Rainbow* (1968), directed by newcomer Francis Ford Coppola *(q.v.)*. The movie died at the box office, but Astaire was as charming and graceful as ever.

Except for his famous TV specials in the 1950s, and his filmic hosting of *That's Entertainment Part I* (1974) and *That's Entertainment Part II* (1976), and an occasional appearance on TV series, Astaire remained in semiretirement until his death in 1987.

See also: The Band Wagon; choreography; musicals; RKO; screen teams

ASTOR, MARY (1906–1988) Though best known as the conniving killer in *The Maltese Falcon* (1941), the actress had a long and tempestuous career that began in the silent era and lasted until the mid-1960s. Astor was best at playing hard-hearted double-crossers but later made a career of playing sweet old mothers; her versatility was admirable. For the most part, she worked as a featured player, commanding attention in strong supporting roles, consciously choosing to remain a working actress rather than trying to become a superstar—a decision that probably accounts for her longevity.

Born Lucille Vasconcellos Langhanke, she was the daughter of two schoolteachers. Contrary to the usual stereotype of the stage mother who pushes her daughter into show business, Astor had a stage father. He was sure he could turn his pretty young child into a movie star. And he was right.

Despite a failed screen test for D. W. Griffith, her father helped her find her way into the movies with a bit part in *Sentimental Tommy* (1921). Her career progressed slowly until John Barrymore insisted that she be his leading lady in *Beau Brummel* (1924). Astor and Barrymore became lovers (without any help from Mr. Langhanke), and the actress became a burgeoning star.

She played opposite Barrymore again in *Don Juan* (1926), but she also appeared on the silent screen with a number of other major stars, including Douglas Fairbanks *(q.v.)* in *Don Q, Son of Zorro* (1925) and George Bancroft and Charles Farrell in *The Rough Riders* (1927).

With her beauty and poise, she seemed destined for a great career in the cinema.

But then came sound, and Astor, inexplicably, did poorly in a talkie screen test. Convinced she didn't have a future in Hollywood, no studio offered her a job until she had a hit in a Los Angeles area stage show for which she received excellent reviews. Suddenly, she was in demand again.

Astor worked steadily during the early and mid-1930s in a host of films for several different studios. The best of the lot was *Red Dust* (1932), in which she played opposite Clark Gable and Jean Harlow *(qq.v.),* and *The Kennel Murder Case* (1933) with William Powell *(q.v.).* In many of her other films during this period, she was either a featured player or a lead in "B" movies—until 1936 when she was involved in a nasty child custody case with her second husband. Information from her personal diary, leaked to the press by her husband's attorney, detailed a wild sex life (her descriptions of the sexual prowess of playwright George S. Kaufman made for particularly tantalizing reading).

The scandal was front-page news throughout the world, and it might have destroyed her career had she not already finished playing a major role in *Dodsworth* (1936), a critical and box office hit. She followed that with two more winners in quick succession: *The Prisoner of Zenda* (1937) and *The Hurricane* (1937). During the latter years of the decade she had begun building her reputation for playing two-faced characters in films such as *Woman Against Woman* (1938), *Midnight* (1939), and her Oscar-winning Best Supporting Actress performance opposite Bette Davis *(q.v.)* in *The Great Lie* (1941). But Astor later wrote in one of her autobiographies, *A Life on Film,* that she wished she had won the award that year for playing Brigid O'Shaughnessy in *The Maltese Falcon,* the role of a lying, murderous woman who uses sex to get her way.

Though she appeared to be typecast as a schemer and a liar, Astor surprised audiences and critics alike with her charming comic performance in Preston Sturges' *(q.v.)* masterful farce, *Palm Beach Story* (1942), after which she soon found herself switching into saccharine matronly roles in films such as *Meet Me in St. Louis* (1944), *Claudia and David* (1946), *Cass Timberlane* (1947), and *Little Women* (1949). She did, however, finally get an opportunity to show her feisty personality in *Act of Violence* (1949), in which she played an aging tart.

Tired of the otherwise insipid roles she was given, Astor begged out of her contract at MGM and the studio obliged. Except for occasional TV shows during the 1950s and a relative handful of minor film roles, Astor's career was winding down. She had a last hurrah during the early 1960s when she gave a strong performance in *Return to Peyton Place* (1961). Thanks to her good reviews, she had a small flurry of interesting, meaty parts in films such as *Youngblood Hawke* (1964)

and *Hush . . . Hush . . . Sweet Charlotte* (1965). But in the later 1960s, with the success of two volumes of memoirs and several novels, she finally retired from the screen.

See also: The Maltese Falcon; scandals

AUTEUR A French term applied to certain film directors, indicating that they are truly "authors" with a distinctive artistic vision, the primary creative force of a motion picture.

The auteur theory, as it has come to be known, was espoused in the 1950s by French film theorist and critic André Bazin, then popularized by his disciples François Truffaut and Jean-Luc Godard. In America, the cause was taken up by film critics Andrew Sarris and Manny Farber.

This combined French and American revolution in the way Hollywood movies were seen and understood helped to elevate the role of the director in the public's eye and, at the same time, opened our eyes to the work of dozens of older Hollywood directors who might have otherwise been wrongly neglected.

Commercial filmmakers who had generally treated their work as a craft rather than an art suddenly found their movies studied in universities all over the world. Howard Hawks, George Cukor, Samuel Fuller, Anthony Mann, Nicholas Ray, and Raoul Walsh *(qq.v.),* to name just a few, were directors who had never been taken seriously by the critical establishment until the advent of the auteur theory.

AUTRY, GENE: (1907–) Orvon "Gene" Autry became a Hollywood "B" movie institution as a singing cowboy. He wasn't the first cowboy to sing on film (Ken Maynard *[q.v.]* holds that distinction), but Autry was the first actor in westerns to achieve stardom on the basis of his musical talents.

After growing up in Texas, Autry's family moved to Oklahoma. It was there that he eventually became a telegraph operator, earning $150 per month. Legend has it that Autry was singing and playing his guitar in the telegraph office to pass the time when a stranger came in to send a message. Hearing the young man, the stranger said, "I think you have something. Work hard at it, and you may get somewhere." That stranger was Will Rogers.

Autry's first success in show business was as "Oklahoma's Yodeling Cowboy" on KVOO radio in Tulsa. His first hit record was "That Silver-Haired Daddy of Mine" in 1930. His radio and record career continued to grow during the early thirties. And like other radio stars such as Jack Benny and Bob Hope, the movies soon beckoned.

The timing could not have been better for Gene Autry's Hollywood debut. Silent stars such as Hoot Gibson and Ken Maynard were well past their prime.

1) A cowboy never takes unfair advantage—even of an enemy.

2) A cowboy never betrays a trust.

3) A cowboy always tells the truth.

4) A cowboy is kind to small children, to old folks, and to animals.

5) A cowboy is free from racial and religious prejudices.

6) A cowboy is helpful and when anyone is in trouble he lends a hand.

7) A cowboy is a good worker.

8) A cowboy is clean about his person and in thought, word, and deed.

9) A cowboy respects womanhood, his parents, and the laws of his country.

10) A cowboy is a patriot.

Gene Autry retired from performing but not from show business. He bought TV and radio stations, as well as the California Angels baseball team. As of this writing, he is still alive and well, and still remembered as Hollywood's quintessential singing cowboy.

AYKROYD, DAN (1954–) A writer and chameleon-like comic actor who has proven to be among the most versatile and talented of all the many "Saturday Night Live" TV alumni who have ventured into the movies. He has not, however, been the most popular of his fellow comic actors, in part because he has not developed á specific comic persona. An intelligent performer, Aykroyd has successfully played everything from good-natured goofballs to hardnosed idiots, with several innocent Danny Kaye types in between. He has also coauthored the scripts for three of Hollywood's biggest comedy hits, exhibiting the underlying depth of his comic sensibility.

Born in Canada, Aykroyd honed his comic talents as a member of Chicago's famous Second City improvisational comedy group. His big break came when he was hired as an original cast member of TV's "Saturday Night Live," on which he and fellow cast member John Belushi introduced the characters of the Blues Brothers. The routine started out as a hip, comic singing act, but the idea caught on and the team began performing as Elwood and Jake Blues at sold-out concerts across the country, eventually leading them to star in the classic movie comedy *The Blues Brothers* (1980), which Aykroyd co-scripted. It was Hollywood's first truly big budget comedy, costing $30 million to produce and, miraculously, it still turned a profit.

The Blues Brothers, however, was not Aykroyd's movie debut. He had appeared earlier in the little-known Canadian movie, *Love at First Sight* (1977), and in a small role in Steven Spielberg's mega-bomb, *1941* (1979). But with the success of *The Blues Brothers,* Aykroyd's career was truly launched and it was followed by splen-

Gene Autry might not have been the first singing cowboy, but he was certainly the most successful. Send him off with his horse, Champion, a guitar, and the most threadbare of plots, and Autry would return with a money-making movie. Photo courtesy of Gene Autry.

The western genre had become repetitive and tired. Something—and someone—new was needed.

The idea of presenting a singing cowboy to the public was attractive for two reasons. The popularity of country and western music on radio and in the record stores had suggested a significant, untapped movie audience. And modest musical numbers were less expensive to produce then big fight scenes.

Autry's first "B" movie was *Tumbling Tumbleweeds* (1933). In a show business career that finally ended in 1956, he ultimately made a total of ninety-three films and ninety-one TV episodes. None of his movies are considered classics, but Autry's contributions to the development of westerns and musicals cannot be minimized. He brought country and western music into the movie mainstream, and—unlike most Hollywood movies—his films often dealt with political and social issues in a direct (if simplified) manner.

Autry was never considered a particularly good actor, but he projected an earnest innocence that younger viewers found appealing. His audience was primarily children, but he imbued several generations of Americans with his particular brand of simple idealism. Autry's "Ten Commandments of the Cowboy" were as follows:

did performances, if modest box office successes, in the weirdly entertaining *Neighbors* (1981) and the more traditional comedy *Dr. Detroit* (1983). When Aykroyd then put together an excellent performance as a stuffy stockbroker in the critically admired and commercially successful *Trading Places* (1983), he was overshadowed by the emergence of Eddie Murphy as a new comic star. It wasn't until the following year, when he co-wrote and starred in the huge comedy hit *Ghostbusters* (1984) that Aykroyd was finally perceived by many as a brilliant comic force.

Since *Ghostbusters,* Aykroyd's career has been uneven. While films such as *The Couch Trip* (1988), in which he played an escaped lunatic posing as a radio talk show psychologist, showed an adventurous comic spirit, fans did not come out to see it. On the other hand, he had a hit with his savagely funny version of *Dragnet* (1987), in which he was partnered with the hot comic actor Tom Hanks. He also coscripted and starred in the successful *Ghostbusters II* (1989).

Finally, it may very well be that Aykroyd, unlike fellow comic actors Eddie Murphy, Bill Murray, Chevy Chase, and Tom Hanks, has yet to develop a strong personal following despite his obvious talents.

AYRES, LEW (1908–   )   An actor whose potential was never fully realized though there were flashes of greatness in his truncated career. A boyishly handsome young man, he became a star at the age of twenty-one and worked steadily until World War II dramatically changed his life, but not in the way it did most Hollywood actors who left the screen during the war to fight.

Born Lewis Ayer, he was a medical student who was discovered in a Hollywood nightclub playing the piano (and several other instruments) with a band. His first film appearance was a miniscule part in *The Sophomore* (1929). Later that same year, though, he burst upon the Hollywood scene in a big way as the recipient of Greta Garbo's *(q.v.)* love in *The Kiss* (1929). And it got better, still, for the actor, when he won the starring role in Lewis Milestone's classic antiwar film, *All Quiet on the Western* Front (1930).

Ayres had become a major star and it seemed as if he could do no wrong. But he found himself sidelined in "B" movies throughout much of the rest of the decade, starring in all but forgotten films with titles such as *Many a Slip* (1931), *Okay America!* (1932), and *Cross Country Cruise* (1934).

He cranked out thirty-one films over seven years before landing a supporting role in George Cukor's "A" movie treat, *Holiday* (1938), and did a credible job as Katharine Hepburn's *(q.v.)* drunken brother. That same year, he was given the role of Dr. James Kildare in the MGM medical series created because the Andy Hardy films had become such a success. Louis B. Mayer *(q.v.)* was especially interested in the Kildare project because Lionel Barrymore could act the part of Dr. Gillespie in a wheelchair even though he had hurt his hip. It was Ayres' big break, and the Dr. Kildare films were a huge hit. *Young Dr. Kildare* (1938) was the first of nine films over a four-year period in which he played the dedicated physician.

Though the world forgot the lesson of *All Quiet on the Western Front,* Lew Ayres did not. His refusal to bear arms in World War II effectively blackballed him from the film industry. He was dropped from the Kildare series; theaters would not show his films and an enraged public wouldn't have gone to see them anyway. Eventually, Ayres volunteered as a medic and won the respect of his fellow soliders by showing his courage in combat.

He returned to the screen in 1946 in *The Dark Mirror,* then made *The Unfaithful* (1947), and costarred as a doctor (a familiar role) with Jane Wyman in *Johnny Belinda* (1948), but the last of these would be his best role for a long time to come. By 1953, he was playing a mad doctor in the interesting but decidely low-budget *Donovan's Brain.*

Ayres faded from Hollywood films during the rest of the 1950s, dedicating himself, in part, to writing, producing, and narrating a documentary about religion called *Altars of the East* (1955), which was based upon a book he had written. Twenty-one years later, he almost singlehandedly created a two-and-a-half hour sequel called *Altars of the World* (1976).

As for his acting career, Ayres began popping up in the 1960s and 1970s in small featured roles in movies such as *Advise and Consent* (1962), *The Carpetbaggers* (1964), *Battle for the Planet of the Apes* (1973), and *Damien—Omen II* (1978). He appeared far more regularly on television, though, in a spate of TV movies during the late 1960s and throughout the 1970s.

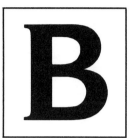

"B" MOVIE During the heyday of the studio system *(q.v.),* "B" movies were those made on a modest budget, usually starring actors who were still on their way up or those who were on their way down. Often, the films were "programmers"—cheap westerns, gangster films, horror movies—that were simply meant to fill out the bill in a double feature. Examples of these films include Gene Autry's *Tumbling Tumbleweeds* (1933) and *Crime School* (1938) with Humphrey Bogart *(q.v.)* before he became a star.

After the studio system crumbled, "B" movies came to mean any cheaply made film. The beach party movies *(q.v.)* (and so many others) produced by American International Pictures to appeal to the youth market are prime examples of latter-day "B" movies.

Regardless of the tag, a fair number of "B" movies have become Hollywood classics. Some were instant hits, elevating lead actors and directors to stardom. *High Sierra* (1940), for instance, catapulted Humphrey Bogart's career, and *Invasion of the Body Snatchers* (1956) galvanized director Don Siegel's reputation. Other "B" movies were discovered only later and became cult favorites, such as Joseph H. Lewis' *Gun Crazy* (1949), Samuel Fuller's *Shock Corridor* (1963), and all of Budd Boetticher's Randolph Scott *(qq.v.)* westerns of the 1950s.

See also: "A" movies; American International Pictures; cult movies; gangster movies; horror movies; westerns

BACALL, LAUREN (1924–) Combining a smokey sex appeal with a tough-as-nails image, Bacall's fame has been due as much to her marriage to Humphrey Bogart *(q.v.)* as her screen appearances. Tall, angular, with an alluringly husky voice, she was popular and effective as the love interest in four of Bogart's movies

"B" movies had to be made cheaply and quickly. Easy to produce and having a loyal following, particularly among children, westerns were ideal for the "B's". Here, Monte Blue, a low-budget western star, goes for his gun in a publicity picture for *Riders of Death Valley* (1940). Photo courtesy of The Siegel Collection.

in the 1940s, but her film career has been uneven ever since.

Born Betty Joan Perske, she studied acting at the American Academy of Dramatic Arts and had performed in a handful of small roles on the New York stage before turning to modeling as a means of making a living. It was director Howard Hawks' *(q.v.)* wife who discovered Bacall, seeing her on the cover of *Harper's Bazaar* and insisting that the model had just the look that her husband was seeking. Mrs. Hawks was right.

Hawks cast the nineteen-year-old Bacall in the Bogart vehicle *To Have and Have Not* (1944). With a peekaboo hairstyle reminiscent of Veronica Lake *(q.v.)* and a seductive manner, Bacall captivated audiences, critics, and Bogart, who married her the following year. She went on to costar with her new husband in *The Big Sleep* (1946), *Dark Passage* (1947), and *Key Largo* (1948), each film drawing power from a palpable chemistry between the two stars that audiences clearly enjoyed.

With few exceptions, Bacall's films without Bogart at her side were far less interesting. Among those rare winners were *Young Man With a Horn* (1950), *How to Marry a Millionaire* (1953), and *Written on the Wind* (1957). In any event, she was not a terribly active actress and by the mid-1960s she had mostly been cast in featured and/or supporting roles such as in *Harper* (1966), *Murder on the Orient Express* (1974), and *The Shootist* (1976). Her only genuine starring role in the last twenty years was in the suspense film *The Fan* (1981).

Despite her Hollywood fame, Bacall's success since the late 1960s has been on Broadway rather than in films. She starred in such stage hits as *Cactus Flower, Applause,* and *Woman of the Year.*

Bacall's private life has been widely reported on. After Bogart's death she nearly married Frank Sinatra but their affair ended badly and she later wed actor Jason Robards, Jr., a marriage that ended in divorce. She is the mother of actor Sam Robards.
See also: dubbing; rat pack

BACK LIGHTING A lighting technique that softens the contours of an object while making it seem more three-dimensional. When lit from behind, a glow of light surrounds the edges of the filmed object, causing it to stand out from a dark background.

Back lighting is generally used for two major purposes. Its primary and more dramatic usage is to light an object (usually an actor) entirely from the rear. The effect can produce a ghostly silhouette rimmed by an ominous outline of light. These images are occasionally glimpsed in thrillers and horror films.

The second use of back lighting is far more pragmatic and can be observed quite regularly in romantic films. As movie stars age, they are often back lit in order to soften their appearance, especially in close-ups. The lighting from behind illuminates their hair and gives their appearance a soft glow. Back lighting throws gentle shadows over an actor's face yet doesn't darken it because of the light surrounding the actor's head.

BACK PROJECTION A technique, also known as process shooting, by which previously shot outdoor footage is projected onto a screen forming a backdrop behind actors being filmed in a studio. It is intended to make it appear as if the actors in the foreground are playing their scene outdoors.

During the heyday of Hollywood—the 1930s and 1940s—back projection was used extensively because the cost of taking an entire crew on location to do a scene was prohibitive. Even though moviemaking has become less studio-bound, back projection has continued as a means of saving both time and money. Perhaps the most gifted back projection specialist was Farciot Eduoart, a special-effects man who spent most of his long career at Paramount. Among his more well-known films where back projection is used are *Lives of a Bengal Lancer* (1935), *Sullivan's Travels* (1941), and *Unconquered* (1947).

BACK LOT Outdoor area on the property of a Hollywood studio where sets representing locations such as western towns, war-torn European villages, New York City streets, etc. were built. The back lot received its name because it was generally a huge tract of land behind the studio's main offices and soundstages where all the indoor scenes were shot.

The back lot existed as an economy measure. It was cheaper to shoot at the studio than to take an entire crew on location where they would have to be fed and housed. The sets that were built on the back lot were rarely torn down; they were used over and over again in countless movies.

All of the major studios: MGM, Paramount, Warner, etc. had huge back lots. Some of them still exist today for television usage. But in an effort to create greater realism, most outdoor scenes shot for movies today are made on location rather than on a back lot.
See also: location shooting

BAKER, CAROLL (1931–) A would-be successor to Marilyn Monroe, she was an actress who showed a great deal of promise as a Hollywood sex symbol. But for one exception, Baker never had roles in the kinds of quality films that might have made her a major star. Nonetheless, Baker worked steadily in Hollywood over a ten-year period in the latter half of the 1950s and the first half of the 1960s before heading for Europe and a long career acting in exploitation films.

Baker started her show business career as a dancer, then showcased herself as a magician's helper. In 1953, she managed to win a small part in an Esther Williams film, *Easy to Love,* but her movie career didn't take at first, and she headed for New York where she found work in TV commercials. Her big break came when she landed a role in the Broadway play *All Summer Long* in 1955. She received additional experience working in television dramas before Hollywood gave her a second chance.

After a small role in *Giant* (1956), she became an instant sensation as the sexy child bride in the hit film *Baby Doll* (1956), winning an Oscar nomination that gave her additional credibility. She appeared in a few good movies after that, such as *The Big Country* (1958), but the serious push to turn her into a sex symbol came when she starred in *The Carpetbaggers* (1964) and as Jean Harlow in *Harlow,* one of two films released in 1965 about the 1930s actress. Both *The Carpetbaggers* and *Harlow* were critical and commercial disasters.

With her career on the rocks, Baker spent the better part of fifteen years making films abroad with titles such as *Orgasmo* (1969) and *The Madness of Love* (1973), most of which were never released in the United States. She did, however, make a bizarre form of comeback in America when she appeared in Andy Warhol's *Bad* in 1977. The comeback was not successful.
See also: sex symbols: female

BAKSHI, RALPH (1939–) A writer/director of adult animated movies, he was among the first filmmakers to break free of the notion that cartoons were solely for children. He also pioneered the use of rotoscoping, an animation procedure that involves the tracing of live-action figures.

Baskshi was born in British-occupied Palestine but grew up in Brooklyn, New York. After surviving a difficult, poverty-stricken childhood, he found work with Terrytoons, drawing cells for cartoon characters such as Mighty Mouse and Hekyll and Jekyll.

Working from his own original script, Bakshi used his experience as an animator to create the comic foul-mouthed, sex-crazed characters in *Fritz the Cat* (1972). This X-rated feature-length movie was a commercial and critical hit that was a landmark in the development of animation as an art form. But while many hailed him as a new force in animated film, others derided him as nothing less than a clever pornographer.

The success of *Fritz the Cat* gave the writer/director the clout to make a still more ambitious, raunchy effort called *Heavy Traffic* (1973), a film that intercut live-action sequences and animation in imaginative, revolutionary new ways.

He faltered with his next film, *Coonskin* (1975), another movie (similar to his first two) that depicted the bizarre, violent years of his youth in phantasmagoric images.

Bakshi finally changed his milieu, if not his themes and imagery, when he turned to the fantasy genre and made *Wizards* (1977), a film he produced as well as wrote and directed. *Wizards,* a message movie about war set in a fantasical future, was a critical and commercial flop. But fantasy seemed to be a fruitful area for animation and Bakshi tried again, directing a lively

adaption of J. R. R. Tolkien's *Lord of the Rings* (1978).

In 1981, Bakshi made his most ambitious movie to date, a multi-generational animated saga that followed the growth and change of popular American music. The film, *American Pop,* was a moderate success with critics, but it was not up to the quality of the comparable Disney classic, *Fantasia.*

If Disney's animated films were essentially for kids, Bakshi's movies seemed ultimately aimed at teenagers. From *Fritz the Cat* to *American Pop,* Bakshi's films tended to be hip rejections of a safe, middle-class America.

In the early 1980s, after directing *Fire and Ice* (1983), an animated fantasy about war that came and went with little fanfare, Bakshi left Hollywood to pursue a career as an artist, working in paint and wood. He has not, however, turned his back on animation, saying that he will someday return to filmmaking.
See also: animation

BALLARD, LUCIEN (1908–) A cinematographer, Ballard was recognized for his excellence rather late in his career. Joseph von Sternberg *(q.v.)* had been his mentor in the early 1930s, and Ballard learned a great deal from him, but he rarely worked on "A" movies *(q.v.)* during the 1930s and 1940s, and his expertise with black-and-white photography didn't receive much notice. Finally, working as a free-lance cinematographer during the 1950s and 1960s, Ballard became fully appreciated both for his excellent black-and-white photography and his abilities in lighting and shooting outdoor action films.

Ballard began working in Hollywood as a roustabout, doing physical labor on a Clara Bow *(q.v.)* film called *Dangerous Curves* (1929). When shooting was finished, Bow invited him and the rest of the cast to her home for a party. As related in Leonard Maltin's excellent book, *Behind the Camera,* Ballard recalled, "I came home three days later, and I said, 'Boy, this is the business for me!' "

He worked his way up over the next five years to assistant cameraman and finally cameraman (a position we now refer to as cinematographer or director of photography). He shared the cameraman credit on his first job as a cinematographer for Josef von Sternberg's *The Devil is a Woman* (1935). He had the job to himself on von Sternberg's version of *Crime and Punishment* (1935). Unfortunately, most of his films during the rest of the 1930s and 1940s are relatively unknown, but Ballard's stark black-and-white photography can be seen to fine effect in films such as *Craig's Wife* (1936), *The Lodger* (1944)—which starred his soon-to-be wife, Merle Oberon (a marriage that lasted from 1945 to 1949)—*Laura* (1944), which he co-photographed, and *Berlin Express* (1948).

It wasn't until Ballard began working on the films of Henry Hathaway, Budd Boetticher, Stanley Kubrick,

Sam Peckinpah *(qq.v.)*, and others that his reputation finally began to soar. He displayed his virtuosity in black and white in films such as Kubrick's *The Killing* (1956), and Boetticher's *The Rise and Fall of Legs Diamond* (1960). When he finally began working in color, lighting and shooting outdoor action films, his work was all the more rich and evocative, most notably in Boetticher's *Buchannan Rides Alone* (1958), Sam Peckinpah's *Ride the High Country* (1960), *The Wild Bunch* (1969), and *The Ballad of Cable Hogue* (1970), and Henry Hathaway's *The Sons of Katie Elder* (1965) and *True Grit* (1969).

In all, Ballard has been the cinematographer of more than one hundred feature films, as well director of photograpbry for television work and comedy shorts (including uncredited work for The Three Stooges and Charley Chase). He has never won, nor has he ever even been nominated for, an Oscar.

THE BAND WAGON A 1953 MGM musical directed by Vincente Minnelli *(q.v.)*, starring Fred Astaire, *(q.v.)*, Cyd Charisse *(q.v.)*, Jack Buchanan, Oscar Levant, and Nannete Fabray. This film, apart from the classic Astaire-Rogers musicals of the 1930s, is among Fred Astaire's greatest triumphs. He considered it one of his best films.

Though the movie had the same title as Astaire's Broadway hit of 1930/31, the only similarities between the two were four songs written by Howard Dietz and Arthur Schwartz, who also contributed the rest of the wonderful new score, which included "Dancing in the Dark," "By Myself," "You and the Night and the Music," and "That's Entertainment."

The script, by Betty Comden and Adolph Green, concerned the fortunes of a has-been movie star (Astaire) trying to make a comeback on Broadway in a play named *The Band Wagon*. The movie was filled with enormous energy, best exemplified by the "Triplets Number" featuring Astaire, Buchanan, and Fabray dressed as infants and literally dancing on their knees. And the Mickey Spillane sendup "The Girl Hunt" is one of the most audacious and clever dance numbers ever put on film. Significantly, the musical's hook song "That's Entertainment" has become a symbolic theme for all movie musicals (as well as the title of two successful movie musical compilation films).

The Band Wagon was one of MGM's big hits of 1953 despite the fact that it was during that fateful year that CinemaScope was introduced and widescreen films became the rage. In order to make it appear as if the film were made by a widescreen process, the bottom of the screen image was masked to make the picture seem wider. At the same time, a new gate was added to the film projector that distorted the film, flattening the image and making it still wider. The effect created the appearance of CinemaScope, but it also cut from view the dancing feet of Fred Astaire and Cyd Charisse!
See also: Comden & Green; musicals

BARA, THEDA (1890–1955) The first movie star to be "created" through an orchestrated publicity campaign even before her first starring role, Bara's debut as a star not only caused a sensation, it added a new word to the language: *vamp*.

Theodosia Goodman (the future Theda Bara) had come to Hollywood from Ohio to break into the movies. At age twenty-six, however, she was still an extra. Meanwhile, Frank J. Powell had decided that he wanted to cast an unknown actress as the evil seductress in his film version of the play *A Fool There Was* (1916). When he set eyes on Theodosia, he decided that she was the woman for the part. But first he meant to prepare the public for his new star.

First came the name change to Theda Bara. Then came the public-relations campaign proclaiming her to

Theda Bara, the original vamp, had a short but sensational career. Her name is supposed to have been concocted as an anagram of "Arab death." Photo courtesy of The Siegel Collection.

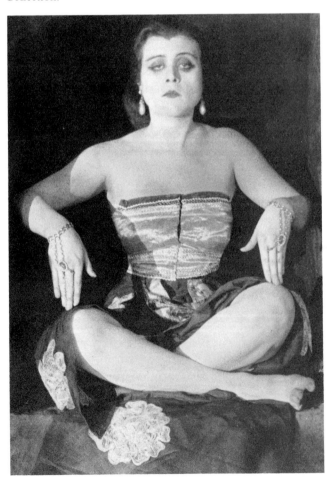

be the daughter of a Middle Eastern potentate. It was reported that she could see into the future and was poison to men. As if that wasn't enough, her press releases proclaimed her name to be an anagram for "Arab death." It was all hype and glitz—and it worked.

A Fool There Was was a mammoth hit, introducing the famous line, "Kiss me, my fool," and making Theda Bara the hottest actress in Hollywood. Her role as the wicked woman enthralled moviegoers with its outrageous sexual overtones. The term *vamp* (short for vampire) was coined to describe her. Without Theda Bara, there might never have been "Dynasty's" Joan Collins; Bara introduced a new type of character who is still with us today.

Theda Bara made forty movies over the next four years; in almost all of them she played the evil temptress. By the end of 1919, however, she was a has-been. Her success unleashed a wave of imitators; vamps filled the world's movie screens and the public simply grew tired of the same old thing. Americans were also more sophisticated and worldly after World War I, and no longer accepting that Theda Bara and her screen imitators destroyed men for no other reason than the fun of it.

It was a long hiatus before Theda Bara reappeared in films in the mid-1920s. By that time, however, she was reduced to burlesquing herself in comic two-reelers. Happily, "The Vamp" had not squandered her money, and she soon retired to a comfortable life with her director husband, Charles Brabin, and became well known in Los Angeles social circles until her death in 1955.

THE BARRYMORE DYNASTY Four generations of this unique family have been actors, and three of its members from the second generation, siblings John, Lionel and Ethel, have had significant movie careers. While the Barrymore name is legend in the theater, it enjoys less renown in Hollywood circles. But while the theater saw the best of the Barrymores, the movies still caught a considerable amount of their talent, charm, and style.

Maurice Barrymore (born Herbert Blythe) and Georgiana Drew were famous actors during their heyday on the American stage in the late 19th century. They gave birth to three children, Lionel (Blythe) Barrymore (1878–1954), Ethel (Blythe) Barrymore (1879–1959), and John (Blythe) Barrymore (1882–1942).

John Barrymore is the most famous of his three siblings, and rightfully so. He had a prodigious talent that was barely captured on screen. Yet this youngest member of the famous acting family originally rejected the theater to become a cartoonist. Eventually, however, he returned to the family business, making his stage debut in 1903 in a play called *Magda*. The handsome actor, who later became known as both the "The

Great Profile" and "The Great Lover," was one of the most admired stage idols of his day, starring over the next twenty-five years in such plays as *The Affairs of Anatol, Peter Ibbetson, The Jest,* and *Richard III.* He was considered one of the great Hamlets, and he even played the melancholy Dane in England, one of the few American actors ever to dare act the role in the home of the Bard.

During the period of his greatest theatrical acclaim, Barrymore starred in silent films with modest success despite being robbed of his greatest gift, his magnificent speaking voice. His first film was *An American Citizen* (1913), and he ultimately appeared in more than twenty silent movies, his most notable being the original film version of *Dr. Jekyll and Mr. Hyde* (1920), in which he used no makeup, relying totally on facial contortions to turn himself into the hideous monster, Mr. Hyde. It was a bravura performance that still amazes to this day.

When the movies learned to talk, Barrymore found himself in great demand, earning in excess of $30,000 per week. Though he was past his prime and suffering from the effects of decades of heavy drinking, he did manage a handful of exquisite performances. In *Grand Hotel* (1932) he was the epitome of the debonair but melancholy jewel thief. In *Counsellor-at-Law* (1933) he lent a finely wrought intensity and a rich humanity to his role of a Jewish attorney who had fought his way out of the slums. And he was utterly brilliant, almost uncontainable, in Hollywood's first screwball comedy, *Twentieth Century* (1934). The best of his other performances were usually parodies of his own well-documented dissolution, such as his painfully realistic portrayal of the drunken, failed actor in *Dinner at Eight* (1933).

With health fading from alcohol abuse, he found himself increasingly unable to remember his lines. Forced to use cue cards, he stumbled his way through many of his later movies. With his drawing power fading at the box office, Barrymore was reduced in the later 1930s to appearing in "B" movies *(q.v.),* often in supporting roles. His last film was *Playmates* (1941). He died the following year, thoroughly broke.

John's brother, Lionel, was never the great star that his brother had been, but he worked far more steadily and successfully in the movies than John did. Lionel took the new moving picture medium far more seriously than either of his siblings. He became involved with the movies as early as 1909 when he joined the Biograph studio and appeared in a good many of D. W. Griffith's early masterpieces, such as *The Musketeers of Pig Alley* (1912) and *Judith of Bethulia* (1914). Lionel also wrote scripts and directed a number of silent films.

Though he was successful on the stage, Lionel began working exclusively in the movies as of the mid-1920s, making solid, credible, but generally ordinary, films.

Of all the theatrical family dynasties, the Barrymore clan is probably the most famous. Seen here are John Barrymore (right) and his wife, along with Lionel Barrymore (center), holding his brother's four-month-old child, Dolores Ethel Mae Barrymore. Photo courtesy of The Siegel Collection.

It wasn't until sound arrived in Hollywood that he emerged as one of the industry's premiere character actors *(q.v.),* winning a Best Actor Oscar for his rousing performance as a clever criminal lawyer whose daughter falls in love with the gangster he's just helped to acquit in *A Free Soul* (1931).

Barrymore was perhaps best known in the late 1930s and 1940s as Dr. Gillespie, playing the older physician throughout all fifteen movies in the *Dr. Kildare* series. It was the kind of role he was best at playing—everyone's kindly but crusty old uncle. And yet he also excelled at portraying parsominous, nasty old men, which he did to perfection in *It's a Wonderful Life* (1946).

From 1938 until his death, the actor was confined to a wheelchair, the result of severe arthritis coupled with a leg injury. But it rarely stopped him from acting. His last appearance was in *Main Street to Broadway* in 1953; he died the following year.

Ethel outlived both of her brothers, rivaling John as a Broadway star in her early years and later rivaling Lionel as a character actor in her later years. She was known as "The First Lady of the American Theater" in her prime, but she followed in her brothers' footsteps, dabbling in silent films beginning in 1914 with *The Nightingale.* She starred in a dozen silent movies over the next five years, finally giving her full attention back to the stage in 1919.

She made but one movie during the 1930s, but it was a dandy, *Rasputin and the Empress* (1933), in which she played the czarina. She was joined in this film by her two brothers, the only time all three siblings starred in the same movie.

After another long stretch on the boards, Ethel came back to Hollywood in 1944 and immediately won an Oscar for Best Supporting Actress in her role as Cary Grant's dying mother in *None but the Lonely Heart.* From then on, she worked steadily in Hollywood in character roles, appearing in a considerable number of fine films such as *The Spiral Staircase* (1946), *The Paradine Case* (1948), *Pinky* (1949), and *The Story of Three Loves* (1953). Her last film was *Johnny Trouble* (1957). She died in 1960.

The next generation of Barrymores didn't fare very well either in life or in their film careers. Diana Barrymore, born Diana Blanche Blythe Barrymore (1921–1960), the daughter of John and his one-time wife, poet Michael Strange, appeared in half a dozen undistinguished films between 1942 and 1944. She is perhaps better known as the author of *Too Much, Too Soon,* which told of her troubled life as the daughter of "The Great Profile." The book was turned into a movie in 1957 starring Errol Flynn (in a bit of inspired typecasting) as her father.

Diana's half-brother, John Drew Barrymore, was born John Blythe Barrymore, Jr. (1932–) to John, Sr. and actress Delores Costello. He fared somewhat better in life than his half-sister did, but he, too, had a disappointing film career. Billed as John Barrymore, Jr., he appeared in his first film, *The Sundowners,* in 1950. But a constantly flaring temper (not unlike Sean

Penn's today) ruined his career in the mid-1950s. Later, as John Drew Barrymore, he worked largely in Europe in the late 1950s and early 1960s, then picked up small parts in American films during the 1970s.

Yet another generation of the Barrymore acting dynasty took to the screen in the early 1980s when John Drew Barrymore's little daughter, Drew Barrymore (1975–), was featured in Steven Speilberg's smash hit, *E.T.—The Extra-Terrestrial* (1982). She followed that success with a far more substantial role as a ten-year-old child suing her parents for divorce in *Irreconcilable Differences* (1984). The pressure of sudden success, however, took its toll. She admitted to alcohol addiction at the age of thirteen.

See also: all-star films; Ayres, Lew; screwball comedy

BARTHELMESS, RICHARD (1895–1963) Though hardly remembered today, he was one of the silent cinema's greatest stars—and deservedly so. His restrained, sensitive acting brought a new dimension to silent film performances, and his association with directors D. W. Griffith and Henry King *(qq.v.)* gave him the vehicles through which his talents could be best expressed.

Raised by a mother who worked as a stage actress (his father died when he was an infant), Barthelmess was born to show business. At his mother's urging, however, he received a college education before embarking full-time on a theatrical career. He started in movies as an extra, but it was thanks to a family association with one-time film star Alla Nazimova that Barthelmess was given an important part in *War Brides* (1916), the film that helped launch his career.

The young actor worked steadily throughout the rest of the teens, beginning a long association with the Gish sisters in 1919, when he worked first with Dorothy Gish in *The Hope Chest.* That same year, having been brought to the attention of D. W. Griffith, Barthelmess became the great director's most well-known male star. He gave sterling performances in two of Griffith's masterpieces, *Broken Blossoms* (1919) and *Way Down East* (1920), playing a broken-hearted Asian in the former, and a rugged farmer's son in the latter. If it had not been clear before, Griffith's films proved that Barthelmess was a versatile actor who had a soulful yet thoroughly masculine appeal.

After leaving Griffith, Barthelmess went on to still greater success, starring in Henry King's *Tol'able David* (1921), followed by a constant stream of various acting triumphs throughout the rest of the silent era, culminating in his nomination for the first Best Actor Academy Award for his work in two films, *The Patent Leather Kid* (1927) and *The Noose* (1928).

There was nothing wrong with Barthelmess' speaking voice, and he made a comfortable transition to

One of the silent era's greatest male stars, Richard Barthelmess, saves Lillian Gish in the famous ice floe scene in D. W. Griffith's classic melodrama, *Way Down East* (1920). Photo courtesy of The Siegel Collection.

talkies. In fact, he was rather popular during the early years of the sound era, opening the new decade with a starring role in one of the great airplane films *(q.v.)* of all time, *The Dawn Patrol* (1930). Unfortunately, this was the high point of his talkie career. He made some interesting films during the next five years, such as *The Last Flight* (1931), *Cabin in the Cotton* (1932), and *Heroes for Sale* (1933), but their generally downbeat nature didn't appeal to audiences during the Depression and his popularity quickly faded.

Barthelmess soon found himself playing villains. Leaving Hollywood in 1935, he made one film in England, then retired from the screen until he made a triumphant return in a strong supporting role in Howard Hawks' *(q.v.) Only Angels Have Wings* (1939). The success of that film, along with Barthelmess' good reviews, brought him three character roles over the next several years, his final movie apperance coming in *The Spoilers* (1942). Retiring for good from the film business, Barthelmess served in the Naval Reserve during World War II, then lived the life of a country gentleman on New York's Long Island. He died of cancer at the age of sixty-eight.

BARTHOLOMEW, FREDDIE *See* child actors.

BAXTER, WARNER (1889–1951) An actor best remembered today for one role, that of the ailing, desperate producer in *42nd Street,* but whose film career spanned more than thirty years. Baxter was a solid, dependable actor with an air of authority and style. He could play a range of characters from fiery Latin types to sober physicians, but he was at his best playing sophisticated, contemporary businessmen. He looked the part.

Warner Baxter's personal life was one melodramatic catastrophe after another, only relieved by one full decade of dazzling Hollywood success. Baxter's father died when he was less than a year old, and as a teenager, he and his mother lost everything they owned in the famous San Francisco earthquake of 1906. When he was a young man, Baxter sold insurance, saved his money, and then lost it all in a bad investment. Later, in the early 1940s, as he slid from the heights of his Hollywood career, he suffered severe psychiatric problems. And, finally, in a bizarre medical move to relieve tortuous arthritic pain, he consented to a lobotomy. Shortly thereafter, he died of pneumonia.

After four years of learning his craft in stock company productions, the young man made his film debut in *All Woman* (1918). He didn't begin acting regularly in the movies, though, until 1921. Baxter worked steadily throughout the rest of the silent era but did not quite reach star status, although he did play Jay Gatsby in the first film version of *The Great Gatsby* (1926).

The part that turned the workaday actor into a star came a dozen years after his first film appearance, and it came quite literally by accident. Raoul Walsh *(q.v.)* was supposed to direct and star in Fox's very first "all-outdoor" sound film called *In Old Arizona* (1930), a film that introduced the character of the Cisco Kid. Walsh, however, was involved in a serious auto accident in which he lost his eye. Baxter was given the role intended for Walsh; the result was an Academy Award for Best Actor, and he became a movie star overnight.

Baxter made serveral Cisco Kid movies during the 1930s in which his dark good looks and winning smile served him well. Yet two other performances during the 1930s also showed him at the top of his form. In the musical *42nd Street* (1933), Baxter neither sang nor danced, yet his aggressive, nervous, near-tragic performance held that movie together. And in John Ford's *(q.v.)* excellent *The Prisoner of Shark Island* (1936), Baxter played Dr. Samuel Mudd, the man who set the broken leg of John Wilkes Booth and was wrongly accused of being part of the Lincoln assassination plot. Baxter gave his character a quiet dignity that was extremely effective.

After suffering a nervous breakdown in the early 1940s, Baxter returned to the screen and spent most of the next decade appearing in "B" movies *(q.v.),* principally in a series of "Crime Doctor" films. His last movie was *State Penitentiary* (1950).

BEACH PARTY MOVIES In the late 1950s and early 1960s, a new kind of movie was born: the teenage beach film. These low-budget films were the first to be aimed directly at the newly emerging baby boom generation. The genre debuted with films like *Gidget* (1959) and *Where the Boys Are* (1960), but it hit its stride with the beach movies made by American International Pictures starring Frankie Avalon and Annette Funicello.

According to a popular story, Walt Disney *(q.v.)* read the original script for *Beach Party* (1963) and told Annette Funicello (she was still under contract to Disney) that it was a good part for her, and that she ought to take it. He had only one proviso: she couldn't show her navel.

Beach Party was a huge success, and six more A.I.P. beach movies with Frankie and Annette followed, among them *Muscle Beach Party* (1964), *Bikini Beach* (1964), *Beach Blanket Bingo* (1965), and *How to Stuff a Wild Bikini* (1965).

In the A.I.P. beach movies, the kids don't defer to adults. If anything, the adults are depicted as fools. The teenagers live in their own world, have their own rules, and solve their own problems. But unlike other earlier teenage movies like *The Wild One* (1954), *Rebel Without a Cause* (1955), and *Blackboard Jungle* (1955), all of the beach movies are about kids who don't get into trouble. The films celebrate an affluent, easygoing life-style of surfing, rock 'n' roll, and romance. It was an innocent ideal that most middle-class teens of that era readily embraced.

But not for very long. The Civil Rights Movement, the Vietnam War, and the drug culture, precipitated a loss of teenage innocence, and the beach movie was washed away. The genre was briefly recalled and satirized in the 1987 nostalgia flick *Back to the Beach,* which starred (once again) that inimitable pair Frankie and Annette. This time they were the parents of a teenager.

BEATTY, WARREN (1937–   ) Principally an actor but also an increasingly sophisticated and successful writer, producer, and director. Virile to a fault, Beatty's long, lean good looks have had women panting in the aisles for three decades. He has often played the part of a rebel, a role he has also enjoyed playing in real life. That rebellious nature led him to buck the Hollywood system and put himself on the cutting edge of commercial viability with movie projects that deal with sexual, cultural, and political issues that many others might have happily chosen to ignore. Beatty's surprising success, however, helped him gain virtually total control over his own projects.

Born Warren Beaty, he is the half-brother of actress Shirley MacLaine. Like MacLaine, he had his start as an actor in amateur productions staged by their mother. After a short spell of aimlessness following high school and a stint at college, Beatty decided to follow in his half-sister's footsteps and become an actor. He studied with Stella Adler and soon began making headway as a television performer, appearing regularly in that medium during the late 1950s, most memorably as a continuing supporting character on the sitcom, "Dobie Gillis."

Beatty's big break came when he appeared on Broadway in *A Loss of Roses,* which eventually led to his movie debut starring opposite Natalie Wood in *Splendor in the Grass* (1961). Women went wild for the handsome newcomer, and his film career was solidly launched. His sex appeal was further enhanced by his playing a gigolo in *The Roman Spring of Mrs. Stone* (1961). He then gave strong, off-beat, and fascinating performances in a string of relatively uncommercial movies, among them *Lilith* (1964) and *Mickey One* (1965). He had a following of loyal film fans by this time but he had yet to become a major star.

That all changed when he chose to produce his own vehicle, *Bonnie and Clyde (q.v., 1967).* The film was a surprise hit both with critics and with filmgoers. Beatty emerged from the enterprise wealthy, respected, and famous. His film appearances in the rest of the 1960s and early 1970s were uneven. He was excellent in *McCabe and Mrs. Miller* (1971) and *The Parallax View* (1974), but thoroughly forgettable in *The Only Game in Town* (1970) and *Dollars* (1971).

When he once again took control of his own films, Beatty hit paydirt, producing, and cowriting the frisky sex farce *Shampoo* (1975), a movie that also poked fun good-naturedly at Beatty's reputation as a womanizer. That same year he starred in Mike Nichols' *(q.v.) The Fortune,* a film that was far better than its ticket sales indicated. But then it was back to controlling his own destiny again, codirecting, coproducing, and cowriting the script for *Heaven Can Wait* (1978), a remake of an old Robert Montgomery *(q.v.)* movie, updating the original hero from a boxer to a football player. The film was a smash. Beatty was honored with three Oscar nominations, for Best Director, Best Actor, and (as producer) Best Picture.

He reached the apex of his career three years later when he directed, produced, cowrote, and starred in *Reds* (1981), the ambitious, epic biopic *(q.v.)* of the American communist John Reed. It was a project that seemed from the very start a totally uncommercial venture, yet Beatty not only made a compelling masterpiece, he also turned it into a moneymaker. Most surprising of all, the Hollywood establishment didn't shy away from his courageous undertaking; they bestowed a Best Director Academy Award upon him for his work.

Since *Reds,* however, neither the critics nor film fans have been kind to Beatty. His clout as a box office draw has been somewhat diminished by his (and Dustin's Hoffman's) flop in Elaine May's hugely expensive comedy *Ishtar* (1987), a film that seemed to confirm that the actor commands a greater following when he is paired with a strong actress (e.g., past co-stars Faye Dunaway *(q.v.),* Julie Christie, Diane Keaton *(q.v.),* etc.) than with a strong actor (e.g., past costars Jack Nicholson *(q.v.),* Dustin Hoffman *[q.v.],* etc.).

BEAVERS, LOUISE (1902–1962) She was one of a mere handful of black actresses who had a long, if compromised, career in Hollywood. Held back from significant roles by racism, she played housekeepers, cooks, and maids throughout scores of movies from the silent era right through to the early 1960s.

Beavers was a singer in a traveling minstrel show before becoming a maid to one-time silent screen star Leatrice Joy. It was through Miss Joy that Beavers received her start in Hollywood in the early 1920s.

Beavers is remembered for *She Done Him Wrong* (1933), in which Mae West calls out to her saying, "Beulah, peel me a grape." But Beaver's best role was in *Imitation of Life* (1934), a film in which she played a moderately realistic character whose daughter, played by Fredi Washington, tries to pass as white. She wouldn't have as good a role again until 1950 when she had a major part in *The Jackie Robinson Story.*

Television gave Louise Beavers a better chance to show off her talents than the movies ever did. She starred in the 1950s TV series, "Beulah," but that, too, was filled with unfortunate racial stereotypes.
See also: racism in Hollywood

BEERY, WALLACE (1886–1949) An actor who had a long and varied career, Beery rose and fell from major stardom three separate times. He was anything but the leading man type, with his big barrel chest, ugly mug, and gravely voice. But the actor had mischief in his eyes and communicated a vulnerability in his oafishness that made him rather lovable in the best of his sound films.

The son of a Kansas City policeman, Beery was the half-brother of actor Noah Beery (1884–1946), who had a notable career as a silent screen heavy and sound-era supporting player. He was also the uncle of Noah Beery, Jr., best known as a TV actor. Among the Beery clan, however, Wallace was the brightest star. He began his show business career by living the old cliché of running away from home to join the circus. Early in the new century, he made his way to the New York stage but his success was limited to a series of female impersonations.

He entered the film business in 1913 as an actor and director for Essanay. Again, he was best known for acting in drag, playing a thick-headed Swedish maid known as "Sweedie" in a number of comic shorts. It was at Essanay that he met Gloria Swanson *(q.v.)*, to whom he was briefly wed.

Beery worked steadily, first as a comedian (including a short stint at Keystone), then as a heavy in movies such as *The Unpardonable Sin* (1919) and *The Virgin of Stamboul* (1920). His first big break came when Douglas Fairbanks *(q.v.)* cast him in the important supporting role of Richard the Lion Heart in the smash hit, *Robin Hood* (1922). His versatility as an actor set to good advantage, Berry was given larger, more significant roles in heftier budgeted movies such as the silent version of *The Sea Hawk* (1924)—the biggest money-maker of its year.

In 1925 Paramount signed him to a long-term contract. Soon thereafter, he became a major star for the first time when he was teamed with actor Raymond Hatton in a military comedy called *Behind the Front* (1926), which spawned far too many sequels and left Beery with a waning popularity.

By the time of the sound era, it appeared as if Beery were washed up. As it turned out, he was only just beginning. MGM took him on and he unexpectedly became one of their biggest stars of the early 1930s when he was cast along with Marie Dressler *(q.v.)* in the surprise hit of the year, *Min and Bill* (1930). Later, he was reteamed with Dressler in *Tugboat Annie* (1933), resulting in another big winner at the box office.

The two Dressler films were a wonderful mix of personalities, and so was his teaming with child star Jackie Cooper in *The Champ* (1931). Despite one of the best scene-stealing performances by a child actor in the history of the movies, Beery's over-the-hill boxer brought him an Oscar in a tie with Frederic March *(q.v., for his performance in Dr. Jekyll and Mr. Hyde)*, and it solidified his image as a gruff but warm-hearted rogue.

Beery was a Victor McLaglen *(q.v.)* type but he was a much better, more versatile actor, which he proved yet again when he played the desperate businessman in *Grand Hotel* (1932), the noveau riche social climber married to Jean Harlow *(q.v.)* in *Dinner at Eight* (1933), and the Mexican revolutionary Pancho Villa in *Viva Villa!* (1934).

Beery's popularity began to flag, however, in the second half of the decade. He had been at his best when paired with strong costars such as Marie Dressler, Jackie Cooper, and Jean Harlow. They brought out his personality the way few other costars could.

Relegated to "B" movies *(q.v.)*—many of them rather fine, such as *Port of Seven Seas* (1938) and *Thunder Afloat* (1939)—Beery seemed to sputter slowly downhill at MGM. Then, unexpectedly, Beery caught on with the public all over again, becoming a top box office draw for a third time, when he was teamed with Marjorie Main in films such as *Wyoming* (1940) and *Barnacle Bill* (1941). The movies with Main recreated (on a smaller scale) the success of his collaborations with Marie Dressler of the early 1930s.

By the mid-1940s, though, Beery's career really slowed down. There were long gaps between films. His last movie, *Big Jack* (1949), was released after he died of a heart attack that same year.

BELOW THE LINE   Below-the-line expenses are all those that must be paid on a daily basis once the film is in production, such as the technical crew's salary, the cost of buying or renting equipment, paying all the actors who have been hired for anything less than the entire shoot (i.e., everyone except the major stars), buying raw film, and paying the location expenses, soundstage rentals, etc.

In addition to the everyday production costs, below-the-line expenses also include the money spent on a daily basis during the post-production period, which includes the cost of renting equipment, space, and the hiring of editor(s), musicians, etc.

The major pre-production expenses constitute the above-the-line costs.
See also: above the line

BENCHLEY, ROBERT   *See* short subjects.

BENDIX, WILLIAM   *See* character actors.

BEN-HUR   Lightning never strikes twice in the same place, except in the movies. Any number of hit films have been remade and turned into new hits. But *Ben-Hur* (1925 & 1959) was the only film whose two incarnations were ever so important to a studio's financial well-being.

Originally, *Ben-Hur* was a best-selling novel by Lew Wallace. The story was adapted to the stage and it became a Broadway hit as well. The Goldwyn Company was so eager to buy the film rights to *Ben-Hur,* that they agreed to pay out fifty percent of the movie's future income to make the deal.

Production on the film began in Rome, and enormous sums of money were spent during the first three months. At the same time, the Goldwyn Company merged with Metro Pictures and Louis B. Mayer Pictures to form Metro-Goldwyn-Mayer (MGM).

Eventually, the cast and crew were fired and the entire production was brought back to Hollywood, where it was shot under the watchful eyes of Louis B. Mayer and Irving Thalberg *(qq.v.)*. But MGM still spared no expense, and the evidence of this can be seen both on the balance sheet (the film cost an astonishing $6 million) and in the elaborate chariot race that remains as thrilling today as in 1925 when heartthrob Ramon Novarro *(q.v.)* as Ben Hur and Francis X. Bushman (q.v.) as the evil Messala sped across movie screens in one of the most popular movies of the silent era.

Despite *Ben-Hur's* box office success, it didn't turn a profit because of its huge cost and the original fifty percent payout that had been agreed to for rights to the story. It remained for MGM's other 1925 blockbuster, *The Big Parade,* to vault the company into financial stablity and prominence. But had *Ben-Hur* been a flop, the loss might have easily sunk the newly formed film studio.

In the late 1950s, in an effort to outflank TV with big screen spectacles, MGM again turned to the story of *Ben-Hur.* The film cost a (then) astronomical $15 million to make and, like its 1925 version, failure at the box office would have brought the studio to the brink of ruin. Directed by the much-respected William Wyler *(q.v.),* and starring Charleton Heston *(q.v.)* in the title role, the 1959 film was both a critical and box office smash, earning more than $80 million. It even garnered twelve Academy Awards (a record), including Best Picture, Best Director, and Best Actor (Heston). *Ben-Hur* saved MGM yet again.
See also: MGM; remakes

BENJAMIN, RICHARD (1938–   )   An actor turned director, Benjamin's work in both areas of film has been uneven but often interesting. For a brief period beginning in the late 1960s, Benjamin was a prospective star, with leading roles in films about none-too-likable yuppies long before the word was coined. By the mid-1970s, he had become a supporting player, generally cast as the diffident and/or neurotic friend of the hero. For the most part, he appeared in comedies, although he has occasionally been quite effective as a villain. His auspicious directorial debut came in 1982 and he has worked steadily as a director ever since.

Benjamin was clear about his career from an early age. Even before attending New York's High School of Performing Arts, as a young actor he had appeared in *Thunder Over the Plains* (1953) and *Crime Wave* (1954). After he finished his education, he worked in the theater until he hit it big on Broadway in *The Star-Spangled Girl* in 1966. Television took notice of his success before the movies did and he was cast with his wife, Paula Prentiss, in the sophisticated TV sitcom, "He and She" in 1967. The series was well-received by the critics but it was not a Neilsen success.

When Philip Roth's best-selling novella *Goodbye Columbus* was turned into a movie in 1969, Benjamin was tapped to play the lead. The film did well and his movie career was finally launched. Good roles were more important to him than stardom, however, and he took the thankless part of the nasty husband in *Diary of a Mad Housewife* (1970). He made other ambitious movies early in the 1970s, such as *The Marriage of a Young Stockbroker* (1971) and the poorly received *Portnoy's*

Complaint (1972), but by the time he graced the entertaining thriller *The Last of Sheila* (1973), Benjamin's ordinary looks and lack of box office pull had finally relegated him to the status of supporting player.

He was well cast and effective during the rest of the 1970s and early 1980s in films such as *The Sunshine Boys* (1975), *House Calls* (1978), and *The Last Married Couple in America* (1979). When he managed a starring role in *Saturday the 14th* (1981), nobody showed up but the critics, and even they weren't all that pleased with this horror spoof.

Fast becoming a second-rate Charles Grodin *(q.v.),* Benjamin finally moved behind the camera and, to the industry's delight and surprise, the actor made a breezy transition to his new career as a director with the critically and commercially successful comedy *My Favorite Year* (1982).

He followed his first hit with another highly regarded film, a teenage dramatic love story set in the early 1940s titled *Racing with the Moon* (1984). His success since then has been tempered by several flops, most notably *City Heat* (1984), starring Clint Eastwood and Burt Reynolds, and the Sidney Poitier vehicle, *Little Nikita* (1988).

BENNETT, CONSTANCE (1904–1965) **& JOAN** (1910–   )   Two popular actresses who were sisters, Constance had several bouts with fame over a turbulent lifetime and Joan enjoyed one long run of screen success lasting more than twenty-five years. Both were glamorous and beautiful, but each had her own special appeal for movie audiences. Constance generally played sharptongued, modern women who were quick with a quip. She reached the peak of her popularity playing the delightful ghost, Marion Kirby, in the hit comedy, *Topper* (1937). Joan tended to star more often in suspense movies and appeared in some of Fritz Lang's better films.

Constance, Joan, and a third actress sister, Barbara, were all daughters of theater star Richard Bennett. Constance was a headstrong young woman who began her film career in a cameo role at age twelve, appearing in one of her father's few films, *The Valley of Decision* (1916). She was wed at the age of sixteen (the first of five marriages), but soon after had the union annulled. The following year she became serious about the movies and began acting regularly in films such as *Reckless Youth* (1922), *Cytherea* (1924), and *The Goose Woman* (1925). She quickly became a star, but left the screen in 1926 to marry a wealthy member of what might have been called the jet set had there been any jets in those days.

The marriage lasted just three years and Constance, with a husky purr that was ideal for the talkies, successfully made her movie comeback in 1929 in *This Thing Called Love.* While she starred in many sophisticated comedies during the ensuing two decades, such as *Rich People* (1930), *Merrily We Live* (1938), and *Topper Takes A Trip* (1939), the actress also showed a flair for drama in films as diverse as *What Price Hollywood?* (1932) and *The Unsuspected* (1947).

After making more than fifty films between 1922 and 1954, Constance retired from the screen and founded the Constance Bennett Cosmetics Company. Later, she returned one last time to the big screen to appear in *Madame X* (1966), but died of a cerebral hemorrhage shortly after filming was completed.

Joan Bennett's life was as eventful as her older sister's. She also married when she was sixteen, but Joan had a child the following year before divorcing her mate. Her adult life had some of the sturm and drang of her youth, as well. In 1952, her husband Walter Wanger *(q.v.)* shot and wounded her agent, Jennings Lang. The whole affair created quite a scandal and Wanger served a number of months in prison, but Joan stuck by her husband during the ordeal, ultimately divorcing him in 1965.

Joan began her film career the same way her sister did hers, with an appearance in a cameo role in *The Valley of Decision*. Unlike Constance, however, Joan didn't pursue a Hollywood career until talkies arrived. Her first significant role on film was in *Power* (1928). The movie did nothing for her, but the following year, playing opposite Ronald Colman *(q.v.)* in *Bulldog Drummond* (1929), she became an instant star.

Joan worked steadily throughout the 1930s, mostly in modest productions, with notable exceptions, including such films as *Disraeli* (1929), *Little Women* (1933), *Private Worlds* (1935), *Mississippi* (1935), *The Man in the Iron Mask* (1939), and *The Housekeeper's Daughter* (1939). After ten years of leading roles, considerable fame, and a marriage to producer Walter Wanger she reached her peak during the 1940s. Wanger, arranged starring roles for her in four of Fritz Lang's *(q.v.)* better films of that decade: *Man Hunt* (1941), *The Woman in the Window* (1944), *Scarlet Street* (1945), and *The Secret Beyond the Door* (1947). These roles gave the actress greater credibility in the Hollywood community and she began starring in prestigious films such as *Nob Hill* (1945), *The Macomber Affair* (1947), and *The Reckless Moment* (1949).

In the 1950s Joan eased into mature roles, most memorably as the wife of Spencer Tracy *(q.v.)* and the mother of Elizabeth Taylor *(q.v.)* in *Father of the Bride* (1950), followed later by *Father's Little Dividend* (1951). She continued acting in films until 1956, and has made few movies since. She was featured in the daytime TV soap opera "Dark Shadows" and starred as well in the theatrical film based on it, *The House of Dark Shadows* (1970). After having starred in more than seventy feature films, Joan began appearing in the occasional TV movie, although in recent years she has been seen on neither the big nor the small screen.

BENNY, JACK (1894–1974) A comedian whose best work was on radio and television but whose Hollywood career was nonetheless noteworthy, Benny's persona of the cheap, vain braggart was a show-business standard for more than fifty years. With his perfectly timed pauses, slightly effeminate hand gestures, and churlish voice, he was a natural screen comedian. But he generally worked best as part of an ensemble, which limited his appeal as a comic movie star.

Born Benjamin Kubelsky in Waukeegan, Illinois, the young man seriously considered a career as a concert violinist. While he was in the Navy during World War I, however, he found himself entertaining his fellow sailors with the violin and getting big laughs for his efforts; it was then that he realized he had the makings of a comedian. Entering vaudeville after the war, he worked the circuits for more than a decade, honing his skills until his fame was such that he was offered the opportunity by MGM to introduce the studio's silent

Jack Benny was a comedy success in several media, with the movies coming in a poor third behind radio and television. Despite mediocre material, Benny was nonetheless quite popular in films. Photo courtesy of Movie Star News.

stars in an early talkie, *The Hollywood Revue of 1929*. He was so engaging in the film that his vaudeville career suddenly skyrocketed. He continued to make film appearances in the early 1930s but most of them were made in the East to accommodate his stage triumphs, which were soon followed by radio fame.

It wasn't until the mid-1930s that he began appearing more regularly in films, splitting his time between guest appearances in movies such as *Broadway Melody of 1936* (1935) and *The Big Broadcast of 1937* (1936), and genuine starring roles in films such as *Artists and Models* (1937) and *Artists and Models Abroad* (1938).

By the early 1940s, it seemed as if Benny was destined for as big (if not bigger) a film career as that of his friend Bob Hope *(q.v.)*. Over a three-year period, from 1940 through 1942, Benny's comedies were the finest and funniest in Hollywood. Far more sophisticated than Abbott & Costello *(q.v.)* (who had just become a hot property), livelier than the tiring and aging Marx Brothers *(q.v.)*, and more eccentrically human than Bob Hope, Jack Benny was at the height of his movie career when he made, in quick succession, *Buck Benny Rides Again* (1940), *Love Thy Neighbor* (1940), *Charley's Aunt* (1941), *To Be Or Not To Be* (1942), and *George Washington Slept Here* (1942).

The sparkling diamond in this set of quality films was Ernst Lubitsch's *(q.v.)* *To Be Or Not To Be,* an hysterical black comedy about the Nazi occupation of Poland. The movie was thought to be in bad taste at the time and it was consequently panned, doing poor business at the box office. Since then it has come to be regarded as a classic, and Benny's career has likewise been more kindly looked upon.

Jack Benny's film career went into a rapid decline in the mid-1940s, pierced through its celluloid heart by the abysmal *The Horn Blows at Midnight* (1945). He appeared in a handful of films after that, mostly in cameo roles, while pursuing his legendary success on radio and TV. His last movie role was in *A Guide for the Married Man* (1967), seven years before his death at the age of eighty.

BERGMAN, INGRID (1915–1982)   While the decade of the 1930s was blessed with hugely talented actresses such as Marlene Dietrich, Greta Garbo, and Bette Davis *(q.v.)*, most of the top female stars of the period were highly stylized performers. Ingrid Bergman's seemingly effortless naturalism was so new and fresh to American moviegoers that she quickly found a large and admiring audience. Her luminous beauty, intriguing accent, and considerable acting talent only added to her allure. In addition to making quite a number of memorable movies, Bergman has the distinction of having inadvertently been one of the first Hollywood performers to help break down the studio contract system. She is also

Ingrid Bergman was perhaps the only actress after Greta Garbo who could be breathtakingly beautiful and agonizingly soulful at the same time. Bergman's acting, however, was far less stylized and audiences prized her accessibility. Photo courtesy of Movie Star News.

remembered as having been, at one time or another, Hollywood's most loved and most hated female star.

Born in Sweden, Bergman's early life was filled with tragedy. Both of her parents died when she was still a young girl; she was raised by relatives. Thanks to her inheritance, however, she was able to pursue a course of study at the Royal Dramatic Theater in Stockholm.

In 1934, she had a small role as a maid in her first film, *Munkbrogreven*. She continued to act in the Swedish cinema, eventually earning leading roles and making a total of twelve films in Europe over a five-year period.

Meanwhile, David O. Selznick's *(q.v.)* trusted story editor, Katherine Brown, saw one of Bergman's Swedish films, *Intermezzo* (1936), and insisted that the producer not only buy the rights to the story but sign the Swedish actress to star in the remake, as well.

Selznick wisely followed Brown's suggestion and brought Bergman to Hollywood on a one-picture deal. *Intermezzo* (1939), with Leslie Howard *(q.v.)* as her costar, was an immediate hit and Selznick wasted no time in calling Bergman back from Sweden, signing her up to a seven-year contract.

After his success with *Gone With the Wind* *(q.v., 1939)*, Selznick made relatively few films and simply didn't have suitable projects for Bergman. Yet, she soon became a gold mine for the producer, who loaned her out to a succession of studios for huge sums of money—but not right away. After a stint on Broadway, she starred in three successful 1941 films before she made the leap to superstardom, including *Dr. Jekyll and Mr. Hyde.*

Bergman had desperately wanted to play the lead role of Maria in the Paramount production of Hemingway's *For Whom the Bell Tolls.* Gary Cooper was already cast and she was terribly disappointed when an actress named Vera Zorina won the part instead. It was unclear what movie she would star in next until Hedy Lamarr *(q.v.)* turned down the role of Ilsa Lund in *Casablanca (q.v., 1942).* The rest, as they say, is history. Playing opposite Humphrey Bogart *(q.v.),* she injected her soulfulness into one of the greatest love stories the movies have ever produced. The film was a smash hit, establishing Bogart as a romantic leading man and Bergman as a sexy, vulnerable star with enormous box-office appeal.

The combination of *Casablanca's* success and Vera Zorina's inability to carry her role in *For Whom the Bell Tolls* (1943) led to a surprise turnaround. Zorina was fired and Bergman was suddenly pursued for the role that she had so vigorously sought nearly a year earlier. The actress was superb in the film and the movie was yet another major box office hit.

Ironically, just as she was not the first choice for her previous two box-office triumphs, Bergman's next two winners also fell to her by default. *Gaslight* (1944) had been originally intended for Irene Dunne *(q.v.),* and later, for Hedy Lamarr, but Bergman not only won the role, she won her first Oscar for Best Actress for her performance as a woman nearly driven insane by her husband (Charles Boyer, *q.v.*). It was Vivien Leigh *(q.v.)* who turned down *Saratoga Trunk* (1945), giving Bergman the opportunity to star in yet another hit film.

She was the hottest female star in Hollywood. Every film she graced was a box office bonanza, including the last three she made under contract to Selznick: *Spellbound* (1945), *The Bells of St. Mary's* (1945), and *Notorious* (1946). Ironically, among all her hit films after *Intermezzo,* only the two Hitchcock films, *Spellbound* and *Notorious,* were Selznick productions.

When the producer tried to re-sign her for another seven years (at considerably better terms than her first contract), Bergman turned him down, choosing instead to make her own deals as a free-lance star. Her ability to free herself of studio domination was an early blow against the studio contract system. Unfortunately, her contractual freedom didn't do her very much good.

A series of poor film choices, such as *Arch of Triumph* (1948), *Joan of Arc* (1948), and a rare Hitchcock dud, *Under Capricorn* (1949), sent her stock spiraling downward. Her descent, however, wasn't fatal until she made *Stromboli* (1950) for Italian film director Roberto Rossellini.

Though Bergman was married to Dr. Peter Lindstrom and had a child by him (Pia Lindstrom, currently a New York TV performing arts critic), she fell in love with Rossellini, had a baby by him, and became a pariah in America virtually overnight. She was even denounced on the floor of the U.S. Senate, where she was called "Hollywood's apostle of degradation." The public flames of indignation and outrage over her infidelity were fanned by the fact that her image had been particularly pure and wholesome. After all, she had played a nun in the *Bells of St. Mary's* and a saint in *Joan of Arc.* It didn't matter that she quickly divorced Lindstrom and married Rossellini. The damage was done.

Not only was Bergman *persona non grata* in America, so were her films. *Stromboli* had limited bookings and so did the subsequent five movies she made in collaboration with her new husband.

Despite the birth of two more children (twins), her marriage to Rossellini collapsed and it appeared as if the same was true of her film career. Jean Renoir tried to help her by giving her the lead in his film *Paris Does Strange Things* (1956). But the real turnaround occured when Twentieth Century-Fox took a chance and hired her to star in *Anastasia* (1957). Not only was the film a huge hit—her first since *Notorious* more than a decade earlier—she even won her second Oscar for Best Actress in the bargain.

Bergman's marriage to Rossellini was annulled in 1958, and the actress eventually married theatrical producer Lars Schmidt. But for film fans, the big news was that the love affair between America and Ingrid Bergman was on again. In fact, over the ensuing decades, despite relatively few significant films, the actress became even more adored and admired by her fans than ever before, perhaps because she survived the scandal with so much dignity.

She enjoyed a short period of good work in fine films such as *Indiscreet* (1957) and *The Inn of the Sixth Happiness* (1958), but by the late 1950s and throughout the 1960s, there were relatively few good roles for her. It wasn't until she joined the all-star cast of *Murder on the Orient Express* (1974) that she had a solid, meaty role, and she won a Oscar for Best Supporting Actress for her efforts.

Perhaps the best performance of her later years was given in her very last film, *Autumn Sonata* (1978), in which her life came full circle. It was made by Swedish director Ingmar Bergman and concerned the coming to terms of a dying concert pianist with her estranged daughter. Ingrid Bergman's haunting, autobiographical performance, for which she was nominated for yet another Academy Award as Best Actress, was a fitting end to her long and illustrious career.

She died of cancer in 1982.
See also: *Casablanca;* scandals

BERKELEY, BUSBY (1895–1976) A choreographer and director who revolutionized the movie musical, Berkeley used the camera not just as a recording device but as an active participant in his wildly creative musical extravaganzas. Berkeley was more successful at directing musical sequences than he was at directing entire films, but his musical numbers, boasting such attractions as one hundred dancing pianos, chorus girls dressed in costumes made of coins, and waterfalls dripping with scantily clad women, were the very reason audiences flocked to see the movies with which his name is so closely associated. His most famous musical numbers appeared in *42nd Street* (1933), *Gold Diggers of 1933* (1933), and *Footlight Parade* (1933). He directed two other films for which he is also well known: *Gold Diggers of 1935* (1935) and *The Gang's All Here* (1943). Though Berkeley worked on many more films, this handful of movies, his most significant contribution, represents the Hollywood musical film at its gloriously gaudy height. In all, Berkeley worked on more than fifty movies, providing the inspiration for a great many musical numbers that rank among the film industry's most entertaining.

Born William Berkeley Enos, he was the scion of a theatrical family in whose footsteps he followed by taking to the stage at five years of age. At roughly that same time, he was tagged with the nickname that would follow him throughout his life, taken from a famous stage actress, Amy Busby.

Although his acting career never took off, his ability as a dance director garnered him much admiration for his work on Broadway during the latter half of the 1920s. His reputation was such that Samuel Goldwyn *(q.v.)* hired him to stage the musical numbers for the film version of Eddie Cantor's *(q.v.)* *Whoopee!* (1930). Once in Hollywood, Berkeley had found his true element. The movie musical was a new form, barely three years old, and he set about doing things that no one had ever imagined before.

After feeling his way through films such as Mary Pickford's *(q.v.)* only musical, *Kiki* (1931), and several other Eddie Cantor vehicles, including *Palmy Days* (1931) and *The Kid From Spain* (1932), Berkeley was hired by Darryl F. Zanuck *(q.v., then at Warner Bros.)* to add some dash to several contemporary (Depression era) backstage musicals. *42nd Street, Gold Diggers of 1933,* and *Footlight Parade* were all made with lavish budgets, and Berkeley made sure that every nickel was well spent.

Unlike the musical numbers in an Astaire/Rogers film, Berkeley's approach was that of mass choreography; he filled the screen full of blonde beauties lost in a swirl of light, motion, and kaleidoscopic effects. Critics have called his work everything from fascisticly dehumanizing to kitsch, but his art is really guided by simple escapism. Yet even in the midst of all his frivolity, the choreographer could deliver a powerful punch, as in the stirring "Forgotten Man" finale of *Gold Diggers*

of 1933, which reminded audiences of World War I veterans who had recently marched on Washington, D.C. in order to receive promised benefits, and the implicit warning against hedonism in his later musical masterpiece, "The Lullaby of Broadway" number in his own *Gold Diggers of 1935.*

Berkeley worked steadily at Warner Bros. from 1933 to 1938, providing that studio with musical numbers in films such as *Dames* (1934), *Wonder Bar* (1934), *Fashions of 1934* (1934), *Gold Diggers of 1937* (1936), *Gold Diggers in Paris* (1938), and many more. At the same time, he also directed a number of films for Warners, among them, *Bright Lights* (1935), *Stage Struck* (1936), and *Hollywood Hotel* (1937).

Berkeley's chief difficulty at Warner Bros. was the studio's loss of interest in musicals by the mid-1930s, resulting in only small budgets with which to work. Berkeley was the Cecil B. DeMille *(q.v.)* of the musical, and "B" movie *(q.v.)* budgets simply wouldn't do. So, he left Warners and went to MGM just as that studio entered its musical golden age. He contributed to the start of that era by directing such films as *Babes in Arms* (1939), *Strike Up the Band* (1940), *Babes on Broadway* (1941), and *For Me and My Gal* (1942), which, incidentally, turned Gene Kelly into a star. In the meantime, Berkeley also continued to direct musical numbers in other directors' films at MGM, including *Born to Sing* (1942), *Cabin in the Sky* (1943), and *Girl Crazy* (1943).

Berkeley had the opportunity to direct his first all-color musical at Twentieth Century-Fox in 1943 and he produced one of Hollywood's most memorable camp classics, *The Gang's All Here,* with Carmen Miranda *(q.v.).* While the movie was mediocre, the musical numbers were awe-inspiring in their incredible outrageousness.

Berkeley's health failed during the mid-1940s and he suffered a mental collapse. He finally returned to filming in 1948, directing the musical numbers of Doris Day's *(q.v.)* first film, *Romance on the High Seas.* His last film was *Take Me Out to the Ball Game* (1949), a hit with Frank Sinatra and Gene Kelly, whose musical numbers, ironically, he did not direct.

He continued to work on the musical direction in other directors' films during the 1950s, most notably in Esther Williams' *(q.v.)* *Million Dollar Mermaid* (1952) and *Rose Marie* (1954). He also added his special touch to *Jumbo* (1962).

Berkeley became a "forgotton man" until he made a triumphant return to the Broadway stage, directing a revival of *No, No, Nanette* in 1970. In the last years of his life he was lionized for work that most agree Hollywood will never be able to duplicate.

See also: musicals

BERLIN, IRVING (1888–1989) A composer and lyricist, he wrote more than one thousand songs, a great many of his most famous tunes for the movies and the theater. Curiously, he could only compose songs in the key of F sharp, but with the help of a transposing device connected to his piano, he created a remarkable number of standards that significantly helped to shape the direction of popular music in the movies for three decades. His songs were sentimental yet a shade short of maudlin, and though the lyrics were generally simple and easy to remember, that didn't mean they weren't often clever and incisive. Movie musicals of the 1930s, 1940s, and 1950s were immeasurably enriched by his compositions.

Born Israel Isidore Baline in Russia's Siberia, he arrived in America with his family when he was five years old. After a youth spent on New York's Lower East Side, Berlin worked as a singing waiter and penned his first published song, "Marie from Sunny Italy" (1907). Success came soon thereafter with his first hit, "Alexander's Ragtime Band" (1911), which later served as the theme song and title of a popular 1938 film.

His song "Blue Skies" was sung by Al Jolson *(q.v.)* in the first talkie, *The Jazz Singer* (1927), and he continued to write for films, with songs appearing in such movies as *Hallelujah!* (1929), *Puttin' on the Ritz* (1930), and *Kid Millions* (1934). Some of his greatest songs were introduced by Fred Astaire in the Astaire/Rogers films of the 1930s, including "Cheek to Cheek" in *Top Hat* (1935), "Let Yourself Go" in *Follow the Fleet* (1936), and "I Used to be Color Blind" in *Carefree* (1938).

When World War II broke out, Berlin recreated his World War I show, *This is the Army,* put it on stage, and then worked as associate producer when it was brought to the screen in 1943. He then went several steps further, acting and singing in the movie, as well. It was during this period that Berlin was awarded the Congressional Gold Medal for his song "God Bless America."

After the war, Berlin provided the songs for films such as *Blue Skies* (1946) and *Easter Parade* (1948). And he didn't slow down in the 1950s either, penning tunes for *Annie Get Your Gun* (1950), *White Christmas* (1954), and *There's No Business Like Show Business* (1954), among others.

Remarkably, Berlin received just one Oscar for Best Song "White Christmas," which he wrote for the film *Holiday Inn* (1942).

BERMAN, PANDRO S. (1905–   ) Though he is most closely associated with the Fred Astaire/Ginger Rogers musicals of the 1930s at RKO, Berman produced top-notch films in every genre in a career spanning nearly forty years. He was honored by the Academy of Motion Picture Arts and Sciences with the prestigious Irving M. Thalberg Award in 1976 for his "outstanding motion picture production." Under his stewardship, a long

list of now famous films were made, first at RKO and later at MGM.

Berman's success in Hollywood is owed to a happy case of nepotism. His father was an executive at Universal Pictures *(q.v.)*, where the younger Berman was given the opportunity to break into the film business at an early age, working as an assistant director during the silent era for the likes of Tod Browning *(q.v.)* and Mal St. Clair. He went on to become a film editor at RKO in the late 1920s, working on such films as *Taxi 13* (1928) and *Stocks & Blondes* (1928). Berman's hands-on moviemaking experience later proved invaluable, giving him the expertise to produce technically excellent movies, a reputation for which he was justly proud.

He began his producing career in 1931 at RKO with *Symphony of Six Million* (1932), going on to make many of that studio's greatest films. In addition to making many of the Astaire/Rogers movies that kept RKO financially afloat during the Depression, Berman produced a number of Katharine Hepburn's *(q.v.)* most memorable 1930s movies, among them *Christopher Strong* (1933), *Morning Glory* (1933), for which she won her first Oscar, *Alice Adams* (1935), and *Sylvia Scarlett* (1936). In addition, he produced the Marx Brothers *(q.v.)* comedy *Room Service* (1938), along with such classics as *Gunga Din* (1939) and *The Hunchback of Notre Dame* (1939).

When he moved to MGM in 1940, Berman at first produced such light musicals as *Ziegfeld Girl* (1941) and *Rio Rita* (1942). It wasn't long, however, before he began making many of MGM's most prestigious movies, among them *The Seventh Cross* (1944), *Madame Bovary* (1949), and *Ivanhoe* (1952). More noteworthy, however, was Berman's success in highlighting new talent. Besides having discovered Katharine Hepburn at RKO, the producer fostered the career of Elizabeth Taylor *(q.v.)* at MGM, making such films with the young actress as *National Velvet* (1944), *Father of the Bride* (1950), and *Butterfield 8* (1960), for which she received her first Academy Award.

After having produced some of the greatest musicals of the 1930s, Berman was called on in the later 1950s to do so again for a new generation, producing what many consider to be Elvis Presley's *(q.v.)* best musical, *Jailhouse Rock* (1957).

Berman continued producing films throughout the 1960s, making such movies as *Sweet Bird of Youth* (1962), *The Prize* (1963), *A Patch of Blue* (1965), and *Justine* (1969). His last film before retiring was *Move* (1970).

BEST BOY Though the name seems to describe a menial position, best boy is in reality one of the more important jobs on a film set. The job title applies to two different people on a film crew: the assistant to the gaffer and the assistant to the key grip. The grip best boy is the second in command of all the grips, and the gaffer best boy is the second in command of all the electricians.

See also: gaffer; grip

BILLING   The order and size of the names listed in the credits of a movie. As a matter of prestige and clout in the film industry, billing has always been a serious consideration among actors, directors, producers, screenwriters, and most everyone else in the film community.

How one is credited in a film is usually a contractual issue. Many stars, for example, insist upon top billing. This has often caused problems when two stars with the identical clause in their contracts are slated to appear in the same film. Usually compromises are made, such as giving one star top billing east of the Mississippi river and the other star top billing west of the Mississippi river. Without a compromise solution, the issue of billing can often scuttle the participation of one or more of the actors.

The most sought-after billing by actors, directors, and producers is the placement of one's name above the title of the film. Some of those who have achieved such status include Charlie Chaplin, Frank Capra, and Steven Spielberg *(qq.v.).*

BIOGRAPH   A film studio of the silent era best known for having nurtured the early career of D. W. Griffith *(q.v.).* Or perhaps it is more accurate to say that Griffith nurtured the success of Biograph until the film studio drove the creative genius out of the company.

Originally called the American Mutoscope and Biograph Company, the fledgeling film studio eventually became known simply as Biograph. The name change, however, didn't help the studio's image. The company was a floundering proposition, selling only twenty films in all of 1907. It wasn't until D. W. Griffith began directing movies for the company in 1908 that Biograph's reputation—and profits—soared.

By 1910, Biograph had become one of the most powerful members of the Motion Picture Patents Company, an organization of film studios created by Thomas A. Edison that attempted to monopolize the movie business and destroy the independents.

The Patents Company had decreed that the names of movie actors would not be released to the public, for fear that the stars would become too popular and demand higher salaries. The public and the press referred to actors by nicknames, such as "The Vitagraph Girl" and "Little Mary." But it was "The Biograph Girl" who was the first to break free of the Patents Company restrictions giving birth to the "star system" that is still with us today.

The real name of the Biograph Girl was Florence Lawrence, and she was lured away from her studio by one of the early successful independents, Carl Laemmle. She went on to become one of the great silent stars of her era, but Biograph survived the blow due to director D. W. Griffith's ability to come up with movies that were more exciting, more inventive, and better made than those of the competition.

In the end, Biograph's success or failure was entirely in the hands of its famous director. As he developed the visual language of film, first shooting one-reelers, and then two-reelers, audiences continued to respond, choosing Biograph films by name. When Griffith wanted to make longer films, however, the studio refused his request, insisting that American audiences wouldn't watch any movie that was longer than twenty minutes in length. Griffith ignored their directive and, while in California during the winter of 1913, secretly made a minor masterpiece in four reels titled *Judith of Bethulia.* So enraged was Biograph that the company refused to release it. So disgusted was Griffith with management's stupidity, he quickly resigned.

It was a terrible blow to Biograph. Not only did it lose its great director, but Griffith also took with him his stock company of actors, which included such soon-to-become fabled names as Dorothy and Lillian Gish *(q.v.),* Blanche Sweet *(q.v.),* and Mae Marsh. Perhaps most important of all, Griffith also took with him Biograph's most innovative cameraman, G. W. "Billy" Bitzer *(q.v.).*

It was the beginning of the end for Biograph. The company disappeared a few years later.

BIOPICS   A contraction of the words "biographical" and "pictures," the term is Hollywood slang for a movie category that has long been a staple of the film industry. Biopics are movie versions of actual people's lives, from honored statesmen to show business personalities. Hollywood film biographies haven't always been terribly accurate in the portrayal of their subjects, but accuracy has never been an explicit goal; a good, dramatic story with strong entertainment value has always been the sought-after result. More often than not, the biopics from the dream factory have managed not only to entertain but to enlighten, as well.

The biopic existed in the silent era, but it came into its own as a film category very early with the talkies thanks to George Arliss' *(q.v.)* stately (if stagey) performances at Warner Bros. in a series of popular historical biographies such as *Disraeli* (1929), *Alexander Hamilton* (1931), *Voltaire* (1933). Arliss set the Hollywood pattern of teaching history through the very palatable medium of filmmaking. He was followed at Warners—a studio that specialized in biopics—by Paul Muni *(q.v.),* who made a strong mark playing historical

The subjects of biopics have been as wide-ranging as famous scientists, statesmen, and baseball players. Hollywood has also had an understandable propensity for making biopics based on the lives of show business people, as evidenced by Clint Eastwood's highly regarded depiction of musician Charlie Parker's life in *Bird* (1988). Photo © Warner Bros., Inc. Courtesy of Malpaso.

characters in films such as *The Story of Louis Pasteur* (1936), *The Life of Emile Zola* (1937), and *Juarez* (1939).

Warners, of course, wasn't alone in making biopics. MGM jumped into the category in a big way in the late 1930s and early 1940s, with Spencer Tracy *(q.v.)* playing the real-life Father Flanagan of *Boys Town* (1938) and the famous reporter Stanley in *Stanley and Livingston* (1939). Then MGM made two film biographies of Thomas Alva Edison in the same year, *Young Tom Edison* (1940), with Mickey Rooney as the inventor, and *Edison the Man* (1940), once again starring Spencer Tracy in the title role.

Biopics have been used by filmmakers as a means of using historical figures to make contemporary political and/or social statements. For instance, as World War II approached, a different sort of biopic appeared that extolled the heroism of famous soldiers, such as *Sergeant York* (1941), and even General George Armstrong Custer in *They Died With Their Boots On* (1942). The films proved popular, and soldier stories have served as biopic fodder ever since in films ranging from Audie Murphy's *To Hell and Back* (1955) to *Patton* (1970).

Finding a perfect blend of melodrama and truth in the lives of America's gangsters, Hollywood has made numerous biopics like *Baby Face Nelson* (1957), *Capone* (1975), and *Bonnie and Clyde* (1967).

Western heroes (and villains) have also been the stuff of biopics, although films such as *I Shot Jesse James* (1949), *Pat Garrett and Billy the Kid* (1973), and *Butch Cassidy and the Sundance Kid* (1969) tend to romanticize their subjects more than biographical films of other personalities.

One of the most popular and logical areas that biopics have mined has been the area of sports. From *Knute Rockne, All American* (1940) to *Jim Thorpe—All American* (1951), and from *Pride of the Yankees* (the Lou Gehrig bio, 1942) to *Fear Strikes Out* (the Jimmy Piersall story, 1957), the movies have found high drama and solid ticket sales in biographies of famous and/or fascinating sports stars.

Hollywood has gone far afield for its biopic subjects, making films in the 1950s about fliers such as *The Court-Martial of Billy Mitchell* (1955) and *The Spirit of St. Louis* (the Lindbergh story, 1957), as well as films about painters, such as Toulouse-Lautrec in *Moulin Rouge* (1952) and Vincent Van Gogh in *Lust for Life* (1956).

But the film industry discovered a gold mine of subject matter in its own backyard when it made a biopic about one of its own, Al Jolson, the famous entertainer who had been the first talkie star. The film, *The Jolson Story* (1946), was a smash hit musical. There had been other show business biopics before, but *The Jolson Story* was such a huge success that, like *Star Wars* in a later generation, it acted as a bellwether for similar projects. The studios assumed that audiences reacted to the music in *The Jolson Story* and commissioned a rash of show business musical biopics based on popular composers such as Cole Porter, in *Night and Day* (1946), and Rodgers and (lyricist) Hart, in *Words and Music* (1947), but the big box office went again to the continuation of the Jolson story, *Jolson Sings Again* (1949).

Show business biopics, particularly musicals, have been popular ever since, making up a significant number of the films in this category in the 1950s with titles including *The Glenn Miller Story* (1954) and *The Benny Goodman Story* (1955), and then reemerging in the last two decades with *The Buddy Holly Story* (1978), Loretta Lynn's saga in *Coal Miner's Daughter* (1980), and the Ritchie Valens biography presented in the recent *La Bamba* (1987).

To some extent, made-for-TV-movies have moved into the biopic arena, making films about historical figures such as Golda Meir, Anwar Sadat, Jimmy Hoffa, etc. Hollywood, it is fair to say, will continue making musical biopics because it is an area in which TV cannot compete as easily because of the better sound offered by theaters. In addition, musical biopics tend to attract younger audiences, which are the film industry's core. *See also:* musicals; sports films

THE BIRTH OF A NATION David Wark Griffith's controversial 1915 masterpiece that revolutionized the

D. W. Griffith's epic *The Birth of a Nation* (1915), was a milestone in the development of film art. President Woodrow Wilson was quoted as saying that it was "like writing history in lightning." Photo courtesy of The Siegel Collection.

art of filmmaking was based on the Reverend Thomas E. Dixon's novel, *The Clansman,* which had been turned into a play. Both the novel and the play, which offered a Southerner's view of Civil War history, enjoyed considerable popularity in the early years of the twentieth century. Griffith, a Southerner, bought the film rights from Dixon for $2,500 and a guarantee of twenty-five percent of the profits (should there be any).

According to one of the stars of the film, Lillian Gish *(q.v.),* there was no script for The Birth of a Nation. "He [Griffith] carried the ideas in his head." Conceived by Griffith and shot by his longtime cameraman, G. W. "Billy" Bitzer *(q.v.),* the movie was an immense undertaking, made on a grander scale than any Amer-

ican movie of the time. But more important, it was the first feature film in which the plot was advanced through a flow of cinematic images; there was nothing static about this film, the camera was not merely the passive recorder of staged scenes. This new, relatively sophisticated form of moviemaking had a stunning impact on the art of the film.

Perhaps the greatest single technique employed by Griffith in *The Birth of a Nation* was his use of editing. In the dramatic conclusion of the film, he constantly intercut between two scenes, showing first a close-up shot of Lillian Gish and Miriam Cooper in dire straits at the hands of an evil black man and his minions (depicted with outlandish rascism by Griffith), and then the ride of the Ku Klux Klan (coming to the rescue, much like the cavalry in later westerns). Content aside, Griffith's juxtaposition of images for various lengths of time, brought a heightened dramatic tension to the climax that only could have been created on film.

Though *The Birth of a Nation* was attacked in some quarters for its rascism, the film brought a new level of respectability to the movie medium. After all, before Griffith's film, very few important people had deigned to comment on the substance of a movie. But that changed forever; *The Birth of A Nation* was the first film ever screened at the White House. In fact, President Woodrow Wilson was quoted as saying, "It is like writing history with lightning."

The public was as mesmerized as the president. The film was a gigantic hit, grossing more than $18 million and earning a profit of $5 million. Its financial success had a marked effect on the business of filmmaking. The feature-length film, as we know it today, had arrived and was embraced by the masses. The era of the two-reeler as a movie mainstay had come to an end.
See also: Bitzer, G.W. "Billy"; Griffith, D. W.

BITZER, G. W. "BILLY" (1874–1944) George William Bitzer, a former electrician, became one of the most important cameramen in Hollywood history. Bitzer was both a technical innovator and an artist who teamed with D. W. Griffith to make some of the most influential movies of the silent era.

A true pioneer in the film business, Bitzer was learning about the camera as early as the 1890s, shooting footage of William McKinley's acceptance of his party's nomination for president in 1896 and capturing on film the famous Jeffries-Sharkey championship boxing match in 1899. Later, he joined the Biograph film company, working as a jack-of-all trades but principally handling the camera.

In 1908, when D. W. Griffith began his directorial career at Biograph, he often relied on Bitzer's advice and expertise. Out of that early association grew a collaboration that lasted sixteen years. Together, Bitzer and Griffith changed the face of filmmaking with movies such as *Judith of Bethulia* (1913), *The Birth of a Nation* (1915), *Intolerance* (1916), *Broken Blossoms,* (1919), *Way Down East* (1921), and *America* (1924).

Bitzer, often at the instigation of Griffith, created original camera techniques such as the close-up, the fade-out, soft-focus photography, and backlighting, to name just a few of his innovations. Bitzer even helped invent a 3-D process that was popular for several years in the early 1920s.

But Bitzer was more than a technical wizard. When he shot *The Birth of a Nation,* he consciously tried to recreate the look of Matthew Brady's famous nineteenth-century photographs. And he succeeded. More

astonishing is the fact that he shot the entire complex epic himself, using just one camera.

Bitzer died in 1944, the acknowledged leading pioneer in cinematography.
See also: Biograph; *The Birth of a Nation;* cinematographer; Griffith, D. W.

BLACHÉ, ALICE GUY (1873–1968) Not only was she the first female director in the history of world cinema, she was also the first woman to own her own film studio in America. This trail-blazing moviemaker began her career in 1896 as a secretary with the Gaumont film company in France. There, she was given the opportunity to write and direct her first film, *La Fée aux Choux (The Cabbage Fairy),* in early 1896. If this date is correct—and there is some dispute on the matter—she might well have directed the very first film story in the history of cinema, preceding Georges Méliés' efforts by several months.

Born Alice Guy, she married Herbert Blaché, an important Gaumont cameraman, in 1907. Together, they traveled to America where Herbert opened a Gaumont office. By 1910, Alice had plunged back into filmmaking, opening her own studio in New York and calling it the Solax Company. Her first U.S. film, made as both a director and a producer, was *A Child's Sacrifice* (1910). Her company was initially successful and her films were highly regarded. In his book *Early Women Directors,* Anthony Slide reported that during the years 1910 to 1914, she either directed or supervised the direction "of every one of Solax's three hundred or so productions."

She had built a new studio in Fort Lee, New Jersey, but was convinced to leave her company and join her husband's new firm, Blaché Features, later to become the U.S. Amusement Company and finally Popular Plays and Players. She continued to direct without significant interference, however, until 1917, after which she occasionally directed for other film companies, making movies such as *A Soul Adrift* (1918) and, her last film, *Vampire* (1920). She was offered other directorial projects, such as *Tarzan of the Apes,* but with her marriage at an end, she chose to leave the U.S. in 1922 and return to France.

Alice Guy Blaché tried to break into the French film industry without success and never directed another movie. It wasn't until 1953 that the French government finally awarded her the Legion of Honor. The American film industry, however, has never bestowed any honor upon one of its most courageous pioneers.
See also: women directors

BLACK COMEDY A provocative form of film humor dealing with subject matter that society generally finds troubling or distasteful. It's no wonder, therefore, that black comedy almost always makes audiences uneasy and disturbed even as they laugh. Black comedy, or dark humor, often revolves around issues of death and dying, but it can also touch upon taboo sexual, social, and political issues. What ultimately differentiates black comedy from farce is that it doesn't undercut or apologize for itself at the end; in order to be a full-blooded black comedy, a film must have the courage of its convictions right through to its darkly comic finale.

The first Hollywood film to approach black comedy was Ernst Lubitsch's *(q.v.)* classic 1942 movie about Nazis in Poland, *To Be Or Not To Be*. Screamingly funny, the film was dark indeed, with a comic character known by the epithet "Concentration Camp Erhardt." Despite a happy ending, the film was condemned as being in bad taste and it bombed when it was released in the early years of World War II.

Another black comedy that opened during the war (although it wasn't about the war at all), became a huge hit. *Arsenic and Old Lace* (1944), based on a hit play of the same name, depicted two sweet old lady murderers who happily buried their victims in their cellar. Made by Frank Capra *(q.v.)* before he became involved in the war effort, and released long after it was made, the film was arguably the first genuine Hollywood black comedy.

Black comedies have rarely been made by Hollywood studios, which have preferred to entertain rather than disturb their audiences. Only an independent filmmaker such as Charlie Chaplin *(q.v.)* could have made such a dark and deeply chilling comedy as *Monsieur Verdoux* (1947), in which he comically murders rich old women for their money. Considered a masterpiece today, the film was reviled at the time it opened.

The 1950s was a time of complacency in America in all manner of things, including black comedy. It wasn't until Stanley Kubrick *(q.v.)* made *Dr. Strangelove or: How I Learned to Stop Worrying and Love the Bomb* in 1964 that black comedy was reborn both critically and commercially. The film remains one of the most successful black comedies in movie history.

Other black comedies followed, but without the same reception at the box office. *The Loved One* (1965), a film version of Evelyn Waugh's novel about Hollywood's peculiar burial customs, drew a great deal of controversy but didn't draw a large crowd.

If there was a golden age of black comedy, it was probably during the 1970s, and it began with the low-budget release of two films that quickly became cult classics, *Where's Poppa?* (1970) and *Harold and Maude* (1971). By the end of the decade, black comedies were being made with big budgets and major stars, and were big box office, as evidenced by the success of such films as the Burt Reynolds movie, *The End* (1978).

The commercial viability of black comedies has spurred their production, making the genre far more accessible in the 1980s, as exemplified by such movies as *Ruthless People* (1986) and *Throw Momma from the Train* (1987).

One might even begin to consider black comedy the normal comic fare of our time.
See also: cult movies; satire on the screen

BLACK MARIA: This is the colorful name given to the world's first movie studio, a unique building designed by William Dickson and constructed in West Orange, New Jersey by Thomas A. Edison *(q.v.)* in 1893. Edison put his invention, the movie camera, inside this large wooden shack that was covered inside and out by black tarpaper to keep out all extraneous light. The Black Maria also had a moveable roof that, when opened, allowed sunlight to pour down directly onto a crude stage, and its entire structure was built on tracks so the building could swivel, following the movement of the sun (providing the necessary light for shooting). The building received its name from Edisons's staff, who likened the dark, hot, claustrophobic structure to the police vans of the day that were known by the same descriptive expression.

BLANKE, HENRY (1901–1981)   A producer who was associated with many of Warner Bros.' best movies of the 1930s and 1940s, often under the leadership of Hal B. Wallis *(q.v.)*. His good taste and cinematic judgment (which came from a solid grounding in filmmaking) helped create an impressive number of intelligent and popular movies.

Blanke, who was born and raised in Germany, recieved his early training working with director Ernst Lubitsch *(q.v.)*. He came to America as Lubitsch's personal assistant in 1922, but only stayed for a couple of years before returning to work in Germany, most notably with Fritz Lang *(q.v.)* on the director's early masterpiece *Metropolis* (1926). Blanke would become associated with a number of great masterworks, particularly after he became a producer at Warner Bros. in 1933.

Before rising to the rank of producer, however, Blanke worked at a number of jobs for Warners. He was the head of the studio's German affiliate and later was put in charge of films made for export to Europe.

Blanke's reputation at the studio was such that he was given both the best and the toughest assignments: the prestigious Max Reinhardt version of *A Midsummer Night's Dream* (1935); the difficult Paul Muni biopics *(qq.v.)* *The Life of Emile Zola* (1937) and *Juarez* (1939); the big technicolor extravaganza *The Adventures of Robin Hood* (1938); John Huston's first film, *The Maltese Falcon* (1941), and the director's most ambitious movie at Warners, *The Treasure of the Sierra Madre* (1948). During his tenure at Warners, Blanke eventually earned the title production supervisor, though usually he still worked under Hal Wallis, with whom he made an excellent team.

Whether at Warners or not, Blanke was often involved in demanding, challenging films, such as the adaptation of Ayn Rand's classic novel *The Fountainhead* (1949), and an excellent movie about alcoholism, *Come Fill the Cup* (1951).

The producer's career, along with the rest of Hollywood, went into a decline during the better part of the 1950s. He made a number of successful films, however, before calling it quits in the early 1960s; among his last efforts were *The Nun's Story* (1959), *The Sins of Rachel Cade* (1961), and *Hell is for Heroes* (1962).

BLIMP A soundproof covering that fits over a camera, dampening its whir so that microphones will not pick up the sound of the camera when dialogue is being recorded as part of a scene. Cameras are designed so that their controls extend beyond the padding of the blimp, leaving the camera fully operational when the blimp is in place. A blimp is generally made of either aluminum or magnesium, and insulated with rubber and plastic foam. More advanced cameras have sound dampening materials built in to their design, and these cameras are known as "self-blimped."

A more flexible form of blimp is known as a "barney." In addition to absorbing sound, a barney is also used to protect the camera from rain and extreme temperatures.

BLONDELL, JOAN (1901–1979) The workhorse of Warner Bros., she was an actress who appeared in more than fifty films during the 1930s, in virtually all of which she had significant supporting or leading roles. She was cast in so many films with good reason: Blondell was not only the quintessential Warner Bros. tough dame who could crack wise without losing audience sympathy, she was a versatile actress who was at home in musicals, crime melodramas, comedies, tearjerkers, and even period pieces. With a large, full face and pop eyes, Blondell was not particularly pretty or sexy, and therefore Warners didn't try to turn her into a romantic leading lady. Instead, she often played the heroine's best friend or a sassy sidekick to a male star. There was hardly any other actress in Hollywood who was better at being second banana.

A member of a successful vaudeville family, Blondell was one of the original Katzenjammer Kids, touring with her parents virtually from birth. She was a seasoned performer long before she reached Hollywood, having worked in Europe, China, and Australia before she quit the act and began appearing in stock productions in the United States. She made it to Broadway in 1927, and over the next three years starred in several plays, including two with James Cagney *(q.v.)*. One of these was *Penny Arcade,* which was bought by Warner Bros. and filmed as *Sinner's Holiday* in 1930 with the original stars.

Blondell and Cagney were often paired together during the rest of the decade, and to great effect in films such as *Blonde Crazy* (1931), *The Crowd Roars* (1932), *Footlight Parade* (1933), and *He Was Her Man* (1934). Other successful pairings were with Pat O'Brien *(q.v.)*, Glenda Farrell, and Dick Powell *(q.v.)* (to whom she was married for ten years, 1936–1945).

The economically depressed 1930s were Blondell's golden years, because she was eminently believable as a streetwise working girl during a period when almost all women had to work to make ends meet. But as is often the case, actors tend to be cited for roles least like the ones they're known for. Such was the case for "tough dame" Joan Blondell. She received her best notices in a precursor to *All About Eve* entitled *Stage Struck* (1936), in which she portrayed a famous actress in danger of losing her star status to an ingenue.

Warners' unwillingness to let her grow into bigger and better roles like that in *Stage Struck* eventually drove Blondell to leave the studio in 1939. She appeared in a great many more films, including a sequel to *Topper* (in which she replaced Constance Bennett), called *Topper Returns* (1941).

Blondell took off a great deal of time during the war to entertain the troops and, as a consequence, crippled her own career. One of her few films during this period was *A Tree Grows in Brooklyn* (1945), in which her performance as Aunt Cissy was one of her last two great triumphs. The other came long after the war was over, when she made a comeback in *The Blue Veil* (1951), a performance for which she received an Oscar nomination for Best Supporting Actress.

By the late 1950s, Blondell was appearing in character parts, which she continued to do throughout the 1960s without very much distinction, although there was a sense of *deja vu* when she appeared in a featured role in *The Cincinnati Kid* (1965) with another old Warner Bros. star, Edward G. Robinson *(q.v.)*.

Blondell always stayed busy, finding her way into a TV series, "Here Come the Brides" during the late 1960s. As one would expect of an actress who had worked almost from the day she was born, Joan Blondell worked virtually until the time of her death, appearing in small roles in *Grease* (1978) and *The Champ* (1979). Her last film was a Canadian film, *The Woman Inside,* that was released in 1981, two years after she died.

BOETTICHER, BUDD (1916–) A director whose life and work have been strikingly intertwined, Boetticher, born Oscar Boetticher, Jr. in Chicago, was an apprentice matador in Madrid in 1941 when he was hired as a technical consultant for Rouben Mamoulian's *(q.v.)* *Blood and Sand,* starring Tyrone Power *(q.v.)*. Seduced by the filmmaking business, Boetticher left the bullring, but the bullring never left Boetticher. The torero's way of life continued to influence the rest of his career both directly and indirectly.

He went to Hollywood and became one of the rare assistant directors to move on to directing his own films. By 1944, at the tender age of twenty-eight, he was making low-budget movies of no special distinction. But in 1951 he made a largely autobiographical film called *The Bullfighter and the Lady*. The success of that film gave him the opportunity to make somewhat higher-budget films with better casts.

The 1950s was the heyday of the western, a genre particularly close to Boetticher because of the link between the lonely gunman and the matador who faces danger all alone. He made several westerns, such as *The Cimarron Kid* (1951), *Horizons West* (1952), and *The Man From the Alamo* (1953).

In 1955, he returned yet again to the bullring for the story of *The Magnificent Matador,* but the movie was not a critical or popular success.

But from 1956 to 1960, Boetticher made his mark as a director of distinction in a series of westerns starring Randolph Scott *(q.v.).* The films, known as the "Ranown cycle" (because the movies were produced by the team of Randolph Scott and his partner Harry Joe Brown), were a distillation of the fundamental elements of the western: honor, pride, and machismo, with a marvelous simplicity that suggests both the style and themes of the work of Ernest Hemingway.

The first film Boetticher made with Scott, *Seven Men From Now* (1956), was not technically a Ranown production, but it set the series tone and style. The rest of the Ranown films were *The Tall T* (1957), *Decision at Sundown* (1957), *Buchanan Rides Alone* (1958), *Ride Lonesome* (1959), and *Commanche Station* (1960).

The westerns were short, simple, and elegantly directed. All of the films were commercially successful, and came to be viewed critically as the apotheosis of the western genre.

At the height of his career, Boetticher suddenly left Hollywood to make a documentary about the famous Mexican matador Arruza. He expected that it would take roughly six months to a year to make this film that was so close to his heart—instead, he worked on it for nearly eight years. During that time he lost his wife and his fortune; he was thrown in jail, spent time in an insane asylum and nearly died. He weathered the deaths of every member of his film crew including that of Arruza, himself, just a few months after filming was finished, but he never gave up on his movie. Later, when asked why he risked everything to make *Arruza,* Boetticher replied: "Wouldn't it have been a wonderful thing if the director of *The Agony and the Ecstasy* had Michelangelo instead of Charlton Heston?"

Though virtually forgotten in Hollywood, he returned there with his finished documentary, *Arruza* (1968), and tried to pick up where he had left off. But

Hollywood had changed in his absence. The western, his speciality, was losing favor as a viable commercial genre. He managed to direct one western, *A Time for Dying* (1969), and was supposed to direct Clint Eastwood and Shirley MacLaine *(q.v.)* in yet another based on his own story, *Two Mules for Sister Sara* (1970), but he was dropped in favor of Don Siegel *(q.v.).*

Boetticher never duplicated the success of his Ranown films. His career stalled, but *Arruza* still stands as a monument to artistic commitment.

See also: westerns

BOGART, HUMPHREY (1899–1957): Born to a prosperous New York family, young Humphrey DeForest Bogart lived a life very dissimilar to that of the hardbitten hoodlums and toughs he later played on the screen. After serving on a merchant ship during World War I (during which he received the distinctive wound to his lip that gave his face so much character), he went into the theater. In his early stage career, he usually played callow society types. Photos of him from the 1920s show a young man with striking Valentino-like good looks. After he attained stardom, Bogart often joked that he was the kind of stage actor who would enter a scene with a tennis racquet in his hand, calling out "Tennis, anyone?"

When the sound revolution hit Hollywood in the late 1920s, the film studios needed actors who could talk: Broadway was the answer. It was in that atmosphere that Bogart was signed by Fox. His first feature-length film was *Up the River* (1930), in which he had a substantial role. But his parts kept diminishing in size. He appeared in a total of ten films between 1930 and 1934; the most interesting among them is *Three on a Match* (1932), in which he played a gangster for the first time. Here one can catch an early glimpse of his tough-guy persona.

With his career seemingly going nowhere, Fox let Bogart go. A failure in the movies, he went back to Broadway. It was here that he had his first big break. He landed the supporting role of Duke Mantee in Robert Sherwood's *The Petrified Forest*. The hit play starred Leslie Howard *(q.v.),* and when Warner Bros. bought the rights to the story, they wanted the famous actor to play the lead. But they didn't want Bogart. Leslie Howard, however, insisted that Bogart be cast or else he wouldn't make the film. Warners finally relented and, when the film was released, Bogart received raves for his electric performance. As a result, Warner Bros. signed Bogart to a long-term contract. Further, Bogart later named his first child (with Lauren Bacall) Leslie, in honor of the man who helped make him a star.

From 1936 through 1940, Bogart played a variety of roles, from gangsters in melodramas such as *Bullets or Ballots* (1936) and *San Quentin* (1937) to well-meaning

Ever the tough-guy, Humphrey Bogart is the desperado Duke Mantee in a publicity still for *The Petrified Forest* (1936), the movie that finally established him in Hollywood. Photo courtesy of Movie Star News.

heroes in films like *Marked Woman* (1937) and *Crime School* (1938). Whenever Bogart had a leading role, it was either in support of another more famous actor or actress or in a low-budget movie for which Warners could find no other actor in their stable. Thus he appeared in *The Oklahoma Kid* (1939) and *Virginia City* (1940), two westerns for which he was thoroughly miscast. Even more striking was his being cast as a zombie with a white streak through his hair, making him look like a skunk, in *The Return of Dr. X* (1939). But when Bogart had a good role during these difficult years, he made the best of it. He gave a strong performance in *Black Legion* (1937) as an ordinary working man who falls under the spell of a hate group patterned after the Ku Klux Klan. As a gangster coming home in the classic *Dead End* (1937), he steals the movie from its star, Joel McCrea (*q.v.*).

Before he became a star, Bogart made a total of twenty-nine films during his second stint in Hollywood. The breakthrough occurred with *High Sierra* (1941). The lead role of gangster "Mad Dog" Roy Earl was first offered to George Raft (*q.v.*), but Raft turned it down because he didn't want to play a character who dies on screen. It was then offered to Paul Muni (*q.v.*), who turned it down because George Raft turned it down. The other Warner stars, James Cagney, John Garfield, and Edward G. Robinson (*qq.v.*), weren't going to star in a film that both George Raft and Paul Muni had refused. That left Bogart. Under the direction of action expert Raoul Walsh (*q.v.*), Bogart created a tough guy of touching vulnerability, a new kind of hero—the antihero.

John Huston (*q.v.*) had written the screenplay of *High Sierra,* and soon thereafter the young writer was given a chance to direct his first film. He chose *The Maltese Falcon* and he requested Bogart for the lead. He got him, and the film was a smash hit.

As Sam Spade in *The Maltese Falcon* (1941), Bogart became a solidly bankable Warner Bros. star. But he was an action star and had yet to prove himself as a romantic leading man. There was some doubt in Hollywood that he could make the leap. But then came *Casablanca,* directed by Michael Curtiz (*q.v.*) in 1942. Starring opposite Ingrid Bergman (*q.v.*) at her most beautiful, Bogart's performance (he was nominated for an Academy Award) further refined the definition of antihero and made him a full-fledged movie star of the first magnitude. It's worth noting, however, that Ronald Reagan (*q.v.*) was offered the part of Rick Blaine but he turned it down. Bogart's career was advanced by default yet again, but the result was what many people consider Bogart's quintessential performance.

Bogart's enduring fame during and after his lifetime is due both to his screen persona and to his good fortune at having worked with some of Hollywood's greatest directors. He worked, for instance, with Howard Hawks in *To Have and Have Not* (1944) and *The Big Sleep* (1946) and Nicholas Ray (*q.v.*) in *In a Lonely Place* (1950). But most important, Bogart worked with John Huston, not only in *The Maltese Falcon* but in five other top-notch films: *Across the Pacific* (1942), *The Treasure of the Sierra Madre* (1947), *Key Largo* (1948), *The African Queen* (1952)—for which he won an Academy Award as Best Actor—and *Beat the Devil* (1954). Every one of the collaborations between Huston and Bogart were either critically or commercially successful, or both.

Bogart took many chances with his career in the late 1940s and up until his death from cancer in 1957. Nonetheless, he had very few flops. In *The Two Mrs. Carrolls* (1947) he played a psychopathic painter trying to kill his wife (Barbara Stanwyck, *q.v.*). In *The Caine Mutiny* (1954) he gave a remarkable performance as Captain Queeg, a bully falling apart under the strain of leadership. And in *The Desperate Hours* (1955) he played a heavy not unlike the character of Duke Mantee that launched his career twenty years earlier.

Bogart's personal life was as rocky as his early film career. In 1926 he married a popular stage actress named Helen Menken. The marriage lasted barely a year. In 1928 he married yet another Broadway actress, Mary Phillips. This union lasted much longer—until 1937. He married Mayo Methot soon thereafter, but the marriage ended in divorce after Bogart met and fell in love with Lauren Bacall during the filming of *To Have and Have Not*. In 1945, Bogart married Bacall and the two collaborated in several hit films (*The Big Sleep, Dark Passage,* and *Key Largo),* as well as in raising their two children.

See also: antiheroes; Bacall, Lauren; *Casablanca; Dead End; The Maltese Falcon*

BOGDANOVICH, PETER (1939–) He was the first American film critic to become a director. Critics Frank S. Nugent and James Agee *(qq.v.)* had previously crossed over to the creative side of the film business to write screenplays, but Bogdanovich made the biggest splash of the three as a writer-director.

It seems only fitting that Bogdanovich, a lover of Hollywood's golden era, was born in 1939, the year most critics claim as Hollywood's greatest. In the early 1960s, he began writing about the movies, creating monographs for the Museum of Modern Art on Orson Welles *(q.v.,* 1961), Howard Hawks *(q.v.,* 1962), and Alfred Hitchcock *(q.v.,* 1963).

His first hands-on work was with Roger Corman *(q.v.)* on *The Wild Angels* (1966). While his screen credit was that of assistant director, he recalled that his actual work on the film was "a twenty-two week paid course on just about everything you could do in a picture: scouting locations, writing script, directing, getting laundry, acting, cutting, and doing sound work."

Like so many others before him, Bogdanovich learned the film business by working for Corman. And it was Corman who also gave him his next big break, the chance to write and direct his own film. Corman even put up his own money for the project: $130,000. the film was *Targets* (1968), staring Boris Karloff *(q.v.).* The film was a sleeper, attaining cult status as a cleverly constructed movie that used the inconography of its star to wonderful effect. Its success brought Bogdanovich to the edge of mainstream filmmaking.

His next movie, *The Last Picture Show* (1971), which he also wrote and directed, was hailed by critics and audiences. Bogdanovich was compared to the young Orson Welles; his career went instantly into high gear. The following year he wrote and directed *What's Up, Doc?* (1972), another huge hit. *Paper Moon* (1973) followed and did equally well. And then the bottom began to fall out.

His next two films starred his girlfriend, actress Cybill Shepherd, whom he had met during the filming of *The Last Picture Show. Daisy Miller* (1974) was murdered by the critics, and audiences stayed away. *At Long Last Love* (1975) was an even greater critical disaster, and it was one of the worst flops of the 1970s. Bogdanovich tried to recoup with *Nickelodeon* in 1976, but it turned into another bomb. A low-budget movie, *Saint Jack* (1979), did even worse business than *Nickelodeon. They All Laughed* (1981) was yet another nail in the director's coffin. Its failure was all the more painful due to the murder of one of the film's stars, Dorothy Stratton, who was also Bogdanovich's girlfriend.

Both professionally and emotionally shattered, the boy wonder was written off as a Hollywood comet that had simply burned out. He struggled for another chance, and finally scored with *Mask* (1985), starring Cher. The film was highly praised and highly attended. *Illegally Yours* (1988) was not. He has since married Stratton's teenage sister.

BONNIE AND CLYDE A controversial hit film of 1967, directed by Arthur Penn *(q.v.),* starring Warren Beatty and Faye Dunaway *(qq.v.).* Based loosely on the lives of the Depression-era bank robbing team of Bonnie Parker and Clyde Barrow, the movie was part comedy and part tragedy. It drew huge audiences and both hostile and glowing reviews because of its startling, violent ending. Some found the violence gratuitous, while others thought it was an honest reflection of American society.

Regardless of its violence, *Bonnie and Clyde* is notable for a great many other reasons. The film's lighting was more textured, darker-hued than most previous Hollywood films, and the cinematographer, Burnett Guffey, won an Oscar for his work. The role of Bonnie Parker made Faye Dunaway a star in her very first year as a movie actress; Gene Hackman *(q.v.)* received his first serious notice for his work in the film, and Gene Wilder *(q.v.)* made his film debut in a small role. Perhaps most interesting of all, *Bonnie and Clyde* was the first of several successful films produced by Warren Beatty.

The Earl and Scruggs score, Dede Allen's *(q.v.)* editing, and the superb supporting players (including Estelle Parsons who won an Oscar and Michael J. Pollard) all made for a top-notch film. The script, by David Newman and Robert Benton, with uncredited assistance by Robert Towne, was right on target, expressing a desperate love story between two people who had nothing in their lives except each other.

It's interesting to note that in the original script Clyde was homosexual. The script was changed to make Clyde heterosexual, with impotence being ascribed to his difficulty in making love to a Bonnie who had a much greater sexual appetite. The change helped make

Clyde a more sympathetic character to mainstream audiences, yet added a note of sexual realism that was rarely exhibited in American movies.

The script for *Bonnie and Clyde* bounced around for five years before Beatty bought the rights for $75,000. But before Beatty owned it, both François Truffaut and Jean-Luc Godard each nearly directed it. The film, as directed by Penn, had a somewhat European sensibility to it, no doubt showing the earlier directors' influence on the script.

BOOM OPERATOR   The person who manipulates the almost infinitely extendable rod (known as a boom) by which a microphone is dangled above an actor (or actors) during a scene. The boom operator must not only have a steady hand, he must also have a considerable knowledge of the script of a scene because he may be called upon to move the microphone from above one actor to another at the precise moment when the first actor finishes his lines. He must also know the lens being used by the cameraman and judge how high or low he can hold the microphone without it dipping into the viewing range of the camera. And, finally, he must be familiar with the principles of lighting, because the boom or the microphone, if moved without proper care, might cast a shadow on the set.

BOOTH, MARGARET (1902–)   If not the most famous editor *(q.v.)* within the industry, she has certainly been the editor with the longest career, having begun as an assistant editor in 1921 at Louis B. Mayer's *(q.v.)* studio before the merger in 1924 that created Metro-Goldwyn-Mayer. She stayed with Mayer, joining MGM and becoming a premier editor there during the late 1920s and throughout the 1930s. Her instincts were so highly regarded that she was promoted to supervising film editor for MGM in 1939. Her influence as a smooth, story-oriented editor can been seen in that studio's fluid, nonintrusive cutting throughout its golden years and right up until 1968, when she finally left MGM not to retire but to successfully free-lance for more than another decade.

Among some of the earliest films for which Booth received sole credit as an editor were *Memory Lane* (1926), *The Gay Deceiver* (1926), and *A Lady of Chance* (1928), the last of which was also the first sound film she cut.

Her reputation continued to grow at MGM as she edited its films' most important female stars such as Greta Garbo in *Susan Lenox–Her Fall and Rise* (1931) and *Camille* (1937), Jean Harlow in *Bombshell* (1933), and Joan Crawford in *Dancing Lady* (1933). Her standing at MGM was such that by 1935, she was handed the assignment of editing the studio's biggest film of the year, *Mutiny on the Bounty,* even though it was not a "woman's movie."

When Booth returned to active editing (as opposed to supervising) in the late 1960s, she masterfully cut John Huston's minor boxing masterpiece, *Fat City* (1972), and edited one of the great love stories of the 1970s, *The Way We Were* (1973). Among her later films were a solid stretch of Neil Simon comedies, *The Sunshine Boys* (1975), *Murder by Death* (1976), *California Suite* (1978), and *Chapter Two* (1979).

In 1977, the Academy of Motion Picture Arts and Sciences belatedly gave Booth a Special Oscar for her impressive body of work.

BORGNINE, ERNEST (1917–)   A barrel-chested character actor/star who came to prominence playing bullies but who soon created an image as an everyman. While he has rarely carried films on his own, he has consistently played lead or important supporting parts. In a movie career that began in 1951, Borgnine has always been in demand, appearing in more than sixty movies, as well as having had a significant career in television.

Born Ermes Effron Borgnine in the United States, his mother brought him to Italy during his early childhood but he returned to finish his education in America. After graduating from high school, Borgnine joined the Navy, rising to the rank of chief gunner's mate after ten years of service. When he decided to become an actor, he enrolled in the Randall School of Dramatic Arts in Hartford, Connecticut. His first professional job was at the Barter Theater in Virginia, where he painted scenery and drove a truck as well as acted.

His career took a leap forward when he made his Broadway debut as the hospital attendant in *Harvey.* His success on the New York stage led to more than two hundred live television performances on such prestigious shows as "G. E. Theater" and "Philco Playhouse."

His first film role was in *China Corsair* (1951), and with his size, fleshy face, and gapped teeth, he was pegged as a villain, a role he assumed in a number of films, most notably (as "Fatso") in *From Here to Eternity* (1953), *Vera Cruz* (1954), and *Bad Day at Black Rock* (1955).

After starring in a TV production of "Marty," the story was made into a motion picture. He played the title role again, and the film was the sleeper hit of 1955, winning four Oscars, including Best Actor for Borgnine. His sympathetic portrayal of the shy, aging butcher who lived at home with his mother established Borgnine as both a versatile and likeable performer with whom audiences have forever felt at ease.

His career began to slide in the late 1950s and early 1960s and he had to go to Italy to find work. But in the early 1960s he rebounded when he starred in the hit TV series "McHale's Navy" as well as a film of the same name based on the show in 1964.

Ernest Borgnine, seen here in his Academy Award–winning role in *Marty* (1955), has usually worked in support of other stars. But his distinctive presence can be seen and felt in a great many of Hollywood's most memorable movies. Photo courtesy of Ernest Borgnine.

At the height of his second wave of popularity during the latter half of the 1960s, Borgnine became a favorite of action directors such as Robert Aldrich and Sam Peckinpah. As a result, he lent his considerable presence to such memorable films as *The Flight of the Phoenix* (1965), *The Dirty Dozen* (1967), *The Wild Bunch* (1969), and *Emperor of the North* (1973).

Borgnine was noteworthy in popular if lesser films such as *Willard* (1971), *The Poseidon Adventure* (1972), *Law and Disorder* (1974), and *Escape From New York* (1981), but his movie appearances grew less frequent during the latter half of the 1970s and during the 1980s as he devoted more time to starring in TV movies and appearing as a guest star on prime-time shows, as well as co-starring in his own TV series "Airwolf."

BORZAGE, FRANK (1893–1962) In a directorial career that began in 1916 and ended in 1959, he was the undisputed master of romantic movies over a fifteen-year span beginning in the late 1920s and lasting until the early 1940s. Borzage pioneered the use of soft-focus photography, giving a shimmering glow and imbuing a romantic aura to his best films. Other directors made love stories, but Borzage's films dramatized the sacrifices, needs, and struggles of young lovers. His films were marked by a richness that put them a cut above the usual sentimental "weepies" of his time.

He began his Hollywood career as an actor in 1912 playing villains. By 1916, he had become a leading man who often directed himself in films such as *That Gal of Burke's* (1916), *The Silken Spider* (1916), and many others. Near the end of the 1910s, he began concentrating on directing and, after making more than thirty movies, had his first major directorial hit with *Humoresque* (1920), which presaged his later success in the romance genre.

Borzage became a major director by the end of the silent era, when he made the lushly romantic *Seventh Heaven* (1927), for which he won his first Best Director Academy Award. It marked the beginning of a long and rarely interrupted streak of films dealing with lovers who often create their own private, desperate worlds against backdrops of war, depression, and illness. In light of the contemporary view that films of the 1930s always seem to have happy endings, Borzage's movies come as a surprise, because they often end in tragedy. Among his many hits were *Bad Girl* (1931), for which he won his second Best Director Oscar, *A Farewell to Arms* (1932), a movie many consider the best film adaptation of any of Hemingway's novels, *Man's Castle* (1933), *Little Man, What Now?* (1934), which was an early anti-Nazi film with a transcendent romance, *History Is Made at Night* (1937), *Three Comrades* (1938), and *The Mortal Storm* (1940).

The harsh, immediate realities of World War II worked against Borzage's particular brand of romanticism. It wasn't acceptable for young lovers to cut themselves off from the war to enter their own little world. The director never fully adapted to the era and movies such as *Seven Sweethearts* (1942), *His Butler's Sister* (1943), and *Till We Meet Again* (1944) weren't up to his usual high standards.

He made just four films during the second half of the 1940s, the best of them a richly romantic love story called *I've always Loved You* (1946). By the end of the decade he was making good, if minor, melodramas such as *Moonrise* (1948), after which he retired from the screen until 1958 when he directed *China Doll,* a critical and box office flop. It was followed by his last movie, *The Big Fisherman* (1959), a biblical tale that barely hinted at Borzage's once great ability as a director of film romance.

BOW, CLARA (1905–1965) The "It" Girl, the movie star who personified the Jazz Age with her emancipated, flapper style, Clara Bow didn't so much act as play herself. And it is only fitting that F. Scott Fitzgerald, the literary lion of the Jazz Age, wrote one of her films, *Grit* (1924).

Bow was born in Brooklyn to a poor family. After winning a movie fan magazine beauty contest, she went to Hollywood. With the nickname of "The Brooklyn Bonfire," she managed to get small parts—and a lot of them. She appeared in fourteen films in 1925, and by the end of the year, she was often working as the lead.

The "It" Girl, Clara Bow, had "it" for only a short while. The Depression brought a swift end to the flapper age that she so wonderfully represented. Photo courtesy of Movie Star News.

Her popularity was growing, but it wasn't until *Mantrap* (1926) that she suddenly became a red-hot star. The "It" Girl was born.

The "It" that Clara Bow possessed was sex appeal. Men went to see her in the movies because she was brazen. At the same time, Bow wasn't a vamp. She wasn't out to destroy men; she only wanted to have a good time. And women in the audience responded to her on that basis, copying her clothes, hairstyle, and makeup.

In subsequent hit films such as *It* (1927), *Rough House Rosie* (1927), and *Dangerous Curves* (1929), she dashed about the screen in search of handsome men, money, and a grand old time. In fact, she was so popular that she was often cast in non-starring roles in some films just so her name could be used on the marquee. For instance, she supported Eddie Cantor *(q.v.)* in his first film, *Kid Boots* (1926), and appeared in the 1927 hit *Wings,* which starred Gary Cooper *(q.v.).*

Clara Bow worked with other stars besides Cooper (with whom she is rumored to have had an affair). In the course of her career, she shared the screen with Lionel Barrymore (see The Barrymore Dynasty), Ricardo Cortez, Warner Baxter *(q.v.),* William Powell *(q.v.),* and Fredric March *(q.v.),* among others.

Her popularity carried her into the sound era with

films such as *True to the Navy* (1930) and *Her Wedding Night* (1930). She was rolling along with an income of $5,000 per week when disaster struck. Leading a life not unlike the heroines of her movies, she was involved in a series of scandals concerning adultery, bribery, blackmail, and drugs that turned her audience against her. Her career took a nosedive. "It" was gone.

Clara Bow appeared in a few films in the 1930s, but otherwise disappeared from view. In 1960, though, she made news when she announced, "I slip my old crown of 'It' Girl not to Taylor or Bardot but to Monroe."

Clara Bow died in 1965. The movies had lost their first sex symbol.

BOYD, WILLIAM (1898–1972)   An actor who enjoyed enormous success in the course of two distinctly different movie careers, playing rugged leading men in big-budget silent films of the 1920s and reemerging in 1935 as a major cowboy star of westerns aimed at a juvenile audience, Boyd is forever linked with his famous character, Hopalong Cassidy.

Boyd was orphaned very early in life and he made his way in the world as a laborer until he found himself in California. He picked up a day job as an extra in Cecil B. DeMille's *(q.v.) Why Change Your Wife* (1920), and his film career was launched. It took only a few short years before he became a star, with leading roles in blockbuster films such as *The Volga Boatman* (1926), *The Last Frontier* (1926), *King of Kings* (1927), *Two Arabian Knights* (1927), and many others.

His career went into decline early in the sound era, not because he lacked an acceptable speaking voice but because another actor with the same name was involved in a sensational scandal. Boyd tried to distance himself from the notoriety by calling himself Bill, but the name change did not help. Though he continued to work, the quality of the films he was offered steadily declined.

His career seemed doomed until he starred in a low-budget western called *Hop-A-Long Cassidy* (1935), based on the Clarence E. Mulford novels about a hero with a limp. Of course, Boyd didn't limp in the film, nor in the sixty-five "Hoppie" features that followed. Geared to children, the Hopalong Cassidy films (the hyphens were eventually removed from the name) were a popular second feature of double bills, offering plenty of action, comedy, and a moral lesson. Despite the obvious good versus evil scenarios of the films, Cassidy was enlivened by certain ironic flourishes. While other western heroes wore white, Hoppie dressed all in black. Thus attired, he appeared all the more heroic, however, on his magnificent white steed, Topper.

Boyd crammed an astonishing fifty-four Hoppie films into an eight-year span between 1935 and 1943, all of them produced by Harry "Pop" Sherman. After Sherman begged off the series, Boyd took over himself, producing and starring in another twelve Cassidy films.

The last original film, *False Paradise*, was released in 1948.

When television needed product in the early 1950s, Boyd shrewdly acquired the rights to all his films and even the Hopalong Cassidy character, making a fortune packaging his movies for TV. He found an entirely new audience of children who cheered his noble bravery and bought an enormous number of "Hopalong Cassidy" licensed products, including his ever-popular lunch boxes.

Boyd's last film appearance, like his first, was in a cameo role directed by his original mentor, Cecil B. DeMille. The film was *The Greatest Show on Earth* (1952).

BOYER, CHARLES (1897–1978) With his deep voice, French accent, and dreamy eyes, he became known to American audiences as "The Great Lover." Boyer, however, was more than dark, handsome, and charming; he was also a very good actor who was capable of playing historical, comical, and villainous characters, as well as his more famous Valentino-types. Later in his career, he was an accomplished character actor *(q.v.)*. Though he appeared in a great many movies outside of the United States (principally in his native France), his international reputation rested on his Hollywood films, the best of which were made during the late 1930s and the first half of the 1940s.

Boyer studied acting at the Paris Conservatory after completing his education at the Sorbonne. While still at the Conservatory, he was offered his first film role, a modest part in *L'Homme du Large* (1920). Throughout most of the 1920s, though, Boyer worked mainly on the stage, becoming a lion of the Paris theater world. His film appearances became more frequent near the end of the decade, when MGM took notice of him and bought his contract from the German film company UFA. At first, he made French versions of American movies, but he was soon given a chance at stardom in the United States with the lead in *The Magnificent Lie* (1931) and *The Man from Yesterday* (1932). Unfortunately, he didn't click with audiences, and he was relegated to playing Jean Harlow's chauffeur in *Red Headed Woman* (1932).

The actor was fed up with Hollywood and he returned to France, where he was a major star. Two years later, after making such films as *Thunder in the East* (1934) and *Liliom* (1934), Boyer returned to America to give Hollywood another try in *Caravan* (1934). The movie bombed and Boyer was ready to return to France once again. However, he was convinced to play a featured role in *Private Worlds* (1935). Finally, he had a hit.

He made several films of ever-increasing popularity, among them *The Garden of Allah* (1936), *History Is Made at Night* (1937), and *Conquest* (1937). But the film that made him a superstar and earned him the title "The Great Lover," was *Algiers* (1938). Though he never said "Come with me to the Casbah" in the movie, that the phrase became legendary suggests something of the impact of Boyer's allure.

Boyer's career continued to thrive in films such as *Love Affair* (1939), *All This and Heaven Too* (1940), and *Back Street* (1941). And despite the fact that he was beginning to show his age, he was perfectly believable as the gigolo husband trying to drive Ingrid Bergman insane in *Gaslight* (1944). It was also one of his last great roles, although he was quite good in the less successful *Confidential Agent* (1945) and *Cluny Brown* (1946).

His movie career dipped in the later 1940s thanks to films such as *A Woman's Vengeance* (1947) and *Arch of Triumph* (1948). Wisely, he turned to character parts, aging gracefully in movies both in the United States and France such as *The Thirteenth Letter* (1951), *The Earrings of Madame de* (1953), *Around the World in 80 days* (1956), *Fanny* (1960), *Is Paris Burning?* (1967), *The April Fools* (1969), and his last movie, *A Matter of Time* (1976).

Boyer was active in areas outside the movies. In 1952 he was one of the founders of TV's Four Star Television, appearing in many of their small-screen productions. In addition, he acted on the stage in Paris, New York, and London.

Disconsolate over the death of his wife, English actress Pat Paterson, Boyer committed suicide two days later, taking an overdose of sleeping pills.

BRACKET, CHARLES: *See* Wilder, Billy

BRANDO, MARLON (1924–   ) Considered by many to be the greatest American actor of the postwar era, Brando's diction and sheer animal magnetism helped to create a new kind of naturalistic movie actor. His success opened the door for such other actors as Paul Newman, James Dean, and Rod Steiger, to name just a few.

Born Marlon Brando, Jr., he was nicknamed "Bud" so as not to be confused with his salesman father. His mother had been an amateur actress who once trod the boards with a young Henry Fonda *(q.v.)* at the Omaha Community Playhouse. After a rebellious childhood and spotty education, Brando left home for New York in 1943, although not, at first, with the intention of becoming an actor. Extreme nearsightedness and a badly damaged knee (from a high school football injury) kept him out of military service and he bounced from one odd job to another. Without any previous theatrical experience, he decided to follow his sister Jocelyn's lead and study acting. Quite by chance, his dramatic coach was Stella Adler, a highly respected teacher who helped develop Stanislavsky's method style of acting in Amer-

Marlon Brando, in his first Oscar-winning performance, as the former boxer/longshoreman who "coulda been a contender" in Elia Kazan's *On the Waterfront* (1954). Photo courtesy of Movie Star News.

ica. Eventually, Brando would become the premier method actor of his time.

His stage career began in 1944 with appearances in plays such as *Morning Telegraph* and *Twelfth Night*. His first important role, however, was Nels in *I Remember Mama*. Later came a series of roles in unsuccessful productions such as *Truckline Cafe, Candida,* and *The Eagle Has Two Heads* (with Talullah Bankhead, who unsuccessfully tried to seduce him and, later, had him fired).

1947 was a critical year for Brando. He met Elia Kazan *(q.v.)*, joined the Actor's Studio, and eventually won the role that catapulted him to stardom. Kazan cast and directed him in the role of Stanley Kowalski in Tennessee Williams' *A Streetcar Named Desire.* The stage role was originally intended for John Garfield but Brando had his chance after the older actor scored a big hit in the movies with *Body and Soul* (1947). Brando soon became the toast of Broadway as the brazenly appealing, torn tee-shirted Stanley. During the run of the play the actor's nose was broken in a backstage accident. He chose not to have it fixed, believing his face to be more masculine with its new flaw.

Brando's critical and popular success in *Streetcar* led to movie offers. He turned down a seven-year contract from MGM, content to pick his own projects on a free-lance basis. His first choice was *The Men* (1950), a serious, downbeat film about crippled war veterans. The movie was admired by the critics but ignored at the box office.

While *Streetcar* turned Brando into a stage star, the movie version in 1951, also directed by Kazan, turned him into a major film star. His association with Kazan during these early years was propicious. Except for *The Wild One* (1954), Kazan directed the actor in his most important early hits, including *Viva Zapata!* (1952) and *On the Waterfront* (1954).

The role of Terry Malloy in *Waterfront,* originally intended for Frank Sinatra, was the high point of Brando's film career. Though nominated for an Academy Award for roles in *A Streetcar Named Desire, Viva Zapata!,* and *Julius Caesar* (1953), he won the Best Actor Oscar for his performance in *Waterfront.*

Always a fascinating actor regardless of the vehicle, Brando surprised audiences by starring in the musical *Guys and Dolls* (1955). In spite of cries of "sell-out" on the tongues of the intelligentsia, the actor went on to choose increasingly eclectic roles ranging from comedies, such as *The Teahouse of the August Moon* (1956), to big-budget spectacles, such as the ill-fated remake of *Mutiny on the Bounty* (1962).

Unlike most other major stars, Brando revelled in playing villains in any number of films, among them *The Ugly American* (1963), *The Chase* (1966), *Burn!* (1969), *Apocalypse Now* (1979), and *The Formula* (1980).

Difficult to direct, he directed himself in *One-Eyed Jacks* (1960) with mixed results. A moody piece, it holds up well today despite its slow pace and self-indulgent touches, principally because of Brando's ever-surprising performance. It was not a hit at the box office, however, and, in fact, neither were many of Brando's later films during the rest of the 1960s. Yet, despite such flops as *Morituri* (1965), and others, his reputation was still such that Charlie Chaplin chose to direct him in *A Countess from Hong Kong* (1967). Unfortunately, it was not a success for either Chaplin or Brando.

In 1972, Brando resurrected his career with his memorable performance as Don Corleone in Francis Coppola's *The Godfather* (qq.v.). Winning the Oscar for Best Actor, he sent an American Indian surrogate to the awards celebration to announce that he would not accept the statuette in protest of America's treatment of its native people, an event that has since become part of Hollywood lore. In that same year, he electrified audiences with his sexual derring-do in Bernardo Bertolucci's X-rated film *Last Tango in Paris.* Since that watershed year, however, the actor has been seen on screen relatively little. Except for a bizarre performance playing opposite Jack Nicholson in *The Missouri Breaks* (1976), he has been content to accept hefty sums for small featured roles in films such as the 1978 *Superman* (for which he was paid more than $3 million for a dozen days' work, a fee that made him—at the time—the industry's highest paid actor). He also had a small but critical role in Francis Ford Coppola's *Apocalypse Now* (1979), heightening the movie's powerful and haunting climax.

After flopping with George C. Scott in *The Formula* (1980), a film in which he reportedly chose to have his lines broadcast into his ear through a hearing aid rather than learn them, he all but disappeared from public view. Amid rumors of his ballooning weight, the actor remained in relative seclusion on his South Sea island until he resurfaced and acted for free in an antiapartheid movie titled *A Dry White Season* (1989).

BRAT PACK   A loose grouping of young, mostly teen-age, actors who rose to fame together in a series of youth-oriented films during the early to mid-1980s. The name "brat pack" was coined in 1985 by writer David Blum in an article in *New York* magazine. The inspiration for the name came from the old Humphrey Bogart *(q.v.)* inspired "rat pack" *(q.v.)* of the 1950s (subsequently taken over by Frank Sinatra *[q.v.]* and his cronies). Of course, "brat pack" inferred that the members of this media-created club were all of rather tender age.

The core of the brat pack came to mass attention in Francis Ford Coppola's *(q.v.)* failed film version of S. E. Hinton's novel *The Outsiders* (1983), which featured the ensemble work of Matt Dillon, C. Thomas Howell, Tom Cruise *(q.v.)*, Ralph Macchio, Emilio Estevez, Patrick Swayze, and Rob Lowe. *St. Elmo's Fire* (1985), another movie of young adulthood angst helped expand the pack with the addition of Ally Sheedy, Judd Nelson, Andrew McCarthy, Demi Moore, and Mare Winningham. Other teenage-oriented films brought young actors such as Timothy Hutton, Sean Penn, and Molly Ringwald into the group.

Unlike members of the earlier rat pack, who met regularly and referred to themselves as members of a clan, the brat packers were merely a large pool of variously talented individuals, some of whom were friends and all of whom tended to resent being referred to as members of the club.

Many of the actors in the so-called brat pack did, however, stick together and help each other's careers, fostering the impression of a closely knit group.

A surprising number of these young actors have put their careers on a solid footing, and many of them may be around for a long time to come.

BREAKAWAY PROP   Any object deliberately created by a property department to be easily broken upon impact without harming anyone coming in contact with it.

Breakaway props are usually items such as bottles, windows, chairs, and tables. They are principally used in action films, such as in westerns, where there are fight scenes involving actors being hit on the head and thrown across rooms.

BREAKDOWN   The job of distilling all the elements of the script and reorganizing them for the purpose of creating the most efficient and economical shooting schedule possible. The breakdown, usually performed by the assistant director *(q.v.)*, consists of taking scenes out of their sequence in the script and grouping them together in categories such as night scenes, crowd scenes, a series of scenes that require a certain actor who may only be available for a short time, scenes that take place on one particular set at different times in the film, etc. The breakdown gives the director the opportunity to choose the order in which he or she will shoot scenes in the film.

BRENNAN, WALTER (1894–1974)   One of the most memorable of Hollywood's character actors *(q.v.)*, he usually played old codgers, even as a relatively young man. Appearing in excess of one-hundred movies in a career that spanned more than fifty years, Brennan made history as the first actor to win three Academy Awards, all of which were won in a five-year stretch between 1936 and 1940.

Although Brennan often played simple country folk, he had studied engineering before finally settling on an acting career. After playing in road shows and appearing in vaudeville without any great success, he decided to give moving pictures a chance. His experience on the stage was only good enough to put him on the fringe of the movie business, working as an extra and occasional stuntman, often in westerns.

In the latter half of the 1920s he finally began to receive billing for small roles in films such as *The Ridin' Rowdy* (1927) and *The Ballyhoo Buster* (1928). For the most part, the roles stayed small and the movies he appeared in were thoroughly forgettable. By the mid-1930s, however, he began to appear in better films. For instance, he had a tiny role in *Bride of Frankenstein* (1935), and still larger roles in *The Man on the Flying Trapeze* (1935) and *Barbary Coast* (1935).

His big breakthrough came in *Come and Get It* (1936), for which he won his first Academy Award for Best Supporting Actor. From that point on, Brennan began to appear more regularly in top-flight movies with good directors and (most importantly) good scripts. He won his second Oscar for his supporting role in *Kentucky* (1938), and was especially poignant as the vulnerable villain Judge Roy Bean in *The Westerner* (1940), for which he won his third Oscar in support of Gary Cooper.

Oscars notwithstanding, Brennan's movie career peaked in the 1940s, not the late 1930s. His most memorable supporting roles were in such classics as *Meet John Doe* (1941), *Sergeant York* (1941), *Pride of the Yankees* (1942), *To Have and Have Not* (1944), *My Darling Clementine* (1946), and *Red River* (1948). Perhaps his most impressive performance was in *Swamp Water* (1941), in which he had a lead role in the first film Jean Renoir directed in America.

Brennan worked steadily throughout most of the 1950s in increasingly minor movies, with the exception of *Bad Day at Black Rock* (1955), *The Far Country* (1955), and *Rio Bravo* (1959). With his film career fading, he wisely agreed to star in the TV series "The Real McCoys" in 1957 (which ran through the 1963 season), a role that brought him more fame than his movies ever had.

Becoming more of a TV star than a movie actor, Brennan's appearances on film throughout the 1960s and the early 1970s were mostly minor affairs except for featured roles in *How the West Was Won* (1962), *Those Calloways* (1965), and *Support Your Local Sheriff* (1969). Brennan's last movie was *Smoke in the Wind* (1975), released after his death.

THE BRIDGES FAMILY A modern acting dynasty founded by father Lloyd Bridges (1913–) and sustained by two of his three sons, Beau Bridges (1941–) and Jeff Bridges (1949–). Lloyd had only modest success as a film actor, becoming far more famous as a TV star, but his two sons have had substantial movie careers, with Beau developing from child actor to leading man to character actor, and Jeff becoming a bona fide movie star almost from the very beginning of his days in front of the camera in the early 1970s.

Lloyd Bridges was a stage actor during the 1930s, making an impressive debut on Broadway in a radical interpretation of *Othello* late in the decade. Tall, blond, and handsome, he was a natural for the movies. By 1941 he was acting in films, making his movie debut in *The Lone Wolf Takes a Chance*. For the most part, he appeared in supporting roles in minor films such as *Two Latins from Manhattan* (1941) and *Alias Boston Blackie* (1942), but also showed promise in more important movies, including *Here Comes Mr. Jordan* (1941), *Talk of the Town* (1942), *Sahara* (1943), and *A Walk in the Sun* (1945).

Bridges was given better roles, if in lesser movies, during the second half of the decade, often in westerns. His most notable role in the early 1950s was in support of Gary Cooper in *High Noon* (1952). It was a role of deep significance because the film was intended as a subtle statement against the paralysis exhibited by the country in the face of McCarthyism. Ironically, Bridges became a witness for the House UnAmerican Activities Committee in the early 1950s. He admitted to being a Communist during the 1930s and he named others in Hollywood who had also flirted with left-wing politics,

many of whom were then blacklisted from the industry.

Bridges went on to make a great many films during the next several decades, few of them of any merit. He earned his fame as the star of the syndicated TV series "Sea Hunt" during the 1950s. His film career was resurrected during the 1980s when he gave two hilarious performances in key supporting roles in the comedy hits *Airplane!* (1980) and its sequel, *Airplane II* (1982), as well as a highly praised performance in *Cousins* (1989).

Beau Bridges, born Lloyd Vernet Bridges III, was very effective as a child actor in, among other films, *Force of Evil* (1948) and *The Red Pony* (1949). But Beau was more interested in basketball than in acting and he pursued an athletic career until his lack of height (he's 5'9″) forced him to reset his goals. He began acting again in the early 1960s but without much success, until the latter part of the decade when he began receiving favorable reviews in films such as *The Incident* (1967), *For Love of Ivy* (1968), *Gaily, Gaily* (1969), and *The Landlord* (1970). Winsome and convincing, the actor displayed a youthful vulnerability in these films, but despite good notices, few were successful at the box office. Although he appeared in fine movies such as *Lovin' Molly* (1974), he was soon being cast in supporting roles in vehicles for other stars, most notably for Richard Pryor in *Greased Lighting* (1977), Dick Van Dyke in *The Runner Stumbles* (1979), and Sally Field in *Norma Rae* (1979).

During the 1980s, he has often appeared in TV movies as well as in feature films. He can be seen in movies such as *Love Child* (1982), *Heart Like a Wheel* (1983), and *The Hotel New Hampshire* (1984), to name just a few.

Meanwhile, Beau's younger brother, Jeff, has had an electric career that began almost from his first performance. After his film debut in *Halls of Anger* (1970) at the age of twenty-one, the taller and more rugged looking Bridges boy gained national recognition in Peter Bogdanovich's sleeper hit, *The Last Picture Show* (1971). Nominated for a Best Supporting Actor Academy Award for his performance in that film as a charming bad boy, he continued to enhance his likable wiseguy image for a good many years to follow.

While not all of Jeff's subsequent movies were hits, a surprisingly large number of them were favorably received and had cult followings, among them John Huston's *Fat City* (1972), *The Last American Hero* (1973), *Rancho Deluxe* (1975), and *Hearts of the West* (1975).

Jeff Bridges is a strong actor who proved he could hold his own with Clint Eastwood in *Thunderbolt and Lightfoot* (1975). His reputation as an actor and as a potential major star were such that he was later given the lead role in the ill-advised remake of *King Kong* (1976). He survived that debacle and went on to solidify his acting credentials in films such as *Stay Hungry,*

(1976), *Somebody Killed Her Husband* (1978), and *Winter Kills* (1979). Then he appeared in yet another disaster, *Heaven's Gate* (1980), but that bomb didn't destroy his career either. Several years of flops during the early 1980s, however, nearly did the trick. *Cutter and Bone* (1981), *Kiss Me Goodbye* (1982), *The Last Unicorn* (1982), *Tron* (1982), and *Against All Odds* (1984) were all box office duds. It wasn't until he gave a charming and effective performance in the science fiction/comedy hit *Starman* (1984) that his career began to soar again.

In more recent years, he has been in several critical and/or box-office winners such as *Jagged Edge* (1985), *The Morning After* (1986), Francis Ford Coppola's *Tucker: A Man and His Dream* (1988), and *The Fabulous Baker Boys* (1989), with brother Beau.

BROADWAY: The relationship between the American theater and Hollywood goes back much farther than the much-ballyhooed talent raids made on the stage with the advent of the talkies. Since the mid-1910s, the American theater—particularly Broadway plays and (later) musicals—has been a significant source of story material, writers, directors, producers, and actors for the movies.

Originally, during the years of the nickelodeons, the legitimate theater and the movie industry had little in common. Plays had rather complex plots and were geared toward an educated, affluent audience. Movies which were no longer than two reels in length, were limited in their storytelling ability, and appealed to the poorer masses who couldn't afford the price of admission to a play. This division between the theater and the movies was changed forever when Adolph Zukor *(q.v.)* bought the rights to show the English production of the filmed play *Queen Elizabeth* (1912), starring the renowned Sarah Bernhardt. He premiered the movie in Broadway's Lyceum Theater and made a fortune. His movie company, Famous Players, with the motto "Famous Players in Famous Plays," began the successful Hollywood onslaught into the domain of the legitimate theater.

Feature-length motion pictures that told intricate stories competed directly with the theater. Their lower admission price was a considerable advantage. Theater road shows were severely affected by the new competition as large, new movie theaters (as opposed to nickelodeons) and ornate movie palaces were built across the country. Robert McLaughlin reports in his book *Broadway and Hollywood* that in 1912 there were two hundred and five road-show companies on tour in the United States. By 1918, that number had dropped to forty-one. And by the mid-1930s, the figure fell to an average of twenty road shows, a number that has remained relatively constant up to the present.

Producing plays without a guarantee of significant road-show income made the financing of plays a good deal more difficult. Enter the motion picture companies, which realized that Broadway was no longer their competition but a relatively inexpensive proving ground for future film stories and talent. During the 1910s and 1920s, a great many hit plays were purchased and filmed with reasonably good box office results, and stage stars such as the Barrymore clan were lured to the coast in great abundance. To be on the inside track of new plays and new stars, film studios had representatives at opening-night performances of virtually every major (and most minor) Broadway plays. By the early 1920s, many studios began putting up their own money to produce plays in New York, thereby obtaining the film rights for much less than they might have to spend in an open bidding war with other studios.

Then came the talkies. The demand for directors who understood the power of the spoken word led to the hiring of a great many Broadway directors such as George Cukor and Rouben Mamoulian *(qq.v.)*. Legitimate stage actors were hired in huge numbers. Actors such as Paul Muni, Edward G. Robinson, Humphrey Bogart, Melvyn Douglas, Leslie Howard, and Katharine Hepburn *(qq.v.)* represent just a few of the countless performers who were discovered on the stage.

Upwards of twenty-five percent of the plays produced during the 1930s were bought by the movie studios. Making a film based on a hit Broadway play improved the status of motion picture companies and it also ensured a certain measure of commercial success.

While many powerful and controversial plays were watered down in their film adaptations, especially during the 1930s and 1940s, the challenge of television in the 1950s made movie moguls rethink their relationship to the theater. The film industry slowly began to realize that the controversial elements in stage plays might be just what was needed to draw audiences away from the pap on TV. Suddenly, there were filmed adaptations of surprisingly sophisticated and controversial plays such as *A Streetcar Named Desire* (1951), *The Member of the Wedding* (1953), and *The Country Girl* (1954).

At the same time, movie companies also attempted to outmaneuver TV by making big-budget musicals. Many of these, such as *Oklahoma!* (1955), *South Pacific* (1958), and *West Side Story* (1961), were based on hit Broadway musicals.

Movies based on Broadway plays and musicals continued to comprise a significant portion of Hollywood's output during the 1960s and early 1970s, with productions such as *The Sound of Music* (1965), *Who's Afraid of Virginia Woolf?* (1966), *Fiddler on the Roof* (1967), and a prodigious number of Neil Simon comedies.

The rights to big Broadway musicals were expensive and the cost of producing the films was high. Though *Funny Girl* (1968) and *Cabaret* (1972) were both critical and box office hits, a series of major flops such as *Finian's Rainbow* (1968), *Sweet Charity* (1969), *Hello,*

Dolly! (1969), *On A Clear Day You Can See Forever* (1970), and *Man of La Mancha* (1972) cooled Hollywood's ardor for Broadway musicals.

But even as Broadway temporarily lost some of its appeal to Hollywood, Off-Broadway provided not only fresh, innovative story ideas, but also a fresh crop of writers and movie stars. For instance, the Off-Broadway movement brought Beth Henley's play *Crimes of the Heart* to the screen in 1986, gave playwright John Patrick Shanley the opportunity to write *Moonstruck* (1987) (and win a Best Original Screenplay Oscar for his efforts), and provided the stepping stone for David Mamet to script the celebrated *The Untouchables* (1987) and write/direct the successful *House of Cards* (1987) and *Things Change* (1988).

Among recent actors to achieve Hollywood stardom after their Off-Broadway successes are William Hurt *(q.v.)*, Christopher Reeve, Al Pacino *(q.v.)*, Jeff Daniels, and Sam Shephard, who is also an acclaimed playwright.

See also: Altman, Robert; the Barrymore dynasty; Famous Players; musicals; Simon, Neil

BRODERICK, MATTHEW (1962–) A charming and engaging young thespian who has proven to be both a popular performer as well as a serious actor. More boyish than handsome, Broderick established himself in the 1980s as a star of youth-oriented movies, but he seems destined to emerge as a young-adult leading man in the years to come. Unlike many of his contemporaries who are film-based brat-packers, Broderick has worked steadily in the theater, gaining immeasureable acting experience as well as the applause of critics who have admired both his talent and his willingness to occasionally eschew Hollywood's riches.

The son of the late actor James Broderick (best known as the father in the TV series, "Family"), he grew up among actors and understood the demands of his craft. He made his film debut in a modest part in Neil Simon's *(q.v.) Max Dugan Returns* (1983), one of the playwright/screenwriter's few flops. In that same year, however, Broderick had the lead role in a surprise hit, *War Games,* propelling the young actor into early stardom.

He followed that success with *Ladyhawke* (1984), a successful fantasy that proved the drawing power of his name at the box office. He surprised many by choosing to star in the clearly uncommercial, low-budget Horton Foote film *1918* (1984) but was well-received by the critics.

Broderick spent a great deal of his time during the 1980s acting on Broadway, playing a supporting role in *Torch Song Trilogy,* and starring in two of Neil Simon's autobiographical plays, *Brighton Beach Memoirs* and *Biloxi Blues.* He also trod the boards Off-Broadway, starring in Horton Foote's, *The Widow Claire,* among other Foote projects.

If Broderick didn't star in a lot of movies, he generally made the ones he did choose to appear in count. He scored big with John Hughes' *(q.v.) Ferris Bueller's Day Off* (1986), a movie that may have been the actor's farewell to teen roles. In addition, after patching up a quarrel with Neil Simon, he starred in the hit film version of Simon's *Biloxi Blues* (1988). He also reprised his role in the film version of Harvey Fierstein's *Torch Song Trilogy* (1988). His only major flop was *Project X* (1987), a rather endearing film that nonetheless failed to win either critical or audience favor.

His career was nearly cut short in 1987 by tragedy, when he was involved in a traffic accident that caused the death of two people while he was on vacation in Ireland. The actor reportedly caused the accident by driving his vehicle on the wrong side of the road. Broderick was later fined for being at fault but was not imprisoned. After recovering from his own injury (he broke a leg), he eventually resumed acting.

BRONSON, CHARLES (1922–) He became a star unexpectedly after his fiftieth birthday, and is living proof that the American public chooses its movie heroes for reasons other than their good looks. Short and muscular, with a threatening visage, Bronson captured the imagination of international movie audiences for being a man who could not be pushed around.

Charles Buchinski was the fifth child in a brood of fifteen. Three years after his debut in *You're in the Navy Now* (1951), the actor changed his name to Bronson because his Eastern European name was a liability in the Red Scare years of the early fifties.

With his menacing look, Bronson was often cast as a villain. But like Humphrey Bogart, James Coburn, and Lee Marvin *[qq.v.],* actors who play bad guys occasionally make the leap to stardom.

Though he didn't know it at the time, Bronson's first big break came when he played a major supporting role in Samuel Fuller's "B" movie *(qq.v.)* production of *Run of the Arrow* (1957). Fuller's films were gaining in popularity in Europe, and the movie's overseas success gave Bronson a modest cult following. European interest in Bronson grew the following year when another "B" movie, Roger Corman's *Machine Gun Kelly* (1958), played in overseas theaters with Bronson in the title role.

In the late fifties and throughout most of the 1960s, Bronson appeared regularly in "A" movies *(q.v.)*, but in supporting roles. For instance, he was one of *The Magnificent Seven* (1960), tried to tunnel his way to freedom in *The Great Escape* (1963), and played a suitably dirty character in *The Dirty Dozen* (1967). Between his movie career and frequent guest shots on TV (he even had his own series in the late 1950s, "A Man With a Camera"), his face had become instantly recognizable, even if most people didn't know his name.

Bronson might have achieved fame much sooner— and he might have aborted Clint Eastwood's *(q.v.)* career in the bargain—had he not turned down the lead in Sergio Leone's international hit western, *A Fistful of Dollars* (1964). But stardom came to him through yet another Leone epic, *Once Upon a Time in the West* (1969). Bronson played the role of "Harmonica," a mysterious man intent upon revenge for a murder committed when he was a boy. The character was cooly dangerous, self-contained yet thoroughly likable. Despite a cast that included Henry Fonda *(q.v.)*, Jason Robards *(q.v.)*, and Claudia Cardinale, Bronson held center stage. The film was a huge hit outside America. In fact, an international poll in 1972 showed that Bronson was the most popular actor in the world! Hollywood finally took notice, and starring roles came flooding in his direction.

The most memorable of his films immediately after his initial success were *Red Sun* (1971), *Chato's Land* (1972), and *The Valachi Papers* (1972). But he also made a number of truly awful films that diminished his star value.

He needed another hit movie. His masterful performance in *Death Wish* (1974), one of the decade's most controversial and successful films, restored his preeminence. The story of a man who takes the law into his own hands by killing New York City muggers, the film was an angry, frustrated audience's dream come true.

Bronson has appeared in only a few good movies since *Death Wish*. *Hard Times* (1975) and *From Noon Til Three* (1976) are certainly among his best. His career has faltered somewhat in the 1980s despite the making of *Death Wish II* (1982) and *Death Wish III* (1985). Yet even in his late sixties, Charles Bronson's strong masculine appeal has not fully diminished.

BROOKS, MEL (1926–) He is an actor/comedian, screenwriter, director, and producer who has mined the vein of vulgar comedy with excellent results. Critics often dismiss his films for their scatological humor, but Brooks has been one of the most outrageously comic film creators of the last twenty-five years, stretching the bounds of film humor and creating several comedy classics in the process. Along with Woody Allen *(q.v.)*, Mel Brooks shapes his own comic vision with virtually complete artistic control.

Born Melvin Kaminsky, he was the son of a process server who died when Brooks was two-and-a-half-years old. He started his show business career at the age of fourteen, entertaining guests around the pool of a Catskill mountains resort hotel in upstate New York. After serving in World War II, Brooks began his stand-up comedy career in earnest, working at several Catskill hotels until he met Sid Caesar, who took Brooks on as a writer on Caesar's influential TV comedy/variety series, "Your Show of Shows" during the early 1950s.

Brooks was earning $5,000 per week as a writer until the program went off the air, and then he soon fell into relative obscurity during the rest of the 1950s, until he and Carl Reiner released a record album of their party routine, The Two Thousand Year Old Man (played by Brooks). The album, *2,000 Years with Carl Reiner and Mel Brooks* (1960), and its sequels, resurrected Brooks' career.

In the 1960s, he and Buck Henry created the hit TV series "Get Smart" and in the 1970s, Brooks tried again with the somewhat less successful TV series "When Things Were Rotten." Despite his long association with TV, Brooks' best, most outrageous, humor has been exhibited in his movies.

Brooks' first film was not *The Producers*, which he made in 1967, but rather a cartoon he created and narrated called *The Critic* (1964), for which he won an Oscar for Best Animated Short Subject. Brooks' failed attempts to write for the legitimate stage during the 1950s and early 1960s were the likely inspiration for *The Producers*, a film many still consider the writer/director's greatest movie. It's inspired lunacy, culminating in the "Springtime for Hitler" (the original title of the film) musical number, remains a cinematic milestone in hilarious bad taste. Brooks won an Oscar for Best Screenplay for his very first feature-length film; and though it was not an immediate success at the box office, it has flourished ever since as a cult favorite.

Brooks wrote and directed *The Twelve Chairs* (1970), another very funny film that flopped. It took Brooks four years to get the financing to make his next movie, *Blazing Saddles* (1974), but it became the most successful comedy of its time, earning $45,200,000 in North America alone.

Brooks played a small role in *The Twelve Chairs* and two parts in *Blazing Saddles,* establishing himself as a screen comedian. But it wasn't until he took a major role in *Silent Movie* (1976) and the lead role in *High Anxiety* (1977) that Brooks appeared center stage in his own films. Yet Brooks has consistently surrounded himself with fine comic actors, using many of the same people in his films, such as Gene Wilder *(q.v.)*, Madeline Kahn, the late Marty Feldman, Cloris Leachman, and Ron Carey.

From the very beginning of his career as a writer/director, most of Brooks' films have been parodies of movie genres. For instance, *The Producers* made fun of backstage musicals, *Young Frankenstein* (1974) horror films, *Silent Movie* silent film conventions (even to the point of eschewing dialogue); *High Anxiety* spoofed Alfred Hitchcock's movies, *History of the World—Part I* (1981) lampooned just about every kind of movie genre, and *Spaceballs* (1987) sent up science fiction films such as *Star Wars.*

His latter films have not been terribly successful at the box office. *History of the World—Part I*, in particular, was a major flop. *To Be or Not To Be* (1983), a remake of the 1942 Ernst Lubitsch *(q.v.)* classic, had mixed results with both critics and ticket buyers. *Spaceballs* was one of the rare Brooks films to be reasonably well received by the critics; it was also his first hit comedy of the decade.

Brooks has shown another side of his personality as a film producer through his company Brooksfilm, making such diverse movies as *The Elephant Man* (1980) and *Solarbabies* (1986), to name just a few.

Brooks has been married to actress Ann Bancroft since 1964. It is his second marriage.

BROOKS, RICHARD (1912–) A writer/director since 1950, usually of movies with a strong masculine ethic, whose commercial success has been erratic. An independent producer of his own films since the early 1960s, he has tended to make intense, low-budget movies that have, on ocassion, become major critical and box office hits. There isn't another Hollywood director who has stayed the course of independent production as long as Brooks has. Like Woody Allen, he is secretive about his work, even to the point of allowing his actors to see scenes from their scripts only on the day of the shooting.

Brooks arrived in Hollywood through a circuitous route, having been trained as a journalist and having worked as a radio news writer. But even as he worked in radio during the early 1940s in Los Angeles, he was writing screenplays (in collaboration) for such minor movies as *Sin Town* (1942) and *White Savage* (1943). Between 1943 and 1945, Brooks served in the Marine Corps, and out of that experience came his first novel, *The Brick Foxhole,* which was turned into the Edward Dymtryk film, *Crossfire* (1947). Brooks would later write two more works of fiction, *The Boiling Point* and *The Producer,* the later novel considered by many to be the best book ever written about Hollywood.

When he was discharged from the Marines, Brooks returned to Hollywood, entering a new phase of his screenwriting career with scripts for such powerful hits as *The Killers* (1946), *Brute Force* (1947), *Key Largo* (1948), *Any Number Can Play* (1949), and *Storm Warning* (1950).

His success as a screenwriter opened the doors for Brooks' entry into the world of writer/director in 1950 with *Crisis.* Unfortunately, most of his early efforts were muddled affairs, except for the solidly made *Deadline U.S.A.* (1952) with Humphrey Bogart. Finally, in 1955, he had his first smash hit, *The Blackboard Jungle* (1955), a movie that helped make Sidney Poitier a star while also bringing rock 'n' roll to America's doorstep with a theme song by Bill Haley and the Comets, "Rock Around the Clock."

Despite his big breakthrough, Brooks made several clunkers until he had some success in adapting Tennes-

Richard Brooks has been a successful writer/director for nearly fifty years. His hard-boiled intellectualism has earned him the respect of many critics and his two-fisted filmmaking has earned him a considerable number of hit movies. Photo courtesy of Richard Brooks.

see Williams' *Can on a Hot Tin Roof* to the screen in 1958. He followed it with what many consider to be his finest film, *Elmer Gantry* (1960), for which he won an Oscar for his screenplay. He also met and married one of the stars of the film, Jean Simmons.

In the mid-1960s, after having produced the ambitious flop *Lord Jim* (1965), Brooks returned to the familiar world of male-oriented action films to make one of Hollywood's rare latter-day hit westerns, *The Professionals* (1966). He hit his stride with the grim adaptation of Truman Capote's *In Cold Blood* (1967). Unfortunately, a string of major bombs followed that nearly bankrupted him, including *The Happy Ending* (1969), *Dollars* (1971), and *Bite the Bullet* (1975). He saved his career and his house (which he had mortgaged to provide financing) with *Looking for Mr. Goodbar* (1977), a cautionary tale cum sex thriller that became a much-discussed hit movie. It turned out to be his last box office winner. His subsequent films to date, *Wrong Is Right* (1982) and *Fever Pitch* (1985) failed to find either critical approval or an audience.

BROWN, CLARENCE (1890–1987) He is best remembered as MGM's glamour director during the late 1920s and throughout the 1930s. But Brown was also a director and sometime producer of movies that dealt with family themes that were often rich in Americana. He was particularly adept at developing and showcasing new talent, including that of Greta Garbo, Clark Gable, and Elizabeth Taylor *(qq.v.)*

An exceedingly bright young man, Brown was given special permission to attend the University of Tennessee at the age of fifteen; he graduated four years later with *two* engineering degrees. At first he was interested in automobiles, eventually opening his own car dealership in 1912. The appeal of the nascent movie business was too strong for him, however, and he sold his dealership and went to work for director Maurice Tourneur as an assistant. He stayed with Tourneur for five years, learning his new craft and gaining particularly valuable knowledge of lighting effects.

In 1920 Brown made his directorial debut with *The Great Redeemer,* produced by Tourneur. It wasn't until 1922, however, that he was recognized as a talent in his own right when he left Tourneur and directed *The Acquittal* (1923) for Universal Pictures.

Brown's reputation continued to grow during the 1920s, making his mark when he saved Rudolph Valentino's fading career with *The Eagle* (1925). He moved to MGM in 1927, directing that studio's most glamorous stars, including Greta Garbo in *Flesh and the Devil* (1927). He went on to direct Garbo in six more films, among them *Anna Christie* (1930), *Anna Karenina* (1935), and *Conquest* (1937). As the preeminent MGM glamour director, he also worked on a great many Joan Crawford *(q.v.)* movies, including *Possessed* (1931), *Sadie McKee* (1934), and *The Gorgeous Hussy* (1936).

Brown stayed at MGM until the end of his career in 1952. His ability to light and direct glamour queens with romantic and mesmerizing chiaroscuro effects was almost a drawback because the stars he was given to direct were often more important than the movies themselves. Therefore, in many respects, his best work could be found not in his star vehicles but in the movies in which he made new stars, such as *A Free Soul* (1931), the movie that helped establish Clark Gable, and *National Velvet* (1944), the film that brought Elizabeth Taylor to the attention of the film audience.

Clarence Brown's glamour projects of the 1930s tend to obscure his warm family films of the 1940s, such as *The Human Comedy* (1943), *The White Cliffs of Dover* (1944), and *The Yearling* (1946). He was also the director of one of Hollywood's earliest anti-racist films, *Intruder in the Dust* (1949), which he valiantly chose to produce.

The last film Brown directed was *Plymouth Adventure* (1952). The following year he produced *Never Let Me Go* and then left the business to enjoy a long and comfortable retirement.

BROWN, JIM (1935–) He was one of football's most exciting stars, becoming an actor near the end of his playing days in the mid-1960s. Ruggedly handsome, Brown quickly turned into a male sex symbol at the same time that he became the first genuine black action-movie star. In his early film career he appeared in movies aimed at both black and white audiences, but he soon found his niche in movies directed solely toward black audiences. His active screen career lasted little more than a decade, after which Brown became an elder statesman for blacks in the film industry. He has

continued to work in Hollywood as an advisor and production executive.

Brown's football career with the Cleveland Browns was near legendary. He was a powerful running back who played for the same National Football League team throughout his entire professional life, from 1957 to 1967, shattering records and gaining national recognition. While still playing football, he took a modest role in a western, *Rio Conchos* (1964), and showed a great deal of screen presence. He was used to good effect in *The Dirty Dozen* (1967) and then became a full-time actor in such mainstream films as *The Split* (1968) and *Ice Station Zebra* (1968). But he gained major attention when he costarred with another sex symbol, Raquel Welch, in *100 Rifles* (1969).

In the early 1970s, Brown had begun starring exclusively in black action films such as *Black Gunn* (1972), *Slaughter* (1972), *Slaughter's Big Rip-Off* (1973), and other low-budget, fast-paced adventure films that, more often than not, showed a modest profit during the period of the bigger hit black films such as *Shaft* (1971) and *Superfly* (1972).

Jim Brown's success opened the door for, among others, such black action stars as Richard Roundtree, Fred Williamson, and another former Cleveland Browns star, Jim Kelly.
See also: racism in Hollywood

BROWN, JOE E. *See* comedians & comediennes.

BROWNING, TOD (1882–1962) He made his reputation as a director and screenwriter of the macabre, making many of Hollywood's most unsettling horror films of the late 1920s and early 1930s, including a significant number of the genre's early classics. He was, in essence, America's answer to the German Expressionist directors of the 1920s, creating a distinctly dark and forbidding homegrown form of horror that was notable for both its sympathy toward its grotesque creatures and its exuberant delight in terrifying the audience.

Browning's early fascination with the grotesque came after he ran away from home to join a circus when he was sixteen years old. Working as a clown and a contortionist, he saw the dark side of the freak shows and understood the audience's lurid interest in all things mysterious and strange. He would later exploit that interest to the fullest extent that Hollywood would allow.

After a stint on vaudeville, Browning worked for D. W. Griffith *(q.v.)* as both an actor and assistant (working on *Intolerance,* 1916). In 1917, he directed his first film, *Jim Bludso.* He continued directing (and often scripting) films without any particular distinction for another eight years. In 1925, however, he found his ideal collaborator in actor Lon Chaney with whom he made *The Unholy Three*. This semi-horror film, using the circus as its backdrop, was a huge success. Browning had found his metier.

The director continued to work with Chaney through the rest of the decade, making such impressive horror films as *The Black Bird* (1926), *The Road to Mandalay* (1926), *The Unknown* (1927), *London After Midnight* (1927), and *Where East is East* (1929).

Together, Browning and Chaney defined the horror film genre, and planned to continue their work with the arrival of sound. Chaney was supposed to star in the director's film version of *Dracula* (1931) but the actor died of throat cancer. Bela Lugosi, who had played the title role on Broadway, was the substitute star. The film was a tremendous hit and has become one of the classic horror films of all time.

After *Dracula*, Browning found himself at the height of his powers as a director, both in terms of his skill and his financial clout within the industry. That power led him to assemble genuine side-show performers from circuses and carnivals all over the world for his most ambitious and most memorable movie, *Freaks* (1932). Audiences were both appalled and repulsed by Browning's sympathetic portrait of nature's grotesques. The film was banned in England and received very poor distribution in America.

Browning's career was dealt a blow by the commercial failure of *Freaks,* and he went on to make just four more films, *Fast Workers* (1933), *Mark of the Vampire* (1935), the highly regarded *The Devil Doll* (1936), and *Miracles for Sale* (1939). He then retired to a reclusive life in Santa Monica, California.

See also: Dracula; horror

BRYNNER, YUL (1915–1985)   An actor who proved that a unique appearance can be far more advantageous than conventional good looks. With his trademark shaved head, Brynner was an international movie star for nearly thirty years. Intense, sharp-featured, with a deep, authoritative voice and mysterious, virtually unplaceable accent, Brynner had a commanding screen presence that was far more memorable than the vast majority of his movies.

Born Youl Bryner on Sakhalin, an island north of Japan (near the Russian coastline), he was of gypsy stock and traveled a great deal in his youth. As a teenager, he was a trapeze artist in Paris before a fall left him badly injured. After his recuperation, he became an actor at the Piteoff Repertory Company in Paris while also studying at the Sorbonne. He came to the United States in 1940 with a Shakespearean company and then stayed in America during the war. Fluent in several languages, he went to work for the U.S. Office of War Information as a foreign-language radio broadcaster.

After the war, Brynner's career seemed destined for the stage and television. He appeared on Broadway in *Lute Song* in 1946 and worked extensively in the evolving TV industry. His early experience with the movies was limited to a single villainous lead role in the low-budget production *Port of New York* (1949), in which he can be seen sporting a full head of hair.

Brynner's breakthrough came when he was cast as the King of Siam in the Broadway musical *The King and I* in 1951. Both the show and Brynner were hits, and he recreated his starring role in the film adaptation in 1956, winning an Oscar for his performance.

The actor had shaved his head for his role in *The King and I* and he kept it bald for the rest of his career. A difficult actor to cast, he was nonetheless seen quite often during the rest of the 1950s in biblical epics and period pieces such as *The Ten Commandments* (1956), *Anastasia* (1956), *The Brothers Karamazov* (1957), *The Buccaneer* (1958), and *Solomon and Sheba* (1959).

His films of the 1950s and early 1960s marked the high point of his popularity, a peak reached thanks to his starring role in the hit western *The Magnificent Seven* (1960). After the big-budget flop *Taras Bulba* (1962), Brynner's career began to slacken. In the middle of the decade he starred in *The Return of the Seven* (1966), a tepid sequel to his earlier smash. Soon thereafter, he moved to Switzerland and began appearing in foreign films with little distribution in America, such as *Triple Cross* (1966), *The Battle of Neretva* (1970), and *The Light at the Edge of the World* (1971).

He made a memorable return to Hollywood movie-making in a supporting role in the hit suspense film *Westworld* (1973), but that success didn't resurrect his career in America. He ultimately triumphed in a revival of his original hit, *The King and I,* playing in sold-out theaters all over America, including a celebrated run on Broadway.

Brynner died of lung cancer. Along with a number of other former heavy-smoking celebrities, the actor recorded a powerful anti-smoking TV commercial that was scheduled to air after his death.

BUCHMAN, SIDNEY (1902–1975)   A gifted screenwriter and successful producer of smart, sophisticated comedies and adroit dramas during the 1930s and 1940s, his career came to a sudden and sad end when he was called before the House Un-American Activities Committee in 1951 and admitted he had once been a communist. When he refused to betray his friends and name others whom he knew had once been party members, he was fined and given a year's suspended sentence. Worse, however, he was blacklisted and denied the chance to work again in the movie industry until the blacklist was finally abolished in the early 1960s.

Buchman, a failed playwright during the 1920s, got his first screen credit when he collaborated on the original script for *Matinee Ladies* (1927). Not long after talkies arrived, so did Buchman. He was hired by Paramount to write dialogue for such films as *Beloved Bachelor* (1931) and *The Sign of the Cross* (1932), but he showed his flair for comedy when he collaborated on the script for the Depression-era hit *If I Had A Million* (1932).

He worked for Paramount until 1934, when he moved to Columbia, the studio that would be his home for the next seventeen years. He blossomed at Columbia, becoming one of the foremost screenwriters of the late 1930s and early 1940s when he either wrote or adapted such films as *Theodora Goes Wild* (1936), *The Awful Truth* (uncredited, 1937), *Lost Horizon* (uncredited, 1937), *Holiday* (1938), *Mr. Smith Goes to Washington* (1939), *Here Comes Mr. Jordon* (1941), for which he won an Oscar, *The Talk of the Town* (1942), and *Sahara* (uncredited, 1943).

After Frank Capra *(q.v.)* left Columbia, Buchman became studio boss Harry Cohn's *(q.v.)* most trusted advisor and friend. The screenwriter was given the added responsibility of producing in 1942 and eventually became Cohn's right-hand man as assistant production chief. Among his triumphs during the latter half of the 1940s were the story for the huge hit *The Jolson Story* (1947), and both the script and production of such films as *A Song to Remember* (1945) and *Jolson Sings Again* (1949).

After Buchman was hounded out of Hollywood in 1951, he made his return as the screenwriter of the thoughtful adult movie made in England about child molestation, *The Mark* (1961). Unfortunately, he followed that project with the troubled *Cleopatra* (1963). He worked very little thereafter, living as an exile in Cannes, France, and writing just two more films, *The Group* (1966) and *The Deadly Trap* (1972).

See also: The Hollywood Ten

BURNETT, W. R. (1899–1982) He was a novelist and screenwriter of considerable influence, particularly in the gangster genre. Most of his novels found their way to the screen, and some were remade twice. A writer of the hardboiled school of fiction, Burnett's dialogue was realistic and gritty—which made his work perfect for adaptation to the screen. Unlike most novelists of his day, Burnett had no trouble writing directly for the movies. In fact, he worked at both careers concurrently, writing novels and screenplays well into the 1960s.

Born William Riley Burnett, the would-be author worked as a statistician throughout the better part of his twenties, becoming a full-time writer in 1928 when he wrote *Little Caesar*. Published the following year, Warner Bros. quickly bought the rights and in 1931 turned it into one of the most famous of the early gangster movies, the kind of film for which the studio was soon to become famous.

Burnett wrote other gangster novels that were turned into such films as *Doctor Socrates* (1935), which was remade as *King of the Underworld* (1939), *High Sierra* (1941), which was remade as *I Died a Thousand Times* (1955), and *The Asphalt Jungle* (1950), remade as *The Badlanders* (1957), and yet again as *Cool Breeze* (1972).

Burnett's impact on the gangster genre was no less impressive when he was writing original screenplays. His scripts included Howard Hawks' *(q.v.)* classic, *Scarface* (1932), and the film that made Alan Ladd *(q.v.)* a star, *This Gun for Hire* (1942).

The variety of Burnett's work sets him apart from other writers of hardboiled fiction who worked for the movies, such as James N. Cain and Raymond Chandler. Burnett wrote westerns that were turned into movies, such as the powerful *The Dark Command* (1940), war stories, including the screenplays for *Wake Island* (1942) and *The Great Escape* (1963) (in collaboration), and even comedies, most notably the original story for John Ford's *The Whole Town's Talking* (1935).

BURNS & ALLEN (George Burns, 1896– , Gracie Allen, 1902–1964) This husband and wife comedy team enjoyed their greatest success in vaudeville, radio, and TV, although they had a notable film career together during the 1930s.

Gracie played a ditsy woman who thought she was smart, while George, the straight man, patiently asked questions that invited her hilarious answers. Their humor derived from absurd misinterpretations of language and common, everyday experiences that Gracie transformed according to a comically inspired logic all her own.

Born Grace Ethel Cecile Rosalie Allen, the young comedienne, the daughter of a show business family, joined her parents' act very early in her life. Meanwhile, George Burns, born Nathan Birnbaum, one of fourteen children, quit school at the age of thirteen to help support his family. He sang in the streets of New York with his group, The Peewee Quartet, for pennies, eventually working his way into vaudeville.

Grace and George met on the vaudeville circuit and formed an act in 1923, marrying in 1926. It's interesting to note that originally George was the comic and Gracie the straight man. When Gracie received laughs just by asking George questions, George wisely decided that they should switch roles. By the time they were married, Burns & Allen had hit the vaudeville big time with their "Lamb Chop" routine.

Their success in vaudeville led them to Hollywood, where they made fourteen comedy shorts during the 1930s. Their first feature film appearance was in *The Big Broadcast* (1932). The pair played important, but supporting characters in virtually all of their twenty feature films. Their most noteworthy roles were in *We're Not Dressing* (1934) and *Big Broadcast of 1936* (1935). Supporting Fred Astaire in *Damsel in Distress*

George Burns has become one of the most beloved entertainers in show business. His suddenly booming movie success as a senior citizen, after his early stardom with his late wife, Gracie Allen, in vaudeville, radio, movies, and television, is just reward for his exquisite comic timing (not to mention his singing). Photo courtesy of George Burns.

(1937), they not only provided comic relief, they also did a splendid dance routine!

Gracie performed without her husband in two films, *The Gracie Allen Murder Case* (1939) and *Mr. & Mrs. North* (1942). In the meantime, Burns & Allen had a radio show that ran from 1933 until 1950, when the program made the move to television. *The Burns & Allen Show* aired on TV until Gracie chose to retire in 1958.

George, who had been in charge of the act and who oversaw their radio and TV show, went on working as a solo performer, starring in two other TV series. Then, after a thirty-five year absence from the big screen, and more than a decade after Gracie's death, George Burns emerged in 1975 as a movie star in Neil Simon's *The Sunshine Boys.* Stepping in to the role originally intended for his best friend, Jack Benny (who had died suddenly), George won an Oscar for Best Supporting Actor. He went on to star in a surprisingly large number of films, receiving his greatest acclaim for *Oh, God!* (1977), in which he played God with endearing comic aplomb. Unfortunately, the many sequels to the film have not been up to George's talents.

In addition to his latter-day film work, he has also written best-selling books, recorded country/western albums, and hosted TV specials.

BURTON, RICHARD (1925–1984)   A gifted actor who rose to fame due to a combination of raw sex appeal, talent, and his grand romance with Elizabeth Taylor. Ruggedly handsome and blessed with a mellifluous baritone that could make the reading of a dictionary sound like poetry, many critics lamented the fact that he didn't live up to his potential. Nonetheless, he managed to garner six Oscar nominations during the course of his Hollywood career, the first as early as 1952 for Best Supporting Actor for *My Cousin Rachel* (1952). Later, he received Best Actor nominations for *The Robe* (1953), *Becket* (1964), *The Spy Who Came in From the Cold* (1965), *Who's Afraid of Virginia Woolf?* (1966), and *Anne of the Thousand Days* (1969).

Born Richard Walter Jenkins, he was the twelfth of thirteen children of a Welsh miner. Raised in dire poverty during the Depression, he took a job as a haberdasher's apprentice. Thanks to his dedicated teacher, Philip Burton, he won a scholarship to Oxford. In tribute to the man who educated him, Richard took his mentor's last name when he embarked upon his stage career, which began in 1943 with his performance in a Liverpool production of *Druid's Rest.*

Military service in the Royal Air Force during the years 1944–47 interrupted his early career, but he quickly returned to acting in 1948. In that year he made his film debut in *The Last Days of Dolwyn,* revealing his propensity to flit back and forth between the stage and the screen, never fully giving himself to one or the other during the rest of his life.

Despite his burgeoning film career, his reputation was made in the theater. He starred in *The Lady's Not For Burning* in London in 1949 and *Hamlet* at the Edinburgh Festival in 1953. Later, in 1960, he starred in the stage musical *Camelot.*

While working on the boards, he starred in English films such as *The Woman With No Name* (1950) and *Green Grow the Rushes* (1951). He arrived in Hollywood in 1952 to star in *My Cousin Rachel.* Other leading roles followed in films such as *Prince of Players* (1955) and *Alexander the Great* (1956), but he was hardly a movie star during the 1950s and early 1960s. That soon changed.

Burton's much ballyhooed affair with Elizabeth Taylor during the making of *Cleopatra* (1963) turned him into an international sex symbol. He was Mark Antony to Taylor's Cleopatra, and the press went wild with the story. Until then, Burton was considered the heir to Olivier as England's greatest actor. In fact, Olivier sent a wire to Burton on the set of *Cleopatra* stating: "Make up your mind, dear heart. Do you want to be a great actor or a household word?" Burton's reply was, "Both."

Burton and Taylor were each married at the time, he to his first wife, Sybil Williams, and she to her fourth husband, Eddie Fisher. They soon divorced their respective spouses and wed in what became the longest-running and most publicized Hollywood romance of all time. They later separated, divorced, and remarried, only to divorce again.

Burton joined Taylor in a number of movies throughout the 1960s and early 1970s, including *The V.I.P.s* (1963), *The Sandpiper* (1965), *The Comedians* (1967), *Boom!* (1969), and *Hammersmith is Out* (1972). Their best collaborations, however, were in *The Taming of the Shrew* (1967) and *Who's Afraid of Virginia Woolf?* (1966).

Burton became a very wealthy man during the 1960s, with he and his wife earning staggering sums of money to appear in movies together. Few of the films were good; despite the dual star appeal, moviegoers finally stopped buying tickets.

In the meanwhile, alcoholism began taking its toll on Burton and, perhaps even more insidiously, his disregard for his craft began to tell. He cared little for his movie projects except for the cash they might earn him, a fact he readily acknowledged. Yet, despite his many mediocre movies, his appeal as an actor was undeniable, and he did occasionally soar in a few of his later movies, particularly in *The Assassination of Trotsky* (1972) and *Equus* (1977), though neither film was a financial success. Otherwise, he plodded through such poorly scripted films as *Villain* (1971), *Bluebeard* (1972), *Jackpot* (1975), *Exorcist II: The Heretic* (1977), *The Medusa Touch* (1978), *Tristan and Isolde* (1980), and *Wagner* (1983).

He died suddenly in 1984 of a cerebral hemorrhage. *See also: Cleopatra;* Taylor, Elizabeth

BUSHMAN, FRANCIS X. (1883–1966) He was Hollywood's first male sex symbol, a heartthrob to millions of female movie fans during the mid-1910s, when he was known as "The Handsomest Man in the World."

Francis Xavier Bushman, a former sculptor's model, was a big, broad-shouldered titan who had worked as a stage actor since adolescence without much success. His rise to stardom in the movies began in 1911 when he started appearing in one- and two-reelers such as *His Friend's Wife* (1911) and *Chains* (1912).

Within just a few years, Bushman's name was on the lips of female moviegoers everywhere, establishing a precedent that would be followed in the 1920s by Rudolph Valentino. During his heyday, Bushman starred in such films as *The Battle of Love* (1914), *The Silent Voice* (1915), and *A Million a Minute* (1916).

The actor's fall from the height of superstardom came when female fans discovered that Bushman had secretly married his costar in *Romeo and Juliet* (1916), Beverly Bayne. No longer able to command the huge salary he had been earning and with his career on the skids, Bushman returned to the stage during the early 1920s.

His most famous role came with his mid-1920s big-screen comeback attempt when he played the villain, Messala, in the colossal hit *Ben-Hur* (1926). More movie work followed, but his career still sputtered along into the early sound era.

Though he appeared to be a victim of the talkies, ironically Bushman made a small fortune as an actor in radio shows! In any event, his later film career consisted of minor roles in a relative handful of films such as *Hollywood Boulevard* (1936), *Wilson* (1944), *David and Bathsheba* (1951), *The Story of Mankind* (1957), and the lamentable *The Ghost in the Invisible Bikini* (1966).

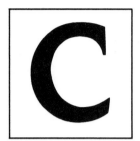

CAGNEY, JAMES (1899–1986) One of the true Hollywood superstars, he is primarily known for playing gangsters, yet he was also a wonderful, idiosyncratic dancer who had precious few opportunities to show off his talents in musicals (although when he got the chance, he shined). Most of his career was spent at Warner Bros., where he was often among the top-ten male draws during the late 1930s and early 1940s. While Cagney is always fascinating to watch on screen, far too few of his sixty-five films are of top-notch quality, and his popularity has waned in recent decades.

Cagney was born on New York's Lower East Side and sought an education beyond learning how to survive in a crime-riddled neighborhood. He was accepted into Columbia University but soon had to drop out because of a lack of money. He took whatever jobs he could find, including working as a racker in a billiard parlor. In desperation, he turned to show business hoping to make a better living.

His first job was in a vaudeville show titled *Every Sailor* (1919), but it wasn't a choice role. He played a female in the chorus line—hardly an auspicious debut for one of the screen's greatest tough guys.

In any event, he went on to appear as an actor/dancer on the vaudeville circuit throughout the early to mid-1920s, until he made it to Broadway. Slowly, he ascended the cast lists, finally becoming the second lead in *Penny Arcade*.

It was his big break. The show was made into a Warner Bros. movie (retitled *Sinner's Holiday*, 1930), and he came with the package. As he said in his autobiography *(Cagney on Cagney)*, "I came out (to Hollywood) on a three-week guarantee and I stayed, to my absolute amazement, for thirty-one years."

Once again he moved up the cast list, but far more quickly than he did on Broadway. He made only three more films in just one year before becoming a major

star. The movie that catapulted him to the top and tagged him forever as a gangster was *Public Enemy* (1931). Ironically, Cagney was originally cast as the protagonist's (Tom Powers) brother. The film's producer, Darryl F. Zanuck *(q.v.)*, switched Cagney's role with another actor's (Eddie Woods) after three days of shooting, and Cagney became the lead.

Cagney's gangster roles rank among the most memorable of that genre. In addition to *Public Enemy*, among the best of his films are *Angels With Dirty Faces* (1938), *The Roaring Twenties* (1939), and *White Heat* (1949).

Though he was typed as a gangster, Cagney excelled in many other parts. In some of his better early roles he played a taxi driver in *Taxi* (1931), a press agent in *Hard to Handle* (1933), and a boxer in *City for Conquest* (1940).

Where Spencer Tracy had Katharine Hepburn and Bogart had Bacall, Jimmy Cagney's steady partner in films at this time was Pat O'Brien *(q.v.)*. Their first movie collaboration was *Here Comes the Navy* (1934). They made eight films together, the last being *Torrid Zone* (1940). They made a wonderful team, each talking faster than the other, their dialogue zipping along like verbal lightning.

Aside from his Pat O'Brien films and gangster efforts (which sometimes overlapped), Cagney is best remembered and most loved for his rare musicals. He first showed his peculiar stiff-legged dancing style in *Footlight Parade* (1933). Given the huge success of the film (it made nearly $2 million), it seems somewhat surprising at first that Cagney was not pushed into more musicals. Musicals, however, have always taken much longer to rehearse and film, and Cagney was more valuable to Warner Bros. when making action films that were faster to produce. In 1935, for instance, Cagney made a total of six movies. But he eventually made three more musicals, two of minor consequence

As hard as he tried, James Cagney could never quite shed his image as the pugnacious gangster. Though he rose to fame as a tough guy in *Public Enemy* (1931), Cagney was a hoofer at heart, and among his own movies, his favorite was *Yankee Doodle Dandy* (1942). Photo courtesy of Movie Star News.

(*Something to Sing About*, 1937, and *Never Steal Anything Small*, 1959), and the masterpiece *Yankee Doodle Dandy* (1942).

Yankee Doodle Dandy was made, in part, because Cagney was accused of being a communist. The charge was ridiculous, but it prompted Cagney to display his patriotism. The flag-waving biography of George M. Cohan was certainly the perfect vehicle. The movie earned Cagney a Best Actor Oscar and it made a fortune in film rentals, earning more than $4 million in its initial release in the United States (except for England, the European market was unavailable because of the war).

Cagney's career slowed down considerably in the mid-1940s. He had left Warners to set up his own production company, producing and starring in only one hit, *Blood on the Sun* (1946), but also turning out (among others) a quiet but endearing film that unfortunately flopped, William Saroyan's *The Time of Your Life* (1948).

The 1950s were a rather uneven decade for Cagney. He made one excellent film about alcoholism in 1951,

Come Fill the Cup, but despite fine performances in the early part of the decade, his popularity had begun to fade. Cagney (ever the city tough) never looked or sounded right in the western *Run for Cover* (1955), a fine Nicholas Ray film that nonetheless was ignored by both audiences and critics. In that same year, however, his career suddenly turned around when he played the aging gangster in the Doris Day vehicle *Love Me or Leave Me*. He emerged yet again with a fine supporting performance as the impossible captain in the Henry Fonda hit *Mister Roberts* (1955).

It was a flurry of activity that unfortunately didn't signal a return to top box office status. Except for an exceptional performance playing Lon Chaney in *The Man of a Thousand Faces* (1957), Cagney's films did not amount to much. He seemingly ended his career on a wonderful high note in Billy Wilder's little seen but highly regarded comedy, *One, Two, Three* (1962).

Cagney walked away from Hollywood, retiring to his farm in upstate New York. He lived there quietly for twenty years, ignoring all entreaties to make yet another film. He had been asked but refused to play Eliza Doolittle's father in the film version of *My Fair Lady* (1964). It wasn't until he suffered a stroke and his doctor suggested acting as good therapy that Cagney consented to return to the movies. He came back to the big screen in a featured role as the police commissioner in *Ragtime* (1981). Though he looked old, there was still that unmistakeable pugnacious rat-a-tat-tat voice punching out his dialogue. And what a thrill it was to see the name James Cagney on the marquee of a theater again, fifty years after *Public Enemy*.

Cagney's idea of good acting was simple and straightforward. He put it best himself when he said, "Never settle back on your heels. Never relax. If you relax, the audience relaxes. And always mean everything you say." Certainly, Cagney was never false in any of his films, whether or not his movies were badly written or directed. He remains a Hollywood treasure, an actor who usually outclassed the vast majority of his films.
See also: gangster films; musicals; screen teams; Walsh, Raoul

CAHN, SAMMY (1913–) A versatile lyricist, Cahn has provided the words to scores of songs in dozens of Hollywood films. Essentially a romantic, he was responsible for such love songs as "Be My Love," "It's Magic," and "I Fall in Love Too Easily." He provided lyrics for tunes in all sorts of films, including many non-musicals, and he was both prolific and talented enough to take home four Oscars for Best Song: "Three Coins in the Fountain," from the 1954 movie of the same name, "All the Way," from *The Joker is Wild* (1957), "High Hopes," from *A Hole in the Head* (1959), and "Call Me Irresponsible," from *Papa's Delicate Condition* (1963).

Born Samuel Cohen, the young man began working in the film industry in 1935 and was soon providing lyrics to songs in a number of minor films such as *Rookies on Parade* (1941) and *Carolina Blues* (1944). He moved up to "A" movies *(q.v.)* when he wrote the lyrics for the entertaining *Anchors Aweigh* (1945). His songs were often better than the movies they were sung in; for instance, he provided the lyrics for the endearing title song of the not so endearing film *The Tender Trap* (1955), as well as songs for movies of the ilk of *Ten Thousand Bedrooms* (1957) and *Thoroughly Modern Millie* (1967).

Frank Sinatra *(q.v.)* starred in eight films for which Cahn supplied lyrics (including two of Cahn's Best Song Oscar winners), linking the lyricist and the singer-actor together in a formidable association. More directly, Cahn has been associated with the composers Jules Styne and James Van Heusen.

CAINE, MICHAEL (1933–) He is a prolific, if non-discriminating, Cockney actor who has appeared in an inordinate number of bad movies, but who has been in many more better ones. His versatility has been the key to his success; he can play charming villains and rogues, flawed action heroes, romantic leads, and comic characters, all with equal ease—and always with a realistic, human touch. Caine is an international movie star who has come to be seen by movie audiences in the United States as "our" Englishman, in much the same way David Niven, Ronald Colman, and Leslie Howard were adopted by American movie fans.

Born Maurice Joseph Micklewhite to a poor family at the height of the Depression, Caine struggled through his youth, eventually going to war in a British combat unit assigned to the United Nations forces in Korea in the early 1950s. After returning to England, he changed his name to Michael Scott when he began his acting career as a bit player in English repertory theaters. Later, when he took on an agent and began appearing in small roles in English films, he was forced to change his name yet again because there already was a Michael Scott in British Equity. The lifelong Humphrey Bogart fan noticed *The Caine Mutiny* playing at a local theater and chose the name Caine.

His first noticeable part in the movies was in *A Hill in Korea* (1956). Between 1956 and 1963 Caine had small roles in thirty films and appeared on the BBC no less than 125 times in various shows. But not until he had a major supporting role in *Zulu* (1963) did his career begin to take off.

It is generally assumed that *Alfie* (1966) was his first major hit, but he actually starred the year before as Harry Palmer in the *Ipcress File* and made a considerable impression, playing the first movie hero (comedians aside) to wear glasses. His glasses have since become his trademark.

Michael Caine seems almost incapable of giving a bad performance. And while many modern stars go often a year or two (or longer) between films, Caine has been a workhorse actor averaging better than two movies per year since the mid-1960s. Photo courtesy of Michael Caine.

As *Alfie*, however, Caine established himself as a sex symbol, thanks to his sympathetic portrayal of a self-centered cad, which received an Academy Award nomination and gave a substantial boost to his career in the bargain. His first American movie was made that same year when he was a surprise choice to play a Southerner in Otto Preminger's *Hurry Sundown,* a movie that bombed but showed his range as an actor to good effect.

Despite the box office failure of an unusually high percentage of his films, Caine is almost always universally praised by critics; the usual line goes something like, "His performance is far better than this movie deserves," etc. The actor's ability to rise above his material has allowed him to continue to receive excellent roles in a variety of films. Despite good personal reviews, however, it appeared as if his star was dimming in the early 1970s after a particularly long spell of losers—until he costarred with Laurence Olivier in the hit mystery *Sleuth* (1972), stealing the notices and winning his second Oscar nomination.

Four years of flops followed, but he ended the skid with his wonderful performance in John Huston's much admired *The Man Who Would Be King* (1976). After another four years of dismal films, he played the psychiatrist/killer in Brian De Palma's smash hit, *Dressed to Kill* (1980). For the most part, he has appeared in better movies during the 1980s, such as *Death Trap* (1982), *Educating Rita* (1983), *Sweet Liberty* (1986) and

Dirty Rotten Scoundrels (1988). But it was typical of the actor's career that he was filming the trashy *Jaws IV* (1987) at the time of his winning a Best Supporting Actor Oscar for his role in Woody Allen's *Hannah and Her Sisters* (1986).

CAMERA (MOVIE) The invention to which Hollywood owes its existence, the motion picture camera records still photographs on long strips of celluloid in such rapid succession that, when developed and projected at the proper speed, it appears as if uninterrupted movement has been captured on film. The perceptual principle behind this visual trick is called "persistence of vision" *(q.v.).*

After the invention of the still camera in the early 19th century, the push to make moving pictures began in earnest. In 1877, Edward Muybridge conducted his famous experiment by making rapid, sequential photographs of a race horse at full gallop. This helped to define in photography the interrelationship of time and motion.

A mere eleven years later, in 1888, the first movie camera was built at Thomas Edison's *(q.v.)* New Jersey laboratory by William Kennedy Laurie Dickson. Edison, however, was not (at first) terribly enthusiastic about the business prospects of the new device, especially given that no dependable source of film had yet been developed for it. Not until George Eastman invented celluloid film in 1889 did the camera become a viable invention.

After Eastman's breakthrough, Auguste and Louis Lumière, two French brothers, demonstrated the commercial potential of their own invention, a combination movie camera and projector. The year was 1895, the year in which the movies were born.

From 1895 until the late 1910s, various early movie cameras were beset by mechanical problems. For the most part, they were crudely made wooden boxes that often caused a jarring jerkiness and flickering in the images they recorded. Worse still, these cameras often jammed. By the time of the golden age of the silent cinema (the 1920s), wooden cameras were finally replaced by more carefully crafted metal machines that have remained essentially the same in design to this day.
See also: Bitzer, Billy; Black Maria; blimp

CAMERA OPERATOR The member of the camera crew who operates the camera during the shoot. This is a job that is often confused with that of the cameraman (also known as the cinematographer or director of photography), who works with the director to light and compose the scenes to be shot. The camera operator (also known as the second cameraman) reports to the cameraman.
See also: cinematographer

A veritable dynamo of energy and talent, Eddie Cantor was a natural movie star in early talkies. More out of a personal choice rather than lack of box office success, he did not appear in a great many films. Photo courtesy of The Siegel Collection.

CANTOR, EDDIE (1892–1964) He was an actor, singer, and comedian with an enormous energy level who could put a song over like Al Jolson *(q.v.)* and throw off comic one-liners like Groucho Marx. He usually played a mousy and seemingly ineffectual type who would find the courage to save the day by the last reel. With his pop-eyes, optimistic attitude, and willingness to do anything for a laugh, Cantor gained a popularity in films that defied the box office doom visited upon other film stars during the worst of the Great Depression.

Born Edward Isidore Izkowitz, he was orphaned at an early age and supported himself any way he could, which included working as a singing waiter, before making his mark in vaudeville. He rose to fame on Broadway in *The Midnight Frolics* (1916) and joined the ranks of popular show business entertainers such as Al Jolson and George Jessel during the 1920s when he starred in the *Ziegfeld Follies,* and later hit shows, including *Kid Boots* (1926) and *Whoopee* (1930).

Cantor made a silent-film version of *Kid Boots* in 1926, but he didn't become a film star until talkies let him show off his unique style. Samuel Goldwyn signed him up and Cantor made five wonderfully silly musical comedies for the producer, including *Whoopee* (1930), *Palmy Days* (1931), *The Kid From Spain* (1932), *Roman*

Scandals (1933), and *Kid Millions* (1934). Cantor also coscripted *Mr. Lemon of Orange* (1931). Goldwyn would later develop the musical comedy star Danny Kaye *(q.v.)* very much in Cantor's image.

Cantor continued acting in films in the 1930s and 1940s, but with considerably less frequency. The movies took a back seat to his immensely popular radio show. Among his later films were *Strike Me Pink* (1936), *Ali Baba Goes to Town* (1937), *Forty Little Mothers* (1940), and *Thank Your Lucky Stars* (1943).

He starred in only two more films, *Show Business* (1944) and *If You Knew Susie* (1948), based on his most famous hit song. He produced both movies and, except for a brief appearance playing himself in the 1952 *The Story of Will Rogers*, he did not appear again on film due to a disabling heart attack that same year. His life, however, was put up on the big screen in a poorly done biopic *(q.v.)* called *The Eddie Cantor Story* (1953), for which the famous entertainer dubbed his own songs.

Cantor was given a special Academy Award in 1956.

CANUTT, YAKIMA (1895–1986) A legendary stuntman who later became a top second unit director, Canutt was an innovator who helped develop the safe yet effective artifice of the Hollywood stunt. In a fifteen-year career as a stuntman, he fell from horses, jumped onto speeding wagons, and fell from buildings in more than 150 films. He was also a stunt double for such stars as John Wayne, Clark Gable, and Gene Autry *(qq.v.)*, to name just a few.

Born Enos Edward Canutt, this native of the state of Washington earned his nickname when he was a champion rodeo rider and a newspaper referred to him as "The Cowboy from Yakima." Though not an Indian from the Yakima Indian Reservation as many people mistakenly supposed, Canutt was a skilled and fearless rider whose exploits on the rodeo circuit (he was a "world champion") brought him to the attention of Hollywood during the early 1920s.

Canutt began as a stuntman, then became a silent-screen western star in his own right. Unable to make the transition to sound, he went back to being a stuntman, while also playing the occasional villain in low-budget westerns. But it was as a stuntman that he became famous within the Hollywood community with his remarkable feats in films such as *Stagecoach* (1939), *Gone With the Wind* (1939), *They Died With Their Boots On* (1940), and *Dark Command* (1940).

He broke both of his ankles in a 1941 stunt, ending this phase of his remarkable career. Canutt directed four "B" movie westerns in the 1940s, but he was in far greater demand as a premier second unit director, where he continued to create many of Hollywood's most remarkable stunts, handling the action scenes in other directors' films for thirty years, including the famous chariot race in *Ben Hur* (1959), the battles in *El Cid* (1961), and the horse-blinding scene in *Equus* (1976), to name just a few.

He was finally honored by the Academy in 1966 with a special Oscar for "creating the profession of stuntman as it exists today and for the development of many safety devices used by stuntmen everywhere."

See also: second unit; stuntman

CAPRA, FRANK (1897–) In addition to being a leading director of the 1930s and early 1940s, his success helped propel one-time minor Columbia Pictures into the ranks of the majors. It is fair to say that Harry Cohn's *(q.v.)* Columbia Pictures would have been a mere footnote in Hollywood history had it not been for the thirteen-year association between the studio and its greatest director. In retrospect the reasons for the mass appeal of Capra's films are obvious. When most other directors made films about "bigger-than-life" heroes, he made films about people with whom the audience could identify—cynics, idealists, working people, out-of-work John Does and small town folks with unfulfilled dreams. There is no mistaking Capra's best films for those of any other director; his good humor, proletarian point of view, sentimentalism, and rollicking pace are unique. His stature and success in the business are evidenced by the fact that even before Cecil B. DeMille, Alfred Hitchcock *(qq.v.)*, or any other studio director, Frank Capra earned the distinction of having his name above the title of his films.

Born in Sicily, he immigrated with his poor family to America when he was six years old. Settling in California, his father worked in the fields picking fruit. Young Capra was an extremely bright young man and he struggled to get a college education, graduating with a degree in chemical engineering from the prestigious California Institute of Technology in 1918.

After a stint in the Army during World War I, Capra led a rudderless existence. When he found himself in desperate need of a job, he talked a small film company into letting him direct a short called *Fultah Fisher's Boarding House* (1922). His fascination with the film medium was born, and he spent the next several years learning everything he could about the movie business, working in a film lab and taking on jobs as a propmaster and editor. Perhaps his most important training came when he worked as a gagman on the *Our Gang* silent comedies for Hal Roach *(q.v.)*, and then as a gagman for Harry Langdon *(q.v.)* at the Mack Sennett *(q.v.)* studio.

Capra's understanding of comedy was displayed in his direction of Langdon's first three touching and very funny feature films, *Tramp, Tramp, Tramp* (1926), which Capra coscripted, *The Strong Man* (1926), and *Long Pants* (1927). Capra's importance to Langdon's career is particularly apparent because the comedian's art dete-

Frank Capra touched the American soul with his beguiling innocence, and no more so than with his classic Christmas fantasy *It's a Wonderful Life* (1946). Seen here are James Stewart and Lionel Barrymore in a scene from that film, a movie that has become one of the most beloved motion pictures ever made. Photo courtesy of Movie Star News.

riorated after he decided he was a comic genius, firing Capra and then directing himself into oblivion.

Out of a job, Capra went to New York to direct Claudette Colbert *(q.v.)* in her movie debut, *For the Love of Mike* (1927), but the film was not a success. He went back to work for Sennett for a short while before Harry Cohn made the smartest decision of his long career at Columbia, hiring Capra in 1928 by what was then a very special arrangement. Capra agreed to be paid the relatively paltry sum of $1,000 per picture in exchange for the right to coscript, direct, and produce his own films without any interference from Cohn. While the amount of money Capra earned would ultimately skyrocket, the other terms of the agreement remained in force for thirteen years.

His first film at Columbia was a delightful comedy, *That Certain Thing* (1928). He worked quickly during the next several years, easily making the transition to

sound, while continuing to learn his craft in a number of minor, but increasingly popular, films such as *Say It With Sable* (1928), *Submarine* (1928), *Dirigible* (1931), *Platinum Blonde* (1931), *American Madness* (1932), and *The Bitter Tea of General Yen* (1933).

Capra was a hitmaker, but his early success at Columbia was nothing compared to what was to come. In 1934 he made the blockbuster of the year, *It Happened One Night,* with Claudette Colbert and Clark Gable *(q.v.).* It became the first film to sweep all five top Oscars: Best Picture, Best Director, Best Screenplay (Robert Risken), Best Actor, and Best Actress. Neither Gable (on loan to Columbia as punishment) nor Colbert (who had worked with Capra without success in her movie debut) wanted to be in the film. The critical and box office reaction was so strong that this single picture not only turned the two actors into superstars, but Capra became the hottest director in Hollywood, turning Columbia, overnight, into a highly respected institution.

Emboldened by his success, Capra went on to make a series of films for which he is justly best remembered. His social comedies, beginning with *Mr. Deeds Goes to Town* (1936) and continuing with *You Can't Take it With You* (1938), *Mr. Smith Goes to Washington* (1939), and *Meet John Doe* (1941), are sometimes known as "Capracorn" for their strong belief in the goodness of man. Despite their apparent naïveté, these films were biting indictments of greed, corruption, and selfishness in their time. In fact, Capra's *Mr. Smith Goes to Washington,* which premiered in the nation's capital with an audience full of congressmen, was roundly booed and criticized by the elected officials for even suggesting that one of their number might be on the take. Nonetheless, *Mr. Smith* was nominated for Best Picture and Capra was nominated as Best Director for the film. The late 1930s were often years of awards for Capra. He won the Best Director Academy Award for *Mr. Deeds Goes to Town,* and both a Best Picture and Best Director Oscar for *You Can't Take it With You.* In addition, his fantasy film, *Lost Horizon* (1937), was nominated for Best Picture.

During World War II, Capra distinguished himself still further when he joined the service and made *Why We Fight,* a stirring explanation of America's role in the war. He won a Best Documentary Oscar in 1942 for his efforts, and went on to make a number of excellent films for the army. Before he left Hollywood, he made *Arsenic and Old Lace,* which was released in 1944 in order to keep his work in front of the American public. It was yet another huge box office success, despite its rather macabre humor.

After the war, however, Capra seemed to lose his touch—not as a filmmaker, but as a hitmaker. Perhaps his greatest film, *It's a Wonderful Life* (1946), while much-loved and revered today as the quintessence of Capracorn, and arguably the greatest Christmas movie of them all, was a box office disappointment when it was released. *State of the Union* (1948) fared somewhat better, but *Riding High* (1950) and *Here Comes the Groom* (1951) were likeable Bing Crosby vehicles not on a par with Capra's earlier works.

After a long hiatus, Capra made his last two films, the underrated *A Hole in the Head* (1959) and the overrated *Pocketful of Miracles* (1961). He subsequently retired from directing, eventually publishing an intriguing and informative autobiography, *Frank Capra: The Name Above the Title,* in 1971.
See also: It Happened One Night; Stewart, Jimmy

CAPTAIN BLOOD The 1935 film that made both Errol Flynn and Olivia de Havilland (qqv.) stars, virtually overnight. At a time when movie studios kept actors under long-term contracts, grooming them for future stardom, the emergence of both stars in Captain Blood deserves special mention.

De Havilland was merely nineteen, and Flynn just twenty-six years old when *Captain Blood* was made. Both were under contract to Warner Bros., having done very little of consequence before they were chosen for a grand action saga about a buccaneer who falls in love with his worst enemy's daughter. Warners had decided that they wanted unknowns in *Captain Blood* after Robert Donat, a popular English actor turned down the part of Peter Blood.

Choosing Flynn as the lead was a courageous move on the studio's part, because *Captain Blood* was not a modest "B" movie. It was an elaborate production with a large cast. Warners also put their best director on the project, Michael Curtiz (q.v.), who did a splendid job in realizing the film's full potential.

Captain Blood had been made as a silent film in 1925, but it was the 1935 version that reestablished the swashbuckler as a viable genre in the sound era and made Flynn the natural successor to Douglas Fairbanks (q.v.). *See also:* swashbucklers

CARPENTER, JOHN (1948–) A writer/director best known for his vivid and ghoulish modern horror films, he has made a number of fine action and science fiction films, as well. If Brian De Palma (q.v.) is the heir to Alfred Hitchcock (q.v.), then John Carpenter is the heir to Howard Hawks (q.v.). Like Hawks, Carpenter shoots his movies with an "invisible" style; the audience is rarely aware of the camera's presence or the editor's splices. Also like Hawks, Carpenter excels at action movies. Most telling of all, at least two of the younger director's films are based on earlier Hawks movies; *Assault on Precinct 13* (1976) is a modern-day version of the Hawks classic western *Rio Bravo* (1959) and Carpenter also remade the 1951 Hawks production of *The Thing* in 1982.

As a youth, Carpenter was interested in both music and movies. In 1962, while still in his early teens, he made the choice to pursue a film career, making short films that culminated in an Academy Award for Best Live Action Short Subject for *The Resurrection of Broncho Billy* (1970). Five years later he made his feature film directorial debut with the low-budget *Star Wars* spoof, *Dark Star* (1975). In addition to directing, he also produced, wrote the screenplay, and penned the score for *Dark Star.*

Carpenter built a reputation on low-budget independent productions that finally could not be ignored, especially when he made the most financially successful independent movie in the history of the motion picture business, *Halloween* (1978), a film that spawned (and that's certainly the right word) a number of highly commercial sequels.

Tentatively accepted by Hollywood, he wrote the

screenplay for the Faye Dunaway (q.v.) horror thriller, *The Eyes of Laura Mars* (1978). Finally achieving financial backing to direct bigger budget movies, Carpenter began making films as diverse as *The Fog* (1981) and *Escape from New York* (1981). After directing the adaptation of the Stephen King novel *Christine* (1983), Carpenter reached the peak of his critical and commercial acceptance with the touching and thoughtful hit science fiction movie *Starman* (1984). He faltered somewhat thereafter, directing the flop action film *Big Trouble in Little China* (1986) and the disappointing horror movie *Prince of Darkness* (1987).

Carpenter is a young man who has already established an impressive body of work. Sure-handed in his direction, his films have always contained excellent pacing, rhythm, and an acute visual style. At the same time, his films seem to be getting richer and more emotionally insightful. It may very well be that his greatest movies are still ahead of him.

CASABLANCA The 1942 Warner Bros. masterpiece starring Humphrey Bogart, Ingrid Bergman, Paul Henried, Conrad Veidt, Claude Rains (q.v.), Peter Lorre (q.v.), and Sidney Greenstreet was directed in spirited fashion by Michael Curtiz, Warners' "A" movie director. With a script by Julius and Philip Epstein and Howard Koch, which was very loosely based on a stage play by Murray Burnett and Joan Alison, the plot centers on cynical Rick Blaine (Bogart), an American who, having fled Nazi-occupied Paris, runs a saloon and casino in the Moroccan port of Casablanca, which is under the nominal control of the Vichy government. The time is December 1940, just before America's entry into World War II. Rick's self-involvement seems to echo pre-war America's isolationist mentality. But Rick once was less misanthropic, before his heart was broken by Ilsa Lund (Bergman). When Ilsa, who believes herself to have been widowed, learns unexpectedly that her husband, an anti-Nazi freedom fighter, is alive, she reluctantly abandons the fleeing Rick at a Paris train station. Later, when Ilsa suddenly shows up at Rick's club, and their smouldering passion threatens to erupt anew, Rick is able to set aside his personal feelings and finally join the fight against the Nazi's as he helps Ilsa leave for America with her husband, Victor Lazlo (Henried).

The film won the Academy Award for Best Picture of 1942, and Bogart was nominated for Best Actor. But unlike many Oscar winners, *Casablanca* has withstood the test of time. The vulnerable hero played by Bogart—a man who could be vindictive and self-centered, yet sympathetic to an audience who understood his pain—was a fresh creation. Bogart's multidimensional portrayal of Rick still seems entirely modern.

Considered a classic Hollywood film, the movie is the perfect amalgamation of music, casting, writing, and direction. The score by Max Steiner (q.v.) had a brooding power, and the Dooley Wilson hit song, "As Time Goes By," added an extra dimension to the film that made its romanticism all the more effective.

Originally, the movie was slated to star Ronald Reagan and Ann Sheridan. When Bogart was finally handed the lead, Warner Bros. was clearly taking a gamble. He had never played a romantic leading man in the movies, and he was paired with the much younger Ingrid Bergman. Ostensibly, one of the reasons he was given the part was that there were relatively few young men left at Warners, the rest having gone off to war. But Bogart was sensational on his own terms, and it was *Casablanca's* huge success that solidified his reputation as a major star.

The making of *Casablanca* has been well-documented. The script was being written even as the film was shooting. None of the actors knew how the story was going to end. For that matter, neither did the writers nor the director. In order to help them make up their minds, they decided to shoot two endings, one where Bogart and Bergman end up together and the other where Bogart sacrifices his love to send Bergman off with Paul Henreid. They filmed the latter ending first, and they liked it so much they never bothered filming the other version. *See also:* Bergman, Ingrid; Bogart, Humphrey; Curtiz, Michael

CASSAVETES, JOHN (1929–1989) A distinguished actor and independent commercial filmmaker, Cassavetes broke into the movies with a small role in *Taxi* (1953) at the age of twenty-four. He continued to find work throughout the rest of the decade, often playing heavies because of his dark, intense appearance. But Cassavetes' creative urge prompted him to make an experimental film. The movie (*Shadows*, 1959), which is about a black family, had no script; the dialogue was improvised. Despite the fact that it was a grainy, black-and-white 16mm film with a meandering pace, it garnered critical praise and a modest audience. Clearly, the time was ripe in America for experimental films; art houses were filled with French New Wave imports.

Based on the success of *Shadows*, Cassavetes was lured into a Hollywood contract to direct. He made two films, *Too Late the Blues* (1961) and *A Child is Waiting* (1962), both of which he considered failures.

He decided to work independently again, but in order to finance his projects, he continued to act, appearing in such movies as *The Dirty Dozen* (1967), *Rosemary's Baby* (1968), and *The Fury* (1978).

The money he earned as an actor helped pay for an extraordinary series of films, a few of which were surprising hits at the box office. His second independent film after *Shadows*, this time with a script he wrote, was *Faces* (1968). The film was nominated for three Academy Awards and made money, fueling the writer-director's ambitions. His next film, *Husbands* (1970), was a stunning success despite some critical carping that Cassavetes' movie was overlong, repetitious, and self-indulgent.

Minnie and Moskowitz (1972) and *A Woman Under the Influence* (1974) were his next two movies, both of which were well received by the critics and art house audiences. The latter film garnered Gena Rowlands (Cassavetes' wife, *q.v.*) an Academy Award nomination as Best Actress, as did the Cassavetes film *Gloria* (1980). For the most part, his films of the later 1970s and 1980s, such as *Murder of a Chinese Bookie* (1976), *Opening Night* (1979), *Love Streams* (1984), and *Big Trouble* (1986) have not achieved the same level of commercial and critical acceptance as his earlier films.

Cassavetes was able to continue his filmmaking, despite commercial failure, because his films were virtual home movies. He used his own home and the homes of his relatives for sets, and he and his wife, family, and friends (such as Ben Gazzara, Peter Falk, and Seymour Cassel) were his actors.

His movies have an intimacy and a spontaneity—as well as a thoughtful intelligence—that mark Cassavetes as an important, if offbeat, director who managed to coexist with Hollywood without succumbing to it.

He died in 1989.

CASTING DIRECTOR: The person or company that is generally responsible for filling all but the most important roles in a film. While sometimes empowered to hire actors, the casting director more often narrows the field of potential actors for particular roles and then suggests those who are selected to the director and/or producer (to whom he reports) so that they may make the final choices. In any event, it is the casting director who usually negotiates the contracts with the actors who are hired.

CASTLE, WILLIAM *See* gimmicks

CHANEY, LON (1883–1930) A silent screen star of horror films known as "The Man of a Thousand Faces," he was born Alonzo Chaney to deaf-mute parents. After years in vaudeville as a comic and a hoofer, he decided in 1914 to try his luck in Hollywood.

Chaney had small roles in unimportant movies over the next several years. His career finally caught fire when he played a character who cleverly pretends to be a cripple in *The Miracle Man* (1919). From that point on, with relatively few exceptions, Chaney used makeup, agonizing body harnesses, and disguises to play a rogues gallery of disfigured and/or grotesque characters. His most famous roles were the hunchback in *The Hunchback of Notre Dame* (1923) and the phantom in *The Phantom of the Opera* (1925).

Chaney added to his mystique by avoiding publicity.

Lon Chaney was "The Man of a Thousand Faces," the most famous face of his illustrious silent film career was that of *The Phantom of the Opera* (1925) seen here. Photo courtesy of The Siegel Collection.

With the hope of keeping his true appearance a mystery, he never volunteered for photo sessions.

By the mid-1920s, Chaney began working with a young director named Tod Browning *(q.v.)* who shared his passion for the macabre. Out of that collaboration came more hits, such as *The Unholy Three* (1925), *The Unknown* (1927), *West of Zanzibar* (1928), and many more.

It's falsely assumed that Chaney couldn't make the transition into the sound era. He made one talkie, directed by Browning, a remake of *The Unholy Three,* in 1930. And he was slated to play the lead in Browning's next horror movie, *Dracula* (1930), but died of throat cancer before filming began.

Chaney was survived by his son, Lon Chaney, Jr. (born Creighton Chaney), who distinguished himself as Lenny in *Of Mice and Men* (1939), but who otherwise traded on his father's reputation, playing mostly in minor horror movies.

See also: Cagney, James; *Dracula;* horror movies; Lugosi, Bela

CHANEY, LON JR.   *See* Chaney, Lon.

CHAPLIN, SIR CHARLES (1889–1977) At the height of his popularity—which lasted twenty-five years—he was the most beloved film personality in the world. Chaplin was a writer/director/actor/producer/ musician without peer.

There is a tendency today to think of Chaplin as merely that funny-looking fellow with the mustache, peculiar gait, and twirling cane. But he was much more. His unique blend of comedy and pathos displayed an artistry that is best described as sublime. Stan Laurel (of Laurel & Hardy *[q.v.]* fame), who understudied Chaplin and saw his rise to stardom, said simply, "He's the greatest artist that was ever on the screen."

Chaplin's childhood in England was early training for his famous characterization of the tramp. He lived a life of punishing poverty. His father died of alcoholism and his mother was often hospitalized. Chaplin spent two years in an orphanage and often lived on the street.

He made his first professional appearance at the age of five, filling in for his mother (who tried to make a living as a musician) and singing one of her numbers. For Chaplin, it was a career born out of desperation. By the age of eight, he was a member of a touring music hall troupe, The Eight Lancashire Lads. He never lacked for work again.

He was seventeen and a seasoned professional when he joined the Fred Karno Pantomime Troupe. He stayed with the Karno company for seven years until he became their star attraction. While on tour in America with Karno in 1913, he was signed up by Mack Sennett's Keystone Studio.

Chaplin's first one-reeler, in support of Keystone's main players, was *Making a Living* (1913). For his second film, *Kid Auto Races in Venice* (1913), he borrowed Fatty Arbuckle's pants, Ford Sterling's massive shoes (putting them on the opposite feet), a tight-fitting jacket, a tiny derby, and one of Mack Swain's mustaches (trimmed down, of course) and the tramp was born. Or at least his costume. Chaplin didn't always dress as the tramp in his early one-reelers at Keystone, but the character slowly began to evolve. By 1914 he was directing himself in his Sennett comedies and according to Gerald Mast in his book *The Comic Mind,* "The most significant lesson that Chaplin learned at Keystone was . . . how to relate to objects and how to make objects relate to him." But Keystone was not a place given to detail and finesse. Chaplin needed to move on and grow.

He left Sennett in 1915 and went to the Essanay Studio. Chaplin had already become popular, but now

Charlie Chaplin, seen here in *The Gold Rush* (1925), was able to generate humor and pathos from the same gesture or movement. He brought the art of pantomime to full flower and became so popular that not even the birth of the talkies could prevent him from making silent film comedy hits well into the 1930s. Photo courtesy of The Siegel Collection.

he had the time to develop his character. Still, the movies were crude. But with *The Tramp* (1915), one of his funniest two-reelers, film comedy was never the same again. He found the heart of his character and the comic means of expressing himself.

From Essanay, Chaplin moved to Mutual in 1916, and it was with this new company that he made some of his most famous two-reelers, consolidating the artistic breakthroughs he had made at Essanay. Two-reelers such as *The Pawnshop* (1916), *The Immigrant* (1916), and *Easy Street* (1916) were so inventive, intimate, and hilariously clever that Chaplin's popularity became a worldwide phenomenon. He was imitated by all sorts of film comedians, but no one was remotely as talented. Though earning $10,000 per week (receiving a $100,000 advance on his salary), he was underpaid in relation to his value to the studio.

His next step took him to First National in 1918 where he was supposed to make eight two-reelers. All of his films for First National were classics, but they weren't all two-reelers. After *A Dog's Life* (1918), *Shoulder Arms* (1919), *Sunnyside* (1919), and *A Day's Pleasure* (1919), Chaplin decided to make his first feature, *The Kid* (1921). It took a year-and-a-half to make; it was six reels long; and, despite the protests of the film company, it became the biggest hit in movie history up until that time except for *The Birth of A Nation* (1915). Thereafter, Chaplin's other films with First National were of any length he chose.

Chaplin wanted more freedom as an artist, so he joined with the other great lights of the silent era, Mary Pickford, Douglas Fairbanks, and D. W. Griffith *(qq. v.)*, to form their own film company. They called it United Artists.

For his first film with his new company, Chaplin wrote and directed (but did not star in) *A Woman of Paris* (1923). His long-time leading lady, Edna Purviance, was the star. It was a serious film that resulted in disappointing box office receipts, but seen today it displays a great deal of sophistication.

Chaplin then took two years to make his next, and perhaps most famous, feature, *The Gold Rush* (1925). This story of the tramp in Alaska was episodic but both moving and very funny. As is the case with most of his work, *The Gold Rush* stands up without apology to the passing of time. Artistry stops all clocks when Chaplin, starving to death in a cabin during a snowstorm, eats his shoe as if it were a delicacy. His "Oceana Roll," otherwise known as the dance of the buns, is one of the most charming moments in the history of the cinema.

Chaplin's output slowed down even further after *The Gold Rush*. It took three years for *The Circus* (1928) to appear, but it became yet another hit. He was awarded a Special Oscar that year for "versatility and genius in writing, acting, directing, and producing *The Circus.*"

When everyone else in Hollywood was making talkies, Chaplin all but ignored the new technology and made another silent film, *City Lights* (1931). Though Chaplin wrote a wonderful musical score for the film and included sound effects, there was no dialogue. The industry pronounced that he was doomed to suffer a terrible disaster. No one, they were convinced, would go to a silent movie. Unless it was a Charlie Chaplin movie—*City Lights* was the fourth-biggest grosser of the year.

Chaplin made yet another silent film in 1936, *Modern Times,* although in this movie he briefly broke the sound

barrier when he sang a song in gibberish. *Modern Times* was a clear attack on the modern world and its dehumanizing machinery. It also had a mildly left-wing point of view that echoed Chaplin's political convictions. But most important, it was both moving and funny. The film was the second biggest money-earner of the year, just behind *San Francisco*.

Nearly fifteen years after the end of the silent era, Chaplin finally decided to make an all-talking movie. And when he started talking, the world was surprised to find he had such a lovely voice. There were some, however, who felt he talked too much. Be that as it may, his next film, *The Great Dictator* (1940), was a savage comic attack on fascism. Chaplin played two roles in the film, a Jewish barber (a character closely resembling the tramp) and Adenoid Hynkel (based on Hitler). The highlight of the film was Chaplin's dance with a globe, as Hyknel dreams of world conquest. Chaplin had put his art on the line, making a striking anti-Nazi film before America entered World War II. And audiences responded, making it the biggest hit of 1941.

But while Chaplin's artistry continued to flourish in his next two films, his popularity (at least in America) did not. Finally relinquishing the tramp persona, Chaplin played a lady killer (literally) in *Monsieur Verdoux* (1947), a black comedy about murder with political overtones. At the time, the film received scathing reviews and did poorly with audiences who were both offended by Chaplin's dark humor and upset that the tramp was no more.

Chaplin's unequivocal left-wing sentiments brought him under fire in America during the red-baiting years of the late 1940s and early 1950s. At the same time, some Americans were fuming that Chaplin had never become a U.S. citizen. When the star left for Europe in order to promote his next film, *Limelight* (1952), he was told that he might not be allowed back into the country. Unwilling to live where he wasn't wanted, Chaplin settled in Switzerland.

Limelight was a hit in Europe but a disaster in the United States. The nostalgic movie recreated the London of the turn of the century with Chaplin playing Calvero the Clown, an aging music hall performer who, much like Chaplin, has lost his audience. It was a sweet film about art and redemption that boasted the hit song "Smile," which Chaplin penned himself.

His last two films, *A King of New York* (1957) and *A Countess from Hong Kong* (1966) were mediocre efforts that never met the high expectations that attended them. The latter film was written and directed by Chaplin and starred Marlon Brando and Sophia Loren, with Chaplin merely making a cameo appearance as a waiter.

Though he was knighted by the Queen of England in 1975, the most memorable moment of Charlie Chaplin's later career was his triumphant return to Hollywood in 1972. A frail old man of eighty-two, he came back to his adopted home to receive an honorary Academy Award. After a splendid film tribute, he appeared on the stage, and the audience of Hollywood's greatest stood up and gave him an extended and tumultuous ovation.

See also: City Lights; Keaton, Buster; Sennett, Mack; United Artists

CHARACTER ACTORS These performers play parts other than those traditional roles of leading man or lady, ingenue, or juvenile. Though they usually act in support of stars, character actors sometimes play leading roles and can (and have) become stars in their own right.

Character actors are often players who are cast repeatedly in certain specific roles. For instance, Elisha Cook, Jr. played small-time losers for more than forty years, his characters being killed in a huge percentage of his films, such as *The Big Sleep* (1946) and *Shane* (1953). Franklin Pangborn is another example of the typecast character actor. He played a seemingly endless series of prissy hotel managers, waiters, and such, most notably in Preston Sturges' *(q.v.)* films of the early 1940s. Among female character actors, Beulah Bondi played old ladies while still in her mid-thirties and continued to do so with astonishing effectiveness for fifty years, most heartwrenchingly in Leo McCarey's *(q.v.) Make Way for Tomorrow* (1937).

Another common role for character actors has been the heavy. One of the premier actors in this type of role was certainly Edward Arnold, who was always well cast as a corrupt businessman or government official. He was director Frank Capra's *(q.v.)* favorite villain in films such as *Mr. Smith Goes to Washington* (1939) and *Meet John Doe* (1941). Other character actors in this category have been Sydney Greenstreet, Claude Rains *(q.v.),* and William Bendix. These actors sometimes had starring roles in films, and William Bendix in particular played a wide range of characters, including average American G.I.s, tough guys, likable comic types, and the hero's best friend.

Character actors often provide comic relief in films, and among the best in such roles were Eric Blore, who was deliciously ascerbic in the Astaire/Rogers musical *Top Hat* (1935), Eugene Pallete, who had the most incredible foghorn voice in Hollywood, and Charles Butterworth, a goofy, idle dreamer in films such as *Love Me Tonight* (1932).

While character actors have generally been overlooked by the public in favor of stars, some of these players have been honored for their work by the Academy of Motion Picture Arts and Sciences with awards for Best Supporting Actor. For instance, one of the most famous character actors in Hollywood history, Walter Brennan, *(q.v.),* took home three Oscars, for

Character actors added personality and style to countless films, often stealing scenes from the stars whom they regularly supported. They became familiar faces to filmgoers, and one such familiar face was Thomas Mitchell (seen here) who played any number of sidekicks, sergeants, drunken doctors, cynical journalists, bumblers, and fathers. Photo courtesy of Movie Star News.

Come and Get It (1936), *Kentucky* (1938), and *The Westerner* (1940). Other character actor Academy Award winners have included, Fay Bainter for *Jezebel* (1938), the enormously versatile Thomas Mitchell for *Stagecoach* (1939), Barry Fitzgerald for *Going My Way* (1944), Martin Balsam for *A Thousand Clowns* (1965), and Olympia Dukakis for *Moonstruck* (1987).

A major source of character actors has been the ranks of fading leading men and women. For instance, Lillian Gish was a major star in the silent film era who became one of the industry's most durable character actresses, and James Mason extended his career by becoming a character actor when he began to age.

Then again, there are some stars who, despite their blling, have *always* been character actors, playing character roles that happen to be the most important parts in their films. For example, Marie Dressler, Charles Laughton, Peter Lorre, Edward G. Robinson, Paul

Muni, George C. Scott, and even Dustin Hoffman *(qq.v.)* have never been considered stars in the traditional sense. The force of their screen personalities however, allowed movies to be built around them if only they had the right vehicle. And with those vehicles, these character actors have been able to build loyal followings.

The number of character actors who have made their mark in Hollywood movies is staggering. From the mousy John Qualen to the brassy Joan Blondell, *(q.v.)* and from the vulgar Burt Young to the sophisticated Clifton Webb *(q.v.)*, Hollywood's character actors have added immeasurable richness to the movies they have graced.

CHARISSE, CYD (1921–) A dancer and actress who was arguably the most technically proficient female dance partner of both Fred Astaire and Gene Kelly at the height of the MGM musical era of the late 1940s and early 1950s. Beautiful, long-legged, and mysteriously sensual in appearance, she exuded sex appeal while moving with the grace of a cat. Unlike Ginger Rogers or Judy Garland *(qq.v.)*, Charisse couldn't sing and her acting was only adequate, but she was a dancer par excellence.

Born Tula Ellice Finklea, she studied ballet from childhood and was a highly regarded dancer while still in her teens. As movie musicals began to grow in popularity in the early 1940s, she was featured in small roles in films such as *Something to Shout About* (1943) under the stage name of Lily Norwood.

Later, after signing with MGM, she took the name Charisse from her first husband (and ballet coach) Nico Charisse and was groomed for stardom. She first appeared in featured roles in such films as *The Harvey Girls* (1946) and *Ziegfeld Follies* (1946), and soon graduated to supporting parts in movies such as *The Unfinished Dance* (1947), *Words and Music* (1948), and *Singin' in the Rain* (1952).

Charisse's received her first important starring role because of her experience as a ballerina. Playing a ballet star trying to make it on Broadway, she was given the enviable opportunity to dance with Fred Astaire in one of the great movie musicals of all time, *The Band Wagon* *(q.v.)* (1953). The film was a major hit and she was a sensation. During the last phase of MGM's musical golden era, she was a star, lending her long legs and seductive charm to such musicals as *Brigadoon* (1954), *It's Always Fair Weather* (1955), *Invitation to the Dance* (1957), and *Silk Stockings* (1957).

After the latter movie, however, the musical virtually disappeared from Hollywood and she began appearing in dramas. She had acted in straight films before, such as *East Side, West Side* (1949) and *Tension* (1949), but there was nothing special about her abilities as an actress

and after appearing in movies such as *Party Girl* (1958) and *Two Weeks in Another Town* (1962), and a number of European films, her movie career began to dissolve. She appeared in very few films during the later 1960s and only one in the 1970s, *Warlords of Atlantis* (1978).

For the most part, she has spent the years since the early 1960s working in nightclubs as a dancer, often sharing the bill with her second husband, singer Tony Martin, whom she married in 1948.

CHASE, CHEVY (1949–) An affable, comic leading man who has starred in films with wildly erratic results for more than a decade. Chase came to prominence on the hit television comedy show "Saturday Night Live," becoming the first star of the program to head for Hollywood with a lucrative multi-picture deal. Among those who eventually followed his lead were Dan Aykroyd, John Belushi, Bill Murray, Gilda Radner, and Eddie Murphy *(q.v.)*.

Chevy Chase (his real name) thought of himself as a writer rather than a comedian, but he was pressed into service before the cameras when *Saturday Night Live* first aired and he quickly became an audience favorite. Tall, good-looking, with a whimsical personal style, he suddenly seemed like promising movie material out on the Coast, though he had already appeared in two low-budget comedies in the mid-1970s, *The Groove Tube* (1974) and *Tunnelvision* (1976).

Chase made his "A" movie *(q.v.)* debut opposite Goldie Hawn *(q.v.)* in the smash comedy, *Foul Play* (1978). He followed that success with an engaging supporting role in *Caddyshack* (1980), only to see his film career go careening off track when he shared top-billing with dog star Benji in *Oh, Heavenly Dog!* (1980). Except for his successful reteaming with Goldie Hawn in *Seems Like Old Times* (1980), many of the actor's subsequent films were (justifiably) berated by the critics and ignored by his fans. Movies such as *Modern Problems* (1981), *Under the Rainbow* (1981), and *Deal of the Century* (1983) were unmitigated disasters.

Chase's once promising career was saved by his starring role in *National Lampoon's Vacation* (1984), a film that brought him back to his eccentric comedy roots. In that same year, he also starred in *Fletch,* a hit comedy/detective piece that solidified his return to box office credibility.

From the very beginning of his movie years, critics have not been terribly kind to Chase. His comic personna has a disdainful element to it that grates on many and his throwaway style can give the impression that he doesn't work very hard at his humor. But after being panned in films such as *National Lampoon's European Vacation* (1985) and *Three Amigos* (1986), he achieved near unanimous praise for his restrained comic performance in *Funny Farm* (1988), a movie that many consider his best work in a prolific career in which he has averaged better than a movie per year, every year since 1978.

CHAYEVSKY, PADDY (1923–1981) He was an influential screenwriter and playwright who wrote with uncommon passion. Considering that he was associated with just eleven movies, his success ratio in Hollywood is truly stunning—he won three Oscars for Best Screenplay. Early in his career, Chayevsky built a reputation for writing about the problems of ordinary people with sympathy and humor. Later, he became a firebrand, writing (some said overwriting) with power and biting wit about "big" issues.

Born Sidney Chayevsky, he took his first stab at show business as a comedian. He turned to writing while recuperating from wounds suffered during his World War II service. Chayevsky continued writing after the war, penning short stories and eventually breaking into radio and TV as a scriptwriter. One of his early works became the basis of a modest movie called *As Young As You Feel* (1951). His first major success, however, came with his teleplay, *Marty,* the story of a middle-aged, none-too-attractive, Bronx butcher who falls in love with a plain and shy woman. It was a much-admired TV production that Chayevksy then rewrote for the screen. *Marty* (1955) was the sleeper hit of the year, winning four Oscars: Best Screenplay, Best Actor (Ernest Borgnine as Marty), Best Direction (Delbert Mann), and Best Film.

It was a long time before Chayevsky had that kind of success again. Still, he saw several of his projects reach the screen, including a teleplay adapted into the film *The Catered Affair* (1956), another teleplay he adapted himself into *The Bachelor Party* (1957), his screenplay from his own story for *The Goddess* (1958), and his adaptation of his play into the movie *Middle of the Night* (1959).

Chayevsky didn't work very much for the movies in the 1960s, writing only the admirable script for *The Americanization of Emily* (1964) and the flop adaptation of *Paint Your Wagon* (1969). The 1970s, though, was Chayevsky's decade. Though he wrote only three screenplays, all were vivid, powerful works. He wrote the sharply satirical exposé of medical practices, *The Hospital* (1971), winning his second Best Screenplay Oscar, and followed with the screenplay for which he is best remembered, *Network* (1976). He won his third Oscar for this bitter and stinging script about the corrupting power of television. His phrase from *Network,* "I'm mad as hell and I'm not going to take it anymore," became a rallying cry even for those who never saw the film. His last script was for *Altered States* (1979), a seductive and fascinating film directed by Ken Russell.

Tragically, Chayevsky died at the height of his powers at the age of fifty-eight.

CHER *See* singer-actors.

CHEVALIER, MAURICE (1888–1972) For audiences all over the world, he was the embodiment of French charm and style. He had two distinct periods of Hollywood stardom, and in both of them he played versions of the same character: a lover with a remarkable combination of sexual suggestiveness and innocence. Chevalier could be earthy and lustful, yet, unlike Mae West *(q.v.),* he was never vulgar. Among his endearing traits were his melodious French accent, a pouting lower lip, his trademark straw hat, and an overwhelming, almost tangible, desire to please his audiences.

Born to an alcoholic house painter, Chevalier was the ninth of ten children. A year after his father died, the then twelve-year-old future star embarked on his first show business venture as an acrobat. He was not a success. He bounced around, even singing in the streets for money, until he got a job performing in a trendy café in 1906. Next, he entered French vaudeville and made a modest success, eventually becoming the partner of the famed Folies-Bergères dancing star Mistinguett. They were lovers as well as dancing partners; Chevalier's sex appeal was already very much in evidence.

During World War I, Chevalier was wounded and became a prisoner of war for two years, during which time he learned English from a cellmate. His second language served him well when, after nearly a decade of success in France as a popular performer in clubs and on the stage, he was offered a screen test by Irving Thalberg *(q.v.)* of MGM in 1927. The "Boy Genius" faltered, seeing no future for Chevalier as a Hollywood star. After viewing the same screen test, Paramount thought differently.

His first film for Paramount, *Innocents of Paris* (1929), made Chevalier a movie star virtually overnight. He had appeared in a number of French shorts as early as 1908, but his talkie debut caused nothing less than a sensation at the box office. And it got better. In the hands of Ernst Lubitsch, *(q.v.),* a director whose touch with light bedroom comedy and operettas became legendary, Chevalier had a string of hits that were as well made as they were successful, among them *The Love Parade* (1929), *The Smiling Lieutenant* (1931), and *One Hour With You* (1932). Very much in the Lubitsch mold was *Love Me Tonight* (1932), directed by Rouben Mamoulian (q.v.), considered by many to be Chevalier's best film.

Teamed with Jeanette MacDonald *(q.v.)* in many of these early pre-Hays Code *(q.v.)* operettas, Chevalier projected a healthy sex drive that was happily played for laughs. Though he is often remembered for his songs such as "Mimi" and "Every Little Breeze Seems to Whisper Louise," above all else, Chevalier was a wonderful comedian.

The laughs, however, were growing thin by 1933. This time Thalberg took a hand and brought Chevalier to MGM. It was a mixed blessing. After the critical success of *The Merry Widow* (1934), again with Lubitsch at the helm, and then a loan-out to Twentieth Century-Fox for *Folies Bergère* (1935), Thalberg made the mistake of insisting that Chevalier take second billing to actress Grace Moore. Insulted, the actor refused and left Hollywood in a huff. He didn't grace another Hollywood movie until 1956.

He did, however, star in a number of French and English films throughout the rest of the 1930s, and in the second half of the 1940s and early 1950s. None of them had the international success of his Hollywood films.

During World War II, Chevalier had performed in Vichy France, singing for German soldiers. When the war was over there was a hue and cry that he had been a collaborator. He defended himself, claiming he sang to the Germans in order to aid Jewish friends; his defense was accepted.

Beginning in the late 1940s, he regained a measure of his earlier fame by putting on one-man shows all over the world. But his second career as a Hollywood film star began when Billy Wilder cast him as Audrey Hepburn's father in *Love in the Afternoon* (1957). It opened the door to his greatest hit as an elder statesman of the cinema: *Gigi* (1958). He might well have been nominated for his splendid role as the aging roué in *Gigi*, but instead, he was honored with a special Oscar that celebrated "his contributions to the world of entertainment for more than half a century."

Chevalier worked steadily throughout the rest of the 1950s and into the 1960s, usually playing charming grandfatherly types in films such as *Can-Can* (1959), *Fanny* (1960), and *I'd Rather Be Rich* (1964). His last screen appearance was in Disney's less than inspired *Monkeys, Go Home!* (1967). His unique voice, however, can be heard singing the title song of Disney's far more charming *The Aristocats* (1970), recorded two years before his death.

CHILD STARS   Though there have been scores of child stars, very few have had that special combination of luck, skill, and emotional stability needed to reach and maintain stardom as adults. Part of the inability of child stars to sustain their careers stems from their very special and intense appeal as youngsters; audiences fall in love with them as they are and cannot abide the swift and inevitable change in the young actors. There is,

therefore, something both innocent and tragic about Hollywood's child actors. They are at once blessed by fame and fortune, and then often discarded before they are old enough to appreciate their success.

Virtually from the beginning of the film industry, child actors have been a cinematic staple. Mary Pickford and Lillian Gish, *(qq.v.)*, among a great many actresses, began their film careers when they were teenagers, and their youth and childlike innocence was accentuated in their starring vehicles.

Among the countless child actors during the silent film era were Baby Peggy, Madge Evans, and even the future director Henry Hathaway *(q.v.)* But the first true child actor superstar was Jackie Coogan (q.v.), who burst into stardom as Charlie Chaplin's young charge in *The Kid* (1920). Coogan was a major box office draw in his own right during the early to mid-1920s, starring in such films as *Peck's Bad Boy* (1921), *Oliver Twist* (1922), and *Little Robinson Crusoe* (1925).

Coogan's phenomenal success led Hal Roach *(q.v.)* to put together an endearing crew of child actors who became the comedy group Our Gang *(q.v.)*. Among the silent stars of the Our Gang shorts were Joe Cobb and Mickey Daniels. Later, during the 1930s and early 1940s, the group was blessed by having among its members, Spanky Macfarland, Carl "Alfalfa" Switzer, Darla Hood, and Buckwheat Thomas.

At one time, young Jackie Cooper was a member of Our Gang, but he left the group and went on to childhood stardom and an Oscar nomination at the age of eight in *Skippy* (1931), followed by *The Champ* (1931). He was particularly affecting in the latter film, crying up a storm and tugging at the heartstrings. In Cooper's autobiography, he wrote that he was told if he didn't cry, his dog would be shot!

Cooper was a star for roughly five years, generally playing tough, lower-class American kids. Though his popularity faded, he continued his acting career throughout most of the ensuing decades, eventually playing Perry White in the *Superman* movies of the late 1970s and 1980s.

At the same time that Cooper played tough kids, Dickie Moore was on the scene playing sensitive children. He started at the age of three and appeared in a total of eighteen films before he turned seven years old. He was Marlene Dietrich's little boy in *Blonde Venus* (1932) but came into his own when he was seven in *Oliver Twist* (1933). The latter film aside, Dickie Moore played mostly supporting parts. But he was among the busiest of child actors during the 1930s. He eventually disappeared from the screen by the time he was fourteen.

Both Cooper and Moore were shunted into the background by the arrival of Freddie Bartholomew, who starred in *David Copperfield* (1935) at the age of ten. Bartholomew was as dignified as a child actor could be. With his English accent, big eyes, and curly hair, he seemed like a young heir to the throne. Over the next four years he did, indeed, rule the male child actor roost, playing Greta Garbo's son in *Anna Karenina* (1935), starring with Wallace Beery in *Professional Soldier* (1935), and playing the title role in *Little Lord Fauntleroy* (1936). Just like Dickie Moore, however, his career ended after the age of fourteen.

While there were plenty of male child stars during the 1930s, there was but one transcendent female star: Shirley Temple *(q.v.)*. Between 1934 and the end of the decade, she was not only the leading child actor of her time, she was also one of Hollywood's biggest draws. In fact, she was the number-one box office star of 1938 when she was only ten years old. A truly talented child who could sing, dance, and act, Shirley Temple was a phenomenon. Her blond curls, dimples, and infectious upbeat attitude were just the antidote for Depression-weary audiences. Among her many memorable films were *Little Miss Marker* (1934), *Captain January* (1936), *Wee Willie Winkie* (1937), and *Heidi* (1937). Unfortunately, despite her genuine talents, Shirley Temple was unsuccessful in her attempt to make the transition to adult stardom.

Even as Shirley Temple was losing her grip on fame at the end of the 1930s, new child actors were emerging. Two of them, Mickey Rooney and Judy Garland *(qq.v.)*, attained stardom together at MGM. Like Temple, they were not only fine actors, they could both sing and dance, as well.

Rooney had been a child actor in silent films at the age of six, appearing in the short *Not To Be Trusted* (1926), and he hasn't stopped working since. He was Puck in the Warner Brothers version of *A Midsummer's Night Dream* (1935), and he achieved stardom in 1937 as the title character in MGM's long-running *Andy Hardy* series.

Judy Garland appeared in the *Andy Hardy* films, too, but her classic performance at the age of seventeen in *The Wizard of Oz* (1939) was her ticket to everlasting stardom.

Deanna Durbin *(q.v.)*, another young actress and singer with a vibrant personality, became a film star at the age of fifteen in *Three Smart Girls* (1936).

The 1930s were clearly the golden age of child stars; even infants became famous. For instance, Baby Leroy, who appeared most notably in four W. C. Fields *(q.v.)* films in the early to mid-1930s, was given a seven-year contract at the age of eight months. He retired at the age of four. Baby Sandy also had a meteoric film career that began in 1939 and ended in 1942 at the age of five.

While the decades after the 1930s offered fewer child stars, the 1940s still managed to yield a bumper crop. For instance, Roddy McDowall and Dean Stockwell were both popular child stars, who like so many others, faded from view by the age of fourteen. Unlike most

others, though, they reemerged years later as working adult actors.

Elizabeth Taylor *(q.v.)* was a young beauty who started in films at ten years of age in *There's One Born Every Minute* (1942). She played mostly supporting roles as a young teenager despite her strong starring performance in *National Velvet* (1944). She didn't achieve true stardom until she was a young adult.

The most affecting and natural of child actresses during the 1940s was pig-tailed Margaret O'Brien. Unlike Shirley Temple, Judy Garland, or the young Elizabeth Taylor, O'Brien seemed like a real child. She was cute rather than pretty, and therefore seemed as if she could be anyone's child, sister, or friend. Her film career began at the age of four in *Babes on Broadway* (1941) and she charmed audiences in supporting roles in films such as *Meet Me in St. Louis* (1944), *The Canterville Ghost* (1944), and *Bad Bascomb* (1946). Her career, unfortunately, ended by the time she was twelve.

Another notable child actor of the 1940s was Natalie Wood, *(q.v.)*, who made her screen debut at the age of four and at seven gave a memorable performance in *Miracle on 34th Street* (1947). Wood, of course, went on to become a major adult star, far outshining her performances as a child.

Beginning in the 1950s, Hollywood began making fewer films, and it became far more difficult for a child actor to build and sustain a career; they simply aged too much in between a mere handful of movies. In addition, television, because of the steady work it offered, became a more fertile area for child actors to practice their craft. Just the same, a handful of child stars made their mark during the 1950s, and the most famous of them was certainly Brandon de Wilde, who, at the age of ten, was nominated for an Oscar for his performance in *Shane* (1953).

Though de Wilde played a young boy who worshipped Alan Ladd *(q.v.)* in *Shane*, Ladd's own son, David, became a child star at the age of eleven in *The Proud Rebel* (1958), playing opposite his father. He was, in fact, a better actor than his dad.

Patty McCormack, another 1950s standout, won an Oscar nomination when she was ten years old for her performance in *The Bad Seed* (1956). Other notable child actors of the 1950s included Billy Chapin, Kevin "Moochie" Corcoran, and George "Foghorn" Winslow.

The 1960s was a relative child actor's desert, although Kurt Russell, Hayley Mills, and Patty Duke were young teenage stars in the early part of the decade. Films such as *To Kill a Mockingbird* (1963), *Mary Poppins* (1964), *The Sound of Music* (1965), and *A Thousand Clowns* (1965) featured children in significant supporting roles, but none of the young actors who appeared in these films became child stars.

With the apparent end of the family movie in the

1960s, it appeared as if there might never be another child star again. But the 1970s saw a resurgence in roles for child actors, led by eleven-year-old Linda Blair who appeared in *The Way We Live Now* (1970). She became a fleeting star and a Best Supporting Actress Oscar nominee three years later for her performance in *The Exorcist* (1973).

In that same year, though, nine-year-old Tatum O'Neal made her film debut in *Paper Moon* (1973) and won the Best Supporting Actress Oscar, becoming Hollywood's youngest Oscar winner. In her second film, *Bad News Bears* (1976), she became the highest paid child star in movie history with a salary of $350,000 and nine percent of the net profit of a very profitable hit film.

In the late 1970s, twelve-year-old Brooke Shields made a splash as a child prostitute in *Pretty Baby* (1978) and has continued to build her career into adulthood. Ricky Schroeder, who played the Jackie Cooper role in a 1979 remake of *The Champ,* proved himself a capably lachrymose moppet and appeared in a few more films in addition to his later work on TV.

Others might have been nominated for and won Oscars, and starred in hit films, but the premier child actor of the 1970s was, without question, Jodie Foster *(q.v.)*. She made her feature-film debut at the age of nine in *Napoleon and Samantha* (1972), making her mark in *Taxi Driver* (1976) and the beguiling *Bugsy Malone* (1976). Unlike most of her contemporaries, Foster shows great range as an actress and recently won a Best Actress Academy Award for her performance in *The Accused* (1988).

E.T.—The Extra-Terrestrial (1982) ushered in two new child stars of the 1980s, Henry Thomas and Drew Barrymore. Of the two of them, Barrymore has had the most screen success during the rest of the 1980s, starring in several other films, including *Irreconcilable Differences* (1984).

More recently, River Phoenix has emerged as a much admired child star in such films as *Stand by Me* (1986) and *Little Nikita* (1988).

CHOREOGRAPHER   The person who designs and then supervises dance numbers. While the choreographer usually consults with the director, he doesn't have any control over filming of the dances; the best dance directors (as choreographers are sometimes known) will therefore create the choreography with the camera in mind.

CINEMASCOPE   By 1952, with television antennas sprouting on rooftops all over America, the number of people attending the movies had nearly halved from eighty million in 1946 to forty-six million. The major studios had been searching for a method to bring au-

Choreographer Hermes Pan diagrams a dance routine for Fred Astaire. What could be simpler? Photo courtesy of The Siegel Collection.

diences back into theaters and hoped to counter television's small picture with a massive screen.

The wide-screen craze began with the introduction of Cinerama *(q.v.)* in 1952, which was a novelty based upon a three-camera/three-projector system. In 1953, Twentieth Century-Fox popularized a system that changed the size of movie screens forever: Cinema-Scope.

The CinemaScope process is based on the use of an anamorphic lens. When a film is shot with such a lens, the image is squeezed to fit on 35mm stock. When that same image is projected back through the lens, it unsqueezes the picture, making it approximately two-and-one-half times as wide as it is high.

This wide-screen system had actually been conceived in 1927 by the Frenchman Henri Chrétien. It was demonstrated several times during the ensuing decades, but there were no takers—until Twentieth Century-Fox made *The Robe* (1953) in a system they called CinemaScope.

The film was rather poor, but the process was a hit and turned *The Robe* into a substantial money-maker. Fox made a commitment to CinemaScope, making virtually all of their new films in the process. And they wisely leased CinemaScope to other studios in order to hasten the building of new screens and projection equipment in theaters across the country and around the world. In fact, by 1955, more than 20,000 theaters worldwide were equipped to show CinemaScope movies. And the movies shown in these theaters were bringing in large audiences. Throughout the mid-1950s, the top moneymaking films were almost always shot in CinemaScope.

Other studios jumped on the bandwagon, leasing the CinemaScope process from Fox, although Warner Bros., Paramount, and RKO eventually came up with their own variations of a wide-screen process, with Paramount's Panavision being the most successful. In fact, many years later, Darryl F. Zanuck *(q.v.)* of Fox admitted, "Cinemascope was all wrong mechanically . . . visual experts told us—not then—but later, that the correct proportion was Panavision. Panavision is the perfect proportion to fit the eyes."

Nonetheless, CinemaScope became the most well-known and commercially successful wide-screen process because Fox brought it out first, and because many of the other studios used it.

CINEMATOGRAPHER Of all the major jobs on a movie set, this is perhaps the most overlooked by both the critics and the public. The cinematographer, not to be confused with the camera operator, is the individual who lights and composes each scene in a film. Working closely with the director, the cinematographer is the technical wizard who is most often responsible for the particular "look" of a film. It is the cinematographer for example, who makes the glamour queen appear her most alluring by backlighting so wrinkles won't show; he lights city streets with deep shadows that make them seem dark and foreboding; and he creates a glow of soft light for a family room in order to make it more warm and inviting.

Originally, the cinematographer (who also goes by the title of cameraman or director of photography) cranked the camera, kept everything in focus, and panned and dollied whenever it was necessary. As the movies became more technically advanced, the cinematographer could no longer handle so many functions and continue visually composing and lighting each shot. It became necessary to assemble a small crew of assistants that included the actual camera operator in their number.

The work of the best cinematographers is as distinctive as that of the first rank of directors; they each have a personal style that leaves their stamp on every movie with which they're associated. Giants such as G. W. "Billy" Bitzer, James Wong Howe, Gregg Toland, Lucien Ballard, Bruce Surtees, and Gordon Willis *(qq.v.)*, to name just a few, have helped to create the language of film through their technical innovations, imaginative lighting, use of color, and unique compositions.

CINERAMA This invention sparked the 1950s revolution in wide screens, which many in the movie business thought would save the industry from losing its audience to television.

Originally developed as Vitarama in 1939 by Fred Waller and shown at the New York World's Fair, this system used eleven cameras to film its scenes and another eleven projectors to show the image on a huge, curved screen with a domelike appendage that hung over the audience. It was a hit at the Fair, but much too cumbersome a system for practical use by film studios and movie theaters.

Waller, however, kept refining his invention until he was able to remove the dome feature and limit the number of cameras and projectors to three of each. He changed the name of his process to Cinerama, enlisted the help of famed newsman Lowell Thomas and Hollywood's Merrian C. Cooper (of *King Kong* fame), and showed his first film, *This Is Cinerama* (1952), at the Broadway Theater in New York.

The film and the process had a galvanizing effect on everyone who saw it, audiences and critics alike. Though it wasn't a perfect system (one could see the lines between the three projected images on the wide, curved screen), the sensations of depth and involvement it created were visceral, especially in the famous roller-coaster sequence that had people screaming in their theater seats.

In order to show *This Is Cinerama* anywhere else in the country, theaters had to be built and adapted for the process. Cinerama theaters sprung up in most major cities, playing *This Is Cinerama* to record-breaking crowds.

It wasn't until February 8, 1955, that Cinerama came out with a second film called *Cinerama Holiday*—another huge hit. It was followed by several other travelogue-style films. But by the early 1960s, the novelty had long worn off; the public was now viewing films in CinemaScope, Panavision, and other wide-screen processes and were tired of watching thin productions meant to thrill but offering no involving story or stars.

In an attempt to save Cinerama, a deal was made with MGM to produce films that could be shown in the Cinerama system and then adapted to 70mm. *The Wonderful World of the Brothers Grimm* (1962) and *How the West Was Won* (1963) were the product of that arrangement, but in 1963 the three camera/projector system became outmoded, replaced with a "single-lens Cinerama" that was similar to the already existing CinemaScope system.

See also: CinemaScope

CITIZEN KANE The 1941 Orson Welles *(q.v.)* classic that many consider the most important movie ever made in Hollywood. The film's impact on the creative people in the motion picture industry can scarcely be overstated. *Citizen Kane* heralded a bold new era in filmmaking thanks to its innovative style and its sophisticated content.

The film starred Orson Welles in the title role, and it introduced a whole new group of stage actors from his Mercury Theater company, among them Joseph Cotton, Everett Sloane, Agnes Moorehead, Ray Collins, and George Colouris. While the entire cast performed splendidly, the power of *Citizen Kane* is its brash, fresh style. Gregg Toland's deep-focus cinematography *(qq.v.)* gave the movie a visual depth that allowed action taking place on several planes to be viewed at once, obviating the need for a great deal of editing within a scene. In addition, Toland's expressionistic lighting and deep shadows signaled the beginning of Hollywood's *film noir (q.v.)* period. Adding to the movie's ambiance was Bernard Herrmann's music, which was wonderfully foreboding, moody, and powerful.

Citizen Kane's plot was imaginatively structured by both Welles and his collaborator, Herman J. Mankiewicz *(q.v.)*. They told Kane's life story in a circuitious patchwork, often detailing the same events from different characters' points of view. The story itself, a study of corruption, power, and loss of innocence, was deeply humanistic. Devoid of any clear-cut heros or villains, it was a tale of fallible people, which made it truly unique in 1941.

The plot of *Citizen Kane* parallels that of newspaper magnate William Randolph Hearst. Like Hearst, the movie's protagonist, Charles Foster Kane, is a man whose immense wealth and power come from his control of newspapers. Kane, like Hearst, influences world events, bringing yellow journalism to new heights as he helps to push the nation into a war with Spain. In addition, Kane, like Hearst, tries to turn his mistress into a major star. The obvious similarities caused Hearst to try to stop the film by offering to compensate Welles' studio, RKO, if it would destroy all copies of the movie and burn the negative. When that failed, Hearst instructed all of his papers to ignore the film by refusing to either review it or take advertisements for it. When *Citizen Kane* finally opened to rave reviews in competing newspapers, however, Hearst took a different tack, ordering that the film be vilified and ridiculed in his own publications.

Whether Hearst gave *Citizen Kane* publicity it might not have had otherwise, or whether he may have truly hurt the movie at the box office cannot be accurately determined.

The fact is, however, that the film did well in the big cities but failed to become a major hit, as audiences ignored it in the all-important second- and third-run theaters. Contrary to popular belief, however, the movie did turn a modest profit at the time of its release.

Nor were the film's artistic merits entirely over-looked at the time, either. In addition to critical praise, *Citizen Kane* won a Best Original Screenplay Oscar, and it was nominated for Best Actor (Welles), Best Director (Welles), and Best Picture.

For Welles, *Citizen Kane* was a stunning achievement. It was, remarkably, the first full-length feature film he wrote, directed, and starred in. He was a twenty-four year old phenomenon who had gained a great deal of notoriety in New York for his radio and theater work. Known as a boy wonder, the troubled RKO studio took a gamble and offered him complete artistic freedom in the hope that he could create box office magic and keep the company solvent. Ironically, *Citizen Kane* was not the movie he had hoped to make for RKO; he had intended to adapt Joseph Conrad's *Heart of Darkness* to the screen. That script was rejected as too expensive to produce, and screenplays for two other films, *The Smiler With the Knife* and *Mexican Melodrama,* were also rejected before he was finally given the go-ahead to make the film that was to become his masterpiece.

CITY LIGHTS　This 1931 film is perhaps Charlie Chaplin's greatest achievement. Chaplin was the producer, writer, director, and star of this cinematic gem that is as funny and touching today as it was when it was first released.

The story, about a tramp (Chaplin) who falls in love with a blind flower girl (Virginia Cherrill), is a perfect blend of comedy and pathos. The tramp's on again/off again friendship with a drunken millionaire (Harry Myers) who doesn't recognize Charlie when he's sober provides the extra twist to the plot that balances the film.

The famous boxing match where the tramp bobs and weaves like a whirling dervish, and the restaurant scene where he slips and slides across the dance floor, are vintage Chaplin comic touches. The climax of the movie, however, approaches the sublime. When Chaplin and the flower girl meet again (with her sight restored, she sees the tramp for what he is), there is long close-up of Chaplin that is one of the most haunting, aching images in all of film history.

There is no sound in *City Lights* apart from some squeaks emanating from a politician and the musical score, (which Chaplin composed). The commercial success of a silent movie four years after the advent of sound is a rousing testament to both Chaplin's artistry and enduring popularity.

See also: Chaplin, Sir Charles

CLAPPER BOARD　The hinged slate held in front of the camera at the beginning or end of a take *(q.v.)* when dialogue is being recorded synchronously with the action. The hinge allows for the attachment of a "clapstick," which is clapped down onto the slate, causing a loud, sharp crack that later gives the editor

Alfred Hitchcock playfully demonstrates the clapper board on the set of *Psycho* (1960). Note the information on the board; the film's title, the number of the production, the director's name, the cinematographer's name, the date, the scene, and the take number. Photo courtesy of Movie Star News.

his synchronization cue when he splices the sound and picture tracks together.

The clapper board goes by several names, including "clapsticks," "clappers," or simply "slate." Technically, however, the latter term merely describes that part of the clapper board on which the names of the film, director, and cameraman, as well as the scene number and take number, are written in chalk. Clapper boards are operated by junior members of camera crews known also as "clappers."

The clapper board has long been a symbol of film-making, but over the last decade it has been made obsolete by new advances in electronics.

CLEOPATRA Two movies depicting the life of the Egyptian queen were made: the first in 1934 starring Claudette Colbert, *(q.v.)* the second in 1963 with Elizabeth Taylor and Richard Burton *(qq.v.)*. The first

version was a first-rate film and a box office hit. The remake nearly bankrupted Twentieth Century-Fox *(q.v.)*, and a tempestuous romance between Taylor and Burton made headlines worldwide.

The second *Cleopatra* plodded through two directors, a change of locations and a suicide attempt by Elizabeth Taylor.

The first hint that *Cleopatra* was going to be the film disaster of the 1960s came when Rouben Mamoulian *(q.v.)*, a highly respected director for more than thirty-five years, resigned in disgust at the millions of dollars being spent to recreate Egypt in England. Heavy rains destroyed the sets and filming had to be begun again in Rome.

Joseph Mankiewicz *(q.v.)* was the second director hired to complete the film. He spent a year and a half on the project, only to be fired after Darryl F. Zanuck *(q.v.)* saw the rough cut. *(q.v.)*. But long before that point had been reached, delays and wild extravagance had sent the film budget spiralling out of control. A Fox executive publicly admitted that the film cost at least $20 million more than was necessary. It was estimated that the movie would have to earn $40 million just to break even—and this was in 1963 dollars.

The shooting was only partially delayed because of the Taylor/Burton affair. But it's certainly true that when Taylor, torn between husband Eddie Fisher and lover Burton, attempted suicide, the movie did temporarily come to a halt. (At the time, the press reported that Ms. Taylor had fallen ill.)

Were it not for the highly publicized affair, *Cleopatra* might not have been nearly as popular with audiences. In spite of the mediocre reviews the movie received when it was finally released, the public rushed to theaters to see the love scenes between the two stars. It was many years later, when Fox finally sold the film to television for $5 million, that *Cleopatra* finally turned a profit. Had there not been the huge success of *The Longest Day* (1962) and *The Sound of Music* (1965), Fox might easily have sunk in a sea of red ink.

CLIFT, MONTGOMERY (1920–1966) An intense, introspective, and hugely talented actor whose fabulous good looks and offbeat acting choices brought him early critical and public acclaim. A child actor who had a substantial career on the stage during his teens and early twenties, he came to the movies as an experienced player. In all, his film career spanned eighteen years but consisted only of a relatively modest seventeen films. Yet Clift still managed to make an enormous impression, gaining four Oscar nominations and the admiration of his peers and a legion of fans.

Born Edward Montgomery Clift, he made his acting debut in an amateur production of *As Husbands Go* in Florida when he was twelve years old. By the age of fourteen he had become a professional, appearing in the

A young Montgomery Clift, seen before his disfiguring traffic accident. Clift was an introspective actor; this dreamy pose seems particularly fitting. Photo courtesy of Movie Star News.

out-of-town production of *Fly Away Home*. The play was a hit and it moved to Broadway, taking Clift with it in the juvenile role. During the later course of his career on the stage, he appeared with the likes of Lunt and Fontanne, Dame May Whitty, Tallulah Bankhead, Frederic March *(q.v.)*, Edmund Gwenn, and many others. Some of the more noteworthy plays in which he starred were Thornton Wilder's *The Skin of Our Teeth* in 1942, the revival of Wilder's *Our Town* in 1944, and Tennessee William's *You Touched Me!* in 1945.

Clift's matinee idol good looks and theatrical fame brought him repeated offers from Hollywood, which he regularly turned down until finally succumbing because he finally found a script he liked. He made his motion picture debut as the star of *The Search* (1948), a hit film that immediately brought him international recognition as well as his first Oscar nomination.

Many were surprised when Clift chose a Howard Hawks *(q.v.)* western starring John Wayne *(q.v.)* as his second vehicle. The film was *Red River* (1948), and it became a Hollywood classic, with Clift giving a strong and assured performance that balanced beautifully with Wayne's.

Clift constantly surprised those who expected him to follow the usual movie star course of playing essentially heroic and dashing characters. He played a clever cad in *The Heiress* (1949), a tragic lover in *A Place in the*

Sun (1951), for which he was nominated for his second Academy Award, a priest in *I Confess* (1953), and a pacifistic, inarticulate soldier in *From Here to Eternity* (1953), a performance for which he received his third Best Actor Oscar nomination. Only occasionally did Clift pick scripts that resulted in flops. His film career seemed limitless—until the making of *Raintree County* (1957). Halfway through production of the big-budget Civil War epic, Clift was involved in a traffic accident. His longtime friend, Elizabeth Taylor *(q.v.)*, rushed to the scene of the wreck near her home and saved the actor's life by removing two of his teeth that had become lodged in his throat. Taylor saved him from choking to death, but saving his badly battered face was another matter. Though disfigured, particularly on the left side of his face, Clift eventually resumed his career. His skill as a performer was not impaired but the effects of the accident lingered.

The actor's constant physical pain and emotional difficulties led to alcohol and drug abuse, but despite this he delivered several brilliant performances.

His movies during the latter half of the 1950s and early 1960s were often interesting, mainly because of his acting. And a few of them were as good as he was, among them *Suddenly Last Summer* (1959) and *The Misfits* (1961). *The Young Lions* (1958) had the appeal of two of the 1950s' actor icons, Brando and Clift, but they didn't have any significant scenes together. Clift was offered a major role in *Judgment at Nuremberg* (1961) but turned it down in favor of a smaller part in the film, which he played for free. His performance—just seven minutes long—was so emotionally charged that he received a Best Supporting Actor Academy Award nomination, his fourth and last Oscar bid.

He made but two more films, neither of them successful, *Freud* (1962) and *The Defector* (1966), the latter film released after his death from a heart attack at the age of forty-five.

COBURN, JAMES (1928–)   In his heyday during the mid-1960s, there wasn't an actor half as hip or as cool as Coburn. Tall, thin, and with the most wonderfully arrogant (toothy) smile in Hollywood, he was America's answer to James Bond. A long-time villain in movies and TV, he was too familiar to audiences in that role to be convincing as the typical good guy, so he played his heroes with a heavy dose of cynicism. Coburn's screen image was somewhat elusive and he was not well received during the bulk of the 1970s; he all but disppeared from the screen by the early 1980s.

While it sometimes appeared as if Coburn's acting was limited to his mannerisms, he was actually well trained, having studied at USC and with Stella Adler. He made his stage debut in *Billy Budd* at the La Jolla Playhouse in San Diego. During the mid-to late 1950s,

Coburn was often seen on TV, becoming a familiar villain in prime-time westerns. He broke into movies at the end of the decade in a modest role in the Budd Boetticher *(q.v.)* directed Randolph Scott *(q.v.)* western *Ride Lonesome* (1959).

He continued to play important supporting roles in action pictures throughout the early 1960s, contributing to the success of such films as *The Magnificent Seven* (1960), *The Great Escape* (1963), *Charade* (1963), and the thwarted Sam Peckinpah *(q.v.)* masterpiece, *Major Dundee* (1965).

Coburn's big break came when he was cast as Derek Flint in a playful, tongue-in-cheek James Bond rip-off, *Our Man Flint* (1966). The movie was a big hit, largely due to Coburn's charming of critics and audiences alike with his breezy, cocky interpretation of the hero. The sequel, *In Like Flint* (1967), wasn't as well realized, although Coburn was just as much fun to watch as he had been in the first film.

Throughout the latter half of the 1960s, the actor starred in a number of clever, sophisticated movies that fell somewhere between thriller and comedy. The best of them undoubtedly was the suspense/satire *The President's Analyst* (1967). Among his other ambitious movies during that peiod were *What Did You Do in the War Daddy?* (1966), *Dead Heat on a Merry-Go-Round* (1966), and *Waterhole No. 3* (1967). Unfortunately, most of Coburn's films from the 1960s seem terribly dated today.

He made a number of poor movies in the late 1960s and early 1970s that crippled his career. In retrospect, however, he had two very good years in the early 1970s, even if audiences didn't come out in great numbers to see his films. He was in Sergio Leone's underrated *Duck, You Sucker!* (1972), Blake Edwards' excellent medical thriller *The Carey Treatment* (1972), Sam Peckinpah's fascinating western *Pat Garrett and Billy the Kid* (1973), the mostly ignored but very satisfying Herbert Ross whodunit *The Last of Sheila* (1973), and the fascinating bomb *Harry in Your Pocket* (1973).

After five films of such relatively high quality, the actor should have been able to make a solid comeback, but instead, his career dipped still further. Coburn was given his last genuinely good role in 1975, when he was teamed with another villain turned hero, Charles Bronson, in *Hard Times*. The film was well reviewed but it was essentially seen as a Bronson vehicle.

Except for Sam Peckinpah's intriguing *Cross of Iron* (1977), Coburn's later films were generally uninteresting. He even returned to form as a western villain in *The Last Hard Men* (1976). He was an appealing actor but had no drawing power, so films such as *The Baltimore Bullet* (1980) and *High Risk* (1981) went mostly unseen.

Silver-haired and distinguished-looking in a rough sort of way by this time, Coburn all but abandoned the movies, becoming a successful television and radio pitchman for beer and other products.
See also: antiheroes

COHN, HARRY (1891–1958)   He was the president and chief of production of Columbia Pictures. He was also one of the most successful of all the Hollywood moguls, leading his company through the shoals of the talkie revolution, the Depression, the end of the studio era, and the advent of television without ever having a losing year. Cohn's reputation as a wily businessman was matched by that as "The Meanest Man in Hollywood." He was legendary for his cruelty to Columbia's actors, directors, and producers, which led to the heaviest personnel turnover of all the major Hollywood motion picture companies. Yet he had a nearly unfailing instinct for what the public wanted to see on the movie screen. The way he tested a film's commercial potential was to sit through it; if he grew restless and scratched his behind, the film wasn't good enough. That comprises Harry Cohn's sophisticated market research.

The second son of a tailor, Harry Cohn had little education but an abiding interest in show business. Among his early jobs were those of chorus boy in the theater, clerk for a music publishing firm, and even a vaudeville act with songwriter Harry Ruby. He had his greatest early success, however, as a song plugger. But Cohn's most important job came when he was enlisted as Carl Laemmle's personal secretary at Universal Pictures. There he learned the workings of the burgeoning film business, and in 1920, he and his older brother, Jack (who also worked for Universal), joined with Joseph Brandt to form CBC Film Sales Company, later to become Columbia Pictures in 1924.

Harry Cohn ran the production side of the business in Hollywood, while Jack Cohn and Joseph Brandt worked the business end of the company in New York. After Jack failed in his attempt to take over the company in 1932, Brandt sold his shares to Harry Cohn, who assumed Columbia's presidency. Despite his brother's power play, the two siblings continued to run Columbia, though they would never cease fighting each other until Jack's death in 1956. For his part, Harry Cohn fought with everybody else as well, earning the title "White Fang," a name given to him by writer Ben Hecht *(q.v.)*.

At Columbia Pictures, Cohn was the absolute ruler. He was unabashedly vulgar and as infamous for spying on his employees as he was for his "casting couch" during the 1930s. Though he enjoyed his image as a tough shark, he was also a generous man who tried to keep his philanthropic activities hidden so as not to be thought weak or sentimental.

Cohn's personality was lampooned in the stage play

Born Yesterday. Characteristically, Cohn bought the play and turned it into a hit movie in 1950, with Broderick Crawford playing the oafish, tyrannical junk dealer. Cohn presided over Columbia right up until his death from heart disease.

See also: Capra, Frank; Columbia Pictures

COLBERT, CLAUDETTE (1905–) An actress, she starred in more than sixty films, making her mark as a star of sophisticated comedies. Considered a great beauty by many in her early years in Hollywood, she seemed destined to be the decoration in big-budget epics before she emerged as a sprightly and witty actress in Frank Capra's *It Happened One Night* (1934 *[qq.v.]*). Her appeal has withstood the test of time due both to her talent and to the fact that she had the good fortune to star in many well-written and well-directed films.

Born Claudette Lily Chauchoin in Paris, she moved to New York City when she was six. Acting was not her goal in life; instead, she hoped to become a successful fashion designer. Discovered at a party, she was convinced that she ought to give the theater a chance, making her stage debut at the age of eighteen in 1923. She worked steadily during the rest of the 1920s in modest stage roles, learning her craft and gaining a growing reputation as a quality player. At one point, she was coaxed into making her film debut in a low-budget silent, *For the Love of Mike* (1927), a film that was little shown due to both the poor quality of the prodution and the new interest in sound films. It was directed by a very green Frank Capra, who later made amends by giving her the biggest hit of her career.

After sound was perfected and Broadway actors became heavily in demand, Colbert tried the movies again, this time with considerably better luck. Her first sound feature was *The Hole in the Wall* (1929). Her ability to speak French came in handy during her early Hollywood stint as she made both the English and French versions of the same movies. She worked steadily but without any particular distinction, save for the camera's love affair with her photogenic face and shapely legs.

Cecil B. DeMille raised her from leading lady to star when he cast her in one of his early sound biblical epics, *The Sign of the Cross* (1932). Not long after, he gave her the title role in *Cleopatra* (1934). She was effective in both, as well as in *Three-Cornered Moon* (1933).

Earning $25,000 per picture from Paramount, she was, nonetheless, lured to star in Capra's *It Happened One Night* while she was on vacation. With the promise that all of her scenes would be shot in four weeks and that she would be paid twice her usual salary, Colbert agreed to work at the then minor studio, Columbia Pictures. *It Happened One Night,* of course, was a staggering hit that put Columbia on the map, earned Colbert her only Best Actress Oscar, and showed off, for the first time, her considerable flair for comedy, a flair that was soon put on display in many of her films during the next fifteen years.

Among her many memorable movies, both dramatic and comic, during the later 1930s and 1940s were *Imitation of Life* (1934), *I Met Him in Paris* (1937), *Tovarich* (1937), *Bluebeard's Eighth Wife* (1938), *Zaza* (1939), *Midnight* (1939), *Drums Along the Mohawk* (1939), *Boom Town* (1940), *Arise My Love* (1940), *The Palm Beach Story* (1942), *Since You Went Away* (1944), and *The Egg and I* (1947).

After a strong performance in *Three Came Home* (1950), her career began to decline. Colbert was not meant for matronly roles, and audiences did not find her quite as appealing in her middle age. She made few films thereafter, *Texas Lady* (1955) being the last before she retired from the screen for six years. She returned to make *Parrish* in 1961, gaining good reviews in a supporting role, but it was the last film for theatrical release that she made. Except for touring on stage and making the rare television appearance (she starred in *The Two Mrs. Grenvilles,* a 1987 mini-series), Colbert has lived a quiet life of leisure.

COLMAN, RONALD (1891–1958) Handsome and aristocratic in manner, he was also an actor who could communicate vulnerability and accessibility; his unique combination of style and warmth made him one of the most beloved of all Hollywood stars. Colman's popularity lasted more than thirty years and, together with Greta Garbo and Charlie Chaplin *(qq.v.),* he was one of only a handful of major stars from the silent era to enjoy equal success in the talkies. His utterly charming speaking voice certainly aided this transition.

Colman was equally adept in action films, comedies, and romances, but he was most often cast in the last. His four Academy Award nominated performances indicate his range if not his talent: the suave detective hero in the title role of *Bulldog Drummond* (1929), as a prisoner on Devil's Island in *Condemned* (1929), as an amnesiac in the classic "weeper" *Random Harvest* (1942), and as an actor playing Othello both on the stage and off in *A Double Life* (1947), for which he finally won his only Oscar.

Born to a middle-class English family, Colman was sixteen when his father died, a tragedy that considerably changed the young man's prospects. He was forced to take a job as an office boy in the British Steamship Company, but he filled his free time during the next five years working in an amateur theater. Finally, at the age of twenty-one, he tried professional acting, but World War I interrupted his nascent career. A broken ankle ended his war service two years later in 1916, after which he returned to the stage. By 1918, he had built a modest reputation as an actor and had even made several English two-reelers such as *The Toilers* (1919) and *A Son of David* (1919). They met with little success.

His acting career stalled, Colman decided to try his luck in America. Without a contract or even a promise of work, he arrived in the United States in 1920, managing to win small parts in New York plays and movies. His big break came with a substantial role in the Broadway production of *La Tendresse* in 1923. Lillian Gish *(q.v.)* had been in the audience and she insisted that Colman was perfect to play her leading man in *The White Sister* (1924). With Gish's help, he quickly became a star, signing soon thereafter with Samuel Goldwyn *(q.v.)*, who featured him in eighteen of the producer's next thirty films between 1924 and 1933. Among the many Colman silent hits were such standouts as *Romola* (1924), *The Dark Angel* (1925), *Stella Dallas* (1925), *Lady Windemere's Fan* (1925), and *Beau Geste* (1926). Also during the late silent era he made five films with vamp Vilma Banky; they were one of the hottest screen teams of the silent era, every bit as sexy together as Greta Garbo and John Gilbert—and just as big at the box office.

Unlike a great many silent stars who were rushed into sound films prematurely, only to see their careers ruined, Goldwyn carefully chose Coleman's talkie debut, waiting until 1929 to present his star in *Bulldog Drummond*. The film was a massive hit, and the actor's immediate future was secured.

The early 1930s were studded with sensitive Colman performances in films such as *Raffles* (1930), *Arrowsmith* (1931), and *Cynara* (1932). But his association with Goldwyn ended in 1933 when Coleman sued his producer who had reportedly said that the actor drank before performing his love scenes. The legal action was settled out of court, but the two men never worked together again.

Coleman acted for a great many studios after that, mostly as a free-lancer. He appeared in fewer movies, but they were generally superior productions. His prize roles during the rest of the 1930s were in *A Tale of Two Cities* (1935), *Under Two Flags* (1936), *Lost Horizon* (1937), *The Prisoner of Zenda* (1937), and *If I Were King* (1938).

It appeared as if his reign as a major star was fast ending when he made several duds in the early 1940s, but then came his classic role as an amnesiac in *Random Harvest* (1942), one of the major hits of the year and one of the most romantic movies ever made. Colman was again a much sought after star, but he knew that he couldn't go on playing lovers much longer. After starring in *Kismet* (1944), he dispensed with hair dye and played an older man in *The Late George Apley* (1947). The following year, he starred in *A Double Life*, winning his Oscar for a movie and a performance that could not match half of his better roles but was no doubt given in recognition of the entire body of his work.

Colman's last star performance was in a delightful hit comedy, *Champagne for Caesar* (1949), which mocked quiz shows with a light but pungent wit. Colman then walked away from Hollywood as a star, returning only twice to make cameo appearances, first in *Around the World in 80 Days* (1956) and then in *The Story of Mankind* (1957).

COLUMBIA PICTURES   Once a barebones film company in the 1920s, this motion picture production and distribution company grew and prospered under the business leadership of Harry Cohn *(q.v.)*, and the creative talent of its top director, Frank Capra *(q.v.)*. Columbia never owned theaters as did the "Big Five" studios, MGM, Paramount, Warner Bros., Twentieth Century-Fox, and RKO. Therefore, like fellow members of the "Little Three," United Artists and Universal, Columbia had to produce the best films possible in order to guarantee exhibition. And to a very great extent, the studio succeeded.

Columbia was originally known as CBC Film Sales Company, founded by Harry Cohn and his brother, Jack, along with Joseph Brandt. All three had worked for Universal Pictures before they began their own film studio in 1920. In 1924, CBC became known as Columbia Pictures, Inc. Harry Cohn eventually rose to become president, as well as chief of production (the only major film mogul to hold both titles), when, in 1932, Brandt sold him his share of the company for $500,000.

Despite Harry Cohn's reputation for crudeness and vulgarity, his company was known during the studio era (1930s and 1940s) for its sophisticated film fare. Part of the reason for this reputation was Columbia's lack of a large back lot, used for outdoor shooting. Unable to make westerns and other action films easily, and confined to shooting on indoor sets, Columbia was led, by necessity, to emphasize stories with contemporary themes.

During the late 1920s and early 1930s, however, Columbia was not known as very much more than a struggling concern. The company's lack of capital and muscle made it slower than its larger competitors in the race to acquire the new talkie technology. Columbia finally began its long climb to respectability with the efforts of Frank Capra, who directed such early studio hits as *Ladies of Leisure* (1930), *Dirigible* (1931) and *Platinum Blonde* (1932).

Columbia's major breakthrough came when Capra directed *It Happened One Night* (1934), starring Clark Gable and Claudette Colbert. The film swept the Academy Awards, winning all of the five top Oscars, including Best Picture, Best Actor, Best Actress, Best Director, and Best Adaptation. The film was also the biggest commercial hit of the year (by far), and suddenly Columbia was no longer a minor studio. Capra continued to direct hits for Columbia throughout the rest of the 1930s, making such memorable films as *Mr. Deeds Goes to Town* (1936), *You Can't Take It with You* (1938), and *Mr. Smith Goes to Washington* (1939). Unfortunately for Columbia, few other of its films were such hits.

Out of necessity, Harry Cohn led the studio toward a greater dependency on "B" movie series such as Blondie, Boston Blackie, and Crime Doctor. In addition, Columbia had a very strong reputation as a producer of comedy shorts, with The Three Stooges one of its staples.

Columbia had relatively few stars on its lot, Cohn preferring to acquire actors and actresses on loan-out from other studios. But during the 1940s he did have one major star, Rita Hayworth *(q.v.)*, who helped bring in profits with films such as *Cover Girl* (1944) and *Gilda* (1946). In addition, the studio's film about a past star, *The Jolson Story* (1946), was a stupendous hit.

By the 1950s, Columbia had developed stars such as William Holden *(q.v.)*, as well their new sex symbol, Kim Novak *(q.v.)*. More importantly, in the face of television competition, the company was willing to make daring films such as *From Here to Eternity* (1953) and *On the Waterfront* (1954), as well as lead the way toward international films, such as the sweeping historical blockbuster *The Bridge on the River Kwai* (1957).

Finally, though, Harry Cohn did not fight television but managed to use the medium to enrich Columbia's coffers. The studio formed a television subsidiary, Screen Gems, and became the first major motion picture company to allow its movies to be shown on the little screen, as well as being the first to jump into the breach to produce television shows.

While Harry Cohn was in charge of Columbia (he died in 1958), the studio never lost money—not even during the Depression. The company's fortunes rose and fell during the 1960s and 1970s, turning out several major hits, such as *Lawrence of Arabia* (1962) and *A Man for All Seasons* (1966), but descending into stretches of heavy losses that threatened the company's existence. In 1968, Columbia was forced to make fiscal changes, and the business changed its name to Columbia Pictures Industries, Inc. Not long after, the new Columbia emerged with the hugely profitable hit, *Easy Rider* (1969).

The studio was bought by Coca-Cola in 1981 and thereby gained virtually unlimited cash resources. Proving to be an erratic money maker, however, the studio was sold again to the Sony corporation in 1989 and became part of a multinational empire.

See also: It Happened One Night; studio system

COMDEN, BETTY (1917–) **& GREEN, ADOLPH** (1915–) A venerable screenwriting team that has also written the lyrics for a number of highly popular Broadway musicals. Not only are Comden & Green closely associated with musicals, some of their best work has been in films *about* musicals. For instance, they wrote the screenplays for such classics as *Singin' in the Rain* (1952) and *The Band Wagon* (1953), as well as the entertaining *The Barkleys of Broadway* (1949).

Comden & Green began their show business careers as cabaret performers in a trio with Judy Holliday, *(q.v.)*, for whom they eventually wrote the Broadway musical *Bells Are Ringing*. The vast majority of Comden & Green's movie work was done under the leadership of Arthur Freed *(q.v.)* at MGM during that studio's musical heyday. Among their other notable works to eventually be turned into MGM musicals were *Good News* (1947), *On the Town* (1949, original book and lyrics), *Take Me Out to the Ballgame* (1949, lyrics only), *It's Always Fair Weather* (1955, script and lyrics), and *Bells Are Ringing* (1960, book and lyrics). Their work in the last three decades has rarely been put on film.

COLOR Though it may appear as if black-and-white movies were the norm in Hollywood for much of its existence, the opposite is actually the case. While full, natural color was long in coming to the movies, color of one kind or another had been used in films virtually from the very beginning of cinema history. In America, Thomas Edison was involved in the hand painting and hand tinting of individual film frames as early as the late 1890s. When more than one color was used on a frame, however, the result was often rather muddy because the application process was so imprecise.

Restored versions of films such as *The Great Train Robbery* (1903) show the effects of hand tinting. When the outlaw fires his gun at the camera at the end of the movie, the frames have a red hue around the barrel of his pistol.

Later, tinting was done not by hand but by bathing the film in the appropriate chemicals to bring out blues for night, yellows for bright sunny days, reds for fire, etc.

A great many silent films that we see today in black and white were originally tinted. For instance, D. W. Griffith *(q.v.)* tinted certain scenes in *The Birth of a Nation* (1915, *q.v.*) and Erich von Stroheim *(q.v.)* tinted parts of *Greed* (1923) yellow to symbolize the characters' lust for gold. In fact, by the early 1920s, the vast majority of feature films made in Hollywood were at least partially hand-tinted. Soon, however, most Hollywood films were colored by virtue of a newer process that involved using tinted film stock.

Color tinting came to a sudden, if temporary, halt when sound films became the rage in 1927. The technology didn't yet exist that would allow the soundtrack to reproduce on tinted film. The problem was soon solved, however, and tinting continued throughout the 1930s and beyond, even when other color processes, such as Technicolor *(q.v.)*, came into vogue for "A" movies *(q.v.)*. For instance, otherwise black-and-white movies such as *The Oklahoma Kid* (1939) and *Portrait of Jennie* (1948) all contained color tinting in their original versions.

Beyond hand painting and one-color tinting processes, attempts to present a richer palette of colors on the screen were constantly being attempted. According to James L. Limbacher in his book, *Four Aspects of the Film,* there were at least twenty-five different companies during the early years in Hollywood that attempted to exploit multicolor systems, among them Prizma, Brewster Color, Kodachrome, Zoechrome, and Color-craft.

The big breakthrough came with the two-color Technicolor system that was first used on a commercial release of the film *Toll of the Sea* (1921). It was a complicated and expensive process, but it worked. The colors in this system weren't natural (they were based on shades of red and green, without using the blue range). A modest number of films were made in this new system such as Douglas Fairbanks' *(q.v.) The Black Pirate* (1926), but, more often, because of the cost, two-color Technicolor sequences only were added to otherwise black-and-white films.

After the arrival of sound, two-color became used more and more as a novelty and its appeal to audiences quickly diminished. Finally, in 1932, the Technicolor company perfected a three-color process that was first used commercially by Walt Disney in his animated short *Flowers and Trees* (1932). Technicolor was a winner with audiences in this experiment and the system was used for parts of other films during the next several years, including the startlingly lush and beautiful finale of Eddie Cantor's *(q.v.) Kid Millions* (1934). *Becky Sharp* (1935) was the first feature film to be made entirely in Technicolor's three-color process.

Because of its cost, full Technicolor was used for only the most important "A" features during the latter 1930s and during the 1940s. A relatively small percentage of Hollywood's total output was made in color. Later, when TV threatened the movie industry's existence during the 1950s, color, along with several wide-screen processes, were seen as panaceas. Color films became far more prevalent until, by the 1960s, more films were being made in color than in black and white. Today, virtually all films are made in color. Black and white movies are exceedingly rare, made mostly by directors with a strong artistic vision, such as Martin Scorsese or Woody Allen *(qq.v.)*.

Despite attempts to supplant it, Technicolor has remained both the company and the process (with improvements) that has provided Hollywood with its rich and vibrant colors to this day.

COMEDIANS & COMEDIENNES Hollywood has been blessed with an enormous number of solo comic actors and actresses, a great many of the more famous, influential, and/or established of whom are discussed in separate entries throughout this volume. A good many others, however, are certainly worthy of mention due to either their place in the development of screen comedy or because they are fast emerging comic stars of the present who may yet become the Bob Hopes, Woody Allens, and Mel Brookses of the future.

The first movie comedy star in the history of the American cinema was John Bunny, a 300-pound ball of comic energy who prefigured the success of Fatty Arbuckle *(q.v.)*. Almost as soon as he began making shorts in 1910 he became an international star. Developing the art of comic pantomime, Bunny made more than two hundred hugely successful one-reelers before his death at the age of 52 in 1915. He laid the groundwork for the golden age of silent comedy, establishing the commercial viability of the genre for such future stars as Charlie Chaplin, Buster Keaton, Harold Lloyd *(qq.v.)*, etc.

Individual comic stars during the early sound era took a back seat to musicals, gangster movies, and dramas. Except for Mae West and W. C. Fields *(qq.v.)*,

Hollywood's first comic star was the somewhat aged and extremely rotund John Bunny. A precursor to "Fatty" Arbuckle, Bunny was a popular comedian who died before his art could be fully appreciated. Many of his more than two hundred one-reelers have been lost. Photo courtesy of The Siegel Collection.

whose careers were erratic in any case, solo comedy stars tended either to play comic relief roles in films or take top billing in "B" movies (q.v.) or shorts. Comic stars often seen in supporting roles were Fred Allen, Jimmy Durante, and ventriloquist Edgar Bergen—with his ever reliable dummies Charlie McCarthy and Mortimer Snerd. Among the leading comic stars of second features was the wide-mouthed Joe E. Brown and the amiable Stu Erwin. In short subjects, no one was more amusing than Robert Benchley.

Comediennes had a much tougher time of it during the 1930s and early 1940s. While female comic stars were fairly plentiful during the silent era, with the likes of Mabel Normand (q.v.) leading the pack, during the better part of the next two decades there were no other female comic stars other than Mae West, who carried their own feature films. Plenty of actresses, such as Eve Arden and Helen Broderick played comic relief characters, but movies were never built around such performers.

Only in the area of short subjects did comediennes have the chance to shine as the stars of their own vehicles; the most notable of such comic stars was Thelma Todd.

Thanks to the growing success in the late 1930s and early 1940s of comic actors Bob Hope and Jack Benny (qq.v.), film studios began grooming new solo comedy stars. By the postwar years, a whole new crop of comic actors, including such talents as Danny Kaye (q.v.) and Red Skelton, began carrying their own vehicles. Even comediennes were given their shot in the late 1940s, with Lucille Ball managing to garner a number of starring comic roles before achieving her stellar success on TV in the 1950s.

The 1950s were a relatively stable period in film comedy for individual performers. Little new talent was introduced to film audiences other than Jerry Lewis' (q.v.) solo act after his split with Dean Martin (q.v.) in the middle of the decade. The advent of TV sitcoms such as "The Honeymooners" and "The Jack Benny Show," plus comedy variety programs such as "Your Show of Shows," seemed to satiate the public's need for new comedy performers.

Things changed in the 1960s with the popular arrival of Peter Sellers (q.v.) and his *Pink Panther* films. And the dam really opened up when Woody Allen (q.v.) left the nightclub scene to make movies in the late 1960s. Mel Brooks (q.v.) soon followed suit, and the solo comedy tradition was in the midst of a solid revival.

Finally, in the mid-1970s, television became the breeding ground for a vast new crop of solo comedy talent. "Saturday Night Live" spawned a remarkable number of comic film actors who have become the nucleus of modern film comedy. Chevy Chase (q.v.), Eddie Murphy (q.v.), Dan Aykroyd (q.v.), John Be-lushi, Gilda Radner, Martin Short, and others were all launched by the late-night show on NBC.

The vast majority of the modern era's film comedy stars have found their way to stardom through television exposure. One route has been the variety and talk-show circuit. Comediennes Lily Tomlin and Goldie Hawn (q.v.) were first introduced to audiences on "Laugh-In," while Rodney Dangerfield became a comic star thanks to repeated guest shots on "The Tonight Show." A good many other comic actors received their big breaks on TV sitcoms. For example, Danny DeVito was a hit on "Taxi," Billy Crystal's first brush with fame came as a character on the controversial sitcom "Soap," and Robin Williams became an instant sensation thanks to his starring role in "Mork and Mindy."

While comedy teams have faded since the 1950s, not since the silent era have solo comedy stars been as popular with the public as they have been during the 1980s. Eddie Murphy and Tom Hanks, for instance, are often more successful at the box office than Sylvester Stallone (q.v.). Long gone are the days when a comedy star has to play second fiddle to dramatic actors in film budgets, distribution, or public adulation.

See also: Burns & Allen; comedy teams; Langdon, Harry; Martin, Steve; Oakie, Jack; Pitts, ZaSu; Pryor, Richard; Semon, Larry; Sterling, Ford; Turpin, Ben; Wilder, Gene

COMEDY TEAMS   Mack Sennett created the first true cinema comedy team when, in 1912, he organized a small group of actors, dressed them in police uniforms, and named them the Keystone Kops after his Keystone Studio. The silent Keystone Kops films were pure slapstick and always culminated with chases. With no character development and precious little plot, these early shorts made a shrewd comic statement, nonetheless, in their irreverent display of authority as incompetent. It was a theme that would continue as a mainstay of many of the comedy teams to follow.

The Keystone Kops faded from the Hollywood comedy scene in 1920, and it wasn't until the middle of the decade that two new comedy teams, Laurel & Hardy (q.v.) and Our Gang, filled the breach.

Stan Laurel and Oliver Hardy both had solo film careers for more than a decade before they teamed up in 1926 in *Slipping Wives*. Their humor was of a quieter sort than that of the Keystone Kops—and it was infinitely more intimate. They made the transition to sound without a hitch, and the continued balance between Hardy's pomposity and Laurel's guileless sweetness made them an endearing—and lasting—comedy team.

The other successful comedy team that emerged out of the silent era was Our Gang (q.v.), an ethnically diverse group of child actors assembled by Hal Roach (q.v.) just a few years after Charlie Chaplin's 1921

Among the more zany comedy teams was Olsen & Johnson, seen here costumed for their roles in *Ghost Catchers* (1944). Wackier than the Marx Brothers, more inventive than Abbott and Costello, Ole and Chic seemed like a couple of Daffy Ducks let loose from Toon Town. Photo courtesy of Movie Star News.

success with *The Kid* (costarring six-year-old Jackie Coogan, *q.v.*). Recognizing that audiences had a soft spot for child actors, Roach created a comedy team that was to last (through innumerable cast changes) into the 1940s.

With the advent of sound, motion picture companies looked to vaudeville and radio for new comedy stars. Out of vaudeville came Wheeler & Woolsey, as well as Gallagher & Shean. Neither team really caught on in the movies despite their stature as live performers.

Though far from headliners in vaudeville, The Three Stooges *(q.v.)* found their niche at Harry Cohn's Columbia Pictures *(qq.v.)*. Moe Howard, Larry Fine, and Curly Howard (Moe's brother) created fast-paced, violent, slapstick comedies that have always been considered low-brow entertainment. Nonetheless, their two-reel films (and they made hundreds of them in the 1930s and 1940s) have withstood the test of time. Many of them, in fact, are now considered classic.

Unlike The Three Stooges, who were never the darlings of the critics, The Marx Brothers *(q.v.)* were the comedy team of the intelligentsia.

At the beginning of their film career, there were four Marx Brothers: Groucho, Chico, Harpo, and Zeppo. Zeppo later left the team after their fifth film, *Duck Soup* (1933). Of all the comedy teams of the sound era, the Marx Brothers were by far the most influential. Harpo was both angel and devil, a mute with a horn and a rubber face who became a link to the glorious

past of silent comedy. Chico, with his preposterous Italian accent, was the link to the immigrant audience of the day. And Groucho was the link to the future. His fast-talking style, laced with insults, sexual innuendo, and an endless stream of puns, was the progenitor of modern comedy.

The Marx Brothers' humor was thoroughly anarchical. It can best be described by one of Groucho's songs in the 1932 film, *Horsefeathers*, titled, "Whatever It Is, I'm Against It." They took on America's taboos: sex, marriage, government, and war. They battled smugness and good taste to the death—and won. They made but thirteen films together, but they were unarguably the most important comedy team in Hollywood history. Without them, there never would have been a Mel Brooks *(q.v.)* or a Woody Allen *(q.v.)*.

The Ritz Brothers were a poor imitation of The Marx Brothers. Al, Jim, and Harry Ritz did have a fair degree of success in the mid to late 1930s but their films were minor affairs that did nothing to advance the art of film comedy.

If there was one comedy team that captured some of the "anything goes" anarchy of the best Marx Brothers films of the early 1930s, it was Olsen and Johnson. The film career of Ole Olsen and Chic Johnson was erratic and brief, but included in their output were two hilarious movies, *Hellzapoppin* (1941) and *Ghost Catchers* (1944). There is a frantic, manic quality to this team's comedy style that still seems eminently modern.

Just as modern in their own way, but far more popular were Burns & Allen *(q.v.)*. They started as a team in vaudeville and made the transition both to radio and film. It was due to their radio success, however, that they began to appear in films with regularity. George, perhaps the world's greatest straight man, and his wife, Gracie, the ultimate scatterbrain, delighted film audiences in the 1930s and 1940s with their supporting roles in features starring other actors.

Radio not only brought Burns & Allen to Hollywood, it also brought Bob Hope *(q.v.)* to the movies. And it was the occasional teaming of Hope with Bing Crosby *(q.v.)* that made possible a string of seven famous Road comedies beginning in 1940 with *The Road to Singapore* and ending with *The Road to Hong Kong* in 1962. Though not a comedy team, per se, Hope and Crosby were perfect foils for each other. Crosby, smooth and hip, and Hope, cowardly and quick-witted, always looked like they were having fun together, and were a joy to watch. While Groucho Marx occasionally talked directly to the camera, Hope and Crosby delighted in letting the audience know that, after all, it was only a movie.

Only one comedy team can be said to have ever developed out of a series of dramatic movies. The teenage actors known as The Dead End Kids were introduced in the classic 1937 William Wyler (q.v.) film *Dead End* (q.v.). After appearing in other hit films, Leo Gorcy, Huntz Hall, and several other Dead End Kids used their fame to form a splinter group known as the Bowery Boys. They made a total of 48 low-budget films between 1946 and 1958. The Bowery Boys' humor was based on slapstick, but without the zany cartoon-like inventiveness of The Three Stooges or the sweetness of Laurel & Hardy. Playing teenagers despite their age was an even more preposterous affect than Chico Marx's Italian accent. Seen today, they are less funny than merely nostalgic.

Abbott & Costello (q.v.) were one of only two comedy teams to become so wildly successful that they were top box office draws (Martin and Lewis was the other). From their first starring roles in *Buck Privates* (1941), Bud Abbott, the manipulative straight man, and Lou Costello, the roly-poly child/man, were Universal Studio's preeminent money-makers until the end of World War II. Bud and Lou traded on slapstick and infantile humor, but their characters suited an America that needed some silliness to help forget the horror of war.

A different kind of silliness became all the rage when Dean Martin and Jerry Lewis (qq.v.) launched their movie career at Paramount in 1949 with *My Friend Irma*. The craze ended in 1956, fifteen movies later, when the team split up to pursue solo careers. A cross between Abbott & Costello and Hope and Crosby, Martin and Lewis were both low-brow and slick at the same time. Dean Martin was the handsome crooner who always got the girl; Jerry Lewis was the gawky nerd who got the laughs.

Since Martin and Lewis, the era of comedy teams in film appears to have ended. There have been tepid attempts in the last three decades by the likes of Allen & Rossi, Rowan & Martin, and Peter Cook and Dudley Moore (q.v.), to take on the mantel of the great comedy teams. Perhaps the closest recent cinema has come to the creation of a new comedy team was the pairing of Dan Aykroyd (q.v.) and John Belushi in *The Blues Brothers* (1980). In this age of the solo performer, however, it would appear as if the last has been seen of the great comedy teams.

COMPOSER During the silent era music was occasionally written specifically for a movie, but generally, whether a film was accompanied by an orchestra in a big New York showplace or by a piano in a small rural theater, its composition was usually of a standard fare: loud and exciting for chase scenes, soft and sweet for love scenes. Not until the talkie era was music regularly composed for individual film soundtracks.

Original film compositions, or scores, soon became an art form that helped to transform many an ordinary movie into a unique cinematic experience. Undoubt-edly, such movies as *Dr. Zhivago* (1965, with an Oscar winning score by Maurice Jarre) and *High Noon* (1952, with an Oscar winning score by Dimitri Tiomkin q.v.) would lose their power without the drama added by their respective scores.

Music is sometimes used to heighten emotion, but more often than not, overreliance on such techniques betrays rather weak filmmaking. A composer would usually much rather score a movie in counterpoint to the action on the screen, with the music telling its own story, commenting and expanding on visual meaning with unique aural statements.

In the production process, the composer reports to the director. His work is generally done after the movie is shot and edited into a rough cut (q.v.), whereupon the composer may begin writing his score for the film. He won't finish the writing, however, until there is a final cut against which he must time his music.

Typically, the composer is given a "timing sheet" by the editor of the film. The timing sheet breaks every image down to one-third of a second. Obviously, the pressure on the composer is quite staggering. He must write the rough equivalent of a symphony in a matter of weeks and have it perfectly timed to fit each edit in the film, as well.

When the score is recorded, there are usually more timing marks on the sheet music than musical notes. The orchestra plays the score with the film projected on a screen behind it, with only the conductor (who is often also the composer) watching the film.

Once the score has been recorded on film, it can still be significantly changed by the sound editor. For the same reason that directors want to edit their own films, many composers will insist upon working with the sound editor, hoping to protect the integrity of their work.

There are a number of deservedly famous film composers whose music has greatly enhanced the motion pictures they have scored. Just a few of the greats include Max Steiner, Dimitri Tiomkin, Bernard Herrmann, John Williams, and Henry Mancini (qq.v.).

CONNERY, SEAN (1929–) A Scottish actor much admired in America for his manly roles in adventure, suspense, science-fiction, and historical films. Long associated with the character of James Bond, which he played to perfection in seven movies, Connery managed to forge his own identity during the mid-1970s as an actor of depth and power.

Born Thomas Connery in Edinburgh, Scotland, to a family of modest means, he joined the Royal Navy at the age of fifteen as World War II finally came to an end. After his stint in the service was over, Connery bounced between jobs as diverse as laying bricks and polishing coffins. A physical fitness addict, the young man was often lifting weights and his impressive physique landed him a job as a male model. Soon thereafter Connery found himself on the London stage in the chorus of *South Pacific*.

Caught up in the acting world, Connery decided to pursue his new calling and found modest work in English repertory theater. Beginning in the mid-1950s, he began appearing fairly regularly on British TV, and in 1956 he made his film debut in *No Road Back*. Other small parts in forgettable English films followed, but he finally showed his talent in a significant supporting role in the Disney movie *Darby O'Gill and the Little People* (1959).

Unfortunately, few good roles came his way during the next few years and he was stuck in such clinkers as *Tarzan's Greatest Adventure* (1959) and *The Frightened City* (1961). Then came a casting call for a low-budget spy film to be based on the popular Ian Fleming character James Bond. Connery was given the part and the film, *Dr. No* (1962), quickly emerged as an international sensation. Connery was suddenly a hot actor, hired to join an all-star cast in *The Longest Day* (1962). But his bread-and-butter role was Bond, whom he played in *From Russia With Love* (1963), *Goldfinger* (1964), *Thunderball* (1965), *You Only Live Twice* (1967), *Diamonds Are Forever* (1971), and after a long hiatus, *Never Say Never Again* (1983).

Even as he earned $1 million per Bond film, Connery complained of being typecast. He considered himself an actor and didn't want to be forever thought of as 007. Nonetheless, the popularity of his spy films brought him the opportunity to star in a host of films, including Alfred Hitchcock's *Marnie* (1964), as well as other notable films such as *A Fine Madness* (1966), *The Molly Maquires* (1970), and *The Anderson Tapes* (1971).

The James Bond films aside, Connery did his best work during the mid-1970s when he starred in the films of several of the cinema's best and/or most interesting directors, lending his talents to John Boorman's controversial *Zardoz* (1974), John Milius' epic *The Wind and the Lion* (1975), John Huston's masterpiece, *The Man Who Would Be King* (1975), and Richard Lester's autumnal romance *Robin and Marian* (1976).

His career began a slow slide in the latter half of the 1970s as he appeared in mostly lesser movies such as *The Next Man* (1976), *Meteor* (1978), *Cuba* (1979), and a disappointing science-fiction remake of *High Noon*, *Outland* (1981). During the early 1980s Connery came close to acting for television, nearly starring in the miniseries *Shogun*. At the last minute other committments kept him from playing the role, which eventually went to Richard Chamberlain.

After several other flops on the big screen, Connery returned to play James Bond in *Never Say Never Again*, producing the picture himself (it was not part of the series that had been continued with Roger Moore in

the role of 007). Fans were left somewhat disappointed, and it was not a major hit.

It seemed as if his stock would rise when he was roundly hailed by critics for his work in *The Name of the Rose* (1986), but the movie was not up to his performance and it failed at the box office. His career didn't pick up again until he accepted a supporting role in Brian De Palma's *The Untouchables* (1987), stealing the movie with a vivid performance that was the talk of the industry. The part brought him a Best Supporting Actor Academy Award and a revitalized career. He played a similar role as the tough older man who must teach the young hotshot the ways of the world in *Presidio* (1988), then outdid himself as Harrison Ford's father in *Indiana Jones and The Last Crusade* (1989). He is presently scheduled to star in *The Hunt For Red October*.

COOGAN, JACKIE (1914–1984)   He was the first major child movie star, a young moppet who rocketed to fame at six years of age in 1920 and remained a hit throughout the silent era. His thick head of unruly hair and big sad eyes made him the child everyone wanted to love.

The son of a vaudeville couple, Jack Leslie Coogan was born to show business. He first appeared in *Skinner's Baby* (1917) when he was three years old. Not long thereafter, Charlie Chaplin discovered Coogan and gave him a role in one of his two-reelers, *A Day's Pleasure* (1919). The great comedian was so impressed with his young charge that he decided to make him his costar in what would be Chaplin's first feature film, *The Kid* (1921).

The movie was a huge success, vaulting Coogan to immediate supercelebrity. The pint-sized actor starred in a number of subsequent films, all of which succeeded handsomely at the box office. Most of Coogans' projects, such as *Peck's Bad Boy* (1921), *Oliver Twist* (1922), *A Boy of Flanders* (1924), and *The Rag Man* (1925), traded on the youth's image as a poor but loveable street urchin.

But Coogan was anything but poor in real life. He had earned $4 million, which he was to receive upon turning twenty-one. Unfortunately, just before his twenty-first birthday, his father was killed in a traffic accident (in which Coogan was also hurt) and his mother and stepfather refused to turn over the money that was Coogan's due. The case wasn't settled until he was twenty-four, by which time the money was virtually gone. He received just $126,000 of the four million he earned. Because of this celebrated case, however, the Child Actors Bill (nicknamed the "Coogan Act") was passed in the state of California, protecting future child stars from the fate that befell Jackie Coogan.

Though he had been a cute child, Coogan was a less than handsome adult. He generally played minor villainous roles in a sporadic acting career that lasted until his death. He became known to a new generation, however, when he played the ghoulish Uncle Fester in the TV series "The Addams Family" in the mid-1960s. *See also:* Chaplin, Sir Charles; child stars

COOPER, GARY (1901–1961) Known as "Coop" to friends and fans alike, he was an actor equally adept in action movies as he was in light comedies. The tall, rangy, and handsome Cooper spent thirty-five years as an actor (almost all of them as a star), and appeared in more than ninety films, surprisingly few of which were losers at the box office. Despite an undeserved reputation as an actor with a dramatic range from "Yep" to "Nope," his performances have been rich and varied—and almost always on target.

Born Frank J. Cooper in Montana to English parents, young Cooper was sent to Britain for his education. He planned to become a cartoonist, but there were no jobs for him when he returned to Los Angeles, then his parents' home. Having been reared in the West, Cooper knew how to ride horses and was able to get a job as an extra in a frontier film, *The Thundering Herd* (1925). In fact, most of his early work in films was as an extra in westerns.

His first significant early role was in *The Winning of Barbara Worth* (1926). He was learning his craft as an actor in the late 1920s but also making a modest name for himself. He had a small role in the Clara Bow *(q.v.)* movie *It* (1927), and after two leading roles in minor films, had an important supporting part in one of the biggest hits of 1927, the Academy Award–winning *Wings*. He had leading roles in eleven more silent films during 1928 and 1929, but he became a major star with his first performance in a talkie, the classic western *The Virginian* (1929). Because of the film's laconic style, Cooper was forever fixed in the minds of many as a monosyllabic actor, but the film managed to single-handedly establish him as the quintessential western star. Cooper would often return to the genre throughout his career, especially during the 1950s when his career needed a boost.

In the 1930s, however, Cooper's career was on a steady upward curve. He was a strong, charismatic leading man for Marlene Dietrich *(q.v.)* in *Morroco* (1930), and he played a simple carnival worker drawn into the underworld in Rouben Mamoulian's *(q.v.)* cleverly directed *City Streets* (1931), one of the biggest box office hits of the year. In 1932, he starred in Hemingway's *A Farewell to Arms* with Helen Hayes, a movie that many consider the best film adaptation of any of Hemingway's works. In fact, when Hemingway's *For Whom the Bell Tolls* (1943) was filmed, the author specifically requested that Cooper star in the movie.

Cooper did not try his hand at comedy until he

Yep, it's Gary Cooper. One of the icons of the cinema, "Coop" was not only tall and handsome, in his own quiet way he was one of Hollywood's most effective screen actors. Photo courtesy of The Siegel Collection.

appeared in Noel Coward's *Design for Living* (1934). It was an awkward attempt and not altogether successful, but he learned from the experience and later became one of Hollywood's most endearing light comedians, using his awkwardness to advantage in the Frank Capra *(q.v.)* social comedies *Mr. Deeds Goes to Town* (1936) and *Meet John Doe* (1941). Cooper once said that the reason he remained popular was because he always played "Mr. Average Joe American." That was certainly true in the Capra films and in most of his comedies. And whether average or not, his comic heroes were always charmingly innocent. For instance, he played a modest rancher in *The Cowboy and the Lady* (1938), an innocuous professor in *Ball of Fire* (1941), and a sweet natured good samaritan in *Good Sam* (1948), to name just a few.

But even as his comic gift became apparent, he continued to please as an action hero, dominating the screen in one impressive picture after another, with hits such as *Lives of a Bengal Lancer* (1935), *The General Died at Dawn* (1936), *The Plainsman* (1936), and *Beau Geste* (1939).

In 1940, Cooper starred in *The Westerner*, a movie about the life of Judge Roy Bean. Walter Brennan *(q.v.)* played the crafty old judge and stole the movie, winning a Best Supporting Oscar. It must have seemed to Cooper that playing historical figures made good sense, and he soon followed with a string of biopics beginning with *Sergeant York* (1941), for which he won his first Best Actor Oscar.

He followed that with *The Pride of the Yankees* (1942), playing baseball great Lou Gehrig, and *The Story of Dr. Wassell* (1944), a movie loosely based on a true story of a hero in the Pacific campaign during World War II.

It seemed as if Cooper was off to a fresh start in the postwar years when he produced and starred in his own western, the agreeable *Along Came Jones* (1945). But, finally, after twenty years, Cooper's popularity began to falter. His performances in the latter 1940s were flacid; even in his more interesting films, such as *The Fountainhead* (1949) based on Ayn Rand's novel, Cooper was oddly miscast (or, more accurately, too old for the part). In the early 1950s, his career went from bad to worse as he suffered through several terrible flops.

It was time for the actor to return to his old faithful genre, the western. The "horse opera" had become quite popular in the 1950s, and no one looked better in buckskin than Cooper—not even John Wayne. Cooper's first two westerns in 1952 did reasonably decent business and kept him afloat as a viable star. But the third film of that year brought him back to the pinnacle of success. The movie was *High Noon*, and it not only cleaned up at the box office, it garnered Cooper his second Best Actor Oscar.

Throughout the rest of the decade he made a mix of films, though the most commercially successful ones were, once again, his westerns: *Vera Cruz* (1954), *Man of the West* (1958), and *The Hanging Tree* (1959). He made some other fine films in the latter 1950s, though few of them turned a profit. The most satisfying was the story of a May/December romance, *Love in the Afternoon* (1957), in which Cooper falls in love with Audrey Hepburn *(q.v.)*. His last film was *The Naked Edge* (1961), in which Deborah Kerr, as his wife, believes his character to be a murderer.

Gary Cooper died of cancer at the relatively youthful age of sixty, and his reputation as an actor has not diminished since. He made an extraordinary number of fine films, and it is no wonder that he was among the top ten draws during nineteen of the twenty-two years between 1936 and 1957. Knowing that he was ill, the Academy of Motion Picture Arts and Sciences properly honored him with a special Oscar in 1960.
See also: westerns

COOPER, JACKIE *See* child actors.

COOPER, MERIAN C. (1893–1973)   Best known as the cowriter, codirector, and coproducer, with Ernest B. Schoedsack, of the classic monster film *King Kong* (1933), he was also a documentary filmmaker of note in the

1920s, as well as a successful producer, particularly in association with John Ford *(q.v.)*.

An adventurer from his youth, Cooper was one among the small coterie of combat pilots during World War I. Later he began making several successful documentaries with his partner, Ernest B. Schoedsack, that explored the exotic worlds of the Far East. The most famous of the documentaries were *Grass* (1925) and *Chang* (1927). He made the transition to Hollywood drama when he coproduced, codirected, and cophotographed the first of three versions of *The Four Feathers* (1929).

Except for *The Four Feathers* and *King Kong,* Cooper's years in Hollywood were spent as a producer. In the 1930s, he worked at RKO before joining Selznick International Pictures in 1936. Among the films he produced during the 1930s were *Son of Kong* (1933), *Little Women* (1933), *Flying Down to Rio* (1933), *The Lost Patrol* (1934), and *The Toy Wife* (1938).

Cooper went off to fight again, in World War II, distinguishing himself in the Army Air Corps, in the Far East where he served as chief of staff to General Claire Chennault and his Flying Tigers. After the war, Cooper formed Argosy Pictures with John Ford. Acting as Ford's coproducer, Cooper was associated with some of the director's best films of the late 1940s and the 1950s, including *Fort Apache* (1948), *She Wore a Yellow Ribbon* (1949), *The Quiet Man* (1952), and *The Searchers* (1956).

It was during this period, though, that Cooper also relived his past by producing another monster movie, *Mighty Joe Young* (1949), a rather tame and pleasantly silly rip-off of *King Kong.* Then Cooper changed directions, showing his adventurous spirit yet again when he lunged into the future by producing the visually overwhelming *This Is Cinerama* (1952).

Both in consideration for his past and his immediate achievements, the Academy of Motion Picture Arts and Sciences honored him that same year with a special Oscar "for his many innovations and contributions to the art of motion pictures."
See also: monster films

COPPOLA, FRANCIS FORD (1939–   )   The first successful director to come out of a film school, he spearheaded a talent renaissance in Hollywood, the results of which are very much with us today.

Coppola, originally known as Francis Ford Coppola before he temporarily dropped the middle name (he came to the conclusion that nobody trusts a man with three names), immersed himself in both the theater and in film, eventually enrolling in UCLA's graduate film program. Like so many others, Coppola (while still at UCLA) worked for Roger Corman *(q.v.)* and received slave-labor wages along with invaluable experience. It was thanks to Corman that Coppola had the chance to make his first film, a "B" movie quickie called *Dementia 13* (1962).

Coppola quit UCLA when he was offered a job for $300 a week to write screenplays. He penned eleven, many of which were never made; one that did make the cut, however, was *Patton* (1970).

While writing screenplays, Coppola fought for the opportunity to direct, and finally had his chance with one of his own works, *You're a Big Boy Now* (1966). The film was a modest success, and it led to his opportunity to direct *Finian's Rainbow* (1968), with Fred Astaire *(q.v.)*. It was Astaire's last musical, and unfortunately for both the famed dancer and the director, the movie was not a commercial success.

Coppola was buoyed by his Best Screenplay Oscar for *Patton* a couple of years later, but it wasn't until *The Godfather* (1972) that the young director became a major force in the industry. Cited by critics for its superb direction, the film became a monster hit, winning an Academy Award for Best Picture and giving Coppola the clout to make a small, personal movie that many consider to be his best, *The Conversation* (1974), starring Gene Hackman. The film is a detailed, incisive character study of a professional wiretapper who overhears too much.

Coppola's next film was *The Godfather, Part II*, and it surprised everyone by being an even richer, more complex film than its predecessor. The film was almost as big a commercial hit as the original, and Coppola was at the height of his Hollywood power.

Unlike many who made it to the top, though, Coppola was more than willing to share his success. From the very beginning, he helped fellow film students such as George Lucas and John Milius *(qq.v.)* reach their own potential. For instance, it was Coppola who produced Lucas' first film, *THX-1138* (1971). He also produced Lucas' breakout film, *American Graffiti* (1973).

Film school graduates could be emboldened by Coppola's trail of box office success combined with personal vision, and the director was an inspirational "godfather" to a new generation of directors, including Martin Scorsese, Brian de Palma, and Steven Spielberg *(qq.v.)*.

Setting Coppola apart from most other directors was his ambition. Wanting to be more than just a filmmaker, he displayed something of the old-style movie mogul in his makeup. He founded several film companies, including Zoetrope Studios, and invested in a distribution network, but his business efforts were thwarted by his notable creative excesses, the first of which was *Apocolypse Now* (1979), starring Marlon Brando *(q.v.)* and Martin Sheen. A landmark movie about the Vietnam War, based on Joseph Conrad's *Heart of Darkness*, the film was shot in the Philippines under horrendous conditions. Typhoons and Martin Sheen's nearly fatal heart attack caused massive delays and the

film nearly bankrupted Coppola. Good reviews and reasonably good box office saved him.

Then came *One From the Heart* (1982), a simple love story set in Las Vegas. Coppola chose to recreate the Nevada gambling city and drove the cost of the film through the roof. The film bombed, despite some positive critical attention, and Coppola was on the ropes.

His big comeback movie was supposed to be *The Cotton Club* (1984), a $30 million musical extravaganza. While the movie was visually stunning, that wasn't enough for either critics or audiences. Nonetheless, Coppola has proved to be a Hollywood survivor. Following Roger Corman's example, Coppola has continued to back young filmmakers, producing and distributing films, and making a handsome profit at it. After a period of relative inactivity (during which time he directed the DisneyWorld 3-D spectacular, *Captain EO*, starring Michael Jackson), he made the less than momentous *Gardens of Stone* (1987). He followed this, however, with a powerhouse production of *Tucker: The Man and His Dream* (1988), a film that received high praise, if only modest box office success. The movie, a true story about a visionary car manufacturer driven out of business by the automotive establishment, was a deeply personal film. It parelleled Coppola's own fight against the Hollywood power structure and was richer for the resonance.

Regardless of the direction of Coppola's future career, it is already quite clear that his influence on the filmmakers of the 1970s and 1980s has been monumental. *See also: American Graffiti*; Arzner, Dorothy; *The Godfather I & II*

CORMAN, ROGER (1926–) A producer-director whose influence on American film goes far beyond his own energetic, creative low-budget exploitation movies of the 1950s and 1960s, most of which were made for American International Pictures, a very successful studio that happily pandered to the youth market. Corman churned out movies at an incredible rate, sometimes shooting his feature-length films in two or three days, yet a surprising number of his movies are enormously fun to watch. He gained his greatest fame as a director for his series of Edgar Allen Poe horror movies during the early 1960s, many of them starring Vincent Price. Though Corman is closely linked with his Poe horror cycle, he worked in a variety of genres with equal ease and style, including science fiction, gangster melodramas, and biker movies. But Corman's most lasting legacy will likely be the legion of modern-day directors, writers, and stars whose careers he actively fostered, among them Jonathan Demme, Peter Bogdanovich *(q.v.)*, Martin Scorsese *(q.v.)*, Jack Nicholson *(q.v.)*, Peter Fonda, Ron Howard *(q.v.)*, John Sayles *(q.v.)*, and Francis Ford Coppola *(q.v.)*.

Corman is anything but the vulgar figure one might

expect from the titles of some of his early movies, such as *Teenage Doll* (1957) and *A Bucket of Blood* (1959). He graduated from Stanford with a degree in engineering and also studied English literature at Oxford. After serving in the Navy, he followed the traditional route to entering the movie business, getting a job as a messenger at Twentieth Century-Fox. He succeeded in being promoted to story analyst. But soon he became dissatisfied with his prospects and eventually joined the newly formed American International Pictures in 1955, becoming its principal director with such films as *Five Guns West* (1955), *The Day the World Ended* (1956), and *Swamp Women* (1956).

Despite the fact that his films regularly turned up in drive-ins and on the second half of 42nd Street double bills, some of his early efforts gained a modest measure of respect from iconoclastic critics. Minor classics such as *Machine Gun Kelly* (1958) and *The Little Shop of Horrors* (1960) presaged the popular and critical applause for Corman's stylish Poe horror films, *The Pit and the Pendulum* (1961), *Tales of Terror* (1962), *The Raven* (1963), *The Masque of the Red Death* (1964), and *The Tomb of Ligea* (1964).

The success of the Poe cycle allowed Corman to work with relatively larger budgets. Though he was still making "B" movies, there were higher production values to such late Corman classics as *"X" the Man with the X-Ray Eyes* (1963), *The Wild Angels* (1966), *The St. Valentine's Day Massacre* (1967), and *The Trip* (1967).

Corman not only directed but produced a great many movies throughout his entire career. As a producer he offered the opportunity to direct to eager if untried talents, giving them invaluable experience that the big studios would never have offered. For instance, among others, he produced Francis Ford Coppola's *Dementia 13* (1963), Peter Bogdonavich's *Targets* (1968), Martin Scorsese's *Boxcar Bertha* (1972), and Ron Howard's *Eat My Dust* (1976).

Corman's reputation for low-brow exploitation films was dealt a serious, if consciously ironic, blow in the early 1970s when he unofficially retired from directing to become an importer/distributor of many of Europe's most esoteric films, among them Ingmar Bergman's *Cries and Whispers* (1972). He continues to produce and distribute through his own company, New World Pictures, and has returned to the director's chair with the upcoming *Frankenstein Unbound* (1990).
See also: American International Pictures; Price, Vincent

COSTUME DESIGNER Unlike his work for the theater, a costume designer for the movies must consider how certain fabrics and colors will photograph. The costume designer, who reports to the director, will usually go to work as soon as he's given the script. Fitting the actors will come long after choosing the proper clothing. Working with the art director, the costume designer will make sure that the clothes under consideration won't clash with the colors of the set.

While the costume designer either creates or chooses the patterns for the actors' clothing, he doesn't make the clothes himself. In the 1930s and 1940s, the studios had dressmakers and seamstresses on staff to do the necessary sewing and stitching, but in recent decades this work has traditionally been hired out. The costumer (not to be confused with the costume designer) is responsible for the care and upkeep of the clothing during the shoot.

It may seem obvious that the costume consists strictly of clothing, but the difference between the responsibilities of the costume designer and the propmaster often appear to overlap. For instance, in a western the gunbelt is considered part of the costume, but the gun that goes in the gunbelt is considered a prop.

When costumes for the extras are needed, they are often rented by the costume designer rather than made. If there is a contemporary crowd scene, it is up to the costume designer to instruct the extras in advance as to how they must dress from their own wardrobe (e.g., for a winter scene, they must bring their own overcoats, hats, etc.).

While famous couturiers have often designed the clothing of individual stars in films (e.g., Givenchy for Audrey Hepburn), they are not necessarily responsible for clothing the entire cast.

Examples of some of the more celebrated costume designers for the movies are Edith Head, Adrian, and Orry-Kelly.
See also: Head, Edith

COSTUMER Not to be confused with the costume designer *(q.v.)*, the costumer is responsible for clothing that has already been bought, made, or rented for the cast.

Originally known by the title of wardrobe mistress or wardrobe master, the costumer not only controls access to the costumes, he and/or she also helps the stars dress for their scenes.

COURTROOM DRAMAS Like the movie musical, courtroom films came of age in Hollywood with the coming of sound. Extremely dependent on dialogue, these films became a minor genre in the late 1920s and early 1930s when a number of courtroom dramas from the stage were bought by Hollywood studios and filmed with gratifying results. But even movies such as William Wyler's *(q.v.)* adaptation of Elmer Rice's *Counsellor-at-Law* (1933), the noble rendering of *The Life of Emile Zola* (1937), and the hard-hitting *Marked Woman* (1937) spent relatively little screen time in a courtroom. Filmmakers recognized that high drama was possible in a courtroom setting but they were reluctant to film an entire feature film on essentially one set. In addition, courtroom dramas were best suited to the portrayal of social and political conflict, and the film industry was anything but adventurous in these areas. It wasn't until the rise of the independent producer in the postwar era that movies with direct political and social implications began to be made.

Beginning in the latter 1940s and continuing through the early 1960s, the courtroom drama had a golden age as America struggled with its values. Movies such as *Force of Evil* (1948) signalled the change, with the judicial system becoming both a plot device and a symbol of the battle between right and wrong. Films in the mode of *Knock on Any Door* (1949) and *I Want to Live* (1958) used the courtroom as a means of making points about societal injustice. Issues of military duty and preparedness were considered in the celluloid courtrooms of *The Caine Mutiny* (1954) and *The Court Martial of Billy Mitchell* (1955). The judicial system itself became the subject matter in courtroom films such as *Beyond a Reasonable Doubt* (1956) and *Twelve Angry Men* (1957).

The biggest explosion of courtroom dramas in film history came in the late 1950s and early 1960s, kicked off with the hugely successful *Witness for the Prosecution* (1958). It was followed by yet another major hit in the category, *Anatomy of a Murder* (1959), after which the doors opened wider for a rush of courtroom films, including the more controversial movies *Compulsion* (1959), *Inherit the Wind* (1960), and *Judgment at Nuremberg* (1961).

The courtroom drama went into eclipse in the later 1960s as government institutions came under attack during the Vietnam War era. But again, in the late 1970s, the courtroom became a place where moral, political, and societal issues could be investigated dramatically. With movies like . . . *And Justice for All* (1979) and *The Verdict* (1982) leading the way, the trend for courtroom dramas continued throughout the rest of the 1980s with the added element of love stories in films such as *Jagged Edge* (1985) and *Suspect* (1987).

COVERAGE   The additional shots of a scene taken at the initial time of filming from several different angles or points of view in order to make sure that when the scene is finally edited there will be at least one viable shot (or a combination of shots) with which the editor can work. It can be very expensive to rebuild or recreate the set and reshoot a scene from scratch if it must be done over again, hence the need to ensure all the potentially necessary footage by providing coverage.

It should be noted, however, that directors like the late Alfred Hitchcock *(q.v.)*, who meticulously plan their shots before the cameras begin rolling never require coverage. Directors who improvise on the set, however, almost always require coverage.

CRABBE, "BUSTER" (1907–1983)   He was an action star who achieved enduring fame in 1930s serials as Flash Gordon and, later, Buck Rogers. In addition to his many serials, which appealed to young filmgoers, Crabbe also starred in low-budget features in a career that lasted more than thirty years.

Born Clarence Lindon Crabbe, the good-looking young man followed in the footsteps (or swimming trunks) of Johnny Weismuller *(q.v.)*, representing the United States in the 1932 Olympic Games and winning a gold medal in the 400-meter freestyle swimming competition. While never as famous as Weismuller either as a swimmer or actor, Crabbe did play Tarzan in his first starring role in *King of the Jungle* (1933), a low-budget quickie designed to take advantage of Weismuller's hit film *Tarzan the Ape Man* (1932).

Unlike Weismuller, Crabbe played a wide variety of action roles, starring in westerns, such as *Desert Gold* (1936), and sports movies, such as *Hold 'Em Yale* (1935) in addition to science fiction serials. His feature film appearances do not trigger the same feeling of nostalgia as his serials, which are simple and innocent (and admittedly silly).

Crabbe starred in serials throughout the 1930s, 1940s, and even into the early 1950s, until his film career began to sputter. He then became famous to a new generation of young viewers in his TV series "Captain Gallant of the French Foreign Legion." Like Johnny Weismuller and Esther Williams *(q.v.)*, Crabbe became associated with a swimming pool company in his later years.

Buster Crabbe's last film was *Arizona Raiders* (1965), in which he played a supporting role.
See also: serials; Tarzan films

CRANE SHOT   Footage filmed using a mobile unit that lifts a camera and a crew of three (the director, camera operator, and camera assistant) above the set for a high-angle shot. A crane can be used to photograph a scene in a long, fluid, multiangled method without any cuts (hence, the crane's nickname "whirly").

One of the most famous and elaborate of crane shots was devised by Orson Welles *(q.v.)* for his film *Touch of Evil* (1958). The shot lasts nearly five minutes as the camera swoops up above a car after a bomb has been placed inside of it. Then, as the car winds its way through a crowded southwestern border town, the camera follows it in one single take from a variety of heights and angles until, several blocks later, the car finally blows up. In their infinite wisdom, the producers decided to put the opening credits over this remarkable bit of filmmaking which, legend has it, nearly exhausted the movie's entire budget.

CRAWFORD, BRODERICK (1910–1986)   Though he acted in more than sixty films in a movie career that lasted well past forty years, even a die-hard movie buff would be hard-pressed to name more than a handful of films in which he appeared. Crawford was a superior actor, but with his burly body, gravelly voice, and mean-looking mug, he spent most of his time on screen playing villains in minor movies. Yet for one brief period, during 1949 and 1950, Crawford was the toast of Hollywood, with two wonderful roles, one of which brought him an Oscar for Best Actor.

Born William Broderick Crawford, he was the son of vaudeville stars Lester (Robert) Crawford and Helen Broderick. His mother became a much-admired co-medienne who played tart-tongued supporting parts in the movies, most memorably in the Fred Astaire/Ginger Rogers *(qq.v.)* musicals *Top Hat* (1935) and *Swing Time* (1936). Helen's son wasted no time getting into show business, making his stage debut in London at the age of 21. He made it to Broadway a few years later, making his mark on the New York stage in 1937 as Lennie in the classic production of John Steinbeck's *Of Mice and Men.*

About this time he began appearing in minor roles as a Neanderthal tough guy in such films as *Woman Chases Man* (1937), *Beau Geste* (1939), and *When the Daltons Rode* (1940). It seemed his genuine talent would forever be kept a secret from film audiences until Robert Rossen *(q.v.)* cast him as the political demagogue Willie Stark in a sizzling adaptation of Robert Penn Warren's *All The King's Men* (1949). The film was a hit, winning the Academy Award for Best Picture, as well as an Oscar for Crawford for Best Actor.

The following year he had the choice role of the millionaire junk dealer (modeled on Columbia Pictures president, Harry Cohn, *q.v.*) in the film adaptation of the Broadway play *Born Yesterday* (1950). It was another hit, but Crawford's movie career began to slide downhill thereafter.

While he no longer had to play the third thug from the left, Crawford was rarely asked to carry a movie. Generally, he was cast in supporting roles, either playing a heavy or a rough-edged lawman. Throughout the second half of the 1950s and most of the 1960s, he acted as often in foreign films as he did Hollywood projects. Most of the European films were as bad as his American movies, although he gave a sterling performance in the early Fellini art-house hit *Il Bidone* (1955).

Crawford's fame during the rest of his career came more from television than movies. He is fondly remembered by baby boomers for his 1950s TV series, "Highway Patrol" (1955–58). He continued to act in movies and TV virtually up to the end of his life, playing in such low-budget bombs as *Terror in the Wax Museum* (1973) and *The Private Files of J. Edgar Hoover* (1977). Yet, despite a virtual lifetime of minor roles in poor movies, he was so well known to film audiences that he was cast as himself in a cameo appearance in the charming George Roy Hill *(q.v.)* film *A Little Romance* (1979).

CRAWFORD, JOAN (1906–1977) There was hardly a less well-liked actress in Hollywood than Joan Craw-

Joan Crawford reportedly loved to be photographed. Unlike many stars, she understood the value of publicity and happily posed for glamour shots such as the one reproduced here. Photo courtesy of The Siegel Collection.

ford. Everyone from Bette Davis *(q.v.)* to George Cukor *(q.v.,* not to mention her adopted daughter Christina) had their problems with her. But never was there such a durable star as Crawford—the only actress to leave the silent era a star and continue with top billing for another forty years. She managed that remarkable feat while being neither a particularly gifted actress nor starring in a great number of excellent movies. In fact, out of eighty motion pictures in which she appeared, barely a dozen have withstood the test of time, and many of them continue to be regarded for reasons other than Crawford's performances.

The actress reached the Hollywood heights primarily because she learned to play one role to perfection: the ruthless girl/working woman from the wrong side of the tracks who would stop at nothing to reach the top. It was a role she played with almost infinite variations. The formula called for her ultimately to appear in gorgeous gowns in every picture, inevitably moving from low life to high life by the last reel. It was every working girl's fantasy, and Crawford had a strong appeal to female fans who flocked to her movies in remarkable numbers, especially in the early to mid-1930s and then again in the latter 1940s, the two eras of her greatest success.

Born Lucille le Sueur, the future actress lived the life that she would later portray so often on the screen. She was poor and ambitious. After working as a waitress and a store clerk, she entered show business by winning a Charleston contest, which eventually led to a job as a chorus girl. She was still a chorus girl three years later, albeit on Broadway, when she was spotted by an MGM bigwig, Harry Rapf.

Under the name Billie Cassin, the nineteen-year-old would-be actress appeared in her first film, *Pretty Ladies* (1925). However, she was still in the chorus. Even though she moved up to an ingenue role in *Old Clothes* that same year, it wasn't until MGM sponsored a fan magazine contest to rename their new star—thus "Joan Crawford"—that her career began to take off.

She was given plenty of work but Crawford didn't break out of the pack as a genuine star until 1928 when she literally stole the script for *Our Dancing Daughters* from the story department and then pigeon-holed the film's producer, insisting that she be given the role of the wild flapper heroine. The movie was a huge success and she was finally a bona fide MGM leading lady.

She became so popular that her silent film *Our Modern Maidens* (1929) did big box office even as the talkie craze took over. She made her talkie debut singing and dancing in *Hollywood Revue of 1929*.

In 1931 she starred for the first of many times with Clark Gable in *Dance Fools Dance*. That film, like almost everything else she starred in until 1937, was a hit. Yet of all her films of that period, only *Grand Hotel* (1932) continues to be remembered: and that was an all-star film boasting stars of the magnitude of Greta Garbo, John and Lionel Barrymore, and Wallace Beery *(qq.v.)*. Nonetheless, Crawford gave a vivid performance in the movie, once again playing a poor girl trying to make her way in the world.

When her career stumbled, Crawford (like Katharine Hepburn) was labeled box office poison by theater owners in 1938. It looked as if they were right when she starred in several big flops in a row. She halted the slide with *The Women* in 1939, but she made just two more hits during the next five years, and MGM dropped her.

It appeared as if Crawford's long career had finally come to an end. But as it turned out, she had only reached its midpoint. Warner Bros. signed her up and Crawford proceeded to make her most memorable pictures, all of them in just a five-year span.

Her career-woman phase began with *Mildred Pierce* (1945), a script she sought out after Bette Davis turned it down. The title role brought her an Oscar for Best Actress, and her career was suddenly back in gear. The evidence of her popularity was clear when the big shoulder pads she wore in *Mildred Pierce* became a fashion staple.

Crawford's next films were *Humoresque* (1946), *Possessed* (1947), *Daisy Kenyon* (1947), and *Flamingo Road* (1949), all of them hits. As a group, these five Warner films undoubtedly represent her best work.

The 1950s weren't kind to Crawford. She returned to MGM briefly for (incredibly) her first color film, *Torch Song* (1953). In retrospect, it seems clear that Crawford's face, with its angles and big, deep eyes was made for black and white.

Except for *Sudden Fear* (1952), *Johnny Guitar* (1954), and *Autumn Leaves* (1956) Crawford's films were either poor or poorly received. She was aging and there weren't many starring roles for fading great ladies—until Robert Aldrich made *Whatever Happened to Baby Jane?* in 1962.

Cast with Bette Davis, the two old warhorses were a sight to see, and people did, indeed, come to see them. The movie was a surprise hit, but much to Crawford's dismay, Bette Davis was nominated for an Oscar. According to Davis, Crawford campaigned actively against her.

During the 1960s Crawford starred in all sorts of horror films, such as *Straightjacket* (1964) and *Berserk* (1967). Her final film was *Trog* (1970).
See also: *Grand Hotel*

CRITICS Some so-called critics simply recount the plot of a movie and announce whether or not they can recommend the film to others, while others try to enlighten potential viewers to the relative qualities of the film. The former are reviewers, the latter are the only ones who deserve the title of critic. Most critics have not had any filmmaking experience, but there are some notable exceptions, among them James Agee *(q.v.)*, Peter Bogdanovich *(q.v.)*, Roger Ebert, Pauline Kael, Frank S. Nugent *(q.v.)*, Paul Shrader *(q.v.)*, and Paul Zimmerman.

There have been many thoughtful American critics who have written about the Hollywood film, among them Otis Ferguson, Robert E. Sherwood, and Dwight Macdonald. These, and others, had a fair degree of influence among intellectuals during the 1930s and 1940s. But it wasn't until James Agee began writing about film in *The Nation* and *Time* during the 1940s that film criticism finally became a respectable occupation for serious-minded people.

After Agee, critics began writing about film with the same rigorous discipline reserved for the other arts. For instance, Robert Warshow began writing about the movies from a sociological point of view, Parker Tyler from a psychological perspective, and Stanley Kauffmann from an aesthetic viewpoint. And Andrew Sarris, a critic for *The Village Voice* helped to define and popularize the *auteur (q.v.)* theory, and probably had more influence on American film criticism than any other critic before or since.

From where the filmmaker stands, the most important critic has always been the one who has the power to shape the opinion of the opinion-makers—and that has almost always meant the critic of *The New York Times.* That powerful newspaper's long-term film critics Bosley Crother and Vincent Canby have wielded enormous influence over the movie industry. As is often said, however, critics have little power to make or break mass audience pleasers of the likes of *Gone With the Wind* (1939) or *Crocodile Dundee II* (1988), but they have the ability to sometimes turn marginally marketed films into hits or flops (certainly Pauline Kael has almost singelhandedly turned several films into art-circuit hits). In addition, when a number of critics praise an actor or director associated with a commercial disaster, that individual has gained a valuable currency among Hollywood producers.

In the last thirty years, film critics have become increasingly important to both the industry and to the audience as the movies and the people who watch them have become far more educated and sophisticated. Critics such as Judith Crist, Rex Reed, and others, have held great sway because they reach so many people through their often syndicated reviews in hundreds of markets. In recent years, though, critics, led by Gene Siskel and Roger Ebert, have taken to television and have had an impact literally from coast to coast. Other critics, such as Jeffrey Lyons, Michael Medved and Richard Brown, have taken to the airwaves, but Siskel and Ebert are clearly the best and the most influential at this new brand of film criticism.

CROSBY, BING (1901–1977) He was arguably the most popular entertainer of the 1930s and 1940s, and his long film career reflected the great affection in which he was held by millions of fans. Blessed with a velvet baritone and an easy, affable manner, the term "crooning" seemed invented for Crosby. Though he was hardly a handsome man with his plain face and "Dumbo" ears, he was so comfortable and natural on film that his looks never seemed to matter. Most of the time he even got the girl. Though he was the leading recording artist of his era, selling more than 30 million records, he was also one of Hollywood's most potent box office attractions, appearing in more than sixty films (most of them as a star) and winning one Oscar for Best Actor. Crosby's fortés were musicals and light comedies, but he also occasionally scored in dramatic roles.

Born Harry Lillis Crosby in Tacoma, Washington, he later took the stage name of Bing from a comic strip character. After a stint at Gonzaga University, Crosby pursued his singing career, joining up with Al Rinker in 1921. They referred to themselves as "Two Boys and a Piano—Singing Songs Their Own Way." Later, he joined the Paul Whiteman Band and became one of "Paul Whiteman's Rhythm Boys." He had already begun recording as a solo act but he was by no means a big star during the 1920s. His modest success as a recording artist, however, did lead to roles in a number of short subjects during the early sound era.

His first feature film appearance was in *King of Jazz* (1930), but it was nothing to write home about; he was merely one of the Rhythm Boys. A few other minor film appearances followed that year, but the big breakthrough for Crosby came not in films but in radio. He was tapped for his own program and it was an immediate sensation. His record sales zoomed and suddenly he was a hot property.

Hollywood pounced on him in much the same way it would later pursue Frank Sinatra and Elvis Presely *(qq.v.).* He was signed by Paramount, the studio with which he has always been most closely associated, and immediately embarked on his new career as a movie star. During the 1930s he mostly made light musicals, although many of them might better be described as light comedies with music. Crosby usually sang approximately four songs in these thinly plotted vehicles, helped along by strong comic supporting players such as Burns & Allen and Jack Oakie *(qq.v.).* These films were consistently popular if rarely memorable. Among the best of them were the all-star *The Big Broadcast* (1932), the utterly charming and often hysterical *We're Not Dressing* (1934), *Mississippi* (1935), *The Big Broadcast of 1936* (1935), Cole Porter's *Anything Goes* (1935), *Pennies From Heaven* (1936), and *Doctor Rhythm* (1938).

Crosby's career went into overdrive during the 1940s when he teamed with Bob Hope and Dorothy Lamour for their first Road picture, *The Road to Singapore* (1940). The vehicle was originally intended for Fred MacMurray and George Burns, but MacMurray backed out. Hope and Crosby seemed like a more suitable duo and the film was a surprise blockbuster thanks to the perfect chemistry of the two stars. They clearly had fun making the movie and their good cheer, irreverence, and obvious ad-libbing made audiences feel as if they were all in on the joke. Six more Road pictures followed during the next twenty-two years, all of them hits.

If Crosby had been popular before, the combination of the Road movies, plus his more ambitious, bigger-budget hits of the 1940s, kept him in the top ten of male box office performers throughout the decade, often in the number-one slot. Then he made the first of what may have become his most beloved classics, *Holiday Inn* (1942), introducing his trademark hit song, "White Christmas," the most popular recording in music business history. Not long after, he continued in the same vein when he starred as a priest in Leo

McCarey's *(q.v.) Going My Way,* winning his only Best Actor Academy Award in the bargain. The movie was a monster hit, leading to an even bigger smash sequel, *The Bells of St. Mary's* (1945). Crosby, playing the same role, was nominated yet again for an Oscar, but didn't win. Thanks to Crosby, aided and abetted by Ingrid Bergman and director McCarey, *The Bells of St. Mary's* became one of the few sequels in Hollywood history to do better box office than its predecessor. At this point in time, Crosby was at the top of his career, a role model of warmth, decency, and puckish good humor.

Among Crosby's films during the second half of the 1940s were *Blue Skies* (1946), *The Emperor Waltz* (1948), and *A Connecticut Yankee in King Arthur's Court* (1949). The last of these films was rather charming but after nearly twenty years audiences were beginning to cool to him. Sinatra was the hot young singer, but Crosby was still a formidable force in the right vehicles; the Road pictures usually came along when he needed a lift and there were several other solid, if unspectacular, entries during the early 1950s, the best of them, *Riding High* (1950), *Here Comes the Groom* (1951), and *Little Boy Lost* (1953).

Then came one of his biggest hits of the 1950s, *White Christmas* (1954). It might have been his last hurrah, but he surprised audiences when, in a striking bit of casting, he played an alcoholic former entertainer in the film version of Clifford Odets's *The Country Girl* (1954). Having to portray an essentially unlikeable pathetic character, he tackled a far more demanding role than any other he had played. He showed enormous range and great courage in the part, winning a much-deserved Oscar nomination for his performance. Grace Kelly *(q.v.),* his costar in the film, won an Oscar, and she joined him, along with Sinatra, in the musical version of *The Philadelphia Story,* titled *High Society* (1956). It was another hit, but Crosby's last major success.

He made several films during the rest of the 1950s, but none of them were particularly distinguished. His last "Road" picture with Hope and Lamour *(q.v.), Road to Hong Kong* (1962), was amusing, but it was a weak sister to its six older brothers. He rarely appeared in movies during the rest of the 1960s, although in a small role he nearly stole *Robin and the Seven Hoods* (1964) from Sinatra and the rest of the Rat Pack *(q.v.).* His last film was the ill-conceived remake of *Stagecoach* (1966), in which he played the part of the drunken doctor.

Throughout the 1960s and right up until his death, Crosby continued to appear in TV specials. He was reportedly one of Hollywood's wealthiest individuals, amassing a fortune estimated at well over $200 million. Like his old friend Bob Hope, he was an avid golfer, and it was on the golf course that he finally died of a heart attack.

See also: singer-actors; Hope, Bob

CRUISE, TOM (1962–) A handsome young actor with a devastating smile, he has become one of the hottest stars of the late 1980s. A combination of boyish charm and sexuality makes him particularly popular with women, and his cool, macho style has also given him a sizeable male audience.

Born Thomas Cruise Mapoother IV, he was the third of four children of what became a broken home when he was eleven years old. His mother, an amateur actress, held the family together for five years before she finally remarried.

Cruise was initially a poor student due to dyslexia. To compensate for his poor showing in class, he was active in sports. Having suffered an injury while in high school and not knowing what to do with his time while he recuperated, he was talked into auditioning for his high school production of *Guys and Dolls.* Cast as Nathan Detroit in the musical, he was immediately hooked on acting.

He kicked around New York, taking any work he could get in order to hone his raw talent until he got a small part in *Endless Love* (1981). He was given a small role that same year in *Taps,* but he was so powerful that the early footage was scrapped and he was given another, bigger part. It was his first important film.

1983 proved to be a banner year for Cruise, who appeared in four films; three of which, however, went nowhere—*All the Right Moves, Losin' It,* and *The Out-*

Tom Cruise has become one of the rising superstars of the late 1980s. Intense, with striking good looks and a smile that could light up Los Angeles (and has), Cruise has consistently picked provocative and (usually) commercial projects in which to star. He is seen here in *Cocktail* (1988). Photo by Rob McEwan, © 1988 Touchstone Pictures.

siders. His fourth film, *Risky Business,* was the sleeper hit of the year, and featured his famous unabashed dance number in his underwear.

Seeming to disappear after his initial success, he surfaced again in 1986, starring in the $30 million fantasy movie *Legend*—a movie that became a monumental bust at the box office. Had he not already filmed what became that year's biggest grossing movie, *Top Gun,* Cruise's career might have been severely crippled. Instead, the actor emerged as a major movie star with the clout that accompanies a $150 million grossing film.

Cruise capitalized on his success by costarring with Paul Newman in *The Color of Money* (1987), playing a young pool player with talent to burn but who needs to learn self-control. It was a formula that recalled *Top Gun,* and was repeated in *Cocktail* (1988), this time with Cruise learning the ropes from an older, more experienced bartender played by Bryan Brown. Cruise continued to share top billing with older stars, giving what many consider to be his best performance to date as Dustin Hoffman's brother in the Oscar-winning hit *Rain Man* (1988).

CUKOR, GEORGE (1899–1983) He began directing in 1930 and amassed a remarkable string of hit movies over a career of nearly fifty years.

Often called a "woman's director" because he elicited top notch performances from many of Hollywood's most famous actresses, Cukor was a sensitive filmmaker who simply understood women in an industry that lacked female directors. It is no wonder, then, that once he demonstrated his ability to work with strong actresses, he was usually the first to be called upon to direct them.

The actresses whose careers he influenced are legion. Prominent among them are Katharine Hepburn *(q.v.),* whom he introduced to movie audiences in *A Bill of Divorcement* (1932) and later redeemed from "box office poison" status with *The Philadelphia Story* (1940). Along the way he directed her in some of her best movies, just a few of which include *Sylvia Scarlett* (1935), *Holiday* (1938), *Adam's Rib* (1949), and *Pat and Mike* (1952).

It is perhaps with Katharine Hepburn that Cukor is most closely associated, but he also directed a number of other actresses in some of their best roles, including Greta Garbo *(q.v.)* in *Camille* (1937), Ingrid Bergman *(q.v.)* in *Gaslight* (1944), Judy Holliday *(q.v.)* in *Born Yesterday* (1950), Jean Simmons *(q.v.)* in *The Actress* (1952), Judy Garland *(q.v.)* in *A Star Is Born* (1954), Ava Gardner *(q.v.)* in *Bhowani Junction* (1956), and Audrey Hepburn *(q.v.)* in *My Fair Lady* (1964).

In addition to his reputation as a woman's director, Cukor is also known as Hollywood's most successful adaptor of books and plays to the screen. From *Dinner at Eight* (1933) to *Travels With My Aunt* (1972), he demonstrated his ability to capture the essence of his sources without being slavishly devoted to the original material.

Above all else, Cukor's movies are about imagination. The characters—both male and female—who people his best films are generally vulnerable souls caught up in their own rendition of the truth. It is a theme that he always handled with touching grace, sympathy, and style.

CULT MOVIES These are films that are ignored by mass audiences upon their initial release but later rediscovered and given a new critical and commercial life by a small and underground audience. Generally movies acquire cult followings in two ways: the first involves the efforts of a small number of film fans who, through word of mouth, build a new following for a picture; the second relies upon critics and/or film scholars who find an overlooked movie and write about it, drawing attention to the movie so that audiences can rediscover its merits.

Surprisingly, many of Hollywood's most beloved movies were panned by reviewers upon their release and shunned by audiences. Two classic examples are Ernst Lubitsch's *(q.v.)* black comedy *To Be or Not to Be* (1942) and the now universally loved Christmas movie, *It's a Wonderful Life* (1946) by Frank Capra *(q.v.).* Both films had a coterie of fans who refused to let the movies disappear, screening them at revival movie theaters and on college campuses until TV stations got wind of the films' popularity and began broadcasting them more regularly. The Lubitsch film was even remade by Mel Brooks *(q.v.)* in 1983. Capra's movie was not only remade as an unfortunate TV film with Marlo Thomas in the Jimmy Stewart *(q.v.)* role, it has become (in its original version) a staple of the Christmas season, shown several times every year on TV.

Films ignored or dismissed by one generation of moviegoers or critics may benefit from reappraisal by another generation with different aesthetic standards. Thus some cinematic treasures that once were overlooked are resurrected. Low-budget movies are the ones most likely to be rediscovered as they are released with the least fanfare. For example, a stylish little film called *Gun Crazy* (1949) by Joseph H. Lewis *(q.v.)* was resurrected by film critics and scholars, as was the brilliant Sam Fuller *(q.v.)* film *Shock Corridor* (1963).

Overlooked movies don't always become cult favorites because of their quality; sometimes a film simply possesses a novelty factor. For instance, Alfred Hitchcock's *Rope* (1948) has acquired a cult following because of its imaginative cinematography. It was shot in such a way as to hide any and all edits, the story taking place in supposed real time. Another cult favorite is Robert Montgomery's *Lady in the Lake* (1946), which is shot entirely in subjective camera.

Other films have become cult classics on the midnight

show circuit of art houses, eventually becoming underground hits. Such was the case of George Romero's horror classic *Night of the Living Dead* (1968), a film shot in Pittsburgh without any stars, and *The Rocky Horror Picture Show* (1975), a film that is probably the most famous midnight show/cult favorite of all time. Watching the latter film, audiences usually mimic the action on the screen, en masse, creating a unique theatrical experience.

Many cult movies become so famous that they eventually lose their cult movie status. Certainly, *It's a Wonderful Life* falls into this category. Other movies, however, are still known only to a relative few and they continue to remain underground cult favorites. One of the best examples of this is the little-known gem *The Projectionist* (1971), a film very much about the movies, featuring a pre-famous Rodney Dangerfield as the villain.

CURTIS, TONY (1925–) An actor who had his greatest popularity during the 1950s and early 1960s. Curtis' early film career was built almost exclusively on his good looks, matched by a strong screen presence. By the latter half of the 1950s, he had proven himself a fine dramatic actor and charming light comedian. Curtis is an excellent example of how important a good script and a good director are to the success of an actor. He has been electric and unforgettable with good scripts and good direction, but he has rarely transcended poor material.

Born Bernard Schwartz, he was the son of a former amateur actor from Hungary who settled into the life of a poor Jewish tailor in the Bronx, New York. The future actor was a gang member who flirted with a life of crime before a truant officer straightened him out at the age of twelve.

After his Navy service aboard a submarine during World War II, Curtis chose the actor's life and studied his new craft at New York's Dramatic Workshop. He had little stage experience before he was discovered by a Universal Pictures talent scout in an Off-Broadway revival of *Golden Boy*.

He was given a seven-year contract as well as a series of name changes. He was originally given the moniker Jimmy Curtis, but that was dropped in favor of Anthony Curtis by the time of his first minor film credit in *Criss Cross* (1949). He used the name Tony Curtis for the first time in *Johnny Stool Pidgeon* (1949), several movies into his new career.

Movie fans took notice of him long before his studio bosses realized his potential popularity. Teenage girls, in particular, wrote hundreds of fan letters to him without even knowing his name. Universal finally understood they had a star in the making and they rushed him into the lead role in a cheaply made swashbuckler, *The Prince Who Was a Thief* (1951). The film

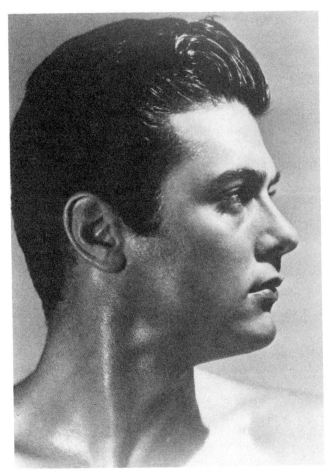

Before Tony Curtis became a master of light comedy, he was a swashbuckling beefcake star. Photo courtesy of Movie Star News.

was a major box office hit and Tony Curtis was fast becoming a household name. In fact, he soon became so popular that he inspired male teenagers to imitate his curly hairstyle.

Curtis had to learn how to act on the job but by the time he starred with his wife Janet Leigh *(q.v.)* in *Houdini* (1953), he had already made much progress. But good movies were scarce and he was rushed into a series of mediocre projects throughout the middle of the decade, including swashbucklers, westerns, light comedies, sports films, and even a musical.

The actor was popular with movie fans but not with the critics. When they weren't panning his movies the critics were panning him. In 1957, however, Curtis finally won his first measure of grudging acceptance from reviewers when he gave a riveting performance in support of Burt Lancaster in *Sweet Smell of Success* (1957). The Academy recognized him the following year by giving him an Oscar nomination for Best Actor for his work in *The Defiant Ones* (1958).

Curtis' career was at its height in the late 1950s and early 1960s. He had the acclaim of both the public and the critical establishment and also the opportunity to work on good scripts with better directors. He starred alongside Marilyn Monroe *(q.v.)* and Jack Lemmon *(q.v.)* in Billy Wilder's *(q.v.) Some Like it Hot* (1959), which was undoubtedly the best movie of his career. He also relived some of his submarine experiences in Blake Edwards' *Operation Petticoat* (1959), and gave a strong performance in Robert Mulligan's *The Rat Race* (1960), among others.

Curtis met his second wife, actress Christine Kaufmann, during the filming of the epic *Taras Bulba* (1962). With just a few other exceptions, however, the actor spent the greater part of the 1960s starring in light comedies such as *Forty Pounds of Trouble* (1962), *Wild and Wonderful* (1964), *Sex and the Single Girl* (1964), and *The Great Race* (1965). A long string of box office flops in the latter half of the decade put his star status in serious question. He recouped, however, with a powerful and highly regarded performance in the title role of *The Boston Strangler* (1968).

It seemed as if Curtis' career had taken a new and richer turn. But three successive mediocre films that failed at the ticket booth drove him to television. He was not terribly successful in that medium either. Curtis has had several abortive big screen comeback attempts, most memorably in *Lepke* (1974), *The Last Tycoon* (1976), and *Little Miss Marker* (1980). He performed admirably in all three films, but none of the movies was a hit.

He has continued to act in the occasional low-budget film, but he gave one of his most stirring performances in recent years in a TV movie, playing mobster Sam Giancana in "Mafia Princess" (1986).

Curtis has appeared in more than seventy films, and leaves a legacy to the American cinema via his talented actress daughter by Janet Leigh, Jamie Lee Curtis.

CURTIZ, MICHAEL (1892–1962)   A director who made more than one hundred Hollywood films, the vast majority of them for Warner Bros., Curtiz is often considered a gifted hack because he worked in virtually every genre, giving his studio exactly what it wanted rather than pursuing a personal vision (as did, say, Howard Hawks, *q.v.*). Upon reflection, however, it would seem as if Warner would have been a much less successful studio, artistically as well as commercially, without the presence of Michael Curtiz. He directed the bulk of Warner's most cherished classics of the 1930s and 1940s.

Born Mihaly Kertesz in Hungary and given his training at the Royal Academy of Theater and Art in Budapest, the young Curtiz began his career as an actor at the age of fourteen. He later worked in Hungarian films beginning in 1912, and not long afterward found his niche behind the camera as a director in Sweden.

World War I brought Curtiz back to Hungary as a soldier. When the war was over, he began an odyssey that took him from Hungary to Austria, Germany, France, Italy, and England, as he enhanced his reputation as an international filmmaker.

As was the custom during the silent era in Hollywood, movie moguls would take trips to Europe in search of talented actors and directors, and thus was Curtiz found by Harry Warner.

According to Jack Warner in his autobiography, *My First Hundred Years in Hollywood,* Curtiz had been told to expect a news conference and gala reception upon his arrival in New York. Warner continues the story: "As the steamer slid up the Hudson River to the dock there were fireboats hurling spears of water high above the ship, there was a band playing martial music on shore, and the sky was on fire with Roman candles and bursting rockets. Mike was so overcome that he wept. 'Ah, thees America!' he cried. 'Vot a vunderful velcome for the great Michael Curtiz. Und these Varner Brothers! I love all five at vunce!'"

As Jack told the story, Harry Warner corrected Curtiz, telling him that there were only four Warner brothers. He did not, however, tell the Hungarian that he had arrived during the hoopla surrounding America's celebration of July 4th.

Curtiz's first film for Warner Bros. was *The Third Degree* (1926). He became the studio's "A" movie director in the early 1930s, a position he never relinquished until he quit Warners over a salary disagreement in 1954.

Curtiz's silent film career at Warners was only moderately successful. But he worked tirelessly and aggressively, earning the respect and admiration of his bosses. Along with a handful of other foreign directors such as Ernst Lubitsch and Fritz Lang *(qq.v.)*, Curtiz managed not only to work but to prosper in the Hollywood dream factory.

During his first six years at Warners, Curtiz directed (among others) such actors as Delores Costello, Al Jolson *(q.v.)*, and even Harry Langdon *(q.v.)*, but not until he made *Dr. X* in 1932 did Curtiz begin to flower.

The director made excellent films in almost every genre he worked in—and he worked in almost all of them. In the horror category, he directed *Dr. X*, as well as the classic *Mystery of the Wax Museum* (1933). He teamed with Errol Flynn *(q.v.)* in most of the actor's best movies, including the top-notch swashbucklers *Captain Blood* (1935) and *The Adventures of Robin Hood* (1938), historical epics such as *The Charge of the Light Brigade* (1936), and Warners' best westerns, *Dodge City* (1939) and *Sante Fe Trail* (1940). He also worked with all of Warner's other great stars, including Paul Muni *(q.v.)* in the powerful, socially-conscious coal mining film *Black Fury* (1935), Edward G. Robinson *(q.v.)* in the memorable boxing movie *Kid Galahad* (1937), and James Cagney *(q.v.)* in the unforgettable gangster film *Angels With Dirty Faces* (1938).

Considering his output in the action genre, it is startling to note that he also directed two of the most beloved musicals of all time, *Yankee Doodle Dandy* (1942) and *White Christmas* (1954, made for Paramount). He put his stamp on strong family films such as *Four Daughters* (1938) and *Life With Father* (1947). And, among other genres, Curtiz begat a whole series of strong women's films with *Mildred Pierce* (1945), saving Joan Crawford's *(q.v.)* career in the bargain.

But of all of his films, Curtiz's greatest achievement was in the combination of romance, intrigue, humor, action, and style he brought to the classic *Casablanca* (1942, *q.v.*), starring Humphrey Bogart and Ingrid Bergman *(qq.v.)*. It was a film for which Curtiz won a richly deserved Oscar for Best Director.

After he left Warner Bros. in 1954, Curtiz went on to make fourteen films for various other studios, working nearly up until the time of his death. Among his better projects in the post-Warners years in addition to *White Christmas,* were *Kid Creole* (1958), *The Proud Rebel* (1958), and *The Comancheros* (1961), which was Curtiz's last film.

All of the movies listed above are truly memorable films, but be assured that Curtiz made his share of stinkers. And yet they cast no shadow on the quality of his movies. It hardly matters that there is no unifying theme in the director's work when one considers the energy, intelligence, and commitment to the best possible filmmaking inherent in his movies. Michael Curtiz was the ideal studio system director, and a craftsman in the very best sense of the word.

CUSTARD PIE   Traditionally, the pie of choice for throwing in actors' faces. However, the famous pies used in silent comedies were not made of custard at all, but filled with blackberries, which showed up better in black and white films.

The first "custard pie" was thrown in *A Noise From the Deep* (1913), a Mack Sennett *(q.v.)* film at the Keystone Studio. Not part of the script, Mabel Normand *(q.v.)* threw the pie in "Fatty" Arbuckle's *(q.v.)* face, creating a bit of comic business that has become a staple in slapstick film comedy.

The custard pie weathered the end of the silent era rather well, finding use in 1930s films by Laurel & Hardy and the Three Stooges, and later, in such films as *Beach Party* (1963) and *The Great Race* (1964).

CUTAWAY   The name given to a cinematic device by filmmakers, which consists of a "cut away" from a scene to show something on the screen that either comments upon or relates to the scene but is not actually a part of the scene. For instance, some cutaways that have become clichés include the moving hands of a clock, the setting (or rising) sun, a crowing rooster, etc. Often, after the cutaway, the scene will pick up again at a later moment of development, allowing the director a certain flexibility in his portrayal of passing time.

The cutaway also provides the opportunity for a visual comment (often symbolic and/or comic) upon the action. For example, filmmakers have cut away to dogs covering their eyes with their paws when two lovers kiss, flowers wilting when a pompous person begins speaking, a volcano erupting when someone loses their temper, etc.

CUTTING ON ACTION   Splicing together a shot of a character in motion taken at one angle and a second shot of that same character while still in motion from a different angle. The purpose of this technique, used by directors and editors, is to make scenes more lively and less visually static. Cutting to a new angle of a character when he is at rest, rather than in motion, tends to create a plodding visual pace. Worse, such an edit is far more readily apparent to the audience. Cutting on action, on the other hand, makes editing far more fluid, seamless, and natural. Even the simple edit to a new angle when a character turns his head enlivens a scene, making it more visually stimulating.

In order to effectively cut on action, a director must shoot the same scene with at least two cameras at different angles, zeroing in on the actor in motion so that he will be in the same place on the set in both shots.

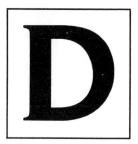

DAILIES A term used to describe the filmed scene(s) rushed to a lab to be processed as soon as the day's work on the set is finished. Also known as "rushes," the film is usually viewed the following day by the producer(s), director, cinematographer, and any other member(s) of the crew who needs to see them. During the height of the Hollywood studio system *(q.v.)*, the dailies were often also viewed by the studio chiefs such as Harry Cohn and Louis B. Mayer *(qq.v.)*.

Because the camera operator is the only person who sees what is being shot, the dailies give the director, his cast, and crew an opportunity to observe and comment on the progress of the picture. Since the advent of video, however, a new step has been added to the viewing process. While viewing the dailies is still essential to see how the images appear on film, an increasingly common practice is to tape the scene on video at the same time (and at the same angle) as it is being filmed. In this way, the scene can be immediately played back in order to check the staging and performances.
See also: video assist

DANIELS, WILLIAM (1895–1970) Best remembered as Hollywood's premier glamour cinematographer, Daniels was the cameraman for that most glamorous of all movie stars, Greta Garbo *(q.v.)*. He worked on the vast majority of her MGM films, such as *The Kiss* (1929), *Anna Christie* (1930), *Anna Karenina* (1935), and *Ninotchka* (1939), to name a mere handful. Norman Zierold, in his 1970 biography, *Garbo*, said, "Daniels studied Garbo's face and body with great care. He saw immediately that she was least attractive in repose, best in close-ups and long-shots, indifferent in the intermediate range. She was better seated or lying down than standing—Daniels later shot some of her best

scenes, in *Flesh and the Devil* (1926) and *Queen Christina* (1933), with Garbo reclining."

The great cinematographer, however, had one regret. He remarked to Norman Zierold, "The saddest thing in my career is that I was never able to photograph her [Garbo] in color. I begged the studio. I felt I had to get those incredible blue eyes in color, but they said no. The process at the time was cumbersome and expensive, and the pictures were already making money. I still feel sad about it."

Because he was MGM's leading glamour cameraman for twenty-two years before he became a free-lancer, it is sometimes overlooked that Daniels was also Erich von Stroheim's *(q.v.)* cinematographer. In fact, after four years as an assistant cameraman at Universal, he started his illustrious career as a cinematgrapher on Von Stroheim's hit silent film *Foolish Wives* (1921) and added his valuable taste and technique to Von Stroheim's masterpiece *Greed* (1923).

In his long, distinguished career, Daniels provided his lighting and composing genius not only to Von Stroheim and Garbo in the 1920s and 1930s, he also showed an ability for hard-edged realism in *The Naked City* (1948)—for which he won an Academy Award.

His career in the 1950s and 1960s highlighted his versatility: the sweet-natured fantasy of *Harvey* (1950), the harsh world of *The Far Country* (1954), and the comedy of *Come Blow Your Horn* (1963). Walter Blanchard, writing in *American Cinematographer* described Daniels' unmistakable signature as "a certain singing smoothness which for all its variety of technique and artistic mood is as distinctive as anything on the screen."
See also: cinematographer

DARK VICTORY A film that owes its place in film history not to its artistry but to its enduring popularity. At first glance, *Dark Victory*'s (1939) story is laughable.

A wealthy and arrogant socialite (Bette Davis, *q.v.*) learns that she has an incurable brain tumor. And, naturally, she falls in love with and marries her doctor (George Brent). A changed woman, she dies gallantly, having shown no serious side effects from her tumor until just minutes before death.

Yet it works. Audiences wept at the end of the film when it premiered as they still do today. The film is an unabashed soap opera that is the grandmother of *Love Story* (1970) and hundreds of other tragic medical romances. Perhaps most important, *Dark Victory*'s startling box office success made Hollywood producers take notice that not every movie had to have a happy ending.

Edmund Goulding directed with flair and, in addition to Davis in one of her best performances and Brent in a sincere portrayal, Geraldine Fitzgerald, Ronald Reagan *(q.v.)*, Cora Witherspoon, and Henry Travers ably supported. Humphrey Bogart *(q.v.)*, in a small role as an Irish stable master, fought his brogue to a standstill.

Dark Victory was remade as *Stolen Hours* (1963) with Susan Hayward *(q.v.)* in the Bette Davis role. It was remade, yet again, as a TV movie with Elizabeth Montgomery in 1976.

See also: women's pictures

DAVIS, BETTE (1908–1989) Though she was not a great beauty in the traditional sense, Bette Davis reigned as Hollywood's most enduring female star because she was more interested in acting than in celebrity status. With her magnificent eyes and intense style, Davis captivated critics, won a devoted fan following, and used all of the above to fight her employers in the most important actor/studio battles of the 1930s.

Born Ruth Elizabeth Davis, Bette always wanted to be an actress. And like the dedicated performer she would always be, Davis worked at her craft in small theater companies in New England until she made it to Broadway in a hit play, *Broken Dishes,* in the late 1920s.

With talkies all the rage, Hollywood was raiding Broadway for actors with good speaking voices. Davis' screen test with Samuel Goldwyn's company went nowhere, but Universal gave the actress a second chance, and offered her a contract. She wasn't welcomed with raves, however. Carl Laemmle, who ran Universal, is said to have dryly commented that Davis had "as much sex-appeal as Slim Somerville."

Davis was, nonetheless, under contract. Laemmle eventually used her as the good sister in *Bad Sister* (1931), and she played a series of minor parts in a string of forgettable movies. When Universal dumped her, Warners was waiting in the wings. George Arliss *(q.v.)*, their early sound star, wanted her to act opposite him in *The Man Who Played God* (1932). Her long association with Warner Bros. had begun, and it would be a tempestuous relationship marked by suspensions, court

Though not considered a great beauty, many a film fan has become lost in Bette Davis' eyes. There has hardly been a more forceful female presence in the movies. Photo courtesy of Movie Star News.

battles, and some of the best made movies of the late 1930s and 1940s.

After several minor films, she sunk her teeth into the part of the young tramp in *Cabin in the Cotton* (1932), riveting the attention of moviegoers everywhere. And her "Bette Davis eyes" were never more in evidence than in *20,000 Years in Sing Sing* (1933), in which she was radiant, costarring with Spencer Tracy *(q.v.)*. It looked like her career was about to take off, but a series of poor films stalled her rise to stardom. And then came the first battle with Jack Warner.

RKO wanted her for *Of Human Bondage* (1934), but Warner refused to loan her to the rival studio. Davis knew it was a fabulous part and she fought for the right to play it, eventually having her way. In the end, Warners benefited handsomely. Besides the considerable fee they were paid for Davis' services at RKO, the movie was a hit, catapulting the actress to stardom. The only surprise was that she wasn't nominated for an Oscar.

In 1935, Davis starred in *Dangerous* and won her first Oscar for Best Actress, but in typical Davis style, she bluntly said that she thought Katharine Hepburn *(q.v.)* should have won instead for *Alice Adams*.

Warner took advantage of her stardom to rush her into several mediocre films, the exception being *The Petrified Forest* (1936). She knuckled under and made the movies, until she was cast in a particularly dreadful film called *God's Country and the Woman*. Davis refused to appear in the movie and was suspended and fined $5,000 per week, but she would not budge. Instead, she decided to make a movie in England. Warners claimed she was in violation of her contract and the two slugged it out in court, with Warners the victor.

In the end, though, Davis was the real winner. Warner Bros. received terrible press, and in order to smooth relations with the public actually gave Davis the money to pay the court damages. The studio also made an effort to give her better scripts. Perhaps most importantly, Bette Davis had established the precedent for actors fighting studios for better scripts, and winning.

After her court battle, the actress made (among others) *Marked Woman* (1937), an early feminist film that costarred Humphrey Bogart *(q.v.)*. But the role Davis really wanted was Scarlett O'Hara in *Gone With the Wind* (1939). Warners didn't have the rights to the book, but David O. Selznick *(q.v.)*, who did, was initially open to the idea of having Davis play the female lead. Jack Warner offered Davis on the condition that Selznick would also use Errol Flynn as Rhett Butler, and Selznick refused. As a consolation, Warner gave Davis her own version of *Gone With the Wind (q.v.)*, *Jezebel* (1938), beating Selznick's film to the theaters and winning Davis her second Oscar.

In 1939, Davis scored again with *Dark Victory (q.v.)*, a movie in which her character dies bravely. The film was so popular that it started a trend for movies with unhappy endings. Her success in the following years was so ironclad that she was constantly among the top ten stars in audience polls; in 1940, she was number one, knocking Shirley Temple *(q.v.)* out of the top spot. With highly regarded hit films such as *All This and Heaven Too* (1940), *The Letter* (1940), and *The Great Lie* (1941), Davis was at the top of her career. And she stayed there with *The Little Foxes* (1941), *Now Voyager* (1942), *Watch on the Rhine* (1943), and *Mr. Skeffington* (1944).

But then Miss Davis faltered, making fewer quality movies in the later 1940s. It appeared as if her career was irrevocably, if quietly on the skids, until she made what many consider to be her best film, Joseph L. Mankiewicz's *(q.v.)* *All About Eve* (1950). This wisecracking, witty film about show business reestablished Davis as Hollywood's preeminent female star, and despite poor film projects throughout the rest of the 1950s, the stature of her performance in that film kept her career alive until 1961, when the offers finally stopped coming her way.

In an unprecedented move, Davis took out full-page advertisements in the trade papers stating that she was available for work. The resulting publicity was a tonic, but more importantly, she was offered the lead role together with Joan Crawford in Robert Aldrich's *What-*

ever Happened to Baby Jane? (1962). The two grand dames of Hollywood chewed up the scenery in this psychological suspense thriller, and audiences loved it. The film resurrected Davis's career and led to yet another Academy Award nomination, but according to Davis, Joan Crawford actively campaigned against her, causing her to lose the Oscar.

The mid-1960s saw Davis continue in horror films that were similar to *Baby Jane*, such as *The Nanny* (1965) and *Hush . . . Hush . . . Sweet Charlotte* (1965). Even when such films ran their course, Davis continued to find work, principally in TV movies. Though she hasn't had a film vehicle to match her talents since the mid-1960s, Davis had a nice turn or two in movies such as *Burnt Offerings* (1976) and *Death on the Nile* (1978). In 1977, Miss Davis was the first woman to be given the American Film Institute Life Achievement Award. Yet at age seventy-six, she wasn't finished achieving. Despite a stroke, she gallantly fought back to continue her acting career, appearing in a starring role with Lillian Gish in the critically acclaimed *The Whales of August* (1987).

DAY, DORIS (1924–   )   An actress and singer, she was one of the biggest stars of the 1950s. In a career that included thirty-nine films, Miss Day was voted the number-one box office attraction in a national poll over a four-year period. Though she often played career woman, she was the personification of American womanhood during the 1950s. Film audiences were drawn to her because she was accessible, warm, bubbly, but not quite saccharine—she was the girl next door but with sex appeal. Starring in a series of sex comedies in the late 1950s and early 1960s that were enormously successful at the box office she reached her apotheosis. When sexual attitudes changed soon thereafter, Day was quickly relegated to the movie star junk heap, forever associated with her "virgin" personna.

Born Doris Von Kappelhoff, Day had originally intended to dance. Though her father was a music teacher her show business career was originally pushed by her mother. At the age of fourteen she planned on moving (with her mother) from her home in Cincinnati to Los Angeles to pursue a dancing career. Just before leaving, her car was hit by a train and her right leg was badly injured. Though told she might not walk again, she responded to treatment. Forced to change career directions, however, she chose music. Within a few short years—by the time she was seventeen—Doris Day became a singer for a big band, Barney Rapp and his New Englanders. Not long after, she sang for the far more well-known Bob Crosby and the Bobcats, and eventually hit the big time as the lead singer with Les Brown and his Band of Renown.

When a star was needed for a Warner Bros. musical, *Romance on the High Seas* (1948), the studio took Betty

Doris Day defined a generation. With her upbeat personality, restrained sexuality, and considerable warmth, she reached her greatest popularity in the late 1950s and early 1960s. Photo courtesy of Doris Day.

Hutton on loan-out. When Hutton had to drop out due to pregnancy, Warners tested and signed Miss Day for the role. The film was nothing special, but it was a hit and it turned the brand new actress into an instant star.

Warners followed that success by putting her in movies not unlike her original hit. Most of her early films, such as *My Dream Is Yours* (1949) and *Tea for Two* (1950), were mildly entertaining but instantly forgettable. The films in which she had supporting roles, such as *Young Man With a Horn* (1950) and *Storm Warning* (1951), usually had better scripts. Nonetheless, she quickly came into her own as a major star, particularly after her lead role in the hit musical *Calamity Jane* (1953). Among her other notable successes during the 1950s were *Young at Heart* (1954), *The Pajama Game* (1957), and *Teacher's Pet* (1958). In addition, it was during the 1950s that she starred in her only dramatic roles, in *Love Me or Leave Me* (1955), with James Cagney (*q.v.*), and *The Man Who Knew Too Much* (1956), directed by Alfred Hitchcock (*q.v.*). She proved her range as an actress in both films, finding her theme song, "Que Sera, Que Sera" in the latter movie.

After more than ten years, during which she played a variety of parts, from dramatic to musical to light comedy, Miss Day embarked on a series of so-called sophisticated sex comedies that were aimed at the American middle class. *Pillow Talk* (1959), with Rock Hudson, started the hugely popular cycle, and it was followed by such films as *Lover Come Back* (1961), *That Touch of Mink* (1962), *The Thrill of It All* (1963), *Move Over Darling* (1963), *Send Me No Flowers* (1964), and *Do Not Disturb* (1965). Along the way, she also starred in several other films, among them the very popular *Please Don't Eat the Daisies* (1960) and the musical *Jumbo* (1962).

After the mildly successful *The Glass Bottom Boat* (1966), she hit the skids with such flops as *Caprice* (1967), *The Ballad of Josie* (1968), and *With Six You Get Eggroll* (1968), which was also her last motion picture. With her film career fading, and her late, third husband (Martin Melcher) having mismanaged and embezzled her $20 million in earnings, Day found herself in a TV series (that Melcher signed her to without her knowledge), "The Doris Day Show," which enjoyed a modest success. Miss Day later won a $22 million judgment against her attorney, who had worked with her late husband.

Miss Day has mostly been absent from show business since the early 1970s. She returned to television in a short-lived series on CBN Cable, "Doris Day's Best Friends," in 1985, but the bulk of her efforts and energies during the 1970s and 1980s has gone to the protection of animal rights, including her formation of the Doris Day Animal League, a lobbying organization designed to bring attention to the inhumane use of animals in laboratory testing.

DEE, SANDRA   *See* teen movies.

DE HAVILLAND, OLIVIA (1916–)   An actress who might merely have been a footnote in film history—as Errol Flynn's (*q.v.*) romantic interest in a wonderful series of movies beginning with *Captain Blood* (1935) and as the other woman in *Gone With the Wind* (1939)—instead she emerged as a superb actress in two of the most emotionally searing films of the late 1940s, *The Snake Pit* (1948) and *The Heiress* (1949).

Olivia de Havilland was born in Tokyo of British parents. Her sister, Joan, was born one year later. Joan de Havilland would later adopt the stage name of Fontaine, and the two sisters would each have long and distinguished Hollywood careers as well as a much-publicized feud.

In 1921, Olivia and Joan were brought to California by their recently divorced mother. Olivia's auspicious cinematic debut was in Max Reinhardt's Warner Bros. version of *A Midsummer Night's Dream* (1935). She was only nineteen years old, with very little stage experience. Her lack of experience didn't seem to matter especially since her *Captain Blood* costar, Flynn, had even less experience. The team of Flynn and de Havilland was a smash, and they were billed together in a total of eight films, including such classics as *The Charge of the Light Brigade* (1936), *The Adventures of Robin Hood* (1938), and *They Died With Their Boots On* (1941).

Though she worked in films without Flynn during her heyday, there was nothing remarkable about them—except *Gone With the Wind* (1939). Despite the protracted debate over who would play Scarlett O'Hara, there was little question about who would play Melanie. De Havilland, given the relatively thankless role early on, managed to imbue the character with sympathy and understanding.

The actress's early 1940s films were modestly entertaining but hardly remarkable. Even *To Each His Own* (1946), for which she won an Oscar for Best Actress, was merely a good soap opera. But when she made *The Snake Pit* in 1948, a stark film about a woman in a mental institution, the sweet, decorative actress suddenly showed her stuff. The courageous performance was not awarded an Oscar; though, the following year she received kudos for her role in *The Heiress* (1949), in which she played a homely, rich woman being courted by a scheming Montgomery Clift *(q.v.)*—This time she won her second Oscar.

De Havilland continued to work throughout the 1950s and 1960s, but only sporadically. Among her later films, she is perhaps best remembered as Bette Davis's costar in *Hush . . . Hush . . . Sweet Charlotte* (1965). In recent years, she has appeared in the occasional all-star disaster movie, such as *Airport 77* (1977) and on TV.

See also: Captain Blood; Fontaine, Joan

DeMILLE, CECIL B. (1881–1959)   A producer/director whose career encompassed seventy films made in nearly every major genre. Eventually, in his later years, he became known for quasi-religious epics exhibiting a surprising amount of sex and violence. The director's favorite ploy was to draw audiences into theaters for displays of "sin," only to redeem the "sinners" by the end of the last reel. Many thought DeMille to be a rather cynical filmmaker, but apparently the director truly believed in the messages of his biblical tales.

DeMille was among the very few filmmakers in Hollywood whose name above the title meant more to movie audiences than the names of the stars in the picture. A DeMille picture combined fast-paced action, old-fashioned storytelling, and a proverbial "cast of thousands." His name became synonymous with spectacle. Yet DeMille made successful epics because he never lost focus of his main characters, despite huge casts and expensive special effects.

DeMille directed a great many entertaining movies that helped define the future direction of Hollywood filmmaking. A pioneer, he established the parameters

of budding genres and created new ones, as well. And whenever speaking of Hollywood as either the physical or spiritual center of worldwide moviemaking, one should never forget DeMille's role in its development. He was the man who made his (and Hollywood's) first feature film, *The Squaw Man,* in 1913 in that sleepy little Southern California village.

Cecil Blount DeMille was the son of a minister who also wrote plays. He was twelve years old when his father died, but his mother (also a playwright) kept the family together by founding a school for girls and, later, a theater company that the young Cecil eventually joined as an actor and manager after making his Broadway debut on stage in 1900.

DeMille continued working in the theater until 1913, when he joined Jesse L. Lasky and Samuel Goldfish (later Goldwyn) to form the Jesse L. Lasky Feature Play Company. Enamored with film and its creative and financial potential, the three partners set about making their grand entrance in the hot new motion picture business by signing the well-known stage actor Dustin Farnum to a lucrative salary to star in a film adaptation of the hit play *The Squaw Man.* Lasky and Goldfish thought the movie would be shot where virtually all westerns were then made: New Jersey. DeMille, as the "director-general" of the triumvirate, insisted that the film be made in the real West, and chose Flagstaff, Arizona for the film's locale. But when DeMille and company arrived in Flagstaff the director felt that the area was too modern looking, and the company hopped back on the train and kept on going until they reached Hollywood, where filming commenced with not a little trouble. According to Charles Higham in his biography of DeMille, previously shot footage of the film was damaged one night by a saboteur. DeMille took to sleeping in a chair in the storage area with a shotgun on his lap in order to protect his work.

When the six-reel *The Squaw Man* opened in 1913, it was an immediate sensation. DeMille, who had never directed a movie before (he codirected *The Squaw Man* with Oscar Apfel), quickly became a creative force in the infant industry with such strong follow-up efforts as *Brewster's Millions* (1914), *The Call of the North* (1914), *The Virginian* (1914), *The Girl of the Golden West* (1915), *The Warrens of Virginia* (1915), *The Trail of the Lonesome Pine* (1916), and a remake of *The Squaw Man* (1918). In addition to producing and directing, DeMille also contributed to his own cause as a screenwriter and an editor on many of his films.

During the silent era, DeMille made everything from westerns to comedies, from romances to morality plays. In the last category he struck oil. His epic version of *The Ten Commandments* (1923) was a box office blockbuster.

Meanwhile, thanks to DeMille's continued success, Jesse Lasky *(q.v.)* had been able to build his company

Cecil B. DeMille was one of the few directors who had long and successful careers in both the silent and sound eras. Here, DeMille is pictured with both old and new motion picture cameras. He shot *all* his silent films with the small wooden camera to his left. Photo courtesy of Movie Star News.

(without Goldfish/Goldwyn) into a major studio that would eventually become known as Paramount Pictures. DeMille not only directed and produced a great many of the Lasky/Paramount pictures during the years between 1913 and 1924, he also oversaw the production of a great many more. In 1925, however, DeMille decided to set up shop for himself. He established The DeMille Studio and made four films, beginning with *The Road to Yesterday* (1925), followed by *The Volga Boatman* (1925), *The King of Kings* (1926), and *The Godless Girl* (1928), the last being a silent film unable to withstand the competitive tidal wave of sound films that began appearing that year. His company collapsing, DeMille became a director at MGM for three pictures, his first sound film, *Dynamite* (1929), *Madame Satan* (1930), and his second remake of *The Squaw Man* (1931). Then it was back to Paramount, his original home, where he stayed for the rest of his working life.

At Paramount, DeMille hit his stride again. He made only fifteen more films but a substantial number of them were major hits, mostly epics based on stories from the Bible, Roman history, the American West, and anything else DeMille could find to turn into a sprawling tale of grand passion and visual spectacle. The religious movies were his stock-in-trade, and none were better during those years in Hollywood than DeMille's *The Sign of the Cross* (1932), *Samson and Delilah* (1949), and his remake of *The Ten Commandments* (1956). *Cleopatra* (1934) and *The Crusades* (1935) are also closely related to the biblical tales. His westerns, such as *The Plainsman* (1937), *Union Pacific* (1939), and *Unconquered* (1947), were nearly as big in scope as his religious films. One of his most endearing extravaganzas, though, *The Greatest Show on Earth* (1952), concerned the circus. It seemed a particularly fitting subject for one of DeMille's last movies, considering that he was often called the greatest showman in Hollywood.

The director died of heart failure in 1959.

See also: Hollywood; Paramount; Quinn, Anthony

DE NIRO, ROBERT (1943–   ) A character actor/star whose career has been closely associated with that of director Martin Scorsese *(q.v.).* De Niro, famous for deeply immersing himself in his roles, has emerged over two decades as one of Hollywood's most dedicated and gifted performers. Lean of build and mildly good-looking, De Niro is not a matinee-idol type; he appears to be an everyman, perhaps of the blue-collar variety, but with an explosive inner core that bubbles just beneath the surface.

A method actor, De Niro received his training from Stella Adler and Lee Strasberg. After working on the stage, he was cast by Brian De Palma *(q.v.),* then a young student director, in three of the filmmaker's early low-budget movies, *Greetings* (1968), *The Wedding Party* (1969), and *Hi, Mom!* (1970). In the period following the independent film success of *Easy Rider* in 1969, De Palma's films, particularly the last, received modest art house distribution.

More film roles came his way, including significant supporting parts in Roger Corman's *Bloddy Mama* (1970), a serio-comic George Segal *(q.v.)* vehicle, *Born to Win* (1971), and the adaptation of Jimmy Breslin's *The Gang That Couldn't Shoot Straight* (1971). None of the films was a hit but his work in them gave him the opportunity to display his talents in his first major costarring role as the dying inarticulate catcher in the baseball movie *Bang the Drum Slowly* (1973). While the movie received mixed notices, De Niro was finally discovered by the critics.

Martin Scorsese discovered him next, casting him in the explosive film *Mean Streets* (1973), a movie that made both the director and actor hot properties in Hollywood. After playing the young Vito Corleone in *The Godfather, Part II* (1974) and winning the Best Supporting Actor Academy Award, De Niro became a star. But his greatest triumphs were still ahead of him. His searing performance as the violent and troubled Travis Bickle in Scorsese's *Taxi Driver* (1976) was one of the most powerful acting displays of the 1970s.

De Niro proved he was nothing if not versatile. Directly after playing Travis Bickle, he essayed the role of Monroe Starr in *The Last Tycoon* (1976), breathing life into the cooly restrained yet romantic Irving Thalberg-like character from F. Scott Fitzgerald's novel. He followed that with his sterling performance in Bernardo Bertolucci's much-admired *1900* (1977).

His willingness (and ability) to give himself totally to his roles led to his learning to play the saxophone for Scorsese's *New York, New York* (1977) and gaining fifty pounds to play the aging Jake LaMotta in *Raging Bull* (1980), a role that brought him his second Oscar

and first Best Actor Academy Award. In between, he was nominated for Best Actor for his role in *The Deer Hunter* (1978).

De Niro dominated the acting scene in the mid to late 1970s but his career has been considerably quieter in the 1980s. Robert Duvall *(q.v.)* stole the show in the moody crime story *True Confessions* (1981), but De Niro was brilliant as Rupert Pupkin in Scorsese's vastly underrated *The King of Comedy* (1983). If the film hadn't been so dark in its comic honesty, De Niro might have been nominated and won another Oscar.

It seemed as if the ultimate match-up of male and female actors was made when De Niro was again teamed with Meryl Streep *(q.v.)* in *Falling in Love* (1984). While the two performers were extremely effective, the movie failed to live up to their talents.

There was yet another disappointment when the big-budget epic *The Mission* (1986) received mixed reviews and poor box office returns. About this time, De Niro returned to the stage after a very long absence to star in the Joseph Papp production of *Cuba and His Teddy Bear,* first Off-Broadway and then in a limited, sold-out, Broadway run.

By choice, he then began appearing again on screen in smallish, but important, featured roles, such as Al Capone in Brian De Palma's hit *The Untouchables* (1987), his first collaboration with the director since they worked together seventeen years before.

Finally, it was time to find a new starring vehicle. He was offered the lead in *Big* (1988) but eventually turned the role down (Tom Hanks played it to perfection).

He continued to pursue the idea of starring in a comedy, finally settling on a comic farce called *Midnight Run* (1988). Considering his reputation for working in serious, dramatic films (even *The King of Comedy* was deadly serious despite its mordant laughs), he surprised a great many people with his choice. Joined by Charles Grodin in the cast, this wonderfully silly comedy went on to become a critical and commercial success, showing yet another side of De Niro's considerable talent. More recently, he gave a powerful dramatic performance in *Jacknife* (1989), but the movie was not a hit.

DE PALMA, BRIAN (1940–   ) A director of suspense who has been called the modern Alfred Hitchcock, De Palma has also been called a derivative director who offers very little in his movies except technical expertise and cheap thrills. Of course, the same was often said of Hitchcock. But a close reading of De Palma's movies, such as *Carrie* (1976), *Dressed to Kill* (1980), and *Blow Out* (1981), suggests a consistent and pervasive point of view, namely that nothing in our world is as we think it is. His masterful cinematic flourishes startle audiences into a visceral understanding of his themes.

De Palma was born in Newark, New Jersey, but

grew up in Philadelphia, where he showed an early aptitude for science. In fact, in his youth, he built a computer based on his own design. While studying physics at Columbia University De Palma's interest in movies developed. He made several short films, including *Woton's Wake,* which won a 1963 Rosenthal Foundation Award.

His career path was set. De Palma left physics behind and went to graduate school in Theater Arts at Sarah Lawrence, where he received his M.A. in 1964. Like the new wave of American directors who came out of film schools in the 1960s, such as Francis Coppola, George Lucas, and Martin Scorcese *(qq.v.),* De Palma had a passion for shooting film. While in graduate school, he wrote and directed his first feature, *The Wedding Party* (shot in 1963 and released in 1969), starring hungry young unknown actors Jill Clayburgh and Robert De Niro *(q.v.).* De Palma's second film was *Murder à La Mod* (1968). But the films that caught the attention of Hollywood were his next two underground hit films, *Greetings* (1969) and *Hi, Mom* (1970), both starring the still unknown Robert De Niro.

The director's first commercial venture, a light satire with Tommy Smothers called *Get to Know Your Rabbit* (1972), was a bust at the box office. But the script hadn't been De Palma's. Falling back on his own material, the writer-director made three psychological suspense films with Hitchcockian elements: *Sisters* (1973), *The Phantom of the Paradise* (1974), and *Obsession* (1976). All three films received mixed critical reactions. The last of these, however, was a significant commercial hit, paving the way for De Palma's big breakthrough movie, *Carrie* (1976).

Carrie made a star out of Sissy Spacek *(q.v.),* and made De Palma a target of outraged critics who objected to the film's violence and accused the director (De Palma did not write the script for this film) of creating a cheap-thrill movie. It was a tag that would stick with him for more than a decade, through critical and commercial disasters such as *The Fury* (1978), *Home Movies* (1980), and *Body Double* (1984), as well as winners, such as *Dressed to Kill* (1980).

Dressed to Kill was his most fully realized thriller, and it seemed as if he had finally answered his critics. But he flopped with *Blow Out* (1981) and *Wise Guys* (1986) despite considerable studio build-up. His film *Scarface* (1983) was a money-maker, but was attacked by the critics. In every case, these failures were laid directly at De Palma's doorstep. The director's career was in jeopardy.

Not until the 1987 smash hit *The Untouchables,* starring Kevin Costner and De Palma's old friend Robert De Niro, was the director's critical and commercial reputation reestablished. He solidified his standing with the highly praised *Casualties of War* (1989).

De Palma, like his contemporaries who came out of film schools, owes much of his knowledge of technique and style to the movies and directors with whom he studied. It's no wonder that De Palma was influenced by Hitchcock, but the younger director's fluid camera work and moody yet sensual ambience full of lurking danger are expressions of a talent that is uniquely his own.

DEAD END   The first movie about gangsters to take a sociological point of view, condemning poverty as the cause of crime. The 1937 movie, which introduced the Dead End Kids, was a hit that led to a spate of films featuring destitute groups in slums who are sliding into a life of crime, including such projects as *Angels With Dirty Faces* (1938) and *Angels Wash Their Faces* (1939). Even *Boys Town* (1938), with its motto, "There is no such thing as a bad boy," owed its existence to the success of *Dead End.*

Besides its effect on the content of future movies, *Dead End* was also a powerful melodrama that was startlingly honest concerning issues that had never been presented in the movies. For instance, Claire Trevor *(q.v.),* in a supporting role, plays a prostitute ill with a sexually transmitted disease.

Dead End was directed by William Wyler *(q.v.)* with a script by Lillian Hellman, and was based on a hit Broadway play by Phillip Kingsley. The film boasted an excellent cast that included Joel McCrea *(q.v.),* Sylvia Sidney *(q.v.),* Humphrey Bogart *(q.v.),* Claire Trevor, Wendy Barrie, Marjorie Main, Ward Bond, Allen Jenkins, and the Dead End Kids.

DEAN, JAMES (1931–1955)   A young actor who starred in just three films in the mid-1950s, he emerged as a powerful symbol of restless, alienated, and misunderstood youth. His tragic death cut short his meteoric rise, but his cult-hero status has grown ever since, and it's fair to say that there has never been a movie star with so few credits who has had such a profound effect on so many filmgoers.

Dean spent most of his youth in Marion, Indiana. Later, he moved to California, where he attended college. After studying acting with James Whitmore, he worked in commercials and played bit parts in minor movies, until he traveled to New York to take a stab at the legitimate theater.

It didn't take long for Dean to catch on. Between 1952 and 1954, he had two important Broadway roles, the first in *See the Jaguar* and the second in *The Immoralist.* Good reviews brought him a movie contract, and he signed to play in the film version of John Steinbeck's *East of Eden* (1955) as the sensitive son who is misunderstood by his father (played by Raymond Massey). Dean's electrifying presence helped to make the literate and serious Elia Kazan *(q.v.)* film into a surprising box office hit. Dean himself was honored

James Dean starred in but three films, but his combination of good looks, sensuality, and vulnerability continue to excite and haunt fans more than thirty-five years after his tragic death. Photo courtesy of Movie Star News.

with an Academy Award nomination for Best Supporting Actor.

Dean's next film was *Rebel Without A Cause* (1955, *q.v.*). As directed by Nicholas Ray (q.v.), this otherwise small film had a powerful impact on the moviegoing youth of America. The movie was a surprise hit, and Dean, as a troubled, tough but vulnerable teenager (again misunderstood by his parents), exhibited a provocative sexual presence combined with a tenderness that appealed to males and females alike.

Giant (1956) was James Dean's last film. It was released after his fatal car crash. In the movie, he costarred with Rock Hudson and Elizabeth Taylor (*qq.v.*), playing a poor Texan who strikes it rich in oil. His performance as a tortured character, in love with Taylor, striving to prove his worth among the old-moneyed ranching elite, is powerful and wrenching.

Despite his fame (both before and after his death), there were those who thought that Dean was merely aping Marlon Brando's insular type of acting, that he

was merely a passing fad. After thirty-five years the fad has yet to pass.

DEEP FOCUS A term used to describe the way in which a shot is made so that foreground and background can be clearly distinguished on film. Deep focus allows the scene being shot to take place on two or more planes, providing the visual opportunity to have the action on one plane comment on the action of another without the need to edit or otherwise disrupt camera movement.

Cinematographer Gregg Toland *(q.v.)* is generally credited with the dramatic advancement of deep-focus photography when he shot Orson Welles' *Citizen Kane* (1941 *qq.v.*). In one of the oft-remarked-upon scenes in the film exemplifying the use of the technique, the young Charles Foster Kane can be clearly seen in the background through a window playing in the snow with his sled ("Rosebud") as he repeatedly calls out the patriotic slogan, "The Union Forever." Meanwhile, in the foreground, Charles Foster Kane's parents are, ironically, ending their union with him forever by agreeing to send him away from home. All the action takes place in one shot, in one scene, without any edits, pans, or dollies, thanks to the use of deep focus.

DEMME, JONATHAN   *See* screwball comedy.

DERN, BRUCE (1936–)   An actor who has been typecast as a lunatic, often playing off-the-wall characters in a variety of films throughout the bulk of the 1960s and 1970s. He was the next generation's Anthony Perkins *(q.v.),* creating a gallery of memorable "psychos," until his versatility as an actor finally began to be tapped in the latter half of the 1970s. He has since proven to be a durable and intriguing leading character actor/star.

Considering the many crazies he has played, Dern's background comes as quite a shock. His roots are deep in America's financial, political, and intellectual bedrock. His grandfather was once governor of Utah, and one of his uncles was the Secretary of War in the F.D.R. administration. Another uncle was the famous writer, Archibald MacLeish. Dern attended the exclusive Choate prep school before becoming an undergraduate at the Ivy League University of Pennsylvania. Drawn to acting, however, he didn't finish his college studies. Instead, he went to New York and began performing on the stage and in television.

He broke into the movies in 1960, appearing in a small role in *Wild River,* but his most important break during these early years was a lead guest role as a lunatic in an episode of TV's "Alfred Hitchcock Presents" series. Dern was chillingly real and his success in the part led to steady, if similar, work playing weird villains for the better part of fifteen years in films such as *Hush . . . Hush . . . Sweet Charlotte* (1965), *The Trip* (1967), *Psych-Out* (1968), *Will Penny* (1968), *The Cycle Savages* (1969), and a great many more.

Dern's career took a turn for the better in 1972 when he gave a bravura performance in the offbeat science fiction film, *Silent Running.* The actor was superb in a virtual one-man show, carrying the film with a combination of vulnerability, wit, and an indomitable spirit. His success opened up other casting possibilities, and he made the best of them, playing strong roles in films such as *The Laughing Policeman* (1973), *Smile* (1975), and Hitchcock's *Family Plot* (1976). He also showed a flair for comedy in the very funny but commercially unsuccessful *Won Ton Ton—The Dog Who Saved Hollywood* (1976), but he then returned to playing disturbed characters again in the late 1970s and early 1980s. Though he was the raving psycho in *Black Sunday* (1977), he was much subtler as Jane Fonda's husband in the anti-war film, *Coming Home* (1978), at the end of which his character committed suicide. This latter role brought Dern an Oscar nomination for Best Supporting Actor.

He continued to play strange characters in films such as *The Driver* (1978) and *Tattoo* (1981), but the odd behavior struck closer to home in *Middle Age Crazy* (1980). Eventually, Dern began to find mellower roles, such as his part in *That Championship Season* (1982). By the late 1980s he was playing supporting roles in such films as *1969* (1988) and *The Burbs* (1989). He also began to work more frequently in the mini-series format on television. In the meantime, his daughter, Laura Dern, has emerged as an interesting young actress in films such as *Smooth Talk* (1985) and *Blue Velvet* (1986).

DETECTIVE FILMS   A genre that flowered in the sound era and became a Hollywood staple with the continuing adventures of an ever-growing number of idiosyncratic detective characters. There are, in broad form, two distinct types of detective film. The first type portrays the deductive detective who cleverly traps the killer by assembling information through interrogations and clues. The second type is the hard-boiled detective who must often use his fists and his handgun to solve his crimes. Both types of detective have been popular in American films, but in recent decades the hard-boiled type has held sway because the sex and violence inherent in these harsher films cannot be duplicated by TV.

Unlike the gangster movie, the detective film is not about hubris and greed, it's about truth. While gangster films often voyeuristically allow us to share in the rise and fall of a Tom Powers, Rico, Rocco, or Tony Camonte (to name a few), the detective film sticks to the high road, allowing the audience to crack the mystery together with the hero and track down the criminal in question.

The first detective film made in the United States was *Sherlock Holmes Baffled* (1903), produced by the American Biograph Company. It was made the same year as the famous western *The Great Train Robbery.* The western was an ideal genre for the silent era because it lends itself to wide open vistas and violent action. The western eclipsed the detective film early on. Requiring a good deal of exposition that was all but impossible in a fast-paced silent movie, it was no wonder, then, that detective films were rarely big box office before sound. The most notable exception was the 1922 *Sherlock Holmes* starring John Barrymore.

If audiences wanted talk in their talkies, they certainly received their share in the 1930s. It was the grand period of the deductive detective, with such entertaining sleuths as Charlie Chan (played by a succession of actors, but most memorably by Warner Oland), Mr. Moto (Peter Lorre), Nick and Nora Charles (William Powell and Myrna Loy *qq.v.*) in the wonderfully sophisticated *Thin Man* series, and Philo Vance (also played by William Powell).

The detective film was a popular genre, but it soon

became fodder for "B" movies (q.v.). Even Bulldog Drummond, a hugely popular character introduced in the talkies in 1929 by Ronald Colman (q.v.), eventually became a "B" movie series in the late 1930s.

The detective literature of Dashiell Hammett and Raymond Chandler had been popular during the 1920s and 1930s, but it wasn't until the third version of Hammett's *The Maltese Falcon* (1941, q.v.), directed by John Huston (q.v.) with Humphrey Bogart (q.v.) as Sam Spade, that the deductive detective gave way to the hard-boiled detective. Though Spade never reappeared in a sequel, he still remains the quintessential modern detective: crafty, violent, distrustful of women, but true to his own moral code.

Raymond Chandler described the modern detective when he wrote, in *The Simple Art of Murder,* "Down these mean streets a man must go who is not himself mean, who is neither tarnished nor afraid." But that didn't mean that the hero couldn't pretend to play both sides of the law. In the latter 1940s and early 1950s, the detective film was the perfect vehicle for the gloomy stories described by the French term *film noir (q.v.).* After the advent of the atom bomb, at the beginning of the Cold War, the dark, rain-splattered streets, swirling mist, and oppressive visual angles of *film noir* mirrored an era of moral confusion and paranoia. The search for meaning—truth—by the detective hero during that time was of considerable relevance to the audience.

Detective films were quite popular during the *film noir* period, but the series detective did not flourish to the same degree as it had in the 1930s. Only one detective hero was brought to the screen again and again: Philip Marlowe. Chandler's hero was first played by Dick Powell in *Murder, My Sweet* (1944), then by Bogart in *The Big Sleep* (1946). Robert Montgomery took a turn as Marlowe in *The Lady in the Lake* (1946). After a long hiatus, he showed up played by James Garner in *Marlow* (1969), Elliot Gould in *The Long Goodbye* (1973), and Robert Mitchum in *Farewell My Lovely* (1975).

Marlow aside, detective films from the 1940s until the present have generally been one-shot affairs, occasionally followed by a sequel. And no longer was the detective film the sole territory of the card-carrying private dick. Insurance agents (Edward G. Robinson [q.v.] in *Double Indemnity,* 1944) and police detectives (Glenn Ford [q.v.] in *The Big Heat,* 1953) entered the scene.

By the mid-1950s, the detective film and most other genres gave way to the western. In the 1960s, however, the private detective made a comeback with Paul Newman (q.v.) in *Harper* (1966) and its 1975 sequel, *The Drowning Pool.* In fact, Newman's films can be said to mark the beginning and end of the modern golden era of the hard-boiled movie detective. Explosive, fast-

paced hits such as *Point Blank* (1967), *Bullitt* (1968), *The French Connection I* and *II* (1971 and 1975, respectively), *Klute* (1971), *Dirty Harry* (1971), and *Chinatown* (1974) were just a few of the impressive films made in the genre during that period of creativity and success, perhaps the richest of the fifty years since the advent of sound. Inevitably, however, there was a decline, marked by the spoof, *The Cheap Detective* (1978), which seemed to indicate that the category had just about played itself out.

It was only a matter of time before the detective film would reemerge, but in the 1980s it has been television, for the most part, that has stolen Hollywood's thunder with shows such as "Miami Vice" and "Moonlighting". Nonetheless, there have been several successful police detective films in the 1980s such as *Lethal Weapon* (1987), *Stakeout* (1987), and *Lethal Weapon II* (1989). *See also:* gangster movies

DIALOGUE DIRECTOR A person hired to help an actor learn his lines. Dialogue directors were hired by all of the Hollywood studios during the talkie revolution of the late 1920s and early 1930s. Film directors, unaccustomed to working with actors who suddenly had to read lines, were usurped by a veritable invading army of theater directors who coached the thespians in the ways of the spoken word. Eventually, just as a great many film directors learned how to deal with dialogue in their movies, a good many dialogue directors learned the secrets of filmmaking and became full-fledged directors in their own right.

In more recent years, the title dialogue director has been modified to that of dialogue coach, a job that usually involves assisting actors in the learning of foreign languages and accents.

DIAMOND, I. A. L. *See* Wilder, Billy

DIETRICH, MARLENE (1901–) Paramount's answer to Greta Garbo (q.v.) at MGM, Dietrich was worldly, sensual, and always mysterious. Though she appeared in relatively few good films beyond the 1930s, Marlene Dietrich's impact has been so powerful, her image so truly unique, that her status as a Hollywood star of the first magnitude has never been questioned.

Born Maria Magdalena von Losch to a middle-class Berlin family, the young girl planned a career as a concert violinist until she suffered a serious wrist injury. The urge to perform, however, was still strong. She worked in the German film industry, starting as an extra. After studying at the Max Reinhardt Drama School, she appeared in quite a number of German and Austrian films and plays, also performing in several stage revues.

It was while she was dancing in a revue that director Josef von Sternberg spotted her. He had come to Ger-

Shaped and molded by director Joseph von Sternberg, Marlene Dietrich was the most exotically dressed and lit movie star of the early 1930s. Photo courtesy of The Siegel Collection.

many to make *The Blue Angel* (1930) with Emil Jannings as the professor ruined by his love for a cabaret singer. Though she agreed to play the part of Lola-Lola, Dietrich later confessed that she thought the role would destroy her growing career.

The result was quite the opposite. Von Sternberg turned her into a blonde, changed her look from that of an ingenue into a world-weary sophisticate, and on the strength of his rough-cut of *The Blue Angel,* Paramount signed Dietrich for one more film. The movie was *Morocco* (1930), in which she and Gary Cooper *(q.v.)* were also directed by von Sternberg. Both films opened in the United States at roughly the same time, and Dietrich became an instant star. She was so popular that her then scandalous propensity for wearing slacks caused a sensation and a fashion revolution among women.

Paramount signed her at the astronomical Depression-era price of $125,000 per picture. Von Sternberg continued to direct her in his own increasingly dreamlike decorative style in films such as *Dishonored,* (1931), *Shanghai Express* (1932), and *Blonde Venus* (1932). The

last of these three did not do well at the box office, and Rouben Mammoulian *(q.v.)* was called in to direct Dietrich in *The Song of Songs* (1933). Bereft over the loss of her svengali, Dietrich reportedly was dazed on the set, and was overheard mumbling, "Joe? Where are you, Joe?"

Apocryphal or not, the story suggests the deep bond between the star and director. They were teamed again in *The Scarlet Empress* (1934), a film that was badly reviewed and poorly received by audiences. Today, however, the film can be seen as a true masterpiece. *The Devil Is A Woman* (1935) was a lesser film and an even worse disaster at the box office, ending forever the collaboration of Dietrich and von Sternberg.

About this time, Hitler demanded that the famous German actress return to the Fatherland. Dietrich, an ardent anti-Nazi, refused, resulting in all her films being banned from Germany. Ironically, at the time Dietrich became a naturalized U.S. citizen, her film career was reaching its nadir. Before the bottom dropped out, she showed a comedic flair in *Desire* (1936), but *The Garden of Allah* (1936), *Knight Without Armour* (1937), and *Angel* (1937) were all disappointments. Worse news for Dietrich was that in a moviegoer poll of favorite actors and actresses, she came in at a dismal 126.

Paramount paid off her contract rather than make another movie with her. She was out of work for two years, until she was offered the role of Frenchie in the comedy western *Destry Rides Again* (1939). The teaming of Dietrich and Jimmy Stewart *(q.v.)* was an inspiration. The film was a big hit, saving Dietrich's career. In the 1940s, she starred in a number of moderately successful movies such as *The Flame of New Orleans* (1941) and *The Spoilers* (1942), but left Hollywood to entertain American troops. When she reappeared in films in the mid-1940s, her roles were either minor or the movies were. Not until 1948, in *A Foreign Affair,* did she have a juicy role in a first-rate film. But even in this Billy Wilder *(q.v.)* movie, she was the second female lead.

Her film appearances became less frequent in the 1950s, but they were memorable, just the same. Teamed again with Jimmy Stewart, she scored a hit in *No Highway* (1951), then played a rather bizarre, but unforgettable, female outlaw in the Fritz Lang *(q.v.)* western *Rancho Notorious* (1952). She had to wait until 1958 for two more decent roles, the first in *Witness for the Prosecution* and the second in Orson Welles' *Touch of Evil,* in which she was on screen for little more than five fabulous minutes.

Dietrich occasionally appeared in films throughout the 1960s and 1970s, and was the subject of a highly regarded documentary by Maximillian Schell in 1986 called, what else, *Marlene.*

See also: Sternberg, Joseph von

DIRECTOR   The person in charge of all the various creative elements of moviemaking. Though the creation of a film is a collaborative effort, it is the director to whom the other creative and technical people must report. And on the set, the director's word is law.

Despite the mythology, it is not the director who yells "action" on the set; it's the assistant director. Working with the producer, writer, cinematographer, and actors, helps the director shape the production in planning sessions, rehearsals, and during shooting. The director is also involved in the editing and scoring of the film in the postproduction process.

In addition to directing, a number of talented and/or successful directors have been known to write their own scripts. Some examples of writer-directors include Preston Sturges, Samuel Fuller, and Billy Wilder *(qq.v.)*. Fewer directors have managed to produce as well as direct. Among their number are such well-known examples as William Wyler and Cecil B. DeMille *(qq.v.)*. Directors also occasionally star in their own films, but in these cases, they generally tend to act as the producer, as well. Some of the best-known examples of these multitalented individuals are Charlie Chaplin, Clint Eastwood, and Warren Beatty *(qq.v.)*.

Directors who make movies about themes of personal interest are known as *auteurs (q.v.)*, a French term denoting creative authorship. Yet a director may be considered an *auteur* without writing, producing, or starring in a production. A few of the directors who are considered *auteurs* are Alfred Hitchcock, Josef von Sternberg, and Martin Scorsese *(qq.v.)*.

See also: actor-director; assistant director; producer-director; writer-director

DISASTER MOVIES   If there were no such thing as a disaster, it would have been created by the movies. No other medium—not fine art, not the theater, not even literature—can capture both the spectacle and the personal horror of a disaster the way a movie can. The huge, ever-changing canvas of the movie screen gives the audience a vicarious sense of danger and tragedy on a massive scale, whether by a volcano burying a city in ashes (*The Last Days of Pompeii*, 1935), an earthquake destroying Los Angeles (*Earthquake,* 1974), or a fire consuming a high-rise building (*Towering Inferno,* 1974). At the same time, in the hands of a skilled writer and director, a disaster film can also capture the human side of what otherwise might be a numbing experience.

With the aid of special effects, Hollywood has been able to recreate the sinking of the *Titanic,* the burning of Chicago, and the destruction of San Francisco. Most disaster movies have a moralistic element in them, at least in that some sort of corruption or hubris usually leads to the disaster. But in the ever-hopeful endings of Hollywood's disaster movies, as in *The Hurricane* (1937), good people always seem to survive to begin anew.
See also: all-star movies; special effects

DISNEY, WALT (1901–1966)   Hollywood's preeminent personality in the world of film animation. Though a mediocre artist, Disney was a visionary creative force as an animator, producer, and businessman. He turned animation into an art form and gave birth to a variety of characters whose names are known to hundreds of millions of people the world over. He built theme parks based on the power and appeal of his film creations, found a niche in Hollywood as *the* provider of family entertainment, and ultimately established a strong enough base so that others could eventually follow in his footsteps and turn the Disney Studio into the most financially successful film company of the late 1980s.

Born to a middle-class family, Disney became interested in drawing at an early age. He began studying his craft at the Kansas City Art Institute when he was fourteen years old. After a stint as an ambulance driver for the Red Cross in France at the end of World War I, Disney worked as a commercial artist back in Kansas City. He entered the infant world of animation when he and his new friend and collaborator, Ub Iwerks, began making crude animated commercials for the Kansas City Film Ad Company. Together, Disney and Iwerks created *Laugh-O-Grams,* animated shorts for local Kansas City theaters, but the company they formed went bust.

Disney went off to Hollywood and pursued his calling (Iwerks would eventually follow and contribute greatly to his friend's success), starting a new company in 1923 with his brother, Roy, and creating a combination of live action and animation shorts called *Alice in Cartoonland.* The pair hardly set the world on fire, but Disney remained in business long enough to try again in 1927 with an *Oswald the Rabbit* cartoon series. These fared slightly better, but Disney's big breakthrough came in 1928 when he and Iwerks created *Plane Crazy* starring a new animated character, Mickey Mouse.

Plane Crazy and the next Mickey Mouse cartoon, *Gallopin' Gaucho,* were both silent shorts. In an effort to stay ahead of the animated competition, he quickly turned to sound and made what became his watershed cartoon starring Mickey Mouse, *Steamboat Willie* (1929), with Disney, himself, providing the little rodent's squeaky voice.

As shown in *Steamboat Willie,* music and animation made a winning combination, and Disney proceeded to create a series of shorts called *Silly Symphonies,* the most famous of which was *The Three Little Pigs* (1933), which introduced the hit tune, "Who's Afraid of the Big Bad Wolf?" In addition to turning his shorts into mini-musicals, Disney also experimented with color, work-

Walt Disney was the "King of Animation." The creator of Mickey Mouse and the dreamer who made *Fantasia* (1940), he was also a businessman who turned cartoon characters into an empire. Photo courtesy of Movie Star News.

ing hand-in-hand with Technicolor to implement their new three-color process in his animated short, *Flowers and Trees* (1933). It was a huge success and soon Disney's Technicolor *Silly Symphonies* were outgrossing his black-and-white Mickey Mouse films, which were later made in Technicolor *(q.v.)*, as well.

Ever the innovator, Disney created not only new characters, such as Donald Duck, Minnie Mouse, Dippy Dawg (later changed to Goofy), and Pluto, he also improved the technology of animation, incorporating the use of Ub Iwerk's multi-plane camera, a device that allowed for greater clarity, depth, and detail in animated filmmaking.

Not content to remain in the relative backwater of short subjects, Disney decided to test the appeal of animation in the feature-length format. Putting his newfound prosperity on the line, he plunged into the making of *Snow White and the Seven Dwarfs* (1937). His gamble paid off in a critical and commercial success, followed by yet another hit, *Pinocchio* (1940). In the hopes of expanding his audience and gaining ever-

greater prestige, Disney then joined with conductor Leopold Stokowski to create an animated feature built around classical music. The result was *Fantasia* (1940), a hugely ambitious work that flopped in its initial release, scorned by the music elite and ignored by children who found it rather boring. It was only later, when reissued, that a more sophisticated audience than young children discovered the film and its startling beauty. It has since become one of Disney's most profitable early features.

In his lifetime, Disney's films earned twenty-nine Oscars, though, curiously, all of them were for his short subjects (except for several special Academy Awards); none of his feature films brought home a statuette.

The early 1940s, after *Fantasia,* were a difficult time for Disney. The company was rocked by labor unrest that finally resulted in mass resignations and the formation of a new competitive company, UPA, by those who quit.

Undaunted, Disney continued making animated features, but with generally lesser ambition as the years rolled on. His more memorable efforts were in the 1940s and early 1950s with films such as *Dumbo* (1941), *Bambi* (1943), *Peter Pan* (1953), and *The Lady and the Tramp* (1956). Among his later animated features only *The Jungle Book* (1967) had any particular flair. For the most part, his animated films became too sweet and simple for anyone but the very young child.

Meanwhile, however, Disney began diversifying out of animation, putting out live-action films beginning with *Treasure Island* (1950). Among his many memorable live-action family entertainment features were *20,000 Leagues Under the Sea* (1954), *Old Yeller* (1957), and *Tonka* (1958). Also during the 1950s Disney produced his highly acclaimed nature movie series, *True-Life Adventures* including *The Living Desert* (1953), *White Wilderness* (1958), and *The Jungle Cat* (1960).

Though he had done so in the past, in the 1960s Disney began combining live action and animation as never before, most memorably in *Mary Poppins* (1964), one of the biggest hits of his last decade. He also went heavily into special effects in the making of such light fare as *The Absent-Minded Professor* (1961) and *Son of Flubber* (1963).

Walt Disney was more than a moviemaker. His Sunday evening television show, "The Wonderful World of Color" (which he hosted) made him known to tens of millions of children. His daring development of Disneyland in Anaheim, California and DisneyWorld in Orlando, Florida resulted in monstrous money-makers that perpetuated the magic he created in his films.

Following Disney's death after lung surgery, the empire continued to thrive by merely feeding off of its founder's original formula for success. But soon the company entered a period of paralysis during the 1970s when profits dwindled and the studio's efforts centered more on real estate than on filmmaking.

The company was close to being taken over and dismantled in the early 1980s when a shake-up brought in Michael Eisner as chairman in 1984. He revitalized the Disney Studio by encouraging the recently established "adult" filmmaking subsidiary of the company, Touchstone Pictures, that had already made *Splash* (1984), the first Disney hit since *The Love Bug* (1969). A constant stream of Touchstone hits under the Eisner team soon followed, including *Down and Out in Beverly Hills* (1986), *Ruthless People* (1986), *Outrageous Fortune* (1987), *Stakeout* (1987), *Good Morning, Vietnam* (1987), *Three Men and a Baby* (1988), and many others.

After being long dormant in the field of animated features, Disney made its grand return with *Who Framed Roger Rabbit* (1988), a film coproduced by Steven Spielberg *(q.v.)*. *Roger Rabbit* combined live action and computer animation with startling visual results. It was a box office bonanza, which Disney followed with the wholly animated movies *Oliver and Company* (1988) and *The Little Mermaid* (1989). The Disney company plans to produce one animated feature every year, putting it once again in the forefront of family entertainment.

As a corporate entity, Disney continues to grow in many directions, including television, theme parks (there is a third Disneyland in Tokyo and a fourth expected to open near Paris, France in 1992), licensing, real estate, and the number and variety of movies that they make.
See also: animation

DISTRIBUTION   The process by which movies are made available to the public. It is one thing to have a good movie "in the can," and quite another to place that film into the best theaters, at the right time, for its optimal audience. From the very beginning of the film business, distribution has been the key to success.

In the earliest years of the twentieth century, the businessman and inventor of moving pictures Thomas Edison nearly succeeded in monopolizing the burgeoning movie industry by controlling its distribution. Along with nine other major film companies, Edison formed the Motion Picture Patents Company in 1909, claiming that it alone had the legal right to make motion pictures. In turn, the Patents Company then created the General Film Company, which announced that any theater showing its films had to pay a licensing fee of $2 per week. According to Richard Griffith and Arthur Mayer in their wonderful book, *The Movies,* "The nickelodeon operators reacted to it much as the colonists of 1760 reacted to the Stamp Act." The independents, led by William Fox and Carl Laemmle, fought the Patents Company and their subsidiary, eventually defeating them by making their own movies in defiance of the

patent laws and distributing them through the independent "exchanges" where films were rented. Later, in 1915, the Patent Company was finally defeated in the courts.

The exchanges proliferated, becoming the device through which films were routinely distributed. Producers sold their product to the middlemen at the exchange, who, in turn, rented the films to theaters. As the studio system solidified in the 1930s, the major film companies had little trouble with distribution because they also owned their own theater chains. Hollywood had become such a dominant force in moviemaking that films made outside the studios or in foreign countries had little appeal in America. Independent producers were no threat to the majors.

In the late 1940s and early 1950s everything began to change. The movie companies were forced to divest themselves of their theater chains; TV was making massive inroads into the moviegoing audience; and foreign films and independent producers began to fight for distribution. Because fees are particularly lucrative, distribution is the one area of the film business that rarely loses money (the distributor doesn't pay any of the usually enormous production costs, yet earns a percentage of the box office gross). It is no wonder, then, that the major studios such as Universal, Warner Bros., and Paramount *(qq.v.)* eventually became distributors for foreign films and the proliferating independents. And though their own film production has drastically diminished during the last four decades, the majors remain the preeminent distributors of motion pictures today.

The actual distribution process begins when the final prints of a film are offered to the distribution company, which, in turn, rents them to theater outlets. The distributor handles all the postproduction publicity, sets up the critics' screenings, and is usually responsible for deciding the release strategy for the film (e.g., should it open with a saturation booking, have a limited run in a few big cities in order to gain word of mouth, be sent to film festivals like Cannes for prestige, etc.). The distribution company may also be involved in the selling of rights to cable TV, the videcassette market, etc., all in an attempt to fully exploit a movie's financial potential.
See also: four-walling

DMYTRYK, EDWARD (1908–   )   A director whose mark in the American film industry was made as much by his unique role in the Hollywood Ten *(q.v.)* scandal as it was by his movies. As a director, he made more than fifty films, only about half-a-dozen of which were especially memorable. Nonetheless, Dmytryk was an effective director in the *film noir* in the late 1940s and early 1950s.

Born to Ukranian immigrants, Dmytryk and his family settled in Los Angeles when he was young. As a teenager, he found work at Paramount as a messenger and, later, as a projectionist. After an aborted college career he went back to Paramount and had a series of jobs at the studio, eventually moving up through the editing department ranks to chief editor, a position he held virtually throughout the 1930s. Along the way, he received his first taste of directing when he made an independent film, *The Hawk* (1935). It was neither a critical nor a commercial success. Finally, he got his big break when he stepped in to direct the troubled Betty Grable *(q.v.)* vehicle, *Million Dollar Legs* (1939). While he didn't receive screen credit for his work on the film, he did receive a contract to direct "B" movies. He was off and running.

In his early years as a director he made such forgettable films as *Television Spy* (1939), *Mystery Sea Raider* (1940), and *Sweetheart of the Campus* (1941). His career took an upswing when he made the anti-Nazi thriller *Hitler's Children* (1943), a film that audiences loved and critics cited for its effective filmmaking. Before long, Dymtryk was working with bigger stars (such as Dick Powell *q.v.*) and more substantial budgets, hitting his stride in the mid-1940s with the adaptation of Raymond Chandler's *Farewell My Lovely,* called *Murder My Sweet* (1944). Other highly regarded *films noir* followed, such as *Cornered* (1945), and *Crossfire* (1947), which was also the first film that decried anti-Semitism.

At what was then the height of his career, Dmytryk was called before the House Un-American Activities Committee, which was investigating Communist influence in Hollywood. The director refused to answer the committee's questions and he, along with nine others, became members of the infamous Hollywood Ten. Unlike the other nine, however, who served a full year in prison and were blacklisted from the industry, Dmytryk eventually admitted to being a member of the Communist Party and agreed to testify for the committee and name others who had been members. His testimony purged him of guilt in the eyes of the industry, and he was allowed to continue working. His actions were not looked upon so kindly by Hollywood liberals who thought he compromised himself and sold his friends down the river in order to get out of jail and continue working.

But work, he did—and quite steadily. Among his few good films during the early 1950s were *The Sniper* (1952) and *The Caine Mutiny* (1954). Because the latter film was such a big hit, Dmytryk received more important, bigger-budget assignments, such as *Raintree County* (1957), *The Young Lions* (1958), and *The Carpetbaggers* (1964). At best, he had mixed results with these and other films during the latter 1950s and early 1960s. After the further box office disappointments of *Alvarez Kelly* (1966), *Anzio* (1968), and *Shalako* (1968),

Dmytryk appeared to have retired, but returned to the director's chair one last time to make *Bluebeard* (1972), which was yet another box office flop.
See also: Hollywood Ten

DOLLY A platform on which the camera and its operator move. The dolly's purpose is to allow the camera to move smoothly in relation to the action of the scene being photographed.

The camera operator doesn't control the dolly; that job belongs to the dolly grip. When the dolly is used, the result is often called a tracking, trucking, or traveling shot, as well as a dolly shot. The most common form of dolly shots are those in which the camera moves toward the action in a scene (i.e., dolly in), moves away from the action (i.e, dolly out), and moves parallel to a scene in motion (i.e., dollying, tracking, etc.). When a camera is placed on the back of a truck to follow an action in motion, it is still called a dolly (or trucking, traveling, etc.) shot, even though the camera isn't on the dolly platform.

There are all sorts of exotic dollies for unusual uses, such as the crab dolly, which can move sideways, in addition to foreward and backward. There is also the western dolly, whose massive rubber wheels provide a steady, smooth ride for the camera over uneven terrain. Yet another kind of tracking device is the elemack dolly (also known as the spider dolly), which is particularly useful in close quarters, such as narrow doorways, because of its adjustable legs.

DONEN, STANLEY (1924–) A former dancer and choreographer, he began codirecting musicals in the 1950s with excellent results. His solo career as a director, however, has had its ups and downs. Known for his sophisticated style, Donen is highly regarded as a link to the glorious past of the MGM musicals of the 1950s, but he has been unable to bring that particular magic to bear during the 1970s and 1980s.

Donen was a dancer who worked in the chorus of the 1940 stage production of *Pal Joey*, which starred Gene Kelly *(q.v.)*. The actor was impressed with the young dancer and gave Donen the job of co-choreographing his next stage musical, *Best Foot Foward*. When the show was turned into a film, Donen went west and co-choreographed the movie version and appeared in the chorus. It was the start of his long Hollywood career.

As a choreographer, he worked on such films as *Cover Girl* (1944), *Anchors Aweigh* (1945), and *A Date with Judy* (1948). 1949 was his watershed year. He wrote the script and choreographed the dance numbers for *Take Me Out to the Ball Game,* and later teamed with Gene Kelly to codirect and choreograph *On the Town.* The latter movie was an innovative milestone because it was the first MGM musical to be partially shot on location (in New York) rather than filmed entirely in the studio.

With Gene Kelly, he went on to codirect *Singin' in the Rain* (1952) as well as choreograph the classic dance routines of that wonderful film. A few years later, he again joined with his old mentor, Kelly, to codirect *It's Always Fair Weather* (1955). He also codirected and coproduced (with George Abbott) *The Pajama Game* (1957) and *Damn Yankees* (1958).

It might seem as if Donen could only do splendid work as a collaborator, but he also had some considerable success as the solo director of *Royal Wedding* (1950), *Seven Brides for Seven Brothers* (1954), and *Funny Face* (1957). He also branched out from musicals to direct and produce such sophisticated comedies and thrillers as *Indiscreet* (1958), *Charade* (1963), and *Arabesque* (1966).

He hit the peak of his urbane style with *Two for the Road* (1967), but he has had nothing but commercial clunkers ever since, suffering with such outright bombs as *Staircase* (1969), *The Little Prince* (1974), and *Lucky Lady* (1975). *Movie Movie* (1978) restored at least a bit of critical shine to Donen's directorial career, but his strikeouts with the box office loser *Saturn 3* (1980) and the roundly hated *Blame it on Rio* (1984) tarnished it anew. With so many box office disasters in a row, even a director with credits including *Singin' in the Rain* has trouble getting films financed. Yet Donen's reputation, built over four decades, remains secure despite the failings that have come at the tail end of his career.

DOUGLAS, KIRK (1916–   )   A movie star for more than forty years, he has rarely played it safe either as an actor, director, or producer. With his muscular body, throaty snarl, and trademark cleft chin, Douglas has always been an imposing presence on screen, usually best cast in action roles. Yet Douglas was never purely an action star. Some of his most memorable roles have been in contemporary urban movies where he plays ambitious, hard-edged, selfish characters who are finally redeemed (or receive their comeuppance) by film's end. That Douglas has been able to win audience sympathy for his oftentimes less than likable characters speaks volumes about the intensity of his performances.

Douglas, the son of illiterate Russian Jewish immigrants, was born Issur Danielovitch, which was changed first to Isidore Demsky then, later, to his stage name. Because of anti-Semitism, Douglas' father could not get a job in his upstate New York hometown. Living a life of poverty, young Douglas worked his way through Saint Lawrence University as a janitor, then won a scholarship to the American Academy of Dramatic Arts in New York City.

He made his Broadway debut as a singing Western Union boy in *Spring Again* in the early 1940s, but when World War II intervened, Douglas enlisted in the U.S.

Navy. Out of the service, he returned to the Broadway stage, where he soon came to the attention of Hollywood. His film career was launched in a lead role opposite Barbara Stanwyck (q.v.) in the hit *The Strange Loves of Martha Ivers* (1946), and his auspicious debut was followed by other meaty roles in some rather good films such as *Out of the Past* (1947) and *A Letter to Three Wives* (1948). The movie that turned him into a major star was Stanley Kramer's *Champion* (1949), in which he played a boxer who would do anything to succeed. The role brought him his first Oscar nomination.

Immensely popular during the 1950s, Douglas was able to make a number of startlingly cynical (and honest) movies without losing his audience. Among his best, most enduring, films of that era were Billy Wilder's *The Big Carnival* (1951), which also goes by the title *Ace in the Hole*, William Wyler's *Detective Story* (1951), Vincente Minnelli's *The Bad and the Beautiful* (1952), for which he won a second Academy Award nomination for Best Actor, and Stanley Kubrick's *Paths of Glory* (1957), a classic antiwar film that the actor also produced.

Douglas exhibited his range when he surprised the industry by choosing to play Vincent Van Gogh in Vincente Minnelli's *Lust for Life* (1956). The film became a hit and Douglas was vindicated with his third and final Oscar nomination.

Wanting more control over his movie projects, Douglas established his own independent film company in 1955, the Bryna Company (named for his mother). It was through the power of this successful enterprise that Douglas was able to take on and defeat the insidious Hollywood blacklist that had kept hundreds of talented people accused of left-wing or Communist ties from ever working in the film industry. He did so by publicly announcing that he was hiring blacklisted screenwriter (and member of the Hollywood Ten) Dalton Trumbo to write the script for *Spartacus* (1960). His bold move was imitated by others and the blacklist soon crumbled.

Douglas' popularity continued to be coupled with good filmmaking throughout the early 1960s with such films as *Town Without Pity* (1961), *Lonely Are the Brave* (1962), *Two Weeks in Another Town* (1962), and *Seven Days in May* (1964). But after *Cast a Giant Shadow* (1966), his movies began to sag at the box office. Mediocre westerns, a gangster movie, and lightweight spy movies sent his career limping into the 1970s. In an attempt to turn things around, Douglas directed himself in *Scalawag* (1973), a western *Treasure Island* that tried too hard to please, and another western, *Posse* (1975), a highly regarded movie that flopped despite good reviews.

It is clear that Douglas owed much of his success during the earlier period of his career to having worked with many of Hollywood's top directors. Wisely attempting to repeat this strategy for success in the late

1970s, he worked with Brian De Palma (q.v.) in *The Fury* (1978) and Stanley Donen (q.v.) in *Saturn 3* (1980). Neither movie caught fire at the box office.

In the early 1980s, Douglas had a sleeper hit with an Australian western, *The Man from Snowy River* (1982), but his opportunities in the film medium were becoming more limited. Still vigorous and unwilling to settle into character parts, he often appeared to be straining to play heroic leading men in his later movies. It was not until he played an old man in a nursing home in a TV movie called "Amos" (1985) that Douglas finally let go of his image. The result was a well-deserved Emmy nomination.

He has begun to appear more regularly on TV in recent years, but the big screen was blessed with a nostalgic teaming of two old friends, Douglas and his pal Burt Lancaster (q.v.), in *Tough Guys* (1986). It was a mediocre film but the two gifted pros clearly delighted in working together and their pleasure was infectious.

Douglas has had other pleasures in his later years, most notably in seeing his son, Michael, win an Oscar for Best Supporting Actor for his work in *Wall Street* (1987). It was a poignant moment knowing that Kirk Douglas, for all his years in Hollywood, had never taken home an Oscar of his own.

See also: Douglas, Michael; Kubrick, Stanley; Minnelli, Vincente

DOUGLAS, MELVYN (1901–1981) In his Hollywood prime, he was a witty and sophisticated leading man, much in the mold of William Powell (q.v.). Far too many of his films were mediocre, but in a handful of well-scripted films, he shone very brightly indeed. In his later film career, Melvyn Douglas lent an awesome dignity to the older men he played, and in many respects his supporting character parts were the highlights of his uneven but intriguing career.

Born Melvyn Edouard Hesselberg, Douglas was the son of a concert pianist. Drawn to the theater after discovering acting in high school, the young man began acting after serving in World War I. After a long apprenticeship, he finally arrived on Broadway in 1928 in *A Free Soul*.

Broadway actors were much in demand at the beginning of the sound era, and Douglas was signed to star with Gloria Swanson (q.v.) in a recreation of his Broadway hit *Tonight or Never* (1931). The play also served as the springboard for his long and happy marriage to Helen Gahagan, who had been a member of the cast. Miss Gahagan would eventually leave show business to become a U.S. Senator from California.

While *Tonight or Never* had been a hit on the stage, the film version didn't catch fire and neither did Douglas. Nonetheless, he was chosen to costar with Greta Garbo (q.v.) in *As You Desire Me* (1932). Garbo's fans didn't latch on to Douglas and his career quickly slumped.

By 1933 he was starring in films like *The Vampire Bat*.

His career began to pick up in 1935 when he joined Claudette Colbert (q.v.) in the cast of *She Married Her Boss*. Columbia Studios was impressed and gave him a seven-year contract. A trail of mediocre films followed until he starred with Irene Dunne (q.v.) in *Theodora Goes Wild* (1936). His career was finally beginning to take off. He was loaned to MGM, which paired him with Joan Crawford (q.v.) in *The Gorgeous Hussy* (1936). By this time it was evident that Hollywood had found a perfect, debonair light comedian to squire the great ladies of film through their better vehicles without upstaging them. In fact, MGM was so taken with his serviceability, that it took the unusual step of making a deal with Columbia to split his contract between the two studios.

Over the course of the next several years he smoothed the way for such stars as Virginia Bruce (twice), Lily Pons, Claudette Colbert (again), Joan Crawford (again), Marlene Dietrich (q.v.), and Deanna Durbin (q.v.). But the role that lifted his career to the Hollywood heights if only for one brief moment was his second starring role opposite Greta Garbo, this time in the classic comedy *Ninotchka* (1939). His bemused capitalist playboy pitted against Garbo's dour Communist was a sheer delight. Douglas was Garbo's perfect foil, and yet he only received the role by default when William Powell (who also would have been marvelous) had to pass on the part due to illness. After *Ninotchka*, Douglas returned to his station, capably playing male leads in movies designed for their female stars.

Despite his age, Douglas enlisted in the army as a private in 1942 and was discharged back into civilian life in 1946 as a major. Hollywood had changed and the seasoned actor never quite regained his leading man status, although he continued acting in films until 1951.

After a long and successful decade on Broadway during the 1950s, Douglas made a triumphant return to the big screen as a character actor in the early 1960s, eventually winning an Oscar for Best Supporting Actor for his harsh, true-to-life portrayal of a demanding father in *Hud* (1963).

His presence in films of the 1960s and 1970s invariably added a measure of class to any production in which he was involved. Whether playing in dramas such as *I Never Sang for My Father* (1970), or comedies such as his last film, *Being There* (1979), nothing rang phony in his portrayals of older men.

DOUGLAS, MICHAEL (1944–) An actor/producer who has boldly succeeded in fighting his way out from behind the shadow of his famous father, actor Kirk Douglas. The younger Douglas, who looks much like his father (including the cleft chin), initially had more success in films as a producer than an actor. Even his best acting roles were in films he produced himself. In recent years, however, he has emerged as a major star both in his own films and those produced by others, proving himself not only a box office draw but a genuinely fine actor.

After graduating from USC—Santa Barbara, he started his film career not as an actor but as an assistant director. The lure of acting, however, was too strong for him and he soon began working on stage and on TV, gaining national recognition in the late 1960s as Karl Malden's young sidekick on the TV cop show, "The Streets of San Francisco."

Douglas' film career started slowly with roles in mostly forgettable films such as *Hail Hero!* (1969), *Where's Jack?* (1969), *Adam at 6 AM* (1970), *Summertree* (1971), and *Napoleon & Samantha* (1972). Though his acting was not making anyone sit up and take notice, his producing certainly did. He bought the film rights to Ken Kesey's novel *One Flew Over the Cuckoo's Nest,* and turned the cult favorite into a blockbuster hit in 1975 with Jack Nicholson *(q.v.)* in the starring role of Randle McMurphy. The film garnered every major Academy Award, including Best Picture, making Douglas' debut as a producer stunningly successful. Ironically, his father had originally bought the rights to the novel in the 1960s, wanting desperately to turn it into a movie starring himself.

Throughout the late 1970s and early 1980s Douglas acted without making much of a ripple in the Hollywood waters in films such as *Coma* (1978), *Running* (1979), *It's My Turn* (1980), and *Star Chamber* (1983). For the most part, the films he produced himself were better received critically and certainly more successful at the box office. Wisely, he gave himself roles in these films, costarring with Jack Lemmon and Jane Fonda in *The China Syndrome* (1979), and finally hitting the big time as an actor with his swashbuckling role in the hit *Romancing the Stone* (1984) and its sequel, *The Jewel of the Nile* (1985).

Fully established as a genuine star, he had his greatest year in 1987 when he starred in two major critical and commercial hits, *Fatal Attraction* and *Wall Street*. For the latter film, in which he played an insidiously charming villian, Douglas was honored with an Academy Award for Best Actor He recently starred in *War of the Roses* (1989) and *Black Rain* (1989).
See also: Douglas, Kirk; Forman, Milos

DRACULA The success of this 1931 film, based on a Broadway play that was, in turn, based on the novel by Bram Stoker, spawned a rash of classic horror films that has never been equaled. *Dracula* also established a new movie star, while providing the movies with a classic character that literally won't die.

Dracula wasn't the first movie about a vampire—that honor belongs to F. W. Murnau's classic German silent film *Nosferatu* (1923). The sound version of the vampire

tale, though, directed by Tod Browning *(q.v.)* and starring Bela Lugosi *(q.v.)* was the film that completely captured the public's imagination.

Tod Browning had already established himself during the silent era as a director of the macabre, working with the great Lon Chaney *(q.v.)* on several films. In fact, the pair was slated to make *Dracula* together until Chaney died of throat cancer. Bela Lugosi, who had played the part on Broadway, stepped in to take Chaney's place and in the process became a screen legend.

When *Dracula* opened, ambulances were stationed at movie theaters to treat people who became hysterical with fright. They were undoubtedly part of a press agent's gimmick, but it worked. The film was a huge hit, and its success led to the making of *Frankenstein* (1931), *The Mummy* (1932), and a host of sequels and other horror films, such as *White Zombie* (1932), and *The Black Cat* (1934).

In every decade since the 1930s there have been new Dracula movies. Since Lugosi, the character has been placed by Lon Chaney, Jr., Christopher Lee, and even George Hamilton, to name just a few of the actors who have essayed the role. The sensual, as well as the horrifying, aspects of the Dracula story continue to fascinate audiences, but it's unlikely that any new rendering of the story will ever have the impact of the original sound version of 1931.
See also: horror movies

DRESSLER, MARIE (1869–1934) One of the most beloved early stars of Hollywood. Her special niche in film history is due to her singular comeback, a return to stardom that very few Hollywood actors before or since have ever accomplished. Unlike Ingrid Bergman, for instance, who fell from grace and made a triumphant comeback, Dressler made her return to glory without the benefit of either youth or a pretty face. Old and overweight, with a voice that sounded like a foghorn, Dressler's resurrection was due to her common touch—and deference to her history. Audiences knew her life story, which inspired them in the Depression era. It was no wonder that she was once called "The Heart of America."

Born Leila Von Koerber in Canada, the future Marie Dressler eventually made her way to New York and became a comic actress. At the turn of the century and beyond, Dressler was a major name in vaudeville, scoring successes in New York and London. In 1914, she joined with Mack Sennett *(q.v.)* to make a film version of one of her hit shows. The movie was *Tillie's Punctured Romance* (1914), a six-reel comedy (the first of its kind) that was a huge critical and financial success.

Though Dressler continued to make silent comedies, none of them was ever again as commercially successful as her first. The downward slide had begun, and her pro-union activities hurt her vaudeville career, as well.

During the early 1930s, at the dawn of the age of glamour queens, Marie Dressler, an older lady with more lines than the Union Pacific, was Hollywood's number-one box office draw. Photo courtesy of The Siegel Collection.

By 1927, Dressler was a has-been who was about to take a job as a maid.

It was then that MGM screenwriter Frances Marion *(q.v.)* wrote *The Callahans and the Murphys* (1927) with Dressler in mind, and won Irving Thalberg's *(q.v.)* permission to sign her for the film. The movie was not a hit. But Frances Marion kept trying, for Dressler had been a great help to the screenwriter earlier in her career. But despite Marion's best efforts, none of the new silent film roles helped Dressler's career.

As a stage-trained actress, Dressler finally had her chance to reach the heights again with the advent of sound. After a series of small roles that established her as a comic personality, Frances Marion once more stepped into the breach, convincing Irving Thalberg to use her in a straight role in Garbo's *Anna Christie* (1930). The film, and Dressler, were hits. MGM eventually signed her to a long-term contract. She was worth every penny; *Min and Bill* (1930), with Wallace Beery *(q.v.)*, brought her an Oscar for Best Actress and it was one of the top-grossing films of the year. In 1933, when she made *Tugboat Annie* (again with Wallace Beery) and the all-star movie *Dinner at Eight*, Marie Dressler was voted Hollywood's number-one box of-fice draw.

Dressler died of cancer in 1934.

DREYFUSS, RICHARD (1948–) Neither tall, dark, nor handsome, Dreyfuss is an actor who is, in fact, short, pale, and slightly tubby—but with a sweet, cherubic face that is immensely likable. Onscreen, he exudes energy and intelligence, along with a rascally charm, all of which helped him to become one of the hottest stars of the 1970s, before he nearly killed himself in a drug-related car accident. He eventually returned to the movies, drug-free, to become one of Hollywood's most accomplished character actor/stars of the 1980s.

Born in Brooklyn, Dreyfuss moved with his well-to-do family (his father was an attorney) to Los Angeles when he was nine years old. He began acting at the Beverly Hills Jewish Center. His professional debut was in a local L.A. production of *In Mama's House* when he was fifteen years old. An agent spotted him and soon found him work in TV shows such as "Peyton Place" and "The Big Valley." He continued working in the theater, as well, during the next several years until he made his film debut in a bit part in *Valley of the Dolls* (1967), which was followed by a tiny role in *The Graduate* (1967). His first important film part, and one that suited his cherubic looks, was in the supporting but splashy role of Baby Face Nelson in *Dillinger* (1969).

After a minor flop in *The Second Coming of Suzanne* (1973), Dreyfuss won the role of Curt in *American Graffiti* (1973), joining a superb cast of future stars. But it was he who stood out from the crowd, bringing a thoughtfulness and integrity to the film that was only partly the result of good writing and direction.

In his next film, *The Apprenticeship of Duddy Kravitz* (1974), he carried the entire production (as opposed to being part of an ensemble in *American Graffiti*), and gave one of the greatest performances of the decade. His kinetic, nervous energy was palpable as the pushy, conniving young man who yearns for success but loses his moral bearings along the way. His Duddy was a richly drawn human being played with remarkable sensitivity. The small-budget movie wasn't a big popular success, but it marked the arrival of a giant talent.

Dreyfuss had one of the three lead roles (as the marine biologist) in *Jaws* (1975). The film's gargantuan success suddenly put the young actor in the category of potential superstar. Instead of making another obviously commercial feature, though, he chose to star in an artsy, low-budget, X-rated film called *Inserts* (1976). The movie was an intriguing tour de force of anguish and angst, but it bombed at the box office.

After appearing in a small role in an all-star TV movie, "Victory at Entebbe" (1976), Dreyfuss' next two films, both released in 1977, brought him to the apex of his pre-accident career. He starred in Steven Spielberg's *(q.v.)* uplifting and enchanting *Close Encounters of the Third Kind,* and then easily shifted gears to play a romantic lead (for the first time) in Neil

Simon's *The Goodbye Girl* (1977), for which he won an Oscar for Best Actor.

His next projects, among them *The Big Fix* (1978), *The Competition* (1980), *Whose Life Is It Anyway?* (1981), and *The Buddy System* (filmed in 1982 but released in 1984) all featured fine performances, but none of them was a big winner at the box office—and some of them were major disasters. He was supposed to have starred in Bob Fosse's *All that Jazz* (1979), but he had quit the project at the last minute (replaced by Roy Scheider). Much of what he did (and did not do) during these years was a result of his growing drug dependency.

When his car hit a tree and overturned one night in late 1982, he not only ended up in the hospital, he was also arrested for cocaine possession. It took him three years to make a comeback in Paul Mazursky's *(q.v.)* hit comedy *Down and Out in Beverly Hills* (1986), but the film marked the debut of a changed, more mature, Dreyfuss who could still take hold of the screen—no mean feat, considering that he shared the screen with Bette Midler and Mike the Dog.

In *Down and Out in Beverly Hills* Dreyfuss had a character part, and it signaled a big change in his approach to the movies. His next film, the critically acclaimed *Tin Men* (1987), was both a splendid, yet touching, comedy that was also built on character portrayals rather than star turns. *Stakeout* (1987) was his third hit in a row, showing that Dreyfuss, in the character part of a regular cop, could be funny, exciting, and sexy. Then, in yet another character part as a middle-aged attorney, he held his own on screen against Barbra Streisand's *(q.v.)* powerful performance in *Nuts* (1988). He stumbled with the critically snubbed *Let It Ride* (1989), yet, like Dustin Hoffman *(q.v.)*, Richard Dreyfuss has become a star character actor of considerable depth and reach.

See also: American Graffiti

DUBBING There are two film-related definitions of this word. The first is the mixing of all the different sound tracks of a film—the music, dialogue, special effects, etc.—which are then edited onto one synchronized master sound track in order to make copies. The second usage of the term, which is more often heard, refers to the recording of sound that will replace what has previously been recorded on film.

When a director sees the dailies *(q.v.)* and is unhappy about the way an individual line of dialogue is delivered, he may ask the actor to "dub," or re-record, his words in the studio, synchronizing his speech to his filmed lip movements (this is also called post-synchronization). When the actor himself doesn't like his reading of a line, the director may not want to spend the time and money to reshoot the entire scene, and he may tell the

actor, "We'll fix it in the studio," by which he means the dialogue will be dubbed.

Another common use of dubbing occurs in musicals where an actor or actress has been hired who lacks an adequate singing voice. In these cases, the musical numbers are dubbed, and the audience hears someone else's voice coming out of the star's mouth. For instance, a very young Andy Williams dubbed Lauren Bacall's *(q.v.)* musical numbers in *To Have and Have Not* (1944); Nan Wynn, not Rita Hayworth *(q.v.)*, sang the sultry lyrics to "Put the Blame on Mame" in *Gilda* (1946); India Adams sang Cyd Charisse's numbers in *The Band Wagon* (1953); and in *West Side Story* (1961), Marni Nixon dubbed all of Natalie Wood/Maria's songs and Jim Bryant dubbed all of Richard Beymer/Tony's lyrics.

The most common form of dubbing takes place when a movie is marketed in a country where a language different from that of the country in which the film was made is spoken. If subtitles are not used, then all of the dialogue may be dubbed in a studio, often by actors other than those who appeared in the film.

DUCK SOUP The 1933 Marx Brothers movie that many critics consider to be their best. No sappy love interests mar the seventy-minute movie as they would in later films at MGM; no interludes halt the movie so that the brothers can show off their musical skills. The film is only powered by fast, furious humor, expertly directed by Leo McCarey *(q.v.)*, the finest director with whom the group would work.

Originally titled Cracked Ice, Paramount changed the film's name so that it would follow the "animal" motif that had begun with their second film, *Animal Crackers* (1930), which had been followed by *Monkey Business* (1931) and *Horsefeathers* (1932).

McCarey was well-trained in movie comedy, having worked with Mack Sennett *(q.v.)* at the Keystone Studio. The script, music, and lyrics were provided by Bert Kalmar and Harry Ruby, with Arthur Sheekman and Nat Perrin providing additional dialogue.

The plot, if you can call it that, involves Groucho becoming the dictator of a Ruritanian country called Freedonia. Ambassador Trentino (Louis Calhern) of the neighboring country, Sylvania, wants to control Groucho's nation and, with the hilarious help of his two spies, Chico and Harpo, the two countries go to war (they have to, says Groucho, because he already paid the rent on the battlefield).

Duck Soup was a masterful comic send-up of dictators, government, nationalism, war, and politics. Made during the height of the Great Depression, and during the same year that Hitler came to power, the film was a welcome and refreshing piece of satire. It's no coincidence that Mussolini banned the film in Italy.

The Marx Brothers (including Zeppo Marx in his last movie role), Margaret Dumont, Louis Calhern, Raquel Torres, and Edgar Kennedy all gave memorable performances.

Though the funniest of their first five films (Groucho thought it was certainly their craziest), *Duck Soup* did poorly with audiences and Paramount didn't renew their contract.

See also: comedy teams; Kalmar (Bert) & Ruby (Harry); The Marx Brothers

DUNAWAY, FAYE (1941–)   A tall, willowy blond actress who, in her best roles, has combined a sense of ruthlessness undercut by self-doubt. In many ways, Dunaway represents the change in the kinds of roles women have received in film; at another time she would have been strictly a romantic lead of the cool, aloof sort. Instead, Dunaway has often played career women or working girls, harkening back to the days of Joan Crawford *(q.v.)* in the 1940s. It's no wonder, perhaps, that she played Crawford (managing an uncanny resemblance to the actress) in *Mommie Dearest* (1981).

An army brat, Dunaway spent her youth traveling from one military base to another with her family. After spending her college years at the University of Florida and, later, Boston University's School of Fine and Applied Arts, Dunaway became a member of the Lincoln Center Repertory Company in 1962. She had excellent stage training, cutting her teeth on such plays as *A Man for All Seasons* and *After the Fall*. She continued to work on the New York stage until making her first film, which, contrary to popular opinion, was not *Bonnie and Clyde* (1967, *q.v.*). She made her debut in *The Happening* (1967), a mild comedy caper movie, several months before she took Hollywood by storm as Bonnie Parker.

Bonnie and Clyde earned Dunaway a Best Actress Oscar nomination and established her as a bright new film star. Although her career has been checkered, she has worked steadily even since, managing either critical or box office hits just often enough to keep from disappearing from the Hollywood map.

She cemented her early stardom by appearing with Steve McQueen *(q.v.)* in the hit thriller *The Thomas Crown Affair* (1968). Despite appearances in a significant number of subsequent films, she didn't resurface as a strong leading lady until 1974 with her nerve-crunching performance in *Chinatown*, a role which brought her her second Oscar nomination. At a new peak of critical and public acceptance, Dunaway did some of her finest work over the next several years, culminating in her high-strung, power-hungry TV executive in *Network* (1976), which finally brought her a Best Actress Academy Award.

In the late 1970s and early 1980s, Dunaway opted for a combination of schmaltz and high camp. The worst of her films in this period of her career was the remake of *The Champ* (1979), and the most fascinating was her remarkable portrayal of Joan Crawford in *Mommie Dearest*. The latter film was decimated by the critics upon its release, but audiences simply devoured Dunaway's happily unrestrained performance, turning the film into a surprise cult favorite.

Dunaway seemed almost to disappear during the rest of the 1980s. Her film appearances became less frequent and the movies she did appear in, such as 1984's *Supergirl* (as campy villainess), didn't do much for her career. It wasn't until her stunning, serious portrayal of a drunk woman in *Barfly* (1987) that she received substantial critical approval for the first time in more than a decade.

See also: Bonnie and Clyde

DUNNE, IRENE (1898–)   A star for more than twenty years in the 1930s and 1940s, she had a poise and dignity that made her serenely indomitable in her dramas and wonderfully brittle in her comedies. Besides being a fine actress, Dunne was also a fine singer, but only used that talent sporadically in her films.

Born Irene Marie Dunn, she grew up in the South. After graduating from the Chicago Musical College, she tried to join the Metropolitan Opera company without success. Undaunted, she won the lead in a touring company of the hit musical comedy *Irene*.

She worked steadily on Broadway during the 1920s and she was a well-established actress by the end of the decade. But she wasn't discovered by Hollywood on the Broadway stage; she was spotted during her road company tour of *Showboat* in 1929 and signed by RKO.

Her first film was a minor musical called *Leathernecking* (1930), but her second movie, *Cimarron* (1931), made her a major star, a distinction she never lost until she voluntarily retired from the movie industry in 1952.

Cimarron, based on the novel of the same name by Edna Ferber, was one of the biggest money-makers of the year, garnering the Oscar for Best Picture and producing a nomination for Dunne as Best Actress. She would eventually be nominated for an Academy Award a total of five times for *Theodora Goes Wild* (1936), *The Awful Truth* (1937), *Love Affair* (1939), and *I Remember Mama* (1948)—but would never win.

Cimarron made her a star but *Back Street* (1932), the film version of the Fannie Hurst novel, defined her image as a tear-jerking actress par excellence. The film was so successful that it spawned two remakes. But after several years of making audiences weep, she made two musicals, *Sweet Adeline* (1935) and *Roberta* (1935), the latter with Fred Astaire and Ginger Rogers *(qq.v.)* in support—and they stole the movie. Neither film did much to enhance Dunne's career, but when she starred in the smash hit film version of *Show Boat* (1936), and her first comedy, *Theodora Goes Wild* (1936), she rocketed to the top of the Hollywood heap.

Seen, finally, as a versatile actress, musical star, and charming light comedienne, she appeared in a wide range of films that included one of Hollywood's most captivating sex comedies, *The Awful Truth* (1937), a Jerome Kern musical, *High, Wide and Handsome* (1937), and one of the great weepies of all time, *Love Affair* (1939).

She lost none of her star power in the early 1940s, performing in such hit comedies as *Penny Serenade* (1941) and wartime tearjerkers such as *The White Cliffs of Dover* (1944). A few mediocre films in the middle of the decade signaled a change in her appeal. The star was getting older and the jilted self-sacrificing woman routine seemed a less and less plausible role for her to play.

Anna and the King of Siam (1946), a dramatic version of the book by Anna Leonowens, seemed to stop Dunne's modest slide. But her career really changed when she began playing more matronly wives and mothers in films like *I Remember Mama* (1947) and *Life With Father* (1948). The latter film was far more successful, but her role was much smaller than that of the film's real star, William Powell *(q.v.)*. The sad truth was that there were few starring roles for aging female actresses in Hollywood.

Dunne's film career wound down rather swiftly. She made just three more films, none of them successful, the last of which was *It Grows on Trees* in 1952. At that point she walked away from Hollywood, became more active in her passion for conservative politics, and was named by President Eisenhower as an alternate delegate to the U.N. General Assembly in 1957. Except for very rare guest appearances on TV shows in the 1950s, and joining the board of directors of Technicolor in 1965, she fully and thoroughly retired from show business.

DURBIN, DEANNA (1921–) A teenage singer/actress who became a star in the late 1930s, she was Universal's answer to Judy Garland *(q.v.)*, saving her studio from bankruptcy in 1937. Durbin's fans were so enamored of her peppy, forthright, and wholesome adolescence that they refused to see her in any other way. Her audience had no trouble watching her grow up, it just did not want her image to change, spelling Miss Durbin's ultimate disillusionment with Hollywood.

Born Edna Mae Durbin in Canada, her family moved to Los Angeles when she was still an infant. Her singing ability as a young teenager was rather well known and, when fifteen years old, she was signed to a contract by MGM. The studio placed her in a short subject with Judy Garland called *Every Sunday* (1936). One of the oft-told show business stories has it that Louis B. Mayer *(q.v.)* saw the short and said, "Drop the fat one." He supposedly meant Judy Garland, but because of miscommunication, the studio fired Durbin.

In the mid-1930s, wholesome Deanna Durbin came along in the nick of time to save Universal Studios from drowning in a sea of red ink. Her effervescent personality and impressive singing were featured in a string of hits that made her one of the most popular stars of her time. Photo courtesy of Movie Star News.

Universal stepped in and hired Durbin, putting her in *Three Smart Girls* (1937). Thanks to her sudden fame as a singer on the "Eddie Cantor Radio Hour," the film was a major hit, saving Universal from bankruptcy. She became the studio's prime star and was given good scripts, a handful of excellent songs, and strong supporting players such as Adolphe Menjou *(q.v.)* in *One Hundred Men and a Girl* (1937), Herbert Marshall *(q.v.)* in *Mad About Music* (1938), and Melvyn Douglas *(q.v.)* in *That Certain Age* (1938).

It was a testament to her immense appeal that in 1938 after just four films she was given a Special Oscar, as was the far more seasoned Mickey Rooney *(q.v.)*, for "setting a high standard of ability and achievement" as juvenile players.

Durbin's studio edged the eighteen-year-old star ever so slightly toward adulthood in *Three Smart Girls Grow Up* (1939). But it was a slow process. She was allowed to have her first screen kiss (Robert Stack did the honors) in *First Love* (1939).

In the early 1940s the star eased into more adult roles with great success, yet was essentially playing the same character. Durbin wanted to expand her range and play in something other than light musical comedies. She was earning $400,000 per film, which indicates how much value Universal placed on her box office clout, and the studio was reluctant to tangle with a successful formula. They finally relented, however, when Durbin insisted, and the result was *Christmas Holiday* (1944), a combination musical and crime story based on a Somerset Maugham novel. Durbin played a "bad girl," and as far as her fans were concerned, it didn't matter that the movie boasted Gene Kelly *(q.v.)* as her costar and had excellent, moody direction by Robert Siodmak *(q.v.)*. Her public was outraged.

Durbin had a few more successful pictures, most of them thin musical comedies, but by the latter 1940s, she was making one dud after another. At the age of twenty-seven, she made her last film, *For the Love of Mary* (1948). She had plenty of opportunities to resume her career but she chose not to.

DUVALL, ROBERT (1931–) A much admired character actor/star who has appeared in films since 1963, often in strong supporting roles, achieving overdue public and critical acclaim in the late 1970s. With his severe looks and balding pate, he has played his share of villains as well as stern, authoritarian figures. In his starring roles, however, he has shown great vulnerability in his effective understated performances. Duvall, adept at accents, has played Englishmen and upper-crust characters, but he has been most memorable in a long string of roles as Southerners.

The son of a naval officer, young Duvall spent his youth traveling around the country as a military brat. Nicknamed "Bodge" as a boy, he nearly flunked out of Principia College before he found his interest in learning rekindled by the school's drama teacher, after which he decided to become an actor.

After military service, Duvall studied the actor's craft with Sanford Meisner at The Neighborhood Playhouse School of the Theater in New York. After two years of study with fellow students Dustin Hoffman and Gene Hackman *(qq.v.)*, Duvall had his first big break in a one-night theater showcase performance of Arthur Miller's *A View From the Bridge*. Miller, himself, was in the audience, along with a number of television and movie people. Before long, the young actor began appearing regularly in TV shows such as "Naked City," "Route 66," "Twilight Zone," and "The Outer Limits."

Duvall made his film debut in the small but important role of Boo Radley in *To Kill a Mockingbird* (1963). The performance set the standard for his work for more than fifteen years; he would so radically transform himself into whatever character he played that he was virtually unrecognizable from movie to movie. Duvall gave strong supporting performances in a host of commercially and critically successful films during the 1960s and 1970s and, even to this day, most people remember the roles but not him! For instance, he played a catatonic officer in *Captain Newman, M.D.* (1964), John Wayne's

(q.v.) nemesis in *True Grit* (1969), Major Frank Burns in *M★A★S★H* (1970), a cold, ruthless TV executive in *Network* (1976), and Dr. Watson in *The Seven-Per-Cent Solution* (1976), to name just a few.

Duvall had acted in Francis Ford Coppola's *(q.v.)* low-budget experimental film, *Rain People* (1969), beginning a professional relationship that eventually helped turn the actor into a star. Early on, Coppola suggested Duvall as the lead (and his first starring role) for George Lucas's *(q.v.)* *THX-1138* (1971). And in 1972, Coppola cast him in the pivotal supporting role as Don Corleone's attorney in *The Godfather* (1972). The film was, of course, a spectacular hit and Duvall was offered a great many other supporting roles in films such as *The Great Minnesota Northfield Raid* (1972), *Badge 373* (1973), as well as three more Coppola films, *The Conversation* (1974), *The Godfather, Part II* (1974), and *Apocalypse Now* (1979), the last of which brought him an Academy Award nomination for Best Supporting Actor.

By this time, film fans were beginning to appreciate the artistry of Duvall's performances. After his long career as a lead supporting actor, he was given top billing in *The Great Santini* (1980) and turned the small-budget family film into a critical and box office hit, as well as a personal triumph, winning an Oscar nomination for Best Actor.

Duvall has been on an upswing ever since, starring with Robert De Niro *(q.v.)* in the controversial *True Confessions* (1981), and finally receiving the full accolades of his profession by winning his first Oscar for Best Actor for his richly humanistic portrayal of a down-and-out country western singer, Mac Sledge, in *Tender Mercies* (1983).

Duvall has been involved in other creative pursuits besides acting. He has put considerable energy, as well as his own money, into two films, both of which he directed: a documentary called *We're Not the Jet Set* (1977), and a feature film, *Angelo, My Love* (1983). The latter received excellent reviews and had a modest success on the art-house circuit.

As often happens after an actor reaches the pinnacle of his or her success, a sudden lull appeared in Duvall's career. He has, for instance, played in support of Robert Redford *(q.v.)* in *The Natural* (1984) and lent his stature to a small family film, *The Stone Boy* (1984), which featured his second wife, Gail Youngs, in a small role, but he didn't reappear in a hit until 1988 when he starred in Dennis Hopper's *(q.v.)* controversial gang warfare film, *Colors*, after which he won raves for his work in the TV mini-series production of Larry McMurty's "Lonesome Dove" in 1989.

DWAN, ALLAN (1885–1981) A director whose film career spanned fifty years and more than four hundred movies, Dwan also received credit for producing, writing, and supervising yet another four hundred films. The vast majority of this movies were one- and two-reelers made during the silent era. But Dwan, who began directing three years after D. W. Griffith *(q.v.)* started making movies at the dawn of the film industry, worked continuously as a director until 1958. He did his best work with action films, directing them with sure-handed speed and style. In addition to his remarkable output and longevity as a film director, Dwan is also remembered as a technical innovator.

Born Joseph Aloysius Dwan in Toronto, the young man earned his college degree in electrical engineering from Notre Dame. While involved in the development of a new mercury vapor arc light (a precursor to the neon light) in 1909, Dwan was approached by the Essanay film company, which thought the arc lamps might be useful for movie lighting. According to Peter Bogdanovich *(q.v.)* in his excellent monograph, *Allan Dwan: The Last Pioneer,* Essanay not only used the lights, they also began buying scripts from the young engineer when he learned they needed more story material. Dwan eventually became their story editor before moving on to the American Film Company, where in 1911 he took over the direction of a one-reel western, *Brandishing a Bad Man,* when the film's ostensible director disappeared on a two-week drunk.

Dwan studied Griffith's films and learned the tricks of the trade from the master, eventually creating some of his own, including a method by which he could follow an actor by mounting a camera on a car, thereby creating film history's first dolly shot in *David Harum* (1915).

Among Dwan's other notable accomplishments during the silent era were his discovery of Lon Chaney *(q.v.)* and a hugely successful collaboration (both artistically and commercially) with Douglas Fairbanks *(q.v.)* that resulted in eleven films, among them *Robin Hood* (1922) and *The Iron Mask* (1929).

Considering Dwan's interest in all things mechanical, it was ironic that he disdained the talkie. Nonetheless, he easily mastered the medium, even managing yet another technical breakthrough in 1929 when he devised a way to dolly with a microphone.

Dwan's big mistake during the early sound era was to leave Hollywood and make three movies in England. During that time he discovered Ida Lupino *(q.v.)*, casting her in *Her First Affaire* (1933). When he returned to America, so much had changed in Hollywood that he had to prove himself all over again.

He directed "B" movies *(q.v.)* for Twentieth Century-Fox throughout the mid-1930s, finally breaking out with the Shirley Temple *(q.v.)* hits *Heidi* (1937) and *Rebecca of Sunnybrook Farm* (1938). His success with those two films gave Dwan the opportunity to direct the big-budget *Suez* (1938), starring Tyrone Power *(q.v.)*. But Dwan never fully escaped the "B" movie circuit.

His best work during the early 1940s was a series of four comedies, most notable among them was *Abroad with Two Yanks* (1944). Soon, thereafter, in 1945, he began a long association with Republic Pictures for which he made low-budget action films, occasionally rising to considerable heights with pictures such as *Rendezvous with Annie* (1946) and *The Sands of Iwo Jima* (1949).

He continued directing throughout most of the 1950s, often working for RKO. Dwan made his last movie in 1958, *Most Dangerous Man Alive* (it was released in 1961).

Allan Dwan was never a great director. He told Peter Bogdanovich, "My weakness was that I'd take anything. If it was a challenge to me, I'd take a bad story and try to make it good. I did what I could to make it a picture." Dwan succeeded far more often than he failed. When he died at the age of ninety-six, one of the last links to the birth of Hollywood was gone.

EASTWOOD, CLINT (1930–) The most consistently popular movie star in the world from the mid-1960s to the present. In addition to his superstardom, Eastwood is also a producer-director with a growing reputation among critics, particularly in Europe.

The young Eastwood led a nomadic life, traveling with his family as his father searched for work during the Great Depression. Over one ten-year span he attended ten different schools. Later, after his uneventful military service as a swimming instructor, he went to Los Angeles to study business administration on the G.I. Bill. It was there that he was talked into getting a screen test at Universal. Three weeks later Universal offered him a contract worth $75 per week for forty weeks.

His movie debut—or at least the first time he received a screen credit—was in a small role in *Revenge of the Creature* (1955). The part wasn't much, but he received valuable training at the Universal Talent School. After eighteen months, though, Universal dropped his option and Eastwood was on his own. He made a few movies for RKO, including some westerns, in the latter 1950s, but nothing of note.

The westerns presaged Eastwood's appearance as Rowdy Yates in TV's "Rawhide," a western series that ran from January 1959 to January 1966. It was Eastwood's first major break, bringing him to the attention of the American public. He reportedly wanted to direct episodes of "Rawhide," but CBS wouldn't let him.

In 1964, while "Rawhide" was on summer hiatus, Eastwood was hired by Sergio Leone for *A Fistful of Dollars,* based on Akira Kurosawa's masterpiece *Yojimbo* (1961). But Eastwood wasn't Leone's first choice. Charles Bronson *(q.v.)* was offered the role first and turned it down. Then James Coburn *(q.v.)* got the nod, but the actor wanted $25,000, which was too much for this low-budget western. Eastwood took the job for $15,000.

A Fistful of Dollars (1964) was a huge hit in Italy and the rest of Europe. During "Rawhide's" summer hiatus of 1965, Eastwood made the sequel, *For A Few Dollars More.* This time, he was paid $50,000 and received a percentage of the profits to play the serape-clad, cheroot-chewing "Man with No Name." Eastwood was a movie star everywhere but in America. In 1967 Leone succeeded in clearing the rights for *Yojimbo* in the United States and Eastwood's first two spaghetti westerns were shown (almost simultaneously) in America. The critics hated them, but moviegoers went wild for these new violent, mythic westerns. Eastwood was paid $250,000 plus a percentage of the profits for *The Good, the Bad, and the Ugly* (1967), his next pairing with Leone, now considered by many to be a classic western epic.

Hang 'Em High (1968) was the first American film in which he had a starring role. With the success of that film, he established his own production company, Malpaso, which is Spanish for "A bad step," the words his manager said when Eastwood agreed to make *A Fistful of Dollars.*

Eastwood's first American non-western, *Coogan's Bluff* (1968), is notable as the first pairing of Eastwood with director Donald Siegel *(q.v.)*, with whom Eastwood would eventually make a total of five films. The actor had but one flop in the 1960s: *Paint Your Wagon* (1969). He costarred with Lee Marvin *(q.v.)* in the Lerner and Lowe musical and, although the movie was a critical and financial disaster, Eastwood surprised those few people who saw the film with his pleasant singing voice.

Interestingly, Eastwood was going to star with Elizabeth Taylor *(q.v.)* in *Two Mules for Sister Sara* (1970), but Taylor withdrew because of other commitments, and Shirley MacLaine *(q.v.)* replaced her. Donald Siegel also replaced Budd Boetticher *(q.v.)* as director. Despite all these changes, the film was another hit.

In 1971, Eastwood made the decision to produce all

Actor/director/producer Clint Eastwood, pictured here directing a scene from *Bird* (1988), has finally, if begrudgingly, been recognized by the critical establishment for his skills behind the camera. Photo © Warner Bros., Inc. Courtesy of Malpaso.

his films through his own company, Malpaso. The first was *The Beguiled* (1971), directed by Donald Siegel. It's a macabre tale that has built a cult following. Bruce Surtees *(q.v.)* supplied the eerie cinematography, and he eventually worked on several other Eastwood films, adding his lush, individualistic look.

Eastwood had watched Don Siegel's directorial work closely and learned enough to direct his first film, *Play Misty for Me* (1971). It was reasonably well received by critics, and was a profitable movie for Malpaso. But the big surprise of 1971 was *Dirty Harry*. The project had originally been slated for Frank Sinatra *(q.v.)*, but a hand injury kept him from playing the part of Harry Callahan. The film elevated Eastwood to superstardom; after *Dirty Harry*, Eastwood was the worldwide number-one male movie star based on a poll conducted by the Hollywood Foreign Press Association. The actor made four more Harry Callahan movies, *Magnum Force* (1973), based on a script by John Milius *(q.v.)* and Michael Cimino, *The Enforcer* (1976), *Sudden Impact* (1983), which Eastwood directed himself, and *The Dead Pool* (1988).

Eastwood's only flop in the 1970s was a movie he directed but didn't appear in. *Breezy* (1973), with William Holden *(q.v.)* and Kay Lenz, was a modest (and

rather good) little film about an older man and a younger woman. It opened and closed in near record time. Significantly, Sondra Locke—who later became Eastwood's regular leading lady and, until recently, long-time girlfriend—had auditioned for the role of Breezy, but had been rejected. Other hits from the 1970s included *Thunderbolt and Lightfoot* (1974), which marked the directorial debut of Michael Cimino (who would later make *The Deer Hunter* and *Heaven's Gate*), and *The Eiger Sanction* (1975).

The Outlaw Josey Wales (1976), which Eastwood directed, remains one of his most satisfying films. It was also his first film with Sondra Locke. But perhaps his worst two movies have also been his most successful. *Every Which Way But Loose* (1978) and *Any Which Way You Can* (1980) were both extremely broad comedies costarring Clyde, an orangutan.

By the late 1970s, however, Eastwood finally began to receive some serious critical attention. His performance was lauded in Donald Siegel's taut thriller *Escape From Alcatraz* (1978). And *Bronco Billy* (1980), which was directed by Eastwood, is arguably his best film and in it he gives his most assured performance. Unfortunately the film, though well received by critics, died at the box office. He garnered accolades again for his performance in *Tightrope* (1984), and many speculated that he would be nominated for an Oscar for the film, though it never happened.

His films of the mid- to latter 1980s have been solidly successful, except for *City Heat* (1984), which paired Eastwood with Burt Reynolds *(q.v.)*. *Pale Rider* (1985) was one of only two commercially successful American westerns of the decade. *Heartbreak Ridge* (1986) was both a critical and popular hit. Most recently, his direction of *Bird* (1988) brought Eastwood a critical ovation, and even the Museum of Modern Art in New York City has begun a collection of his work and memorabilia.

Eastwood's career as an actor, director, film company mogul, and former mayor (he was elected to that office in his hometown of Carmel, California in 1986), has marked the development of one of the relatively few long-lasting star personalities of the modern Hollywood era. Of the three major action stars of the last twenty years (Burt Reynolds and Charles Bronson being the other two), only Eastwood has sustained a high level of quality in his films and an ever-increasing popularity.

EASY RIDER   The small-budget, independently produced 1969 hit movie had several startling effects on the moviemaking establishment. *Easy Rider* changed the kinds of movies Hollywood made, as well as who made them and how much they cost. In addition, the film made a star of Jack Nicholson *(q.v.)*, who took the movie's acting honors in a flashy supporting role.

Easy Rider was a road movie, but nothing like the films made by Bob Hope and Bing Crosby *(qq.v.)*. The story was deceptively simple: two drug dealers, Wyatt (Peter Fonda) and Billy (Dennis Hopper, *qq.v.*), made a sale that nets them a lot of money. They decide to go in search of America and themselves on their motorcycles, traveling from California to New Orleans for Mardi Gras. Along the way, they experience the best and the worst that America has to offer, with both suddenly murdered by rednecks at the end of the film, ostensibly for being long-haired motorcycle freaks.

Wyatt's and Billy's doomed search for meaning in their lives touched a chord among young moviegoers. The film became *The Rebel Without a Cause* of a new generation. *Easy Rider* was a descendant of Roger Corman's A.I.P. (American International Pictures) motorcycle film, *The Wild Angels* (1966), as well as his LSD movie, *The Trip* (1967). Yet where the two earlier movies focused on the bikers and the drug culture, *Easy Rider* depicted two bikers from the drug culture but focused on America.

At a time when huge amounts of money had been spent and lost on colossal flops such as *Dr. Doolittle* (1967) and *Star!* (1968), the startling critical and financial success of the low-budget *Easy Rider* stunned the film industry. The movie had been produced by Peter Fonda

with his own money (not even A.I.P. would give him the money to make the film) and the script was written by Fonda, Hopper, and Terry Southern. Dennis Hopper made his directorial debut, as well, winning the "New Director" first prize at the Cannes Film Festival for his work.

Easy Rider had two immediate affects on the Hollywood establishment. It unleashed a lot of money for small-budget films to independent filmmakers (most of whom didn't make the grade), and Hollywood turned ersatz radical in the hope of capitalizing on the sudden popularity of the counterculture. The films that came in *Easy Rider's* wake, such as *The Strawberry Statement* (1970), *The Revolutionary* (1970), and *Getting Straight* (1970), were some of Hollywood's failed attempts to cash in on a trend.

More significantly, though, the major studios learned a lesson from *Easy Rider* that they have not forgotten: the movie audience is no longer a family audience (if, indeed, it ever was). Since *Easy Rider*, the movies of the 1970s and 1980s have been largely geared toward the young.

EDENS, ROGER (1905–1970)   An important composer, lyricist, and producer at MGM during that studio's musical golden age of the 1940s and 1950s. Often overlooked because of his subordinate position to MGM's musical kingpin Arthur Freed *(q.v.)*, Edens' tunes for more than a dozen musicals were among the greatest achievements of their era. Edens also worked as associate producer on more than twenty-five MGM musicals, composing, writing lyrics, and scoring many of them. He is also noteworthy as the one person at MGM who believed in Judy Garland's *(q.v.)* talent before she became a star. He was her biggest booster at the studio and helped her with her "Dear Mr. Gable" rendition of "You Made Me Love You," which gave Garland her big break. He would remain closely associated with Garland throughout their years together at MGM.

Edens was born in Texas, making his early living playing the piano for ballroom dancers. He went to Hollywood in 1934 to arrange music for Ethel Merman. The following year he moved to MGM, where he stayed for virtually the rest of his career. There, he arranged and adapted music and worked as an accompanist during most of the 1930s, but in 1939 he wrote the music and lyrics for *Babes in Arms,* a hit musical starring Mickey Roony *(q.v.)* and Judy Garland.

Among the many musicals for which he wrote songs were *Strike Up the Band* (1940), *Little Nelly Kelly* (1940), *Babes on Broadway* (1941), *Ziegfeld Follies* (1946), *On The Town* (1949), the classic *Singin' in the Rain* (1952), with Comden & Green, *Funny Face* (1957), which he also produced, and *Jumbo* (1962).

Edens began working as an associate producer in 1945, assisting in the production of many of the films mentioned above. Musicals he helped produce include, *The Harvey Girls* (1946), *The Pirate* (1948), *Easter Parade* (1948), *Annie Get Your Gun* (1950), *Royal Wedding* (1951), *Show Boat* (1951), *An American in Paris* (1951), *The Band Wagon* (1953), and *Brigadoon* (1954). For his work in scoring, Edens was honored with three Oscars (in collaboration) for *Easter Parade, On the Town,* and *Annie Get Your Gun.*

After MGM's glory years were over, Edens worked on but two more musicals as associate producer before his death, *The Unsinkable Molly Brown* (1964) and *Hello, Dolly!* (1969).

EDESON, ARTHUR (1891–1970) A cinematographer best known for his superb atmospheric black-and-white films. He started in the film business in 1911 with the now forgotten Eclair Company after gaining some experience as a portrait photographer.

Edeson cut his teeth as a camera operator on Douglas Fairbanks' *(q.v.)* early comedy hits such as *Wild and Woolly* (1917) and *Mr. Fix-it* (1918), finally rising to prominence as the cinematographer of Fairbanks' swashbuckling epics *The Three Musketeers* (1921), *Robin Hood* (1922), and the visually stunning classic *The Thief of Bagdad* (1924).

When sound arrived, a great many cinematographers found their art shackled by the needs of the sound technicians. But Edson helped prove that films need not be studio-bound when he expertly photographed the first major outdoor sound film, *In Old Arizona* (1929), for which we won an Academy Award nomination for Best Cinematographer. It was the first of three nominations (regretably, he never won the Oscar).

If he demonstrated his craft with *In Old Arizona,* he confirmed it when he photographed the breathtaking antiwar film *All Quiet on the Western Front* (1930), for which he received his second Academy Award nomination. His ability to light and shoot complicated scenes led to his work in early sound horror films such as *Frankenstein* (1931), *The Old Dark House* (1932), and *The Invisible Man* (1933), films in the style for which German Expressionist cinematographers such as Karl Freund are famous.

Edeson's skills in black-and-white photography where put to their ultimate test when he finally went to work for Warner Bros. in the late 1930s and early 1940s. The content of the dark melodramas made at Warner were a perfect match for his crisp, yet moody, visual style. His works on films such as *They Drive By Night* (1940) and *The Maltese Falcon* (1941) would provide much of the visual idiom for *film noir (q.v.).* His cinematography reached its peak in *Casablanca* (1942, *q.v.*), for which he was again nominated for an Oscar.

Edeson worked throughout the 1940s, but with less

impact in the latter half of the decade. He retired in 1949.

EDISON, THOMAS A. (1847–1931) Though he had just three months of formal education, "The Wizard of Menlo Park," as he was known, the man who invented the incandescent lamp, the stock ticker, and the phonograph, was also the man who was largely responsible for the invention of motion pictures.

Even more than an inventor, Edison was a clever and resourceful businessman who improved and adapted the work of other inventors, turning their devices and machines into viable commercial products—and then taking all the bows for their creation. Such was the case of the first motion picture camera, the kinetograph, which Edison's associate, William Kennedy Laurie Dickson, built in 1888. The following year, Edison and Dickson invented the kinetescope, a viewing device capable of showing what had been filmed on the kinetograph. The kinetescope became a popular rage as a peep show novelty after Edison introduced it to the public in 1893.

In order to supply a steady stream of moving pictures for the invention, Edison's wizard, Dickson, built the world's first movie studio in 1893, nicknaming it the Black Maria *(q.v.).*

With both the hardware and the software at hand, nickelodeons *(q.v.),* sprung up all over the country as individuals flocked to low-rent storefronts to watch a simple scene unfold before their eyes on film.

Unable to see beyond the limited money-making potential of his peep show machine, Edison watched his invention fade in popularity after a few short years. Meanwhile, he had neglected to perfect his kinetescope so that it could project a film onto a screen for a larger audience. Others, however, saw the potential that Edison did not. Finally, the clever inventor bought the rights to the Jenkins-Armat Vitascope, renamed it the Edison Vitascope, and demonstrated it on April 23, 1896 at the Koster & Bial Music Hall on the site of what is now Macy's department store in New York City. With the magic of Edison's name and reputation behind it, the Vitascope, in one fell swoop, gave new life to the infant mass entertainment medium.

His Edison Company, a filmmaking enterprise, was the most prominent of the early studios and was responsible for one of the fledgling industry's most popular and influential early dramas, Edwin S. Porter's *The Great Train Robbery* (1903). Porter, in fact, gave D. W. Griffith *(q.v.),* who would become the father of movies as an art form, his start at the Edison Company.

But Edison, himself, saw the movie business strictly as a cash cow. He had invented the new industry and he meant to control it. He had, unfortunately, been uncharacteristically lax in applying for worldwide patents on his inventions and he found himself in competition with upstart film companies that were using variations of his own technology. By 1909, he felt the keen edge of competition from a total of nine film companies, which included, among others, Selig, Biograph, Vitagraph, and Essanay. He knew he couldn't fight them, and cleverly offered them the opportunity to join together in the Motion Picture Patents Company, effectively barring any other companies from competing against their trust. The arrangement worked for a while until the small independents, led by Carl Laemmle's IMP company, fought back and eventually, in 1917, broke the monopoly that Edison had created in the production and distribution of motion pictures. That same year, Edison bowed out of the movie business.

See also: Biograph

EDITOR   The person who, after a film is shot, edits the individual scenes together, usually under the instructions of either the director or the producer. Sometimes, when an editor has an established reputation and the director does not, the producer may give great latitude to the editor to put the movie together as he or she sees fit. However, the editor can only work with the footage that the director has already provided.

The editor's craft evolved slowly during the early part of the silent era when movies were single-reel affairs that were nothing more than recorded events. At that time, editors were known as cutters, people who simply cut excess film from the end of one setup and spliced it to the beginning of the next. Later, however, when moviemaking became more sophisticated, so did the need for more creative editing. By the time films such as D. W. Griffith's *Birth of a Nation* (1915) were made, editing had already evolved into a burgeoning art form. Cross-cutting of chases scenes, reaction shots, and multiple camera setups all required creative editing after a movie was shot.

For the most part, editors are unsung heroes in the filmmaking process. As important as it is to the creation of a movie, editing was only slowly given its due. It wasn't until 1934 that the Academy of Motion Picture Arts and Sciences decided to give an Oscar for such work, awarding its first editing Academy Award to Conrad Nervig for *Eskimo* (1934).

Some directors have come to trust their editors and have chosen to collaborate with them on film after film. Such teamwork often results in a truly exceptional body of work, as evidenced by the collaborations of director Arthur Penn *(q.v.)* and editor Dede Allen *(q.v.)*, as well as the long-term success of writer/director/star Woody Allen *(q.v.)* with his editor, Ralph Rosenblum.

An understanding of editing is so central to good filmmaking that it is surprising that there have not been more editors who have made the leap to directing.

Nonetheless, some well-known directors who were once editors include Dorothy Arzner *(q.v.)*, Hal Ashby *(q.v.)*, David Lean, Mark Robson, John Sturges, and Robert Wise *(q.v.)*.
See also: Booth, Margaret

EDWARDS, BLAKE (1922–   )   One of the few modern writer-directors who has become a specialist in the area of comedy, Edwards is so associated with comedies, such as the *Pink Panther* films (he wrote and directed all five, four of which he produced himself), that it is easy to forget that he has also been responsible for thrillers and high dramas such as *The Tamarind Seed* (1974) and *Days of Wine and Roses* (1962). A probing, serious filmmaker who finds humor (as well as suspense) in the commonplace, Edwards has created his own niche in the film business, and has rather consistently provided laughter in an area where most modern directors fear to tred, namely slapstick comedy.

Edwards, who was born William Blake McEdwards, had his first taste of Hollywood when he was a mere twenty-year-old. He appeared in a small role in *Ten Gentlemen from West Point* (1942), but World War II cut short his career as a thespian. When he returned to the popular arts after the war, his first important break came not in the movies but in radio. He created the successful "Richard Diamond: Private Detective" series, which later also had a run as a TV series. He would go on to create "Dante," and "Peter Gunn" for TV as well. (*Gunn,* based on his TV show, was a 1967 movie directed by Edwards.)

His success on radio gave him the opportunity to write screenplays. He wrote seven of them, including *Operation Mad Ball* (1957), that were all directed by Richard Quine. His own first directorial effort was in 1955 with *Bring Your Smile Along.* He showed nothing more than solid professionalism in the several films that followed his debut, until he directed *Operation Petticoat* (1959). The film, with Cary Grant and Tony Curtis *(qq.v.),* was an inspired comedy set on a submarine. Its success gave Edwards the chance to direct *Breakfast at Tiffany's* (1961) and *Days of Wine and Roses* (1962)*.* These two movies were among the more popular films of the early 1960s, and they established Edwards as a directorial star.

His glittering career in the early part of the decade shone even brighter when he made *The Pink Panther* (1963), *A Shot in the Dark* (1964), and *The Great Race* (1964).

These three smash hits established his reputation for humor, but his venture into a more modish sort of sophisticated comedy during the latter 1960s left his career in a shambles. Movies such as *What Did You Do in the War, Daddy?* (1966) and *Waterhole 3* (1967) were just a few of his ambitious failures.

In 1969, Edwards married actress Julie Andrews (q.v., it was his second marriage), and she began appearing in a great many of his movies. But the presence of his famous wife in these films did not save his career so much as his clever reuniting with Peter Sellers (q.v.) to make three more *Pink Panther* movies. All three were hits, and Edwards' revitalized reputation for comedy gave him the opportunity in 1979 to direct *10*, which was one of the biggest hits of the year. In addition to proving that Edwards could make a hit film without Peter Sellers, it also made a star out of Dudley Moore (q.v.) and introduced Bo Derek to the world.

Edwards still pursued a bitter, melancholy sort of humor in films such as *S.O.B.* (1981), *That's Life* (1986), and *Skin Deep* (1989) with rather poor results at the box office. But the director's work was nonetheless seen as worthy of serious discussion. And in between his dour comedies he offered audiences more commercial fare such as *Victor/Victoria* (1982), a hit for Julie Andrews as well as Edwards, and *Blind Date* (1987), a slapstick farce which introduced Bruce Willis to the big screen.

After more than three decades, Edwards' reputation as one of a vanishing breed of modern American comedy directors seems solidly assured.

EPICS Films that attempt to deal with real or imagined events in a grand, sweeping visual style. Known for casts of thousands and action on a massive scale, these are tales set against a panoramic backdrop dealing with the weighty issues most appropriate to the form, generally the fate of nations, morality, politics, religion, and the struggle between man and nature.

Movies are an ideal vehicle for the epic—the stage simply cannot offer the same kind of physical reality and television screens (and TV network production budgets) are too small to effectively capture the sweep of the genre.

There were two periods in American movie history when the epic reigned supreme: the last half of the silent era, from 1915 until the introduction of sound in 1927, and the bulk of the 1950s and the early 1960s. D. W. Griffith (q.v.) brought the Hollywood epic film to life with *The Birth of a Nation* (1915) depicting the battles of the American Civil War. He raised the epic to even grander heights with *Intolerance* (1916), a movie that still leaves viewers awestruck by its magnificent sets and colossal tableaux.

If Griffith created the Hollywood epic, Cecil B. DeMille (q.v.) made it his life's work, and he, more than any other director, has been associated with the genre. While none may have been brilliant, most were commercially successful. From his two versions of *The Ten Commandments* (1923 and 1956) to *Cleopatra* (1934), and from *Sign of the Cross* (1932) to *Samson and Delilah*

(1949), DeMille gave most of his attention to sin-and-salvation films set in ancient, usually biblical, times.

Despite the fact that films such as *Ben Hur* (1925 and 1959), *Salome* (1953), and *Solomon and Sheba* (1959) are considered typical of the genre, epics need not be concerned with biblical or classical themes. The American West has proven to be a particularly fertile source of epics. Movies such as *The Covered Wagon* (1923), *Duel in the Sun* (1946), *How the West Was Won* (1961), *Little Big Man* (1970), and even the commercial and critical disaster *Heaven's Gate* (1980) dealt with the great issues of the frontier in epic proportion.

Big-budget war movies have also contributed to the epic, a few of the more memorable examples being *The Longest Day* (1962), *Tora! Tora! Tora!* (1970), and King Vidor's (q.v.) *War and Peace* (1956). In the same vein as the war epic is the national epic, including such films as *El Cid* (1961), which depict the heroism that helps to galvanize nations to combat terrible threats against impossible odds.

There have been biographical epics such as *Lawrence of Arabia* (1962), built around the majesty of a single person who changed history. Science fiction epics such as *2001, A Space Odyssey* (1968) and *Star Wars* (1977), offered a view of the future filled with epic themes, which were presented with stunning visual grandeur. Adventure epics like *The Wind and the Lion* (1975) and fantasy epics such as *The Thief of Bagdad* (1924), and even gangster epics like *The Godfather* (1972, q.v.) have delighted audiences. Finally, there have been epic love stories, with none more beloved by film fans than *Gone With the Wind* (1939, q.v.).

In recent years, it has ultimately become too expensive to produce a true "Hollywood epic." This is not to say that epic films will no longer be made, but when an otherwise simple action film like *Rambo III* (1988) can cost $64 million, the epic is no longer cost-effective. Epic themes will abound, but epic budgets for massive casts and magnificent sets have already been dealt the same treatment as Samson's hair.
See also: disaster movies

ESTABLISHING SHOT An early shot that allows the audience to see the physical relationship of everything of importance that may come into play within a scene. In other words, the actors and the important elements on the set or location are all shown at one time—generally in a long shot—in order that future shots within the scene make spatial sense to the viewers. The angle of the establishing shot, as well as the way it's lit and photographed, all contribute to the initial mood and tone of the scene to follow.

The establishing shot is a heavily used cinematic storytelling device, but directors have been known to avoid using it, either to conceal information or to purposefully disorient the audience.

EXECUTIVE PRODUCER   Since the 1950s, the title has come to signify the person responsible for providing or arranging to provide the money for a film's production. The executive producer may also be the person who made the deal to pull the star(s), director, and the story property together. Whatever way the executive producer comes by his title, he is always the individual who sets everything in motion, and is responsible for hiring the producer to oversee the technical and logistical elements of the filmmaking process. Some of the more well-known executive producers of the modern era are Dino de Laurentis and (more recently) Steven Speilberg *(q.v.)*.

In Hollywood's golden era, executive producer credits were rarely given as it was assumed that people like Irving Thalberg at MGM, Jack L. Warner at Warner Bros., and Harry Cohn at Columbia *(qq.v.),* etc. were the ultimate executives in charge of production. By the 1940s, however, there began to be exceptions, and producers with clout sometimes received recognition by being given executive producer status on certain pictures. For instance, at Warner Bros. Hal B. Wallis *(q.v.)* was sometimes granted that rarified title. But it didn't happen often.

See also: associate producer; producer

F

FAIRBANKS, DOUGLAS (1883–1939) The singularly most successful action star of the silent era, Fairbanks changed both the style and the substance of Hollywood's silent movies, both as an actor and as a producer. He was, in many ways, the cinematic personification of America before the Great Depression: enormously energetic, optimistic, and eager to take risks.

Fairbanks was the scion of a wealthy family, but higher education didn't appeal to him; he quit Harvard after just a few months and became enamored of the theater. In 1902 he made his Broadway debut and soon thereafter began playing juveniles with growing success. By 1914, he was a well-known and popular actor on the Great White Way.

It was at this time that expanding movie companies, wanting to shed their nickelodeon image, made their bid for greater respectability by hiring famous theater actors. As a curiosity, these attempts were successful with the public for a short while. The actors also benefited. Sarah Bernhardt, for example, made a fortune by performing her stage plays on film—without dialogue. Fairbanks, eager for new challenges and lured by the staggering salary of $2,000 per week, took the plunge and went west to Hollywood. His first film was *The Lamb* (1915).

Almost from the beginning, Fairbanks brought a healthy, vigorous, *physical* presence to his film roles. He was in constant motion, leaping and diving, and audiences loved it. By 1916—just one year later—he was earning $10,000 per week.

In 1917, Fairbanks established the successful Douglas Fairbanks Pictures Corporation in order to make even more money. Films such as *Wild and Woolly* (1917) and *A Modern Musketeer* (1918) were hugely popular in a society flushed with war fever. In 1919, Fairbanks joined the giants of the movie industry, Charlie Chaplin,

D. W. Griffith and Mary Pickford *(qq.v.)*, to form a film studio to produce and distribute their own movies. The studio still bears the name they chose: United Artists *(q.v.)*.

There was yet another merger of stars. In 1920, Fairbanks and Mary Pickford were married, a match made in Hollywood heaven. The union did not last as long as United Artists, but long enough (until 1935) to offer a star-struck generation the comforting impression that the movies and real life weren't quite so far apart. As Alistair Cooke once wrote, "They were a living proof of America's chronic belief in happy endings."

Fairbanks had achieved remarkable popularity, and he meant to hold onto it. In a more sophisticated postwar United States, he realized he could no longer play his usual spunky hero. So instead, he turned to epic adventures such as *The Mark of Zorro* (1920), *The Three Musketeers* (1921), and *Robin Hood* (1922). The films were enormous hits. Lavishly produced by Fairbanks, they showed off the actor's dashing athleticism and wild exuberance in settings that were perfect for his bigger-than-life characterizations. Forevermore, Fairbanks established the standard by which swashbuckling heroes would be defined.

The highlight of Fairbanks' film career is without question his magnificent production of *The Thief of Bagdad* (1924). The incredible sets, costumes, special effects, the huge cast—and Fairbanks' smiling, barechested, and courageous hero—made the movie irresistible. While most of his films before 1920 don't hold up very well by modern standards, his costume adventures of the 1920s, and particularly *Robin Hood* and *The Thief of Bagdad,* are as thrilling today as they were when they were first released nearly seven decades ago.

Fairbanks continued making swashbucklers with considerable success. *Son of Zorro* (1925), *The Black Pirate* (1926), and *The Gaucho* (1927) were all well

Douglas Fairbanks was Hollywood's foremost hero of the swashbuckler. He is seen here in his most famous film, *The Thief of Bagdad* (1924). Photo courtesy of The Siegel Collection.

received. Even the silent *The Iron Mask* (1929) did well despite the talkie craze.

Throughout the decade, Fairbanks and Pickford never made a movie together. But with the advent of sound, they teamed up to make their first talking picture, *The Taming of the Shrew* (1929). Their fans wanted action and romance, not poorly performed Shakespeare; the movie was a flop. It was a terrible shock to the two stars to see their first effort together in the new era fail.

Fairbanks had a pleasant speaking voice, but he never again created the magic of *The Thief of Bagdad*. The thirties were a grim decade, and Fairbanks, with his smile and ever-present optimism, seemed like a star from another time. And he was. He made several more movies, but stopped producing in 1931. His last film, *The Private Life of Don Juan* (1934), was a valiant, though failed, attempt to recapture his past glory. He retired from acting in 1936.

His sudden death from a heart attack in 1939 shocked a world that adored him as only few other actors have been.

Fairbanks' son (from his first marriage before Mary Pickford), Douglas Fairbanks Jr., had a long, moderately successful Hollywood career. Resembling his father and a swashbuckler in his own right, he is a likable actor with charm and a melifluous voice. He would have made his father proud had the elder Fairbanks seen

him in his two best roles, *Gunga Din* (1939) and *Sinbad the Sailor* (1947).

FAIRBANKS, DOUGLAS, JR.   *See* Fairbanks, Douglas.

FAMOUS PLAYERS   This film company eventually became Paramount Pictures. Founded by Adolph Zukor *(q.v.)* in 1912, The Famous Players Company was born out of the brief success in France of Film d'Art, a company that brought well-known novels and plays to the screen with stage stars in lead roles in order to appeal to a more sophisticated audience. Zukor bought the American rights to the Film d'Art production of *Queen Elizabeth* (1912) with Sarah Bernhardt. Bolstered by the commercial success of the movie, Zukor formed Famous Players, trumpeting the slogan, "Famous Players in Famous Plays."

Among the many famous players signed by Zukor were John Barrymore and Lily Langtry. Among the famous "plays," which more often than not were actually famous novels, he produced were *The Prisoner of Zenda* (1913) and *The Count of Monte Cristo* (1913). The success of the company during the tumultuous 1910s was due in large part to the fact that Zukor had Mary Pickford *(q.v.)* under contract. Ironically, she was a genuine movie star rather than a famous "stage" player. She did star in a great many popular vehicles for her employer, however, having hits with films such as *Tess of the Storm Country* (1914), *Cinderella* (1915), and *Rebecca of Sunnybrook Farm* (1917).

Of course, nothing succeeds like success, and Famous Players had competition from companies such as Popular Plays and Players, Paralta Plays, and Jesse L. Lasky's Feature Play Company. Lasky was strong enough competition to force a merger with Famous Players in 1916, with the company renamed Famous Players-Lasky. Meanwhile, in 1914, a powerful distribution company called Paramount Pictures was created. Adolph Zukor bought it in 1917 and folded in into Famous Players-Lasky. The company continued to prosper and, a decade later, Zukor changed the name of his firm to Paramount Famous Lasky Corporation. It was a mouthful, and the name was changed yet again in 1930 to Paramount Publix Corporation. Famous Players finished its evolution to the name of Paramount Pictures, Inc. in 1935 after Paramount Publix was reorganized under U.S. bankruptcy laws.
See also: DeMille, Cecil B.; Goldwyn, Samuel; Lasky, Jesse; Paramount Pictures

FANTASY FILMS   Hollywood has supplied us with prehistoric monsters, aliens from outer space, and other unspeakably ghoulish creatures. In the broadest sense, the movies in which these beings might appear fall within the category of fantasy, but for the sake of clarity, we have broken the category into four parts, three of which can be found elsewhere in this volume. (See: horror movies, monster movies, and science fiction.) That which we more narrowly call fantasy here is any film that either amuses or charms us with its either magical or fantastical premise (e.g., *The Wizard of Oz,* 1939) or is inspired, however remotely, from myth or legend and conspires to fill us with a marvelous sense of wonder and awe (e.g., *The Thief of Bagdad,* 1924). Baird Searles in his excellent book, *Films of Science Fiction and Fantasy,* distinguishes between amusing "light fantasy" and the more mythologically based category of "high fantasy."

Light fantasy often deals with ghosts and similar such apparitions, usually in either a comic or a romantic fashion. While light fantasy existed during the silent era, it came to fruition with talkies, especially during the Great Depression of the 1930s when the need to lose oneself in flights of fancy was greatest. *Peter Ibettson* (1934), *Night Life of the Gods* (1935), and *Topper* (1937) all tapped into this genre.

If light fantasy had its heyday during the 1930s, it had its second coming during and after World War II when many such films touched upon the issues of death and dying. *Here Comes Mr. Jordan* (1941), *A Guy Named Joe* (1943), *The Horn Blows at Midnight* (1945), and *It's A Wonderful Life* (1946) all portrayed characters coming to terms with their mortality in a light, fantastical fashion.

There was little light fantasy during the 1950s. Notable exceptions, however, were *You Never Can Tell* (1950), in which Dick Powell played a dog, the classic *Harvey* (1950), in which Jimmy Stewart's best friend is a six-foot invisible rabbit, the musical *Carousel* (1956), and *Bell, Book, and Candle* (1958). The 1960s were even lighter on light fantasy, but at least there were *Mary Poppins* (1964) and *The Seven Faces of Dr. Lao* (1964). The 1970s was a desert insofar as light fantasies were concerned, managing little more than Warren Beatty's *Heaven Can Wait* (1978), which was a remake of *Here Comes Mr. Jordan.* But the subgenre came alive again in the 1980s with such films as Woody Allen's *The Purple Rose of Cairo* (1985), *Labyrinth* (1986), *Mannequin* (1987), as well as a spate of films in which children were magically transformed into adults (and sometimes vice versa), the best and most popular example of which is *Big* (1988).

High fantasy, which finds its roots in legend and folklore, had a richer silent film history than did its sister subgenre. Douglas Fairbanks' *The Thief of Bagdad* (1924) was one of the greatest fantasy films in the history of Hollywood. If there were precedents for Fairbanks' opus, they could be found in D. W. Griffith's *Intolerance* (1916) and Thomas H. Ince's *Civilization* (1916), both of which had sweeping, epic, fantastical settings and events.

High fantasies often touch off deep primal emotions in their audience. Certainly, such was the case in the 1930s when one considers Frank Capra's *Lost Horizon* (1937) and Walt Disney's *Snow White and the Seven Dwarfs* (1937). On a smaller, more personal, level, there was also the unforgettable *Death Takes a Holiday* (1934).

High fantasy took the low road in the 1940s with cheaply made Arabian Nights tales starring Sabu, Maria Montez, and Turhan Bey. Bordering on high fantasy, however, was the ever-so-charming Douglas Fairbanks, Jr. gem, *Sinbad the Sailor* (1947).

The subgenre showed some life in the 1950s with films as different as *Pandora and the Flying Dutchman* (1950), *Ulysses* (1955), and *Brigadoon* (1954). As with light fantasy, high fantasy had little to show for itself in the 1960s aside from such fare as *Jason and the Argonauts* (1963) and *Camelot* (1967), but that began to change in the 1970s.

High fantasy began to appear far more regularly, if not terribly successfully, on the big screen in the late 1970s with Ralph Bakshi's animated version of *The Lord of the Rings* (1978).

The 1980s saw a veritable rash of sword and scorcery films that are at the very heart of high fantasy, dealing as they do with legend and myth. Movies such as *Dragonslayer* (1981), *Conan the Barbarian* (1982), *The Beastmaster* (1982), *Red Sonja* (1985), and *Ladyhawke* (1985) filled movie screens with great spectacle, but with few exceptions the films were not big box office. Given their often large budgets, some of them, such as *The Dark Crystal* (1983) and *Legend* (1985), were out-and-out disasters. One of the biggest disappointments of the decade, however, was George Lucas' *Willow* (1988).

Curiously, a combination of both light and high fantasy, Rob Reiner's *The Princess Bride* (1987) proved to be both highly praised and commercially viable.

Whether the subject matter is mermaids, dancing caterpillars, ghosts, spirits, leprechauns, would-be Santa Clauses, barbarians, ancient kings, visitors from Atlantis, or hobbits, both the light and high fantasy traditions remain firmly rooted in American cinema.

FARMER, FRANCES (1913–1970) An actress who rose to stardom in the latter half of the 1930s only to suffer a dramatic reversal in fortune, her story has become a bleak parable of Hollywood fame gone awry. Farmer's troubled life has been the subject of the feature biopic *Frances* (1982), starring Jessica Lange, and a TV movie titled "Will There Ever Be a Morning?" (1983).

Farmer was the daughter of a well-to-do family. Bright, beautiful, and talented, Farmer made but fifteen films, her first a "B" movie (q.v.), *Too Many Parents* (1936). After another low-budget quickie, *Border Flight* (1936), she was cast in a modest Bing Crosby musical, *Rhythm on the Range* (1936). Groomed for stardom,

Farmer was given her big chance in *Come and Get It* (1936), starring in a dual role that brought her high praise and the full star treatment. Her career seemed poised to skyrocket.

In 1937 she solidified her acting credentials by joining the Group Theater in New York and starring on stage as the female lead in Clifford Odets' *Golden Boy*. Despite continuing to work in the theater and in film, her career soon began to falter. Movies such as *Exclusive* (1937) and *The Toast of New York* (1937) were strong starring vehicles, but self-destructive behavior, principally in the form of alcoholism, led to bad publicity and legal tangles. Becoming an unreliable performer, she was banished to the "B's" and began appearing in films such as *South of Pago-Pago* (1940), *Badlands of Dakota* (1941), and *Among the Living* (1941). A particularly telling indication of how low Farmer had sunk was when she was cast alongside fellow enfant terrible, John Barrymore in *World Premiere* (1941), a film designed to capitalize on their mutual bad reputations.

After appearing in a supporting role in the "A" movie production of *Son of Fury* (1942), the emotional bottom fell out and Farmer began a long and harrowing journey through mental institutions, receiving questionable care and undergoing a lobotomy. She was briefly in the limelight again during the latter half of the 1950s when she was deemed well enough to host a TV show in Indianapolis and appear in a modest role in a low-budget teen film, *The Party Crashers* (1958).

Farmer died of cancer at the age of fifty-seven.

FAYE, ALICE (1912–)
One of Twentieth Century-Fox's greatest assets during the latter half of the 1930s and early 1940s, Faye had a lovely singing voice, beautiful eyes, and a warm, appealing style. She appeared in a long series of light musicals that were distinguished mostly by her presence in them. Nonetheless, nearly all of her movies were big hits, and her following was extremely loyal. Faye perfected the role of the woman who, though jilted, perseveres to win back the foolish object of her affections in the end. Among those foolish men were Tyrone Power *(q.v.)*, whom Faye discovered and with whom she starred in three films. But her most frequent costar was Don Ameche *(q.v.)*, with whom she shared top billing in six films.

Born Alice Jeane Leppert, Faye was the daughter of a New York City policeman. After quitting school at the age of thirteen to pursue a show business career, she got an early break that same year with the Ziegfeld Follies. When her true age was discovered, however, she was fired. Undaunted, she was dancing professionally in vaudeville by the time she was fifteen.

Faye's career began to zoom by the time she was seventeen. She was hired that year to appear in *George White's Scandals* in New York. Still known only as a dancer, she was cajoled into singing at a private party

Alice Faye was Twentieth Century-Fox's greatest female star during the latter half of the 1930s and early 1940s. Despite her absence from the screen for more than forty years, she continues to have active fan clubs all over the world. Photo courtesy of Alice Faye.

at which *Scandals* star Rudy Vallee was in attendance. A short time later, she was given the opportunity to sing on Vallee's radio show. According to W. Franklyn Moshier in his book, *The Films of Alice Faye*, she sang "Honeymoon Hotel" during the show and "as the notes died out at the song's conclusion, fainted dead away from sheer fright." Duly discovered, Faye sang regularly on Vallee's show, toured with his orchestra, and developed her own successful recording career. Later, she was also named in divorce proceedings initiated by Mrs. Vallee.

When *George White's Scandals* was turned into a movie in 1934, Faye was supposed to play a small role. Instead, in true movie-cliché fashion, when Lilian Harvey, the intended female star of the film, refused to play her part because it was too small, the relatively unknown Faye was given the role, which led to her instant stardom.

During the first few years of her film career, Faye was molded into a Jean Harlow *(q.v.)* type; her hair was bleached a platinum blond and she was cast in films with such titles as *She Learned About Sailors* (1934) and *365 Nights in Hollywood* (1934). Her singing, however, set her apart from the horde of Harlow imitators and she soon emerged with her own style and personality in musicals such as *Sing, Baby, Sing* (1936) and *King of Burlesque* (1936).

Despite her films in support of Twentieth Century-Fox's biggest star, Shirley Temple *(q.v.)*, Faye was emerging as a sure-fire money-maker in her own right. Singing Irving Berlin tunes in *On The Avenue* (1937), her popularity continued to grow, reaching a peak when she starred in two of her biggest hits, both of them

Best Picture Oscar nominees, *In Old Chicago* (1937) and *Alexander's Ragtime Band* (1938).

Other hits followed, such as *Rose of Washington Square* (1939), *Lillian Russell* (1940), and *Tin Pan Alley* (1940), but after her second marriage in 1941 to orchestra leader Phil Harris (her first marriage to singer Tony Martin lasted from 1936 to 1940), Faye took time to have a family. She appeared infrequently on film during the early 1940s, yet scored one of her biggest and most memorable hits in 1943 with *Hello, Frisco, Hello,* which was a remake of *King of Burlesque.*

It was also during the early 1940s that Fox chief Darryl F. Zanuck *(q.v.)* brought Betty Grable *(q.v.)* to the lot to challenge Faye's standing as the studio's number-one female star. The ploy worked far too well. In 1945, distraught over the studio's editing of her role in the Otto Preminger *(q.v.)* drama, *Fallen Angel* (1945), Faye fled the studio and never returned. She retired from the screen to raise her family (two daughters) and spend time with her husband in their perdurable marriage. They also performed together on radio on "The Phil Harris-Alice Faye Show" between the years 1946 and 1954.

Faye didn't appear in another movie until she supported Pat Boone in *State Fair* (1962). Her other latter-day film roles have included a cameo appearance in *Won Ton Ton, The Dog That Saved Hollywood* (1976), and supporting parts in *Every Girl Should Have One* (1978) and *The Magic of Lassie* (1978). She occasionally appeared on TV variety shows during the late 1950s and 1960s, and has also taken to the boards in shows such as the revival of *Good News.* In recent years, she has traveled tirelessly to speak on health issues of concern to the elderly.

FETCHIT, STEPIN (1902–1985) A black actor who has become a symbol of Hollywood's racist attitudes during the studio era of the 1930s and 1940s. Throughout his acting career, Fetchit was cast in comic relief roles that called for him to play slow-talking, dim-witted, lazy, and constantly frightened characters. He was given to pop-eyed double-takes and much eye-rolling in scores of films, a number of them rather good except for their now painful scenes with Fetchit. In an industry that offered little opportunity to black actors, Fetchit managed to become the first black to receive featured billing in otherwise all-white Hollywood movies. It was a dubious distinction, reflecting the movie industries racism.

Born Lincoln Theodore Monroe Andrew Perry, the actor took his stage name from a horse he once bet on that came in a winner. He had kicked around vaudeville as a young man and found his way to Hollywood at around the time Al Jolson *(q.v.)* was singing in blackface in *The Jazz Singer* (1927). Some of his early appearances on film can be found in *In Old Kentucky*

Stepin Fetchit was early Hollywood's most successful black actor. He worked constantly, playing comical parts that were racial stereotypes. Given the racism of his era, he had little opportunity to do otherwise. Photo courtesy of Movie Star News.

(1927), *The Ghost Talks* (1929), and an early version of *Show Boat* (1929). Though it is not to his credit, director John Ford *(q.v.)* used Fetchit fairly often in demeaning roles in such films as *Salute* (1929), *Judge Priest* (1934), and *Steamboat 'Round the Bend* (1935).

If a movie was set in the rural Deep South, Fetchit was likely to have a part in it. While he usually played minor roles, he did get top billing in an all-black film, *Miracle in Harlem* (1947). But by then, his career was already on the wane.

Fetchit was a popular comic actor, at least among whites, and he was much in demand during the 1930s, a decade in which he may have earned as much as $2 million. But he eventually spent more than he had, going bankrupt in 1947.

With the advent of socially conscious films in the late 1940s such as *Pinky* (1949), racial attitudes were finally beginning to change. Fetchit's personna was so deeply ingrained in the public consciousness, though, that despite his less outlandish performances in films such as *Bend of the River* (1952) and *The Sun Shines Bright* (1953), he was essentially finished as an actor.

Perhaps in reaction to the image his name conjures up among movie fans, he joined the Black Muslims in the latter half of the 1960s. His last hurrah was a cameo appearance in an all-black movie comedy called *Amazing Grace* (1974).

See also: racism in Hollywood

FIELD, SALLY (1946–) An actress who came out of lightweight TV sitcoms to win two Oscars for Best Actress. Diminutive and perky, Field's most successful portrayals have generally been of poor rural woman. Neither glamorous nor especially attractive, Field overcame low expectations for her Hollywood career to triumph as a major star for more than a decade.

Field was born to a theatrical family. Her mother was the movie actress Margaret Field, who later married actor Jock Mahoney and changed her stage name to Maggie Mahoney. With the knowledge and experience absorbed from her mother and stepfather, Field achieved early success in television as the star of two mind-numbing 1960s sitcoms, "Gidget" and "The Flying Nun." During this period she also made her film debut in a modest supporting role in the failed western. *The Way West* (1967). She didn't appear in another movie for nine years.

Struggling to be taken seriously as an actress during the 1970s, Field received good reviews for her performance in the well-received low-budget film about body building, *Stay Hungry* (1976), but her big breakthrough came in 1977 in the title role of the TV movie "Sybil," playing a woman with multiple personalities. Field won an Emmy for her performance and new-found respect among filmmakers.

She also began a much publicized relationship with actor Burt Reynolds *(q.v.),* who cast her as his love interest in what turned out to be some of his most popular movies, including *Smokey and the Bandit* (1977) and *The End* (1978). She was also the female lead in Henry Winkler's debut movie, *Heroes* (1977). In each case, however, she was secondary to the male stars of these films.

After joining an all-star cast in *Beyond the Poseidon Adventure* (1979), Field had the part of her life, playing the title role in *Norma Rae* (1979). As a poor working-class Southerner inspired to better herself through the influence of a Northern labor lawyer, Field stunned the Hollywood establishment with her strong, gutsy performance and won her first Academy Award for Best Actress.

She reteamed with Burt Reynolds for *Smokey and the Bandit II* (1980), which she followed with *Back Roads* (1981); the latter film flopped. She recouped smartly, however, when she played a journalist, costarring with Paul Newman *(q.v.)* in *Absence of Malice* (1981).

Despite the failure of the light comedy *Kiss Me Goodbye* (1982), her career has been on the upswing thanks to her second Oscar-winning performance in *Places in the Heart* (1984), once again in the role of a tough rural character. Her success, however, was somewhat militated by her unfortunate acceptance speech on national television, which remains one of the most embarrassing moments in Academy Award history. Taking the Oscar in her hands, Field cried out to the audience, "You *really* like me!" in a manner that made untold millions all over the world cringe.

In recent years she has continued to receive grudging respect from her peers thanks in part to her willingness to play second fiddle to the talented Tom Hanks in *Punchline* (1988), a movie Field also produced.

FIELDS, W. C. (1879–1946) The misanthrope of the movies, Fields created a character hilariously put-upon by virtually every institution in American society from marriage to Hollywood itself. With his bulbous nose, portly body supported by skinny legs, and his inimitable raspy voice, Fields played dupe to a hostile world. Like all great comedians, he knew that the underdog gets the laughs. The master of the throwaway line, he made his cinematic reputation through the use of wry asides tossed slyly under his breath. He said what a great many people were afraid to say, and audiences loved him for it.

Born William Claude Dunkinfeld, Fields came from a poor family in Philadelphia. He ran away from home when he was eleven years old. At the age of fourteen he had perfected enough skill to land a job as a juggler in an amusement park. At the bottom of the vaudeville circuit, Fields began a climb toward the top that took just six short years; at age twenty he was a headliner.

The next twenty years of Fields' life were prosperous and productive. He toured the world with his comic juggling and billiard acts, and eventually joined the Ziegfeld Follies. His only film during this period was a silent short made of his vaudeville act called *Pool Sharks* (1915).

He was the star of the Broadway hit *Poppy* in 1923, and the character he played, a con man with good intentions, established his stage, film, and radio persona for the rest of his career. When *Poppy* was bought by Paramount and rewritten, Fields was given a much-reduced part in the newly named *Sally of the Sawdust* (1925), which was directed by D. W. Griffith *(q.v.).* Fields was a hit in the movie, finding his film career launched at the advanced age of forty-six.

In most of his subsequent silent films, the critics

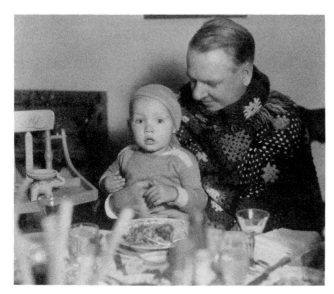

W. C. Fields had a reputation for hating children, but he was caught here in a benevolent off-screen moment with his on-screen nemesis, Baby Leroy. Photo courtesy of Movie Star News.

lauded him and the public collectively shrugged its shoulders. Fields was not a movie star yet. The tide began to turn in his favor, though, when he made his first sound shorts, the most successful of which were made for Mack Sennett *(q.v.)* in 1932–33: *The Dentist, The Fatal Glass of Beer, The Pharmacist,* and *The Barber Shop.*

At Paramount, Fields appeared in a succession of films that were moderately successful. Although he often had top billing, movies such as *Million Dollar Legs* (1932) and *International House* (1933) were not adequately built around his unique comic personality.

Nonetheless, while steadily building a cult following, Fields starred in his most suitable vehicle to date, *It's a Gift* (1934). Finally, Fields had Baby Leroy to bemoan and a wife against whom to direct caustic comments; the result was a minor masterpiece. His reputation grew still further thanks to his affecting, restrained performance as Mr. Micawber in MGM's production of *David Copperfield* (1935).

He completed only a few more films before illness kept him idle for nearly two years. The hard-drinking screen comic made one of his funniest films, *The Man on the Flying Trapeze* (1935), and then, finally, *Poppy* (1936), in a version closer to the original play that he had starred in more than a decade earlier.

After leaving Paramount in 1938, Fields entered his short but intensely creative period with Universal. The studio gave him virtual carte blanche to make any movie he wanted, just so long as it could be done on the cheap. Finally with the freedom to create his own films, Fields made four comedies that are considered among his best. Written under pen names such as

Mahatma Kane Jeeves and Otis J. Criblecoblis, Fields penned *You Can't Cheat an Honest Man* (1939), *My Little Chicadee* (1940), with Mae West, *The Bank Dick* (1940), and *Never Give a Sucker an Even Break* (1941). Legend has it that the last of these scripts was written on the back of an envelope by Fields while he sat on a toilet.

Never Give a Sucker an Even Break was Fields' most outlandish movie. It's threadbare plot concerned the making of a movie by Fields, playing himself, and it was surrealism at its most comicly potent, taking a slap at Hollywood, filmmaking, and all sorts of movie clichés. While sometimes more astonishing than funny, the film acutely captures Fields' sour outlook and expresses it in wildly imaginative style.

It was the last great film of his career. He appeared in a few more minor movies in the early to mid-1940s, but his drinking and failing health combined to keep him from being active. He died on Christmas Day in 1946.

See also: West, Mae

FILM NOIR: A term meaning "black film," coined by French film critics to describe a certain type of moviemaking that became prevalent in America during the 1940s and early 1950s. In content and theme, *films noir* are concerned with corruption, betrayal, cynicism, and disillusionment. The look of the films match their mood: odd angles, oppressive compositions, indoor scenes shot either in dark or dimly lit rooms, and outdoor scenes inevitably shot at night, often on rain-drenched streets.

While many *films noir* were made by directors with European backgrounds, such as Billy Wilder, Michael Curtiz, Otto Preminger, and Robert Siodmak *(qq.v.),* to name just a few, the genre was actually ushered in by Orson Welles when he made *Citizen Kane* (1941), a pensive and gloomy movie that owed much to German Expressionism.

The *film noir* changed audience expectations concerning heroes; it was the movement that gave birth to the Hollywood antihero, one of the earliest examples of which was Humphrey Bogart's Sam Spade in John Huston's version of *The Maltese Falcon* (1941). Certainly, Bogart was the classic *film noir* antihero.

America lost its innocence during World War II and that change was reflected in the *films noir* that began to proliferate during the early 1940s, such as *This Gun For Hire* (1942), *Double Indemnity* (1944), *Laura* (1944), and *Phantom Lady* (1944). But *films noir* soon exploded in popularity in the second half of the decade due to millions of disillusioned soldiers returning home with a harsher view of life, coupled with the new apocalyptic presence of the atom bomb. That troubled, disturbing world view was very much in evidence in scores of dark and somber movies such as *Spellbound* (1945), *The Killers* (1946), *Out of the Past* (1947), *Body and Soul* (1947), and *Ride the Pink Horse* (1947).

As deeply pessimistic as the 1940s *films noir* were, they had nothing on the violence and gloom and doom of their early 1950s counterparts. For instance, *The Enforcer* (1951) presented a society in which it seemed as if criminals ruled everywhere except inside police headquarters. In *The Big Heat* (1953) Lee Marvin, the villain, displayed unprecedented sadism by scarring Gloria Graham's face with scalding coffee. Finally, the darkest *film noir* of them all was *Kiss Me Deadly* (1955), a movie containing one of the most nihilistic climaxes in Hollywood history.

Fewer *films noir* were made in the later 1950s and they all but disappeared during the 1960s. But there have been occasional intentional (often darkly nostalgic) recreations of that style of moviemaking in the 1970s and 1980s, most memorably in *Chinatown* (1974), *Farewell, My Lovely* (1975), *Body Heat* (1981), and *Blood Simple* (1984).
See also: antiheroes

FINAL CUT The fully edited work print to which the negative is made to conform, and from which the release prints are made. Copies of the final cut are what audiences see on the big screen.

Since the demise of the studio system *(q.v.)*, the question of who determines the final cut of a film has become an important contractual point. In Hollywood's glory days, directors never had the right of final cut; it was the prerogative of the producing studio. In the last several decades, however, directors with commercial clout invariably insist upon (and receive) the right of final cut. Nonetheless, this right is still jealously guarded by the producers of most motion pictures.
See also: rough cut

FLYNN, ERROL (1909–1959)   He was one of the most dashing, charismatic leading men of the sound era. Both on screen and off, Flynn was the epitome of reckless, romantic masculinity. But perhaps Jack L. Warner *(q.v.)* described Flynn best when he wrote in his autobiography, "He had mediocre talent, but to the Walter Mittys of the world he was all the heroes in one magnificent, sexy, animal package. . . . Actor or no actor, he showered an audience with sparks when he laughed, when he fought, or when he loved."

Unlike most actors who primarily appeal to either men or women, Flynn was equally attractive as a character to both sexes. Women found his virile attitude, charming accent, handsome face, and lithe body thoroughly alluring. Men saw him as an ideal of strength, courage, and quick-wittedness. Considering the depth of his appeal, Flynn's success in Hollywood lasted a brief but spectacular ten years.

While many believe that Flynn was Irish, he was actually from Tasmania, an island near the Australian continent. His family was well-to-do, but Flynn was

Errol Flynn was just as handsome and dashing without his mustache as he was with it. This early publicity shot reveals the exuberance and charm that helped make him a star. Photo courtesy of The Siegel Collection.

too restless for traditional schooling. Among a great many youthful adventures, he prospected for gold, smuggled diamonds, hunted rare tropical birds, managed a plantation, and worked as a policeman. At one time, living in New Guinea, he was even tried for murder (he was aquitted).

It was while he was still in New Guinea that he had his first acting experience, appearing in a travelogue that essentially served as a screen test. It landed him the role of Fletcher Christian in a modest little version of *Mutiny on the Bounty* that was titled *In the Wake of the Bounty* (1933).

Flynn decided to explore an acting career further and went to England, where he landed work in the Northampton Repertory Company. Spotted on the stage by a Warner Bros. scout, he was signed up for his first film in Great Britain, *Murder in Monte Carlo* (1934), at $150 per week, and then shipped off to Hollywood.

In his first American film, *The Case of the Curious Bride* (1935), he played a corpse. He made just one more film in a modest supporting role, and then opportunity not only knocked, it pounded.

Warner Bros. was planning a big costume adventure epic, *Captain Blood* (1935, *q.v.*), with the well-known

English actor Robert Donat expected to play the lead. At the last minute, Donat decided not to take the part. Warner Bros., more well known for their hardboiled crime movies than their costume dramas, had stars under contract such as Edward G. Robinson, James Cagney, and Paul Muni *(qq.v.)*. They were hardly the types to play the buccaneer Peter Blood. It was decided, therefore, to gamble with two unknowns as the leads. Errol Flynn was tapped for Blood, and nineteen-year-old Olivia de Havilland *(q.v.)* was given the role of his love interest. With director Michael Curtiz *(q.v.)* in charge, they were in excellent hands.

The film was an immediate hit and Flynn was catapulted into instant stardom. Not since Douglas Fairbanks *(q.v.)* in the mid-1920s had audiences thrilled to such swashbuckling derring-do. Flynn and de Havilland made an excellent team, and were regularly paired together in movies through 1941.

Flynn's starring role in yet another hit, *The Charge of the Light Brigade* (1936), made it clear that his appeal was no fluke. Soon thereafter he proved adept at comedy as well, starring in *The Perfect Specimen* (1937), a clever reworking of *It Happened One Night* (1934). Flynn played the spoiled, rich society character and Joan Blondell played the tough reporter.

His crowning achievement, however, was *The Adventures of Robin Hood* (1938), directed with zest and style (as were so many of Flynn's early pictures) by Michael Curtiz. Filmed in Technicolor, the movie was a stupendous hit and Flynn was at the height of his popularity.

When westerns became popular again in the late 1930s, Flynn was outfitted with a cowboy hat, boots, and a six-shooter. More often than not, he seemed rather silly in western garb, but audiences didn't seem to care. Movies such as *Dodge City* (1939), *Virginia City* (1940), and *Sante Fe Trail* (1940) were all successful Flynn vehicles. Only when he was in uniform, playing George Armstrong Custer in Raoul Walsh's *(q.v.)* *They Died With Their Boots On* (1941), did Flynn seem genuinely right for the part. More than that, it was an excellent movie and one of his best performances of the 1940s.

In 1942 Flynn was accused of statutory rape. He went to trial and was acquitted of the charges, but the press coverage was sensational. One byproduct of the legal proceedings was the expression, "In like Flynn." The phrase entered the American vernacular, much to the actor's chagrin.

Unlike other celebrities involved in sex scandals, Flynn didn't suffer a loss in popularity. From 1942 onward, though, most of his movies were directed more consistently toward the male audience. From the clever and vibrant Raoul Walsh film *Gentlemen Jim* (1942), where Flynn played a boxer, to a spate of war movies such as *Desperate Journey* (1942), *Northern Pursuit*

(1944), and *Objective Burma* (1945), the actor was doing much more fighting than loving.

After the war, Flynn's films had no focus or fire. His westerns seemed sillier than ever, and his light comedies and dramas were rather poor vehicles. *The Adventures of Don Juan* (1948) had a little fire but not enough to rekindle Flynn's sagging career. By 1951, he was reduced to starring in a Republic feature, *The Adventures of Captain Fabian*. Flynn was certainly trying (the movie was based on his own original screenplay) but his hard living, alcohol swigging, and drug taking were catching up to him. His looks were fading, and movie fans were no longer interested in him.

Flynn tried to recapture his past glory with several swashbucklers in the early 1950s, even going overseas to find the financing. It wasn't until he began playing parodies of himself as a drunken has-been that he resurrected his career as a supporting player. Appearing in *The Sun Also Rises* (1957), *Too Much Too Soon* (1958), and *The Roots of Heaven* (1958), Flynn received good reviews.

He died of a heart attack at the age of fifty, but not without having the last word. His autobiography, *My Wicked, Wicked Ways,* was published the year he died (1959), and in it he proudly admitted, without apologies, all his faults and foibles. He was everything he appeared to be, and he left a true-life legacy just as spectacular as his years in the Hollywood sun.

FONDA, HENRY (1905–1983)   An actor who embodied the plainspoken, yet unassuming character of the American midwesterner. He was an actor first and a movie star second in a career that spanned six decades.

Fonda came by his middle-American image honestly, as a born-and-bred Nebraskan. Drawn to acting at an early age, he worked as an amateur in the Omaha Community Playhouse (along with Marlon Brando's mother). By 1928, he had turned professional and while in New England, joined the University Players and worked with future theater and Hollywood luminaries Joshua Logan, James Stewart *(q.v.),* and Margaret Sullavan *(q.v.).* He not only made a lasting friendship with Jimmy Stewart, he married Margaret Sullavan. It was the first of his five marriages.

His career on Broadway was rather modest through the early 1930s, until he found a major hit in *The Farmer Takes A Wife,* which ultimately became his first film vehicle in 1935. In 1936, Fonda appeared in the hit movie *The Trail of the Lonesome Pine.* His role in that film became the basis not only for Al Capp's character L'il Abner, it also brought Fonda's persona more into focus. Throughout the rest of his career, he would usually play a variation on the man of intergrity that he portrayed in only his third motion picture.

Fonda worked steadily as both a leading man and supporting player in the latter 1930s. His leads, however, were usually against better-known female stars, such as Bette Davis *(q.v.)* in *Jezebel* (1938). Nonetheless, a few fine movies saw excellent performances by Fonda in this period, particularly *You Only Live Once* (1937) and *The Story of Alexander Graham Bell* (1939). The film that changed his career wasn't a terribly big hit, but the director, John Ford *(q.v.),* was very much impressed with Fonda, and their association over the next fifteen years transformed the actor's career. After their first film together, *The Young Mr. Lincoln* (1939), Ford used him again in *Drums Along the Mohawk* (1939), which was the huge hit that solidified Fonda's image as a star.

Just the same, in order to get the plum role of Tom Joad in John Ford's next film, *The Grapes of Wrath* (1940), Fonda had to agree to a seven-year contract with Twentieth Century-Fox. The film is the quintessential Henry Fonda movie, in which he plays an idealist who stands for right and is willing to fight for it. Fonda expressed an inner strength and a quiet resolve that struck a deep, responsive cord in audiences, who found him to be especially credible because of his restraint.

Except for four other great films, the rest of the 1940s were a washout for Fonda. He showed a deft light comedic touch in Preston Sturges' *(q.v.)* delightful comedy *The Lady Eve* (1941). He also proved his devotion to progressive causes when he starred in the anti-lynching film *The Ox-Bow Incident* (1943). After his World War II Navy service, Fonda teamed up with John Ford again to make the classic western *My Darling Clementine* (1946). And then, in deference to Ford, he joined the great director's other star player, John Wayne, and played his first bad guy, a stuffed shirt army officer in *Fort Apache* (1948).

Fonda had made four wonderful movies while under contract to Fox, but not enough to make up for all his poor ones during his tenure at the studio. Fonda did what few movie stars have ever done before or since. He simply walked away from the movies to pursue his first love, the theater. For the next six years, Fonda appeared in three long-running hit plays on Broadway, *Mr. Roberts, Point of No Return,* and *The Caine Mutiny Court Martial.*

Fonda might never again have appeared in the movies had it not been for John Ford. The director was to make the film version of *Mr. Roberts,* but Warner Bros., claiming that Fonda had been off the screen for too long, did not want the actor. Ford insisted that he would only direct the film if Fonda played Roberts, even though the role had already been offered to William Holden and Marlon Brando, with Brando already having accepted the part. But Warner backed down and let Ford have his way. Ironically, during the filming of *Mr. Roberts,* Fonda and Ford literally came to blows over how the play was to be filmed and never worked together again.

Mr. Roberts was one of the top-grossing films of the year, and Fonda's film career was once more in full flower. He found new roles in Hitchcock's *The Wrong Man* (1956), *Twelve Angry Men* (1956), a film that Fonda was particularly proud of, and an Anthony Mann western, *The Tin Star* (1958).

After a successful return to Broadway in *Two for the Seesaw* and a TV series, "The Deputy," in the late 1950s, Fonda tended toward elder statesmen roles, playing noble politicians and/or presidents in movies such as *Advise and Consent* (1961), *The Best Man* (1963), and *Fail-Safe* (1964). In the latter 1960s, he became a supporting actor in other stars' films, keeping his name before the public but no longer carrying movies on his own. Yet he was often wonderfully effective even in smaller roles. One of the best of these was his portrayal of a villain in Sergio Leone's epic masterpiece *Once Upon a Time in the West* (1969).

When he was offered leading roles, however, Fonda did well with them. He scored a hit with *Yours, Mine and Ours* (1968) in which he costarred with Lucille Ball, once again showing his sly comic touch. But such roles were relatively rare; most of his other starring roles were in minor westerns such as *Firecreek* (1968) and *The Cheyenne Social Club* (1970), in which he costarred with his old friend Jimmy Stewart.

In the 1970s, Fonda did very little film work. He had once again returned to Broadway, scoring a huge success in a one-man show based on the life of the famous attorney Clarence Darrow. Fonda toured with *Clarence Darrow* all over the country and eventually filmed the production as a TV special. But the aging actor had been felled during this time with heart trouble.

He was a sick and dying man when he agreed to film *On Golden Pond* (1981), a movie produced by his daughter, Jane. Based on a Broadway play, *On Golden Pond* teamed Fonda with Katharine Hepburn *(q.v.)* as his wife and Jane Fonda as his embittered daughter. The elder Fonda was magnificent, and won his first and only Academy Award for Best Actor. Some said it was an Oscar given out of sympathy; others said it was an Oscar given for the achievements of a lifetime. Regardless, Henry Fonda was proud to receive the honor, dying with the same dignity he had exhibited throughout his long, honorable career.

Fonda's two children, Jane and Peter, both entered show business, and both have had a significant impact on the movie business, Jane as a major Hollywood star, and Peter mostly for his short-lived success as a producer and star in the influential movie, *Easy Rider* (1969, *q.v.*). His granddaughter, Bridget Fonda (daughter of Peter), has also recently emerged as a potential new star in films such as *Scandal* (1989) and *Frankenstein Unbound* (1990).

See also: Fonda, Jane; *The Grapes of Wrath*

FONDA, JANE (1937–) The daughter of Hollywood icon Henry Fonda and sister of actor-director-producer Peter Fonda, she has been a movie star since the early 1960s. Fonda is an accomplished, if mannered, actress who has won two Best Actress Oscars and has garnered an additional five Best Actress Academy Award nominations in a career that has included more than thirty movies. There is hardly another modern screen star who has had a more adventurous film career than Fonda.

Though brought up in the movie business, young Jane had little interest in acting, preferring the art world to Hollywood. Though she made her stage debut at the age of sixteen, acting with her father in the Omaha Community Theater production of *The Country Girl* in 1954, Fonda ignored the applause of the audience and continued her formal education at Vassar, later attending an art school in Paris.

After returning from Europe, she found it relatively easy—thanks to the Fonda name and her striking good looks—to build a career as a model in New York. She became a cover girl but found little satisfaction in the work and soon began exploring her father's profession at the Actors Studio.

She made her film debut in Joshua Logan's *Tall Story* (1960), playing the female lead. (Incidentally, Logan was an old friend of her father's from their youth.) Audiences liked her and her career continued apace with such films as *Walk on the Wild Side* (1962), *The Chapman Report* (1962), and *Sunday in New York* (1963). Fonda then began starring in European films that she interspersed with her Hollywood projects. For instance, in 1964 she starred in a French production titled *The Love Cage* as well as *La Ronde,* which was directed by Roger Vadim, whom she married the following year.

After strong performances in hits such as *Cat Ballou* (1965), *Any Wednesday* (1966), and *Barefoot in the Park* (1967), she shocked the film industry by starring in her director/husband's erotic sexual fantasy movie *Barbarella* (1968). The film was no masterpiece but it was an amusing romp that has since become something of a cult favorite.

From a career perspective, however, Fonda's credibility as a serious actress was seriously undermined by her flamboyant success in Vadim's film. She quickly restored her respect in Hollywood and gained an Oscar nomination for her performance in the bleak drama *They Shoot Horses, Don't They?* (1969). She followed that critical success with yet another much-admired performance, this time in the hit *Klute* (1971), winning her first Best Actress Academy Award.

It was to be the last box office winner she would have over the next six years as Fonda expanded her outspoken opposition to the war in Vietnam. She went so far as to travel to North Vietnam and allow herself

There are few modern actresses who have had as varied a career as Jane Fonda. She has played everything from light romantic comedy to heavy drama, from westerns to sexy science fiction. Photo by Harry Langdon, courtesy of Jane Fonda.

to be photographed sitting behind an antiaircraft gun. Known as "Hanoi Jane" by American soldiers in South Vietnam, there were serious calls in the United States to try her for treason. Nothing came of such threats because America was not technically at war with North Vietnam.

During these emotionally charged years, Fonda either starred in or helped produce, write, and direct a number of antiwar documentaries, such as Jean Luc Godard's *Tout va bien* (1972), *Free the Army* (1972), and *Introduction to the Enemy* (1974).

When Fonda returned to commercial filmmaking, it was to appear in an all-star version of *The Blue Bird* (1976), a joint Russian and American film venture that bombed.

Finally, with Vietnam less prominent in the American psyche, Fonda starred in an impressive number of hit films that dealt with serious political, cultural, and social issues, but she did so within the bounds of solidly commercial entertainment. Movies such as *Fun With Dick and Jane* (1977), *Julia* (1977), *Coming Home* (1978), for which she won her second Best Actress Oscar, *The Electric Horseman* (1979), *The China Syndrome* (1979), and *Nine to Five* (1981) turned Fonda into one of the most bankable female stars in Hollywood during the late 1970s and early 1980s.

The emotional highlight of her career was surely

working with her father in a film for the very first and last time. The movie, which she produced, was *On Golden Pond* (1981) and the elder, ailing Fonda won the Best Actor Oscar just a short time before he died.

During much of the 1980s, Fonda became involved in producing exercise/fitness books and videotapes that became huge best-sellers. Her biggest success in this area was *The Jane Fonda Workout* book, which was at the top of best-seller lists for over two years.

Her acting during the mid- to late 1980s has been limited but effective. She won an Emmy for her TV performance in "The Dollmaker" (1984), and was nominated for an Oscar when she played an alcoholic in *The Morning After* (1986). Fonda geared up to make more movies at the end of the decade when her own production company, Fonda Films, produced her first film in three years, *Old Gringo* (1989).

Divorced from her long-time husband, former radical activist and California state senator Tom Hayden, Fonda continues to be equally committed to both her movie career and any number of political and social issues.
See also: Fonda, Henry

FONTAINE, JOAN (1917–) A year younger than her sister, Olivia de Havilland, she became a star when she was almost ready to quit the movie business. Though she appeared in more than fifty films, she is best remembered for a handful of roles calling for her to play plainlooking, frightened women in dangerous circumstances.

Like her sister, Joan was born to the de Havilland family in Tokyo. After Olivia's sudden fame in *Captain Blood* (1935), Joan decided to try her luck in the movies as well. Having a famous sibling didn't hurt, but her climb to the top was still painfully slow.

Originally acting under the name of Joan Burfield, she appeared in a Joan Crawford film, *No More Ladies* (1935), but her part was so small she was barely noticed. While gaining more stage experience, she dropped Burfield, chose her stepfather's last name, and became Joan Fontaine. RKO gave her another chance at the movies in 1937 and the actress appeared without distinction in several films. Nonetheless, because she had an English accent (her parents were English), she was given the opportunity to become Ginger Rogers' successor as Fred Astaire's dancing partner in *Damsel in Distress* (1937). Fontaine didn't really dance, and the movie was only mildly successful, accomplishing little for her career. She continued making inconsequential movies until she had a chance to shine in a modest role in *Gunga Din* (1939) as Douglas Fairbanks Jr.'s fiancée.

Though Olivia de Havilland was quickly cast in the supporting role of Melanie in *Gone With the Wind* (1939), Joan had a chance to test for the leading role of Scarlett O'Hara. And though virtually everybody in Holly-

wood tested for that role, the film's original director, George Cukor (*q.v.*), was impressed with Fontaine, and he cast her in the *The Women* (1939).

After five years of acting, though, Fontaine felt that she was running in place and was prepared to quit the profession and marry actor Brian Aherne. Then at a party, David O. Selznick (*q.v.*) asked her to test for a role in Alfred Hitchcock's (*q.v.*) first American film. The movie was *Rebecca* (1940) and both Joan Fontaine and the film were smash hits. Her portrayal of the shy, circumspect (and endangered) second wife of Max deWinter (Laurence Olivier) was enormously appealing. She repeated that same sort of characterization in Hitchcock's *Suspicion* (1941) and won a Best Actress Oscar for her efforts. As the title character in *Jane Eyre* (1944), she gave yet another stellar performance.

Her other films of the 1940s were considerably lesser vehicles, except for *Letter from an Unknown Woman* (1948), which may very well be her best film. Again, she played a shy woman, this time taken advantage of by a worldy playboy (Louis Jourdan).

A well-publicized feud between Fontaine and her sister during the height of their careers kept their names in the newspapers even when their films weren't worthy of mention. Fontaine's films, especially in the 1950s, were more and more often not worth mentioning. *September Affair* (1950) and *Something to Live For* (1952) were two of her rare good movies. She made a noble attempt in *Island in the Sun* (1957), a film about racism, in which she played Harry Belafonte's lover.

Hollywood isn't as kind to aging female beauties as it is to aging male actors, with very few good parts available for older women. Fontaine was finally reduced to doing a horror film in England called *The Witches* (1966).

Joan Fontaine retired from the movie business, wealthy and with a handful of movie performances for which she can be justifiably proud.
See also: de Havilland, Olivia

FORD, GLENN (1916–) A leading man of the postwar era who became a star due to his stoic style. Ford, who appeared in more than eighty movies, was a versatile actor who was equally adept in light comedies, crime films, and westerns. Pleasant looking—though hardly handsome—audiences responded to his "everyman" features and his down-to-earth warmth.

Born Gwyllyn Samuel Newton Ford in Quebec, Canada, his well-to-do family moved to southern California when he was still a child. He began acting while in high school in Santa Monica and continued to act with small theater groups until he was noticed by Columbia Pictures, which signed him to a contract in 1939.

Ford was given leading, if not starring, roles from the very start; for instance, he was the young male love interest in his motion picture debut in *Heaven With a Barbed Wire Fence* (1939). Though the films he was featured in were often low-budget affairs, such as *Babies for Sales* (1940) and *Blondie Plays Cupid* (1940), Ford was clearly being groomed for bigger things.

World War II, however, altered Columbia's plans for their young comer. After appearing in fourteen films released between 1939 and 1943, Ford joined the war effort by enlisting in the Marine Corps. The studio, in an effort to reestablish the actor as a viable box office force after his discharge from the service at the end of the war, paired him with their hottest female star, Rita Hayworth *(q.v.)*. The result was a huge hit, *Gilda* (1946). Ford followed that success by playing opposite another strong female star, Bette Davis *(q.v.)*, in yet another hit, *A Stolen Life* (1946). His career was back on track.

A workhorse actor, Ford appeared steadily in films until the late 1960s when he finally turned to television. If he seemed indiscrimate in his choice of material (the quality was extremely variable), he was fortunate enough to appear in so many films that the odds of landing in a genuinely good movie were finally in his favor. Regardless of quality, though, Ford remained quite popular and enjoyed a particularly successful string of films in the 1950s, which include *The Big Heat* (1953), *The Blackboard Jungle* (1955), *The Teahouse of the August Moon* (1956), and *3:10 to Yuma* (1956). It's worth noting, though, that in most of his big hits he was often upstaged by his supporting cast.

The actor's career held steady into the early 1960s thanks to the success of *The Courtship of Eddie's Father* (1963). It was, however, his last big hit. After the modest success of *The Rounders* (1966), he found himself being cast in lower budget movies such as *Day of the Evil Gun* (1968).

By 1970, Ford had begun starring in TV movies, even trying his luck at a TV series, "Cade's County" in 1971, without success, and again with "Holvak" in 1975. His big-screen appearances have been few and far between during the 1970s and 1980s, the most memorable was as Superman's human stepfather in the original *Superman* (1978).

FORD, HARRISON (1942–) This ruggedly handsome actor has starred in four of the ten top-grossing films of all time, an unprecedented achievement. Associated with action roles, Ford brings depth to his characterizations with a world weary style reminiscent of Humphrey Bogart *(q.v.)*. He often plays cynical, antiheroes who manage to win audience sympathy thanks to his energetic and intelligent performances. In a career that has been closely tied to two of America's most gifted modern directors, George Lucas and Steven Spielberg *(qq.v.)*, Ford has created a hip action image

Harrison Ford is a modern-day Gary Cooper. A rugged, masculine appearance and a gruff, no-nonsense style—leavened with a sense of humor—have made him a popular star of adventure films. He is seen here in *Indiana Jones and the Temple of Doom* (1984). Photo courtesy of Harrison Ford.

that appeals to a wide cross section of the moviegoing public.

Born in Chicago, Ford spent his youth in the Midwest, obtaining his first serious taste of acting in theater productions at Ripon College in Wisconsin. After a short stint playing in stock, he decided to break into the movie business. He had a promising beginning, signing contracts with Columbia and (later) Universal, but the studio system *(q.v.)* in the 1960s was no longer capable of grooming new stars.

His first significant film role was a small part in the James Coburn *(q.v.)* film *Dead Heat on a Merry-Go Round* (1966). But with his square-jawed, raw-boned good looks, he was a natural for westerns. And though cowboy roles were fast becoming a thing of the past, he managed to land guest starring roles on TV shows such as "Gunsmoke" and "The Virginian" and small parts in films such as *Journey to Shiloh* (1968). But his career was floundering.

After a modest role in the Elliot Gould flop *Getting Straight* (1970), Ford quit acting to become a professional carpenter. Then George Lucas turned Ford's career around by giving him a small part in the sleeper hit of 1973, *American Graffiti*. The film yielded a bumper crop of new stars, but Ford was not immediately one of them. Lucas remembered the actor, though, and gave him the plum role of Han Solo in *Star Wars* (1977) after the actor had been struggling for several years. The film was a smash hit and Ford became an instant star. He moved quickly to solidify his position in the industry, but his follow-up films, *Heroes* (1977), *Force 10 From Navarone* (1978), and *Hanover Street* (1979), received a tepid response at the box office. The latter film, however, received good reviews, particularly for Ford. He costarred with Gene Wilder in his next film, the western comedy *The Frisco Kid* (1979), which also received favorable notices. His reputation as an actor was growing.

Ford once again played Han Solo in the George Lucas production of the second *Star Wars* film, *The Empire Strikes Back* (1980). The film's gargantuan success revitalized Ford's box office appeal. Lucas then produced the Steven Spielberg movie *Raiders of the Lost Ark* (1981) with Ford in the lead as the archaeologist/adventurer Indiana Jones. By this time, Ford had starred in three super blockbusters in a period of just five years. After playing a futuristic Bogart type in the visually stunning box office flop *Blade Runner* (1982), he got back on track again with the 1983 *Return of the Jedi* (*Star Wars III*, his fourth top-ten grosser) and 1984's *Indiana Jones and the Temple of Doom*, eventually starring in yet another monster hit, *Indiana Jones and the Last Crusade* (1989).

Since the mid-1980s, however, Ford has starred in several films that have displayed the wide range of his talents, most notably *Witness* (1985), for which he received a Best Actor Oscar nomination. His more recent performances in films such as *Mosquito Coast* (1986), *Frantic* (1988), and *Working Girl* (1988) have continued to add to his stature as an actor.

See also: American Graffiti; Star Wars

FORD, JOHN (1895–1973) When Orson Welles *(q.v.)* was asked what American directors he favored, the man who made film history with *Citizen Kane (q.v.)* replied, "The old masters, by which I mean John Ford, John Ford, and John Ford." In his long career in Hollywood, Ford made one hundred and twelve feature films, a good many of them becoming cherished classics. Among his many achievements, Ford became the cinematic chronicler of the American West, elevating the western genre to poetic heights, and discovering John Wayne *(q.v.)* and making him a star. Ford also was a director of conscience who made the landmark films *The Grapes of Wrath* (1940, *q.v.*) and *Cheyenne Autumn* (1964).

Born Sean Aloysius O'Feeney in a small town in Maine, Ford grew up in a traditional Irish family. When he graduated from high school, he immediately went west to join his elder brother, Francis, in Hollywood. Francis, thirteen years John's senior, had changed his

last name to Ford, and the kid brother did the same. Francis was a writer-director-actor for Universal, and he helped John get his start.

According to Peter Bogdanovich *(q.v.)* in his book, *John Ford,* the young man began his distinguished film career in 1913 as a laborer, stunt man, actor, and third assistant prop man. By 1917, however, he was already directing two-reel westerns starring Harry Carey. During his early apprenticeship, he called himself Jack Ford, but he changed his name to John Ford when he directed *Cameo Kirby* (1923), although his friends continued to call him Jack until the day he died.

His first important film was *The Iron Horse* (1924), an epic western about the building of the railroads. It was heavily influenced by D. W. Griffith's earlier work, but having directed a big-budget hit gave the young filmmaker a higher level of credibility in the business. He worked steadily throughout the rest of the silent era and made a relatively easy transition to sound films.

In the 1930s, Ford made movies of every kind, from comedies such as *Up the River* (1930) to action films such as *Submarine Patrol* (1938). He worked with actors as disparate as Boris Karloff (*The Lost Patrol*, 1934) and Shirley Temple (*Wee Willie Winkie*, 1937). Yet Ford's films of this period, despite their obvious differences, had much in common. Specifically, they were about codes of conduct (*Mary of Scotland*, 1936), moral expectations (*Stagecoach*, 1939) and, more often than not, they were also about the creation of myths (*Young Mr. Lincoln*, 1939).

Ford's reputation reached new heights in 1935 when he won a Best Director Oscar for *The Informer*. Critics lauded the film's impressionistic Irish streets full of mist and dark shadows. Ford, who didn't care very much for critics, shrugged off the praise, admitting that he filled the set with mist and kept the star, Victor McLaglen *(q.v.)*, in shadows because he didn't have a big enough budget for sets.

It was typical of Ford to ignore high-fallutin' praise of his movies. He didn't claim to be an artist, though he clearly was one despite his protestations. And in the late 1930s, Hollywood saw him as its premier director, leading Darryl F. Zanuck of Twentieth Century-Fox *(qq.v.)* to choose Ford to direct *The Grapes of Wrath* (1940).

Hollywood had never taken on a social issue in quite the grand manner as this film version of John Steinbeck's novel about the Great Depression and the Okies who fled the Dust Bowl. Ford's feeling for the land and for the downtrodden Joad family was communicated in the carefully directed gestures of the actors, giving the movie a powerful emotional charge.

Ford's empathy for the Joad family was similar to his feelings for his Irish roots, and the director made "Irish" movies throughout his career. The best of these include *How Green Was My Valley* (1940) and *The Quiet Man*

(1952), which captured the feelings that many an immigrant American felt for the land of their forebears, no matter what country they may have come from.

After serving as a filmmaker for the government during World War II and making, among others, the classic documentary *The Battle of Midway* (1942), Ford returned to Hollywood and soon began a series of western movies that were to become the crowning achievement of his career.

Ford hadn't made a western since his silent days, except for *Stagecoach* in 1939, the film that briefly brought westerns back into vogue before World War II, and made a star out of a "B" movie actor, John Wayne, whom Ford believed had major star potential.

My Darling Clementine (1946), an intelligent, thoughtful movie about civilization coming to an untamed land, was Ford's first postwar western. It was a theme to which Ford would return time and again throughout the rest of his career.

Fort Apache (1948), *She Wore a Yellow Ribbon* (1949), and *Rio Grande* (1950) constituted the director's cavalry trilogy. But Ford's acknowledged masterpiece among his westerns is *The Searchers* (1956). One movie that is best representative of the theme underpinning Ford's westerns is *The Man Who Shot Liberty Valance* (1962). At the end of the film, a reporter learns that the oft-told story of who shot the outlaw Liberty Valance is based on a lie. But the reporter, caught between the truth and a legend, chooses to "print the legend." It was always Ford's belief, exemplified in so many of his films, that people need heroes and heroism in order to inspire them, even if it's at the expense of truth.

Toward the end of his magnificent career, Ford made a point of correcting some of the racial stereotypes he had fostered in many of his earlier films. In *Sergeant Rutledge* (1960), which starred black actor Woody Strode, he dealt with racial bigotry. In 1964, he gave Indians their due in *Cheyenne Autumn*. And long before it was fashionable, he made a strong feminist film, *7 Women* (1966).

Ford was famous for his use of Monument Valley for nine of his westerns, a majestic setting on the border between Arizona and Utah. Perhaps the other dependable element in his films was the presence of John Wayne, who was the archetypal Ford hero. But Wayne wasn't the only actor who consistently showed up in John Ford movies. The director had an unofficial stock company made up of Ward Bond, Ben Johnson, Harry Carey, Jr., Woody Strode, and Victor McLaglen. Henry Fonda *(q.v.)* appeared in quite a number of Ford films, beginning in 1939, but their relationship ended in 1955 when they fought over the direction of *Mr. Roberts*.

Ford, of course, was not alone in making his great movies. He has been closely associated with a handful of screenwriters who helped shape his vision, including Frank S. Nugent, Dudley Nichols, and Nunnally Johnson *(qq.v.)*.

See also: Stagecoach; westerns

FORMAN, MILOS (1932–   )   A Czech writer-director who fled to America after the Russians invaded his homeland after the "Prague Spring" of 1968. Though Forman has made relatively few movies, those he has made have often been enormously popular with both critics and audiences. A rebellious sort, Forman is clearly in tune with the young. But his identification with the youthful outsider is not cynical or fashionable posturing; Forman's cinema celebrates commitment and positive action.

Born to a Jewish professor father and a Protestant mother, Forman was orphaned when his parents perished in Hitler's concentration camps. Raised by relatives, he later attended Prague's Academy of Music and Dramatic Art. After penning a number of screenplays in the 1950s, he wrote and directed *Audition* (1963), followed by the short *If There Were No Music* (1963). His first feature, *Black Peter* (1964), won first prize at the Locarno Film Festival. Forman's next two projects, *Loves of a Blonde* (1965) and *The Firemen's Ball* (1967), were wry comedies that became international art-house hits.

Luckily, Forman happened to be in Paris when the Soviets invaded Czechoslovakia to quell dissident uprisings. In exile, he soon arrived in the United States and made his American directorial debut with the successful comedy *Taking Off* (1971). After participating as one of the directors of a documentary about the 1972 Olympics in Munich, *Visions of Eight* (1973), he was hired by Michael Douglas to direct *One Flew Over the Cuckoo's Nest* (1975), which was the only film he did not at least cowrite. The picture swept the Academy Awards, becoming the first film since Frank Capra's *It Happened One Night* (1935) to take all five top Oscars—Best Picture, Best Actor, Best Actress, Best Screenplay, and Best Director.

Forman went on to adapt the Broadway hit *Hair* to the screen in 1979, but the film's content was badly outdated by the time of its release. In any event, the movie was highly praised by the critics if lightly attended by audiences. Forman stumbled slightly yet again when he turned the hit novel *Ragtime* into a movie in 1981. Though the reviews were generally positive, the box office response was not. But the critics and the public agreed that *Amadeus* (1984) was well worth the price of admission. This unlikely popular musical about the life of Mozart and his chief rival, Salieri, was a soaring masterpiece, a magical blend of music and visual virtuosity. Filmed in the land of Forman's birth, the movie won eight Oscars, including Best Director and Best Picture.

Since 1978, Forman has been codirector of Columbia University's Film Division.

42nd STREET This 1933 movie introduced a new, outlandish form of movie musical.

Though Warner Bros. made the first movie musical, *The Jazz Singer* (1927), by the early 1930s the genre was dying due to the production of too many mediocre films. In order to revive the category, Warner Bros. turned to Busby Berkeley *(q.v.)*, a talented Broadway musical director who had shown flair in Goldwyn's *Whoopee* (1930), starring Eddie Cantor. The result was the wildly successful *42nd Street*.

Unlike the classy Astaire/Rogers musicals at RKO, or the clever, sophisticated operettas at Paramount, Busby Berkeley and Warner Bros. contrived a string of the gaudiest, kitschiest musicals ever made. The spectacle of huge sets, hundreds of scantily clad women, and mammoth overhead camera shots revealing kaleidoscopic effects became the hallmark of the Berkeley/Warners musical. And no other musical director or studio put on shows like *42nd Street* and its immediate successors, *Gold Diggers of 1933* (1933) and *Footlight Parade* (1933).

Ironically, the underlying plot of *42nd Street* and the follow-up films it spawned were based on the desperation caused by Depression unemployment. At the center of *42nd Street,* Warner Baxter plays a famous theater producer who has gone broke in the stock market crash. He's also very ill, and his doctor tells him he's got to quit or he'll drop dead. But Baxter needs the money and goes ahead with his show anyway.

The movie introduced songs such as "Young and Healthy," "You're Getting to be a Habit With Me," and "Shuffle Off to Buffalo." The music was written by Al Dubin, with lyrics by Harry Warren. The movie also introduced Dick Powell *(q.v.)* in the first of his decade-long string of boy ingenue roles, and it also made a star out of Ruby Keeler. Of perhaps more interest, though, is the fact that *42nd Street* offered an enormous number of lines that turned into instant clichés, such as Baxter's famous line to Keeler, "You're going out a chorus girl, but you're coming back a star." In fact, the plot device of the unknown actress becoming a star overnight by subbing for the injured lead has become the very height of clichédom.

It should be noted that only the musical sequences in *42nd Street* were directed by Berkeley. The rest of the film was ably directed by Lloyd Bacon, with a cast that included Bebe Daniels, George Brent, Guy Kibbee, Una Merkel, and Ginger Rogers (in a modest supporting role).

FOSSE, BOB *See* musicals.

FOSTER, JODIE (1963–) A child actress of remarkable poise and maturity who has since grown up to become a significant adult performer. She and Brooke Shields were the two hottest young actresses during the 1970s, but Foster has since proved to be the more talented and versatile artist. It must be acknowledged, however, that Foster has had the advantage of far more experience than Shields, having begun her acting career at the age of three.

Born in the Bronx, New York, Foster spent her early childhood working in Walt Disney television shows. She was all of nine years old, but a veteran, nonetheless, when she made her motion picture debut in a starring role in *Napoleon and Samantha* (1972). Other early roles included Becky Thatcher in *Tom Sawyer* (1972) and a bit part in the Raquel Welch film *Kansas City Bomber* (1972). She might just as easily have been a TV actress during these years, having had roles in two different failed television series: "Bob and Carol and Ted and Alice" (1973) and "Paper Moon" (1974).

Foster's most important break came when she met director Martin Scorsese *(q.v.)*, who first cast her in a small part in his film *Alice Doesn't Live Here Anymore* (1973). Impressed with the precocious actress, he cast her three years later in the pivotal role of the child prostitute in *Taxi Driver* (1976), the film that vaulted her to national prominence. The controversy surrounding her portrayal of the drug-addicted teenage streetwalker who befriends a potential assassin (Robert De Niro) tended to overshadow her utterly convincing performance. But in that same year, her tongue-in-cheek playing of a Mae West-like character in the bizarrely amusing *Bugsy Malone* opened a lot of eyes to her talent.

Foster seemed on the verge of a major career but there were relatively few roles for thirteen-year-old girls in Hollywood. She ended up in another Disney movie, *Freaky Friday* (1977), and then a dark murder thriller, *The Little Girl Who Lives Down the Lane* (1977), in which she played the ever-so-cute but deadly murderess.

Having studied at the bilingual Lycée française in Los Angeles, Foster easily made the transition to international films, making movies in France and Italy during the late 1970s. These did not find audiences in America nor did *Foxes,* released in the United States in 1980. She registered a rich and intriguing supporting performance in the underrated movie about carnival life, *Carny* (1980), but Foster could not escape her difficulty in finding the right roles in the right movies; she seemed all at once to be too smart and too young and was a challenge to cast.

The actress solved her problem by taking a hiatus from her career to go to Yale University. While at Yale, her past came back to haunt her when a deranged young man named David Hinckley attempted to reenact a scene from *Taxi Driver* in order to win Foster's affection. Hinckley wounded then-President Ronald Reagan in a nearly successful assassination attempt.

Foster stayed out of the public eye during much of the early 1980s. She pursued her studies and wasn't seen again on the big screen until she joined the ensemble cast of *Hotel New Hampshire* (1984). The film was roundly panned and quickly disappeared. A number of other films followed over the next several years, none of them successful. *The Blood of Others* (1984), *Mesmerized* (1986), and *Siesta* (1988) were all rather poor and some of them were never even theatrically released in America.

It appeared as if Foster was going to be yet another child actress who could not make the transition to adult roles. But then came three films in a row, all of which garnered her excellent reviews. The first two, *Five Corners* (1988) and *Stealing Home* (1988), were not commercial hits but critics raved about her performances. And the third, *The Accused* (1988), not only won critical raves, it brought Foster her first Best Actress Oscar.

FOUR-WALLING The distribution strategy of renting movie theaters at a set fee in order to exhibit a motion picture. The practice is called four-walling because the usually small, independent filmmakers or companies that follow it buy all four walls of the theater for the length of the run. In normal distribution, the theater owners generally receive a percentage of a film's box office gross. Due to the fact that four-walled films are almost always unknown commodities, theater owners protect themselves with the flat fee and the filmmakers, by paying for the theaters themselves guarantee their movies much needed exposure.

The purpose of the practice is to build interest and word-of-mouth for a film with the hope that a good showing will convince a powerful distributor to buy the movie and show it nationally.

Sometimes, though, four-walling can be so successful that a national distributor might not even be needed.

Saturation booking (renting as many theaters as possible in a concentrated area) on a four-wall basis can make a small independent movie appear to be a major release. If a movie does good box office on that basis, the same procedure can be repeated over and over again in different areas of the country. An example of an independent movie that was successfully four-walled into a national hit is *Billy Jack* (1971).

FRANKENHEIMER, JOHN (1930–) A former TV director whose early film career in the 1960s made him one of Hollywood's new shining lights, Frankenheimer's seering studies of alienation have marked him as a visually acute director of somber, often depressing movies. He has most successfully directed thrillers; his other films have generally been plodding affairs that have been attacked by critics and ignored by audiences.

Frankenheimer came from a well-to-do family, finding his interest in the movies whetted by his experience in making several short films for the "Film Squadron" while he served in the U.S. Air Force during the early 1950s. He went on to become a TV director, eventually winning recognition for his work on the prestigious "Showcase 90" program.

He was briefly among the first wave of TV directors to take the plunge into feature filmmaking when he made *The Young Stranger* (1956). Though the movie was well received, Frankenheimer didn't return to the big screen again until 1961 when he directed *The Young Savages*. It was the start of a short-but-sweet streak of critical and commercial success that briefly vaulted him to the top of the directorial heap in the early 1960s. His strong handling of *All Fall Down* (1962), *Birdman of Alcatraz* (1962), *The Manchurian Candidate* (1962), *Seven Days in May* (1964), and *The Train* (1964) made him one of the hottest directors in Hollywood.

His descent from the top was as quick as his rise. Curiously, the film that started his tumble was actually, in retrospect, one of his most stunning achievements. The movie was *Seconds* (1966), a daring and visually adventurous film about a man who finds a way to become young again and has a second chance at a new life. Despite its virtuoso direction, the movie was scorned by the critics and audiences were put off by its depressing climax. *Grand Prix* (1966) was a more successful movie but critics called it a sell-out.

Frankenheimer had had enough. He moved to Europe and made a number of interesting flops, the best among them *The Fixer* (1968), *The Gypsy Moths* (1969), and *I Walk the Line* (1970). By the early 1970s, his once promising career was in a shambles. He inched his way back with the ponderous if critically acclaimed film version of *The Iceman Cometh* (1973), followed by several thrillers. His biggest films of the later 1970s were *The French Connection II* (1975) and *Black Sunday* (1977), after which he fell into obscurity with another series of sometimes interesting flops, such as *Prophecy* (1979), *The Challenge* (1982), and *The Holcroft Covenant* (1985).

In 1988 Frankenheimer was rediscovered by many critics with the re-release of the *The Manchurian Candidate*. Frank Sinatra, who starred in the film and owned the rights to it, had refused to let it be shown since the 1960s due to its eerie similarities to President Kennedy's assasination. When Sinatra finally allowed *The Manchurian Candidate* to be seen, it was newly hailed as a masterpiece and did surprisingly big business at the box office despite the fact it was more than twenty-five years old and shot in black and white. Frankenheimer's career was consequently given a shot in the arm, the result of which was the disappointing *Dead Bang* (1989).

FREED, ARTHUR (1894–1973) He was Hollywood's most accomplished and successful producer of musicals and, less well known, a very fine lyricist. Freed was principally responsible for MGM's musical golden era that lasted from 1939 through 1958. His "Freed Unit" became a virtual hitmaker for the studio, giving him an unusual degree of independence within MGM. He used that freedom well, gathering around himself an enormously talented group that included composer/arranger Roger Edens *(q.v.)*, who was his associate producer on a great many films, and directors such as Vincente Minnelli, Stanley Donen, and Busby Berkeley *(qq.v.)*. He had access to Hollywood's greatest musical talent, with stars such as Judy Garland, Mickey Rooney, Fred Astaire, and Gene Kelly *(qq.v.)*. Most importantly, he passed along the creative freedom he had been given to his directors, stars, and choreographers, allowing them to make fresh, innovative musicals over a remarkable twenty-year period.

Born Arthur Grossman, Freed seemed more likely in his early years to have had a career on the stage than to have become a powerful movie producer. He worked the vaudeville circuit, even appearing with the Marx Brothers *(q.v.)*, but finally settled into writing song lyrics during the 1920s. By the late 1920s, he had had minor success as a lyricist and as a stage director of musical revues and shows.

In 1929, when the musical film was the premier form of the new talkies, Irving Thalberg *(q.v.)* hired Freed to go to work at MGM as a lyricist. Freed stayed for more than thirty years. During his first decade at the studio, he worked largely in collaboration with composer Nacio Herb Brown, writing tunes for the films *The Broadway Melody* (1929) and *Broadway Melody of 1936* (1935), among others.

Freed was the associate producer of *The Wizard of Oz* (1939), a job that catapulted him to producer later that year. His first musical as a producer was *Babes in Arms* (1939). The list of films he went on to produce is a virtual movie musical hall of fame. Among his most memorable films are *For Me and My Gal* (1942), which made Gene Kelly a star, *Cabin in the Sky* (1943), a rare all-black musical that introduced Lena Horne, *Meet Me in St. Louis* (1944), an unusual and effective family musical (with Freed also dubbing the singing voice of Leon Ames), *The Pirate* (1948), which gave Vincente Minnelli the chance to experiment with studio-bound theatricality, *An American in Paris* (1951), for which Freed garnered a Best Picture Oscar, *Singin' in the Rain* (1952), whose lyrics, including the title tune, were largely written by the producer himself, and *Gigi* (1958), for which Freed took home another Best Picture Academy Award.

To understand the full extent of his impact on the musical genre, here is just a sampling of some other Freed-produced musical hits: *Girl Crazy* (1943), *Easter Parade* (1948), *On the Town* (1949), *Annie Get Your Gun* (1950), *Royal Wedding* (1951), *Show Boat* (1951), *The Band Wagon* (1953), *Brigadoon* (1954), and *Bells Are Ringing* (1960).

In all, he produced more than forty films, the vast majority of them musicals. When the demand for movie musicals finally abated in the early 1960s, Freed produced two non-musicals, *The Subterraneans* (1960) and *The Light in the Piazza* (1962), and then gracefully retired.

See also: musicals

FREUND, KARL (1890–1970) Germany's greatest cameraman during the 1920s, he arrived in Hollywood in 1929 and became a top-flight cinematographer and occasional director of low-budget films, particularly stylish horror movies. Known for his abilities with lighting effects and creative camera movement, Freund was a master of moody, psychological cinema.

As a fifteen-year-old Czech in need of a job, Freund became an assistant projectionist at a Berlin movie theater. Mesmerized by the technical elements of the film industry, he quickly learned as much as he could about the workings of a movie camera and latched onto an opportunity to become a cameraman. Resourceful and clever, his trick photography helped turn *The Golem* (1920) into a classic of early German Expressionism. His later contributions as a cinematographer include F. W. Murnau's *The Last Laugh* (1924), E. A. Dupont's *Variety* (1925), and Fritz Lang's *Metropolis* (1926).

Freund was initially brought to Hollywood to continue his masterly work as a cameraman, and he did so with considerable skill in films such as *Dracula* (1931), *Murders in the Rue Morgue* (1932), *Back Street* (1932), and *The Kiss Before the Mirror* (1933). Meanwhile, his visual flair was so strongly in evidence that Freund was given the chance to direct. He made just eight movies, but two of them are considered minor classics of the horror genre, *The Mummy* (1932) and *Mad Love* (1935).

Despite his modest success, Freund gave up directing these low-budget films and concentrated on his cinematography. "A" movie projects soon followed such as the two Garbo vehicles, *Camille* (1937) and *Conquest* (1937), and the only film for which he won an Oscar, *The Good Earth* (1937).

Though he photographed his share of soft-hued romances and comedies such as *Rose of Washington Square* (1939) and *Du Barry was a Lady* (1943), Freund was at his best with the dark paranoia of films such as *Golden Boy* (1939), *The Seventh Cross* (1944), *Undercurrent* (1946), and *Key Largo* (1948). Nonetheless, ever the creative adventurer, Freund opted for something new in the early 1950s: television situation comedy. He became the director of photography for the "I Love Lucy" show, soon becoming the supervising cinematographer of every show shot at the Desilu Studios. He retired from television work in 1959 and did not return to the movies. Instead, he gave his full attention to the Photo Research Corporation, a company he created in 1944 to make light-measuring equipment.

FULLER, SAMUEL (1912–   )   A "B" movie director "discovered" by the French critics of the 1950s, such as Jean-Luc Godard, and then hailed by Andrew Sarris and other American critics who appreciated Fuller's dynamic visual style. It is fair to say that Samuel Fuller is one of the most cinematic of filmmakers, a director of primitive emotions who, at the same time, posseses a sophisticated expressive style. As a writer-director, whose best films appeared in the 1950s and early 1960s, Fuller amassed a body of work that was meant for the second half of double features, but is now shown in museums and revival houses all over the world.

One might have expected that Fuller would have been an artist or photographer considering his vivid visual sense, but the director began his career as a copy boy for a newspaper and quickly worked his way up at the *New York Journal* to become at seventeen the youngest crime reporter in the city. In the 1930s, he had several novels published, but also wrote a handful of screenplays that were turned into minor movies. After fighting in World War II in a unit nicknamed "The Big Red One," (he would someday make a movie of the same name), he returned to the United States to begin an iconoclastic film career as a director of his own work.

His first film, *I Shot Jesse James* (1949), was dramatically filmed with an enormous number of close-ups. The visual effect was stunning: nothing this innovative had ever been attempted before in what was ostensibly a "B" movie western.

Fuller usually worked in four basic genres: westerns, war movies, crime films, and newspaper stories. His westerns, such as *The Baron of Arizona* (1950), *Run of the Arrow* (1957), and *Forty Guns* (1957), never took the audience where convention demanded. For example, in *Forty Guns,* when the villain grabs the heroine and uses her for a shield, the hero actually shoots her to get a clear shot at the bad guy!

Fuller's war movies are probably the most realistic war films ever made, not because they're naturalistic but because the director understood the emotions of the fighting man, and his films were true to those feelings. In movies such as *The Steel Helmet* (1950), *Merrill's Maurauders* (1962), and *The Big Red One* (1980), Fuller managed to make films that were violent and exciting without glorifying war. His point of view was made clear in *Merrill's Maurauders* when his camera panned a battlefield of dead soldiers without distinguishing the enemy casualties in any way.

Fuller's crime films, such as *Underworld USA* (1960), *The Naked Kiss* (1964), and *Dead Pigeon on Beethoven Street* (1972) were each, in turn, angrier statements about American society. In *The Naked Kiss,* for instance, the prostitute heroine eventually spurns hypocritical small-town American life and returns to the life of a hooker.

Many consider Fuller's best movie to be *Shock Corridor* (1963), the story of an ambitious reporter who pretends to be crazy in order to discover a murderer in an insane asylum. By the end of the film, the reporter discovers the killer but becomes insane himself. The spectacular use of sound and riveting visual images has made *Shock Corridor* a cult classic. The climactic scene in the mental institution corridor when the hero hallucinates being struck by lightning in a thunderstorm is one of the most awesome creative moments in Hollywood history.

There is nothing subtle about Fuller's cinema, however. *The Naked Kiss,* for instance, begins with a beautiful woman in a physical fight with a man. Suddenly, the woman's wig comes off revealing that she's completely bald! After she knocks the man out, the bald woman puts her lipstick on using the camera lens as a mirror. No other director except Fuller would think of such an audacious scene; and this all happens before the opening credits!

Fuller rarely worked with stars. His stock company of actors consisted of Constance Towers (at one time Fuller's wife), Gene Evans, Gene Barry, and Barry Sullivan. The real star of Fuller's movies, though, was the camera.

GABLE, CLARK *(1901–1960)* Known as "The King of Hollywood," he was an actor of limited skill but almost limitless popularity. Despite his prominent ears and a thin mustache, Gable was adored by women. And males liked him because he was not a softy who would let women push him around. But MGM loved him the most, because he brought more money to the famed studio than any other actor in their vast stable of stars. He had the astonishing record of having made thirty-nine films in the 1930s with only one box office dud (*Parnell*, 1937).

Born William Gable in Cadiz, Ohio, the future movie star entered the theater working as a backstage handyman for a series of touring stock companies. Occasionally, he would fill in for an ailing actor, but that was the extent of his early acting experience.

Gable would have five wives, but his first wife, a drama coach by the name of Josephine Dillon, helped him get a start in the movie business in the mid-1920s. He appeared in a handful of silent films (including *The Merry Widow*, 1925), but in miniscule parts. He gave up on Hollywood and went back to the theater.

His reputation as an actor started to grow in the latter 1920s, but he was by no means a big Broadway star. Thanks to his friendship with another theater actor, Lionel Barrymore, he was given a screen test at MGM. For no apparent reason, Gable was dressed like a South Seas native, complete with a flower behind his ear for the test. MGM didn't want him. Neither did Warner Bros., which gave him their own screen test when they considered him for the role of Rico in *Little Caesar* (1930). But with the sound film revolution, Hollywood was hungry for Broadway actors with good voices. Gable just barely grabbed hold of the brass ring, winning the role of the villain in a minor western, *The Painted Desert* (1931).

Irving Thalberg *(q.v.)* at MGM had a change of heart. Perhaps seeing Gable in western garb helped, but whatever the reason, Hollywood's premier studio signed Gable to a two-year contract for $350 per week.

They got their money's worth.

After just four films in supporting roles, Gable was the talk of the industry. And not just for his acting. His highly publicized romance with Joan Crawford *(q.v.,* who was already a major star) galvanized fan interest in Gable. The lovers were paired in a number of films, such as *Dance Fools Dance* (1931), *Laughing Sinners* (1931), and *Possessed* (1931). MGM rushed him from one film to the next to take advantage of his sudden popularity. It was in *A Free Soul* (1931) that his rough-hewn masculinity came to the fore as he pushed his leading lady, Norma Shearer *(q.v.),* around on the screen (much like James Cagney *[q.v.]* had done to Mae Clarke in *Public Enemy* earlier that same year).

Though he hardly seemed the type, Gable was called the second Valentino in the early 1930s. His sexy image was enhanced by his risqué movies with Jean Harlow *(q.v.), Red Dust* (1932) and *Hold Your Man* (1933).

Meanwhile, Gable was becoming annoyed with the way MGM was casting him. He felt he was being run into the ground by repeatedly playing the same kind of role. He refused to act in his next movie for MGM, and the studio retaliated (they thought) by loaning him out to Columbia Pictures, a small, poverty row studio, for Frank Capra's film *It Happened One Night* (1934, *qq.v.*). The movie was the biggest hit of the year, winning Gable a Best Actor Oscar. The impact of his performance can best be gauged by the fact that T-shirt sales plummeted when he took off his shirt in the film revealing a bare torso.

Gable was bigger than ever, and even without his mustache in *Mutiny on the Bounty* (1935), he had women

Clark Gable was the "King" of Hollywood, and he is seen here surveying his domain from the set of *Gone With the Wind* (1939), the film with which he has been most closely associated. Photo courtesy of Movie Star News.

With the Wind. Every time that picture is re-released a whole new crop of young movie-goers gets interested in me.' "

Also in 1939, Gable married the popular and talented movie star, Carole Lombard *(q.v.)*. It was his third marriage, and this one seemed like a perfect match— even his fans approved. Her tragic death in a plane crash in 1942 was a terrible blow to Gable, and it came just as he left Hollywood to go to war.

After he returned in 1945 he had two hit films, *Adventure* (1945) and *The Hucksters* (1947). But after 1947 he was no longer the sure box office bet he had been during the 1930s. A number of duds led MGM to drop Gable after his contract ran out in 1953. But Gable's *Mogambo* (1953), which was a lesser remake of his 1932 hit *Red Dust,* was a surprise money-maker. MGM decided they wanted Gable back after all. The actor, however, would have none of it. Bitter over the treatment he had received at the hands of the studio, he decided to free-lance.

Gable's films in the mid- to late 1950s, such as *The Tall Men* (1955), and *Run Silent, Run Deep* (1958), were well received by critics and fans. Though the star was aging, he still had the magic in his voice, his eyes, and in that wonderful smirk.

His last film, *The Misfits* (1961), was also Marilyn Monroe's last. Gable had been paid $750,000 with a guarantee of $58,000 per week in overtime. It was by far his highest salary for a film (excluding percentage arrangements), and he was the perfect, lover/father figure for Monroe. But Gable insisted on doing his own stunts for the film and the strain apparently brought on a heart attack that killed him just a few weeks after shooting was completed.

GAFFER The head electrician on the set of a movie. Not to be confused with a "gofer" (an errand boy who "goes for" things), the gaffer is a highly respected member of the crew, who is responsible for making sure that the cinematographer, to whom he reports, has all the lighting he will need for each individual scene. The gaffer, therefore, inspects locations ahead of time in order to gauge what specific lighting equipment (and how much of it) will be needed. On each day of a shoot, the gaffer will direct his often substantial staff— whom he hires—in the setting up of the lamps, cables, and other electrical equipment.

The gaffer, his best boy (assistant), and the rest of his crew are principally charged with either finding or creating a source of electrical power in order to make sure the lights will function—not an easy task when working on location. Power sources are often at a considerable distance from where a scene is being shot, and it is necessary in these cases for the gaffer to instruct his crew in the most efficient, least disruptive way to

swooning in the aisles. Among his many projects, several excellent movies followed, including *Too Hot to Handle* (1938) and *Idiot's Delight* (1939).

Gable was not David O. Selznick's *(q.v.)* first choice to play Rhett Butler in the film version of Margaret Mitchell's best-seller *Gone With the Wind* (1939, *q.v.*) but Gable was the public's first choice. Wisely, Selznick listened to the fan magazine polls and changed his mind. Ironically, however, Gable didn't want the part. MGM owned his contract and insisted that he play Rhett. Gable would never regret his forced hand. According to author David Shipman, in *The Great Movie Stars,* "Clark Gable once said to David O. Selznick: 'The only thing that kept me a big star has been revivals of *Gone* run their cable between the power source and the lighting equipment. When there is no power source nearby, the gaffer is responsible for setting up independent generators.

The derivation of some of the technical crew's titles (such as best boy) are lost to history. But one theory as to the origin of the title of gaffer goes back to the early silent era when the main lighting source was the sun. Studios were fitted with canvas roofs, and in order to control the amount of light, the canvas would be moved back and forth with gaffing hooks (normally used to snag fish). Apparently, the person using the gaffing hooks became known as a gaffer and the name stuck.

See also: best boy

GANGSTER MOVIES Violent action films, usually with contemporary urban settings, that tend to focus on society's outsiders and their perverse pursuit of the American dream, the gangster movie is often a dark tragedy with flawed but sympathetic heroes who break the law and ultimately pay for their transgressions. The genre has been enduring and profitable because it can be easily adapted to today's headlines. It has also, at times, been controversial because it tends to glorify hoodlums and the brutality they often employ in their rise to power. Though by no means a perfect definition, a character in *The Petrified Forest* (1936) described the difference between a gangster and a desperado by saying that a desperado was an American and a gangster was a foreigner. For the most part, that rough distinction has held true—at least in gangster movies—with tragic heroes of ethnic descent, usually either Italian or Irish.

The gangster movie's antecedents can be found in D. W. Griffith's *The Musketeers of Pig Alley* (1912), a film that portrayed the criminal life. America, however, saw itself as essentially a rural nation in the early twentieth century, and showed little interest in the trials of the urban dispossessed until 1927 when the first real gangster film, *Underworld,* was made. The film established the fundamental elements of the gangster movie: a hoodlum hero; ominous, night-shrouded city streets; floozies; and a blazing finale in which the cops cut down the protagonist.

Other seminal gangster films followed, such as *Thunderbolt* (1929), *Doorway to Hell* (1930), and Warner Bros.' *Little Caesar* (1930), starring Edward G. Robinson (*q.v.*) as Rico Bandetti. The film was a smash hit, and not only made Robinson a star, it spawned the Warner cycle of gangster movies throughout the early 1930s.

Little Caesar, together with *Public Enemy* (1931), with James Cagney (*q.v.*), and *Scarface* (1932), with Paul Muni (*q.v.*), were hugely violent pre-Hay's Code (*q.v.*) gangster films that galvanized public interest in a new sort of hero. The box office success of these three films set off a storm of imitations (most of them by Warners) as well as a storm of protest. Civic leaders were outraged that people like Al Capone—the obvious inspiration for Scarface—were being cheered in movie theaters all across the nation. By the same token, moviemakers knew that the elements of the gangster film—the blasting tommy-guns, car chases, molls, and clever slang of the mobsters—made for a potent box office mix.

So the studios adapted. Warner produced *G-Man* (1935), in which the hero became the law-enforcement official and the gangster became the villain. But the same tommy-guns and car chases were much in evidence. America's fascination with gangsters, however, could not be denied forever. By the end of the 1930s, the genre began to evolve in several different directions. Sociological gangster films, such as *Dead End* (1937) and *Angels With Dirty Faces* (1938), attempted to blame criminal behavior on societal factors; nostalgic gangster movies harked back to the prohibition era with films such as *The Roaring Twenties* (1939); and gangster elegies such as *High Sierra* (1941) portrayed the modern-day gangster as the last of a dying breed.

The gangster film went into eclipse during World War II only to return in the bleak form of *film noir* in the postwar years. The dark, moody gangster films of that era, such as *The Killers* (1946), were pessimistic and cynical far beyond their 1930s counterparts. And in movies such as *Key Largo* (1948), the gangster, as played by Edward G. Robinson in his role as Rocco, became a symbol of everything evil that America fought against in the war but had somehow failed to eradicate.

Other postwar gangster movies began to depict criminal behavior expressed by large, faceless, organized forces rather than by individuals. Movies like *The Enforcer* (1951) gave the impression that the mob was everywhere and one could not hide from them for long. And in *The Big Heat* (1953), a police officer (Glenn Ford) had to work from outside the constraints of government to defeat the corruption brought on by organized crime.

Scientific methods of crime detection were coming to the fore in the late 1940s and early 1950s, but the same attention to science that brought the world the atom bomb also brought the apocalyptic end of crazed gangster Cody Jarrett (James Cagney) in *White Heat* (1949).

Throughout the 1950s and early 1960s, the predominant theme of gangster films involved a powerful organized criminal elite, as in movies such as *Underworld USA* (1961), though there were the occasional low-budget recreations of old-time gangster movies such as *Baby Face Nelson* (1957) and *Machine Gun Kelly* (1958).

The gangster film faded into relative obscurity during most of the 1960s, replaced by spy films. *Bonnie and Clyde* (1967), however, harked back to the theme of criminals as misunderstood outsiders and tragic heroes and was a great success. The real high point of the gangster film came with the release of *The Godfather* (1972) and its sequel, *The Godfather, Part II* (1974). The gangster as tragic outsider and the faceless yet all-powerful organization were beautifully melded in Francis Coppola's Oscar-winning masterpieces. Just as Hollywood copied the success of *Little Caesar,* forty years later filmmakers copied Coppola's new hit gangster formula, resulting in a spate of movies such as *The Valachi Papers* (1972).

Gangster films have always been adaptable to contemporary situations and so it came as no surprise to see *Scarface* remade in 1983 with illicit cocaine instead of prohibition alcohol at the core of the film's plot. Ever-mindful of its roots in the Chicago underworld, the Hollywood gangster film lives on in works such as *The Untouchables* (1987), the hit-movie version of the TV series.

See also: Bogart, Humphrey; *Bonnie and Clyde;* Coppola, Francis Ford; *Dead End; The Godfather I & II; Little Caesar*

GARBO, GRETA (1905–) Known to her fans simply as "Garbo," she remains the quintessential female movie star. No other actress of either the silent or sound era has had such a profound and lasting effect on audiences. She is, as David Shipman wrote in *The Great Movie Stars,* "the standard against which all other screen actresses are measured."

Born Greta Louisa Gustafson to a poor family in Stockholm, Sweden, she began making her living in a barber shop, lathering mens' faces with shaving cream. Her film career began when she later worked for a department store and was used in a short film advertising the company wares.

After appearing in several other short films, she won a scholarship to the Royal Stockholm Theater School. It was there that she began her association with Mauritz Stiller, who cast her in his movie *The Atonement of Gosta Berling* (1924).

While traveling in Europe, MGM's Louis B. Mayer *(q.v.)* saw the film and tried to hire Stiller. The great L. B. Mayer wasn't impressed with Garbo, however, whom he thought to be too overweight for American audiences. Stiller insisted that he wouldn't go to Hollywood without her—if Mayer wanted him as a director, he would have to have Garbo as an actress. Reluctantly, Mayer agreed to hire both of them.

Once in Hollywood, MGM tried to find a way to promote her, so the studio called Garbo "The Norma Shearer of Sweden." It was "sheer" hype, until they cast her in what they thought would be a minor movie, *The Torrent* (1926). The film proved to be a sensation, and Garbo received excellent reviews, becoming a star in America with her very first production.

Garbo. She was the purest of movie stars: a pretty woman made ravishing by the magic of the camera. Mysterious, exotic, and always bigger-than-life, Garbo cemented her image as the ultimate unattainable heroine when she walked away from Hollywood. Photo courtesy of The Siegel Collection.

Stiller hadn't directed her in *The Torrent* but he planned to direct her in her next feature, *The Temptress* (1926). To both his and Garbo's dismay, he was fired from the film and never made another movie with the star he had discovered. He died in 1928. Garbo's career, however, continued to flourish. She often played a wronged woman who nobly submits to her fate, usually dying at the end of the movie.

1927 was a banner year for Garbo. *Flesh and the Devil* (1927) was a massive hit, thanks to her pairing with John Gilbert *(q.v.).* The reported off-screen romance between the two stars helped ticket sales to soar. MGM wisely paired them again in *Love* (1927). Her several films in the late 1920s included another match-up with John Gilbert, *A Woman of Affairs* (1929). But when the sound revolution hit Hollywood, Garbo's career was at a crossroads.

After considerable coaching of their star, MGM released *Anna Christie* (1930) with the advertising slogan "Garbo talks!" Her first lines were, "Gimme a vwisky vwith chincher ale on the side—and don't be stinchy, beby."

Garbo had already established her aloof personal style, rarely giving interviews to the press. Called the "Swedish Sphinx" by some, the air of mystery that surrounded her made her that much more intriguing to the public. Rumored affairs with famed conductor Leopold Stokowski and director Rouben Mamoulian *(q.v.)* fueled the gossip columnists' fires. The enigma of Garbo is, of course, one of the elements that has contributed to the world's lasting fascination with her.

It would be wrong to suppose that all of Garbo's movies were box office bonanzas. Her first few sound movies did respectable business but she was by no means MGM's biggest money-maker. Audiences, however, did line up to buy tickets to see her with brash new star Clark Gable *(q.v.)* in *Susan Lenox: Her Fall and Rise* (1931). And she was at the peak of her popularity in 1932 when she made *Mata Hari* and *Grand Hotel (q.v.)*.

The latter part of Garbo's career saw some of her best films, but fewer people went to see them. Her modest appeal at the box office, coupled with her huge salary, made her a liability at MGM. The studio stuck by her, though, because of her popularity in Europe. *Queen Christina* (1933), in which she costarred with John Gilbert for the last time, was highly praised but was not the gigantic hit MGM was hoping for. *Anna Karenina* (1935) and *Camille* (1936) also won accolades from critics but merely respectable audience response.

Her next film, *Conquest* (1937), was a bomb. Like Marlene Dietrich *(q.v.),* she was labeled "box office poison" in a theater owners' poll. And, like Dietrich, she turned to comedy to save her career. If the decade had begun with "Garbo talks," it ended with the advertising slogan "Garbo laughs! The film was Ernst Lubitch's *Ninotchka* (1939, *qq.v.*), and her performance as the Communist who is wooed and won by the dashing capitalist (Melvyn Douglas) ranks among her best movies.

Based on the success of *Ninotchka,* Garbo starred in another comedy, *Two-Faced Woman* (1941), but the movie was neither funny nor successful. At this time Garbo decided to retire—but not forever, as is generally supposed. She merely intended to wait until the war in Europe was over and theaters there (where she was most admired) reopened.

But the war lasted much longer than she expected. She came close to remaking *Flesh and the Devil* in 1945, and tentatively considered several other film projects throughout the rest of the 1940s and early 1950s all of which were eventually aborted. In one case, she was actually signed to star in a 1949 Max Ophuls film, but the movie was never made because Garbo would only agree to meet the film's producers in a dark room where they would not be able to see her face clearly.

Garbo had been nominated during her career for Best Actress Oscars for *Anna Christie* (1930), *Romance* (1930), *Camille* (1936), and *Ninotchka* (1939), losing every time. But Hollywood finally paid tribute to Garbo in 1954 with a special Oscar for her "unforgettable performances."

GARDNER, AVA (1922–   ) A star more famous for her off-screen love affairs than her film roles, she was one of the last studio-created sex sirens. Called the most beautiful woman in the world by no less a beauty than Elizabeth Taylor *(q.v.)*, Gardner's sultry eroticism was a powerful antidote to saccharine stars like June Allyson *(q.v.)*. And though Hollywood had a hard time casting her, in the right films, she was the woman every man wanted and the woman every woman wanted to be.

Ava Lavinia Gardner was born in Grabtown, North Carolina, to a poor tenant farmer family. She showed no inclination toward acting while she grew up, and her ambition was merely to get a good job as a secretary in New York. With a shorthand speed of 120 words per minute, her ambition was quickly realized. But Hollywood lightning struck when her picture, taken by her photographer brother-in-law, was seen by an MGM scout.

The beautiful nineteen-year-old girl with a thick Southern accent was given a screen test at the MGM studio in 1941. According to John Daniell in his book, *Ava Gardner,* after Louis B. Mayer *(q.v.)* saw the test, he exclaimed, "She can't act, she can't talk, she's terrific!"

MGM gave her speech and drama lessons, but the studio didn't use her very much. Her first tiny film appearance was in a Norma Shearer movie, *We Were Dancing* (1942). Her marriage that year to MGM's number-one star, Mickey Rooney, received more attention than her movie debut. Neither the marriage nor her career did very well, but she later stated that Rooney taught her a good deal about acting in front of a camera.

Her big break came in *Whistle Stop* (1945), her first leading role in a United Artists movie (she had been loaned by MGM for the part). And then Gardner was loaned out yet again, this time to Universal, where she made the movie that put her over the top, *The Killers* (1946). She starred with a young Burt Lancaster (in his debut *q.v.*), and both of them burned up the screen. Gardner had finally found her niche in the *film noir* movies of the latter 1940s, projecting a dark, dangerous sensuality. Unfortunately, MGM was dedicated to family entertainment rather than dark melodramas, and the studio found it difficult to take advantage of their new sex star.

Gardner had a few good roles in films such as *The Hucksters* (1947) and *One Touch of Venus* (1948), but for the most part, MGM wasted her talents in lackluster movies until the studio decided to make a musical version of *Showboat* (1951). Against great opposition, she was given the role of Julie Laverne, the black woman who tries to pass as white. Remarkably, Judy Garland had been originally cast but she was ill and had to withdraw. The film, of course, was a huge hit and represented the best work of Gardner's career.

Meanwhile, her personal life was becoming increasingly notorious. Her short marriage to bandleader Artie Shaw, a romance with Howard Hughes, and a torrid affair and eventual marriage to Frank Sinatra were a boon to the gossip columnists.

Her films of the 1950s were more successful than her private life. The best of the lot were *Mogambo* (1953), a remake of *Red Dust,* in which she played the Jean Harlow role, *The Barefoot Contessa* (1954), and *Bhowani Junction* (1956). She finally fulfilled her contract with MGM in 1959, and the last of the studio sex sirens was on her own.

Since the 1960s, Gardner's films have been rather poor, with the exception of *On The Beach* (1960) and *The Night of the Iguana* (1964). In more recent years, she has made modest supporting or cameo appearances in movies.

See also: sex symbols: female

GARFIELD, JOHN (1913–1952) An explosive actor who projected a unique balance of sensitivity and violence. In some respects, Garfield was the next generation Humphrey Bogart (q.v.), but he didn't appear in nearly as many good films as his talents warranted. The quality films in which he did appear, however, were stamped by his greatness.

Born Julius Garfinkle in the slums of New York City, Garfield pursued a serious acting career, eschewing the glamour of Broadway to work with the more avant garde and left-leaning Group Theater. But when Warner Bros. spotted him in Clifford Odet's *Golden Boy,* a hit play for the Group Theater, he signed with the film company and left for the West Coast.

Some of his former colleagues thought the actor had "sold out," but Garfield never stopped believing in the ideals of the Group Theater, and he would forcefully demonstrate his beliefs both in his art and in his life before his tragic early death.

His film career began in 1938 with *Four Daughters,* which was an immediate hit and, because it spawned several mediocre rehashes, was probably the worst thing that could have happened to him. Soon thereafter, his tough guy image was shaped by films such as *They Made Me a Criminal* (1939) and *Dust Be My Destiny* (1939).

The Sea Wolf (1941), directed by Michael Curtiz (q.v.) and costarring Edward G. Robinson (q.v.) was his breakthrough movie. *Tortilla Flat* (1942) and Howard Hawks' *Air Force* (1943) followed and helped to build his reputation. A few years later he burned up the screen with Lana Turner (q.v.) in the classic version of James N. Cain's thriller *The Postman Always Rings Twice* (1946).

Garfield was forced to appear in many more poor movies, but the actor had higher aspirations than to play the parts that Warner Bros. kept offering him. He refused to renew his contract in 1947, and putting his money and his reputation on the line, made *Body and Soul* (1947), an independent film about the boxing

world that is now considered a classic.

Next, the committed Jewish actor agreed to play a supporting role in Hollywood's first major film concerning anti-Semitism, *Gentlemen's Agreement* (1947). The film won an Academy Award for Best Picture.

The following year, Garfield starred in Abraham Polonsky's ambitious *Force of Evil* (1948), a no-holds-barred movie about corruption. Unfortunately, the film did not do well at the box office. In fact, none of his next few films were hits, either, although he gave an excellent performance in *The Breaking Point* (1950).

Due to Garfield's left-wing associations, he was called before the House Un-American Activities Committee in the early 1950s and asked to name the names of people in Hollywood he knew to be Communists. The actor refused, and was blacklisted from the film industry. He died soon thereafter of a heart attack.

See also: Gentlemen's Agreement

GARLAND, JUDY (1922–1969) This supremely talented actress and singer was the studio system's greatest achievement as well as its greatest victim. Though never a great beauty, Judy Garland radiated a warmth and sensitivity that tugged at the heartstrings and her strong yet tremulous voice gave her an air of vulnerability that touched her many fans. She was the top female musical star at MGM at a time when the studio was reinventing the movie musical.

Though it seems as if Judy Garland grew up in front of the camera, she began her life as Frances Gumm in Grand Rapids, Michigan. At three she made her vaudeville debut singing "Jingle Bells" in a theater managed by her father and was soon teamed with her two older sisters in an act. "The Gumm Sisters" worked in vaudeville until one of them married and broke up the trio.

When Garland was thirteen years old her mother pushed to get her a screen test at MGM; the studio recognized the girl's talent and signed her up. She first appeared in a Deanna Durbin (q.v.) short, *Every Sunday* (1936). A small role in a very minor musical, *Pigskin Parade* (1936), followed, but it was clear that MGM didn't quite know how to use her. Garland, however, had a mentor in Roger Edens (q.v.), the highly respected musical talent supervisor at MGM. He had played the piano at her screen test and recognized her star potential. In an effort to help her get noticed, Edens wrote new lyrics to the song, "You Made Me Love You," and gave it to Garland to sing at Clark Gable's birthday party on the MGM lot.

She was such a big hit that the studio immediately put her (and the song) in *Broadway Melody of 1938* (1937). Leading roles in several films followed, including her first opposite Mickey Rooney (q.v.), in *Thoroughbreds Don't Cry* (1937). In 1938, she joined Rooney in the first of many Andy Hardy films, *Love Finds Andy*

Hardy. *The Wizard of Oz* (1939), however, was the film that put Garland on the Hollywood map.

It is not uncommon in movie history to find actors and actresses who have emerged as stars in vehicles originally intended for other, already established, stars. The man who was ultimately responsible for the gigantic success of MGM's movie musicals in the 1940s and 1950s, Arthur Freed, *(q.v.)*, wanted Garland for the role of Dorothy in *The Wizard of Oz*. But this was a major production, unlike her handful of previous films, and the rest of the MGM brass was opposed to using the relatively unknown and inexperienced young actress in such an important film. They wanted Shirley Temple *(q.v.)*. Plans fell through, however, when Twentieth Century-Fox refused to loan their biggest star to their competitor, and Judy Garland got the part by default.

The Wizard of Oz was a hit, and has become one of the most beloved movie classics of all time. The film made Judy Garland an international star, brought her a special Oscar in 1939 "for her outstanding performance as a screen juvenile," and provided her with her lifelong theme song, "Over the Rainbow." It's curious to note, however, that before the movie was released, "Over the Rainbow" had almost been cut from the film.

Garland continued in the Andy Hardy films but, more significantly, she starred in *For Me and My Gal* (1942), which also introduced Gene Kelly *(q.v.)*, and *Meet Me in St. Louis* (1944), a landmark film that did not use a show business background as a pretext for its musical numbers. Thanks to Garland's luminous performance, the movie became MGM's second most lucrative film at that time, topped only by *Gone With the Wind* (1939). Garland married Vincente Minnelli *(q.v.)*, the director of *Meet Me in St. Louis*, and later had a child, Liza Minnelli, who has ably followed in her mother's footsteps.

Garland proved her dramatic ability in the touching World War II home-front film, *The Clock* (1945), and launched into more musicals, such as *The Harvey Girls* (1946) and *The Pirate* (1948). 1948 also saw her team up with Fred Astaire *(q.v.)* in *Easter Parade*. The movie was a mammoth hit (Astaire had come out of retirement to make it), and MGM planned on teaming the two in *The Barkley's of Broadway* (1949). But for the first time, Garland pleaded ill health and was dropped from the film. Failing health, and her subsequent pattern of making and then breaking commitments began that fateful year.

Garland had been a money-making machine for MGM, and in an effort to help her sleep at night and perk her up during the day, studio doctors prescribed an assortment of pills to which she eventually became addicted. Later when she began to drink the combination proved devastating.

Nonetheless, she eventually went back to work, appearing in several films, such as *Words and Music* (1948),

In the Good Old Summertime (1949), and *Summer Stock* (1950), but soon she became more famous for the films she didn't make rather the ones she did. Garland failed to complete *Annie Get Your Gun* (1950) and had to be replaced by Betty Hutton. She was suspended for not showing up to film *Royal Wedding* (1950) and she bowed out of playing Julie in *Showboat* (1951). MGM tore up her contract. After fifteen years as a movie star, it looked as if Garland was through—at only twenty-eight.

Sid Luft, the third of her five husbands, arranged a concert career that kept her in the public eye, and she then made one of the greatest—if shortest—comebacks in movie history, when she starred in the Warner Bros. musical remake of *A Star Is Born* (1954). The movie was both a critical and box office winner, putting Judy Garland back on top. But her reputation for unreliability still haunted her and no more serious projects were offered to her.

Garland didn't appear on film again until 1961, in a small dramatic part in *Judgment at Nuremberg*. The role led to an Oscar nomination for Best Supporting Actress, but she didn't win the award. That same year she starred in *A Child Is Waiting* with Burt Lancaster *(q.v.)*. It was a touching, if flawed, film directed by John Cassavetes *(q.v.)*. Garland's last film was the aptly titled *I Could Go On Singing* (1963). She sang in concerts and caberets until her death from an accidental drug overdose in 1969. Ray Bolger, who played the Scarecrow in *The Wizard of Oz,* once said, "Judy didn't die of anything, except wearing out. She just plain wore out."

GARMES, LEE (1897–1978)   A gifted cinematographer who was a master of "north light," a lighting effect that resulted in a distinct yet soft contrast between bright and dark areas within the same frame. Like many early cameramen, he was responsible for important technical innovations, including the crab dolly *(q.v.)*. From his long and varied career, Garmes is probably best known for his dreamlike, romantic lighting of several of the better Joseph von Sternberg *(q.v.)* films starring Marlene Dietrich *(q.v.)* and his cinematography and codirection of a number of fascinating if flawed films in which he worked in collaboration with screenwriters Ben Hecht *(q.v.)* and Charles MacArthur.

Garmes began working in Hollywood in 1916, serving his apprenticeship in a variety of jobs for director George Fitzmaurice. By 1924 he graduated to the position of cameraman and quickly made his mark by lighting such silent masterworks as *The Grand Duchess and the Waiter* (1926) and *The Garden of Allah* (1927).

In the 1930s, Garmes worked closely with Josef von Sternberg on such films as *Morocco* (1930), *Dishonored* (1931), and *Shanghai Express* (1932), the last of which earned him an Oscar. The cinematographer showed his versatility in these early years, creating the gossamer images of von Sternberg's movies as well as the slick sheen of Rouben Mamoulian's *City Streets* (1931) and the harsh, violent shadows of Howard Hawks' *Scarface* (1932).

In the 1930s Garmes worked in the dual capacity of cinematographer and associate director for three films shot in Astoria, New York that were ostensibly to be directed by Hecht and MacArthur for Paramount. The two screenwriters blithely ignored the technical demands of filmmaking and left the movies largely in the hands of Garmes, who shot the peculiar scripts with style and panache. The best of the three movies was *Crime Without Passion* (1934), which was made all the more fascinating by the inclusion of a bizarre montage sequence shot by the Salvador Dali of the movies, Slavko Vorpkapitch. The other two Hecht/MacArthur films for which Garmes took charge were *The Scoundrel* (1935) and *Once in a Blue Moon* (1935).

Despite the fact that he worked until the end of the 1960s, Garmes' best, most interesting, work was done in the 1930s. Among his more noteworthy efforts as a cinematographer in his later years were *Duel in the Sun* (1946), on which he collaborated, Alfred Hitchcock's experimental *Rope* (1948), and Max Ophuls' *Caught* (1949). Lesser efforts near the end of his career, usually in color rather than in black and white, included *Hemingway's Adventures of a Young Man* (1962) and *How to Save a Marriage and Ruin Your Life* (1968).

GARSON, GREER (1908–   ) Noble and dignified even as her characters suffered rejection, loneliness, and other tragedies, Garson projected exactly the kind of image America needed during the war years. Though the bulk of her Hollywood career spanned fifteen years, she had her greatest impact from 1939 to 1945.

Born in Ireland, Garson intended to become a teacher, but the theater captured her interest and she successfully reached the London stage in the mid-1930s. When Louis B. Mayer *(q.v.)* of MGM was in England looking for talent in 1937, he saw her in a play called *Old Music* and immediately signed her up. Once in Hollywood, she languished for more than a year until she was given the part of Mrs. Chips opposite Robert Donat in *Goodbye, Mr. Chips* (1939). The movie was box office gold and Garson was instantly established as a credible movie actress.

Much of Garson's early success in the 1940s was due inadvertently to Norma Shearer *(q.v.)*, who turned down the roles that made the new Hollywood actress famous. Shearer said no to and Garson accepted the lead roles in *Pride and Prejudice* (1940) and *Mrs. Miniver* (1942). Garson had not wanted to play Mrs. Miniver for the same reason Shearer turned down the role; she didn't want to be cast as a mother. But Garson did not have Shearer's clout, and much to her eventual delight, she not only became a major star because of *Mrs.*

Miniver (winning an Oscar for Best Actress), she also met her first husband. As it turned out, the man she fell in love with was the actor who played her son (Richard Ney), and they agreed, after studio pressure prevailed, not to marry until after the film had finished its run.

Random Harvest (1942) was another spectacular success for Garson. In this grand tear-jerker she played the understanding and longsuffering wife of an amnesiac (Ronald Colman).

Madame Curie (1943) showcased her acting talents, but just as Garson had feared when she made *Mrs. Miniver,* she was becoming typecast as a mother, and MGM put her in a series of family movies, including, *Mrs. Parkington* (1944) and *The Valley of Decision* (1945).

Audiences were greeted in 1946 with the slogan, "Gable's back and Garson's got him." The movie was *Adventure,* and it was no family saga. Gable's first film since returning from wartime service, it drew huge numbers of fans but it was a rather poor movie. It seemed that each time Garson tried to establish an image beyond that of a beautiful matron, the movie in which she starred was either a critical disaster or a financial flop (or both).

Plagued by mediocre movie scripts, she eventually begged out of her MGM contract in 1954. Yet she still had her moments: as Calpurnia in *Julius Caeser* (1953) and Eleanor Roosevelt in *Sunrise at Campobello* (1960). But her career never recovered from its downward slide. Despite a paucity of good movies after 1945, she still managed to receive a whopping total of seven Oscar nominations over the course of her career, leaving her mark as one of the great ladies of Hollywood.

GAYNOR, JANET (1906–1984) Nearly forgotten now, she was once one of Hollywood's greatest stars, winner of the first Best Actress Academy Award and a highly successful performer for over a decade in both the silent and talkie eras. Petite and wholesome looking, she was the perfect waif, and was often cast as an innocent girl forced by circumstances to live a dissolute life (before being redeemed in the last reel, of course).

Born Laura Gainor, she set her sights on the movies when she was a teenager, heading for Hollywood right after her graduation from high school. Stardom didn't come immediately, and she held a series of odd jobs, among them the ever-popular position of usher(ette) in a movie theater. She soon received work as an extra, leading to small roles in a number of Hal Roach *(q.v.)* comedies.

Her big break came in 1926 when she landed an important supporting role in *The Johnstown Flood.* Steady work followed in a handful of movies, but she suddenly struck paydirt the following year when she was teamed for the first of twelve times with actor Charles Farrell in Frank Borzage's *Seventh Heaven (1927),* a romantic tale of a poor, love-starved prostitute. It was a massive hit, second only that year to the Al Jolson talkie, *The Jazz Singer.* Gaynor was quickly reteamed with Farrell in a similar story that was just as big a smash as the first, *Street Angel* (1928). Her skills as an actress were also much in evidence in what many consider to be one of the greatest silent movies ever made, F. W. Murnau's *Sunrise* (1927). During the first Academy Award ceremony in 1928, she was proclaimed the best actress of 1927–28 for the three movies (awards were originally given for a body of work rather than a single film).

Gaynor remained a top box office draw throughout the early 1930s. Unfortunately, few of her films have withstood the test of time, but among her better known movies of the early sound era are *Sunny Side Up* (1930), *Daddy Long Legs* (1931), *Delicious* (1931), and *State Fair* (1933). She and Farrell (who later played the father in the 1950s TV sitcom, "My Little Margie") probably went to the well too often, and by 1933 ticket sales for their films began to plummet; their last film together was *Change of Heart* (1934). Worse yet, Gaynor's studio, Fox, had merged with Twentieth Century to create Twentieth Century-Fox, and she did not figure in the new company's future plans.

After *The Farmer Takes a Wife* (1935) with Henry Fonda, the actress was little used at Twentieth Century-Fox. She took her famous name and talents elsewhere, making several films for others, including MGM and David O. Selznick *(q.v.).* Among her last films were two major hits, both admired by critics and audiences—the original version of *A Star Is Born* (1937) and the delightful comedy *The Young In Heart* (1938). With these two successes, including an Oscar nomination for her performance in *A Star is Born,* Gaynor could have easily continued starring in movies for many years to come. Instead, she married one of Hollywood's leading dress designer's, Adrian (her second husband), and promptly retired while she was still on top.

She later claimed that she might have returned to movie acting had she not enjoyed her married life so much. Nineteen years later, however, she briefly returned to the big screen to play Pat Boone's mother in *Bernadine* (1957), but it was her last film performance. When Adrian died in 1959, Gaynor began to appear occasionally on the stage and on television. She died in a car accident in 1984.
See also: screen teams

GENTLEMEN'S AGREEMENT The 1947 landmark movie that made a frontal assault on American anti-Semitism. Based on the best-selling novel of the same name by Laura Z. Hobson, *Gentlemen's Agreement* was courageously produced by Darryl F. Zanuck *(q.v.)* at Twentieth Century-Fox despite opposition from many prominent Hollywood Jews who were afraid of a backlash.

From Moss Hart's script, Elia Kazan *(q.v.)* directed an impressive cast. Gregory Peck *(q.v.),* an actor possessing quiet dignity, played the role of the Gentile reporter who poses as a Jew to write about anti-Semitism and learns firsthand how Jews are treated in America. John Garfield *(q.v.),* who was Jewish, played a Jewish soldier. Dorothy McGuire, Celeste Holm, Anne Revere, June Havoc, Albert Dekker, Jane Wyatt, and Dean Stockwell rounded out the cast.

Gentlemen's Agreement came out the same year as a melodrama, *Crossfire,* that also dealt with anti-Semitism, but the Fox film was released first and focused more attention on the issue. Both movies were winners at the box office, but *Gentlemen's Agreement* received more press because it won Oscars for Best Picture, Best Director, and Best Supporting Actress (Celeste Holm). Gregory Peck and Dorothy McGuire won nominations for Best Actor and Best Actress, respectively.

The success of Gentleman's Agreement led directly to *Pinky* (1949), a movie about racial-discrimination.

Seen today, *Gentlemen's Agreement* seems terribly dated, but the film's impact at the time of its release was significant.
See also: message movies;

GERSHWIN, GEORGE (1898–1937) **& IRA** (1896–1983) They were sibling songwriting collaborators who brought a greater respectability to popular music. Their work was mostly heard on Broadway, where, together, they composed the songs and lyrics for fourteen musicals. George Gershwin wrote an additional nine musicals for the New York stage, bringing their combined total to twenty-three. The two wrote the first Broadway musical to ever win a Pulitzer Prize, *Of Thee I Sing* (1932). The brothers' impact on movie musicals resulted from many of their Broadway shows being adapted to film, and the large number of their songs that were used in various movie musicals. The Gershwins also provided original scores for several Hollywood films, including the wonderful Astaire/Rogers musical, *Shall We Dance* (1937).

George, who was born Jacob Gershvin, and Ira, born Israel Gershvin, saw their Broadway show *Girl Crazy* adapted for the big screen three times, first in 1932, then (in the most famous version) in 1943, followed by the renamed adaptation, *When the Boys Meet the Girls* (1965). Some of their other famous stage plays later adapted to the screen include, *Lady Be Good* (1941) *Funny Face* (1957), and *Porgy and Bess* (1959).

George's "Rhapsody in Blue" and "An American in Paris" (which was used in the Oscar-winning 1951 film of the same name) have made him more famous than Ira, yet Ira had considerable impact on movie musicals. After George's untimely death from a brain hemmorage, Ira continued his work as a lyricist, his clever words appearing in the songs of films such as *Cover*

Girl (1944), *The Barkleys of Broadway* (1949), and *A Star is Born* (1954).

George was the subject of a biopic, *Rhapsody in Blue* (1945), with Robert Alda playing the composer. It was a poor drama but was peppered with terrific Gershwin music.

GIBBONS, CEDRIC (1893–1960)   The dean of Hollywood art directors, he designed movie sets for more than forty years. Of more significance than his longevity, however, was the impact he had on setting the standard for art directors throughout the industry. From his early beginnings as an art director for Edison (1915–17), for Samuel Goldwyn (1918–24), and finally for MGM (for the rest of his career), Gibbons was a leader in production design.

As the principal designer of hundreds of films and the chief art director of many hundreds more at MGM, Gibbons was involved in the "look" of every MGM movie during that studio's golden years. Largely due to his talents, MGM's films consistently had the highest production values of all the major studios.

Gibbons was nominated for Best Art Direction Academy Awards with almost monononotous regularity. He won eleven times, taking home the Oscar (which statuette he had also designed for the Academy) for *The Bridge of San Luis Rey* (1929), *The Merry Widow* (1934), *Pride and Prejudice* (1940), *Blossoms in the Dust* (1941), *Gaslight* (1944), *The Yearling* (1946), *Little Women* (1949), *An American in Paris* (1951), *The Bad and the Beautiful* (1952), *Julius Caesar* (1953), and *Somebody Up There Likes Me* (1956).

The famous art director only once tried his hand at direction, codirecting *Tarzan and His Mate* (1934). While the movie was successful, Gibbons did not enjoy the experience and he chose not to pursue that career.
See also: art director

GILBERT, JOHN (1897–1936)   He was the classic example of a popular and expressive silent film star who could not make the adjustment to talkies. Gilbert's voice was rather tinny and high-pitched, and when he opened his mouth to speak, he lost the dashing, impressive presence that had been his mainstay in silent films.

Born John Pringle, he came from a theatrical family and broke into the movie business as an extra in the William S. Hart *(q.v.)* western *Hell's Hinges* (1916). He continued in small parts for many years, slowly moving up the cast list. His first big break came in 1920 when he wrote the script with director Clarence Brown *(q.v.)* for *The Great Redeemer* (1920), and managed to wrangle the lead. He continued writing and starring in his own films throughout the early 1920s, and soon he was offered the opportunity to direct films, as well. Instead, he pursued his acting career, which continued to build.

He had several big hits, such as *He Who Gets Slapped*

The talkie revolution destroyed the careers of many, but John Gilbert's fall was among the most tragic. He is seen here while still in his heyday as one of the silver screen's great lovers. Photo courtesy of The Siegel Collection.

(1924) and *The Snob* (1924), but he became a superstar in 1925 when he played the lead in two of that years biggest grossers, *The Merry Widow* and *The Big Parade*.

The Merry Widow, directed by Erich von Stroheim *(q.v.)*, was a movie musical without music. Such was the magic of von Stroheim's direction and Gilbert's magnetic performance that the film made $1.5 million. *The Big Parade*, an antiwar film masterfully directed by King Vidor *(q.v.)*, was the biggest hit of its time, bringing in a staggering $15 million. Gilbert was at the height of his career and the popular equal of Valentino.

In 1927, when Gilbert began his famous acting liaison with Greta Garbo *(q.v.)* in *Flesh and the Devil*, both he and his costar sizzled on screen. Rumors of a love affair between the two actors heightened interest in their pairing, which continued in *Love* (1927) and *A Woman of Affairs* (1929).

His talkie debut in *The Hollywood Revue of 1929* is

legend. In a short scene with Norma Shearer *(q.v.),* he performed the balcony scene from *Romeo and Juliet,* and audiences laughed out loud at him. His career seemed doomed, but he gallantly tried to forestall the end in films such as *His Glorious Night* (1930) and *Way for a Sailor* (1930). Every film was a box office loser except *Queen Christina* (1933) in which he was paired again with Greta Garbo, who asked for him when Laurence Olivier was dropped from the lead male role. The film was a hit, due largely to Garbo's popularity.

His last film was *The Captain Hates the Sea* (1935), in which he played a drunk; in his despair, he had become a heavy drinker in real life as well. He died the following year.

See also: Garbo, Greta

GIMMICKS There is often a thin line between innovation and gimmickry. New technological developments in the cinema initially perceived as gimmicks but later accepted as important new storytelling tools include sound, color, and various widescreen processes. Other ideas, however—some of which were serious concepts that simply didn't catch on with the public and others that were obviously gimmicks—have peppered the history of Hollywood.

Today, 3-D *(q.v.)* films are generally considered a gimmick, but a considerable number of serious movies were filmed in the process during the 1950s in the hope of luring audiences away from their television screens. Ultimately, the 3-D systems proved to be visually unacceptable, and the novelty wore off. Nonetheless, the occasional 3-D film is still made in the hope of luring the curious into movie theaters.

Color and sound had long been a part of the film-going experience, when some decided the sense of smell had been neglected. In a battle of gimmicks, two different scent oriented systems were tried out on a bemused public in late 1959 and early 1960. The first accompanied a movie called *Behind the Great Wall,* offered in AromaRama. According to James L. Limbacher in his book, *Four Aspects of Film,* AromaRama offered "72 odors capable of being transmitted by the triggering and timing mechanism in the theater. The odors are fed to the audience through the regular air circulating system." A critic from *The Detroit Free Press* called AromaRama "A real stinker."

A competing system named Smell-O-Vision was introduced with the film *Scent of Mystery* (the later, unscented, version was retitled *Holiday in Spain*). This system differed from its competitor in that the odors were piped separately to each seat in the theater. Neither system ever resulted in a follow-up effort.

Psychorama, another, more insidious, gimmick came (and went) in 1960. Purposefully using subliminal images (scenes flashed on the screen too quickly for the eye to consciously register them) in order to enhance the effect of horror films, the movies appealed to audiences' growing awareness of psychology. There were two such films made, *My World Dies Screaming* (a.k.a. *Terror in the Haunted House*) and *A Date With Death.*

Also in 1960, another novelty thriller called *The Hypnotic Eye,* produced by Allied Artists, tried to hypnotize the audience. The gimmick involved having ushers pass out balloons to the theater patrons, then an actor in the film dared them to try and use their arms to raise the balloons.

Often, gimmicks used to lure customers into a movie theater have nothing to do with the way a film is made. For instance, the famous producer/director William Castle offered free life insurance to those who went to *Macabre* (1958), a film he claimed to be so scary that patrons might die of a heart attack while watching it. And he was the same man who had a fake skeleton shoot out across the audience at a critical moment in *House on Haunted Hill* (1958) in a process called Emergo. But his most famous gimmick, Percepto, literally shocked people in the theater by wiring selected seats and giving those customers a small dose of electricity during showings of *The Tingler* (1959).

For the most part, gimmicks have always come from either small studios that lack big name stars or independent producers who lack both big name stars and a decent script. A true gimmick, as opposed to an innovation, has nothing to do with the quality of the film but only the quantity of the box office take.

GISH, LILLIAN (1896–) One of the most popular and influential screen stars of the silent era, Gish has practiced her craft in what has become the longest acting career in show business history.

Born Lillian de Guiche, she was the eldest of two sisters in a home in desperate financial straits. Her father had walked out on the family and her mother tried to earn a living as an actress. Mrs. Gish had better luck placing her children in juvenile acting roles, so "Baby Lillian" (as she was billed) started her show business career at the age of five in a play called *In Convict's Stripes.* Soon, the entire family began touring the country with various acting companies.

Mary Pickford *(q.v.)* had been a child actress during this time and knew the Gish family. Later, when she began working for D. W. Griffith *(q.v.),* she talked the director into hiring the two teenaged Gish sisters. Often called the Sarah Bernhardt of the movies, Gish's frail, child/woman persona fit her mentor D. W. Griffith's ideal of pure womanhood, and her expressive, angelic face made the image complete.

Lillian's first acting stint in film was in a two-reeler directed by Griffith, *An Unseen Enemy* (1912). Over the next three years she appeared in more than twenty Griffith films, culminating in her starring role in his epic masterpiece *The Birth of a Nation* (1915, *q.v.*),

Lillian Gish has been called "The First Lady of the Silent Screen." She is seen here (on the left) with her sister, Dorothy Gish, in a scene from D. W. Griffith's classic *Orphans of the Storm* (1922). Photo courtesy of The Siegel Collection.

which vaulted her to international celebrity. Interestingly, Blanche Sweet *(q.v.),* had been Griffith's first choice for the female lead, but he was delighted with Lillian's performance. Between 1915 and 1922, Gish was Griffith's main actress, and she starred in his most impressive films, including *Broken Blossoms* (1919), *Way Down East* (1920), and *Orphans of the Storm* (1922).

After she left Griffith over a salary dispute, Lillian eventually signed with MGM, where her best films were *La Bohème* (1926) and *The Scarlet Letter* (1926). As the 1920s came to an end, she found herself losing popularity. She was seen as old-fashioned compared to other MGM stars like Norma Shearer and Greta Garbo *(qq.v.).*

She made the transition to sound in *One Romantic Night* (1930) with but one problem: nobody wanted to see Lillian Gish in a romantic leading role. She was thirty-one years old and a has-been—or so the Hollywood establishment thought.

Except for an occasional film appearance in the 1930s and early 1940s, Gish continued her career on Broadway with considerable success. She returned to the screen with a splash in a supporting role, in *Duel in the Sun* (1946), and performed magnificently in a leading role

in *The Night of the Hunter* (1955). She has continued to act in the movies from time to time, and her later films include Robert Altman's *A Wedding* (1978) and *The Whales of August* (1987).

Lillian Gish was honored in 1970 with a much-deserved special Oscar "for her superlative and distinguished service in the making of motion pictures."

Her younger sibling, Dorothy *(q.v.),* also had an illustrious, if not quite as spectacular, screen career, as Lillian's. The two sisters often appeared in films together, particularly early in their movie careers. In fact, Lillian once directed her sister in *Remodeling Her Husband* (1921). The two sisters were very close. Dorothy died in 1968.

GODDARD, PAULETTE *See* Chaplin, Sir Charles.

THE GODFATHER (1972) and **THE GODFATHER, PART II** (1974) Francis Ford Coppola's *(q.v.)* stunning, allegorical epic masterpieces set in the world of modern American organized crime. Alternately nostalgic and cold-blooded in their observations of family relationships, these two films were provocative and deeply resonant achievements that managed also to be enormously popular.

The two *Godfather* sagas presented the story of the Corleone family. The original film told the tale of elderly Mafia patriarch Vito Corleone's (Marlon Brando *[q.v.]*), death and the struggle for power by his son. The sequel, thanks to a clever structure, managed to be two movies at once, traveling both forward and backward in time, explaining the young Vito's (Robert De Niro *[q.v.]*) rise to power while also detailing the expanding role of the mob through the story of Vito's son (Al Pacino *[q.v.]*).

The Godfather was originally slated to be a modest little gangster film, without a name cast and made on a budget of less than $2 million. The film rights to Mario Puzo's blockbuster best-seller had actually been bought by Paramount for a mere $35,000 before the novel became a hit. The decision to use non-name actors in major roles held firm except for the pivotal, if modest, part of Don Vito Corleone. As the budget escalated to more than $6 million to meet the growing expectations of the public, the studio considered Edward G. Robinson *(q.v.)* and Danny Thomas. Coppola's first choice, however, was Laurence Olivier *(q.v.),* who turned it down. His second choice, Marlon Brando, wanted the role, but Paramount didn't want Brando. The studio was afraid the actor's sometimes erratic behavior might send the movie overbudget, not to mention Brando's diminishing drawing power after a number of recent box office failures. But Coppola held firm and Brando won the role after performing in a makeshift screen test the actor shot himself at his home.

Coppola would seem an odd choice for such an

increasingly important movie. His track record as a director was anything but impressive. He had had one modest success, *You're a Big Boy Now* (1967), and two highly publicized flops, *Finian's Rainbow* (1968) and *The Rain People* (1969). His biggest claim to fame was his Oscar for the screenplay of *Patton* (1970). James Monaco, writing in *American Film Now,* astutely speculated that "[Coppola] was the only thinkable choice with an Italian surname. The producers were already having trouble with the Mafia and with Italian-American lobbying groups. A director named Coppola would (and did) take some of the heat off." Just the same, Coppola was reportedly nearly fired at least three times during filming.

The Godfather was, for a short while, the highest grossing film in Hollywood history. In addition to making the otherwise struggling young writer-director Francis Coppola a household name, the films also made stars of such performers as Al Pacino, Robert De Niro, and Robert Duvall *(q.v.).* The original movie also resurrected the career of Marlon Brando.

Besides its critical and popular success, *The Godfather* also won the acclaim of the industry, winning three Oscars for Best Film, Best Actor (Marlon Brando), and Best Screenplay (Mario Puzo and Francis Coppola). It also won three nominations for Best Supporting Actor (Al Pacino, James Caan, and Robert Duvall). It was the only gangster film, before being joined by its sequel, to win a Best Picture Oscar.

The Godfather, Part II won six Academy Awards, for Best Film (Coppola producing), Best Direction (Coppola), Best Supporting Actor (Robert De Niro), Best Screenplay Adaptation (Coppola and Puzo), Best Art Direction (Dean Tavoularis & Angelo Graham, George R. Nelso—set direction), and Best Original Dramatic Score (Nino Rota and Carmine Coppola—the director's father). Also nominated for Best Supporting Actor Oscars were Michael V. Gazzo and Lee Strasberg. *Part II* remains the only sequel ever to win a Best Picture Oscar in Hollywood history.

The cast list of *The Godfather* includes Marlon Brando, Al Pacino, James Caan, Richard Castellano, Robert Duvall, Sterling Hayden, John Marley, Richard Conte, Diane Keaton, Al Lettieri, Talia Shire, John Cazale, Abe Vigoda, Al Martino, Morgana King, Alex Rocco.

The cast list of *The Godfather, Part II* includes Al Pacino, Robert Duvall, Diane Keaton, Robert De Niro, John Cazale, Talia Shire, Lee Strasberg, Michael V. Gazzo, G. D. Spradlin, Morgana King, Mariana Hill, Troy Donahue, Joe Spinell, Abe Vigoda, Fay Spain, Harry Dean Stanton, Danny Aiello, James Caan.
See also: gangster films

GOLDWYN, SAMUEL (1882–1974) An independent producer whose Hollywood tenure was marked by momentous events and excellent filmmaking. In a ca-

reer spanning nearly sixty years, he discovered and fostered the talents of a great many actors, directors, and writers. He was also one of very few independent producers to successfully survive during the studio era and beyond. In fact, Goldwyn holds the record for the longest career as an independent producer in Hollywood.

Born Shmuel Gelbfisz in Poland, he immigrated first to England when he was eleven and then to America when he was thirteen. Broke and without any skills when he arrived in the United States, he learned the glove-making trade and began to prosper. By this time he was known as Samuel Goldfish. At the age of twenty-eight, he married Blanche Lasky (whom he divorced in 1919), sister of the vaudeville performer and producer Jesse L. Lasky, who introduced Goldfish to show business. The two men joined with Cecil B. DeMille *(q.v.)* to form the Jesse L. Lasky Feature Play Company in 1913, which promptly began making movies. Their first venture was *The Squaw Man* (1913), which was a spectacular box office success.

Events moved quickly during the early years of the film industry. After the Lasky company merged with Adolph Zukor *(q.v.)* in 1916, Goldfish was soon forced out in a $900,000 settlement. That same year, Goldfish joined with Edgar Selwyn, merging not only their capital and experience but also their names to create The Goldwyn Company. Goldfish liked the ring of the new company's name and changed his own to match it in 1918.

During the late 1910s, Goldwyn began establishing his reputation for producing films from high-quality scripts. One of these efforts, *Polly of the Circus,* became one of the biggest hits of 1917, but not until the sound era would Goldwyn's reverence for writers and their world translate into a consistent hit-making formula.

Meanwhile, The Goldwyn Company limped into the 1920s, which saw the ever-increasing consolidation of the industry into a handful of major studios. In 1922, amid bickering and squabbling, Goldwyn was once again forced out of a company of his own creation. A short while later, his namesake studio was merged with Metro and Mayer to form Metro-Goldwyn-Mayer, which quickly became the colossus of Hollywood. Goldwyn never was involved with the famous studio that still bears his name.

In 1923 the mogul formed Samuel Goldwyn Productions, embarking on a career as an independent producer, foreswearing partners so that he would always be in charge of his own operation. During the silent era, he numbered among his hits such memorable films as *Stella Dallas* (1925) and *The Winning of Barbara Worth* (1926). But he had his first real breakthrough in the late 1920s with his initial sound film, *Bulldog Drummond* (1929). Goldwyn proved a crafty businessman by capitalizing on the growing influence of newspaper critics, becoming the first producer to provide an all-expenses-paid junket to Hollywood for New York journalists. It paid off in good press and substantial box office for the film.

In the years following, Goldwyn generally produced two types of film: the serious, prestige drama and the musical comedy . Many of his best and most famous dramas were directed by William Wyler *(q.v.)*. The director's credits are attached to such Goldwyn classics as *Dodsworth* (1936), *Dead End* (1937), *Wuthering Heights* (1939), *The Westerner* (1940), *The Little Foxes* (1941), and *The Best Years of Our Lives* (1946). Among Goldwyn's other famous productions were *The Hurricane* (1937), *Pride of the Yankees* (1942), *The Bishop's Wife* (1947), *Guys and Dolls* (1955), and *Porgy and Bess* (1959).

Of Goldwyn's musical comedies, most have centered around the same kind of charming, daffy, comic hero personified by his two greatest comedy stars, Eddie Cantor *(q.v.)* and Danny Kaye *(q.v.)*. Between those two performers, Goldwyn produced more than a dozen films, among them *Whoopee!* (1930), *The Kid From Spain* (1932), *The Secret Life of Walter Mitty* (1947), and *Hans Christian Andersen* (1952).

Goldwyn was famous for more than his movies. His malapropisms became legend in Hollywood. Memorable "Goldwynisms" include "Let's bring it up to date with some snappy nineteenth-century dialogue," "I had a great idea this morning, but I didn't like it," "A verbal contract isn't worth the paper it's written on," and the ever quotable, "Include me out." It would be a mistake, however, to conclude that Goldwyn was not intelligent. He may have lacked a formal education but knew enough to always surround himself with the finest in available directorial talent in the properties he bought for filming, and in the screenwriters who were hired to adapt them.

While he generally worked with already established directors and writers, Goldwyn was more than willing to develop new acting talent for the screen. Among his discoveries were Lucille Ball, Ronald Colman *(q.v.)*, Gary Gooper *(q.v.)*, David Niven *(q.v.)*, Will Rogers *(q.v.)*, and Susan Hayward *(q.v.)*, to name but a few.

Goldwyn's films won innumerable Oscars and he was personally honored at the 1946 Academy Award dinner with the prestigious Irving G. Thalberg Award for his "outstanding motion picture production."

GONE WITH THE WIND (1939)   Until it was overtaken by *The Sound of Music, Star Wars, E.T.—The Extra-Terrestrial, Raiders of the Lost Ark,* and several other modern-day films, it was the most financially successful movie of all time. It remains one of Hollywood's most beloved films, often topping popularity polls as the greatest movie ever made. Based on Margaret Mitchell's best-selling novel, this slickly told love story set against the Civil War starred Clark Gable, Vivien Leigh, Leslie Howard, and Olivia de Havilland *(qq.v.)*. The super-production was guided from start to finish by producer David O. Selznick *(q.v.)*.

In many respects *Gone With the Wind* was an unlikely hit. It had long been a maxim in Hollywood that films about the Civil War don't do well at the box office; after all, half of the country is not going to like the outcome. Beyond marketability, the movie was troubled from the start by production problems. For instance, Clark Gable didn't want to play Rhett Butler despite the fact that he was the overwhelming choice for the role among movie fans. Only after strong studio pressure did he agree to accept the part. The other male star of the film, Leslie Howard, was dead set against playing Ashley Wilkes; he was cajoled into taking the role by being given the chance to produce (and star) in *Intermezzo* (1939). Nor did *Gone With the Wind* have a leading lady—even after production began. Vivien Leigh was hired to play Scarlett O'Hara *after* the "burning of Atlanta" (one of the film's most famous scenes), and after a much-ballyhooed talent search had been conducted. Among the actresses seriously considered for the lead female role were Paulette Goddard, Katharine Hepburn, Bette Davis, Loretta Young, and Miriam Hopkins. Among the enormous numbers of less serious contenders were Jean Harlow, Jean Arthur, Talullah Bankhead, and, believe it or not, Lucille Ball!

There were even more strikes against this production: Selznick went through three directors (George Cukor, Sam Wood, and Victor Fleming), three cinematographers (Lee Garmes, Ernest Haller and Ray Rennahan—the latter two stayed with the production), and interminable script revisions (by the likes of Ben Hecht, John Van Druten, F. Scott Fitzgerald, Jo Swerling, and Sidney Howard, who received the sole screen credit). The film came out to two hundred nineteen minutes, the longest movie ever released theatrically in America up to that time (and for several decades after).

Selznick acquired the rights to *Gone With the Wind* in a most unusual way. In Mel Gussow's biography of Darryl F. Zanuck, *Don't Say Yes Until I Finish Talking,* the Twentieth Century-Fox boss is quoted as saying there was a bidding war among the studios for the popular novel . . . "To end the bidding, at the suggestion of L. B. Mayer, we met in Thalberg's bungalow, the heads of the studios, about five . . . Someone suggested, let's put our names on slips of paper and put them in a hat and draw one slip out and whosoever's name is on the slip will purchase it—whatever the price . . . the first paper touched had Selznick's signature on it. That's how he got *Gone With the Wind*."

Selznick didn't get off easy, however. He had the property but he had to agree to distribute through MGM in order to get the services of Clark Gable. MGM bought Selznick's rights to the film during the

1940s and every seven years reaped a bonanza on reissues of the movie.

Gone With the Wind won the Best Picture Oscar for 1939 along with eight other Academy Awards. At the time, it was the record holder for the most Oscars ever awarded to any one film. It broke other ground, as well, by having in its cast the first black performer, Hattie McDaniel *(q.v.)*, to ever win an Oscar. Less well known is the fact that Vivien Leigh was the first British performer to win a Best Actress Academy Award for her portrayal of Scarlett. The film also put just the slightest dent in the Hay's Code by virtue of the inclusion of Rhett's famous line, "Frankly, my dear, I don't give a damn."

GORDON, RUTH (1896–1985)   An actress, screenwriter, and playwright who had a unique career in Hollywood, becoming the only scriptwriter in the industry's history to sandwich several stints as a film performer between a string of memorable screenwriting hits. As an actress, she had some success on Broadway but flopped twice in the movies, first in the silent era, then in the early 1940s. She finally hit it big on the silver screen in her seventies when she began playing an assortment of eccentric old ladies, usually in comedies. As a playwright and screenwriter, she generally collaborated with her husband, Garson Kanin *(q.v.)*, penning a number of delightful theatrical comedies during the late 1940s and early 1950s.

Born Ruth Gordon Jones, she tried to break into the legitimate theater during the 1910s and first appeared in the movies in small roles in films such as an early and otherwise forgotten version of *Camille* (1915). After enjoying some success on the stage, Gordon was lured back to Hollywood in the early 1940s to play character parts in such films as *Abe Lincoln in Illinois* (1940, well cast as Mary Todd Lincoln), *Dr. Erlich's Magic Bullet* (1940), and *Edge of Darkness* (1943).

When an earlier play she had written, *Over 21,* was turned into a movie in 1945, she decided to write directly for the screen, going on to pen such hits as *A Double Life* (1948), *Adam's Rib* (1949), *The Marrying Kind* (1952), and *Pat and Mike* (1952). She also wrote the screenplay for *The Actress* (1953), based upon her autobiographical play, *Years Ago.*

Gordon disappeared from the screen as both an actress and a writer for more than a decade before she returned for her last unlikely stab at stardom in 1965 when she appeared in *Inside Daisy Clover*. The following year she also appeared in *Lord Love a Duck* (1966), but it wasn't until her startling Oscar-winning Best Supporting Actress performance in *Rosemary's Baby* (1968) that critics and audiences began to take notice. But the best was yet to come. Gordon's baroque characters in the cult hits *Where's Poppa?* (1970) and *Harold and Maude* (1971) made her a favorite among young filmgoers.

Ruth Gordon became Hollywood's favorite "little old lady" in films such as *Where's Poppa?* (1970), *Harold and Maude* (1971), and *Every Which Way But Loose* (1978), but she was also a highly respected screenwriter and playwright when this photograph was taken. Photo by Dorothy Wilding.

There were few good roles written for actresses her age but she had memorable turns in Clint Eastwood's two broad comedies *Every Which Way But Loose* (1978) and *Any Which Way You Can* (1980). She continued appearing in films during the early 1980s, such as the hit *My Bodyguard* (1980) and the flop *Jimmy the Kid* (1982). After a long and creative life, she died at the age of eighty-nine.

GOSSIP COLUMNISTS   A blend of journalism, show business, and plain old dirt was the stock-in-trade of the first national celebrity gossip columnist, Louella Parsons (1893–1972). She began her gossip column in the 1920s, employed by the Hearst newspaper chain, in part to help boost the film career of actress Marion Davies, William Randolph Hearst's mistress. Parsons' column was such a success, however, that others soon followed the same practice of reporting on the latest tinsel town news. Eventually, as many as four hundred writers covered the Hollywood gossip beat for papers, radio stations, and magazines all over the world.

For the most part, Hollywood easily controlled the press, giving anxious reporters whatever tidbits they wanted to leak out—the publicity machines of the major studios were well-oiled and enormously sophisticated. Nonetheless, several gossip columnists wielded so much personal power due to their wide readerships that they could significantly affect Hollywood careers and the financial success of almost any movie.

Louella Parsons was one of these, together with her two greatest compeititors, Hedda Hopper (1890–1966) and Sheila Graham (1908–   ). While Louella Parsons had been a reporter before arriving in Hollywood, Hopper had been a sometime film actress and Graham had been a model. Journalistic skills, however, weren't necessarily the key to success in the gossip game. A keen sense of what ones readership wanted to know and the ability to push the right buttons to get that information were all that mattered.

Hedda Hopper was known for her wildly eccentric hats and her sadistic nature. She began writing her column in 1938 and it was soon syndicated all over the country. While both Parsons and Hopper enjoyed their immense power, Hopper was much more likely to use it to hurt and humiliate her enemies. Hopper and Parsons were cutthroat in their competitiveness and many a powerful Hollywood figure quivered at the thought of bad press in one of their columns. (Incidentally, Hopper's son, actor William Hopper, played the investigator, Paul Drake, on the old "Perry Mason" TV show; his mother was instrumental in launching his modest career).

Shiela Graham, on the other hand, was the least vindictive of the influential three. She began her column in 1935 and actually appeared in more papers than the other two women, but they weren't the "right" papers and she didn't reach the diehard fans the way Parsons and Hopper did. Unlike the other two columnists, Graham tended to report facts rather than rumor. Perhaps her love affair with the ailing F. Scott Fitzgerald during the last four years of his life also made her far more aware of the fact that people live in exceedingly fragile glass houses.

The power of all three of these women was such that the movies themselves could hardly ignore them. Parsons appeared as herself in *Hollywood Hotel* (1937), *Without Reservations* (1946), and *Starlift* (1951). Hopper played herself in *Breakfast in Hollywood* (1946), *Sunset Boulevard* (1950), and *The Oscar* (1966). Graham did them both one better by having Deborah Kerr *(q.v.)* play her in the film version of her relationship with Fitzgerald in *The Beloved Infidel* (1959).

The power of these three gossip columnists began to

wane with the end of the studio system *(q.v.)* in the late 1940s and 1950s. Or, rather, it was diminished by fierce competition from newer, younger gossip columnists who were in touch with the changing nature of celebrity worship. A younger generation was interested in TV stars, rock 'n' rollers, and sports personalities as well as movie stars.

Columnists such as Walter Winchell, Earl Wilson, Ed Sullivan, Dorothy Kilgallen, Cholly Knickerbocker, and others grew in popularity during the 1940s and 1950s.

In more recent years, gossip columnists such as Liz Smith, Rona Barrett, Cindy Adams, Suzy, and Claudia Cohen have held sway. None of them are gossip columnists who concern themselves solely with the movies as did the big three of gossip's golden era.

Ironically, however, gossip has never been more widely disseminated than it is today. From tabloids such as *The National Enquirer* and *The Star* to slick magazines such as *People* and *Us,* and from TV shows such as "Entertainment Tonight," the amount of gossip emanating out of Hollywood is staggering. It is, however, rather tame compared to the often outlandish and mean-spirited stories that were written during the days of Parsons and Hopper.

GRABLE, BETTY (1916–1973)   Though neither a great talent nor a ravishing beauty, her famous pin-up pose during World War II helped her to become an unlikely sex star. Her persona as the slightly sexy girl-next-door made her a popular actress/singer/dancer in 1940s light musicals, as well as Hollywood's highest paid female star.

Her stardom didn't come easily. Grable and her mother left St. Louis for Los Angeles when the young girl was twelve years old. She studied dance and, pushed by her mother, appeared in the chorus of her first musical, *Let's Go Places,* in 1930. She can be spotted in dozens of films of the 1930s, either in the chorus or in speciality numbers, but none of the studios thought she had sufficient star quality to carry her own films.

At one time or another during the decade, she danced and sang for Goldwyn, RKO, and Paramount, but not until she married former child star Jackie Coogan *(q.v.)* in 1937 did she begin to receive press attention. The marriage ended in 1940, but her career began its upswing from about the time she appeared on Broadway in the hit musical *Du Barry Was a Lady*. This time, Twentieth Century-Fox took a gamble on her, and it paid off handsomely.

Down Argentine Way (1940) and *Tin Pan Alley* (1940) launched her starring career. Much was made of her legs by the press and the public, and she obliged both during World War II by posing for a photo that became a favorite of American G.I.s. It was so popular, in fact, that Fox titled one of her films *Pin Up Girl* (1944). As a major publicity stunt, Fox also insured Grable's gams for $1 million with Lloyd's of London.

Grable's films were mostly backstage musicals, such as *Coney Island* (1943) and *Sweet Rosie O' Grady* (1943). The films don't hold up very well, but they were extremely successful at the time of their release. After the war ended, she was still at the top of the heap with *The Dolly Sisters* (1946). But the end for Grable was coming. After a series of pleasant, if nondescript, musicals that paired her with Dan Dailey, MGM reached the height of its golden musical period with stars such as Judy Garland, Fred Astaire, Gene Kelly, and Frank Sinatra *(qq.v.)*, and directors of the calibre of Vincente Minnelli and Stanley Donen *(q.v.)*. Neither Fox nor Grable could compete, and box office fell off drastically.

Grable's last shining moment was in *How to Marry a Millionaire* (1953), in which she appeared with Lauren Bacall and Marilyn Monroe *(qq.v.)*. According to the 1960 biography *Marilyn Monroe*, written by Maurice Zolotow, Grable reportedly told the blond bombshell, "Honey, I've had it. Go get yours. It's your turn now."

She appeared in just a handful of films in the 1950s, and made her living in nightclubs and dinner theaters thereafter, making a triumphant return to Broadway as a replacement Dolly in *Hello, Dolly!* before dying of lung cancer at the age of fifty-six.

GRAHAM, SHEILA *See* gossip columnists.

GRAND HOTEL Though there had been several earlier "revue" films with all-star casts, this 1932 movie was the first narrative film to break the "one star-one picture" rule—with a vengeance. With seven name actors in leading roles (five of them major box office stars), *Grand Hotel* launched the all-star movie *(q.v.)*, a concept that is still with us today.

After much negotiation on the subject of billing, the illustrious cast was listed in the credits in the following order: Greta Garbo, John Barrymore, Joan Crawford, Wallace Beery, Lionel Barrymore *(qq.v.)*, Lewis Stone, and Jean Hersholt *(q.v.)*. The movie was based on the novel and successful play of the same name by Vicki Baum; the screenplay was written by William Drake; and the film was artfully directed by Edmund Goulding.

The idea of presenting *Grand Hotel* as an all-star film belonged to MGM's Irving Thalberg *(q.v.)*. At a time when other movie studios such as Paramount, Warners, and Fox were losing millions of dollars, MGM, the studio with "more stars than there are in the heavens," used its multitude of stars to keep audiences coming to theaters even as the Great Depression deepened into its worst years.

Thalberg, the so-called "boy genius," was right on target. *Grand Hotel* was a major hit, winning both an Oscar for Best Picture and a huge audience response. And MGM, because of its stable of stars, was the only studio in a position to follow up the success of *Grand Hotel* with more all-star vehicles, such as *Dinner at Eight* (1933) and *The Women* (1939).

With *Grand Hotel's* shifting stories of desperation—John Barrymore's need for cash; Lionel Barrymore's terminal disease; Wallace Beery's company going broke; Joan Crawford's poor secretary trying to move up in the world; and Greta Garbo's high-strung, terrified, ballerina—the film was a beautifully crafted and acted soap opera. It holds up wonderfully well, with Joan Crawford and Lionel Barrymore stealing the film from the other stars.

GRANT, CARY (1904–1986) Possessing an exquisitely charming voice, dashing good looks, and rakish nonchalance, Cary Grant was the epitome of sophistication, yet he never came across as effete or snobbish. He was also a comforting screen presence whose image never seemed to change. In a variation on *The Picture of Dorian Gray,* Cary Grant seemed to preserve his youth while his audiences grew older. And if never considered a versatile or masterful actor, he played "Cary Grant" to perfection.

Born Archibald Leach in Bristol, England to divorced parents, the future actor lived in extreme poverty, scraping for a living like a character out of a Dickens novel. It has often been said that Archie Leach deliberately turned himself into the urbane Cary Grant as a means of obliterating any memory of his past.

While a teenager, he joined an acrobatic act and came to America with them in 1920. He quit the act in the U.S. and hit the vaudeville circuit with a mind-reading routine. None too successful in America, he returned to England in 1923 and broke into the theater, playing modest roles in musical comedies. Spotted on the London stage, he was hired for an Oscar Hammerstein musical on Broadway called *Golden Dawn.*

His stage career was soon well established. With the advent of sound motion pictures, Grant (like so many other stage-trained actors) saw an opportunity to make big money. He went to Hollywood, but only managed to get a job at Paramount feeding lines to an actress who was being screen-tested. The actress remains unknown; Grant was discovered. He had been right—there was big money to be made in Hollywood; his starting salary was $450 per week.

His first film was a musical, *This is the Night* (1932), in which he had a modest role. In a string of films he had supporting parts, including the heavy who nearly destroys Marlene Dietrich *(q.v.)* in *Blonde Venus* (1932) and Mae West's *(q.v.)* foil in *She Done Him Wrong* (1933) and *I'm No Angel* (1933). He kept getting plenty of work, but he hadn't truly become a star as evidenced by his having to wear a moustache in *The Last Outpost* (1935).

1936 was the year that Grant suddenly began to shine

at the box office. As is often the case, a combination of the right script, the right chemistry between costars, and the right director made an actor who had previously appeared in twenty films suddenly catch on with the public. The movie was *Sylvia Scarlett;* his costar was Katharine Hepburn; and the director was George Cukor.

But Grant's contract was finished with Paramount before *Sylvia Scarlett* was released. He was a free agent when he suddenly became a major star. In a unique arrangement, Grant signed a nonexclusive contract with *two* studios, Columbia and RKO, and he even managed to win script approval. He was now master of his own fate, and very few stars have ever chosen their films more wisely than Cary Grant.

Grant worked with Hollywood's most inspired directors. As a consequence, the actor starred in a substantial number of top-notch movies. For instance, Grant appeared in Howard Hawks' *(q.v.)* wonderful screwball comedies *Bringing Up Baby* (1938) *His Girl Friday* (1940), *I Was a Male War Bride* (1949), and *Monkey Business* (1952). He also distinguished himself in a Hawks drama, *Only Angels Have Wings* (1939).

When it came to drama, though, Grant was at his best in the films of Alfred Hitchcock, appearing in some of the master's best films, *Suspicion* (1941), *Notorious* (1946), *To Catch a Thief* (1955), and *North by Northwest* (1959).

Grant worked with other great directors as well, such as George Stevens (*Gunga Din,* 1939), George Cukor (*Holiday,* 1938 and *The Philadelphia Story,* 1940), Leo McCary (*The Awful Truth,* 1937 and *An Affair to Remember,* 1959), and Frank Capra (*Arsenic and Old Lace,* 1944).

The number of quality films that Cary Grant starred in is staggering, and he was rarely between hit movies during his long career—with only one exception. In 1953–1954, after one mediorce film, *Dream Wife* (1953), he disappeared from movie screens for nearly two years; it was generally assumed that none of the studios wanted a fifty-year-old leading man (despite his youthful appearance). But the real reason he was absent from movie screens for two years had nothing to do with his lack of appeal: he had agreed to star in two films, but both deals fell through because of Grant's own ambivlance about the parts. Had he actually played those two roles, there may have been that many more quality films to add to his already impressive list. The movies he was supposed to appear in were *Sabrina* (1954) and *A Star is Born* (1954).

Grant remained immensely popular throughout the late 1950s and well into the 1960s. His last film, *Walk Don't Run* (1966), was a money-maker. But Grant was offered the directorship of the Fabergé cosmetics company, and he opted to leave his movie career while he was still on top.

Very few actors have walked away from the limelight

as Grant did. Even Jimmy Cagney *(q.v.)* returned to films after a twenty-year retirement. But not Grant. He was America's best-looking senior citizen, and movie fans the world over lamented his abandoning the silver screen.

Somehow, in all his years in Hollywood, Grant had never received an Oscar. But the Academy belatedly rectified that error by presenting the actor with a special award "for his unique mastery of the art of screen acting." Certainly, there was hardly another actor who made it seem so easy.

Once, a few years before his death, he had forgotten his ticket to a charity fund-raiser, so he went to the ticket-taker and explained his problem, telling the woman that he was Cary Grant. She shook her head, saying "That's impossible. You don't look like Cary Grant." To which the imperturbable actor replied smiling, "Who does?"

See also: screwball comedy

THE GRAPES OF WRATH　The socially and politically conscious classic 1940 film that proved controversy could be big business. The movie was both a courageous undertaking, because of its pro-labor stance, and also a beautifully written, acted, photographed, and directed work of lasting power.

Based on the John Steinbeck novel of the same name, *The Grapes of Wrath* was bought outright by Darryl F. Zanuck of Twentieth Century-Fox *(qq.v.)* for $100,000. Unlike most authors, who generally despise the film versions of their work, Steinbeck had a grudging respect for the adaptation of his Puliltzer Prize-winning book by Zanuck, director John Ford *(q.v.)*, and screenwriter Nunnally Johnson *(q.v.)*.

The Grapes of Wrath documented the devastation of the early 1930s drought that carved the Dust Bowl on large areas of the lower midwest and the poor Okies who lost their land in cruel foreclosures. The movie version of the story was necessarily trimmed, with characters eliminated and a long flood scene removed. Nonetheless, the spirit of the novel was maintained by following the fortunes of one Oklahoma family, the Joads.

Few in the film industry felt that a movie could be made from such a controversial novel. Zanuck, to his credit, felt otherwise, and hired one of the best directors available, John Ford, once he had a script he liked. Ford, himself, was attracted to the story because it was so much like the famine in Ireland that had affected his own family.

Casting the film was the next problem. Ford wanted the thin and brittle Beulah Bondi for Ma Joad, but Zanuck wanted the film cast with Fox contract players, and Jane Darwell was his choice for the Joad family matriarch; Zanuck had his way. Though Darwell won an Oscar for Best Supporting Actress as Ma Joad, there are critics who still feel that she's the weakest member of the cast. Zanuck, however, also wanted either Don Ameche or Tyrone Power *(qq.v.),* Fox's two biggest male stars, to play Tom Joad, the idealistic hero of the movie. Ford wanted Henry Fonda *(q.v.),* and Fonda wanted the part, as well. In order to get the role, the actor had to agree to a seven-year contract with Fox.

The final cast for *The Grapes of Wrath* included Henry Fonda (Tom Joad), Jane Darwell (Ma Joad), John Carradine (Casey), Charley Grapewin (Grampa Joad), Dorris Bowdon (Rosasharn), Russell Simpson (Pa Joad), and John Qualen (Muley).

Ford sought an artful authenticity in *The Grapes of Wrath,* which he more than received from his actors, none of whom wore make-up. Cinematographer Gregg Toland *(q.v.),* captured the poverty of the Okies in harsh black-and-white shots that seemed almost documentary-like. At the same time, he showed the destruction of the land by dust storms in a series of startlingly bleak scenes.

After the movie was shot, Zanuck added a new ending to the film. Originally, it was to have ended with Tom Joad heading up over a hill, a symbol of (among other things) the labor movement. That scene was kept, but Zanuck wrote Ma Joad's final speech that included the memorable sentiment: "We're the people that live. Can't nobody wipe us out." The original ending was more ambivalent. Zanuck's change added a bit of hopefulness.

When the movie opened, it met with immediate and unequivocal praise. That praise has never diminished. The movie represents one of Hollywood's shining moments of courage coupled with cinematic expertise and art.

In addition to Jane Darwell's Academy Award, the movie brought John Ford the Oscar for Best Director. The film was nominated for Best Picture and made Henry Fonda, nominated for Best Actor, a star of the first order, firmly establishing his noble, honest, and upright image.

THE GREAT TRAIN ROBBERY: This seminal film in the development of the art of moviemaking was directed by Edwin S. Porter in 1903. *The Great Train Robbery* was the longest movie of its day at twelve minutes and it told a cohesive story using intercutting, a panning shot, and a famous close-up, during which a cowboy shoots his gun into the camera lens, at the end of the film. None of these filmmaking techniques were new—Porter, himself, had pioneered their use in his earlier films—but it was the first time that they had been used all at once and to such dramatic effect. *The Great Train Robbery* was a huge hit and remained one of the most popular movies of the early silent era, shown and reshown for more than a decade before its artistry was finally overshadowed by the growing so-phistication of directors such as D. W. Griffith *(q.v.).*

The Great Train Robbery told a simple story of a band of villains who sneak aboard a train, rob it, and are then chased on horseback by a posse until they are gunned down in the woods while dividing up their loot. Shot in the wilds of New Jersey with what was then a massive cast of forty, the movie established the direction and content of future westerns, incorporating the classic elements of the chase and the showdown.

Porter, though a genuine innovator, was ultimately more concerned with the mechanics rather than the art of moviemaking. Yet his contribution to the early growth of the cinema cannot be underestimated.

GREENSTREET, SYDNEY   *See The Maltese Falcon.*

GRIFFITH, D. W. (1875–1948)   Unquestionably, the single most important filmmaker in Hollywood history, Griffith understood the potential for artistic expression in the fledgling movie business, and with a ready supply of creativity and ingenuity, fashioned a visual language for telling stories in moving pictures.

David Wark Griffith was the son of Colonel "Roaring Jake" Griffith, a Confederate hero of the Civil War who went bankrupt and died when Griffith was ten years old. The boy had to do his best to help his family survive, working as a clerk in a store and at several other odd jobs. But he wanted to be a writer and a dramatist. His luck in those arenas was not very great, and he had to make his living as an actor. Calling himself Lawrence Griffith because he was ashamed of the way he earned his money, he toured the country in small stock companies, often supplementing his meager income with odd jobs.

In 1907, broke and in desperate need of employment (he had married in 1906), Griffith took a stab at the movie business, hoping to sell his story ideas. He went first to the Edison studio and sought out Edwin S. Porter, a pioneering director who, four years earlier, had made *The Great Train Robbery (q.v.).* Porter wasn't interested in Griffith's stories, but he offered him a job as a movie actor.

For a stage actor, working in the movies was the ultimate humiliation. But Griffith swallowed his pride and took the job, appearing in *Rescued from an Eagle's Nest* (1907).

In 1908, Griffith was still trying to sell his story ideas, this time to the Biograph *(q.v.)* company. They bought his stories and hired him as an actor, as well.

Biograph was a small, not terribly successful film company in 1908. But Griffith took an interest in directing and was given the opportunity with a film called *The Adventures of Dolly* (1908). G. W. "Billy" Bitzer *(q.v.)* wasn't Griffith's cameraman on the film, but he did offer helpful advice. And the two men worked together afterwards for sixteen years in unarguably

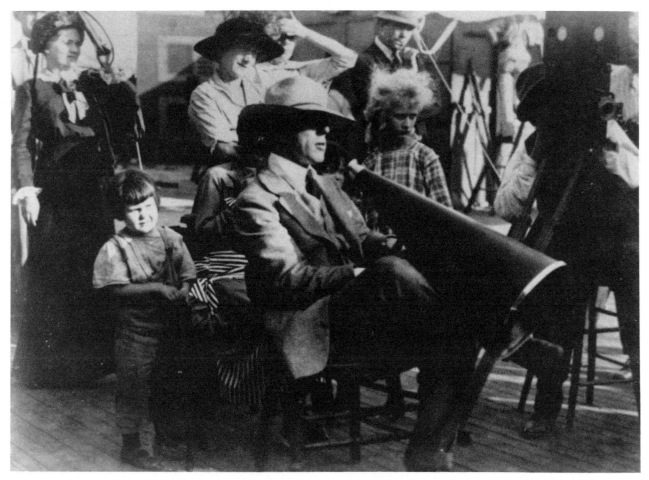

The most influential director in the history of film is D. W. Griffith, who almost single-handedly invented the language of the cinema. Photo courtesy of Movie Star News.

cinema's most important artistic union. At the time, however, Bitzer didn't think very much of Griffith. "Judging the little I had caught from seeing his acting," Bitzer later remarked, "I didn't think he was going to be so hot."

The Adventures of Dolly, however, became a hit and Griffith quickly took over the creative reins of Biograph. According to Iris Barry's famous monograph on Griffith published by The Museum of Modern Art, "all of Biograph's films from June 1908 until December 1909 were made by Mr. Griffith, and all the important ones thereafter until 1913."

Biograph prospered like never before. By 1911, Griffith had dropped the name Lawrence and forever after used his full name David Wark Griffith; he was finally proud of his work.

From the very beginning at Biograph, Griffith experimented and developed the language of film. In *For Love of Gold* (1908), he changed the camera setup in the middle of a scene, bringing it closer to the actors. It had never been done before. With Bitzer, he also created the fade-in and fade-out, and numerous other technical storytelling tools.

As he directed Bitzer to take more and more close-ups, Griffith understood that the new art form needed a new kind of actor whose face could stand the scrutiny of the camera. He hired teenagers, such as Mary Pickford *(q.v.)*, Mabel Normand *(q.v.)*, Mae Marsh, Blanche Sweet *(q.v.)*, and Dorothy and Lillian Gish *(q.v.)*, all of whom would become major movie stars.

In 1909, he further developed the use of cross-cutting between scenes in *The Lonely Villa.* It was a technique that would come to glorious fruition in Griffith's masterpiece, *The Birth of a Nation* (1915, *q.v.*).

Griffith not only extended the language of motion pictures, he also extended their length. He was the first to shoot a two-reel film (each reel was ten minutes long), and he kept making his films longer until *The Birth of a Nation* reached the unheard of length of twelve reels.

Griffith had to leave Biograph in 1913 in order to continue his artistic growth. When he left, he took Bitzer with him, as well as his loyal stock company of actors. He soon began work on the film that would change the course of moviemaking, *The Birth of a Nation.*

He had budgeted *The Birth of a Nation* at $30,000, but it cost nearly $100,000. It was of no matter; Griffith's movie was a colossal hit, earning an estimated $18 million. But because of attacks on the film due to its racist elements, Griffith felt compelled to show his tolerance by making *Intolerance* (1916), a hugely expensive epic on the evils of hatred.

For all its grandeur, the film was a financial disaster. A pacifist movie made just as America was being primed to enter World War I, it didn't stand a chance. Griffith lost a fortune. The film, however, remains a testament to his incredible vision. The sets, the huge cast, and the enormous spectacle of the movie were truly awesome and remain so even by today's standards. Though *Intolerance* was a failure in America, the film played for ten continuous years in the USSR, and it clearly influenced the work of Cecil B. DeMille *(q.v.)*, Abel Gance, and Fritz Lang *(q.v.)*.

In 1919, Griffith joined with the other great silent-screen giants Charlie Chaplin *(q.v.)*, Mary Pickford, and Douglas Fairbanks *(q.v.)* to form United Artists *(q.v.)*. Griffith's first film for the new company was *Broken Blossoms* (1919) with Lillian Gish and Richard Barthelmess *(q.v.)*. It was an achingly simple story of interracial love that played to large audiences and excellent reviews. It is considered an important movie in the development of film art because of its subtle attention to visual detail.

He followed that success with several other films, the most popular being *Way Down East* (1920) and *Orphans of the Storm* (1922). In 1924, he made *America,* a sweeping story of the Revolutionary War, but financial considerations finally drove him out of independent production and his career went into serious decline.

One would think that the coming of talkies would have literally sounded the death knell for any hope of a Griffith comeback, but he made *Abraham Lincoln* in 1930, and the film received good reviews and did respectable business. However his next film, *The Struggle* (1931), was a bomb. Griffith retired from the movie business, though he reputedly had some involvment in *One Million Years B.C.*, a 1940 film.

He died a forgotton man in 1948, but he has since been remembered and honored. As critic Andrew Sarris wrote in *The American Cinema,* "The cinema of Griffith, after all, is no more outmoded than the drama of Aeschylus."

GRIP   The crew of a film is divided into two groups, the electricians and the grips. Electricians are responsible for providing power for the lighting equipment, and the grips handle everything else. In the theater, a grip would be referred to as a stagehand. In essence, grips are laborers who carry out a multitude of jobs on a movie set. Often, the grips are subdivided by their job functions, such as construction grips, lighting grips, dolly grips (the people responsible for laying the dolly tracks and also moving the dolly during the shoot), and so on.

The origin of "grip" is rather prosaic. The word was first used to describe laborers who literally "grip" scenery, scaffolding, lighting diffusers, etc. in the course of their job.

The person in charge of all the grips is known as the key grip. His assistant is the grip best boy.

The key grip's relative station on the set of a film is equal to that of the gaffer, who is the chief electrician. The key grip works in tandem with the gaffer and reports to the cinematographer (or director of photography). The key grip's job title did not come into being because it is a key position (though it is), but because the key grip has traditionally been the person who carries the keys for various locked storage spaces.

See also: best boy; dolly; gaffer

GRODIN, CHARLES (1935–   )   An appealingly comical actor with a subtle, deadpan delivery, he has worked consistently in films since the late 1960s. Grodin has easily shuttled back and forth between starring and supporting roles, usually playing either neurotic everymen or middle-class prigs. The key to Grodin's humor has been his dry, sincere style; his characters would be the last to be amused by his performances.

Grodin made his film debut in a supporting role in *Rosemary's Baby* (1968), but his big breakthrough was as the callow young husband in Elaine May's hit comedy *The Heartbreak Kid* (1972). It appeared as if he was destined for stardom, but his particular style of restrained acting wasn't suited for such later films as *11 Harrowhouse* (1974) or *King Kong* (1976).

His career seemed to sputter in the mid- to late 1970s, until he slowly emerged as an attention-getting supporting player. His presence in such movies as Warren Beatty's *Heaven Can Wait* (1978) and Albert Brooks' *Real Life* (1979) added immeasurably to their success.

Having found his niche, Grodin has received nearly universal praise from critics. Even in poor films such as *Sunburn* (1979), *The Couch Trip* (1987), and even the mega-flop *Ishtar* (1987), he has been admired for evincing small truths in the midst of major fiascos. But in good films, such as *Seems Like Old Times* (1980) and *The Lonely Guy* (1984), he has been brilliant. Only once has he been seriously panned in recent years, and that was for *Movers and Shakers* (1985), a satire about the movie business he wrote, coproduced, and starred in, that left the critics cold and audiences frigid. Grodin recouped smartly from that disaster and, in the late 1980s, nearly realized the promise of *The Heartbreak Kid* to become a full-fledged star thanks to his wonderfully fussy performance opposite Robert De Niro *(q.v.)* in the acclaimed hit comedy *Midnight Run* (1988).

HACKMAN, GENE (1931–)   A prolific character actor/star, Hackman has quietly become one of Hollywood's most highly regarded performers. If it seems as if the actor has always been middle-aged, it's because he didn't emerge as a star until he was nearly forty years old. Despite a haggard, everyman appearance—or rather because of it—he has been Hollywood's actor of choice in a wide variety of films over nearly two decades. Though he hasn't been in a great many box office blockbusters, even in commercial failures he wins the plaudits of critics because he plays his roles so skillfully.

Hackman grew up in a lower-middle-class household in Illinois and quit school when he was sixteen to join the Marines. After his stint in the service, he spent years doing everything from driving trucks to selling shoes before eventually settling into a vagabond existence working as an assistant director for a series of small TV stations. Meanwhile, Hackman had been nurturing his dream of acting. He had obviously seen the talent on many a local TV show and had been unimpressed.

In his early thirties, long after most aspiring actors have given up their show business quests, Hackman decided to take the performing plunge. He studied at the famous Pasadena Playhouse, where he and fellow student Dustin Hoffman were voted "least likely to succeed." Undaunted, he went to New York to try and break into the theater. Thanks to his unactorish looks, he soon found modest success in small Off-Broadway productions and in television, eventually leading to a starring role in *Any Wednesday* on Broadway in 1964.

His good reviews in the hit comedy brought the offer of a small role in *Lilith* (1964). It was his first important film role (his debut movie was a tiny role in *Mad Dog Call,* 1961). Other small character parts followed in films such as *Hawaii* (1966) and *First to Fight* (1967). The big breakthrough, however, came when Warren

Beatty, who had starred in *Lilith,* chose Hackman to play his brother, Buck, in *Bonnie and Clyde* (1967, *q.v.*). The controversial film was a hit that boosted the careers of a great many people, and Hackman garnered a nomination for Best Supporting Actor for his performance.

Hackman had emerged as a legitimate character actor but he had yet to achieve star status. After working in support of such luminaries as Robert Redford (*q.v.*) in *Downhill Racer* (1969) and Burt Lancaster (*q.v.*) in *The Gypsy Moths* (1969), he was given a rare costarring role with Melvyn Douglas (*q.v.*) in *I Never Sang for My Father* (1970). The critics raved about Hackman's complex performance, and he was honored yet again with an Oscar nomination for Best Supporting Actor.

Finally, in 1971, when he played obsessed, uncouth New York cop "Popeye" Doyle in *The French Connection,* everything fell into place. The movie was a smash with both critics and filmgoers and, suddenly, at the age of forty, Hackman had become a star and the recipient of an Oscar for Best Actor. He had found the secret of his future success: play both heroes and villains as vulnerable, human characters.

After *The French Connection,* Hackman's career in the early 1970s consisted mostly of good roles in good films that did not fare well with anyone but the critics. The all-star disaster film *The Poseidon Adventure* (1972) aside, he starred in such highly regarded movies as Michael Ritchie's *Prime Cut* (1972), *Scarecrow* (1973), and Francis Ford Coppola's post-*Godfather* masterpiece, *The Conversation* (1974). Despite good notices, however, Hackman was in need of a hit. He went back to the well to recreate Popeye Doyle in *French Connection II* (1975), which proved to be a success.

Unfortunately, the second half of the 1970s became a relative wasteland for Hackman. Except for *Night Moves* (1975), a good movie that failed at the box office, most of his other vehicles were often poor films that were also big commercial losers. By the end of the decade he was playing Lex Luthor in *Superman* (1978) and *Superman II* (1980).

In the early 1980s Hackman starred with Barbra Streisand in the little-known but wonderful comedy *All Night Long* (1981). Again, he was well-reviewed but the film went nowhere. Finally, in 1983, Hackman fired up the public in one of the first Vietnam-related movies, *Uncommon Valor* (1983), which became a sleeper hit. Since then, whether successful or not, either his films or his performances (or both) have generally been critically acclaimed. With a prodigious output during the mid-to-late 1980s, he has delighted filmgoers with brilliant characterizations in films as varied as *Under Fire* (1983), *Misunderstood* (1984), *Twice in a Lifetime* (1985), *Hoosiers* (1986), *Bat 21* (1988), *Another Woman* (1988), *Mississippi Burning* (1988), and *The Package* (1989).

HANKS, TOM (1956–): An actor specializing in comedy who has become one of the great young talents of the 1980s. Compared to the likes of James Stewart and Jack Lemon, Hanks is an everyman with whom audiences can easily identify. A gifted light comedian, he can break your heart just as easily as make you laugh. Good looking in a boyish, unthreatening way, he has starred in an average of two movies per year since 1984, when he made his film debut in the hit comedy *Splash*.

Hanks began his acting career as an intern at the Great Lakes Shakespeare Festival in Cleveland, Ohio, acting in such plays as *The Taming of the Shrew* and *The Two Gentlemen of Verona*. After brief stints on the stage in both New York and Los Angeles, he won a starring role in the ABC-TV sitcom "Bosom Buddies," which ran for two years in the early 1980s.

After scoring in *Splash*, a film that earned more than $60 million, Hanks went on to star in a series of movies that were extremely variable in both their quality and their box office appeal. Though *Bachelor Party* (1984) earned $40 million, *The Man With One Red Shoe* (1985) and *Every Time We Say Goodbye* (1986) were box office failures. *Volunteers* (1985) and *The Money Pit* (1986) both found a modest following, but the film that got the attention of both the critics and the paying public was *Nothing in Common* (1986), which was the first movie that showed Hanks capable of reaching deeper, richer emotions underneath his comic persona.

During this period of growth, Hanks often worked with other strong comic performers, such as John Candy in *Volunteers*, Jackie Gleason in *Nothing in Common*, and Dan Aykroyd in *Dragnet* (1987). When given the opportunity to carry a major motion picture on his own shoulders, he did not disappoint. After Robert De Niro could not settle on contractual terms to play Josh Baskin in *Big* (1988), the role fell to Hanks, and it brought him both a blockbuster hit that earned more

than $100 million and his first Academy Award nomination for Best Actor. In that same year, he electrified the critics with his dazzling performance as a self-destructive stand-up comedian in *Punchline*. Unfortunately, the movie was not the commercial success its producer (and costar) Sally Field had hoped it would be. Equally disappointing for critics was *Burbs* (1989), but Hanks continues to impress even when his films don't quite match his talent.

JEAN HARLOW (1911–1937): Previously in films, the vamp usually had dark hair, while the "good" girl was blonde. But Harlow added a new dimension. Her platinum blonde hair was so unique, and (for the 1930s) her gowns so low-cut, the expression "blonde bombshell" was coined to describe her. She was modern, vulgar, and wonderfully funny. Here was a woman who seemed to want sex as much as a man. Harlow brought a healthy sex appeal to the movies, that was both shocking and liberating in its time.

Born Harlean Carpenter to a middle-class family, she ran away from home to get married at sixteen. After the marriage failed, she went to Hollywood and worked as an extra, eventually winning a small part in *Moran of the Marines* (1928). Other tiny roles followed, most notably in *The Love Parade* (1929).

Nothing came of her work until Howard Hughes got a glimpse of her. Hughes wanted her for *Hell's Angels* (1930), his epic airplane movie *(q.v.)* that had been two years in the making but had to be reshot because of the advent of sound. Hughes, always quick to spot a beauty, saw her potential and signed her to star in his film as the woman who comes between the two heroes.

Hell's Angels was a big hit, partly because of the remarkable aerial display in the movie, and partly because Harlow, was so sexy. Hughes had her under a long-term contract and proceeded to loan her to other studios for lead roles, notably to Warner Bros. for *Public Enemy* (1931). She was also loaned to Columbia, where she starred in Frank Capra's *Platinum Blonde* (1931), a movie clearly titled to best take advantage of her peculiar hair color.

Hughes finally sold her contract to MGM for $60,000. She appeared in two MGM films without causing much of a ripple until *Red Dust* (1932) with Clark Gable *(q.v.)*. The two stars ignited sexual fires, making the rather daring movie a blockbuster hit. Harlow and Gable were a hot team; they were paired together a total of five times in just six years, and all of their films drew big crowds.

After *Red Dust*, Harlow was *the* Hollywood sex goddess. And, as such, she was a perfect foil for the purposefully stuffy cast in MGM's all-star film *Dinner at Eight* (1933), just as she was the perfect victim in the aptly titled *Bombshell* (1933).

Jean Harlow was the sound era's first major sex symbol. She brought an earthiness to the screen to which audiences responded—especially when she played her roles for laughs. Photo courtesy of The Siegel Collection.

She could play tough *(Riff Raff,* 1935), or she could play funny *(Suzy,* 1936). But no matter what she played, the slinky star had one hit after another. There was no reason to believe she might not have an extremely long career. Tragedy struck, however, when Harlow was only twenty-six years old. She had been filming *Saratoga* (1937) when she fell ill and then suddenly died of uremic poisoning. The movie was finished with a double, and went on to become a great hit precisely because it was the sex star's last movie.
See also: sex symbols: female

HART, WILLIAM S. (1870–1946)   There were quite a few silent western movie stars, but William S. Hart was the first to bring a sense of authenticity to the genre.

Hart grew up in the West, counting many Sioux Indians among his childhood friends. He hated the misrepresentation of the West in the early one- and two-reelers that had become so vastly popular. After touring as a stage actor, he went to Hollywood to make the kinds of westerns he thought ought to be made.

He played the bad guy in his first film appearance. The movie was a two-reeler titled *His Hour of Manhood*

(1914). He was already forty-four years old, but with rugged good looks and a seriousness of purpose that bespoke integrity, it didn't take him long to catch on. In the same year as his debut, he starred in his first film, *The Bargain* (1914).

One of his best early movies was *Hell's Hinges* (1916), and audiences responded to it (and most of the rest of his films) because of the gritty details, the credible action, and Hart's no-nonsense persona (although he sometimes looked as grim as Buster Keaton's old stoneface). Hart's dedication to his subject matter led him not only to star in his own films, but often to write, direct, and produce them. Except for Clint Eastwood *(q.v.),* Hart was the last major western star to take such complete control of his movies.

Hart was the number-one western star in the late teens and early 1920s. By the mid-1920s, his popularity began to fade. He decided to make one last movie, *Tumbleweeds* (1925), and it was his masterpiece. The movie was a major hit, but Hart, discouraged with the movie business and the general direction of the western, decided to retire. His last film appearance was in 1939 when he filmed an introduction for the reissue of *Tum-*

Silent western star William S. Hart brought a gritty realism to his films, but he was not without a sense of humor. That old chestnut about cowboys kissing their horses can finally be put to rest: clearly, it was the horses who did the kissing. Photo courtesy of The Siegel Collection.

bleweeds. He had an excellent speaking voice and surely could have had a talkie career, but Hart had left the business while he was still on top and he never expressed any regrets.

See also: westerns

HATHAWAY, HENRY (1898–1985) He was a dependable, efficient, and unpretentious director of mostly "A" movies *(q.v.)* for more than forty years during the sound era. Though never in the same league as such directors as John Ford and Howard Hawks *(qq.v.),* Hathaway brought a direct and lively competence to large-scale action films (especially westerns), and a gritty, no-nonsense style to mystery/suspense/crime films.

Born into a theatrical family in California (his father was a theater manager and his mother was an actress), Hathaway began his career in the movies as a child actor in 1908, appearing in more than four hundred one- and two-reelers, many of them for director Alan Dwan *(q.v.).* After a stint in the Army during World War I, Hathaway returned to Hollywood and began working behind the camera as a property man and later as an assistant director for the likes of Paul Bern, Joseph von Sternberg *(q.v.),* and Victor Fleming.

He began his directorial career with a string of Randolph Scott *(q.v.)* "B" movie westerns in 1932, the first of which was *Heritage of the Desert.* His big break came in 1935 when he was assigned to direct Gary Cooper *(q.v.)* in *The Lives of a Bengal Lancer.* It was the first major Hollywood movie about India, and Hathaway's grasp of the difficult project and his solid storytelling abilities garnered him not only a big box office success but the respect of his bosses at Paramount.

Hathaway established a well-earned reputation for dealing with unusual or difficult films. He had a way of keeping his stories on track despite all the peripheral razzmatazz. He demonstrated his ability time and again in films such as the bizarre romantic fantasy *Peter Ibbetson* (1935) and the first of many Hollywood pseudo-documentary thrillers, *The House on 92nd Street* (1945). He directed the untried Marilyn Monroe *(q.v.)* in her first major starring role in *Niagara* (1953), and took on the responsibility to direct the majority of the episodic epic *How the West Was Won* (1962).

Hathaway's success as a director was erratic. In a career that included more than sixty films, he had streaks of fine work, such as in the second half of the 1930s when he made (among others) *The Trail of the Lonesome Pine* (1936), *Souls at Sea* (1937), and *Spawn of the North* (1938), the second half of the 1940s when he initiated the Hollywood docudrama with *The House on 92nd Street,* *13 Rue Madeleine* (1947), and *Call Northside 777* (1948).

Despite his knowledge and ability as a director of westerns, the 1950s was a period of decline for Hathaway. While directors such as Anthony Mann, John Ford, Budd Boetticher *(qq.v.),* etc. were redefining and expanding the genre, Hathaway made only a few mediocre horse operas. After his involvement in *How the West Was Won* (a job that brought considerable attention to an otherwise old, forgotten director), Hathaway seemed reinvigorated and he emerged in the second half of the 1960s with a series of finely made big-budget westerns that included *The Sons of Katie Elder* (1965), *Nevada Smith* (1966), and *True Grit* (1969). With the latter John Wayne Oscar-winner, Hathaway reached the height on his roller coaster career. He continued to direct, making several more films in the early 1970s, his last a minor crime film, *Hangup* (1974).

HAWKS, HOWARD (1896–1977) Long one of the most underrated directors in Hollywood, he began his career in the silent era, and worked constantly and successfully until 1970. Hawks was a quiet director who thought of himself as a craftsman, rather than an artist, and for whom movies were meant only to be entertaining. But to students of Hollywood, he is an *autuer (q.v.)* on a grand level, a director who worked within the studio system *(q.v.)* to project a consistent point of view no matter what kind of film he might have been making.

Hawks was the eldest of three sons of a well-to-do paper manufacturer. He spent much of his youth in Southern California but went to college in the East, receiving a degree in mechanical engineering from Cornell University. After serving in World War I, Hawks put his mechanical engineering to use, building his own cars and planes. His fascination with machinery brought him into the movie business.

He got his start as a prop man in 1918 with the Mary Pickford Company, eventually getting experience in the script and editing departments. With an inheritance he received at the age of 26, he wrote, directed, and produced his own comedy shorts. He continued building his reputation (and his skill), and was finally given the opportunity to direct his first feature film for Fox in 1926, *The Road to Glory,* which was based on his own story.

Unlike most other directors, who tended to specialize in one or two different areas, Hawks worked in almost all of the popular genres. And, more significantly, he mastered many of them. For instance, although Hawks is sometimes best regarded as a director of westerns, he made only four horse operas, two of which became classics: *Red River* (1948) and *Rio Bravo* (1959). Hawks produced (and some say directed) only one science fiction film, *The Thing* (1951), which has long been a cult favorite. He made several gangster films, including one of Hollywood's most heralded, *Scarface* (1932), and one of its most loved, *The Big Sheep* (1946). He also made quite a number of airplane movies *(q.v.),* including the first version of *The Dawn Patrol* (1930) and the highly regarded *Only Angels Have Wings* (1939). Hawks

Among Howard Hawks' many claims to fame is his invention of the screwball comedy. He is seen here with actress Rosalind Russell, who starred along with Cary Grant in *His Girl Friday* (1940), one of Hawks' most delightful romps. Photo courtesy of Movie Star News.

even made one biblical epic, *The Land of the Pharaohs* (1955), and a couple of musicals, including the top-notch *Gentlemen Prefer Blondes* (1953).

But Hawks outdid himself and the rest of Hollywood when it came to directing comedies. He invented the screwball comedy *(q.v.)* in 1934 when he made *Twentieth Century,* starring John Barrymore and Carole Lombard *(qq.v.)*. Nobody made screwball comedies better than Hawks. Every one of his fast-paced, eccentric romps holds up as well today as when it was made. *Bringing Up Baby* (1938), *His Girl Friday* (1940), *Ball of Fire* (1941), *I Was a Male War Bride* (1949), and *Monkey Business* (1952) are the cream of Hawks' comedy crop.

Hawks' themes were consistent. In particular, he believed that the correct execution of a job was a sacred duty of all men and women. In fact, he was so incensed with the work ethic evidenced in Stanley Kramer's *High Noon* (1952) that he made *Rio Bravo* (1959) in direct response. Hawks was peeved that the film's protagonist, played by Gary Cooper *(q.v.)*, town marshall, begged everyone in his community to help him fight the bad guys who were arriving on the noon train. In Hawks' opinion, fighting the bad men was Cooper's job, and his job alone. In *Rio Bravo,* John Wayne *(q.v.)* is the

sheriff is in similar straits, but when several people volunteer to help him, Hawks sees to it that Wayne, the professional law man, purposefully turns them down.

In Hawks' comedies, men were chronically incapable of doing their jobs correctly, usually because of women. He often made his professional male characters charmingly ineffectual as they struggled against an increasingly female dominated society. Cary Grant was Hawks' ideal foil because he could be confused and appealing at the same time.

Hawks never won an Oscar and except for discovering Lauren Bacall and Angie Dickinson *(qq.v.),* he didn't establish any new stars. He was certainly never known for his fancy camera work or intricate story construction. Hawks made an art of telling his stories in a straightforward manner. And it worked. As a result, Hawks enjoyed one of the longest and most successful directorial careers in Hollywood history.
See also: screwball comedies

HAWN, GOLDIE (1945–   )   One of a relative handful of powerful female stars of the late 1970s and 1980s who has produced some of her own movies. Hawn combines a ditzy manner with an endearing vulnerability, which has resulted in her consistent personal popularity despite an uneven film career.

Born to a musically inclined family—her father was a musician and her mother a dancing teacher—Hawn pursued a show business career from an early age. Though she acted on stage as early as 1961 in a Virginia Stage Company presentation of *Romeo and Juliet* (she was Juliet), her passion was dancing. At the age of eighteen she arrived in New York and worked at the World's Fair, then danced as a go-go girl in a sleazy, New Jersey strip joint. Not long after, she became a chorus girl in Las Vegas, but was so fed up with her life that she gave herself two weeks to get a break or she was going home to Maryland. She got the break, being cast in a small role in an Andy Griffith TV special. Noticed on the air by an agent, she was offered a three-week stint on the new "Laugh-In" TV show, and her career quickly took off from there.

Though she had a short, unhappy run in the TV series "Good Morning World" in 1967, her early show-business persona was formed on the enormously popular "Laugh-In," where she played a goofy, childlike airhead who giggled incessantly. Audiences loved her. And so did film director Billy Wilder *(q.v.)*, who saw her on the show and thought she would be just right for his film *Cactus Flower* (1969). Hawn was cast in the movie and came away with an Oscar for Best Supporting Actress. In an interview with Rex Reed, she candidly admitted, "My greatest regret is that I won an Oscar before I learned how to act."

Before hitting it big in the movies with *Cactus Flower,* Hawn could have been seen in a bit role in the Disney production of *The One and Only Genuine Original Family Band* (1968). After *Cactus Flower,* she worked steadily in the movies as a comedienne in such films as *There's a Girl in My Soup* (1970), *Dollars* (1971), and *Butterflies Are Free* (1972), all of which traded on Hawn's kooky image. In 1974, however, the actress surprised filmgoers by starring in *The Sugarland Express,* a stark drama directed by the then unknown Steven Spielberg *(q.v.).* The film and Hawn received a shower of praise from the critics but her fans seemed hesitant to accept her as a dramatic actress.

Hawn turned back to light comedy in such films as *The Girl From Petrovka* (1974), *Shampoo* (1975), and *The Duchess and the Dirtwater Fox* (1976). She entered her most successful period when she joined with Chevy Chase in *Foul Play* (1978). After stumbling with *Travels with Anita* (1979), she produced and starred in *Private Benjamin* (1980), a film that earned more than $100 million and vaulted her into the top echelon of female movie stars.

The hits kept coming. *Seems Like Old Times* (1981) reunited her with Chevy Chase and *Best Friends* (1982) was a favorite of the critics. Subsequent efforts in the mid- to late 1980s, however, have been less well received. Her production of *Swing Shift* (1984) was a box office disappointment, and *Protocol* (1984) was a pallid imitation of *Private Benjamin.* She has appeared on screen with considerably less frequency in recent years, making little impact in such light comic fare as *Overboard* (1987), in which she starred with boyfriend Kurt Russell. However, she may be heading in a new, somewhat more serious direction with the upcoming *Bird on a Wire.*

HAYDEN, STERLING (1916–1986) A ruggedly handsome actor whose air of melancholy permeated his performances, making them richer than anything one might have expected from his generally inferior starring vehicles. Hayden, a genuine salt with a passion for the sea, was never consumed by his acting career; he was just as happy (if not happier) to be away from Hollywood, sailing somewhere in the South Pacific. Tall and blond, Hayden was a slow-talking, physical actor who fit the Gary Cooper *(q.v.)* mold. Unfortunately, he lacked both the scripts and the versatility to fill Coop's shoes, but in the right films Hayden proved to be a strong and imposing actor. When his starring days were over in the 1960s, he slipped comfortably into character roles, which he continued playing until shortly before his death.

Born John Hamilton, Hayden quit school at the age of sixteen to run away to sea. By the age of 22 he was a bona fide captain with a surprising degree of fame due to his well-publicized sailing exploits. Urged to take advantage of his chiseled good looks, and in need of money to buy his own boat, he began modeling and

quickly found himself with a movie contract at Paramount. He made his screen debut as one of the two male leads (Fred MacMurray *[q.v.]* was the other) in the western *Virginia* (1941). His female costar was Madeleine Carroll, whom he would soon marry and then divorce four years later. Hayden made but one more movie, *Bahama Passage* (1941), before turning his back on Hollywood to join the Marines when the Japanese attacked Pearl Harbor.

Hayden was off the big screen until 1947, when he had to start virtually from scratch. Without much studio support, he seemed destined for obscurity. Paramount soon dropped him and he began looking for work on his own, landing the prize role of the down-and-out tough guy who joins the other doomed criminals in John Huston's classic *The Asphalt Jungle* (1950). His character was both harsh and not a little dumb, but Hayden infused him with a dignity and vulnerability that made audiences care about his ultimate downfall. It was the greatest performance of his career.

Most of his films during the rest of the 1950s were routine action films, with but two notable exceptions. The first was *Johnny Guitar* (1954), Nicholas Ray's intense psychological western, in which he portrayed the title character, a laconic gunslinger. The second was Stanley Kubrick's *The Killing* (1956), in which he virtually reprised his role in *The Asphalt Jungle.* In fact, the film bore a striking resemblance to Huston's movie. In any event, both the film and Hayden's performance were widely admired by the critics, if not the public.

Hayden had harbored deep feelings of guilt concerning his testimony to the House Un-American Activities Committee in 1951. He had named names of Communist sympathizers in Hollywood, destroying their careers, and he later came to believe that he had made a terrible moral mistake. In the late 1950s, his emotional distress was compounded by divorce proceedings and a custody battle for his children. In defiance of a court order, he took his kids with him and set sail to the South Seas.

His career was in a shambles. Slowly, he put it back together again, first by writing a thoughtful autobiography, *Wanderer,* that was centered around his highly publicized "kidnapping" of his own children. The book was published in 1963 and it brought him a measure of sympathy and respect. The following year, he returned to the screen as a character actor, playing an insane general in Stanley Kubrick's *Dr. Strangelove* (1964). He worked only sporadically during the rest of his career but his supporting character roles in films such as *Loving* (1970), *The Godfather* (1972), *The Long Goodbye* (1973), and *Winter Kills* (1979) were often memorable.

In the last decade of his life, Hayden demonstrated both his love for the sea and a talent for writing fiction when he penned a best-selling novel, *Voyage: A Novel of 1896.* He died of cancer.

THE HAYS CODE   The film industry's rules for self-censorship, also known as the Production Code, that were designed in 1930 and originally administered by Will H. Hays. During the first four years of the code's existence, it was almost universally ignored because there was no enforcement mechanism.

Will Hays, former chairman of the Republican National Committee and U.S. Postmaster General during President Harding's administration, was originally hired by the movie bigwigs in 1922 to head a newly formed industry watchdog organization, the Motion Picture Producers and Distributors of America, Inc. The organization was brought into being as a response to the public outcry following a long string of Hollywood scandals, most notably the Fatty Arbuckle *(q.v.)* rape case. The MPPDA soon came to be known simply as The Hays Office. It was an organization with little clout during the 1920s, created merely as a smokescreen to keep the federal government from imposing its own brand of censorship or control over the wild and woolly film business.

In the early 1930s, however, filmmakers pushed the more conservative members of the moviegoing audience too far. Mae West's suggestive humor, Jean Harlow's harlotry, and a rash of violent gangster films all led to a public outcry that the film industry was corrupt and had to be censored. Fearing that their power might be circumscribed by Congress, the movie moguls went into action first, censoring themselves by putting genuine teeth in Will Hays' strengthened new production code in 1934. Any movie shown in any movie theater owned by the studios (which were the vast majority of the most successful, most profitable, theaters in the country) had to have the Hays Code seal of approval. Without that seal, a movie simply could not survive commercially.

The Hays Code was stringent, particularly in matters pertaining to sex. The code stated that "no picture shall be produced which will lower the standards of those who see it." To see to this, the code held that, "Seduction or rape should should never be more than suggested . . . sex perversion or any inference to it is forbidden . . . sex hygiene and venereal diseases are not subjects for motion pictures. . . . indecent or undue exposure is forbidden," etc.

Language was another area of concern. Certain words could not be used in films if said in a "profane" manner. While there was a faintly liberal impulse behind the Hays Code's dictates concerning religion; it stated that no film "may throw ridicule on any religious faith," in the application of that rule, one could not present any member of the cloth as a villain—or for that matter, even a bumbler or a fool—thereby impicitly upholding the institution of religion rather than merely protecting it from abuse.

As for violence, the guiding principle came to be known as the "Law of Compensating Values." Characters could be terribly evil and violent just so long as they were properly punished for their sins by movie's end. Films suffered from this dictum because audiences could always guess the ending; the bad guy would get his just deserts and the hero would always win. As a result, movies that purported to be realistic often had tacked-on happy endings that were anything but.

The examples of censorship imposed by the Hays Code are legion. Some of them, at least by today's standards, seem particularly ludicrous. For instance, the Hays Office ruled out the use of "razzberries" as an epithet in *Bedtime for Bonzo* (1951); W. C. Fields could not use the expression "Nuts to you," in *The Bank Dick* (1940). One of the great early battles between a producer and the Hays Office occurred over the famous line in *Gone With the Wind* (1939), when Rhett Butler says to Scarlett O'Hara, "Frankly, my dear, I don't give a damn." The line was so well known to the millions who had read the book that the movie's producer, David O. Selznick *(q.v.),* fought for its inclusion, and won his case at the cost of a modest $5,000 fine. It would be many years before such a victory would come again.

The Hays Code stayed in effect long after Mr. Hays' departure from Hollywood in 1945. The cracks in the code finally began to show ever so slightly in the 1940s, and particularly during the 1950s. Howard Hughes titillated audiences with his sexy western *The Outlaw* (1943), skirmishing with the Hays Office for three years before finally rereleasing the movie in 1946 to a wider audience anxious to see what all the fuss was about.

Otto Preminger *(q.v.)* was the next rebel, making two films that challenged basic tenets of the code during the 1950s. *The Moon is Blue* (1953) dealt explicitly with the issue of virginity, but Preminger managed to get distribution for his film thanks to the publicity generated by his breaking of the Production Code taboo. Two years later, Preminger made a film about drug addiction—another taboo—when he directed *The Man With the Golden Arm* (1955). And again, Preminger came away with a hit. The code began to crumble soon after.

By the 1960s, thanks to a more liberal moviegoing public, the incursion of successful foreign films on Hollywood's turf, and the softening of obscenity laws by the courts, the once all-powerful Hays Code was markedly changed. In 1966 a new production code was created by the MPPDA that made it a rating rather than a censoring device. The rating system and the criteria used to rate films has been adjusted since 1966 to reflect society's changing values. The code is now essentially designed to protect children from sex, violence, or dialogue that might be too explicit in certain films. For the most part, however, the code still seems to be far more concerned with sex than any other issue.
See also: Valenti, Jack

HAYWARD, LELAND   *See* agents.

HAYWARD, SUSAN (1918–1975) A popular actress, particularly during the 1950s, who specialized in playing plucky women who fight life's cruel blows. Her inspirational roles made her a favorite of female movie fans, and her talent brought her five Best Actress Academy Award nominations, one of which resulted in an Oscar. Auburn-haired and husky-voiced, Hayward was a stunning beauty whose film career spanned thirty-five years and fifty-eight films.

Born Edythe Marrener to a nontheatrical family, she went to a vocational school to learn secretarial skills. Her striking good looks, however, led to a job as a photographer's model. When David O. Selznick *(q.v.)* began his highly publicized search for an actress to play Scarlett O'Hara in *Gone With the Wind,* Hayward volunteered for the role. While the inexperienced nineteen-year-old obviously didn't get the part, she did get a Hollywood contract.

She began appearing in films in 1937, making her debut in a tiny role in *Hollywood Hotel.* Except for a good ingenue role in the otherwise all male *Beau Geste* (1939), Hayward was mostly saddled with parts in mediocre movies such as *Girls on Probation* (1938), *$1,000 a Touchdown* (1939), and *Young and Willing* (1942). Though it would be hard to tell from the titles, her scripts started improving in the early 1940s. Movies such as *I Married a Witch* (1942) and *The Hairy Ape* (1944), proved she was a capable actress. But not until she starred in *Smash-Up: the Story of a Woman* (1947) could the depth of her talent truly be seen. Her bravura portrayal of an alcoholic in the film brought Hayward her first Oscar nomination. The movie also established the kind of troubled characters the actress would often play throughout the peak years of her career.

While Hayward starred in a number of biblical epics during the 1950s, such as *David and Bathsheba* (1951) and *Demetrius and the Gladiators* (1954), her impact was greatest in contemporary women's movies dealing with disease, heartbreak, and struggle. The best examples of her work from this period are her Oscar-nominated films *My Foolish Heart* (1950), *With a Song in My Heart* (1952, a biopic *[q.v.]* of Jane Froman), *I'll Cry Tomorrow* (1956, a biopic of Lillian Roth), and *I Want to Live* (1958), for which she finally won her Best Actress Oscar.

Her films during the early 1960s were cut from the same cloth as her 1950s vehicles. Unfortunately, the quality of their scripts and direction had deteriorated and the audience's taste for them was declining as well. Her remakes of the old tear-jerker *Back Street* (1961), and *Dark Victory,* this time called *The Stolen Hours* (1963), were not big winners at the box office. After *Where Love Has Gone* (1964), another flop, she briefly retired from the screen.

Hayward made the first of her two comebacks in 1967 when she starred in *The Honey Pot* (1967) and played a supporting role in *The Valley of the Dolls* (1967). After the latter experience, Hayward didn't return to the movies again until 1972 in a very poor western, *The Revengers.*

During her long career, Hayward's personal life was at times as harrowing as those of the characters she played. She tried to kill herself in the mid-1950s after an ugly courtroom battle with actor Jess Barker, to whom she had been married for ten years (1944–1954), for the custody of her twin boys. Then, in the early 1970s, in a tragically ironic twist, it was discovered that Hayward had a brain tumor, the same ailment that befell her character in *The Stolen Hours.* She died two years later.

HAYWORTH, RITA (1918–1987) Long-legged, with a striking face, beautiful complexion (particularly in Technicolor), and long auburn hair, Hayworth was the sex goddess of the 1940s, bridging the gap between Harlow and Monroe *(qq.v.).*

Born Margarita Carmen Cansino, she was Ginger Rogers' first cousin (their mothers were sisters), and it seems only fitting, therefore, that Hayworth eventually had the opportunity to dance with Fred Astaire *(q.v.).*

Dancing came easily to Hayworth, whose father was a dancer. The family talent proved to be her avenue into show business. Dancing at a popular Hollywood nightclub, The Agua Caliente, she was discovered by a scout from Fox.

At first, Hayworth was simply a chorus dancer in films such as her debut movie, *Under the Pampas Moon* (1935). But Fox had big plans for her and intended to give her the lead in a film called *Ramona* (1936). But when Fox merged with Twentieth Century, Hayworth not only found herself bumped from *Ramona* but was soon dropped from the new studio altogether.

After some "B" movie roles, she landed a contract at Columbia, but still played in lesser films such as *Criminals of the Air* (1937) and *Who Killed Gail Preston?* (1938). Her big break came when she was tested by George Cukor *(q.v.)* for the role of Katharine Hepburn's sister in *Holiday* (1938). Though the director did not cast her, he was impressed enough to use her in *Susan and God* (1940), a picture that brought her some serious attention by the press and the public. It also didn't hurt that pin-up pictures of the striking beauty were starting to have an impact as well. She started receiving lead roles in important movies, most notably in *Strawberry Blonde* (1941) and *Blood and Sand* (1941). The success of these films brought Hayworth to the next, most glamorous phase of her career—and the most ironic.

Hayworth became a musical star in *You'll Never Get Rich* (1941) with Fred Astaire. The musicals *My Gal*

Sal (1942), *You Were Never Lovelier* (1942), with Astaire, and *Cover Girl* (1944), with Gene Kelly, followed. Hayworth, who was a trained dancer, could not sing. In all her musicals, including her most famous, *Gilda* (1946), her songs were dubbed.

Meanwhile, Hayworth's personal life soon spilled over into her professional life. She was married five times, and her second husband, Orson Welles *(q.v.)*, made one of his best movies, *The Lady From Shanghai* (1948), with Hayworth as the femme fatale. Though the movie is highly regarded today, at the time of its release it was a box office failure. After her marriage to Welles ended, she tied the knot with one of the richest men in the world, Prince Aly Khan, causing her to turn her back on Hollywood for several years. When the marriage ended in 1951, though, she quickly returned. Unfortunately, her audience didn't.

In the 1950s, her career was uneven. *Pal Joey* (1957) and *Separate Tables* (1958) are perhaps her best movies of that decade, but her films were no longer built around her. Hayworth continued to act in the 1960s and into the 1970s, but her appeal had waned. Her last film appearance was in a minor featured role in *The Wrath of God* (1972). She suffered from Alzheimer's disease for a very long time before her death in 1987.
See also: sex symbols: female

HEAD, EDITH (1907–1981) A costume designer whose name appeared in the credits of more than one thousand movies. She was the chief costume designer at Paramount from 1938 until 1967, after which she worked at Universal until her death. As Joseph McBride points out in *Film Makers on Film Making, Volume Two,* though Edith Head was best known for her high-fashion designs, her versatility was the real key to her success. During the late 1930s and 1940s, she was one of the few costume designers to clothe both women and men. More significantly, she also designed costumes for a wide variety of movies, including romances, epics, westerns, period pieces, horror and science fiction films.

Edith Head didn't originally intend to design clothes. She had been a Spanish teacher and an art instructor before becoming a sketch artist at Paramount in 1923. She became the assistant to then chief costume designer at the studio, Howard Greer, whom she succeeded in 1938. Head soon had a major effect on American fashions when women began copying the Latin look she gave Barbara Stanwyck *(q.v.)* in *The Lady Eve* (1941). Her designs continued to influence American dress throughout the rest of her career.

Head was not only recognized on Fashion Avenue, she was also appreciated in Hollywood, receiving an astounding thirty-four Academy Award nominations for costume design, and walking away with a total of eight Oscars. Her awards were for her work in *The Heiress* (1949), *All About Eve* (1950), *Samson and Delilah*

(1950), *A Place in the Sun* (1951), *Roman Holiday (1953),* *Sabrina* (1954), *The Facts of Life* (1960), and *The Sting* (1973).

Head had the particular distinction of designing the costumes for a great many Alfred Hitchcock *(q.v.)* films and all of the Hope/Crosby "Road" pictures (including Dorothy Lamour's sarong). She may also be the only costume designer in Hollywood history to have appeared in two films, *Lucy Gallant* (1955) and *The Oscar* (1966), playing herself.

Ironically, her last film (which was released after her death) had the fashion-conscious title *Dead Men Don't Wear Plaid* (1982).
See also: costume designer

HECHT, BEN (1893–1964) One of the most talented and certainly the most prolific of Hollywood's screenwriters. Ironically, he only worked in Hollywood part time; he was more interested in writing plays and novels than he was in writing screenplays, yet the movie industry paid him such extravagant sums of money—and he lived in such a grand style—that he traveled to Los Angeles virtually every year to replenish his bank account. Despite his low regard for Hollywood, it is even more ironic that his reputation as a writer rests firmly on his rich, well-plotted, witty screenplays. In the course of nearly forty years, he either wrote the screenplays or provided the stories for more than seventy films, a great many of them classics. Incredibly, he won but two Oscars for his work.

Hecht's life was as melodramatic as many of his films. He was a child prodigy at age ten, seemingly on his way to a career as a concert violinist, but two years later he was performing flips as a circus acrobat. That career was short-lived, but his next was not. He ran away from his home in Racine, Wisconsin at the age of sixteen and started his writing career by becoming a cub reporter for a Chicago newspaper. He later became a war correspondent and a tough crime reporter while also becoming known in Chicago's literary circles.

Intent on a career as a playwright and novelist, Hecht traveled to New York. In need of money, however, he was convinced that there might be some cash to be earned in Hollywood. He arrived in Los Angeles and began his remarkable career at the very beginning of the sound era by providing the story for Josef von Sternberg's early gangster movie, *Underworld* (1927), for which Hecht won Hollywood's first Academy Award for Best Original Story.

The talkie era put writers like Hecht at a premium because they could write dialogue in the quirky, idiosyncratic style of the common man. Hecht, in particular, was wonderful with slang and he peppered his films with the argot of the streets. He also had a lively sense of humor and an uncanny ability to successfully ground even the most outrageous stories with credible, fast-paced plots.

Hecht wrote scripts or supplied stories for virtually every genre, from adventures such as *Gunga Din* (1939) to science fiction such as *The Queen of Outer Space* (1958), and from musicals like *Jumbo* (1962) to impassioned romances such as *Wuthering Heights* (1939). Ultimately, however, he was best known for two specific types of films: crime thrillers and screwball comedies. Among crime thrillers, Hecht was responsible for such films as *The Unholy Night* (1929), the classic gangster movie *Scarface* (1932), *Notorious* (1946), and *Ride the Pink Horse* (1947). Among his comedies one finds such winners as *The Front Page* (1931) and its many remakes, *Design for Living* (1933), about which Hecht once proudly said there wasn't a line of Noel Coward's left in the screenplay, *Twentieth Century* (1934), *Nothing Sacred* (1937), and *Monkey Business* (1952).

Hecht also cowrote, codirected, and coproduced films with his favorite theater and film collaborator, ex-Chicago reporter Charles MacArthur. Their *Crime Without Passion* (1934) and *The Scoundrel* (1935) are far more interesting today as curiosity pieces than they are as important films. Hecht and MacArthur actually took little interest in them and left much of the actual directing credit to their cameraman, the talented Lee Garmes *(q.v.)*. Nonetheless, Hecht and MacArthur received Oscars for Best Original Story of the year for the latter film.

The influence of Ben Hecht's prolific pen touched many of Hollywood's most loved movies, including, among others, Rouben Mamoulian's *Queen Christina* (1933), John Ford's *The Hurricane* (1937), David O. Selznick's *Gone With the Wind* (1939), and several Hitchcock films, including, *Lifeboat* (1944), *The Paradine Case* (1948), and *Rope* (1948). He received no screen credits for his work on these and a considerable number of other well-known films that he either rewrote or revised.

Five years after he died, a portion of his memoir, *A Child of the Century,* was turned into the movie, *Gaily, Gaily* (1969). In that charming film, in the person of Beau Bridges, Hecht comes to life again as a young reporter in Chicago.

HENIE, SONJA (1910–1969)   In the days before TV's "Wide World of Sports," Hollywood offered this three-time Olympic Gold Medal winner a chance to become a movie star. Famous athletes such as Johnny Weismuller and Buster Crabbe had previously made their way to star status, but only Sonja Henie (and later, Esther Williams *q.v.*) built their movie careers specifically around their respective sports.

In an effort to prove she was movie-star material, Henie rented a skating rink in Los Angeles to show producers both her skating ability and her crowd ap-

peal. It worked. Twentieth Century-Fox was suitably impressed and put the Norwegian in her first film, *One in a Million* (1936) She was a sensation, and so were the films she made that quickly followed up her initial success. Henie's movies put the skater in the list of top-ten money-earners of the late 1930s, and she was soon the highest paid film star in Hollywood.

By the early 1940s, however, audiences grew tired of the same old plots and Henie's career went into a quick decline. She continued making films for lesser studios throughout the 1940s, eventually retiring a wealthy woman, having reigned as queen both of the sporting world and the movie world.

HEPBURN, AUDREY (1929–)   Thin, long-legged, with an exquisite fragility, Hepburn possesses a pixieish charm that is tempered by unmistakable class. Ironically, she emerged as a star in the early 1950s when America seemed to favor more buxom stars in the mold of Marilyn Monroe *(q.v.)*. Versatile, despite her seemingly relentless poise, she was effective in period pieces, musicals, thrillers, and especially love stories. She was nominated five times for an Academy Award for Best Actress, winning once for her very first starring role.

Born Audrey Hepburn-Ruston in Belgium to a well-heeled English banker and a Dutch baroness, she looked and acted like the member of the aristocracy that she was. Educated in London, she was caught in the Netherlands when the Nazi's invaded that country and was forced to spend the duration of World War II there. She returned to London at the war's end to continue her study of the ballet, which she had begun in Holland. Her striking beauty and slim figure, however, led to a successful fashion modeling career instead.

As many models do, Hepburn took acting classes and began appearing in a number of English films in minor roles, making her debut in *One Wild Oat (1951)*. Her only notable film during that early period before stardom was *The Lavender Hill Mob* (1951). Her acting career didn't take off, though, until she met Colette, the author of *Gigi*. Colette became the young girl's champion, insisting that Hepburn play the title role in the soon to be produced stage version of her book. Colette had her way and Hepburn was a smash on Broadway, gaining the attention of Hollywood in the process and being cast in her first major film role in *Roman Holiday* (1953).

Success came quickly. *Roman Holiday* was a box office winner and Hepburn took top honors with an Academy Award for Best Actress. Over the next dozen years she made only fifteen films, but a great many of them were either critical or box office smashes, or both.

Curiously, the actress was often cast with much older men as her love interests. Perhaps her fragile, childlike quality seemed to require the balance of a more powerful fatherly figure. For instance, there was Humphrey

Audrey Hepburn possessed a delicate, utterly feminine beauty that was nothing less than radiant on the big screen. And she was a marvelous actress, proving herself especially adept in romantic roles. Photo courtesy of Movie Star News.

Bogart *(q.v.)* in *Sabrina* (1954), which brought her a second Oscar nomination, Fred Astaire *(q.v.)* in *Funny Face* (1957), Gary Cooper *(q.v.)* in *Love in the Afternoon* (1957), Cary Grant *(q.v.)* in *Charade* (1963), and Rex Harrison in *My Fair Lady* (1964).

Hepburn reached the height of her fame with a series of major hits, including *The Nun's Story* (1959), for which she received her third Oscar nomination, *The Unforgiven* (1960), *Breakfast at Tiffany's* (1961), bringing her a fourth Best Actress nomination, *Charade, Paris When It Sizzles* (1964), and *My Fair Lady,* her biggest hit.

It was two years before she appeared in another film, the slight caper movie *How to Steal a Million* (1966), but then she played in the sophisticated marital drama *Two for the Road* (1967), and surprised audiences still further with her effective portrayal of a blind woman fighting for her life in the thriller *Wait Until Dark* (1967), for which she won her fifth Oscar nomination for Best Actress.

In 1968 Hepburn's marriage to actor Mel Ferrer (they married in 1954) came to an end and, with it, so ended her Hollywood career for nearly a decade. The following year she wed a doctor and retired from the film business, living a relatively quiet life in Rome. She was finally lured back to the big screen in 1976 to play Maid

Marian to Sean Connery's *(q.v.)* Robin Hood in *Robin & Marian,* a gentle comedy about heroes who grow old. Her return to the movies was ballyhooed in the press but she didn't pursue her acting career with much vigor thereafter. She made the mistake of starring in *Bloodline* (1979) and followed it with yet another poor choice when she joined the cast of Peter Bogdanovich's *They All Laughed* (1981). She has recently been cast in Steven Spielberg's *Always* (1989).

HEPBURN, KATHARINE (1907–   )   One of the few true superstars of American film, she has had a long, distinguished career, winning an unprecedented four Oscars for Best Actress. With her crisp New England accent, high cheekbones, and aristocratic manner, Hepburn played everything from light comedy to high tragedy. She was feisty and independent yet vulnerable and endearing. In all, she epitomizes America's idea of free-thinking womanhood.

Born to a wealthy Connecticut family, Hepburn pursued theater in college and made her acting debut in Baltimore as a lady-in-waiting in *The Czarina* (1928). But she had precious little theater training and her career was anything but smooth sailing.

After landing the lead in a play called *The Big Pond* (1928), she made a shambles of her opening night performance and was fired. In fact, most of her early stage career consisted of one disaster after another.

Discouraged, she briefly gave up the theater and married Ludlow Ogden Smith (known to Kate as "Luddy") in 1928. Neither her marriage nor her career fared very well over the next few years. She eventually divorced in 1934, but the marriage had long since ended amicably. In the meantime, Hepburn persevered in learning her craft in spite of little success on stage.

Finally, in 1932, she appeared in *The Warrior's Husband,* a play that won her critical acclaim. She was offered a screen test from Fox, and a long-term contract from Paramount. She turned down both because she did not want to leave the theater for any length of time. But when David O. Selznick *(q.v.)* wired requesting her to test for his film version of *A Bill of Divorcement* (1932), she assented because it was a one picture deal. Hepburn made the test and although everyone else in the screening room thought she was terrible, director George Cukor *(q.v.)* and Selznick were pleased with the results. This first film began a lifelong association with Cukor, who almost always brought out the best in Hepburn. The pair would eventually work together in eight movies and two TV films.

A Bill of Divorcement made Hepburn an instant star. It seemed that Broadway could wait, after all. She made three more films in rapid succession—all of them hits. *Morning Glory* (1934), the third film of her career, won Hepburn her first Best Actress Oscar.

She reached her peak of popularity in the early to

mid-1930s, after which the actress's upper-class bearing finally began to wear on Depression-era audiences. Two of her most beloved films today, *Bringing up Baby* (1938) and *Holiday* (1938), were flops in their day. By this time, she was labeled "box office poison" by a group of theater owners.

Nonetheless, David O. Selznick, who had launched her career with *A Bill of Divorcement,* offered Hepburn the part of Scarlett O'Hara in *Gone With the Wind* (1939). She was only one of three actresses to whom Selznick offered the plum role. To be fair to Selznick (and not wanting to be fired later if he changed his mind), Hepburn told him that she'd take the part at the last minute if he couldn't settle on anyone else to play Scarlett. Vivien Leigh *(q.v.)* ended that tantalizing offer.

By 1939, however, Hepburn, who had commanded $175,000 per film, was offered $10,000 to star in an Ernst Lubitsch *(q.v.)* vehicle (which she declined). It appeared as if her Hollywood career had come to a crashing end.

It was back to Broadway for Hepburn, and she commissioned Phillip Barry (who had penned *Holiday,* among a great many other popular Broadway plays), to write something for her. The result was *The Philadelphia Story.* It was a smash on Broadway and Hepburn wisely bought the film rights. Despite her box office poison label, any studio that wanted to adapt the hit play had to use her in the lead.

MGM took a chance on the actress, adding Cary Grant and Jimmy Stewart *(qq.v.)* to the cast for insurance and putting George Cukor behind the camera. The movie, released in 1940, was a popular hit and Hepburn was back in Hollywood to stay.

It is interesting to note that while Hepburn's fans are loyal, they are limited in number, and while her later career has been a series of acting triumphs, she rarely received top billing after the 1930s. One reason for this is her pairing with the costar of her next film who had a contract that ensured top billing in all his films. That actor was Spencer Tracy *(q.v.).*

Hepburn and Tracy initiated one of the great screen teamings, as well as a long love affair when they starred together in *Woman of the Year* (1942). The story of their first meeting bears retelling. Hepburn said to Tracy, "I'm afraid I'm too tall for you, Mr. Tracy." To which he replied, "Don't worry, Miss Hepburn. I'll soon cut you down to my size." On the basis of this film with MGM, the studio offered her a long-term contract. But of all the movies she made at MGM, the nine Tracy-Hepburn films were the most consistently successful, especially *Keeper of the Flame* (1942), *State of the Union* (1948), and *Adam's Rib* (1949), which was also directed by George Cukor.

Perhaps her most well-known costar besides Tracy only appeared with her in one film—but what a film it was. She played the psalm-singing spinster in *The Af-*rican Queen* (1951) against Humphrey Bogart's irascible Charlie Alnut. The movie was a huge hit, and it became her most successful film up to that time.

Except for her continued teamings with Tracy, the rest of the 1950s found her playing variations on the spinster role she had done to perfection in *The African Queen.* One of the best of these roles was in *The Rainmaker* (1956), with Burt Lancaster doing the impossible—stealing the movie from her.

Hepburn has appeared in relatively few films from the 1960s to the present. *Guess Who's Coming to Dinner* (1967) was generally more interesting for being the last Tracy-Hepburn vehicle than a film about interracial marriage. And though Hepburn seemed to cry throughout the movie—perhaps because of it—she won her second Best Actress Academy Award. She was superb in *The Lion in Winter* (1968), winning yet another Oscar for Best Actress.

Hepburn tried a western version of *The African Queen* with John Wayne *(q.v.)* called *Rooster Cogburn* (1975) and appeared occasionally on TV in highly regarded productions, such as *Love Among the Ruins* (1975). But her final triumph came in 1981, when she starred with Henry Fonda and Jane Fonda *(qq.v.)* in *On Golden Pond.* She won her fourth Oscar, setting a record, and showing no inclination to retire. Hepburn has continued to act, adding laurels to a career that has no equal in Hollywood.

HERRMANN, BERNARD (1911–1975)   The composer of nearly fifty film scores, he was closely associated with the works of directors Orson Welles and Alfred Hitchcock *(qq.v.).* Ominous, moody, and sinister music was his trademark and there was no one in Hollywood who was his equal at such scores.

Julliard-trained, Herrmann made his mark early as a conductor of a chamber orchestra that he founded at the age of twenty. He continued to conduct orchestras and to compose operas and ballets, but by the age of thirty he had arrived in Hollywood, making his debut as a film composer for the same movie that marked Orson Welles' directorial debut, *Citizen Kane* (1941, *q.v.*). His rich, inventive score deeply affected the film's visual impact as few scores had done for films before and it was one of the important ingredients in what some consider to be the greatest movie ever made. In that same year, Herrmann also wrote the powerful score for *All That Money Can Buy,* winning an Oscar for his music in his second film. The composer had clearly made an impressive entrance to the film industry.

Herrmann's work set just the right tone in Welles' *The Magnificent Ambersons* (1942) and the Welles starring vehicle, *Jane Eyre* (1944). But except for films like *The Ghost and Mrs. Muir* (1947), and, to a modest extent, *The Day the Earth Stood Still* (1951), he lacked the right directorial collaborator for whom he could focus his talents. Finally, in 1956, Herrmann was hired to work with Alfred Hitchcock, writing the score for *The Trouble With Harry* (1956). Though the movie was not a success, the team of Hitchcock and Herrmann was very much a winner. The composer went on to write the scores for such Hitchcock classics as *The Man Who Knew Too Much* (1956), *Vertigo,* (1958), *North by Northwest* (1959), *Psycho* (1960), and *Marnie* (1964). He was also the sound consultant on Hitchcock's *The Birds* (1963).

He became so identified with the master of suspense, that Herrmann was hired by François Truffaut to write the score for the French director's Hitchcockian thriller *The Bride Wore Black* (1967). Brian De Palma, *(q.v.),* among the most Hitchcockian of modern directors, also hired Herrmann for two of his films, *Sisters* (1973) and *Obsession* (1976). Even director Martin Scorsese *(q.v.),* another student of film history, couldn't pass up the opportunity of hiring the man who wrote the music for *Citizen Kane* and *Psycho* for the film that many consider to be his own masterpiece, *Taxi Driver* (1976).

HERSHOLT, JEAN (1886–1956) A man far better known today for the award associated with his name, the Jean Hersholt Humanitarian Award, than for his reputation as an actor. But Jean Hersholt was a popular and much respected character actor during the silent era who made the transition to sound, appearing in, with a few exceptions, small roles in more than fifty films, mostly during the 1930s.

Hersholt, the son of a Danish acting couple, came to the United States in 1914 and wasted little time making his reputation in Hollywood. He made his first film appearance in *The Disciple* (1915). Some of the more well-known silent films in which he appeared were *The Four Horsemen of the Apocalypse* (1921), *Greed* (1924), and *Stella Dallas* (1925).

Hampered by his accent, Hersholt had a more limited choice of (smaller) character roles in the talkie era, but he worked consistently in films such as *Susan Lenox: Her Fall and Rise* (1931), *The Painted Veil* (1934), and *Heidi* (1937). On occasion, Hersholt assumed lead roles, usually playing a kindly doctor in films such as *Men in White* (1934) and the Dr. Christian series, which the actor also performed on radio, that included the films *Meet Dr. Christian* (1939), *The Courageous Dr. Christian* (1940), *Remedy for Riches* (1940), and *Melody for Three* (1941).

Though he was hardly a famous actor, Hersholt was a tireless worker in the fight against poverty and suffering during the Great Depression and was the founder and president of the Motion Picture Relief Fund, an endeavor that brought him a special Oscar in 1939. His good works brought credit not only to himself but to the Hollywood community and he was, therefore, given a second special Oscar in 1949 in recognition of his "distinguished service to the motion picture industry."

Hersholt appeared in just two films after his Dr. Christian series ended, *Dancing in the Dark* (1949) and *Run for Cover* (1955), but his impact in Hollywood was such that in the year of his death from cancer in 1956, the Jean Hersholt Humanitarian Award was established to honor other members of the motion picture community who give of themselves in the manner of Mr. Hersholt. Winners of the award are chosen by the Board of Governors of the Academy of Motion Picture Arts and Sciences. Though not presented every year (there must be a worthy recipient), those who have been given the Jean Hersholt Humanitarian Award include, among others, Samuel Goldwyn (1957), Bob Hope (1959), George Jessel (1969), and Frank Sinatra (1970).

HESTON, CHARLTON (1923–) An actor whose name is synonymous with movie spectaculars, his having played a range of epic characters from Ben-Hur to Moses and from Michelangelo to El Cid. With his large, muscular body and strong facial features, he has an imposing presence that lends authority to his acting, matched by an inner dignity that shines through in his best work. In a career that includes more than fifty films, Heston has also found time to star in TV and theater projects throughout the roughly four decades of his professional acting life. In addition, he has been active in Hollywood politics as a six-term past president of SAG (Screen Actor's Guild).

Born Charlton Carter in Michigan's backwoods, he studied acting at Northwestern University and made his way to New York to break into theater. To make ends meet, he posed in the nude for art students at a $1.50 per hour. After gaining experience in regional theater, he got his first big break in a supporting role in *Antony and Cleopatra* on Broadway in 1947.

Heston then became one of the first major movie stars to come to national prominence through his work in television. He starred in highbrow live TV specials in the late 1940s such as "Julius Caesar" (as Antony, 1948), "Of Human Bondage" (1948), "Wuthering Heights" (1949), and "Macbeth" (1949).

Although he acted in two 16mm amateur films, Heston made his professional film debut in Paramount's *Dark City* (1950), a low-budget movie that did not set Hollywood afire. Not until his second film the star-studded *The Greatest Show on Earth* (1952), for which he was chosen by Cecil B. DeMille *(q.v.)* for an important role, was Heston's movie career given a jolt.

He acted steadily throughout the early 1950s in films such as *Ruby Gentry* (1952), *Pony Express* (1952), and *The Private War of Major Benson* (1955). Though he was playing leading roles, he was hardly a major star. That changed overnight when Cecil B. DeMille cast him as Moses in the stellar remake of the director's silent classic, *The Ten Commandments* (1956).

There is no other film actor who has starred in more epics (biblical or otherwise) than Charlton Heston. His spectaculars were seen and enjoyed by huge audiences during the late 1950s and early 1960s. Photo courtesy of Charlton Heston.

The film was a colossal hit, putting Heston in a position to pick and choose his projects. And much to his credit he chose *Touch of Evil* (1958) and insisted that Orson Welles *(q.v.)* direct it. The movie has since been recognized as one of Welles' great films.

That same year Heston agreed to accept the modest role of a heavy in *The Big Country* (1958) for the chance to work with famed veteran director William Wyler *(q.v.)*. Wyler appreciated both Heston's gesture and his talent, and offered him the role of the villain in the director's next movie, *Ben-Hur* (1959). Later, after Burt Lancaster *(q.v.)* chose not to play the title character, Wyler eventually handed it to Heston, who ultimately won an Oscar for Best Actor for his work in the blockbuster hit.

Though he was associated with DeMille's two epics and the Wyler *Ben-Hur* in the 1950s, Heston actually starred in more epic films in the 1960s than in the previous decade. But *El Cid* (1961), directed by Anthony Mann, was to be the last of his major hits in these spectaculars. His subsequent epics, *55 Days at Peking* (1962), *Major Dundee* (a massacred epic, 1965), *The Agony and the Ecstasy* (1965), *The War Lord* (1965), and *Khartoum* (1966) were all box office failures that garnered, at best, faint critical praise, though his performance in a low-budget western, *Will Penny* (1967), led critics to remark on Heston's reserved dignity and vulnerability in a thoughtful, quiet film. The movie was a disappointment at the ticket window, however.

It appeared as if Heston's movie career was in a serious slide until he starred in a most unlikely hit, *Planet of the Apes* (1968). He followed that success with a starring role in the sequel, *Beneath the Planet of the Apes* (1969), committing the producing studio, Twentieth Century-Fox, to kill off his character so he couldn't be called back for further sequels (of which there were three).

Except for a couple of intriguing low-budget science fiction cult films, *The Omega Man* (1970) and *Soylent Green* (1973), Heston buried himself during the 1970s in a series of all-star films such as *Skyjacked* (1972), *Earthquake* (1974), *Airport 1975* (1975), and *Two Minute Warning* (1976), until his credibility as a serious actor began to erode. By the end of the 1970s and throughout the 1980s, he has surfaced in occasional movies, often scripted by his son, Fraser Heston, but they have not been particularly successful or noteworthy.

In the 1980s, he starred in a miniseries on TV and then succumbed to the lure of prime time TV soap operas, starring for a short while in "The Colbys." He has been active on the stage when not filming.

HILL, GEORGE ROY (1922–) A director who has had a great deal of commercial success but who has only lately been accorded a commensurate degree of critical acceptance. Though often regarded as a director of action films, it is perhaps more accurate to call Hill a director of comedies. In 1969 he popularized what became known as the "buddy film" when he directed Paul Newman and Robert Redford *(qq.v.)* in the hit comedy/western *Butch Cassidy and the Sundance Kid*. He is also noted for being the director who brought back old-fashioned story structure to the movies after the sometimes ramshackle efforts of more avant garde directors during the 1960s.

Born in 1922 to a family with a background in journalism and business, Hill grew up with a passion for airplanes. That passion eventually led to his serving as a pilot during World War II and as an instructor during the Korean War, emerging from the military with the rank of captain. His interest in aviation eventually led to the making of one of his more personal film projects, *The Great Waldo Pepper* (1975), a nostalgic movie about stunt pilots who barnstormed around the country during the years of his youth.

Hill's original career direction took him to Yale University, where he studied music, and later to Trinity College in Dublin, Ireland, where he took up acting. He made his first professional stage appearance in a bit part in G. B. Shaw's *The Devil's Disciple* at Dublin's Gaiety Theater in 1948.

Hooked on the stage, Hill continued his acting career in the United States, working in a radio soap opera, becoming a member of a Shakespearean repertory company and, later, acting on television. In the early 1950s, Hill also began writing and directing for television, soon winning both a writing and directing Emmy for "A Night to Remember" in 1954. His success in tele-

George Roy Hill directed mega-hits *Butch Cassidy and the Sundance Kid* (1969) and *The Sting* (1973). He still makes popular movies, such as the recent Chevy Chase comedy *Funny Farm* (1988). Photo courtesy of George Roy Hill.

vision led to directing efforts on Broadway, where he made a decidedly strong impression with *Look Homeward, Angel* in 1957. The play won both the New York Drama Critics Circle Award and the Pulitzer Prize. He continued directing many plays for the stage during the late 1950s and early 1960s, most notably *Period of Adjustment* in 1960. Hill made his directorial debut in films with the cinematic version of that same play in 1962—to generally good reviews.

His movie career during the 1960s was marked by great peaks and valley. As was often to be the case, his best films of the decade were comedies, including *The World of Henry Orient* (1964), *Throughly Modern Millie* (1967), and his first big blockbuster, *Butch Cassidy and the Sundance Kid* (1969). The less successful films were the dramas *Toys in the Attic* (1963) and *Hawaii* (1966), a commercial and critical flop. In an interesting footnote, Hill was temporarily fired from *Hawaii* while the movie was in production, but the large Polynesian cast refused to work for anyone but Hill and he was quickly reinstated.

The 1970s were Hill's golden period. With the clout that came from directing *Butch Cassidy,* he was able to make what many considered an "unmakeable" movie, Kurt Vonnegut's surrealistic *Slaughterhouse Five* (1972). This dark comedy was well received by most critics and it found a loyal, enthusiastic audience among young people. He followed that with the most popular movie

of his career, *The Sting* (1974). Once again pairing Newman and Redford, this slick comedy caper film brought Hill a Best Director Oscar while also winning the Best Picture Academy Award. At the time, it was also the fourth biggest grossing movie in Hollywood history, just behind *The Godfather* (1972), *The Sound of Music* (1965), and *Gone with the Wind* (1939).

Hill continued to create seriocomic hits, although of a more modest variety. *Slap Shot* (1977) was a controversial comedy because it dealt with the violence and blood lust inherent in the game of hockey. Critics didn't know quiet what to make of it, but the film has become more highly regarded in recent years. There was no controversy, however, about *A Little Romance* (1979), a lovely film that has enjoyed modest success. The director's next movie, *The World According to Garp* (1982), received a mixed reaction both from reviewers and audiences. Then came Hill's straight dramatic effort, *The Little Drummer Girl* (1984), which was dismissed by the critics and spurned by audiences. In more recent years, however, Hill has gone back to what he does best, comedy, fashioning the highly regarded Chevy Chase vehicle, *Funny Farm* (1988), a movie that featured Hill's particular talent for combining commercial viability with comically pungent observations on human behavior.

HITCHCOCK, ALFRED (1899–1980)   One of the cinema's greatest directors, he is known as "The Master of Suspense." He once remarked, "There is no terror in a bang, only in the anticipation of it," and the underlying tension in his movies comes from placing ordinary people in extraordinary circumstances. The audience is made to relate almost palpably to his characters' anxieties, in part because of Hitchcock's masterful use of montage. How he intercuts a scene to emphasize what is truly fearful creates suspense, heightening our awareness of impending danger.

Ironically, his dark themes and striking visual style lent themselves to such entertaining films that audiences and critics alike tended to dismiss their artistry. How could Hitchcock's films be art, after all, if they were so much fun? Yet in a fifty-year directorial career that also included the producing and scripting of many of his own films, Hitchcock proved, beyond a shadow of a doubt, that his movies could withstand the test of all art: time.

Born to a poultry dealer and fruit importer in England, the middle-class Hitchcock received a rigorous Jesuit education, eventually pursuing a career in electrical engineering. But not ardently. He had studied art and, after taking the transitional step of working in advertising as an artist, took the plunge into filmmaking in 1920 as a title designer.

Hitchcock actually began his film career working for an American firm, Famous Players-Lasky, which would

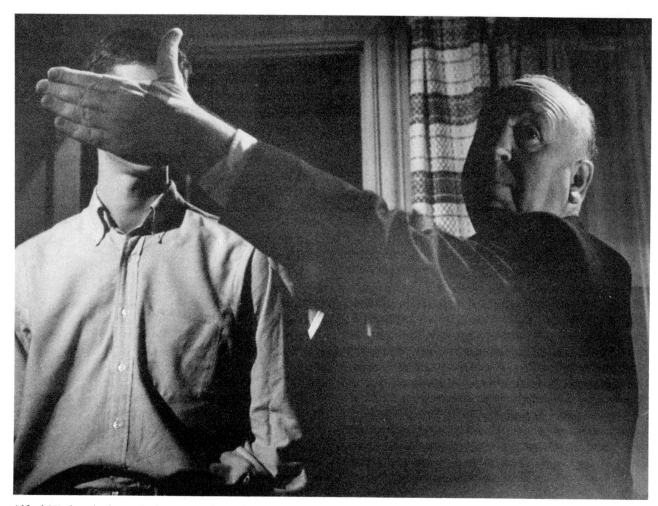

Alfred Hitchcock always had a wonderfully perverse sense of humor. He is seen here on the set of *Psycho* (1960), purposefully covering Anthony Perkins' face. Photo courtesy of Movie Star News.

later become Paramount Pictures. Not long after, however, the company was taken over by a British concern and Hitchcock was given greater responsibilities. Soon he was involved in all aspects of production, from art direction to screenwriting. Eventually, he was promoted from assistant director to director, making his official debut in that capacity with *The Pleasure Garden* (1925).

The director's first thriller was *The Lodger* (1926), but he would not become known for his work in the genre for nearly another decade, although he made a splash with the suspenseful *Blackmail* (1929), Britain's first all-talking picture. Hitchcock made everything from musicals to romances, finally finding his niche and sticking to it when he made *The Man Who Knew Too Much* (1934). It was an international hit, and he followed it with other thrillers, among them *The Thirty-Nine Steps* (1935), *Sabotage* (1937), and *The Lady Vanishes* (1938). By the second half of the 1930s he had become England's leading director, and that meant that Hollywood had to have him.

David O. Selznick *(q.v.)* signed Hitchcock to a contract and brought him to America. Over the next thirty-six years, almost all of which were spent making movies in America, Hitchcock built and enhanced his reputation as an immensely talented storyteller, provoking a lively debate as to whether his English or his Hollywood period was best. To most observers, though, there can be no doubt as to the answer; Hitchcock reached the height of his powers in Hollywood, especially during the 1950s.

It didn't take long for the director to win the respect of his peers. His very first Selznick film, *Rebecca* (1940), brought Hitchcock the first of his five Best Director Academy Award nominations. Regrettably, he would never win an Oscar, although he was later honored with an Irving Thalberg Award in 1967.

For the most part, the 1940s was a period of experimentation for Hitchcock. Many of the films he made during the decade were brilliant, others were flops, but all were interesting. *Suspicion*'s (1940) depiction of paranoia pushed the audience to new limits; *Shadow of a*

Doubt (1943) uncovered evil in small-town rural America like no other film before; *Lifeboat* (1944), a cinematic tour de force of montage, rhythm, and pacing—the camera was confined to a small lifeboat for virtually the entire length of the film—brought him a second Oscar nomination; *Spellbound* (1945) allowed him to experiment with dream sequences and gave him his third Academy Award nomination; *Notorious* (1946), a sexually charged tale of masochism, was daring even for the *film noir (q.v.)* era; and *Rope* (1948), filmed in such a way as to make it appear as if there were no cuts in the action at all, was a fascinating novelty then as now.

Rich and provocative as Hitchcock's work was in the 1940s, he surpassed himself in the 1950s, directing many of his greatest films, including *Strangers on a Train* (1951), *Rear Window* (1954), for which he garnered his fourth Oscar nomination, *To Catch a Thief* (1955), *The Man Who Knew Too Much* (1956, a remake of his own earlier film), *Vertigo* (1958), and *North by Northwest* (1959). In these films he refined his earlier themes, crystallizing the sense of corruption that is part and parcel of the human condition.

In 1960 Hitchcock won his fifth and last Oscar nomination for the classic suspense thriller *Psycho*, a film that influenced the showering habits of a whole generation. Unfortunately, the rest of the 1960s was more problematic for the director. He made fewer films, most of which were neither critically nor commercially successful. After *The Birds* (1963), which was a hit despite mixed reviews, *Marnie* (1964), *Torn Curtain* (1966), and *Topaz* (1969) were not immediately appreciated.

Finally, though, Hitchcock returned to his usual mold in the 1970s to make two more films, *Frenzy* (1972) and *Family Plot* (1976), both of which displayed a macabre sense of humor, playful use of film techniques, and edge-of-the-seat suspense.

The two actors who are most associated with Hitchcock are Jimmy Stewart and Cary Grant *(qq.v.)*, both of whom appeared quite often in the master's films during the 1940s and 1950s. But despite their excellent performances in Hitchcock's films, he was not an actor's director. He thought of actors as "cattle," who were merely to be manipulated on the set just as the audience's emotions were to be manipulated in the movie theater. Actors merely had to do what they were told; he wasn't interested in their interpretations of their roles. Before filming even began, Hitchcock already knew who his characters were.

The director was famous for having planned every shot of his films in advance, drawing them on storyboards. As a consequence, he was often bored during filming, figuring the movie was essentially finished, except for the nuisance of actually having to shoot it. One of the happy results of his filmmaking system was that there was so little extra film shot that producers couldn't edit a Hitchcock movie in any other way except as it was designed; he left no room for alternatives in the cutting room.

There has never been a director whose image was more well known than that of Hitchcock. That familiarity was due in part to his two long-running TV series, "Alfred Hitchcock Presents" (1955–1961) and "The Alfred Hitchcock Hour" (1962–1965), both of which featured the rotund director as the on-camera host. (He did, in fact, direct as many as a twelve hours worth of shows.) But Hitchcock had already been introduced to viewers thanks to cameo appearances in his own films, a tradition that began with *The Lodger* in 1926 when he helped fill out an insufficiently peopled crowd scene. When the film was a hit, superstition took hold and he appeared in subsequent films until he became a steady feature—audiences seeking him out and he finding amusing ways to enter and exit scenes.

The director died in 1980.

See also: De Palma, Brian; Herrmann, Bernard; Leigh, Janet

HOFFMAN, DUSTIN (1937–) A character actor/star since the late 1960s, Hoffman is talented, adventurous in his choice of roles, and fully dedicated to his craft. A perfectionist, directors and producers have often referred to him as "difficult," but his perfectionism has paid off in a great many unique and often exhilarating film portrayals. In the course of his first eighteen starring roles, Hoffman has garnered six Academy Award nominations for Best Actor, winning the Oscar twice.

Hoffman was not, as legend has it, named for the silent screen cowboy star Dustin Farnum. His mother merely liked the name Dustin and gave it to her son. There was, however, an early family connection to the movies. His father was a one-time prop man at Columbia Pictures and the film business always loomed large in the young Hoffman's consciousness. In fact his older brother, Ronald, briefly broke into the movies as a child actor playing a tiny role in Frank Capra's *Mr. Smith Goes to Washington* (1939).

Hoffman was originally interested in a music career, enrolling at the Los Angeles Conservatory of Music. But his acting experiences in school plays made him rethink his decision and he switched career paths, first studying at the Pasadena Playhouse, then coming to New York and enduring five rejections from the Actors Studio before finally being admitted.

His success was long in coming. He supported himself with an assortment of jobs, such as weaving Hawaiian leis, working in a mental institution, and the ever-popular waiting on tables. Meanwhile, he slowly made his reputation in the theater with roles in such productions as *Harry, Noon, and Night*, *The Journey of the Fifth Horse* (for which he won the coveted Obie Award), and *Eh?* His success in the last of these led to his first film role, in *The Tiger Makes Out* (1967), for which he received 19th billing. Soon thereafter he played the lead in a low-budget Spanish/Italian coproduction, *Madigan's Millions*, a film that wasn't released in the United States until 1970, after both Hoffman and another actor in the movie, Jon Voight *(q.v.)*, became big stars.

Eh? also led to the biggest break in Hoffman's career. Director Mike Nichols *(q.v.)* saw him in the show and decided to cast him in his new film, *The Graduate* (1967). Hoffman was paid $17,000 to play Benjamin Braddock in what became a blockbuster hit, instantly establishing Hoffman as a major new star and bringing him the first of his Oscar nominations.

He proved his success was not a fluke by wowing the critics and the public with his portrayal of Ratso Rizzo in *Midnight Cowboy* (1969), garnering yet another nomination for Best Actor. Hoffman might have been a star with a loyal following, but he didn't choose conventional starring roles. Except for the contemporary love story *John and Mary* (1969), he has played such characters (in starring roles) as the 121-year-old Jack Crabb in *Little Big Man* (1970), the nerdy prisoner who befriends the Steve McQueen *(q.v.)* character in *Papillon* (1973), and a down-on-his-luck ex-con in *Straight Time* (1978).

The mid-1970s was Hoffman's most consistently successful period. Among the top box office films in which he gave winning performances were the controversial Sam Peckinpah movie *Straw Dogs* (1972), his Oscar nominated portrayal of Lenny Bruce in Bob Fosse's *Lenny* (1974), the real-life political thriller in which he played Carl Bernstein, *All the President's Men* (1976), and his last hit of the 1970s, *Marathon Man* (1976).

Having been nominated several times for Academy Awards, the actor was overdue when he finally won his Oscar for *Kramer vs. Kramer* (1980). Had Ben Kingsley not taken the statuette for *Gandhi* in 1982, Hoffman might have won again for his tour de force in *Tootsie* (1982), one of the actor's most successful movies.

After *Tootsie,* he was not seen on the big screen for several years, having a smash success on Broadway as Willy Loman in an acclaimed revival of Arthur Miller's *Death of a Salesman,* a production that was later adapted for television, with Hoffman recreating his role. When he finally returned to the movies, however, it was in the $50 million megaflop *Ishtar* (1987). Neither Hoffman nor his costar Warren Beatty *(q.v.)* were big enough box office draws to compensate for the negative press of this mediocre comedy. But Hoffman quickly recouped in 1988 when he played the autistic savant brother of Tom Cruise in *Rain Man,* a film that brought Hoffman his second Best Actor Oscar.

HOLDEN, WILLIAM (1918–1981) An actor who became one of Hollywood's leading romantic sex symbols of the 1950s, his career spanned more than forty years and nearly seventy starring roles. He brought a virile humanity to his performances that satisfied the public even when his films did not. With his tall, athletic physique and open-faced good looks, there was something likable about Holden even when he played cynics and soreheads.

Born William Franklin Beedle, Jr., he came from a well-to-do family. He went to Pasadena Junior College with the expectation of studying chemistry and joining his father's chemical company. But while in school he was spotted by a Paramount talent scout and given a standard seven-year contract. His first film appearance was as a member of a road gang in *Prison Farm* (1938). After just one more bit part in the Betty Grable *(q.v.)* musical *Million Dollar Legs* (1939), he won the role of the boxer/violinist in *Golden Boy* (1939). Despite his lack of acting polish, the film was a moderate success and, though Holden didn't become a major star, he did jump from bit player to leading juvenile actor virtually overnight.

More than most actors, Holden had to learn on the job. After *Golden Boy,* he appeared in supporting roles in films such as *Invisible Stripes* (1940) and *Our Town* (1940) as he continued to learn his craft. His career improved steadily, if unspectacularly, in films such as *Arizona* (1941), *I Wanted Wings* (1941), and *Texas* (1941). At this time, he married actress Brenda Marshall, a union that lasted until their divorce in 1970. After starring in a few more minor films, he enlisted in the Army in 1942, the first married star to join up.

He didn't appear in a Hollywood film again until 1947, when he starred in *Blaze of Noon.* He worked steadily thereafter but he neither excited film fans nor critics, until he filled in for Montgomery Clift *(q.v.),* who was supposed to star in Billy Wilder's *Sunset Boulevard* (1950). The film was not a box office hit, but it was critically acclaimed, and Holden finally established himself as a reputable actor with the added bonus of a Best Actor Oscar nomination for his performance in the film.

Holden reached the peak of his career during the 1950s. Not long after *Sunset Boulevard* reached movie theaters, he was in another big hit, *Born Yesterday* (1950), a movie that made fun of Holden's studio boss, Harry Cohn *(q.v.).* But the true turning point in Holden's path to major stardom was his tough, cynical performance in Billy Wilder's *Stalag 17* (1953). This time Holden was not only nominated, he won the Academy Award for Best Actor.

With exceptions, Holden appeared far more regularly in excellent films, such as the Hays Code-challenging *The Moon is Blue* (1953), *Sabrina* (1954), *The Country Girl* (1954), *The Bridges at Toko-Ri* (1955), *Love Is a Many Splendored Thing* (1955), *Picnic* (1956), and the biggest blockbuster of them all, *The Bridge on the River*

Kwai (1957). In many of these films, Holden played lovers, cads, and the occasional reluctant hero. Considering that the 1950s represented a period of marked decline in Hollywood, Holden's long string of hit films was particularly impressive.

His film success began to slowly diminish during the late 1950s and early 1960s. Though he worked steadily, he didn't have a hit in over a decade. His star status and credibility as an actor were saved by a strong, convincing performance as Pike Bishop in Sam Peckinpah's controversial film, *The Wild Bunch* (1969). Holden's career throughout the 1970s was full of ups and downs. The actor seemed more interested in his conservation work in Africa than in the movies, but he managed a sensitive performance in the flop *Breezy* (1973), and was effective as Faye Dunaway's lover in the hit *Network* (1976). His last movie, *S.O.B.* (1981), a bitter Blake Edwards (q.v.) satire of Hollywood, was a fitting finale for an actor who cared little for the industry.

Holden, who fought a drinking problem for more than twenty years, died of an alcohol-related injury in his home.

HOLLIDAY, JUDY (1922–1965) A talented comedienne, Holliday projected vulnerability even as she chewed up the scenery in a series of brilliant performances in many of the better comedies of the 1950s. Her appearance allowed her to play both prim, repressed comic heroines as well as saucy, femmes fatales. Although she starred in only seven films, with noteworthy appearances in but four others, she had a considerable impact in the course of a ten-year Hollywood career that ended in her untimely death at the age of forty-three.

Born Judith Tuvim, she derived her stage name from *tuvim*, which means holiday in Hebrew. Her first important show business break came when she teamed with Betty Comden and Adolph Green (qq.v.) to form a cabaret act. Later, after a few small roles in films during the mid-1940s, Holliday gave up on Hollywood and concentrated on a Broadway career, soon starring in the hit stage comedy *Born Yesterday* in 1946. She came to the attention of film audiences in 1949 when she played the comically addled murder suspect in the hit Hepburn-Tracy vehicle, *Adam's Rib* (1949).

Holliday lit up the screen in 1950 when she reprised her role as Billie Dawn in *Born Yesterday,* playing the seemingly vapid and common broad who has more upstairs than anyone gives her credit for; her performance brought her an Oscar for Best Actress. In spite of her success in films, she continued to work as much on Broadway during the 1950s as she did in Hollywood. Her screen credits during the 1950s included a subtle and sensitive performance in the drama *The Marrying Kind* (1952), followed by the comedies *It Should Happen*

to You (1954), *Phffft* (1954), *The Solid Gold Cadillac* (1956), *Full of Life* (1957), and *Bells Are Ringing* (1960).

HOLLYWOOD Today, it is a somewhat seedy Los Angeles suburb, bereft of its one-time glamour as the titular capital of the movie world. But to most movie fans, past and present, Hollywood—also known as "The Dream Factory" and "Tinsel Town"—was never so much a place as a state of mind. Even during Hollywood's golden era of the 1930s and 1940s, the studios were spread far and wide across the Los Angeles basin.

"Hollywood" was originally the name of a ranch that existed on the site of the world's future film mecca. It was owned (and named) by a Mr. and Mrs. Wilcox, late of Kansas, who had retired there in 1886. Mr. Wilcox had been a successful real estate man and he put his skill to work again in 1891 when he began subdividing his ranch and selling homesites. In 1903, the sleepy little community was incorporated as a village, taking the name of the ranch as its own.

Meanwhile, the American film industry was growing by leaps and bounds in New York. It was, essentially, an East Coast business. But in 1907, movie production on a small scale began in the Los Angeles area when Colonel William N. Selig (q.v.) began shooting films there. The area of southern California appealed to filmmakers for a variety of reasons: Abundant year-round sunshine allowed more time to shoot movies, and the wildly varied terrain was suitable for making various genres of films outdoors. In 1908 when the Edison-inspired Motion Picture Patents Company began trying to put their competitors out of business, Southern California became a haven for upstart film companies trying to stay as far away from New York as they could. In addition, the Mexican border was close by for a quick escape from the law.

Hollywood became part of greater Los Angeles in 1910, but was still a backwater. That changed dramatically when Cecil B. DeMille (q.v.) arrived in 1913 with the intention of making his first movie there. He had planned to shoot his film in Flagstaff, Arizona, but he didn't care for the locale and kept on traveling by train until he reached the end of the line: Hollywood. There he made the feature-length hit *The Squaw Man* (1914), and suddenly, thanks to DeMille (who is sometimes referred to as the Father of Hollywood), filmmakers arrived in droves. By the time the Motion Picture Patents Company was dissolved in 1917, most major studios had come out to the Coast to make movies, keeping their business offices in New York.

Despite the fact that the big studios had built their massive soundstages and back lots in places as divergent as the San Fernando Valley and Culver City, Hollywood was the name that stuck to describe the home of the movie business. To movie audiences all over the world, the words "Made in Hollywood" ensured the most opulent, most professionally made, and most exciting movies available.

And so it remained until the late 1940s and early 1950s when the studio system (q.v.) finally ended. Forced to divest themselves of their movie theater chains in an anti-trust case and suffering big box office losses due to the newly expanding television medium, studios began to crumble. Films that would once have been routinely made in Hollywood were now shot overseas for tax reasons. In addition, stars, directors, and producers became independents, merely renting studio space to make their movies. Finally, the studios became largely distribution networks rather than genuine film producers. As this erosion took place, Hollywood's image as a film capital suffered.

Hollywood was saved by what had, at first, killed it: television. The film industry's soundstages and back lots continue to hum with activity today thanks to the steady production of TV series and TV movies where once the great classics of the silver screen were made. Yet, all these years later, "Hollywood" remains a synonym for "movie."

HOLLYWOOD ON FILM It was a natural step for moviemakers to exploit audience interest and fascination with the people and workings of the "Dream Factory" itself. And as the Hollywood studio system (q.v.) solidified during the 1920s, clever writers, directors, and producers began to make films that provided an upbeat and amusing glimpse of life in the moving picture business. *Ella Cinders* (1926), about a girl who wins a contest and takes off for Hollywood to make her fortune, is a perfect example.

There have been any number of amusing and endearing films that have painted a rosy, if goofy, view of Hollywood. Movies such as *Going Hollywood* (1933), *Hollywood Party* (1934), and *The Youngest Profession* (1943), presented the movie mecca as a loony bin full of quirky, funny, creative types. Often, however, the movies served merely as a convenient novel backdrop. Such was the case for W. C. Fields' *Never Give a Sucker an Even Break* (1941) and *Abbott and Costello in Hollywood* (1945).

Despite their often light touch, films about Hollywood began to express a more cynical vision as early as the 1930s. For instance, *Merton of the Movies* (1932), *What Price Hollywood?* (1932), *Boy Meets Girl* (1938), and *A Star Is Born* (1937) all took a jaundiced view of the emotional flim-flam that existed beneath tinsel town's surface. Perhaps the only movie that tried to come to terms with the gap between the commerce and the art of moviemaking was Preston Sturges' classic, *Sullivan's Travels* (1941). In that film, a successful director of inane comedies such as "Ants in Your Pants of 1939" decides he wants to make a serious statement in his next film, "Brother, Where Art Thou?" By the end of the film, Sullivan discovers that making escapist movies that allow people to forget their troubles is no small achievement.

Eventually, two decidedly different strains of movies about Hollywood emerged during the 1940s and continued into the 1950s. There were warm, nostalgic recreations of the past, such as *Singin' in the Rain* (1952) and the show business biopics (q.v.) that blossomed after the success of *The Jolson Story* (1946). Then there were the contemporary condemnation movies that not only bit the hand that fed them but chewed vigorously. After Billy Wilder's *Sunset Boulevard* (1950), the floodgates opened wide, releasing movies such as *The Bad and the Beautiful* (1952), *The Barefoot Contessa* (1954), the Judy Garland musical remake of *A Star is Born* (1954), and *The Big Knife* (1955). When the studios began to crumble during the 1950s, stars, writers, and directors were able to finally strike back at their tormentors.

Beginning in the 1960s, harsh contemporary views of Hollywood became few and far between, no doubt because the city's centrality to American film no longer existed except in symbol. But such dark movies as *Two Weeks in Another Town* (1962), *The Oscar* (1966), and *S.O.B.* (1981) did offer a biting comment on American film culture. And movies demythologizing old-time Hollywood such as *The Carpetbaggers* (1964), *Harlow* (two versions, both 1965), *The Day of the Locusts* (1975), *Inserts* (1976), and *Frances* (1982), painted a bleak vision of movieland corruption and decadence.

Finally, however, a less hysterical, if sardonic, view of Hollywood has recently emerged on the big screen. These movies about filmmaking are more accepting of the fact that there is a price to pay for creating illusions. Films of this kind include *The Comic* (1969), *The Purple Rose of Cairo* (1985), *Sweet Liberty* (1986), and even *Hollywood Shuffle* (1987).

HOLLYWOOD TEN The ten individuals who refused to testify before the House Un-American Activities Committee (HUAC) in 1947. Found in contempt of Congress, they were all eventually sentenced to one year in jail and fined $1,000. As a result, the Hollywood Ten became a symbol of the Communist witch-hunt mentality that swept through the entertainment industry (and the rest of America) during the height of the Cold War in the late 1940s and early 1950s. Paranoia concerning Russian intentions to undermine and destroy American society led to a Hollywood purge of vast proportions, with left-leaning actors, directors, and particularly writers, seeing their careers—and often their lives—destroyed.

Nine members of The Hollywood Ten, Alvah Bessie, Herbert Biberman, Lester Cole, Ring Lardner, Jr., John Howard Lawson, Albert Maltz, Samuel Ornitz, Adrian Scott, and Dalton Trumbo, were blacklisted—locked out from all work in the film industry—after they were released from jail. The tenth member of the group, director Edward Dmytryk *(q.v.)*, broke while in prison and agreed to cooperate with the committee, confessing his past affiliation with the Communist Party and offering the names of others who had also been members.

A great many people in the entertainment industry during the 1930s had seen communism as a viable form of government during the Great Depression. A parade of friendly witnesses, such as Sterling Hayden *(q.v.)*, Lloyd Bridges *(q.v.)*, Budd Schulberg, and Elia Kazan *(q.v.)*, admitted their past involvement in the Communist party, rejected that past, and then told of friends and associates who had been members of the party. With rumors and accusations flying—many of them unfounded—people who were named, and many who were not (and who had no history as Communists), were blacklisted.

HUAC returned to Hollywood in 1951 to continue its highly publicized hearings, calling on a parade of famous names to testify. It was a circus. Among those linked to the Communist Party were Sidney Buchman, Jules Dassin, Will Geer, Dashiell Hammett, Lillian Hellman, Joseph Losey, Abraham Polonsky, Robert Rossen *(q.v.)*, and many more. It seemed as if anyone was fair game. Among those testifying was author Ayn Rand who went so far as to describe Louis B. Mayer, the right-wing head of MGM, as being "no better than a Communist."

HUAC ran roughshod over Hollywood because everyone in the industry was afraid of being labeled a "red" if they spoke out against the committee. Eventually, however, in the early 1950s, a courageous group of filmmakers, led by John Huston and Humphrey Bogart *(qq.v.)*, publicly denounced HUAC's tactics and motives. But in the end, more than one thousand people were smeared with the Communist label and found that they were unable to defend themselves; many didn't even know they were on the blacklist until they suddenly couldn't find work.

Among others, the blacklist effectively destroyed the acting careers of Larry Parks and John Garfield *(q.v.)*, forced such directors as Joseph Losey and Jules Dassin to work in Europe, and sent scores of writers such as Dalton Trumbo into hiding, writing screenplays under assumed names and at cut-rate prices. Trumbo, in fact, won an Oscar for his screenplay of *The Brave One* (1956) under the name of Robert Rich!

At the movies, themselves, the red scare produced a spate of films during these years that mirrored the paranoia of the times. The most deeply right-wing of the lot was Leo McCarey's *My Son John* (1952), a film that detailed the horror a mother experiences upon learning her son is a "commie." While the western *High Noon* (1952) indirectly attacked American reluctance to stand tall against the bullying of HUAC and the red-

baiting Senator Joseph McCarthy, the movies generally kept a safe distance from material considered left wing throughout the rest of the 1950s, until the blacklist was finally abolished.

Hollywood, which had been torn apart by the political upheaval of the red-scare years, looked at its past in two modern films, *The Way We Were* (1973) and *The Front* (1976). The latter film was particularly noteworthy because its director, Martin Ritt, was a blacklist victim, as was one of its costars, Zero Mostel.
See also: Douglas, Kirk

HOPE, BOB (1903–   ) His screen character was usually that of a fast-talking, wisecracking, con man who ran scared at the first sign of trouble. He also thought he was God's gift to women and couldn't understand why he never got the girl. From his solo hits to his legendary partnership with Bing Crosby *(q.v.)* in the famous Road movies, Hope fashioned a remarkable film career that made him Hollywood's most successful comic actor for a period of nearly fifteen years. And it's no accident that he has been admired and studied for his comic timing by a great many subsequent film comedians, including Woody Allen *(q.v.)*.

Born Leslie Townes Hope in London, his family imigrated to America and settled in Cleveland when he was four years old. After winning several Charlie Chaplin impersonation contests he found the courage to try his hand at vaudeville. Starting with "Songs, Patter and Eccentric Dancing," he eventually made his way to Broadway, appearing in the hit show *Roberta* (1933).

Several other successful Broadway shows followed and his reputation as a comic actor led to his own radio show. When Paramount decided to continue their series of Big Broadcast movies with *The Big Broadcast of 1938,* they hired a great number of radio personalities, including Hope. It was his first film and he acquitted himself well, singing with Shirley Ross the song that was to become his theme, "Thanks for the Memories."

Hope continued in movies, participating in several minor efforts until he made *The Cat and the Canary* (1939), a funny horror film in which he began perfecting his special brand of comic cowardice. The movie was a hit, but it was just the beginning.

The 1940s, Hope's richest decade in terms of hits and quality comedies, began with his first teaming with Bing Crosby and Dorothy Lamour *(q.v.)* in the original Road movie, *The Road to Singapore* (1940). There were seven Road movies in all, and the Hope/Crosby team became one of the most beloved duos in all of film comedy; because it seemed as if the two stars were having the time of their lives.

There is a tendency to forget the enormous number of films Hope made because of his long television career beginning in the 1950s. But he was a bona fide movie star of long duration who entered the top-ten list of

While modern audiences might think of Bob Hope as a TV star, he was actually an extremely potent box office personality during the 1940s, thanks in part to the Road movies he made with his pal, Bing Crosby (pictured right). Photo courtesy of The Siegel Collection.

money-makers in 1941, and stayed in the top ten every single year until 1953, with hits such as *Monsieur Beaucaire* (1945), *My Favorite Brunette* (1947), and a good many others. In 1949, he was voted the number-one box office star in the country, thanks to his hit comedy, *Paleface* (1948), with Jane Russell *(q.v.)*.

In the mid-1950s, however, Hope's film comedies began to falter. Except for a few solid efforts such as *The Seven Little Foys* (1955), *Beau James* (1957), and the last of the Road movies with Crosby, most of Hope's movies of the latter 1950s and 1960s were rather stale. By this time he had become more of a television star than a film star. But if Bob Hope is an American institution, the foundation of that institution was laid with his classic comedies of the 1940s.

See also: comedy teams

HOPPER, DENNIS (1936–   ) The wayward actor and director whose thirty-five-year film career has been subject to steep peaks and deep valleys. Known to have been an obstinate, impossible young actor early in his career, he became a director notorious for his drug use. Perhaps best known for having directed, coscripted, and costarred in *Easy Rider* (1969, *q.v.*)—a landmark movie that temporarily changed the face of Holly-

wood—Hopper later emerged in the 1980s from a hell of his own creation to shine as a brilliant character actor and imaginative director.

Hopper thought he was hot stuff until he met James Dean *(q.v.)* on the set of *Rebel Without a Cause* (1955). Hopper played Goon, a minor character in that classic film, but found himself mightily impressed with Dean and his "method" style of acting. Hopper continued to appear in minor roles, including one in Dean's *Giant* (1956). Hopper displayed his own rebelliousness while filming *From Hell to Texas* (1958) when he refused to play a scene as ordered by veteran director Henry Hathaway *(q.v.)*. In a famous test of wills, Hopper finally relented after an incredible 85 takes. Word of Hopper's stubborness spread quickly through the film industry and he soon found himself persona non grata in Hollywood—at least until he married Brooke Hayward, the daughter of actress Margaret Sullavan and top film agent Leland Hayward.

By virtue of his wife's connections, Hopper began appearing in movies again (even those of Henry Hathaway), including *The Sons of Katie Elder* (1965), *Cool Hand Luke* (1967), *Hang 'Em High* (1968), and *True Grit* (1969). He had small roles in the Hollywood establishment movies but leading roles in teen exploitation films such as *Queen of Blood* (1966), *The Trip* (1967), and *The Glory Stompers* (1967). His marriage to Hayward ended in 1969.

Itching to direct, Hopper talked fellow actor Peter Fonda into producing a motorcycle movie that the pair eventually cowrote and starred in. Made for $370,000, *Easy Rider* grossed more than $40 million. Hopper had proven that an independently made movie directed at the baby boom generation could be a huge commercial success, prompting studios to scramble to give young filmmakers the opportunity to make youth-oriented movies, most of which failed. Hopper's next film, *The Last Movie* (1971), also funded by a major studio was no exception: the film went way over budget and, due to Hopper's drug use, was virtually incomprehensible when finally edited.

Zonked out on drugs, Hopper drifted through the 1970s in a fog, occasionally appearing in foreign films, most memorably in Wim Wenders' *The American Friend* (1977).

In the early 1980s he began to clean up his act. He appeared in *Rumble Fish* (1983) and directed *Out of the Blue* (1983), a sort of "son of *Easy Rider*" that did not repeat the earlier movie's stunning success. Hopper relapsed and was ultimately committed to a mental hospital, where he finally kicked his drug and alcohol dependencies. Since then, he has been nothing short of astonishing, winning an Oscar nomination for Best Supporting Actor for his evocative performance in *Hoosiers* (1986), and gaining raves for his acting in *Blue*

Velvet (1986) and *River's Edge* (1987). He has also finally hit the top again as a director with the critically acclaimed *Colors* (1988).

HOPPER, HEDDA *See* gossip columnists.

HORNE, LENA *See* racism in Hollywood.

HORROR FILMS In their purest sense, movies based on the sinister supernatural or events that occur when "man meddles in things better left untouched." Therefore, scary science fiction films, such as *Invasion of the Body Snatchers,* movies about creatures from a prehistoric past, such as *King Kong,* and psychological suspense movies, such as *Psycho,* are not classified here as "horror" films. But horror does include just about everything else capable of raising goose bumps.

The horror film is not a distinctly American genre in the way the western and gangster films are. While the German Expressionists, for example, were making sophisticated horror films such as *The Golem* (1914), *The Cabinet of Dr. Caligari* (1919), and *Noseferatu* (1921), filmmakers in the U.S. made only the rare horror movie, such as John Barrymore's *Dr. Jekyll and Mr. Hyde* (1920).

In fact, it wasn't until the 1920s that Hollywood even began to compete with the Europeans in the lucrative horror market. While there were, for instance, many Hollywood comedy stars of the silent era, there was only one true horror star: Lon Chaney *(q.v.).* He specialized in the macabre and the horrific, making movies such as *The Phantom of the Opera* (1925) and *The Monster* (1925).

Soon after the talkie revolution, Hollywood reigned supreme in the horror genre. And yet, even after doing so, the horror film quickly became a Hollywood stepchild, reduced to "B" movie *(q.v.)* status, and rarely taken seriously as a means of cinematic expression.

Nonetheless, when the horror film was suddenly revived in 1931 with the presentation of Tod Browning's *Dracula* starring Bela Lugosi *(q.v.),* Hollywood took notice. The movie was a sensation, assuring a spate of sequels that have conferred a certain cinematic immortality that not even a celluloid spike could end. Lugosi often reprised his role as the vampire, and he was not the only actor to do so.

Lugosi might have gone on to even greater fame had he not turned down the role of *Frankenstein* (1931), giving Boris Karloff *(q.v.)* his chance at stardom. *Frankenstein,* directed by James Whale *(q.v.),* was just as big a hit as *Dracula* had been, and these two films formed the basic core of all future Hollywood horror films. In fact, Lugosi and Karloff became a virtual two-man horror acting unit, often appearing together in the same movies.

Both *Dracula* and *Frankenstein* had been made at Universal Studios. Just as Paramount was known for comedies, Warners for gangster films, and MGM for romantic gloss, Universal in the 1930s was known for its horror films.

The golden period of the horror film was certainly the early to mid-1930s. Tod Browning and James Whale continued directing horror films, creating some of the genre's best, such as Browning's *Freaks* (1932), and Whale's *The Invisible Man* (1933) and *The Bride of Frankenstein* (1935). They were joined by other directors such as Karl Freund *(q.v.),* who made *The Mummy* (1932), and Rouben Mamoulian *(q.v.),* who directed the definitive version of *Dr. Jekyll and Mr. Hyde* (1932), starring Fredric March *(q.v.)* in an Oscar-winning role (remade with Spencer Tracy *[q.v.]* in the title role in 1941). Stuart Walker directed *Werewolf of London* (1935), *Halloween* (1978) and *Friday the 13th* (1980), plus all of their respective bloody spawn.

By the latter 1930s, the genre was already declining with inferior sequels and remakes. The slide was halted in the early 1940s by producer Val Lewton *(q.v.)* at RKO who was responsible for a number of low-budget but atmospheric horror films such as *Cat People* (1942) and *I Walked With a Zombie* (1943).

The familiar 1930s horror characters were eventually lampooned in *Abbott and Costello Meet Frankenstein* (1948). The film was both funny and scary—as well as hugely popular, leading to its own inferior sequels in which Abbott & Costello *(q.v.)* met the Invisible Man (1951), Dr. Jekyll and Mr. Hyde (1953), and so on.

By this point it might have appeared that the horror film was dead. And by the early 1950s, it also seemed as if Hollywood was dead. In the search to bring people back into theaters, 3-D was offered to the public, which enjoyed the novelty. And there was no better effect with which to scare people than 3-D; e.g., a slimy hand seemingly extended into the audience had a frightening effect. It is no wonder, then, that 3-D movies such as a remake of *House of Wax* (1953) and *The Creature From the Black Lagoon* (1954) brought the horror movie back with a vengeance.

By the late 1950s, American International Pictures *(q.v.)* and their prime director, Roger Corman *(q.v.),* had taken up the torch of the horror film. They made their movies fast and cheap—and usually it showed. Films such as *I Was a Teenage Werewolf* (1957) starring Michael Landon were directed specifically to the teenage drive-in theater market. Corman ultimately made a series of movies starring Vincent Price *(q.v.)* that were based on the writings of Edgar Allen Poe. These films, such as *The Pit and the Pendulum* (1961) and *The Raven* (1963), lifted the A.I.P. films to a stylized, campy height that most latter-day horror films have never quite achieved.

The violent, gory horror film had its birth in 1968 when George Romero *(q.v.)* made his now classic *Night of the Living Dead* in Pittsburgh with an unknown cast and a miniscule budget. Based on the success of that shocking movie, the 1970s and 1980s have witnessed a boom in the horror genre with enormous hits such as *Halloween* (1978) and *Friday the 13th* (1980), plus all of their respective bloody spawn.

The horror movie hasn't been entirely relegated to the exploitation market. The 1970s and 1980s have seen some big-budget "A" films *(q.v.)* in this area, such as *The Exorcist* (1973), *The Omen* (1976), and *Poltergeist* (1982). But even these serious, successful films were followed by exploitive poorly done remakes.

There isn't another genre that has so fed upon itself as horror. Any creature, monster, or supernatural apparition that succeeds on screen is bound to return time and again. Yet there is something comforting about the recycled nature of the horror film. The images of Dracula, the Mummy, and Frankenstein, are part of our collective nightmares, and their continuing permutations in the movies let us know with a (dread) certainty that there is always something out there in the dark waiting to grab us and make us scream. Horror on film has been especially effective because movies are so similar to dreams; the best of them are nightmares that we experience with our eyes wide open in a dark theater.

HOUSEMAN, JOHN (1902–1988) A renaissance man who successfully wrote, produced, and directed entertainments in radio, theater, and film. Late in life, Houseman became an Oscar-winning actor and a highly recognized personality. He was involved in the writing of two motion pictures, one of them an unequaled masterpiece. As a producer, he has been associated with a great many quality movies of the late 1940s and 1950s.

Born Jacques Haussmann to a prosperous Alsation father and an English mother, he was educated in England and arrived in New York in the mid-1920s to represent his father's grain business. Not long after coming to America, Houseman began his increasingly influential work in the theater, at first translating German and French plays into English, and soon writing, directing, and producing plays directly for the stage—with considerable success.

His story took a fateful turn when Houseman befriended the "boy wonder," Orson Welles *(q.v.)*. Together, they founded the famous Mercury Theater in 1937. They also worked together in radio, including the historic Halloween eve broadcast of H. G. Wells' *The War of the Worlds*.

Unbeknownst to most, *Citizen Kane* (1941) was not Orson Welles' first movie. Houseman produced and had a small role in *Too Much Johnson* (1938), a film Welles never completed. In any event, Houseman's

influence on Welles' masterpiece, *Citizen Kane,* was also significant. Though uncredited, he helped devise the story and he supervised the script revisions. Unfortunately for Welles, their fruitful association—and their friendship—ended in 1941. Houseman went on to work briefly for David O. Selznick Productions before quitting to join the war effort in radio communications in early December of 1941.

When he returned to Hollywood, Houseman co-scripted one film, *Jane Eyre* (1944), which ironically starred Welles. He then went on to produce such hits as *The Blue Dahlia* (1946), Max Ophul's classic *Letter From an Unknown Woman* (1948), the first film of his young protégé, Nicholas Ray *(q.v.), They Live By Night* (1949), then Nicholas Ray's *On Dangerous Ground* (1952), Vincente Minnelli's *The Bad and the Beautiful* (1952), Joseph L. Mankiewicz's Shakespearean all-star *Julius Caesar* (1953), and two more Vincente Minnelli winners, *Lust for Life* (1956) and *Two Weeks in Another Town* (1962).

In the mid-1960s, Houseman took his first acting role (*Too Much Johnson,* aside) in *Seven Days in May* (1964). But it was for his second film appearance, as the autocratic, tyrannical Professor Kingsfield in *The Paper Chase* (1973), that he received a great deal of attention, stealing the movie and winning an Academy Award for Best Supporting Actor as well. He went on to recreate the role in a TV series of the same name.

Houseman later appeared in many TV movies as well as in such theatrical films as *Rollerball* (1975), *Three Days of the Condor* (1975), *St. Ives* (1976), *The Cheap Detective* (1978), *My Bodyguard* (1980), *The Fog* (1980), *Bells* (1980), *Ghost Story* (1981), and others. In the years before his death, he became best known to the mass audience as a TV pitchman for several different products, all of which benefited from his no-nonsense delivery.

HOWARD, LESLIE (1893–1943) He was among the most charming of English actors ever to grace a Hollywood soundstage. With his long, thin face, sensitive eyes, high forehead, and delightfully musical speaking voice, Howard was an upper-crust hero who was at his best playing clever but kindly intellectuals and idealistic dreamers. Though English by birth and beloved in his home country, most of his movies were either made or financed by Hollywood studios. And as far as American audiences were concerned, he was *their* Englishman.

Born Leslie Stainer in London to Hungarian parents, Howard was a first-generation Englishman who fought for his country in World War I only to be sent home in 1917 suffering from shell shock. It was his mother's idea that he get involved in the theater to get his mind off his troubles. He learned his trade on the stage over the next five years before becoming a Broadway notable in 1922, when he made his New York debut in *Just Suppose*.

He was a major star of the stage throughout the rest of the 1920s and it led to the filming of one of his stage hits *Outward Bound*, for Warner Bros. in 1930. The bizarre film about people on an ocean liner who eventually discover that they are all dead was a surprise hit and Howard became a hot property in Hollywood.

He starred in films for MGM, RKO, and Paramount over the next two years, the best of his films being *Service for Ladies* (1932). He had been considered for the part of Dr. Henry Frankenstein in the 1931 film *Frankenstein,* but the role went to Colin Clive, instead. And perhaps both actors were best served by that decision.

Howard also nixed the role of Garbo's lover in *Queen Christina* (1933) because he thought, and rightly so, that he'd be overshadowed by the actress. But he scored a hit in *Berkeley Square* that same year and signed a nine-film contract with Warner Bros. that led to his starring with Bette Davis *(q.v.)* in the critical success *Of Human Bondage* (1934). Warner then loaned him to Alexander Korda in England for what became one of Howard's biggest triumphs of the 1930s, *The Scarlet Pimpernel* (1935).

Howard, meanwhile, had starred on Broadway in the *Petrified Forest*. When Warner Bros. bought the rights to the play with the intention of having Howard star as the dreamy idealist hero, the actor balked unless his costar in the play, Humphrey Bogart *(q.v.),* was allowed to play Duke Mantee in the film version. The studio eventually agreed and Bogart's film career was established.

A picture Howard should have refused at all costs, however, was *Romeo and Juliet* (1936). He was too old to play Romeo but he spoke the lines beautifully, nonetheless, and the critics were kind.

In the latter 1930s, Howard found his way into a couple of delightful light comedies, *It's Love I'm After* (1937) and *Stand-In* (1937), but his three best-remembered roles from the end of the decade were in *Pygmalion* (1938), *Intermezzo* (1939), and *Gone With the Wind* (1939).

Howard starred in and codirected *Pygmalion* with Gabriel Pascal in England, and his performance as Professor Henry Higgins is a gem. He was offered *Intermezzo* by Selznick if only the actor would play Ashley Wilkes in *Gone With the Wind,* a role that Howard detested. The actor agreed and Howard's portrayal of Ashley is the one by which most casual movie fans remember him today.

When war broke out in Europe, Howard returned to England to star, direct, and produce rousing pro-English/anti-Nazi films that cheered his countrymen, the most memorable of them being *Pimpernel Smith* (1941) and *Spitfire* (1942). As a symbol of England's steadfast courage, Howard was sent to Spain and Portugal by his government on a secret mission to help keep those two countries from joining forces with the Axis powers. On his return trip, his plane was shot down by Nazi fighters who thought they were attacking Winston Churchill's plane returning from Algiers that same day. Leslie Howard was killed and his loss was mourned by millions on both sides of the Atlantic.

HOWARD, RON (1954–) Originally a child actor in movies (and later on TV) known as Ronny Howard, he has developed into one of Hollywood's most successful young directors. With a commercial touch leavened with a surprising sensitivity, he has fashioned an enviable record of critical and box office hits during the 1980s.

Howard began acting at two years of age when he appeared on stage with his parents in a Baltimore production of *The Seven Year Itch*. The first of his handful of early film appearances was in *The Journey* (1959). He was more noticeable in *The Music Man* (1962) and finally the very center of attention in *The Courtship of Eddie's Father* (1963). He was best known, however, as Opie on TV's long-running "Andy Griffith Show" and later as Richie on "Happy Days." His Richie was a reprise, of sorts, of the ordinary high school senior he played in George Lucas' *(q.v.)* hit film *American Graffiti* (1973, *q.v.*).

The actor didn't fare very well as Ron Howard, a name he preferred after becoming an adult. Typed by his success in "Happy Days," he had few roles of note until he played the young man who learned a few lessons about life from John Wayne *(q.v.)* in *The Shootist* (1976) and then starred in a low-budget but fast-paced racing movie, *Eat My Dust!* (1976). His success in the latter film gave him the opportunity to cowrite, direct, and star in a similar film, *Grand Theft Auto* (1977), which turned a profit at the box office and received some admiring nods from the critics for its competence and energy.

During the 1980s, Howard emerged from low-budget crash and cash films with *Night Shift* (1982), the sleeper comedy hit of the year, which he followed with yet another comedy hit surprise, *Splash* (1984). Howard then made the ambitious science-fiction drama, *Cocoon* (1985), and won universal praise for his sensitive direction of one of the year's biggest box office winners. It appeared as if he could do no wrong until he directed *Gung Ho* (1986), a badly calculated flop. Yet producer and writer George Lucas had plenty of faith in Howard and invited him to direct *Willow* (1988), a big budget fantasy film that was a box office disappointment. He rebounded smartly, however, with his direction of *Parenthood* (1989).

HOWE, JAMES WONG (1899–1976) One of the giants of cinematography, his career in Hollywood spanned fifty years. Howe's black-and-white photography, in

James Wong Howe, one of Hollywood's greatest cinematographers, was given the nickname Low Key Howe. His low-key lighting style gave a distinctively dark and moody look to the *films noir* of the 1940s. Photo courtesy of Movie Star News.

particular, was always sensitive and ingenious. He worked for virtually all of the major studios, but in the late 1930s and 1940s, he did some of his best work for Warner Bros., or so it seemed until his artistry was put on full view in his two Oscar-winning films, *The Rose Tattoo* (1955) and *Hud* (1963).

Howe's original name was Wong Tung Jim. Drawn to the fledgling movie business, he began working in Hollywood in 1917 as an assistant cameraman to Cecil B. DeMille *(q.v.)*, eventually becoming a second cameraman. His promotion to director of photography in 1923 was the result of a fluke.

Howe had taken some still photographs of one of DeMille's great stars, Mary Miles Minter. She loved the pictures and insisted that he become her cameraman on all her movies. He found out specifically why she wanted him when he was called into her dressing room. In Leonard Maltin's interview book, *Behind the Camera,* Howe relates the story as follows: " 'You know why I like these pictures, Jimmy? Because you made my eyes go dark.' She had pale blue eyes, and in those days the film was insensitive to blue, and they washed out. And I didn't realize how I'd made her eyes go dark! I walked and stood where I took the pictures, and there was a

huge piece of black velvet. Something told me, 'Well, it must be a reflection. The eye is like a mirror. If something is dark, it will reflect darker.' So I cut a hole in it (the velvet), and put my lens through, and made all her close-ups that way . . . that's how I became a cameraman . . . Everybody who had light blue eyes wanted to have me as their cameraman!"

It was a time of innovation. Movies were young and the camera was often a mystery, even to those who depended upon it for their living. But Howe was a master of unlocking the camera's secrets, and his contributions to the one hundred eighteen feature films he worked on is incalculable.

His first was *Drums of Fate* (1923) starring, of course, Mary Miles Minter. He photographed all genres of films, from swashbucklers such as *The Prisoner of Zenda* (1937) to war movies such as *Air Force* (1943). He was just as sensitive to boxing movies, such as the stunningly photographed *Body and Soul* (1947), as he was to musicals, such as his crisp *Yankee Doodle Dandy* (1942). And one of his most memorable movies, a film that benefited from his knowledge and expertise with shooting in black and white, was John Frankenheimer's *Seconds* (1967).

Howe dabbled with directing, making one movie, *Go Man Go,* in 1952. Happily, he returned to cinematography, working until 1975 and ending his illustrious career that year with *Funny Lady.*

HUDSON, ROCK (1925–1985)   A performer whose career in the late 1940s and early 1950s was based strictly on his good looks, but who slowly emerged as a competent and popular actor. Hudson began in action pictures and westerns, moved on to romantic dramas in the mid-1950s, and then flowered in light romantic comedies in the late 1950s and early 1960s. His career was heavily based on his strong masculine image but, ironically, it was well known within the Hollywood community that he was a homosexual. His secret finally emerged in the media when he fell ill and then died of AIDS.

Born Roy Scherer, Jr., he later took his stepfather's last name of Fitzgerald. After graduating from high school he became a mailman, and then a mechanic in the Navy during World War II. He drifted from job to job after the war, unsure of his direction. Told that with his looks he ought to be in pictures, he drifted to Hollywood and found that the movie people agreed. His name was changed to Rock Hudson (as fake a name as the industry has ever conjured), and he was given his chance in a small role in *Fighter Squadron* (1948). Thoroughly green, with no training as an actor whatsoever, he required thirty-eight takes before the director was satisfied with his very first line. It got easier after that, but his was a long learning process that took several years.

Audiences liked him, though, and he continued to learn his craft in ever larger roles in low-budget action movies and westerns such as *Undertow* (1949), *I Was a Shoplifter* (1950), *Winchester '73* (1950), *The Desert Hawk* (1950), and *Tomahawk* (1951).

By late 1951 and early 1952, Hudson had become a leading man in a number of films, rounding out the casts of modest movies of the ilk of *Bright Victory* (1951), and two Budd Boetticher *(q.v.)* westerns, *Horizons West* (1952) and *Seminole* (1953). His big break came in 1954 when he played the male lead in *Magnificent Obsession,* a romantic movie that scored heavily at the box office, propelling him to matinee-idol status. While he continued acting in occasional action films, his career veered toward movies such as *One Desire* (1955), aimed primarily at female fans, and several Douglas Sirk films, including *All That Heaven Allows* (1956), *Written on the Wind* (1957), and *Tarnished Angels* (1958), films that were dismissed as mere "women's pictures" in the 1950s but which have since become considered minor classics. Nonetheless, Hudson's most important role of the mid-1950s was in the epic *Giant* (1956), in which he starred with Elizabeth Taylor and James Dean *(qq.v.),* and for which Hudson was honored by his peers with an Oscar nomination for Best Actor.

After a decade in Hollywood, Hudson entered the most memorable phase of his career when he costarred with Doris Day *(q.v.)* in *Pillow Talk* (1959), a bright, breezy comedy that, for its day, was considered mildly risqué. The film was a huge hit and Hudson and Day were teamed together in *Lover Come Back* (1961) and *Send Me No Flowers* (1964). They made just those three films together but the impact they had was so great that it is often assumed that they acted together far more frequently. Hudson did go on to make other light comedies, including *Man's Favorite Sport* (1964) and *Strange Bedfellows* (1965), but they did not feature Day.

Hudson surprised audiences and critics alike when he starred in John Frankenheimer's brilliant *Seconds* (1966). It was unarguably the actor's best performance in his nearly twenty years in the movie business. The film, unfortunately, was ahead of its time and it wasn't the hit it should have been. No other major box office winners followed and, despite his still youthful good looks, his film career was suddenly in jeopardy.

He continued to make the occasional movie during the 1970s but with little effect. Instead, he wisely put his efforts into developing a television career. He starred in the hit show "McMillan and Wife" from 1971 through 1975. In the last decade of his life, he tried starring in two other TV series, neither of which caught on, and, later, made a modest comeback in a recurring role in the prime-time TV soap "Dynasty." In the end, however, he will probably be remembered by many as the first major Hollywood star to die of AIDS.

HUGHES, HOWARD (1905–1976)   This eccentric billionaire remains one of the most fascinating figures in Hollywood history despite the relatively few movies he is closely associated with. But in spite of his modest output as a producer, Hughes is directly responsible for having created three movie stars and four landmark films. He is also the man who presided over the demise of RKO *(q.v.)* Radio Pictures, Inc.

Hughes began life with a silver spoon in his mouth; he was the son of the man who revolutionized the oil industry with the invention of a new, powerful drill bit. But he proceeded to turn that spoon to platinum. Tragically, both Hughes' parents died within two years of each other while he was in his teens. The orphan millionaire took over the Hughes Tool Company at the age of eighteen and decided soon thereafter to go into the movie business.

Hughes' Uncle Rupert was one of Hollywood's most successful screenwriters, and it was through this relation that Hughes had become acquainted with the movie business. His Uncle Rupert, however, advised him to stay out of Hollywood and was of no help to him, except inadvertently to spur the stubborn twenty-year-old on to success.

Hughes' career as a producer started badly. He made *Swell Hogan* (1925), starring Ralph Graves, a movie so poor that Hughes refused to ever let it be shown. The second film he produced was *Everybody's Acting* (1926), which was a modest hit. His third film, however, brought him a measure of respect in a town that had written him off as a naive rich kid. The movie was *Two Arabian Knights* (1927), and it won the Academy Award for Best Director of a Comedy for Lewis Milestone *(q.v.)*.

With his early success, Hughes was emboldened to make a film that was close to his heart. The young man was fascinated by airplanes, and his next movie, *Hell's Angels* (1930), was devoted to them. The film project was begun in 1928, but this time Hughes was intimately involved in the production. It was with *Hell's Angels* that he was deservedly tagged with the reputation of being both a meddler and a perfectionist. Two other Hughes productions would be released while this movie, a labor of love, was being filmed. After two directors quit because of his interference, Hughes finally took over the directorial chores of *Hell's Angels* himself.

The movie was shot as a silent film, but most of the footage had to be tossed out (except for the aviation scenes) because of the talkie revolution. For the reshooting, one important addition was made by Hughes; he hired a virtually unknown actress, Jean Harlow *(q.v.)*, as his new leading lady. In the process, he turned her into a star.

The film was a hit, thanks to Harlow and the aviation footage. The total cost of the film (excluding the human toll—three fliers died in crashes during the production) was nearly $4 million. Despite its box office pull, the movie was so expensive that it barely broke even.

Hughes went on to produce other films in the early 1930s, and two of them were truly memorable. The first of these was *The Front Page* (1931), directed by Lewis Milestone and based on the hit play by Ben Hecht *(q.v.)* and Charles MacArthur. This comedy about journalists established the still-existing cultural perception of newspapermen as tough, wisecracking, and resourceful loners.

The second important film Hughes produced in the early 1930s was *Scarface* (1932), the gangster movie that launched Paul Muni's *(q.v.)* film career as well as hastened the strict enforcement of the Hays Code *(q.v.)*.

After *Scarface*, Hughes temporarily ended his career as a producer. He later resurfaced, making *The Outlaw* (1943), the first "sexy" western. In the process, he turned busty, nineteen-year-old Jane Russell *(q.v.)* into a star, just as he had Jean Harlow a decade earlier. The racy film was an enormous success despite its poor quality, but more important, it was a breakthrough in the effort against movie censorship.

Through the balance of World War II, Hughes once again stopped making pictures, this time concentrating on aviation projects for the war effort.

He returned to Hollywood in the latter half of the 1940s, producing, among other things, *Mad Wednesday* (1947), with Preston Sturges *(q.v.)* directing. The film, starring the former silent screen comedian Harold Lloyd *(q.v.)*, had its moments but it was poorly received by audiences.

Hughes then stunned Hollywood by purchasing the ailing RKO studio in 1948, which he proceeded to run into the ground over an eight-year period before selling it in 1955. He made very few quality movies during his RKO period, although there were some modest money-makers. The best of the lot were *Flying Leathernecks* (1951) and *Split Second* (1953). At the end of his Hollywood career, he tried to top the success of *Hell's Angels* with *Jet Pilot* (1957), but the film was both an artistic and commercial failure.

The enigmatic Hughes meant more to Hollywood than the movies he produced. He was a symbol of its excesses and eccentricities—and also of its glamour. He dated some of the movie capital's most famous stars, including Katharine Hepburn, Olivia de Havilland, Ginger Rogers, Linda Darnell, Lana Turner, Bette Davis, Yvonne De Carlo, Elizabeth Taylor, Ava Gardner, and Jean Peters, whom he married in 1955.

Hughes, who had been living outside of the United States, died while being transported to Texas by airplane. For a man who loved airplanes as much as Hughes, to die while in flight was certainly an ironic end.

HUGHES, JOHN (–) A screenwriter, director, and sometime producer who has cornered the 1980s youth market, making both thoughtful and entertaining movies about teenagers that are very much from their point of view. Less well known is the fact that Hughes has also been a successful writer-director of outlandish comedies, responsible in large measure for many of the National Lampoon films of the last decade.

Hughes began his show business career as a gag writer before succumbing to the lure of advertising. When his unusual sense of humor could no longer be contained, he began writing for the *National Lampoon* magazine, eventually becoming a contributing editor. His association with the magazine brought him the opportunity to pen the screenplay for *National Lampoon's Class Reunion* (1982). It was not well-received by the critics, but it did well enough at the box office to successfully launch Hughes' screenwriting career.

Though he was half responsible (he cowrote the screenplay) for the bomb *Nate and Hayes* (1983), he came into his own as a screenwriter with two major critical and box office hits, *Mr. Mom* (1983) and *National Lampoon's Vacation* (1983). His subsequent zany comedies have fared less well with the critics but have generally been winners at the box office. His later hits of this kind have been *National Lampoon's European Vacation* (1985), which was based on his story, *Planes, Trains, and Automobiles* (1987), which he also directed, *The Great Outdoors* (1988), and *Uncle Buck* (1989).

His reputation as "the voice of the younger generation," however, has come from another set of movies. They, too, have been comedies, but are sympathetically focused on the trials and growing pains of teenagers, and lack any trace of condescension. Hughes has directed and occasionally produced a string of these films, making his directorial debut with *Sixteen Candles* (1984).

He followed that success by writing, directing, and producing *The Breakfast Club* (1985), a bold and somewhat innovative movie for the teen market that had the audacity to simply let a handful of young people speak their minds on film. It was a major hit, highlighting the talents of several young actors and helping to turn them into major teen stars, among them Molly Ringwald, Anthony Michael Hall, Judd Nelson, Emilio Estevez, and Ally Sheedy.

Hughes has written several other youth-market movies, including the pleasantly silly *Weird Science* (1985), and a joyous celebration called *Ferris Buehler's Day Off* (1986). He followed those films with a new departure, *She's Having a Baby* (1988), a movie that challenged his teenaged audience to face the prospects of marriage and parenthood. The film was neither a critical nor a commercial success, suggesting that Hughes will have to find another way to address his loyal following.

See also: brat pack; Broderick, Matthew; teen movies

HURT, WILLIAM (1950–) A gifted, versatile, and unpredictable actor who has made a strong impression on the screen in a relatively modest number of starring roles since beginning his film career in 1980. Tall and handsome, he could have easily been a romantic Hollywood leading man. Instead, he has chosen to portray an odd and intriguing assortment of characters, establishing himself as a serious actor who cares little for the trappings of stardom.

Hurt's father was a U.S. State Department official, and the young boy lived in a number of exotic South Pacific locales before his parents finally divorced. As a teenager, he lived briefly in New York City before his mother married Henry Luce 3rd, the son of the founder of *Time* magazine. Hurt then found himself continuing his education at the elite Middlesex School in Massachusetts. It was there that he started to act.

He began his college career at Tufts University as a theology major but soon switched to theater. Upon graduation, he attended Julliard to further his study of acting.

Next, he traveled to Oregon, where he acted in a theater festival presentation of *Long Day's Journey into Night* in 1975. Hurt later made his major breakthrough in the Circle Repertory Company production of *My Life* in 1977, winning an Obie (Off-Broadway) Award for his performance.

Hurt continued acting for Circle Rep. through the rest of the 1970s, refusing film offers until finally taking a leading role in Ken Russell's *Altered States* (1980). The movie received mixed reviews but the actor was acknowledged by the critics. He was next cast as the hero in the thriller *Eyewitness* (1981), and both he and the movie enjoyed a modest success. His third feature, the *film noir* suspense film *Body Heat* (1981), written and directed by Lawrence Kasdan, was a solid success for both Hurt and his costar, Kathleen Turner (*q.v.,* in her film debut).

Hurt, for his part, wasn't terribly interested in stardom, except for the clout it gave him to help get good roles. He happily joined the large ensemble cast of Lawrence Kasdan's highly regarded *The Big Chill* (1983), deliberately played down his role as the Russian detective in the disappointing *Gorky Park* (1983), and then took the off-beat role of a daydreaming homosexual prisoner in the low-budget *Kiss of the Spider Woman* (1985), an art-house hit that brought Hurt an Oscar for Best Actor for his unconventional portrayal.

The actor has continued to pursue good roles wherever he can find them, often returning to the stage to work. In films, he has continued to take on challenging roles, such as in *Children of a Lesser God* (1986), knowing that actress Marlee Maitlin would inevitably be the movie's focal point, and *Broadcast News* (1987) in which he played an anchorman of mediocre intelligence, knowing that actress Holly Hunter and actor Albert Brooks would steal the show. Happily, a number of critics commented on Hurt's understated performance. He has also recently reteamed with his *Body Heat* director Lawrence Kasdan and costar Kathleen Turner to give yet another quietly powerful performance in *The Accidental Tourist* (1988).

HUSTON, JOHN (1906–1987) A director, screenwriter, and actor who made many of Hollywood's most admired films during a long directorial career that spanned more than forty-five years. Huston directed several kinds of films but did his best work with serious adventure movies. He elevated such genres as the crime drama, the detective film, the war movie, and the boxing film to new heights of artistry. He was also an excellent screenwriter who was a skillful adapter of other writers' works. In fact, the vast majority of the feature films Huston wrote and directed were adaptations. He was among the first wave of talented writer-directors to come into prominence in Hollywood in the early 1940s.

During his first twelve years as a director, Huston was one of Hollywood's golden boys, but his reputation was later attacked by auteurist critics who found no unifying theme in his work. In the 1970s, however, critics rediscovered Huston's unique and highly creative ability to direct films whose heroes show a quixotic sort of courage, and Huston's entire career underwent a substantial reevaluation. Regardless of questions of theme, however it has always been clear that Huston was a gifted filmmaker who made his movies with intelligence, wit, and considerable style.

The son of actor Walter Huston, he began and ended his life as an actor. Huston made his stage debut at the age of three and worked quite often with his father on the vaudeville circuit in his youth. He nearly died when he was twelve years old from an enlarged heart and kidney, but fully recovered. Two years later he quit high school to become a prize fighter, winning twenty-three of twenty-five amateur bouts, and garnering the Amateur Lightweight Boxing Championship of California.

If his childhood wasn't colorful enough, Huston's early adult life was nearly blinding in its eccentricity. He became a professional stage actor in his late teens, enjoying some success, but ended that to join the Mexican Army, becoming a cavalry officer. He later performed in horse shows, wrote a musical play for puppets, and then made his film debut as an actor in a small role in William Wyler's *The Shakedown* (1928). He went on to appear in two other early sound features but walked away from that opportunity as well, becoming a short story writer and a reporter. The obviously talented but unfocused Huston continued his career changes throughout the early to mid-1930s, collaborating on several screenplays, most notably two that starred his father, *A House Divided* (1931) and *Law and Order* (1932). Later, he ran off to Europe to study art, nearly starving on the streets of Paris.

Finally, after short stints in America as a magazine editor and, again, as a stage actor, Huston returned to Hollywood to begin his film career in earnest. He tried his hand at screenwriting again. This time he had a real impact, collaborating on the screenplays of a number of major hits, among them *Jezebel* (1938), *The Amazing Dr. Clitterhouse* (1938), *Dr. Ehrlich's Magic Bullet* (1940), and *Sergeant York* (1941). His most important early screenplay, though, was for *High Sierra* (1941). He had struck a deal with mogul Jack Warner *(q.v.)* that he would be allowed to both write and direct a movie of his own if the film was a success. *High Sierra* was, of course, a smash hit and Huston had his chance.

For his first film as a writer-director, Huston decided to remake Dashiell Hammett's *The Maltese Falcon,* a novel that had been turned into a film twice before. With perfect casting, tight direction, and adroit screenwriting (he was the first to realize that Hammett's

dialogue was perfectly suitable for the screen), Huston turned *The Maltese Falcon* (1941, *q.v.*), into one of Hollywood's all-time classics.

He directed two more films of only modest distinction before heading off to war as a filmmaker in the Signal Corps. During World War II he made a number of stirring documentaries, two of which are considered landmark films, *The Battle of San Pietro* (1945) and *Let There Be Light* (1946), the latter so shattering in its depiction of the effects of shell shock that it was kept under wraps by the Pentagon for several decades.

Upon returning to Hollywood, Huston made what many consider his greatest film, *The Treasure of the Sierra Madre* (1948). One of the first films of the studio era to be made largely on location (in Mexico), the movie brought Huston's father an Oscar for Best Supporting Actor, and earned the director his only Academy Award.

The decade following *The Treasure of the Sierra Madre* was a rich and rewarding one for Huston. During that time he made many of his best movies, among them *Key Largo* (1948), *The Asphalt Jungle* (1950), for which he was nominated for an Oscar for Best Director, *The Red Badge of Courage* (1951), *The African Queen* (1951), for which he was again nominated, *Moulin Rouge* (1953), for which he gained yet another nomination, *Beat the Devil* (1954), a latter-day cult favorite, *Moby Dick* (1956), an ambitious undertaking that was much better than critics of the day realized, and *Heaven Knows Mr. Allison* (1957), an underrated minor masterpiece that had much in common with his earlier *African Queen.*

1956 was a turning point in Huston's career; *Moby Dick* was harpooned by the critics and sank at the box office. Used to one hit after another, Huston's erratic commercial success in the late 1950s and 1960s seemed like a fall from grace. His first genuinely bad movie was *The Barbarian and the Geisha.* Some fascinating critical and/or commercial flops followed, including *The Roots of Heaven* (1958), *Freud* (1962), *The Bible* (1964), *Reflections in a Golden Eye* (1967), *Sinful Davey* (1969), and *A Walk with Love and Death* (1969), the latter film starring his young daughter, Anjelica Huston.

But very good movies were to be found as well, a few of them hits, during that period: *The Unforgiven* (1960), *The Misfits* (1961), *The Night of the Iguana* (1964), and *Casino Royale* (1967)—all had much to recommend them.

In spite of these successful movies, it seemed as if the great director was in serious decline. But Huston fooled those who thought his best days were behind him when he directed one of the finest films about boxing ever made, *Fat City* (1972). Suddenly rediscovered, Huston went on to make, among other movies, the much-admired *The Man Who Would Be King* (1975), the art-house hit.*Wise Blood* (1979), and *Prizzi's Honor* (1985), for which he won his fifth Oscar nomination for Best Director and for which his daughter, Anjelica, won an Oscar for Best Supporting Actress. With Anjelica's award, the Huston family, became the first Hollywood dynasty to have three generations honored by the Academy.

The final film Huston directed was James Joyce's *The Dead* (1987), a lovely effort that served a fitting end to an illustrious career.

But John Huston was not content to stop working. He acted far more often in his later years. His long, evocative face and sonorous voice made him a much-in-demand character actor, and in addition to making appearances in some of his own films, he also acted in others, including *The Cardinal* (1963), *Candy* (1968), *Chinatown* (1974), *The Wind and the Lion* (1975), *Winter Kills* (1979), and many more. His last performance was in his adopted son director Danny Huston's *Mr. North* (1988), but he collapsed during the production and asked Robert Mitchum *(q.v.)* to replace him. John Huston died of emphysema before the picture was completed.

HUSTON, WALTER (1884–1950) An actor who could always be counted on to give an intelligent, thoughtful performance. Though he came to the movies in middle age and was a rather ordinary looking man, there were few film actors who could hold an audience's attention like Huston; he had a magnetic screen presence. Huston knew how to underplay a role and he was enormously versatile, playing everything from historical figures to romantic leads, to villains and kindly old characters in a film career that lasted more than twenty years.

Born Walter Houghston in Toronto, he tried to lead a "normal" life but was ultimately drawn to acting. Trained as an engineer, he chose to work on the stage, and did so with modest success until marrying his first wife in 1905 (with whom he had a son, the future writer-director John Huston). With a wife and child to care for, Huston soon deserted the stage for a series of jobs as an engineer.

The regular working life did not appeal to Huston and he eventually returned to acting in 1909, becoming a bigger star than ever before. He was a hit in vaudeville during the 1910s and his career soared even as the first of his three marriages soured. His reputation was such that Huston was offered starring roles on Broadway in the mid- to late 1920s and he scored major successes on the Great White Way in such plays as *Mr. Pitt* and *Desire Under the Elms.*

Lured to Hollywood during the sound film revolution, he made his movie debut in *Gentlemen of the Press* (1928), soon making an impact in the title role of D. W. Griffith's final masterwork, *Abraham Lincoln* (1930). The early 1930s was Huston's best era. He gave vivid performances in such memorable movies as *The Crim-*

inal Code (1931), *A House Divided* (1932), *American Madness* (1932), and *Rain* (1932). After returning to Broadway and scoring rave reviews in *Dodsworth,* he reprised his role for the 1936 film version of the play and was nominated for a Best Actor Academy Award.

Huston was seen less on the screen in the later 1930s, but had a major triumph in *All That Money Can Buy* (1941), garnering his second Academy Award nomination as Best Actor. It was also in 1941 that Huston's son, John, emerged as a hot young writer-director with *The Maltese Falcon,* a film in which the elder Huston made a cameo appearance as Captain Jacoby, dying on Sam Spade's couch with the falcon in his arms. He also made a cameo appearance in Huston's second film, *In This Our Life* (1942).

By this time, Huston had settled into character parts and he could be seen to fine effect playing such roles as James Cagney's father in *Yankee Doodle Dandy* (1942), for which he was honored with an Academy Award nomination for Best Supporting Actor, ambassador Joseph E. Davies in the ill-fated *Mission to Moscow* (1943), and Ling Tau in *Dragon Seed* (1944). Huston continued to give strong performances in major hit films throughout the rest of the decade, shining in such movies as *And Then There Were None* (1945), *Dragonwyck* (1946), and *Duel in the Sun* (1947).

Modern audiences undoubtedly remember Huston best for his role as the wise old prospector in his son's classic *The Treasure of the Sierra Madre* (1948). His performance brought him a Best Supporting Oscar just three years before his death in 1950. Huston's last film was *Furies* (1950), but his recorded talk-singing rendition of "September Song" from the stage production of *Dodsworth* became a posthumous hit for the actor when it was used in the film *September Affair* (1950). *See also:* Huston, John

HUTTON, BETTY (1921–) A big, bright, brassy star—mostly in musicals—over a ten-year period from 1942 to 1952, Hutton self-destructed and her film career came to an abrupt end. Hutton was known for her incredible exuberance and energy, which earned her the nickname "The Blonde Bombshell." It was a moniker that had little to do with her looks (which were fine), but a lot to do with her implacable personality; she didn't merely perform, she bulldozed. Among her other nicknames were "The Huttentot" and "The Blonde Blitz."

Born Betty June Thornburg, she was the younger sister of Marion (Thornburg) Hutton who later became a big band vocalist with the Glenn Miller orchestra. Their father died when the sisters were young, and both girls were forced to fend for themselves. Betty began by singing on street corners, eventually becoming a band singer and then working her way into vaudeville. Broadway beckoned and Hutton made her

The irrepressible Betty Hutton was known as "The Blonde Bombshell," and for good reason, as seen here. Photo courtesy of Movie Star News.

big breakthrough as the star of the stage musical *Panama Hattie* in 1940. Paramount took notice and signed her to a contract.

Her first film was *The Fleet's In* (1942), in which she filled a supporting comic-relief role. She scored with audiences and critics as a man-crazy female, a role she played in a string of musicals, such as *Star Spangled Rhythm* (1942), *Happy Go Lucky* (1943), and *Here Come the Waves* (1944). Hutton proved that she did not need to sing in films to succeed when she starred with her long-time costar Eddie Bracken in Preston Sturges' *(q.v.)* classic comedy *The Miracle of Morgan's Creek* (1944). And then she went a step further, proving her ability as a dramatic actress playing the once famous

nightclub impressario Texas Guinan in the hit movie *Incendiary Blonde* (1945).

Hutton's career slowed down in the later 1940s, with just a few memorable films, including her biopic *(q.v.)* about the silent serial queen Pearl White, called *The Perils of Pauline* (1947). *Dream Girl* (1948) and *Red, Hot and Blue* (1949) followed. Finding the right roles for a talent such as Hutton's was not an easy task, but the ideal vehicle came along when Judy Garland was forced to drop out of *Annie Get Your Gun* (1950) due to illness. Paramount loaned Hutton to MGM for the film and she scored a major triumph.

MGM wanted to buy her contract but Paramount had plans of their own for their new superstar. She was teamed with Fred Astaire *(q.v.)* in *Let's Dance* (1951) and Paramount gave her the lead in its biggest film of 1952, Cecil B. DeMille's *The Greatest Show on Earth*. It was yet another hit, winning a Best Picture Oscar. With her career at its height, Hutton followed her success with a musical star turn in *Somebody Loves Me* (1952), the story of vaudeville star Blossom Seely.

Then disaster struck. Hutton married her choreographer, Charles O'Curran, and demanded that he be made her director. Paramount said no, and Hutton walked. She broke her contract and her Hollywood fame and fortune came to a dead stop. She didn't appear in a movie again for another five years, and then only in a small, overlooked film called *Spring Reunion* (1957). She performed ably in it, but didn't elicit any other offers.

Plagued by four unsuccessful marriages, a drug problem, fights with managers, and, finally, bankruptcy, Hutton slid from nightclub work to stock production, to a failed Broadway comeback to walking out on a low-budget western in 1966. In 1974, she was discovered working as a housekeeper in a Catholic rectory in Rhode Island. Later, she took a job as a hostess at a Connecticut jai-alai complex. Eventually, in a daring and nostalgic move that brought theater audiences to their feet, she returned to Broadway in 1980 for three weeks to replace the vacationing Alice Ghostley as Mrs. Hannegan in the hit musical *Annie*. The thunderous applause and warm critical attention she received had little effect on her; she returned to working for the Catholic church and little has been heard from her since.

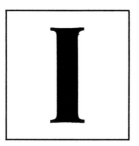

I AM A FUGITIVE FROM A CHAIN GANG The 1932 classic starring Paul Muni *(q.v.)* and directed by Mervyn Leroy *(q.v.),* that proved movie entertainment could be a source of powerful social commentary. The film was based on the true story of Robert E. Burns who had been unjustly convicted of a crime and sent to work on a chain gang in Georgia. When he escaped, he reached New Jersey and told his story to his brother, a priest. The incredible tale eventually made it to the screen as one of the most courageous movies ever made, with a finale that is among the most haunting in film history.

With Paul Muni playing Robert Burns, the movie showed the brutality of life on the chain gang and Burns' desperate attempts to escape. Muni played a decent man being hunted like a wild animal with no place to turn for help. In the end, while still on the run, he visits his wife. He hides in the garage, his face edging forward into the light to make his final farewell.

Suddenly there is a sound outside. Fear fills his face. He has to go.

"How do you live?" his wife plaintively calls out to him.

He pulls back into the shadows. The screen is dark as you hear Muni's chilling answer: "I steal." And the movie ends.

According to Michael Freedland in his book, *The Warner Brothers,* "It turned out that the screen went dark because the lights failed; if that was so it was one of the most fortunate accidents ever to occur in a studio."

The movie was so effective in its condemnation of the Southern chain gang system that Warner Bros. was threatened with a boycott of its films by several Southern states. But *I Am A Fugitive From a Chain Gang* also led to prison reform, and for that Warner Bros. was justly proud. Most important for the studio, the film was a huge success, confirming its decision to make movies of social significance from the headlines of the day in order to set it apart from its competitors.

INCE, THOMAS H. (1882–1924) A writer, director and producer who was a seminal figure in the development of film production. A contemporary of D. W. Griffith *(q.v.),* Ince was a shrewd and talented filmmaker who insisted that fully written shooting scripts be prepared rather than the customary rough outlines from which directors improvised. In addition to his tight supervision over the preparation of screenplays, he also oversaw the work of other directors and editors, establishing the position of studio production chief, which would become the norm during the studio system's golden era. Thanks to his penchant for planning and efficient organization, Ince, as both a director, and later as Hollywood's first true producer, made many of the early industry's best paced, most tightly made movies.

Born Thomas Harper Ince to a show business family, he began acting at the age of six. When he grew older, Ince aspired to an acting career in theater, but the often out-of-work thespian appeared in the movies as early as 1906, when he acted in *Seven Ages.* In 1910, without any prospects for success on the stage, he finally succumbed to the lure of motion pictures and, like D. W. Griffith, began acting regularly in front of the camera.

Shortly thereafter, he had the good fortune to begin his directorial career making several films that starred Mary Pickford *(q.v.),* among them *Their First Misunderstanding* (1910) and *Artful Kate* (1911). He learned his trade well and soon developed a reputation for making fluid, fast-paced, realistic movies—many of them westerns. Ince also developed a reputation as a smart showman who spared no expense to give his films a high production gloss. He had a studio built in Los Angeles that covered 20,000 acres, and hired a Wild West show for his westerns.

Within two years, Ince was so busy, that he finally began to largely supervise other directors, rarely directing films himself. He prepared scripts in great detail for his subordinate directors and made sure that they followed his orders explicitly. When he did produce and direct his own films, the results were often thrilling, as was the case with his version of *Custer's Last Fight* (1912) and *Civilization* (1915), an epic that won more plaudits and more patrons than Griffith's *Intolerance* (1916).

In one of the more ironic twists of fate in early Hollywood, three great filmmakers of the era, Thomas Ince, D. W. Griffith, and Mack Sennett *(q.v.)* found themselves working for the same company, Triangle Film Corporation, in 1915. Ince's production methods were put into effect, with all three heavyweights largely supervising the busy output of the studio. Triangle failed due to the hiring of high-priced Broadway stars who were unknown outside of New York. Even Ince's production methods could not save the company from insolvency.

Ince left Triangle and continued producing movies with excellent critical and commercial results throughout the rest of the 1910s and early 1920s. Among his most notable achievements as a producer/director during this later era were *Human Wreckage* (1923), *Anna Christie* (1923), and *Idle Tongues* (1924).

The idle tongues of gossip mongers certainly had occasion to wag after the events of November 19, 1924. Thomas Ince, then just forty-two years old, died on William Randolph Hearst's yacht under extremely suspicious circumstances. The official cause of death was listed as a heart attack induced by acute indigestion but rumor had it that Hearst shot Ince because the producer was having an affair with his lover, actress Marion Davies. An official investigation was launched into the death but no new evidence was uncovered; many believed that Hearst's power quashed any hope of the truth being revealed.

IT HAPPENED ONE NIGHT Frank Capra's *(q.v.)* 1934 sleeper became the year's biggest hit, swept the Academy Awards (winning all five major Oscars, including Best Picture, Best Director [Frank Capra], Best Screenplay [Robert Risken, *q.v.*], Best Actor [Clark Cable, *q.v.*] and Best Actress [Claudette Colbert, *q.v.*]), and changed Hollywood history.

The film was produced by Columbia and therefore Harry Cohen *(q.v.)* accepted the film's Best Picture Academy Award. It was the only film to ever win all five top awards until *One Flew Over the Cuckoo's Nest* was equally honored in 1975.

The movie, for all its impact, was a modest romantic comedy about a spoiled, runaway heiress (Colbert) who falls in love with a wisecracking, down-on-his luck reporter (Gable) while traveling together with him on a long bus ride. The film's natural, idiosyncratic dialogue, the genuine sparks between the macho Gable and the headstrong Colbert, and location shooting that gave the natural feel of the open road added immeasurably to the movie's appeal. Capra's uncanny knack for telling a story with visual flair was very much in evidence from the famous "Walls of Jericho" scene to the equally famous hitchhiking sequence.

In his splendid autobiography, *Frank Capra: The Name Above the Title,* the director explained how the movie came into being. The film was based on a short story called "Night Bus" by Samuel Hopkins Adams, which Capra read in *Cosmopolitan* while sitting in a barbershop. He had Columbia buy the film rights to the story for $5,000.

As it happened, two previous "bus-trip" films had been made by other studios and both had been flops. Columbia studio boss Harry Cohn ordered that the word "Bus" be stricken from the title and so the name of the film was changed to *It Happened One Night.*

After repeated failures in signing up a female lead for the film, Capra decided to go after the male lead in the hope of getting a star whose presence in the cast would help attract a formidable leading lady. MGM owed Columbia the use of one of its stars, and though Capra asked for Robert Montgomery, Montgomery refused. MGM's L. B. Mayer forced Columbia to take one of his up-and-coming actors, Clark Gable, who was known to be demanding more money from Mayer. The mogul tried to show Gable who was boss by humiliating him and sending him to lowly Columbia on loan.

With Gable set for the film, Capra went after Claudette Colbert for the female role because she was on vacation from Paramount and could make her own deals without studio interference. She received double her salary, receiving $50,000.

The film's entire budget was a mere $325,000, with a shooting schedule of four weeks. When the film opened, it received only mildly positive reviews. But the word of mouth on the film was stupendous. Every week the crowds at theaters all over the country grew larger. Before long the film was the talk of the industry and critics went back to see the film to find out what it was they missed the first time around.

The film's overwhelming success wrought great changes in Hollywood. Columbia was catapulted into the ranks of the major studios. Clark Gable's supposed punishment ended up turning him into MGM's major male star and Louis B. Mayer had to triple the actor's salary. And from a filmmaking perspective, the movie was significant because, in script doctor Myles Connolly's words, as reported by Capra, "You [Capra] took the old classic four of show business—hero, heroine, villain, comedian—and cut it down to *three,* by combining hero and comedian into one person." This immensely important change in story and character structure has continued to this day.

Proving that lightning rarely ever strikes twice in the same place, the film was remade in 1956 as *You Can't Run Away From It* with June Allyson and Jack Lemmon *(qq.v.).* It was not a hit.

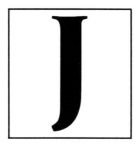

THE JAZZ SINGER The first feature-length "talkie" that rendered silent pictures obsolete. Made in 1927 by Warner Bros. (a relatively minor studio at the time), directed by Alan Crosland, and starring Al Jolson *(q.v.),* *The Jazz Singer* saved Warners from bankruptcy and revolutionized the motion picture business.

The Jazz Singer began its artistic life as a short story called "The Day of Atonement" by Samson Raphaelson and was later turned into a Broadway musical starring George Jessel. When Warner Bros. bought the film rights to the musical, the studio meant it to be a silent film with Jessel as its star. But when the studio decided to gamble in making *The Jazz Singer* its first feature-length sound film, Jessel demanded more money. He had been offered $30,000 but wanted $10,000 more if he was going to risk his career on a new invention. Jack Warner agreed, but when Jessel demanded that Warner put the agreement in writing, Warner raged that his word ought to be enough and the deal fell apart.

Jack Warner then turned to Eddie Cantor to play the lead, but Cantor refused in deference to his friend, Jessel. And then Al Jolson was approached, agreeing to star at a cost of $75,000. But part of the deal also included Jolson's purchase of Warner Bros. stock. That proviso only served to further enrich Jolson when the studio made a fortune on *The Jazz Singer.*

That Jolson was the studio's third choice for *The Jazz Singer's* lead is supremely ironic because "The Day of Atonement" was originally written by Raphaelson with Jolson in mind. It would be hard to argue that Jolson was not playing himself—a cantor's son who runs away to become a vaudeville star.

The Jazz Singer was not an all-talking, all-singing film; large parts of it were mute. But it caused a sensation nonetheless and grossed a staggering $3.5 million. The movies would never be the same again.

The Jazz Singer has been remade twice, first in 1953 starring Danny Thomas, and in a rock 'n' roll version in 1980 starring Neil Diamond.

JEWISON, NORMAN (1926–) A versatile producer-director since 1963, he has provided popular entertainments in a wide variety of genres for nearly thirty years. Jewison's strengths are his strong storytelling ability and a flair for visual composition. On the negative side, his work has been criticized for a lack of intellectual depth. His best decades have been the 1960s and 1980s, suffering a modest critical and box office slump in the '70s.

Born and raised in Toronto, Jewison gained his first valuable experience as a writer and actor for the BBC in London. He later began directing for Canadian television before crossing the border to work in the United States for CBS-TV. His initial claim to fame was his work as the director of the acclaimed musical TV specials of Judy Garland in the early 1960s.

Jewison made the leap to directing feature films in 1963 with the juvenile comedy *40 Pounds of Trouble*. He followed it with the last of Doris Day's best vehicles, *The Thrill of It All* (1963) and *Send Me No Flowers* (1964). After the mild *The Art of Love* (1965), Jewison moved from light comedy to drama with *The Cincinnati Kid* (1965) and to satire with *The Russians Are Coming, the Russians are Coming* (1966), which he also produced.

It seemed as if everything Jewison touched turned to gold at the box office. And his streak of hot films continued with the popular racial drama *In the Heat of the Night* (1967), for which he won an Oscar nomination for Best Director. *The Thomas Crown Affair* (1968) was another winner made doubly so by virtue of the fact that he had produced this movie, as well. Jewison has produced virtually all of his movies since the late 1960s.

After faltering with two small films, *Gaily Gaily*

(1969) and *The Landlord* (1970), which he only produced, Jewison made two big production musicals, *Fiddler on the Roof* (1971), for which he garnered his second Best Director Academy Award nomination, and *Jesus Christ Superstar* (1973). Both turned a profit. His next three films, however, were flops: *Billy Two Hats* (1974), which he only produced, *Rollerball* (1975), and *F.I.S.T.* (1978). He didn't recoup until he teamed with Al Pacino to make . . . *And Justice for All* (1979).

Many of Jewison's films of the 1970s tended to be big, ambitious projects. He scaled down somewhat in the 1980s with positive results. The warm *Best Friends* (1982) was a more honest romantic comedy than any of his earlier Doris Day movies; *A Soldier's Story* (1984) dealt more thoughtfully with racial issues than *In the Heat of the Night;* and *Agnes of God* (1985) explored religious questions more deeply and personally than *Jesus Christ Superstar.*

Jewison's biggest hit of the decade, however, was unlike any other movie he had made before. For *Moonstruck* (1987), he marshaled all of his storytelling skills to make a seamless and endearing social comedy that pleased audiences, critics, and even the Academy, which honored him with his third Oscar nomination for Best Director.

JOHNSON, NUNNALLY (1897–1977)   He was a prolific and talented screenwriter who sometimes donned the hat of producer and director. In a movie career that spanned four decades and more than sixty films, his story construction, realistic dialogue, and wit contributed mightily to some of Hollywood's best films. Johnson penned period pieces, westerns, light comedies, satires, thrillers, war movies, psychological suspense films, and more—all with intelligence and skill.

Johnson began his writing career as a journalist in his home city of Columbus, Georgia, at the *Enquirer Sun.* He later plied his trade at several other daily papers until he landed a job at the New York *Herald Tribune.* By this time he was already writing short stories for *The Saturday Evening Post,* and one of these stories was made into the silent film *Rough House Rosie* (1927).

The screenwriter began his Hollywood career in 1933 with the adaptation of *A Bedtime Story* (for which he did not receive screen credit). He wrote the screenplays for several films in the mid-1930s, including *The House of Rothschild* (1934) and *Kid Millions* (1934). Johnson's most important movie of this period was *Thanks a Million* (1935), which was produced by Darryl F. Zanuck *(q.v.)* and was Twentieth Century-Fox's second film. The movie's success saved the company from financial failure and cemented the screenwriter's relationship with the studio.

Johnson spent most of his career at Twentieth Century-Fox and was involved with some of John Ford's *(q.v.)* better films at the studio, particularly as associate

producer for *The Prisoner of Shark Island* (1936) and *The Grapes of Wrath* (1940).

Johnson was writer and producer of such other famous films as *Roxie Hart* (1941), *The Moon is Down* (1943), *The Woman in the Window* (1943), and *How to Marry a Millionaire* (1953). As a producer, he made *The Senator Was Indiscreet* (1948) and *The Gunfighter* (1950). In the role of writer, producer, and director, Johnson was responsible for *The Three Faces of Eve* (1957). As a writer/director, he left his stamp on *The Man in the Gray Flannel Suit* (1956) and *The Angel Wore Red* (1960). And his name appeared in the credits as the writer of such memorable movies as *Mr. Hobbs Takes a Vacation* (1962), *Take Her She's Mine* (1963), and *The World of Henry Orient* (1964). His last screenwriting credit was for *The Dirty Dozen* (1967).

Whether writing an original screenplay or adapting a work from another medium, Johnson was that rare screenwriter who wrote with sound and sight in mind. While not all of his films were commercial or critical hits, he had an unusually large percentage of both. There are a great many stars who never acted in as many films as Nunnally Johnson wrote, produced, and directed. In short, Johnson achieved a level of quantity and quality that is unique.

JOHNSON, VAN (1916–)   An actor who became a major MGM star in the 1940s by trading on his boyish good looks and charming, easy-going manner. Johnson did not have great range as an actor but was at the right place at the right time, filling a vacuum left in Hollywood by more established stars who had gone off to war.

Born Charles Van Johnson, he worked on Broadway as a hoofer in the chorus of various musicals during the late 1930s. His first Hollywood film was *Too Many Girls* (1942), in which he had a tiny role. But he was photogenic and natural on screen and he quickly found himself replacing Lew Ayres *(q.v.)* as Dr. Kildare in *Dr. Gillespie's New Assistant* (1942). He continued to play Kildare in two more films over the next few years.

In the meantime, Johnson was brought along carefully, if quickly, in supporting roles in major films such as *The Human Comedy* (1943), *Madame Curie* (1943), and *The White Cliffs of Dover* (1944). During 1944 he emerged as a star in *Two Girls and a Sailor.* It was a breezy musical with plenty of guest performers, but Johnson proved he was capable of handling a leading role.

Between 1944 and 1950 he enjoyed his period of greatest popularity, starring in films such as *Weekend at the Waldorf* (1945), *The Romance of Rosy Ridge* (1947), *In the Good Old Summertime* (1949), and *Battleground* (1950). He was so popular with young girls, in fact, that he earned the nickname, "the voiceless Frank Sinatra."

Johnson's career flagged in the early 1950s, but he came back strong as a surprisingly effective supporting player in some of the best films of 1954. He was the sincere officer egged on to mutiny against Humphrey Bogart in *The Caine Mutiny*, Gene Kelly's morose friend in *Brigadoon*, and the man caught between Elizabeth Taylor and Donna Reed *(qq.v.)* in *The Last Time I Saw Paris*.

Unfortunately, with the exception of *23 Paces to Baker Street* (1956), he had few other fine moments during the 1950s. But even when the films were good, the box office take usually was not. His star status was waning and he left Hollywood to make several films in England, with equally poor results.

In the 1960s, he starred in *Wives and Lovers* (1963), again without success, and had a modest role in *Divorce American Style* (1967) as well as appearances in a handful of European films. In the 1970s, he showed up on TV in the miniseries "Rich Man, Poor Man" (1976). In recent years, he has taken to working on the stage in everything from dinner theater to Broadway, where he appeared briefly in *La Cage aux Folles*.

JOLSON, AL (1886–1950) Born Asa Yoelson, his was the first voice heard in a feature-length motion picture. He originally achieved fame as a vaudeville and Broadway singer and was America's first genuine pop-recording sensation. Because of his popularity as a singer, he was hired to make several sound shorts for Warner Bros. in 1926. At the time, however, talking short subjects were considered nothing more than novelties. That attitude was to change dramatically the following year when Jolson sang and spoke in Warner's *The Jazz Singer* (1927, *q.v.*).

Jolson was paid $75,000 to act and sing in the first "talkie" feature although he was not the first choice for the lead. His performance proved electric and the movie took in $3.5 million, revolutionizing the motion picture business.

More astounding, but less well known today, was the success of Jolson's second feature film, *The Singing Fool* (1928). That movie made $15.5 million setting a record for profits that stood for eleven years, until it was finally broken by *Gone With the Wind* in 1939.

Jolson was the movies' first musical star, but his subsequent films met with much less success. His most interesting movies were *Hallelujah I'm a Bum* (1933) and *Rose of Washington Square* (1939), but his career was in eclipse from the very early 1930s. The musical had become far more sophisticated, and Jolson was considered passé.

After spending World War II entertaining the troops, he found his career rejuvenated, thanks to the hit biographical film, *The Jolson Story* (1946). Though he did not appear in the movie (or its sequel, *Jolson Sings Again*, 1949), Jolson sang all its songs. The film re-

Al Jolson's blackface act, which grew out of the minstrel tradition of the nineteenth century, was extremely popular both on stage and in his early films, like *The Jazz Singer* (1927). Photo courtesy of The Siegel Collection.

minded audiences that Jolson was the man who first said in *The Jazz Singer*, "You ain't heard nothin' yet." Those were prophetic words in 1927, because the movies have been talking ever since.

JONES, JENNIFER (1919–) An actress capable of projecting great sensuality while retaining a high degree of dignity. She was beautiful if moderately talented, and under the guidance of producer David O. Selznick *(q.v.)*, who later became her husband in 1949, she became one of Hollywood's major female stars during the 1940s and 1950s. Her film career spanned thirty-five years and twenty-five movies, and won the recognition of the film community with an Academy Award for Best Actress.

Born Phyllis Isley, she was a child of show business who worked in her youth in vaudeville and in traveling road shows as a teenager. In an effort to go "legit," she attended the American Academy of Dramatic Arts. It was there that she met her first husband, actor Robert Walker (whom Jones divorced in 1945).

Jones and Walker traveled to Hollywood together in 1939 and she soon made her movie debut as a leading player in a low-budget western, *New Frontier* (1939). Finding work was not hard for the young beauty, but she hardly landed top roles, as witnessed by her next job in the serial *Dick Tracy's G-Men* (1939). Again in 1939, through an incredible stroke of good luck, David O. Selznick *(q.v.)*, who that year released his epic masterpiece *Gone With the Wind,* the most popular movie in film industry history at the time, picked her to become his protégée.

Selznick changed Isley's name to Jennifer Jones. Over the next three years he instructed her in the art of movie acting, while skillfully using the press to build interest in the debut of his new star in a film carefully chosen to match her talents. That movie was *The Song of Bernadette* (1943), for which Jones won her first and only Oscar for Best Actress.

Whether in his own films or those of others, Selznick kept a watchful eye on his most valuable asset. Jones went on to star in such mid-1940s films as *Since You Went Away* (1944), *Love Letters* (1945), and *Cluny Brown* (1946). Then came *Duel in the Sun* (1947), Selznick's attempt to achieve another *Gone With the Wind* in the form of an epic western. Jones was the female lead in this fascinating if overwrought movie. It was followed, however, by what many consider to be Jones' best movie, the lusciously romantic fantasy *Portrait of Jennie* (1949).

In the years thereafter she starred in a number of good movies and gave strong performances in most, including *Madame Bovary* (1949), *Ruby Gentry* (1953), and *Love Is a Many Splendored Thing* (1955). She worked consistently during the 1950s, spending most of the latter half of the decade in prestigious movies such as *A Farewell to Arms* (1957) and *Tender is the Night* (1962). But both her career and personal life were struck a blow by the death of her husband and mentor in 1965. She made just three more movies after Selznick's death: *The Idol* (1966), *Cult of the Damned* (1969), and *Towering Inferno* (1974). She remarried in 1971, becoming the wife of famed businessman Norton Simon.

JUMP CUT   An abrupt, unnatural gap in the action of a scene created by either the removal of a series of continuous frames or by stopping the camera during filming and then moving it closer or further away from the action (keeping the same angle) and then resuming the shot. The effect of a jump cut is startling; for instance, a character in the background running toward the camera can suddenly appear in the foreground.

Traditional Hollywood directors considered the jump cut to be the mark of sloppy filmmaking. As a consequence, jump cuts didn't appear in American movies (except as visual gags) until the 1960s. It wasn't until French New Wave films of the late 1950s and early 1960s reintroduced the jump cut in a fresh new way that Hollywood directors began to reuse it.

Contemporary directors tend to avoid the jump cut, regarding it as a 1960s cliché. It is, however, sometimes used today as a means of depicting dreams, as well as drug and illness-related hallucinations.

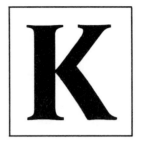

KALMAR, BERT (1884–1947) **& RUBY, HARRY** (1895–1974)   A team that wrote clever and amusing music and lyrics, as well as comic screenplays. Kalmar was the lyricist and Ruby the composer, but they collaborated on their Broadway shows and film projects.

Three of their nine Broadway shows were turned into movies: *The Cuckoos* (1930), *Top Speed* (1930), and the Marx Brothers' *Animal Crackers* (1930). They continued their collaboration with Groucho, Chico, Harpo, and Zeppo, writing the scripts and the music for two of the Marx's funniest films, *Horsefeathers* (1932) and *Duck Soup* (1933), including such witty songs in the former as "Whatever It Is, I'm Against It," and, in the latter, the outrageous adaptation called "All God's Chillun' Got Guns."

In addition to writing comedy scripts and music for the Marx Brothers, Kalmar & Ruby also provided Eddie Cantor *(q.v.)* with one of his best vehicles, *The Kid From Spain* (1932). Their later scripts were not quite up to their early successes, but their music was still quite memorable in films such as *Hips, Hips, Hooray* (1934) and *Walking on Air* (1936).

Ruby went on to write the music and scripts for several other modest films without Kalmar in the mid- to late 1940s and early 1950s, but the two collaborators were recognized by Hollywood in *Three Little Words* (1950), a biopic—the genre appropriate for movie royalty—in which Fred Astaire *(q.v.)* played Kalmar and Red Skelton portrayed Ruby. The film featured many of the team's songs in the score.

KANIN, GARSON (1912–   )   A former actor turned screenwriter, director, playwright, and author, Kanin's work in various fields is distinguished by a high level of playfulness, energy, and intelligence. Most of his work for Hollywood was done in the late 1930s, during which he directed a string of hit social comedies, and

the late 1940s and early 1950s when he scripted (often with his wife, Ruth Gordon, *q.v.*) a number of wonderfully adroit, sophisticated comedies—several of them Hepburn/Tracy vehicles. In addition, a number of his plays have been adapted to the screen.

Kanin was a high school dropout who helped support his family as a musician and comedian during the early years of the Depression. Eventually, he received formal training at the American Academy of Dramatic Arts and embarked on an acting career in 1933, appearing in such Broadway plays as *Little Ol' Boy* (1933), *Boy Meets Girl* (1935), and *Star Spangled* (1936). During the mid-1930s he doubled as an assistant director for the famed Broadway director George Abbott. Not long after, Kanin began directing for the Broadway stage in his own right, putting on such shows as *Hitch Your Wagon* (1937) and *Too Many Heroes* (1937).

Kanin received the call to Hollywood in 1938 and worked steadily on the coast until World War II. In his first few short years in the movie business, though, he directed a steady stream of charming, funny films that predated the rise of Preston Sturges *(q.v.)*. Like Sturges, Kanin made movies that played on social issues and social conventions, such as *The Great Man Votes* (1939), *Bachelor Mother* (1939), *My Favorite Wife* (1940), and *Tom, Dick and Harry* (1941).

During World War II, Kanin went on to produce and direct a number of highly regarded documentaries for the government, among them a collaboration with Jean Renoir, *A Salute to France* (1944), and a collaboration with Sir Carol Reed, *The True Glory* (1945), a film that won an Oscar for Best Documentary.

At the close of World War II, Kanin returned to Broadway rather than Hollywood. His success on the Great White Way was almost immediate with *Born Yesterday* in 1946 (later turned into a hit film of the same name in 1951). Also in 1946, he returned to writing screenplays, and in 1948 he and his wife, Ruth Gordon, coscripted *A Double Life* (1948), for which they shared an Academy Award nomination for Best Original Screenplay. Among his other fine screenplays were several Hepburn/Tracy comedies including *Adam's Rib* (1949) and *Pat and Mike* (1952).

Since the mid-1950s, Kanin has been largely absent from Hollywood. He directed two unsuccessful films in 1969, *Where It's At* and *Some Kind of a Nut,* but was otherwise involved in the theater during the late 1950s and 1960s. Though he had written books during the 1950s, he developed a moderately successful career as a writer of both fiction and nonfiction during the 1970s and 1980s, many of his stories using Hollywood as a background.

KAPER, BRONISLAU (1902–1983) A film composer known for both his vibrant, infectious music as well as his haunting, romantic scores. In a career that began in Poland, the Warsaw Conservatory graduate eventually moved to Germany, where he wrote music for early talkies. Like so many of his contemporaries, Kaper wisely fled Germany when Hitler came to power.

Kaper arrived in the U.S. during the mid-1930s and eventually became an important composer for MGM. He often collaborated with lyricist Gus Kahn, writing songs that enlivened several Marx Brothers movies, including the hit tune "Alone" from *A Night at the Opera* (1935), as well as songs for *San Francisco* (1936), *Lillian Russell* (1940), and *The Chocolate Soldier* (1941), among others. But Kaper is best known for his full scores of films such as *Mutiny on the Bounty* (1935 & 1962), *Comrade X* (1940), *Bataan* (1943), *Gaslight* (1944), *The Courage of Lassie* (1946), *The Red Badge of Courage* (1951), *Lili* (1953), for which he won his only Oscar, and *Home from the Hill* (1960).

KARLOFF, BORIS (1887–1969) Often billed simply as "Karloff," his is one of the best-known names in movie history, yet he was rarely the star of the films he appeared in. His reputation was made in *Frankenstein* in 1931, and he spent most of the rest of his life playing monsters on one kind or another.

Born William Pratt in England, Karloff changed his name long before he reached Hollywood. He had imigrated to Canada in 1909 and taken his stage name when he began touring in a Canadian stock company. After ten years on the road he found himself unemployed in Los Angeles. There was more work in Hollywood than in vaudeville, and he became an extra in *His Majesty the American* (1919).

It was an inauspicious beginning and Karloff's film career remained so during the course of the silent era—the actor took a variety of small roles (often as a minor villain) in roughly fifty films through the twenties. Happily, however, Karloff possessed a silky, cultured speaking voice that adapted easily to sound films, and he continued to find work with the advent of the talkies.

His first big break came in 1931 in Howard Hawks' *(q.v.) The Criminal Code,* in which he (naturally) played a killer. If only in a small way, his performance finally put him on the Hollywood map. The actor had modest featured roles in a slew of 1931 movies, but among them was *Frankenstein*—his career-maker.

Because of the success of Universal Pictures' *Dracula* in 1931, the film company was in a hurry to cash in on the new horror craze. Their lead ghoul, Bela Lugosi *(q.v.)* of *Dracula* fame, was originally tapped to play the Frankenstein monster. But Lugosi refused, planning to do a movie called *Quasimodo.* That film never saw the light of day (at least not with Lugosi), but his unavailability for *Frankenstein* brought Karloff his big break.

Karloff imparted a pathetic humanity to the monster—the actor managed to elicit from viewers fear mingled with sympathy. Concealed by an elaborate makeup job, and barely having any dialogue, Karloff's portrayal brought him stardom nonetheless. Universal signed him up immediately to a seven-year contract.

The actor appeared in supporting roles, in non-horror movies such as *Scarface* (1932) and *The Lost Patrol* (1934), but such instances were rare. He was quickly and forever typed as a horror actor, and like Bela Lugosi before him, was expected to take on the mantle of the great Lon Chaney *(q.v.),* who had died in 1930.

After *Frankenstein,* Karloff brought *The Mummy* (1932) to life, and he was Fu in *The Mask of Fu Manchu* (1932). His greatest triumph in the 1930s, however, was playing the monster again in *The Bride of Frankenstein* (1935), one of the rare instances when a sequel proved better than the original.

But as horror films became "B" movie *(q.v.)* fodder for Universal in the latter 1930s, Karloff found his films doing poorly and he was in increasingly less demand. *The Son of Frankenstein* (1939), a disappointing (second) sequel, didn't help.

Yet Karloff was not without other options. He left Hollywood for a priceless role on Broadway in the comedy *Arsenic and Old Lace.* He played a killer who has plastic surgery done on his face and ends up looking like Boris Karloff! The character becomes enraged whenever anyone tells him he looks like himself. It was a wonderful send-up of Karloff's own image and a terrible shame that he wasn't cast in the Frank Capra *(q.v.)* film version of the play. (Raymond Massey played the part.) In any event, Karloff's triumph on Broadway brought him more work when he returned to Hollywood, most significantly Val Lewton's *(q.v.)* horror films at RKO, including *The Body Snatcher* (1945) and *Isle of the Dead* (1945).

By the late 1940s, however, Karloff's career was truly in decline. *Abbott and Costello Meet the Killer, Boris*

Karloff (1949), despite being an amusing and scary film, made the actor a target for spoofing—though obviously his name had enough value to be used in the title of the film. For the next five years, he continued to appear in rather poor horror films, while also appearing on TV, where his name brought modest ratings.

Karloff's movie image was finally enhanced by American International Pictures, which used him in many of the Roger Corman *(q.v.)* horror movies, such as *The Raven* (1963) and *A Comedy of Terrors* (1964). Another A.I.P. film, *Targets* (1967) (this one directed by Peter Bogdanovich *[q.v.]* in his film debut), allowed Karloff to make a graceful departure from the movies in a role of dignity and self-esteem. He died soon thereafter.

KASDAN, LAWRENCE (1948–   ) A remarkably successful young screenwriter, director, and producer who has been involved in several of Hollywood's most commercially successful films. Like so many other talented film people, Kasdan was discovered by Steven Spielberg *(q.v.)*. But unlike many of Spielberg's protégés, Kasdan has gone on to make films without his mentor's help or influence. In the process, he has made a number of memorable movies with the promise of many more to come.

Kasdan was raised in West Virginia, attending college at the University of Michigan, where he began writing original screenplays. After receiving his B.A. in 1970, he went on to earn an M.A. in education in 1972. But writing, rather than teaching, appealed to the young man, so over the next five years he worked as an advertising copywriter. He plied his trade in Detroit and Los Angeles, continuing to pen screenplays until his sixth effort, *The Bodyguard*, was bought in 1977.

His big break, however, came later that year when his screenplay for *Continental Divide* was purchased by Universal with Steven Spielberg anxious to produce. That would have been excellent news all by itself, but a happy confluence of events occurred when George Lucas *(q.v.)* wanted Spielberg to direct a very special adventure story. Lucas needed a writer for the project, so Spielberg suggested Kasdan, who was almost immediately hired to write the screenplay for what would become *Raiders of the Lost Ark* (1981). Lucas was so impressed with Kasdan's work, he was hired to write the second and final draft of *The Empire Strikes Back* (1980), the second installment in the *Star Wars* trilogy.

The early 1980s were especially good for Kasdan. In addition to having screenwriting credits on two huge hits, he also saw *Continental Divide* make it to the big screen in 1981. On the basis of his screenwriting kudos, he convinced the Ladd Company to let him direct *Body Heat* (1981), based on his original screenplay, a modern *film noir (q.v.)* that not only catapulted Kasdan into the ranks of up-and-coming new directors but helped es-

tablish William Hurt and Kathleen Turner *(qq.v.)* as bright new stars.

As the 1980s unfolded, Kasdan continued on his roll, writing the screenplay for yet another installment in the *Star Wars* series, the blockbuster *Return of the Jedi* (1983). Most significantly, though, he proved his success as a director was no fluke when he made *The Big Chill* (1983), a film that helped define the experience of the 1960s for the upwardly mobile of the 1980s. In addition to coscripting the film with Barbara Benedek, Kasdan also showed his business acumen and independence by working as executive producer of *The Big Chill*.

With six hits in a row, Kasdan took on the moribund western genre, producing, coscripting (with his brother, Mark), and directing *Silverado*, a lavish, sprawling epic. His ambitious effort received generally good reviews, but the movie lost the gunfight at the box office getting shot down by disappointing ticket sales. Kasdan's career has slowed since but has hardly come to a stop: among his more recent projects, he has produced *Cross My Heart* (1987), and has coscripted, directed, and produced Anne Tyler's *The Accidental Tourist* (1988), the latter film nominated for an Oscar as The Best Picture of the year.

KAYE, DANNY (1913–1987) An attractive and engaging comic talent who was a Hollywood star for nearly twenty years. His unique brand of comedy was perhaps closest to that of Eddie Cantor *(q.v.)*; he usually played befuddled but lovable simpletons who, if less than courageous, were capable of the most hysterical forms of indirect bravery. Also like Cantor, Kaye was an inventive and lively singer. He rose to fame thanks to his rapid-fire delivery of wonderfully idiotic lyrics, many of which were written by his wife, Sylvia Fine.

Born David Daniel Kaminski to a poor tailor and his wife, the young man quit school at the age of thirteen to enter show business. He got his start as a comic in what became known at the "Borscht Belt," an enclave of resort hotels in the Catskill Mountains where New York City Jews often went to vacation during the summer. From there, Kaye traveled the dying vaudeville circuit, gaining experience and trying out new material.

Spotted for the rising young comedian that he was, Kaye made several two-reel shorts for the small independent Educational Pictures, but they didn't immediately bring him fame and fortune. They were, however, later compiled into a film inaccurately titled *The Danny Kaye Story*.

After Kaye's several successes on Broadway in the late 1930s and early 1940s, Hollywood took another chance on him. Samuel Goldwyn, the famous producer who had once made Eddie Cantor's movies, recognized

Was there anyone who didn't like Danny Kaye? The versatile performer is seen here (bird in hand) with director Norman Z. McLeod on the set of Kaye's most famous film, *The Secret Life of Walter Mitty* (1947). Photo courtesy of Movie Star News.

the same genius in the young Kaye and signed him to a film contract.

The following year, Kaye began his long and illustrious association with Goldwyn as the star of *Up in Arms* (1944), the first of many bright, witty, and thoroughly entertaining comedies. In all, Kaye starred in only seventeen feature films, but while not all of them were gems, most of them were hits. And a number of them have become minor classics.

Kaye's most fondly remembered movies are *Wonder Man* (1945), *The Secret Life of Walter Mitty* (1947), *The Inspector General* (1949), *Hans Christian Andersen* (1952), *Knock on Wood* (1953), *The Court Jester* (1956), and *Merry Andrew* (1958). Kaye occasionally shared top billing with other stars, most notably with Bing Crosby *(q.v.)* in *White Christmas* (1954), and in his last feature film, the all-star drama *The Madwoman of Chaillot* (1969).

Long associated with his devotion to the world's children, Kaye was an early and passionate advocate of UNICEF. He made a serious short called *Assignment Children* for the United Nations in 1954, and in that year was also given a special Oscar for "his unique talents, his service to the Academy, the motion picture industry, and the American people."

Occupied with his highly regarded TV variety program, "The Danny Kaye Show" (1963–1967) and his

continued commitment to UNICEF, his film career virtually came to a halt. He didn't seem to mind. He starred in the Broadway musical *Two by Two* in 1970 and traveled the country as a popular comic guest conductor of various city symphony orchestras. Later, he made occasional forays back into television, most memorably as Captain Hook in a new version of "Peter Pan" (1975), and in "Skokie" (1981), giving a stunning dramatic performance as a concentration camp survivor facing the nightmare of neo-Nazis marching in his hometown near Chicago.

KAZAN, ELIA (1909–   )   An actor's director best known for films with a political point of view. The theme that he explored throughout his career is the tortuous balance of the individual's needs against the dictums of society. His period of greatest activity was from the late 1940s through the early 1960s, during which time he usually directed (and later also produced) movies based on either plays or books; rarely did he work with untried material. While many of Kazan's films seem dated today, the works he adapted were often on the cutting edge of what was acceptable to the mass audience when they were released.

In addition to breaking new ground with his movies, Kazan also helped revolutionize modern acting as a cofounder of the Actors Studio, temple of the Stanislavsky Method approach to acting. Among the actors whom Kazan has greatly influenced are Marlon Brando *(q.v.)*, James Dean *(q.v.)*, Lee J. Cobb, and Rod Steiger *(q.v.)*. His success in bringing out the best in his performers is evidenced by the fact that in his mere eighteen Hollywood productions, twenty-one of his actors received Academy Award nominations and nine of them were honored with an Oscar.

Born to a Greek family living in Turkey, Elia Kazanjoglou immigrated to America with his family when he was four years old. After graduating Williams College in 1930, he went on to the Yale School of Drama and began his career in the theater as an actor, eventually turning to writing and especially directing. In 1932, he joined Lee Strasberg and Harold Clurman's Group Theater. Also during this time Kazan joined the Communist Party, later being expelled from its ranks because he refused to betray Strasberg and Clurman, whom the local party wanted ousted from their Group Theater leadership positions.

Because of his abiding interest in the mass audience, Kazan was drawn to the mass entertainment medium— the movies. He had had minor acting roles in two films, *City for Conquest* (1940) and *Blues in the Night* (1941), but they did not lead to bigger projects. While still active in the theater (which he would continue to be into the early 1960s), Kazan began directing films, making the documentaries *People of the Cumberland* (1937) and *It's Up to You* (1941). But it was his success during the 1940s as a Broadway theater director (with stage hits such as *The Skin of Our Teeth* in 1942 and *One Touch of Venus* in 1943), not his experience making documentaries, that finally brought him to Hollywood.

Kazan eased his way into commercial filmmaking with *A Tree Grows in Brooklyn* (1945) and *Sea of Grass* (1947), but he then began directing a streak of enormously popular, socially relevant films that brought him to the attention of the public. The first of these films was *Boomerang* (1947), a gritty, semi-documentary style movie about a prosecutor torn between professional obligation and his belief that his case is a sham. Kazan followed *Boomerang* with one of the surprise hits of the year, *Gentlemen's Agreement* (1947), an indictment of anti-Semitism in America. The movie not only won the Best Picture Academy Award, it also brought Kazan a Best Director Oscar. Taking up the liberal cause yet again, Kazan directed the hit *Pinky* (1949), this time taking on racism.

The only work Kazan ever directed for the movies that he had also directed for the stage was *A Streetcar Named Desire* (play 1947, movie 1951). Kazan's direction helped make Marlon Brando a star in both mediums. It also led to their collaboration on two other critically acclaimed and popular movies, *Viva Zapata!* (1952) and *On the Waterfront* (1954), the latter film sweeping the Academy Awards with eight Oscars, including Best Picture, Best Director, and Best Actor (Brando).

Kazan is remembered by many for his appearance before the House Un-American Activities Committee (HUAC) in the early 1950s. The HUAC, convinced that Hollywood was riddled with Marxist ideologues trying to spread propaganda, rode roughshod over the industry and caused the blacklisting that resulted in the destruction of hundreds of careers and the ruin of many innocent lives. Many called before the HUAC refused to cooperate and inform on their friends and were promptly jailed (*see*: Hollywood Ten). Kazan named the names of people whom he knew to have been Communists, many of them having left the party in the 1930s.

On the Waterfront was widely viewed by critics as Kazan's way of rationalizing his betrayal of his friends, for the hero of the film, Terry Malloy (Brando), turns on his friends in the corrupt longshoreman's union and acts as a stool pidgeon for the federal authorities. Kazan has not disputed this interpretation.

After *On the Waterfront's* critical box office success, Kazan wielded the power to produce and direct his own movies, and his next project also proved to be a major winner, introducing the then unknown James Dean in John Steinbeck's *East of Eden* (1955). Except for *Splendor in the Grass* (1960), it was Kazan's last major hit. Subsequent movies were adventurous in their subject matter, such as his pre-*Lolita* movie, *Baby Doll* (1956), and his anti-television/antifascist *A Face in the Crowd* (1957).

Unfortunately, the public began to lose interest in his work and the films sold few tickets.

Kazan turned to writing fiction in the 1960s, penning three best-sellers, two of which he adapted for the screen, produced, and directed. Despite their time on the best-seller lists, the film versions of *America, America* (1963) and *The Arrangement* (1969) were flops. His third novel, *The Assassins,* was never turned into a movie.

Later, Kazan made an anti-Vietnam War film in 16mm, *The Visitors* (1972), that communicated more about Kazan's inability to find financing than it did about the conflict in Southeast Asia. It seemed as if the filmmaker's career was over. But he returned to the screen one last time to direct the adaptation of F. Scott Fitzgerald's *The Last Tycoon* (1976) with Robert De Niro. The film received generally good reviews but did poor business. He has not directed a major motion picture since.

KEATON, BUSTER (1895–1966) Depending on one's taste in film comedy, Keaton is either the greatest movie comedian of all time or the second greatest, behind Chaplin. While Chaplin's comedy was essentially theatrical, Keaton's was utterly cinematic. Chaplin's humor was warm and Keaton's cool, but both were enormously funny and richly deserving of their reputations.

But where Chaplin remained famous and was revered throughout most of his life, Keaton faded from view in the early 1930s. Happily, both Keaton and his artistry were rediscovered before he died, and new audiences came to know Keaton, "The Great Stone Face." Wearing his pork-pie hat, Keaton was the indomitable foe of fate—a modern everyman who locked horns with nature and machines, somehow (but not always) surviving the comic disasters that came hurtling his way.

Born Joseph Francis Keaton to a vaudeville family, he received his famous nickname from an old family friend, the famous escape artist Harry Houdini. It seems that at the age of six months, the infant Keaton fell down a long flight of stairs without so much as a scratch. "Buster" was a vaudeville term for a comic fall; Houdini tagged Keaton with the name and it stuck.

By the age of three, Keaton had joined his family in vaudeville, and "The Three Keatons" became a popular act. Young Keaton, himself, was soon the star attraction. Later, after his father began drinking heavily, making their acrobatic act terribly dangerous, the trio disbanded. Buster went to New York to appear as a solo act for $250 per week in *The Passing Show of 1917* at Broadway's Winter Garden Theater. There he bumped into an old vaudeville friend who was with Roscoe "Fatty" Arbuckle (*q.v.*). The meeting not only changed Keaton's plans, it changed his life.

Keaton was invited to watch the filming of a comedy short at Arbuckle's studio. Mesmerized by the camera,

The key to Buster Keaton's comic sensibility was his absolute fortitude in the face of every imaginable obstacle. He is seen here in his classic Civil War adventure comedy *The General* (1926), unaware that the mortar he is firing has tilted the wrong way. Photo courtesy of The Siegel Collection.

that very day he turned down the guaranteed $250 per week vaudeville salary to accept a $40 per week offer from Arbuckle.

Keaton learned everything he could about film comedy from Arbuckle, working for the popular comedian for four years (minus a stint in the army). His first film was *The Butcher Boy* (1917). From the very beginning, his persona was that of the unsmiling stone face. Keaton had developed his stoic expression very early on in his vaudeville career, noting that audiences laughed when he didn't smile. Nonetheless, Keaton laughed once on film, in *Fatty at Coney Island* (1917).

Keaton took over Arbuckle's studio in 1921 when his rotund friend went to another company. And it should be noted that he remained loyal to his mentor in the worst days of the famous Arbuckle rape case.

Just before he took over the studio, Keaton appeared in his first feature, *The Saphead* (1920), a film he did not write or direct, but a movie whose success would soon pave the way for his own features. The features, however, came soon after Keaton's classic two-reelers, such as *The Playhouse* (1921), *The Boat* (1921), and *Cops* (1922), all movies with an absurdist quality that seems thoroughly modern today. Keaton was a huge popular

success, and by the early 1920s he and Chaplin ruled the comedy roost.

Keaton shared his directorial chores with Eddie Cline, but Cline himself graciously conceded that 90 percent of the comic inventions in their films belonged to Buster. Their first feature together was *The Three Ages* (1923), an amusing takeoff of *Intolerance* (1916), but Keaton really hit his stride with his second feature, *Our Hospitality* (1923). Virtually all of his silent features through 1928 were as good or better.

He presaged Woody Allen's *The Purple Rose of Cairo* (1985) with his *Sherlock Junior* (1924), a film in which Keaton, as a film projectionist, jumps in and out of the movie he's projecting in the film. *The Navigator* (1924) was his biggest box office success. But *The General* (1926) is considered his masterpiece, with one of the greatest chase scenes in all of film comedy. It was so good, in fact, that the Marx Brothers stole it for their climax in *Go West* (1940).

Keaton was his own boss, making movies the way he wanted to make then when suddenly everything fell apart. In his book, *My Wonderful World of Slapstick,* Keaton explained, " 'I made the worst mistake of my career. Against my better judgement I let Joe Schenck talk me into giving up my own studio to make pictures at the booming MGM lot in Culver City.' " The other great comics of the day, Chaplin and Harold Lloyd, begged him not to do it. But Keaton was not a businessman and he relented under Schenck's offer of a $3,000 per week salary.

From the very beginning, MGM tried to change the way Keaton made his films. The first movie he made at his new home was *The Cameraman* (1928). It was an excellent comedy and a hit, but Keaton had to battle for every gag. He made two more comedies for MGM that were hits, including his first talkie, *Free and Easy* (1930), but the quality was already falling off.

His films thereafter were bombs. In an attempt to make him a dramatic actor, Keaton was screentested for the Lionel Barrymore role in *Grand Hotel* (1932, *q.v.*). Nothing came of that, and his subsequent comedies at the studio continued to do terrible business. But by this time, Keaton was drinking heavily, divorced, and broke. In 1933 MGM fired him.

During the next two decades, Keaton only occasionally appeared in films, usually in minor roles. He was the proverbial forgotton genius until Chaplin made *Limelight* in 1952, featuring Keaton in a small role. Slowly, the rediscovery of Keaton's artistry began. In 1957, Donald O'Connor starred in *The Buster Keaton Story,* a movie of minor merit except that it introduced a new generation to the once famous silent star. His fee for the rights to his life story also finally ended Keaton's poverty, allowing him to live comfortably for the rest of his life.

In 1959, Keaton was given a Special Academy Award "for his unique talents which brought immortal comedies to the screen."

Finally recognized for his contribution to film comedy, Keaton spent the rest of his years making guest appearances in movies as diverse as *It's a Mad, Mad, Mad, Mad World* (1962) and *How to Stuff a Wild Bikini* (1965). More important Keaton's silent films (which had been found and restored during the 1950s), reached new audiences in the ensuing decades who laughed just as loudly as audiences had back in the 1920s.

KEATON, DIANE (1946–   ) An actress who has surprised many critics with the depth of her talent in a film career that has been going strong for nearly two decades. Originally a discovery of Woody Allen *(q.v.),* who directed her in many of his films of the 1970s, she emerged in her own right as an effective dramatic actress in the late 1970s and throughout the 1980s. Tall, gawky, with a vulnerable off-center style, Keaton has slowly become one of Hollywood's major actresses.

Born Diane Hall to a middle-class family in California, she dropped out of college to become an actress. After traveling to New York she studied at the well-known Neighborhood Playhouse. Her rise was meteoric by show business standards; after mere months of playing in stock, she won a modest role in a show that became the hottest ticket on Broadway during the 1960s, *Hair.* She also had the job of understudying the lead, eventually inheriting the role in 1968 after the star left the show.

As big a break as starring in *Hair* might have been, it wasn't half as big as when Woody Allen tapped her to be the female lead in his Broadway production of *Play it Again, Sam* in 1969. The two subsequently became lovers and he later featured her in a great many of his films.

Before Woody introduced her to filmgoers, however, Keaton made her movie debut in a small role in *Lovers and Other Strangers* (1970), and played a more important supporting role as Al Pacino's wife in *The Godfather* (1972), later reprising her role in the sequel, *The Godfather, Part II* (1974). Her real film fame, however, came not from Francis Coppola's hits but from her neurotic and endearing performance in the film version of *Play it Again, Sam* (1972).

Critics and audiences loved the film and, though it was clearly a Woody Allen vehicle, Keaton was singled out for considerable praise. Though she starred in other non-Allen films during the 1970s, such as *I Will, I Will . . . for Now* (1976) and *Harry and Walter Go to New York* (1976), her early reputation was built on her costarring leads in the Woody Allen classics *Sleeper* (1973), *Love and Death* (1975), *Interiors* (1978), and *Manhattan* (1979). Her most important Allen film was *Annie Hall* (1977), which was loosely based on Keaton's relationship with her director/lover—even to the point of giving the title character her actual last name. She won the Best Actress Oscar for her performance in that film, while also starting a fashion trend known as the "Annie Hall look."

In the same year as *Annie Hall,* Keaton also starred in what was then her most important dramatic role, the lead in *Looking for Mr. Goodbar* (1977). The provocative and much-discussed film concerning sexual repression highlighted Keaton's acting versatility and surprised a great many critics.

After her amicable breakup with Woody Allen, she went on to make mostly dramatic movies, including *Reds* (1981), a hit romantic film of ideas, with her new lover, Warren Beatty *(q.v.),* and a powerful, critically acclaimed movie about divorce, *Shoot the Moon* (1982). But then she hit a rough spot in her career with two major bombs, *The Little Drummer Girl* (1984) and *Mrs. Soffel* (1984). Keaton bounced back, though, with several highly regarded films, among them *Crimes of the Heart* (1986), *Baby Boom* (1987), and *The Good Mother* (1988).

In the late 1980s, Keaton also made her directorial debut with the rather controversial *Heaven* (1987), putting together a melange of interviews and film clips concerning people's ideas of the hereafter.

KELLY, GENE (1912–) A dancer, actor, choreographer, director, and producer whose contributions to the Hollywood musical made him the unquestioned heir of Fred Astaire *(q.v.)*. Kelly's impact on the movie musical was due in particular to his innovative dancing style and choreography. In the postwar era, his exuberant athleticism was just right for a nation anxious to jump back to life. He was square-jawed and handsome, with a smile as winning and winsome as ever graced a big screen. Like Astaire, Kelly did not possess a beautiful singing voice but he knew how to put a song over. He had a thin, reedy voice, but it had a pleasing rasp to it. While his dramatic acting and his directing of films in the 1960s and beyond did not stir critics or audiences, his achievements in the years between 1942 and 1957 were certainly worthy of the special Oscar he received in 1951, given "in appreciation of his versatility as an actor, singer, director, and dancer; specifically for his brilliant achievements in the art of choreography on film."

Born Eugene Curran Kelly, the young future movie star was a dance instructor in his home town of Pittsburgh before he left for New York to make his way in the theater. He was a success almost from the first, quickly landing a role in the chorus of the Broadway show *Leave It to Me* in 1938. He became a Broadway luminary as a result of his dramatic portrayal of the young hoofer in William Saroyan's *The Time of Your Life* (1939) and soon had the opportunity to show his wide-ranging talents when he won the starring role in the 1940 production of *Pal Joey*. David O. Selznick *(q.v.)* saw Kelly on stage and immediately signed him for Hollywood. In the end, however, it was MGM that bore the fruit of Selznick's discovery.

Kelly was loaned by Selznick to MGM for his film debut in *For Me and My Gal* (1942), costarring Judy Garland. The film and Kelly were instant hits. He first began to do the choreography for his own films with *Cover Girl* (1944), and he became a major star and a force in movie musicals when he made *Anchors Aweigh* (1945), for which he won an Academy Award nomination for Best Actor.

Kelly entered his golden era during the late 1940s and 1950s, starring in many of MGM's best-loved musicals, including *The Pirate* (1948), *Take Me Out to the Ballgame* (1949), *Summer Stock* (1950), *Brigadoon* (1954) and *Les Girls* (1957). Among his musicals of that era were three films that he codirected with Stanley Donen *(q.v.)*, two of which have become classics, the innovative *On the Town* (1949), the first MGM musical to be shot on location (in New York), and *Singin' in the Rain* (1952), which was a delight from start to finish and provided Gene Kelly with his theme song in the title number.

Gene Kelly sang and danced his way into Hollywood immortality in *Singin' in the Rain* (1952), but his reputation could have been made by any number of other classic performances during the height of the MGM musical era of the 1940s and 1950s. Photo courtesy of Gene Kelly.

Yet many consider his greatest achievement the Oscar winner for Best Picture of 1951, *An American in Paris,* beloved for its ballet, which was, of course, also choreographed by Kelly.

Kelly went on to direct, choreograph, and star in *Invitation to the Dance* (1956), an experimental film without dialogue in which three stories were told by means of dance only. It was, in some respects, his last great dancing film.

While Kelly's importance as film star rests mostly on his achievements in the musical, he was also effective in dramatic roles, including such films as *The Cross of Lorraine* (1943), *Marjorie Morningstar* (1958), *Inherit the Wind* (1960), and many others.

In his later years, he directed such films as *Gigot* (1962), *A Guide for the Married Man* (1967), *Hello, Dolly!* (1969), and *The Cheyenne Social Club* (1970). All were done competently but none of them had the flair of his earlier work with Stanley Donen.

Kelly has not limited himself to the movies. He has, among other things, directed for the theater, putting his stamp on the 1958 Broadway show *Flower Drum Song*. Beginning in the late 1950s, he also did a great deal of work in television, including a number of classic dance specials. Though few may remember it, he was also Father O'Malley in the 1962 prime time TV series version of the Academy Award winning Bing Crosby vehicle *Going My Way* (1944).

He was last seen dancing on screen (or, rather, skating) in an awful Olivia Newton-John musical, *Xanadu* (1980). He was, as one might expect, the best thing in the film, making one wish for the magical days of MGM's movie musicals.

KELLY, GRACE (1928–1982)   She was an actress whose cool, aloof exterior belied an alluring sexuality. Her Hollywood career was brief—just five years—but her impact was considerable, due to both the quality of her work and the manner in which she left the film industry, exchanging the make-believe royalty of Hollywood for a real-life prince—Rainier III of Monaco.

Kelly came from an accomplished family. Her father, Jack Kelly, was a rich businessman and a one-time world champion oarsman. Her mother had been a model and cover girl. Her uncle, George Kelly, a playwright, won a Pulitzer Prize for penning *Craig's Wife*.

The young girl was first touched by the acting bug when she was ten years old, appearing in a local (Philadelphia) play. After her education in elite private schools, Kelly set off for New York to follow in her mother's footsteps and become a model. At the same time, she also took acting classes. After appearing in cigarette commercials on TV, she had her first big break, appearing in a 1949 Broadway revival of August Strindberg's *The Father*.

Kelly's first film appearance was little more than a walk-on in *Fourteen Hours* (1951). But in spite of her inexperience as a film or theater actress, she was next thrust into the female lead as Gary Cooper's Quaker wife in *High Noon* (1952). The film was a major hit, saving Cooper's career and launching Kelly's. In her very next movie, *Mogambo* (1953), a remake of *Red Dust* (1932), she played the part of the prim wife, which had once been played by Mary Astor, and garnered a Best Supporting Actress Oscar nomination. Her career was in high gear and moving ever faster.

1954 was the best year of her career. She starred in four films, all successful at the box office, three critically acclaimed. Though *Green Fire* was forgettable, she triumphed in two Alfred Hitchcock hits, *Dial M for Murder* and *Rear Window*, plus the film for which she won an Oscar for Best Actress, *The Country Girl*, playing against type as the bitter wife of an alcoholic (Bing Crosby, in what was also one of his best performances).

Kelly starred in but four more films, *The Bridges at Toko-Ri* (1955), *To Catch a Thief* (1955), *The Swan* (1956), and her only musical, *High Society* (1956). During location shooting in the south of France for Hitchcock's *To Catch a Thief*, Kelly met Prince Rainier III of Monaco. Her storybook wedding might have provided the perfect ending for a Hollywood movie but Kelly's real end was tragic. Princess Grace died in an automobile accident along the treacherous roads of the French Riviera near her principality. A question remains concerning whether she or her daughter, Princess Stephanie, was actually at the wheel when the car went out of control and plunged off the road.

KERN, JEROME (1885–1945)   An influential composer whose music graced more than twenty movie musicals. He wrote a staggering thirty-eight Broadway musicals, eight of which were turned into movies, many of them more than once. In addition to his shows that were adapted to film, Kern also wrote expressly for the movies.

Unlike many of his self-taught contemporaries, Kern was a trained musician who had studied at the New York College of Music. But he was firmly drawn to popular music, as evidenced by his first song hit in 1905, "How'd You Like to Spoon with Me?" His later show tunes during the 1910s and 1920s influenced future composers for the Broadway stage, including George Gershwin and Richard Rodgers, who, in turn, influenced the direction, style, and substance of what became the modern, popular Broadway and Hollywood musical comedy.

Kern began writing for the movies as early as 1916 when he wrote a film score designed to accompany the silent serial *Gloria's Romance* (1916), but not until 1930 did he move to Hollywood to stay.

Kern's lyricist was usually Oscar Hammerstein II, and together, they wrote, among others, the shows *Show Boat* (filmed in 1929, 1936, and 1951), *Sunny* (filmed in 1930 and 1941), and *Roberta* (filmed in 1935 and, under the title *Lovely to Look At*, in 1952).

Working with other lyricists, he also composed the music for such popular musicals as *Swing Time* (1936), *High, Wide, and Handsome* (1937), and *Cover Girl* (1944).

Kern won two Oscars for Best Song, first for "The Way You Look Tonight" from *Swing Time*, and the second for "The Last Time I Saw Paris" from *Lady Be Good* (1941). The latter tune was created in reaction to the fall of Paris to the Nazis in 1940.

Like several other famous popular composers who died during the late 1930s and 1940s, Kern was made the subject of a biopic called *Till the Clouds Roll By* (1946), with Robert Walker as Kern.

KERR, DEBORAH (1921–)   An actress known for her poise and cool restraint, she often played high-toned characters in a film career that spanned forty-four films and three decades. In her long and distinguished career, she was nominated for six Academy Awards for Best Actress but never won the Oscar.

Born Deborah J. Kerr-Trimmer, she was a trained

ballerina who danced on the London stage. Feeling more attuned to the theater than the dance, however, she began acting on the stage in small parts in the late 1930s. In 1941 she made her film debut in a modest role in the British production of *Major Barbara*. Eight increasingly larger roles in English movies followed, the most memorable being in *The Life and Death of Colonel Blimp* (1943) and *Black Narcissus* (1947).

On the basis of the latter film, MGM signed her up and whisked her to Hollywood to star with Clark Gable (*q.v.*) in *The Hucksters* (1947). Except for a number of English productions in the 1960s, Kerr continued to make most of her movies in Hollywood over the next twenty-two years. In all that time she was a leading lady, making her early mark in *Edward, My Son* (1949), for which she garnered her first Oscar nomination.

If the film industry wasn't doing well in the 1950s, Kerr was not affected, and she appeared in a large number of hits, among them *King Solomon's Mines* (1950), *Quo Vadis* (1951), *The Prisoner of Zenda* (1952), and the Joseph L. Mankiewicz all-star production of *Julius Caesar* (1953). But even so, her biggest hits were yet to come.

In many of her early Hollywood films Kerr had played the upper-crust lady, but her torrid love scene in the surf with Burt Lancaster in *From Here to Eternity* (1953) brought her down from her pedestal. The film won eight Oscars and was a huge hit. It also brought Kerr her second Oscar nomination for Best Actress.

Both hits and Oscar nominations kept coming her way during the rest of the 1950s. Between 1956 and 1960, she was nominated every year but one (1959). Her Oscar-nominated performances were in *The King and I* (1956), *Heaven Knows, Mr. Allison* (1957), *Separate Tables* (1958), and *The Sundowners* (1960). In addition to her performances in highly regarded Oscar-nominated films, she also scored with audiences in such movies as *Tea and Sympathy* (1956), *An Affair to Remember* (1957), and *Bonjour Tristesse* (1958).

Kerr's career began to wane in the 1960s when she appeared in few hits and even fewer good movies. She worked as steadily as she had in the past but without the same success. Her best work of the decade was in *The Innocents* (1961), *The Night of the Iguana* (1964), and *Prudence and the Pill* (1968). But few good roles were being written for older actresses and the turbulent 1960s simply wasn't the decade for reserved, well-bred actors in any case.

Kerr's last film before semiretiring was Elia Kazan's *The Arrangement* (1969). She has since been seen occasionally on television.

KING, HENRY (1888–1982)   A director for nearly fifty years, from 1915 to 1962, he was the epitome of the solid, efficient craftsman. King made a significant number of hit films in a wide variety of genres, but relatively few of them have withstood the test of time. King rarely shaped his material to fit any sort of personal vision and the lack of deep commitment to his movies shows in a languid, plodding, visual style. Nonetheless, King is representative of a large number of talented directors who worked best under the yoke of strong-minded studio producers who gave purpose to their filmmaking.

King's youth was spent on the family plantation in Virginia, but an interest in acting led him to shuck work and hit the boards. King appeared in everything from burlesque to legitimate theater but was not a terribly successful actor, which led him, in 1912 to condescend to appear in the movies. By 1915, he had begun directing one-reelers for Pathé, usually acting in these as well. Among his action-oriented movies during that era were *Who Pays?* (1915), *Told at Twilight* (1917), *The Ghost of Rosy Taylor* (1918), *When a Man Rides Alone* (1918), and *This Hero Stuff* (1919). Though his films were consistently successful, he didn't score a genuinely big hit until *23 1/2 Hours Leave* (1919), a service comedy that suggested King could direct more than just action films.

Other strong efforts followed and King was emboldened to join silent film superstar Richard Barthelmess (*q.v.*) in establishing their own production company, Inspiration Films. Together, they made *Tol'able David* (1921), a critical and box office milestone that glorified rural America and won the praise of the Russian director and film theorist Vsevolod Pudovkin, as well. While Inspiration Films didn't last, King's career continued to grow with films such as *Sonny* (1922), *Romola* (1924), *Stella Dallas* (1925), and *The Winning of Barbara Worth* (1926). By the end of the silent era, King was one of Hollywood's most consistently successful directors.

The director began working for Fox in 1930, and he would continue to work for that studio for the rest of his career. At first, the association did not bode well. Without a strong hand at the wheel of the tottering studio, King's movies were nothing special. His best efforts were those in which a major star held the film together, as was the case with the Will Rogers vehicles *Lightnin'* (1930) and *State Fair* (1933). Once Fox and Twentieth Century merged and Darryl F. Zanuck (*q.v.*) took over, King's fortunes also rose.

King became one of Zanuck's most trusted directors, receiving many of the studio's "A" movie assignments. Among King's triumphs during the second half of the 1930s and into the 1950s were such films as *Lloyd's of London* (1936), *In Old Chicago* (1938), *Alexander's Ragtime Band* (1938), *Stanley and Livingstone* (1939), *Chad Hanna* (1940), *The Black Swan* (1942), *Song of Bernadette* (1943), for which he received an Academy Award nomination for Best Director, *Wilson* (1944), for which he got his second—and last—Best Director Oscar nomination, *Margie* (1946), *Twelve O'Clock High* (1949), *The*

Gunfighter (1950), *Love Is a Many Splendored Thing* (1955), and *Carousel* (1956). In the 1950s he also began directing more literary works, most notably *The Snows of Kilimanjaro* (1952), *The Sun Also Rises* (1957), and *Tender is the Night* (1962), the last of these marking the end of his directorial career.

KRAMER, STANLEY (1913–   )   Despite his reputation as a producer and director of sometimes heavy-handed message movies, Kramer brought social issues to the screen when many others lacked the courage to do so. Though some may be loathe to admit it, Kramer has also been both critically and commercially successful in selling his liberal messages, particularly in mid-career. If one occasionally winces at his films today, it is likely because the issues he addressed have either changed or become far more complex. To his credit, Kramer has never been accused of being insincere and, having been an early pioneer in independent producing, he certainly has put his money where his beliefs are. In all, he has produced thirty-five movies, directing fifteen of them. Six of his films have received Academy Award nominations for Best Picture and he has been nominated for Best Director four times. Though he never won an Oscar for any of his films, he was honored as early as 1961 with the Irving Thalberg Award for outstanding motion picture production.

Born in New York City, Kramer traveled to Hollywood not long after his graduation from New York University. After working as a film editor at Twentieth Century-Fox, he moved to the story department at MGM where he also wrote "B" pictures. He gained modest experience as an associate producer working for independent producers David Loew and Albert Lewin before leaving to join the service during World War II.

When Kramer was mustered out, his old job was no longer available, and he took the gamble of starting his own company, Screen Plays, Inc. His first independently produced film was *So This Is New York* (1948). It hardly portended the success that would immediately follow when he produced the hit boxing movie *Champion* (1949), a film nominated for six Oscars.

Early in his producing career, Kramer often looked to the theater for his films, and many of his memorable productions were adapted from hit plays. For instance, he was responsible for the film versions of *Cyrano de Bergerac* (1950), *Death of a Salesman* (1951), *Member of the Wedding* (1953), and *The Caine Mutiny* (1954); the last won a Best Picture Oscar nomination. He also began making his message movies during the early 1950s with films such as *The Men* (1950), which introduced Marlon Brando *(q.v.)* to the movies in a film detailing the plight of wounded war veterans, and *High Noon* (1952), a western that was also a subtle attack upon those who refused to stand up and fight McCarthyism and which was nominated for Best Picture.

Director Stanley Kramer is the king of the message movie. More than any other modern director of commercial cinema, Kramer has used his films to educate and influence the moviegoing public. While Kramer has his critics, no one has ever doubted his sincerity. Photo courtesy of Stanley Kramer.

Once he began directing his own films in 1955, Kramer soon made many more message movies. He dealt with all sorts of issues, from racism, in two of his Best Picture and Best Director nominated films *The Defiant Ones* (1958) and *Guess Who's Coming to Dinner* (1967), to nuclear war, in *On the Beach* (1959), and from war crimes, in yet another Best Picture and Best Director nominated film, *Judgement at Nuremberg* (1961), to saving animals from extinction, in *Bless the Beasts and the Children* (1971).

Between 1958 and 1967, Kramer seemed to have his finger smack dab on the pulse of the American public. Serious issues were in vogue and with big budgets and all-star casts, he combined entertainment with socially conscious filmmaking to memorable effect. Among his other films during this, his most successful, period were *Inherit the Wind* (1960), *A Child Is Waiting* (1963), and yet another Best Picture and Best Director nominated movie, *Ship of Fools* (1965). Kramer was also not above merely having a cinematic good time; he produced and directed *It's a Mad, Mad, Mad, Mad World* (1963).

Kramer was less successful in the 1970s; he lost touch with younger audiences when he tried to make a statement about the youth culture in *RPM* (1970). None of his later films caught on either, despite strong performances by George C. Scott in *Oklahoma Crude* (1973) and Dick Van Dyke in *The Runner Stumbles* (1979). Kramer shot the latter film in Seattle, and the director stayed in the city teaching and writing for six years thereafter. He had all but abandoned the movie business. In recent years, however, he has returned to filmmaking, announcing plans to produce and direct a new message movie called *Polonaise* about Polish labor leader Lech Walesa.

KUBRICK, STANLEY *(1928–   )* One of the few contemporary American directors who did not serve an apprenticeship with a studio nor gain his training at a film school. Almost entirely self-taught, Kubrick soon became one of a handful of directors (beginning in the 1960s) whose name alone was as much of a selling point as the stars who appeared in his films. While some critics have complained that the director is merely a cold technician, many others have called him one of the great film artists of our time.

Born in the Bronx, Kubrick was a poor student who was encouraged by his physician father to take up photography as a hobby. By the time he graduated from high school, young Kubrick was so accomplished as a photographer that he landed a job with *Look* magazine. His interest in all things visual led him to pursue a budding interest in filmmaking by writing, directing, editing, and producing (with borrowed funds from relatives) a one-reel documentary called *Day of the Flight* (1950). It cost $3,900 to make, and he eventually sold it to RKO-Pathé for a $100 profit. He sold a second documentary, *The Flying Padre* (1951), to RKO-Pathé and then quit his job at *Look*. He was hooked on filmmaking.

At the age of twenty-five, he was virtually the entire creative *and* technical crew for his first feature film, a privately funded (by family and friends) movie called *Fear and Desire* (1953). It found modest distribution in the art-house circuit, and encouraged yet other small investors to help Kubrick make *Killer's Kiss* (1955). Neither film turned a profit.

Kubrick's movies caught the attention of producer Jim Harris, with whom he formed a production company. Still on a low budget, but with enough money to hire stars and a crew, Kubrick wrote and directed the taut, suspenseful crime movie *The Killing* (1956). The film received good reviews, though it bore more than a passing resemblance to John Huston's *The Asphalt Jungle* (1950), to the extent that it even starred the same actor, Sterling Hayden *(q.v.)*.

His next movie, however, was a genuine, original masterpiece: *Paths of Glory* (1957), still considered by many to be Kubrick's finest achievement. Yet this bitter and deeply touching antiwar film, set against the backdrop of World War I, was almost never produced.

Kubrick pedaled the script around Hollywood, but no one was willing to finance it until Kirk Douglas *(q.v.)* agreed to be the film's star.

Kubrick had chosen to retain a percentage of the profits of both *The Killing* and *Paths of Glory* rather than take a salary. And as both films failed at the box office he didn't make a dime.

He had worked on the script of *One-Eyed Jacks* (1961) and was supposed to direct it, but at the last moment Marlon Brando *(q.v.)* decided to work both sides of the camera. At that point, Kubrick was hired to replace director Anthony Mann *(q.v.)* on the troubled epic *Spartacus* (1960). He did a credible job and the film was successful, but the director doesn't include it among his own works, the rest of which he was far more deeply involved in as a writer, director, and often as a producer.

After *Spartacus*, Kubrick left America to make *Lolita* (1962) in England. Though the film was set in the United States, the only funding he could get was British because American studios were afraid of the sexual nature of Nabokov's story. *Lolita*, however, was a critical and box office hit that stretched the acceptable limits of sexual material allowed in the movies, no doubt because it was a comedy (albeit a dark one).

No other comedy of its time, however, was as dark as Kubrick's next film, *Dr. Strangelove or: How I Learned to Stop Worrying and Love the Bomb* (1964). Clearly, Kubrick was not interested in a mass audience, but his film was a surprise hit and Kubrick's reputation as a director was growing.

Kubrick made *Dr. Strangelove* in England because Peter Sellers, one of his principal stars of the film, could not leave the country. And Kubrick, who found England an agreeable place to work, decided to continue making his films there, which he has done ever since.

Kubrick's next film was, in some ways, even more controversial than *Dr. Strangelove*. *2001: A Space Oydessey* (1968) was a science-fiction epic that divided critics into those who thought it was empty-headed and silly or those who found it provocatively prophetic. But both critical camps agreed that the film was visually stunning. And young audiences in particular flocked to the film to experience its stunning visual images, often under the influence of various drugs.

Kubrick successfully married both style and substance in *A Clockwork Orange* (1971), a futuristic fable about a violent, sex-crazed society. The movie was another smash hit, further enhancing his image as a thinking person's director who could deliver commercially.

His interest in visual composition, however, got the better of him in *Barry Lyndon* (1975). An overwhelmingly beautiful film to watch, the story moves along so ponderously, however, that it failed to draw an audience beyond Kubrick's devoted fans. It was the director's first commercial flop since *Paths of Glory*.

It appeared as if Kubrick was back on track when he adapted Stephen King's horror novel *The Shining* (1980) and hired Jack Nicholson *(q.v.)* to star. King's novels, however, have not often been transferred successfully to the screen, and *The Shining* did not turn into the hit that many expected it would be.

Kubrick's last film to date, *Full Metal Jacket*, was both a critical and box office success, although it would have undoubtedly drawn larger audiences had it not been released after *Platoon* (1986), the much ballyhooed Academy Award–winning Vietnam War movie.

The length of time between each of Kubrick's films is due to his intense involvement in every element of his films' development, from conception to promotion. The long hiatus between pictures has also added to his mystique, making each of his films a much-anticipated event.

See also: antiwar films; black comedy

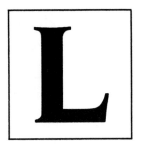

LADD, ALAN (1913–1964)   Though as an actor he had very little range, he did have presence. Playing either a contemporary tough guy in the 1940s or a western hero in the 1950s, Ladd enjoyed nearly two decades of stardom, but he is largely remembered for only one film, *Shane* (1953). But even if his films were not memorable, his tough guy image survives: Ladd in his trenchcoat, holding a pistol, with Veronica Lake *(q.v.)* smirking into his handsome face.

Ladd was only twenty years old when he broke into the movies. He was signed by Universal Pictures, which intended to groom him for stardom but decided to drop him six months later. After a series of odd jobs that included a stint as a grip at Warner Bros. and some extra work, he met Sue Carol, a former actress-turned-agent, who made it her job to turn Ladd into a star. Eventually, she also turned him into a husband.

At first he was cast in mostly "B" movies, such as *Rulers of the Sea* (1939) and *Petticoat Politics* (1941). He had a small role as a reporter (seen only in shadow) in *Citizen Kane* (1941) and a more significant part in *The Black Cat* (1941). The latter film brought him some attention and a chance to play an even larger role in *Joan of Paris* (1942), in which he showed genuine star quality.

Paramount was impressed and the studio gave him a plum part in *This Gun for Hire* (1942), pairing him with another relative newcomer, Veronica Lake. The two clicked on screen (though Ladd would later say he never liked working with her), and a new team was born. The pair would only act together in four films, but they were the definitive 1940s screen couple until Bogart and Bacall.

Ladd was rushed into more tough guy roles and both he and the audience responded. The remake of Dashiell Hammett's *The Glass Key* (1942), with Lake, was a solid hit. And then he showed he could carry a film

without Lake when he played the cynical hero in *China* (1943).

With films like *The Blue Dahlia* (1946) and *Whispering Smith* (1948), Ladd maintained his popularity throughout the 1940s, until he overreached and played Jay Gatsby in *The Great Gatsby* (1949). His fans didn't want to see him in a "serious" film, and neither did the critics. He tried to recoup with several action films, but his career appeared to be on a slide.

Then came *Shane* (1953), which many feel to be the best film that Ladd made, and which was undoubtedly his most successful, earning more than $9 million. The actor might have been associated with yet another classic if he hadn't turned down the role eventually taken by James Dean in *Giant* (1956).

Alan Ladd spent the rest of the 1950s and early 1960s in films of lesser and lesser quality, the best of which was probably *The Proud Rebel* (1958). Unfortunately, he didn't age well and heavy drinking made his face look puffy. His drinking, coupled with pills, led to his death in 1964, just before the release of *The Carpetbaggers* (1964), in which he made his last film appearance.

One of Alan Ladd's sons, Alan Ladd, Jr., became a major force in Hollywood as a producer in the late 1970s and 1980s.

LAEMMLE, CARL: *See* Universal Pictures.

LAKE, VERONICA (1919–1973)   She had a short, meteoric career as a tough blonde in the early 1940s, based more on her looks than her acting ability. Yet despite her limitations as an actress, Lake had a come-hither quality that made her especially appealing when teamed with an "I don't give a damn" actor, who was, in most cases, Alan Ladd *(q.v.)*.

Born Constance Ockelman, she had very little acting training but riveting looks. After making the beauty contest circuit, she went to Hollywood to take some acting classes, quickly managing to land a few roles in local plays. Spotted by RKO, she made a screen test, and her film career was soon under way. After her debut in a small role in *Sorority House* (1939), Paramount tried the actress in minor parts in a few more films, but then the studio gambled and gave her a major role in *I Wanted Wings* (1941). The gamble paid off.

With her "peek-a-boo" hairstyle (long blond hair curled on one side partially obscuring her face), Lake became an instant star. Her next film was unquestionably her best. She played a tough, down-on-her-luck beauty who befriends Joel McCrea *(q.v.)* in Preston Sturges' *(q.v.)* classic comedy *Sullivan's Travels* (1941).

If *Sullivan's Travels* was her best film, *This Gun For Hire* (1942), co-starring Alan Ladd was the most important to her career. Lake's four films with Ladd would define her Hollywood image, one of vulnerability balanced by taunting sensuality, which made the most of Ladd's limited romantic appeal. Their other films together were *The Glass Key* (1942), *The Blue Dahlia* (1946), and *Saigon* (1948).

Veronica Lake's star, however, began to fade even before she finished her four movies with Ladd. One factor in her slide can be traced directly to the U.S. government. Her hairstyle, copied by so many women during World War II, was causing an alarming number of women to get their long hair caught in defense-industry machinery. Lake was asked, for the good of the war effort, to change her hairstyle. She did, and her popularity plummeted.

The actress continued to appear in minor movies throughout the rest of the 1940s, saved from total oblivion by her last two pairings with Alan Ladd. Her last film in Hollywood was *Slattery's Hurricane* (1949). She made a movie in Mexico in 1952 and then a couple of cheapies in 1966 and 1970 after she had been discovered by a New York newspaper working as a cocktail waitress.

LAMARR, HEDY (1913–　) An actress, she came to the United States from Austria in 1938 with the unofficial title of "The World's Most Beautiful Woman." With her delicate features, aquiline nose, alluring eyes, sensuous mouth, perfect skin, and exquisite figure, it was a title well-deserved. Unfortunately, her acting ability wasn't the equal of her good looks. And having had little emotional rapport with her audiences, it was inevitable that her career would fade with her beauty.

Born Hedwig Eva Maria Kiesler in Vienna, Lamarr was the daughter of a well-to-do banker. Discovered by Max Reinhardt, she went on to appear in Central and Eastern European films in the early 1930s, culminating in the 1933 Czech film *Ecstasy*, which featured her infamous nude swimming scene. She was typecast forevermore as a sex goddess.

Hedy Lamarr may not have been much of an actress, but her exquisite looks and scandalous reputation (she filmed a nude scene in the 1933 European film *Ecstacy*) brought her a high degree of publicity and a decade of Hollywood stardom. Photo courtesy of Movie Star News.

Following such European actresses who conquered Hollywood as Greta Garbo and Marlene Dietrich *(qq.v.)*, Hedy Lamarr arrived in America with a contract and a major build-up from MGM. She had her first starring role opposite Charles Boyer *(q.v.)* in *Algiers* (1938), a solid hit, which was followed by several other successful films, such as *Lady of the Tropics* (1939), *Boom Town* (1940), and *Comrade X* (1940).

Considering her Germanic roots, Lamarr's career didn't suffer unduly during the war years. Cast as an exotic beauty, she seemed less German than merely foreign. She appeared in some fine films, such as *H. M. Pulham, Esq.* (1941), *White Cargo* (1942), in which she was a delight to behold as a native girl, and the gripping mystery *Experiment Perilous* (1944). One could therefore forgive such clunkers as *The Heavenly Body* (1944) and *Her Highness and the Bellboy* (1945). Her career, however, would have been much better served—in fact, she might have become a superstar—had she not refused to star in *Casablanca* (1942), *Gaslight* (1944), and *Laura* (1944).

In most of her earlier films, Lamarr was cast with strong male stars such as Clark Gable, Spencer Tracy, and William Powell *(qq.v.)*. After the war, she was made to carry her own films and her career faltered as a result. Then she was offered the part of Delilah in Paramount's production of *Samson and Delilah* (1949) and scored her greatest success; it represented the pinnacle of her Hollywood career. She suffered a swift descent, immediately falling into "B" movies such as *A Lady Without a Passport* (1950) and *Copper Canyon* (1950). Playing second banana to Bob Hope in his comedy *My Favorite Spy* (1951) signaled the end of Lamarr's glamour era and she fled Hollywood to make European films, coming back to America in the later 1950s to appear in just two more movies, *The Story of Mankind* in 1957 (as Joan of Arc) and as Jane Powell's mother in *The Female Animal* (1958).

Lamarr left the limelight only to resurface in 1965 when she was arrested for shoplifting. In 1966 she published her autobiography, *Ecstasy and Me,* then sued her collaborator on the book before finally fading into obscurity.

See also: sex symbols: female

LAMOUR, DOROTHY (1914–   )

The actress who made the sarong famous. Lamour—her real name was Dorothy Kaumeyer—had a dark, exotic look that brought her stardom (and typecasting) as a "native girl."

Lamour was born and grew up in Louisiana, becoming "Miss New Orleans" in 1931. After a short career as a band singer, she was signed by Paramount and immediately cast in the title role of *The Jungle Princess* (1936); the movie did rather well. In the latter 1930s she worked steadily, although she rarely starred in her own pictures.

Her career took a fateful turn when she was loaned to Samuel Goldwyn for the John Ford *(q.v.)* film *Hurricane* (1937). She played the young native girl with whom Jon Hall fell in love. The movie caused a tidal wave at the box office. Lamour and her sarong (which she wore the first time in that film) became sensations.

Her image had been set. Movies like *Her Jungle Love* (1938) and *Tropic Holiday* (1938) were natural followups. Of course, not all of her films required her to wear a sarong—witness *Spawn of the North* and *St. Louis Blues* (1939).

Finally in 1940, Lamour was teamed with Bob Hope and Bing Crosby *(qq.v.)* in their first Road picture, *The Road to Singapore*. She wore her sarong yet again, but it was all in good fun. Just as Margaret Dumont was considered by many to be the fourth Marx Brother, Lamour was very much a part of the Hope/Crosby team. She appeared in all seven of the Road movies.

Lamour's career in the 1940s and early 1950s—apart from the *Road* films—was relatively minor. Her best movies were *My Favorite Brunette* (1947) with Bob Hope and *The Greatest Show on Earth* (1952). She did little else of quality.

But the Road films were something special and La-

Dorothy Lamour can look back at a career that included more than fifty films. She is best remembered as the woman whom Bob Hope and Bing Crosby fought over in their seven Road movies. Photo courtesy of Dorothy Lamour Howard.

mour was more than mere decoration. She had a playful sexiness, never taking herself too seriously. She struck the right balance between the two male stars, and could handle a quip and toss it back at either Hope or Crosby with élan.

Going into semi-retirement in 1953, she appeared not only in the final Road movie but also in small parts in *Donovan's Reef* (1963) and *Pajama Party* (1965), as well as occasionally on TV.

Lamour often made fun of her own image; after all, she was never really a sex symbol and she knew it. The sarong image, in fact, embarrassed her. But the sarong—and Lamour—have been forever linked.

LANCASTER, BURT (1913–   )

An actor with a commanding screen presence who has succeeded at being both a star of action films and a sensitive, thoughtful player in art-house fare. In fact at the height of his popularity he would alternate between more and less commercial projects. Even into his seventies, Lancaster's masculine good looks have made him a favorite of both male and female fans in a film career that began with immediate success in 1946. Though critics tended to disparage him initially—perhaps because he was so popular—he has come to be recognized not only as a unique movie personality but a truly talented performer whose work on film seems better with each viewing.

Lancaster has also been a producer; he formed a production company in 1948 that went on to make a number of important movies, chief among them the Oscar-winning sleeper hit of 1954, *Marty*.

He was born Burton Stephen Lancaster to a lower middle-class family in New York City and grew up on the rough-and-tumble streets of East Harlem. Tall and athletic, Lancaster excelled at sports and won a scholarship to New York University. His college career ended abruptly, however, when he decided to become a professional acrobat, teaming up with his childhood friend, Nick Cravat, who later appeared in a number of Lancaster's swashbuckler films.

Lancaster and Cravat led a grueling life, working for circuses and appearing in vaudeville with only sporadic success. Finally, they gave up and Lancaster took a series of conventional jobs, including refrigerator repairman. World War II soon saw him overseas and in combat. By the time he mustered out in 1945, he was thirty-two years old and without a career.

The story goes that Lancaster's re-entry into show business was precipitated by an encounter with a Broadway producer who happened to be sharing an elevator with the handsome and dashing ex-soldier. The producer simply assumed that Lancaster had to be an actor and asked him to audition for a role in a play he was putting on. Lancaster obliged, won the role, and later that year made his Broadway debut in *The Sound of Hunting* (1945). The play was a flop; Lancaster was not.

His matinee-idol looks seemed perfect for the movies and Hollywood immediately beckoned. He was given the role of Swede in *The Killers* (1946) and leaped to stardom with a powerful, brooding performance in what was a low-budget movie that became the surprise hit of the year. In his next starring role, Lancaster proved to be a fiery actor whose energy and audacity helped turn Jules Dassin's prison picture, *Brute Force* (1947), into a minor masterpiece.

Lancaster's athleticism led him almost singlehandedly to revive the swashbuckler genre in the early 1950s. Films such as *The Flame and the Arrow* (1950), *The Crimson Pirate* (1952), and *His Majesty O'Keefe* (1953) brought favorable comparisons to Douglas Fairbanks and Errol Flynn *(qq.v.)*. In addition to his swashbucklers, Lancaster also showed off his athletic prowess in other hits, most notably in the biopic *(q.v.)* *Jim Thorpe— All American* (1951) and *Trapeze* (1956). His versatility also extended to westerns, many of them especially top-notch, including, *Apache* (1954), *Vera Cruz* (1954), the not-so-terrific *The Kentuckian* (1955) (which was his one attempt at directing himself), *Gunfight at the O.K. Corral* (1957), *The Unforgiven* (1960), *The Professionals* (1966), *Ulzana's Raid* (1972), and *Cattle Annie and Little Britches* (1980). As a romantic lead, there could be no doubt as to his abilities after his rousing love scene in the surf with Deborah Kerr *(q.v.)* in *From Here to*

Eternity (1953), a film that brought the actor his first nomination for Best Actor.

But Lancaster also surprised and often delighted more serious audiences with his restrained performances in such seemingly noncommercial films as *All My Sons* (1948), *Come Back, Little Sheba* (1952), (in which he played very much against type), *The Rose Tattoo* (1955), *The Rainmaker* (1957), *Sweet Smell of Success* (1957), *Separate Tables* (1958), *The Devil's Disciple* (1959), and *Elmer Gantry* (1960), for which he won an Oscar for Best Actor.

Even as his popularity began to wind down in the 1960s, Lancaster continued to give inspired performances in many an off-beat film. for instance, he was wonderful in *The Birdman of Alcatraz* (1962), gaining his third Best Actor Academy Award nomination, *The Leopard* (1963), and *The Swimmer* (1968). His decline in popularity that began in the 1960s accelerated during the early- to mid-1970s and even his better films—of which there were few—did not do well at the box office. Nonetheless, such movies as *Twilight's Last Gleaming* (1977) and *Go Tell the Spartans* (1978), seemed to suggest that Lancaster was far from through. He proved it in 1980 with his rich and complex portrayal of an aging small-time hood in the Louis Malle-directed hit *Atlantic City* (1980). He garnered a richly deserved Oscar nomination for Best Actor for his performance, the fourth such honor of his career.

During the 1980s, Lancaster has tended to play mostly eccentric supporting roles in films such as *Local Hero* (1983) and *Little Treasure* (1985). He has, however, been known to come out full throttle, showing the old magic, such as when he and longtime friend and oft-time screen partner Kirk Douglas *(q.v.)* shared top billing in *Tough Guys* (1986), a film admired more for the acting of its old pros than for the quality of its script.

Ill health in his later years has not prevented Lancaster from appearing on stage as well as in the occasional television movie and miniseries during the 1980s. His presence in any medium continues to be a powerful reminder of old-time Hollywood star quality.

LANG, FRITZ (1890–1976) He was a leading director during Germany's golden age of cinema in the 1920s and then one of Hollywood's most gifted filmmakers for more than twenty years. No matter where or when he made his films, Lang's themes were consistent; he was a determined anti-fascist whose movies often communicated moral warnings of both a political and personal nature. Forces of fate, revenge, power, and lust were at the heart of his films, and he expressed himself on these subjects with a fluid visual style that was dramatic and evocative, resulting in an impressive, emotionally haunting body of work.

Born and raised in Vienna, Lang was expected to

follow in his father's footsteps and become an architect. Instead, at the age of twenty, he ran off to Paris to become an artist. He became a vagabond, traveling all over the world, living the life of a bohemian until he returned to Paris to continue his painting. But when World War I broke out, Lang fled to Austria and served in his homeland's army. Severely wounded near the end of the fighting, he spent a full year in a hospital, where he began writing screenplays, selling some of them to German directors, among them Joe May, a major force in the new German cinema. Soon after his health was restored, Lang became a force in his own right in the emerging German film industry, writing and directing as he would throughout the rest of his film career.

The first film Lang directed was *Halbblut/The Half-Breed* in 1919. He was slated to direct the now-famous Robert Weine German Expressionist film, *The Cabinet of Dr. Caligari* (1919), but was tied up making what was to become his own first hit, *Die Spinnen/The Spiders* (1919), a two-part film about a criminal organization trying to take over the world. The concept of world domination, which would later become so dear to the Nazis, was a subject Lang repeatedly dealt with in his films, particularly his famous Dr. Mabuse movies (a sort of Dr. No character), of which he made several throughout his lifetime.

One of Lang's two most famous films during his German era was *Metropolis* (1927), a film inspired by a short trip to New York City. *Metropolis* was a dazzling movie about the future that dealt with the loss of freedom in a mechanized society. The visual effects, created with models and magnificent set design, are as staggering today as they were in the late 1920s. In fact, as proof of its timelessness, *Metropolis* was re-released as a theatrical film in 1984 with a new musical score and color tinting.

Lang's other internationally famous film was his first sound motion picture. The film was *M* (1931), an elegantly directed movie that detailed the pursuit of a child murderer by both the Berlin police and the underworld. Peter Lorre *(q.v.)* made his movie debut in the role of the murderer, and soon both Lang and Lorre, along with a great many other German-speaking artists, fled Europe when the Nazis came to power.

Lang, in particular, was vulnerable to Hitler's legions. He made a straightforward anti-Nazi film in 1933, which was banned by the party. When he was ordered to see Goebbels, Hitler's minister of propaganda, Lang was stunned to be offered the opportunity of coordinating and directing all films made under the Nazi regime. Lang, whose mother was Jewish, made his decision that very day, fleeing the country that night by train and leaving virtually all of his savings and belongings behind.

He made one film in France, and was then signed by David O. Selznick *(q.v.)*, representing MGM, for a one picture deal in Hollywood. Once in America, he immediately applied for U.S. citizenship and set about both learning the language and discovering as much about his new home as possible.

Having seen firsthand in Germany the result of mob psychology, Lang was determined to wake up his audience. His first film in America was *Fury* (1936), a movie about an innocent man (Spencer Tracy) who is accused of being a murderer and is nearly lynched by an angry small-town mob. The film was a hit but MGM let Lang go. Over the next twenty years, the director worked for several studios, often as an independent.

All of his films of the late 1930s, right into the new decade, centered on persecuted individuals and their attempts to avoid being destroyed by an intolerant society. *You Only Live Once* (1937), *You and Me* (1938), and *The Return of Frank James* (1940) all dealt with this same theme.

Considering his relatively recent arrival in America, Lang was particularly adept at westerns. Besides *The Return of Frank James*, he made two other horse operas, *Western Union* (1941) and *Rancho Notorious* (1952), all of them memorable, intelligent movies, the last of which is especially noteworthy as the first western to use a ballad as a thematic thread all the way through the movie.

The war years seemed to galvanize Lang into a frenzy of creativity. His anti-Nazi films were not mere propaganda efforts, but richly drawn, suspenseful, thought-provoking films that detailed the differences between totalitarianism and democracy. For instance, his excellent thriller *Manhunt* (1941) concerned the moral dilemma of a skilled hunter (Walter Pidgeon) who has the opportunity to stalk and kill Adolph Hitler. Among his other powerful anti-Nazi films were *Hangmen Also Die* (1943), a film whose screenplay he wrote in collaboration with Bertold Brecht (though Brecht is not credited), and *Ministry of Fear* (1944), one of Lang's most highly regarded thrillers.

But not all of Lang's work during World War II was anti-Nazi films. In fact, two of his best movies concerning the tragic consequences of uncontrolled sexual desires were made during this period, *The Woman in the Window* (1944) and *Scarlet Street* (1945).

After a nearly unbroken decade-long string of hits and quality films, Lang suffered a long dry spell of poor films and bad box office that lasted until 1952. He reemerged with the previously mentioned revenge western *Rancho Notorious*, a gripping story of lust and betrayal, *Clash by Night* (1952), and one of the best *film noir (q.v.)* crime thrillers of the 1950s, *The Big Heat* (1953). Then came a rash of mediocre movies, followed by a film reminiscent of *M* called *While the City Sleeps* (1956).

Unfortunately, his last film in America, *Beyond a Reasonable Doubt* (1956), was rather poor and showed signs of studio interference that had always been a thorn in Lang's side. Fed up with the Hollywood system, he went to India to make a movie that never came to fruition. On his way home, however, he stopped in Germany and ultimately made three films there, the last one his final Dr. Mabuse movie, *The Thousand Eyes of Dr. Mabuse* (1960).

Lang returned to America and, apart from appearing in Jean-Luc Godard's *Contempt* (1963), led a quiet, financially secure retirement in the country that he had adopted as his home.

LANGDON, HARRY (1884–1944) During the mid-1920s, he was an enormously popular silent comedian. With his almost other-wordly baby face, Langdon played at a peculiar form of humor that contrasted his childlike looks with adult desires. The result was funny, but with a disturbing edge.

Langdon was a rather non-athletic actor, and in his way he was different from his three acrobatic and physical comic contemporaries—Charlie Chaplin, Buster Keaton, and Harold Lloyd. Nonetheless, Langdon was a compelling star, proving that physical comedy wasn't a necessary ingredient for silent screen success.

From a very early age, Langdon began working in the circus, vaudeville, burlesque—in short, wherever he could earn a living in show business. As his body grew older, though, his face didn't seem to age. He looked strangely like a child with a man's body.

When Langdon, who had a reputation as an entertainer, came to Hollywood, he was signed up by Mack Sennett *(q.v.)* and was eventually teamed with gagwriter (soon to become famous director) Frank Capra *(q.v.)*, and Harry Edwards *(q.v.)*, a director. With the help of these two talented gentlemen, Langdon flourished on film.

He started with two-reelers, making his first film in 1924, *Picking Peaches*. There were, altogether, twenty-five two- and three-reelers, virtually all of which were hits.

In 1926, Langdon made his first feature. He had left Sennett and had gone to Warner Bros. Wisely, he had taken Capra and Edwards with him. Three excellent full-length comedies followed: *Tramp, Tramp, Tramp* (1926), *The Strong Man* (1927), and *Long Pants* (1927). All three movies were massive hits.

But then Langdon virtually destroyed his own career by firing Capra and Edwards in order to write and direct his own movies. He made several films for Warner Bros. over the next year and a half, and one was worse than the other. His movies were a form of box office suicide. By 1931 he was bankrupt.

Except for the occasional role in a feature, Langdon spent most of the 1930s and early 1940s making sound

Harry Langdon was the silent era's version of Pee Wee Herman. Unlike Herman, though, Langdon was as childlike in real life as he was on screen. His naivete finally led to his downfall. Photo courtesy of The Siegel Collection.

shorts of no particular distinction. He died in 1944 of a cerebral hemorrhage.

LANGE, JESSICA (1950–) A blonde actress, she seemed destined to become a mere trivia question after her film debut in the critically pounded remake of *King Kong* (1976), but she rebounded in the 1980s to become one of Hollywood's premiere female stars. Lange's open, Midwestern features have made her an ideal pick for a number of uniquely American films, many of which have either been critical or commercial successes (or both).

Raised in Minnesota, Lange flew the coop after two years at the University of Minnesota to study mime in Paris, eventually returning to the U.S. to embark on a modeling career in New York.

Intent on becoming an actress, she received what appeared to be her big break when she was chosen to play the Fay Wray role in Dino De Laurentis' ill-advised remake of *King Kong*. Thought of as a mere sex object, she was dismissed by the critics, only to turn up again in a leading role in Bob Fosse's much-admired *All That Jazz* (1979). After flopping in *How to Beat the High Cost of Living* (1980), she was cast in yet another remake, this time playing the Lana Turner role opposite Jack Nicholson *(q.v.)* in *The Postman Always Rings Twice* (1981). Though this film was also considered inferior to the original 1946 version, the sex scenes between Lange and Nicholson were so steamy that the film managed a successful, if controversial, run in theaters. At this point, Lange was finally being touted as an actress with genuine star potential.

She fulfilled that potential the following year when she showed her range in two decidedly different roles, playing the doomed actress, Frances Farmer, in the biopic *Frances* (1982) and the bubbly ingenue in *Tootsie* (1982). Though she won a Best Supporting Actress Oscar for her performance in the latter film, it was clearly the total sum of her acting that year that brought Lange the Academy Award.

Her career has since been a series of triumphs. She has wisely played characters with deep roots in middle America, such as the heroine in *Country* (1984), a film she coproduced and for which she gained an Oscar nomination for Best Actress, *Sweet Dreams* (1985), a biopic of country western singer Patsy Cline in which she gave another Oscar-nominated performance, *Crimes of the Heart* (1986), based on Beth Henley's Pulitzer Price–winning play set in the Deep South, and *Everybody's All-American* (1988), a story about a football hero's marriage.

Lange has had a long, personal relationship with playwright/actor Sam Shepherd, who has also appeared in a number of her films.

LASKY, JESSE L. (1880–1958)   He was a pioneering film executive and, later, an independent producer of note. A former vaudeville musician, Lasky's major contributions to the developing movie industry came as a result of his partnership with Samuel Goldfish (later Goldwyn) and Cecil B. DeMille *(qq.v.)* in 1913. The three enterprising young men established the Jesse L. Lasky Feature Play Company with Lasky as president. Their first film, *The Squaw Man* (1914), was shot in Hollywood by the company's neophyte director, DeMille. Its huge success put both Lasky's company and the sleepy little Southern California town in which it was made on the map.

Lasky's business was eventually folded into Adolph Zukor's Famous Players *(q.v.)* film company in 1916, the two firms becoming known as Famous Players-Lasky. Zukor was president of the new company and Lasky was relegated to vice president in charge of production, where he was instrumental in developing the producer system, i.e., the delegation of responsibility to individual "supervisors" who reported to him. As feature-length films became the norm, Lasky pioneered the use of original screenplays, hiring writers to concoct fresh scenarios for a fraction of what it would

have cost him to secure the film rights to famous plays or novels.

Lasky stayed aboard Adolph Zukor's ever-expanding conglomerate (which ultimately became Paramount Pictures) until the early 1930s when he was forced out by Depression-era business reversals. He continued on in Hollywood as an independent producer for many of the industry's major studios, making such films as *The Power and the Glory* (1933), *Sergeant York* (1941), *Rhapsody in Blue* (1945), and *The Great Caruso* (1951).

Lasky's son, Jesse Lasky, Jr., was a moderately successful screenwriter, novelist, and poet. His most noteworthy screenplays were written for his father's old partner, Cecil B. DeMille, among them, *Union Pacific* (1939), *Samson and Delilah* (1949), and *The Ten Commandments* (1956).

LASSIE   Perhaps the most famous dog in the history of the movies. The collie starred in a total of eight films plus another feature that was compiled from four TV shows. Also featured in a radio program, the canine star is probably best remembered today for her long-running TV series.

Lassie was trained by Rudd Weatherwax, who also trained Asta from the Thin Man mysteries and Daisy from the Blondie movie series.

Lassie has always been referred to as "she," but in actual fact was male. In true Hollywood fashion (in what might be called a canine version of *42nd Street*), the intended star of the first Lassie movie, *Lassie Come Home* (1943), could not perform (it was summer and she was shedding too heavily for the role). Pal, her male double, stepped in with all four feet and became a star.

While male dogs aren't as smart as female dogs, they are better-looking and Pal and his male descendants have played Lassie ever since.

Lassie Come Home featured Elizabeth Taylor *(q.v.)*, Roddy McDowall, Edmund Gwenn, Dame May Whitty, and Elsa Lanchester. Despite the talented cast, it was the dog who emerged as a star.

Between 1945 and 1951 there was a Lassie film every year except 1947. All of these MGM films turned a profit, although the box office was diminishing by the end of the cycle.

The last serious attempt to revive Lassie's career on the big screen took place in 1978 when the collie was paired with James Stewart *(q.v.)* in *The Magic of Lassie*. The film was not a success.

Just as Lassie assumed the title of leading dog star from Rin-Tin-Tin, she passed it on to Benji.
See also: animals in film

LAUGHTON, CHARLES (1899–1962)   He was, without question, the foremost character actor/star of the 1930s and 1940s. With his fleshy face and roundish physique he seemed an unlikely film actor, let alone a major star, but his talent was so striking that for the better part of two decades, audiences regarded his films as sure-bet, quality entertainment.

Laughton was not always the easiest person to cast, and a good number of his movies were poor vehicles, but even in these he was a pleasure to watch as he chewed up the scenery in delightfully hammy performances. In his better films, however, Laughton never even appeared to be acting; his technique was seamless, and he could truly breathe life into his creations.

Born in England, Laughton seemed destined for a career in hotel management. His father, who was in the hotel business, got his gawky son a job as a desk clerk. But after serving in the military during World War I, Laughton joined an amateur theater group. Soon thereafter he was accepted in the Royal Academy of Dramatic Arts where his talent finally had a chance to grow and flourish.

He worked steadily and successfully on the London stage, married Elsa Lanchester (who would later play the title role in *The Bride of Frankenstein* in 1935), and joined her in his first film, a comic two-reeler, *Bluebottles,* in 1928.

Laughton made a few films in England, but his stage success on Broadway in *Payment Deferred* and a revival of *Alibi,* in which he played Agatha Christie's Hercule Poiret in 1931, brought him to the attention of Hollywood. On the strength of his acting reputation, Paramount signed him to play supporting character parts.

He was loaned to Universal for his first Hollywood film, *The Old Dark House* (1932). It was an excellent horror movie directed by a master of the genre, James Whale, and the film boasted a remarkable cast that included Raymond Massey, Boris Karloff *(q.v.),* and Melvyn Douglas *(q.v.).* It was an auspicious beginning for the newly arrived actor.

Laughton had a few memorable eccentric roles over the next few years, such as Dr. Moreau in *Island of Lost Souls* (1932). His breakthrough, however, came not in Hollywood, but in an English film, *The Private Life of Henry VIII* (1933). The Alexander Korda movie was a surprise international hit, setting the groundwork for a newly revived British film industry, and it launched Laughton's career to genuine star status when he won an Oscar for Best Actor for his portrayal of Henry.

When he returned to Hollywood in 1934, he began a series of remarkable performances that included the tyrannical father in *The Barretts of Wimpole Street* (1934), the prissy English butler in *Ruggles of Red Gap* (1935), the relentless Inspector Javert in *Les Miserables* (1935), and the cruel Captain Bligh in *Mutiny on the Bounty* (1935). In an act of professional graciousness, he turned down yet another marvelous role, Micawber in *David Copperfield* (1935), insisting that W. C. Fields was the only actor who could do the part justice.

Though he had starring roles in the two biggest hits of 1935, *Mutiny on the Bounty* and *Les Miserables,* Laughton left Hollywood, frustrated by the fact that he had become typed as a heavy. He had wanted a greater range of parts, and he had especially wanted to play more likable characters.

The next several years were relatively fallow ones for Laughton. He gave a marvelous, understated performance as the painter in Alexander Korda's *Rembrandt* (1936). Then came the famous Korda disaster, *I, Claudius,* which was never finished. His film career stumbled along throughout the rest of the 1930s until, at the end of the decade, he returned to Hollywood to give one of his greatest, most touching performances as Quasimodo in *The Hunchback of Notre Dame* (1939). This remake of the Lon Chaney *(q.v.)* silent film was a magnificent spectacle, with Laughton displaying an exhaustive range of emotions.

His career should have skyrocketed after *Hunchback,* but few roles were important enough for his massive talent. Not until he played the painfully shy French school teacher in Jean Renoir's anti-Nazi film, *This Land is Mine* (1943), did he have an opportunity to really shine. Following this, he appeared in other excellent films, such as *The Canterville Ghost* (1944), *The Suspect* (1945), *The Paradine Case* (1948), and *The Big Clock* (1948), but good roles in good films were becoming scarcer for Laughton. A sharp downward slide in his career in the late 1940s and early 1950s culminated in his embarrassing appearance in *Abbott and Costello Meet Captain Kidd* (1952).

In 1955, Laughton briefly turned his attentions to directing, working behind the camera in *The Night of the Hunter.* A stylish thriller with a screenplay by James Agee *(q.v.),* the film received good reviews but it languished at the box office. It was the only film Laughton ever directed.

Laughton had stayed away from the movies during long stretches of the 1950s, but he returned to give a brilliant performance in Billy Wilder's *Witness for the Prosecution* (1957). He and his wife were nominated for Best Supporting Actor and Actress Oscars for their peerless work in that movie. It was a marvelous comeback, but he appeared in only three more films before he died of cancer in 1962, his last being *Advise and Consent* (1962), in which he played a sly Southern senator to great effect.

LAUREL & HARDY (Stan Laurel, 1890–1965; Oliver Hardy, 1892–1957) Thin, shy Stan Laurel, and rotund, overbearing Oliver Hardy were a comedy team that milked laughs out of a Mutt & Jeff relationship. The audience was always way ahead of them, knowing full well that any of their schemes was always doomed to failure. But just how the pair would fail was always in doubt.

Laurel & Hardy were one of the very few comedy teams to make a totally successful transition from the silent to sound era. Photo courtesy of Movie Star News.

Laurel & Hardy reacted to the failures predictably. For instance, Laurel had his famous whining cry; Hardy had his perfectly timed complaint: "Here's another fine mess you've gotten us into." It was the sheer repetition of their set pieces that made them comfortably familiar while also limiting their growth. Yet they were a popular team for roughly twenty years, and have regained a measure of popularity thanks to TV, revival houses, and more recently, videotape.

Laurel and Hardy, however, weren't always a team. Stan Laurel, who was born Arthur Stanley Jefferson in England, was a member, along with Charlie Chaplin (q.v.), of Fred Karno's Company. After Chaplin became a movie star, Laurel (who did a fine job of imitating him—and why not, he had been Chaplin's understudy), was hired by Hollywood to make his first appearance on film in a Chaplinesque short subject: *Nuts in May* (1918). He was in the movie business to stay, soon working for the former cowboy star turned producer "Broncho Billy" Anderson (q.v.). In 1919 Laurel appeared in a film, *Lucky Dog,* with an actor

named Oliver Hardy—but nothing came of it. Stan Laurel would make more than fifty one- and two-reelers as a solo comedian.

Hardy, the heftier member of the team, was born in Atlanta, Georgia. He began his career as an extra in 1913, and because of his size, often played villains. Also because of his size, he picked up the nickname "Babe."

In 1926, when both comedians were under contract to Hal Roach (q.v.), they played together in *Slipping Wives,* followed by a number of large-cast comedy all-star films. There was a certain chemistry between the two, and Hal Roach (not the two comedians) decided to turn them into a team. Under the inspired direction of Leo McCarey the new team of Laurel & Hardy turned out more than thirty shorts that immediately captured a loyal audience. After McCarey left to pursue his directorial career, Stan Laurel became the creative force in the comedy team. Much of the inventiveness of their humor is due solely to his comic imagination.

Laurel & Hardy coped rather effectively with the arrival of sound in films in the late 1920s by ignoring it. The team simply continued doing their same brand of humor, only adding the language that seemed appropriate and nothing more.

They made their first feature in 1931, *Pardon Us*, which did only moderate business. With their main work still in comedy shorts, they reached their apogee of critical acceptance in 1932 when they won an Oscar for *The Music Box*. It was the first Oscar ever given in the category of Short Subjects, Live Action—Comedy.

For several years the pair made both shorts and features. It is their features of this era, however, that are now best remembered, for they include their two most loved films, *Sons of the Desert* (1933) and *Babes in Toyland* (1934). As the 1930s rolled on, so did Laurel & Hardy, making a number of other funny films, such as *Way Out West* (1937), *Blockheads* (1938), *The Flying Deuces* (1939), and *A Chump at Oxford* (1940), their last quality comedy.

The team continued making movies in the 1940s, but Laurel had little control of their material and the films were rather poor. Their last movie together was *Utopia* (1950), a French production that didn't serve them (or the audience) well.

Hardy had made a couple of supporting appearances in films without Laurel, specifically in *Zenobia* (1939) and *The Fighting Kentuckian* (1949).

After Oliver Hardy died in 1957, Hollywood realized that one of its treasures had passed away without proper recognition. In 1960 the Academy awarded Stan Laurel a Special Oscar for "his creative pioneering in the field of cinema comedy."
See also: comedy teams

LEE, SPIKE   *See* racism in Hollywood.

LEHMAN, ERNEST (1920–) A highly successful screenwriter who has also dabbled as a producer and director. He has either provided the stories or written the screenplays for sixteen films, many of them enormous hits. One of Lehman's unique talents has been his ability to pen solid scripts for big-budget movies, particularly musicals. Lehman has also been a particularly effective adapter of other writers' works. If he has a specialty, it would be fair to say that it is the suspense film, two of which he wrote for Alfred Hitchcock *(q.v.)*.

Lehman was a business editor and writer of short stories before the latter enterprise introduced him to Hollywood. A short story he coauthored became the basis of *The Inside Story* (1948). But his film-writing career began in earnest six years later when he wrote scripts for *Executive Suite* (1954) and *Sabrina* (1954), given the assignments, one might assume, because of his business writing background.

Lehman's streak of successful screenplays for blockbuster Hollywood musicals began in 1956 with *The King and I*. He followed that triumph with *West Side Story* (1961), *The Sound of Music* (1965), and then stumbled somewhat with *Hello, Dolly!* (1969), a film he also produced.

Among his suspense films, Lehman wrote *The Prize* (1963), *Black Sunday* (1977), and two excellent Hitchcock thrillers, the classic *North by Northwest* (1959) and *Family Plot* (1976).

Lehman took a number of chances, among them, writing *Sweet Smell of Success* (1957), which was based on his own story, and the script for *Who's Afraid of Virginia Woolf?* (1966), a highly controversial but much-praised film that he also produced. His biggest gamble, however, did not pay off. He wrote the screenplay, directed, and produced *Portnoy's Complaint* (1972), a film based on Philip Roth's best-selling novel. The movie was widely panned by the critics and had a short, unhappy commercial life.

In recent years he has been relatively inactive.

LEIGH, JANET (1927–) A popular actress of the 1950s and early 1960s, Leigh built a reputation as an attractive star of light entertainments. Though she appeared in nearly fifty films, she is best remembered today for only a few dramatic roles in the latter half of her career.

Born Jeanette Helen Morrison, she grew up in Stockton, California, the daughter of a ski lodge receptionist. While Leigh was away studying music at the College of the Pacific, actress Norma Shearer *(q.v.)* saw a photo of the young girl at The Sugar Bowl Ski Lodge and immediately contacted her studio, MGM.

Reacting to their star's enthusiasm, MGM sent for "Miss Morrison"; she was immediately tested, signed to a contract, renamed Janet Leigh, and, in a matter of weeks, was making her motion picture debut starring opposite Van Johnson *(q.v.)* in *The Romance of Rosy Ridge* (1947).

She took to her new job with surprising ease, becoming a full-fledge star in her own right in the early 1950s. Her marriage in 1951 to up-and-coming actor Tony Curtis *(q.v.,* they divorced in 1962) increased the couple's popularity and helped rocket both of their careers to new highs. They costarred in a number of successful movies, such as *Houdini* (1953), *The Vikings* (1958), and *Who Was That Lady?* (1960). Among her best movies of the 1950s, however, were *The Naked Spur* (1953), *Pete Kelly's Blues* (1955), and her most important film of the decade, Orson Welles' *Touch of Evil* (1958).

Her work in *Touch of Evil* suggested that Leigh was a much better actress than Hollywood had ever suspected. As a result, Alfred Hitchcock *(q.v.)* wanted her for the pivotal role of Marion in perhaps the director's most famous film, *Psycho* (1960). She was the only genuine star in the picture, and Hitchcock stunned the audience by killing her off in the famous shower se-

Janet Leigh was discovered by Norma Shearer and molded into a successful star of light, sexy comedies during the 1950s. Her reputation as a serious actress rests on her solid performances in *Touch of Evil* (1958) and *Psycho* (1960). Photo courtesy of Janet Leigh.

quence quite early in the film. Her performance was such, however, that the Academy of Motion Picture Arts and Sciences gave her a Besting Supporting Actress nomination. There were two other consequences resulting from her sexy, vulnerable performance in *Psycho:* she was voted the most popular actress of 1961 by the Associated Theater Owners of America and she never took a shower again; to this day she will only take baths.

Leigh capped off her career with a starring role in the highly regarded John Frankenheimer thriller, *The Manchurian Candidate* (1962), and followed it up with a fine musical performance in *Bye Bye Birdie* (1963) and a witty turn in the sophisticated comedy *Wives and Lovers* (1963). Then, inexplicably, she appeared in a poor Jerry Lewis vehicle, *Three on a Couch* (1963), and her career never quite recovered.

After a stint on Broadway, she returned to the movies in films like *Harper* (1966) and *An American Dream* (1966), but she was no longer considered a major draw and by the early 1970s she had moved on to sporadic television appearances and a life of pleasant semi-retirement. Among her last movie appearances was a role in John Carpenter's horror film, *The Fog* (1980), in which she costarred with her daughter by Tony Curtis, Jamie

Lee Curtis. In the ensuing years, Miss Leigh has had the pleasure of watching her youngest of two daughters with Curtis turn into a popular new movie star.

LEIGH, VIVIEN (1913–1967)   An English actress who made only a handful of films in Hollywood, yet became known as the quintessential Southern belle thanks to her two most famous, Oscar-winning roles, Scarlett O'Hara in *Gone With the Wind* (1939 *q.v.*) and Blanche du Bois in *A Streetcar Named Desire* (1951). One of the most beautiful women ever to grace the screen, the delicate Leigh suffered from both physical and psychological problems that ultimately crippled her career and ended her life at an early age.

Born Vivian Mary Harley in India, she took her stage name from her first husband, Leigh Holman, whom she later divorced to marry Laurence Olivier *(q.v.)* after a much-publicized love affair. (She and Olivier were wed in 1940 and divorced in 1960.) Because of her stunning beauty, Leigh had no difficulty finding roles in English films, though she had yet to make her stage debut. Her first movie role was in *Things Are Looking Up* (1934) and the actress continued making films throughout the 1930s, gaining notoriety when she and Olivier, who were both married, met and fell in love on the set of *Fire Over England* (1937).

Visiting Olivier in Hollywood while he was making *Wuthering Heights* (1939), Leigh was taken by her agent, Myron Selznick, to meet producer David O. Selznick (the agent's brother) who had yet to cast Scarlett O'Hara in *Gone With the Wind* even though the film had already gone into production. Taken with Leigh, Selznick quickly gave her the role almost every major (and many minor) American actress had coveted. Her portrayal of Scarlett turned Leigh into an international movie star overnight.

She stayed in Hollywood long enough to make *Waterloo Bridge* (1940), a touching romance, and, with Olivier, *That Hamilton Woman* (1941). In the meantime, she also starred on Broadway with Olivier in *Romeo and Juliet,* which turned into a theatrical debacle.

After returning to England, more stage disasters followed—at least for her. Constantly compared to Olivier, and found wanting, her confidence was shaken and her emotional problems grew worse. In and out of hospitals and sanitariums, she made few movies during the rest of her career, among them *Caesar and Cleopatra* (1945), *Anna Karenina* (1948), the previously mentioned *A Streetcar Named Desire, The Deep Blue Sea* (1955), *The Roman Spring of Mrs. Stone* (1961), and her last film, *Ship of Fools* (1965).

LEMMON, JACK (1925–   )   An accomplished actor, he made his reputation in light comedy but has also proved to be an affecting performer in dramatic roles. Lemmon's forte, whether in comedy or drama, is playing contemporary middle-class everymen. His characters have generally reflected the anxieties of the mass audience; they are often skittish about sex, fearful of authority, and full of self doubt. His physical appearance is also perfect for the Hollywood version of an everyman: handsome without being too good looking, and average in height, weight, and build. In other words, he is a realistic, yet idealized, replica of the man on the street.

Born John Uhler Lemmon III, he grew up in a family that was anything but average. His father was a wealthy businessman, the owner of a large doughnut company. The young Lemmon had the advantages of a prep school and Harvard education. His first important experience as an actor was at Harvard, where he became involved in the drama club.

Lemmon, however, put his acting on hold until after his service in the Navy. When he returned to civilian life, he began paying his dues as an actor, working on radio, Off-Broadway, and especially in television, where he honed his craft in more than four hundred appearances during one five-year stretch. By the time he made his movie debut opposite Judy Holliday (q.v.) in It Should Happen to You (1954), Lemmon was already a seasoned performer despite his baby face and relative youth (he was twenty-nine).

Lemmon's rise to stardom was swift. His supporting performance as Ensign Pulver in only his fourth film, Mr. Roberts (1965), won him an Oscar. Many other strong performances followed in Operation Mad Ball (1957), Cowboy (1958), and Bell, Book, and Candle (1959).

Finally, it was his association with director Billy Wilder (q.v.) that turned him into a major star. The first of their seven movies together was Lemmon's breakout film, Some Like it Hot (1959). Not yet a household name at the time he made the film, Lemmon's agreement to join Tony Curtis and Marilyn Monroe (qq.v.) in the cast was a controversial career move because he would have to pretend to be a woman for much of the film. His gamble paid off in a major hit and Wilder rewarded Lemmon with the starring role in what many consider both the director's and the actor's greatest film, The Apartment (1960), a seriocomic movie in which Lemmon showed great emotional depth in his portrayal of a man torn between his own confused desires.

The 1960s was Lemmon's most successful decade. Virtually every one of his films during that ten-year span was a hit. And during that long string of box office winners, the actor showed great range, starring in, among others, the bleak drama The Days of Wine and Roses (1962), the bawdy sex comedy Irma La Douce (1963), the black comedy The Fortune Cookie (1966), which was also the first of his many acting collaborations with Walter Matthau (q.v.), and the purely entertaining The Odd Couple (1968), which not only continued Lemmon's acting relationship with Matthau, it also launched another long and fruitful association with playwright and screenwriter Neil Simon (q.v.).

Lemmon had fewer hits in the 1970s as his comic persona, which best suited the late 1950s and the early 1960s, became passé. He was, nonetheless, able to help turn the The Out-of-Towners (1970) and The Prisoner of Second Avenue (1975) into hits, helped also by two very funny Neil Simon scripts. From a commercial standpoint, he was less successful with films such as The War Between Men and Women (1972), Avanti! (1972), The Front Page (1974), and Alex and the Gypsy (1976). He received excellent reviews for his performance in the TV film "The Entertainer" (1976), but was reduced in 1977 to joining the all-star cast of Airport '77. Also during the 1970s, Lemmon tried his hand at directing, working behind the camera in the Walter Matthau comedy Kotch (1971). The film was generally well received by both the critics and the public, but Lemmon has not directed again.

If there were two high points in Lemmon's career during the 1970s, they were two dramatic roles that gave the actor new stature at the beginning and at the end of the decade. He won the Academy Award for Best Actor for his performance as a desperate factory owner in Save the Tiger (1973), and then stole the show from Jane Fonda and Michael Douglas (qq.v.) in The China Syndrome (1979).

For the most part, Lemmon has continued to lean more heavily toward drama in his later years, playing a dying man in Tribute (1980), a concerned father in Missing (1982), and a cynical priest in Mass Appeal (1984). Two comedies in which he appeared in recently, Buddy, Buddy (1982) and Macaroni (1985), were both critical and commercial flops.

As Lemmon moves comfortably into his later years, he seems destined for the kind of adulation that has been bestowed upon actors whom audiences have enjoyed over a lifetime.

LENSES There are all sorts of lenses, but they can be classified essentially into three basic types: a non-distorting lens, a long lens, and a short lens.

The vast majority of scenes within any movie are filmed through a non-distorting lens. For the most part, a director and his cinematographer want the audience to see a scene more or less the way they see it with the naked eye. But not always.

Long lenses (also known as telephoto lenses) are a handy tool in the cinematographer's bag of tricks because they "flatten" the image they photograph. An example of this flattening effect seen in countless movies is where an actor runs toward the audience, seemingly getting nowhere. The long lens freezes the actor in time and space, giving the impression that he or she is trapped.

There are, of course, many other uses for the long

lens. For instance, if a director wants to film an actor walking down New York City's Fifth Avenue surrounded by a sea of humanity, rather than hiring thousands of extras and closing the street to traffic, the director can instruct the cinematographer to shoot the actor with a long lens from a discreet distance. Those sharing the sidewalk with the actor are unaware of being filmed.

The short lens (also known as a wide-angle lens), tends to cause the greatest sense of distortion because it is often used in close-ups. A face photographed in close-up through a short lens will distort much like an image in a funhouse mirror. This effect is often used in horror films or in scenes where a character is either drunk or high on drugs.

The short lens is used to more subtle effect to create visual clarity both in the foreground and background of a scene. This allows for more than one action to be played out on the screen at the same time. The most famous example of this effect is in *Citizen Kane* (1941), where Orson Welles and his cinematographer, Gregg Toland *(q.v.)*, used the short lens to create depth of field with enormous artistic success.

LE ROY, MERVYN (1900–1987) A director and producer responsible for more than seventy-five films, Le Roy made more than his share of commercial hits, managing in the process to make a surprising number of highly regarded classic motion pictures. Despite having directed and produced landmark movies in several different genres, he has had only a modest reputation among film historians and critics. Lacking a consistent visual style and having no discernible thematic unity to his work, he has been dismissed as a mildly likable filmmaker. There being relatively few directors, however, whose films have had such a strong impact on audiences and on Hollywood trends, it might be that Mervyn Le Roy's films deserve a reappraisal.

Born and raised in San Francisco, he survived the famous 1906 earthquake and went on to become a child actor at the age of twelve. He spent much of his adolescence pursuing a career in show business, gaining a foothold in vaudeville when he won a Charlie Chaplin imitation contest in 1915. Four years later he decided to try his luck in Hollywood and began working both behind and in front of the cameras at Famous Players-Lasky (see Famous Players). He performed all sorts of functions, from assistant cameraman to gag writer during the early 1920s. At the same time, he appeared in films such as *Double Speed* (1920), *Little Johnny Jones* (1923), and *Broadway After Dark* (1924).

When his acting career seemed to be going nowhere fast, he began concentrating more heavily on the business of filmmaking. After coscripting *Ella Cinders* (1926), a hit comedy about a girl who comes to Hollywood to make her fortune, Le Roy was given a promotion to director, making his directorial debut with *No Place to Go* (1927). There was nothing special about the film, and it seemed the only place for Le Roy to go was up.

Several years and a dozen films later, Le Roy finally hit the big time when he directed Edward G. Robinson in *Little Caesar* (1930 *q.v.*). The film launched the famous Warner Bros. gangster cycle and has since become a classic. Another Le Roy classic was *I am a Fugitive from a Chain Gang* (1932 *q.v.*), a film of such searing power—with an ending as haunting today as it was nearly sixty years ago—that it helped bring about significant prison reforms. Among his other early hits were *Hard to Handle* (1933), *Gold Diggers of 1933* (1933), *Tugboat Annie* (1933), and *Anthony Adverse* (1936).

In 1937 Le Roy began to occasionally produce his own films, sometimes producing without directing. But a falling out with Warner Bros. sent him to MGM where he entered an entirely new and equally productive phase of his career. He produced the timeless *The Wizard of Oz* (1939) as well as the amusing Marx Brothers *(q.v.)* vehicle, *At the Circus* (1939). He then returned to directing, making several of his most successful films that were aimed primarily at the female market, among them *Waterloo Bridge* (1940), *Blossoms in the Dust* (1941), the ultimate "weepie," *Random Harvest* (1942), for which Le Roy received his one and only Oscar nomination for Best Director, and *Madame Curie* (1943).

After scoring with *Thirty Seconds Over Tokyo* (1944) and winning a special Oscar in 1945 for an anti-prejudice short he produced and directed called *The House I Live In,* his career began to falter. It wasn't until 1951 that he returned with a big hit, the overblown but enjoyable *Quo Vadis.*

Le Roy returned to Warners in the mid–1950s and his projects improved almost immediately, thanks in part to John Ford's begging off the direction of *Mr. Roberts* (1955), which Le Roy took over and turned into a hit. He followed with a couple of solid efforts amid some clinkers, the winners being *The Bad Seed* (1956) and *No Time for Sergeants* (1958).

Le Roy worked steadily into the 1960s, making such films as *The Devil at 4 O'Clock* (1961) and *Gypsy* (1962). His last film was *Moment to Moment* (1966), after which he retired.

Le Roy, who was once married to Doris Warner, daughter of Harry M. Warner, one of *the* Warner brothers, clearly had the career advantage of family connections. He nonetheless made his opportunities count. In recognition of his achievements, the Motion Picture Academy honored him with the Irving Thalberg Award in 1975.

LEVINE, JOSEPH E. (1905–1987) A producer and showman who was among the last of the great independents during the conglomeratization of the movie business. As a producer and distributor he brought nearly five hundred films to American movie screens. Ironically, the films with which his name has become associated tend to be either serious and artful or pure, unadulterated shlock.

Levine, who came from a poor Boston family, dropped out of school at the age of fourteen and slowly built a small nest egg, which he invested in a Connecticut movie theater in 1938. In the 1940s, he enlarged his holdings and began to build a small theater empire in New England. Soon thereafter he bought the American rights to a number of foreign films and began distributing them in the art-house circuit. In that fashion, he introduced American audiences to such movies as *Open City* (1945), *Paisan* (1946), and *The Bicycle Thief* (1948).

He made his mark as a promoter/distributer when he bought the American rights to the Japanese monster film *Godzilla* (1956) for $12,000 and turned it into a "monster" hit. But that was nothing compared to his success in importing cheaply and then promoting expensively the Italian "muscle movie" *Hercules* (1959) with Steve Reeves, turning it into a huge money-maker by pioneering the use of saturation booking.

Not long after, he was responsible for the American releases of such popular imports as *Divorce, Italian Style* (1961), *8 1/2* (1963), and *Romeo and Juliet* (1968). He acquired roughly 150 films from Italy and France alone for distribution in the U.S., eleven of them starring Sophia Loren, whom he thereby helped to become a star in America.

Levine also produced many of his films, and he was often adventurous. For instance, he gave both Mike Nichols and Mel Brooks *(qq.v.)* their first chance to direct with *The Graduate* (1967) and *The Producers* (1967), respectively. After *The Graduate* became a huge hit, Levine sold his company, Embassy Pictures, to the Avco Corporation, forming Avco Embassy in 1968, and becoming the new firm's CEO. Avco Embassy was successful under his tutelage, with films such as *Carnal Knowledge* (1971), *A Touch of Class* (1972), and *The Day of the Dolphin* (1973), but Levine chafed at having to answer to others and resigned in 1974, establishing a new independent company, Joseph E. Levine Presents. He was successful again, presenting foreign-made films such as *The Night Porter* (1974) and producing such controversial films as *. . . And Justice for All* (1979).

LEVINSON, BARRY (1932–   ) A gifted writer-director, Levinson has blossomed in the 1980s with an impressive streak of energetic, intelligent, and idiosyncratic films. As of this writing he has directed only six movies but they have been of such high quality that Levinson seems to have clearly established himself as a major American director.

Raised in Baltimore, Levinson did his earlier writing for TV. In the late 1970s, however, he began penning the screenplays for such films as *First Love* (1977), *. . . And Justice for All* (1979), and *Inside Moves* (1981). With a growing reputation as a screenwriter, Levinson opted to direct his own screenplay for *Diner* (1982), a story that was close to his heart. The movie was a nostalgic coming-of-age tale of a group of friends who hang out together at a local Baltimore diner. The film was the sleeper hit of the year, launching the acting careers of Mickey Rourke, Steve Guttenberg, and Kevin Bacon, as well as the directorial career of Levinson.

After directing an intimate low-budget movie with no stars, Levinson next found himself hired to direct Robert Redford in the big-budget adaptation of Barnard Malamud's novel *The Natural* (1984), which he pulled off with considerable aplomb. It is regarded by many as one of the best baseball movies ever made, capturing a childlike view of the myth and grandeur of sports heroism.

He faltered with *Young Sherlock Holmes* (1985), his only stumble of the 1980s, and then scored with three substantial hits, *Tin Men* (1987), a blue-collar comedy of manners, *Good Morning, Vietnam* (1987), one of the biggest commercial blockbusters of its year, and *Rain Man* (1988), for which Levinson won an Academy Award for Best Director. He was, in fact, the fourth director of *Rain Man,* the three previous directors having quit the project in frustration. In collaboration with Dustin Hoffman, who fought to make the movie for several years, *Rain Man* became a surprise commercial hit as well as a highly regarded critical success.

LEWIS, JERRY (1926–   ) He is, at once, one of the most reviled and revered film comedy stars in the world. Looked down upon in America as a hopelessly juvenile and uninspired comedian, he is exalted in Europe (particularly France), where he is seen as a modern-day Chaplin. His place in the Hollywood canon falls somewhere between the two extremes. A comic actor, director, writer, and producer, Lewis' film persona of the childlike goofball has sustained him through more than forty movies. His film career can be divided neatly into three periods: the amusing Martin & Lewis movies, the brilliant solo years, and the startlingly rapid decline.

Born Joseph Levitch to a show business family, Lewis joined his parents' act, singing with them on stage when he was five years old. But his real training came from performing in the Catskill Mountains resort area north of New York City known as the "Borscht Belt," where he honed his stand-up comedy routine. Lewis didn't have much success as a solo performer, but in 1946 he joined with another young also-ran, Dean Martin, to form a team in Atlantic City; they became an overnight sensation.

Lewis was the comic to Martin's crooning straight man, and the team's nightclub success led with surprising speed to a supporting role in their first film, *My Friend Irma* (1949). The movie was mediocre but it was a big money-maker, thanks to the popularity of Martin & Lewis, who were a zanier version of Abbott & Costello. They were quickly rushed into a starring vehicle of their own, *My Friend Irma Goes West* (1950), and continued making films together until 1956. There were sixteen Martin & Lewis films altogether, every one of which was a commercial hit. Among the better efforts were *Living it Up* (1954), *Artists and Models* (1955), and *Pardners* (1956).

When Martin quit the team, Lewis began taking greater control of his solo career. He had a hit record (*Rockabye Your Baby*—later the title of one of his films) and soon began producing, writing, and directing his own movies. His first solo effort was *The Delicate Delinquent* (1957), a movie not unlike his films with Dean Martin. But Lewis began to experiment and grow as a filmmaker, learning from director Frank Tashlin (*q.v.*), and in the early 1960s he wrote, directed, and produced a handful of excellent comedies, including two masterpieces, *The Ladies' Man* (1961) and *The Nutty Professor* (1963). His other fine films of that era were *The Bellboy* (1960), *The Errand Boy* (1961), and *The Patsy* (1964).

After the *The Family Jewels* (1965), an overripe film in which Lewis played seven roles, the quality of his movies dropped precipitously. Nonetheless, his comedies continued to be profitable for a short while longer, adding to a remarkable record of more than thirty-seven straight hits (a streak that includes his Martin & Lewis movies). His later films, such as *Hook, Line and Sinker* (1969) and *Which Way to the Front?* (1970) were pale imitations of his early 1960s works and they were part of a series of commercial flops that made it difficult for him to find financing.

One reason commonly given for Lewis' demise as a comic film star is that he played a character who had to be young. Playing his sincere idiot as a middle-aged man became embarrassing rather than amusing. There was, therefore, something infinitely sad about Lewis' return to film comedy in the same old role in *Hardly Working* (1979).

More recently, however, Lewis has begun playing dramatic parts to great effect. His portrayal of a Johnny Carson-like talk show host in Martin Scorsese's *The King of Comedy* (1983) and a dramatic TV movie role as the father of a dying child, finally brought him good reviews from American critics.

In addition to his film work, Lewis has three times tried and failed as the host of a television series. He has also consistently worked in nightclubs. Though his film career has faded, he is universally known in America as the host and driving force of The Jerry Lewis Telethon which raises money to fight muscular dystrophy. Lewis and his telethon have become a television insti-

tution. Broadcast every Labor Day weekend, the show has been on the air since 1965.

LEWIS, JOSEPH H. (1900–) A director of "B"-movies during the 1940s and 1950s, he was later rediscovered by auteurist critics and film historians. With generally poor scripts, unheard of actors, and miniscule budgets, Lewis managed to make a number of vivid, atmospheric action/suspense movies that have become minor classics.

Lewis learned the business from the technical side, working as a camera assistant at MGM and later as an editor at Republic. He graduated from second-unit director to feature director in 1937 when he codirected *Navy Spy*. The scripts he was assigned to direct during the rest of the 1930s and early 1940s were dreadful. He directed films such as *Singing Outlaw* (1937), *Border Wolves* (1938), *Boys of the City* (1940), and *The Invisible Ghost* (1941) that were billed as the bottom half of double features and promptly forgotten.

After making twenty-four movies, he finally had a hit with his twenty-fifth, *My Name is Julia Ross* (1945). The film was the sleeper hit of the year. A tightly made suspense thriller, audiences and critics responded in tandem and Lewis rose a peg in the Hollywood hierarchy. While he never had a big budget, his access to minor stars increased, and he made a number of compelling little movies, including *The Undercover Man* (1949), *The Big Combo* (1955), and *The Halliday Brand* (1957). But the movie that remains his masterpiece is the startling *Gun Crazy* (1949). With totally unknown actors John Dall and Peggy Cummins, Lewis made a stylized and vivid action movie that prefigured Arthur Penn's *Bonnie and Clyde* (1967). In *Gun Crazy*, Lewis pulled off an elaborate bank robbery scene and getaway in one long, incredible take that is as visually astonishing as anything ever done by any other director in Hollywood.

Lewis made a total of thirty-nine movies before finally turning to television directing in the late 1950s. His last motion picture was *Terror in a Texas Town* (1958).

LEWTON, VAL (1904–1951) A producer at RKO who put his stamp on a series of low-budget horror films, creating a new kind of terror in the movies in the 1940s. Lewton's fresh approach to the genre was in *suggesting* horror rather than showing it.

The first Lewton "B" horror movie was *The Cat People* (1942). It was an unexpected hit starring Simone Simon and was followed by the memorably titled *I Walked with a Zombie* (1943). Altogether, he made eight horror films between 1942 and 1946.

There was a great visual flair to Lewton's films that belied their low budgets. For the most part, his movies didn't feature stars, except for the ever-reliable Boris

Karloff (q.v.) in *The Body Snatcher* (1945), *Isle of the Dead* (1945) and *Bedlam* (1946). But one doesn't think of these movies as Karloff vehicles. The stars were really the dark shadows, the stylish camerawork, and the often forbidden sexual subject matter.

Unlike most horror films, Lewton's have the feel of a clever calculating mind behind them, and a horror all the more terrifying for its subtlety.

See also: horror films

LITTLE CAESAR Though by no means the first gangster film, this controversial 1930 hit movie turned the genre into a major commercial force. *Little Caesar* was the right movie at the right time. A poll taken by a Chicago newspaper not long after the film opened showed that Americans were more familiar with the names of gangsters than any other group—except for movie actors.

Based on the novel of the same name by W. R. Burnett (q.v.), *Little Caesar* was a box office bonanza for Warner Bros. and a trendsetter not only as the first of a spate of gangster movies but also the first of the studio's dramas based on current events. Its success encouraged Warners to become the provider of streetwise movies for (and about) the common man, a cycle of films that lasted through the 1930s and for which the studio is best known.

Little Caesar depicted the rise and fall of Caesar Enrico Bandello (Edward G. Robinson, q.v.), who went from small-time hood to top mobster, only to be killed at the end of the movie in a dark alley muttering the now famous line, "Mother of Mercy, is this the end of Rico?" Tightly directed by Mervyn Le Roy (q.v.), and filled with a strong supporting cast, including Douglas Fairbanks, Jr., Glenda Farrell, Stanley Fields, Sidney Blackmer, Ralph Ince, and George E. Stone, the movie bristled with violence, tension, and a refreshing grubbiness that rang absolutely true to life.

The film's ability to speak the language of the people, both in its realistic dialogue and in its dim-eyed view of society, had a great deal to do with its appeal. Edward G. Robinson brought Rico to life, imbuing the character with depth and pathos. One might be repelled by Rico but one couldn't help but feel a certain grudging respect for him too, thanks to Robinson's portrayal. And as Robert Warshow wrote in his famous essay, "The Gangster as Tragic Hero," Rico, despite his cruelty and stupidity, is a character of tragic dimensions. The very qualities that bring him to the top—his vanity chief among them—also seal his doom.

See also: gangster movies

LLOYD, HAROLD (1893–1971) After Chaplin and Keaton, he was the most accomplished of the silent screen comedians. In fact, during the better part of the 1920s, Lloyd was actually more successful at the box office than either of his two rivals. Lloyd was a superb comic actor who created an American go-getter character to whom jazz age audiences could easily respond.

Lloyd was nineteen years old and living in San Diego, California, when a camera crew from the Edison Company arrived to shoot some location footage. He picked up work playing an extra and was immediately hooked on the movies. He teamed up with Hal Roach (q.v.) to form a fledgling production company and starred in a primitive comedy one-reeler, *Just Nuts* (1915).

In 1916, Lloyd invented a character called Lonesome Luke, whom he patterned after Charlie Chaplin (q.v.). Instead of wearing baggy cloths like the tramp, Lloyd dressed his Lonesome Luke in particularly tight-fitting togs. The character was immediately popular and Lloyd made more than one hundred Lonesome Luke comedy shorts.

Not satisfied, he had an idea for a new character whom he called "Glasses." This character was the epitome of the upwardly mobile young American. He was a young college man with a seemingly meek-and-mild disposition who simply would not give up until he met with success. Glasses first appeared on film in a one-reeler titled *Over the Fence* (1917).

By 1918, Lloyd had dropped the Lonesome Luke character completely, such was the public acceptance of his new persona. One-reelers gave way to two-reelers during the next few years, and by this time, the only obstacle to Lloyd's growing fame was a bomb—but not necessarily of the celluloid variety. In 1920, while posing for a publicity still, he leaned on "prop" explosives. They were not props after all, and Lloyd spent six months in a hospital, and lost two fingers on his right hand when the explosives blew up.

When he returned to work Lloyd continued to expand the scope of his films. With complete artistic control of his movies, he made three-reelers, four-reelers, and five-reelers. By 1922, he was making full-fledged features, the first of which was *Dr. Jack*. His second feature became his most famous, *Safety Last* (1923), in which he was literally suspended from the hands of a clock on a high tower in one of film comedy's grandest stunts.

From this point on, Lloyd's humor tended more toward the awe-inspiring than the belly-laugh. His breath-taking stunts (done without benefit of a stuntman) remain unequaled to this day.

The hits came fast and furious, including *Girl Shy* (1924), one of the top money-makers of the year. *The Freshman* (1925) was his most successful movie at the box office and one of the biggest grossers of the entire silent era, with receipts of over $2.5 million. *For Heaven's Sake* (1926), *The Kid Brother* (1927), and *Speedy* (1928) were also highly successful.

After the shock of the Great Depression, Glasses no

longer seemed quite believable as a character. Nonetheless, Lloyd continued making films throughout the 1930s and had modest success. His best films of this era were *The Milky Way* (1936) and *Professor Beware* (1938). After the latter movie, he retired from the screen until he attempted a curious comeback in 1947 in the Preston Sturges *(q.v.)* film *Mad Wednesday,* which began with the end of Lloyd's silent hit *The Freshman.* Unfortunately, the film was not a success, and Lloyd retired for good.

In 1952, Lloyd was given a special Oscar, honoring him as a "master comedian."

LOCATION SHOOTING   Filming that takes place outside a studio soundstage or back lot *(q.v.).* A location shoot of a scene might be made within a few hours' distance of a studio and might therefore require only a day trip by select members of the cast and crew, or it might require the entire cast and crew to travel for a week or several months to one or more distant locations, adding the cost of feeding and housing everyone to the film's budget.

In the silent era, location shooting was extremely common. In fact, the desire to make films on location was one of the reasons that led to Hollywood becoming the center of American filmmaking. Southern California was an ideal place to make movies because of its geographical variety. Within a short distance filmmakers could find an ocean, mountains, deserts and forests. And, of course, the warm, sunny weather allowed for prolonged outdoor shooting as well.

The talkies brought about a massive reversal in the number of movies shot on location. The difficulties of sound filming were such that it forced most movies to be made in the studio.

At the same time as the sound revolution, the film industry solidified into a relative handful of major companies which, in the late 1920s and early 1930s, established a streamlined method for turning out movies for an entertainment-hungry public. For the most part, it was less expensive to shoot in the studio or the back lot than to send the cast and crew all over the country to make a film. Just as significantly, studio moguls such as Louis B. Mayer and Jack L. Warner *(qq.v.)* felt they had less control over costs if a film was made outside the walls of their fiefdoms. In fact, later financial debacles such as *Cleopatra* (1963, *q.v.*) and *Heaven's Gate* (1980) were a direct result of poor studio/producer supervision.

Films were made on location during the studio heyday of the 1930s and 1940s but were more the exception than the rule. Generally, exteriors of big-budget outdoor films were shot on location but interiors were still done in the studio. One of the most famous examples of location shooting during this period occurred in 1939 in John Ford's *Stagecoach (qq.v.).* Part of the movie was shot in Monument Valley and it became the location of a great many of Ford's later westerns of the 1940s and 1950s.

But even Ford only shot exteriors on location in 1939. Making most of a film on location was still extremely rare in Hollywood when John Huston *(q.v.)* convinced Warner Bros. to let him take the entire cast and crew to Mexico for two months to shoot *The Treasure of the Sierra Madre* (1948). The film was a critical though not a box office hit, but it was successful enough to crack open the door to more location shooting.

The advent of television in the 1950s, however, brought a resurgence of location shooting to the movies. Most TV shows were studio-bound and movies could make a visual distinction between the product on the big screen and the little box, providing a greater sweep and realism with location shooting.

With the demise of the studio system *(q.v.)* and the rise of independent producers, location shooting has become as common in recent years as it was during the silent era. In an effort to avoid high union labor costs in Hollywood and New York, many films are shot on location with nonunion crews. It's ironic that for a great many filmmakers, shooting on location has become less expensive than shooting in a studio.

LOESSER, FRANK (1910–1969)   Unlike the majority of famous Hollywood composers and lyricists, Loesser actually got his start in Los Angeles, in 1930. He worked with a great many composers, including Burton Lane ("The Lady's in Love with You"), Hoagy Carmichael ("Small Fry"), and Arthur Schwartz ("They're Either Too Young or Too Old"). During his years as a lyricist, his work appeared in twenty films, including the fondly remembered *Destry Rides Again* (1939), famous for Marlene Dietrich's number, "The Boys in the Back Room."

After a long tenure as a lyricist, in 1947 Loesser began composing music for the screen, as well. His first film was *The Perils of Pauline* (1947), but he gained Hollywood's attention in 1949 when he won a Best Song Oscar for "Baby, It's Cold Outside," from *Neptune's Daughter.* In that same year, he had his one and only screen appearance playing the gangster Hairdo Lempke in *Red, Hot and Blue,* a film for which he also wrote the music and lyrics.

In the early 1950s, while composing the minor Fred Astaire and Betty Hutton *(qq.v.)* vehicle, *Let's Dance* (1950), and the ever-popular Danny Kaye film, *Hans Christian Anderson* (1952), Loesser also embarked on a Broadway career, writing *Where's Charley,* which was a hit on the stage and then a film in 1952 (it featured the song, "Once in Love with Amy"). Loesser went on to write a great many Broadway musicals, many of which were later turned into movies, including *Guys and Dolls* (1955) and the Pulitzer Prize–winning *How to Succeed in Business Without Really Trying* (1966).

LOMBARD, CAROLE (1908–1942) An actress who seemed destined for a career as a glamour queen but who surprised everyone by proving to be a consummate comedienne. A more upscale version of Jean Harlow *(q.v.)*, she could be both sexy and funny without being vulgar. She appealed not only to movie audiences but to movie stars as well: during the 1930s she married, in succession, William Powell and Clark Gable *(qq.v.)*.

Born Jane Peters, she was raised in a broken home. Her first appearance in the movies came as a fluke. She was spotted in her backyard by director Alan Dwan *(q.v.)* who was visiting nearby. He decided she had the ideal look for a part in *A Perfect Crime* (1921). The thirteen-year-old girl had her first screen credit.

Once having appeared in the movies, she set out to learn her craft. When she was sixteen she tested for the role of Georgia (the female lead) in Charlie Chaplin's *The Gold Rush* (1924), but she didn't get the part. The following year, however, finally brought her back into the film business with a starring role in *Marriage in Transit*. Eventually, in 1927, she joined Mack Sennett's studio and received a valuable two-year education in silent film comedy playing in a number of comic two-reelers.

Lombard mostly played vamps or glamorous sophisticates in the early 1930s. She had achieved a certain level of popularity in mediocre movies but was hardly a major star. As David Shipman wrote in his book *The Great Movie Stars,* she was "noted more for her slinky blonde looks, good legs and daring gowns than for anything else."

That all changed when she starred with John Barrymore in Howard Hawks' *(q.v.)* first screwball comedy, *The Twentieth Century* (1934). Barrymore was fabulous in one of his last great roles, but Lombard was the revelation. Her comic abilities were on grand display and suddenly audiences (and film studios) saw a great talent behind the beauty.

Unfortunately, that talent was trapped in a number of mediocre movies over the next few years, but there were also several films that gave Lombard a chance to shine. *My Man Godfrey* (1936), in which she starred with her then ex-husband, William Powell, was a standout. So was *Nothing Sacred* (1937). That year she was Hollywood's highest paid actress, earning $465,000.

Dramatic roles came her way along with comedies. She was winsome in *Made for Each Other* (1939) with Jimmy Stewart *(q.v.)*, and wonderfully tough-minded in *They Knew What They Wanted* (1940) with Charles Laughton *(q.v.)*.

Her last movie was Ernst Lubitsch's anti-Nazi film *To Be Or Not To Be* (1942). She starred opposite Jack Benny *(q.v.)* in what is now considered a classic com-

Carole Lombard showed her superb talent for comedy in films such as *Twentieth Century* (1934), but she was originally groomed to be a glamour queen, as evidenced by this 1932 publicity shot. Photo courtesy of The Siegel Collection.

edy. At the time, however, it was poorly received by the critics.

In that same year, Lombard died in a tragic plane crash near Las Vegas while returning home to her husband, Clark Gable, after a successful war bond drive. The nation mourned along with Gable.

Lombard engendered a new sort of female star: beautiful without being brittle, her wit, style and feistiness did not compromise her glamour.

LOOS, ANITA (1893–1981) Though best known as the author of the novel, play, and movie versions of *Gentlemen Prefer Blondes* (filmed in 1928 and 1953), she was actually one of Hollywood's wittiest screenwriters in an active film career of thirty years. Discovered by D. W. Griffith *(q.v.)*, who bought her first story idea for $15 in 1912 and turned it into *The New York Hat,* Loos went on to write scores of one- and two-reelers as well as features. She was one of the rare breed of women who worked steadily in the film business as a screenwriter.

Loos had a talent for creating unusual stories and amusing subtitles. Griffith, however, was not well known for his sense of humor, so it was a happy circumstance that she was assigned to write scripts in 1916 for the relatively unknown Douglas Fairbanks *(q.v.)*. With a series of exuberant, clever comedies such as *Manhattan*

Madness (1916), *The Matrimaniac* (1916), and *Wild and Woolly* (1917), Loos helped define Fairbanks' star personality and helped launch his spectacular career.

Her success with Fairbanks gave her considerable clout in Hollywood, and with her fine working relationship with director (and later, husband) John Emerson, Loos went on to write and occasionally produce successful female-oriented films during the 1920s such as *The Perfect Woman* (1920), *Woman's Place* (1921), and *Learning to Love* (1925).

While a great many screenwriters of the silent era were pushed aside with the advent of sound, Loos had no trouble finding work due to her playwriting success with *Gentlemen Prefer Blondes.* As she had in the 1920s, Loos fashioned most of her sound films for the female audience, writing movies such as *Hold Your Man* (1933), *The Biography of a Bachelor Girl* (1935), and *The Women* (1939). But like any adaptable Hollywood screenwriter, she was capable of writing melodramas, too, penning *Riffraff* (1936) and (with her husband) the most popular film of 1936 *San Francisco.* While her last official screenplay was *I Married an Angel* in 1942, she was rediscovered by the public yet again when *Gentlemen Prefer Blondes* was remade as a musical with Jane Russell and Marilyn Monroe *(qq.v.)* in 1953.

A prolific author, Loos wrote a number of nonfiction books, including two with her husband, *How to Write Photoplays* (1919) and *Breaking into the Movies* (1921). After John Emerson's death in 1956, she wrote a series of autobiographies: *A Girl Like I* (1966), *Kiss Hollywood Good-Bye* (1974), and *Cast of Thousands* (1977). She also wrote a biography of her silent screen contemporaries, *The Talmadge Girls* (1978).

LORRE, PETER (1904–1964)   Though small of stature, his talent was of a tall order and he was one of the most distinctive actors in Hollywood. With his large sad eyes, mysterious and menacing voice, and his coiled body, Lorre could play villains, heroes, or fools with equal ease. It was not uncommon for the actor to steal scenes from bigger stars, not because he chewed the scenery as a conventional ham might but because his voice, movements, and languid style riveted the eyes and the ears of his beholders.

Born Lazlo Lowenstein in Hungary, the young man began his adult life as a bank clerk but studied acting in Vienna before commencing his career on the stage in Switzerland. A theater actor for seven years, he had little film experience and only a minor reputation in Central Europe before winning the part of the child murderer in Fritz Lang's *M* (1931). The film was an international success both for the director and the young star who gave a splendid performance. It remains among Lorre's greatest triumphs.

After the Nazis' rise to power in Germany, Lorre fled to France and England, stopping along the way to

Peter Lorre was among Hollywood's most intriguing character actors. He played everything from Asians to Russians, to Arabs and Europeans. He could play sniveling or implacably sinister characters as easily as he could heroes. Photo courtesy of The Siegel Collection.

made two films, including Alfred Hitchcock's *The Man Who Knew Too Much* (1934). Lorre's European reputation preceded him when he arrived in the United States. In 1935, he was given his first role in a Hollywood film, the lead in a horror thriller called *Mad Love.* He was electric in the film, and he followed it up with the role of Raskolnikov in Joseph von Sternberg's nearly forgotten version of *Crime and Punishment* (1935).

After a trip back to England to appear in Hitchcock's *Secret Agent* (1936), Lorre returned to America and soon began appearing in a low-budget but eminently entertaining series of detective mysteries, playing the title character, Mr. Moto. Though he was of Eastern European descent, Lorre was adept at playing vaguely oriental types, and Mr. Moto was an obvious attempt at cashing in on the success of the Charlie Chan movies. Unlike Chan, Moto not only used his wits to solve crimes, he also used ju-jitsu and a gun (when necessary). Action-packed and well-plotted, the *Moto* films were popular "B" movies and Lorre made eight of them between 1937 and 1939 before anti-Japanese sentiments spelled the end of the series.

Though he continued working, his career lacked focus until he became a member of the Warner Bros. stock company in the 1940s. Often featured along with Sydney Greenstreet, Lorre made his mark on film history with a wonderfully subtle performance as the effeminate Joel Cairo in *The Maltese Falcon* (1941). He was also memorably oily as Ugarte in *Casablanca* (1942), and compelling as the writer/protagonist of *The Mask of Dimitrios* (1944). Perhaps his best film—and most unusual starring vehicle—was the Donald Siegel–directed minor classic, *The Verdict* (1946).

By the latter part of the 1940s, Lorre's career seemed to flounder, and in lesser films the actor seemed to camp up his roles. Then he briefly left Hollywood for Germany to write, direct, and star in *Der Verlorene/The Lost One* (1951). It was to be his only directorial credit.

The 1950s was a period of marked decline for Lorre. He was off the screen for three years with health problems, and when he returned, bloated and heavy, he gave but a handful of charming supporting performances in films such as *Beat the Devil* (1954), *Silk Stockings* (1957), and *The Big Circus* (1959). There was a suggestion of his earlier fame when, in the early 1960s, he appeared in more major roles in Roger Corman's Edgar Allen Poe movies *Tales of Terror* (1962) and *The Raven* (1963), as well as Jacques Tourneur's *Comedy of Terrors* (1964). He made his last film appearance playing a heavy in the Jerry Lewis vehicle, *The Patsy* (1964). During that same year Lorre died of a heart attack.

LOY, MYRNA (1905–) She was an actress who appeared in roughly sixty movies before she became a star, spending much of her early career playing oriental vamps. (It hardly seemed to matter that she wasn't Asian.) When she finally became a star after her long apprenticeship, there was hardly a more accomplished actress in Hollywood. Once she became famous, Loy was quickly typecast as the ideal wife, playing the role to perfection for nearly two decades before making a slight change and becoming the ideal mother.

Born Myrna Williams, she began her show business career as a dancer, making it to the chorus line at Grauman's Chinese Theater in Hollywood. She was spotted there and given a tiny role in *What Price Beauty* (1925). She can also be seen in a small role in the original *Ben Hur* (1926).

During the next eight years, Loy jumped up and down the credit list, having lead roles and bit parts, but without making a strong impression on movie audiences. Her most interesting appearances are in films such as *Ham and Eggs at the Front* (1927), in which she played a spy in blackface, *The Jazz Singer* (1927), in the small role of a showgirl, and *Crimson City* (1928) in a lead role and playing her first oriental vamp character. Her last such role was as the daughter of Fu Manchu in *The Mask of Fu Manchu* (1932).

Loy worked steadily, even during the transition to sound. And when she finally received a meaty role in *The Animal Kingdom* (1932) opposite Leslie Howard (*q.v.*), she showed flashes of star quality.

A former dancer at Grauman's Chinese Theater, Myrna Loy eventually became known as "the perfect wife," thanks to her lively teaming with William Powell in the many successful Thin Man mystery movies. In 1936, she was the country's number-one female box office draw. Photo courtesy of Myrna Loy.

MGM, which owned her contract, began using Loy in "A" movies, hoping to turn her into a star. Several successful films followed, one of which, *Manhattan Melodrama* (1934), was a hit for unexpected reasons. The film received enormous publicity as the movie that the gangster John Dillinger had seen right before he met his end in a deadly shootout in front of a Chicago theater where the film was playing.

More important for her career, however, she starred in *Manhattan Melodrama* with both William Powell and Clark Gable (*qq.v.*), her two most important leading men. She had already appeared in two other films with Gable, but this was her first with Powell. The film's director, W. S. Van Dyke, thought that Loy and Powell would make a wonderful comic team. The result was *The Thin Man* (1934).

The film was a huge hit. As Nora Charles, Loy became the quintessential modern wife: clever, resourceful, and very much the equal of her husband Nick Charles (Powell) both in sleuthing and in quipping. And Loy played her character with charm, wit and warmth. The two stars were a delightful pair and they clearly enjoyed working together. The two of them reprised their roles five times in subsequent Thin Man movies, the final one being *Song of the Thin Man* (1946).

As famous as she was for playing Nora to Powell's Nick, Loy actually acted just as often with Clark Gable. In fact, she was voted the Queen of Hollywood at the same time (1937) that Clark Gable was voted King.

But Loy wasn't terribly interested in lording it over Hollywood. She made only one movie (*The Thin Man Goes Home,* 1944) during the war years, choosing instead to work for the Red Cross. She returned to full-time acting after the war, and soon appeared in the Oscar-winning movie, *The Best Years of Our Lives* (1946), playing both wife and mother to perfection.

Loy finished out the 1940s with a succession of polished performances in several films, including *The Bachelor and the Bobby Soxer* (1947) and *Mr. Blandings Builds His Dream House* (1948), both with Cary Grant (*q.v.*).

The actress chose to slow down her film career in the 1950s and apart from *Cheaper by the Dozen* (1950) and *Lonelyhearts* (1958), made no movies of note. She barely appeared on screen in the 1960s, and was wasted in *The April Fools* (1969). Except for featured performances in films such as *Airport 1975, The End* (1979), and *Just Tell Me What You Want* (1979), Loy appeared far more often in TV movies.

From Asians to blacks, and from sophisticates to drunken mothers, Myrna Loy has probably played a greater variety of roles in her career than any other screen actress. But it is for the intelligent, witty wives she portrayed that she will be best remembered.

LUBITSCH, ERNST (1892–1947) A director-producer who set the standard for sophisticated sex comedies during both the silent and sound eras. He became known for "The Lubitsch Touch," clever visual innuendos about events occurring behind closed doors. Yet despite this wittiness, many critics have commented on an undercurrent of melancholy and nostalgia that deepens Lubitsch's comedy, some of this feeling perhaps was due to the European locales in which the German director set most of his Hollywood films. But there can be no doubt about Lubitsch's real home: he once said, "I've been to Paris, France and I've been to Paris, Paramount. Paris, Paramount is better."

Born to a well-to-do Berlin tailor, Lubitsch became enamored of the stage while an adolescent. In 1911 he became a member of Max Reinhardt's legendary Deutsches Theater, quickly establishing himself in important roles. But the theater didn't pay very well and, in order to make extra money, he took a job with a Berlin film company in 1912. The following year he began acting in films, starring in a series of comedy shorts in which he played a Jewish character named Meyer. The Meyer comedies proved to be quite pop-

ular, and Lubitsch furthered his film education and career by writing his own scripts and directing himself in subsequent movies.

When the Meyer shorts finally faded in popularity, Lubitsch stopped acting and became one of Germany's leading directors in the late 1910s and early 1920s with several huge international hits, among them *Gypsy Blood* (1918), *The Oyster Princess* (1919), and *Deception* (1920). His great reputation led Mary Pickford to insist that he direct her. Lubitsch turned down one Pickford project before finally making his American debut directing her in *Rosita* (1923). Lubitsch stayed on in Hollywood for the rest of his life.

Among his silent film succcesses were such milestones as *The Marriage Circle* (1924), *Forbidden Paradise* (1924), and *Lady Windemere's Fan* (1925). Critic Andrew Sarris has said of the this last film that it "was an improvement over [Oscar] Wilde's original."

While many foreign directors were defeated by the coming of sound, Lubitsch thrived. For instance, his continental operettas, *The Love Parade* (1929), *One Hour With You* (1932), and *The Merry Widow* (1934), all with Jeanette MacDonald and Maurice Chevalier (*qq.v.*), were witty soufflés that advanced the emerging art of the movie musical. And he was just as entertaining without music, making *Trouble in Paradise* (1932) one of the cleverest, most satisfying bedroom farces that has ever graced the big screen.

Lubitsch began producing his own films in the latter half of the 1930s when he became production manager at Paramount. His new duties did not stop him from continuing to add to his seemingly endless string of quality productions with *Angel* (1936), *Bluebeard's Eighth Wife* (1938), *Ninotchka* (1939), *The Shop Around the Corner* (1940), and *That Uncertain Feeling* (1941).

His first major critical and commercial flop also happened to be one of his greatest films, *To Be Or Not To Be* (1942), a movie that starred Jack Benny and Carole Lombard (*qq.v.*). There was a storm of protest against the film because Lubitsch had made an anti-Nazi farce that showed Hitler and company to be buffoons and fools rather than starkly evil men. *To Be Or Not To Be* has since come to be regarded as a classic, and was even remade virtually scene-for-scene by Mel Brooks (*q.v.*) in 1983.

Lubitsch shrugged off the failure, but could not shrug off his declining health. He managed to direct just two other critical and commercial hits, *Heaven Can Wait* (1943) and *Cluny Brown* (1946), before succumbing to his sixth heart attack. He died while directing *That Lady in Ermine* (1948), a film that was completed by Otto Preminger (*q.v.*).

In a film career spanning nearly thirty-five years, twenty-five of them in America, where he became one of the industry's most revered (and copied) directors, Lubitsch nevertheless failed to win a Best Director

Academy Award. [He had been nominated for *The Patriot* (1928), *The Love Parade* (1929), and *Heaven Can Wait* (1943).] Aware that he was a very sick man, the Academy moved quickly to honor him while he was still alive with a Special Oscar in 1946 "for his distinguished contributions to the art of the motion picture."

LUCAS, GEORGE (1945–) A writer, director, producer who in one capacity or another has been involved in the making of six of the most commercially successful movies in Hollywood history.

Lucas grew up in Modesto, California, with a penchant for car racing. This passion was considerably cooled after his miraculous survival of a serious car accident. After two years of junior college, he began studying film at USC, where he made a science fiction short titled *THX-1138* that won first prize at the 1965 National Student Film Festival. A scholarship followed that allowed him the opportunity of watching Francis Ford Coppola (*q.v.*) direct *Finian's Rainbow* (1968). Coppola took Lucas under his wing and doors soon began to open.

Lucas gained valuable experience as a production associate on Coppola's *The Rain People* (1969), and later he was a cameraman for the Rolling Stone's rock concert documentary *Gimme Shelter* (1970). He made his first film, a feature-length version of *THX-1138* in 1971, with the unknown Robert Duvall (*q.v.*) in the lead. The movie was visually stunning and it was admired by critics, but it didn't create much of a sensation at the box office.

With the help of Coppola, Lucas eventually received the funding to make an autobiographical film set in a small California city not unlike Modesto, and he called the movie *American Graffiti* (1973, *q.v.*). He cowrote the screenplay, based on his own story, and directed the film on a tiny $700,000 budget. It turned out to be the year's biggest hit film.

Despite the success of *American Graffiti,* Lucas had trouble finding financing for his next film, a science fiction movie with a $9 million budget. It was to be a film without stars in a genre that had been box office poison since the early 1960s. Twentieth Century-Fox finally gave Lucas the money, and *Star Wars* became the biggest grossing film of all time (since supplanted by *E. T.—The Extra-Terrestrial*).

The success of *Star Wars* (1977) has had an enormous impact on the American movie industry. For example the May 25 release of the gargantuan hit extended the summer movie season forevermore (it now begins on "George Lucas Day," two weeks before its earlier traditional beginning). Lucas' *Star Wars* also drove home the point that young people, in particular, would pay to see a film over and over again, and that special effects would bring massive numbers of people into movie theaters.

Star Wars elevated Lucas to the very height of directorial power. Yet Lucas has not directed a movie since. He has chosen, instead, to either write and/or produce his films. He provided the original stories and acted as executive producer for the two other *Star Wars* epics, *The Empire Strikes Back* (1979) and *Return of the Jedi* (1983). Along with Steven Spielberg (*q.v.*), Lucas conceived and produced the Spielberg-directed *Raiders of the Lost Ark* (1981), *Indiana Jones and the Temple of Doom* (1984), and *Indiana Jones and the Last Crusade* (1989). The *Star Wars* trilogy and the *Indiana Jones* films became six of the top-grossing films of all times.

The overwhelming commercial success of *Star Wars* allowed Lucas to make *The Empire Strikes Back* (1979) with his own money. The huge bankroll earned on the second *Star Wars* film made it possible for Lucas to establish his own company, Lucasfilm, and its special-effects subsidiary, Industrial Light and Magic, both of which are located on 3,000 acres in Northern California on Lucas' Skywalker Ranch, named for the hero of the *Star Wars* films, Luke Skywalker.

Lucas' touch hasn't always been golden. He was the executive producer of *More American Graffiti* (1979), a minor misstep compared to his involvement in the cataclysmic flop *Howard the Duck* (1986). But Lucas didn't write either of those failures. Recently, after five years without a writing credit, Lucas returned to the creative wars, penning the script and producing the fantasy epic *Willow* (1988), directed by Ron Howard (*q.v.*), which was disappointing. His script for *Indiana Jones and the Last Crusade,* however, was particularly well received by the critics. And as for the much-discussed six remaining installments of the *Star Wars* opus (the previously made trilogy represents the middle segment of a nine part serial), Lucas will only say that he's thinking about them.

When asked to describe the themes of his films, Lucas once told journalist Aljean Harmetz, "The underlying issues, the psychological motives, in all my movies have been the same: Personal responsibility and friendship, the importance of a compassionate life as opposed to a passionate life."

See also: science fiction films; special effects; *Star Wars*

LUGOSI, BELA (1882–1956) An actor who will be forever associated with the role of Dracula, though he had a long film career both before and after he played the famous vampire. Bela (pronounced Bayla) Lugosi's deep baritone voice with its aristocratic Slavic texture was both his acting signature in Hollywood and the main reason he never progressed beyond his success as Dracula.

Born Bela Ferenc Dezso in Hungary, Lugosi was a classically trained actor who learned his craft at the Budapest Academy of Theatrical Arts. Occasionally using the stage name of Ariztid Olt, he was a serious

Probably the most typecast actor in Hollywood, Bela Lugosi was so tied to his role as Count Dracula that he was rarely offered significant non-horror parts. And yes, it's true: he was buried in his Dracula cape. Photo courtesy of The Siegel Collection.

and successful stage actor in Hungary for more than a decade before he appeared in his first silent film in 1915.

After a political upheaval in Hungary, he made his way to Germany where he made several more films. But America was the land of opportunity for movie actors, particularly in the silent era, and Lugosi arrived in the United States in 1921 to pursue his career. He found work in the theater and in the movies, making his first U.S. appearance on screen in *The Silent Command* (1923). He went on to make a handful of other films during the 1920s but, ironically, given his thick accent, his greatest success was on the stage.

By 1927, Lugosi had garnered the lead in the Broadway production of *Dracula.* It was a huge hit and a personal success for the actor. He wisely stuck with the show and went on the road playing his most famous part for another two years.

When Universal Pictures bought the rights to *Dracula,* Lugosi, with his black cape, dark menacing eyes, and velvet voice, became an instant sensation. The film, directed by Tod Browning *(q.v.)* and released in 1931, was the first huge horror hit of the sound era.

Lugosi was slated to star as the monster in *Frankenstein* (1931), but he passed on the film to pursue another

that was never made. In doing so, he created his own horror competition by giving Boris Karloff *(q.v.)* the chance to become a star. From then on, the two actors were linked in the public consciousness as the leading horror personalities of their time and the dual heirs to the late Lon Chaney *(q.v.).*

Lugosi appeared in dozens of horror films during the 1930s and 1940s. The quality of his projects didn't seem to matter to him, just so long as he worked. Some of his better films were *Murders in the Rue Morgue* (1932), *The Black Cat* (1934), *Mark of the Vampire* (1935), *The Raven* (1935), and (as Dracula) *Abbott and Costello Meet Frankenstein* (1948). His only significant supporting role outside of the horror genre was in the delightful Greta Garbo comedy *Ninotchka* (1939).

Lugosi became increasingly strange during his later years. He took his horror image rather seriously and often gave interviews while lying in a coffin. Yet his campy quality survived more than fifty mediocre—sometimes awful—movies. His last film was *Plan 9 From Outer Space* (1956). As per his instructions, when he died he was buried in his Dracula cape.
See also: Dracula; horror films

LUMET, SIDNEY (1924–   )   One of the most prolific directors of the modern era, he has made more than one movie per year on average since his directorial debut in 1957. His ability to draw major actors to his projects has allowed Lumet to make some ambitious movies—which have resulted in the occasional resounding failure. He has more than made up for them, however, with a number of highly regarded films during the 1970s and 1980s.

Born to a theatrical family, Lumet began his show business career at the age of four as a radio performer. His acting career continued throughout his childhood, with stints on Broadway in plays such as *Dead End.* World War II interrupted and forever altered the course of his career. When he returned from the service in 1946, Lumet turned his back on acting in favor of directing. After gaining valuable experience working Off-Broadway and in summer stock, he began directing in the new medium of television in 1950. In his six years as a TV director of such top-notch showcases as the "Alcoa Theater" and the "Goodyear Playhouse," Lumet gained a considerable reputation for being talented and resourceful. That reputation, along with having also been the director of a TV show called "Best of Broadway," led to his directing the film version of the hit Broadway play *Twelve Angry Men* (1957). The movie, starring Henry Fonda *(q.v.),* was well received by both critics and audiences, and Lumet was honored with his first Best Director Oscar nomination. As a result, he also led the first wave of directors who made a successful transition from TV to movies.

Lumet's work during the late 1950s and early 1960s

continued to be largely in the area of film dramatizations of Broadway plays, such as Arthur Miller's *A View from the Bridge* (1960) and Tennesse Williams' *Long Day's Journey into Night* (1962). He ventured into the area of grim thrillers with *Fail Safe* (1964), in which New York City is blown up at the end. He would later use New York time and again as the backdrop—if not the symbol—of his preoccupation with America's decline.

The director brought a dark visual flair to the unexpected art-circuit hit *The Pawnbroker* in 1965, but not long after his career began to falter. He was producing and directing films such as *The Deadly Affair* (1967), *Bye Bye Braverman* (1968), and (another theater adaptation) *The Last of the Mobile Hot Shots* (1970) with modest critical praise and very little audience support.

In 1973 Lumet finally broke out of his tailspin by directing Al Pacino (*q.v.*) in one of the year's biggest hits, *Serpico,* based on the true story of a New York City cop. After directing *Murder on the Orient Express* (1974), based on Agatha Christie's novel, with professional polish, he returned to the streets of New York to direct Pacino yet again in *Dog Day Afternoon* (1975), gaining another Best Director Academy Award nomination. He then hit the peak of his career when he brought Paddy Chayefesky's brilliant, if overwrought, screenplay of *Network* (1976) to life. He was again nominated for Best Director, and again, did not win an Oscar.

Unexpectedly, Lumet returned to adapting plays to the screen, but this time with less optimum results. *Equus* (1977) was poorly received, and the big-budget all black version of *The Wizard of Oz, The Wiz* (1978), was a major bomb, both critically and commercially. Lumet went back to the kind of film with which he had enjoyed his greatest success, the New York crime drama, and he hit it big yet again with *Prince of the City* (1981). *Deathtrap* (1982) redeemed his reputation as a director of filmed stage plays but was not a major box office winner.

In recent years, Lumet's social concerns have been increasingly on display in films such as *The Verdict* (1982), *Daniel* (1983), *Power* (1986), and *Running on Empty* (1988).

LUPINO, IDA (1918–) An actress, she excelled at playing tough tarts and later became Hollywood's only female director of the 1940s and 1950s, managing to write and produce her own films, as well. She experienced her greatest popularity as an actress in the early to mid-1940s when her smokey good looks and hard-edged performances laced with a hint of vulnerability made her a standout. Her artistic success in the latter 1940s and early 1950s as a Hollywood screenwriter and director were limited, but her pioneering efforts are

historically important as they eventually opened the door to future female screenwriters and directors.

Lupino was born in England to a well-known British actor, Stanley Lupino, and was, in fact, a member of a family with an acting tradition going back to the seventeenth century. The young actress was trained at the Royal Academy of Dramatic Arts and, after assorted bit parts in the movies, made her official film debut at the age of fifteen in an American film shot in England, *Her First Affair* (1933).

When she was brought to America in 1934, Lupino appeared in a number of films, but none of the studios with which she worked were able to turn her into a star. The only film she really shined in during the 1930s—and there was really only one—was *The Gay Desperado* (1936).

It would have seemed that with her beauty and English accent she could have become another Greer Garson (*q.v.*) during the war years. Instead, Lupino became a sexier, sultrier version of Joan Blondell (*q.v.*), costarring in a series of hardboiled adventure yarns at Warner Bros. that finally tapped her gaminelike qualities. Her run at stardom began with *They Drive By Night* (1940), in support of Humphrey Bogart and George Raft (*qq.v.*). Though she played the wayward wife of Alan Hale in the film, there was good chemistry between her and Bogart, and she was cast as his moll in the surprise hit film *High Sierra* (1941). It was a movie that helped launch not only Lupino, but Bogart and screenwriter John Huston (*q.v.*).

1941 also saw her star with John Garfield (*q.v.*) in *The Sea Wolf* and *Out of the Fog*, two of her better efforts. She hit the top of her acting career with *The Hard Way* (1943), a film about a poor but determined beauty who would do anything to escape her poverty-stricken life. It was pure soap opera, but she was good at it, earning The New York Film Critics Award as Best Actress of the year.

With Bette Davis (*q.v.*) as queen of the lot, it was Lupino's bad luck to be under contract to Warners during the 1940s. Unable to get the better scripts that were handed to Davis, her career suffered. But the actress was as tough as the characters she portrayed, and she decided to work behind the camera, writing and producing a low-budget film about pregnancy called *Not Wanted* (1949). It was a minor success, leading to the opportunity to write and direct a story about a polio victim's struggle, *Never Fear* (1950). Both films had a female protagonist. RKO was sufficiently impressed with her work to offer her the chance to act, write, and direct. Her output as a director was small—seven films—and of no particular artistic merit, but movies such as *Outrage* (1950), *Hard, Fast and Beautiful* (1951), *The Bigamist* (1953), and *The Trouble with Angels* (1966) worked well enough at the box office to prove to

Hollywood that a woman could sit in the director's chair.

Lupino continued to act on a regular basis during the early to mid–1950s, but she never starred in any of the films she directed. Once she began appearing on television in 1956 (she starred with her third husband, Howard Duff, in her own series, "Mr. Adams and Eve"), she also began directing in that medium, as well. Her film appearances since the 1950s have been limited to a few supporting roles.

McCAREY, LEO (1898–1969)   A director, screenwriter, and producer who, at the height of his career in the late 1930s and early 1940s, found an ideal balance between humor and sentiment, creating a string of memorable hit movies.

McCarey's background was rather unusual for a director who started in the silent era. Many early movie directors had backgrounds either in engineering or the theater, but McCarey had been a lawyer—a bad one. He once told Peter Bogdanovich *(q.v.)* that he had been literally chased out of a courtroom by one of his clients, and he kept on running until he reached Hollywood in 1918. He received his training in the early 1920s as an assistant to director Tod Browning *(q.v.)*. He was given the opportunity to direct his first feature film at Universal Pictures, *Society Secrets* (1921). Unfortunately, the young director wasn't quite ready to handle such a responsibility and the movie was a dismal failure.

During the balance of the 1920s—from 1923 through 1929—McCarey wrote, supervised production, and directed comic short subjects at the Hal Roach Studio, gaining expertise as a gag man and learning how to fashion cinematic comedy. During those years he either wrote, directed, or supervised the production of Laurel & Hardy's greatest shorts, including their classic, *Big Business* (1929).

McCarey took a second stab at feature-film directing in 1929 with a minor effort called *The Sophomore*. This time, he passed muster and continued directing feature films until 1962. There was nothing special about his earliest work until he began directing comedy stars such as Eddie Cantor *(q.v.)* in *The Kid From Spain* (!932), the Marx Brothers *(q.v.)* in *Duck Soup (q.v.)* (1933), and Mae West *(q.v.)* in *Belle of the Nineties* (1934). He directed a different kind of star in 1935 when he chose Charles Laughton *(q.v.)* as the lead in *Ruggles of Red Gap*. The film was a critical and box office hit, firmly establishing McCarey as a director of note.

After a noble but failed attempt at resurrecting Harold Lloyd's *(q.v.)* career with *The Milky Way* (1936), McCarey went on to produce and direct the most unflinchingly honest film ever made in the 1930s about the American family and the Great Depression. The movie was *Make Way for Tomorrow* (1937), and it had surprisingly good humor despite its heart-wrenching story of an aging couple who lose their home and discover that their grown children are either unwilling or unable to help them live the last few years of their lives together. The two old people are parted forever in one of Hollywood's most haunting film endings.

Beginning with *Make Way for Tomorrow*, McCarey produced every movie he directed save one, and from 1939 onward, he either supplied the stories for his own films or cowrote the screenplays. For a solid decade, he had hit after hit.

He started his hit parade after *Make Way for Tomorrow* with a delightful screwball comedy starring Cary Grant and Irene Dunne *(qq.v.)*, *The Awful Truth* (1937), a movie that boldly and quite comically dealt with the issue of divorce. McCarey won an Academy Award as Best Director for 1937, ostensibly for *The Awful Truth*, but most likely because he had shown such remarkable directorial range that year.

He showed still more range when he directed his most lushly romantic movie, *Love Affair* (1939), a film rarely seen today because McCarey remade it himself in 1957 as *An Affair to Remember* and the earlier version was removed from circulation. Those who have seen both consider *Love Affair* the superior film.

McCarey's career was building to a high point when he made *Once Upon a Honeymoon* (1942). He reached the apex when he directed *Going My Way* (1944), staring Bing Crosby *(q.v.)*. The movie was a spectacular hit and McCarey won Academy Awards for his story and for his direction. He followed that success with a sequel to *Going My Way, The Bells of St. Mary's* (1945), and it, too, was a smash hit.

McCarey began making movies less often, directing only one in the late 1940s, the moderately successful and sweet-natured *Good Sam* (1948), starring Gary Cooper *(q.v.)*. Four years later, McCarey's career took a nosedive when he made *My Son John* (1952), an incredibly heavy-handed anticommunist film that is almost unwatchable today. He recouped with *An Affair to Remember* in 1957, but McCarey's humor—his greatest asset—was sadly lacking in *Rally Round the Flag, Boys!* (1958), and the drama was flat in his last film, *Satan Never Sleeps* (1962).

McCREA, JOEL (1905–) In a career spanning five decades, he is best remembered as an agreeable light comic actor who had his heyday in the late 1930s and early 1940s. In the early 1930s, he usually had the less important male lead opposite bigger female stars. From the mid-1940s until his retirement, he appeared almost exclusively in westerns. But whatever he played in, Joel McCrea's easy, likable manner made him a bankable if not altogether exciting film star throughout his career.

McCrea grew up in southern California and set his sites on the movie business from a very early age. He pursued theater in college and acted in local community productions, all the while working as an extra in Hollywood whenever he got the chance.

He found his first non-extra role in *The Jazz Age* (1929) and proceeded to work at many of the major studios, principally MGM, RKO, and Goldwyn, during the 1930s. McCrea made a lot of movies, some of them of reasonable quality, but nothing that made him stand out. Even when he starred in the William Wyler *(q.v.)* classic *Dead End* (1937, *q.v.*), he was upstaged by Humphrey Bogart *(q.v.)*, cast in a lesser role. That same year, however, he starred in his first western, *Wells Fargo* (1937), and carried the film, turning it into a major hit. *Union Pacific* (1939) ensured his standing as a credible western star.

The early 1940s brought McCrea his highest level of popularity. He showed his dramatic range as an actor in Alfred Hitchcock's *Foreign Correspondent* (1940), and then teamed up with Preston Sturges *(q.v.)* at Paramount in that director's golden period, starring in the delightful comedies *Sullivan's Travels* (1941) and *Palm Beach Story* (1942), as well as the lesser Sturges comedy/drama, *The Great Moment* (1944).

Beginning in 1946, McCrea acted almost exclusively in westerns, none of which are worth mentioning other than Sam Peckinpah's highly regarded *Ride the High Country* (1962). As an aging lawman with nothing left

but his principles, McCrea was truly superb. Nonetheless, his costar, Randolph Scott, stole the picture from him.

McCrea temporarily retired after *Ride the High Country,* returning to the big screen just a few more times over the next two decades in low-budget westerns.

Though generally considered in his day a second-string Gary Cooper in action films and a second string Cary Grant in contemporary comedies, in his open, honest style, McCrea was probably closest to Henry Fonda. In any event, he was a serviceable and attractive actor.

McDANIEL, HATTIE (1895–1952) A black actress who breached the color barrier in a number of significant ways in the film, radio, and TV industries. Limited opportunities for blacks in films resulted in few roles other than demeaning stereotypical ones, but McDaniel made the best of a bad situation, making her presence felt in a great many films from the 1930s until the early 1950s.

The daughter of a Baptist minister, McDaniel was accustomed to singing in church. She began her show business career as a band singer, becoming the first black woman to perform on radio. She began her acting career in the early 1930s, often in the role of a maid. With her warm, friendly style, she was often chosen to play in support of sharp-edged performers such as Marlene Dietrich (in *Blonde Venus* [1932]) and Mae West (in *I'm No Angel* [1933]). In the latter film, she was the recipient of Mae West's famous line, "Beulah, peel me a grape."

McDaniel worked steadily in films, often (although not exclusively) in either contemporary or period pieces that were set in the South. For instance, she played supporting roles in *Judge Priest* (1934), *The Little Colonel* (1935), *Show Boat* (1936), *Maryland* (1940), and *Song of the South* (1946). Her most famous role was in *Gone With the Wind* (1939), for which she won an Oscar for Best Supporting Actress, the first black actor in Hollywood history to be so honored.

McDaniel also acted on radio, appearing on the "Eddie Cantor Show," "Amos 'n' Andy," and eventually her own show, "Beulah," later turned into a TV show in 1952 in which she briefly held the limelight before her death.

See also: racism in Hollywood

MacDONALD, JEANETTE (1901–1965) A star of 1930s movie musicals, MacDonald is generally remembered today for her teaming with Nelson Eddy in a series of endearing operettas for MGM. MacDonald was also a fine light comedienne, and both her voice and her humor were put on display early in her film career in a number of clever bedroom farces directed by Ernest

Lubitsch *(q.v.)*. In fact, these earlier movies, in which she starred with Maurice Chevalier *(q.v.),* represent some of the best musicals of the early sound era.

The young singer originally worked in the theater during the 1920s, building a considerable reputation. With the advent of sound, studios showed a great interest in Broadway stars, and MacDonald was given a screen test at Paramount. Lubitsch liked what he saw and signed her up for *The Love Parade* (1929). She costarred with Chevalier, with whom she would appear in four films.

Musicals were the first successful talkies, and MacDonald made her share of them, including *Monte Carlo* (1930) and *Love Me Tonight* (1932), the latter being one of the most outstanding musicals of all time.

After falling out of favor at Paramount she was dropped, only to be reunited with her mentor, Lubitsch, at MGM. After making her last film with Chevalier *(The Merry Widow,* 1934), MacDonald was teamed with a rising young singing star of dubious acting ability, Nelson Eddy. The movie was *Naughty Marietta* (1935), and a new musical love match was made whose romantic harmonizing thrilled audiences.

They appeared together in eight films, in the most memorable of which, *Rose Marie* (1936), Eddy serenaded her with "The Indian Love Call." Some of their other films were *The Girl of the Golden West* (1938) and *Sweethearts* (1938), which was their most successful pairing in terms of box office receipts. Their last film together was *I Married an Angel* (1942).

Whether MacDonald starred with Maurice Chevalier or Nelson Eddy, she generally played a rich, spoiled, and sophisticated woman who eventually came to her senses and fell in love with the poor but charmingly sincere hero. It was a formula that worked because MacDonald, with her soprano voice and high-toned style, played female aristocrats convincingly.

While most of MacDonald's film career was spent in musicals, she did have a noteworthy dramatic role in *San Francisco* (1936) with Clark Gable *(q.v.)*. But by the early 1940s she was wanted for neither dramatic nor musical roles. With her career waning, she received mostly minor parts in a handful of films, ending her Hollywood career in a Lassie movie, *The Sun Comes Up* (1949).

See also: screen teams

McLAGLEN, VICTOR (1886–1959) A big, barrel-chested former boxer who became a raw, though popular, actor first in England and then in the United States. McLaglen was a long-time favorite of John Ford *(q.v.)* who directed him a dozen times, often giving him a good role just when the actor's career needed a shot in the arm. He was a major (if unlikely) star in the latter 1920s and through most of the 1930s before he became a serviceable character actor.

McLaglen was born in Great Britain and spent a colorful youth as a soldier, miner, and professional prize fighter, going six rounds with the then world heavyweight champion, Jack Johnson. In 1920, he was spotted in England by a producer who thought the fighter could make a dashing film star. Cast in *The Call of the Road,* a surprise hit, McLaglen suddenly became a bankable actor. Within just two years, he was one of England's biggest stars. But when the bottom dropped out of the English film market, the actor suddenly found himself in need of work.

When Hollywood beckoned, McLaglen quickly responded. His first American feature was *The Beloved Brute* (1925), an aptly named movie that also defined the actor's film personality. Among his silent films were *The Unholy Three* (1925), in which he costarred with Lon Chaney *(q.v.), The Fighting Heart* (1925), his first film under the directorial guidance of John Ford, and *What Price Glory* (1926), in which he had his most important silent screen role, playing Captain Flagg. The latter film made $2 million at the box office and spawned several sequels with McLaglen good-naturedly battling his friend Sergeant Quirt (played by Edmund Lowe).

John Ford directed McLaglen in his first talkie, *The Black Watch* (1929). But after a few successes, such as *Dishonored* (1931) with Marlene Dietrich *(q.v.),* his career began to fade. Ford, as always, was there to help him, giving him a starring role in *The Lost Patrol* (1934). The film was a hit and it led Ford to cast McLaglen in *The Informer* (1935). McLaglen was at his boozy, brawling, brutish best, turning his character, Gypo Nolan, into a sympathetic man tortured by guilt. He won a Best Actor Oscar for his performance.

The latter 1930s were uneven for McLaglen. He starred in several pictures and played supporting roles in others. His best films of this period were *Professional Soldier* (1936), *Wee Willie Winkie* (1937), the Ford-directed Shirley Temple *(q.v.)* film, and the magnificent *Gunga Din* (1939).

Though McLaglen worked fairly regularly, his career began a steady slide in the 1940s. He was soon playing villains in "B" movies. Though he continued to appear in "B" movies throughout the rest of his life, he did manage to appear in a handful of quality films, all of them directed by his friend and protector John Ford. The director cast him as a tough, hard-drinking but lovable sergeant in *Fort Apache* (1948), *She Wore a Yellow Ribbon* (1949), and *Rio Grande* (1950). Ford used him again as John Wayne's foil in *The Quiet Man,* although a double stood in for McLaglen in the long fight scene that concludes the film.

The actor continued to appear in small character parts throughout the 1950s, and he lived long enough to be directed by his son, Andrew V. McLaglen, in *The Abductors* (1957). He died two years later of a heart attack.

MacLAINE, SHIRLEY (1934–   ) An actress of unconventional beauty with even more unconventional interests, she has been in show business for nearly forty years, a movie star for more than three decades. For much of her early screen career, MacLaine was typed as a prostitute with a heart of gold; she has played variations of the part in fourteen films, many of which count among her most well-known movies. Originally a dancer, she has appeared in few musicals, but her long leggy look has been as much of an asset as her pixieish manner.

Born Shirley MacLean Beatty to a middle-class family in Virginia, she is the older half-sister of actor/director/producer Warren Beatty (q.v.). But her show business training began even before Warren was born. She was given dancing lessons at the age of two and a half in order to firm up her weak ankles. Dancing appealed to her and, aided by her amateur drama coach mother, she pursued a show business career, venturing to New York at the age of sixteen. It paid off, at least temporarily, in a chorus job in a revival of *Oklahoma*. She went home to finish high school before finally returning to New York two years later with the new stage name Shirley MacLaine.

If the way in which she rose to fame had been made into a movie, its screenwriter would have been accused of plagiarizing the 1933 movie classic *42nd Street*. MacLaine had been in the chorus of *Me and Juliet* for 358 performances before getting another job in the chorus of a new musical, *The Pajama Game*. She had also been hired to understudy the star, Carol Haney. Haney broke her ankle and, with only four days' rehearsal, MacLaine had to go on. When she dropped her hat during the famous "Steam Heat" number, she reportedly swore loud enough for everyone in the theater to hear. But by the end of the show, the audience loved her, and MacLaine was an overnight sensation. Hal Wallis (q.v.), the famed movie producer, caught her performance and immediately signed her to a five-year movie contract.

Her film debut in Alfred Hitchcock's macabre comedy, *The Trouble With Harry* (1955), was auspicious. Though the film was a commercial failure, MacLaine received good reviews. Except for a sexy and amusing performance in the Martin and Lewis comedy *Artists and Models* (1955), the young actress didn't attract much attention again until she delivered a riveting performance as the poor, love-starved Ginny in *Some Came Running* (1958). Her portrayal brought her the first of her five Oscar nominations.

The early 1960s were her best, most productive screen years. She started the decade singing and dancing in *Can-Can* (1960) and gave what many consider to be her best performance in *The Apartment* (1960), for which she won her second Oscar nomination. Not long after, she stepped into the title role in *Irma La Douce* (1962),

substituting for Elizabeth Taylor (q.v.), and had another big hit, plus her third Oscar nomination. But then came a long string of flops. Even her return to musicals in *Sweet Charity* (1969) was a bust. She didn't star in another hit film until *Two Mules for Sister Sara* (1970), which was essentially a Clint Eastwood (q.v.) vehicle.

Though she wasn't big box office in the early 1970s, MacLaine's reputation was enhanced by her performance in *Desperate Characters* (1971). She had the chance to recoup her star status when she played a mature mother tortured by what might have been had she continued her dancing career in *The Turning Point* (1977). The film was a hit and it garnered MacLaine yet another Oscar nomination.

The actress gave a charming supporting performance in *Being There* (1979), but she was truly triumphant in *Terms of Endearment* (1983). Her portrayal of Aurora Greenwood, the proud and difficult mother who must help her dying daughter, brought her her fifth Academy Award nomination and, finally, her first Best Actress Oscar.

Except for *Madame Souzatzka* (1988), MacLaine has not been seen very often on the big screen in recent years. She has, however, been active as an author, writing autobiographical books leavened with New Age insights and philosophies. She has even starred in a TV miniseries based on one of her best-sellers, *Out on a Limb*.

MacMURRAY, FRED (1907–   ) An actor who has had a remarkably long career despite appearing in few first-rate films. Though he had mostly starring roles in over eighty movies, MacMurray never carved out a unique film personality. In fact, his image throughout the 1930s and early 1940s was generally of a likably callow fellow, and his acting, with a few notable exceptions, has rarely challenged that perception.

The son of a concert violinist, MacMurray's original career ambition was to play the saxophone. He joined a few bands, vocalized, and had a growing career as a musician. A tall and handsome young man, he worked as an extra (appearing in *Girls Gone Wild,* 1928), but not until 1934 did the movies hook him for good. His first film was *Friends of Mr. Sweeney* (1934), but it wasn't until Claudette Colbert took a liking to him that his career began to soar. They played together for the first time in the comedy *The Gilded Lily* (1935); the film was a considerable hit.

MacMurray was a good foil, and Hollywood's top actresses often requested him as a costar, most notably Katharine Hepburn who starred with him in *Alice Adams* (1935). Throughout the 1930s he played genial leading men, usually in comedies, although he also acted in westerns such as *The Texas Rangers* (1936) and musicals such as *Cocoanut Grove* (1938).

He continued floating through the early 1940s without much distinction until he starred with Barbara Stanwyck and Edward G. Robinson in Billy Wilder's *Double Indemnity* (1944). In the best role of his career, he played a deceitful insurance salesman who commits murder. Interestingly, he was the twelfth actor approached for the part, all others having turned it down. Even MacMurray, afraid the role would ruin his image, did not want to play it at first. Instead, it established him as a credible actor.

Later in the 1940s, MacMurray had one of his most successful films, *The Egg and I* (1947), another comedy with Claudette Colbert as his costar. Then came a period of steady activity in consistently mediocre movies. The only exception was MacMurray's sterling performance as the cowardly writer in *The Caine Mutiny* (1954).

By the latter 1950s he was starring in cheap westerns, and it appeared as if his career was petering out. MacMurray was saved by Walt Disney, who offered him the lead in *The Shaggy Dog* (1958). The movie was a surprise hit, eventually leading to a string of starring roles in Disney family pictures such as *The Absent-Minded Professor* (1961) and *Son of Flubber* (1963).

Both MacMurray and the Disney movies were beyond any sort of serious criticism. But the actor was recruited by director Billy Wilder *(q.v.)* one more time to play a cad in *The Apartment* (1960). And again, MacMurray rose to the occasion, giving an excellent supporting performance. But it was the last time he would play a bad guy in the movies.

As a comic actor, Fred MacMurray was pleasant, but he was at his best playing against type, which he did far too infrequently. As a result, MacMurray never seriously stretched his talents. He reached the apex of his fame not in the movies but as the father in the popular TV series "My Three Sons." At the beginning of his career he seemed destined for superstardom; he seems to have settled comfortably for longevity.

McQUEEN, STEVE (1930–1980) An actor who was the personification of "cool," he built his considerable reputation in the 1960s and 1970s around a macho, loner image. His weathered good looks made him a sex symbol to women and his tough action roles earned him the admiration of men. McQueen was never considered an accomplished actor (although he was very effective within his limitations), but he was every bit the movie star, with a charisma that was unmistakable on the big screen. In addition to being one of the highest paid actors of the late 1960s and early 1970s, he also had the distinction of being among the first television stars to make what was then the very difficult leap to major movie-star status.

McQueen had a difficult childhood, having been abandoned by his father when he was three years old. He spent much of his youth in trouble, getting the

What Steve McQueen lacked in acting ability, he more than made up in charisma. Playing vulnerable loners and tough guys, he won audience sympathy. And with his piercing stare and weathered good looks, he also won the admiration of men and the adoration of women. Photo courtesy of Movie Star News.

better part of his education in a reform school. He held a variety of jobs, such as carnival worker, sailor, and lumberjack, before joining the Marines. He was not the perfect soldier, going AWOL at one point and spending a portion of his military service in jail.

Directionless and headed for hard times when he left the Marines, McQueen drifted from job to job, making money as a poker player when all else failed, until an aspiring actress girlfriend suggested he become an actor. He was accepted at New York's Neighborhood Playhouse and began learning his craft there on the G.I. Bill in 1951, later studying with Uta Hagen.

McQueen had on-the-job training in stock and on television. His big break came in 1956 when he replaced Ben Gazzara as the star of the Broadway production of *A Hatful of Rain*. That same year he finally broke into the movies in a bit part in *Somebody Up There Likes Me* (1956).

He first became known to the mass audience when he was cast as Josh Randall in the TV series "Wanted: Dead or Alive." He played a bounty hunter in the western action show, and its success over three-and-a-half years (1958–1961), made him a famous TV personality. McQueen continued to act in movies and make TV guest appearances during the run of his own show. For instance, he had the lead role in the low-budget science fiction film *The Blob* (1958), and he also appeared in *The Great St. Louis Bank Robbery* (1959) and *Never So Few* (1959). But the film that suggested he might have a career beyond television was *The Magnificent Seven* (1960), in which he gave a strong supporting performance.

The film industry saw McQueen's potential and he was cast in several films in the hope that he'd emerge a star. After such flops as *Hell Is for Heroes* (1962) and *The War Lover* (1962), he finally clicked in *The Great Escape* (1963), the film with which he is still most closely identified.

Again, McQueen's career stalled with several interesting failures, among them *Love with the Proper Stranger* (1963) and *Baby the Rain Must Fall* (1965). He finally hit his stride with *The Cincinnati Kid* (1965), a poker version of Paul Newman's pool-hall saga, *The Hustler* (1961), and nearly as successful. (For the rest of McQueen's career, he and Newman would be considered Hollywood's top male action/sex symbols.) The hits kept coming for McQueen: *Nevada Smith* (1966), *The Sand Pebbles* (1966), for which he won his only Best Actor Oscar nomination, *The Thomas Crown Affair* (1968), *Bullitt* (1968), and an off-beat comedy, *The Reivers* (1969).

After *The Great Escape*, McQueen's love for motorcycles and fast cars became well known to film fans. The automotive fast track seemed to suit him in *Bullitt*, a movie full of chase scenes, and racing cars were at the heart of *Le Mans* (1971), his first major flop as a mega-star.

After having made a number of films through his own production company, Solar Productions, including the *Le Mans* fiasco, he decided to join a more powerful organization, becoming, in 1971, a founding member of First Artists, together with Barbra Streisand, Sidney Poitier, and Paul Newman *(qq.v.)*. Dustin Hoffman *(q.v.)* joined First Artists the following year, which led to his teaming with McQueen in *Papillon* (1973), which was one of McQueen's last compelling movies. In fact, the early 1970s marked the final flowering of the actor's worldwide appeal to film audiences. He scored with such Sam Peckinpah *(q.v.)* films as *Junior Bonner* (1972) and *The Getaway* (1972), meeting and later marrying and divorcing his costar, Ali McGraw. His appearance in the all-star *The Towering Inferno* (1974) brought him a staggering $12 million.

He was off the screen for several years after *The Towering Inferno*, returning in 1977 in a film that surprised but did not delight his fans or the critics, an adaptation of Henrik Ibsen's *An Enemy of the People*.

He was again off the screen for several years, returning in 1980 with his last two movies, *Tom Horn* and *The Hunter*, neither of which were major hits.

McQueen died of a heart attack after a long fight against terminal cancer with what many in the traditional medical community considered to be unorthodox methods.

MAKE-UP ARTIST   According to union regulations, a make-up artist can apply make-up only to the head and neck, going no lower than the top of the breastbone. He or she is also restricted to making up the arms no higher than the elbows. Any other make-up that is needed must be done by a body make-up artist. A make-up artist on a union production generally must be licensed for the job.

Sometimes, make-up treads close to the area of special effects, as in providing the appearance of wounds and scars, or when an actor's face is dramatically changed, such as Charles Laughton's in The *Hunchback of Notre Dame* (1939) and Dustin Hoffman's in *Little Big Man* (1970).

THE MALTESE FALCON   There are three film versions of Dashiell Hammett's detective novel; the third attempt released in 1941 did the trick, turning the story into a major hit. In its definitive version, the film confirmed Humphrey Bogart's star status, established John Huston *(q.v.)* as a force to be reckoned with in his directorial debut, and introduced Sydney Greenstreet to movie audiences. *The Maltese Falcon* was also one of the earliest *film noir* movies, helping to usher in a dark, cynical period in 1940s filmmaking that came to its fruition in the second half of the 1940s.

Briefly, the story of *The Maltese Falcon* concerns an eccentric group of duplicitous characters in search of an ancient statue (the falcon) full of priceless gems. Detective Sam Spade becomes involved in the hunt in order to clear himself of murder charges after his partner is killed by one of the villains.

The Maltese Falcon was a highly regarded novel that was first filmed by Warner Bros. in 1931, starring Ricardo Cortez as Sam Spade and Bebe Daniels as Brigid O'Shaughnessy. Interestingly, the first version of the movie generally followed the plot of the novel but didn't use Hammett's crisp dialogue. It had a minor success.

The movie was remade in 1936 with the title *Satan Met a Lady*. It starred Warren William as the hero and Bette Davis as the double-crossing female. It otherwise bore precious little resemblance to either the novel or the original film. Despite Bette Davis' presence, the movie was a flop.

Meanwhile, John Huston had been working for Warner Bros. as a screenwriter in the latter 1930s. He was finally promised an opportunity to direct if his coauthored screenplay for *High Sierra* (1941) was a success. It was, and Huston decided to try his hand on a new rendition of *The Maltese Falcon*. The studio, however, balked at the title since it had been used a decade earlier. The brass wanted to name it *The Gent from Frisco,* but Huston insisted on keeping the original title and the studio finally relented.

George Raft *(q.v.)* was tapped to play the role of Sam Spade, but not wanting to work for a neophyte director, he declined the part. The role fell to Bogart who had just starred in *High Sierra* and seemed primed for stardom if cast in the right vehicle. And with *The Maltese Falcon,* he got it. The rest of the cast included Mary Astor *(q.v.)* as the lying Brigid O'Shaughnessy, Peter Lorre *(q.v.)* as the effete but dangerous Joel Cairo, Elisha Cook Jr. as the ineffective gunsel, Wilmer, and Sydney Greenstreet as "The Fat Man," his first film role (at the age of sixty-one). Huston cleverly made a point of filming Greenstreet from low angles in order to accentuate his girth as well as his power.

Huston was also clever about his script. He didn't make the mistake his two predecessors had. He stuck close to the novel and used as much of Hammett's wonderfully pithy dialogue as he could ("I'll wait for you angel. Unless they hang you. Then I'll always remember you.").

The film, made for less than $300,000, was an immediate hit. Critics and audiences were stunned and delighted by its tough cynicism. The movie was nominated for an Academy Award as Best Picture of 1941. *See also:* Bogart, Humphrey; detective films; *film noir;* remakes

MAMET, DAVID   *See* writer-directors.

MAMOULIAN, ROUBEN (1897–1987) One of Hollywood's most innovative directors, his clever use of sound at the beginning of the talkie era liberated filmmaking from the tyranny of the microphone. He pioneered the use of color, special effects, and music, and he did so in a manner that was highly entertaining.

Born to an Armenian family, Mamoulian received his early stage training in the London theater, eventually arriving in New York in his mid-twenties. He continued working in the theater, bringing the original (nonmusical) *Porgy and Bess* to the stage. After more theatrical successes as a director, he was finally enticed into bringing his skills to motion pictures.

The first film he directed was *Applause* (1929), a backstage musical with Helen Morgan. Mamoulian came up with a dual-channel microphone, enabling two characters to be recorded at the same time, with one speaking softly and the other loudly. It had never been done before.

In the early talkie era, the camera was left stationary while attention was paid almost exclusively to the sound recording. Mamoulian, however, insisted that the camera move in *Applause*—and indeed it swooped and soared.

Applause was a landmark film, though it didn't set any box office records.

Mamoulian's next film, however, was a much bigger hit, though it is less well remembered now than his first movie. *City Streets* (1931), with a script by Dashiell Hammett, was an early gangster film starring Gary Cooper *(q.v.)* and Sylvia Sidney *(q.v.)* (in her debut). The film's distinctions include a clever and persuasive use of music and a rather European style of symbolism uncommon to most Hollywood movies (for example, two feline figurines are shown in close-up while two female characters are heard to argue on the soundtrack).

Mamoulian was on a creative winning streak when he followed his first two films with the definitive version of *Dr. Jekyll and Mr. Hyde* (1932) with Fredric March in the Oscar-winning title role. In an interview that appears in *The Celluloid Muse, Hollywood Directors Speak* by Charles Higham and Joel Greenberg, Mamoulian explained one of the early sound era's greatest mysteries:

"The secret of the transformation of Dr. Jekyll into Mr. Hyde in one continuous shot—without cuts and without winding the film backwards in the camera to permit the application of additional make-up—lay in the use of color transparencies, which gradually revealed more and more of the actor's make-up. As you know, a red filter will absorb and reveal all the other colors, and a green filter will do the reverse. Working on that principle, we held graduating color filters one by one before the camera, thus allowing successive portions of March's colored make-up to register on film. It was all rather primitive—the filters were handmade—but it worked."

Next was *Love Me Tonight* (1932), one of Hollywood's most charming and cleverly directed early musicals. The film starred Maurice Chevalier and Jeanette MacDonald *(qq.v.)*. It's opening musical number (which starts in Paris and ends in the French countryside) is one of the creative glories of the American musical.

Mamoulian was much in demand and went on to direct Greta Garbo *(q.v.)* in *Queen Christina* (1933) and Marlene Dietrich *(q.v.)* in *Song of Songs* (1934). In the former film, Mamoulian gave Garbo the famous direction to think of absolutely nothing when the camera made its final close-up of her at the end of the picture.

Mamoulian went on to direct ten more films, but except for *Becky Sharp* (1935), Hollywood's first three-color Technicolor *(q.v.)* feature, most of them were not quite up to the innovative brashness of his early efforts. Nonetheless, warmly remembered are *Golden Boy* (1939) and the remakes of *The Mark of Zorro* (1940) and *Blood and Sand* (1941). His last film, *Silk Stockings* (1957), starring Fred Astaire and Cyd Charisse *(qq.v.)*, was a musical remake of *Ninotchka* (1939).

His later original films and remakes have been intelligent and satisfying, but it's Mamoulian's early creative

Many of Henry Mancini's movie theme songs have become classics, and his long collaboration with director Blake Edwards has paid rich dividends for both. Photo courtesy of Henry Mancini.

efforts that have given him his special place in Hollywood history.

MANCINI, HENRY (1924–)   Hollywood's most famous composer/arranger, Mancini is also among the industry's most honored musical artists, having garnered eighteen Academy Award nominations and won the Oscar four times. Mancini has written the scores for more than eighty films, a significant number of them for writer/director Blake Edwards *(q.v.),* who gave Mancini his first big break, inviting the composer to write the theme song for the TV series, "Peter Gunn." He is a prolific and versatile composer who has had success with lush romantic scores, jazz, and satirical music.

Mancini was first introduced to music at the age of eight when his father taught him to play the flute. At twelve he took up piano and a few short years later he became interested in arranging. After studying at The Julliard School for one year (1942), Mancini served in the army. Honorably discharged in 1945, he joined the Glenn Miller-Tex Beneke Orchestra as a pianist/arranger.

In 1952 Mancini joined the music department of Universal-International Studios. During the next six years he contributed to over 100 films as both a composer and arranger, most notably *The Glenn Miller Story* (1954, for which he received his first Academy Award nomination), *The Benny Goodman Story* (1955), and Orson Welles' *Touch of Evil* (1958).

The "Peter Gunn" theme song came soon after Mancini left Universal-International. The composer has continued to write music for television ever since, but his film career has been nothing less than a series of triumphs. In 1961 he won two Oscars—one for Best Original Score for Blake Edwards' *Breakfast at Tiffany's* (1961) and the other for Best Song, "Moon River" (with lyrics by Johnny Mercer). That same year, he was also nominated for an Oscar for his song "Bachelor in Paradise" (lyrics by Mack David). The following year he had yet another hit Oscar-winning song, "Days of Wine and Roses," from the Blake Edwards film of the same name. In addition, his theme for Edwards' *Pink Panther* films remains as popular today as when it was first introduced. And Mancini has continued his winning ways in Edwards-directed films, receiving his fourth Oscar in 1983 for the original song score for *Victor/Victoria* (lyrics by Leslie Bricusse).

In addition to his long-standing collaboration with Blake Edwards, Mancini is also known for his scores for films such as *Charade* (1963), *Two for the Road* (1967), *Sometimes a Great Notion* (1971), *Silver Streak* (1977), *Mommie Dearest* (1981), and *The Glass Menagerie* (1987).

MANKIEWICZ, HERMAN J. (1897–1953) A screenwriter and producer who made great contributions to the art of the film despite long stretches of involvement in merely commercial enterprises. He is best remembered today as Orson Welles' collaborator on the Oscar-winning screenplay for *Citizen Kane* (1941)—indeed, a controversy still reigns as to how much of that work Welles actually wrote. Less well known is the fact that Mankiewicz was the executive producer of such early sound comedy classics as *Million Dollar Legs* (1932), and three Marx Brothers (*q.v.*) gems, *Monkey Business* (1931), *Horsefeathers* (1932), and *Duck Soup* (1933). The elder brother of Joseph L. Mankiewicz (*q.v.*), his arrival in Hollywood preceded that of his ultimately more famous sibling.

Mankiewicz came to the attention of Hollywood through his theater reviews for the influential *New York Times* and *New Yorker*. Invited to Hollywood in 1926, he began his prolific career by providing story ideas for films such as *The Road to Mandalay* (1926), writing titles to silent films during the latter days of the silent era for the likes of *Gentlemen Prefer Blondes* (1928), writing dialogue for early sound films such as Josef von Sternberg's *Thunderbolt* (1929), and penning screenplays (either alone or in collaboration), for such hits as *Girl Crazy* (1932), *Dinner at Eight* (1933), *The Pride of the Yankees* (1942), *The Enchanted Cottage* (1945), and many more.

MANKIEWICZ, JOSEPH L. (1909–) A writer/director/producer who had one of the most unusual careers in Hollywood. He started out as a screenwriter in the late 1920s and early 1930s, contributing to a number of historically important movies before becoming a producer in 1936 and overseeing the production of several courageous and hard-hitting commercial films. He might have remained a successful producer but, instead, chose to become a director, often penning his own screenplays. As a consequence, he reigned in the late 1940s and throughout the 1950s as the premier writer-director of Hollywood's most literate and sophisticated fare, many of his movies highly successful at the box office, as well. If he had a plodding and uninspired visual style as a director, his witty, biting scripts more than made up for the lapse.

Born Joseph Leo Mankiewicz, he followed in his older brother's (Herman J. Mankiewicz, *q.v.*) footsteps, becoming a correspondent for the Chicago *Tribune's* Berlin office. While Herman gained access to the movies

through his position as a respected theater critic for the *New York Times*, Joseph began his career by writing subtitles for German films that were exported to English-speaking countries. Eventually, he joined his brother in Hollywood in 1929, making his one and only on-camera appearance that year in *Woman Trap*.

Mankiewicz continued writing subtitles for his first assignments in Hollywood. By the early 1930s, however, he had begun writing dialogue as well as screenplays. Among his more memorable early efforts were *Skippy* (1931), *Million Dollar Legs* (1932), *If I Had A Million* (1932), *Alice in Wonderland* (1933), *Manhattan Melodrama* (1934), and, significantly, King Vidor's independent production of *Our Daily Bread* (1934).

Mankiewicz's willingness to take chances was evidenced by his work with Vidor on the politically progressive and controversial *Our Daily Bread*. When he became a producer in 1936, he made such films as Fritz Lang's antilynching movie, *Fury* (1936), the poignant *Three Comrades* (1938), which was scripted by F. Scott Fitzgerald, and Katharine Hepburn's comeback film, *The Philadelphia Story* (1940).

By the mid-1940s, after rewriting a number of scripts by other authors, Mankiewicz decided to write for the screen once again, this time controlling his own work by directing it.

Mankiewicz had his first chance to direct when Ernst Lubitsch (*q.v.*) took ill and he took over directorial chores for *Dragonwyck* (1946), a film for which he wrote the screenplay. His new career was off and running.

Among the films he directed from scripts other than his own were *The Late George Apley* (1947), *The Ghost and Mrs. Muir* (1947), *House of Strangers* (1949), and *Suddenly Last Summer* (1959). But his reputation rests on the films he wrote as well as directed, his most famous being *All About Eve* (1950), the richly sardonic movie about behind-the-scenes theater life. The film won the Oscar for Best Picture of the Year and brought Mankiewicz Best Director and Best Screenplay Academy Awards as well. Less well known but equally impressive was Mankiewicz's work of the previous year, *A Letter to Three Wives* (1949), for which he also won Oscars for Best Director and Best Screenplay.

At the top of his craft in the late 1940s and 1950s, he wrote and directed such admired films as *No Way Out* (1950), *People Will Talk* (1951), *Julius Caesar* (1953), *The Barefoot Contessa* (1954), *Guys and Dolls* (1955), and *The Quiet American* (1958). Not all of his films were hits, but nothing seriously hurt his career until it was nearly destroyed by the initial box office disaster of *Cleopatra* (1963, *q.v.*). He made just three films thereafter, *The Honey Pot* (1967), *There Was A Crooked Man* (1970), and *Sleuth* (1972).

MANN, ANTHONY (1907–1967) A director best known for his action films—principally westerns—during the

1950s. His collaboration with Jimmy Stewart *(q.v.)* in a much-admired and commercially successful series of hard-edged psychological westerns eventually helped lift the genre to a greater respectability among thoughtful critics.

Mann had a strong pictorial sense and a keen ability to depict emotional turmoil. While he tended toward symbolism, he was rarely heavy-handed in his imagery. Though closely associated with the western, Mann also had a significant impact in the *film noir (q.v.)* era of the late 1940s and early 1950s. Toward the end of his career he directed epics with somewhat less success.

Born Anton Bundsmann in San Diego to two schoolteachers, the future director fell in love with the theater after moving to New York City with his family when he was ten years old. Later, quitting high school after his father's death, he changed his name to Anton Mann and became an actor, often working in other jobs in the theater as well. During the 1930s, he garnered a modest reputation as a stage director of shows such as *So Proudly We Hail* (1936) and *The Big Blow* (1938). Hollywood took notice.

David O. Selznick *(q.v.)* hired Mann as a talent scout and director of screen tests, the latter function giving him greater familiarity with directing actors for the camera. His assignments during this era included screentesting the would-be stars of such films as *Gone With the Wind, Intermezzo,* and *Rebecca.* In 1939, Mann moved on to become an assistant director at Paramount, learning his craft and eventually winning his first directorial assignment on the low-budget *Dr. Broadway* (1942).

Throughout most of the 1940s, Mann continued directing low-budget films with minor stars, making his first real splash with *T-Men* (1947). Slightly bigger budgets and better-known actors came his way in a string of tough-minded, gritty *films noir,* movies including *Raw Deal* (1947) and the excellent *Border Incident* (1949).

Mann made his first western, *Winchester '73,* in 1950. The movie, starring Jimmy Stewart, was a surprise hit and it reestablished the actor's fading career. Out of that success came a bond between Mann and Stewart, linking the two men together in a long and rewarding series of movies. In all, the actor and the director worked together in eight films in a five-year period. The best of their movies were *Bend of the River* (1952), *The Naked Spur* (1953), and *The Man from Laramie* (1955).

With his reputation growing as an action director, Mann went on to make such other highly regarded westerns as *The Tin Star* (1957) and *Man of the West* (1958). The latter film portended the director's interest in epic themes. The movies he directed subsequently were almost all epics, including *Cimarron* (1960), *El Cid* (1961), *The Fall of the Roman Empire* (1964), and *The Heroes of Telemark* (1965). Among these films, only *El*

Cid was a major hit. Mann's last film was *A Dandy in Aspic* (1968), a muddled spy story set during the cold war. Mann died of a heart attack during filming and it was completed by the movie's star, Laurence Harvey.

MARCH, FREDRIC (1897–1975) A highly respected actor whose sober, direct style was so "unactorish" that he often seemed uncommonly natural on screen compared to other stars. Yet many of his best-remembered roles are of wonderfully flamboyant characters, made believable by his admirable restraint.

Born Frederick McIntrye Bickel, March was preparing for a career in the banking industry when he became seriously ill. His brush with mortality apparently helped him decide to do something more brash with his life, and he raced off to New York to become an actor.

A tall man with piercing dark eyes, March landed some modeling work and a few stints as an extra in New York–produced movies, but his real experience was gained on the stage, learning his craft on Broadway during the years 1920 to 1927. In 1927, he went to Los Angeles to appear in the road version of *The Royal Family,* a thinly veiled play about the Barrymore family. Spotted as a potential star of the new sound era, he was immediately signed by Paramount.

March's first film was the *The Dummy* (1929), and he appeared in roughly a dozen more movies before he truly made his mark on audiences, reprising his stage role in (what was now titled) *The Royal Family of Broadway* (1930). When he starred in Rouben Mamoulian's classic version of *Dr. Jekyll and Mr. Hyde* (1932), March became a bona fide Hollywood star, winning an Oscar for Best Actor in the bargain.

Beside the inevitable duds, March added his talents to several fine films in the early 1930s, such as *Design for Living* (1933) and *Death Takes a Holiday* (1934). Yet he demonstrated his best work in *Les Miserables* (1935), *The Road to Glory* (1936), and the non-musical version of *A Star is Born* (1937).

In the late 1930s and early to mid-1940s, March's screen career slowed, principally because he and his actress wife, Florence Eldridge, spent a great deal of time acting on Broadway. But he returned to the movies in 1946 as one of the principal stars of William Wyler's post–World War II hit, *The Best Years of Our Lives* (1946). March shared in the flood of seven Oscars bestowed upon the film, picking up a second Best Actor Award.

By 1950 March was no longer the leading man type, and good roles were becoming harder for him to find. But he did manage to land the role of Willy Loman in the film version of Arthur Miller's play *Death of a Salesmen* (1952). Unfortunately, his performance wasn't appreciated by the critics, and audiences never showed up to see the movie and decide for themselves.

March then found a comfortable niche as a character

actor (with star billing) surrounded by other actors with greater audience appeal. His powerful, intelligent performances in *Executive Suite* (1954), *The Desperate Hours* (1955), *The Man in the Gray Flannel Suit* (1956), and his superb performance in the relatively unknown Paddy Chayevsky (q.v.) film, *The Middle of the Night* (1958), were highlights of an enormously talented actor at the height of his mature powers.

March continued to act right through the 1960s and into the early 1970s. His impassioned portrayal of William Jennings Bryan in *Inherit the Wind* (1960) gave way to smaller, less flashy roles in films such as *Seven Days in May* (1964), *Hombre* (1967), and his last film, *The Iceman Cometh* (1973).

Unlike most movie stars, Fredric March isn't associated with a handful of hit films that defined his personality (as was the case with stars as divergent as John Wayne, Humphrey Bogart, and Jimmy Stewart). Yet, just like the greatest Hollywood stars, March's place in film history is secure because his talents helped to create a substantial number of memorable movies.

MARION, FRANCES (1887–1973) One of the film industry's rare female screenwriters, she was among the most successful, particularly during the 1930s. In a career that spanned both the silent and sound eras, Marion either created the stories or wrote the screenplays (or both) for nearly one hundred and fifty films. She was prolific without sacrificing quality, and many of the movies with which she is associated are among Hollywood's best. Remarkably versatile, Marion was adept at penning romances, comedies, and domestic dramas that tugged at the heart strings.

Born Frances Marion Owens in San Francisco, she was uncommonly courageous for a woman of her time. A reporter for the San Francisco *Examiner,* she was a combat correspondent during World War I. When she returned to the United States in 1915, film director Lois Weber took her on as protégée, giving Marion her introduction to the film business. She worked on rare occasions as an actress, and soon made her mark as a scenario writer. Among her early film-writing efforts were *Esmerelda* (1915) and *The Foundling* (1916). It wasn't long, however, before she began writing and adapting some of the silent era's greatest hits, including *Rebecca of Sunnybrook Farm* (1917), *Polyanna* (1920), *Stella Dallas* (1925), and *The Son of the Sheik* (1926).

Her artistic and commercial touch made her a sought-after screenwriter and she worked with many of Hollywood's best directors, including John Ford (q.v.), Frank Borzage (q.v.), James Cruze, George Cukor (q.v.), and Maurice Tourneur, among others. She even directed three films herself, *The Love Light* (1921), *Just Around the Corner* (1922), and *The Song of Love* (1923).

She had no trouble making the transition to scriptwriting for the talkies, and her success in the 1930s

even outstripped her silent era triumphs. She became one of Hollywood's best paid screenwriters thanks to a string of hits that included *The Big House* (1930), for which she won her first screenplay Oscar, *Min and Bill* (1930), *The Champ* (1931), for which she won her second screenplay Oscar, *Dinner at Eight* (1933), and *Camille* (1937).

Because of her top-rank status as a screenwriter, Marion was one of the few women with power in Hollywood. She used her influence with great generosity and compassion, helping other women, such as Marie Dressler (q.v.), whose career she saved, and her mentor Lois Weber, whose burial she paid for.
See also: women directors

MARSHALL, HERBERT (1890–1966) An English actor, Marshall came to America in the early 1930s and became a star immediately. With his elegant, silky voice and masterful way of projecting suffering, particularly at the hands of adulterous wives, Marshall was a favorite of female movie fans.

Marshall had a long career on the stage that was nearly aborted when he was badly wounded while serving in World War I. The actor's right leg had to be amputated and thereafter he walked with the aid of a wooden leg, a fact which remained relatively unknown to stage and movie audiences.

Marshall's screen career began in England with an appearance in a silent film, *Mumsie* (1927). In 1929, he appeared in *The Letter,* based on the work by Somerset Maugham, a writer with whom Marshall would again be associated. The film was a hit and he followed it up with a sterling performance in one of Alfred Hitchcock's early sound films, *Murder* (1930).

By this time, Marshall had already been acting for nearly twenty years, and considered the stage his true home. But when he made *Secrets of a Secretary* (1931) with Claudette Colbert (q.v.) in Hollywood, everything changed. He was in great demand and Paramount was ready to turn him into a 1930s version of Rudolph Valentino.

Although he never did become a huge star, Marshall was a much valued leading man for two decades and a dependable supporting actor for another two decades after that, always adding a measure of class to the films in which he appeared.

The start of Marshall's sad-eyed, long-suffering husband roles began with *Blonde Venus* (1932), where Marlene Dietrich (q.v.) abandons him for Cary Grant (q.v.). That same year Marshall was superb as the debonair thief in Lubitsch's wonderfully amoral comedy *Trouble in Paradise.* It was unquestionably the best role (and the best film) of his career. Then came more cuckolded husband roles in films such as *Riptide* (1934), *The Painted Veil* (1934), *The Good Fairy* (1935), *Dark Angel* (1935), and others.

He was cast against type in some films, the best of which was a tearjerker about two spies, *Till We Meet Again* (1936), and *Foreign Correspondent* (1940), in which he was a villain. But by the 1940s, Marshall often found himself playing fathers rather than lovers. He was still capable of playing the wronged husband, however, as he did in *The Little Foxes* (1941).

In 1942, Marshall returned once again to the work of Somerset Maugham, playing the writer as the narrator of *The Moon and Sixpence* (1942). In *The Razor's Edge* (1946) he played Maugham yet again in a film that starred Tyrone Power *(q.v.)*.

Even as his age caught up with him, Marshall's mellifluous voice continued to charm. By the mid-1940s, however, he was generally cast in small supporting roles. Unfortunately, most of the movies in which he later appeared weren't worthy of his talents. Among the handful of better movies he appeared in during the last twenty years of his life were *Duel in the Sun* (1946) and *Stage Struck* (1958). His last film was *The Third Day* (1965), made one year before his death. In all, Marshall made seventy films in his long and distinguished film career.

MARTIN, DEAN (1917–)

An actor, singer, and comedian, Dean Martin's movie career can be divided into three distinct phases: that of his partnership with Jerry Lewis, his serious acting roles, and his self-parodying. The third and longest phase, is less notable.

Born Dino Crocetti, the young crooner teamed up with aspiring comedian Jerry Lewis and together they became a nightclub sensation. They were soon tapped for the movies and became the hottest comedy team in Hollywood since the heyday of Abbott & Costello *(q.v.)*. Lewis played the innocent (almost retarded) sidekick to Martin's handsome and suave ladies' man.

The Martin and Lewis films, beginning with *My Friend, Irma* (1949) and ending with *Hollywood or Bust* (1956), were consistently popular. The team made a total of sixteen films together, with Martin singing a few numbers in each and playing straight man to Lewis. Their best films together include *Scared Stiff* (1953), *Artists and Models* (1955), and *Pardners* (1956). Eventually, Lewis began to overshadow Martin in their films and the straight man wanted out.

It was widely assumed in show business circles that Martin would quickly disappear after the breakup of the team. And it certainly seemed likely after he starred in the silly *Ten Thousand Bedrooms* (1957). But Martin recovered his career and his standing in the industry with a mixture of strong starring and supporting performances in *The Young Lions* (1958), *Some Came Running* (1958), *Rio Bravo* (1959), and *Bells are Ringing* (1960).

Except for a handful of rat-pack *(q.v.)* movies with Frank Sinatra *(q.v.)*, and his mildly entertaining Matt Helm films that spoofed James Bond, Martin's film career degenerated as his TV career blossomed in the 1960s.

MARTIN, STEVE (1945–)

A multitalented comedian who has written and produced, as well as starred in, some of the most imaginative and daring comedies of the 1980s. Unlike many former stand-up comedians, Martin has effectively melded his club and concert persona with an impressive array of comic cinematic characters.

Born in Waco, Texas, and raised in Southern California, Martin found his entry into show business through magic. He performed his act at nearby Knott's Berry Farm, eventually adding comedy routines. Martin became a television comedy writer when he was still very young and he won an Emmy for his work on the "Smothers Brothers Comedy Hour." Later he wrote for Sonny and Cher, Pat Paulsen, Glenn Campbell, and John Denver. Finally he decided to perform his own material.

Martin worked as a stand-up comic during the late 1960s and most of the 1970s, gaining recognition from appearances on "The Tonight Show." He soon became a major comedy star and made several guest-host appearances on "Saturday Night Live." Whatever he touched during the 1970s turned either to gold or platinum. He won two Grammy awards for his first two albums (which went platinum), *Let's Get Small* and *Wild and Crazy Guy*, and he even had a hit novelty single, "King Tut," which sold over 1.5 million copies. At the height of his popularity as a TV, club, and concert performer, he even had a best-selling book, *Cruel Shoes*.

Martin's first venture into film was a short he wrote and starred in called *The Absent-minded Waiter*, which was nominated for an Academy Award. In 1979, he graduated to features, cowriting and starring in *The Jerk*, directed by Carl Reiner *(q.v.)*, who became his frequent collaborator. *The Jerk* was a collossal hit, grossing over $100 million. It instantly established Martin as a major movie star, with critics suggesting that he was the new Jerry Lewis *(q.v.)*. Surprisingly, that was meant in a nice way.

Pennies From Heaven (1981), his next film, was an innovative and striking musical comedy directed by Herbert Ross *(q.v.)*. Martin learned to tap dance for the film and gave a virtuoso performance in what was a smart and ambitious movie. Unfortunately, his audience wasn't thrilled by a film so startlingly different from *The Jerk;* it failed badly at the box office.

Martin quickly reteamed with director Carl Reiner for two wild and crazy comedies, *Dead Men Don't Wear Plaid* (1982) and *The Man with Two Brains* (1983). He gave yet another excellent performance in *The Lonely Guy* (1984).

Steve Martin may be among the most underrated of film comedians. His willingness to take chances and expand his art in such films as *Pennies From Heaven* (1981), *All of Me* (1984), and *Roxanne* (1987) bespeaks superior talent and vision. Photo courtesy of Steve Martin.

The roundly admired and commercially successful *All of Me* (1984), in which he costarred with Lily Tomlin, marked the fourth pairing of Steve Martin and Carl Reiner. *All of Me* showcased Martin's remarkable physical comedy, and he received the Best Actor award from the New York Film Critics for his performance. Many thought he was wrongfully overlooked for an Oscar nomination.

Martin was overlooked by the Academy yet again for a stirring supporting performance as the demented dentist in the movie version of the hit off-Broadway musical *Little Shop of Horrors* (1986). After coscripting and starring with Chevy Chase *(q.v.)* and Martin Short in the poorly received *Three Amigos* (1986), the ever-ambitious Martin was the executive producer, co-scripter, and star of the marvelously imaginative romantic comedy *Roxanne* (1987), a clever modern version of Edmond Rostand's classic *Cyrano de Bergerac.* Once again, the Academy ignored Martin's work, but the Los Angeles Film Critics honored him with their Best Actor citation and the Writers Guild of America gave him their award for best screenplay based on material from another medium.

After *Roxanne,* Martin starred with John Candy in a more frivolous yet satisfying comedy, John Hughes' *Planes, Trains and Automobiles* (1988). He then teamed with Michael Caine in the much-admired remake of

Bedtime Story (1964) retitled *Dirty Rotten Scoundrels* (1988). Most recently he starred in the hit comedy *Parenthood* (1989).

In ten years, Steve Martin has become not only one of Hollywood's most successful new comedy stars, he has also become one of the industry's most creative and audacious comedians.

MARTY The 1955 Academy Award–winning movie was the cinematic version of the Paddy Chayevsky *(q.v.)* story originally produced for TV. Its success on television prompted its precedent-making remake on film for theatrical release. *Marty* became the sleeper box office hit of the year, winning a total of four Oscars.

At first glance, a movie about a shy, lonely, middle-aged and none-too-attractive Bronx butcher, Marty, played by Ernest Borgnine, *(q.v.)* who finds love with a plain-Jane schoolteacher (Betsy Blair) would hardly seem like a sure-fire money-maker. But the sensitively written screenplay by Chayevsky (who had also written the teleplay) turned Marty's tentative attempt to find love into a universal experience.

The success of *Marty* caused Hollywood to look to television as a source of future films and as a source of talent. Actors, directors, and writers soon graduated from TV to movies, in large part thanks to *Marty*.

The movie's four Oscars were for Best Picture (Harold Hecht, producer), Best Director (Delbert Mann), Best Actor (Borgnine) and Best Screenplay. The movie also was honored with Best Supporting Actor/Actress nominations for Joe Mantell and Betsy Blair.

MARVIN, LEE (1924–1987) He was the roughest, meanest, toughest of Hollywood's heavies during the 1950s. When he took on heroic roles in the mid-1960s, he was at his best unleashing the sinister charisma that characterized his earlier screen successes. With his wolfish grin and deep, growly voice, Lee Marvin ultimately had as powerful a screen presence as any other star of the modern era.

Though one might assume from his performances that he grew up in rough circumstances, Marvin was actually born to an upper-middle-class family in New York City. His hard-boiled attitude came from a stint in the Marine Corps during World War II. After the war, while working as a plumber's assistant in a summer stock theater, he found himself filling in for a sick actor—and so his acting career began.

He studied his craft and worked on the stage in New York, eventually making his film debut (along with Charles Buchinski/Bronson) in *You're in the Navy Now* (1951). Marvin worked steadily in the movies, gaining a reputation as an effective villain. By 1953 he was fourth-billed in the explosive Fritz Lang *(q.v.)* crime drama, *The Big Heat,* in which he was at his vicious best throwing scalding coffee in Gloria Graham's face.

hen he wasn't stealing scenes as a heavy, Marvin was aying corrupt authority figures to the hilt in films ch as the underrated Robert Aldrich *(q.v.)* war movie *ttack!* (1956).

Marvin was the avatar of villainy as the title character John Ford's masterpiece, *The Man Who Shot Liberty alance* (1962). He was the only Hollywood actor of s era who could have successfully played a heavy to lance the combined heroic status of his two costars, hn Wayne and James Stewart *(qq.v.)*.

After his Oscar-winning portrayal of twins—one a unk and the other a gunfighter with an artificial se—in the comedy western *Cat Ballou* (1965), Marvin as finally offered more conventional starring roles. In e best of these roles, Marvin was only marginally od-hearted; his heroic status was relative to how tten the other characters were. In films like *The ofessionals* (1966), *The Dirty Dozen* (1967), and *Point lank* (1967), he played characters that were hard and uel, but they were fighting for higher ideals in an moral world.

Marvin's career was going so well that it seemed like thing could diminish his popularity—until the non-nging actor agreed to star (with Clint Eastwood) in e movie musical version of *Paint Your Wagon* (1969). he film was a critical and financial disaster. In retro-ect, it marked a turning point in Marvin's career. He d some fine roles after that, such as in *Prime Cut* 972) and *Emperor of the North* (1973), but even his tter films didn't often succeed at the box office. And e bad ones were often bombs. The best role of his er career brought him back to World War II, starring a tough sergeant in Sam Fuller's biographical war ovie, *The Big Red One* (1979).

There were even fewer good roles for the aging tough y in the 1980s. In the end, he received more press r his involvement in a landmark palimony case than r his acting during the last decade of his life.

HE MARX BROTHERS

The funniest and most influ-tial comedy team in Hollywood history, their humor aved the way for such later film comedians as Mel rooks and Woody Allen *(qq.v.)*.

In a mere thirteen films, only a handful of which ere consistently good from beginning to end, the arx Brothers—Groucho, Chico, Harpo, and (in their st five movies) Zeppo—were a veritable comedy tack force, slinging a wild, anarchic style of humor movie audiences, the likes of which they had never perienced. Their movies' plots, weak as they are, are f small concern; the real attractions of any Marx rothers' film are Groucho's rapid-fire punning and his ver-present leer, Chico's lame-brained Italian accent d his inventive piano playing, and Harpo's silent chery and coat that doubles as a Sear's warehouse.

Chico (1891–1961), born Leonard Marx, acquired his nickname from a strong and persistent interest in "chicks"; Harpo (1893–1964), born Adolph Marx, came by his nickname from his playing the harp; Groucho (1895–1977), born Julius Marx, picked up his nickname as a result of his moody behavior; Zeppo (1901–1979) was Herbert Marx until, according to Harpo, he picked up his nickname from constantly doing chin-ups like "Zippo," a popular monkey act in vaudeville; and a fifth brother, Gummo (1893–1977), born Milton Marx, was tagged with his nickname because he wore gumsole shoes. Gummo, however, left the act early on and never appeared in any of the Marx Brothers' films.

The boys were the children of a poor tailor, Sam Marx, and an aggressive mother, Minnie Marx, who pushed her kids into show business with the consider-able help of her brother, vaudeville star Al Shean, of the team of Gallagher and Shean.

The brothers' individual comic personalities evolved over a long stretch spent in vaudeville. Harpo's mute clown, for instance, was the result of an act written by their Uncle Al in which Harpo was given but three lines. In a review of the act published the day following its opening, a local critic wrote that Harpo was brilliant as a mime, but that the magic was lost when he spoke. Harpo never spoke in character again (except for a sneezed "achoo" in *At the Circus* (1939).

When the Marx Brothers arrived on Broadway in a loosely written play called *I'll Say She Is* in 1924, the knockabout vaudevillians suddenly became the toast of the Great White Way. A year later they opened in *The Coconuts*, a play written for them by George S. Kauf-man and Morrie Riskind, with music and lyrics by Irving Berlin *(q.v.)*. The play was another hit, and was eventually filmed in Astoria, Queens, even while the team was performing in another hit play, *Animal Crack-ers*.

Paramount put the Marx Brothers under contract, releasing *The Coconuts* in 1929 and *Animal Crackers* in 1930. The latter film contained the tune that would become Groucho's theme song, "Hooray for Captain Spaulding."

The brothers made three more films for Paramount, all of them in Hollywood. These included *Monkey Business* (1931) and the hilarious send-up of higher education, *Horsefeathers* (1932), followed by *Duck Soup* (1933), in which the team turned politics and the insti-tution of war into sheer hilarity. These last two films are arguably their finest.

Unfortunately, *Duck Soup* was not a rousing success at the box office. Paramount chose not to renew the Marx Brothers' contract, and Zeppo quit the team to become a theatrical agent. Though Paramount no longer wanted the Marx Brothers, Irving Thalberg *(q.v.)* at MGM did. He proposed, however, that they be paid twenty-five percent less than before because Zeppo had quit the team. Groucho retorted that they were twice

The Marx Brothers (from left to right) Harpo, Groucho, Zeppo, and Chico, have long been cult favorites, but they were also heralded in their own time, as evidenced by the hoopla over their making hand and footprints in cement at what was then Grauman's Chinese Theater in Hollywood. Sid Grauman, the famous movie exhibitor, looks on. Photo courtesy of The Siegel Collection.

as funny without Zeppo; Thalberg relented and a deal was struck. In any event, Margaret Dumont, who played the perfect dowager foil to Groucho in seven Marx Brothers movies, was ultimately more important to their films than Zeppo ever was.

Believing the brothers to be actually *too funny,* Thalberg sought to slow their movies down and attract a female audience by adding a love interest. He also thought it would be a good idea for the boys to take their comic bits out on the road in order to hone them for their pictures. The result of Thalberg's brainstorm was *A Night at the Opera* (1935), the most commercially successful of the Marx Brothers' movies. *A Day at the Races* (1937) was only a slightly lesser follow-up, but

MGM seemed to lose interest in the team after Thalberg died, and their films were soon beset by sillier romantic subplots. Nonetheless, there were still wonderful moments in their movies, particularly in *At the Circus* (1939) and *Go West* (1940).

Among other later movies were the film version of the hit play *Room Service* (1938), *The Big Store* (1941), an independent production of *A Night in Casablanca* (1946), and *Love Happy* (1949), the team's last movie together and the only one in which Harpo had top billing. *Love Happy* also featured future female superstar, Marilyn Monroe *(q.v.),* and was produced by the first female superstar, Mary Pickford *(q.v.).*

The Marx Brothers never made another movie toether as a team after *Love Happy*—though they each appeared in separate segments of the all-star film *The Story of Mankind* (1957). Of the three brothers, only Groucho remained fully active in show business. In addition to his hit radio and TV series, "You Bet Your Life" during the 1950s, he also appeared solo in several films, including the Carmen Miranda vehicle *Copacabana* (1947), *Double Dynamite* (1951) with Jane Russell, *A Girl in Every Port* (1952), and, finally, *Skidoo* (1969). Groucho also cowrote a screenplay with Norman Krasna for *The King and the Chorus Girl* (1937), a film starring Joan Blondell *(q.v.)*.

See also: agents; comedy teams; *Duck Soup*

MASON, JAMES (1909–1984) An actor with one of the richest, most evocative speaking voices in the history of the cinema. A one-time matinee idol in England, he came to Hollywood in the late 1940s but never became the superstar that many predicted. Though he had a number of triumphs, particularly in the early 1950s, he eventually became a reliable and highly valued character actor. In his later years, his smooth acting style and mellifluous voice brought him a measure of the fame and praise that had eluded him in earlier decades.

Born in England and educated as an architect, he nonetheless chose a career in the theater, making his debut in *The Rascal* in 1931. He continued acting on the stage throughout the 1930s and the very early 1940s, but he was one of the few stage-trained actors who publicly professed to prefer the camera to the boards. He began working in film in the mid-1930s, starring in a number of low-budget English movies, the first of which was *Late Extra* (1935). His first important film role was a small part in Alexander Korda's *Fire Over England* (1937).

Clearly interested in pursuing a movie career, however, Mason helped produce and script his own starring vehicle on a shoestring budget called *I Met a Murderer* (1939). The critics liked the film but it didn't go over well with the public. Mason would later produce several films on his own, none of them commercial hits.

By 1941 he had begun acting in films full time, making his big breakthrough in *The Man in Grey* (1943). Mason specialized in playing hard-hearted men who treated their women badly, but were redeemed by the end of the movie. Women moviegoers couldn't get enough of this handsome young man who was such a rotter. During the next three years he became England's most popular movie star. He made his reputation as a serious actor in a top-notch drama, Carol Reed's *Odd Man Out* (1946).

Hollywood wanted Mason. He arrived in America in 1947, but was unable to act on film in the U.S. by court order due to contractual problems. He was forced to bide his time. Unfortunately, it was time ill-spent:

He went on to flop in a Broadway show and made inadvertent unkind remarks about the American film industry that were made public. By the time he starred in his first Hollywood vehicle, *Caught* (1949), he was tarnished goods.

Mason struggled along in mediocre movies, his stock diminishing every year, until he had a short streak of strong roles in good movies, most notably in *The Desert Fox* (1951), *Five Fingers* (1952), and in Joseph Mankiewicz's highly-regarded, all-star version of *Julius Caesar* (1953), in which he had perhaps the greatest role of his career, Brutus. His most famous role, however, was that of the fading star, Norman Mane, in George Cukor's *A Star Is Born* (1954). The film was obviously a Judy Garland vehicle, but Mason was the character who held the emotional center of the story. Originally, Humphrey Bogart *(q.v.)* was slated for the part and, later, Cary Grant *(q.v.)* actually signed to play Norman Mane, but when the dust settled Mason ended up with the meaty role, winning an Oscar nomination for Best Actor.

Mason went on to play challenging roles in only a handful of notable films from then on. He was memorable as a victim in Nicholas Ray's *Bigger than Life* (1956), as the villain in Alfred Hitchcock's *North by Northwest* (1959), and, in a tour de force that should have resurrected his fading fortunes, as Humbert Humbert in Stanley Kubrick's *Lolita* (1962).

After several flops, however, Mason had become solidly entrenched in supporting character parts—many of them in English films. Though his roles were smaller, at least his films were good, as were his reviews. Among his better films during that era are *The Fall of the Roman Empire* (1964), *The Pumpkin Eater* (1964), *Lord Jim* (1965), *The Blue Max* (1966), and *Georgy Girl* (1966).

His film choices became considerably more indiscriminate in the later 1960s and throughout the rest of his career; he was an actor who simply kept working regardless of the material. Still, there were a number of good films amid the schlock. The best of them were *The Last of Sheila* (1973), *11 Harrowhouse* (1974), *Voyage of the Damned* (1976), *Heaven Can Wait* (1978), *The Boys From Brazil* (1978), *The Verdict* (1982), and *The Shooting Party* (1984), his final film.

MASTER SHOT An entire scene photographed from beginning to end as recorded by a single camera, and without any edits. While the master shot may be used in a film exactly as it is photographed, it is more often intercut with close-ups, reactions shots, etc., all of which are photographed separately in order to correspond to the master.

For example, a master shot of a typical gunfight in a western might have the camera recording the scene from slightly behind the hero and off to his right.

Whether the camera itself moves or not, the film must run continuously as the hero and villain approach each other, size each other up, then draw and shoot their guns, with (let us suppose) the bad guy crumpling to the ground. If the director likes this particular take, he has his master shot.

The director might then establish new set-ups and roll the cameras again in order to get close-ups of the two men's facial expressions as they approach each other. He might also choose a subjective shot capturing one gunman from the other's point of view as well as a close-up of a hand reaching for a gun. Finally, the director might have a medium close-shot of the villain as he falls to the ground. All of these scenes would be carefully shot so as to "match" the visual information recorded on the master, otherwise the fully edited scene would be full of visual inaccuracies.

MATTHAU, WALTER (1920–) A late-blooming star, Matthau came to prominence in the latter half of the 1960s and has been a much-loved actor ever since, specializing in comedy but equally adept in action and the occasional romantic role. With his beat-up looking face and body, a shuffling gait, and a decidedly ethnic-sounding vocal quality, Matthau hardly seemed a candidate for movie stardom, but thanks to an abundance of talent, the right roles, and a receptive audience, he became a top box office attraction and an Oscar-winning performer.

Born Walter Matuschanskayasky to a former Catholic priest and his Russian-Jewish wife, Matthau grew up in poverty on New York's Lower East Side. His job at the age of eleven of selling soda in a Yiddish Theater during intermission led to his acting on stage in bit parts.

After serving in the Air Force as a gunner, Matthau studied acting on the G.I. Bill at the New School's Dramatic Workshop. With his peculiar mug, he seemed best suited for character parts, and he played them with ever-increasing success on stage until he made his film debut in *The Kentuckian* (1955). He played the villain—as he would in virtually all of his films during the next decade.

Matthau worked constantly from 1955 to 1965, appearing on Broadway, starring in a short-lived TV series, "Tallahassee 7000" in 1959, and playing bad guys in the movies, most memorably in *A Face in the Crowd* (1957), *King Creole* (1958), and *Charade* (1963). He even directed himself in a film, a low-budget affair called *Gangster Story* (1958).

A highly respected actor, Matthau merely needed the right vehicle to show off his abilities. Director Billy Wilder *(q.v.)* wisely cast Matthau in his black comedy *The Fortune Cookie* (1966). Matthau's brilliant performance as a sleazy ambulance-chasing lawyer brought him a Best Supporting Actor Academy Award. He also

Walter Matthau proves that one need not be handsome to [be] a movie star. Audiences have responded to his W. C. Field[s-] like comedy performances, his earthy dramatic roles, an[d] even his few romantic parts. Photo courtesy of Walter Ma[t-] thau.

came away with a lasting personal and profession[al] relationship with his costar Jack Lemmon *(q.v.)*.

Playwright/screenwriter Neil Simon provided Ma[t-] thau with another important vehicle, penning the ro[le] of Oscar Madison in the play *The Odd Couple* express[ly] for him. The critical and public response to his perfor[-] mance as Madison made Matthau an undisputed sta[r,] at least in New York. And when he later reprised t[he] role in the film version of the play in 1968 (costarri[ng] with Lemmon), he solidified his standing as a majo[r] comic film talent. Simon has since provided a gre[at] many other excellent roles for Matthau in such films [as] *Plaza Suite* (1971), *The Sunshine Boys* (1975), whic[h] garnered him one of his two Best Actor Oscar nom[i-] nations, and *California Suite* (1978). Jack Lemmon d[i-] rected him in *Kotch* (1971), and Matthau received h[is] other Oscar nomination for Best Actor.

Matthau's portrayal of a modern-day W. C. Fiel[ds] ([*q.v.*] playing cranky comic characters) has led to eith[er] critical or commercial success in such films as *A Ne[w] Leaf* (1971), *The Bad News Bears* (1976), and *Little Mi[ss] Marker* (1979). Having proved himself not only in com[-] edy, Matthau has exhibited a wider range of actin[g] talents. He first showed his dramatic potential in t[he] seriocomic film *Pete 'n' Tillie* (1972). His next thr[ee] films were pure action movies, all well reviewed, an[d] all of them hits: *Charley Varrick* (1973), *The Laughi[ng] Policeman* (1973), and *The Taking of Pelham One T[wo] Three* (1974). In yet another display of versatility, Ma[t-] thau, then in his late fifties, starred in *House Calls* (197[8,] a light romance with Glenda Jackson. The film w[as] such a hit the pair was reunited in another romant[ic] comedy, *Hopscotch* (1980).

Due to ill health, Matthau has appeared with less frequency in the movies during the 1980s—and also with less commercial success than in the past. Despite generally good personal notices, films such as *First Monday in October* (1981), *Buddy, Buddy* (1981), *The Survivors* (1983), and *The Couch Trip* (1988) have not been hits.

MATURE, VICTOR   *See* sex symbols: male.

MAY, ELAINE (1932–)   An actress, writer, and director specializing in humorous subjects, she was one of the first women in the modern Hollywood era to write and direct major motion pictures. Unfortunately, her career took a serious tumble in 1987 due to her direction of the failed *Ishtar,* the biggest bomb of the late 1980s.

Born Elaine Berlin to a theatrical family, she performed in several plays in the Yiddish Theater with her father, Jack Berlin. While at the University of Chicago she met Mike Nichols *(q.v.),* another aspiring young actor, and the pair formed a comedy team that proved to be enormously popular during the 1950s. The act broke up in 1961 and May began writing and directing for the theater, though she soon found herself temporarily drawn back into performing, appearing in *Luv* (1967) and *Enter Laughing* (1967).

During the 1970s May was one of a rare breed: a female screenwriter and director. She wrote the script of *Such Good Friends* (1971) under the pen name Esther Dale and wrote, directed, and starred in the hit comedy movie, *A New Leaf* (1971). When she followed that success with yet another hit, *The Heartbreak Kid* (1972) (directing her daughter, Jeannie Berlin, to a Best Supporting Actress nomination), it appeared as if May were going to become a major new directorial force. But her next film, *Mikey and Nicky,* went considerably over-budget (presaging her greatest disaster), spent years being edited, and didn't arrive on movie screens until 1976. It was not a success.

In 1978, she cowrote the smash hit *Heaven Can Wait* and stepped in front of the cameras again in *California Suite,* but she was little heard from again until she directed Warren Beatty and Dustin Hoffman *(qq.v.)* in the colossal flop *Ishtar* (1987). A comedy that went stupendously overbudget, it was ripped apart by the critics and ignored by audiences despite the film's star power. Beatty and Hoffman took a lot of the critical heat for the disaster, but Elaine May's reputation suffered a terrible beating nonetheless.

MAYER, LOUIS B. (1885–1957)   The studio chief at Metro-Goldwyn-Mayer, the famous film company that bore his name. Like all the Hollywood moguls, he was a ruthless, demanding executive with a paternalistic style of doing business. As John Douglas Eames has noted in *The MGM Story,* Mayer saw his studio as a family, with himself as the patriarch. He therefore treated everyone beneath him—and there were as many as 6,000 employees at the studio—like children.

Born in Minsk, Russia, Mayer grew up in Canada after his family immigrated there when he was still very young. He was no sooner out of elementary school when he joined his father's scrap metal business, eventually opening a similar business of his own in Boston. Successful, Mayer put his profits into a failing movie theater, managing to turn it into a money-making proposition. He soon bought other theaters until he owned New England's largest chain of movie houses. A powerful exibitor in the growing film business, Mayer then involved himself in the distribution of movies, becoming an officer of Metro Pictures until he resigned to form his own production company in 1917. His first film under the banner of Louis B. Mayer Pictures was *Virtuous Wives* (1918).

Mayer continued to make movies but was one of the smaller players in a business that was beginning to solidify into larger concerns. His company was finally bought in 1924 by Loew's, Inc., which added the studio to two recent purchases to form Metro-Goldwyn-Mayer. Mayer's company was bought by Loews largely to obtain the business acumen of its president. Mayer was quickly made vice president and general manager of the new MGM.

Mayer's influence as studio chief was muted by the acknowledged brilliance of Irving Thalberg *(q.v.),* MGM's head of production, who received most of the credit for the studio's better offerings during the latter 1920s and early 1930s. But after Thalberg died, Mayer put his own stamp on MGM's films, turning the company toward wholesome family films such as the Andy Hardy series that starred Mickey Rooney *(q.v.).*

While virtually all of the Hollywood moguls were tyrannical, Mayer was the most visible of the pack·due to his station as the head of the most powerful studio. And his compensation reflected his power and influence; he earned more than $1.25 million per year, making him the highest paid executive in America.

In 1951, with revenues falling at MGM and across all of Hollywood due to the inroads of television, Mayer was finally replaced by his assistant, Dore Schary. The mogul went on to become a consultant to Cinerama before making a desperate attempt to regain his job at MGM via a stockholder insurrection. His bid failed, and he died the following year.
See also: Metro-Goldwyn-Mayer

MAYNARD, KEN (1895–1973)   An exciting cowboy star who was arguably the greatest trick rider ever to appear in westerns *(q.v.).* He is also noteworthy for being the original singing cowboy, introducing musical interludes into his films in the early 1930s, several years before the advent of the king of the singing cowboys, Gene Autry *(q.v.)*, whom Maynard introduced in *In Old Santa Fe* (1934). Maynard became a star in the late 1920s and the early 1930s, his career lasting into the 1940s. His remarkable horse, Tarzan, was nearly as famous as he was; the animal even starred in his own movie, *Come on Tarzan* (1932).

Maynard, like so many of his fellow cowboy stars, was a former rodeo champion. He started appearing in bit parts in westerns in 1923, quickly rising in popularity thanks to his daredevil stunt riding, so similar to that of the hugely successful Tom Mix *(q.v.)*. By the end of the 1920s Maynard was a major western star, having made such hit films as *Gun Gospel* (1927) and *Wagon Master* (1929).

The years 1929 to 1934 marked the peak of Maynard's career. He often wrote, produced, directed, and starred in his own "B" movies, among them *Sons of the Saddle* (1930) in which he sang for the first time, *King of the Arena* (1933), and *Gun Justice* (1933).

Unfortunately, Maynard had a severe drinking problem that undermined his ability to perform. His younger brother, Kermit Maynard, sometimes doubled for him, before becoming a serviceable "B" movie western star in his own right in the mid-1930s.

Ken Maynard continued to work in low-budget westerns until the end of the 1930s. After making personal appearances at rodeos in the early 1940s, he returned briefly to Hollywood to make a handful of additional minor horse operas, such as *Arizona Whirlwind* (1944). But the magic was gone. And so was Tarzan; the horse had died in 1940.

Maynard was all but forgotten when he was given a bit part in the low-budget *Bigfoot* (1971). Soon thereafter, though, his drinking caught up to him and he was put in The Motion Picture Country Home. He died of stomach cancer in 1973.

MAZURSKY, PAUL (1930–) A one-time actor, he has become a writer-director-producer sharply attuned to popular taste, infusing his usually comic films with trenchant observations on our times. Sometimes criticized for merely skimming the surface of timely issues, it would be fair to say in Mazursky's defense that he is one of the few commercial filmmakers willing to make cultural statements of any kind in his movies.

Mazursky began performing while in school and, after graduation from Brooklyn College, continued to pursue his career, though with little success. He first appeared on film in Stanley Kubrick's *Fear and Desire* (1953) and later had a significant role in *The Blackboard Jungle* (1955). Though he continued to find occasional roles in films and on TV throughout the 1950s and into the 1960s, he made his first important breakthrough as a writer, penning sketches for the high-quality comedy/

variety TV series, "The Danny Kaye Show." His writing credits helped him sell his first screenplay (written in collaboration with his early writing partner, Larry Tucker), *I Love You, Alice B. Toklas!* (1968).

Given a chance to direct his own script (written with Larry Tucker), Mazursky hit a home run his first time up with his lively comedy about wife-swapping, *Bob & Carol & Ted & Alice* (1969). The film didn't quite have the courage of its convictions but it dealt with what was still a shocking subject for a Hollywood comedy in the late 1960s.

Averaging a film every two years since his debut as a director, Mazursky has only seriously flopped when he has been either obviously autobiographical or pretentious. Among his critical or box office failures are *Alex in Wonderland* (1970), *Next Stop, Greenwich Village* (1976), *Willie and Phil* (1980), and *The Tempest* (1982). None of these films, however, are disasters—Mazursky has the uncanny ability to make even his poor films interesting.

He began producing as well as writing and directing his movies with his third film, *Blume in Love*. It was with this movie that he hit his stride, establishing an intimate visual style. He followed that success with the warm yet unsentimental *Harry and Tonto* (1974). His biggest success of the 1970s was the seriocomic *An Unmarried Woman* (1978). Mazursky was the first mass-market filmmaker to focus on the social and emotional upheaval divorce inflicts on women. The film was nominated for a Best Picture Oscar.

During the 1980s, Mazursky has excelled as a director of out-and-out comedies, making several critical and commercial hits, including *Moscow on the Hudson* (1984) and *Down and Out in Beverly Hills* (1986), as well as the less successful *Moon Over Parador* (1988).

Mazursky, it should be noted, is a student of the cinema. A number of his films have been based on foreign film classics. For instance, his *Willie and Phil* is an American version of François Truffaut's *Jules and Jim* (1961), and *Down and Out in Beverly Hills* is similar to Jean Renoirs' *Boudu Saved from Drowning* (1932).

Interestingly, the acting bug still bites the director. In addition to occasionally appearing in small roles in other directors' films, such as *A Star Is Born* (1976), Mazursky is visible in small roles in many of his own films, including *Alex in Wonderland, Blume in Love, An Unmarried Woman, Down and Out in Beverly Hills,* and *Moon Over Parador*. In the latter film he goes so far as to play Richard Dreyfuss' mother. As a director who so loves acting, Mazursky has been able to elicit top-notch performances from the stars of his films, many of whom have done some of the best acting of their careers with him, including Jill Clayburgh, Richard Dreyfuss, Bette Midler, Natalie Wood, and Robin Williams.

MENJOU, ADOLPHE (1890–1963) A dapper leading man during the silent era who went on to be one of Hollywood's most polished character actors in seventy-six sound films. Known for his black waxed mustache and sartorial splendor—his reputation as one of Hollywood's best dressed men sometimes overshadowed his reputation as an actor—Menjou became the quintessential "other man" in celluloid love triangles. He excelled at playing the rich, sophisticated, somewhat decadent older gentleman who threatens the romantic bliss of hero and heroine.

Of French extraction, Menjou was born in Pittsburgh and grew up to become an engineer, a profession he found little time for when he stumbled upon his acting career. He appeared in one film in 1916, *The Blue Envelope Mystery,* and several others in 1917 before heading off to war in Europe. When he returned, he pursued his acting career in the theater, acquiring the poise that would later mark his acting style.

Menjou returned to Hollywood in 1921 and was immediately cast in significant roles in such major films as *The Three Musketeers* (1921) and *The Sheik* (1921). The film that brought him stardom, however, was Charlie Chaplin's *A Woman of Paris* (1923). The movie was a serious drama that Chaplin wrote and directed as a vehicle for Edna Purviance, his longtime leading lady. Menjou shined in the film as a suave, sophisticated boulevardier, a role he never fully abandoned, playing variations on it throughout much of the rest of his career.

Despite having a wonderful speaking voice, Menjou could not quite hold onto his star status after the advent of sound in the late 1920s. Nonetheless, he gracefully made the transition to being an excellent supporting player in *Morocco* (1930), in which he tempts Marlene Dietrich *(q.v.)* with his wealth and power to forget her love for Gary Cooper *(q.v.).*

Despite his continued success, largely as a major character actor, Menjou did have several important leading roles in the 1930s, the most memorable of which came in *The Front Page* (1931), for which he won a Best Actor nomination. But even in a leading role, he usually supported a more popular star, such as Katharine Hepburn *(q.v.)* in *Morning Glory* (1933), Shirley Temple *(q.v.)* in *Little Miss Marker* (1934), and Deanna Durbin *(q.v.)* in *One Hundred Men and a Girl* (1937).

Though he was usually cast against major talent, Menjou was not above stealing a few scenes when he had the chance, as he did in *Roxie Hart* (1942), playing a wildly dramatic lawyer defending Ginger Rogers *(q.v.).* Among his other fine performances during the 1940s and 1950s were those in *State of the Union* (1948), *The Sniper* (1952), and Stanley Kubrick's classic antiwar film *Paths of Glory* (1957), in which he had his last great role, as an imperious French officer in World War I.

His final film was *Pollyanna* (1960), once more in support of a child actress, this time Hayley Mills.

MENZIES, WILLIAM CAMERON (1896–1957) He was an imaginative and innovative art director whose striking visual style helped to elevate the status of set designers and art directors within the film industry. His lavishly designed sets were feasts for the eye, and his work during both the silent and sound eras—from the 1920s into the 1950s—is legendary.

Menzies' set decoration can best be appreciated in such silent films as the Douglas Fairbanks' epic *The Thief of Bagdad* (1924), Rudolph Valentino's *The Son of the Sheik* (1926), and his Academy Award winners (for which he received one Oscar) *The Dove* (1927) and *Tempest* (1927). In the sound era, he demonstrated his flair in D. W. Griffith's *Abraham Lincoln* (1930), *Alice in Wonderland* (1933), *Gone With the Wind* (1939), for which he won a special Oscar for his outstanding achievement in the use of color, *King's Row* (1941), and *For Whom the Bell Tolls* (1943).

Menzies also worked without much distinction as a director of low-budget films from the 1930s through the early 1950s, for many of which he also designed sets and provided art direction. The most famous film he directed was *Things To Come* (1936), a futuristic tale still admired with something approaching awe by both science fiction buffs and film designers, made in England and boasting his stunning art direction. He also directed a film sadly overlooked by the critics, *Invaders From Mars* (1953).

Late in his career, Menzies also worked as a producer of several films. As an associate producer he found great success with his last project, *Around the World in 80 Days* (1956), a movie that also showed his marvelous talent for art direction.

MEREDITH, BURGESS (1912–) In a career spanning approximately fifty years, he has proven himself a tireless actor, director, writer, and producer in virtually every area of popular entertainment.

Meredith had any number of colorful jobs in his youth, among them reporter, vacuum cleaner salesman, tie clerk at Macy's, Wall Street runner, and seaman. By 1930, however, he began working steadily in the theater, gaining glowing reviews and the award for "Best Performance of the Year" by the New York Drama Critics for his work in *Little Ol' Boy* (1933) and *She Loves Me Not* (1933). A small, elfin man, he commanded attention, thanks in large part to his distinctive speaking voice. It was his 1936 starring role on Broadway in *Winterset,* though, that brought him to the attention of Hollywood. He recreated his role of Mio for the film version of the play in 1937.

A good deal of film work followed, most notably in

Burgess Meredith's impish smile has graced dozens of films in a long and extremely varied career. Despite his starring role in many classic films he is probably best known for his recent performances as Sylvestor Stallone's manager in the first three *Rocky* movies. Photo courtesy of Burgess Meredith.

major supporting parts in movies such as *Idiots Delight* (1938), *Second Chorus* (1941), *That Uncertain Feeling* (1942), and *Tom, Dick and Harry* (1942). On the rare occasions when he had true starring roles, Meredith was riveting. He gave what many consider to be his most memorable performance as Lenny in *Of Mice and Men* (1939), but he also earned raves for his portrayal of Ernie Pyle in *The Story of G.I. Joe* (1944).

Meredith wrote, coproduced, and costarred with his wife, Paulette Goddard, in the Jean Renoir-directed version of *Diary of a Chambermaid* (1945), which remains one of his most admired works. In 1947, Meredith directed (for the first and last time) and starred in *Man on the Eiffel Tower*.

During the 1950s, Meredith was little seen in the movies. He directed plays, starred in the theater, and gave his talents to television, until finally he made an impressive comeback on the big screen in *Advise and Consent* (1962). He has appeared regularly in films ever since, making noteworthy contributions in modest roles in such films as *The Cardinal* (1963), *Madame X* (1965), *Big Hand for a Little Lady* (1965), *The Reivers* (1969), *Day of the Locust* (1973), *Foul Play* (1977), *Clash of the Titans* (1979), and *Full Moon in Blue Water* (1988).

Though his face might be best remembered from his

strong and memorable performances in the first three *Rocky* films, Meredith's voice is still better known due to his work in countless commercials.

MESSAGE MOVIES *See* Kramer, Stanley.

METRO-GOLDWYN-MAYER MGM, as it was more popularly known, was the most famous of all the movie studios. It was also the most consistently profitable film company during the heyday of the studio system. The company was born out of the need for films that could be shown at Marcus Loew's growing theater chain during the 1920s, without his having to pay the high prices demanded by such producers as Paramount and Fox. Loew's therefore engineered the purchase of Metro Pictures in 1920, and Goldwyn Pictures and Louis B. Mayer Productions in 1924, hiring Mayer to oversee the production of motion pictures by the newly formed Metro-Goldwyn-Mayer studio.

Unlike the other four members of the "Big Five," Paramount, Twentieth Century-Fox, Warner Bros., and RKO, Loew's/MGM owned the smallest number of theaters. Because of this, MGM, more so than their competitors, had to find ways to make their pictures especially desirable to exhibitors outside their own orbit. They did so by aggressively building a stable of stars, later proclaiming that MGM had "more stars than there are in the heavens." It was an advertising slogan that worked, thanks to a lineup of talent that included, to name just a few, Greta Garbo, Norma Shearer, Marie Dressler, Wallace Beery, Joan Crawford, Jean Harlow, Clark Gable, Spencer Tracy, Judy Garland, Mickey Rooney, Gene Kelly, Elizabeth Taylor, and even Lassie.

In addition to stars, Irving Thalberg *(q.v.),* the studio's boy wonder producer, made it a point to make epic and/or prestige pictures, such as *Ben-Hur* (1925), *The Big Parade* (1925), and *The Crowd* (1927), in order to draw attention to the MGM product line. That tradition was continued during the sound era with films such as *Grand Hotel* (1932), *David Copperfield* (1935), and *Romeo and Juliet* (1936). After Thalberg died in 1936, Louis B. Mayer shifted the production strategy into pure mainstream, middle-American entertainment, pushing such profitable enterprises as the Andy Hardy series starring Mickey Rooney, and the Dr. Kildare series that featured Lew Ayres, both major moneymakers. In addition, Louis B. Mayer negotiated for the distribution rights and half the profits of *Gone With the Wind* (1939) when David O. Selznick *(q.v.)* wanted MGM star Clark Gable to play Rhett Butler. Later, in the 1940s, MGM bought all rights to the film and prospered mightily with its rereleases and television sales over the next several decades.

The fact that MGM owned a modest number of theaters was a blessing in the 1930s when business was bad throughout the industry. The company raked in money while their competitors struggled (and sometimes failed) to pay the mortgages on their huge real estate investments. Flush with cash, MGM invested in their movies, creating exquisite production values and producing the glossiest films in Hollywood during the Great Depression.

It was a different story during the industry boom years of the 1940s. MGM continued to be in the black, but the company's lack of movie theaters in which to showcase their films caused them to lose their preeminent position as Hollywood's most profitable studio, sending them to fourth place, ahead of ever-sickly RKO. Many of MGM's male stars had gone off to war, but the studio found new stars in performers such as Greer Garson, Van Johnson, and Margaret O'Brien.

It is the musicals that remain the most beloved of MGM's contributions to American film. With the likes of Judy Garland, Gene Kelly, Fred Astaire, and Frank Sinatra as talent, a producer who understood the genre in Arthur Freed, and directors such as Vincente Minnelli and Stanley Donen, MGM created the golden era of the movie musical with such classics as *The Pirate* (1948), *Easter Parade* (1948), *On the Town* (1949), *Royal Wedding* (1950), *Show Boat* (1951), *An American in Paris* (1951), *Singin' in the Rain* (1952), *The Band Wagon* (1953), and many others.

One of the reasons for MGM's long and successful reign had been the stability of its management team. But in the 1950s, the company's aging leaders began to fall by the wayside. Louis B. Mayer was forced out as head of MGM in 1951, replaced by Dore Schary who was, in turn, fired in 1956. Meanwhile, Nicholas Schenck, who had run the parent company, Loew's Inc., ever since the death of Marcus Loew in 1927, was forced out in 1955. The company lost money for the very first time in its corporate existence in 1957.

There were more bad years to come, with some good periods in between, such as in 1959 when the company remade its silent hit, *Ben-Hur*—yet 1959 was also the year that MGM and Loew's finally parted company as a result of the government's long-standing antitrust action. With constant management changes during the 1960s, MGM made fewer and fewer films, and depended heavily on big-budget movies that would either make or break the studio every year. MGM took heavy losses when *Mutiny on the Bounty* failed in late 1962. But the company made a fortune on *Dr. Zhivago* in 1965.

Kirk Kerkorian bought MGM in 1969 and kept the company in the black by selling off its assets (i.e., real estate, MGM Records, movie memorabilia, etc.) and by venturing into the hotel business with the MGM Grand Hotel in Las Vegas. Then came what seemed to be the final blow: MGM stopped distributing films in 1973, turning that function over to United Artists. The company finally reasserted itself as a distributor in 1979, absorbing United Artists. Later, after Turner Broadcasting bought the MGM/UA film library, Kerkorian hired Lee Rich to run the newly named MGM/UA Communications in 1986. The reborn MGM/UA had had some notable early successes, including Mel Brooks' *Spaceballs* (1987) and *Moonstruck* (1987), but the studio has not been a major player in the movie business for the last several years.

MEYER, RUSS (1923–) Known as "The King of the Nudies." Meyer built a reputation for making surprisingly slick "sexploitation" films on a small budget and turning a very large profit. His early independent nudies established "softcore" pornography: plenty of skin but no sex. Other innovations brought by Meyer to the evolution of the sexploitation movie were a storyline and a sense of humor.

Meyer began making films of neighborhood children, pets, and sports events when he was a boy in his native Oakland, California, using an 8mm Univex bought for him by his mother, who pawned her engagement ring to pay for the camera. In 1942, after six months of college, he became a combat photographer at the age of eighteen, eventually shooting some of the most famous combat newsreels of World War II, including D-Day footage at Normandy and battles at Bastogne and Saar.

After the war, Meyer drifted into still photography, shooting layouts for *Playboy* magazine and other skin books of the 1950s. His experience led him to making his first nudie *The Immoral Mr. Teas* (1959). It was shot in four days at a cost of $24,000, and grossed more than $1 million. The film is now considered a minor classic of its kind with a place in the archives of New York's Museum of Modern Art. While his early films, including *Eve and the Handyman* (1960), *Erotica* (1961), and *Europe in the Raw* (1963) were crude (in more ways than one), Meyer soon produced quality work, giving his movies a high-gloss look. Later films, such as *Mondo Topless* (1966), *Faster Pussycat, Kill Kill!* (1966), and *How Much Loving Does a Normal Couple Need?* (1967), all set the stage for his breakthrough film, *Vixen* (1968). *Vixen* was a surprising mainstream box office winner, and Meyer followed it with yet another high camp sex farce hit, *Cherry, Harry and Raquel* (1969).

In 1969, then Twentieth Century-Fox president Richard D. Zanuck saw *Vixen* and asked Meyer to come in for a conference. The production chief offered Meyer a $1 million budget to make *Beyond the Valley of the Dolls* (1970). Meyer summoned Roger Ebert, critic for the *Chicago Sun Times* (and the future partner of Gene Siskel in the widely admired and much copied TV show about the movies), and the two produced a shooting script of a softcore teaser that went on to make roughly $15 million dollars worldwide.

Sexploitation writer/director/cameraman/producer Russ Meyer has always had a penchant for bosomy females. He might have remained a relatively unknown fringe filmmaker had he not had such a financial success with his independently produced *Vixen* (1968). Photo courtesy of Russ Meyer.

Meyer subsequently made another studio film, *The Seven Minutes* (1971), but the rest of his work, including films such as *Supervixens* (1975) and the imaginatively titled *Beneath the Valley of the Ultravixens* (1979), was done independently. Since 1979 he has been consumed with a magnum opus, a seventeen-and-a-half-hour sexual extravaganza called *The Breast of Russ Meyer*, still in production as of this writing.

MIDLER, BETTE   *See* singer–actress.

MILESTONE, LEWIS (1895–1980)   A director of more than three dozen movies spanning the silent era to the 1960s. Yet for all of his many and varied projects, only a handful of his films have survived the test of time. One of these is *All Quiet on the Western Front* (1930), Hollywood's most powerful antiwar film.

Milestone had his first exposure to filmmaking during World War I when he served in the Signal Corps. After his discharge, he headed for Hollywood, where he continued his education as an editor. In 1925 he directed his first film, *Seven Sinners*. The script was written by Darryl F. Zanuck *(q.v.)*.

In 1927, Milestone won an Academy Award as Best Director for the Howard Hughes produced *Two Arabian Knights*. Five films later, he won his second Best Director Academy Award for *All Quiet on the Western Front* (1930).

Though not a genius of the stature of Orson Welles, Milestone suffered a fate similar to the great director's. Every project he completed after *All Quiet on the Western Front* was compared unfavorably to his earlier effort.

But Milestone still had some triumphs during the 1930s and 1940s, though they were relatively few. He directed the original film version of *The Front Page* (1931) with dash. In 1939 Milestone turned John Steinbeck's novel *Of Mice and Men* into a hit movie, though most of Hollywood was sure audiences would stay away in droves. And the director made several more noteworthy films, among them *The Strange Love of Martha Ivers* (1946) and another Steinbeck project, *The Red Pony* (1948).

A Walk in the Sun, which Milestone directed in 1946, brought him a new measure of respect and success. It was a thoughtful, introspective film about a soldier's experience in battle. The movie was the first to introduce the idea of a ballad weaving in and out of the storyline. The much-copied device would find its way into films such as *High Noon* (1952) and reach its apotheosis in *Cat Ballou* (1965).

Milestone's career plummeted in the 1950s with such minor works as *Melba* (1953), *They Who Dare* (1954), and *Pork Chop Hill* (1959). After directing the "rat pack" *(q.v.)* vehicle *Ocean's Eleven* (1961), he bowed out with a gargantuan flop, *Mutiny on the Bounty* (1962).

If not for *All Quiet on the Western Front* and a few other films, Milestone would have been long forgotten. But the power of this director at his best has sustained his reputation.
See also: antiwar films

MILIUS, JOHN (1945–   )   A highly underrated writer/director whose right-wing politics and macho themes have made him a pariah to the more liberal critical establishment. His beliefs aside, Milius is a gifted screenwriter and a dynamic and often inspired director.

Born to a well-to-do shoe manufacturer, Milius spent most of his youth in Southern California, where he was known to spend his days surfing. Later, studying film at USC, he met and befriended future *Star Wars* director George Lucas and future screenwriters Walter Huyck and Gloria Katz. After leaving college, Milius got a job at American International Pictures, for whom he later cowrote his first screenplay, *The Devil's 8* (1969). He went on to collaborate on the script of *Evel Knievel* (1971) before receiving serious recognition as the co-screenwriter of the Robert Redford hit *Jeremiah Johnson* (1972). He also provided the story and screenplay for John Huston's *The Life and Times of Judge Roy Bean* (1972). Milius had previously worked on the script for Clint Eastwood's *Dirty Harry* (1971), receiving no screen credit, but he later provided the story for the sequel, *Magnum Force* (1972), cowriting the film's screenplay.

Milius was a hot commodity in Hollywood in the early 1970s. He parlayed his screenwriting success into a chance to direct his own screenplay of *Dillinger* (1973). Made on small budget, it was a fast-paced, intelligent, and quirky film that caught the attention of the critics. He followed that modest success with a huge leap forward, making the sweeping, nostalgic adventure film *The Wind and the Lion* (1975).

Milius was hailed as a brilliant new director—until he wrote and directed his third film, *Big Wednesday* (1978), a movie loosely based on his own life as a young surfer. The critics called it a wipeout and it sank almost instantly beneath the critical waves. Yet the film was a breathtaking masterpiece about friendship and the tides of time.

Big Wednesday didn't destroy Milius' film career but it did send him briefly in different directions. He produced and collaborated on the original story for Steven Spielberg's *1941* (1979). Milius was also executive producer of Paul Schrader's *Hardcore* (1979) and later producer of the sleeper hit of 1983, *Uncommon Valor*. In the meantime, he had returned to screenwriting, coscripting Francis Coppola's brilliant *Apocalypse Now* (1979).

Milius didn't reenter the directorial ranks until 1981 when he wrote and directed *Conan the Barbarian* with Arnold Schwarzenegger *(q.v.)* in the title role. It was the film that turned Schwarzenegger into a credible box office attraction, and despite mixed-to-poor reviews from the critics, it was a sizeable commercial success.

If the critics were not wild about *Conan,* they absolutely detested *Red Dawn* (1984), a movie that dramatized the resistance of teenage Americans to a Russian/Cuban invasion. Again, despite poor press, the film did moderately well at the box office.

After a long hiatus from directing, Milius made a bold, if commercially unsuccesful, return to the screen with *Farewell to the King* (1989).

MILLAND, RAY (1905–1986) An actor who appeared in films for more than forty years, his greatest success being in the 1940s in contemporary roles. Handsome and suave, but with a tough edge, and possessed of a mild and pleasing welsh accent, Milland was good at light comedy and even better in hard-boiled roles. Unfortunately, the actor rarely had good material to

work with, and of his more than 120 movies (in more than ninety of them he was a leading man), a mere dozen, at best, are distinguished films.

Born Reginald Truscott-Jones in Neath, Wales, Milland first used his stepfather's surname, Mullane, as his show business moniker. After a tour of duty as a Royal Guardsman, and thanks to the intercession of an actress friend, he made his acting debut, under the name Spike Milland, in the English film *The Plaything* (1929). Having a screen credit led to more work in England but no spectacular successes. Anita Loos *(qiv.)* spotted the actor and put in a good word for him at MGM.

At first, Hollywood was not thrilled to have him. His first American film appearance was in *The Bachelor Father* (1931) and he was offered only smallish roles in seven subsequent films before heading back to England, an apparent flop. Work in two English films followed, but Milland had begun to get a good public response for his work in some American movies and he returned to Hollywood.

He was given small parts again in films such as *Bolero* (1934) and *We're Not Dressing* (1934), but soon graduated to featured roles in films such as *Next Time We Love* (1936) and *Wings Over Honolulu* (1937). In 1940 he had a breakthrough with a starring role in *French Without Tears.* Showing a genuine flair for comedy, he was finally established as a box office draw. A number of light comedies followed, such as *Irene* (1940), *The Doctor Takes a Wife* (1940), and *The Major and the Minor* (1942), which confirmed and solidified his star status. Yet, except for the last of these films, none of his vehicles was particularly memorable.

Things finally began to change in 1944 when Milland began starring in movies with a more cynical point of view such as *The Uninvited* (1944), Fritz Lang's *Ministry of Fear* (1944), and the movie for which he is most well known, *Lost Weekend* (1945), in which he gave his Oscar-winning tour de force as an alcoholic. Despite his Oscar and newfound respect as an actor, Milland rarely received good scripts. His good films during the rest of the 1940s were far and few between, the best being *The Big Clock* (1948) and *Alias Nick Beale* (1949).

His record was even more uneven in the 1950s but had notable peaks in the western *Bugles in the Afternoon,* (1952), *The Thief* (1952), and Hitchcock's *Dial M for Murder* (1954), in which he played Grace Kelly's murderous husband. In the second half of the decade, Milland tried his hand at directing as well as acting in the off-beat western *A Man Alone* (1956); his efforts were well-received. Milland's best films of the late 1950s and early 1960s were often the ones in which he directed himself, among them *The Safe-Cracker* (1958) and *Panic in Year Zero!* (1962).

Milland had a successful turn on TV with his own series, "Markham," and made several good cheapie horror films in the early 1960s, such as *Premature Burial*

(1961) and *X—The Man With the X-Ray Eyes* (1963). His career faltered during the rest of the 1960s, however, until it was resurrected by a strong character part in *Love Story* (1970).

Throughout the 1970s Milland made some truly ghoulish (and foolish) horror movies. Some did rather well at the box office and were respectable efforts, while others were excruciatingly bad. Milland's more interesting work in the genre was in *Frogs* (1972) and *The Man With Two Heads* (1972). Later, he had small roles in classier (though not much better) films such as *The Last Tycoon* (1976) and *Oliver's Story* (1978).

When his health began to decline Milland finally stopped working. He died having amassed a truly eclectic body of work.

MILLER, ARTHUR C. (1895–1970) Noted for his exquisite composition, he was an accomplished cinematographer who photographed more than one hundred thirty feature films between 1915 and 1951. His early fame rested on having shot *The Perils of Pauline* (1914), the original blockbuster serial. But in a long and distinguished career, he had many triumphs, the most memorable achieved during his tenure at Twentieth Century-Fox in the 1940s.

Miller grew up fascinated by cameras, but his introduction to the motion picture business was purely accidental. As related in an interview with Leonard Maltin in his book, *Behind the Camera,* Miller explained that when he was thirteen years old, "I went to work for a horse dealer, delivering horses . . . one day I saw this crowd gathered outside a German beer garden, and I sat there astride this horse bareback. A guy came over and asked me if I wanted to work in moving pictures. I said, 'Doing what?' He said, 'You can ride a horse bareback, can't you?' " Miller was hired as an extra, but found a greater interest in the technical side of the business. In that same year, 1908, he got a job in a film laboratory. Though he was still a teenager, he soon began working as a cameraman on shorts for Edwin S. Porter and others.

At Bay (1915) was the first feature film he photographed, beginning a long, nearly exclusive, collaboration with director George Fitzmaurice that lasted through thirty-six films, until 1925. His films of the later 1920s and early 1930s were relatively minor, but he came into his own when he began working at Fox in 1932. His importance to the studio is evidenced by the fact that he was assigned to photograph Shirley Temple, Fox's most important asset. He was the cinematographer of several of the moppet's hits, such as, *Bright Eyes* (1934), *The Little Colonel* (1935), *Wee Willie Winkie* (1937), *Heidi* (1937), and *Rebecca of Sunnybrook Farm* (1938).

In the 1940s, Miller won three Oscars for *How Green Was My Valley* (1941), *The Song of Bernadette* (1943), and *Anna and the King of Siam* (1946). Examples of other Miller-photographed films during his golden era are *The Mark of Zorro* (1940), *Tobacco Road* (1941), *Man Hunt* (1941), *Gentlemen's Agreement* (1947), and *The Gunfighter* (1950).

On doctor's orders, Miller retired from cinematography in 1951 after shooting *The Prowler.* He remained active, however, working in various capacities for the American Society of Cinematographers until his death in 1970.

MINNELLI, VINCENTE (1910–1986) MGM's preeminent director of musicals during the 1940s and 1950s, his ability to integrate musical numbers naturally into the framework of his films began a trend that continues to this day. Conversely, Minnelli also pioneered the sublime artificiality of the musical genre.

As is often the case with directors of musicals, Minnelli's early training was in the theater. He had become a respected designer and later a director of Broadway shows before MGM's premier producer of musicals, Arthur Freed *(q.v.),* persuaded Minnelli to give Hollywood a try.

Among his earliest work at MGM was the direction of individual musical sequences in other directors' films. (For instance, he often directed Lena Horne's musical numbers.) Minnelli's first solo directorial credit was the all-black film *Cabin in the Sky* (1943). The movie was well received by white audiences and Minnelli was on his way to a long and successful career.

He directed *Ziegfeld Follies* (1944), a variety film that presented a long roster of great stars, including Fred Astaire and Judy Garland *(qq.v.).* Minnelli later married Garland and fathered their daughter, Liza.

His first real breakthrough as a director came with *Meet Me in St. Louis* (1944), in which Minnelli told a nostalgic family story with warmth and feeling, weaving the musical numbers in and out of the film with a grace and style that seemed effortless.

With films such as *The Pirate* (1948), *An American in Paris* (1951), *The Band Wagon* (1953), and his Academy Award–winning direction for *Gigi* (1958), Minnelli put his stamp on the movie musical, filming them almost exclusively in the studio in bright, lively colors. Many of his films were criticized for being unnaturally stylized, but this was a deliberate technique used to emphasize the dreamlike quality of the musical.

Not all of Minnelli's musicals were classics, but even his lesser efforts stand out, such as *Yolanda and the Thief* (1945), *Brigadoon* (1954), and *Bells are Ringing* (1960).

Because Minnelli is known primarily as a director of musicals, it is often forgotten that roughly two-thirds of his nearly three dozen films are comedies and dramas. Some of the best among them are the taut thriller *Undercurrent* (1946), the charming comedy *Father of the Bride* (1950), the great biopic of van Gogh *Lust for Life* (1956), and the gritty Southern drama *Home from the Hill* (1960).

Minnelli worked with the top people in the musical

field—Arthur Freed, Fred Astaire, Gene Kelly, and Judy Garland among them. In his dramas, his most memorable work was with Kirk Douglas *(q.v.)*, who starred in four of Minnelli's movies, including his wonderfully acerbic attack on Hollywood, *The Bad and the Beautiful* (1952).

Minnelli's powers as a director seemed to fade rather abruptly after the early 1960s. He ended his career with *A Matter of Time* (1976), a poorly received film made primarily as a family affair, starring his daughter Liza. Unfortunately, none of his later films had the panache of his earlier efforts. But the quality of the vast majority of his work is undeniable. Vincente Minnelli's name remains synonymous with the great MGM musicals.

MIRANDA, CARMEN (1909–1953) The "Brazilian Bombshell" whose memorable comic caricature of South American sensuality made her a hit virtually from the beginning of her relatively short Hollywood career.

Born Marie de Carmo Miranda de Cunha in Portu-gal, she moved with her family to Brazil while still a youngster. By her mid-twenties, she was a popular radio and film star well beyond her country's borders. She was imported to America in 1939, singing "South American Way" in the Broadway show *Streets of Paris*. The number was a show stopper and she was asked to reprise it in a Betty Grable movie musical, *Down Argentine Way* (1940).

Miranda stole the movie from Grable and American audiences went crazy over this outrageous singer with wild costumes, fruit basket hats, thousand watt smile, and garish make-up. Despite a seemingly ridiculous appearance (or because of it), she won legions of fans.

While Miranda was never the heroine of a romance (Hollywood was still too close-minded for that), she often played the friend of the love interest, giving her advice in fractured English and in song. And even though her acting ability was woefully inadequate, the sheer force of her personality was enough to sustain her career as a leading lady for the better part of a decade.

Carmen Miranda, the "Brazilian Bombshell," is seen here on the set of her last film, the Martin and Lewis vehicle *Scared Stiff* (1953). Photo courtesy of Movie Star News.

Her most memorable movies are *That Night in Rio* (1941) and *The Gang's All Here* (1943). The latter film was directed by Busby Berkeley *(q.v.);* though it is a rather poor movie, it is without a doubt the ultimate in kitsch, and it was appreciated even then for its good-natured silliness.

Miranda's movies were rarely any good, though they were never boring. The singer was much too bizarre a presence ever to be dull. Musicals such as *Greenwich Village* (1944) and *Something for the Boys* (1945) kept her before the public, but her novel appeal suffered the inevitable decline. Nonetheless, she was an amusing and offbeat costar to Groucho Marx in *Copacabana* (1947).

In all, Miranda graced just fourteen films in the United States. In her last comedy, *Scared Stiff* (1953), she had a featured role. She died that same year of peritonitis, closing a colorful if brief chapter in Hollywood musical history.

MITCHELL, THOMAS *See* character actors.

MITCHUM, ROBERT (1917–) A laconic, sleepy-eyed actor who survived a long string of villainous roles in low-budget westerns and an equally long stint playing psychopaths, as well as a controversial drug bust early in his career, finally to emerge a star and male sex symbol. Yet even as a star, Mitchum received little respect from critics until more recent years, when he was finally seen as one of the few remaining screen giants (along with Kirk Douglas and Burt Lancaster *[qq.v.]* of Hollywood's golden studio era. With his sardonic manner, bedroom eyes, and a deep, commanding drawl, Mitchum epitomized the new breed of rebellious movie tough guy.

Mitchum lost his father when he was two years old and was raised by his mother and stepfather. His older sister was the first to enter show business, working as a nightclub entertainer when she was a teenager. Mitchum came around to the acting profession much later. After a rough adolescence in New York's Hell's Kitchen, the young man took a wide assortment of jobs from ditch digger to factory worker. After trying his hand as a professional boxer, Mitchum joined a local theater group at the urging of his sister. His wandering days had finally come to an end.

In addition to acting, Mitchum also began writing everything from children's plays to song lyrics. He even penned a piece about Jewish refugees fleeing Hitler's Germany that Orson Welles *(q.v.)* used in a 1939 benefit at the Hollywood Bowl. During the late 1930s, however, Mitchum made his living working as a flack for the famous astrologer of the day, Carroll Richter.

Later, after his 1940 marriage, he took a job as a sheetmetal worker in Burbank, California. In order to keep his sanity (he hated the job), he spent several evenings a week acting for a little community theater. Unhappy with his life, his mother suggested he take a stab at the movies. Mitchum thought he might manage to find some work as an extra and gave it a whirl.

From the start, Mitchum was more than an extra. His first film was *Border Patrol* (1943), a Hopalong Cassidy western in which he played a bad guy. Mitchum would go on to appear in six more "Hoppie" movies and a whopping total of twenty-three films during his first year and a half as a movie actor, most of them either westerns or war movies. Among the more well-known films in which he had small parts were *The Human Comedy* (1943), *Gung-Ho!* (1943), and *Thirty Seconds Over Tokyo* (1944).

Mitchum began receiving leading roles in low-budget horse operas such as *Nevada* (1944) and *West of the Pecos* (1945), but his biggest break came when he was given a major supporting role in the "A" movie *The Story of G.I. Joe* (1945). His work in that film earned him a Best Supporting Actor Oscar nomination.

The postwar years were perfect for Mitchum's gritty style of acting. He came into his own in hard-edged movies such as *Crossfire* (1947), *Pursued* (1947), and *Out of the Past* (1947). Toward the latter half of the 1940s, he was fast evolving from leading man to major star—until he was arrested for possession of marijuana in 1948. Ultimately he spent fifty days in jail after being found guilty.

Surprisingly, this didn't hurt the actor's career. Viewed as a rebel, Mitchum became an even bigger star in films such as *The Big Steal* (1949) and *The Racket* (1951).

The 1950s were full of extreme highs and lows for Mitchum. While he tended to walk through a large number of poor movies, his work with strong directors was quite impressive. His best movies during that era were Nicholas Ray's *The Lusty Men* (1952), Otto Preminger's *River of No Return* (1954), the Charles Laughton–directed *The Night of the Hunter* (1955), John Huston's *Heaven Knows Mr. Allison* (1957), and Arthur Ripley's *Thunder Road* (1958).

The 1960s started well for Mitchum with his strong performances in *Home from the Hill* (1960) and *The Sundowners* (1960). He also began taking chances with his career, playing a sinister and chilling villain to Gregory Peck's hero in *Cape Fear* (1962), taking on comedy in *The Last Time I Saw Archie* (1961), and starring in the movie adaptation of the play *Two for the Seesaw* (1962). Though he worked steadily throughout the rest of the decade, after big-budget films such as *The Longest Day* (1962), his vehicles became more and more forgettable, and he often found himself playing in secondary roles to actors such as John Wayne in *El Dorado* (1967), Dean Martin in *Five Card Stud* (1968), and Yul Brynner in *Villa Rides!* (1968).

Mitchum made a comeback playing against type, in David Lean's lush romance, *Ryan's Daughter* (1970).

Critics finally took notice of the actor's ability and the movie scored well at the box office. Thanks to his success in *Ryan's Daughter,* Mitchum found a whole new audience and he slowly developed an art-house following, starring in such films as the highly regarded *The Friends of Eddie Coyle* (1973) and *Farewell, My Lovely* (1975) and *The Big Sleep* (1978), based on two Raymond Chandler Philip Marlowe detective novels.

Despite his success in these films, the aging actor was offered few other substantive roles and his career began to wane until he hit it big once again in such 1980s TV miniseries as "North and South" and "The Winds of War."

Though rarely seen on the big screen during the 1980s, he was impressive in *That Championship Season* (1982) and *Mr. North* (1988). He stepped in at the last moment to take the late John Huston's part in the latter movie, winning high praise for his work.

MIX, TOM (1880–1940)   The most popular of all the silent cowboy stars, he rode supreme on the celluloid range in the late 1910s and throughout most of the 1920s. Unlike the gritty westerns of William S. Hart *(q.v.),* which preceded his, Mix's horse operas were patently unrealistic. Thanks to magnificent location shooting, excellent cinematography, tight direction by many of Hollywood's better directors (he rarely directed himself during his most popular period), and

Tom Mix, seen here in the foreground wearing the white cowboy hat, was among the most popular of all the silent screen cowboys. Mix's escapist entertainments provided the simple format that was used in thousands of future Hollywood westerns. Photo courtesy of The Siegel Collection.

big-budget production values, Mix's films became the westerns by which other oaters were judged.

Born in Mix Run, Pennsylvania, young Tom led an adventurous life long before becoming a movie star. Though his studio biography made him appear to be a combination of Colonel Frémont and Wild Bill Hickock, Mix was actually a sergeant in the U.S. Army (although he deserted in 1902) and was a member of the Texas Rangers in 1906. Yet it was his rodeo fame that served him best when he found his way into the movies, appearing in a William N. Selig (q.v.) production, *Ranch Life in the Great South West* (1910). In addition to performing several stunts, he had supplied the horses from his own ranch for the film.

Selig was impressed with Mix and he was hired to continue working as a combination wrangler, stuntman, and actor. Before long, however, Mix was starring in and directing his own one- and two-reel light western comedies with modest success. In fact, he made more than one hundred films for Selig before he finally left the company for Fox, where he (and his famous horse, Tony) catapulted to stardom in 1917 in action-oriented features such as *The Daredevil* (1920), *Just Tony* (1922), and *The Rainbow Trail* (1925).

Mix made more than sixty features at Fox, becoming that studio's biggest draw. But his star faded with the coming of sound. He made a few silent westerns for FBO (Film Booking Offices of America) in 1928 and 1929, and then retired from the screen to tour with Ringling Bros. Circus. With the rise of the "B" western in the early 1930s, though, Mix was lured back to Hollywood, where he made a handful of low-budget films between 1932 and 1934, the most well-known among them an early version of *Destry Rides Again* (1932).

Mix died in an automobile accident in 1940.

See also: westerns

MOHR, HAL (1894–1974) A cinematographer who pioneered the use of dollys, booms, and other innovations in a long and varied film career. He shot well over one hundred feature films, the vast majority of them during the sound era. In fact, Mohr has the distinction of being the cinematographer of the very first sound film, *The Jazz Singer* (1927, q.v.).

The son of a well-to-do San Francisco family, Mohr built his own camera as a young man and began to make primitive newsreels that he sold to the nickelodeons sprouting all over the Bay area. At one point, he was actually put out of business by the infamous Patents Company, which confiscated his camera. Mohr continued making films, however, eventually making his way down to Hollywood, where he codirected two Harold Lloyd (q.v.) comedies before heading off to battle in World War I.

After returning to Hollywood, Mohr decided to concentrate on becoming a cinematographer. He had previously held every function imaginable, including director, producer, writer, and actor, and as he related to Leonard Maltin in his interview book, *Behind the Camera,* Mohr felt that the most creative job in the industry was that of the cameraman.

Mohr began photographing feature films in the early 1920s, shooting such movies as *Little Annie Rooney* (1925), *Sparrows* (1926), and *Old San Francisco* (1927). His startling visual effects on early sound films are evident in *Broadway* (1929), the impressive Technicolor movie *The King of Jazz* (1930), and the elegant fantasy *Outward Bound* (1930).

Mohr jumped from studio to studio, working on a wide variety of films from program fillers like *Charlie Chan's Courage* (1934) at Fox to "A" movies such as *Destry Rides Again* (1939) at Paramount. At Fox, he photographed leading lady Evelyn Venable in *David Harum* (1934) and then promptly married her.

Though he worked at most of the studios, Mohr did his most memorable work of the 1930s at Warner Bros. For *A Midsummer Night's Dream* (1935), he won the first of his two Oscars. Curiously, he hadn't been nominated that year for an Academy Award but won in a write-in vote, the only Oscar winner ever to receive the statuette in that fashion. After he won, the Academy did away with the right of members to vote for anyone but the official nominees. Among his other fine Warner Bros. movies during that decade were *Captain Blood* (1935) and *Bullets or Ballots* (1936). Mohr tried his hand at directing in 1937, making *When Love Is Young.* The experience wasn't a fully satisfying one and he went back to cinematography.

In the 1940s, Mohr brought a cool, crisp honesty to the sober anti-Nazi film *Watch on the Rhine* (1943) and a delicious eeriness to *The Phantom of the Opera* (1943), for which he won his second and last Oscar. In the latter 1940s, however, he worked steadily but the films he shot were less important.

Mohr turned the tide in the 1950s with Fritz Lang's offbeat western *Rancho Notorious* (1952). Among his starkly shot and powerful films during the next decade were *The Wild One* (1954), *Baby Face Nelson* (1957), and *Underworld USA* (1961).

The aging cinematographer slowed down in the 1960s, but he demonstrated his skill one last time as the photographic consultant on Alfred Hitchcock's *Topaz* (1969), a movie more noteworthy today for its visual effects than its plot.

MONROE, MARILYN (1926–1962) She was Hollywood's legendary sex goddess, the voluptuous blonde bombshell with an outrageously sexy walk and little-girl innocence and vulnerability. Her film career was relatively short—less than fifteen years—and her major starring roles numbered only eleven, but her impact was enormous. After she became a star, every studio in Hollywood tried to come up with their own bosomy blonde version of Monroe. Among the actresses molded in her image were Kim Novak (q.v.), Jayne Mansfield, and Mamie Van Doren. Monroe was never nominated for an Oscar nor did she receive any other major acting award—in fact, only a handful of her films are worthy of note—yet nearly three decades after her death she remains among Hollywood's most enduring and compelling screen personalities.

Born Norma Jeane Mortenson to the then unmarried Gladys Mortensen, a film cutter and movie fanatic who possibly named her daughter after her favorite movie star, Norma Talmadge, Monroe was raised mostly by foster parents. Due to a history of mental illness, Mrs. Mortensen spent a large part of her adult life in sanitariums.

Norma Jean's adolescent years were full of loneliness and trauma. According to her one-time maid and confidante, Lena Pepitone, Monroe was raped by one of her foster parents. Finally, at the age of sixteen, in an effort to escape to a better life, she married twenty-one-year-old Jim Dougherty. Not long after they were wed, Dougherty joined the merchant marine. The couple was divorced four years later.

Meanwhile, in order to help the war effort and earn extra money, Monroe began working in a defense industry plant, packing parachutes. David Conover, an army photographer, arrived at the factory to take pictures of women working in support of the boys overseas. His shots of Marilyn for *Yank* magazine brought her a great deal of attention, leading to a career as a model. It was her modeling agency that decided to change Monroe's hair color from its natural brown to blonde.

Long interested in the movies due to her mother's involvement in the film industry, Monroe began auditioning at several studios. The actress's first break came when Ben Lyon, the casting director of Twentieth Century-Fox signed her to a contract. Lyon gave her the name Marilyn, taking it from Marilyn Miller, an actress he knew who had died in 1936 at the age of thirty-seven, a victim of poisoning. The actress took her mother's maiden name for her surname, because she liked the way it sounded with Marilyn.

Monroe was given acting lessons at Fox and was eventually cast in tiny roles in two movies, *Scudda Hoo! Scudda Hay!* (1948), in which she can be seen in a canoe for a short moment, and *The Dangerous Years* (1948). Seeing no potential in the actress, Fox promptly dropped her option. As it happened, however, Marilyn had been keeping company with sixty-nine-year-old Joseph M. Schenck, a powerful producer at Fox with connections all over Hollywood. Schenck, as a favor to Marilyn, called the president of Columbia Pictures, Harry Cohn, and asked him to give her a contract. Cohn signed her

up, gave her the lead in a "B" movie musical, *Ladies of the Chorus* (1949), and then dropped her from the company. According to Monroe, Cohn let her go because she rebuffed his sexual advances.

With no steady work and trying to make a living, Monroe posed nude for a calendar spread, earning $50.00 for her efforts. When she became famous and the photos resurfaced, the calendar sold more than one million copies. The publicity actually helped her career rather than hurt it.

In the immediate aftermath of her lost opportunity at Columbia, Marilyn free-lanced, hoping to catch on somewhere. She had a small role in the last Marx Brothers movie, *Love Happy* (1949), and got the attention of William Morris agent Johnny Hyde. He went on to become both her lover and her mentor, guiding her career and getting her small but important parts in such films as *The Asphalt Jungle* (1950) and *All About Eve* (1950).

Monroe was starting to get press attention and Hyde succeeded in garnering for her a seven-year contract at Twentieth Century-Fox, just before he died of a heart attack in 1951. The studio groomed her for stardom, giving her modest roles in films such as *As Young As You Feel* (1951), *Love Nest* (1951), *Let's Make It Legal* (1951), *Clash by Night* (1951), *We're Not Married* (1952), and *Monkey Business* (1952). In most of these early films she was cast as a dumb blonde, with the studio banking on her sex appeal rather than her acting abilities.

Finally, Monroe had her first major role in *Niagara* (1953), and despite the film's mediocrity, her presence in the movie turned it into a hit. The actress's career suddenly blossomed. Her follow-up film, *Gentlemen Prefer Blondes* (1953), teamed her with another busty movie star, Jane Russell (q.v.), and the hit musical proved that Marilyn could do more than look beautiful. She could sing in her own inimitable breathy, sexy style, and she could dance with provocative bravado. But the real surprise was that she was a surprisingly adept comedienne.

Monroe continued her successful role as an improbably innocent gold digger in *How to Marry a Millionaire* (1953). She continued to play a variation on the dumb blonde in *There's No Business Like Show Business* (1954) and *The Seven Year Itch* (1955). She played a somewhat wiser dramatic character in the mediocre *River of No Return* (1954). Although all of her films were big hits, Monroe was unhappy at not being given an opportunity to play a wider variety of roles. Attempting to save her integrity as an actress, she walked out on her contract and went to New York to study acting with Paula and Lee Strasberg.

Monroe made headlines for her personal life as well as for her fight with Twentieth Century-Fox. After her nine-month marriage to former baseball hero Joe DiMaggio, she met and fell in love with America's leading playwright, Arthur Miller, who became her third and last husband.

Meanwhile, Fox finally capitulated and gave Marilyn a new contract with the right to approve scripts and directors. Her next film under that contract was the hit *Bus Stop* (1956), proving Marilyn knew what she was doing. For the first time, critics who had previously scoffed at her acting ability began to change their tune.

Unfortunately, her next film was the rather weak *The Prince and the Showgirl* (1957) with Laurence Olivier. She bounced back strongly with Billy Wilder's hugely successful *Some Like It Hot* (1959). *Let's Make Love* (1960) was not as successful a film, but it attained a certain notoriety because of Monroe's affair with costar Yves Montand.

By this time, though, Marilyn's inconsistent professional behavior was becoming more and more a topic of discussion in the movie industry. She was often late to arrive on the set and sometimes didn't show up at all. Monroe was considered extremely difficult to direct; a number of her directors publicly complained about both her tardiness and the constant need to retake her scenes because she could not give a consistently credible performance.

Well aware of her reputation, John Huston *(q.v.)* agreed to direct Monroe in a film that Arthur Miller had written for her: *The Misfits* (1961). Because of delays caused by her emotional problems and dependence on sleeping pills, the film went way over budget. Nonetheless, the star delivered a powerful and elegant performance as an ethereal child/woman. Though generally well-received by the critics, *The Misfits* was not a winner at the box office (at least not upon its initial release). A week before the movie opened she announced her divorce from Miller.

Monroe began making *Something's Got to Give* (1962), but the film was never finished. After two box office failures, her unprofessional behavior became intolerable. When the film fell hopelessly behind schedule, she was fired.

Through her acquaintance with Frank Sinatra and Peter Lawford, the actress had met and had become intimately involved with President John F. Kennedy as well as his brother Robert, the attorney general. Monroe grew increasingly ill, depending heavily on sleeping pills. She died of a drug overdose under mysterious circumstances, with some reputable journalists claiming that Robert Kennedy was in some fashion involved in her death.

See also: sex symbols: female

MONSTER MOVIES   In a narrow definition that excludes sister genres horror and science fiction, these are the movies that present huge and terrifying creatures that are not otherwise humanoid, supernatural, or extraterrestrial. Monster movies, more so than any other films, depend upon special effects. Horror can be expressed through make-up, lighting, and camera angles, and science fiction comes alive on film due to, in large part, costumes, props, and sets (although special effects have played a large role since *Star Wars [q.v.]* in 1977). Monster movies, however, depend almost entirely upon visual tricks to work. Monsters must be created and then made to seem awesome, real, and as fierce-looking as possible.

In 1925, the first major monster movie was made, *The Lost World,* with startling special effects work by Willis O'Brien. The film shocked audiences with massive creatures of another age, forever establishing dinosaurs as the standard monster of the genre.

In 1933, a new monster emerged to do battle with both man and dinosaur, King Kong. Again, the genius behind the special effects was Willis O'Brien. *King Kong,* a beauty-and-the-beast story featuring a surprisingly sympathetic giant gorilla, remains to this day, the most realistic, expressive, and intelligent monster movie ever made. Unfortunately, it spawned a mediocre sequel, *Son of Kong* (1933), and a very weak cousin, *Mighty Joe Young* (1949). It should be noted that the Japanese, who created one of the most popular of all monster dinosaur movies, *Godzilla* (1956), eventually pitted "their" creature against "ours" in *King Kong vs. Godzilla* (1963). Not so surprisingly, in the Japanese version, Godzilla wins; in the American release print, King Kong is the victor.

The dinosaur has thrived in monster movies throughout the decades, making its appearance in films such as the Victor Mature vehicle *One Million B.C.* (1940) and its 1966 remake, *One Million Years B.C.,* starring Raquel Welch, with dinosaurs brought to life by Willis O'Brien disciple Ray Harryhausen. Dinosaurs have also reared their massive heads in movies such as an unlikely combination of western and monster movie called *The Beast of Hollow Mountain* (1956), as well as *Dinosaurus* (1960), and *The Valley of Gwangi* (1969).

The height of monster movie popularity was the 1950s, an era dominated by fear of the atomic bomb. Monster movies played on that fear with plots suggesting that nuclear testing might awaken sleeping giants from their rest, as in *The Beast From 20,000 Fathoms* (1953), or that radiation from atomic tests might create giant mutant life forms that would destroy civilization. In *Them* (1954) the monsters were giant ants, in *It Came From Beneath the Sea* (1955) a giant octopus threatened mankind, and in *The Beginning of the End* (1957) the world lived in fear of massive marauding grasshoppers.

Monster movies have become virtually extinct during recent decades, helped along in their demise by the colossal flop of the remake of *King Kong* (1978). Audiences tend not to be so amazed or frightened by giant creatures on the screen anymore; perhaps we've become too sophisticated for such make-believe.

MONTAGE Generally, the art of editing together the scenes of a movie. Montage has also come to mean the layering of a great many images in rapid succession, often dissolving one on top of the other. Montage of that sort is usually meant to convey the passing of time, such as pages falling off of a calendar, or of places visited all in one wild night, which might include a series of shots of neon-lit nightclub signs dissolving into one another.

Hollywood's acknowledged master of montage was Slavko Vorkapitch, who created some truly incredible montages within the films of other directors. One must see his montage—a surrealistic opening sequence—in *Crime Without Passion* (1934) in order to appreciate the colossal visual impact that a few mere moments of film can create.

MONTGOMERY, ROBERT (1904–1981) A debonair leading man at MGM during the 1930s, known then more for his glamorous co-stars than for his own cinematic personality. But that changed in the late 1930s and 1940s when Montgomery stopped playing in light comedies and became a tough guy. Looking back on his career today, it seems his best work was as an actor-director of a handful of films in the mid- to late 1940s. In any event, Montgomery had a fascinating and multifaceted career.

He was born Henry Montgomery, and his one ambition was to be a writer. However, he found self-expression as an actor in the 1920s, playing in a repertory company in Rochester, New York. He made his way to Broadway in the late 1920s and was whisked away to Hollywood to appear in *So This Is College?* (1929).

Soon thereafter, the handsome and self-effacing actor was the leading man and foil for MGM's greatest female stars. He made six movies with Joan Crawford, five with Norma Shearer, and supported Greta Garbo, Tallulah Bankhead, Constance Bennett, Myrna Loy, and Rosalind Russell.

He might have gone on in that fashion had he not been active in Hollywood politics, helping to organize the Screen Actors Guild. MGM was none too pleased with his union activities and sought to ruin his image (and by extension, his career) by casting him as an especially loathsome villain in *Night Must Fall* (1937). The result, however, was a hit movie and a greater level of critical and audience respect for Montgomery as an actor.

MGM didn't want anything to do with their star if they could help it, and they proceeded to loan him out to other studios whenever they could. Still, both at MGM and elsewhere, Montgomery turned in a number of fine performances in films such as *Yellowjacket* (1938), *The Earl of Chicago* (1940), and *Here Comes Mr. Jordan*

(1941), which was later remade as *Heaven Can Wait* (1978) with Warren Beatty in Montgomery's role.

After finishing his World War II military service as a Lieutenant Commander in the U.S. Navy, he made a triumphant comeback in John Ford's *They Were Expendable* (1945). He then starred and directed for the first time in a movie that still sparks comment today, *The Lady in the Lake* (1946). In the film, he played Raymond Chandler's famous detective, Philip Marlowe. Montgomery made the entire movie using a subjective camera technique. The entire film was shot as if the camera were Marlowe, with the audience seeing everything through his eyes. Montgomery/Marlowe was only seen whenever the character looked into a mirror or into a clear pool of water.

Clearly, the one-time struggling writer had found a new avenue of self-expression as a director. And he continued to direct and star with flair, making *Ride the Pink Horse* (1947), a moody, atmospheric gangster film that ranks as a classic of late 1940s *film noir*. The movie's unfortunate failure at the box office kept him working in front of the cameras for other directors, but he returned to his dual profession in 1949, with two lesser films, *Once More My Darling* and *Your Witness*. Montgomery then walked away from the movie business, finding more freedom to act and direct material of his own choosing in television. He returned only once more to the big screen to direct Jimmy Cagney in *The Gallant Hours* (1960).

See also: subjective camera

MOORE, DICKIE
See child actors

MOORE, DUDLEY (1935–) The diminutive English actor surprisingly became a Hollywood star well into his forties. But long before he emerged as a comic and romantic movie personality, Moore lent his considerable talents to the movies as a comedian, composer, screenwriter, and singer. Very much a movie cult favorite during the second half of the 1960s and through most of the 1970s, his stardom came suddenly in 1979 in Blake Edwards' hit film *10*, which was soon followed by his bravura performance in the smash success *Arthur* (1981). Unfortunately, his film career since those two blockbusters has been considerably less successful.

Music was Moore's early preoccupation. He learned to play the violin at an early age, but his later mastery of the organ earned him a scholarship to Oxford's Magdalen College. There he received a B.A. in music in 1957 and a degree in composition in 1958.

Moore's first big show business break came in the university review he helped write and in which he also performed called *Beyond the Fringe*. It was so successful that it played on the London stage and was brought to

Broadway, where he was introduced to the American audience.

During the 1960s, he and Peter Cook teamed up to become a popular, if cerebral, comedy team. The two appeared in *The Wrong Box* (1966). It was Moore's first film and was quickly followed by *Bedazzled* (1967), in which he and Cook starred. In addition, Moore cowrote the story, composed the film's musical score, and also sang. The hip comedy became a cult classic and it still holds up very well today.

Bedazzled may have been the most enjoyable of Moore's early films, others of note include *30 Is a Dangerous Age, Cynthia* (1968), for which he also cowrote the script and provided the score, *The Bed Sitting Room* (1969), *Those Daring Young Men in Their Jaunty Jalopies* (1969), and *Alice's Adventures in Wonderland* (1972).

After spending a large part of the 1970s on the stage, Moore charmed movie audiences with his supporting performance in the hit Goldie Hawn and Chevy Chase film comedy *Foul Play* (1978). *10* (1979) turned him into a major romantic comedy star, earning him the nickname "Cuddly Dudley." After the flop *Wholly Moses* (1980), Moore scored again in *Arthur* (1981), playing a drunk millionaire with great charm and considerable humor. The hit comedy turned him into a major star and a flurry of films followed, each of them trying to capitalize on Moore's cuteness. But *Six Weeks* (1982), *Romantic Comedy* (1983), *Lovesick* (1983), and *Unfaithfully Yours* (1984) were at best, mediocre. For the most part, Moore was consistently better than his material, charming his way through films that he might have been wiser to avoid.

1984 saw a resurgence in Moore's box office clout when he starred in *Micki & Maude* (1984), a clever, frenetic comedy. Unfortunately, he starred in the stinker *Best Defense* that same year and followed it with his (literally) elfin performance in the poorly received *Santa Claus, The Movie* (1985). After disappearing from movie screens for two years, he starred in *Like Father, Like Son* (1987), yet another box office loser. But, as always, he garnered sympathetic notices from critics.

Finally, in an effort to recoup his popularity, Moore agreed to star in *Arthur 2, On The Rocks* (1988). The film received mixed reviews and an equally mixed response at the ticket window.

M.O.S An abbreviation of the words, "mit out sound," this is a German/English expression meaning "without sound." A scene shot without dialogue or sound effects is said to be M.O.S., and also known as a "wild picture." Conversely sound recorded without a picture is known as "wild sound."

The expression mit out sound and its subsequent abbreviation came into common Hollywood usage in the early sound era. Lothar Mendes, a Hungarian director who worked in Austria and Germany before coming to the U.S., is commonly credited with introducing the quaint expression into the Hollywood vocabulary when, working on a picture, he asked for a scene "mit out sound." The American crew was amused and the expression caught on.

Today, whenever a wild picture is being shot, the letters M.O.S. are written on the clapper board *(q.v.)* to indicate to the editor that the scene to follow is intended as silent.

MOTION PICTURES PATENT COMPANY
See Edison, Thomas A.

MUNI, PAUL (1896–1967) He was Warner Bros.'s class act during the 1930s, a star with the stature to pick his own roles at a studio notorious for shoving its actors into any available project. Though he certainly was a star, Muni was a powerful character actor who immersed himself in his roles to such an extent that he was sometimes unrecognizable from one movie to the next. But his undeniable talent was always apparent.

Born Muni Weisenfreund in Austria, he came to America with his family when he was still quite young. His parents had a theatrical background so it wasn't very strange for Muni to become active in the New York Yiddish theater. He made the leap to Broadway in 1926 when he replaced Edward G. Robinson *(q.v.)* in *We Americans*. His next Broadway play, *Four Walls*, made him a genuine stage star.

Muni was not ignored in Hollywood's rush for Broadway actors during the talkie revolution of the late 1920s. He starred in the Fox film *The Valiant* (1929), which did poorly at the box office but showcased Muni's talent, garnering him an Academy Award nomination for Best Actor. He made another film that same year for Fox, *Seven Faces*, in which he played seven different characters. That, too, failed to find an audience, and Muni seemed to lack the broad appeal needed to sustain a Hollywood career.

He returned to Broadway in 1931, scoring a major success in Elmer Rice's play about a Jewish lawyer, *Counsellor-at-Law*. The play was later made into a movie starring John Barrymore.

When producer Howard Hughes *(q.v.)* decided to make a gangster picture, he was looking for a fresh face to play the vicious Al Capone-like protagonist. He and director Howard Hawks *(q.v.)* settled on Muni, bringing him back to Hollywood for *Scarface* (1932). The movie was a gigantic hit and the actor's film career was firmly established.

Soon thereafter, Warner Bros. gambled on Muni to star in their controversial exposé of the Southern penal system, *I Am a Fugitive from a Chain Gang* (1933, *q.v.*). It was a gamble that paid off both at the box office and in prestige both for the studio and the actor.

Muni was given a long-term contract at Warner Bros.

Paul Muni was a powerhouse actor who liked to change both his appearance and his voice from film to film. He was the leading dramatic actor at Warner Bros. during the 1930s, particularly in that studio's successful cycle of biopics. Photo courtesy of The Siegel Collection.

that lasted until the end of the 1930s, during which time he starred in (among other projects) a famous series of biographical films. He was Pasteur in *The Story of Louis Pasteur* (1936), a movie Warners was hesitant to make but which earned a fortune and won Muni a Best Actor Oscar. Muni was Zola in *The Life of Emile Zola* (1937), a film that won Best Picture honors, and Benito Juárez in *Juarez* (1939), perhaps his most impressive performance.

In addition to the various nationalities he assumed in biopics *(q.v.),* Muni played a Chinese in his starring role in *The Good Earth* (1937). But Muni never played in comedies or farces; he was far too strong a force for such films and instead played characters such as the angry striking miner in *Black Fury* (1935).

While Muni was the most prestigious actor on the Warners lot, he wasn't always the most successful at the box office. By the late 1930s, his films were losing money. The studio wanted Muni to play a gangster again, harking back to his original success in *Scarface,* but Muni refused. He turned down the tough guy role in *High Sierra* (1941); the part eventually went to Humphrey Bogart *(q.v.)* and turned him into a star.

Muni and Warner Bros. parted company at the end of the 1930s and the actor went back to Broadway.

He starred in any number of plays, including *Key Largo,* which eventually became another Bogart starring vehicle in 1948.

He starred in a handful of other films during the 1940s and early 1950s, but nothing of the caliber of his 1930s movies. Muni did, however, make one final triumphant return to the big screen in *The Last Angry Man* (1959) as an aging doctor fighting disease and despair in the slums. Though it didn't make waves at the box office, both he and the movie were well received by the critics. It was an effective and memorable swan song.

MURPHY, AUDIE (1924–1971) His fame as the most decorated soldier of World War II brought the boyish-looking G.I. a Hollywood career that lasted more than twenty years. Murphy, who gave a sense of realism to his action roles, had a surprisingly long career, especially in "B" movie westerns.

Born the son of a poor Texas sharecropper, Murphy's fame as a war hero brought him to the attention of James Cagney *(q.v.),* who suggested that he consider making a living as an actor.

Murphy took Cagney's advice. The slightly built veteran appeared in a small role in *Beyond Glory* (1948). His first starring role came shortly thereafter in *Bad Boy* (1949), a movie about juvenile delinquents. In fact, throughout much of his acting career, Murphy played teen-aged characters because of his baby face.

Out of his forty-four films, Murphy appeared in thirty-three westerns. But two of his non-westerns are worth special mention. He starred in the John Huston *(q.v.)* production of *The Red Badge of Courage* (1951), a cult favorite that Murphy considered his best movie. He also starred in a film version of his autobiography, *To Hell and Back* (1955), a smash box office hit and the biggest money-maker in Universal-International's history.

During the course of his career, Murphy almost single-handedly kept the "B" western alive, making them long after Alan Ladd, Randolph Scott and Joel McCrea *(qq.v.)* either died or retired. Despite a general impression that he was only a mildly popular actor, Murphy was voted the top western box office draw by theater owners in 1955. And that was during the heyday of John Wayne *(q.v.).*

While most of his films received little recognition, there were some gems among them, such as *No Name on the Bullet* (1959) and *Arizona Raiders* (1965). Because of his box office appeal, he occasionally appeared in "A" westerns, such as *The Unforgiven* (1960), with Burt Lancaster and Audrey Hepburn.

Murphy also produced two westerns, both of which he appeared in, *The Guns of Fort Petticoat* (1957) and his last movie, *A Time for Dying* (1971). The latter film, directed by Budd Boetticher *(q.v.),* was released after

Murphy's own sudden and tragic death in a plane crash in North Carolina.

Murphy made it a point never to trade directly on his war record. He wouldn't allow mention of it in the publicity for any of his films. But the audience knew who he was and what he stood for. Despite his cherubic face there was a hint of menace about him. John Huston referred to Murphy during the making of *The Red Badge of Courage* as "my gentle little killer." That combination of innocence and danger was a large part of his appeal. *See also:* westerns

MURPHY, EDDIE (1961–) An actor/comedian who zoomed to Hollywood superstardom in the early 1980s on the basis of just three films. Clearly, Murphy has become one of the very few talents whose name on a marquee ensures a box office hit (as of this writing he has not had a single flop). His brash, cocky humor, coupled with a disarming personal charm, has brought him a legion of fans. While Murphy's comedy is often harsh and jarring, it has much of the crude honesty of the early Richard Pryor *(q.v.),* who he has overtaken as Hollywood's leading black comedy star.

Murphy was born in the Bushwick section of Brooklyn, New York. His father was a New York City cop and amateur comedian who died when the future star was eight years old. Raised by his mother and step-father, Murphy soon showed a flair for comedy. He began writing and performing his own routines at youth centers and local bars when he was fifteen. When Murphy performed at The Comic Strip, a showcase that has launched many a comedian's career, owners Robert Wachs and Richard Tienken were so impressed that they agreed to manage him. Events moved swiftly after that.

At the tender age of nineteen, Murphy landed an audition for the new cast of TV's "Saturday Night Live" and was signed as a featured player for the 1980–81 season. He was an instant hit on the show, staying with the program for four years and creating such memorable characters as the prison poet Tyrone Green, the grownup Buckwheat, the grumpy Gumby, and the TV huckster/pimp Velvet Jones.

"Saturday Night Live" had already served as a springboard for movie comedy stars Chevy Chase, Dan Aykroyd, John Belushi, Bill Murray, and Gilda Radner. It seemed logical for Murphy to try his luck in the movies, as well. His first film was *48 Hours* (1982), in which he costarred with Nick Nolte; it was a smash hit and Murphy was highly praised as a natural actor. For his second film, he teamed with Dan Aykroyd in *Trading Places* (1983), which was another winner.

Though Murphy shared top billing and did not carry either of his first two films, that changed with his third film, *Beverly Hills Cop* (1984). The movie established him as one of Hollywood's biggest box office draws.

Eddie Murphy has become the most commercially successful comedian in Hollywood history, with several of his most recent films taking in well over $100 million at the box office. Photo courtesy of Eddie Murphy.

Murphy had generally received good reviews from the critics for his first three films. That changed with *The Golden Child* (1986) and *Beverly Hills Cop II* (1987), but it didn't keep his fans away. Both films made a bundle at the box office.

Meanwhile, Murphy continued to appear on TV, make records, and tour. Two of his comedy concerts were recorded on film and edited into a motion picture that was released to theaters as *Raw* (1988), the biggest money-maker in concert-film history. He followed that success with his most ambitious project to date, *Coming to America* (1988), a major hit and a highly regarded movie by critics who were impressed with Murphy's growth as an actor and his willingness to play a character rather than simply play himself as he had done in most of his previous work.

The actor/comedian has not been content to merely perform. He has become a one-man conglomerate, establishing Eddie Murphy Productions (for film projects), Eddie Murphy Television Productions, and Eddie Murphy Tours (a concert producing company).

MUSICALS The first talkie, *The Jazz Singer* (1927, *q.v.),* was also Hollywood's first musical. It's well known that the Al Jolson *(q.v.)* vehicle ignited the sound revolution, but it is less well known that its success also led to a deluge of musicals over the next several years that nearly killed the genre in its infancy. Every studio advertised their "all talking, all singing, all dancing" films as they desperately tried to take full commercial advantage of the new sound technology. As a result, so many mediocre musicals were made in such a relatively short period of time that box office returns soon began to fall precipitously. It was the flowering of the classic movie musicals in the early 1930s that resurrected the genre, but even before that happy event, two basic kinds of musicals had already emerged, the singing musical and the dancing musical. All other subcategories fall within these two major groups.

The singing musical is the broader of the two groups because there have been very few dancers with large enough popular appeal around whom films could be built. Though often containing at least some dancing, the singing musical primarily focuses on musical numbers, comedy, and, on occasion, drama—but almost always they hinge on romance. Among early singing musicals one finds the charming and risqué Ernst Lubitsch (q.v.) operettas *The Love Parade* (1929), *Monte Carlo* (1930), and *The Merry Widow* (1934), Rouben Mamoulian's (q.v.) brilliant *Love Me Tonight* (1932), as well as the more dramatic operettas of Nelson Eddy and Jeanette MacDonald (q.v.), such as *Naughty Marietta* (1935) and *Rose Marie* (1936).

Many out and out comedies were also leavened with songs and can also be considered singing musicals, among them the films of Eddie Cantor, and many Marx Brothers, Abbott and Costello, Martin and Lewis, and Danny Kaye movies.

A lesser form of the singing musical could be found in the westerns of Gene Autry and Roy Rogers (qq.v.). The popularity of these singing cowboys during the 1930s and 1940s was quite substantial. The country-western and hillbilly music of the singing cowboy merged in the 1950s with the rockabilly sound of Elvis Presley (q.v.) and a subsequent boom in rock 'n' roll musicals. Presley, alone, made thirty-three movies, the vast majority of them formula musicals that earned in excess of $150 million at the box office.

With rare exceptions, such as *Yankee Doodle Dandy* (1942) *and The Story and Vernon and Irene Castle* (1939)—films about dancers—most musical biopics were essentially singing musicals, such as *Night and Day* (1945), *The Jolson Story* (1946), *Words and Music* (1948), *The Great Caruso* (1951), *The Helen Morgan Story* (1957), *The Buddy Holly Story* (1978), and *La Bamba* (1987).

Great though many of the singing musicals are, the glory of the genre ultimately belongs to the dance musicals. When one thinks of the movie musical, images of Fred Astaire and Gene Kelly (qq.v.) come immediately to mind. Or perhaps one thinks of the Busby Berkeley (q.v.) spectaculars of the 1930s or the Broadway musical extravaganzas of the 1950s and early 1960s. For most people, these films are the pinnacle of movie musical art.

The dance musical had its start in the musical review films of the late 1920s and early 1930s, including movies such as *The Hollywood Revue of 1929* (1929) and *Paramount on Parade* (1930). Though dance numbers did not dominate these movies, audiences responded with great enthusiasm to the sights and sounds of dancing feet.

By the early 1930s, the time was ripe for full-scale dancing movies. Busby Berkeley breathed new life into the musical and created a dynamic visual style when he choreographed and directed the musical numbers in *Footlight Parade* (1933), *Gold Diggers of 1933* (1933), and *42nd Street* (1933). These lavish, audacious works have never been duplicated. For instance, the very idea of putting one hundred dancing pianos on screen (which Berkeley presented in *Gold Diggers of 1935*) was both wonderfully silly and thoroughly awe-inspiring. His work at Warner Bros. reaffirmed that studio's leadership in the musical genre after its initial success with Al Jolson.

Berkeley's "mass" extravaganzas, with scores of scantily clad women creating kaledioscopic effects (e.g., forming images of violins, flowers, etc.) were in contrast to the "intimate" musicals that were characterized by the subtle, graceful, and elegant dance numbers of Fred Astaire and Ginger Rogers, (q.v.), whose musicals were equally popular during the 1930s. Astaire and Rogers, in films such as *The Gay Divorcée* (1934), *Top Hat* (1935) and *Swing Time* (1936), created the yardstick by which intimate dance films would be measured forevermore. Astaire, in particular, whose dancing career on film spanned four decades, was Hollywood's preeminent dance musical star; he was the only musical performer who had a major impact during both the flowering of the musical in the 1930s and its golden era during the late 1940s and early 1950s.

With varying degrees of success, each studio pursued its own course in the profitable musical genre. And more often than not, a musical performer helped save several studios from bankruptcy. For instance, RKO avoided Chapter 11 thanks to the enormous success of Fred Astaire and Ginger Rogers in the 1930s, helped greatly by the unheralded but extremely bright producer Pandro S. Berman (q.v.). Also in the 1930s, Deanna Durbin (q.v.) sang Universal out of near-insolvency, just as Shirley Temple (q.v.) kept the wolf from the door at Twentieth Century-Fox until they developed such other popular musical stars as Alice Faye and Betty Grable (qq.v.). Of course, not every leading musical performer was a savior, but many were immeasurably important to their studio's bottom line. For example, Dick Powell (q.v.) warbled very profitably for Warner Bros. in innumerable musicals during the bulk of the 1930s. Bing Crosby (q.v.) was a major asset at Paramount, just as Rita Hayworth *(q.v.)* was worth millions to Columbia. Even the independent Samuel Goldwyn had his musical stars: Eddie Cantor *(q.v.)* in the 1930s and Danny Kaye *(q.v.)* in the 1940s and 1950s. And then there was MGM, which boasted "more stars than there are in the heavens"; by the late 1930s, a good many of them were musical stars. The studio produced few musicals during most of the 1930s but finally began to emerge as a powerhouse in the genre with such films as *The Wizard of Oz* (1939) and *Babes in Arms* (1939), eventually becoming the predominant creator of musicals in the 1940s and 1950s.

One of MGM's performers was Gene Kelly *(q.v.),* whose exuberant and acrobatic dance style, especially in films such as *The Pirate* (1948), *On the Town* (1949), and *Singin' in the Rain* (1952), gave the musical a shot in the arm (or leg?). After Fred Astaire, Kelly has been the most influential of movie musical performers, often co-choreographing and codirecting many of his greatest triumphs.

Astaire and Kelly, as well as such talents as Judy Garland, Mickey Rooney *(qq.v.),* Mario Lanza, and Cyd Charrise *(q.v.)* were all part of MGM's famous "Freed Unit." Arthur Freed *(q.v.),* a noted songwriter and producer, put together an awesome assemblage of musical talent, presiding over the creation of many of the film industry's most illustrious musicals. With the assistance of such innovative directors as Vincente Minnelli and Stanley Donen *(qq.v.),* the Freed Unit produced such memorable hits as *Meet Me in St. Louis* (1944), *Ziegfeld Follies* (1946), *Till the Clouds Roll By* (1946), *Easter Parade* (1948), *Summer Stock* (1950), *An American in Paris* (1951), and *Show Boat* (1951). It was also during this time that MGM pioneered the so-called "wet musical" featuring Esther Williams *(q.v.)* in elaborate aquatic production numbers.

The musical was ever-changing. The movie industry was under siege during the 1950s, losing patrons and revenue to television. Just as Hollywood turned to epics and spectaculars in order to compete with the little box,

so did the movie musical become more epic in its scope, adapting big Broadway musicals to the screen such as *Seven Brides for Seven Brothers* (1954), *Oklahoma!* (1955), and *West Side Story* (1961).

The movie musical—both the singing and dancing varieties—finally collapsed under their own budgetary weight. After a spate of hugely successful singing Broadway musical adaptations, including, *My Fair Lady* (1964), *The Sound of Music* (1965), and *Funny Girl* (1968), film companies poured massive amounts of money into a series of very poor musicals, such as *Doctor Dolittle* (1967), and *Star!* (1968), which were staggering box office failures, souring the movie industry on the genre.

The musical, however, is resilient, and Bob Fosse fought the tide with three innovative dance musicals that had force and subtlety: *Sweet Charity* (1968), *Cabaret* (1972) and *All That Jazz* (1979). But Fosse's films were too idiosyncratic to reestablish the genre to its former popularity. This was accomplished, however, by the success of the "disco" musical *Saturday Night Fever* (1977), which proved there was a strong and vibrant youth market for dance musicals. Since then, teen dance musicals have been extremely popular, as evidenced by such hits as *Flashdance* (1983), *Footloose* (1984), and *Dirty Dancing* (1987).

Outside of the youth market, there has been little in the way of big movie musicals. Small-scale musicals such as *Tap* (1989) keep the musical tradition alive, while today's leading movie musical stars tend to ignore the genre. Barbra Streisand *(q.v.)* and Liza Minnelli, for instance, prefer to make non-musicals (when they make films at all) because of the enormous time and effort required to make elaborate musicals such as Streisand's *Yentl* (1983).

In recent years, the one Hollywood personality who has worked most consistently in musicals has not been a star, but a director, Herbert Ross *(q.v.),* who has made such musicals as *Funny Lady* (1975), *The Turning Point* (1977), *Nijinsky* (1980), *Pennies from Heaven* (1981), and *Dancers* (1987).

NEAL, PATRICIA (1926–   ) Tall, willowy, with patrician features, she has starred in twenty-six theatrical films and, in her later years, a number of made-for-TV movies. In the course of a film career that began in 1949, Neal has starred in several minor classics and a number of fascinating near misses.

Neal studied acting at Northwestern University and then supported herself as a model before making her debut on Broadway at the age of twenty-one in *The Voice of the Turtle*. Her big stage hit came shortly thereafter in *Another Part of the Forest*. Hailed as a beautiful and bright new star, Hollywood plucked her for the female lead in *John Loves Mary* (1949). That same year, she was chosen to play opposite Gary Cooper *(q.v.)* in the oddly compelling film version of Ayn Rand's *The Fountainhead* (1949). She and Cooper had a torrid off-screen love affair that, when it ended, left Neal shattered by a nervous breakdown.

The films she made subsequently did not enhance her career. Her only truly memorable movie during the early 1950s was the minor science fiction classic *The Day the Earth Stood Still* (1951). After Neal married author Roald Dahl, she temporarily quit movie acting. She didn't appear on film again for three years until Elia Kazan *(q.v.)* cast her in his perceptive attack on television, *A Face in the Crowd* (1957).

Though Neal was much in demand, she didn't work very often in films thereafter. When she did, however, she gave strong performances both in leading and supporting roles, lending her presence to such films as *Breakfast at Tiffany's* (1961), *Hud* (1963), for which she won a Best Actress Oscar, and *In Harm's Way* (1965).

It was after working in the last of these films that she suffered a massive stroke that left her paralyzed and unable to speak clearly. After a herculean effort she successfully recouped her health, and in 1968, made her comeback in *The Subject Was Roses*. She received a Best

Actress Academy Award nomination, which was no doubt a testament to her personal courage.

Neal has made relatively few theatrical films since her comeback; her most recent is *An Unremarkable Life* (1989). She has been seen occasionally in TV movies, the best known of them being "The Homecoming" (1971), which was the pilot for the TV series, "The Waltons." In 1981, she was the subject of a TV biopic, "The Patricia Neal Story," starring Glenda Jackson.

NEGRI, POLA (1894–1987) Before Garbo and Dietrich, there was Pola Negri—the original femme fatale from the Continent. The green-eyed, raven-haired beauty brought a sensual and exotic presence to Hollywood. Unfortunately, her American films tended to use her as a conventional leading lady, smothering the spark that had ignited audience interest in her in the first place.

Born Barbara Apollonia Chalupiec in Poland, Negri entered the theater world in Russia as a dancer. After some considerable success in cabaret, she returned to Poland, where she wrote and produced her first film, whose English title is *Love and Passion* (1914). Quickly becoming Poland's most successful film star, she was convinced by producer Max Reinhardt to travel to Germany, where she conquered yet another audience. More significantly, she demanded and received directorial guidance from a relative unknown, Ernst Lubitsch *(q.v.)*. The two teamed to make a remarkable series of hit movies, many of which were well received in America.

Negri was deluged with offers from Hollywood studios. She finally accepted an $8,000 per week contract from Paramount and made her first film in the United States in 1923 *(Bella Donna)*. Neither her first nor many of her subsequent films were successful. Rather surprisingly, critics liked her but audiences did not. Happily, Ernst Lubitsch was also brought to America, and he directed her in *Forbidden Paradise* (1924), a movie that was highly regarded by both critics and the public.

Though she continued making movies, her hits became fewer. Even Negri's personal life took a beating with the sudden death of Rudolph Valentino, with whom she was engaged in a romantic affair.

Sound dealt the final blow. Negri made a few talkies (she even sang in two of them) but her accent was considered too heavy by Paramount executives. When her contract ran out in 1928, so did she—back to Europe.

The singing success of Marlene Dietrich *(q.v.)*, however, offered Negri new encouragement. She returned to America in 1932 and made *A Woman Commands* at RKO. She sang again—and rather well—but the movie was an especially bad vehicle and Negri left Hollywood.

She returned to Germany, reestablished her film career there, and (rumor had it) became romantically involved with Adolf Hitler. Nevertheless, Negri fled Germany during World War II and returned to America. She made just two more films, *Hi Diddle Diddle* (1943) and Disney's *The Moonspinners* (1964).

NEWMAN, PAUL (1925–   ) An actor/director/producer who has been a movie mainstay for more than thirty years. Blessed with strikingly handsome features, talent, and the bluest eyes in Hollywood, Newman has generally opted for challenging roles rather than typical matinee-idol parts. His popularity as an actor has been matched by the appreciation of his peers, who have nominated him a total of seven times for the Best Actor Academy Award; he has won the statuette once.

Born to a well-to-do Cleveland family, Newman served in the Navy during World War II before attending Kenyon College as an economics major. While in school, he developed an affinity for acting and he eventually continued his education at the Yale School of Drama. His most important training, however, took place at the Actors Studio, where he became one of a number of influential performers to emerge as devotees of the "Method" approach to acting.

Newman's rise to fame was meteoric. Not long after his stint at the Actors Studio he landed a leading role in the 1953 production of the hit play *Picnic*. He was immediately tapped for the movies. Because of his looks and his Actors Studio training, Newman found himself in constant competition with James Dean *(q.v.)*, another actor who seemed cut from the same cloth. Hoping to make his film debut as the misunderstood son yearning for love in Elia Kazan's *East of Eden* (1955), Newman saw the role given to Dean. In fact, Newman was able to make his movie debut in *The Silver Chalice* (1955) only when Dean declined the offer. (Dean, it should be said, made the wiser choice—the biblical epic was panned by the critics.) The two actors' careers continued to be

Paul Newman has been both a male sex symbol and one of the film industry's most accomplished leading men since the mid-1950s. His deep blue eyes can't be seen in this black-and-white picture, but most female movie fans can describe them in great detail. Photo courtesy of Movie Star News.

linked; the role of Rocky Graziano in *Somebody Up There Likes Me* (1956) had been slated for Dean until he died in a car accident. Newman took over the part and it became his first hit film.

It was the first of many. During the next fifteen years Newman was the hottest actor in Hollywood. He peaked at the end of the 1960s, had a rather poor decade in the 1970s, but reemerged in the 1980s with some of the best performances of his career. In fact, his Oscar nominations tend to uphold that assessment. He was nominated for *Cat on a Hot Tin Roof* (1958), *The Hustler* (1961), *Hud* (1963), *Cool Hand Luke* (1967), *Absence of Malice* (1981), *The Verdict* (1982), and finally took home the honor for a reprise of his Fast Eddie role from *The Hustler* in *The Color of Money* (1986).

Newman's hits defined the emerging Hollywood of the late 1950s and 1960s. In an effort to outshine television, Hollywood turned to adult dramas, and Newman could be seen in *The Long Hot Summer* (1958), *The Left-Handed Gun* (1958), and *Sweet Bird of Youth* (1962). The 1960s were a time of growing alienation, and

Newman reflected the zeitgeist with such films as *The Outrage* (1964), *Harper* (1966), *Hombre* (1967), and *Cool Hand Luke* (1967). And yet Newman could also be the typical Hollywood leading man, as evidenced by his starring roles in *A New Kind of Love* (1963), *The Prize* (1963), *Torn Curtain* (1966), and the ultimate crowd pleaser, *Butch Cassidy and the Sundance Kid* (1969), which marked his popular highpoint. The film also made a mega-star out of his costar, Robert Redford *(q.v.)*, the man who supplanted Newman as Hollywood's romantic ideal.

As one of the original cofounders of First Artists, along with Barbra Streisand, Sidney Poitier, and Steve McQueen *(qq.v.)*, Newman was in a position to control more of his work and he did so during the 1970s, producing and directing a number of films. He had begun directing in the late 1960s, making *Rachel, Rachel* (1968), a film starring his wife, Joanne Woodward *(q.v.)*, that was well received, if not a major box office success. He went on to produce and direct several other films, including the highly underrated *Sometimes a Great Notion* (1971), in which he also starred, and three other vehicles for his wife, *The Effect of Gamma Rays on Man-in-the-Moon Marigolds* (1972), "The Shadow Box" (1980), and *The Glass Menagerie* (1988).

Newman also produced, but did not direct, many of his own films during the early 1970s, among them, *WUSA* (1970), *Pocket Money* (1972), *The Life and Times of Judge Roy Bean* (1972), and *The Drowning Pool* (1975). None of them were big hits. He had a string of real duds at the end of the decade and the very beginning of the 1980s, including *Buffalo Bill and the Indians . . . or Sitting Bull's History Lesson* (1976), *Quintet* (1979), and *When Time Ran Out* (1980). His only big winners as an actor during the 1970s were *The Sting* (1973), in which he reteamed with Robert Redford, the all-star *The Towering Inferno* (1974), and *Slap Shot* (1977).

He recouped smartly in the 1980s, becoming once again the powerful box office force he had been in his early years, and making much better movies in the bargain. *Fort Apache, The Bronx* (1981) was a controversial hit that put Newman back in the spotlight. His troubles with the media during that film led him to make the intelligent and thought-provoking *Absence of Malice* (1981), a film that dealt with the power of the press to destroy innocent people. He continued making quality films throughout the 1980s, including his semi-autobiographical *Harry and Son* (1984), which he wrote, produced, and directed. It was a film that touched on the difficult relationship between a man and his son, and it owed much to Newman's experience with the death of his son by drug overdose in 1978.

Outside of the film industry, Newman has been politically active in liberal causes, and has become well-known for his various food products, the profits of which he donates to charity. He is also a highly visible

race car driver who became especially interested in the sport during the making of *Winning* (1969).

In 1985, Paul Newman was given a special Oscar in honor of his fine work. In his acceptance speech he told the Academy not to write him off, that he wasn't through yet. The following year he won the Best Actor Award for *The Color of Money*. Well into his sixties, he remains a stunning actor both in his looks and ability.

NEWSREELS Nonfiction film footage once shown in movie theaters on a regular basis, newsreels became a form of movie journalism that lasted for more than sixty years. While never as timely nor as comprehensive as the news one might find in daily newspapers, America's newsreels supplied not only facts but unforgettable images. The newsreel was a standard part of movie fare, presented to audiences along with a cartoon or short subject, as well as coming attractions and at least one (if not two) feature films.

A few current events films were made before the advent of newsreels, such as the Bob Fitzsimmons and Jim Corbett heavyweight bout in 1897, Queen Victoria's funeral in 1901, and the San Francisco earthquake of 1906 (some of which was faked through the use of miniatures). As Raymond Fielding reports in his excellent book, *The American Newsreel,* the first ongoing series of news shorts produced in America were made in 1911 by the French-owned Pathé's Weekly. The success of Pathé's Weekly was such that competition blossomed in the form of companies such as Fox News, which went into business in 1919.

The talkie revolution slowed the newsreel business down for a short while because of the difficulty of recording sound on film in sometimes treacherous situations that were hardly suited for moviemaking. Nonetheless, sound newsreels soon flourished, the most powerful and far-reaching of them being Fox Movietone News. Lowell Thomas later become the voice of Fox Movietone News and his name, face, and voice became famous worldwide. Other newsreel companies included Hearst Metrotone, Universal Newsreel, Paramount News, and in 1935, the famous March of Time newsreel begun by Time, Inc.

The March of Time was the forerunner of the TV newsmagazine and therefore the predecessor of such shows as "Sixty Minutes" and "20/20." It differed from its newsreel competition in focusing its full twenty minutes on only one subject, examining it in considerable depth. Though the newsreel did not pretend to be neutral in its point of view, its passion made it rich and fascinating. The March of Time won a special Oscar in 1937 for "having revolutionized one of the most important branches in the industry—the newsreel." The March of Time remains one of the best remembered of all the newsreels because Orson Welles mimicked it so well in his masterpiece, *Citizen Kane* (1941).

Newsreels captured some of the best-remembered events of the century, such as the Lindbergh flight, the startling assassination of King Alexander of Yugoslavia in 1934, and the famous Hindenburg catastrophe in Lakehurst, New Jersey, in 1937. But newsreels also covered such areas of interest as fashion, sports events, celebrities, political campaigns, and natural disasters.

The stories of daredevil cameramen who often risked their lives to shoot dangerous footage became the stuff of legend. They worked their way into Hollywood features when Clark Gable and Myrna Loy starred in *Too Hot to Handle* (1938), a movie using the world of newsreels as its backdrop. Yet the most dangerous news footage, shot during war, was usually handled by army cameramen. During both World War I and World War II, civilians were rarely permitted to film at the front. But no matter who was filming, relatively little of what was shot was ever seen by audiences on the home front; most of the images were too terrifying for civilians to witness and the military banned their showing.

The newsreel began to fade in importance during the 1950s because it couldn't compete with television's ability to report the news almost instantly. But contrary to popular belief, the newsreel did not die an early death due to TV, and continued on well into the 1960s. The fact is, many of the newsreel companies began shooting their footage for TV news rather than theater distribution. But with video replacing film, even that source of revenue began to dry up. The king of the newsreels, Fox Movietone News, stopped producing in 1963. Hearst Metrotone lasted until November 30, 1967. And the last holdout, Universal Newsreel closed their doors on December 26, 1967.

NICHOLS, DUDLEY (1895–1960) An Oscar-winning screenwriter who wrote literate, intelligent movies for a variety of wildly diverse first-class directors. Though he wrote, directed, and produced three movies himself, Nichols is remembered as one of Hollywood's most influential and successful screenwriters.

A former reporter for the New York *World*, he arrived in Hollywood in 1929 when studios were in dire need of writers to script the new talking pictures. He wrote his first screenplay, *Men Without Women*, (1930) directed by John Ford (*q.v.*), with whom Nichols would collaborate over the course of nearly two decades. All told, Nichols scripted fifteen Ford films, including *The Lost Patrol* (1934), *Judge Priest* (1934), *Stagecoach* (1939), and *The Long Voyage Home* (1940). He also wrote the screenplay for Ford's *The Informer* (1935), a film that won Oscars for both Ford (Best Director) and Nichols (Best Screenplay). His last screenplay for Ford was *The Fugitive* (1947).

Nichols had no trouble finding work when he wasn't

writing for Ford. He scripted Howard Hawks' (*q.v.*) wonderful screwball comedy *Bringing Up Baby* (1938), along with two other Hawks classics, *Air Force* (1943) and *The Big Sky* (1952). He wrote the screenplays for Jean Renoir's best American films, *Swamp Water* (1941) and *This Land Is Mine* (1943). The clever and disturbing thriller *Man Hunt* (1941) and the *film noir* *Scarlet Street* (1945) were projects he scripted for Fritz Lang (*q.v.*), and *The Bells of St. Mary's* (1945) is a fondly remembered film penned for Leo McCarey (*q.v.*). For Elia Kazan (*q.v.*), he wrote the anti-racist *Pinky* (1949), and for Anthony Mann (*q.v.*), he scripted the fine western, *The Tin Star* (1957). Nichols wrote his last film (not counting the 1966 remake of *Stagecoach*, which used his original script), the offbeat western *Heller in Pink Tights* (1960), for George Cukor (*q.v.*).

Nichols wrote, produced and directed three films: *Government Girl* (1943), *Sister Kenny* (1946), and *Mourning Becomes Electra* (1947). All were well received by the critics, even if they weren't particularly successful at the box office.

NICHOLS, MIKE (1931–   ) A director who has made a number of intelligent, entertaining, and often hard-hitting movies since beginning his film career in 1966. Nichols is also a very successful stage director who has not deserted Broadway for Hollywood. He has continued to move back and forth between film and stage with gratifying results in both. A former cabaret performer, Nichols is known for working very well with actors. He is also a good judge of talent, having discovered Dustin Hoffman and Whoopi Goldberg.

Born Michael Igor Peschkowsky in Berlin, Germany, he was seven years old when he emigrated with his Jewish family to the U.S. to avoid persecution at the hands of the Nazis. Nichols was twelve years old when his father died, but he managed to continue his education, eventually attending the University of Chicago thanks to a series of scholarships and a succession of jobs as varied as janitor and jingle contest judge.

After college, he studied acting with Lee Strasberg in New York, but learning the "Method" theory of acting didn't land him a job, and he returned to Chicago with as little acting experience as when he left. Back in his hometown, however, he teamed up with friends Barbara Harris, Paul Sills, Alan Arkin (*q.v.*), and Elaine May (*q.v.*) and began an improvisational theater group that performed for three straight years at Chicago's Compass club.

In the late 1950s, Nichols and May began their two-person comedy act, which culminated in a hit Broadway show in 1960, *An Evening With Mike Nichols and Elaine May*. The team broke up in the early 1960s, and Nichols eventually took a stab at directing for the theater, making his debut with Neil Simon's *Barefoot in the Park* in 1963. The show was a smash hit, and Nichols directed six more plays consecutively, all of them major hits.

His success on Broadway made it inevitable that he would be asked to direct a movie. The first film he agreed to direct was *The Graduate* (1967), but he delayed production on that movie when he had the opportunity to direct *Who's Afraid of Virginia Woolf?* (1966). The film based on the Edward Albee play is judged by many to be the best movie that Elizabeth Taylor and Richard Burton ever starred in together. And for his part, Nichols came away with both a box office winner and an Oscar nomination for Best Director.

The Graduate became an even more successful movie. It was one of the biggest grossers of the 1960s, earning in excess of $60 million. It made Dustin Hoffman a star and brought Nichols the Best Director Academy Award and a nomination for Best Picture.

With the clout that came from two previous hits, Nichols was given an $11 million budget to direct the movie version of Joseph Heller's *Catch-22* (1970), a novel that was generally considered unfilmable. The result was a flawed masterpiece. Equally ambitious was *Carnal Knowledge* (1971), a film about sexual and social relationships that showed its audience no quarter; it was a provocative and extremely controversial movie that proved to be popular, as well.

Nichols seemed to pull back from tough-minded filmmaking to direct *The Day of the Dolphin* (1973), *The Fortune* (1975), and *Gilda Live* (1980), but he returned to more socially conscious content when he took on *Silkwood* (1983), a film based on the true story of a whistle-blower in a nuclear power plant.

In the last several years, Nichols has begun directing movies not unlike his earliest film efforts. *Heartburn* (1986) and *Biloxi Blues* (1988) are both about love ·relationships, the first about one that doesn't work out, the second about the youthful hope that one will. In addition, his touch for social comedy is as sure as ever, as evidenced by his direction of *Working Girl* (1988) for which he received an Oscar nomination for Best Director.

NICHOLSON, JACK (1937–   ) An actor who has made an art out of playing alienated loners. He has been a major star of offbeat, intelligent movies since emerging from relative obscurity in a supporting role in *Easy Rider* (1969). The oft Oscar-nominated Nicholson had a fascinating decade-long film career before being discovered by the critics and the mass audience, during which time he acted, wrote screenplays, directed, and even produced low-budget movies. Like Robert De Niro *(q.v.),* Nicholson has been willing to radically change his appearance from film to film, even if it means looking distinctly un-star-like. Also like De Niro, superstar Nicholson has been open to playing supporting roles in films that have offered him meaty scenes.

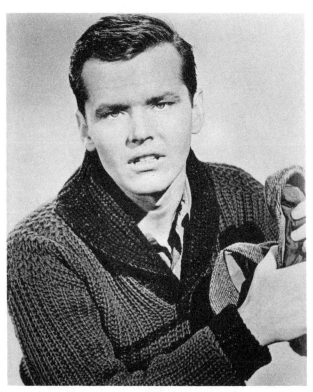

Jack Nicholson's persona of alienated outsider has served him well over more than twenty years of film stardom. Seen here in his younger days, Nicholson has grown into a supremely accomplished and versatile actor who has, ironically, become a Hollywood insider. Photo courtesy of Movie Star News.

Born to an alcoholic father who abandoned his family before he was born, Nicholson was raised by his grandmother, who owned a New Jersey beauty parlor. Unlike many modern actors who received their early training in college, Nicholson never got past high school. He drifted into the movies while visiting his mother in Los Angeles when he was just seventeen years old. His first job in the film industry was working as a gopher at MGM. Acting appealed to him and he joined the Players Ring Theater group and began studying his new craft.

After some minor stage and TV experience, Nicholson began appearing in the movies, making his film debut in a lead role in the low-budget Roger Corman *(q.v.)* production *The Cry Baby Killer* (1958). Nicholson would continue working on and off with Corman during the next ten years. Curiously, while any number of writer/directors, including Francis Ford Coppola *(q.v.),* Peter Bogadanovich *(q.v.),* Jonathan Demme, and others, have emerged from Roger Corman's school of cinema hard knocks, Nicholson is the only major acting star to have done so. Among Nicholson's Corman-related projects are *The Wild Ride* (1960), *The Little Shop of Horrors* (1961), *The Terror* (1963), *The Raven* (1963), and *The St. Valentine's Day Massacre* (1967). He worked strictly as a screenwriter for *The Trip* (1967).

Nicholson didn't act exclusively for Corman during his long trek through the cinema wilderness. He was occasionally seen in small roles in more mainstream films, such as *Studs Lonigan* (1960) and *Ensign Pulver* (1964). His real growth, however, came as a combination actor/screenwriter/sometime producer, working in collaboration with director/producer Monte Hellman. Together, they made several interesting cheapie films, among them *Flight to Fury* (1964), *Ride in the Whirlwind* (1965), and *The Shooting* (1965).

After cowriting and coproducing the rock group the Monkees' vehicle, *Head* (1968), Nicholson found himself a last-minute fill-in for actor Rip Torn, who was supposed to play the alienated lawyer in *Easy Rider*. Having acted in more than his share of low-budget motorcycle/psycho/drug movies, there was no reason for Nicholson to expect that this film would be any different from the others. Yet *Easy Rider* became the huge sleeper hit of 1969, catapulting Nicholson to the brink of stardom with an Oscar nomination for Best Supporting Actor.

A symbol of the youth market, Nicholson was quickly hired to play a supporting role in the Barbra Streisand musical *On a Clear Day You Can See Forever* (1979). The film was such a bomb that Nicholson has stayed clear of such ponderous mainstream vehicles ever since. He had found his niche as a rebellious outsider and he has continued to play variations on that character ever since, including in the film that finally brought him legitimate star status and his first nomination for Best Actor, *Five Easy Pieces* (1970).

Since attaining the clout of a star, Nicholson's projects have mostly been intelligently ambitious films that have challenged his audience. If anything, his commercial failures have resulted from being too far ahead of their time. *Carnal Knowledge* (1971), *A Safe Place* (1971), *The King of Marvin Gardens* (1972), *The Last Detail* (1973), *The Passenger* (1975), and *The Border* (1982) were all chancy projects, and only *Carnal Knowledge* was a success at the box office, although he did win an Oscar nomination for *The Last Detail*. Nicholson has also directed two films: *Drive He Said* (1971) and *Goin' South* (1978). He starred in the latter, but both were box office losers that have since become minor cult favorites.

If Nicholson's flops were adventurous, so too were his hits. Roman Polanski's *Chinatown* (1974) saved Nicholson's flagging career and brought him yet another Oscar nomination. Then he was brilliantly cast as Randle McMurphy in the film version of Ken Kesey's *One Flew Over the Cuckoo's Nest* (1975). The film won all five top Oscars, including a Best Actor Academy Award for Nicholson.

The actor began appearing in smaller roles in interesting movies during the latter half of the 1970s and early 1980s. For instance, he sang in a small role in the rock musical *Tommy* (1975), played in support of Robert De Niro in *The Last Tycoon* (1976), Warren Beatty in *Reds* (1981), and Shirley MacLaine in *Terms of Endearment* (1983). The last of these performances brought him a Best Supporting Actor Academy Award.

Nicholson began choosing his starring vehicles even more carefully during the late 1970s and throughout the 1980s. He was teamed with Marlon Brando *(q.v.)*—one of his early idols—in *The Missouri Breaks* (1976), worked with one of the cinema's leading directors, Stanley Kubrick *(q.v.)*, in *The Shining* (1980), made a hot-blooded remake of *The Postman Always Rings Twice* (1981), and starred with one of the cinema's most talented female stars, Meryl Streep *(q.v.)*, in *Heartburn* (1986). Unfortunately, none of these films was terribly successful commercially although his performances in all of them were much praised.

Nicholson's commercial standing rose to meet his critical reputation during the mid- to late 1980s with his Oscar-nominated performance in the hit *Prizzi's Honor* (1985), as well as his starring role in the successful romp *The Witches of Eastwick* (1987). Though *Ironweed* (1987) was not a money-maker, his Oscar-nominated performance in this prestigious picture was so strong that it further enhanced his reputation as one of Hollywood's most serious and valued actors. Finally, he topped off the decade with a tour-de-force portrayal of *The Joker* in the megahit *Batman* (1989).

NICKELODEON   The humorous name given to makeshift movie theaters built in converted storefronts during the early 1900s that charged an admission price of a mere nickel. According to Green and Laurie in their book, *From Vaude to Video,* "In 1904 not a single nickelodeon sullied the land. But three years later, over 2,000,000 people a day . . . were jamming into movie shows."

Nickelodeons were known as "the poor man's amusement," and at a nickel per show, the movies were soon killing off vaudeville. Geared for low-cost, no frills entertainment, nickelodeons prospered because they were small, seating less than 300 patrons, the magic number at which most theaters had to be licensed. This allowed them to avoid city bureaucracies and the consequent cost of bribing local officials.

The lifespan of the nickelodeon era was very short: little more than ten years. As the new star system made millionaires out of actors and as films became longer and more expensive to produce, it became inefficient for film companies to make costly prints of each film to rent to thousands upon thousands of such small "theaters." The only way the producers could turn a profit was to sell their movies to fewer but bigger houses, which could, in turn, show the films to larger audiences at a higher price.

As Green and Laurie report, the beginning of the end of the nickelodeon era came with the building of the Strand Theater in New York City in 1914. The first movie palace sat 3,300 people. The top admission price was twenty-five cents. Not long after, when safety laws all across the country concerning buildings that housed public entertainment were tightened, the nickelodeon could no longer survive.

A perceptive handful of men who owned nickelodeons and could see the bright future of the movies went on to become powerful moguls in Hollywood. Some of the early owners of such establishments were the Warner brothers, Louis B. Mayer, and Adolph Zukor (qq.v.).

In more modern times, Peter Bogdanovich (q.v.) made a charming movie, Nickelodeon (1976), that captured some of the energy and excitement of the early film business, when movies could be seen for just five cents.

NIVEN, DAVID (1909–1983)   An urbane Scottish actor who specialized in playing light comedic and romantic leads in both Hollywood and England for more than forty-five years. Niven wasn't a formally trained actor like so many of his British colleagues, but he imparted a dashing enthusiasm to his roles that sufficed until he finally learned the tricks of the trade. Niven was not a terribly handsome man but he did have charm and a soothing upper-class accent that made him seem all the more sophisticated to American audiences.

He was born James David Graham Niven to a military family. He attended Sandhurst Military Academy, England's equivalent of West Point, and went on to serve in the Highland Light Infantry. Restless and adventurous, Niven left "the family business" of soldiering and began an around-the-world odyssey, working as a reporter, mercenary, bartender, and at a host of other jobs, whenever he needed money.

When he finally landed in Hollywood in 1934, Niven thought he'd pick up some pocket money working as an extra. And soon enough he could be glimpsed in such films as Mutiny on the Bounty (1935), Barbary Coast (1935), and Splendor (1935). His affair with actress Merle Oberon (q.v.) brought him into the right circle of powerful Hollywood producers and directors and he soon began moving up the cast list, making his breakthrough as Major Clyde Locket in Dodsworth (1936). He also gave winning supporting performances in the latter half of the 1930s in such action/adventure films as The Charge of the Light Brigade (1936), The Prisoner of Zenda (1937), and The Dawn Patrol (1938).

Holding his own with Laurence Olivier (q.v.) in Wuthering Heights (1939) and playing comedy in Bachelor Mother (1939), Niven was fast becoming a major star. But when war broke out in Europe, and England joined the fray, Niven quickly finished making Raffles (1940) and hurried back to Britain to join the war effort as a lieutenant in the Commandos (he was a colonel by war's end).

With the war over, Niven returned to acting and made one of his best films, the English production of Stairway to Heaven (1946). It was a hit in America, as well. Niven traveled back and forth between the two countries during the rest of his career. On the whole, he did not make a great many fine or memorable films, but he was always much in demand. His English films were particularly bland, the best of them being Court Martial (1955), Bonjour Tristesse (1958), and Prudence and the Pill (1968). He also made the James Bond spoof Casino Royale (1967) in England; it's worth noting that the suave Niven was Ian Fleming's first choice to play 007.

Niven's American films were variable. He had some early success after the war with films such as The Bishop's Wife (1947) and Enchantment (1948), but his career took a dip in the early 1950s. During that time he turned to television, joining with Dick Powell (q.v.) and others in the formation of Four Star Productions, a successful venture that later led to his starring in the TV shows "Four Star Playhouse" and "The David Niven Show."

By the mid-1950s, rather late in his career, Niven suddenly found himself with a burst of major movie hits that brought him to a new level of stardom. The big breakthrough was his playing of Phileas Fogg in the international blockbuster, Around the World in 80 Days (1956). He went on to win his one and only Best Actor Academy Award with his intelligent and subdued performance in Separate Tables (1958). And then he had the last of his major hits with Please Don't Eat the Daisies (1960) and The Guns of Navarone (1961).

Niven had his moments during the rest of the 1960s but his star was definitely fading. In the early 1970s he published his engaging memoirs The Moon's a Balloon (1971) and its sequel, Bring on the Empty Horses (1975), both of them best-sellers that brought him a new wave of celebrity.

Opportunities to act were still available to him but the roles were seldom good. He seemed in his element in the all-star film Death on the Nile (1978), but he was sadly out of place in films such as Old Dracula (1974), Better Late Than Never (1982), and Curse of the Pink Panther (1983), which was his last movie. He died before the final dialogue had been looped and his voice was dubbed by impressionist Rich Little.

NORMAND, MABEL (1894–1930)   She was the only female star equal in popularity as well as talent to such silent screen comedy giants as Chaplin, Keaton, Lloyd, and Arbuckle. Often working both ends of the camera

Mabel Normand was the leading comedienne of the silent era and a staple of Mack Sennett's Keystone stock company. Athletic, adventurous, and yet supremely feminine, she was enormously popular until she became a suspect in the 1922 murder of director William Desmond Taylor. Photo courtesy of The Siegel Collection.

as an actress/director, the pretty and lithesome Normand had considerable impact on early film comedy. Her career, however, was cut short by scandal and ill health.

Normand was introduced to show business by her father, who was a piano player on the vaudeville circuit. At the age of sixteen, she landed a job at the Biograph company. The studio was enjoying a renaissance under the stewardship of D. W. Griffith (q.v.), but it was the director Mack Sennett (q.v.) who took Normand under his wing.

Normand's first leading role was in *The Diving Girl* (1911). She became a star quickly thereafter, her name often included in her one-reel comedy titles, such as *Mabel's Adventures* (1911), *Mabel's Strategem* (1911), *Mabel's Heroes* (1912), and *Mabel's Awful Mistake* (1912).

When Sennett left Biograph to establish his Keystone Studio in 1912, Normand followed. She became one of his biggest stars, leading casts that included Charlie Chaplin, Ford Sterling, Fatty Arbuckle (qq.v.), and the rest of the Keystone company. She directed and codirected a number of her own films with excellent results.

Her comedy was very much in the Keystone tradition: enormously energetic and extremely slapstick. Like her comic contemporaries, she was as much an acrobat and gymnast as she was an actress. Her starring performance in Sennett's ambitious 1914 feature *Tillie's Punctured Romance* displayed her thespian skills, and

more feature-length movies were in store for her. But they didn't happen right away.

In the meantime, Normand and "Fatty" Arbuckle made a successful series of shorts as a rather mismatched husband and wife in films such as *Mabel and Fatty's Wash Day* (1915), *Mabel and Fatty's Simple Life* (1915), and *Fatty and Mabel Adrift* (1916).

Her popularity was such that Sennett (who nearly married Normand on several occasions) finally created The Mabel Normand Feature Film Company in 1916. She starred in *Mickey* that same year which inexplicably was not released until 1918. *Mickey* was a huge hit when it was finally presented to the public and it gave proof that Normand was a multitalented actress who could express a range of emotions. But by then Normand had already left Sennett's employ in frustration and had signed with the Samuel Goldwyn Company.

Though Normand made several successful features during the next few years, such as *Molly O* (1921), her wild personal life had already begun to interfere with her professional life. But it wasn't until 1922 when her lover, director William Desmond Taylor, was murdered that her career began to sputter seriously. She was a suspect in the highly publicized killing but was never charged with the crime. That scandal was followed by the murder of a prominent millionaire by Normand's chauffeur, who used a gun that the newspapers of the day claimed belonged to the actress. Audiences no longer laughed at Mabel Normand's screen antics after all that bad publicity and the comedienne no longer seemed to have her heart in her work.

She made a few more films, but the combination of her high living and a worsening case of tuberculosis finally caught up with her. She died of pneumonia at the age of thirty-six.

NOVAK, KIM (1933–) She was among the last of the studio-manufactured sex goddesses. An actress with an alluring combination of naiveté and smoky sensuality, Novak was one of the leading blonde bombshells of the 1950s, second only to Marilyn Monroe (q.v.). Novak was never a great actress, but she had a certain reserve that set her apart from the other buxom sex symbols of her time, such as Mamie Van Doren and Jayne Mansfield.

Born Marilyn Pauline Novak, she had no aspirations to become a movie star. She made some money as a model in her teens and later hit the road as Miss Deepfreeze, demonstrating refrigerators in a touring kitchen appliance show. Extremely shy and somewhat overweight as a young woman, she possessed a marvelous face that made her stand out from a crowd of extras in her first two screen appearances in RKO's *The French Line* (1954) and *Son of Sinbad* (1955).

A Columbia talent scout signed her up when his studio was in desperate need of a sexy female star. Rita

Kim Novak was one of the few Marilyn Monroe clones of the mid-1950s to become a legitimate star in her own right. Blonde and buxom, she learned to act on the job, developing a cool sensuality that suggested just the right touch of vulnerability. Photo courtesy of Kim Novak.

Hayworth *(q.v.)* was making trouble for Columbia, and Harry Cohn *(q.v.),* the studio's president, wanted to pull her into line by developing a new star capable of replacing her. In addition, Cohn had the opportunity of signing Marilyn Monroe and had turned her down. Six months later, when Monroe became a major star, Cohn was embarrassed and felt he needed to create his own version of Marilyn.

Novak lost weight, was turned into a blonde (her natural hair color was light brown), and was given acting lessons. More importantly, a publicity campaign was launched on her behalf and she made a big splash as a seductress in her first important role in *Pushover* (1954). The next few years were heady ones for Columbia's new star as she quickly rose through the ranks of female sex symbols in films such as *Phffft* (1954), *Five Against the House* (1955), and *The Man with the Golden Arm* (1955).

The best was yet to come. In 1956, she starred with William Holden *(q.v.)* in the smash hit *Picnic* and was subsequently voted the number-one box office draw of that year. Harry Cohn had succeeded beyond his wildest dreams.

Badly cast in *Jeanne Eagels* (1957) and *Pal Joey* (1957), Novak's career slowed down. But that didn't keep her

out of the headlines when rumors spread that she and black entertainer Sammy Davis, Jr. were romantically involved. In those years, the gossip was enough to destroy both of their careers. The furor died down after Davis married another woman (whom he quickly divorced).

In 1958 Novak rebounded with two of her best films, Hitchcock's classic *Vertigo* (1958) and the amusing *Bell, Book and Candle* (1958), both of them costaring James Stewart *(q.v.).*

Although often slammed by critics as being blonde and bland, Novak's performances in the majority of her films have held up very well. Movies such as *Strangers When We Meet* (1960), *Boy's Night Out* (1962), *The Notorious Landlady* (1962), *Kiss Me Stupid* (1964), and *The Amorous Adventures of Moll Flanders* (1965) attest to her sensual star power.

Unfortunately, Novak was never fully at ease in Hollywood and acted in fewer and fewer films during the early 1960s. In addition, she had become temperamental on the set of several productions, such as the ill-fated *Of Human Bondage* (1964). Finally, in 1965, Novak simply turned her back on Hollywood. She didn't make a film until she was wooed back to star in Robert Aldrich's *The Legend of Lylah Clare* (1968), an acerbic film that poked fun at Hollywood in general and sex goddesses in particular.

Married to Dr. Robert Malloy, Novak has subsequently built a life in Northern California surrounded by a veritable menagerie of her favorite animals. She has appeared in a small number of uninspired movies and TV series over the last two decades, usually in featured roles.

See also: sex symbols: female

NOVARRO, RAMON (1899–1968) An actor best known for his performance in the title role of *Ben Hur* (1926), he rivaled Rudolph Valentino *(q.v.)* as a Latin lover throughout the 1920s. But Novarro never aroused the same passion as did Valentino. Though Novarro's career spanned both the silent and sound eras, the period of his greatest popularity was from 1923 to 1929.

Born Ramon Samaniegos in Mexico, Novarro moved to Los Angeles as a teenager and eventually made a modest living as a singing waiter, breaking into the movie business as an extra in 1917. His first big chance came in 1922 when he starred in a minor film company's version of *The Rubaiyat of Omar Khayyam* (released in 1925 as *A Lover's Oath).* Director Rex Ingram saw the film in 1922, however, and he immediately signed Novarro to a contract at Metro (which later became part of Metro-Goldwyn-Mayer), turning him into a star.

After Valentino's incredible success in *The Sheik* (1921), Hollywood became full of Latin-lover types. But Novarro was one of the best, as he proved in *The Arab*

(1924). After Valentino's death in 1926, Novarro seemed poised to fill the void. And certainly after his great success in *Ben Hur* (1926), MGM seemed sure they had a major star on their hands.

It was not to be. His films through the rest of the silent era were money-makers but nothing on the order of Valentino's success. Clearly, MGM's expectations had been too high.

The sound revolution was less a factor in Novarro's decline than his acting skills. While his best role in the 1930s was the male lead in Greta Garbo's *Mata Hari* (1932), her assured performance exposed his weaker talents. Later, after a failed comeback attempt in the late 1930s, Novarro faded into obscurity. He appeared in small character roles a decade later, retired in 1950, and then graced the screen one last time in *Heller in Pink Tights* (1960).

The forgotton movie star made headlines one last time when he died. He was beaten to death by two young men, his naked body found in his ravaged apartment.

See also: Ben Hur

NUGENT, FRANK S. (1908–1965)   An influential film critic for *The New York Times* during the 1930s, he became a script doctor and screenwriter who had a long and impressive association with John Ford *(q.v.),* writing many of the director's most memorable films.

Mel Gussow's highly entertaining biography of Dar-ryl F. Zanuck, *Don't Say Yes Until I Finish Talking,* suggests that the Twentieth Century-Fox mogul hired Nugent away from the *Times* in 1940 at triple the critic's salary in order to keep him from constantly panning the studio's films. Nugent's job over the next four years included writing critiques of Fox's screenplays and a bit of script doctoring. Nugent, himself, was quoted as saying, "Zanuck told me he didn't want me to write . . . that he just thought the studio would save money if I criticized the pictures before they were made."

Nugent left Fox (and Zanuck) in 1944 to begin his screenwriting career in earnest, and most of his scripts were written for his father-in-law, John Ford. Nugent scripted a total of eleven Ford films, many translated into the director's best work, including *Fort Apache* (1948), *She Wore a Yellow Ribbon* (1949), *The Quiet Man* (1952), *The Searchers* (1956), and *The Last Hurrah* (1958).

Nugent was a careful craftsman, and his plotting was rich and intricate. But perhaps most importantly, he had a thorough understanding of his characters, who were both tough and vulnerable.

Nugent's screenplays for films that were not directed by John Ford were much less effective. He had a well-deserved reputation, however, as a screenwriter of westerns and his best non-Ford work is found in movies such as *The Tall Men* (1955) and *Gunman's Walk* (1958). Nugent's last film was also a western, *Incident at Phantom Hill* (1966), which was released after his death at fifty-seven.

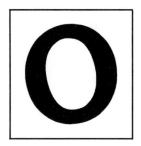

OAKIE, JACK (1903–1978) As a comic movie star and later as a supporting actor, Oakie made a career out of portraying good-natured oafs. The characters he played were usually dumb but friendly, and always falsely confident of their own supposed intelligence. With his chubby body, round face, and fast-talking style, Oakie was an amusing personality who found a congenial niche in the Hollywood of the 1930s and early 1940s. His comic speciality was the double take, which he eventually extended into a triple take to great comic effect.

Born Lewis Delaney Offield, the actor took his stage name from the term "Okie," used to describe someone from Oklahoma, where Offield spent most of his youth. After a stint as a clerk on Wall Street, Oakie became an actor, making his theatrical debut in the chorus of *Little Nellie Kelly* (1922). He honed his craft both on Broadway and in vaudeville until he arrived in Hollywood in 1928. But the rotund Oakie hardly looked like star material and he began his movie career in minor roles in films such as *Finders Keepers* (1928) and *The Fleet's In* (1928).

By the early 1930s, however, Oakie had become a comic leading man, sharing top billing with W. C. Fields *(q.v.)* in *Million Dollar Legs* (1932). Considering that he was in his thirties, it was somewhat surprising that Oakie starred in a rash of college movies such as *College Humor* (1933), *College Rhythm* (1934), and *Collegiate* (1936), just to name a few. But his best film of the decade was a dizzy romantic comedy called *Murder at the Vanities* (1934).

Jack Oakie reached the height of his career playing Benzini Napaloni in Charlie Chaplin's *The Great Dictator,* (1940). As the dictator of Bacteria, Oakie did an hysterical takeoff of Mussolini. The role won him an Oscar nomination for Best Supporting Actor and it is the one for which Oakie is still best remembered.

Oakie was popular in the early 1940s but his career began to wind down after World War II. During the decade he played mostly small comic parts. He retired in 1951 only to return for brief appearances in a handful of movies, the last being *Lover Come Back* (1962).

OBERON, MERLE (1911–1979) A mysterious and beautiful actress who starred in a great many British and American movies, particularly during the late 1930s and the early 1940s. Oberon's regal bearing and dark beauty were greater assets than her acting skill, but she had such a striking appearance on screen that her limited ability as an actress was often overlooked.

Born Estelle Merle O'Brien Thompson to an Indian mother and an Indo-Irish father, she kept her background a secret, claiming, instead that she was born in Tasmania and raised in India. With little hope of a secure future in India and being beautiful and ambitious, she decided to make a new life for herself in England, where she arrived at the age of seventeen.

Oberon was known as Queenie O'Brien during her early years in England, a name remembered by author Michael Korda who wrote a novel based on her life called *Queenie,* which was later turned into a TV mini-series in 1987. Young Michael Korda knew Oberon because she had become first the protégée and then the wife (from 1939–1945) of his uncle, famed producer Sir Alexander Korda.

Oberon was twenty years old when she made her first tentative appearance on film in *Alf's Button* (1930). She continued receiving bit parts until late 1932, when Alexander Korda first spotted her and recognized her cinematic potential. He made her into a star by casting her in increasingly larger roles in such important British films as *The Private Life of Henry VIII* (1933), in which she played Anne Boleyn, *Thunder in the East* (1934),

The Private Life of Don Juan (1934), and *The Scarlet Pimpernel* (1935).

In order to propel her into the lucrative U.S. market, Korda sold half of his Oberon contract to Samuel Goldwyn in 1935. The actress shuttled back and forth between London and Hollywood making some of her best films during the late 1930s, particularly *The Divorce of Lady X* (1938), *The Cowboy and the Lady* (1938), and *Wuthering Heights* (1939).

She continued to be in vogue during the 1940s but appeared in films of lesser quality as the decade wore on until finally she lost her audience. Oberon's best films of the 1940s were *That Uncertain Feeling* (1941), *The Lodger* (1944), and *A Song to Remember* (1945). She married the famous cinematographer Lucien Ballard in 1945 (the were divorced in 1949), but his talents were of little help to her. She began appearing in films less frequently during the late 1940s and her Hollywood career all but ended in the 1950s.

Oberon made the occasional cameo appearance during the 1960s in films such as *The Oscar* (1966) and *Hotel* (1967), but was essentially living in semiretirement with her third husband, Bruno Pagliai, a rich Italian businessman. When that marriage ended in 1973, she produced, coedited, and starred in her own film, *Interval* (1973). It was not remarkable except for the fact that it costarred Robert Wolders, her future husband. It was her last film.

O'BRIEN, MARGARET (1937–   ) She was the ultimate child actress, a pig-tailed, freckle-faced charmer. Unlike Shirley Temple *(q.v.),* she did not sing or dance, but many film scholars and critics consider her the most gifted of all the Hollywood child actors because she seemed completely natural on screen.

Born Angela Maxine O'Brien, she was the daughter of a former dancer. Discovered and signed by MGM when her face was seen on the cover of a local magazine (she had been a child model since the age of three), she made her first film appearance at four years of age in *Babes on Broadway* (1941). Soon after, she changed her name to that of the title character she played in *Journey for Margaret* (1942).

O'Brien worked steadily throughout the 1940s, having her greatest success as the star of *Lost Angel* (1943) and in compelling supporting roles in *Jane Eyre* (1944), *The Canterville Ghost* (1944), and *Meet Me in St. Louis* (1944). Her work was such that the Academy of Motion Picture Arts and Sciences honored her with a special Oscar as the outstanding child actress of 1944.

While child actors often acted in secondary roles, O'Brien's box office pull garnered her leading roles in films such as *Our Vines Have Tender Grapes* (1945), *Bad Bascomb* (1946), and *Tenth Avenue Angel* (1947). After the age of ten, she began losing her appeal, but her acting was no less superb in the performance she gave

Margaret O'Brien was a natural child actress who was equally adept at drama and comedy. If there was a competition for the greatest of all child performers, O'Brien would certainly be among the finalists. Photo courtesy of Movie Star News.

in *Little Women* (1949). In an attempt to break into adolescent roles, she received her first big screen kiss in *Her First Romance* (1951), but audiences didn't want little Margaret O'Brien to grow up and the film was not a success.

A 1956 comeback attempt in a movie called *Glory* was a failure. O'Brien has made rare appearances in films since, including *Heller in Pink Tights* (1960), the Peruvian-made *Annabelle Lee* (1972), and TV movies. *See also:* child stars

O'BRIEN, PAT (1899–1983)   An actor who overcame plain features to become a minor star with frequent leading roles in the 1930s and 1940s, O'Brien's ace in the hole was a warm and sincere countenance that endeared him to audiences even when he played unlikeable characters. O'Brien was usually cast as a fast-talking, tough, yet ultimately good-natured, Irishman in a film career that spanned nearly fifty years. Though he went to school, to war, and into the theater alongside his childhood pal Spencer Tracy *(q.v.),* O'Brien's movie career has been forever linked with that of a later close friend, James Cagney *(q.v.),* with whom he was very often paired in Warner Bros. films of the 1930s.

Born William Joseph Patrick O'Brien, the future actor began his show business career as a hoofer. Except for a single role in a silent Western called *Shadows of the West* (1921), O'Brien's acting was restricted to the stage. With the introduction of sound films, however, he was summoned once more to do movies, appearing as early as 1929 in *Fury of the Wild*.

Fame and fortune in Hollywood were never a sure thing, even for trained stage actors with suitable voices. O'Brien proved his mettle, however, when he played the fast-talking reporter in the first film version of the Hecht and MacArthur stage hit *The Front Page* (1931).

His ability to deliver his dialogue in a rapid-fire manner was put to constant use when he was later teamed with Jimmy Cagney in such films as *Devil Dogs of the Air* (1935), *The Irish in Us* (1935), *Ceiling Zero* (1936), *Boy Meets Girl* (1938), *The Fighting 69th* (1940), and *Torrid Zone* (1940). Their most famous film together, however, was *Angels with Dirty Faces* (1938), in which O'Brien plays a priest who is a childhood friend of Cagney's criminal. In this film, as well as all the others, there was an undeniable chemistry between the two stars that is as visible today as it was in the 1930s.

Of course, O'Brien didn't always play in support of Cagney. He also carried plenty of his own movies, such as, *Oil for the Lamps of China* (1935), *Knute Rockne, All American* (1940), in which he played his most famous role as the title character, and *Fighting Father Dunne* (1948) among many others.

O'Brien began to assume smaller character roles during the 1950s, having a notable turn in John Ford's wonderful *The Last Hurrah* (1958), in which he also had the opportunity to act with his old friend Spencer Tracy. In 1960 O'Brien starred in the TV series "Harrigan and Son." He appeared in only a few films thereafter. His last movie role was a minor one in the Burt Reynolds comedy *The End* (1978).

O'CONNOR, DONALD (1925–) A cheerful, exuberant performer who made the transition from child actor to adult star. He was at his best as a musical comedy entertainer but was rarely given the kind of material that would have allowed him to properly show off his talents. Except for his strong supporting singing and dancing role in *Singin' in the Rain* (1952), O'Connor's reputation rests on his charming light comedy work in the Francis, the Talking Mule series during the 1950s.

Born into a family of circus performers, O'Connor was no stranger to show business. He joined his parents and siblings when they began working in vaudeville, and by the tender age of eleven had made his film debut in *Melody for Two* (1937). Except for a short return to vaudeville during the early 1940s, O'Connor worked steadily in the movies until the late 1950s.

O'Connor was not a star as a child actor, but he had his moments in such films as *Sing You Sinners* (1938), *Tom Sawyer—Detective* (1938), in which he played Huck Finn, and *Boy Trouble* (1939). During the early 1940s, when musicals were not terribly popular, he starred in

a number of low-budget films that featured his singing and dancing; few were well received. Nonetheless, they include a number of small, if flawed, gems such as *Mister Big* (1943), *Chip Off the Old Block* (1944), and *Patrick the Great* (1945).

During the latter half of the 1940s, O'Connor's career began a slow decline that ended when he was cast as the human lead playing opposite a talking mule in *Francis* (1950), a low-budget, nonmusical movie that caught fire at the box office. Suddenly, O'Connor was a hot actor again, and he starred in five more of the six Francis films during the early and mid-1950s (Mickey Rooney starred in the final movie in the series). Between his Francis films, O'Connor appeared in one of Hollywood's greatest musicals, *Singin' in the Rain*, creating a lasting impression with the classic number "Make 'em Laugh." He also starred in several other musicals, including *Call Me Madam*, (1953), *Walkin' My Baby Back Home* (1953), and *There's No Business Like Show Business* (1954).

He landed the title role in *The Buster Keaton Story* (1957), but the film was a critical and commercial disappointment. In retrospect, O'Connor was much too upbeat an actor to play The Great Stoneface. In any event, by the late 1950s his movie career had virtually come to an end. He pursued work as a composer and made only a handful of film appearances, *That Funny Feeling* (1965) and *Ragtime* (1981) among them. In more recent years, he has taken to the nighclub and dinner theater circuit.

O'HARA, MAUREEN (1920–) A statuesque actress discovered by Charles Laughton and prominently featured in many of John Ford's films, O'Hara, beautiful but somewhat aloof, had a strong screen presence that overshadowed a modest talent.

Born Maureen Fitzsimmons in Ireland, she worked in show business from an early age, performing in radio programs as well as on stage. She received formal training as an actress at the Abbey School in Dublin. It was her good looks, however, rather than her budding talent, that attracted film producers. She made her movie debut at the age of eighteen in a minor role in *Kicking the Moon Around* (1938). Not long after, Charles Laughton *(q.v.)* took notice of her and, with his partner Erich Pommer, signed her to a contract.

She starred with Laughton in Alfred Hitchcock's *Jamaica Inn* (1939) and then was brought to Hollywood to costar with him again in the classic film rendition of *The Hunchback of Notre Dame* (1939). It was Laughton's movie, but her sultry, conniving, yet innocent portrayal of Esmeralda, the fiery beauty who is Quasimodo's devotion, was eminently convincing. She was to work with Laughton only once more, in the truly affecting Jean Renoir movie *This Land is Mine* (1943).

Hollywood had claimed O'Hara, but during her early

years the studios didn't know quite what to do with her. She made several mediocre films before finally being cast as Angaharad Morgan in John Ford's evocative *How Green Was My Valley* (1941). Ford, unlike most directors, was capable of bringing out O'Hara's warmth. Later, she became a member of Ford's stock company and her alluring presence graced such films as *Rio Grande* (1950), *The Quiet Man* (1952), *The Long Gray Line* (1955), and *The Wings of Eagles* (1957).

Her specialty, however, was playing exotic beauties, bringing her striking good looks and bright red hair to bear in such escapist fare as *The Spanish Main* (1945), *Sinbad the Sailor* (1947), *Bagdad* (1949), *Tripoli* (1950), *Flame of Araby* (1951), *The Red Head From Wyoming* (1953), and *Lady Godiva* (1955), to name just a few.

O'Hara settled into more matronly roles in the 1960s, starring in such films as *The Parent Trap* (1961), *Mr. Hobbs Takes a Vacation* (1962), *Spencer's Mountain* (1963), and *McLintock!* (1963). Good roles were few and far between for O'Hara during the ensuing years and she appeared in only a handful of films, most notably *The Rare Breed* (1966). Her last theatrical film was the John Wayne vehicle, *Big Jake* (1971).

OLIVIER, LORD LAURENCE (1907–1989) An actor whom many consider to be the greatest in the English-speaking world during the twentieth century. Though Olivier was based mostly in England, he made a significant number of Hollywood films. He was nominated for Academy Awards as an actor, producer, or director twelve times, winning twice, while also being honored with two special Oscars. In his long and varied career, Olivier appeared in more than one hundred twenty stage roles, nearly sixty films, and more than fifteen television productions. He directed and produced thirty-eight stage productions, directed six films, and six plays for television.

Son of a clergyman, he was well educated, and introduced to the arts at an early age. He made his acting debut at the age of fifteen at the all-boys All Saints Choir School, Marleybone, playing Katharine in *The Taming of the Shrew*. He continued playing Shakespearean and other classical roles while in training, first at St. Edwards School, Oxford, then at the Central School of Speech Training and Drama.

Olivier's next big step was joining The Birmingham Repertory Company in 1926; the experience he gained there led to his movie debut in 1930 in *The Temporary Widow*. Olivier had also acted on Broadway in 1929 and was not unknown to the American film industry, which was just then raiding Broadway for potential "talkie" film stars. He had his chance at early Hollywood stardom when he played the lead in *Yellow Ticket* (1931). Olivier made more films in America in the early 1930s, but he was as yet just another actor whose appeal and talent had not been recognized. The final indignity

occurred when he was replaced by John Gilbert (*q.v.*) in the Greta Garbo (*q.v.*) vehicle *Queen Christina* (1933).

Olivier returned to England and finally broke through as a Shakespearean actor and film star in his homeland during the mid- to late 1930s. By the time he made *Fire Over England* (1937) he was a hot commodity, made even hotter by his well-publicized affair with his costar, the beautiful and talented young Vivien Leigh (*q.v.*). Tongues wagged wilder than usual because both Olivier and Leigh were married to other spouses at the time. They later freed themselves in order to marry, a union that lasted from 1940 to 1960.

As a sought-after actor, Olivier heeded the clarion call to Hollywood a second time, but this go around was considerably more successful. He starred as Heathcliff in the scintillating romance, *Wuthering Heights* (1939), based on the Brontë novel, and became an international matinee idol. He followed that hit with several others, including *Rebecca* (1940), *Pride and Prejudice* (1940), and *That Hamilton Woman* (1941).

During World War II, Olivier returned to England and took up active service in the Fleet Air Arm of the Royal Navy. He also made some propaganda films during the war.

When he was discharged from the service in 1944, Olivier began his most productive period, producing, directing, and starring in a film version of *Henry V* (1944). The movie displayed stunning innovations and resulted in Olivier's being honored with a special Academy Award for his achievement. (Foreign films were not at that time eligible for Academy Award consideration.) Later, Olivier went on to produce, direct, and star in *Hamlet* (1948), and was nominated by the Academy of Motion Picture Arts and Sciences in all three categories, winning in two, Best Film and Best Actor. Among his other directorial achievements have been *Richard III* (1956), *The Prince and the Showgirl* (1958), and *Three Sisters* (1979).

During the 1950s, Olivier worked on the stage a great deal, often with Vivien Leigh, and did not make a great many movies. What movies he did make were more often British than American productions. Among his better Hollywood entries were *Carrie* (1952) and *The Devil's Disciple* (1958). His later noteworthy films include *The Entertainer* (1960), *Uncle Vanya* (1963), *Othello* (1965), *Oh! What a Lovely War* (1969), *Sleuth* (1972), *The Seven Percent Solution* (1976), *Marathon Man* (1976), *The Boys from Brazil* (1978), *A Little Romance* (1979), *The Jigsaw Man* (1984). No matter what country has produced his films, Olivier remains an international star whose talent belongs to all nations.

Burdened by ill health for more than a decade, Olivier fought cancer and other ailments working at a furious pace in his old age. He was knighted in 1947 and in 1970 he was made a life peer, Baron Olivier of Brighton, for services to the theater, which allowed him to sit in the House of Lords. If that wasn't enough, in 1981 he was given the Order of Merit. In America, the Academy of Motion Picture Arts and Sciences bestowed its version of knighthood and peerage on "Lord Larry," awarding him a special Oscar "for the full body of his work, the unique achievement of his entire career and his lifetime of contribution to the art of the film."

OLSEN & JOHNSON
See comedy teams.

OPERETTAS   *See* musicals

OUR GANG   For twenty-two years, from 1922 to 1944, a small, ever-changing group of children were part of this charming and very funny comedy team. Clearly inspired by the unprecedented public interest in Jackie Coogan after his winning performance in Charlie Chaplin's *The Kid* (1921), Hal Roach *(q.v.)* put together a group of children and began filming one-reel comedies that detailed their antics.

The children were chosen by Roach based on their physical appearance rather than their acting ability. Among the first child actors in Our Gang were Joe Cobb, Mary Kornman, Mickey Daniels, Jackie David, Jackie Condon, and Allen Clayton Hoskins. Yapping at their heels was Pete, the dog with the painted black circle around his right eye.

It's worth noting that the inclusion of a black child (Hoskins, who played Farina), who mixed freely on screen with his white friends, raised few racist protests. Though Hoskins and his later counterparts, Mathew "Stymie" Beard and "Buckwheat" Thomas, were presented in stereotypical fashion, they were allowed to show more range than any other black actors in commercial vehicles during the three decades of the series' existence.

Very little happened in an Our Gang comedy short; the appeal of the films was based on the idiosyncracies of the characters rather than gags or elaborate chases. Cast changes (as kids grew too old to be cute), however, helped reinvigorate the series.

After sound arrived, new cast members were added, including child actors Jackie Cooper and Dickie Moore, who would later become major stars in their own right. Cooper and Moore didn't stay with the group for very long, unlike George Emmett "Spanky" McFarland, Carl "Alfalfa" Switzer, and Darla Hood. These last three cast members, along with "Stymie," formed the nucleus of the group during its golden period in the 1930s.

In 1936, an Our Gang comedy, *Bored of Education,* won an Academy Award for Best Short. Roach decided to capitalize on the group's popularity by making their one and only feature film that same year, *General Spanky.*

The Our Gang comedies had been distributed by MGM, and in 1938, Hal Roach sold the series to his distributor. MGM churned out the shorts for another six years before finally laying the series to rest.

But Our Gang returned in 1955 when Roach sold 100 of his pre-1938 sound shorts to TV, introducing the kids to a new generation of viewers as "The Little Rascals" (because MGM still held the rights to the "Our Gang" name).

PACINO, AL (1939–) An intense and exciting actor who attained stardom during the 1970s. Dark and thin, with a fiery temperament, Pacino was nominated for an Oscar four years in a row but never won the coveted statuette. Though he didn't have a hit film in more than a decade, Pacino's talent is such that he is still considered a major star.

Born to a lower-middle-class Sicilian-American family, Pacino was abandoned by his father at the age of two. Displaying an early aptitude for acting, he was admitted to New York's High School of Performing Arts but quit at the age of seventeen to try and break into the theater—with little initial success. The actor made his living doing odd jobs while studying his craft at the Herbert Berghof acting school and, later, at the Actors Studio.

Pacino's career began slowly with minor roles in little-known plays. In 1968 he had a breakthrough, winning an Obie (Off-Broadway) Award for his lead performance in *The Indian Wants the Bronx.* The following year he starred on Broadway and won a Tony Award for *Does a Tiger Wear a Necktie?*

On the strength of his theater credentials, Pacino was given a small role in the Patty Duke vehicle, *Me, Natalie* (1969), making a rather inauspicious film debut. Two years later he had the lead role in the small, low-budget *Panic in Needle Park* (1971) and won critical raves. The film, however, was not much of a commercial success. Nonetheless, director Francis Ford Coppola *(q.v.)* had seen the film and chose Pacino to play the role of Michael Corleone in his upcoming *The Godfather* (1972). This greatest of gangster films was originally intended as a low-budget movie, but when the Mario Puzo book upon which it was based became a mega-best-seller, the budget doubled and the film took on new impor-

tance—as did the casting of Michael Corleone. The studio (Paramount) wasn't enthusiastic about the unknown Pacino, but Coppola insisted on keeping him and the director had his way. As a result, Pacino's brooding, intelligent performance in the huge hit turned him into a star overnight and brought him an Oscar nomination for Best Supporting Actor.

Pacino never seriously faltered throughout the rest of the 1970s, scoring either critical or commercial successes (or both) in *Scarecrow* (1973), *Serpico* (1973), for which he received a Best Actor Oscar nomination, *The Godfather, Part II* (1974), for which he received another Best Actor nomination, *Dog Day Afternoon* (1975), culminating in a third Best Actor Academy Award nomination, *Bobby Deerfield* (1977), which was, perhaps, his weakest film of the decade and . . . *And Justice for All* (1979), which was the last hit he would have for a very long time.

Pacino's first film of the 1980s was the controversial *Cruising* (1980), a movie about gay life in New York City that was blasted by the critics and avoided by filmgoers. *Author! Author!* (1982) garnered the actor better reviews but was a small, sentimental movie that was not well attended. His next film, Brian De Palma's remake of *Scarface* (1983), got lots of attention—mostly negative. There was a virtual tidal wave of criticism against the film's violence, and Pacino's riveting performance in the title role was generally overlooked amid a storm of controversy. The failure of *Scarface* was nothing compared to the big-budget disaster *Revolution* (1985). Pacino's voice and acting style did not lend themselves to the portrayal of an 18th century American. The actor took much of the criticism for this badly scripted and poorly done epic. He was little seen until he made his comeback movie, *Sea of Love* (1989).

See also: The Godfather I & II

PAGE, GERALDINE (1924–1987) An actress who has often played vulnerable, eccentric women, Miss Page's riveting screen performances in a relatively modest number of films brought her a staggering eight Academy Award nominations and one Best Actress Oscar. Essentially a character actress for most of her film career, she assumed an impressive variety of roles in everything from Clint Eastwood films to Woody Allen dramas.

The daughter of a doctor, Miss Page was determined to become an actress, beginning her quest at the age of seventeen by working in stock. A modest reputation in the theater led to her movie debut in the forgettable *Out of the Night* (1947). She returned to the stage and eventually achieved theatrical stardom with her critically acclaimed Off-Broadway performance in Tennessee Williams' *Summer and Smoke* in 1952.

Thanks to her newfound celebrity as a stage actress, she was invited back to Hollywood and starred in two films, *Taxi* (1953) and the John Wayne hit *Hondo* (1953), garnering the first of her Academy Award nominations for the latter, this one for Best Supporting Actress. Despite the nomination, Miss Page was not immediately enamored of the movie business and, instead, pursued her stage career. She didn't return to the movies until she reprised her role in *Summer and Smoke* in a film version of the play in 1961, gaining her second Oscar nomination, this time in the Best Actress category. It was at this point that she began acting in the movies on a semi-regular basis.

Appearing in character roles, Miss Page also gained Oscar nominations for Best Supporting Actress for her work in *You're a Big Boy Now* (1967), *Pete 'n' Tillie* (1972), and *The Pope of Greenwich Village* (1984). Her additional Best Actress Oscar-nominated performances were for *Sweet Bird of Youth* (1962), *Interiors* (1978), and *The Trip to Bountiful* (1985), the latter film finally bringing her a much-deserved Oscar for her portrayal of a crotchety old lady who simply has to see her old home again before she dies.

Altogether, Page appeared in less than twenty-five films. Among those relatively rare performances for which she was not nominated were ones in *Toys in the Attic* (1963), *The Happiest Millionaire* (1967), *What Ever Happened to Aunt Alice?* (1969), *The Beguiled* (1971), *J.W. Coop* (1972), *Day of the Locust* (1975), *Nasty Habits* (1976), *The Three Sisters* (1977), *Honky Tonk Freeway* (1981), and *I'm Dancing as Fast As I Can* (1982).

Miss Page also worked in television, winning two Emmys, but was most devoted to the theater throughout her career, as evidenced by her election to the Theater Hall of Fame. She was long married to her second husband, the noted stage, screen, and TV actor Rip Torn.

PAKULA, ALAN J. (1928–) A highly successful producer/director who makes films about social and political issues. He has displayed a unique visual style that uses architecture to conjure up feelings of impending doom and terror in his audience.

Pakula was interested in show business from a very early age. After graduating from Yale School of Drama, he went to Hollywood and gained a foothold in the industry with a low-level job at Warners' cartoon factory in 1949. By 1951 he was working at Paramount in the production department, learning the technical aspects of moviemaking. Pakula was being groomed as a future producer and he fulfilled his promise by producing his first film in 1957, the Jimmy Piersall baseball biopic *Fear Strikes Out*.

Later, Pakula formed a production company in association with director Robert Mulligan. Together, they collaborated on six films with Pakula producing and Mulligan directing. Their very first venture was the critical and box office smash hit *To Kill a Mockingbird* (1962). It was followed by *Love with the Proper Stranger* (1963), *Baby, the Rain Must Fall* (1965), *Inside Daisy Clover* (1965), *Up the Down Staircase* (1967), and *The Stalking Moon* (1969).

A proven success as a producer, Pakula decided in 1969 to try his hand at directing his own production of *The Sterile Cuckoo*. The film, which gave Liza Minnelli her first starring role, was a modest success. He followed it with a major hit, producing and directing the thriller *Klute* (1971), the first of his atmospheric, visually ominous movies.

His ability to render an oppressive physical reality on film was even more evident in *The Parallax View* (1974), a stark depiction of political corruption and manipulation that Pakula also produced. Despite the fact that *The Parallax View* failed at the box office, Pakula was clearly the perfect director for the big-budget movie version of Robert Woodward and Carl Bernstein's book *All the President's Men* (1976). In this case, the air of paranoia heightened by the director's visual flair seemed perfectly in keeping with the realities of the Watergate coverup that it depicted. A sense of fear and tension was maintained throughout the movie thanks to his direction, which was honored with a Best Director Oscar nomination.

Pakula has continued to make films that place his characters in a harsh and often overwhelming world of deceit, violence, and apprehension. Whether in the old West, as in *Comes a Horseman,* the world of high finance, as in *Rollover* (1981), or in the minds of those crippled by the cruel forces of society, as in *Sophie's Choice* (1982) and *Orphans* (1987), Pakula has expressed a deeply felt empathy for his seemingly doomed heroes who struggle against the dark.

Happily, Pakula hasn't been relentlessly somber in his concerns. He has also demonstrated a fine sense of humor, producing and directing a couple of witty and biting love stories, *Love and Pain and the Whole Damned Thing* (1973), *Starting Over* (1979), and *See You in the Morning* (1989).

PAN, HERMES (1910–) One of Hollywood's greatest dance directors, he enjoyed a long and fruitful collaboration with Fred Astaire *(q.v.)*. Pan also created imaginative dance routines for Betty Grable *(q.v.)* in her most enjoyable movies of the 1940s, as well as for many of Hollywood's big-budget musicals of the 1950s and early 1960s.

Born Hermes Panagiotopulos in Tennessee, Pan was an assistant dance director at RKO when he helped Astaire work out his dance numbers in his first film, *Flying Down to Rio* (1933). The two not only became fast friends but partners, with Pan intimately involved in the choreography of the majority of Astaire's greatest dance numbers in many of his films, including all of the Astaire/Rogers movies. He won an Oscar for his work on *A Damsel in Distress* (1937) as well as for later Astaire films such as *Blue Skies* (1946), *Silk Stockings* (1957), and *Finian's Rainbow* (1968).

His choreography for Betty Grable in films such as *Coney Island* (1943) and *Sweet Rosie O'Grady* (1943) took advantage of the star's legs without overtaxing her talents.

If one looks closely, Pan can be seen dancing in a number of films, including *Moon Over Miami* (1941), *My Gal Sal* (1942), and *Pin Up Girl* (1944). He's the one with an uncanny resemblance to Fred Astaire.

Pan was superb at choreographing intimate dance numbers, but he showed surprising versatility late in his career when, in the late 1950s, he created lavish production numbers for *Porgy and Bess* (1959), *Can-Can* (1960), and *Flower Drum Song* (1961). Pan continued to choreograph into the 1970s, bringing his talents to *Darling Lili* (1970) and the musical remake of *Lost Horizon* (1973).

Considering how much popular dance had changed in his forty years of choreographing and directing dance numbers, Pan's longevity in Hollywood is particularly astonishing.

See also: choreographer

PARAMOUNT PICTURES A film studio whose ancestry goes back further than that of any other presently active movie company. Its roots were in Adolph Zukor's Famous Players *(qq.v.)* company, founded in 1912. With the success of Mary Pickford *(q.v.)*, its biggest star in 1913, the company was off and running. Paramount was founded in 1914 by William H. Hodkinson

as a distribution company. Famous Players and Jesse L. Lasky Production Company supplied films to Paramount for distribution and, in 1916, the three companies merged with Zukor at the head of the organization, then called Famous Players-Lasky. In 1925, the name changed to Paramount-Famous-Lasky. Among the company's greatest creative assets during the silent era were actors Gloria Swanson, John Barrymore, Pola Negri, and Rudolph Valentino *(qq.v.)*. Among their important directors were Cecil B. DeMille and Ernst Lubitsch *(qq.v.)*.

During the 1920s the company went on a buying spree, purchasing theaters all over the country, particularly in the South, New England, Canada, and the upper Midwest. In an effort to create brandname identification, many of the showcase theaters in the larger cities were renamed "Paramount," leading to the eventual change of the corporate name to Paramount Publix Corporation in 1930.

The transition to sound did not prove to be a problem for the then most powerful of all the film companies. The Great Depression, however, was another story. Because of the company's huge investment in its theater chain (it owned more than 1,200 theaters in 1930), the debt service on those theaters became unmanageable when audiences no longer attended movies in the same numbers they had during the 1920s. Revenues fell sharply and the company went into receivership in 1933, reorganizing itself and emerging from bankruptcy as Paramount Pictures, Inc. in 1935.

Yet Paramount was one of the most interesting film companies during its most troubled years because in its financial panic, it was willing to try most anything to get people into its theaters. For instance, Paramount brought the Marx Brothers and Mae West *(qq.v.)* to the screen, hoping they would catch fire. In addition, Paramount hired Josef von Sternberg *(q.v.)*, who made the most visually sensual movies of the early 1930s and a star of Marlene Dietrich *(q.v.)*. Other directors, such as Rouben Mamoulian *(q.v.)* were given the opportunity, amid all the financial confusion, to experiment and develop the art of the sound film.

Paramount had been a rudderless company during the early 1930s. At one point, while in receivership, director Ernst Lubitsch was briefly put in charge of production. It was one of the rare moments in film history when a creative person, rather than a businessman, held such a position. In 1936, Barney Balaban took over the studio reins and, with Y. Frank Freeman soon coming in to oversee film production, Paramount finally began to stabilize and prosper.

Unlike most other film companies, Paramount created few stars, rather it followed the original concept of Famous Players and took stars from other mediums, such as radio, recording, and vaudeville, and put them into the movies. It worked. Entertainers such as Maurice Chevalier *(q.v.)*, the Marx Brothers, and Mae West, as well as Bing Crosby, Bob Hope, and Martin & Lewis *(qq.v.)*, were already famous in their respective arenas before Paramount put their names on movie marquees. One of the few Paramount stars who hadn't been plucked from another medium was Gary Cooper *(q.v.)*, and the studio eventually lost his services because they didn't know how to best take advantage of his talents.

Just as important as the stars they held under contract, the studio fostered talented directors such as Cecil B. DeMille, who made most of his hits during the silent and sound eras for the studio, as well as directors Leo McCarey *(q.v.)*, Mitchell Leisen, Preston Sturges *(q.v.)*, and Billy Wilder *(q.v.)*.

Under the leadership of Balaban and Freeman, Paramount became one of the most profitable of the "Big Five" film companies in the 1940s and 1950s. Virtually all the film studios made money during the 1940s, but Paramount was the leader thanks, in part, to its continued ownership of a great many movie theaters, as well as the phenomenal success of the Crosby/Hope Road movies. The studio continued to be successful during the 1950s thanks to the success of the Martin & Lewis films and blockbuster hits such as *Shane* (1953), *Stalag 17* (1953), and *The Ten Commandments* (1956), to name just a few.

The company fell on hard times, just as other film studios did, in the late 1950s and early 1960s. Paramount was purchased by Gulf & Western in 1967, and has subsequently become, yet again, one of the most profitable of all the film companies, with hits during the 1970s such as *Grease* (1978), and in the 1980s with the Indiana Jones films and its ownership of properties such as *Star Trek*.

PARSONS, LOUELLA
See gossip columnists

PATSY AWARDS
The "Academy Awards" for animals, the name being an acronym for Picture Animal Top Star of the Year. The award for best animal performance in a film has been given every year since 1951. Television animal stars were later included in 1958. The awards might appear to be a publicist's joke, but the Patsys are actually given by the American Humane Association. The first winner of the Patsy Award was Francis the (talking) mule. All forms of animal life have been winners in the ensuing years, from jungle cats to fish. Dogs, however, have been the perennial big winners.
See also: animals in film

PECK, GREGORY
(1916–) He has starred in more than fifty movies in a film career spanning five decades. Tall, lean, and handsome, Peck is often compared to

Gregory Peck's image of moral rectitude has been gained through performances in such films as *Gentlemen's Agreement* (1947), *Captain Horatio Hornblower* (1951), and *To Kill a Mockingbird* (1962). Ironically, he originally came to the movies as a heartthrob. Photo courtesy of Gregory Peck.

Gary Cooper *(q.v.)*, and, with his strong image of integrity and dignity, Henry Fonda *(q.v.)*. Curiously, Peck's screen persona is more brittle than that of either actor, yet his distance, his aloofness, coupled with his deep, authoritative voice, gives him a bigger-than-life quality well suited to many of the heroic roles he's assumed.

Born Eldred Gregory Peck in La Jolla, California, the young man was a pre-med student and athlete before a spinal injury left him temporarily paralyzed. During his recovery, he turned to the theater and was encouraged to become an actor. Armed with a letter of introduction to a business friend of his stepfather's, he set out for Broadway in 1939. The letter got him a job—as a barker at a concession in the amusement zone at the New York World's Fair. Later he became a guide at Radio City Music Hall. Meanwhile, Peck won an audition for a scholarship at the respected Neighborhood Playhouse School of Dramatics. He cut his actor's teeth on a road tour of *The Doctor's Dilemma*, getting his big break when he was signed for the Broadway production of *Morning Star* in 1942.

He worked on Broadway throughout the early 1940s until he was hired to star in his first movie, *Days of Glory* (1944). The film was a flop, but critics singled him out for praise and his career took off with his second film, *The Keys of the Kingdom* (1944), for which he won an Oscar nomination for Best Actor.

Peck had the good fortune of working with a great many of Hollywood's leading directors, starring in such films as Alfred Hitchcock's *Spellbound* (1945), Clarence Brown's *The Yearling* (1946), which brought him his second Academy nomination for Best Actor, and Elia Kazan's *Gentlemen's Agreement* (1947), for which he received yet another Oscar nomination. It was a heady time for the young actor, especially when he was paired with Jennifer Jones *(q.v.)* in the David O. Selznick *(q.v.)* production of *Duel in the Sun* (1946), an epic western directed by King Vidor *(q.v.)*. Virtually over-night, Peck had become one of Hollywood's most versatile leading men, having the best of both worlds as a matinee idol and serious dramatic actor.

Of all the directors Peck worked with, the one with whom he is most closely associated is Henry King *(q.v.)*, who guided the actor through many of his biggest critical and commercial hits, including *Twelve O'Clock High* (1949), which brought him his fourth Oscar nomination, and the highly praised psychological western, *The Gunfighter* (1950).

Peck developed a reputation as a western star thanks to his roles in *Duel in the Sun, The Gunfighter,* and other horse operas such as *Yellow Sky* (1948) and *Only the Valient* (1951). In one of his rare career mistakes, the actor turned down the lead role in *High Noon* because he feared he was getting typed as a cowboy star. Gary Cooper took the role and won an Oscar.

Throughout the 1950s, Peck continued to work with primarily top-flight directors, often in challenging films. Among his most ambitious movies were Raoul Walsh's lively version of *Captain Horatio Hornblower* (1951), Henry King's adaptation of Hemingway's *The Snows of Kilimanjaro* (1952), William Wyler's *Roman Holiday* (1953), Nunnally Johnson's *The Man in the Gray Flannel Suit* (1956), and John Huston's *Moby Dick* (1956).

Peck had as many hits as he did misses, but no one could accuse him of choosing obviously commercial projects. He became more aware of financial considerations, however, when he began producing his own films, among them *The Big Country* (1958), *Pork Chop Hill* (1959), *The Guns of Navarone* (1961), which was one of his biggest hits, *Cape Fear* (1962), and *To Kill a Mockingbird* (1962), the film that finally brought him a Best Actor Academy Award.

To Kill a Mockingbird marked the pinnacle of Peck's career, both critically and at the box office. He would have a number of hits in the years to follow, but nothing of that magnitude. As the decade wore on, he made the mistake of starring in westerns when such films were no longer very popular. Nonetheless, at least he made a good one, *The Stalking Moon* (1969). But after-ward his career went into a slump that continued well into the 1970s.

It wasn't until Peck added his considerable stature to a big-budget horror movie hit, *The Omen* (1976), that his career was resurrected. Unfortunately, he followed that success with the mega-flop *MacArthur* (1977). Then, in a surprise move, Peck took a role against type playing the Nazi Dr. Josef Mengele in *The Boys From Brazil* (1978). The film brought him his best notices in more than a decade. He has appeared in relatively few movies since, although his work pace accelerated somewhat in the latter half of the 1980s when he appeared in such films as *Amazing Grace and Chuck* (1987), in which this Lincolnesque actor found himself playing the president of the United States, and *Old Gringo* (1989) in which he starred with Jane Fonda.

If Peck's film career has been variable in the last two decades, his work for the film industry has not. He was president of the Academy of Motion Picture Arts and Sciences between 1967 and 1970, winning the Jean Hersholt Humanitarian Award in 1968. In addition, he was the first chairman of the American Film Institute and he still sits on the AFI's Board of Trustees. In 1989 he was honored with the AFI's Life Achievement Award.

PECKINPAH, SAM (1926–1984) Probably the most controversial American director of the 1960s and early 1970s, in fourteen films Peckinpah's propensity to de-pict graphic mayhem led to a highly charged public debate about violence in the movies. Complicating the debate was the fact that Peckinpah clearly had a consis-tent personal vision and was not an exploitative film-maker. Violence was central to a Peckinpah story be-cause his misfit heroes had to fight to find the human heart within their savage souls.

Born Samuel David Peckinpah he grew up in Cali-fornia and received a M.A. in Drama from USC. He went on to work in the theater as both a director and an actor, eventually taking a job at a Los Angeles TV station.

Peckinpah made the transition to the movies in the mid-1950s when he became the dialogue director on several Donald Siegel *(q.v.)* films, beginning with *Riot in Cell Block 11* (1954). Peckinpah learned a great deal about directing action films by working with Siegel, and he gained writing experience as well, rewriting the script for one of that director's most admired movies, *Invasion of the Body Snatchers* (1956).

In the later 1950s, Peckinpah returned to television, achieving success as a writer. He penned scripts for a host of prime-time shows, a preponderance of them westerns, such as "Gunsmoke," "The Rifleman," and "Broken Arrow."

Peckinpah's reputation with westerns led to his op-portunity to direct a low-budget horse opera in 1961, *The Deadly Companions*. There was nothing in this film to suggest the brilliance he would later demonstrate. His sophomore effort, *Ride the High Country* (1961), was the sleeper hit of the year, a film that lovingly brought together two screen legends, Joel McCrea and Randolph Scott *(qq.v.)*, in an evocative and deeply felt movie about the value of friendship and honor.

The director's next film, *Major Dundee* (1965), nearly destroyed his career but showed him to be a man of ambitious artistic vision. Peckinpah coscripted as well as directed *Major Dundee,* a movie considered by many to be a near masterpiece tragically destroyed by its producer, who substantially shortened the movie in the editing process. Bloody but unbowed, Peckinpah fought back to make *The Wild Bunch* (1969), the movie that catapulted him to a place among the top directors of his era. This film was his fully realized masterpiece, but it was attacked by critics because it seemed to glorify violence. The film was so complex, however, that to merely emphasize its violence was to miss the point entirely.

He followed *The Wild Bunch* with the highly underrated *The Ballad of Cable Hogue* (1970), a movie that showed a gentler side of Peckinpah. But the director stunned movie audiences with his next film, *Straw Dogs* (1971), depicting in a contemporary setting the violence and brutality associated with his westerns. Critics and audiences were shocked but the movie was a hit and Peckinpah weathered the storm of protest, explaining his viewpoint that modern man was not only capable of acts of brutality but that such acts were often necessary.

Peckinpah's career held steady in the early 1970s with the pleasant *Junior Bonner* (1972), the action film *The Getaway* (1972), and the somewhat muddled but entertaining *Pat Garrett and Billy the Kid* (1973). Then, suddenly, Peckinpah seemed to lose his touch. *Bring Me the Head of Alfredo Garcia* (1974), *The Killer Elite* (1975), *Convoy* (1978), and *The Osterman Weekend* (1983) were mediocre to awful. Peckinpah did make one solidly intelligent and engrossing film during this period of decline, *Cross of Iron* (1977), but it received little attention at the box office.

PENN, ARTHUR (1922–) A director whose protagonists are often outsiders and loners searching for a place in a society that often ignores them. Penn has been a movie director since the late 1950s, but he had his greatest impact during the late 1960s and early 1970s. Heavily influenced by the cinema of the French New Wave, particularly the movies of Truffaut and Godard, Penn's films are rarely straightforward narratives. His movies, especially the later ones, have tended to be loosely structured character studies set against the backdrop of an indifferent, if not hostile, world.

The product of a broken home, Penn had an unhappy youth. He was briefly apprenticed to a clockmaker after graduating from high school, but developed an interest in the theater after serving in the armed forces during

World War II. It was during the war that he was befriended by the producer/directors Fred Coe and Joshua Logan. After a stint as a student at the Actors Studio in the late 1940s, Coe gave Penn a job in television in 1951. Within two years, Penn had begun directing TV dramas. At the same time, he began directing for the stage, building a major reputation with Broadway hits such as *Two for the Seesaw* and *Toys in the Attic.*

He directed his first film in 1957, *The Left-Handed Gun,* but edited without his input, it was disappointing. As a consequence, Penn became determined not to return to filmmaking until he had full artistic control, which he was given when he directed the film version of his Broadway smash, *The Miracle Worker (1962).*

The Miracle Worker earned Penn a Best Director Oscar nomination, the first of three that he would ultimately receive. His next two efforts were failures, the complex, Kafkaesque *Mickey One* (1965) and the star-studded but muddled *The Chase* (1966).

Penn found his voice and initiated lively debate with his next movie, *Bonnie and Clyde* (1967), based loosely on the lives of the Depression-era bank robbing team of Bonnie Parker and Clyde Barrow. Penn was the third choice to direct the film, getting the assignment only after François Truffaut and Jean-Luc Godard (his two idols), had turned it down because of prior commitments. The movie was a huge success at the box office, though critics were shocked by its violence. In retrospect, *Bonnie and Clyde* was a seminal movie of the late 1960s, the first in a torrent that reflected the growing violence in American society. The power of the movie could not be denied and Penn was honored with his second Academy Award nomination as Best Director.

Alice's Restaurant (1969), based on a popular song by Arlo Guthrie, was Penn's view of the search for new societal alternatives. It was a gentle, loving, if erratic, movie that achieved a modest cult following. It's audacious and creative disregard of form, coupled by its deep regard for content, brought Penn a surprise third nomination for Best Director.

In many ways, Penn's most ambitious movie was the offbeat western *Little Big Man* (1970), starring Dustin Hoffman, a film that was both a comedy and a serious allegorical indictment of America's role in Vietnam. It was, perhaps, his most fully realized film, a critical and box office winner that marked the apex of his career in Hollywood.

Penn's subsequent films have been fascinating and insightful, but they haven't stirred very much interest among film fans or film scholars. The best of his later movies was *Night Moves* (1975), followed by the flawed *The Missouri Breaks* (1976), and the intense but little seen *Four Friends* (1981), a movie that owed more to Steve Tesich's script than Penn's inconsistent direction.

Target (1985) missed the mark entirely; it was poorly written and equally poorly directed. He attempted to come back with the suspense film *Dead of Winter* (1987), a movie that failed to find an audience.

See also: Allen, Dede; *Bonnie and Clyde*

PERKINS, ANTHONY (1932–   )   An actor who has appeared in more than forty films since his movie debut in 1953. But despite his many film credits, Perkins will probably best be remembered as Norman Bates—in Alfred Hitchcock's *Psycho* (1960). Perkins began playing deranged characters in films before *Psycho,* but his performance in that film typecast him and he has played a host of troubled individuals ever since.

Born to an acting family (his father, Osgood Perkins, was a well-known thespian), fifteen-year-old Tony Perkins spent summer vacations performing in stock companies. At twenty-one, learning that MGM was making a film called *The Actress* (1953) based on a play in which he had the juvenile lead in summer stock, he hitchhiked to Hollywood, where he got a screen test opposite the film's star, Jean Simmons *(q.v.).* When no offer was forthcoming, he went back to Rollins College in Florida. Six months later, out of the blue, he was notified to report to wardrobe—he had the part.

Surprisingly there was little subsequent interest in Perkins despite his impressive debut, but he kept busy in New York, where he was signed by Elia Kazan *(q.v.)* to play the young boy in the Broadway production of *Tea & Sympathy* (1954) and where he appeared in a number of live TV drama showcases.

His movie career began in earnest in 1956 when he played Gary Cooper's son in *Friendly Persuasion,* making his strongest impression during the latter half of the 1950s as Jimmy Piersall in *Fear Strikes Out* (1957), the first time he played a disturbed character, and as a young deputy in *The Tin Star* (1957).

When Perkins played Norman Bates in *Psycho,* the actor's career hit a peak, but it was a mixed blessing; he has worked consistently ever since but he hasn't been offered a very wide range of roles and most of his movies have been mediocre. And for the most part, he has had important supporting parts rather than star roles. Nonetheless, Perkins has had no regrets about playing Norman Bates, a part he has referred to as "the Hamlet of horror roles."

After twenty-three years, Perkins reprised his Bates role again in *Psycho II* (1983), turning in an excellent performance in a surprisingly satisfying sequel. The film did excellent business at the box office and spawned yet another sequel, *Psycho III* (1986), this time with Perkins directing as well as starring. Played for humor as much as for suspense, the movie was reasonably well received by both critics and audiences.

Other than his *Psycho* movies, Perkins' most memorable films have been Orson Welles' *The Trial* (1962),

To many film fans, Anthony Perkins will always be Norman Bates of *Psycho* (1960) fame. Yet he has starred in a wide variety of roles in his long career and has had a substantial career in music as well. Photo courtesy of Anthony Perkins.

Pretty Poison (1968), *Play It As It Lays* (1972), and *Crimes of Passion* (1984).

In addition to his movie roles, Perkins has recorded eight albums. He has also worked steadily in the theater since the 1970s, both as an actor and, increasingly, as a director.

PERSISTENCE OF VISION   The principle of perceptual psychology that explains why a succession of sixteen or more still frames per second appears to the human eye as one continuous, uninterrupted image. The visual portion of the brain retains images for an instant after they disappear from actual sight. This "persistence" in seeing what is no longer there allows subsequent still pictures—changed ever so slightly from one image to the next—to appear to the eye as part of one movement.

PICKFORD, MARY (1893–1979)   The most popular film star in the history of Hollywood, Pickford was also Hollywood's most successful businesswoman, building a large personal fortune and a film studio (United Artists) almost half a century before the advent of the women's liberation movement. It didn't seem to matter that Pickford was a mediocre actress; her image was transcendent. She spoke to a worldwide audience, consistently presenting herself in a sympathetic light as an energetic, plucky child/woman.

Born Gladys Smith in Toronto, her father died in a construction accident when she was just four years old. In order to help support her mother, sister, and brother, she began acting in a small traveling theater company. Billed as "Baby Gladys," she graduated to starring roles by the age of nine, and reached Broadway four years later in David Belasco's production of *The Warrens of Virginia*. It was Belasco who gave Gladys Smith the stage name Mary Pickford.

In 1909, when there was little stage work to be had, Pickford took a chance on the dubious film industry and was given a per diem salary by D. W. Griffith at Biograph. But even at the beginning she showed her business acumen. Griffith offered her the going rate of $5 a day but she insisted on $10. Griffith capitulated. Over the next decade, Pickford continued to double her salary until it reached astronomical proportions.

Pickford's first film at Biograph was probably *Her First Biscuits* (1909). Soon thereafter she had her first starring role in *The Violin Maker of Cremona* (1909). Her costar was actor Owen Moore, her first husband, who appeared in a great many films with her during her early stardom. His alcoholism reportedly destroyed their marriage.

Pickford's first major hit film was *The Little Teacher* (1910), in which she had a full head of curly hair and was referred to in the titles as "Little Mary." Film studios didn't want to reveal the names of actors for (the justified) fear that the actors would want more money if they became famous. Hollywood, however, was destined to have stars, and audiences soon clamored for films with "Little Mary" and "The Girl with the Curls."

Pickford's fame made her a much desired commodity, and she left Biograph for Carl Laemmle's IMP studio in 1910, went to the Majestic film studio in 1911, followed by a quick stint back at Biograph that same year, and then joined Adolph Zukor's Famous Players company in late 1912. In those two years, she managed to raise her salary from $40 to $500 per week.

Boosted by such hits as *Tess of the Storm Country* (1913), *Cinderella* (1914), and *Rags* (1915), Pickford's salary leapt to a princely $10,000 per week. As evidenced by the above titles, her image as a poor downtrodden waif who finds happiness by picture's end was already well established. It was a formula that worked to perfection. But it was also quite limiting. Whenever the actress tried another kind of character, audiences stayed away. Captive to her persona, Pickford went on to make *A Poor Little Rich Girl* (1917) and *Rebecca of Sunnybrook Farm* (1917), two of her greatest hits of the teens. By the end of the decade, when she left Zukor to make three films for First National, she earned a handsome $350,000 per movie.

Pickford was more than a money-making machine. She fostered the careers of a great many film artists, among them screenwriter Frances Marion (*q.v.*), who wrote twelve of the actress's movies. She also brought Ernst Lubitsch (*q.v.*) to America to direct her in *Rosita*

(1923), which, unfortunately, was a bomb. Pickford was also a talented producer. And, in 1919, her abilities as both a businesswoman and a producer led her to join D. W. Griffith, Charlie Chaplin (*q.v.*), and Douglas Fairbanks (*q.v.*) in founding the film studio United Artists (*q.v.*), still in operation today.

The following year she married Douglas Fairbanks, giving America its closest approximation of a royal couple. The two stars were at the height of their popularity, and to audiences worldwide their pairing was magical. They even resided in an American version of a fairy-tale castle, a magnificent home they called Picfair.

Pickford's first film for United Artists, *Pollyanna* (1920), was significant not so much in that she was a twenty-seven-year-old woman playing a twelve-year-old girl (although that was remarkable in itself), but because it was the first movie ever sold to exhibitors on a percentage basis. The film was a hit, but it was one of Pickford's last smash successes, although the majority of her films throughout the 1920s made money.

In 1927, she starred in *My Best Girl*, notable for being her last silent film and also the movie in which Buddy Rogers, her future husband, was her costar. The talkie revolution was nearly two years old before Pickford appeared on screen in her first sound venture, *Coquette* (1929). Though the film was a success and she won an Academy Award that year for Best Actress, she was no Helen Hayes (who had played the role of Coquette on Broadway).

She and husband Fairbanks then made perhaps the biggest mistakes of their careers when they starred together for the first and only time in *The Taming of the Shrew* (1929). Neither of them had any experience playing Shakespeare, and the giddiness of the tale was at odds with their images. The film was a major flop, best remembered today for its astounding credit, "Additional dialogue by Sam Taylor."

Pickford appeared in two more box office failures, *Kiki* (1931) and *Secrets* (1933), and then abruptly retired from the screen. In 1935 she and Fairbanks ended their marriage. Two years later, Pickford married Buddy Rogers; their union lasted until her death at Picfair at the age of eighty-seven.

In the years between her retirement and her death, Pickford wrote books, had radio shows, produced a couple of films, built a cosmetics company, sold her share of United Artists (in 1953), and nearly made a comeback in *Storm Center* (1956), but wisely passed, allowing Bette Davis to get stuck in that clunker. With equal wisdom, Pickford bought the rights to a great many of her silent films during the 1930s when no one appreciated the historic value of the nontalking films. It was her intention, however, to have the movies burned upon her death. Happily, she had a change of heart and many films that might have otherwise been lost have been saved for posterity.

Known during the silent era as "America's Sweetheart," Pickford was actually "The World's Sweetheart," so dubbed by the international press. In 1975, both America and the world paid homage to her when she received a special Academy Award "for her unique contributions to the film industry and the development of film as an artistic medium."

PIDGEON, WALTER (1897–1984) A distinguished leading man who appeared in films from the late silent era to the end of the 1970s. Though he did not possess a commanding personality on screen, his gentlemanly style and precise speech made him a serviceable foil for more imposing leading ladies; he rarely upstaged them. Despite a long career that included appearances in more than one hundred movies, there are very few one thinks of as Walter Pidgeon films. Nonetheless, his starring roles in the 1940s and character parts in the 1950s were effective examples of solid screen acting.

A Canadian by birth and a musician by training, Pidgeon pursued an acting career and achieved quick success. He had barely begun acting on the stage when Hollywood snatched him and put him to work in his first film, *Mannequin* (1926). He continued acting in silent films but the arrival of sound was hardly troublesome for the young thespian. He possessed a rich and resonant baritone voice that was quickly put to use; he can be seen singing in a number of early musicals.

Pidgeon appeared in nearly thirty movies during the 1930s, few of them of any distinction. In big-budget movies, such as *Saratoga* (1937), *The Girl of the Golden West* (1938), and *Too Hot to Handle* (1938), he generally played the second male lead. He only tended to star in low-budget films of the ilk of *Nick Carter—Master Detective* (1939).

The turning point came in the early 1940s with two strong performances, the first as a villain in Raoul Walsh's *Dark Command* (1940) and then as a hero in Fritz Lang's *Man Hunt,* a hit film about a sportsman who decides to hunt Hitler, but who instead becomes the hunted. In the former movie Pidgeon showed surprising depth and passion; his performance in the latter movie turned Pidgeon into a credible "A" movie star.

As the 1940s unfolded, Pidgeon settled into roles of dignity and stature, playing the helpful Mr. Grufydd in John Ford's *How Green Was My Valley* (1941), the man behind Greer Garson in *Mrs. Miniver* (1942), and the man once again behind Greer Garson in *Madame Curie* (1943), and so on. He was ever the supportive, gentle, caring man who effectively stayed in the shadows, doing his job as an actor to make the actress the focal point of so many of his movies.

In the 1950s he became a valued character actor in such films as *The Bad and the Beautiful* (1952), *Executive*

Suite (1954), and *The Last Time I Saw Paris* (1954). But his most famous film of the 1950s, and perhaps of his entire career, was in the science fiction classic *Forbidden Planet* (1956), in which he played the part of Dr. Morbius.

After disappearing from the big screen during the latter part of the 1950s, he returned in two surprisingly strong commanding roles in *Voyage to the Bottom of the Sea* (1961) and *Advise and Consent* (1962). But Pidgeon did not appear in very many Hollywood films thereafter. He made mostly cameo or special guest star appearances, most notably in *Funny Girl* (1968), as Florenz Ziegfeld, *Harry in Your Pocket* (1973), and *Sextette* (1978), in support of Mae West in her last movie. It was Pidgeon's last movie, as well, and it seemed fitting that he should have gone out in support of yet another major female star.

PITTS, ZASU (1898–1963) An actress/comedienne who had two very distinct film careers. During the 1920s she was one of Hollywood's most intensely dramatic actresses, but during the sound era she delighted audiences as a scatterbrained cuckoo in comic-relief roles and as a star of low-budget comedy features and shorts.

ZaSu was given her memorable name at birth; it was a combination of the last two letters in Eli*za* and the first two in *Su*san, the names of her aunts.

She had the good fortune to break into the movie business in a popular Mary Pickford (q.v.) vehicle, *The Little Princess* (1917). Audiences took to her and she worked steadily thereafter in a variety of genres, including adventures, comedies, and romances. But her claim to fame during the silent era was her association with Erich von Stroheim (q.v.) in two of his most ambitious, artful films, *Greed* (1924) and *The Wedding March* (1928). Known for serious drama, she had also starred as the female lead in the silent version of *All Quiet on the Western Front* (1930), but she was replaced by Beryl Mercer for the sound version; Pitts was so effective in her early talkie comedies that preview audiences who saw the stark antiwar film immediately started laughing when they saw her on film.

Pitts did occasionally appear in supporting roles in a number of serious movies such as *Bad Sister* (1931) and *Back Street* (1932), but her forte during the rest of her career was, indeed, comedy, playing ditzy characters in films such as Ernst Lubitsch's *Monte Carlo* (1930), *Love, Honor, and Oh Baby!* (1933), *Mrs. Wiggs of the Cabbage Patch* (1934), *Ruggles of Red Gap* (1935), *The Plot Thickens* (1936), *Forty Naughty Girls* (1937), *52nd Street* (1937), *So's Your Aunt Emma* (1942), and many others.

In the late 1940s, she surprised audiences with her restrained character performance in *Life with Father* (1947), but she went on to appear in only a relative handful of films thereafter during the 1950s and early 1960s. She occupied herself, instead, with television,

ZaSu Pitts not only had one of the most memorable of Hollywood names, she also had one of the industry's most unusual careers. She made the transition from dramatic roles during the silent era to become a much-admired comedienne during the talkies, right up until the early 1960s. Photo courtesy of Movie Star News.

appearing in support of Gale Storm in her series "Oh, Susanna" between 1956 and 1959.

ZaSu Pitts' last movie appearance was in the all-star comedy film *It's a Mad, Mad, Mad, Mad World* (1963). She died of cancer the year it was released.

POLANSKI, ROMAN (1933–   ) He is a director of technical virtuosity whose themes have centered on obsession, moral corruption, and violence. If ever there was a director whose preoccupations complemented the alienation of the 1960s and 1970s, it was Polanski. Both in America and abroad, he made several dark and moody hit films, garnering two Oscar nominations, the first for what many consider his best film, *Chinatown* (1974), and the other for *Tess* (1980).

Born to Polish-Jewish parents in Paris, Polanski grew up in Cracow from the age of three. His was not a pleasant youth. Both his mother and father were sent to a concentration camp when he was eight years old. He never saw his mother again. He lived the life of a street urchin and survived in the midst of terrible suffering and cruelty. He found what little solace he could in the movies, which he attended with near religious fervor.

His father survived the camps and found his twelve-year-old son in Cracow selling newspapers on the street.

The elder Polanski sent Roman to a trade school, but the budding entertainer was soon acting on a radio show. During his latter teenage years, he worked in the theater as an actor and in 1954 joined the Polish Film School at Lodz after being turned down at the state acting school. The theater's loss was the cinema's gain.

He began making award-winning short films, including *Two Men and a Wardrobe* (1959), often writing his own screenplays and acting in his movies, as well. After film school he made several other shorts, but finally made his first feature film, the internationally acclaimed *Knife in the Water* (1962). Not long after, he went to England to make *Repulsion* (1965) and *Cul-de-Sac* (1966). He received Hollywood support for the British production of the black comedy *The Fearless Vampire Killers* (1967). All three of these films became substantial art-house circuit hits in America, prompting Paramount Pictures to give him the financing to make the sinister horror movie *Rosemary's Baby* (1968). The film was a huge mass-market hit, even as it was admired by the critics for its creepy ambiance and visual flair.

Polanski seemed destined for a long and prosperous Hollywood career when in 1969 his eight-months-pregnant bride of one year, Sharon Tate, was savagely murdered by Charles Manson and his deranged followers. Shocked and reeling from yet another blow of seemingly random cruelty, Polanski fled to England and made a cathartically violent version of *Macbeth* (1971).

He returned to America to make *Chinatown;* his two subsequent movies, *Che* (1973) and *The Tenant* (1976), were made abroad. It was after making *The Tenant,* while staying in Jack Nicholson's California home on a visit, that he was arrested for allegedly drugging and raping a thirteen-year-old girl. He pleaded innocent at first, then later agreed to reduced charges. Free on bail, however, he hurriedly left the country and refused to return to stand trial. He continued making movies in Europe, including the widely admired *Tess,* with which he turned his teenaged protégée, Nastassia Kinski, into an international star. After a long absence from the screen, Polanski went on to make the poorly received *Pirates* (1986), but rebounded with the hit thriller *Frantic* (1988).

There have been moves afoot to allow Polanski back into the United States but so far no arrangement has been worked out.

POITIER, SIDNEY (1924–   ) Hollywood's first major black film star whose popularity crosses racial boundaries. Tall and goodlooking, Poitier presented 1950s and 1960s film audiences with a new view of black people, often portraying professionals such as doctors, lawyers, and teachers. In a career spanning forty years, he has become not only a highly respected and bankable actor, he has also become an extremely successful actor-director with a string of hit films to his credit.

Born in Florida to Bahamian parents, young Poitier and his family returned to Cat Island in the Bahamas and was raised there. His formal education consisted of a year and a half of schooling. After serving in the Army, he moved to New York and worked at a series of odd jobs before joining the American Negro Theater, where he received his early training. His first public performance was in an all-black version of Aristophanes' *Lysistrata* (1946). He had only a dozen lines, but on opening night he blew them. Ironically, the critics applauded his jumbled delivery of his lines while panning the rest of the production. His career was launched.

Poitier continued to act on the stage and was soon offered the opportunity to play a doctor in one of Hollywood's earliest studio-financed antiracist films, *No Way Out* (1950). It was not his first film appearance, however. He was in a U.S. Army documentary called *From Whom Cometh My Help* (1949).

Good roles for black actors have always been hard to come by, but Poitier was Hollywood's choice for virtually all of them in the 1950s. Unfortunately, even an actor of Poitier's growing reputation was cast only in films about bigotry. It rarely occurred to casting directors that he might star in a film that had nothing to do with race. Nonetheless, he played an important role in changing America's stereotyped views of blacks with movies such as *Cry, The Beloved Country* (1952), *The Blackboard Jungle* (1955), and *The Defiant Ones* (1958). For his performance in the last, he received a Best Actor Oscar nomination.

He won the Oscar five years later for his performance in *Lilies of the Field* (1963), but the 1960s didn't differ much from the 1950s with regard to the kinds of roles he played. Movies such as *A Raisin in the Sun* (1961), *Pressure Point* (1962), and *A Patch of Blue* (1965) dealt with the issue of racism in America. There were, happily, a few exceptions, such as his roles in *A Slender Thread* (1966) and the sleeper hit of 1967, *To Sir with Love*.

When Stanley Kramer decided to make the controversial film *Guess Who's Coming to Dinner?* (1967), a movie about an interracial couple, Poitier was, again, the obvious casting choice for the male lead. The film was a media event and a box office success, and along with *To Sir With Love* and a third hit in that same year, *In the Heat of the Night* (1967), the actor had finally become a Hollywood superstar.

His movie roles began to widen slightly but, with the exception of *They Call Me Mister Tibbs!*, his later films didn't fare well at the ticket booth. His image as the black man most acceptable to whites rankled the more militant members of the black community and his popularity began to fade despite some excellent films, particularly *Brother John* (1971), a film Poitier also produced.

Never known for comedy, Poitier expanded his talents in two directions, becoming both a director and a comic actor in a series of three popular films with Bill Cosby, *Uptown Saturday Night* (1974), *Let's Do It Again* (1975), and *A Piece of the Action* (1977). He also directed other films without appearing in them, most notably *Stir Crazy* (1980) and *Hanky Panky* (1982).

As an actor, Poitier took a decade's sabbatical before reappearing on the big screen in a flurry of activity in 1988 with *Little Nikita* and *Shoot to Kill*. The films received a great deal of media attention because of Poitier's return to acting, but both were critical and box office flops.

See also: racism in Hollywood

POLLACK, SYDNEY (1934–) One of the most critically acclaimed and commercially successful directors of the 1970s and 1980s, he owes part of his success to his close and rewarding professional association with Robert Redford (*q.v.*), who has starred in six of his films to date. Pollack's movies have received a staggering 43 Oscar nominations, including four for Best Picture. Pollack, himself, has been nominated as Best Director three times, winning an Academy Award in that category for *Out of Africa* (1985). The central theme of Pollack's works clearly suggests why his films have been so popular; his stories usually center on heroes and heroines trapped in an often hostile society.

Born in South Bend, Indiana, Pollack traveled to New York to pursue an acting career. He was a student at the famous Neighborhood Playhouse, from which he emerged a competent actor, working in television and on the stage in the mid-1950s. He went on to teach drama at New York University and to direct for television before getting the opportunity to direct his first feature film, *The Slender Thread* (1965).

He began his association with the young Robert Redford when he directed *This Property Is Condemned* (1966), a film that did not set the world on fire. Pollack made a couple of action films with Burt Lancaster (*q.v.*) without much distinction before the director emerged as a serious and provocative filmmaker with *They Shoot Horses, Don't They?* (1969), a creative Depression-era drama centering on the trials and tribulations of participants in a dance marathon. He followed that three years later with the hit saga about a mountain man, *Jeremiah Johnson* (1972). The film renewed his collaboration with Robert Redford.

Pollack's best and most successful films during the rest of the 1970s all starred Redford. *The Way We Were* (1973) teamed Redford with Barbra Streisand (*q.v.*) in one of the most celebrated casting coups of the decade. The movie was an intelligent examination of the red scare in Hollywood during the late 1940s and early

Producer-director Sydney Pollack has worked with the biggest names in contemporary Hollywood, among them Jane Fonda, Robert Redford, Barbra Streisand, Paul Newman, Dustin Hoffman, and Meryl Streep, bringing out many of these actors' best performances in a long list of critical and commercial hits. Photo courtesy of Sydney Pollack.

1950s, which succeeded at the same time as a love story. Later came *Three Days of the Condor* (1975) and *The Electric Horseman* (1979), both with Redford. Pollack's non-Redford movies during the 1970s, *The Yakuza* (1975) and *Bobby Deerfield* (1977), were flops. They also happened to be the only two films during that time period that Pollack also produced.

The director has consistently worked with Hollywood's biggest stars. In 1981 he directed Paul Newman in the journalism thriller *Absence of Malice.* In 1982 he directed Dustin Hoffman in the superhit *Tootsie,* also appearing in the film himself, playing the Hoffman character's agent. In 1985 he asked Redford to play the thankless role of Meryl Streep's love interest in *Out of Africa* and the actor, out of loyalty to Pollack, obliged. One suspects it will not be the last time these two will work together in the movies.

PORTER, COLE (1892–1964)   A major composer/lyricist of twentieth-century popular music. Famous for his haunting melodies and sophisticated lyrics, Porter wrote twenty-three Broadway musicals, twelve of which were brought to the screen. A number of those musicals, however, used only a few (or even none) of

Porter's songs. Among those that used much or all of his music were *Panama Hattie* (1942), *Kiss Me Kate* (1953), *Silk Stockings* (1957), and *Can-Can* (1960). While Porter did not write music specifically for movies, he did contribute songs to eleven films in addition to his filmed stage musicals.

The composer was born to a wealthy family and had a comprehensive education, attending Yale University and Harvard Law School. But music was always a part of his life (he wrote his first song when he was eleven). After a short stint in the French Foreign Legion in 1916, Porter settled down to write for the Broadway stage. His success came quickly, but it wasn't until 1929, after the talkie revolution occurred, that there was a rush to adapt his musicals to the big screen and to use his songs in various films.

His music was first heard in the movies in *The Battle of Paris* (1929) when Gertrude Lawrence sang "They All Fall in Love," but he is better remembered for "Night and Day" in *The Gay Divorcée* (1934), and for his many hits in films such as *Born to Dance* (1936), *Rosalie* (1937), *DuBarry Was a Lady* (1943), *The Pirate* (1948), *Anything Goes* (1936 & 1956), *High Society* (1956), and *Les Girls* (1957).

Ever the image of 1920s sophistication and style, but crippled by a tragic horseback riding accident in 1937, Porter made an excellent subject for a biopic. He was played by Cary Grant in *Night and Day* (1947), a film that featured Porter's music but had an unfortunate script. Long after his death, Porter's music was still fodder for the movies and his tunes were used in the Peter Bogdanovich flop *At Long Last Love* (1975), with Burt Reynolds and Cybill Shepherd massacring the music.

PORTER, EDWIN S.   *See The Great Train Robbery.*

POWELL, DICK (1904–1963)   A singer, actor, director, producer, and business executive who had surprising durability as a film star. Powell warbled through nearly a decade's worth of musicals, the best of them very early in his career, yet his popularity with movie fans was substantial, thanks to a pleasant and pleasing onscreen personality. In the mid-1940s, desperate to change his image, Powell emerged a hard-boiled, tough guy with a power and range many critics found surprising. When the movies finally gave him the cold shoulder in the early 1950s, he became a powerhouse in the burgeoning TV medium as one of the cofounders of Four Star Television, eventually branching out to produce and direct films in the mid-1950s.

Born Richard E. Powell, he had an early interest in music, singing in his church choir and becoming a versatile musician. He worked for a telephone company after graduating from college, but quit to join a band. He was on the road for several years, playing instruments and vocalizing until he was discovered by Warner Bros. It was 1932; the studio was the early leader in movie musicals and it was in search of fresh new talent. Powell was first cast in a small role in *Blessed Event* (1932). Several other films followed before he shot to stardom in Warner's classic backstage musical, *42nd Street* (1933). He appeared with Ruby Keeler in the film, the first of seven such pairings.

Powell went on to play juvenile leads and (later) starring roles in the best of all the Warner musicals of the early and mid-1930s, including *Gold Diggers of 1933* (1933), *Footlight Parade* (1933), *Wonder Bar* (1934), *Dames* (1934), and *Gold Diggers of 1935* (1935). Unfortunately, he continued to star in Warner musicals long after they became pedestrian vehicles with little flair and only minor box office appeal. He acted and sang in an endless array of films such as *Colleen* (1936), *The Singing Marine* (1937), *The Cowboy from Brooklyn* (1938), and *Naughty But Nice* (1939), to name just a few.

At the end of the decade, Powell refused to renew his Warner Bros. contract. Looking for meatier roles in better films, he had only middling success at first. He scored a hit in Preston Sturges' delightful comedy, *Christmas in July* (1940), played straight drama in *I Want a Divorce* (1940) with his then (second) wife (from 1936–1945), Joan Blondell (*q.v.*), but soon ended up in light musicals such as *Star Spangled Rhythm* (1943), *Riding High* (1943), and *Meet the People* (1944).

His career finally began to change when he starred in Rene Clair's *It Happened Tomorrow* (1944), a fantasy film about a man who receives the daily newspaper a day early, learning the news twenty-four hours before the rest of the world. It was a clever film and Powell was effective enough to win the tough guy role of Philip Marlowe in the screen adaptation of Raymond Chandler's novel *Farewell, My Lovely*, retitled *Murder, My Sweet* (1945) so that audiences wouldn't think it was yet another Dick Powell musical. He played Marlowe as gritty and grubby, and it worked. During the rest of the 1940s, the actor mostly starred in *films noir*, movies such as *Johnny O'Clock* (1947), *Pitfall* (1948), and *Right Cross* (1950).

By the early 1950s, however, moviegoers had had enough of Powell as either a singer or a tough guy. Wisely, he turned to television, forming Four Star Television, a production company that presented "Four Star Playhouse," "The Dick Powell Show," and a number of other TV series to an ever-growing audience. He acted, directed, and produced for television, becoming an early giant in the new medium.

His success was such that he was again solicited for the movies, appearing in *The Bad and the Beautiful* (1952) and *Susan Slept Here* (1954), which was his last big-screen acting credit. In the meantime, however, he began directing and producing feature films, making a number of run-of-the-mill movies including *Split Sec-*

ond (1952), *The Conqueror* (1956), *You Can't Run Away from It* (1956), *The Enemy Below* (1957), and *The Hunters* (1958).

He succumbed to cancer at the age of fifty-nine in 1963, survived by his third wife, actress June Allyson (*q.v.*).

POWELL, WILLIAM (1892–1984) A debonair actor graced with wit and charm, he became a star playing sophisticated heroes. Though best remembered as the urbane detective Nick Charles in half a dozen Thin Man movies, Powell's long and illustrious career comprised ninety-five films made over thirty-three years. His Hollywood career can be neatly divided into three periods according to the parts he played: villain, leading man, and character actor; he was superb at all three. Though not possessed of conventional good looks, Powell had a distinctive face with a trademark mustache and was blessed with a marvelous, resonant speaking voice. Powell received three Oscar nominations for Best Actor, but never won the coveted statuette.

Born to a middle-class family, Powell decided to become an actor against his father's wishes. According to Lawrence J. Quirk in *The Complete Films of William Powell*, the young would-be actor borrowed $700 from an aunt in order to attend the American Academy of Dramatic Arts in New York. He struggled to make ends meet throughout most of his twenties, making his New York stage debut in 1912 in *The Ne'er Do Well* and finally having his first Broadway hit in *Spanish Love* in 1920.

Powell took a chance on the movies when he was invited to play a villain in the John Barrymore version of *Sherlock Holmes* (1922). It was a memorable role in a hit film, and Powell was on his way to playing a series of villains throughout the rest of the silent era, most notably in *Romola* (1924), *Beau Geste* (1926), and *The Last Command* (1928).

Powell worked steadily throughout the silent era but he was never the star of his films. That soon changed with the advent of sound. His stage training finally paid off in a big way when Powell's voice rang clear on the primitive soundtrack of *Interference* (1928). Paramount decided to try him out in more heroic roles, starring him as the detective Philo Vance in *The Canary Murder Case* (1929). The film was a hit, and Powell went on to star in three more Philo Vance movies during the next few years. In addition to playing a hero, the actor established himself as a versatile light comedian as well as a romantic leading man. His comic ability was demonstrated in *Charming Sinners* (1929) and as a romantic lead he came to the fore in *Behind the Make-Up* (1930), in which he costarred with Kay Francis, with whom he was successfully paired in a number of films before he began his more famous screen partnership with Myrna Loy (*q.v.*).

Powell had been well paid by Paramount and, later, Warner Bros., but during the early years of the Depression his drawing power didn't appear to justify his large salary. MGM took a chance on him, making him the second male lead after Clark Gable (*q.v.*) in *Manhattan Melodrama* (1934). The film did excellent business at the box office but, more important, the chemistry between Powell and leading lady Myrna Loy was so obvious director W. S. Van Dyke decided to put the two actors together again in his next film, *The Thin Man* (1934). Playing Nick and Nora Charles, ably abetted by their dog, Asta, Powell and Loy turned the Dashiell Hammett mystery into a blockbuster hit. Powell was nominated for his first Oscar, and audiences so loved his pairing with Loy that the two stars eventually appeared together in a total of thirteen movies, five of them sequels to *The Thin Man*.

Perhaps Powell's best year of the 1930s was 1936. In that year he scored in the title role of the Best Picture Academy Award winner, *The Great Ziegfeld* (1936), the title role of *My Man Godfrey* (1936), for which he won his second Oscar nomination, and in the hit comedy *Libeled Lady* (1936). By this time he had already divorced his second wife, Carole Lombard (*q.v.*), and was deeply involved with Jean Harlow (*q.v.*), who died before they could wed. It was shortly after Harlow's death that Powell, himself, nearly died of cancer. His life was saved by two major surgeries and he was off the screen for nearly two years, missing the opportunity to play opposite Greta Garbo (*q.v.*) in *Ninotchka* (1939).

Powell returned to the screen in *Another Thin Man* (1939), rebuilding his career as he gained his strength. Except for his teamings with Myrna Loy in the early 1940s and an amusing comedy with Hedy Lamarr (*q.v.*), *The Heavenly Body* (1944), Powell's films were becoming second rate. Well into his fifties, he was content to play character roles if only there were decent ones to be had. Happily, one came along in 1947 in *Life with Father*. Playing the patriarch of a turn-of-the-century New York family, Powell was brilliant; at once taciturn and vulnerable, his performance was the triumph of his career. The film, based on a hit Broadway play, was a critical and box office winner, bringing Powell renewed prestige, along with his third and last Best Actor Oscar nomination.

He followed *Life with Father* with another hit, *The Senator Was Indiscreet* (1947). His films thereafter were generally minor affairs, except for movies such as *The Girl Who Had Everything* (1953) and *How to Marry a Millionaire* (1955), in which he had featured appearances. In his last movie, Powell gave a warm, charming performance in the supporting role of Doc in the hit, *Mr. Roberts* (1955). He retired from the movie business and with his third wife, former actress Diana Lewis (whom he married in 1940), settled in Palm Springs, California, where he lived until his death at the age of 91.

Was there ever a more handsome man in Hollywood than Tyrone Power? Some might have been sexier or had more personality—and there were certainly better actors—but on sheer good looks, Ty Power was the ultimate image of a male movie star. Photo courtesy of The Siegel Collection.

POWER, TYRONE (1913–1958)   A strikingly handsome actor of modest skill who appeared in nearly fifty films, mostly in starring roles. His reserved personal style balanced his intimidating good looks, and he remained a favorite of female fans even when his face began to grow jowly. During his early years of stardom, however, he was a potent matinee idol and top box office attraction. Power was among Twentieth Century-Fox's handful of major stars and he was used in many of their most important films, more than a dozen of them directed by Henry King (*q.v.*).

Born Tyrone Power, Jr. to a theatrical family, he was the great grandson of the legendary Irish actor Tyrone Power (1797–1841) and the son of the popular stage and silent screen performer also named Tyrone Power (1869–1931). The young Power wanted nothing more than to follow in the footsteps of his elders and, with help from his father, made his theatrical debut in a Chicago production of *The Merchant of Venice* (1931). Also thanks to his father, he was given the opportunity to make a brief film appearance in *Tom Brown of Culver* (1932). But before the film's release his father died of a heart attack and the young actor had to fend for himself.

Power struggled in Hollywood and made only one more film, *Flirtation Walk* (1934), before leaving to make his way on the stage. A short while later, though, a Twentieth Century-Fox scout spotted him in a play and he was signed to a contract. His first two films at Fox, *Girls Dormitory* (1936) and *Ladies in Love* (1936), were of little consequence, but they did display his powerful screen presence and handsome (some might say pretty) face. Fox, in desperate need of stars, gave him a leading role in the big-budget production of *Lloyds of London* (1937) and the result was instant stardom for Power.

He went on to make many of his most memorable films during the next five years, a great many of them period pieces, such as *In Old Chicago* (1938), *Alexander's Ragtime Band* (1938), *Suez* (1938), *Rose of Washington Square* (1939), *Brigham Young* (1940), as well as swashbucklers, including *The Mark of Zorro* (1940), *Blood and Sand* (1941), and *The Black Swan* (1942). While he was successful in the contemporary gangster film *Johnny Apollo* (1940), many critics thought his soft features made him a poor choice for such a tough guy role.

He was nonetheless tough enough to join the Marine Corps as a pilot during World War II. In 1946 he returned to Hollywood in a pretentious version of Somerset Maugham's *The Razor's Edge*, which was a hit. His next film, the bleak *Nightmare Alley* (1947), brought him the best reviews of his career, but it was a flop at the box office.

Over the better part of a decade, Power's career drifted downward. He was in a few good films and some commercial successes, however, among them *Captain from Castile* (1947), *Rawhide* (1950), and *The Eddie Duchin Story* (1956). In the absence of good movie scripts, he had taken to working on the stage during the 1950s with equally modest results.

Finally, his film career seemed to be on a upswing in the latter half of the 1950s when he starred in *The Sun Also Rises* (1957) and *Witness for the Prosecution* (1958). His reteaming with Rouben Mamoulian (*q.v.*), who had directed him in two of his best films of the early 1940s, *The Mark of Zorro* and *Blood and Sand,* to make *Solomon and Sheba* (1958) augered well, but Power died of a heart attack during the shooting after a strenuous fencing scene with George Sanders.

Power was married three times, including unions with actresses Annabella (1939–1948) and Linda Christian (1949–1955). His children, Taryn, Romina, and Tyrone Power, Jr., have subsequently appeared in films.

PREMINGER, OTTO (1906–1986) A producer-director whose films do not dramatize a clear conflict between right and wrong so much as a conflict between flawed points of view. Such a sophisticated attitude did not always bring viewers to Preminger's movies, but it wasn't for want of his trying. He was a consummate showman who made thirty-six films and well understood the need to make a profit if he was going to be able to keep on making movies.

Born the son of Austria's chief prosecutor (equivalent to attorney general of the U.S.), the young Preminger followed in his father's footsteps and took his law degree from the University of Vienna in 1928. But even as he studied law, Preminger fell in the love with the stage, working as an actor, and later as a producer and director under the tutelage of the famous Max Reinhardt. While still in Europe, he made his motion picture directorial debut with *Die Grosse Liebe* (1931).

Preminger's reputation as a director was such that he was invited to New York to direct *Libel* in 1935, a play he had put on in Vienna. With Hitler on the rise, the Jewish Preminger wisely stayed in America, heading next for Hollywood and Twentieth Century-Fox, where he made two minor films, *Under Your Spell* (1936) and *Danger—Love at Work* (1937). After a fierce argument with Darryl F. Zanuck (*q.v.*), however, Preminger was fired. He returned to Broadway to direct *Margin for Error,* and with his bald pate, accent, and strutting manner, acted as the play's villainous Nazi. The production was a hit, but it was Preminger's acting that brought him back to Hollywood—and Fox—to play a Nazi in *Pied Piper* (1942). When Fox then wanted him to recreate his role in the film version of *Margin for Error* (1943), he refused unless he was also allowed to direct. With Zanuck away from the studio helping the war effort, Preminger was given his chance and he turned in a winner.

He continued directing at Fox until Zanuck returned in 1944 and was outraged to find Preminger on the lot. Preminger was supposed to direct *Laura* (1944) but Zanuck ordered him to produce the film instead. Later, when the film's director, Rouben Mamoulian (*q.v.*), didn't pan out, Zanuck reluctantly turned the picture over to Preminger, who finished it. *Laura* became a major hit, bringing Preminger the first of his two Best Director Oscar nominations.

Preminger stayed at Fox for roughly another decade, directing and usually producing his own films, but never quite living up to the success of *Laura.* Among his better Fox films were *Fallen Angel* (1945), *Daisy Kenyon* (1947), *The Fan* (1949), *Whirlpool* (1950), and *Where the Sidewalk Ends* (1950).

In the early 1950s, he joined the growing number of directors who became independents, making a big splash when he fought the Hays Office over the use of banned words such as "virgin" and released *The Moon Is Blue* (1953) without the production code seal. The notoriety surrounding the film turned it into a hit. He later made *The Man with the Golden Arm* (1955), which dealt with another production code taboo, drug abuse, and again he scored at the box office.

The 1950s and early 1960s marked Preminger's richest and most adventurous period. In addition to his scrapes with the Hays Office, which eventually led to a complete overhaul of the production code, Preminger also courageously produced and directed two all-black musicals, *Carmen Jones* (1954) and *Porgy and Bess* (1959). He also began adapting big, best-selling novels to the screen in the late 1950s with mixed artistic and commercial results. For instance, he made *Bonjour Tristesse* (1958), *Anatomy of a Murder* (1959), *Exodus* (1960), *Advise and Consent* (1962), and *The Cardinal* (1963), the last of which brought him his second Best Director Oscar nomination.

After *In Harm's Way* (1965) and *Bunny Lake Is Missing* (1965), Preminger began to lose his commercial touch. Always known as a frugal producer, he managed to keep making films until the end of the 1970s despite his poor track record at the box office. Films such as *Skidoo!* (1968), *Tell Me That You Love Me Junie Moon* (1970), and the rest of his movies through to his last, *The Human Factor* (1979), failed to excite either critics or filmgoers.

See also: Hays Code

PRE-PRODUCTION The elements of filmmaking that involve all tasks short of principal photography (*q.v.*). When a movie is in pre-production, it means the producer has hired his or her key people and they are all beginning their assignments: The producer prepares the budget for the film, the screenwriter either adapts or writes the script, the assistant director breaks down (*q.v.*) the script, and the director oversees the preparations of the set and costume designers. Locations are scouted by the director (often with the cinematographer in tow). When pre-production ends, it is finally time for the camera to begin to roll.

PRESLEY, ELVIS (1935–1977) The "King of Rock 'n' Roll" and the eye of a musical hurricane, Elvis popularized a sexually charged new beat. His recording success was astounding and his personal appearances caused near-riots. The so-called moral leaders of the nation condemned his blasphemous music and objected to his legendary hip gyrations, which earned him the nickname "Elvis the Pelvis." But it wasn't just his swinging hips and rockabilly sound that drew audiences. Presley also had personal charm, counterbalanced by bedroom eyes and a sexy sneer. His overwhelming appeal to the teenage market could hardly be ignored by Hollywood. Previous singing sensations such as Bing Crosby and Frank Sinatra (*qq.v.*) had become major movie stars, and Presley certainly had the same potential. In a career that included thirty-three movies, his potential—at least commercially—was well realized with ticket sales of roughly $150 million. His movies, in fact, represent the most commercially successful series of musicals ever produced by Hollywood.

Born in Tupelo, Mississippi, Presley had an identical twin who died at birth. The family later moved to Memphis, Tennessee, and the young Presley seemed destined for a career as a truck driver until he hit it big at Sun Records. RCA quickly signed him in 1955 and his career began to soar. He had one hit song after another and in 1956 he made his movie debut in *Love Me Tender,* a post–Civil War western in which he played a supporting role and sang four songs, including the title tune.

He starred in a total of thirty musicals, most of them formulaic and inexpensively produced. They were generally dismissed by the critics, and Elvis was considered a poor actor. While the majority of his musicals were indeed insipid, it must be said in Elvis's defense that he moved through them with considerable charm and an amiable lack of concern for their nonsensical plots. After all, the films were mere excuses for musical numbers, and there were usually a few good songs per film. There were, however, a handful of genuinely good Presley musicals, among them *Jailhouse Rock* (1957), *Viva Las Vegas* (1964) and *Frankie and Johnny* (1966).

Presley also starred in a few nonmusicals: *King Creole* (1958), *Flaming Star* (1960), and *Wild in the Country* (1961), the last based on a Clifford Odets piece. He was quite good in the first two, but out of his depth in the third. Nonetheless, it is worth noting that under the guidance of a good director such as Donald Siegel (*q.v.*), who put him through his paces in *Viva Las Vegas* and *Flaming Star*, Presley could be quite impressive.

While Presley's music and film careers dipped during the Beatles-led British invasion of the mid-1960s, his films were still commercially viable, although they were soon made with even less attention to plot and production values, making them almost painfully unwatchable. In his last film, *Change of Habit* (1969), Presley actually plays a doctor who falls in love with a nun (Mary Tyler Moore); it was an embarrassing exercise.

Presley went into semi-seclusion after his film career ended and he didn't reemerge until a Las Vegas comeback gig caused a sensation. While he continued to tour and perform, he delved heavily into prescription drugs, which ultimately led to his death at the age of 42.

PRESTON, ROBERT (1917–1987) An actor who worked in the movies for over six decades, rarely emerging as a star but, nonetheless, leaving his imprint on a host of films. In his younger days, Preston's sharp-featured face often led him to be cast as a scroundrel or a coward, but with age (and familiarity) his visage softened into that of a friendly rapscallion, the kind of lively gent who might egg someone on to do something adventurous (though he'd hardly do the same himself). Despite his long career in the movies—usually as a second male lead—he achieved his greatest fame on Broadway during the 1950s when he erupted on stage with previously untapped energy as Professor Harold Hill in *The Music Man,* later recreating his success in the 1962 film version of the hit musical.

Born Robert Preston Meservey, he took an early interest in the theater. At fifteen he joined a Shakespearean acting troupe that was directed by Tyrone Power's mother. By the age of twenty-one he had broken into the movies, making his acting debut in a small role in *King of Alcatraz* (1938). Often cast as a heavy, he appeared in a mix of "A" and "B" movies, the more well-known films being *Union Pacific* (1939), *Beau Geste* (1939), *Northwest Mounted Police* (1940), *This Gun for Hire* (1942), and *Wake Island* (1942).

After World War II, Preston gave strong performances in *The Macomber Affair* (1947) and *Tulsa* (1949), but most of his movies were lesser efforts and his roles didn't improve. After a few minor movies in the early 1950s, he all but disappeared from the big screen but scored on the Broadway stage.

Despite the rousing success of *The Music Man* when it appeared in movie theaters, Preston found that he was not very much in demand for new film roles. In any event, he made the most of his limited film appearances, giving memorable performances in movies such as *All the Way Home* (1963), *Junior Bonner* (1972), *Semi-Tough* (1977), *Victor/Victoria* (1982), for which he garnered a nomination for Best Supporting Actor, and *The Last Starfighter* (1984).

PRICE, VINCENT (1911–) An actor who has appeared in more than 100 films since 1938. While he is best remembered for his villainous roles in horror movies of the 1950s and 1960s, he has played in everything from romances to comedies, and from period pieces to contemporary dramas. Through the better part of his career, the tall, intense-looking thespian has been a character actor, using his wonderfully resonant baritone voice either to suggest a haughty superiority or to portend evil.

Born to a wealthy St. Louis family, Price received an excellent education that was weighted heavily with an appreciation of the arts. He toured Europe after graduating from high school and then went on to study art history and English at Yale. Enamored of the theater, he decided to try his luck on Broadway—with little success. He returned to his studies, choosing to get his master's degree in fine arts at the University of London. But the theater continued to beckon him and, this time, he had the good fortune to be cast in a modest role in a play called *Chicago* at London's Gate Theater in 1935. Cultured and sophisticated beyond his years, he was soon chosen for a lead role in *Victoria Regina,* an English play that was then brought over, with Price, to Broadway. He starred opposite Helen Hayes, launching his career with considerable impetus. Price appeared in a number of important Broadway plays throughout the

One of the cinema's most engaging villains, Vincent Price earned the title of "master of the macabre" after starring in Roger Corman's Edgar Allen Poe series in the early 1960s. Photo by Dan Umstead, courtesy of Vincent Price.

next several years before Hollywood decided to take a chance on him.

The actor made his film debut in *Service de Luxe* (1938) and, during the first decade of his film career, was often cast in gentlemanly and/or aristocratic leads because of his well-bred manner and formal speaking style. He was, for instance, Sir Walter Raleigh in *The Private Lives of Elizabeth and Essex* (1939), the Duke of Clarence in *Tower of London* (1939), Clifford Pyncheon in *The House of the Seven Gables* (1940), and Dutour in *The Song of Bernadette* (1943).

As a byproduct of playing decadent aristocrats, he was cast in more sinister roles. Movies such as *Shock* (1946), *Dragonwyck* (1946), *The Bribe* (1949), and *The Baron of Arizona* (1950) laid the groundwork for his quintessential villain in *House of Wax* (1953).

It's ironic that though his stock as a major actor in important features had been slowly descending during the 1940s and early 1950s, his reputation as an actor and cinematic presence would finally be made in exploitation "B" movies such as *The Fly* (1958), *Return of the Fly* (1959), *The Tingler* (1959), and most importantly, Roger Corman's "Poe Cycle," *The House of Usher* (1960), *The Pit and the Pendulum* (1961), *Tales of Terror* (1962), *The Raven* (1963), *The Masque of the Red Death* (1964), and *The Tomb of Ligeia* (1964).

The Corman/Price collaboration would not be appreciated by many critics until some time later and the actor's career continued to slide despite the commercial success of his horror films. He continued making movies, most of them overseas, and none of them drew any attention until he starred in *The Abominable Dr. Phibes* (1971), the sequel, *Dr. Phibes Rises Again* (1972), and *Theater of Blood* (1973). More bad films followed. Finally, in 1987, he received some small measure of acclaim from critics when he joined Lillian Gish, Bette Davis, and Ann Southern in *The Whales of August,* a contemporary film about four aging friends.

In addition to his movie work, Price busies himself writing books and lecturing about art and cooking, and, since 1980, hosting the popular PBS television series *Mystery!*
See also: Corman, Roger

PRINCIPAL PHOTOGRAPHY   Whether on a set or on location, this is the filming of all the speaking parts indicated in the shooting script of a movie. If inserts of any kind are needed, such as second unit footage of a crowd scene, a montage of newspaper headlines, etc., these may be shot either before, during, or after principal photography.

PRISON PICTURES   Audiences have had an on-again, off-again interest in movies dealing with prison life. There are two fundamental reasons underlying the popularity of such films. First, prison pictures deal in a very direct way with our primitive desire for freedom. From a psychological point of view, incarcerating (usually unjustly) the hero and forcing him to break out of prison reenacts a deeply felt human need to escape, to break free of social and societal bonds. In this sense, prison pictures are deeply antiauthoritarian. Second, prison pictures have served a political purpose, dealing, as they often have, with issues of social injustice and corruption.

While prison pictures have long been made, they have had their greatest vogue in two eras, the 1930s and the decade between 1945 and 1955. When it seemed as if society was crumbling during the Great Depression and otherwise honest men and women were sometimes forced to steal to stay alive, films about prison and the injustices that took place there began to take a firm hold on the public consciousness.

While MGM had the first major prison picture hit with the stark and powerful *The Big House* (1930), neither Irving Thalberg nor Louis B. Mayer *(qq.v.)* had the stomach to continue with the genre, leaving a vacuum that was quickly filled by Warner Bros., the one studio that spoke directly to the lower classes. Warner went on to make the best and the most important, not to mention the most, prison pictures of any other studio during the 1930s. Warner started its popular prison cycle with *I Am A Fugitive From a Chain Gang* (1932, *q.v.*), a shocking indictment of brutality and injustice that actually led to prison reforms in several Southern states. Through the rest of the decade, Warner and other studios continued making prison pictures, many of which dealt, in part, with social issues. Examples of such films are *The Last Mile* (1932), *The Mayor of Hell* (1933), later remade as *Crime School* (1938), *Twenty Thousand Years in Sing Sing* (1933), *San Quentin* (1937), *King of Alcatraz* (1938), and *Each Dawn I Die* (1939).

In the postwar era, the issue of freedom stood paramount in the minds of many, and prison—as a symbol—was a barrier to such freedom. Authority began to be viewed in movies not as benign or, at worst, occasionally corrupt (as it was often shown in the films of the 1930s), but as inherently evil. As a result, films such as *Brute Force* (1947) and *Riot in Cell Block 11* (1954) began to proliferate. These were films that were built around the issue of escape. The breakout movie finally overcame the social consciousness film, and that attitude has prevailed ever since in all sorts of prison films, including such diverse movies as *Stalag 17* (1953), *The Great Escape* (1963), and *Escape From Alcatraz* (1979).

There have been a relative handful of prison pictures concerning women. Some of them have been mere exploitation films, such as *Girls in Prison* (1956), but there have also been some serious films, including *Caged* (1950), that have detailed the humiliations and traumas that women suffer in prison. More recently, in *Mrs. Soffel* (1984), prison served as the backdrop for a fascinating love story between the wife of a warden and one of his prisoners.

There have been modest attempts during the last few decades at recreating the social consciousness prison picture. Paul Newman had a hit with *Cool Hand Luke* (1967), a hipper version of *I Am a Fugitive From a Chain Gang,* and Robert Redford played a crusading warden in *Brubaker* (1980), but neither film spawned a new cycle of prison pictures. A recent attempt to revive the genre was *Lock Up* (1989), starring Sylvester Stallone.

PRODUCER   The person who has the overall financial responsibility for a movie. Whether the producer chooses the project or has it assigned by a studio executive, he or she is the one who then sets all the production wheels in motion, and is responsible for hiring the screenwriter and director.

Even before the director is hired, the producer will be intimately involved in the preparation of the script because it is his job to ascertain the film's budget based on the content of the screenplay. If the necessary budget appears to be too high, the producer will order a rewrite, probably excluding more expensive scenes.

Once the screenplay and budget are tentatively approved, the producer will then work with the director to fill the most important roles in the film, and to hire other personnel such as the cinematographer, the composer, the editor, and key members of the technical crew. At this early time decisions concerning the shooting schedule and shooting locations will be made by the producer in consultation with the director, balancing artistic and financial considerations at every turn.

Once the film goes into production, the director takes over and the producer will usually keep his distance, carefully monitoring the dailies to see if the film is on schedule. He will also act as the arbiter of conflicts between the director and any other major players on the team.

When the movie is finished, the producer becomes more active in the process again, becoming intimately involved in the oversight of sound mixing, music, editing, and the ultimate exploitation of the film through its distribution, advertising, and sale to other markets, including cable and video.

During the studio era, producers were hired hands who were assigned their films and answered to either an executive producer or the studio production head. Independent producers either put up their own money or raised the funds to make movies. Today, independent producing usually involves finding a property, obtaining a committment from a hot director and a bankable star, and then taking that package to either a studio or some other source of financial backing in order to get the movie made.

Some of the more successful directors (e.g., Howard Hawks, John Ford, Steven Spielberg, etc.) have also produced their own films, thereby gaining greater control of their projects. A number of major actors have become producers as well, choosing their own projects and shepherding them to the screen through their production companies (e.g. Clint Eastwood, Sally Field, Mel Brooks, etc.). However one comes to producing, though, the job function remains essentially the same: to make the best, most successful movie possible while spending the least amount of money.

See also: actor-director; producer-director

PRODUCER-DIRECTOR   Those who both produce and direct their own films aren't quite as rare as they were during the height of the studio era. In those days there was a strict delineation of responsibilities and it was deemed inefficient for either a director to burden himself with production chores or a producer to become overly involved in the artistic decisions that were the director's province. During the 1930s and 1940s, only the most successful Hollywood directors were able to wangle more control by producing their own films. For instance, Howard Hawks performed both chores for *Twentieth Century* (1934), as did John Ford when he made *Stagecoach* (1939). These directors and a relative handful of others often produced their own movies.

When the studio system began to crumble in the late 1940s and early 1950s, a much larger percentage of directors began producing their own films. As independent contractors, no longer on staff at a studio, they began choosing their own projects and lining up financing—often from their former studio bosses.

In the last several decades, however, as the film business has fragmented and budgets have risen to astronomical proportions, it has become rather difficult for a director to raise the money to produce his own films. The exceptions to this rule are famous actors who also produce and direct their own vehicles, such as Warren Beatty, Clint Eastwood, Mel Brooks, and Robert Redford, all of whom produce through their own production companies.

As a general rule, it has always been far more common for a director to produce his own films than for a producer to suddenly start directing. The flow tends to usually be in the direction of the artist wanting more control of his own work. One of the rare exceptions to that rule is Stanley Kramer, who began producing in the early 1940s and added the extra hat of the director in 1955, continuing in both capacities during most of the rest of his Hollywood career.

PROPERTY MASTER   The individual charged with the responsibility of providing all the necessary props for a film's production. The property master, who is also known simply as the "prop person," must not only provide the props for specific scenes, but must also place them on the set in accordance with the instructions in the script. In other words, if the screenplay calls for an actor to pick up a brick from the sidewalk in front of a store and throw it through a window, the property master is the one who must place the brick on the sidewalk in front of the store.

PRYOR, RICHARD (1940–)   A comedian and actor who has also written, directed, and produced a number of his own films. Pryor's comic technique—projecting a comic machismo while at the same time showing abject fear—is reminiscent of Bob Hope. But unlike Hope, Pryor proudly carries his color and culture into his best roles, parodying racial stereotypes and turning those images inside out for laughs.

Born in Peoria, Illinois, and raised by his grandmother, who ran a brothel, Pryor rose to fame as a nightclub and TV comic during the 1960s. He parlayed that success into a number of small movie roles in films such as *The Busy Body* (1968), *You've Got to Walk It*

Like You Talk It or You'll Lose That Beat (1971), and *Dynamite Chicken* (1972). He had played mostly comic turns in his early films, but when he played the more serious supporting role of Piano Man in the biopic of Billie Holiday, *Lady Sings the Blues* (1972), Pryor was honored with a Best Supporting Actor Oscar nomination.

He appeared in (among other films) the highly regarded documentary *Wattstax* (1973), supported Sidney Poitier and Bill Cosby in the hit *Uptown Saturday Night* (1974), and showed his screenwriting ability by coscripting (with Mel Brooks) *Blazing Saddles* (1974), before finally hitting it big as a star in his own right in the second half of the 1970s. His breakthrough film was *The Bingo Long Travelling All-Stars and Motor Kings* (1976), and he quickly followed that with movies of the caliber of *Silver Streak* (1976), *Blue Collar* (1978), *Richard Pryor—Live in Concert* (1979), and *Stir Crazy* (1980). Most of his films during this period were either commercial or critical successes (such as *Blue Collar*), or both.

Pryor was among the biggest box office draws in Hollywood heading into the 1980s until he accidentally set himself on fire in what was reported to be a drug-related accident. Badly burned, Pryor set about to reclaim his health and his career. He's done well with the former but has had mixed results with the latter. Movies such as *Bustin' Loose* (1981), which he coproduced and scripted, *Some Kind of Hero* (1982), and the concert film *Richard Pryor Live on the Sunset Strip* (1982) have been solid successes. But he faltered with two major bombs in a row, *The Toy* (1982) and *Superman III* (1983), the latter film earning him a cool $4 million, which was a testament to his drawing power.

Just as Pryor was slipping at the box office, Eddie Murphy *(q.v.)* came on the movie scene with the hit *Trading Places* (1983), seeming to edge out the older star, as the premier American black comedian. But Pryor's box office appeal was still strong enough to allow him to bring to the screen an autobiographical film he starred in, coscripted, directed, and produced, *Jo Jo Dancer, Your Life is Calling* (1986). The film received mixed reviews from the critics but it brought him renewed attention as a serious filmmaker. Except for the ambitious comedy *See No Evil, Hear No Evil* (1989), Pryor's recent films have lacked the inspired satiric anger and energy of his best work of the late 1970s and he has settled for making minor comedies such as *Moving* (1988).

PUBLICIST Unlike the advertising company that may run radio and television commercials and pay for newspaper ads for a film, the publicist is the person responsible for bringing a movie to the attention of the public strictly on the basis of a film's subject matter, stars, or events surrounding its production.

A publicist, also known as a press agent, tries to generate free publicity for a film. He or she may do so in any number of ways, from merely sending out press releases to staging elaborate stunts to generate TV news coverage.

When a publicist works on a motion picture, he or she is referred to as a "unit publicist." In the past, publicists were often ex-newspaper people with contacts in the media. Contacts are just as important today, but one must be a member of the Publicist's Guild in order to work as a publicist for a union shop motion picture.

QUINN, ANTHONY (1915–) An actor of commanding stature who has appeared in more than one hundred and twenty movies. While not a conventionally handsome man, Quinn projects a strong, almost menacing, masculinity that initially brought him a great many minor roles as a villain. He rose to fame, however, by virtue of his combined machismo and vulnerability, demonstrating his acting skills in a number of impressive supporting roles during the 1950s, later graduating to starring character parts.

He was born Anthony Rudolph Oaxaca Quinn in Chihuahua, Mexico, to a Mexican mother and Irish father. His family moved to the United States while he was still a child, his father eventually finding work as a cameraman in Hollywood.

Quinn's first taste of acting came when he was a high school student on the east side of Los Angeles. His first professional acting job was in the 1935 Los Angeles theater production of *Clean Beds,* starring Mae West. The following year he began appearing in bit parts in low-budget films such as *Parole!, Night Waitress,* and *Sworn Enemy.* He soon made a modest breakthrough, however, when he played a Cheyenne warrior in Cecil B. De Mille's *The Plainsman* (1936). Quinn married De Mille's daughter soon after in 1937 (they divorced in 1965), but the marriage did not seem to affect his career. The actor continued to play small roles, usually native characters of one kind or another, in roughly twenty films during the next decade without attracting much attention.

It wasn't until he left Los Angeles and headed for Broadway that his career began to improve. He starred in *The Gentleman from Athens* and scored a critical success. He topped that with a highly praised run as Stanley Kowalski in the Chicago production of *A Streetcar Named Desire,* after which he went on the road with the play for nearly two years.

By the time he returned to Hollywood, Quinn had earned a reputation as a good actor. He landed a significant role in *The Brave Bulls* (1950), but really came into his own as a film actor when he starred along with Marlon Brando in *Viva Zapata!* (1952) and won his first Best Supporting Actor Academy Award.

Despite his Oscar, starring roles were still eluding Quinn, and he decided to try his luck in Europe's burgeoning film industry.

It was Federico Fellini's *La Strada* (1954) that made him an international star and led to a new appreciation of Quinn's talents.

Back in Hollywood the actor played the painter Paul Gauguin in *Lust for Life* (1956) and won another Best Supporting Actor Oscar. He went on to play important supporting roles in films such as *Last Train from Gun Hill* (1958), *Guns of Navarone* (1961). *Becket* (1961), and *Lawrence of Arabia* (1962). Quinn's father-in-law even gave him a break by offering him the chance to direct Charlton Heston and Yul Brynner in *The Buccaneer* (1958), but the Cecil B. De Mille production was a bomb.

Quinn's solid performances and good reviews in a string of hit films during the late 1950s and early 1960s led to starring character roles in movies such as *Barabbas* (1962), *Requiem for a Heavyweight* (1963), *Zorba the Greek* (1964), *The Shoes of the Fisherman* (1968), and *The Secret of Santa Vittorio* (1969). These and other films propelled him to the critical and popular apogee of his movie career during the 1960s.

He continued to star in films throughout the 1970s and 1980s, but the movies weren't as good and the box office receipts were usually worse. At best the films were mediocre, e.g., *A Walk in the Spring Rain* (1970), *Across 110th Street* (1971), and the poor but popular *The Greek Tycoon* (1978). At worst they were truly awful, e.g. *R.P.M.* (1970), *The Don is Dead* (1973), and the

In a long film career that began in 1936, Anthony Quinn has been associated with a number of fine films, including *Viva Zapata!* (1952) and *Lust for Life* (1956), but the one movie with which he is most closely associated has been *Zorba the Greek* (1964), in which he is seen here with his costar, Alan Bates. Photo courtesy of Anthony Quinn Productions.

big-budget disaster *Mohammed, Messenger of God* (1977).

Quinn has appeared much less frequently in films during the 1980s, mostly starring in foreign productions such as *The Salamander* (1983) and *Valentra* (1984). Though the actor worked on live television during the late 1940s and in prime time TV in the early 1970s, he has ignored the medium in the 1980s, instead returning to the stage to star in a musical version of *Zorba the Greek* (1983–1986); including a triumphant run on Broadway. During the last decade he has come to be a highly regarded sculptor and painter, exhibiting his work throughout the United States.

RACISM IN HOLLYWOOD Like many facets of American society, Hollywood has been guilty of gross prejudice against minority groups, particularly blacks. Systematic, institutionalized racism in the movie business allowed no opportunities for blacks behind the camera, and it relegated talented performers to demeaning roles, forcing movies to be structured and edited not for quality but for racial content.

Early attempts by filmmakers to address the inequities in our society might have been awkward and embarrassing—and sometimes misguided—but they remained tentative steps in the right direction. Such steps were well in advance of those in other media, including radio, TV, mainstream newspapers and magazines, and, for that matter, most political and social institutions. For all its faults, for all the shame of decades of deliberate bigotry, Hollywood—in the persons of individual courageous filmmakers—did have a conscience. Unfortunately, as a longtime shaper of public opinion, the movie business had a great deal to compensate for.

D. W. Griffith's *The Birth of a Nation* (1915 *qq.v.*) was certainly not the first example of racism in Hollywood, but it was the most infamous, if not the most blatant. Incredibly, the heroes of the film were Ku Klux Klansmen, riding to the rescue of a white girl threatened with rape by a black villain and his cronies. The hue and cry of outrage by groups such as the NAACP at such inflamatory racism did nothing to curtail the widespread popularity of the movie. Griffith, embarrassed at the charges of racism leveled against him, tried to counter the criticism through his paen to understanding, *Intolerance* (1916), and promptly lost a bundle.

The minstrel show tradition of the nineteenth century had, of course, perpetuated racial stereotypes long before *The Birth of a Nation*. Distorted images of blacks were carried over from the minstrel shows into the movies and were reinforced by popular performers,

such as Al Jolson in his blackface appearance in the first talkie, *The Jazz Singer* (1927).

While the Hal Roach Our Gang comedy series of the 1920s and 1930s showed black children mixing freely with their white counterparts on generally equal terms, it was the exception to the rule. Nonetheless, racial stereotypes abounded in the Our Gang series in the persons of Buckwheat and Stymie. The predominant cinematic view of blacks at the time was represented more accurately by performers such as Stepin Fetchit and Hattie McDaniel *(qq.v.)* who appeared in movies usually as porters, maids, an cooks. Fetchit, in particular assumed the archetypal black stereotype: slow-talking, lazy, cowardly, and superstitious. The closest black Americans came to being honorably recognized by Hollywood was when Hattie McDaniel received a Best Supporting Actress Academy Award for her role as Scarlett O'Hara's mammy in *Gone With the Wind* (1939), the first black performer to win an Oscar.

There were few dignified roles for black actors or actresses in Hollywood movies, as Ethel Waters *(q.v.)*, Butterfly McQueen, and others would have readily attested. The one partial exception to this lack of self-expression was in the world of the Hollywood musical. Black performers could sing and dance in otherwise white films, as evidenced by Bill "Bojangles" Robinson dancing in a number of Shirley Temple films, the Nicholas Brothers wowing audiences with their incredible choreography, Lena Horne singing her heart out in musical revues, etc. In many cases, however, such numbers were structured within films to be easily excised without disturbing the flow of the scenes around them. The purpose of this was to allow the scenes with black performers to be edited out when the movies were shown in the South.

A rarer, but more cohesive, means of expression for black performers occasionally availed itself in the form of all-black musicals, such as *Hallelujah* (1929), *Cabin in the Sky* (1943), *Carmen Jones* (1954), and *Porgy and Bess* (1959), all of which, however, were written and directed by whites and, despite the best of intentions, contained crude racial stereotypes.

At the height of the studio era there were films for whites and films for blacks, separate and terribly unequal. Movies created strictly for black audiences were cheaply made with virtually no production values. Nonetheless, a few notable independent movies were made in this era, thanks to the towering personality of Paul Robeson.

Robeson had been a star athlete turned singer and actor. He starred in the screen adaptation of his stage success *The Emperor Jones* (1933), but it was not a hit. After the original film version of *Showboat* (1936) in which he gave his impressive rendition of "Ole Man River," the only films that allowed him any dignity were those made in England.

Showboat was the crude beginning of a very slow reexamination of race in America. The story dealt with a girl of mixed race passing as white. It dealt with serious issues despite its musical trappings, and it was a hit. So was the 1951 remake. In both versions, though, the heroine was played by a white rather than a black actress. In fact, Lena Horne wanted very much to play the part but she was denied the opportunity because she was black, though it was obvious that she would have been ideal.

World War II slowly accelerated the pace of black acceptance in the movies. Blacks and whites were shown together fighting a common enemy. The typical configuration of an Irishman, an Italian, a Jew, and a black as part of a combat team ultimately became something of a cliché. Nevertheless, it was a step in the right direction.

After the war, a few filmmakers began to deal with the issue of racism head-on. Elia Kazan's *Pinky* (1949) dealt with the same issue of passing as *Showboat* had done but in a more direct fashion. Again, however, the lead role was played by a white actress, Jeanne Crain.

Despite the latter-day criticism leveled against Stanley Kramer for his pretentious "message" movies, he was the first producer-director to consistently deal with the issue of racism. His late 1950s and 1960s films, *The Defiant Ones* (1958), *Pressure Point* (1962), and *Guess Who's Coming to Dinner* (1967), were attempts not to convince the committed but to educate while entertaining a mass audience that found the idea of racial harmony relatively novel.

It was partly through the efforts of Kramer that Sidney Poitier *(q.v.)* became the first black leading man in Hollywood films and the first to win a Best Actor Oscar, taking the Academy Award for *Lillies of the Field* (1963). Unfortunately, Poitier was also the only black Hollywood star of the late 1950s and 1960s.

Finally, Hollywood realized that a potentially huge black audience existed that would buy millions of dollars worth of tickets if only their needs would be respected. Melvin Van Peebles opened the door with *Sweet Sweetback's Baadassss Song* (1971), a low-budget film he wrote, directed, produced, and starred in that was a sleeper hit in black communities all over the country. His breakthrough led to a revolution in movies aimed at blacks, most of them known as "Black exploitation" films, for example *Shaft* (1971) and *Superfly* (1972). Eventually, the trend died out due to poor product and repetitiveness.

But if the black exploitation film was defunct, the concept of black filmmaking was still alive and well. It soon flourished in the hands of more committed filmmakers, such as Harry Belafonte, Sidney Poitier, and Bill Cosby, who collaborated on a number of hit comedies, most memorably *Uptown, Saturday Night* (1974). Finally, blacks were working both behind the camera and in front of the camera in "A" movies with well-known stars capable of reaching a crossover (i.e., white) audience.

It's been more difficult for younger blacks without the financial clout of such stars as Belafonte, etc. to get the financing they need to make movies, but some, such as Spike Lee and Robert Townsend, have persevered and succeeded, making not only entertaining and provocative films, but continuing to point out in their movies the lingering racial inequities in our society. A case in point is Spike Lee's *Do the Right Thing* (1989). And certainly the major on-camera crossover successes of first Richard Pryor *(q.v.)* and then Eddie Murphy *(q.v.)* indicate that not only movies, but movie audiences, are becoming ever-increasingly color blind.

Racism in Hollywood, however, has not been exercised strictly against blacks. Most minority groups have suffered the slings and arrows of outrageous misrepresentation. During the late 1940s, when "message" movies came into their own, *Crossfire* (1947) and *Gentlemen's Agreement* (1947), films decrying anti-Semitism, were both hits. Up until that time, Jews weren't so much distorted in Hollywood movies (many of the major studios were run by Jews) as ignored, at least insofar as Jewish characters and concerns were rarely shown on screen, except as comic relief.

Italian-Americans have been offended by the fact that most gangsters in films, since the days of Enrico Bandello (Edward G. Robinson) in *Little Caesar* (1930) through Don Corleone (Marlon Brando) in *The Godfather* (1972) and beyond are given Italian surnames.

The Hollywood stereotype of the inscrutable oriental in films such as the Charlie Chan and Mr. Moto series dogged Asian–Americans. Films of this nature were all the more insidious because the heroes were always played by white men.

To a larger degree, racist depictions of Native Americans, particularly in westerns, has been blatant. At the time few balked at such dialogue as, "The only good Indian, is a dead Indian." For decades the Native American was the all-purpose villain. Beginning in the 1950s, the realization began to set in that Native Americans were victims of genocide, and filmmakers tried to set the record straight in movies such as *Broken Arrow* (1950), *Cheyenne Autumn* (1964), and *Little Big Man* (1970).

See also: Brown, Jim; Ford, John; *Gentlemen's Agreement; The Godfather I & II;* Kazan, Elia; Kramer, Stanley; Our Gang; Preminger, Otto; Vidor, King

RAFT, GEORGE (1895–1980)   He was an actor of little range and poor judgment, but he played tough guys as well as any actor outside of the Warner Bros. lot. Except for a short-lived attempt by Paramount to turn him into the next Valentino, Raft played gangster types almost from the very beginning of his career. And during most of the 1930s and early 1940s that was just fine with Raft, who enjoyed a heady success even though he was well aware of his shortcomings as an actor.

It was only fitting that Raft was typed as a gangster since he was an up-and-coming hood in Owney Madden's mob in New York, where he grew up. He started out as a boxer, and later became a dancer with a reputation for doing a spectacularly fast Charleston. After dancing in a few Broadway shows, he went to Hollywood and was supported by his pal Madden until he became a star.

Raft's debut came in a bit part as a gangster in *Queen of the Night Clubs* (1929). After a short lull, he played similar roles in several other films in the early 1930s, but it was his supporting performance as Guido Rinaldo, the coin-flipping hood in *Scarface* (1932), that turned him into a star.

When he wasn't playing gangsters, Raft was usually playing a tough guy of some other sort—a taxi driver, a detective, or an ex-con. But his best starring vehicle of the 1930s was *Bolero* (1934), in which he played a dancer. It didn't hurt that he costarred with Carole Lombard *(q.v.)*. It was the success of *Bolero,* soon followed by *Rumba* (1935), that made Paramount believe they had the next Valentino among their stable of stars, but the public was more interested in Raft as a tough guy than as a sex symbol.

In 1939, when his contract was up at Paramount, Warner Bros. eagerly sought him out. He seemed as if he was just their kind of tough guy actor. Among his better Warner films of that period were *They Drive by Night* (1940) and *Manpower* (1941). He might have gone on to become one of Warner's most important stars of the 1940s had his own lack of good sense not thwarted him.

David Shipman in *The Great Movie Stars* reports Raft

George Raft wasn't one of the brightest or the most talented actors in Hollywood but he did have screen presence. The one actor who owed the most to Raft was Humphrey Bogart, who rose to fame in films that Raft turned down. It's only fitting, therefore, that Raft be seen here next to an advertisement for a 1939 Bogart movie. Photo courtesy of The Siegel Collection.

saying in 1937, "I'm not a good enough actor to trust myself to any but the best director, best cameraman, best story." He didn't think *High Sierra* (1941) was a good story and he turned it down because he didn't want to die at the end. Humphrey Bogart *(q.v.)* got the role and it established him as a star. Then he turned down *The Maltese Falcon* (1941) because he didn't want to work with first-time director John Huston *(q.v.)*. Again, Bogart received the role on the rebound and solidified his star standing in a film that has become a classic. Then, finally, Raft was one of the actors (along with Ronald Reagan) who was offered the lead in *Casablanca* (1942). He didn't like the script and Bogart, again, stepped into the breach and became a romantic leading man in one of Hollywood's greatest films. Raft's decisions over that three-year period virtually killed his own career and helped create Humphrey Bogart's.

In his autobiography, Jack Warner related yet another example of Raft's less than keen mind: In 1943 he offered Raft the opportunity of being bought out of his contract. Raft asked how much? Jack Warner said $10,000. The actor, who also wanted his freedom, immediately wrote a check for the amount and gave it to Warner, who rushed to the bank to cash it. Raft didn't understand that Warner was offering to pay *him*.

Most of Raft's films during the rest of the 1940s were of no distinction. After working in Europe in the early 1950s, he had a minor Hollywood revival in films such as *Black Widow* (1954) and *Rogue Cop* (1954), but by the end of the 1950s and throughout the rest of his career, he tended to make only cameo appearances playing a caricature of his coin-flipping Guido Rinaldo character. Most notable among his later films were *Some Like It Hot* (1959), *The Ladies Man* (1961), and *Casino Royale* (1967). His final appearance was in Mae West's last movie, *Sexette* (1978).

RAINS, CLAUDE (1889–1967) He was one of the screen's most debonair villains, particularly during the 1940s. His expressive face, wonderfully modulated baritone voice, and deft manner with a wry riposte made him that all-too-infrequent film character: a likable bad guy. He didn't always play villains; he occasionally garnered heroic leading roles in addition to his character parts, but regardless of the size of his role, Rains almost always seemed to steal the show. Nominated four times for Academy Awards as Best Supporting Actor, he was denied the Oscar but his performances have hardly diminished with time.

Born in London, he began his theatrical career as a child actor when he was eleven years old. He arrived in the United States in 1914 and had considerable success both on the stage and later on radio. It appeared as if his film career would be limited because of his slight stature and average looks, but he became a film star in 1933 when he played the title role in *The Invisible Man,* despite the fact that he was barely seen in the film.

He starred in the Hecht-MacArthur film, *Crime Without Passion* (1934), but his career dipped soon thereafter and he didn't fully take hold in the public consciousness until he played the wonderfully venal King John in Warner Bros.' splendid version of *The Adventures of Robin Hood* (1938). He continued to work steadily, and his roles quickly became richer, as did his performances. He received his first Academy Award nomination as the corrupt senator in *Mr. Smith Goes to Washington* (1939); his second nomination was for his portrayal of the suave and charming collaborator, Captain Renault, in *Casablanca* (1942); his third Oscar bid came from his role as a loving husband of Bette Davis, *(q.v.)* in *Mr. Skeffington,* and his fourth nomination was for his role as the Nazi who can't help falling in love with Ingrid Bergman *(q.v.)* in Hitchcock's *Notorious* (1946).

If Rains came into his own at the end of the 1930s, he flourished in the 1940s, with plum starring roles in films such as *The Phantom of the Opera* (1943), *Deception* (1946), and *The Unsuspected* (1947). Unfortunately, he didn't find suitable roles in the 1950s and his career

suffered a deep decline. Rains was the ideal actor for the studio system; he was suited to a variety of character roles. All that ended in the 1950s and Rains made only the occasional film thereafter. He was memorable in a small role in *Lawrence of Arabia* (1962) and he finished his acting career as Herod the Great in *The Greatest Story Ever Told* (1965).

RAT PACK A loosely organized group of rebellious show business personalities. According to Lauren Bacall in her book, *By Myself,* the charter members of the pack were Humphrey Bogart (founder and leader), Bacall, David Niven and his wife, Hjorids, restaurateur Mike Romanoff and his wife, Gloria, agent Irving "Swifty" Lazar, Frank Sinatra, Judy Garland and her then husband, Sidney Luft. Others were later invited to join, but only with unanimous approval of the original rat packers.

The group was purely social, though it gained a great deal of notoriety during the early 1950s because of its exclusive membership and fun-loving attitudes. As Bacall wrote, "one had to be addicted to noncomformity, staying up late, drinking, laughing, and not caring what anyone thought or said about us."

After Bogart's death in 1956, Frank Sinatra ascended to the position of unofficial leader of the group. The Rat Pack was soon transformed into a Sinatra clique that included Dean Martin, Sammy Davis, Jr., Joey Bishop, and Peter Lawford. Unlike the original Rat Pack, Sinatra and his "clan" often appeared together in movies, among them, *Ocean's Eleven* (1960), *Sergeants Three* (1962), and *Robin and the Seven Hoods* (1964).

The concept of the Rat Pack has carried on through the years, finding fresh applications (at least in the media) in a loose confederation of young 1980s actors known as the Brat Pack *(q.v.),* and a group of successful black performers called the Black Pack.

RATHBONE, BASIL (1892–1967) Tall, gaunt, and possessed of a delightful English accent, he was an actor best known for his worthy portrayals of villains opposite the likes of Errol Flynn and Tryone Power *(qq.v.),* as well as for his depiction of one of the screen's most admired detective heroes, Sherlock Holmes.

Born Philip St. John Basil Rathbone in Johannesburg, South Africa, to British parents, he was sent to England for his schooling. Rathbone was to have gone into the insurance business but he followed his instincts and entered the acting profession instead, later becoming a much-admired Shapespearean actor.

His first film appearance in England was in *The Fruitful Vine* (1921). Meanwhile, his stage work brought him across the Atlantic and eventually to Hollywood, where he was seen in *Pity the Chorus Girl?* (1924). He made several other silent films in the United States while continuing to act on the stage. His big-screen

It's "elementary, my dear Watson" that despite all the actors who played Sherlock Holmes, the only one worthy of the name was Basil Rathbone. He was also an exquisite villain in swashbucklers, and one of Hollywood's best fencers (yet only in one film, *Romeo and Juliet,* 1936, was he allowed to win a duel). Photo courtesy of Movie Star News.

breakthrough came early in the sound era when he costarred opposite Norma Shearer *(q.v.)* in *The Last of Mrs. Cheyney* (1929). Soon thereafter the future Sherlock Holmes received some early training in film sleuthing when he played Philo Vance in *The Bishop Murder Case* (1930).

Though he appeared in a considerable number of films both in America and Britain in the early 1930s, Rathbone kept returning to the stage. It wasn't until he played Mr. Murdstone in MGM's version of *David Copperfield* (1935) that the actor put down roots in Hollywood and stayed for eleven years.

From 1935 till the end of 1939, Rathbone played a marvelous succession of villains, highlighted by performances as Greta Garbo's husband in *Anna Karenina* (1935), the rapacious buccaneer who dueled Errol Flynn in *Captain Blood* (1935, *q.v.*), and the memorably corrupt Sir Guy, the Sheriff of Nottingham, who dueled with Flynn yet again in *The Adventures of Robin Hood* (1938). If this were not enough, he played the title role in *The Son of Frankenstein* in 1939. One of his rare reprieves from playing scoundrels was *The Dawn Patrol* (1938), in which he portrayed an officer cracking up under the pressure of having to send his men off to certain death. It was a reminder of what this fine actor could do when given the chance to demonstrate his considerable skills.

What distinguished Rathbone's villains from the usual black hats was the superior attitude they usually affected. Rathbone was a cerebral actor, and that quality was set to the cause of justice when he played Sherlock Holmes in *The Hound of the Baskervilles* (1939). It was the first and best of an astonishing fourteen Holmes films in which Rathbone starred along with Nigel Bruce as his ever-faithful Dr. Watson.

The Holmes films were made during a seven-year stretch, during which Rathbone continued to play villains, including in *The Mark of Zorro* (1940) and *Fingers at the Window* (1942), among others.

By 1946, tired of playing Holmes in ever more dreadful films, Rathbone left Hollywood. He worked on the stage and made only occasional films during the 1950s, most notably John Ford's *The Last Hurrah* (1958). In the 1960s, he appeared in more films but they were of lesser quality. He traded on his villainous image in movies such as Roger Corman *(q.v.)* quickies *Tales of Terror* (1962) and *Comedy of Terrors* (1963), and even stooped to appearing in *The Ghost in the Invisible Bikini* (1966). His last film was *Hillbillys in a Haunted House* (1967).

RAY, NICHOLAS (1911–1979)   As critic Andrew Sarris noted in *The American Cinema,* "every relationship establishes its own moral code and . . . there is no such thing as abstract morality [in a Nicolas Ray film]." This ambiguous approach caught on with the disaffected youth of the 1950s, particularly as expressed in Ray's most famous film, *Rebel Without a Cause* (1955). The director's style is frenetic and his camera movements and editing heighten the nervous energy of his desperate and troubled heroes.

Born Raymond Nicholas Kienzle, he first showed his flair for dramatics in a radio script he wrote at the age of sixteen that he sent to the University of Chicago. The school promptly offered him a scholarship. While in college, he studied architecture with Frank Lloyd Wright. Later, he was influenced by the socially conscious left-wing attitudes of The Group Theater for whom he worked as an actor, appearing in director Elia Kazan's first play, *The Young Go First,* in 1935. He went on to become a member of John Houseman's Phoenix Theater Company in 1938.

Ray was active in both radio dramas and the theater during the late 1930s and early 1940s. He wrote and directed *Back Where I Came From* for the Broadway stage in 1943. In 1946 he directed *Lute Song,* which featured a young Yul Brynner. Meanwhile, Ray got his first taste of Hollywood when his old mentor from the Group Theater, Elia Kazan, invited him to work as his assistant director on *A Tree Grows in Brooklyn* (1945).

Production chief Dore Schary's interest in developing new young directors at RKO gave Ray the chance to direct *They Live By Night* (finished in 1947 as *The*

Twisted Road, but released in 1949). A film about two young outsiders trying to find love in a bleak world, its theme was one Ray would return to often, most memorably in his classic youth movie *Rebel Without a Cause,* for which Ray also provided the story.

The director's career was in its most creative phase during the late 1940s and early 1950s. Among his most interesting films of that era were a powerful Hollywood psychological suspense thriller starring Humphrey Bogart and Gloria Grahame (Ray's second wife), *In a Lonely Place* (1950), the deeply moody crime film *On Dangerous Ground* (1952), the socially conscious *The Lusty Men* (1952), the psychological western, *Johnny Guitar* (1954), and another underrated western, *Run For Cover* (1955), with James Cagney.

Except for *Bigger than Life* (1956), he slumped in the second half of the 1950s with mediocre films such as *Hot Blood* (1956), *The True Story of Jesse James* (1957), and *Wind Across the Everglades* (1958). Ray made a strong artistic comeback in 1960 with *The Savage Innocents,* an international production starring Anthony Quinn and Peter O'Toole. In addition to directing, Ray wrote the screenplay.

By this time he had already become a hero of the French film critics and his reputation was on the rise. Wanting to become an independent, and needing the money to do so, he chose to make two epics for which he was extremely well paid. Neither lent itself to Ray's intimate and intense style of filmmaking, but he nonetheless turned *King of Kings* (1961) into a critical and commercial success. Unfortunately, he lost control of *55 Days at Peking* (1963), which had to be finished by his second unit director, Andrew Marston. It unexpectly turned out to be Ray's last Hollywood project.

He spent six frustrating years in Europe trying to get new projects off the ground without success. In the early 1970s he began teaching filmmaking at Harpur College of the State University of New York. As a supervisor of his students, he oversaw the production of *You Can't Go Home Again* (1976). He was not, however, altogether finished with the movies; he played an important role in front of the cameras in Wim Wenders' *The American Friend* (1977). He died of cancer two years later.
See also: auteur; Dean, James

REAGAN, RONALD (1911–) An actor of modest talent whose Hollywood career consisted mostly of "B" movies. Pleasant, easy-going, and amiable were all terms that described Reagan, along with warm, comfortable, and affable. He was good-looking in a wholesome sort of way, and he was a serviceable leading man in most of his more than fifty films, though few of them were memorable.

He had far greater impact in Hollywood as president of the Screen Actor's Guild (1947–1952 and 1962) than

Though he didn't look it in this publicity still from *Tugboat Annie Sails Again* (1940), Ronald Reagan was preparing for his role as "The Great Communicator." In a modest acting career, he projected the same amiable sincerity on film as he did when he was president of the United States. Photo courtesy of Movie Star News.

as an actor. It was during his tenure as president that the House Un-American Activities Committee investigated the film industry for Communist infiltration. Depending upon one's viewpoint, Reagan was instrumental in either saving the Screen Actor's Guild or selling out its more liberal members. In either case, he was deeply involved in the politics of his time. He later left the movies to enter government, ultimately ascending to the presidency of the United States in 1980. He held that position for eight years and in that capacity was far more popular than he had been during his more than twenty-five years in Hollywood.

In his youth, Reagan was more interested in sports than in either movies or politics. Born in Illinois, he was known in his younger days as "Dutch" Reagan when he had his first significant brush with show business as a play-by-play radio announcer for the Chicago Cubs baseball team. Handsome and personable, he was encouraged to give Hollywood a try. He went West and signed with Warner Bros. in 1937, making his debut in the leading role of *Love Is on the Air* (1937), a "B" movie that tried to take advantage of his experience as a radio personality.

He worked steadily throughout the rest of the 1930s and early 1940s, starring mostly in low-budget light romances, thin comedies, and action/adventure films such as *Sergeant Murphy* (1938), *Secret Service of the Air* (1939), and *Tugboat Annie Sails Again* (1940). Happily, not all of his films were quite so forgettable. He showed some flair in better movies, such as *Brother Rat* (1938), *Knute Rockne, All American* (1940), *King's Row* (1942), and *Desperate Journey* (1942), although in many of these films he played in support of bigger stars.

During World War II, as a captain in the U. S. Army Air Force, Reagan made training films. When he was discharged from the service he resumed his acting career, starring in mildly amusing comedies such as *John Loves Mary* (1947) and *The Girl From Jones Beach* (1949), but by the early 1950s he was slogging through movies of the ilk of *Hong Kong* (1952), *Tropic Zone* (1953), and *Cattle Queen of Montana* (1954). The only bright moments of his postwar film career were *Hasty Heart* (1950) and the unfairly maligned comedy *Bedtime for Bonzo* (1951).

With his movie career slumping badly, Reagan turned to television with considerable success, hosting the TV shows "Death Valley Days" and "General Electric Theater." Meanwhile, he divorced actress Jane Wyman (*q.v.*, the marriage lasted from 1940 until 1948), and married actress Nancy Davis in 1952, with whom he also costarred in *Hellcats of the Navy* (1957). Reagan was long off the big screen when he was signed to play the conniving villain in Don Siegel's *The Killers* (1964). Cast against type, he delivered one of his best screen performances; it was also his last.

A former Roosevelt New Deal Democrat, Reagan became a staunch and active conservative Republican during the 1950s and finally entered the political fray to run for governor of California, winning two terms of office (1966–1974). In 1976 he auditioned for the job of president of the United States, didn't get the part, but received a callback in 1980, finally winning two terms to the highest office in the land. He left the White House in January 1989 having presided over some of the most revolutionary changes in the federal government since the Great Depression.

REDFORD, ROBERT (1937–) A handsome superstar actor, Redford's reputation as a director is growing. Ironically, his dazzling, clean-cut good looks have sometimes prevented him from getting roles in movies with contemporary settings thought to be better suited to more ethnic types. For instance, the majority of his starring roles of the last twenty years have been in period pieces, except when he portrays specific, recognizable types, such as a glamour boy politician in *The Candidate* (1972) or a cowboy in *The Electric Horseman* (1979). Redford has chosen his vehicles wisely and, in the process, he has established himself as one of Hollywood's most bankable stars since the late 1960s.

Born Charles Robert Redford to a well-to-do Los Angeles accountant, the young man had no apparent interest in the movies. He was an athlete earning a baseball scholarship to the University of Colorado when he quit college to become a vagabond artist, painting and sketching his way across Europe. At twenty he returned to the States and decided to become a scenic designer for the theater. With that thought in mind he first enrolled at the Pratt Institute in Brooklyn and then the American Academy of Dramatic Arts in the belief that if he understood the requirements of the theater more fully he could better design for the stage.

Instead, he ended up *on* the stage. His striking good looks could not be ignored for long, and he found himself with one line of dialogue in a 1959 Broadway play, *Tall Story*. He continued working intermittently in the theater and in television, appearing on several different prime-time series such as "Perry Mason," "Naked City," "Route 66," and "Alfred Hitchcock Presents." At one point, he was considered for the title role in the TV series "Dr. Kildare" later won by Richard Chamberlain.

Redford's first film appearance was as the lead in *War Hunt* (1962), a low-budget action film. More importantly, he met future director Sydney Pollack (*q.v.*), who had a small role in the film. Redford and Pollack would ultimately make many of their best movies together.

From the very start, Redford had leading roles in his films. But he didn't blossom into a movie star overnight. Interesting though flawed films such as *Inside Daisy Clover* (1965), *The Chase* (1966), and his first Pollack-directed movie, *This Property Is Condemned* (1966), kept him in front of the public.

Redford still had an interest in the theater and starred on Broadway in Neil Simon's *Barefoot in the Park*, reprising his role in the 1967 hit film version. He was poised to make his mark as a film star and, in his next movie, *Butch Cassidy and the Sundance Kid* (1969), a huge critical and financial success, he made his big breakthrough.

Redford has consistently worked with good directors, leading to the occasional critical hit that doubles as a commercial failure, such as Michael Ritchie's *Downhill Racer* (1969) and Sidney J. Furie's *Little Fauss and Big Halsy* (1970). But he has been enormously successful with Sydney Pollack, who directed him in *Jeremiah Johnson* (1972), *The Way We Were* (1973), *Three Days of the Condor* (1975), *The Electric Horseman* (1978), and *Out of Africa* (1985), although the actor did not receive good personal reviews for the last effort.

Surprisingly, Redford has had only one colossal flop, *The Great Gatsby* (1974), and one surprising loser, *The Great Waldo Pepper* (1975). Otherwise he has had an outstanding number of highly regarded hits in addition to those directed by Sydney Pollack. For instance, he appeared in Michael Ritchie's *The Candidate*, George Roy Hill's *The Sting* (1973) for which he received an Oscar-nomination, Alan J. Pakula's *All the President's Men* (1976), and Barry Levinson's *The Natural* (1984).

Redford has been more than an actor; he has taken an active role in his projects, establishing his own production company, Wildwood, and using his star clout to get certain movies made, such as *All the President's Men*.

He has also been creatively involved behind the scenes, surprising Hollywood and a great many critics and fans by choosing to direct (and not star in) *Ordinary People* (1980). Even more shocking to most was how good a job he did, good enough, in fact, to win Best Picture and Best Director Oscars. Ironically, he had been acting for twenty years without winning a major award, and then he won one his first time out as a director.

His second directorial effort, *The Milagro Beanfield War* (1987), was also well received by critics but only modestly attended by moviegoers. At his superstar level, Redford can continue to act or direct as he so chooses. Yet his extracurricular activities as a conservationist and liberal activist have fueled rumors of a possible political career.

REED, DONNA (1921–1986) An actress with an attractive, wholesome appearance who starred in films during the 1940s and early 1950s with only a modest impact. Though she appeared in more than forty movies, Reed is best remembered for only a few performances that were in support of bigger stars.

Born Donna Belle Mullenger in Iowa, she was every bit the mid-American beauty that audiences saw on screen. After moving to Los Angeles, she was voted Campus Queen at Los Angeles City College and acted in school productions before being spotted and signed by an MGM talent scout in 1941.

Reed made her film debut in a minor role in *The Getaway* (1941) and proceeded to be groomed for stardom in ingenue roles in films such as *Shadow of the Thin Man* (1941), *The Courtship of Andy Hardy* (1942), and *Dr. Gillespie's Criminal Case* (1943). She had a chance to shine in more serious films such as *The Human Comedy* (1943) and finally graduated to leading roles in *The Picture of Dorian Gray* (1945), *They Were Expendable* (1945), and *It's a Wonderful Life* (1946). Her characters were not, however, the focus of any of those pictures.

The latter half of the 1940s found her in such dreary films as *Green Dolphin Street* (1947), and a couple of Alan Ladd films, *Beyond Glory* (1948) and *Chicago Deadline* (1949). Her career was going nowhere fast, and she finally left MGM for Columbia where her husband (Tony Owen) worked as studio boss Harry Cohn's assistant. Nothing much changed at Columbia; she played the same bland characters in equally bland films—with one exception. She fought to play the role of Alma (the prostitute) in *From Here to Eternity* (1953). Her decision to perform against type brought her a great deal of attention, plus an Academy Award for Best Supporting Actress.

Surprisingly, it didn't help her career. She finished out the better part of the 1950s appearing in a number of westerns, such as *Gun Fury* (1953), *They Rode West* (1954), and *The Far Horizons* (1955), as well as a handful of more expensive productions, including *The Last Time I Saw Paris* (1954), *The Benny Goodman Story* (1956), and *The Whole Truth* (1958), after which she left the film business and ultimately became far more successful as the star of "The Donna Reed Show" on television than she ever was in the movies.

REEL The device around which film is wound. But the reel is more than a mere film holder; it is also a unit of measurement. Whether a film was made in the silent era or the sound era, in sixteen, thirty-five, or seventy millimeters, a standard reel has always added up to ten minutes of screen time. Of course, reels are much bigger today and can hold more film, but in Hollywood jargon, a reel is still ten minutes.

REINER, CARL(1922–) A versatile actor/writer/director who has put his stamp on modern film comedy. As an actor Reiner rarely had starring roles, but his modest output was always cheerfully effective. It has been his writing and directing that have earned him his considerable reputation as a consistently funny and entertaining filmmaker. It is hard to say where he has had his greatest impact, on television or in film.

Born to a Bronx watchmaker, Reiner went to work as a machinist's helper at the age of sixteen before enrolling in the WPA Dramatic Workshop. At age eighteen, he got his first acting job at the Rochester Summer Theater.

When World War II broke out, Reiner enlisted in the Army Signal Corps and was soon transferred to Maurice Evans' Special Services Unit, which toured the South Pacific entertaining G.I.s. A fellow soldier in that division was writer-comedian Howard Morris, who later introduced Reiner to Sid Caesar.

Reiner worked as a writer on Caesar's landmark TV comedy program "Your Show of Shows," later teaming with fellow writer Mel Books (q.v.) in the creation of the 2,000-Year-Old-Man records that won three Grammy nominations and became top-selling comedy albums. Reiner next created, wrote, produced, and occasionally acted in the long-running TV sitcom hit "The Dick Van Dyke Show."

Even while he was working in television, Reiner ventured into movies, working first as an actor during the early 1960s in films such as *Happy Anniversary* (1959), *The Gazebo* (1960), and *Gidget Goes Hawaiian* (1961). Probably his most well-known acting role was in *The Russians Are Coming, the Russians Are Coming* (1966). It was also during the 1960s that Reiner also began to write for the big screen, penning movies such as *The Thrill of It All* (1963) and *The Art of Love* (1965).

More well known for his television work than his films, Carl Reiner has quietly directed a substantial number of excellent movie comedies, many of them starring Steve Martin. Photo courtesy of Carl Reiner.

In the late 1960s, Reiner made the leap to film directing, beginning with *Enter Laughing* (1967), a movie based on his own autobiographical novel, which he also turned into a play. He made two more movies, a nostalgic recreation of the silent film era, *The Comic* (1969), and the ferociously funny and irreverent *Where's Poppa?* (1970). Both movies have become cult classics, particularly the latter film, but neither did well at the box office during their initial releases.

Reiner's prestige in the industry plummeted after the two commercial flops and he didn't direct another movie until he made *Oh, God!* (1977), a much gentler comedy than his previous movies, which was a hit.

Once again bankable, Reiner coscripted and directed one of Hollywood's all-time biggest comedy hits with a box office take of over $100 million, Steve Martin's *(q.v.)* first movie, *The Jerk* (1979). Reiner and Martin made such a good team that they worked together three more times in *Dead Men Don't Wear Plaid* (1982), *The Man With Two Brains* (1983), and *All of Me* (1984). He directed John Candy with nearly equal aplomb in the mildly successful *Summer Rental* (1985), only to stumble with the Mark Harmon vehicle *Summer School* (1987).

Among his other productions, Reiner also produced a son who is fast becoming another important director of film comedies, Rob Reiner (1945–   ). The younger Reiner, after his stint as Michael Stivic on the Norman

Lear TV sitcom, "All in the Family" has evolved as a sensitive, insightful director of such films as *This Is Spinal Tap* (1984), *The Sure Thing* (1985), *Stand by Me* (1986), *The Princess Bride* (1987), and *When Harry Met Sally* (1989).

REMAKES There are entirely new film versions of older movies. Before the advent of television, Hollywood often remade its more successful films at least once, if not twice. The major studios during the 1930s, 1940s, and 1950s rarely re-released their older films (*Gone With the Wind* and the Disney movies being the major exceptions). Movies were made to be seen at the time of their release and then consigned to a vault where they were all but forgotton. Therefore, with the coming of a new generation, a previously successful film could be remade with new stars and, perhaps, a different or updated point of view. By the early 1960s, after older films were sold en masse to TV; Hollywood remakes became far less common.

In the last decade or so, American moviemakers have been accused of timidity, falling back on endless sequels of previously popular films such as *Jaws* (1975), *Rocky* (1976), *Police Academy* (1984), *Beverly Hills Cop* (1984), etc. The criticism contemporary producers endure for making sequels hardly seems fair when one considers the enormous numbers of remakes made during Hollywood's golden years.

Great numbers of silent film hits were remade after the talkie revolution. These remakes, with the added dimension of sound, were truly changed films. The list of silent films that were remade as talkies is enormous, but some of the more celebrated examples include *The Phantom of the Opera* (1925, 1943, 1962, 1974), *The Mark of Zorro* (1920, 1940), *Rebecca of Sunnybrook Farm* (1917, 1938), and *Ben-Hur* (1926, 1959).

Once a studio owned a property—be it a book, a play, or a short story, there was a tendency to milk it for everything it was worth. In fact, studios used the same stories over and over in movies of different genres. For example, *Sahara* (1943), a World War II combat film, was remade as a western, *Last of the Comanches* (1952).

Films that were remade from hugely successful box office hits were usually released with the same title as the original. For example *Back Street* was made three times (1932, 1941, and 1961), always with the same famous title taken from the Fannie Hurst novel. Remakes of less popular movies were often given titles different from the original. Often, the audience wouldn't know beforehand it was seeing a remake. Such was the case with *High Sierra* (1941), remade as *I Died a Thousand Times* (1955).

Remakes were occasionally given an entirely different look and feel when the sex of a leading character was changed from one version to the next. For instance, the

Carole Lombard role in *Nothing Sacred* (1937) was played by Jerry Lewis in *Living It Up* (1954). Also, the leads in the original film version of the Ben Hecht and Charles MacArthur play *The Front Page* (1931) were Adolphe Menjou and Pat O'Brien. When the film was remade as *His Girl Friday* (1940), the leads were played by Cary Grant and Rosalind Russell. The change helped turn a good film into a great film. (*The Front Page* has subsequently been remade two more times: in 1974 with Jack Lemmon and Walter Matthau and as *Switching Channels* in 1988 with Burt Reynolds and Kathleen Turner.)

The film industry was less derivative when it turned "straight" movies into musicals. Curiously, the comedies were often more successful than the dramas when they were remade as musicals. For instance, the drama *Lost Horizon* (1937, 1973) was a critical and box office flop in its later musical version. On the other hand, a comedy such as *The Philadelphia Story* (1940) was a pleasant, entertaining commercial success when remade as the musical *High Society* (1956). This is the case with any number of other comedies, including the film in which Garbo laughed, *Ninotchka* (1939), when it was remade into the Fred Astaire musical *Silk Stockings* (1957).

On rare occasions, directors have chosen to remake their own films. For instance John Ford remade with sound his silent film *Three Bad Men (1926) as Three Godfathers* (1949); Alfred Hitchcock remade his black-and-white production of *The Man Who Knew Too Much* (1934, 1956) in color; and Howard Hawks remade his comedy *Ball of Fire* (1941) as the musical *A Song Is Born* (1948).

Hollywood has often looked beyond its borders when searching for a new movie to remake. Foreign films have often been remade in American versions, as evidenced by Fritz Lang's adaptation of Jean Renoir's *La Chienne* (1931) as *Scarlet Street* (1945) and the recent remakes of *Three Men and a Baby* (1987) and *Cousins* (1989) from popular French films.

Hollywood versions of foreign movies aside, the last surge of remakes occurred at the end of the 1970s and early 1980s when producers tried to cash in on nostalgia for some of the old Hollywood chestnuts such as *The Champ* (1931, 1979), *Little Miss Marker* (1934, 1949, 1963, 1980), and *The Jazz Singer* (1927, 1953, 1980). There are bound to be more remakes in the future, but one can expect that they will tend to be TV movies rather than feature films. TV movie versions of *Stagecoach* (1939, 1966, 1986-TVM), *It's a Wonderful Life* (1946, 1977-TVM retitled *It Happened One Christmas*), *Suspicion* (1941, 1988-TVM), and many others have proliferated wildly on the little screen.

REPUBLIC PICTURES Founded in 1935, it was one of the great "B" movie companies of the 1930s and 1940s. Republic was created by Herbert J. Yates, whose base of operations was a film-processing laboratory business. In the early 1930s he absorbed several failing production companies that owed his company money and created a new firm called Republic Pictures. Two of the more famous companies he took over were the original Monogram (not to be confused with the "new" Monogram formed in 1936; *see* Allied Artists), and Mascot Pictures. Both had been active in "B" movies and serials, and Republic continued the tradition with great profitability.

Republic was best known for its westerns and serials. Among its stars were Gene Autry, John Wayne, Johnny Mack Brown, Rex Allen, Roy Rogers, and Vera Hruba Ralston (who later became Mrs. Herbert Yates).

The company's best years were during World War II and, newly confident and cash-rich, Republic made an attempt to make the leap to "A" movies in the latter 1940s by hiring top-notch directors and stars. For example, Orson Welles directed and starred in *Macbeth* (1948); Allan Dwan directed *Sands of Iwo Jima* (1949); and John Ford made *Rio Grande* (1950) and *The Quiet Man* (1952) at Republic. The last of these films won two Academy Awards. But Republic was already fading during the 1950s. "B" movies and serials, the backbone of the company, were becoming obsolete in the face of television and the demise of the double feature. In 1958, Republic closed its doors.

REYNOLDS, BURT (1936–) An action and light comedy star who became one of Hollywood's biggest draws during the 1970s and early 1980s. Athletic and rambunctious, with a ready grin and breezy manner, Reynolds exudes a macho charm that spells his formula for stardom.

Born in Georgia, Reynolds grew up in Palm Beach, Florida, where his father was the local police chief. His high cheekbones (which led to his early casting in a number of Indian roles) are due to Cherokee ancestry on his father's side of the family. Active in sports, Reynolds won a football scholarship to Florida State University. He was a sensation as a halfback and it seemed as if a professional football career was in the offing when he was drafted by the (then) Baltimore Colts. When he injured his leg in an automobile crash, all hopes of a sports career ended and he reluctantly tried acting in college to fill the void, finding, to his surprise, that he enjoyed it.

Reynolds quit college in 1955 and went to New York to break into the theater. He found few acting opportunities and was forced to take many of the jobs struggling actors usually do. Finally, rather than making it in the theater, he found his first big break in television, winning a recurring role in the series "Riverboat" (1959–1960). Later he became a regular supporting character on the long-running "Gunsmoke" (1965–1967), and starred in two short-lived series of his own, "Hawk" (1967) and "Dan August" (1970).

While most of his efforts were being expended on his television career, Reynolds was also trying to make the transition to the movies. He had made his feature film debut in *Angel Baby* (1961) and had drifted relatively unnoticed through such other 1960s movies as *Operation CIA* (1965), *Navajo Joe* (1967), *Shark* (1968), and *100 Rifles* (1969).

Reynolds' film career began to turn around due to several unusual factors. He was probably the first movie star to find his audience on the late-night talk show circuit. He was such an affable, glib, and amusing guest on programs like "The Tonight Show" that he became popular even before he had a hit movie. In addition, his semi-nude centerfold spread in a 1972 issue of *Cosmopolitan* made him the talk of the industry. He had posed for it to get publicity and there was no denying that it worked. During that year he starred in two hit movies, a police comedy called *Fuzz* and the film that many still consider his best, *Deliverance*.

He became increasingly popular throughout the rest of the decade, making some rather good movies including *The Longest Yard* (1974), *Semi-Tough* (1977), *The End* (1978), which he also directed, *Hooper* (1978), and *Starting Over* (1979), all of which were hits. It was also during this period that he established his down-home, good-ole-boy image in a series of car chase dramas and comedies set in the South, chief among them *White Lightning* (1973), *Gator* (1976), in which he also made his directorial debut, and his biggest hit of all, *Smokey and the Bandit* (1977).

Reynolds was not without his bombs during the 1970s, in fact he starred in a number of major box office disasters, including the reviled *At Long Last Love* (1975) and the lamented *Lucky Lady* (1976).

While such 1980s films as *Smokey and the Bandit II* (1980) and *Canonnball Run* (1981) were solid hits, Reynolds soon began to run into trouble. His last well-received film was *Best Friends* (1982), in which he co-starred with Goldie Hawn. But not even Dolly Parton could help him in *The Best Little Whorehouse in Texas* (1982), yet another big-budget bomb. Normally, the car chase films or the action films bailed him out when all else failed, but audiences suddenly stopped showing up at these. Film after film was lambasted by the critics and ignored by the folks who had once made him a top box office attraction. Movies such as *Sharkey's Machine* (1982), *Stick* (1985), which Reynolds directed, and several others came and went with startling rapidity. Even Clint Eastwood's box office muscle couldn't help when the two teamed up to make *City Heat* (1984), and the flops continued unabated through the 1980s with films like *Heat* (1987), *Rent-a-Cop* (1988) and *Switching Channels* (1988), although the last of these at least received some positive reviews. Finally, at the end of 1988, he announced that in addition to his movie roles he would also be returning to television to play a policeman in Florida, "B. L. Stryker." In 1989, however, he made a modest comeback in *Breaking In*.

Reynolds' personal life has also been news during his long movie career. After a tempestuous marriage to Judy Carne of TV's "Laugh-In," he became involved in a May-December romance with Dinah Shore, followed by a long affair with Sally Field, who costarred in a number of his movies. Finally, he married TV actress Loni Anderson.

REYNOLDS, DEBBIE (1932–) An actress with a perky, wholesome image who found success in sentimental romances and light comedies during the 1950s and early 1960s. Though she was a popular performer in her era and remains well-known today, she actually starred in surprisingly few memorable movies. But if for no other reason, her place in film history is secure thanks to her leading role in the classic musical *Singin' in the Rain* (1952).

Born Mary Frances Reynolds, the future star had a childhood befitting her later all-American image; as a Girl Scout she won forty-eight merit badges. After becoming Miss Burbank of 1948, she was signed by Warner Bros. and made her debut in *June Bride* (1948). By 1950, she had moved to MGM and went on to star in such mild entertainments as *I Love Melvin* (1953), *The Affairs of Dobie Gillis* (1953), *Susan Slept Here* (1954), *The Tender Trap* (1955), and one of her biggest hits, *Tammy and the Bachelor* (1957), for which she also recorded the theme song, "Tammy," a tune that resulted in the best-selling record of the year.

Her personal life soon became more dramatic than any of her films. She had married pop singer Eddie Fisher in 1955, but that marriage fell apart with a great deal of publicity when her husband left her for Elizabeth Taylor in 1959. Reynolds persevered with her career and found that audience sympathy was with her, sustaining her through a number of mediocre films in the early 1960s. Finally, her movies improved in the mid-1960s with roles in *The Unsinkable Molly Brown* (1964) and *The Singing Nun* (1966), but by then the times were changing and the sweet, wholesome Reynolds persona had become passé with the advent of the counterculture. By the end of the 1960s, her film career was essentially over.

She tried television with minor success, starring in "The Debbie Reynolds Show" in 1969, and then turned to the stage, scoring a hit on Broadway with *Irene*. Reynolds took the show on the road for several years before working up a nightclub act. She returned to the screen on rare occasion, such as when she co-narrated *That's Entertainment* (1974), and appeared in *Aloha, Paradise* (1981). In more recent years, she has produced a very successful line of exercise videotapes. She has also basked in the success of her daughter, Carrie Fisher, who became a star as Princess Leia in *Star Wars* (1977) and, later, a successful novelist.

RIN-TIN-TIN (1916–1932)   Lassie *(q.v.)* may be more famous, but "Rinty" was the most important early animal star in Hollywood. The male German shepherd was "discovered" in a trench during World War I by Captain Lee Duncan. The American Army officer befriended the dog and brought him home to Los Angeles. After an intensive training period, Rin-Tin-Tin became a sensation in silent features and serials, beginning in 1922 in *The Man from Hell's River*.

Today, Warner Bros. is best remembered as the studio of James Cagney, Bette Davis, Humphrey Bogart, and Edward G. Robinson, to name just a few, but during the 1920s, it was Rin-Tin-Tin who kept the studio going. The dog was their biggest star and was usually billed above his human supporting players.

With scripts penned by Darryl F. Zanuck *(q.v.)*, the future head of Twentieth Century-Fox, Rin-Tin-Tin's movies were well paced and stylish, presenting an admirable combination of adventure and humor.

The emergence of sound films posed no problem for the dog, of course, and his career continued to flourish until his death in 1932. Rin-Tin-Tin, Jr., took on the mantle of America's bravest, most resourceful canine until the latter 1930s. A new Rin-Tin-Tin became a star on TV in the 1950s.

The success of Rinty not only led to Lassie's long career, but opened the eyes of producers and audiences alike to the possibility of animal actors such as Cheetah, Asta, Francis the Talking Mule, and Benji, to name just a few.
See also: animals in film

RISKIN, ROBERT (1897–1955)   A screenwriter whose career was closely tied to that of director Frank Capra *(q.v.)*, Riskin's adventurous ideas, coupled with a strong flair for dialogue, made him a top scriptwriter at Columbia throughout the 1930s. He was the winner of a Best Screenplay Academy Award for *It Happened One Night* (1934, *q.v.*).

Riskin began writing in his teens, becoming a successful playwright in his twenties. He was brought out to Hollywood to try his hand at screenwriting after two of his plays were turned into films, *Illicit* (1931) and *Miracle Woman* (1931), the latter a Capra-directed movie.

Capra hired Riskin to write dialogue for *Platinum Blonde* (1931), and the two collaborated on many of Capra's biggest hits, including *American Madness* (1932), *Lady for a Day* (1933), *It Happened One Night, Broadway Bill* (1934), *Mr. Deeds Goes to Town* (1936), *Lost Horizon* (1937), *You Can't Take It with You* (1938), and *Meet John Doe* (1941).

While Riskin's best work was with Capra, he also wrote excellent screenplays for others' films, including *The Whole Town's Talking* (1935) for John Ford and *The Real Glory* (1939) for Henry Hathaway. He also wrote and directed his own script for *When You're in Love* (1937), which had only modest success.

Riskin and Capra went their separate ways in the early 1940s; neither of them had quite the success alone that he had enjoyed as part of a team. Curiously, Capra's greatest achievement of his post-Riskin era was *It's a Wonderful Life* (1946), a film that owed much to the structure of Riskin's *American Madness* script. By the same token, Riskin's best screenplay of his post-Capra era was *Magic Town* (1947), which was a distinctly Capraesque story.

Riskin's career slowed considerably in the late 1940s and early 1950s. Several of his scripts, however, were the basis of films made after his death, including a remake of *It Happened One Night* called *You Can't Run Away from It* (1956), and Frank Capra's remake of his own *Lady for a Day*, which was retitled *A Pocketful of Miracles* (1961).

RITT, MARTIN (1920–   )   A director blacklisted during the McCarthy era, he later directed several successful socially conscious dramas. A former actor, Ritt has been particularly effective in eliciting first-rate performances from his casts. In a directing career spanning more than thirty years and twenty-five movies—many of them both critical and commercial hits—he has been nominated only once for Best Director.

Ritt was born in New York City but went to college in the South, which led him to set a surprisingly large percentage of his films in that region of the country. As a young man he intended to pursue an athletic career, but when that seemed unlikely, he decided to study law—until he met Elia Kazan *(q.v.)*, who convinced him to join the theater instead.

Ironically, Ritt's knowledge of sports smoothed the way for his entry into the world of the theater; his first job was to teach Luther Adler how to box for his role in the stage production of Clifford Odets' *Golden Boy* in 1937. Ritt also made his theatrical debut in a small role in the same play.

Though deeply involved as an actor with the Group Theater, when World War II broke out, Ritt joined the Air Force. While in the military, he made his directorial debut, putting on a stage production of *Yellow Jack*. When the war was over, Ritt moved comfortably back and forth between acting and directing, first for the theater, then for television. He acted in more than one hundred fifty teleplays and directed more than one hundred shows in a relatively short period before it all came to a crashing end in 1951. He was blacklisted from television because of his previous membership in the Communist party. It became impossible for him to find work. Among his lost opportunities was the chance to play the title role in the television production of "Marty," which Paddy Chayevsky had written specifically with Ritt in mind. Lean years followed. He taught at the Actors Studio and had a few roles in the theater, but it wasn't until he directed the hit show *A Very Special Baby* on Broadway that his prospects began to improve.

On the basis of his success in theater, he was summoned to Hollywood and given the opportunity to direct his first film, the low-budget but powerful drama about racism, *Edge of the City* (1956). He was in Hollywood to stay.

Ritt's subsequent early films, *No Down Payment* (1957) and *The Long Hot Summer* (1958) were critically praised and moderately successful at the box office. He then went into a brief but sharp decline with movies such as *The Black Orchid* (1959), *Paris Blues* (1961), and the particularly poor *Hemingway's Adventures of a Young Man* (1962).

He made his comeback with *Hud* (1963), gaining his one Oscar nomination for Best Director, and enhancing his reputation by having also coproduced the film. From that point, with only an occasional flop, Ritt has been remarkably consistent in both his choice of material and in his generally favorable critical acceptance.

A large percentage of his films have dealt with either social or political issues. For instance, Ritt's films dealing with racism include *Hombre* (1967), *The Great White Hope* (1970), *Sounder* (1972), and *Conrack* (1974). Among his political films are *The Spy Who Came in from the Cold* (1965), *The Molly Maguires* (1970), *The Front* (1976), and *Norma Rae* (1979).

Ritt has had a tendency in a number of his films to wax a bit sentimental, undermining his characters. Such was the case in *Pete 'n' Tillie* (1972), *Casey's Shadow* (1978), and *Back Roads* (1981). In recent years, however, a tougher edge has emerged and he has made some of the best films of his career, including *Cross Creek* (1983), *Murphy's Romance* (1985), and *Nuts* (1987).
See also: Hollywood Ten

RITZ BROTHERS   *See* comedy teams.

RKO (Radio-Keith-Orpheum)   One of the "Big Five" motion picture companies (along with MGM, Paramount, Warner Bros., and Twentieth Century-Fox), the studio produced some of the most beloved and most innovative films of the 1930s and early 1940s. A fully integrated film company, RKO owned production facilities and theaters and controlled distribution of its films. But it was not well run, and was the least successful of the major studios.

The brainchild of David Sarnoff of RCA (Radio Corporation of America) RKO was a hastily built company. When Western Electric convinced the "Big Four"

movie companies to use its sound system, RCA was left with no takers for its own sound-on-film system called Phonofilm. So it bought the Film Booking Office (FBO) to provide it with a movie studio and distribution system and the Keith-Albee-Orpheum theater chain, which had fallen on hard times, to be its exhibition outlet. With these two strokes, RCA, using its Phonofilm system, built a major film company in 1928 that was prepared to capitalize on the talkie revolution.

RKO started production with few stars, but it managed to create the occasional hit, such as *Rio Rita* (1929) and *Cimarron* (1931). In 1932, the studio was blessed with the guiding hand of David O. Selznick *(q.v.)*, who brought such stars to the company as Leslie Howard, John Barrymore, and Katharine Hepburn (who made her debut in the RKO production of *A Bill of Divorcement*, 1932). But Selznick was forced out in 1933 and Merian C. Cooper *(q.v.)* took over for a while, producing the memorable RKO classic *King Kong* (1933).

Amid the financial chaos of the Depression, a succession of weak managers failed to give the company firm direction. Nonetheless, the studio survived during the 1930s, due largely to the success of the Fred Astaire/Ginger Rogers musicals produced by Pandro S. Berman *(q.v.),* such as *The Gay Divorcée* (1934), *Top Hat* (1935), and *Swing Time* (1936). In addition, RKO took over the distribution of Walt Disney's films from United Artists in 1938, earning the company a significant income over the next several years.

In the late 1930s and early 1940s, the studio made some of its most memorable pictures, such as *The Hunchback of Notre Dame* (1939), *Abe Lincoln in Illinois* (1940), and the film that many consider to be the greatest movie ever made, Orson Welles' *Citizen Kane* (1941). But RKO had much better financial success with low-budget films during the war years, the best of them a much-admired horror series produced by Val Lewton *(q.v.)* in the early 1940s that began with *Cat People* (1942). During World War II, RKO became highly profitable—as did all the other studios.

In the early postwar years, under the production supervision of Dore Schary *(q.v.),* RKO made some of Hollywood's darkest *films noir,* such as *Out of the Past* (1947), before it turned as bleak as its product when, unexpectedly, Howard Hughes *(q.v.),* the eccentric billionaire, bought the company in 1948. Hughes quickly ran RKO into the ground releasing a mere handful of films per year until he sold off all the pieces, finally turning a profit on his initial investment. The production facilities were sold to Desilu in 1953, and what was left of RKO was then sold to General Tire.

Known as RKO General ever since, the company stopped making movies and its reign as a major motion picture company came to an end. RKO General has since been involved in various television, cable, and video operations.

After Mack Sennett, Hal Roach was the most influential comedy producer of the silent era. Unlike Sennett, however, Roach changed with the times and moved from making Our Gang, Laurel & Hardy, and Charley Chase comedy shorts to feature film production and eventually television. Photo courtesy of The Siegel Collection.

ROACH, HAL (1892–   )   His name is forever associated with film comedy. Most of his work as a screenwriter, director, and producer was spent creating comedy shorts, many of which are beloved classics.

Hal Roach and Mack Sennett *(q.v.)* were the two giants of comedy production during the silent era, but only Roach prospered after the advent of sound films. The Hal Roach Studio depended less on slapstick and broad farce than did Sennett's and more on character humor. As American audiences lost their fascination with stunts, Sennett's brand of humor yielded to Roach's in popularity.

Roach was an adventurer who saw a good deal of life as a young man. He skinned mules, prospected for gold (in Alaska), and traveled widely. When fate dropped him in Hollywood, he took work as an extra and stuntman. It was during this early apprenticeship that he met Harold Lloyd *(q.v.),* who was no further along in his film career than Roach. They eventually formed a partnership that led to Roach's producing and often directing a series of one- and two-reel comedies starring Lloyd as Lonesome Luke. The movies became popular immediately and were the springboard of both Roach's and Lloyd's future successes.

Lloyd eventually went off on his own and Roach continued to develop new comedy talents for his growing studio. In the 1920s, Roach hit paydirt with Our Gang and Laurel & Hardy *(qq.v.).* He also had comedy

talents such as Harry "Snub" Pollard, Charlie Chase, and Edgar Kennedy under contract. Remarkably, Roach not only oversaw production on all of his films but often cowrote and directed many.

In the 1930s, Roach was rewarded for his work in comedy when Laurel & Hardy won an Oscar for their short *The Music Box* (1932). In 1936, Our Gang also won an Oscar for Best short for *Bored of Education* (1936).

Not content merely to make comedy shorts, Roach branched out in the 1930s to make comedy features as well. Laurel & Hardy led the way with *Rogue Song* (1930) and *Pardon Us* (1931). Eventually Roach even made an Our Gang feature (their only one) in 1936, *General Spanky.*

Roach had no distribution system of his own and depended upon MGM to disseminate his movies. In 1938, as he moved out of shorts to concentrate solely on feature films, he sold his Our Gang rights to MGM.

In the late 1930s, Roach not only left shorts, he left comedy, to produce the highly acclaimed hit film version of John Steinbeck's *Of Mice and Men* (1939). After producing and/or directing nearly a dozen other films and serving as a filmmaker for the Army during World War II, Roach—ever the adventurer—left movie production for TV while the new medium was in its infancy. In 1967 he produced a film compiled from the best of Laurel & Hardy shorts called *The Crazy World of Laurel and Hardy.*

ROBARDS, JASON, JR. (1922–   )   A respected character actor/star of the stage who has lent substance to more than thirty films. He had lead roles in a number of prestigious movies during the 1960s, then settled into important supporting roles, winning two Academy Awards during this later period of his career. Long-faced with drooping eyes and a voice tinged with a soothing drawl, he has become a gentle authority figure without being sentimental.

The son of actor Jason Robards, Sr., the younger Robards witnessed the deep disappointments that clouded his father's professional life and early on decided against an acting career. Instead, he joined the Navy and spent seven years in the service, including a stint at Pearl Harbor at the time of the Japanese surprise attack. During his time at sea, Robards picked up a copy of Eugene O'Neill's *Strange Interlude* from the ship's library and became intrigued. The play sparked his interest in the theater and his father advised him to go to the American Academy of Dramatic Arts.

Robards did as his father suggested and went to New York to study his craft. He toiled for a decade in stock, radio, and TV, finally getting the attention of the critics at the age of thirty-five when he starred in the 1956 Off-Broadway production of O'Neill's *The Iceman Cometh.* The following year, he enhanced his stage reputation with his starring role in O'Neill's *Long Day's Journey Into Night,* later recreating his part in the acclaimed film adaptation of the play in 1962. He has since become the leading American interpreter of O'Neill's work.

Long Day's Journey was not, however, Robard's first film. He made his debut in 1959 in *The Journey* with Yul Brynner. He received better reviews in *Tender Is the Night* (1962), and by the mid-1960s he had become a minor star of art-house movies, making his greatest hit as a middle-aged dropout in *A Thousand Clowns* (1965). Robards continued to win accolades for his performances in films that ranged from the light romantic comedy *Any Wednesday* (1966) to the grim western *The Hour of the Gun* (1967). He reached the height of his short stretch of cinematic starring roles in Sam Peckinpah's highly underrated *The Ballad of Cable Hogue* (1970) and as Brutus in the poorly received *Julius Caesar* (1970).

Robards was excellent in support of Henry Fonda and Charles Bronson in *Once Upon a Time in the West* (1969), and his quiet stability became a valuable asset in supporting roles during the 1970s and beyond. His two most famous Oscar-winning roles were, in fact, supporting parts, as Ben Bradlee in *All the President's Men* (1976) and as Dashiell Hammett in *Julia* (1977). Though his roles might have been small, he appeared in a number of interesting, off-beat films, among them *A Boy and His Dog* (1976), *Comes a Horseman* (1978), *Melvin and Howard* (1980), *Bright Lights, Big City* (1988), and *Parenthood* (1989).

Robards has frankly admitted to having had problems with alcohol, which began to be particularly troublesome after his initial success on the stage. Undoubtedly contributing to the breakups of his four marriages (one of them to actress Lauren Bacall), his drinking threatened at one point to keep him from the stage. Luckily, he was able to recover, and had a hit on Broadway with *The Moon for the Misbegotten* that resurrected his standing within the industry.

Robards has occasionally taken to acting for television, making his greatest impact as the star of "The Day After" (1983), the controversial made-for-TV-movie that dealt with the consequences of nuclear war on one small city. The program was the highest rated TV movie in television history.

ROBERTSON, CLIFF (1925–) An actor and sometimes writer-director who never quite achieved major stardom, though he was an effective and steadily employed leading man in films from the mid-1950s. Given the right script, Robertson was able to demonstrate his abilities as an actor, but that didn't happen often.

Born Clifford Parker Robertson III, the future performer had no intention of becoming an actor. After growing up in the well-to-do San Diego, California

suburb of La Jolla, he gradated from Antioch College and pursued a career as a reporter, writing for a daily newspaper. He went to New York in order to break into the theater as a playwright, but ended up getting a job in summer stock, doing everything from building sets to acting. He soon began making his living as an actor and put his writing aside until, much later, he began penning screenplays.

Before he made it in Hollywood, Robertson played the title role in the children's TV show "Rod Brown of the Rocket Rangers" in 1953. Later, his success on the stage led to his film debut in a major role in the hit *Picnic* (1955), and he continued working in Hollywood, appearing in a wide range of movies from *Autumn Leaves* (1956) and *The Naked and the Dead* (1958) to *Gidget* (1959) and *All in a Night's Work* (1961). He did some of his best acting of the period, however, in the low-budget Samuel Fuller *(q.v.)* film *Underworld USA* (1961).

Robertson appeared to be poised for major stardom when he played John F. Kennedy in *PT-109* (1963)—he was chosen for the role by the president himself—but the movie was rather disappointing. He followed that up with major roles in bigger-budget films such as *Sunday in New York* (1964) and *The Best Man* (1964), but failed to gain many fans.

Again, Robertson seemed certain to achieve a new level of stardom when he played the title role in *Charly,* the story of a retarded man who, through experiments, suddenly becomes a genius, only to gradually regress to his previous state. His performance brought raves and an Oscar, but his career didn't improve appreciably afterwards. He was later given the chance to produce, direct and star in *J. W. Coop* (1972), a film that he had also written. The movie was well received by the critics, but he didn't write, direct and star in another film until *The Pilot* (1979). In the meantime, he gave solid performances in such films as *The Great Northfield Minnesota Raid* (1972), *Man on a Swing* (1974), *Three Days of the Condor* (1975), and Brian De Palma's thriller, *Obsession* (1976).

1979 marked a turning point in Robertson's career. His accountant pointed out that he had received a 1099 tax form indicating that he had been paid $10,000 by Columbia Pictures. The actor had no recollection of having worked for Columbia in recent years and asked to see a copy of the check; it was a forgery. When he pursued the matter, it was discovered that the powerful and very successful president of Columbia Pictures, David Begelman, had not only forged Robertson's name on a check but had also forged others' names on checks and had cashed them as well. Robertson was warned by important Hollywood figures not to go to the authorities, but he did so anyway and consequently found himself out of work for the next three and half years. He was finally given a job by director Douglas Trum-

tinued working the vaudeville circuit alone during the late 1920s and had a few roles in film shorts, but her first big break came on the stage, not the screen, when she was chosen for a significant role in a Broadway musical, *Top Speed,* (1929), followed by a good role in Gershwin's *Girl Crazy* (1930). Her success on the boards brought her to the attention of Paramount, and the studio hired her to play leading roles in a few low-budget films shot at their Astoria, Queens studio in New York. Her first significant role was in *Young Man of Manhattan* (1930).

In 1931 Rogers set out for Hollywood and worked for several studios, including Pathé and Warner Bros. It was at Warners that she began to emerge as a musical star to watch, appearing with Dick Powell in Busby Berkeley's spectaculars *42nd Street* (1933) and *Gold Diggers of 1933* (1933). She had her astonishing moment in *Gold Diggers of 1933* when she sang "We're in the Money," in pig latin, dressed in a flimsy costume made entirely of coins.

Rogers became a star at RKO when she was chosen to be Fred Astaire's dance partner (both of them were second leads) in *Flying Down to Rio* (1933). The public response was such that RKO quickly teamed them up again, this time starring them in *The Gay Divorcée* (1934). The popular success of their films during the mid-1930s reportedly saved RKO from bankruptcy during the Depression.

While Astaire performed only in musicals during the 1930s, Rogers was busy in all sorts of other films, but met with only modest success. After a total of nine musicals with Astaire, which included *Roberta* (1935), *Top Hat* (1935), *Swingtime* (1936), *Follow the Fleet* (1936), *Shall We Dance* (1937), *Carefree* (1938), and *The Story of Vernon and Irene Castle* (1939), the two stars parted company, not to be reunited again on film until 1949.

Rogers had long wanted to be taken seriously as a dramatic actress and, in 1940, she accomplished just that, winning a Best Actress Oscar for her portrayal of the title character in the soaper *Kitty Foyle.* The early 1940s were her golden solo years, when, without Astaire, she starred in a number of popular, amusing comedies such as *Tom, Dick, and Harry* (1941), *Roxi Hart* (1942), and *The Major and the Minor* (1942). Her career tailed off, however, in the latter part of the decade, only to be saved by her reunion with Astaire in their final film together, *The Barkley's of Broadway* (1949), a movie that also poked good-natured fun at Rogers' desire to be a serious actress.

Rogers worked steadily until 1957, appearing in a few amusing movies, most notably Howard Hawks' *Monkey Business* (1952), but when there was little work to be found in the movies, she went back to the stage, where she triumphed during the 1960s as Carol Channing's replacement in the Broadway production of *Hello, Dolly!* and in a London run of *Mame.* One of her rare film appearances during the 1960s was as Carol Lynley's mother in *Harlow* (1965). She spent the 1970s and 1980s in semi-retirement, making an occasional TV appearance.

See also: Astaire, Fred; musicals; screen teams

ROGERS, ROY (1912–)   He was the heir to Gene Autry's title of "King of the Cowboys." A popular singing cowboy in low-budget western films, principally during the 1940s, he later reached the height of his fame as a TV star in a long-running series that bore his name during the 1950s. Like Autry, Rogers appealed to the juvenile audience, but he was never quite as awesomely successful in the movies as was his predecessor. Earnest, rather than playful, Rogers had a somewhat staid image that was brightened by his perky wife, Dale (who appeared in many of his films); the amusing sidekick, Gabby Hayes; Roger's remarkable horse, Trigger; and his well-trained dog, Bullet. One suspects that, alone, Rogers might not have had the success he did.

Born Leonard Slye, Rogers made his way to California as a migrant farm worker, picking fruit. He was a singer (using the name Dick Weston) long before he became an actor, but he eventually formed The Sons of the Pioneers, a singing group that appeared in a great

Roy Rogers succeeded Gene Autry as "King of the Cowboys" during the 1940s, gaining his greatest fame on TV during the 1950s. The debate still rages between men of a certain age as to who was a greater hero, Roy or Gene. Photo courtesy of Roy Rogers.

many westerns, including several of John Ford's films.

His first film appearance was in a tiny part in Gene Autry's *Tumbling Tumbleweeds* (1935). He sailed along in small roles throughout the rest of the 1930s, deep in the shadow of Autry's success. As a means of keeping Autry in line, worried producers ultimately pushed Rogers into the limelight as a potential new singing star. With his pleasant voice and warm manner, he took hold in films such as *Sons of the Pioneers* (1942), *Romance on the Range* (1942), and finally the one that established him as Autry's successor, *King of the Cowboys* (1943).

Rogers worked steadily in thoroughly forgettable light western musicals with simple plots and clichéd stories until the early 1950s. He went on to star, with Dale Evans, in "The Roy Rogers Show" on television, making his last film appearance to date in *Mackintosh and TJ* in 1975.

Rogers, like Autry, invested his money very well and is a wealthy man. And, yes, it is true that Rogers did have Trigger stuffed after the horse's death.
See also: Autry, Gene; westerns

ROGERS, WILL (1879–1935)   Rarely has there been an actor more beloved by American movie audiences than Will Rogers. There were actors who were more dashing, sexy, and dynamic, but none matched his folksy wit, wisdom, and charm. Rogers was the uncle everyone wished he had.

Born William Penn Adair Rogers in Colagah, Indian Territory (which later became the state of Oklahoma) of reputedly Irish and Cherokee Indian ancestry, he learned his roping and riding tricks very early in life.

Those tricks served him in good stead when he joined a Wild West show in Johannesburg, South Africa, after delivering mules to the British there during the Boer War. Rogers continued working in Wild West shows until he made his way to New York and took a stab at vaudeville. His act consisted entirely of rope tricks; he had yet to speak on stage. It wasn't until he got a laugh ad-libbing a joke to cover a failed trick that he suddenly became a humorist.

Over the next several years Rogers began making amusing comments on politics, politicians, and human nature. By 1912, he had become a well-known vaudevillian and was able to make the leap to Broadway. Five years later, he was a star attraction in the Ziegfeld Follies.

The movies beckoned in 1918 and Rogers made his first film, *Laughing Bill Hyde,* for Samuel Goldwyn. The movie did reasonably well and it seemed as if Will Rogers was about to become a silent screen star. But after twelve more features between 1918 and early 1922, the rope-twirling star had failed to find an audience. His appeal was in what he said and how he said it, and silent films simply couldn't project his personality.

But neither Hollywood nor Rogers were willing to give up. He made *One Glorious Day* (1922) for Paramount, and an independent version of *The Headless Horseman* (1922). He even produced, wrote, and directed three films himself that same year and proceeded to go broke.

Except for two pre-talkie features in 1927, Rogers' only other film experience during the silent era was in a series of a dozen shorts he made for Hal Roach in the mid-1920s, but they weren't terribly successful either.

Though his film career appeared to be a bust, Rogers' popularity continued to grow thanks to his humor columns in the newspapers. He had also written two successful books. With the coming of sound, Hollywood gave Rogers another chance with *They Had to See Paris* (1929). And he was a hit.

From that moment his film career never seriously faltered. He was an American Everyman who managed to ridicule and satirize without ever offending. His movies, coupled with his radio performances and newspaper columns, made him a commanding popular figure. His support of Franklin Delano Roosevelt was generally credited with helping FDR win the presidency in 1932. Rogers, himself, was offered the nomination for Governor of Oklahoma but declined it. (He did, however, serve as the honorary mayor of Beverly Hills.)

Though his movies were almost all formulaic, they were immensely successful, making Rogers the second most popular film star in 1933 (after Marie Dressler, *q.v.*), and the number-one draw in 1934.

Rogers made a total of twenty sound films, but only a handful hold up reasonably well today. His best were *A Connecticut Yankee in King Arthur's Court* (1931), *State Fair* (1934), *Judge Priest* (1934), and *Steamboat 'Round the Bend* (1935), the latter two directed by John Ford.

When Rogers died in a plane crash in Alaska in 1935, his audience didn't wail and shriek as they had over Valentino's death. Americans went into a deep, introspective mourning, as if they had lost a family member.

ROMERO, GEORGE A. (1940–   )   A director of mostly low-budget horror films who burst on the filmmaking scene in 1968 with his shockingly violent, no-holds-barred *Night of the Living Dead*. Based in Pittsburgh, Pennsylvania, Romero has shot most of his films in and around his home state, relishing his reputation as a movie maverick. Though most of his films have rarely reached a wide audience, the director has had a significant impact on the movie industry. His debut film has often been cited as the spur that led to the MPAA rating system. In addition, Romero, via *Night of the Living Dead,* can be credited with being the father of the blood-and-gore cycle of horror films that spawned such later entries (by other filmmakers) as *The Texas Chainsaw Massacre,* the *Friday the 13th* series, the *Halloween* series, etc.

Born in the Bronx, New York, Romero received his

higher education at the Carnegie Institute of Technology (later the Carnegie-Mellon Institute of Technology) in Pittsburgh, and he stayed in that area ever since.

He made *Night of the Living Dead* on a miniscule budget with money invested by friends. He could afford to shoot only on weekends, when his cast and a rented farmhouse were available. Soon after its release, however, the film became a top attraction at midnight shows and quickly attained cult status.

Among Romero's later films, only the long-awaited sequel to *Night of the Living Dead, Dawn of the Dead* (1979), and *Creepshow* (1982), a bigger-budget film scripted by Stephen King and boasting a well-known cast, have garnered box office honors. One of Romero's most interesting films, however, was his prophetic movie about a biological plague in a small town. The film was called *Crazies* (1973), but it failed after being re-released under the title *Code Name: Trixie*. Some of Romero's other films include *Day of the Dead* (1985) and *Monkey Shines: An Experiment in Fear* (1988), this last another rare big-budget, major-studio production. *See also:* horror films

ROONEY, MICKEY (1920–)

A prodigiously talented actor who began his career as a child star, becoming one of Hollywood's most popular teenagers, a role he was able to assume well into his twenties because of his short stature and baby face. Although he had a bumpy career in adult films, he has continued to act in movies ever since the silent era. Though he reached the peak of his fame in the late 1930s and early 1940s, Rooney has never been long out of the limelight. Married eight times, most memorably to Ava Gardner (1942–1943), he has made and lost a fortune, tinkered in the business world, conquered the stage, the nightclub circuit, and TV, but his boundless energy and talent has best been captured by the big screen.

Born Joe Yule, Jr., the son of a vaudeville couple, he began performing at the age of fifteen months in his parents' act. His first film was a silent short, *Not to be Trusted* (1926). The following year he took the name of Mickey McGuire, the same moniker as the comic strip character he played in a long-running series of comedy shorts made between 1927 and 1933. Beginning in 1932, when he began to appear in films other than the Mickey McGuire movies, he changed his name to Mickey Rooney.

In small roles in films such as *The Big Cage* (1933) and *The Chief* (1933), Rooney bounced around from studio to studio until MGM finally signed him to a long-term contract in 1935. He was promptly loaned out to Warner Bros., where he made a lasting impression as Puck in *A Midsummer Night's Dream* (1935). He was in three films supporting child star Freddie Bartholomew, and his brashness was the perfect foil for the young English actor's reserve. After *Little Lord Fauntle-*

The multitalented Mickey Rooney has spent most of his life in show business and has acted in films since 1926. He is seen here with one of his longtime costars, Judy Garland, with whom he appeared in many of his Andy Hardy films as well as in some of the most exuberant musicals of the early 1940s. Photo courtesy of The Siegel Collection.

roy (1936), *The Devil Is a Sissy* (1936), and *Captains Courageous* (1937), Rooney's star began to rise just as Bartholomew's began to fade.

In 1937, MGM produced a "B" movie called *A Family Affair,* the first of a series of Andy Hardy films that featured Rooney as the affable teenager in an archetypal American family. The film was a surprise hit and it was followed by fifteen more.

When Judy Garland *(q.v.)* was featured in *Love Finds Andy Hardy* (1938), Rooney found his perfect female counterpart (although the "love" Hardy found in the film was Lana Turner). The two MGM teenagers starred together in three Andy Hardy films but more notably in a series of charming musicals including *Babes in Arms* (1939), *Strike Up the Band* (1940), *Babes on Broadway* (1941), and *Girl Crazy* (1943).

At the same time that Rooney was playing light comedy in the Andy Hardy films and singing and dancing in musicals, he was also playing heavy dramatic roles in films such as *Boy's Town* (1938) and *Young Tom Edison* (1940). It was eminently clear that Rooney was an immensely talented young man with a remarkable acting range. And the public could hardly get enough of him. He appeared in anywhere from three to eight films per year during the latter 1930s and early 1940s, becoming the recipient of a special Academy Award, along with another teenage star, Deanna Durbin *(q.v.),* for their "significant contribution in bringing to the screen the spirit and personification of youth and as a juvenile player setting a high standard of ability and achievement." Rooney reached the apex of his career in 1939 when he became the nation's number-one box office draw, a title he held for three straight years.

After starring with Elizabeth Taylor in *National Velvet* (1944), Rooney joined the army. It was hard for audiences to accept the young baby-faced actor as Andy Hardy after his return from the service, and *Love Laughs at Andy Hardy* (1946) was a commerical flop. So, too, were the rest of his movies during the late 1940s. By 1949, MGM bought out his contract and Rooney was on his own. He set up an independent film company that produced a string of box office and critical failures throughout the early part of the new decade, and eventually he was forced to declare bankruptcy.

Though Rooney worked in nightclubs and on TV, he continued making films, usually undistinguished "B" movies, until he reestablished himself with three important character roles: as a soldier in *The Bold and the Brave* (1956), for which he was nominated for an Oscar as Best Supporting Actor; as a tough sergeant in the service comedy *Operation Mad Ball* (1957); and as a vicious gangster in the title role of *Baby Face Nelson* (1957). Then MGM brought Rooney temporarily back into the fold, starring him in the last Andy Hardy film, *Andy Hardy Comes Home* (1958). It was a bomb and a career mistake for the actor.

Rooney was nothing if not irrespressible; he continued to find work in a variety of poor films until he once again played a character role as Audrey Hepburn's Japanese neighbor in *Breakfast at Tiffany's* (1961), and nearly stole the movie. From comedy to drama, he was once again searing in a supporting role in *Requiem for a Heavyweight* (1962), but the actor couldn't parlay his good reviews into starring roles. In addition to a stream of appearances in minor films throughout the 1960s, he managed to create some memorable moments in a few bigger-budget films such as *It's a Mad, Mad, Mad, Mad World* (1963) and *The Comic* (1969).

Rooney's comeback picture was the surprise hit film of 1979, *The Black Stallion,* for which many thought he deserved an Oscar nomination as Best Supporting Actor for his role as the aging horse trainer. Despite his success in the movie, Hollywood didn't come calling. His film work has been scarce in the 1980s, but he hit it big on Broadway in the revival of *Sugar Babies* in 1979, and found an outlet for his dramatic talents on television, starring in several powerful TV movies, including his

Emmy-award-winning performance in the title role of *Bill* (1981).

Rooney continues to perform in TV films and in the theater, most recently in a revival of *A Funny Thing Happened on the Way to the Forum* (1987).
See also: child stars

ROSS, HERBERT (1927–) He is Hollywood's current leading director of dance movies. The former actor and dancer has deep roots in the theater that go back to the 1950s and 1960s, but his success as a film director of musicals and non-musicals alike has been quite extraordinary. For instance, the films with which he has been associated through 1988 have accumulated a stunning 44 Oscar nominations. In one year alone, 1977, two of his movies were nominated for Best Picture, *The Turning Point* and *The Goodbye Girl.* Those two pictures garnered a total of fifteen nominations, including a Best Director nod for Ross for *The Turning Point.*

Ross was a choreographer for the American Ballet Theater and, at the age of 23, had his first ballet per-

Herbert Ross is a former choreographer who is regarded today as the premier contemporary director of dance movies, having made such commercial hits as *The Turning Point* (1977) and *Footloose* (1984). He has also proven himself to be an adroit director of comedic and dramatic films. Photo courtesy of Herbert Ross.

formed. Later, he became the resident choreographer for the American Ballet Theater and married the company's prima ballerina, Nora Kaye. He had an early inauspicious experience with the big screen when he directed the musical portions of *Summer Holiday* (1963).

It was during the 1960s that Ross began directing for the theater. An important milestone in his career came when he directed Barbra Streisand's show-stopping number as Miss Marmelstein in the musical *I Can Get It for You Wholesale.*

He then went on to direct the musical numbers in the stage version of *Funny Girl,* the play that turned Streisand into a Broadway star. He was asked to direct Miss Streisand's screen test for the film version of the play and eventually he also directed the film's dazzling musical numbers.

Ross attained full director status in films with *Goodbye, Mr. Chips* (1969). Among his other musicals are *Funny Lady* (1974), *Pennies from Heaven* (1981), and *Footloose* (1984). It is Ross's dramatic dancing films that have earned him accolades. For instance, he directed *Nijinsky* (1980), *Dancers* (1987), and his most famous film, *The Turning Point* (1977), a movie about the ballet and about those who must choose between the world of art and a normal life.

Ross' reputation for musical/dance films has overshadowed his accomplishments in comedy. He directed a number of memorable hits, including *The Owl and the Pussycat* (1970), *Play It Again, Sam* (1972), *The Sunshine Boys* (1975), *The Goodbye Girl* (1977), and *The Secret of My Success* (1987).

Ross has rarely had long fallow periods, although he has had his share of critical and box office fiascos including Goldie Hawn's *Protocol* (1985). But one should also remember that Ross directed the critically admired *The Last of Sheila* (1973), scripted by Anthony Perkins and Stephen Sondheim, and *The Seven Percent Solution* (1976).

ROSSEN, ROBERT (1908–1966) A talented writer-director-producer who made hard-hitting, socially conscious films during the late 1930s through the early 1950s but was crippled artistically by the politics of the McCarthy era. Rossen continued to make films until his death, but with just a couple of exceptions, his career was never the same after his run-in with the House Un-American Activities Committee in 1951.

Born Robert Rosen and raised on the Lower East Side of New York, he struggled to get his college degree from New York University and, in the process, became enamored of the theater. He wrote and directed plays, gaining experience in stock and eventually making his way to Broadway. He was not, however, a major success on the Great White Way. When his play

The Body Beautiful closed on Broadway after four performances, Rossen decided that he had suffered enough and it was time to heed the clarion call of Hollywood. He went west and found that the movies were a far better vehicle through which to express his social concerns—and there was no better studio for a liberal-minded screenwriter than Warner Bros.

Rossen wrote a number of memorable scripts for Warner Bros., including *Marked Woman* (1937), *They Won't Forget* (1937), *Racket Busters* (1938), *Dust Be My Destiny* (1939), and *The Roaring Twenties* (1939). He made his liberal points about justice and corruption through character, rarely opting for easy solutions. But he was also a showman, and his films were well-paced, with crackling good dialogue.

It wasn't surprising that World War II inspired Rossen to write films that touched on the broad issues of freedom such as *Edge of Darkness* (1943) and *A Walk in the Sun* (1946). But those horrific times also stimulated him to write scripts of a more psychological nature, focusing not so much on the injustice of society as on personal moral choices. Powerful films from this period include *A Child Is Born* (1940), *The Sea Wolf* (1941), *Out of the Fog* (1941), *The Strange Love of Martha Ivers* (1946), and his uncredited work on the screenplay of *The Treasure of the Sierra Madre* (1948).

In the late 1940s, Rossen began to take more control of his own scripts, and he got off to a stunning start writing and directing the hit *film noir Johnny O'Clock* (1947) and a powerful and provocative boxing drama, *Body and Soul* (1947). He rose to the very top of his profession as a writer, director, and producer when he made the compelling anti-fascist *All the King's Men* (1949), a film that took top honors with a Best Picture Academy Award.

Rossen had demonstrated his liberal and reformist political convictions by joining the Communist party during the late 1930s. He left the party in 1945, but was not spared from brutal and intrusive questioning when the House Un-American Activities Committee investigated Communist influence in Hollywood in 1951. Yet he refused to name others in the movie industry who had also been party members.

Rossen's principled stand caused him to be blacklisted in Hollywood. Two years later, he finally buckled under to the Committee and named names. He was removed from the blacklist and went back to work, but Rossen was never quite the same. His spirit had been broken and films such as *Mambo* (1955), *Alexander the Great* (1956), and *Island in the Sun* (1957) weren't nearly as powerful as his earlier efforts, either as a writer or director.

It was not until the early 1960s that he regained some of the fire of his earlier years, writing, producing and directing the highly regarded hit *The Hustler* (1961), as well as *Lilith* (1964), which was the last film he made. *See also* The Hollywood Ten

ROUGH CUT The first version of a movie after the shooting is completed. Though the film's individual scenes are almost never shot in the order that they appear in the script, in the rough cut, the scences are edited together so that they flow in the general manner in which they were originally intended to be seen.

From this point on, the movie is edited toward its final version. New scenes may have to be shot; other scenes may have to be reshot; dialogue may still have to be dubbed; etc., but the editing process has begun. The end result will be the final cut—that which will be seen in movie theaters.
See also: final cut

ROWLANDS, GENA (1934–   ) An actress of considerable range who has become one of Hollywood's most respected performers. In a film career that spans more than thirty years, she has gracefully made the transition from leading lady to character actress. The widow of actor/director John Cassevetes, Miss Rowlands' roles have often been in her husband's independent films. These parts have been both a bane and a deliverance—limiting her exposure to the "art" crowd while giving her some of the best female roles in recent American film.

Born and raised in Wisconsin, Miss Rowlands traveled to New York to attend the American Academy of Dramatic Arts while she was still in her teens. Cassevetes, then at the beginning of his acting career, saw her in one of her early productions and they were married soon after.

Her big professional break came when she was discovered by Joshua Logan, who gave her the lead opposite Edward G. Robinson in Paddy Chayefsky's *The Middle of the Night* in 1956. The play ran eighteen months on Broadway and her career was launched.

MGM's Dore Shary brought her to Hollywood, where she made her film debut in the comedy *The High Cost of Loving* (1958). Important screen credits followed, including the now minor classic *Lonely Are the Brave* (1962) and *A Child is Waiting* (1963), in which she appeared under the direction of her husband for the first time.

In 1968 Rowlands starred in Cassevetes' film *Faces,* followed by further collaborations, including *Minnie and Moskowitz* (1971) and *A Woman Under the Influence* (1974) (in which Rowland's gave a searing performance and received a Best Actress Oscar nomination), *Opening Night* (1978), *Gloria* (1980) (which brought her yet another Academy Award nomination), and *Love Streams* (1984).

Miss Rowlands hasn't appeared in many films other than her husband's, at least not until recently. She gave

Gena Rowlands is a riveting actress who has mostly been seen in the films of her independent filmmaker husband, the late John Cassevetes, often to excellent effect. Photo courtesy of Gena Rowlands.

a strong performance as the mother of Joan Jett and Michael J. Fox in *Light of Day* (1987) and was riveting in Woody Allen's *Another Woman* (1988). Those two roles aside, she has found richer work of late in TV. For instance, she garnered an Emmy nomination for playing the mother of a person with AIDS in *An Early Frost* (1985), and she took home an Emmy for her portrayal of Betty Ford in *The Betty Ford Story* (1987). *See also:* Cassevetes, John

RUSSELL, JANE (1921–   ) A voluptuous actress made famous by her debut in Howard Hughes' sexy western *The Outlaw* (1943). She made few memorable movies among the two dozen of her career, yet she remains an important figure in Hollywood because she was the first of the bosomy sex symbols that dominated the film industry throughout the 1950s and beyond.

Born Ernestine Jane Geraldine Russell, she was not an unschooled actress when Hughes chose her to star in his racy western. Russell had studied acting at the prestigious Theatrical Workshop founded by Max Reinhardt and had taken acting lessons from longtime Hollywood character actress and teacher Maria Ouspenskaya.

Unfortunately for Russell, *The Outlaw* was deemed too salacious by the Hays Office as originally shot in 1941. The film was released briefly in 1943, gained notoriety, and was then put on the shelf until it was finally given a general release in 1946. Russell's career was in limbo during that six-year period. Hughes, who owned her contract, was reluctant to let her appear in other films, fearing that if she bombed, *The Outlaw,* when finally released, would be worth nothing. As a result, Russell starred in just one film during that time, *Young Widow* (1946).

In a recent autobiography she expresses little bitterness over the fact that what might have been her prime years during the 1940s had been wasted by Howard Hughes.

After *The Outlaw* became a box office sensation, Russell appeared in a number of films that exploited both her fame and physical attributes. The most obviously exploitative of these is *Double Dynamite* (1951). She showed comedic flair in *The Paleface* (1948) and in *Son of Paleface* (1952), both with Bob Hope, but she really demonstrated her versatility and talent in the Howard Hawks musical *Gentlemen Prefer Blondes* (1953), in which she costarred with Marilyn Monroe.

Gentlemen Prefer Blondes was the high point of her career. Until 1957 she continued to work steadily in a string of mostly forgettable films, the best of them being *The Tall Men* (1955), *Gentlemen Marry Brunettes* (1955), and *The Revolt of Mamie Stover* (1956). During the late 1950s and throughout much of the 1960s, she performed a singing and dancing act in nightclubs.

After a seven-year absence from the screen, Russell returned to films in a supporting role in *Fate is the Hunter* (1964). She appeared in just four more movies, among them *Born Losers* (1967), the precursor to the low-budget sleeper hit, *Billy Jack,* in which surprisingly she portrays Tom Laughlin's mother. Russell was last seen on film in a supporting role in *Darker than Amber* (1970).

In the 1970s she became famous to a whole new generation as the spokesperson for a company selling bras for "full-figured gals."

See also: Hughes, Howard

RUSSELL, ROSALIND (1908–1976)

A talented and popular actress who served as a role model for women during the late 1930s and 1940s. In a film career spanning nearly forty years and comprising more than fifty films, Russell often outclassed her material. Although relatively few of her films have weathered the test of time, Russell's appeal endures for having proved that pretty women could be smart and resourceful, as well as sexy and desirable. If Joan Crawford's career women suffered for their choices, Rosalind Russell's were healthy, confident, and fun-loving.

Born to a wealthy family, Russell had the advantage of a good education, at Marymount College and the American Academy of Dramatic Arts, before the beginning of her acting career. She acted first on the stage in the late 1920s, gaining valuable experience, before heading to Hollywood. Her film debut was in an important supporting role in *Evelyn Prentice* (1934). After nearly a dozen mediocre movies, she made her critical breakthrough playing the non-too-likable title character in the hit *Craig's Wife* (1936). With her stock rising, she was given better scripts and she starred in such strong dramatic films as *Night Must Fall* (1937) and *The Citadel* (1938).

Russell's first major break in sophisticated comedy was her role in the all-star, all-female *The Women* (1939). More comedies followed, such as *His Girl Friday* (1940) and *No Time for Comedy* (1940), in which she proved to be the match of any man—even Cary Grant—in trading quips and sly rejoinders. Her wonderfully brittle comedic style brought her a Best Actress Oscar nomination in 1942 for *My Sister Eileen.* She played the lead in the biopic *Sister Kenny* (1946), about the nurse who helped discover the cure for polio. It brought her a second Oscar nomination and led to additional dramatic roles. The following year she garnered her third Oscar nomination for her work in *Mourning Becomes Electra* (1947). Her subsequent films during the late 1940s and early 1950s, by which time she was playing second leads, were neither notable nor successful, except for *Picnic* (1955).

In 1958 Russell made a comeback in the title role of *Auntie Mame,* winning her fourth and last Best Actress Academy Award nomination. Despite her success, she didn't appear in films again until 1962, when she blitzed the nation's movie screens in three movies, the most memorable of them being *Gypsy.*

Russell appeared in few movies during the rest of her career, usually playing strong supporting roles in films such as *The Trouble with Angels* (1966), *Rosie!* (1968), and *Where Angels Go, Trouble Follows* (1968). Her last theatrical film was the unfortunate *Mrs. Pollifax—Spy* (1971), an embarrassing movie that Russell also scripted under a pseudonym. She then turned to television, starring in a TV movie, "The Crooked Hearts" (1972). That same year, Russell became one of the few actors, and only the second woman, to be honored by the Academy with the Jean Hersholt Humanitarian Award. She died four years later after a long bout with cancer.

SANDERS, GEORGE (1906–1972) No one played cads, scoundrels, and cynics more effectively than this actor, who appeared in more than one hundred films. With his acerbic and sardonic style, stylized snobbishness, and mellifluous voice, Sanders played characters audiences loved to hate. Though his reputation rests on his elegant characterizations of heels, it should be noted that he was also quite capable of playing heroes, as evidenced by his work in both the Saint and Falcon action/mystery series, in which he played the debonair title characters.

Born in Russia to an English family, Sanders was educated in Britain with the intention of becoming a businessman. It wasn't until he was well into his twenties that he was bitten by the acting bug. He quickly found his way from the stage to the screen, making his debut in *Find the Lady* (1936), an English movie. Within a year, he shipped off to Hollywood, where he first appeared in the Twentieth Century-Fox hit *Lloyds of London* (1937).

It wasn't long before he settled into starring roles in "B" mysteries, taking over for Louis Hayward in the second Saint film, *The Saint Strikes Back* (1939). He played the Saint four more times before playing the Falcon in *The Gay Falcon* (1941), the first of three such films. In a brilliant gimmick, Sanders turned the role over to his brother, Tom Conway, who played the hero in nine more films, in a movie called *The Falcon's Brother* (1942).

When he wasn't playing heroes, Sanders added his waspish and evil characterizations to a substantial number of very fine films, including *Confessions of a Nazi Spy* (1939), *Rebecca* (1940), *Foreign Correspondent* (1940), *This Land Is Mine* (1943), and many others. But his quintessential performance, for which he won an Oscar for Best Supporting Actor, was as the vicious drama critic in *All About Eve* (1950).

Sanders worked steadily in leading villainous roles throughout the 1950s and 1960s, though an increasingly large number of his films were made overseas. Most of his 1950s movies were hardly memorable, exceptions being *Ivanhoe* (1952) and *Death of a Scoundrel* (1956). Age suited him well in his later character parts during the 1960s and he flourished anew in films such as *Village of the Damned* (1960), *A Shot in the Dark* (1964), *The Amorous Adventures of Moll Flanders* (1965), *The Quiller Memorandum* (1966), and *Warning Shot* (1967).

Sanders was married four times, once each to Gabor sisters Zsa Zsa (1949–1957) and Magda (1970), and was the author of an autobiography, *Memoirs of a Professional Cad* (1960). He took his own life in 1972, claiming in his suicide note that he was bored.

SATIRE ON THE SCREEN Playwright George S. Kaufman once described satire as "that which closes on Saturday night." The intelligent use of wit and irony to cut fools and folly down to size has rarely been an audience-pleaser among those seeking simple entertainment, whether in the theater or at the movies. Relatively few out-and-out satirical films have been made and few of these have been box office winners. Ironically, many of the best satires—whether or not they succeeded with the public in their day—tend to stand up very well decades later.

The satiric tradition began in earnest in the early 1930s when America was in the grip of the Great Depression. There was certainly plenty to satirize in those bleak days and Frank Capra (*q.v.*) was among the first to capitalize on popular discontent in *American Madness* (1932). Later in that decade *Nothing Sacred* (1937) poked fun at American gullibility. But nobody satirized American society or its institutions better during the 1930s than the Marx Brothers (*q.v.*), who attacked everything from higher education in *Horse-*

feathers (1932) to government and war in *Duck Soup* (1933).

The leading movie satirist of the 1940s was unquestionably writer-director Preston Sturges *(q.v.),* whose hit comedies made fun of politics, in *The Great McGinty* (1940), for which Sturges won a best Original Screenplay Oscar; marriage, in *The Palm Beach Story* (1942); and small-town American values, in *The Miracle of Morgan's Creek* (1943). In the case of Sturges and many others who were successful with satire, the biting humor of their films seemed less satirical than merely zany with an acerbic touch.

Hollywood took itself very seriously during the late 1940s and 1950s and there were very few satires during those years. The postwar era and early cold war years were filled with such angst that most comedies, as an antidote, tended to be extremely light. Even when *Nothing Sacred* was remade in 1954, it was designed as an innocuous vehicle for Martin and Lewis and renamed *Living It Up.* One major exception to the rule was Charlie Chaplin's *Monsieur Verdoux* (1947), a film so bleak in its harsh humor, satirizing, as it did, religion and justice, that it brought cries of outrage, and many theaters refused to run it.

The tumultuous 1960s saw the return of the satire with surprising box office strength. The rise of the "counterculture" and a shift in the focus of the movies toward a younger, less conservative, baby-boom audience, allowed films to be outrageous. Among the filmmakers who responded were Stanley Kubrick *(q.v.),* whose *Dr. Strangelove* (1964) satirized the military and the threat of nuclear destruction with pungent black humor. Later in the decade, *The President's Analyst* (1967) took potshots at everything from the government to the phone company with hilarious results.

The leading film satirist of the 1970s was screenwriter Paddy Chayefsky *(q.v.),* whose angry comedies were noted for both their humor and their truth. His screenplays for the hits *The Hospital* (1971) and *Network* (1976) were winners; the latter movie brought him an Oscar for Best Screenplay. Other notable satires during the decade were the powerful *Catch-22* (1970) and *Little Murders* (1971), plus the mild *Fun with Dick and Jane* (1977).

The self-indulgent 1980s should have provided fertile ground for satirist filmmakers but the offerings were surprisingly lean from mainstream directors. Satire bubbled up with a vengeance, however, from the underground cinema, most notably in the work of writer-director John Waters, who made such iconoclastic social satires as *Polyester* (1981) and *Hairspray* (1988).
See also: black comedy

SAYLES, JOHN (1950–) A quirky writer-director of independent motion pictures who has carved a niche for himself as a creator of low-budget movies for the art-house audience. A former novelist and award-winning author, he has approached the movie business with refreshing resourcefulness and humor—and has even managed to create a modest reputation for himself as an actor in many of his own films.

Born to a family of educators, initially Sayles was more interested in sports than in writing. He once said, "Most of what I know about style I learned from Roberto Clemente." Nonetheless, after doing some college acting, he eventually embarked on a writing career, penning two acclaimed novels, *Pride of the Bimbos* and *Union Dues.* He also won two O. Henry awards for short stories.

On the basis of his unusual writing style, Roger Corman hired Sayles to write the screenplay for a low-budget rip-off of *Jaws* (1975) called *Piranha* (1978), in which Sayles was also given a small acting role. Critics noted that the film, for all its foolishness, was cleverly written. Meanwhile, Sayles continued to learn his new craft on-the-job by writing the scripts for *The Lady in Red* (1979) and *Battle Beyond the Stars* (1980).

In the late 1970s, Sayles decided to use his $40,000 in savings (earned from his work-for-hire screenwriting) to make a film of his own. The result was *The Return of the Secaucus Seven* (1980), a forerunner of *The Big Chill* (1983) and a film that delighted the critics, becoming a sleeper hit on the art-house circuit. In order to fully pay for its production, however, Sayles had to come up with another $20,000, which he earned writing the TV movie "A Perfect Match" (1980), and the low-budget feature films *The Howling* (1981) and *Alligator* (1981).

The success of *Secaucus Seven* allowed Sayles to raise $300,000 (a very minor sum by movie standards) to make *Lianna* (1983), a courageous, thoughtful drama about lesbianism. In that same year, Sayles won the MacArthur Foundation "genius" award, which granted him $30,000 tax-free every year for five years.

His growing reputation as a filmmaker got him studio backing for his third film, *Baby, It's You* (1983), a movie made with a $3 million budget. It received mixed reviews and was not a major commercial success.

Sayles went back to independent filmmaking, preferring to have greater control of his projects, and proceeded to make such provocative and highly regarded movies as *The Brother from Another Planet* (1984), *Matewan* (1987), and *Eight Men Out* (1988).

SCANDALS American royalty doesn't reside in Washington, it reigns from Hollywood, where the rich, powerful, and famous frolic both in the sun and the public eye. Ultimately, in true democratic fashion, it is the American people who make or break the kings and queens of Tinsel Town, and the perpetual scandals that rock the film industry only destroy those whom audiences have grown tired of. But nothing sells newspapers and magazines like a scandal, and the stars, with their inflated bank accounts and often equally inflated egos and passions, have given the scribes plenty to write about.

There have been scandals over all sorts of peccadillos, but, until recently, sex has been number one. Mary Astor's diary made headlines when it was submitted as evidence in her mid-1930s divorce proceedings. It went into great detail about her adulterous sexual liaisons with a number of famous men, including playwright George S. Kaufman. But Astor not only survived the scandal, she later flourished as a femme fatale in *The Maltese Falcon* (1941) and enjoyed a long career in character roles, as well.

Audiences have rarely been outraged by sexual excesses as long as no one gets hurt. In fact, film fans have rather enjoyed sex scandals, getting a vicarious thrill from the escapades of such stars as Errol Flynn, and Marilyn Monroe *(qq.v.)*—especially when they have been compatible with the on-screen image of the actor involved. In Flynn's case, it mattered little that he was brought to trial for statutory rape. Once he was acquitted of all charges, his devil-may-care attitude was condoned by the public and the expression "in like Flynn" entered the language as a euphemism for sexual conquest. As for Monroe's famous nude calendar, it didn't hurt her at all; it actually helped turn her into a star.

In contrast to the likes of Flynn and Monroe, actors and actresses who are perceived to be innocent tend to be hurt much more by scandalous publicity. In addition, when either children or other innocent parties are involved in a scandal, the repercussions are often quite severe. One need only think of the outcry against Ingrid Bergman *(q.v.)* when she left her husband and child for director Roberto Rossellini. Her career was temporarily shattered and it took quite some time for American audiences to forgive and forget. Another example of this phenomenon was the Elizabeth Taylor *(q.v.)* and Eddie Fisher marriage. When Fisher left his then wife, Debbie Reynolds *(q.v.)*, for Taylor, the world sympathized with the wronged wife who had been done in by her close friend Liz. Ironically, when Taylor humiliated Fisher with her highly publicized affair with Richard Burton *(q.v.)* on the set of *Cleopatra* (1963), there was little public sympathy for Fisher, who most watchers felt deserved what he got for leaving Debbie Reynolds in the first place.

Sex is one thing, but murder is quite another. When the two are combined in a scandal, the result is often a ruined career. Among the most famous sex and murder scandals was the 1921 "Fatty" Arbuckle *(q.v.)* case. He had been accused of rape and manslaughter in the death of Virginia Rappe, but while he was acquitted on all counts, the publicity resulting from the trial ruined

him. Unlike Errol Flynn, Arbuckle was seen not as a dashing man-about-town but a monstrous villain. His crime was that he was not the same man offscreen as he was on, and audiences made him pay for the "duplicity" with his career.

On the heels of the Arbuckle case was yet another murder case with sexual overtones. William Desmond Taylor, a handsome and charismatic director, was shot and killed in his palatial mansion. When it became known that two popular actresses, Mabel Normand *(q.v.)* and Mary Miles Minter, had both been his lovers and had seen him the day of his death, they suddenly found their fame and glory compromised. Though neither actress was ever accused of the killing—in fact, no one was ever brought to trial—their names were dragged through the mud and the mud stuck.

Another victim of a mysterious end was the powerful director-producer Thomas H. Ince *(q.v.)*. He supposedly died of "heart failure brought on by acute indigestion" while on William Randolph Hearst's yacht in 1924. Rumor had it that Hearst shot and killed Ince because of the director's dalliance with the newspaper magnate's mistress, Marion Davies. Though an investigation was belatedly made by the authorities, it was quickly dropped, some say because of Hearst's immense clout. Because of Hearst's control of the media, the scandal was very much underground, and kept alive in whispers.

There are some Hollywood scandals involving sex and murder that are more shocking than titillating. In 1958, Lana Turner's daughter, Cheryl Crane, stabbed mobster Johnny Stompanato to death, claiming she was defending her mother. The nation took pity on the young girl, and, despite Turner's intimate association with Stompanato, audiences preferred to think of Turner as having simply fallen for the wrong man; her career didn't suffer.

Most Hollywood scandals involve private events that become public knowledge. A rare on-set scandal that shocked the industry in the 1980s took place during the making of *Twilight Zone, The Movie* (1983), when actor Vic Morrow and two children were killed in a helicopter accident. The director of the segment, John Landis *(q.v.)*, was brought to trial on charges that he had been careless and reckless in the shooting of the helicopter scene and was therefore responsible for the three deaths. Landis was acquitted and he has continued to direct, but his once hot career has never been quite the same.

When a major star dies under mysterious circumstances, that kind of scandal never fully disappears. Marilyn Monroe's sexual involvement with President John F. Kennedy and, later, Attorney General Robert F. Kennedy, has been well documented. Robert Kennedy's possible role in her death in 1963, however, remains one of Hollywood's most enduring scandals because it links the two scandal capitals of America, Hollywood and Washington, as well as the most charismatic actress and politicians of our time.

The Hollywood/Washington connection has evolved a great many other scandals besides Marilyn Monroe's. Jane Fonda's visit to North Vietnam during the Vietnam War of the 1960s and early 1970s provoked accusations of treason from a large segment of the American public. She survived in Hollywood because the moviegoing public was generally young and antiwar. But during the red-scare years of the late 1940s and early 1950s, even a movie idol as beloved as Charlie Chaplin was hounded out of America because of his leftist political beliefs, and that came after he had overcome the scandals of a lurid divorce case, a paternity suit, and a federal morals charge.

Hollywood, itself, suffered one of its worst scandals when, in the late 1940s and early 1950s, the House Un-American Activities Committee (HUAC) investigated Communist infiltration of the movie industry. At the time, it seemed the scandal was that there were, indeed, a number of Communists among writers, directors, and actors in Hollywood. With hindsight, however, the real scandal was that hundreds of innocent lives were ruined by innuendo and unsubstantiated charges. The insidious blacklist was the outgrowth of the HUAC hearings and the damage that list wreaked on Hollywood was incalculable.

Due to a far more permissive society, genuine scandals have been hard to come by in recent decades. Actors involved in illicit sex, having children out of wedlock, and becoming drug addicts aren't big news. Sexual conduct is merely a matter of gossip, not scandal, and celebrity drug addicts announce their treatment at the Betty Ford Clinic almost as a rite of passage. Perhaps the only recent shocking scandal concerning drugs in Hollywood was when thirteen-year-old Drew Barrymore admitted that she had an alcohol and drug problem that had begun when she was nine years old.

Perhaps the only potential ingredient for scandal that can really shake the jaded members of the film industry is the one that fuels all their other passions: money. When the then president of Columbia Pictures David Begelman was prosecuted for forging checks in the late 1970s, there were headlines and head-shaking. The scandal toppled Begelman from his perch—for all of four months. The actor who blew the whistle on Begelman, Cliff Robertson (q.v.), didn't work again for three and a half years. But that was another, quieter, scandal.

SCHARY, DORE (1905–1980) He rose from lowly contract scriptwriter of "B" movies to become the head of MGM. Along the way, he won an Oscar for his writing, became an executive producer, and was the

vice president in charge of production at not one, but two, major studios. Schary is perhaps best known for spearheading, along with Darryl F. Zanuck (q.v.), the rush into "message" movies in the late 1940s (i.e., films dealing with social issues such as bigotry) and replacing Louis B. Mayer (q.v.) at the helm of MGM in 1951.

Schary's original ambition was to become an actor, and he reached Broadway when he was just twenty-five, playing a supporting role in *The Last Mile*. Fancying himself a writer, he also worked as both a journalist and a playwright, with little success in either field. He had done enough writing, however, to latch on in Hollywood as a screenwriter, penning such "B" movies as *He Couldn't Take It* (1932), *Chinatown Squad* (1935), and *Silk Hat Kid* (1935).

Schary landed in the big leagues when he began writing for MGM, sharing a best Original Story Academy Award with his cowriter, Eleanor Griffin, for *Boys Town* (1938). He continued writing, but showed even more promise as a producer, and so was promoted to the post of executive producer of MGM's "B" movie list. Opinionated and strong-willed, he quit after a fracas and went to work for David O. Selznick (q.v.), producing such films as *The Spiral Staircase* (1946) and *Till the End of Time* (1946).

Schary kept rising up the Hollywood ladder, being named head of production at the troubled RKO studio. He hoped to bring RKO back from the edge of bankruptcy and he was off to a good start with *Crossfire* (1947), a sleeper hit and one of the first movies about prejudice to be made by Hollywood. It came out the same year as *Gentlemen's Agreement* and the two films started a rash of "adult" message movies. Unfortunately, not long after Schary arrived at RKO, Howard Hughes (q.v.) bought the company. Far too liberal in his politics for the extremely conservative Hughes, Schary was quickly out on his ear.

But, again, Schary found himself being kicked higher up the ladder. Due to skyrocketing costs at MGM, Nicholas M. Schenck (q.v.), the president of MGM-Loew's, insisted that Louis B. Mayer find a new Irving Thalberg (q.v.) to oversee the production process and boost MGM profits. With Schenck's blessings, Mayer picked Schary in 1947.

During the next four years it was war between Mayer and Schary, with Schenck often having to act as peacemaker. Meanwhile, in the face of inroads from TV, Schary was effectively doing his job as head of production. He was also producing hits such as *Battleground* (1949). In 1951, when Mayer finally forced Schenck to pick between Schary and the man whose name was part of the title of the company, Schenck stunned both Mayer and Hollywood by choosing Schary.

During the next five years, Schary ran MGM until the company posted its first losing year in its entire history in 1956. He was promptly fired. He went back to Broadway, which he had left with his tail between his legs nearly twenty-five years earlier, and wrote and produced the critically acclaimed hit *Sunrise at Campobello,* which was later turned into a 1960 movie with a Schary screenplay. He continued to dabble in the movies during the late 1950s and early 1960s, scripting and producing such films as *Lonelyhearts* (1959) and *Act One,* (1963) which he also directed.

A longtime liberal activist, Schary was one of the few major studio heads to speak out against the Hollywood blacklist in the early 1950s. In fact, his left-leaning attitudes were so well known that gossip columnist Louella Parsons once referred to MGM in print as "Metro-Goldwyn-Moscow" during the height of the red-baiting era. Staunch in his beliefs, however, Schary withstood the attacks and in his later years became a well-known defender of civil and human rights.

SCHENCK, JOSEPH M. (1878–1961) **& NICHOLAS M.** (1881–1969) Two brothers who, between them, at one time wielded more power in Hollywood than anyone. The two brothers controlled two of the five major studios, with Joseph as chairman of the board of Twentieth Century-Fox and Nicholas as president of the theater chain and parent company of MGM, Loew's, Inc. Though neither man was well-known to the public at large, within the industry they were the equivalent of royalty.

Both brothers were born in Rybinsk, Russia, arriving in the United States when they were small children. Joseph, the elder of the two, became a pharmacist and then, with his brother, bought several drugstores. Again it was Joseph, ever the risk taker, who convinced his kid brother to join him in a new venture, opening up an amusement park at Fort George in upstate New York. Later, in 1912, they joined with Marcus Loew in buying the famous Palisades Amusement Park in New Jersey.

During these years Loew was building his theater chain and he invited the two brothers into his business, making them senior executives. They took to the theater business like racehorses on a fast track, helping build the Loew's chain into one of the most powerful in the country. But it was Nicholas who continued the job for Loew, staying with the company until 1956, becoming president upon his mentor's death in 1927. Nicholas was instrumental in the acquisition of MGM in 1924, and he was the power and the financial brains behind the studio's ascent to the top of the heap during the 1930s through the early 1950s. It was Nick Schenck to whom Irving A. Thalberg and Louis B. Mayer *(q.v.)* had to answer. And when he was no longer pleased with Mayer's reign on the West Coast, he replaced him with Dore Schary *(q.v.).* When that move failed to stem MGM's fall from grace, Schenck, himself, was

forced into the figurehead position of chairman of the board in 1955, retiring the following year from the company he had guided to preeminence.

Joseph Schenck took a different route to Hollywood power. Unlike his brother who ruled from the East Coast, Joseph "went Hollywood," quitting Loew's in 1917 to become a producer. And he was a successful one from the outset, producing the films of a tightly knit group of talented and popular performers, including those of his wife, Norma Talmadge (whom he married in 1917), as well as the films of the other Talmadge sisters, Constance and Natalie. In addition, he produced "Fatty" Arbuckle's popular films, and those of Arbuckle's buddy (and Natalie Talmadge's husband), the great Buster Keaton, including all of the "Great Stoneface's" most important and successful movies.

Joseph Schenck was the man everyone turned to in Hollywood to get things done. When the founders of United Artists, Douglas Fairbanks, Mary Pickford, D. W. Griffith, and Charlie Chaplin, needed the strong hand of management to keep their enterprise afloat, they turned to Schenck to become the company's chairman of the board. Later, when Darryl F. Zanuck left Warner Bros., he went Schenck to get the backing to form a new company during the depths of the Depression. So, Twentieth Century was formed in 1933, later to merge with Fox in 1935, at which time Schenck became chairman of the board of Twentieth Century-Fox *(q.v.),* a post he held until 1941 when he went to prison for four months in a tax and payola scandal.

He returned to his studio as executive producer but made few films of distinction. Among his minor accomplishments during the late 1940s and early 1950s was befriending Marilyn Monroe, who was known to be one of his "girlfriends." He was instrumental during her early career at Fox and in later getting her a contract at Columbia.

Hollywood ignored Schenck's prison record and later honored him in 1952 with a special Academy Award "for long and distinguished service to the motion picture industry." But the risk taker was not quite ready to sit on his laurels. He promptly joined with Michael Todd in forming the Magna Corporation in 1953 to publicize and sell the new widescreen process, Todd-AO, to both the industry and the public.

By the end of the 1950s, both Joseph and Nicholas Schenck had come to the end of their movie careers.

SCHRADER, PAUL (1946–   ) An intense screenwriter and director whose films are often challenging and controversial. Schrader intends to entertain, but his films are never mindless excursions into fantasy; unlike many Hollywood writers and directors, he rarely makes concessions to the marketplace. For the most part, he has been far more successful as a screenwriter than as a writer/director. In particular, his talents have been best brought out through his collaboration with strong, independent directors such as Brian De Palma and Martin Scorsese (qq.v.).

Raised as a strict Calvinist, Schrader saw his very first film at the age of eighteen. After graduating from Calvin College, he traveled to Los Angeles and took an M.A. degree from U.C.L.A. Falling in love with the movies, Schrader eventually became a film critic for the *L.A. Weekly Press* and also served as editor of *Cinema Magazine.* In 1972 his book *Transcendental Style in Film: Ozu, Bresson, Dryer* was published.

Meanwhile, Schrader toiled at writing screenplays, finally hitting it big when (in collaboration with Robert Towne) he sold *The Yakuza* (1974) for a reported $400,000. It was an important sale because it highlighted a new trend in Hollywood for paying large sums of money for original screenplays. *The Yakuza,* however, was a flop at the box office.

Schrader quickly became a hot screenwriter, though, when he penned two major hits, Martin Scorsese's *Taxi Driver* (1976) and Brian De Palma's *Obsession* (1976). The success of these two films gave Schrader the clout to shoot his own screenplay of *Blue Collar* (1977), a critically applauded movie that did not do great business.

Moving back and forth between strictly writing, and writing and directing, Schrader has amassed an impressive body of work. His movies are often violent and harsh, dealing with both the physical and psychological underworld. Though he has rarely had commercial success as a writer/director, his films, such as *Hardcore* (1978), *American Gigolo* (1979), and *Mishima* (1985), have been consistently compelling. His direction of other writers' work in *Cat People* (1981) and *Patty Hearst* (1988) is also strong and provocative. Yet it is his screenwriting, with films such as *Raging Bull* (1980), *The Mosquito Coast* (1986), and Scorsese's controversial masterpiece, *The Last Temptation of Christ* (1988), that have marked Schrader as a major Hollywood talent.

SCHWARZENEGGER, ARNOLD (1947–) A former world champion bodybuilder who has become the most consistently popular action star of the 1980s. Unlike Sylvester Stallone, his closest competitor in both body mass and acting style, Schwarzenegger has starred in tightly made lower-budget movies that have been remarkably reliable money-makers. In his rise to stardom, he overcame such obstacles as an impossibly long last name, a thick Austrian accent, and a gap-toothed appearance. He attained his goal thanks to public fascination with his massively muscled body, his undeniable star presence, and his savvy in recognizing his weaknesses and picking his projects accordingly.

Born to a policeman in a small Austrian village, Schwarzenegger began lifting weights as a form of training for soccer and swimming. By the age of fifteen, however, he had become seriously involved in what was then the fringe sport of bodybuilding. At the age of eighteen, he won his first title, Junior Mr. Europe. He would go on to win a great many other titles including Mr. Olympia. In fact, by the time he appeared as the focus of the highly regarded documentary *Pumping Iron* (1977), he had been world champion for eight consecutive years.

Schwarzenegger arrived in the United States at twenty-one to continue his pursuit of bodybuilding fame. In order to make a living, he formed a construction company in Los Angeles called Pumping Bricks. Later, when he became a modestly well-known name outside of the bodybuilding world due to the success of *Pumping Iron,* Schwarzenegger decided to become an actor. The consensus of many at the time was that the good reviews Schwarzenegger received while playing himself in *Pumping Iron* had gone to his head. His effort to break into the movie business was considered a joke.

Five years later, however, Schwarzenegger was cast in the perfect vehicle, playing the title character in John Milius's *Conan the Barbarian* (1982). He had just a few lines of dialogue, but he was the center of the film, showing off his magnificent torso in a lively, if violent, sword-and-sorcery action film. The critics might have sneered, but *Conan* and its sequel, *Conan the Destroyer* (1984), grossed a combined total of $100 million. Schwarzenegger was fast becoming a force to be reckoned with.

The turning point in Schwarzenegger's acting career came with his mesmerizing villain's role in *The Terminator* (1984). It was a sleeper hit made on a low budget; the key factor in Schwarzenegger's favor was that he held the screen without taking off most of his clothes and rippling his muscles.

Red Sonja (1985) was a modest disappointment—mostly due to the poor acting by the two female stars, Brigitte Nielsen and Sandahl Bergman (both of whom made Schwarzenegger look like Laurence Olivier). But that one film aside, Schwarzenegger's movies have been box office winners. His ability to be likable despite his imposing bulk has made him a film favorite of a great many male moviegoers. With a string of hits that includes *Commando* (1985), *Raw Deal* (1986), *Running Man* (1987), *Predator* (1987), and *Red Heat* (1988), his films have taken in more than $500 million in box office receipts. And that was before he ventured into comedy, playing diminutive Danny DeVito's twin brother in the hit farce *Twins* (1988).

Schwarzenegger, an active conservative Republican, married a member of the liberal Democratic Kennedy clan in 1986, broadcast journalist Maria Shriver.

SCIENCE FICTION A genre that grew and matured rather late by Hollywood standards. While gangster films, musicals, westerns, etc. all had at least their first blossoming as viable commercial categories by the 1930s, science fiction features didn't have their initial heyday until the 1950s, and this despite the fact that George Melies' science fiction movie *A Trip to the Moon* (1902) was one of filmdom's earliest sensations.

There was little in the way of films in the genre made during the silent era in Hollywood. With technology racing ahead during the first decades of the new century, it must have seemed as if the future had already arrived. The present was fascinating enough for the masses. Nonetheless, D W. Griffith tinkered with the genre in films such as *The Flying Torpedo* (1916).

It wasn't until Fritz Lang's classic *Metropolis* (1926), a futuristic film about man's loss of freedom in a technological society, that science fiction appeared as a brand new subject for the movies. Unfortunately, the elaborate models and special effects required to make *Metropolis* nearly bankrupted UFA (the German film company that produced Lang's masterpiece) and the movie was a beautiful and intelligent box office failure.

In England, the much admired *Things To Come* (1936), directed by William Cameron Menzies *(q.v.)* with a script by H. G. Wells, not only suggested a future that might come to pass but was the precursor of the science fiction films of the 1950s and beyond. In the meantime, however, back in Hollywood the science fiction film was born as a bastard child of the horror genre.

It was during the 1930s, when horror was at the height of its popularity, that the mad scientist film came into vogue, spinning off a peculiar form of science fiction film that found its roots in *Frankenstein* (1931). The result was a hybrid horror/science fiction film such as *The Invisible Ray* (1936), in which the line: "There are some things man is not meant to know," was uttered for the very first time in the movies. Knowledge of science was growing at a pace far beyond society's ability to digest it, and the backlash (in the form of distrust of scientists) was apparent in movies such as *Dr. X* (1932), which dealt with the creation of synthetic flesh, *The Island of Lost Souls* (1932), in which a mad doctor tries to turn animals into humans through vivisection, and *The Invisible Man* (1933), concerning a scientist who tries to rule the world.

If horror movies present our personal primal fears, than science fiction presents, like no other genre, the fears and anxieties of society as a whole. The political, cultural, sociological elements of science fiction are often visceral statements of the hopes, fears, and values of our species.

The closest thing in the 1930s to what we generally call modern science fiction could be found in the serials that featured Buck Rogers and Flash Gordon, but these were simplistic movies based on comic-strip characters and made for children.

Science fiction films virtually disappeared during World War II, but the advanced weapons of the conflict—principally, the V-2 rocket and the atomic bomb—eventually unleashed both the imagination and the interest of a terrified audience in a genre that suddenly seemed quite relevant.

In 1950, producer George Pal struck a commercial mother-lode when he made *Destination Moon*. This unexpected low-budget hit, based on a Robert Heinlein novel called *Rocket Ship Galileo,* combined a good story and believable special effects to rivet audiences to their seats. The film won an Oscar for Best Special Effects; the science fiction film was finally on the map.

George Pal went on to produce several other science fiction classics during the next decade, including *When Worlds Collide* (1951) and *War of the Worlds* (1953). The first golden age of science fiction was under way when Pal's films were joined by Howard Hawks' *The Thing* (1951), Robert Wise's *The Day the Earth Stood Still* (1951), and Jack Arnold's *It Came from Outer Space* (1953).

This initial wave of science fiction was generally made with relatively unknown actors and with modest budgets. But in 1956, MGM took a chance and put one of their better-known (if aging) stars, Walter Pidgeon, in the serious and intelligent *Forbidden Planet*. The movie, based on Shakespeare's *The Tempest,* introduced an entirely new sort of evil creature: the Monster from the Id. At the same time, Donald Siegel *(q.v.)* directed the classic *Invasion of the Body Snatchers* (1956), a movie that was just as much a political attack on right-wing American society as it was about pods from outer space. Science fiction wasn't just for kids anymore.

At their simplest level, movies such as *Invasion of the Body Snatchers* spoke to humankind's sense of wonder about the stars. But in the 1950's, the answer to the question "Is there life in outer space?" was a frightening "yes,"not only in the Don Siegel film, but in movies such as *Them!* (1954), *The Twenty-Seventh Day* (1957), *The Monolith Monsters* (1957), and *I Married a Monster from Outer Space* (1958).

As science fiction replaced horror in the 1950s, children and teenagers lined up to see "B" movies that exploited their unique fears of annihilation. The first generation to live under the threat of the bomb spent the better part of the 1950s watching science fiction films dealing with the issue of science running amok on a global rather than an individual level, as in 1930s movies. In film after film, such as *The Beast from 20,000 Fathoms* (1953), *Attack of the Crab Monsters* (1957), and *Attack of the Giant Leeches* (1959), nuclear explosions and scientific experiments caused either the resurrection or the creation of huge, deadly creatures that threatened to destroy humanity. (Movies about monsters either created or unleashed by science fall for our purposes, within the science fiction category. Films about dinosaurs and other similar creatures are categorized as *Monster Movies.*)

With the advent of the so-called "Missile Gap" during the 1960 presidential campaign and the subsequent Cuban Missile Crisis, science fiction films reflected more pointed fears of outright nuclear devastation in movies such as *The Last Woman on Earth* (1960), *Panic in the Year Zero* (1962), and *The Day the Earth Caught Fire* (1962).

With the easing of the fear of nuclear extermination, science fiction turned in the latter half of the 1960s to explore a broader range of ideas. For instance, *Fantastic Voyage* (1966) was a journey through the human body, while *Planet of the Apes* (1968) was a moralistic parable about human behavior.

It was Stanley Kubrick's *2001: A Space Oydessey* (1968), however, that changed the face of science fiction forever, turning what had heretofore been a fringe genre into a mainstream mainstay due to a combination of special effects and intellectual appeal. It enjoyed a spectacular success at the box office.

Science fiction films were made rather consistently during the decade after *2001.* Movies such as *The Andromeda Strain* (1971) and *Silent Running* (1972) achieved a very high level of artistic success, but they didn't truly catch fire at the box office.

It wasn't until George Lucas *(q.v.)* made *Star Wars* (1977, *q.v.*) that the promise of *2001* was realized, with a rousing adventure yarn, spectacular special effects, and a simple, yet elegant, mysticism ("May the force be with you.") that appealed to kids of all ages. *Star Wars* was an unabashed salute to Buck Rogers and Flash Gordon, but was made with such lavish detail, love, and cinematic flair that it became one of the most commercially successful movies of all time.

Star Wars was such a huge hit that it ushered in a second golden age of science fiction. In its wake, Lucas produced two more Star Wars epics; a continuing series of *Star Trek* movies spawned from a TV series made hundreds of millions of dollars; and Steven Spielberg *(q.v.)* followed with two of his most beloved films, *Close Encounters of the Third Kind* (1977) and *E.T.—The Extra-Terrestrial* (1982). These latter two films are of particular significance because they presented aliens not as enemies, as was so often the case in the science fiction films of the 1950s, but as friendly, benign creatures. These films offered a comforting, less paranoid view of the cosmos.

It's been postulated that science fiction has replaced the western as the genre of choice for those interested in movies about the frontier. And that is certainly true; one need only watch *Outland* (1981), an obvious remake of *High Noon,* to see how science fiction has subsumed a great many of the western concerns. But science fiction, in more recent years, has incorporated the police procedural genre as well, in films such as *Blade Runner* (1982) and *Robocop* (1987). The trend appears to be continuing.

SCORE   The music written to accompany a motion picture. Music was part of the moviegoing experience long before the advent of sound films. When one- and two-reelers were first shown in vaudeville houses, the orchestras that played for the various acts also played background music for the movies. A short time later, when movie houses began dotting the American landscape, the musical tradition continued; piano players were hired to supply generic romantic music, chase music, etc.

The breakthrough in the scoring of American films came, as did so many early cinematic innovations, from D. W. Griffith. He prepared a specific film score for a full orchestra for *The Birth of a Nation* (1915). The power of that score, which was mostly adapted from previously existing music, so enhanced the picture that many subsequent feature-length films followed the master's lead. But whether full orchestras in the big cities played music written specifically for each scene of a film or piano players in small rural towns played the main themes of a film's score, there was music in abundance during the silent era.

Ironically, the talkies proved to be a hindrance to musical scores, at least in the late 1920s and very early 1930s. Early sound technology was such that getting the words on film was hard enough without worrying about music as well. Only unobtrusive musical accompaniment could be heard in the background of most comedies and dramas during those difficult transitional years.

By the mid-1930s, however, the technology had advanced enough to allow significant musical scores to be added to most motion pictures. While many were often adaptations of existing melodies, the art of composing original music for the screen was coming into full flower, thanks to such composers as Max Steiner, Erich Wolfgang Korngold, and many others.

There have been three separate Academy Award categories for scoring: Best Original Music for a Drama or Comedy, Best Music Adaptation for a Drama or Comedy, and Best Scoring for a Musical. In recent years, the latter category has been dropped due to the paucity of musical films.

The importance of "mood" music in films cannot be taken lightly. The scores of such films as *Gone with the Wind* (1939), *The Treasure of the Sierra Madre* (1948), *The Pink Panther* (1964), *The Godfather* (1972), *The Sting* (1973), *Jaws* (1975), and *Star Wars* (1977) all attest to the power of music to affect the audience in the most fundamental ways.

See also: composers; Herrmann, Bernard; Mancini, Henry; Steiner, Max; Tiomkin, Dimitri; Williams, John

SCORSESE, MARTIN (1942–   ) One of the first—as well as one of the most creative and adventurous—of a new breed of film school–trained directors who came to prominence in the late 1960s and early 1970s. Scorsese has a reputation for making films about violent people who live on the fringe of society. But his themes run deeper: his heroes are people desperate for redemption. Religion rarely helps them, and they channel their violent temperaments in directions that point to deep flaws in our culture.

Scorsese, a sickly child growing up in New York's Little Italy, found a refuge in the movies. He had intended to become a priest but found his true calling to be the screen rather than the cloth. He went to New York University and received his undergraduate degree in film communications in 1964, following it up with an M.A. in the same subject from New York University in 1966. While still a student, he made a number of prize-winning films, among them *What's a Nice Girl Like You Doing in a Place Like This?* (1963), *It's Not Just You* (1964), and *The Big Shave* (1967).

His knowledge and skill as a filmmaker were fully appreciated at New York University, where he found employment as an instructor. While teaching at his alma mater, Scorsese made his first full-length film, *Who's That Knocking at My Door?* (1968), a personal film that presaged his breakout movie, *Mean Streets* (1973). Between those two films, however, Scorsese continued to learn his craft by working as an editor on the famed rock-concert movie *Woodstock* (1970) and directing a Roger Corman (*q.v.*) quickie, *Boxcar Bertha* (1972).

Hollywood took notice of the intense young director when his autobiographical film *Mean Streets* was shown at the 1973 New York Film Festival. Made on a shoestring budget in Little Italy, the movie not only launched Scorsese's directorial career, it also brought actors Harvey Keitel and Robert De Niro (*q.v.*) to the public's attention. And Scorsese used both actors extensively in his later films, particularly De Niro.

Mean Streets was a critical success but not a box office winner. His next two films, however, *Alice Doesn't Live Here Anymore* (1975) and *Taxi Driver* (1976), were huge hits. The former movie struck a nerve as one of the first popular films concerning a woman's desperate struggle to financially and emotionally survive without a man in modern society. After the violence of *Mean Streets,* it seemed an unlikely project for Scorsese, but survival has often been the theme of many of the director's films. Laced with comedy, *Alice Doesn't Live Here Anymore* was eventually adapted into the TV sitcom, "Alice."

Taxi Driver was undoubtedly the most controversial film of the 1970s. Inspired by Harry Chapin's popular song "Taxi," this dark portrait of a loner driven toward violence was a riveting tour de force of writing (Paul Schrader), acting (Robert De Niro in the title role), and especially directing. Scorsese's affinity for outsiders was never more vividly revealed than in this film. While the child prostitute played by Jodie Foster and the bloodbath finale outraged some segments of society, no one questioned the power of Scorsese's filmmaking. In short order, Scorsese had arrived as one of America's premier young directors.

His willingness to experiment was in evidence when he tried to bring back the lavish movie musical with *New York, New York* (1977) and when he changed gears altogether to make a documentary about the rock group The Band's final tour called *The Last Waltz* (1978).

Scorsese almost always receives good reviews from the critics but has had middling support at the box office. *Raging Bull* (1979), for instance, was an artful attempt at making a movie about a real-life character (boxer Jake La Motta) whom the audience couldn't easily like. *The King of Comedy* (1983) was an audacious movie that satirized show business paths to success, once again creating a fascinating hero for whom film fans felt little empathy. But the director managed to express his themes and find commercial success once again in *After Hours* (1985), a hard-edged comedy set in New York City with a sympathetic hero.

While his films have often been controversial, Scorsese outdid himself with *The Last Temptation of Christ* (1988), a religious opus that offended a great many conservative Christians with the depiction of a brief erotic reverie, while Jesus is on the cross, suggesting that Christ might have considered sleeping with (and marrying) Mary Magdalene. The storm of protest engendered by the film helped turn what was a thoughtful, quiet, art-house movie into a cause célèbre—and a hit. The film also brought Scorsese a best Director Academy Award nomination.

While making Hollywood features, Scorsese has filmed low-budget documentaries, such as *Italianamerican* (1974), a movie about his parents, and *American Boy* (1978), a film about a friend from the 1960s. It would seem that Scorsese is a truly independent filmmaker who just happens to make Hollywood movies.
See also: Foster, Jodie; Schrader, Paul

SCOTT, GEORGE C. (1927–   ) A talented actor whose relentless intensity dominates the screen. Imposing and barrel-chested, he has a face that resembles a well-fed American eagle and a raspy voice that might just scare off such a bird. For all his ability, Scott has been admired by movie critics more often than audiences, particularly in the two decades since he leaped to stardom with his Oscar-winning portrayal of General George S. Patton in 1969.

If George Campbell Scott sometimes looks and sounds

like a marine, it's because he was in the Corps for four years. Determined to become an actor, he served a long apprenticeship in summer stock and Off-Broadway, finding character roles befitting his less than matinee idol looks. There was TV work in the 1950s, where he learned to act in front of a camera, finally culminating in a lead role in a late 1950s prime-time cop series, "East Side, West Side." He finally had enough exposure to gain good supporting parts in his first films, *The Hanging Tree* (1959) and *Anatomy of a Murder* (1959).

Scott came into own soon thereafter, and he was nominated for a Best Supporting Actor Oscar for his villainous role in *The Hustler* (1961). He followed up with the lead in John Huston's *The List of Adrian Messenger* (1963) before returning to supporting parts, most memorably as a war-hungry general in the classic antiwar black comedy *Dr. Strangelove* (1964).

Scott's work was so strong that more starring roles came his way. There was the charming *Flim Flam Man* (1967), *Petulia* (1968), and then, finally, *Patton*. After he announced before the Oscar telecast that he thought acting awards ceremonies were a foolish exercise, the Academy promptly awarded him the statuette—in his absence.

Over the next decade Scott starred in sixteen films, but few were either critically or commercially successful. Like Paul Muni, Scott seemed to be an actor who was simply too overpowering for most stories. Among the movies that seemed to fit him—and not all of them were successful—were *The New Centurions* (1972), *Hospital* (1972), *Rage* (1972), which he also directed, Mike Nichols' *The Day of the Dolphin* (1973), Stanley Donen's *Movie, Movie* (1978), and Paul Schrader's *Hardcore* (1979).

The actor, formerly married to stage actress Colleen Dewhurst, later married actress Trish Van Devere, with whom he costarred in many of his movies during the '70s, such as *The Last Run* (1971), *The Savage is Loose* (1974), which he also directed, and *The Changeling* (1980). The chemistry (at least on screen) was not successful. By 1982, he was playing second fiddle to Brat Pack *(q.v.)* actors Timothy Hutton, Sean Penn, and Tom Cruise in *Taps*. It was at this point that he began to devote more attention to television and the Broadway stage, the latter being the most effective showcase for his prodigious talent.

SCOTT, RANDOLPH (1903–1987) An actor best remembered as a star of westerns. With his square jaw, piercing eyes, weathered features, and Southern drawl, he was the perfect embodiment of the rugged frontier hero. Though he was never a star of the magnitude of John Wayne or Gary Cooper *(qq.v.)*, the sheer quantity and quality of his westerns make him a standout in the genre. Scott brought a decency and a tough-minded morality to the western that made many of his movies— particularly those of the 1950s—memorable.

Randolph Scott was the quintessential cowboy hero: tall, gentlemanly, and tough as nails. If many of his films were mediocre, he ended his career well, with a string of memorable low-budget westerns directed by Budd Boetticher, topped off by the classic Sam Peckinpah movie *Ride the High Country* (1962). Photo courtesy of The Siegel Collection.

Born Randolph Crane to a well-to-do Virginia family, the young man lied about his age and went overseas to fight during World War I when he was just fourteen years old. After attending Georgia Tech and the University of North Carolina, where he received a degree in engineering, he worked briefly at his father's textile company before heading off to Hollywood to try his hand at acting.

He worked as an extra and bit player in films such as *The Far Call* (1929), and picked up additional experience as Gary Cooper's dialogue coach in *The Virginian* (1929). He had previously joined the Pasadena Community Playhouse, a jumping-off point for many a future star, and it paid off when Paramount signed him to a seven-year contract.

During the early to mid-1930s Scott had a bumpy career. He had everything from a tiny role as a half-animal/half-human creature in *The Island of Lost Souls* (1933) to co-leads as Fred Astaire's buddy in *Roberta* (1935) and *Follow the Fleet* (1936) on loan-out to RKO. Most notably, though, he starred in a low-budget, but highly successful, series of nine westerns based on Zane Grey stories between 1932 and 1935, seven of them directed by Henry Hathaway *(q.v.)*.

Scott's break came in 1936, when he played Hawkeye in a film version of James Fenimore Cooper's *The Last of the Mohicans*. The film was a hit and Scott appeared more frequently in "A" movie productions. After his Paramount contract ended in 1938, he signed non-exclusive contracts with Twentieth Century-Fox and Universal. It didn't help his career at first because he often found himself supporting other stars such as Shirley Temple in *Rebecca of Sunnybrook Farm* (1938), and Tyrone Power and Henry Fonda in *Jesse James* (1939). It wasn't until 1941 that he emerged as a full-fledged star of "A" movies in *Western Union* (1941). But then he briefly put the western behind him to make combat films during World war II such as *To the Shores of Tripoli* (1942), *Bombardier* (1943), and *Gung Ho!* (1943).

When the war was over, Scott went back to westerns with a vengeance. He made a total of forty-five films after World War II, forty-two of which were westerns. In fact, he made more westerns after World War II than any other star. But he never had a major hit such as Alan Ladd's *Shane* (1953), Gary Cooper's *High Noon* (1952), or John Wayne's many 1950s westerns. His films, such as *Abilene Town* (1945), *Colt .45* (1950), and *Hangman's Knot* (1952) were made inexpensively but not shabbily. They were solid action films that were appreciated by afficionados of the genre—and by his legion of fans. Despite a lack of tremendous hits, he was a top-ten draw at the box office for four consecutive years from 1950.

Scott worked with producer Harry Joe Brown on a great many of his postwar westerns, with the actor often doubling as associate producer. Finally, the pair formed their own company, Ranown (a combination of Randolph and Brown), that produced the Ranown series of westerns directed by Budd Boetticher *(q.v.)*, considered by many critics to be the perfect distillation of the western. There were seven Scott/Boetticher collaborations between 1956 and 1960, and six (all but *Westbound,* [1959] are among the finest westerns made during the heyday of the genre. The six films are *Seven Men from Now* (1956), *The Tall T* (1957), *Decision at Sundown* (1957), *Buchanan Rides Alone* (1958), *Ride Lonesome* (1959), and *Comanche Station* (1960).

He might have retired after his last Boetticher film, but Scott made one more movie, *Ride the High Country* (1962), and it was the perfect vehicle for his exit. He joined Joel McCrea (another aging star who found a comfortable niche in westerns) in Sam Peckinpah's early classic, playing two over-the-hill former lawmen on a last job delivering a payroll. Scott played against type, his character seeking to steal the money with which the two were entrusted. (In the end, however, Scott gives his word to the dying McCrea that he will deliver the money.)

Scott gave a clever, irracible, and resonant performance as the wily old would-be thief, and then he rode off into retirement. One of the richest actors in show business, he amassed a fortune in real estate, oil, and stocks estimated between $50 and $100 million.

SCREEN The flat surface upon which films are projected. Screens are almost always made of a reflective plastic material (e.g., polyvinyl chloride) and have a matt white surface. Invariably, a screen is perforated with tiny holes. Speakers placed behind the screen send sound through these holes.

Older screens may suffer from oxidation, which turns the surface yellow and diminishes the amount of light it will reflect, causing a less sharp picture. One of the primary causes of detoriation of movie screens is the residue left by cigarette smoke that stains the screen. While screens can be resurfaced with a new coat of paint, the tar stains from cigarette smoke are not easily covered. In any event, when a screen is resurfaced there is often a subsequent loss of sound quality because the screen's performations are made smaller.

When Thomas Edison established the frame size, he also inadvertantly established the size of the screen that it would be shown upon. Based on Edison's frame-size ratio of 4:3, a screen twenty-feet in width had to be fifteen feet high in order to properly accommodate the image of the frame projected on it. Except for big-city movies palaces, twenty by fifteen foot screens were standard in most American theaters.

Screen size went through a number of changes in the later 1940s and 1950s. Because television took such a large chunk of the moviegoing audience, studios and exhibitors fought back with various widescreen inventions, including Cinerama and CinemaScope.

In addition, drive-in movies began dotting the landscape in the 1950's with screens that were often bigger than the movie palaces'—even that of Radio City Music Hall in New York. Though the drive-in was a successful enterprise for less than two decades, its explosive popularity was unprecedented. There were only a few hundred drive-ins in the immediate postwar era, but according to film historian Kenneth Macgowan, "By 1962, the 'hard top' houses had shrunk from 20,000 to 15,000 while there were almost 6,000 drive-ins."

Despite experiments with multiple screens, circular screens and translucent screens used for back projection, the movie screen—even considering CinemaScope—has not changed all that significantly in the nearly 100 years of its existence.
See also: CinemaScope; Cinerama

SCREENPLAY The written blueprint for a movie that provides the structure of the story to be told (in scenes) and the film's dialogue. When it comes time to actually make a motion picture, the screenplay is revised into a shooting script that outlines specific shots, camera angles, and directions (e.g., pan, zoom, track, etc.).

The screenplay began in the silent era with Georges Méliès, whose films were so complicated that he was known to plan his works on paper before actually shooting them. For the most part, however, films during the early twentieth century didn't have scripts of any kind. The director would merely have an idea, gather his actors and crew, and improvise. Even as late as 1915, the great D. W. Griffith created *The Birth of a Nation* without a written script.

Griffith aside, as films became longer and producers began buying the rights to novels and plays, it became necessary to carefully figure out how these works from other media would be adapted to the screen. Thus were born scenarios, which are loose adaptations of the source material without dialogue or camera angles that essentially pinpoint the main thread of the original story and suggest the order of scenes.

It was director/producer/writer Thomas H. Ince *(q.v.)* who significantly developed the scenario during the silent era, creating detailed shooting scripts for the many projects he supervised.

But the real change came with the coming of sound films, which revolutionized the way movies were created, making it necessary to write what has become known as the screenplay. Films could no longer be reshaped easily in the editing room when the spoken word was so important to the plot. Ever since the advent of sound films, the screenplay has usually been completed in advance of filming in order to minimize expensive reshooting.

See also: script supervisor; screenwriting

SCREEN TEAMS Hollywood has paired thousands of actors in the hope of creating that special chemistry that yields big box office. Only a small number of those teamings have borne fruit, but what sweet fruit it has been.

There were a number of famous screen teams during the silent era; one of the foremost was that of the Gish sisters, Dorothy and Lillian. They starred in several films and Lillian once even directed her sister, in *Remodeling Her Husband* (1920). Perhaps the most famous film in which the sisters starred was *Orphans of the Storm* (1921).

A majority of the great screen duos have been of a romantic nature, capturing the sexual spark between two well-matched performers.

The most sizzling screen team of the silent era was that of Greta Garbo and John Gilbert. Before the talkies destroyed Gilbert's career, the pair starred in three movies, *Flesh and the Devil* (1927), *Love* (1927), and *A Woman of Affairs* (1929). All three films were major hits, helped along by the widely circulated rumor that Gilbert and Garbo were lovers. After the coming of sound films, Gilbert had but one good role (of course, opposite Garbo), in *Queen Christina* (1933).

One of the most famous screen teams in Hollywood history was that of Spencer Tracy and Katharine Hepburn, who starred together in nine films over a twenty-five-year period. Photo courtesy of Movie Star News.

When Janet Gaynor *(q.v.)* and Charles Farrell were first teamed in *Seventh Heaven* (1927), they made such a stir that they were paired another eleven times until the magic finally wore off in 1934. At the height of their popularity, they were billed as "America's favorite lovebirds." The two were the only major screen team to successfully make the transition from the silent to the sound era.

The 1930s saw the rise of screen teams that took their cue from the provocative pairing of Clark Gable and Joan Crawford *(q.v.)* in *Dance Fools Dance* (1931). The tough, macho Gable and the "loose" flapper Crawford were a gold mine for MGM, and the two costarred in six films. But if Gable had one female star during the 1930s who was his match, it was Jean Harlow *(q.v.)*. Harlow worked with Gable in only three movies between *Red Dust* (1932) and *Saratoga* (1937), but the pair was electric on screen; funny and flirtations, they traded quips and barbs that bounced off each other like rubber bullets—they were both tough enough to take it.

Warner Bros. claimed a more chivalrous teaming—between swashbuckling hero Errol Flynn and demure Olivia De Havilland. The pair attained instant fame in *Captain Blood* (1935). De Havilland seemed the perfect leading lady to Flynn's exuberant hero, and she continued to be paired with him throughout the rest of the 1930s and early 1940s in eight movies, many of them Flynn's best. Unfortunately, she had little to do in these adventures, but audiences expected her to be the object of Flynn's attentions.

A more modern pairing, perhaps the most sophisticated of all the classic screen teams, was that of William Powell and Myrna Loy *(q.v.)*. They first appeared as a screen team in *The Thin Man* (1934) and their lively, loving, equal, and *fun* relationship as Nick and Nora Charles struck a responsive chord with the public. As it happened Powell and Loy also enjoyed acting together, and the two were paired thirteen times.

Another extremely modern screen team was that of Spencer Tracy and Katharine Hepburn *(q.v.)*. The two were intimate friends off-screen, and their genuine affection for one another was obvious—and infectious—from their very first film together, *Woman of the Year* (1942), to their ninth, and last, teaming in *Guess Who's Coming to Dinner* (1967). It was a personal and professional partnership that continued until Tracy's death.

In the 1940s, *film noir* screen teams came to the fore with the likes of Alan Ladd and Veronica Lake *(q.v.)*. They were both tough and laconic, but a sexual chemistry between them made each seem much sexier than when they appeared with other actors.

The sexiest of all the 1940s teams was unquestionably that of Humphrey Bogart and Lauren Bacall *(qq.v.)*. After their first film together *To Have and Have Not* (1944), they were soon married. Their sexy repartee on film, especially in *The Big Sleep* (1946), made them a special favorite of film fans past and present. After *Dark Passage* (1947), the pair made the last of their four films as a team, *Key Largo* (1948).

The 1950s brought both new stars and new screen teams. The good-looking young stars Janet Leigh and Tony Curtis happened to fall in love and were married. They were immediately paired in *Houdini* (1953), and went on to star in five movies together until their divorce in 1962.

Though Rock Hudson and Doris Day never married, they certainly seemed like the perfect couple. Ironically, they costarred in only three "bedroom comedies," but those movies—*Pillow Talk* (1959), *Lover, Come Back* (1962), and *Send Me No Flowers* (1964)—became instant pop culture classics.

One of the only screen teams to flourish almost purely on the basis of publicity rather than the quality of their films was that of Elizabeth Taylor and Richard Burton *(qq.v.)*, otherwise known to the public as "Liz and Dick." They met and conducted a torrid (and highly publicized) affair during the making of *Cleopatra* (1963) and scored box office successes in most of their early outings together, though the films were often mediocre. The best of their ten theatrical features together was *Who's Afraid of Virginia Woolf?* (1966). On the whole, they made better copy than they did movies.

Diane Keaton eventually grew large in the estimation of both the critics and the public and became so integral to Woody Allen's movies (witness *Annie Hall*, 1977) that she eventually became a full partner in one of the most intelligent, provocative, and hysterical screen teamings of the last several decades.

In addition to dramatic and comedic screen teams, there have also been very popular musical pairings. Maurice Chevalier and Jeannette MacDonald *(qq.v.)* were among the first, making music together in a series charming and often funny operettas, beginning with *The Love Parade* (1929) and ending with *The Merry Widow* (1934). Chevalier left Hollywood but MacDonald found a new partner in Nelson Eddy, and they sang their way through eight films between *Naughty Marietta* (1935) and *I Married an Angel* (1942), the best of their collaborations being *Rose Marie* (1936). Their films were enormously popular and, due to their lush, if saccharine, romantic quality, the two stars were dubbed "America's sweethearts."

As popular as were Nelson Eddy and Jeannette MacDonald, the most enduring musical screen team was (and is) Fred Astaire and Ginger Rogers *(qq.v.)*. Their ten films together represent a dazzling body of work that includes innumerable hit songs, stunning dance routines, and many of the most entertaining musicals in Hollywood history. As Katharine Hepburn remarked, Astaire gave Rogers class and Rogers gave Astaire sex appeal. Together, they made magic.

All of the screen teams mentioned so far, except for the Gish sisters, are male/female pairings. There has not, as yet, been another female duo to have established itself as a screen team, although Bette Midler seems to work best with other female stars, such as Shelley Long, Barbara Hershey, and Lily Tomlin. Should one of these emerge a steady partner for Midler, the first sound female screen team will have been created.

As for strictly male screen teams, there have been a number of memorable pairings. For instance, there was the inimitable teaming of James Cagney and Pat O'Brien *(qq.v.)* during the 1930s. Their obvious friendship and good humor saw them through a great many Warner Bros. movies, not the least of which was *Angels with Dirty Faces* (1938).

In later years, Walter Matthau and Jack Lemmon *(qq.v.)* teamed up in a handful of comedies, the first of them being Billy Wilder's *The Fortune Cookie* (1966), and the most popular, surely, *The Odd Couple* (1968). Lemmon later directed Matthau in *Kotch* (1971), helping his pal earn a Best Actor Academy Award nomination.

Though Paul Newman and Robert Redford teamed up only twice in *Butch Cassidy and the Sundance Kid* (1969) and *The Sting* (1973), both were so popular that a new term was derived for much male screen teamings, "buddy" films.

SCREENWRITING The craft of writing the script and shooting directions for a story that is intended to be filmed. Screenwriting first developed out of the need to adapt plays and novels to the silent screen and was called scenario writing. Original scenarios were also first written during the silent era, as original stories could be bought far more cheaply than the rights to expensive Broadway hits and famous novels of the day.

With the coming of the talkie revolution, most scenario writers took a back seat to the invading hordes of playwrights and novelists who could write dialogue for talking pictures. The advent of sound films made screenwriting a vital link in the creative filmmaking process.

Screenwriting may either be done alone or in collaboration with others. No matter who writes the script, however, it is the director who usually has ultimate control over the details of story and dialogue. Where novelists, playwrights, poets, and painters all have considerable control over their work up until its public presentation, screenwriters either adapt or create a story and are then often shunted aside while others interpret and/or change their work. Other screenwriters may even be called in (more than once) to rewrite an original script. Screenwriters who also manage to become directors—a trend that began in the early 1940s and continues to this day—are in the best position to protect their work.

The film credit that is given to a writer who adapts someone else's work from another medium is "screenplay by." If the story is conceived by the person who writes the screenplay, then the credit is "written by."
See also: screenplay; treatment; writer-directors

SCREWBALL COMEDY A special kind of film humor that had its heyday in the 1930s. If farces are known for their improbable plots, screwball, or crazy, comedies, are marked by improbable characters and their outlandish antics. The genre received its name after a baseball pitch known as a "screwball," which breaks in the opposite direction of the traditional curveball. A screwball comedy, then, is filled with characters who act differently than you might first expect, which explains why so many of these movies are set in high society, where eccentric behavior is tolerated more. Another characteristic of screwball comedy is the breakneck speed at which characters deliver their lines often in overlapping dialogue; the language in a screwball comedy can be just as dizzy as the characters.

The father of the screwball comedy was director Howard Hawks, who perfected and popularized the genre. Hawks gave birth to the screwball comedy with *Twentieth Century* (1934), a hilarious film peopled with such wild characters that it seemed as if there was hardly a sane person in the cast. He went on to make the most famous screwball comedies in Hollywood history, namely *Bringing Up Baby* (1938), *His Girl Friday* (1940), which was a reworked version of *The Front Page, Ball of Fire* (1942), *I Was a Male War Bride* (1949), and *Monkey Business* (1952).

Hawks was the premier director of screwball comedies, but not its sole practitioner. Among other directors who dabbled in the genre were Gregory La Cava (*My Man Godfrey,* 1936) Leo McCarey (*The Awful Truth,* 1937), and George Cukor (*Holiday,* 1938).

Except for Hawks' efforts, the screwball comedy faded away in subsequent decades, although one could argue that a number of the Martin and Lewis films of the 1950s were modified crazy comedies. It seemed as if the screwball comedy was a thing of the past, however, until Peter Bogdanovich *(q.v.)* made a conscious effort to revive it with *What's Up, Doc?* (1972), a film that owes a great deal of its energy and structure to *Bringing Up Baby.*

In recent years there have been films that flirt with the concept of the screwball comedy, such as Hawks devotée Jonathan Demme's two romps *Something Wild* (1986) and *Married to the Mob* (1988), but the pure form seems rooted forever in a madcap 1930s sensibility.
See also: Grant, Cary; Hawks, Howard; Lombard, Carole

SCRIPT SUPERVISOR The person whose job it is to keep meticulous track of a myriad of details during the shooting of a film in order to ensure the movie's "continuity," i.e., the perfect continuation of all the details recorded on film from scene to scene. Originally known as the script girl, the job is also known as continuity girl, continuity clerk, and script clerk. Essentially a secretarial job, this is one of Hollywood's most demanding and important work assignments.

The scenes of a film are almost always shot out of sequence; therefore, the script supervisor must keep track of what has transpired during each take of every scene, logging such information onto continuity sheets as the camera angle, the lense used, changes in dialogue from the script, physical gestures made by the actors, the actors' clothing, etc. For example, if a character approaches a door wearing a jacket and tie, it is the script supervisor's responsibility to make sure that the character is wearing the same jacket and tie (in the same condition) when he opens that door and steps inside a room, even though the two scenes might be shot weeks apart.

The precise and thorough work of the script supervisor comes into play not only during filming but during the editing process. When the shooting is finished, the continuity sheets prepared by the script supervisor are far more important to the director and the editor than the original shooting script because they represent a log of what was actually filmed, making editing (from an organizational standpoint) considerably easier.

SECOND UNIT A production crew that shoots footage in which the principal actors do not appear. For instance, a second unit might shoot a crowd scene or exotic location shot (e.g., a jungle scene of wild animals), or footage that will be used for back-projection *(q.v.)* purposes. The second unit might also shoot scenes for a montage *(q.v.)* used to help bridge a time gap.

The second unit crew, headed by a second unit director, often shoots their material at the same time as the rest of the movie is being made, but they may also film well before or after the time set aside for principal photography *(q.v.)*.

Second unit work has, on rare occasions, been elevated to a special status when the work involves major action scenes in big-budget films. In movie spectaculars such as *Ben-Hur* (1926, 1959), *The Charge of the Light Brigade* (1936), *El Cid* (1962), etc., the famous action scenes were all filmed by second unit directors and their crews.

The most famous of the second unit directors are Andrew Marton, who directed the chariot race in the silent version of *Ben-Hur,* and Yakima Canutt *(q.v.),* who directed the same chariot race in the sound version of *Ben-Hur* as well as the massive battle scenes in *El Cid,* to name just two of his better-known efforts.

Many modern directors disdain the use of second units, maintaining that they don't want any footage in their films that they haven't shot.

SEGAL, GEORGE (1934–   ) A major box office magnet principally during the 1970s, his mischievous grin and sense of comic timing brought him great success as a light comedian, but he has been effective in dramatic and romantic roles as well. Segal is also noteworthy because he was among the first of a new wave of ethnic-looking and sounding actors (after the more conventional stars of the 1950s such as Rock Hudson, Gregory Peck, and Charlton Heston) who came into prominence in the 1960s and early 1970s, leading the way for such future stars as Dustin Hoffman, Robert De Niro, and Al Pacino.

Born in New York City and educated at Columbia University, Segal was just as interested in music as he was in acting. Among the many musical groups he formed were Bruno Lynch and his Imperial Jazz Band and Corporal Bruno's Sad Sack Six (while in the Army). He later worked for The Circle in the Square theater as a janitor, ticket-taker, usher, and, finally, an understudy in the hope of getting a chance to act. He finally made his theatrical debut with a different theater company in Molière's *Don Juan.* The production closed after one performance.

However, Segal soon found acting opportunities on Broadway in such plays as *The Iceman Cometh, Antony and Cleopatra,* and *Leave It to Jane.* But he received his most important training as one of the original cast members of the long-running improv show *The Premise.*

Segal made his film debut in a small role in *The Young Doctors* (1961). Throughout the rest of the early 1960s, he shuttled between the theater, TV, and the movies, appearing in modest roles in such films as *Act One* (1963) and *The New Interns* (1964). His career began to pick up substantially in the mid-1960s when he scored a hit as the lead in *King Rat* (1965), a part that was turned down by both Paul Newman and Steve McQueen *(qq.v.).* He joined the all-star cast of *Ship of Fools* (1965), played Biff in the television version of *Death of a Salesman* in 1966, and received a Best Supporting Actor Oscar nomination for his role in *Who's Afraid of Virginia Woolf?* (1966).

Segal seemed well on his way to stardom and did, indeed, star in a number of interesting and relatively good movies during the rest of the 1960s, but he didn't quite take off. Films such as *The Quiller Memorandum* (1966), *The St. Valentine's Day Massacre* (1967), *Bye, Bye Braverman* (1968), *The Southern Star* (1969), and *The Bridge at Remagen* (1969) were, more often than not, mediocre or poor performers at the box office despite their many worthy attributes.

During the 1970s, however, Segal found his niche as the contemporary everyman, struggling, with comic effect, to deal with many of the foibles of modern society. He showed his seriocomic range in the highly regarded *Loving* (1970), nearly stole the hit comedy *The Owl and the Pussycat* (1970) from his powerful costar Barbra Streisand *(q.v.),* and gave a tour de force performance in the cult favorite *Where's Poppa?* (1970). Finally, in 1973, he hit his commercial stride with several box office winners, the sophisticated romantic comedy *A Touch of Class* (1973), Paul Mazursky's *(q.v.)* poignantly funny *Blume in Love* (1973), and Robert Altman's *(q.v.)* manic *California Split* (1974).

While his material was considerably less interesting in the latter half of the 1970s, Segal did manage a couple of winning films that examined middle-class values: *Fun with Dick and Jane* (1977) and *The Last Married Couple in America* (1979).

The 1980s have been less kind to Segal. He has not been in a great many movies; those he has starred in have not been hits, as evidenced by *Carbon Copy* (1981) and *All's Fair* (1989). Like many a film star in decline, he has taken to appearing in television movies, such as "The Cold Room" (1984), and starring in his own TV series, "Murphy's Law." (1988).

SELIG, WILLIAM N. (1864–1948) A leader and innovator among the early film producers, he entered the brand new movie business in 1896. Selig's Polyscope Company was among the largest and most successful of the early film companies, joining the ranks of the Edison Company, Biograph, and Pathé.

Selig's place in film history is assured by a number of his accomplishments. Desiring exterior shots that could be used in *The Count of Monte Cristo* (1908) Selig became the first producer to send a film unit west to California.

An audacious producer with the blood of a showman (he had been a magician), Selig became famous in the film industry for his bogus version of a Teddy Roosevelt African safari. Selig had asked and been denied permission to send a cameraman along with the president. So, the canny producer hired an actor who bore a mild resemblance to Roosevelt, bought a lion from a local zoo, and filmed his own version of the hunt. When Roosevelt actually bagged a tiger, making headlines across the nation, Selig immediately released his film, called *Hunting Big Game in Africa* (1909), and made his own killing at the box office.

Selig's success with his fake safari film ignited his interest in jungle movies, and he set about making several with actual location footage—a first.

Among his other notable firsts, Selig discovered western star Tom Mix *(q.v.)* and made Hollywood's first serial, *The Adventures of Kathlyn* (1913). He was among the very first, as well, to make feature films, producing the then mammoth nine-reel *The Spoilers* (1914).

Selig was a pioneer who created new stars and new genres, but he rarely developed and nurtured the stars and film categories he created. He was always onto something new, and when in 1922 he could no longer finance his creative filmmaking, he retired from the movie business.

SELLERS, PETER (1925–1980)   Unlike most comedy stars, who make their mark by becoming recognizable comic characters (e.g., Chaplin as the Tramp, Keaton as the Great Stone Face, Woody Allen as the neurotic schlemiel, etc.), this English comic actor became an international star on the basis of playing a wide variety of comic types. He was, in essence, both a talented slapstick artist and a gifted impersonator, and his skills brought him a screen career that lasted thirty years.

Born Richard Henry Sellers to a show business family, he began working on stage with his parents when he was a child. He continued playing in English music halls throughout his adolescence and then spent a tour of duty with the Royal Air Force entertaining the troops. After World War II, Sellers attained a modest level of fame as a member of the popular madcap BBC radio program "The Goon Show,"' which would later inspire the BBC television series "Monty Python's Flying Circus." On the basis of being one of "the goons," Sellers got a role in his first feature film, *Penny Points to Paradise* (1951).

Sellers' film career was steady if unspectacular during most of the 1950s, with solid supporting performances in such movies as *The Ladykillers* (1955) and *Man in a*

Cocked Hat (1959), but he came into his own as a star both in England and America with *The Mouse That Roared* (1959), playing three roles in the hit comedy about a tiny country that declares war on the United States in order to gain foreign aid.

His film career had extreme ups and down during the next twenty years. Far too often he starred in mediocre movies, but when he had good material—particularly during the mid-to-late 1960s (largely Hollywood productions)—Sellers was a delight to watch. His best performances during that high point were in *Dr. Strangelove* (1964), *The World of Henry Orient* (1964), *What's New Pussycat?* (1965), *The Wrong Box* (1966), *After the Fox* (1966), *The BoBo* (1967), *I Love You Alice B. Toklas!* (1968), and *The Party* (1968).

Sellers' portrayal of Inspector Clouseau, the role for which he became most famous, also began in the mid-1960s with *The Pink Panther* (1964), followed by *A Shot in the Dark* (1964), and was then finally resurrected again in 1975 with *The Return of the Pink Panther* (1975), *The Pink Panther Strikes Again* (1976), and *Revenge of the Pink Panther* (1978). The Pink Panther films—all done under the direction of Blake Edwards *(q.v.)*—saved Sellers' floundering career in the mid-1970s after his starring roles in such poor movies as *Where Does It Hurt?* (1972) and *The Blockhouse* (1974).

His revival in the latter 1970s gave him the opportunity to star in what many consider to be his greatest role, the TV-watching hero of *Being There* (1979). He died not long after its release. Unfortunately, out–takes from his *Pink Panther* movies found their way to the screen in 1982 in the form of *Trail of the Pink Panther* (1982), a travesty of a film that did not honor his memory.

SELZNICK, DAVID O. (1902–1965)   He stands among the handful of major independent producers who thrived during the studio era. Known for writing voluminous memos that bespoke his intense and thorough involvement in each of his productions, Selznick was the final author of all his films, save for those movies directed for his company by Alfred Hitchcock *(q.v.)*. Though he was known to be humorless and full of hubris, hardly anyone else in Hollywood worked as hard as Selznick. His lasting claim to fame is, of course, *Gone With the Wind* (1939).

Born David Oliver Selznick to one-time movie mogul Lewis J. Selznick (1870–1933), he began working in the industry for his father. When the elder Selznick was forced into bankruptcy in 1923, the opulent world David knew suddenly vanished. In his early twenties, he produced two documentaries independently and used his earnings to start other non-movie enterprises, but he flopped as an entrepreneur and returned to Hollywood in 1926 to start near the bottom as an assistant story editor for one of the men who helped put his father out of business, Louis B. Mayer, at MGM.

Selznick's abilities could not be denied and he quickly progressed through the MGM ranks, becoming associate producer of a number of MGM's "B" movies. But his real coup was marrying Mayer's daughter, Irene, which did not please the mogul.

In any event, Mayer had no control over Selznick, who left MGM to become an associate director at Paramount, where he was involved in the production of such films as *Spoilers of the West* (1927) and *The Four Feathers* (1928). Ever anxious to move ahead, he made the big leap to vice president in charge of production at the troubled RKO studio in 1931 and helped to create such enduring films as *Bill of Divorcement* (1932), *What Price Hollywood?* (1932), and *King Kong* (1933).

By this time, Selznick had become a major figure in Hollywood and, given his familial relationship to Mayer, found himself invited to return to MGM to step in for the ailing Irving G. Thalberg and oversee production. Selznick leaped at the chance and proceeded to make films very much in the Thalberg mode: classy movies, often based on either famous plays or books, with lush production values. *Dinner at Eight* (1933), *David Copperfield* (1935), *Anna Karenina* (1935), *A Tale of Two Cities* (1935), *Little Lord Fauntleroy* (1936) and others were among his triumphs during this period at MGM.

Rather than face a power struggle with the returning Thalberg or continue to work for the often tyrannical Mayer, Selznick surprised the industry by becoming an independent producer, establishing his own company, Selznick International, in 1936. Under that banner he made such movies as *The Prisoner of Zenda* (1937), *The Adventures of Tom Sawyer* (1938), *Made for Each Other* (1939), *Intermezzo* (1939), and the movie that assures his place in Hollywood history, *Gone With the Wind* (1939).

Selznick's problem after the huge success of *Gone With the Wind* was that he could never top it. Nonetheless, he was responsible for a number of fine movies during the 1940s, notably *Since You Went Away* (1944), *The Paradine Case* (1948), and the overblown but mesmerizing western *Duel in the Sun* (1946), all of which he scripted. The latter film was his grand attempt to repeat the success of *Gone With the Wind*. Among his other accomplishments were bringing Alfred Hitchcock to America to make his first Hollywood film, *Rebecca* (1940), and discovering and grooming Jennifer Jones for stardom (they eventually married in 1949).

Though he continued producing films into the 1950s—all of them European ventures—he was considerably less successful than he had been in the past. A number of projects fell through and those that he made, such as *Gone to Earth* (1950) and his final film, *A Farewell to Arms* (1957), were neither critical nor commercial winners. He subsequently retired from the motion picture business. Still relatively young, he lived a life of considerable comfort thereafter.

See also: agents; *Gone With the Wind;* Jones, Jennifer

SEMON, LARRY (1889–1928)   An all but forgotten silent comedian who, in the early 1920s, was nearly as popular as Buster Keaton and Charlie Chaplin *(qq.v.).* Semon's humor was based on chases and stunts, strung together in a hodge-podge of gags. He excelled at playing a grotesque character; Semon accentuated his less than handsome features to make himself appear as idiotically ugly as possible, and he walked like a marrionnette on strings, in a weird herky-jerky fashion. Other comics of the day thought very highly of Semon's ability to construct a gag or a stunt. Semon, however, did not develop any interrelationship between

Over a period of roughly five years, between 1917 and 1922, Larry Semon was the popular equal of Chaplin, Keaton, and Lloyd. He was world famous, but he lost his stature almost as quickly as he had won it by vastly exceeding his budgets. Photo courtesy of The Siegel Collection.

humor, story, and characters. It's no wonder, therefore, that Semon's films have not weathered well.

Semon grew up in a show business environment; his father was a magician known as Zera the Great. Later, after working as a cartoonist for a New York newspaper, Semon began writing and directing one- and two-reel comedies for Vitagraph in 1916. Soon he started casting himself in his own films, such as *Spooks and Spasms* (1917). Semon became immensely popular for playing a bizarre version of the young romantic lead who pursues the girl. The humor, of course, came from a freaky looking man acting as if he were a macho type.

After his success in one- and two-reelers, Semon began making features. He often wrote, directed, and starred in his films, but he was well known for requiring lavish budgets that could not be sustained by the profits from his movies. Nonetheless, his best feature film, *Kid Speed* (1924), was made during his otherwise declining years. He was also the scarecrow in a silent version of *The Wizard of Oz* (1925), a film he directed as well as coscripted.

When his comedy career went bust in 1927 with the commercial failure *Spuds,* a film he produced as well as directed, scripted, and starred in, Semon turned to drama, appearing in Joseph von Sternberg's excellent early gangster film, *Underworld* (1927). It was not enough to save Semon's film career. In relatively quick succession during 1928, he went bankrupt, suffered a mental breakdown, and died of pneumonia.

SENNETT, MACK (1880–1960) The father of Hollywood slapstick film comedy, he created a healthy tradition of irreverence; nothing was immune from his good-natured jabs. As director, producer, and film executive, Sennett was the first to make comedy his sole preoccupation, building Keystone, one of early Hollywood's most successful speciality studios. His frenetic comedies launched many of the silent era's greatest comic stars, among them Charlie Chaplin *(q.v.),* Mabel Normand *(q.v.),* "Fatty" Arbuckle *(q.v.),* Ford Sterling *(q.v.),* Edgar Kennedy, and the Keystone Kops, and later, Harry Langdon *(q.v.),* Ben Turpin *(q.v.),* Billy Bevan, and even Gloria Swanson *(q.v.).*

The comedies for which Sennett is best known weren't so much clever as they were outrageous. His films were solidly based on well-timed but unpredictable physical comedy: crashing buildings, comic chases, double-takes, and the pie in the face were constant features. Though lacking in subtlety, his movies were bold and fresh in their wild abandon; there was absolutely no telling what would happen next in a Sennett comedy—except that whatever happened was bound to surprise you and make you laugh.

Born Mikall Sinnott of Irish parentage in the French-Canadian province of Quebec, he grew to be a sturdy young man who worked with his hands as a laborer;

his only apparent talent was a strong and deep singing voice. When he was seventeen, not long after his family moved to New England, he happened to meet Marie Dressler *(q.v.)* and charmed her into giving him a letter of introduction to the theatrical impresario David Belasco. The letter worked insofar as he got to meet Belasco, but it didn't result in a job. Undaunted, Mikall, then Michael, and eventually Mack, decided to try his luck in burlesque, making his debut in 1902 playing the rear end of a horse, an inauspicious yet somehow appropriate beginning for the future iconoclast who took such fierce delight in poking fun at society's customs and institutions.

Sennett was not a terribly successful performer but he persevered, eventually joining the Biograph *(q.v.)* company in 1908 as a comic film actor. He appeared in movies during the next several years, often as a minor star, but his on-camera histrionics did not auger well for a long acting tenure. Happily, Sennett had begun writing his own scripts at Biograph and was soon directing them under the tutelage of cinema pioneer D. W. Griffith *(q.v.).*

By 1912, Sennett was a major director of comedies (Griffith cared little for comedy and happily relegated such films to his eager protégé) and had already established the style and content of his knockabout farces with such Biograph players as Mabel Normand and Ford Sterling. He left Biograph to establish Keystone later that year with two former bookies who provided the financing, and many of his comedy stars went with him.

Sennett's first Keystone film was *Cohen Collects a Debt* (1912), and it picked up right where he left off at Biograph; the film was inventive and full of motion and mayhem. It was no coincidence that the first custard pie thrown in an actor's face took place in a Keystone comedy. Another of Sennett's most memorable inventions was the Keystone Kops, a goofy crew of policemen who somehow always managed to catch their man (or woman) at the end, but only after innumerable hysterical blunders and misadventures.

The raucous physical humor of the Keystone comedies delighted the mass audience, but so did the Keystone Bathing Beauties, who represented the other side of Sennett's wonderfully vulgar imagination. He was wise enough to know that pretty girls in skimpy (for their day) bathing suits would sell tickets, and he provided his bathing beauties with just enough comic business to make the films risqué rather than salacious.

Sennett often provided the ideas for his comedies, although he made little use of scripts. He would first send his crew and comics off to an actual event (a car race, parade, etc.) and have them film scenes "on location;" later he would figure out how to meld these scenes into a story and fill in the transitions. But invariably his movies ended with a comic chase, a topsy-

No, this is not MGM—it's Mack Sennett's Keystone Studio, a place where anything could happen. Mack Sennett, seen here with the King of the Jungle, was royalty in his own right, with the title King of Slapstick. Photo courtesy of The Siegel Collection.

turvey rendition of what Sennett had learned about editing and pacing at D. W. Griffith's knee.

Sennett was in the forefront when the film industry moved toward consolidation. He joined the other two giants of the silent screen, his mentor Griffith and Thomas H. Ince, to form a new studio called Triangle in 1915. Triangle was not a success and Sennett pulled out of the arrangement in 1917—but at a cost. He had to give up the name Keystone. It was a symbolic loss, but it also marked the beginning of the end of Sennett's reign as the king of comedy.

Under the new corporate name, Mack Sennett Comedies, he continued making movies with many of his established stars, but he made shorts almost exlusively. Though he had pioneered comedy features with success when he made *Tillie's Punctured Romance* (1915), he was ultimately more comfortable with the shorter form. Given his mastery of physical comedy rather than story structure or character development, it was, perhaps, wise for Sennett to avoid making many features. Nonetheless, slapstick was becoming passé during the 1920s, and audiences began to favor the more sophisticated comedy of character that could be found in Hal Roach's comedies such as Our Gang, Laurel & Hardy, and others.

Sennett finally began presenting more polished, less anarchic, movies, but by then he had already lost many of his best stars, including his one-time fiancée, Mabel Normand. (His relationship with Normand was the basis of the critically acclaimed 1974 Broadway musical, *Mack and Mabel,* with Robert Preston as Sennett and Bernadette Peters as Normand.) His last great star during the silent era was Harry Langdon, certainly a comic of character, but unfortunately his career was short-lived. In any event, the talkies literally sounded the death knell for Sennett's brand of fast-paced humor.

During the early sound years, action and chases were superseded by a static camera and clever repartee.

Sennett continued making shorts during the first half of the 1930s, producing, among other films, W. C. Fields' *(q.v.)* most cherished two-reelers, *The Dentist* (1932), *The Fatal Glass of Beer* (1933), *The Pharmacist* (1933), and *The Barber Shop* (1933). By 1935, however, Sennett's long and wondrous career in Hollywood was over. Slapstick had become a low-brow art form left to the likes of The Three Stooges, and it was no longer appreciated by the masses as an original form of film comedy.

Sennett virtually retired from making movies, returning briefly to work on a couple of films. He received a special Academy Award in 1937 that honored "the master of fun, discoverer of stars, sympathetic, kindly, understanding comedy genius, Mack Sennett, for his lasting contribution to the comedy technique of the screen, the basic principles of which are as important today as when they were first put into practice."
See also: custard pie; slapstick

SERIALS   A cinematic saga told in installments; each installment almost always ends in a cliff-hanger. The concept of the movie serial was borrowed from newspapers and magazines that published serials to encourage a steady readership. In this same fashion, films of one, two, and three reels were made and released on a weekly basis as parts of a grand tale. Almost always produced on a much smaller budget than a feature film, the serial became a popular mainstay of the silent cinema, and a low prestige but profitable endeavor during the sound era for Hollywood's more hard-pressed studios.

The serial, in embryonic form, came into existence with *What Happened to Mary?* (1912), a twelve-chapter entertainment that concerned Mary's life story. Each one-reel installment was a complete story in itself and taken together they more closely resembled a series than a serial, but the seeds were planted for the serials to come. The first bona fide serial arrived on movie screens just one year later when William Selig *(q.v.)* produced thirteen chapters of *The Adventures of Kathlyn* (1913) in an episodic format. Selig's serial was a mild success. In early 1914, however, the serial became big box office for the first time with the landmark, twenty-chapter Pathé production, *The Perils of Pauline,* starring Pearl White *(q.v.).* The commercial impact of *The Perils of Pauline,* with the newly devised concept of cliff-hanger endings and dangerous stunts, was such that within the next twelve months almost every single major film company in the United States released at least one serial, many of them cranking out several. One company, Kalem, holds the record for the longest serial, *The Hazards of Helen* (1914), that ran a phenom-

enal one hundred nineteen chapters at one reel per chapter.

Pearl White was the "Queen of the Serials," but she was hardly the only star of this fast developing genre. Other actors of note who appeared in silent serials included the popular Francis X. Bushman *(q.v.),* William Desmond, Elmo Lincoln, the first Tarzan, and even Jack Dempsey, the prize fighter.

It appeared as if serials were dead and buried when the talkies arrived. Serials were low-budget outdoor adventures and sound equipment forced most movies in the late 1920s and early 1930s to be studio-bound. According to Kalton C. Lahue in his excellent book about the serials, *Continued Next Week,* the first sound serial, *The Indians Are Coming* (1930), was made at a cost of $160,000 and brought in $1 million, proving that the format was worthy of renewed interest.

Serials began evolving into juvenile entertainment in the 1920s and were almost exclusively for kids by the 1930s. The action was rarely realistic but the thrills were nonstop. In the sound era, the major studios virtually abandoned the serial, leaving them to the poorer companies such as Mascot and Monogram, which churned them out regularly in the 1930s and 1940s. Among the most famous serials of the 1930s were those that followed the exploits of Buck Rogers and Flash Gordon, with Buster Crabbe *(q.v.),* the form Olympic swimming champion, interpreting both roles. While Crabbe never effectively made the transition from serials to feature films, John Wayne *(q.v.)* who starred in cheapie Western serials throughout the 1930s was turned into a star by John Ford in *Stagecoach* (1939).

Movie serials continued to be made into the 1950s, but television ultimately put an end to the peculiar art form by providing similar weekly thrills for young audiences with shows such as "Captain Video."

It is worth noting that the spirit of the serials, if not the actual episodic cliff-hanging style and format, inspired the making of both the *Star Wars* trilogy and the *Indiana Jones* films of more recent years.

SERIES   An open-ended set of films having the same character or characters and following a tried-and-true formula with only minor variations from movie to movie. Unlike serials, with episodes that end in a cliff-hanger, series consist of complete films having a beginning, middle, and end.

In America the series was born with the Mr. Jones films (1908–9) made by D. W. Griffith. These one-reelers starred John Compson, Florence Lawrence, and Mack Sennett *(q.v.).*

Series films, largely westerns and comedies, soon began to multiply. For instance, there was G. M. Anderson's *(q.v.)* long series of hugely popular "Broncho Billy" westerns (1910–16). Among silent comedians, John Bunny played a character with no false humility called "Bunny" in a series between 1912 and 1914. Then there was the Fatty series (1913–1917) starring Roscoe "Fatty" Arbuckle *(q.v.),* and the Sweedie series (1914–15) starring Wallace Beery *(q.v.),* among many others.

Though feature films dominated the silent era in the later teens and 1920s, the film series tended to remain in the realm of the two-reeler. There were, of course, exceptions, such as feature-length movies of the The Cohens and Kellys series, which had a long life in the talkie era as well.

While series films were modestly popular during the silent era, they became a veritable Hollywood mainstay during the 1930s and 1940s. Most, but not all, series films were feature-length "B" movies, made on low budgets and designed to fill the lower half of double bills. Over time, the average series film proved to be a steady, if not spectacular money-maker. Many of the more well-known series, however, were actually exceedingly profitable and proved to be cash cows for the lucky studios who owned and exploited them.

Series films in the sound era went far beyond just westerns and comedies. In fact, a large majority of series featured mystery/detective heroes such as Sherlock Holmes, the Thin Man, Mr. Moto, Bulldog Drummond, Charlie Chan, Boston Blackie, and the Falcon, to name just a few. The domestic series also flourished, featuring the likes of Henry Aldrich, Blondie, and the greatest, most successful series of them all, Andy Hardy. There were also jungle series with heroes such as Tarzan; medical series with men in white such as Dr. Kildare; animal series that featured Rin-Tin-Tin, Francis the Talking Mule, and Lassie; monster series of undying popularity with ghouls such as Dracula, Frankenstein, and the Wolf Man; not to mention the still-popular western series such as Hopalong Cassidy. The list goes on and on.

Series films were not only cheaply produced and reliable sources of income, they also offered the major studios vehicles into which they could put fading stars who still had name value but who no longer had the drawing power necessary for leading roles in "A" movies. On more than one occasion, though, the supposedly washed-up star's career was resurrected by a series (as in the case of William Boyd who played Hopalong Cassidy).

More often, however, studios used their series as a safe means of introducing new actors to the mass audience. Audiences could be counted on to show up irrespective of any raw, unpolished performances from minor "guest" actors. A great number of stars received their early training in the Andy Hardy films at MGM. Lana Turner, Judy Garland, Kathryn Grayson, and Donna Reed, among others, all had early roles in Andy Hardy movies. In fact, in addition to her appearance in an Andy Hardy film in 1942, Donna Reed was also featured in the Dr. Kildare and Thin Man series, all in the same year. Even Clint Eastwood made one of his earliest screen appearances in a Francis the Talking Mule film.

The series as a Hollywood staple died hard and fast in the 1950s with the rise of television and its multitude of prime-time series.

Surprisingly, though, the concept of the series has survived in a big-budget format with such latter-day offerings as James Bond, Indiana Jones, Superman, Rocky, etc., although one might justifiably refer to some of these movies as sequels rather than films in a series.

See also: Ayres, Lew; Lassie; Rin-Tin-Tin; Rooney, Mickey; "Tarzan" films: Weismuller, Johnny

SET DECORATOR   The person responsible for the detailed dressing of all the sets created for a film after they have been conceived by the art director and built by the set designer. The set decorator, much like an interior designer, chooses the specific furnishings for a set. Very often, the modern set decorator is an interior designer.
See also: art director; set designer

SET DESIGNER   A somewhat misleading title for the person responsible for building a film's various sets based on designs suggested by the art director. The set designer takes the art director's concepts and turns them into reality, using his practical skills as a builder. He knows what is physically possible and will draw blueprints of the sets to match (as much as possible) the art director's vision. After these more detailed sketches are approved by the art director, director, and producer, the set designer will then oversee the building of the sets.
See also: art director; set decorator

SEX IN THE MOVIES   A short scene taken from a play called *The Widow Jones* became the *May Irwin-John C. Rice Kiss* (1896), the first intimate moment shown on screen. The closeup kiss shocked audiences; one wonders what those audiences would have thought, for example, of the ultra steamy coupling of Jack Nicholson and Jessica Lange on a kitchen table in *The Postman Always Rings Twice* (1981). But sex in the movies has not ridden a racy upward curve since 1896. The acceptable limits of what could and could not be shown on the screen has changed according to forces often— but not always—beyond Hollywood's control.

For the most part, movies during the early twentieth century were rather tame. America was a culturally isolated country during these years, until soldiers returned home from Europe after World War I with considerably different ideas about sex. Relaxed moral standards led to bawdier movies in what became known as the Jazz Age. Films of the 1920s and early 1930s were risqué, with nudity and suggestive sex scenes far more explicit than anything that was to be seen either before or during the rigidly enforced Hays Code *(q.v.)* years between 1934 and the early 1960s.

The filmmaker most responsible for daring films during the 1920s was Cecil B. DeMille *(q.v.)*. His sophisticated sexual dramas, such as *Male and Female* (1919), many of them with Gloria Swanson *(q.v.)* in the lead, were big box office winners and hastened the acceptance of such behavior on film. Even after the creation of the Hays Office in 1922, DeMille continued to make sexy movies, using the new self-censorship dictum of "compensating values" to go even further than he had before. He simply "punished" those characters by the end of a film who had "sinned" during its course. Thus *The Ten Commandments* (1923) had more sex and debauchery in it than any of DeMille's previous pictures.

The personification of the new attitude toward sex was Clara Bow, the "It" Girl, who defined the flapper as an independent woman capable of sensual enjoyment. A more intense sexuality could be seen in the films of Rudolph Valentino, Greta Garbo, and, later, Marlene Dietrich.

Sex and sexual themes ran rampant during the early sound era. Ernst Lubitsch's sly operettas were loaded with clever innuendos, both verbal and visual. The famed "Lubitsch touch" was a subtle means of getting a sexual message across to his audience, such as having the shadows of a man and woman fall across a bed as if they were sprawled there together in a lover's embrace.

While Lubitsch's approach to sex was sophisticated, others took a more direct approach. And none was more direct than that of Jean Harlow, the reigning sex symbol of the 1930s. Her characters reveled in their sexuality. In addition, she has been generally credited with shifting sexual attention from the legs to the breasts, where it remains today.

When rigid enforcement of the Hays Code began in 1934, attitudes toward sex in the movies changed dramatically, and stayed changed for approximately three decades. One need only compare the 1932 version of *Red Dust* to its 1953 remake, *Mogambo,* to see that the earlier film was infinitly more erotic and clear about the sexual nature of the characters' relationships.

American sexual attitudes, at least as they were expressed in the movies, seemed frozen in time. Characters had their fun offscreen after the dissolves and fadeouts. Sexuality was only subtly alluded to and one had to be fairly sophisticated to pick up the references. For instance, it's doubtful whether many who saw *The Maltese Falcon* (1941) knew that the Joel Cairo character (Peter Lorre) was intended to be homosexual.

Challenges to the Hays Code during the 1940s and 1950s slowly chipped away at the restrictive industry self-censorship. By the late 1960s, a film like *Midnight Cowboy* (1969), with open references to homosexuality could be made with major stars in leading roles and win a Best Picture Oscar. *Midnight Cowboy* was rated "X" but by today's standards it would, at worst, be rated "R."

Controversial films that had sex as their main themes, such as *Carnal Knowledge* (1971) and *Pretty Baby* (1978), continued to break new ground in the 1970s. One of the most important films in this trend was the pornographic film *Deep Throat* (1973), which was a surprise hit with mainstream audiences. Ultimately, sex in the movies began to catch up with the sexual revolution in American society. By the end of the 1970s and during the 1980s, sex on the big screen finally became *almost* as acceptable as violence.

There have, of course, been limitations. Films concerning gay people have been far more circumspect than those depicting heterosexuals. For example, *Crossfire* (1947) was originally a story about a homosexual, but when the film was made it was changed to a Jew, turning it into a movie condemning anti-Semitism rather than attacking homophobia. It has been the rare Hollywood film that has dealt directly with homosexuality, the most famous of them being *The Boys in the Band* (1970) *Cruising* (1980), and the recent *Torch Song Trilogy* (1989). Even less attention has been paid to lesbianism with a mere handful of films led by *The Children's Hour* (1962), *Rachel, Rachel* (1968) and *Lianna* (1983).

See also: sex symbols: female; sex symbols: male; screen teams

SEX SYMBOLS: FEMALE Movie moguls have often been referred to as "flesh peddlers" with good reason, but if Hollywood films have sometimes been gratuitously salacious, they have also been exhilaratingly sensual. In the right vehicles, and through the collaboration of writer, director, producer, cinematographer, and costume designer, certain actresses have been able to transcend their roles to become symbols of sensuality, viewed by audiences as the ultimate objects of sexual desire. Audiences need and want an ideal image to long for. In the case of the male moviegoer, that desire has been elicited by an ever-changing and evolving company of female sex symbols.

The first Hollywood sex symbol, Theda Bara *(q.v.),* played upon the fear of sex. She was the original vamp, an exotic seductress whose brand of sensuality in films during the mid-1910s was both alluring and dangerous; men would pay if they fell into her clutches. It wasn't long, though, before a healthier attitude toward sex and women emerged. The Jazz Age introduced the flapper, a sort of unihibited girl next door who was sexy without being threatening. Clara Bow *(q.v.),* the

Jayne Mansfield, seen here in a publicity still, was one of the more outrageous Marilyn Monroe clones in the 1950s sex symbol sweepstakes. If Monroe formalized the big bosom look, Mansfield turned it into a cliché. Photo courtesy of Movie Star News.

"It" Girl, epitomized this dominant sex symbol of the 1920s.

The early sound era of the late 1920s and early 1930s featured the last of the flapper sex symbols in the person of Joan Crawford (q.v.). But Crawford, like Greta Garbo and Marlene Dietrich (qq.v.), soon crossed the fine line from sex symbol to glamour queen. The real sex symbol of the 1930s was Jean Harlow (q.v.). With her platinum hair and blowsy style, she was a wonderfully vulgar icon of her age. What distinguished her from the glamour queens was that her appeal was based not on romance or sophistication but on her sexual magnetism. Moviegoers went to the movies not to see how she was dressed, but how she was undressed, and how she slinked and purred. Harlow's impact was so great that a great many up-and-coming actresses, including Carole Lombard, Bette Davis, and Barbara Stanwyck (qq.v.), were forced to dye their hair to match her platinum marcelled waves.

After Harlow's tragic death in 1937, the sex symbol

mantle was available to all comers, and there was a growing number of contenders, among them the beautiful and exotic Hedy Lamarr (q.v.), the G.I.'s favorite pin-up girl, Betty Grable (q.v.,) the peekaboo hairstyled Veronica Lake (q.v.), the ravishing Rita Hayworth (q.v.), sweater girl Lana Turner (q.v.), and the smoldering Ava Gardner (q.v.). All of them were popular but none was the dominant sex symbol of the 1940s.

Jane Russell, under the tutelage of Howard Hughes, made a splash in the 1940s, personifying a new breed of more blatant sex symbol, her cleavage creating a stir in The Outlaw (1943). But Russell was merely a precursor of the 1950s sex symbol personified by Marilyn Monroe.

Monroe was the vulnerable child/woman, blonde, big breasted and naive; she set the standard in the 1950s as Harlow had done during the 1930s. In fact, she was asked to play the title role in Harlow (1965), but turned it down repeatedly. Like Harlow, Monroe had clones such as Jayne Mansfield, Mamie Van Doren, Kim Novak (q.v.), and many others. Marilyn was warm, sexy, and provocative; every move she made, every sound she uttered, seemed to have a sexual connotation, yet she communicated much more than her typical "dumb blonde" roles allowed and that set her above the competition.

If Monroe was hot, Grace Kelly was cool, representing a more aloof version of the 1950s blonde sex symbol. Somewhere between the two was the dark-haired Elizabeth Taylor, a child of Hollywood who grew up to become a violet-eyed temptress.

The 1960s saw the rise of a new sort of sex symbol, or "sex kitten," as dubbed by the media. These were often pouty young starlets who, after Monroe's death, were touted as her successors, among them Carol Lynley, Carroll Baker, Ann-Margret, and even Jane Fonda.

During the late 1950s and throughout the 1960s an influx of foreign actresses came to Hollywood to seduce American moviegoers. Sophia Loren led the pack, followed by such beauties as Virna Lisi, Gina Lollobrigida, Ursula Andress, and Elke Sommer, among others.

The sexual revolution of the sixties and the feminist movement of the seventies made sex symbols somewhat obsolete. It was no longer acceptable to view women merely as sex objects. The 1960s' emphasis on individuality also altered the public's perception as to what constituted sexy. Sex-appeal became less a matter of physical appearance.

Cybill Shepherd in The Last Picture Show (1971) and Kathleen Turner in Body Heat (1981) exemplify the new screen siren, but often they play down the sensual side of their screen personalities to receive a wider range of roles. Even Raquel Welch, who worked at becoming a sex symbol in her early years, found that she received too few good roles in films and abandoned the movies for a nightclub and video career.

Among the current crop of actresses, Darryl Hannah and Kim Bassinger seem to be heading in the sex symbol direction, but neither has established herself as a major box office attraction strictly on the basis of her sex appeal. Perhaps the only bona fide sex symbol of the 1980s has been Bo Derek; her screen image is based purely on sex, but it remains to be seen if she's capable of sustaining any sort of box office after the disappointing reception to her X-rated *Bolero* (1984).

SEX SYMBOLS: MALE One can roughly divide male sex symbols into three categories: sensitive, "beautiful" men, such as Tyrone Power and Montgomery Clift *(qq.v.)*, charismatic types who exude style and perhaps a devastating charm, such as Rudolph Valentino, Charles Boyer, and Cary Grant *(qq.v.)*, and the beefcake star, exemplified by Rock Hudson and Sylvester Stallone *(qq.v.)*. No matter what category the male sex symbol might fall into, however, the career of such a star generally lasts longer than that of most female sex symbols, perhaps because women fans respond less to transient qualities in their cinematic ideals than do men.

Francis X. Bushman *(q.v.)* was the first of Hollywood's male sex symbols. Known as "The Handsomest Man in the World," he was a barrel-chested he-man with a well-fed look that drove women wild during the first half of the 1910s. He might have remained the most famous of the silent screen's lovers had not Rudolph Valentino emerged in the 1920s to elicit the kind of adulation that would later go to rock stars. Valentino established a new kind of sex symbol; he was sensual, almost effeminate, and could be cruel, but mostly he seemed to have a rapport with women that no screen actor ever had before.

While Valentino was the greatest of the silent screen sex symbols, he wasn't the only heartthrob of the 1920s. John Gilbert *(q.v.)* became one of the leading sex symbols of the late silent era, particularly when teamed with Greta Garbo *(q.v.)*.

Male and female sex symbols were teamed throughout the rest of Hollywood history. For instance, Clark Gable *(q.v.)* was often paired with female sex symbols such as Joan Crawford, Jean Harlow, and Hedy Lamarr *(qq.v.)*. Even in his final movie, *The Misfits* (1961), he was paired with the last great female sex symbol, Marilyn Monroe *(q.v.)*.

Gable had modest competition as the reigning male sex symbol of the decade from Charles Boyer, who was nicknamed "The Great Lover." Certainly the dashing Errol Flynn also had his following, as did Tyrone Power and Robert Taylor *(q.v.)*.

As a new decade began, the muscular and swarthy Victor Mature showed off his physique in *One Million B.C.* (1940), entering the beefcake sweepstakes with a studio publicity campaign that referred to him as a "beautiful hunk of man." His sex symbol heyday was

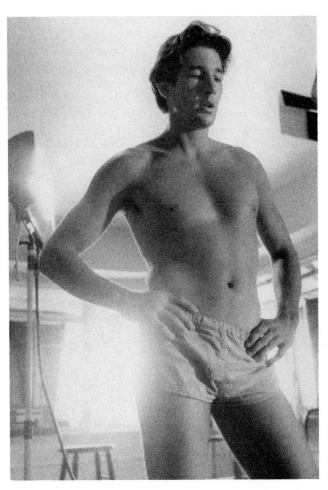

Richard Gere became the reigning male sex symbol of the late 1970s and early 1980s in films such as *Looking for Mr. Goodbar* (1977), *American Gigolo* (1979), and *An Officer and a Gentleman* (1982). He certainly left a great many female fans *Breathless* (1983) when he disrobed for the camera. Photo courtesy of Movie Star News.

in the late 1940s and early 1950s thanks to the hit *Samson and Delilah* (1949) and several similar biblical epics.

Just as Mature came into his own as a sex symbol in the postwar years, so did a great many other actors, including Burt Lancaster *(q.v.)*, Rock Hudson, and Montgomery Clift. Lancaster was a truly gifted actor whose magnificent body and striking good looks weathered as well as his talents into the late 1980s. Ironically, both Hudson and Clift were sex symbols who also happened to be homosexuals. With some exceptions, such as *Giant* (1956), Hudson was principally a beefcake presence in films, especially in his younger days, but Clift was a genuinely talented actor, and women responded not just to his good looks (before his automobile accident) but to his sensitive performances.

Lancaster, Clift, and the newest sex symbol of the 1950s, Marlon Brando *(q.v.)*, were that rare blend of sensual performer and immensely talented actor. It was a combination that became more frequent, beginning in the 1940s and continuing to the present. Female fans liked the dumb brute just as much as men liked the dumb blonde, but female fans also found a place in their palpitating hearts for the handsome charmer, too, leading to the rise of such latter-day sex symbols as Paul Newman (q.v.), Robert Redford (q.v.), Warren Beatty (q.v.), Kevin Costner, and Tom Cruise (q.v.).

Of the more macho types, men who acted more with their shirts off, one must include John Travolta (q.v.), Richard Gere (pants off, as well as shirt), and Sylvester Stallone.

The feminist movement has freed women to express an interest in sex more openly and the numbers of male sex symbols seems have increased. In fact, male sex symbols outnumber female sex symbols by a wide margin, with new contenders steaming up movie screens almost every year; witness the success of such actors as Dennis Quaid, Patrick Swayze, and Rob Lowe, to name just a few.

See also: sex symbols: female

SHEARER, NORMA (1900–1983) She was billed by MGM as the "The First Lady of the Screen," and the publicists were not far wrong: Shearer was the queen of the Metro lot, and Metro was the number-one studio. The actress compensated for a relative lack of talent through the force of her personality; she had an unmistakable screen presence and admirable poise, both of which helped her to accumulate six Academy Award nominations and one Oscar for Best Actress. Attractive, though not a beauty, Shearer nonetheless cut a striking figure through a canny understanding of film lighting and how it affected her appearance. And not least among her assets was her marriage to MGM's head of production, Irving Thalberg (q.v.), who personally guided her career. With Thalberg's help in choosing her vehicles, she was among the most popular actresses of her day, at or near the top of most popularity polls during the first half of the 1930s.

Born Edith Norma Shearer in Montreal, she studied the piano as a child. She broke into the movies in front of the screen, tinkling the ivories in a nickelodeon. In desperate need of money after her father went broke, her mother trundled Shearer and her sister to New York. Mrs. Shearer was hoping she could get her two daughters into the movies.

Norma edged into her film career as an extra in *The Flapper* (1920), quickly working her way up to a featured role in *The Stealers* (1920). She worked steadily thereafter in mostly unimportant movies, moving to Metro Pictures right before it became Metro-Goldwyn-Mayer. She ended up staying with MGM for the rest of her film career.

Shearer had her breakthrough in 1924 when she starred in *He Who Gets Slapped*. Over the next several years she played a large number of sophisticated ladies; becoming a favorite of female movie fans, who copied her clothing and hairstyles. She was not, however, MGM's biggest star in the last years of the silent era—Garbo had that distinction. That soon began to change after Shearer married Thalberg in 1927.

Thalberg, known as "the boy wonder" for his ability to spot talent and produce quality hit productions, picked Shearer's scripts with his vaunted commercial and critical sense. She catapulted to the top of the MGM heap in such silent films as Lubitsch's *The Student Prince* (1927) and *The Latest from Paris* (1928), and then in sound films, including *The Trial of Mary Dugan* (1929) and *The Divorcee* (1930), which brought her a Best Actress Academy Award. Oscar-nominated performances in *Their Own Desire* (1929) and *A Free Soul* (1931) soon followed, by which time Shearer was among the highest paid actors in Hollywood, earning a reported $6,000 a week.

Shearer then entered her highbrow period with rich roles in such sophisticated fare as *Private Lives* (1931), *Strange Interlude* (1932), *The Barretts of Wimpole Street* (1934), and *Romeo and Juliet* (1936) the last two of which garnered her Best Actress nominations. Then the ailing Thalberg died in 1936. Shearer was cut adrift—in more ways than one; besides losing her husband, she also lost her mentor and her protector.

Thalberg had laid the groundwork for her starring role in *Marie Antoinette* (1938), which brought Shearer her final Best Actress Oscar nomination. But without the late mogul's unfailing intuitive knack for picking scripts, she soon began appearing in poor vehicles. At first, she did well in chosing *Idiot's Delight* (1939) and *The Women* (1939), but she stumbled badly when she turned down leading roles in *Gone With the Wind* (1939) and *Mrs. Miniver* (1942). Her later films such as *Escape* (1940) and *We Were Dancing* (1942) were disasters. When what became her final film, *Her Cardboard Lover* (1942), bombed at the box office, Shearer decided to retire.

As a stockholder in MGM, though, she still wielded power and influence at the studio. For instance, she was instrumental in establishing Janet Leigh's career.

Shearer remarried after leaving MGM, taking a former skiing instructor as her husband. In her later years she became blind and lived at the Motion Picture and Television Lodge in Woodland Hills, California.

There is a building named for her at MGM, the last legacy of the First Lady of the Screen.
See also: Leigh, Janet

SHEEN FAMILY DYNASTY An acting family headed by patriarch Martin Sheen (1940–), who has quietly built a significant body of work in both movies and television. Sheen possesses a dignity and sincerity on screen that makes him instantly likable. He is not, however, a warm character; he displays an aloofness

Martin Sheen is the patriarch of a popular acting family. Sons Emilio and Charlie are stars already, and two more potential stars are on the way, Ramon and Renee. Photo courtesy of Martin Sheen.

that tends to lend him an air of mystery. Still in the midst of his career, his four children have also joined the acting ranks, and two of them have become stars.

Born Ramon Estévez of a Spanish father and Irish mother in Dayton, Ohio, he later changed his name to Sheen to avoid racism and typecasting. Upon graduation from high school, he knew exactly what he wanted to do. He traveled to New York to become an actor and soon made his stage debut in the Off-Off Broadway show *The Connection* in 1959, followed by his Broadway debut in *Never Live Over a Pretzel Factory*. But his big breakthrough came in a later Broadway show, *The Subject Was Roses,* in which he starred in 1964. Among his other important stage appearances were the rock version of *Hamlet* presented by Joseph Papp, the New York Shakespeare Festival's production of *Romeo and Juliet,* and *Death of a Salesman,* in support of George C. Scott in a Broadway revival.

Even with those sterling credits, Sheen did not have an easy time of it in the movies. Though he made his film debut as early as 1967 in *The Incident* and starred the following year in the film version of *The Subject Was Roses,* he didn't catch on with the public. The critics hailed him in *Badlands* (1973), but he gained more attention for his excellent work in a great many TV movies during the 1970s, especially his performance in

the title role of "The Execution of Private Slovik" (1974). A modest level of movie stardom finally came his way as a result of his performance in Francis Ford Coppola's *Apocalypse Now* (1979), but the role nearly killed him; he suffered a heart attack during the grueling filming in the Philippines.

He not only survived the heart attack but began to thrive thereafter, working far more often on the big screen in parts large and small in such fine films as *Gandhi* (1982), *That Championship Season* (1982), *The Dead Zone* (1983), *Firestarter* (1984), *The Believers* (1987), *Wall Street* (1987), and *Da* (1988).

The first of Sheen's children to follow in his footsteps was his eldest son, Emilio, who used the original family name of Estévez. One of the original members of the brat pack *(q.v.),* Emilio Estévez (1963–) became a favorite of teenage fans thanks, in part, to his role as a vulnerable jock in John Hughes' film *The Breakfast Club* (1985). Estévez has starred in a number of films throughout the mid-to-late 1980s, including the hit brat pack western *Young Guns* (1988). Unfortunately, he also chose to write, direct, and star in *Wisdom* (1987), which proved to be anything but a wise career move.

In the meantime, Emilio's kid brother, Charlie, also began acting, using the more familiar family name of Sheen. Charlie Sheen (1966–) has since eclipsed his older brother, catapulting to fame in a role originally written for Emilio in the Academy Award winning *Platoon* (1986). He has since gone on to greater fame in films such as *Wall Street* (1987), *Eight Men Out* (1988), and *Major League* (1989).

Two other Sheen children, Ramon and Renee, are actors, primarily in television. All four Sheen children have worked at one time or another with their father, although they have yet to appear en masse.
See also: family dynasties

SHERIDAN, ANN (1915–1967) A much-admired performer in hardboiled dramatic roles in the late 1930s and 1940s. In addition to possessing an earthy beauty, she was also a versatile actress adept in screwball comedies, romances, and musicals. Though her film career spanned the years 1934 to 1957 and comprised more than seventy-five movies, Sheridan rarely had the opportunity to carry a film on her own, but she was consistently a strong performer who was no weak sister opposite the likes of James Cagney, Humphrey Bogart, and Cary Grant *(qq.v.).*

Born Clara Lou Sheridan, she won a "Search for Beauty" contest in 1933 that entitled her to an appearance in a 1934 Paramount movie named for the contest. She might have easily disappeared from view as did so many other contest winners during the gimmick-ridden Depression, but the camera liked Sheridan and Paramount thought it might just have lucked into something. Using her own name, she acted in bit parts in all sorts of films over the next two years, the best of them being *Murder at the Vanities* (1934), *Mrs. Wiggs of the Cabbage Patch* (1934), and *Bolero* (1934).

By the time she changed her name to Ann Sheridan, she had sensed that Paramount was exploiting, rather than developing, her, so she went to Warner Bros. and was given a publicity push as the "Oomph Girl." More importantly, she was given increasingly larger roles in many of Warners' gritty urban films, in which she often played a worldly-wise woman who "knew the score." Her reputation grew with strong supporting, and later leading, performances in such films as *Angels With Dirty Faces* (1938), *They Made Me a Criminal* (1939), *Torrid Zone* (1940), *They Drive by Night* (1940), and *City for Conquest* (1940).

Sheridan's popularity peaked in the 1940s when tough but feminine women were very much in vogue. She became a full-fledged star thanks to her impressive performance in *King's Row* (1942), and she remained popular thanks to good box office in a wide mix of movies that included *George Washington Slept Here* (1942), *Edge of Darkness* (1942), *Shine On, Harvest Moon* (1944), *Nora Prentiss* (1947) and *The Unfaithful* (1947). Unquestionably one of her best films from this period is the Howard Hawks gem *I Was A Male War Bride* (1949), in which she trades quips with Cary Grant.

Poor scripts did Sheridan in during the 1950s; her popularity plummeted after being wasted in movies such as *Appointment in Honduras* (1953). In 1957 the actress made her last big screen appearance, in a British production called *Woman and the Hunter*. Sheridan kept busy working in the theater and was among the first of Hollywood's major stars to appear in a daytime soap opera when she became an ongoing character in "Another World." She regained her popularity and later moved to a prime time TV series, "Pistols and Petticoats." She died of cancer in 1967.

SHORT SUBJECTS These are films under thirty minutes long. When all movies consisted of only one or two reels, "short subjects" were the only films the industry produced. But the term didn't come into use until well after the establishment of the feature-length motion picture.

By the 1920s, most Hollywood fare was full-length, except for serials, comedies, newsreels, and cartoons. Serials were made up of short episodes shown (usually) on a weekly basis until the story was completed. Serials became enormously popular during the 1910s and they continued to fill out movie bills until they petered out in the 1950s. A number of actors achieved fame in serials, among them Pearl White and Buster Crabbe *(qq.v.)*. Only one major movie star made the leap from serials to starring in feature-length movies: John Wayne.

Comedies remained popular as short subjects during the 1920s and beyond because they served as a successor to vaudeville. At the beginning of the talking-film era,

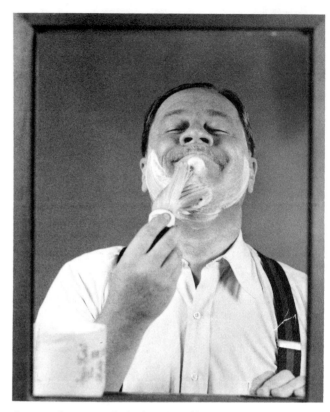

Among the most admired series of live-action short subjects were those written and performed by Robert Benchley. He made a total of forty-six clever shorts, with such titles as *The Sex Life of a Polyp* (1928), the Oscar-winning *How to Sleep* (1935), and *How to Eat* (1939). Photo by Fred Hendrickson, courtesy of Movie Star News.

major vaudeville comedy acts were signed by Warner Bros. to make short subjects with their new sound-on-disc system—*before* the release of *The Jazz Singer (q.v.)* in 1927.

Among the biggest producers of early short subjects were independents such as Mack Sennett and Hal Roach *(qq.v.)*, who made comedy shorts starring the likes of Laurel & Hardy, Our Gang, Charley Chase, Edgar Kennedy, and many others. By the time the studio era began in earnest, however, the majors developed their own short-subject departments. Their shorts were usually comedies, but sometimes musical acts were featured as well.

Newsreels were flashes of history caught on film. Ironically, while documentary movies held little appeal to filmgoers, newsreels, such as The March of Time series, were quite popular and became a genuine source of information for the mass audience before TV news finally put them out of business in the late 1950s and 1960s.

The most popular short subjects, particularly during the sound era, were cartoons. Led by Walt Disney with Mickey Mouse, the boom in animation brought several studios into the animated short subject arena. Animation remained the cornerstone of the short subject market into the 1960s until the competition from animated television shows finally proved too strong.

In the end, serials, live-action comedy shorts, newsreels, and cartoons, passed from the movie scene because of economics. They proved handy during the Depression when film studios did everything in their power to draw audiences to movie theaters. Like double features, short subjects were bonuses offered to audiences in the hope of increasing business. During the flush 1940s there was no reason to change, but during the 1950s, as ticket receipts plummetted, cost-saving measures had to be taken. Short subjects were rarely big money-makers, so they were among the first to go. Live-action shorts were axed first, followed by serials, newsreels, and finally the cartoons.

Short subjects, however, continue to be made, mostly as vehicles for directors and producers trying to break into feature films. These are independent productions without studio backing. Very few regular moviegoers ever see these shorts in theaters because they usually receive poor distribution; they are more often seen in film festivals than in film theaters. Yet they are voted on by Academy members and the winners not only have an Oscar to show for their efforts but also a foot in the door of the industry. One such young filmmaker who got his start making shorts was Steven Spielberg *(q.v.)*, whose twenty-four-minute *Amblin'* (1969) brought him to the attention of Universal Pictures. Spielberg later named his production company Amblin Entertainment in homage to the short subject that launched his career.

See also: animation; newsreels; serials

SIDNEY, SYLVIA (1910–   )   An actress, she has appeared in films since 1927, achieving her greatest fame during the 1930s. Delicate and pretty, she starred in many films in which she played a victim, but these usually weren't her best movies. Sidney was a talented and versatile actress but had little opportunity to display her skills on screen because of her being typecast.

A gallery of shots of the lovely Sylvia Sidney, among them two stills from her most famous films, *You Only Live Once* (1937), with Henry Fonda, and *Madame Butterfly* (1933). Photos courtesy of Sylvia Sidney.

Born Sophia Kosow, she overcame poverty and became an actress, making her Broadway debut at the age of seventeen, the same year that talkies arrived. She soon made her way to Hollywood, making a cameo appearance in *Broadway Nights* (1927), followed by a slightly larger part in *Thru Different Eyes* (1929). She reappeared on Broadway for a short while before returning to Hollywood to begin her film career in earnest as the female lead in Rouben Mamoulian's dazzling *City Streets* (1931), which made her a star.

Among her many fine films during the 1930s were Josef von Sternberg's *An American Tragedy* (1931), *Street Scene* (1931), *Madame Butterfly* (1932), *Fury* (1936), *Sabotage* (1936), *You Only Live Once* (1937), and *Dead End* (1937).

She married Bennett Cerf, the wealthy publisher in 1935 (the marriage ended the following year), and later wed actor Luther Adler (1938–1947), who was the second of her three husbands.

By choice, she began acting far less often in films from the 1940s. Her best films in these later years were *Blood on the Sun* (1945), *Les Miserables* (as Fantine, 1952), *Summer Wishes, Winter Dreams* (1973), for which she was honored with a Best Supporting Actress Oscar nomination, *Damien: Omen II* (1978), and *Hammett* (1983).

When not in films, Sidney has been active in the theater, has appeared in TV movies, such as "Raid on Entebbe" (1977), and has done guest shots on TV series such as the 1988–89 sitcom "Dear John" with Judd Hirsch.

SIEGEL, DONALD (1912–   )

Considered by many to be among the best of the "B" movie directors of the late 1940s through the early 1960s, he entered the commercial mainstream in the early 1970s through his association with Clint Eastwood (*q.v.*). Siegel had always shown a special flair for crime and action/adventure movies, and consistent with the male orientation of his films, his characters have often been (in the American tradition) loners facing impossible odds. In a directorial career spanning more than thirty-five years and thirty-six feature films, he has made a considerable number of minor classics in several different genres.

Despite his rough-and-tumble image and a childhood spent in Chicago, Siegel received his higher education at Cambridge University in England and, after deciding to become an actor, continued his studies at London's Royal Academy of Dramatic Art. He went nowhere as an actor, though he eventually appeared in a number of films, including many of his own in cameo roles. Unable to make a living in front of the camera, he went to work for Warner Bros. in 1933, spending the next thirteen years moving up the ladder from assistant film librarian to assistant cutter and montage director. As head of the montage department at Warner Bros. in the

early 1940s, he was responsible for the powerful sequence at the beginning of *Casablanca* (1942).

His excellent montages brought him the opportunity to direct short subjects in the mid-1940s and he responded with two Oscar winners, *Star in the Night* (1945) and *Hitler Lives?* (1945). Having won two Academy Awards in the same year, he was finally given a chance to direct feature films. Ironically, he would never win another Oscar; in fact, he would never be nominated for another Academy Award.

Siegel's first feature was *The Verdict* (1946), a solid crime melodrama that featured Warner stock company performers Peter Lorre and Sydney Greenstreet. He worked without much distinction for a number of years as he mastered his new craft. Siegel then drew a good deal of attention from his prison film, *Riot in Cell Block 11* (1954), which depicted explosive violence and used real prisoners as extras. The movie had a powerful impact and remains a minor masterpiece among prison pictures.

The director's most famous film of the 1950s was his one and only science fiction movie, *Invasion of the Body Snatchers* (1956). The film depicts alien pods infecting humans and stealing their forms, and a number of critics saw the film as a political statement against McCarthyism. It was remade by director Philip Kaufman in 1978 with both Siegel and the film's star, Kevin McCarthy, appearing in minor roles.

Siegel continued making low-budget films of merit without getting very much attention either from the critics or the industry. Among his other memorable films of the later 1950s and early 1960s were the excellent Mickey Rooney movie *Baby Face Nelson* (1957), one of Elvis Presley's most satisfying films, *Flaming Star* (1960), and one of Ronald Reagan's best movies—and also the future president's last—*The Killers* (1964).

With the demise of the Hollywood-supported "B" movie, Siegel was forced to begin directing for television in the mid-1960s. He reemerged a few years later in feature films with the well-reviewed *Madigan* (1967) and the first of his Clint Eastwood hits, *Coogan's Bluff* (1968), which Siegel also produced. He went on to direct and often produce the Eastwood vehicles *Two Mules for Sister Sara* (1970), *The Beguiled* (1971), the mega-hit *Dirty Harry* (1971), and *Escape From Alcatraz* (1979). During the course of his newfound success, he officially changed his name from Don Siegel to Donald Siegel.

In addition to Siegel's work with Eastwood, he also directed most of the top action stars in Hollywood, displaying his technical skill in the slick, if silly, Charles Bronson thriller *Telefon* (1977), saving the Burt Reynolds caper film *Rough Cut* (1980, he was the fourth director on the project), and directing John Wayne in his final movie, *The Shootist* (1976), sending that legendary actor out on a high note.

Siegel's one major flop was his last movie, the Bette Midler disaster *Jinxed* (1982).

SIMMONS, JEAN (1929–   ) A delicately beautiful English actress, Simmons has stared in more than fifty films, the majority of them Hollywood productions. She was nominated twice for Academy Awards.

Simmons was a dance student in London when her life took an unexpected turn; without any serious acting experience, she was chosen to play Margaret Lockwood's sister in *Give Us the Moon* (1944), launching her film career at the tender age of fourteen. She looked so fine on film and was such a self-possessed young performer that other roles quickly came her way, the most notable of which were in *Great Expectations* (1946), *Black Narcissus* (1947), and as Ophelia, opposite Laurence Olivier, in *Hamlet* (1948), the film that brought her international stardom, a Best Supporting Actress Oscar nomination, and the interest of Hollywood.

After marrying actor Stewart Granger in 1950 (a union that lasted until 1960), Simmons followed her husband to America but found herself entangled in contractural problems with Howard Hughes. As a result, she didn't appear on film for three years until she starred in her first Hollywood production, *Androcles and the Lion* in 1953. It was the first of an astonishing total of six vehicles in which she starred that year. Among her most memorable early Hollywood films were the aptly titled *Angel Face* (1953), *Young Bess* (1953), the achingly theatrical rendition of Ruth Gordon's autobiographical *The Actress* (1953), *Desiree* (1954), *Guys and Dolls* (1955), and *The Big Country* (1958).

Married to writer-director Richard Brooks in 1960, she was cast in his screen version of *Elmer Gantry*. Burt Lancaster won an Oscar for his work in the title role of that film, but Simmons was every bit his match. She gave other excellent performances during the 1960s in movies such as *The Grass Is Greener* (1960), *All the Way Home* (1963), and *Life at the Top* (1965). Simmons was offered little in the way of good films or interesting roles in the latter half of the decade, however, until she collaborated with her husband on *The Happy Ending* (1969), for which she was honored with her second Best Actress Academy Award nomination.

The actress has appeared in only a few films in the 1970s and 1980s. Ms. Simmons turned both to the theater and to television in her later years. She starred in the New York and London stage productions of *A Little Night Music,* and she has been in a number of TV movies and miniseries, mostly notably "Beggarman Thief," "North and South" (Parts I & II), and "The Thorn Birds," winning an Emmy Award for her performance in the latter series.

SIMON, NEIL (1927–   ) America's most popular playwright, Simon has penned more than twenty plays,

Jean Simmons, seen here in a recent photo, was both a great beauty and an accomplished actress who never reached the superstar status many predicted for her. She rose to fame in English films and then proceeded to have a variable career in Hollywood, highlighted by stunning performances in such films as *The Actress* (1953), *Desiree* (1954), and *Elmer Gantry* (1960). Photo courtesy of Jean Simmons.

many of which have been turned into movies, many also having a screenplay by Simon. Simon has also written more than ten original screenplays, most of which have also been major commercial and critical successes. His speciality is comedy, and his films are a potent mix of witty lines and finely wrought characters. The writer has been a veritable font of creativity and big box office with both plays and films.

After graduating from New York University in 1946, Simon honed his skills writing for television programs such as "The Tallulah Bankhead Show" in 1951, "Caesar's Hour" in 1956–57, and "The Phil Silvers Show" in 1958–59. He left television in 1961 after having his first hit play on Broadway, *Come Blow Your Horn,* a comedy that found its way to the movies in 1963.

Simon continued writing plays, but broke into the movie business with the original screenplay for the Peter Sellers comedy *After the Fox* (1966). The critical and commercial success of that film opened doors for him and he wrote the screenplays for many of his hit plays, such as *Barefoot in the Park* (film 1967) and *The Odd Couple* (film 1968), the latter movie winning the only Oscar nomination of his long and remarkable career.

While maintaining his prodigious output for Broadway, Simon alternated between adapting his own work for the screen and writing original screenplays. Among his adaptations have been *Plaza Suite* (film 1971), *Last of the Red Hot Lovers* (film 1972), *The Prisoner of Second Avenue* (film 1975), *The Sunshine Boys* (film 1975), *Chapter Two* (film 1979), *Brighton Beach Memoirs* (film 1986), and *Biloxi Blues* (film 1988). On one rare occasion he adapted the work of another author, writing the screenplay for the Steve Martin vehicle *The Lonely Guy* (1984).

Among Simon's original works for the screen have been *The Heartbreak Kid* (1972), *Murder by Death* (1976), *The Cheap Detective* (1978), *Max Dugan Returns* (1983), and *The Slugger's Wife* (1985).

In recent years, Simon's work has been autobiographical, deepening the texture of his stories and bringing warmth to his sometimes brittle humor. For instance, *Chapter Two* dealt (in fictionalized form) with his coming to terms with the death of his first wife and his second marriage to actress Marsha Mason. He subsequently wrote a highly acclaimed trilogy for the theater (all three plays becoming films) *Brighton Beach Memoirs, Biloxi Blues,* and *Broadway Bround,* which have detailed, in turn, his coming of age, army experience, and beginnings as a writer.

SINATRA, FRANK (1915–) A singer, actor, producer, and one-time director who has scaled the heights of show business as few before or since. Known as "The Voice," "The Chairman of the Board," and "Old Blue Eyes," Sinatra has become one of the wealthiest and most powerful people in the entertainment industry. Music has been the main focus of his career, but he has, nonetheless, appeared in more than fifty films, mostly in starring roles. Sinatra has twice been nominated for Academy Awards, winning once in the Best Supporting Actor category for his portrayal of Maggio in *From Here to Eternity* (1953). He has been effective in musicals, particularly those in which he costarred with Gene Kelly, and has shown considerable skill as a dramatic actor and charm in light romantic comedy. Though his physique has filled out during the years, he came to fame as a skinny, young man with a winning combination of street-wise toughness and beguiling innocence.

Born Francis Albert Sinatra in Hoboken, New Jersey, he had visions of a sportswriting career when he was a youngster and worked briefly as a copy boy for a local newspaper. Upon hearing the music styles of Billie Holiday and Bing Crosby, however, he decided to pursue a singing career. He started with a local group called the Hoboken Four, and when the quartet broke up, the young singer took the solo route and toured the vaudeville circuit. Eventually, Sinatra landed a job as a singing MC at the Rustic Cabin, a roadhouse in Englewood, New Jersey. It was there that Harry James heard him sing in 1939 and immediately hired him as a band vocalist. A year later he joined Tommy Dorsey and began recording with the band's vocal group, The Pied Pipers.

Sinatra soon went out on his own and appeared on radio's "Your Hit Parade" and then his own show, "Songs by Sinatra." The turning point came in late 1942 when he appeared at the Paramount Theatre in Times Square. When Sinatra was introduced, the place went wild with bobby-soxers swooning and crying out for him in an explosion of emotion. The event became show business legend and Sinatra soon became his generation's most popular entertainer.

While still a band singer, Sinatra appeared in several films featuring Tommy Dorsey's group, making his movie debut as part of the band in *Las Vegas Nights* (1941). He had his first starring role in the breezy, if inconsequential, musical *Higher and Higher* (1943). He went on to star in or make cameo appearances in at least one film per year throughout the rest of the decade, winning a special Oscar for *The House I Live In* (1945), a documentary condemning bigotry. His best vehicles were those in which he was teamed with Gene Kelly, *Anchors Aweigh* (1945), *Take Me Out to the Ball Game* (1949), and the groundbreaking *On the Town* (1949). In all of these films he showed a surprising dancing talent, but Kelly was clearly the main attraction.

After the initial excitement of seeing Sinatra on the big screen wore off, movie fans began to judge Sinatra more critically. Poor films such as *The Kissing Bandit* (1948), *The Miracle of the Bells* (1948), *Double Dynamite* (1951), and *Meet Danny Wilson* (1952) led to a considerable drop in his popularity. When he suffered from severe vocal chord problems in 1952, it appeared as if his career was shattered.

Sinatra pleaded for the role of the scrappy Angelo Maggio in the film version of James Jones's *From Here to Eternity* (1953). The movie was a Columbia production and the studio's boss, Harry Cohn, was always on the look-out for down-and-out talent he could hire cheap. He got Sinatra for a mere $8,000, but when the movie became a hit and earned Sinatra an Oscar, the singer was back on top.

Sinatra went on to make many of his best films during the 1950s, starring in an eclectic mix of musicals (when his voice was restored in the mid-1950s), comedies, and dramas. His musicals included *Guys and Dolls* (as Nathan Detroit, 1955), and *High Society* (1956); the highly underrated Frank Captra film *A Hole in the Head* (1959) was among his comedies. Sinatra's reputation as an actor, however, was ultimately based on his serious roles in such films as the controversial Otto Preminger movie *The Man with the Golden Arm* (1955), for which he was nominated for a Best Actor Academy Award, plus his strong performances in *The Joker is Wild* (1957) and *Some Came Running* (1959).

Sinatra gained notoriety in Hollywood for his leadership of the cliquish rat pack *(q.v.)*, a group that previously had been led by Humphrey Bogart. During the early 1960s he was particularly active in Hollywood, often starring with rat pack cronies Dean Martin, Sammy Davis, Jr., Peter Lawford, and others in lightweight entertainments of the ilk of *Ocean's Eleven* (1960), *Sergeants Three* (1962), *Four for Texas* (1963), and *Robin and the Seven Hoods* (1964) and producing a number of these films, as well. He also made a few serious movies during the first half of the decade, most notably *The Manchurian Candidate* (1962), and the only film he directed, produced, and starred in, *None But the Brave* (1965).

He slowed down in the latter 1960s, putting his best movie efforts into a number of somber and serious thrillers: *The Naked Runner* (1967), *Tony Rome* (1967), *The Detective* (1968), and *The Lady in Cement* (1968). In 1971, after the failure of the comedy *Dirty Dingus Magee* (1970), Sinatra announced not only his retirement from the movies but his farewell to show business. He didn't stay away for long, however, returning to recording and concert tours, and, rarely, the movies. His last major starring role was in *The First Deadly Sin* (1980).

Sinatra's personal life has been a rollercoaster ride. He was romantically involved with Laren Bacall as well as having been married four times, twice to famous actresses. His first wife, Nancy, is the mother of his three children, Nancy, Tina, and Frank, Jr. Ava Gardner was spouse number two, followed by Mia Farrow, and finally Barbara Marx, the ex-wife of the fourth Marx Brother, Zeppo.

See also: singer-actors

SINGER-ACTORS Major recording stars have often attempted to make the transition to films, and a number have had considerable success. Certainly, movie studios and producers have actively courted the most popular recording artists in the hope that their fans will plunk down the price of admission to see them act on the big screen. For the most part, the money-men have been right. From the entertainer's point of view, making it in the movies is the ultimate achievement. One can be the biggest recording star in the world but, for some reason, it doesn't have the same panache as having one's name on a movie theater marquee.

Until the sound revolution, when Al Jolson's voice was heard in *The Jazz Singer* (1927), there was little demand in Hollywood for famous singers. Jolson became the first singer-actor and he was enormously popular in movies throughout the late 1920s and early 1930s. Jolson's popularity prompted the signing of several other top singer/entertainers, including Eddie Cantor, Rudy Vallee, Maurice Chevalier, and Bing Crosby.

All of them performed exclusively in musicals during their early film careers. Later, Vallee became a fine character actor, but only Crosby managed also to become a major star of comedies and dramas. Due to his versatility, Crosby also built the longest and most sustained Hollywood career of this early bunch of singer-actors, ultimately opening the door for future singer-actors to become well rounded Hollywood performers.

The success of Bing Crosby was followed by the sensational appeal of Frank Sinatra. Thanks to Sinatra's recording success, he made his first appearance in the movies in the early 1940s and quickly became a star, working both in musicals and in light romantic comedies. Ironically, when he was nearly washed up in the early 1950s, it wasn't his singing but his acting in *From Here to Eternity* (1953) that saved his career. He went on to regain his popularity, becoming the first singer-actor to direct, produce, and star in his own film *(None But the Brave,* 1965). Unfortunately, Sinatra didn't sing on camera in any of his films after the 1950s.

Not all popular singers make it in the movies. Dick Haymes, for instance, was a singer very much in the Sinatra mold, and he was enormously popular as a recording artist. Handsome and appealing in person, he lacked that special screen charisma and he never developed into a credible motion picture actor.

Mario Lanza wasn't a famous singer when he went to Hollywood, but he was a notable young concert artist. His meteoric rise and equally fast fall from grace as a star of 1950s movie musicals was marked by at least one great performance in the title role of *The Great Caruso* (1951).

While male singer-stars have received more attention, several female band singers have used their musical fame to break into films, the most notable of them being Lena Horne and Doris Day. Unfortunately, because of rampant racism in Hollywood, Horne's film career was severely limited. Doris Day, on the other hand, became a major star who, like Frank Sinatra, ultimately passed muster as an actor but rarely sang in her later films. After she became a top box office attraction as a romantic light comedienne, she attracted a legion of young fans who weren't aware that she could sing.

Each generation, from the 1930s through the 1950s, has seen its most popular singer become a movie star. In the 1950s, Elvis Presley became the only major rock 'n' roller to have a long, if relatively undistinguished, movie career. Almost all of his films were formulaic musicals but they were sufficiently popular to continue being made for more than a dozen years.

The only other "top-forty"-style singer to have any sort of serious movie career has been Diana Ross, who became famous as a Motown recording star with The Supremes in the 1960s. She had the opportunity that Lena Horne was denied, starring in a few films, including *Lady Sings the Blues* (1972), *Mahogany* (1976), and *The Wiz* (1978), the last of these featuring Lena Horne in a small supporting role that stole the movie.

Broadway was the source of the most gifted singer-actor to come along in a very long time: Barbra Streisand. Though she was equally an actress and singer before hitting it big first in the play then the movie version of *Funny Girl* (1968), her vocal talent was so integral to her rise that one could hardly imagine she would be a superstar without that soaring, majestic voice. Nonetheless, once Streisand became a major star of movie musicals, many of her later films dispensed with her singing, and she was soon regarded as a talented comedienne and dramatic actress. Streisand also went on to produce, direct, and star in her own musical, the commerical hit *Yentl* (1983).

The country-and-western circuit was also a source of Hollywood stars. Besides Gene Autry, who had been a modest radio and recording star before becoming a famous singing cowboy in 1930s and 1940s movies, the down home sound has also propelled writer-singer Kris Kristofferson to an acting career in more recent years. Rugged and masculine, Kristofferson rarely sang in films, even from the outset of his movie career.

Kristofferson's nonmusical acting career portended the future of later singer-actors. Though Cher sang in her first film, *Good Times* (1968), when she was still teamed with Sonny Bono, her subsequent movies roles during the 1980s have all been non-singing—by design. Having won a Best Actress Oscar for her performance in *Moonstruck* (1987), one wonders if she might finally be willing to star in a musical.

Like Cher, pop star Madonna has been adamant about not singing in her films. She reportedly lost the title role in the forthcoming musical *Evita* (based on the Broadway musical hit of the same name) because she wouldn't sing in the film. As of this writing, however, she has relented and has agreed to sing in a future movie.

See also: Autry, Gene; Cantor, Eddie; Chevalier, Maurice; Crosby, Bing; Day, Doris; *The Jazz Singer;* Jolson, Al; musicals; Presley, Elvis; racism in Hollywood; Sinatra, Frank; Streisand, Barbra

SIODMAK, ROBERT (1900–1973)   A director for four decades, he worked in Hollywood for approximately a dozen years, but during the 1940s he helped to establish the *film noir* genre in a number of atmospheric moody movies full of deep shadows and dark secrets.

The son of a German banker, Siodmak was born in the U.S. (his parents were in America on a business trip). He was raised in Germany and found himself attracted to the theater, beginning a stage career as an actor. When that effort failed, Siodmak began working in motion pictures as a title translator in 1925. He quickly graduated to the job of editor, and in 1929 was the codirector, with Edgar G. Ulmer, of the greatly admired *Menshen am Sonntag* (U.S. title: *People on Sunday*). It was one of those rare films that brought together a number of great talents at the beginning of their careers. In addition to Siodmak and Ulmer, it boasted Fred Zinnemann as cocinematographer and Billy Wilder as cowriter with Robert's brother, Curt Siodmak (1902–   ).

After Hitler's rise to power and persecution against Jews in 1933, the Siodmak brothers fled Germany. While Curt arrived in Hollywood in 1935, Robert stayed in France, directing films there through the rest of the 1930s. He left Paris at the last possible moment as the city fell to the Nazis in 1940.

Siodmak's first Hollywood film was *West Point Widow* (1941), a "B" movie of little consequence. After a few more forgettable films, he began to hit his stride, recreating the Germanic visual tradition in the horror film *Son of Dracula* (1943) and continuing with that style in a series of early *film noir* thrillers that included *Phantom Lady* (1944), *Christmas Holiday* (1944), *The Suspect* (1945), and *The Spiral Staircase* (1945). By this time, his "B" movies were showing considerable box office punch, and he was handed the job of turning the Hemingway short story *The Killers* into a movie. The result was a knockout, becoming a sleeper hit of 1946 and turning Burt Lancaster, in his movie debut, into a star. The film did not hurt Ava Gardner's career, either, and Siodmak was awarded an Oscar nomination for Best Director.

He continued making exciting thrillers, and among his better efforts during the balance of the 1940s were *The Dark Mirror* (1946), *Cry of the City* (1948), and *Criss Cross* (1949). He didn't fare so well in the early 1950s, although he directed the lively swashbuckler *The Crimson Pirate* (1953), a film that was dissimilar to the body of his work.

Siodmak left Hollywood after making *The Crimson Pirate* and returned to Europe, making films mostly in France and Germany throughout the rest of his career. He made only two more Hollywood films, a German/American coproduction, *Escape From East Berlin* (1962), and a Spanish/American coproduction, *Custer of the West* (1968). Neither film set the world on fire.

SIRK, DOUGLAS (1900–1987)   A Danish-born director of exquisite style whose American career during the 1940s and 1950s was handicapped by a seemingly endless stream of lightweight screenplays. To his enduring credit, however, Sirk managed to transcend the content of his films with virtuoso direction.

Born Claus Detliv Sierk, he grew up intending to pursue a career in the theater. While still in his teens, Sirk traveled to Berlin, the center of theater in northern Europe. He eventually became a widely respected director and producer but began running afoul of the

Nazis and their xenophobic attitudes after they came to power in 1933 (even though he had changed his name to the more German-sounding Detlef Sierck). In 1934 Sirk began directing movies, hoping that the German authorities would interfere less with his work on a soundstage than the theater stage. This switch worked for a short while—many of his German movies were widely admired for their visual artistry—but Sirk soon realized he was doomed if he were to stay within Hitler's reach. He fled in 1937, taking a circuitous route through Spain, South Africa, and Australia before finally arriving in America. Along the way, he even directed a film, *Wilton's Zoo* (1938), in South Africa.

German expatriates in Hollywood such as Fritz Lang, Conrad Veidt, Peter Lorre and Billy Wilder could not vouch for Sirk because he had begun directing after they had left Germany. Sirk therefore, had to reestablish himself in America. It took five years before he was given a directorial assignment, *Hitler's Madman* (1943); it was the first of a long line of "B" movies with foolish stories and minimal production values, but the director worked with what he was given. If he didn't make gold out of straw, he often made silver; *Summer Storm* (1944), *A Scandal in Paris* (1946), *Lured* (1947), and *Sleep, My Love* (1948) were among his better early films in Hollywood.

Sirk's talents were noticed, and he began to win assignments in the 1950s for bigger budgeted movies with better known stars. Unfortunately they were often turgid romances or over-muscled action movies. He was better with romances, directing such lush and visually exciting movies as *All I Desire* (1953), *Magnificent Obsession* (1954), *All That Heaven Allows* (1956), and three of his very best, *Written on the Wind* (1957), *Tarnished Angels* (1958), and *Imitation of Life* (1959), his last film.

Sirk retired due to ill health in 1959 and moved to Germany, living long enough to see his movies saved from obscurity by attentive and vocal auteurist-inspired critics who praised the visual accomplishment of his American films.
See also: women's films.

SLAPSTICK Physical humor consisting, for example, of chases, pratfalls, seemingly dangerous comic collisions, and other roughhouse antics. The term denoting this kind of comedy is taken from a paddle—a slapstick—once used in knockabout farces to whack the actors and make a loud, comic noise.

Slapstick is usually considered a low-brow form of humor, using, as it does, exaggerated depictions of characters undergoing pain and humiliation. Archetypal slapstick gags entail victims falling on a banana peel or being hit in the face with a custard pie. Because the film medium was originally silent, humor depended on outrageous visual stunts, and although the tradition has

fallen on hard times in recent decades, it has not altogether disappeared.

All of the great silent comics, as well as the lesser ones, built their art out of rudimentary slapstick. Mack Sennett's Keystone Kops and his other comedians practiced slapstick in its most extreme form. Chaplin, Keaton, Lloyd, and Langdon, among others, all eventually practiced a more inventive style of slapstick, adding a human element that gave their comedy depth and their characters resonance.

Slapstick became a less pure comedy form during the sound era as verbal humor became possible. Comedians such as Laurel & Hardy, The Three Stooges, and Abbott & Costello still depended heavily on slapstick for their humor; the Stooges, in particular, relied on hitting and slapping each other in ever more elaborate fashion and with highly unique sound effects. More verbal comics such as W. C. Fields, Eddie Cantor, and even the Marx Brothers still relied on a certain amount of slapstick to enliven their comedy.

Slapstick saw the continuation of its legacy in Danny Kaye's gentle physical humor and Jerry Lewis' raucous bumbling. It seemed as if it reached its apotheosis in Stanley Kramer's slapstick epic, *It's a Mad, Mad, Mad, Mad World* (1963). Later comic talents, such as Mel Brooks and Woody Allen, despite their work's sophistication have cleverly wrought a great many laughs from slapstick humor; Brooks, in particular, has used slapstick humor in most of his films.

Recently, actor comedian Chevy Chase has brought a touch of physical humor to the movies in such vehicles as *Fletch* (1985), but perhaps the last great practitioner of the art of slapstick in Hollywood isn't a star but a director. Blake Edwards appears to be keeping the tradition alive singlehandedly in many of his recent films, most notably in the Pink Panther movies, *10*(1979), and *Blind Date* (1987).
See also: Abbott & Costello; Brooks, Mel; Chaplin, Charles; custard pie; Edwards, Blake; Keaton, Buster; Laurel & Hardy; Lewis, Jerry; Sennett, Mack; Three Stooges, The

SMITH, ALEXIS (1921–   ) A tall, cool, blonde actress who is the veteran of more than forty films, and who excelled at playing "the other woman" especially during the 1940s and 1950s. While she never attained top star status, she was a dependable and glamorous actress with considerable sex appeal.

She was born Gladys Smith (which is also Mary Pickford's real name), and was raised in Los Angeles after spending the first five years of her life in Canada. She was discovered by a Warner Bros. talent scout while appearing in a student production of *The Night of January 16th* at Los Angeles City College. Immediately after the studio screen-tested the blond, blue-eyed beauty, she was signed to a long-term contract and

The still youthful Alexis Smith was the sultry and conniving "other woman" in a great many movies during the 1940s at Warner Bros., but she also had occasion to prove that she had considerable warmth and a deft touch with light comedy. Photo courtesy of Alexis Smith.

quickly became an asset in such films as *The Lady with Red Hair* (1940), in which she made her debut, *Dive Bomber* (1941), *Gentlemen Jim* (1942), *The Constant Nymph* (1943), *The Adventures of Mark Twain* (1944), and *The Horn Blows at Midnight* (1945).

Smith continued at Warner Bros. to the end of the decade, making a modest mark in *Of Human Bondage* (1946) and *The Two Mrs. Carrolls* (1947). Though she had plenty of work, her career continued to smolder rather than burn during her free-lance period in the 1950s, when she starred in such films as *Split Second* (1953), *Beau James* (1957), and *This Happy Feeling* (1958). She gave one of her best performances, however, in a low-budget British film, Joseph Losey's psychological drama, *The Sleeping Tiger* (1954). Overlooked at the time of its release, the movie has since acquired a cult following.

After appearing in a supporting role in *The Young Philadelphians* (1959), Smith left Hollywood, seemingly at the end of a long, if modest, career. After more than a decade out of the public eye, however, she achieved her greatest triumph in 1971 when she won the Tony Award for her singing and dancing performance on the Broadway stage in *Follies*. She continued winning praise in the hit Broadway plays *The Women* and *Summer Brave*.

Smith's stage successes led her back to Hollywood and starring roles in the films *Once Is Not Enough* (1975), *The Little Girl Who Lives Down the Lane* (1977), *Casey's Shadow* (1978), and others. In addition to touring in plays such as *The Best Little Whorehouse in Texas,* she has also spent a year as a guest star on the "Dallas" TV series.

Ms. Smith has been married to actor Craig Stevens since 1944.

SOFT FOCUS   A cinematography technique that uses diffused lighting to make images less distinct on film. Diffusion filters placed in front of lamps, as well as earlier makeshift diffusers such as gauze and vaseline placed on a camera lens, reduce harsh shadows and can soften the facial features of actors being photographed. Soft focus has long been a trick of cinematographers who must shoot aging movie actors without revealing their lined and wrinkled faces. In addition, soft focus has often been used to create dreamy, romantic effects.

SOUND   Without question, the most revolutionary development in the history of the motion picture industry was the invention and commercialization of the "talkies." The wedding of sound to film, however, was not an entirely new development when Al Jolson proclaimed, "You ain't heard nothin' yet" in the first talking and singing sound feature, *The Jazz Singer* (1927).

Experiments and patents had waxed and waned for nearly thirty years before the talkies became a reality. Outside the U.S., filmmakers such as the Italian Leopold Fregoli provided sound tracks for his movies by speaking and making sound effects from behind the projection screen. As James L. Limbacher reports in his excellent study, *Four Aspects of the Film,* this technique was practiced all over the world, and was used for such American films as *Uncle Tom's Cabin* (1910) and *The Birth of a Nation* (1915).

The mechanical age, however, was in full swing during the early twentieth century and inventors plied their trade in the hope of bringing sound more fully to the movies. One such invention was Laurie Dickson's Kinetophone, created in 1889 for Thomas A. Edison. A forerunner of the Walkman, the Kinetophone was designed with earplugs. A phonograph machine synchronized to a Kinetoscope, the Kinetophone was perfected just as the peep show era ended. Later, a tragic fire destroyed the Edison complex in 1914 and continued development of the Kinetophone was abandoned. Edison had never been a strong believer in talking motion pictures; had he felt differently, the talkie revolution might have come considerably earlier.

Other inventions came and went, such as Cameraphone, Synchronophone, and Vi-T-Phone. But the big breakthrough was the invention of Phonokinema that was used for D. W. Griffith's *Dream Street* (1921). The film was a hit and so was the process, which was somewhat similar to Edison's original Kinetophone (e.g., dialogue and music recorded on a phonograph record and synchronized to the motion picture), except in this case earplugs were not necessary. According to Limbacher, "everyone had thought the 'talkies' had arrived, but lack of financial backing and Griffith's philosophy that sound films would only confine the movies to English-speaking people caused the entire idea to be abandoned."

It was, of course, the sound-on-disc system developed by Western Electric for Warner Bros. that finally launched the talkies. Warner Bros. began using the sound-on-disc system to present short subjects as early as 1926, recording a great many famous vaudeville acts. It was the "all talking, all singing" feature-length film *The Jazz Singer* (1927), however, that signaled the start of a new era.

Unfortunately, sound-on-disc was a fallible system that, like Phonokinema, relied on the perfect synchronization of a moving picture with a separate phonograph recording of music and dialogue. Ironically, Warner Bros. created a revolution with the wrong invention. Sound-on-disc was soon replaced by a sound-on-film process that was based on the Movietone system developed at Fox.

Movietone grew out of the Phonofilm system that was developed as early as 1924. In fact, Fox shot several scenes with this new sound system for *Retribution* (1926), a feature-length film. Only partially shot with sound, the movie did not receive much fanfare at the time. In addition, William Fox did not (at first) see the full potential of the invention and merely used it for his Fox Movietone Newsreels in 1927. By the end of the 1920s, however, the Movietone sound-on-film process, by which sound signals are imprinted on a portion of the film known as the sound track, came to be the standard for the industry. It is essentially the same process that is used today.
See also: The Jazz Singer; Jolson, Al; screen; sound track; Warner Bros.

SOUND TRACK If you hold the emulsion side of a strip of sound film toward you, the sound track can be found on the left side of the frame: it is made up of jagged lines not unlike the tracks in a phonograph record. Called "optical recordings," motion picture sound tracks are converted from electrical recordings into such jagged lines. When a film is projected, a beam of light is directed at the sound track and is modulated into varying intensities as it passes through the track. The changing light patterns activate a photocell or "sound head," within the movie projector, which then converts the light into electricity, which in turn activates a loudspeaker. The sound track is usually divided

into four specific tracks, one each for dialogue, music, sound effects, and the fourth for whatever extra sound might be needed (essentially a reserve track).

The sound that one hears when a film is projected is not printed on the frame next to the image. Each frame of a film reaches the picture gate at a different time than it passes next to the sound head. Therefore, in order to synchronize sound and image, the sound is printed 26 frames ahead of the corresponding image on 16mm film, and 20 frames on 35mm film.

Another definition of the term sound track refers to the record album made from the musical score of a film, such as "the sound track album of *The Buddy Holly Story.*"

SPACEK, SISSY (1949–) An open-faced, innocent-looking character actress who came to prominence during the 1970s and has been a star ever since. Spacek's choice of roles has been limited by a Texas twang to her voice but she has excelled in playing Southern girls and women in everything from musical biopics to comedies, and from psychological studies to horror.

Born Mary Elizabeth Spacek, she studied at the Actors Studio, which perhaps accounts for her natural and apparently effortless acting style. She made her film debut in a supporting role in *Prime Cut* (1972) and received major critical attention the following year for her performance in *Badlands* (1973). It was 1976, though, before the public joined the critics in appreciation of her talents, when she played the title character in Brian De Palma's hit shocker, *Carrie*.

Spacek seemed unable to immediately capitalize on the success of *Carrie* and starred in several off-beat films that were not successes. After a modest role in *Welcome to L.A.* (1977), a starring part in Robert Altman's much-admired art circuit hit *Three Women* (1977), and the female lead in the disappointing *Heart Beat* (1979), she finally hit it big playing Loretta Lynn in the biopic *Coal Miner's Daughter* (1980). The film was a box office sensation and Spacek won both critical huzzahs and a Best Actress Academy Award.

Her husband, art director Jack Fisk, made his directorial debut putting Spacek through her paces in *Raggedy Man* (1981), a film that garnered generally good reviews but only modest audience support. *Missing* (1982) was one of her major hits of the 1980s but the movie really belonged to Jack Lemmon. Except for her Oscar-nominated performance in the film version of Beth Henley's Pulitzer Prize winning play, *Crimes of the Heart* (1986), Spacek has not had a major hit during the rest of the 1980s, despite good work in such films as *The River* (1984), *Marie* (1985), and *Violets Are Blue* (1986).

SPECIAL EFFECTS In its broadest film definition, any visual effects not achieved through the use of conventional cinematography. In the silent era, many of the photographic effects that we take for granted today, such as the fade in and fade out, were considered special effects. As special effects have become considerably more sophisticated, the term tends to be used to describe "tricks" that are fairly elaborate and complicated.

There are three basic types of special effects: those that are accomplished "in the camera," those that are achieved through laboratory processes (i.e., in the printing), and those that are a combination of the first two.

An example of an "in the camera" special effect is the glass shot, in which one section of a glass plate is painted to simulate part of a scene. The painting represents what might otherwise be an expensive set or location shot. The painting is then photographed along with the actors and/or action in the unpainted portion of the glass plate, leaving the effect that the action is taking place in the midst of a realistic milieu.

An example of a special effect that can be accomplished "in the lab" is a traveling matte, which combines into one image shots that are filmed in the studio with those that are filmed on location. The combination of the two approaches is in evidence whenever back projection or front projection are used.

Special effects are used in most films, although they can be found in greatest abundance in horror, fantasy, and science fiction movies. Throughout much of Hollywood's early history there was hardly a better example of the use of special effects than *King Kong* (1933), which used miniatures to create the great ape. In the 1950s, when special effects were widely used in the burgeoning science fiction genre, the state of the art was represented by *The War of the Worlds* (1953), which won an Oscar in that category. Stanley Kubrick's *2001: A Space Odyssey* (1968) brought a new interest in special effects, but it was George Lucas' *Star Wars* (1977) that set the standard for excellence through the use of miniatures, optical printing, and many other devices that were newly created to make the movie as realistic as possible.

Lucas' special effects company, Industrial Light and Magic, now hires out its services to other filmmakers. Many films, however, neither create nor subcontract their special effects, instead they simply borrow them already on film, for a modest fee, from a special effects library. It's for this reason you may think you saw the same building collapse in two different movies.
See also: back projection, Lucas, George; monster movies; science fiction; *Star Wars*

SPIEGEL, SAM (1901–1985) Also known as S. P. Eagle, he was the consummate independent producer. Though he worked in films from 1927 until his death, he had his greatest success during the 1950s and early 1960s, when three of his films won Best Picture Oscars.

Born in what was then Jaroslau, Austria (later, Poland), Spiegel's early life was nomadic; he spent part of his youth in Palestine, then came to Hollywood at the age of twenty-six to work as a story translator. A quick study, he learned enough about the film business to travel back to Europe and produce foreign-language versions of Hollywood films for Universal Pictures. When Hitler came to power in 1933, Spiegel went on the run, producing films elsewhere in Western Europe before arriving in America in 1935.

Using the name S. P. Eagle in order to sound both more patriotic and less ethnic, Spiegel began producing such films as *Tales of Manhattan* (1942), Orson Welles, *The Stranger* (1946), and *We Were Strangers* (1949).

With the rise of independent producers during the 1950s, Spiegel came into his own with such major hits as *The African Queen* (1952), the Oscar-winning *On the Waterfront* (1954), for which he used his original name in the credits for the first time in America, the Oscar-winning *The Bridge on the River Kwai* (1957), *Suddenly Last Summer* (1959), and the Oscar-winning *Lawrence of Arabia* (1962).

Spiegel's films were as artistically ambitious during his later years but they did not often enjoy the same box office success. He began backing movies that fell somewhere between the commercial and art house categories, thereby losing the audiences of both; this was the case with *The Chase* (1966) and *The Happening* (1967). Spiegel landed more firmly in the commercial camp with *The Night of the Generals* (1966), and his last full-blown epic, *Nicholas and Alexandra* (1971). But he also scored quite impressively, at least with the critics, with the cult favorite *The Swimmer* (1968), starring Burt Lancaster and based on a story by John Cheever.

Spiegel's production fell off in the 1970s and early 1980s. He did, however, make a credible attempt at bringing F. Scott Fitzgerald's *The Last Tycoon* to the screen in 1976 and his version of Harold Pinter's *Betrayal* (1982) was extremely well received by the critics and art house audiences.

Spiegel was honored by his peers in 1963 with the Irving Thalberg Award for "outstanding motion picture production."

SPIELBERG, STEVEN (1947–) As both a director and a producer, he is an extraordinary modern Hollywood success story. Spielberg is the "suburban" director—he is a baby boomer whose films reflect both the tender warmth and clear-eyed innocence of childhood. In fact, a large percentage of Speilberg's films—both those he has directed and those he has produced—have children as their protagonists or as significant supporting players. As a director, Spielberg has demonstrated a vivid visual style, but more importantly he has been a consummate strategist, marshaling script, music, acting, special effects, editing, set design, etc. into an astonishing streak of intelligent, entertaining, and enormously successful motion pictures.

Born in Cincinnati, Ohio, and raised in Phoenix, Arizona, Spielberg was the product of a broken home. He funneled his energies into the movies, making his first film when he was twelve years old—an 8-mm western lasting a little over three minutes with a budget of $10. He made several other films while a teenager, each more ambitious than the one before. By the age of sixteen, he had made *Firelight,* a two hour and twenty minute 8-mm science fiction spectacular made on a budget of $500.00.

Contrary to popular belief, Spielberg was not part of the new wave of "film school directors," which includes Francis Ford Coppola, George Lucas, and Martin Scorsese *(qq.v.).* Spielberg, a poor student, broke into Hollywood when a producer backed his twenty-minute short, *Amblin'* (1969). Universal was so impressed with the young man's work that he was signed to a seven-year contract by the studio when he was just twenty-one. Spielberg later named his production company "Amblin' " in recognition of his big break.

It seemed as if the young director simply appeared out of nowhere when he had his first major film successes, but in fact he served his apprenticeship working in television. He was responsible for directing several TV movies, including the highly regarded "Duel" (1971) and "Something Evil" (1972), as well as episodes of TV series such as "Columbo," "Night Gallery," and others.

Spielberg's opportunity to direct feature films came when "Duel" was turned into a theatrical release in Europe and became both a critical and box office hit. His first movie was the acclaimed *The Sugarland Express* (1974). This downbeat story starring Goldie Hawn failed miserably at the box office, but by the time that had happened, he had already begun filming the suspense film *Jaws* (1975), the movie that was to catapult him into the directional stratosphere, a height from which he has yet to descend.

Jaws became the biggest money-maker in Hollywood history until it was overtaken by a number of other films, some of them Spielberg creations. Though *Jaws* was a well done, suspenseful action film, Spielberg's next movie, *Close Encounters of the Third Kind* (1977), was much closer in feeling to the director's heart. His personal vision, combining a sense of optimism and an interest in the way children view the world—a theme that predominates in his movies—was eloquently set to film. The movie was a critical and commercial hit, solidifying the young director's place among the directorial elite. His place was so secure, in fact, that it withstood the big-budget bust of his *1941* (1979), a comedy that was more awe-inspiring for its special effects than laugh-inducing. He got back on track, however, when he made *Raiders of the Lost Ark* (1981),

a massive success at the ticket windows and a charming throwback to movie serials of the 1930s. His sequel, *Indiana Jones and the Temple of Doom* (1984) wasn't quite as good nor as successful as the original but was still a major hit. The third (and supposedly final) installment in the series was the critical and box office smash *Indiana Jones and the Last Crusade* (1989).

Between the making of his three Indiana Jones films, Spielberg made *E.T.—The Extra-Terrestrial* (1982). The movie was the perfect blend of innocence and adventure, without evil villains, sex, violence, or even knock-out special effects. But it had more than its share of heart and humor, making it the most commercially successful movie in Hollywood history.

Since the mid-1980s, Spielberg has taken on directorial projects with an eye toward projects that allow him more creativity. He had the clout to adapt the Alice Walker novel *The Color Purple* (1985) and turn it into a hit, but the Academy of Motion Picture Arts and Sciences neglected to nominate him for a Best Director Oscar, raising a number of eyebrows in the Hollywood community. The Academy was silent, yet again after he made the highly regarded *Empire of the Sun* (1987). Some have whispered that the Academy is too envious of Spielberg's incredible financial success to honor him further with an Oscar.

In any event, the huge sums of money Spielberg has earned have allowed him to make whatever movies he might choose, in whatever capacity he chooses. His golden touch at the box office has been just as strong when he has produced films as when he has directed them. While Spielberg started off as a producer with amusing commercial flops such as *I Wanna Hold Your Hand* (1978), *Used Cars* (1980), and *Continental Divide* (1981), he soon began producing hit after hit with films such as *Poltergeist* (1982), *Gremlins* (1984), and *The Goonies* (1985). As big as these films were at the box office, though, they could not match the success of *Back to the Future* (1985), which Spielberg produced, and *Who Framed Roger Rabbit?* (1988), which he coproduced, each film earned in excess of $100 million in ticket sales.

Spielberg has become Hollywood's most celebrated director and producer of the modern era. His name, when associated with any movie, automatically suggests a high level of competence and entertainment value. His name on a film also suggests that it is very likely to become a hit.

See also: Ford, Harrison; Lucas, George; Zanuck-Brown

SPORTS FILMS Along with the growth of professional sports came a greater awareness by filmmakers of both the commercial and cinematic potential of making movies set in an athletic milieu. Sports movies are a natural for the film industry because athletic contests are inherently dramatic.

A serious obstacle to sports films, however, is the

There have been sports movies dealing with almost every conceivable athletic endeavor, but the boxing film remains the champion. Seen here are Anthony Quinn and Mickey Rooney in a still from one of the more serious boxing movies, *Requiem for a Heavyweight* (1962). Photo courtesy of Anthony Quinn Productions.

inability to match the excitement of real competition. Why watch a movie about boxing when you can go to a boxing match? That challenge has been met by making movies that go beyond the sport to an inside story of athletic life—sometimes truthfully, sometimes with a large dose of fantasy.

Sports films have traditionally been geared to the male audience, but they have been most successful at the box office when male sex symbols play leading roles or love stories are included thereby luring women into theaters.

Of all sports films, movies about the world of boxing have been the most numerous and the most successful. The drama of two men battling it out in front of a cheering crowd is utterly cinematic and easy to follow whether one is a boxing fan or not. *The Champ* (1931) was an early boxing film and a huge hit. Its power at the ticket window was demonstrated anew when it was remade in 1979. The 1930s and 1940s saw a proliferation of boxing movies, among the most famous *Kid Galahad* (1937, later remade as a musical in 1962 with Elvis Presley in the title role), *Golden Boy* (1939), *City for Conquest* (1940), *Gentleman Jim* (1942), and *Champion* (1949). The 1950s saw *Somebody Up There Likes Me* (1956), the story of Rocky Graziano. But with the rise of black boxing champions, Hollywood betrayed its racist attitudes by giving little attention to the genre in the 1960s and the first half of the 1970s. In fact, Hollywood seemed to be saying farewell to the boxing film by making the somber *Requiem for a Heavyweight* (1962).

Then came Sylvester Stallone's sleeper hit of 1976, *Rocky*. The film galvanized interest in the sport and made Stallone a star. Rocky has had three sequels (1979, 1982, and 1985), all of which have been monster hits.

For all the success of boxing films, baseball was long regarded by industry insiders as box office poison. America's favorite pastime is a team sport and has a slow pace, both of which make it less cinematic. Nonetheless, filmmakers have occasionally tried (and succeeded) at hitting critical and commercial home runs with baseball films. *The Pride of the Yankees* (1942) a biopic adapted from Lou Gherig's life story, has long been considered the greatest baseball movie of all time, and few directors attempted to duplicate its success. However, most baseball films have been biopics, extolling the virtues of famous or courageous ballplayers; among them are *The Babe Ruth Story* (1948), *The Stratton Story* (1949), and the fine examination of Jimmy Piersall's life, *Fear Strikes Out* (1957). There were even fewer baseball films in the 1960s and 1970s as the sport fell out of favor in relation to football. But both the sport and the films about it have enjoyed a major resurgence in popularity in the 1980s with several major box office winners, including *The Natural* (1984) based on a novel by Bernard Malamud, *Bull Durham* (1988) starring Kevin Costner and Susan Sarandan, and *Major League* (1989).

While baseball was fading in the 1960s and 1970s, football came of age in the movies. With its violence and intensity, football garnered audience attention in a big way. Of course, the sport had often been featured in earlier movies such the Marx Brothers' romp *Horse Feathers* (1932) and *Knute Rockne, All American* (1940), but it exploded on the screen in the 1970s in such hits as *The Longest Yard* (1974), *Semi-Tough* (1977), and *North Dallas Forty* (1979).

The latter 1970s and 1980s have been a golden age for sports films, principally due to the overwhelming success of the *Rocky* movies. They spawned a host of clones set against a variety of sports. Many of these films were rather good despite their obvious contrivances. Most notable among them are the bicycle racing film *Breaking Away* (1979), the basketball films *One on One* (1977) and *Hoosiers* (1986), and the martial arts movie *The Karate Kid* (1984) and its sequel, *The Karate Kid, Part II* (1986), both directed by *Rocky*'s original director, John G. Avildsen. Less notable was the arm wrestling movie *Over the Top* (1987), a surprisingly misguided attempt by the progenitor of the formula, Sylvester Stallone, and a major box office disaster.

See also: Stallone, Sylvester

SPY MOVIES A film genre whose popularity generally has been tied to national and international events. Most spy films are fictional accounts; a relative handful have been based, however loosely, on true stories, such as *Mata Hari* (1932) with Greta Garbo, *The House on 92nd Street* (1945), *13 Rue de Madeleine* (1946), and *Scandal* (1989). But even when spy movies are essentially fictional, they are often inspired by real incidents, people, or organizations, as was the case with *O.S.S.* (1946). But whether or not the story or characters in a spy movie are real, the underlying appeal of these films lies in their dramatization of a very real and dangerous

world at the underbelly of our so-called civilized nation-states.

Spy films had their first commercial success during World War I and immediately thereafter. Spies were alternately seen as either heroes (if they were on our side) or fiends (if they were on the other side). There were few truly memorable spy movies made in Hollywood during the silent era. And even during the 1930s spies were rarely a hot subject in Hollywood, and were often presented only in the most outlandish fashion. Witness the exotic *Dishonored* (1931) with Marlene Dietrich as a captured spy putting on lipstick as she stands before a firing squad; and the Marx Brothers' *Duck Soup* (1933), with those two master spies Chico and Harpo trying to steal war plans from Groucho in what has to be the greatest send-up of spies ever made.

Though Hollywood wasn't much interested in spies, the British film industry was, particularly Alfred Hitchcock. He was a one man spy-movie industry, directing the hits *The Man Who Knew Too Much* (1934), *The Thirty-Nine Steps* (1935), *Secret Agent* (1936), *Sabotage* (1937), and *The Lady Vanishes* (1938). These films were not without an audience in the U.S. But the fact that Hollywood didn't follow Hitchcock's lead throughout most of the 1930s was an indication of how insulated the American film industry was from the realities of a world heading into war. It wasn't until 1939 that the American film industry produced a riveting spy thriller, *Confessions of a Nazi Spy,* and even then it was considered a rather courageous statement.

Once America entered World War II, however, the film factories began cranking out spy films, with Hitchcock (now in America) leading the way with *Foreign Correspondent* (1940). Others followed, such as *All Through the Night* (1942), *Across the Pacific* (1942), *Ministry of Fear* (1945), and *Confidential Agent* (1945).

After the war, Hollywood continued to turn out its fair share of spy films. In fact, many of the spy movies made near the end of the war and in the later 1940s were far more sinister than those made during the conflict, possibly because the studios had been afraid of panicking their customers. In any event, dark, paranoid spy thrillers joined the *film noir* ranks in the latter half of the 1940s, with titles including *Cloak and Dagger* (1946), Hitchcock's *Notorious* (1946), and *Spy Hunt* (1950).

By the late 1940s and in the decades that followed, the cold war introduced the communists as the new enemy be they Chinese, Russian, East German or Cuban. A proliferation of anti-red spy films hit movie screens with titles such as *I Married a Communist* (1949) and *I Was a Communist for the FBI* (1951).

In the late 1950s and 1960s, filmmakers discovered that the most effective enemy was simply "them." No country or specific ideology needed to be identified; it was enough that some foreign, evil "them" was trying to destroy "us." Spy films entered a new realm of paranoia and psychological suspense, touching audiences not with national fears but with deep, personal anxieties. Hitchcock—ever the master of the spy film—began the trend with *North by Northwest* (1959). Then the genre accelerated wildly with the surprise success of the Ian Fleming inspired James Bond series beginning with *Dr. No* (1962).

The James Bond movies, made in England, were such massive hits that they touched off an explosion of copies. If the western was the genre of choice in the 1950s, the spy movie was the hands-down winner of the 1960s (followed by science fiction in the 1970s). The Derek Flint films starring James Coburn, (e.g., *Our Man Flint,* 1966), the Matt Helt series starring Dean Martin (e.g., *The Silencers,* 1966), and the Harry Palmer series starring Michael Caine (e.g., *The Ipcress File,* 1965) all leaped into the fray.

In addition to the series, there were a number of sophisticated spy thrillers during the 1960s, such as *The Manchurian Candidate* (1962), *Charade* (1963), *The Spy Who Came in from the Cold* (1965) *Arabesque* (1966), Hitchcock's *Torn Curtain* (1966), and *The Naked Runner* (1967).

Spy movies became so prevalent that it was soon time to mock the genre, as several movies did in the late 1960s and early 1970s. Among these were the notable *Casino Royale* (1967) and several other lesser films, such as *The Liquidator* (1966).

The spy movie epidemic finally spent itself by the end of the 1960s, with a few interesting latecomers, such as two by John Huston, *The Kremlin Letter* (1970) and *The Mackintosh Man* (1973), Sydney Pollack's *Three Days of the Condor* (1975), and Don Siegel's *Telefon* (1977). The 1980s have seen even less in the way of spy films, except of course for the regularly released James Bond movies that remind us of how things used to be.

With relations between the U.S. and Russia warming, a recent attempt to revive the genre, *Little Nikita* (1988), did not meet with success. In this atmosphere, there seems to be room for the more buoyant silliness of films like *Boris & Natasha* (1989), a comedy spy film based not on real life but on cartoon characters from the old "Rocky and Bullwinkle" TV show.

STAGECOACH The classic 1939 movie directed by John Ford that established the western as a format for serious filmmaking, and, in the bargain, turned John Wayne into a major star. In a year that produced what many consider the greatest crop of movies in the history of Hollywood, *Stagecoach* garnered a number of top Oscar nominations, including Best Picture and Best Director. It won a Best Supporting Actor Oscar for Thomas Mitchell as the drunken Doc Boone, and it also won the Best Music Score Academy Award.

Stagecoach was John Ford's first film shot in Monument Valley, Utah, an eerie desert punctuated by towering, majestic buttes; there is no other place like it in the world. Ford made the region his own in *Stagecoach* (and in many of his subsequent westerns) and it was an unwritten rule in Hollywood that no one else could make movies there.

The film was based on the Ernest Haycox short story *Stage to Lordsburg,* which was, in turn, based on a Guy de Maupassant story called *Boule-de-suif.* The screenplay, written by Dudley Nichols, concerned a band of disparate and desperate people who must travel together across hostile Indian country. Very much a work of ensemble acting, the film featured John Wayne, Claire Trevor, John Carradine, Thomas Mitchell, Andy Devine, George Bancroft, Louise Platt, Donald Meek, Berton Churchill, and Tim Holt.

John Wayne was the film's hero, and he made the most of it. Having been a "B" movie actor in cheap second features and serials throughout the 1930s, starring in a Ford movie was his chance of a lifetime. The director had originally given Wayne his start in the movies, but, even so, Wayne was not Ford's first choice for the role of the Ringo Kid. The role was originally offered to Gary Cooper, who was unsure about the part. Cooper's wife read the script and told him to turn it down, which he did. When Wayne was given the chance to read the script, he was so sure he would never be cast as the Ringo Kid that he suggested Lloyd Nolan for the role.

Stagecoach turned Wayne into a star and Ford and his protégé made many of their best movies together through the 1940s, 1950s, and early 1960s.

Other epic historical westerns had been made during the 1920s and 1930s, from *The Covered Wagon* (1923) to *Cimarron* (1931), and Ford himself filmed *The Iron Horse* (1924). But *Stagecoach* outstripped all others in its genre by emphasizing themes of character, honor, and the conflict between the dying West and the encroachment of civilization (themes Ford would later explore in even greater depth). The film's critical and commercial success opened the door to a boom in serious, adult westerns after World War II.

The film was noteworthy for a great many other reasons, not least among them the dazzling stunt work choreographed and staged by Yakima Canutt. The famous climactic fast-tracking chase across the desert floor as the Indians attack the fleeing stagecoach is one of the most thrilling action scenes in movie history and much of the credit belongs to Canutt.

Stagecoach was remade twice, first as a theatrical release in 1966 and later as a TV movie. Both versions were far inferior to the original.
See also: Canutt, Yakima; Ford, John; Trevor, Claire; Wayne, John; westerns

STALLONE, SYLVESTER (1946–) An actor, screenwriter, and director who became an overnight star

The combination of Sylvester Stallone's soulful bedroom eyes and muscled torso—not to mention his often overlooked talents as a screenwriter and director—have propelled him to the forefront of modern-day movie stars. Photo courtesy of Sylvester Stallone.

when he wisely negotiated the starring role in his own screenplay of *Rocky* (1976) rather than selling the rights to the story for a bundle of money. Since *Rocky,* Stallone has become the highest paid actor in Hollywood, receiving as much as $12 million per picture. His career, however, has been a rollercoaster ride of huge hits and stunning disasters. As an actor, Stallone has relatively little range because his voice is capable of little more than the growl of a latter day tough guy. But his swarthy good looks, bedroom eyes, and impressive physique, have allowed him to become both a rousing physical actor and potent sex symbol.

Born in New York City, Stallone grew up in the infamous Hell's Kitchen area. Later, after attending a boy's school in suburban Philadelphia (where he first started acting), Stallone spent two years at the American College of Switzerland in Geneva. While there, he became serious about his desire to become an actor.

Returning to the United States, he enrolled as a drama major at the University of Miami but left college before graduation to pursue an acting career in New York. In order to make ends meet, he once worked as an usher at the Baronet movie theater. It seemed that was as close to the movies as he was going to get. In desperation, he took a role in a pornographic film before

finally getting a tiny part as a young hood terrorizing Woody Allen in *Bananas* (1971).

Stallone struggled without success for three more years, often spending his time writing screenplays that didn't sell. Finally, in 1974 he was cast as one of the leads in the low-budget New York-based movie *The Lords of Flatbush,* a film that received some good reviews; it was Stallone's ticket to Hollywood. More tough guy roles followed in films such as *The Prisoner of Second Avenue* (1975), where, in a miniscule role, he was mistaken for a thief by Jack Lemmon. The parts weren't much bigger in *Capone* (1975), *Death Race 2000* (1975), *Farewell My Lovely* (1975), and *Cannonball* (1976).

Unable to get a meaty role in a major movie, Stallone decided to write one for himself. The result was *Rocky,* a film about a boxing hopeful who triumphs against impossible odds. Several producers offered to buy the screenplay, wanting to cast a name star in the title role. In true Rocky fashion, Stallone refused to sell. Although his bank balance was reportedly $100.00 and he had a pregnant wife to take care of, the actor held fast, determined to play the lead himself. In the end, he made a brilliant deal that not only gave him the starring role, it also gave him a large chunk of the profits in lieu of a very modest payment for the screenplay. He ended up both a star and a very wealthy man when *Rocky* opened to excellent reviews and boffo box office. The storybook finish was nearly perfect when he was nominated for Best Actor and Best Screenplay by the Academy of Motion Picture Arts and Sciences. He didn't win either award, but he was perfectly satisfied when the movie won the Oscar for Best Picture.

The question in 1976 was whether or not Stallone was a flash in the pan. Could he play anything other than Rocky? He wrote, directed, and starred in *Paradise Alley* (1978), a visually creative movie that deserved a much better fate than it received at the hands of both critics and filmgoers. In that same category was the ambitious *F.I.S.T.* (1978), directed by Norman Jewison based on a Stallone script, with the actor playing a Jimmy Hoffa–type labor leader.

With his career jeopardized by two flops in a row, *Rocky II* (1979), which Stallone wrote, directed, and starred in, bailed him out. In fact, the *Rocky* movies, including *Rocky III* (1982) and *Rocky IV* (1985), have been his one consistently successful series.

Stallone's work outside of the *Rocky* movies has been more problematic. He had major hits with his first two Rambo movies, *First Blood* (1982) and *Rambo: First Blood Part II* (1985), but *Rambo III* (1988) cost more than $60 million to produce (becoming the most expensive movie ever made) and failed to make it into the black.

Except for the entertaining cop movie *Nighthawks* (1981), Stallone's other movies have not sat well either with the critics or with audiences. *Victory* (1981), *Cobra* (1986), *Lock-up* (1989), and especially his ill-conceived arm wrestling movie *Over the Top* (1987) have been flops. Curiously, his directing of John Travolta in *Staying Alive* (1983), a *Rocky*-like sequel to *Saturday Night Fever* (1977), was roundly panned by the critics but fared reasonably well with the public, suggesting that as long as Stallone sticks with *Rocky* he can't go too far wrong.

See also: sex symbols: male; sports films

STAND-IN A person who takes the place of a star or actor in a film, allowing himself to be properly lit for a scene, a process that can be quite time consuming. The stand-in is hired because he bears a resemblance in size, build, face shape, and coloring to the star for whom he is substituting. The stand-in should not be confused with a double, a stuntman who replaces the star in scenes that require a dangerous activity.

STANWYCK, BARBARA (1907–) A husky-voiced actress who starred in eighty-three movies in a long and illustrious career. Small and thin, with bird-like features, Stanwyck has been a dynamo throughout her years in show business, gaining a reputation as one of the hardest-working actresses in the industry. If not a brilliant actress, she brought a great deal of style to her roles and managed to win four Oscar nominations. She was finally recognized by the Academy in 1982 when she was given an Honorary Award, stating that she was "an artist of impeccable grace and beauty, a dedicated actress, and one of the great ladies of Hollywood."

Born Ruby Stevens, she was orphaned at four years of age and spent much of her early life in foster homes. Influenced by her older sister who was a chorus girl, Stanwyck decided on a career in show business and was working in the chorus of a nightclub called The Strand Roof by the age of fifteen. Not long after, she moved up a grade to dancing in Broadway revues and stage musicals. Her first big break came after she was cast in the chorus of a play called *The Noose,* in which she had a few lines of dialogue. According to Ella Smith in her biography of the actress, *Starring Miss Barbara Stanwyck,* when the show had trouble out of town, its producer, director, and writer, Willard Mack, rewrote the third act and decided that Stanwyck's character was the logical one to carry the burden of the play's emotional climax. Suddenly, without any experience, the young hoofer was asked to become a dramatic actress. Tutored by Mack, Stanwyck gave a stirring performance that had the New York critics raving. Incidentally, it was Mack who gave her the stage name of Barbara Stanwyck.

Playing on Broadway in *The Noose* for nine months, she was discovered by the movies. She had a modest role in *Broadway Nights* (1927), a silent film shot in New York. It flopped and Stanwyck gave no more thought to the movies until her first husband, Frank

Fay, a popular vaudeville comic, was given a contract by Warner Bros. Stanwyck went to Hollywood with him, also signing with the studio.

Her first two talkies were disasters. Both *The Locked Door* (1929) and *Mexicali Rose* (1929) were bombs whose causes she did little to help. It looked as if her career was over before it had begun. Enter director Frank Capra, who went wild over a screen test of Stanwyck's he happened to see. Capra used her in four of his early films, *Ladies of Leisure* (1930), *The Miracle Woman* (1931), *Forbidden* (1932), and *The Bitter Tea of General Yen* (1933), and in the process helped turn her into a formidable screen actress.

One of the keys to Stanwyck's success over the years, particularly in the 1930s and 1940s, was her association with many of Hollywood's better directors. She may not have worked with them at the pinnacle of their careers (e.g., Capra) but Stanwyck had the good fortune to be cast in the films that helped to establish their reputations. For instance, she worked with the young William Wellman in three films during the 1930s, including the excellent *Night Nurse* (1931). She also worked with George Stevens in *Annie Oakley* (1935), the hit movie that shaped her public persona as a tough-as-nails woman who could hold her own against any man. After George Stevens, she worked with George Marshall in *A Message to Garcia* (1936), King Vidor in *Stella Dallas* (1937), for which she received her first Oscar nomination, Cecil B. DeMille in *Union Pacific* (1939), and Rouben Mamoulian in *Golden Boy* (1939). The latter three films were not only major hits, they helped turn a dependable leading lady into one of Hollywood's top female stars as she entered the 1940s.

When she began the new decade, Stanwyck also had a new husband. She had divorced Frank Fay in 1935, taking on a new mate, actor Robert Taylor, *(q.v.)* in 1939. The marriage lasted until 1952.

Newly married and with her career in high gear, Stanwyck found the early 1940s to be her grandest years in Hollywood. She demonstrated her ability in a wide range of roles and showed a decided flair for comedy. Again, working with top-notch directors she made such classics as Preston Sturges' delightful comedy *The Lady Eve* (1941), *Meet John Doe* (1941), in which she was reunited with director Frank Capra, the riotously funny screwball comedy directed by Howard Hawks, *Ball of Fire* (1942), a film in which she gave one of her best performances and received her second Oscar nomination, and Billy Wilder's classic *film noir, Double Indemnity* (1944), the movie in which she plays the symbolic spider to Fred MacMurray's fly. For her performance in this film, she captured her third Academy Award nomination.

The second half of the decade had bright spots for the actress in films such as *The Strange Love of Martha Ivers* (1946) and *Sorry, Wrong Number* (1948), which brought Stanwyck her fourth and last Oscar nomination. But she appeared in a greater number of lesser films as her career seemed to begin to fade.

The postwar years were not kind to a great many stars. A new generation was rising and aging movie queens were often the first to be cast aside. Nevertheless, Stanwyck held her own through the greater part of the 1950s, managing to work with good directors between a number of very minor films. Her best work could be seen in Fritz Lang's *Clash by Night* (1952), Douglas Sirk's *All I Desire* (1953), and Robert Wise's *Executive Suite* (1954).

By the mid-1950s, however, in the midst of the western craze, the actress joined the boots and saddles movement and began showing up regularly in films such as *Cattle Queen of Montana* (1955), *The Violent Men* (1955) and *The Maverick Queen* (1956). Stanwyck liked performing in westerns, but her movies were of variable quality. She did make one minor classic in the genre, starring with Barry Sullivan in Sam Fuller's low-budget *Forty Guns* (1957). It was, however, her last motion picture until she returned to the big screen in 1962 in *Walk on the Wild Side* (1962). In the meantime, she spent part of her time working in television, starring in "The Barbara Stanwyck Show." She would later get her wish to star in a "women's western" on TV when she headed the cast of "The Big Valley" during the second half of the 1960s.

Miss Stanwyck made just two more motion pictures during the 1960s, the Elvis Presley vehicle *Roustabout* (1964) and *The Night Walker* (1965). The rest of her work throughout the 1970s and 1980s has been on television, most notably in the miniseries *The Thorn Birds* (1983), for which she won an Emmy.

STAR WARS Released on May 25, 1977, this film written and directed by George Lucas *(q.v.)* was one of the most influential movies of the modern Hollywood era. Its stupendous success materially changed the kinds of movies that were made in its aftermath—how they sounded, when they were released—and established the huge potential of licensing arrangements. The success of its original story also helped to emancipate movies from necessarily being adapted from books and plays.

Inspired by 1930s serials, George Lucas conceived of *Star Wars* as a stylish space opera pitting clearly demarcated forces of good and evil against one another. Its story follows the young Luke Skywalker (Mark Hamill) as he learns how to use "the force" from Obe Wan Kenobee (Alec Guinness) in order to fight the evil space empire that is aided by a rogue Jedi knight, Darth Vader (voice supplied by James Earl Jones). Skywalker's principal allies are Princess Leia (Carrie Fisher) and Han Solo (Harrison Ford). The heroes are ably abetted by two ever-charming robots, R2D2 and C3P0.

Curiously, among the young actors in the cast, only Harrison Ford *(q.v.)* emerged from *Star Wars* and its sequels as a full-fledged movie star. The film was hardly a star vehicle; it was that rare film that used the mediums of sight and sound to their fullest and did not depend upon brilliant performances to carry the story along.

Despite Lucas' previous surprise hit with *American Graffiti,* the director's original studio, Universal, as well as United Artists, turned down his screenplay for *Star Wars.* The very successful producer/film executive Alan Ladd convinced Twentieth Century-Fox to spend $9 million on Lucas' project. The result was the then biggest box office hit of all time (it has since been bested by *E.T.—The Extra-Terrestrial*). *Star Wars* earned a stunning $400 million in North America alone. Altogether, the *Star Wars* trilogy has earned an incredible $1.2 billion at the box office.

The impact of George Lucas' science fiction film, however, goes beyond money. Before *Star Wars,* the traditional summer season for film releases was mid-June. The overwhelming success of Lucas' film, which was released during the last week of May, had the net effect of expanding the important summer season by more than two weeks. The new beginning of the movie summer season—the Wednesday before Memorial Day—is now known in the industry as "George Lucas Day."

Star Wars also changed Hollywood's image of science fiction from a backwater genre that had been out of favor since the late 1960s—and a category that was considered to appeal to a rather narrow audience—to the hottest genre in Hollywood. Also, thanks to John Williams' inspiring score, the film reestablished the importance and appeal of symphonic music in movies. In addition, the movie's spectacular special effects became the benchmark of excellence in the field, as well as a strong influence on dozens of producers who saw special effects as a pivotal new element in filmmaking.

If all of that wasn't enough, *Star Wars* and its sequels caused a marketing revolution. The films actually earned more in licensing agreements than at the box office, bringing in an estimated 1.5 billion in the merchandizing of *Star Wars* books, T-shirts, toys, lunchboxes, etc. And, finally, the film proved that a hugely profitable movie could be made both without stars and with an original screenplay (i.e., a story not based on a hit book or play).

Originally conceived by Lucas as a nine-part opus, the original *Star Wars* was actually *Episode IV: A New Hope.* What followed were *The Empire Strikes Back (Episode V)* and *Return of the Jedi (Episode VI)*. Lucas hasn't yet abandoned the idea of making future installments in the series.

See also: science fiction

STARK, RAY (1909?–) One of the last of the great independent producers, he came to his calling rather late in life, but made up for it with a string of big-budget hit movies that began in the late 1960s. Though he has had his share of critical and commercial disasters, Stark has always rebounded smartly, wisely investing in proven talent time and time again.

Stark graduated from Rutgers University and fell into the rough-and-tumble work of show business public relations. In the latter half of the 1940s he changed careers and became a talent agent, representing radio writers, novelists, and eventually show business personalities when he joined Famous Artists during the 1950s. Among his clients were Marilyn Monroe and Kirk Douglas.

Stark left the agency business in 1957 to become the cofounder of Seven Arts Productions, a company that became a highly successful producer of shows for television; Stark was in charge of production. He stayed with the company until 1966, but even before he left he had begun producing theatrical films, making his big screen producing debut with *The World of Suzie Wong* (1960). In 1964, he began his association with Director John Huston, with whom he collaborated on a number of films, among them *The Night of the Iguana* (1964), *Reflections in a Golden Eye* (1967), *Fat City* (1972), and *Annie* (1982).

When Stark found someone he liked, he stuck with them—and they with him. He hit it big as an independent producer with Barbra Streisand when he produced the film that made her a star, *Funny Girl* (1968), and he continued to produce many of her most famous early triumphs, including *The Owl and the Pussycat* (1970), *The Way We Were* (1973), and *Funny Lady* (1975). His most enduring collaboration, though, has been with playwright/screenwriter Neil Simon who has provided the material for Stark hits for fifteen years, some of them being *The Sunshine Boys* (1975), *The Goodbye Girl* (1977), *California Suite* (1978), *Chapter Two* (1979), *Brighton Beach Memoirs* (1986), and *Biloxi Blues* (1988).

STEIGER, ROD (1925–) An actor who has aptly been compared to Paul Muni. Like Muni, Steiger has played a wide variety of ethnic types, while also performing in a grandly dramatic style. Certainly Steiger, like Muni before him, has often been accused of overacting. Criticism aside, Steiger rarely goes unnoticed in his films no matter how small his role might be. As one of the prime adherents of "The Method" style of acting he has a brooding, electric quality; one never knows when he's going to explode on screen. That dangerous element in his acting style has kept him working with relative steadiness in films since the 1950s. While he usually plays villains, he has also made a reputation (à la Muni) as a biopic star, playing a considerable number of historical characters with flair and intensity.

Raised in Newark, New Jersey, young Steiger en-

In addition to playing a long list of historical characters, Rod Steiger has also exhibited a volcanic power on screen that often overwhelms his fellow players, making him a true successor to the late, great Paul Muni. Photo courtesy of Rod Steiger.

listed in the Navy at the start of World War II and spent five years in the service. Later, he took a civil service job and joined a Veterans Administration drama group. He took to acting so well that fellow employees suggested he go into it full time. Using the G. I. Bill to pay his way, he joined the New York Theatre Wing, then the Dramatic Workshop, followed by Elia Kazan's Actors Studio. Meanwhile, he found work in stock and made his Broadway debut in a revival of Clifford Odets' *Night Music*. At roughly this time he also began acting in television dramas. Steiger played the title role in the TV production of "Marty," a role that later brought Ernest Borgnine an Oscar when it was turned into a movie in 1955.

Steiger made his film debut in a small role in Fred Zinnemann's *Teresa* (1951), but he made his mark in his second film, Elia Kazan's *On the Waterfront* (1954), playing Marlon Brando's brother, Charlie, and winning a Best Supporting Actor Oscar nomination for his efforts. He was later nominated for Best Actor in *The Pawnbroker* (1965) and he finally won the Best Actor Academy Award for his racist police chief in *In the Heat of the Night* (1967).

Steiger's wide-ranging abilities were put to the test early on. Although he had never sung or danced professionally, he sang the "Pore Jud" number in the film version of *Oklahoma!* (1955) and was the only principal member of the cast to be in Agnes DeMille's ballet for the Rodgers and Hammerstein musical.

Nobody plays villains with greater intensity than Steiger. He has created a rich gallery of bad guys in films as wide-ranging as *The Harder They Fall* (1956), *Dr. Zhivago* (1965), and *F.I.S.T.* (1978). Among his distinctive biographical performances have been the title role in *Al Capone* (1959), Napoleon in *Waterloo* (1970), and the Fields in *W. C. Fields & Me* (1976).

Whether in starring roles or in major supporting parts, Steiger has proven to be a powerful and unpredictable actor. His roles in films such as *The Mark* (1961), *The Illustrated Man* (1969), and *The Chosen* (1981) show a breadth of talent that makes him unique among modern character actors.

STEINER, MAX (1888–1971) He was a prodigiously talented and prolific composer of film scores who enjoyed his greatest success during the 1930s and 1940s. Steiner was very much appreciated during his own lifetime, garnering eighteen much-deserved Oscar nominations and winning three Academy Awards for his scores for *The Informer* (1935), *Now Voyager* (1942), and *Since You Went Away* (1944). He didn't win the Oscar for his most famous score, however, which he composed for *Gone With the Wind* (1939). Despite his association with *Gone With the Wind* and his Oscar-winning films, the bulk of Steiner's best work was written for sweeping action films. His dramatic style was best suited to such movies and they were immeasurably enhanced by his music.

Born in Vienna, Steiner was a musical wunderkind who finished an eight-year course of study at Vienna's Imperial Academy of Music in just one year, graduating at the age of thirteen. He conducted major orchestras when he was sixteen, finally choosing to come to America at the outbreak of World War I when he was a well-established twenty-six-year-old.

Steiner spent the next decade and a half conducting and orchestrating Broadway musicals. His true talents might have never been fully appreciated had sound not come to the movies. Seeing a fresh opportunity, he went to Hollywood and quickly became one of the film industry's leading composers for the screen. Much of his early film career was spent at RKO where he wrote the highly charged score for *King Kong* (1933). Late, in the mid-1930s, he moved to Warner Bros. where he spent most of his next fifteen years, writing the thrilling scores for such classics as *The Charge of the Light Brigade* (1936), *The Dawn Patrol* (1938), *They Died With Their Boots On* (1941), *Casablanca* (1942), *The Big Sleep* (1946),

The Treasure of the Sierra Madre (1948), *Key Largo* (1948), and *White Heat* (1949).

Steiner continued to show his versatility in the 1950s with swashbuckling music for *The Flame and the Arrow* (1950), fragile, gentle music for *The Glass Menagerie* (1950), martial music for *Battle Cry* (1955), and nostalgic strains for *The Searchers* (1956).

Steiner wrote film scores well into the 1960s. By the time he died, he had composed the music for more than two hundred movies, leaving an indelible musical mark that will likely never be equaled.

STERLING, FORD (1883–1939) A silent film comedian who made his mark as one of Mack Sennett's slapstick stars. Sterling had a memorable appearance, highlighted by heavy dark eyebrows, a miniscule goatee, and thin, rubbery legs. Sterling was a wonderful comic heavy, who is best remembered as Chief Teheezal, head policeman of the famous Keystone Kops.

Born George Ford Stitch, the young Wisconsin lad joined the circus as a teenager and became known as Keno, the Boy Clown. He was twenty-eight, and a mildly successful veteran of both vaudeville and the legitimate theater when he joined Mack Sennett's comedy group at Biograph in 1911, appearing that year in *Abe Gets Even with Father*. Not long after, however, Sennett left Biograph to form Keystone and Ford Sterling went with him, making history in a variety of fast-paced adventurous slapstick comedies.

Sterling occasionally directed his own one- and two-reel comedies. He also often acted in the Keystone ensemble, which included Mabel Normand and Fatty Arbuckle (*qq.v.*), among others. At the height of his popularity during the teens, he had his own series of shorts, the Sterling Comedies. But perhaps Ford Sterling's greatest contribution to film comedy was his shoes. Among the items Charlie Chaplin borrowed from different Keystone performers to create his classic tramp outfit were Ford Sterling's enormous shoes, which Chaplin wore on the wrong feet.

After leaving Sennett in 1921, Sterling continued acting with mixed success. The age of slapstick humor had passed its peak. Nonetheless, he worked steadily throughout the 1920s and made the transition into sound films, appearing in a modest number of early 1930s movies, including *Alice in Wonderland* (1933), in which he played the White King. His last film was *Black Sheep* (1935). The comedian, who was so adept at impossible twirls, suffered the loss of a leg in an accident in the 1930s and died not long after.
See also: Chaplin, Sir Charles; Sennett, Mack

STERNBERG, JOSEF VON(1894–1969) The ultimate director of light and shadow whose languid, dreamlike films sprang from a highly exotic vision. It was not von Sternberg's artistic purpose to accurately depict

Hoping for a repeat of their successful teamwork in the hit *The Last Command* (1928), the great Emil Jannings made a personal request that Josef von Sternberg direct him in *The Blue Angel* (1930). Lightning struck again, but not for Jannings. Von Sternberg introduced Marlene Dietrich to the world in *The Blue Angel,* seen here with Jannings (seated). Photo courtesy of Movie Star News.

reality; according to Andrew Sarris' *The Films of Josef von Sternberg.* when the Pasha of Marrakesh insisted to the director that *Morocco* (1930) so captured the look of his nation that von Sternberg must have shot it on location (which he had not), von Sternberg replied that it "was no more than an accidental resemblance, a flaw due to my lack of talent to avoid such similarity." The choice of Morocco, like most of von Sternberg's locales, merely provided him with an excuse to take free rein in creating a mood of visual enchantment. The unique and exquisite beauty of the director's films have been somewhat overlooked due to von Sternberg's famous Svengali-Trilby relationship with Marlene Dietrich, an association that led to both his greatest triumphs as well as to his downfall. He discovered and molded Dietrich into his image of mysterious femininity in seven films between 1930 and 1935, and these movies remain quitessential von Sternberg.

Born Josef Sternberg, the "von" was added to his credits as assistant director in *The Mystery of the Yellow Room* (1919). The addition was made without his knowledge by the film's director and its star, both of whom decided that the aristocratic "von" would add more dignity to the credit list. Sternberg chose to keep the name despite the anti-German feelings of the immediate post World War I era. In fact, he was an Austrian Jew who had spent three years of his adolescence living in New york.

Von Sternberg's entrance to the movie business was as a film patcher when he was seventeen years old. He learned a good deal about the technical side of the emerging new art form by later working as a cutter, editor, a signal corps photographer for the U.S. government during World War I, and finally as an assistant director on a number of films between 1919 and 1924.

He directed his first film, *The Salvation Hunters* (1925),

when a well-to-do aspiring actor asked him to make a film in which he could star. With $5,000 in hand from the actor, von Sternberg wrote, produced, and directed this film that was smuggled into Charlie Chaplin's house where it was seen by the great comedian as well as his United Artists partners, Douglas Fairbanks and Mary Pickford, all of whom were enormously impressed. Later, Chaplin hired von Sternberg to direct a film he had conceived called *The Sea Gull* (1926), starring his one-time leading lady, Edna Purviance. The film was never commercially released, however, for unknown reasons.

Von Sternberg's early directorial career was full of several disappointments and false starts, such as his episode with Chaplin. Finally, however, he hit his commercial stride with one of Hollywood's early gangster films, *Underworld* (1927), a movie that was characteristically long on mood and style and short on action and plot. He quickly went on to make the highly regarded hit *The Last Command* (1928), but found himself the following year during the rush to sound with a silent masterpiece, *The Docks of New York* (1929), and no audience.

Once he began working with sound, von Sternberg proved to be inventive and clever, making another top-notch gangster film, *Thunderbolt* (1929). By this time, he was seen in Hollywood as a talented and innovative director with a great deal of promise. That promise was immediately fulfilled when he went to Germany to make *The Blue Angel* (1930). In need of a suitable temptress to destroy the film's professor character (played by Emil Jannings), he discovered Marlene Dietrich in Berlin and cast her as Lola Lola. *The Blue Angel* was an international hit and von Sternberg returned to Hollywood with Dietrich in tow.

Von Sternberg and Dietrich made six more films together: *Morocco* (1930), *Dishonored* (1931), *Shanghai Express* (1932), *Blonde Venus* (1932), *The Scarlet Empress* (1934), and *The Devil Is a Woman* (1935). Each of these collaborations was a triumph of style and imagery. Dietrich was photographed behind veils, fishnet, smoke, feathers, etc. in a cluttered mise en scène that was often backlit and cloaked in shadow. The films were about beauty, sex, and the infinite mysteries of womanhood, no matter if the woman was a spy, a desperate mother, or the czarina of Russia. However, von Sternberg's films were not paced like other movies of the period, and filmgoers, as well as critics, began to complain that his movies weren't about anything, didn't go anywhere, that they were merely decadent exercises in making Dietrich (whom many thought to be his lover) beautiful. His studio finally denied him the opportunity of directing her any more and he went on to make *Crime and Punishment* (1935) and several other films of only modest distinction. His time had past.

After the aborted *I, Claudius* (1937), and the fasci-nating *The Shanghai Gesture* (1941), he made only three more films, none of them coming close to the majesty of his Dietrich films. The last movie he directed was *Anatahan* (1953), although *Jet Pilot,* made for Howard Hughes in 1950, wasn't released until 1957.

Von Sternberg lived long enough to see his reputation redeemed. He died of heart disease at the age of seventy-five.

See also: Dietrich, Marlene

STEVENS, GEORGE (1904–1975) A scrupulously professional director whose career in Hollywood spanned six decades. As a former cameraman, he brought a strong visual sense to his films, and as a producer of many of his own movies, he was involved in almost every detail of pre- and postproduction, a rather uncommon occurrence among studio directors of the 1930s, 1940s, and 1950s. His zealous attention to detail, and a propensity to shoot miles of extra footage in order to ensure coverage of every scene, account for his tally of only twenty-five feature-length movies during his thirty-seven years as a director (from 1933–1970). Though he made relatively few movies, he worked in a surprisingly wide variety of genres, making classic Hollywood musicals, comedies, westerns, and adventure films.

Part of a theatrical family, George Stevens joined his actor parents on the stage when he was five years old. Not a terribly talented performer, he found work in the movie industry as an assistant cameraman in 1921. His vaudeville background came in handy, though, when he graduated to cameraman and worked for the Hal Roach Studio shooting (among other shorts) Laurel & Hardy comedies such as *The Battle of the Century* (1927) and *Big Business* (1929).

In the early 1930s Stevens began directing short subjects for Hal Roach, Universal, and RKO. Finally, in 1933, he was given his first opportunity to direct a feature, albeit a "B" movie comedy programmer, *The Cohens and the Kellys in Trouble.* He continued directing "B" movie comedies until 1935 when RKO gave him a chance to direct Katharine Hepburn in *Alice Adams.* The film was both a critical and box office hit, solidifying Stevens's position as an "A" director, a distinction he never relinquished.

Stevens' films of the latter 1930s and early 1940s had a "can-do" attitude about them. His deft handling of adventures such as *Gunga Din* (1939), comedies of the quality of *Woman of the Year* (1942), and musicals, including what many consider the best of the Astaire/Rogers musicals, *Swingtime* (1936), all had a thoroughly uplifting style. His last film before heading off for war service in the signal corps was the good-natured romantic comedy *The More the Merrier* (1943), for which he received his first Oscar nomination for Best Director.

As an officer in the Signal Corps, he shot the Allied footage of the liberation of the Dachau concentration camp. By the time he returned to Hollywood, Stevens' outlook had become tinged with a melancholy that soon enriched and deepened his work. His films of the late 1940s and particularly the 1950s were his best movies, achievements that were recognized by the critics, the public, and his peers in the industry.

Stevens began his postwar era with the richly evocative *I Remember Mama* (1948). His next film was the classic adaptation of Theodore Dreiser's novel *An American Tragedy,* retitled *A Place in the Sun* (1951) for the big screen. His work on the film earned him his first Oscar for Best Director. In 1953, he directed *Shane,* which many consider to be *the* classic western, and was yet again nominated for Best Director. Stevens did not win the Academy Award that year but was instead given the even greater honor of being presented with the Irving Thalberg Award in recognition of the high standards of his work.

The director's next great achievement was the blockbuster *Giant* (1956) for which he won his second Oscar for Best Director. It seemed as if he was destined to make one sweeping saga after another, but he changed gears and made the small, intimate, and touching story, *The Diary of Anne Frank* (1959), and was rewarded with another Oscar nomination for Best Director.

Stevens made but two more films, the biblical epic and colossal flop *The Greatest Story Ever Told* (1965), on which he spent five years of his life, and the all-but-ignored *The Only Game in Town* (1970), which failed despite its cast, including Elizabeth Taylor and Warren Beatty.

Beginning in 1938 with *Vivacious Lady,* Stevens produced all but two of his own movies *(Gunga Din* and *Woman of the Year).* His control over his own film projects left no doubt as to who was responsible for the style, substance, and quality of his productions.

The director imbued his son, George Stevens, Jr. (1932–) with a love of Hollywood. The younger Stevens was put to work as associate producer on *The Diary of Anne Frank* and *The Greatest Story Ever Told.* In the mid-1960s he headed the Motion Picture Service of the United States Information Agency. But he became well-known to film buffs and film students as the director of The American Film Institute, a post he held from 1967 through 1979. While George Stevens created some of Hollywood's most memorable movies, his son helped to preserve them.

STEWART, JAMES (1908–) Awkward yet charming, youthful yet serious, and courageous yet modest, Jimmy Stewart has embodied America at its best. Film audiences have trusted him to entertain them ever since 1935. He has rarely ever let them down.

Stewart has been a star in essentially two distinct incarnations. He was a light comedy leading man of the late 1930s and much of the 1940s and then a western

One of the most beloved Hollywood superstars, Jimmy Stewart has become an American icon, due to his idiosyncratic style, ineffable charm, plus the good fortune of having worked with many of the greatest directors in Hollywood, including Frank Capra, Ernst Lubitsch, George Stevens, Anthony Mann, Alfred Hitchcock, and John Ford. Photo courtesy of James Stewart.

and action star of the 1950s. In 1952, he became the first major star of the modern era to put his popularity on the line, working for a small salary against a significant percentage of each of his film's profits.

Jimmy Stewart had intended to live life quietly as an architect. Though he had acted while in college in the Princeton (University) Triangle Club, he did not take his performing seriously until his fellow classmate Joshua Logan convinced him to give the theater a try after graduation. Stewart agreed and joined Logan's University Players. With members like Henry Fonda and Margaret Sullavan, it was quite a group.

Stewart had a short and modest career in the theater before Hollywood gossip columnist Hedda Hopper discovered him, touting his naturalness to MGM. After a screen test, the studio signed him and gave him a small part in *The Murder Man* (1935). He was soon helped along by his old friend, Margaret Sullavan, then a star at Universal, who requested him for a large part in *Next Time We Love* (1936).

Stewart's first starring role was in a "B" movie, *Speed* (1936); it was clear that MGM didn't know how to cast him. He was a sailor in a musical, *Born to Dance*

(1936), a villain in *After the Thin Man* (1936), and a lower-class Frenchman in *Seventh Heaven* (1937).

It took two directors outside of MGM to recognize Stewart's talent and appeal. Loaned out from MGM, George Stevens put him in two romantic comedies at RKO, the first with Ginger Rogers, *Vivacious Lady* (1938), and the second, *The Shopworn Angel,* with old pal Margaret Sullavan (1938). Both were hits and Stewart had become a bona fide Hollywood leading man. But it was Frank Capra at Columbia who turned the leading man into a star with *You Can't Take It with You* (1938) and *Mr. Smith Goes to Washington* (1939). The latter film brought Stewart his first Oscar nomination.

In the meantime, the only movie MGM could offer its new star was *Ice Follies of 1939.* MGM continued to loan him out, this time for the comic western *Destry Rides Again* (1939), another hit and another feather in Stewart's cap.

The actor's remarkable string of hits was finally abetted by MGM, which happily paired him with Margaret Sullavan in two excellent films, *The Shop Around the Corner* (1940) and *The Mortal Storm* (1940). That same year he also joined Katharine Hepburn and Cary Grant in *The Philadelphia Story* (1940), this time winning his one and only Best Actor Oscar.

Stewart made several other films before leaving Hollywood to join the war effort, but none were hits, presaging the difficulties he would have upon his return to the movie business.

When Stewart returned from the service (he was a bomber pilot who made twenty sorties over Germany), he found that his charming innocence no longer appealed to movie audiences. His first film after the war, Frank Capra's inspiring *It's a Wonderful Life* (1946), was a box office disappointment. He won another Oscar nomination for his performance in the film but audiences simply were not interested. *Magic Town* (1947) was much in the mold of *It's a Wonderful Life* and it, too, failed to find paying customers.

Finally, in 1948, Stewart stopped his slide by playing a tough detective in *Call Northside 777.* But with his career still lacking focus, he made several more films of questionable quality. It wasn't until 1950 that he not only found his focus, but also began on a path that brought him to his highest level of stardom. The change began when he starred in the surprise hit Western directed by Anthony Mann, *Winchester 73.*

Between 1950 and 1955, Stewart starred in six Westerns, all but one of them directed by Mann. Every one was a hit, and they presented a new Stewart persona. Instead of the sweet innocence of the 1930s and 1940s, he exhibited a hard edge of cyncism, anger, and violence. Stewart excelled at playing heroes with little interest in heroics; only when either shamed or pushed by circumstances beyond their control would they finally go into action. In films such as *Bend of the River*

(1952) and *The Far Country* (1955) his characters were intensely human, troubled loners. Stewart's mature, intelligent performances helped to lift the western to a new level of respectability.

Instrumental to Stewart's success in the 1930s was his work with quality directors like Capra, Borzage, Cukor, and Stevens, and the same held true in the 1950s and early 1960s when he acted for Anthony Mann, Alfred Hitchcock, and John Ford.

The actor starred in the first of his four Hitchcock thrillers in *Rope* (1948). The movie was an experiment of Hitchcock's in which he attempted to hide discernible edits and breaks, pacing the film in real time. The gimmick did not appeal to audiences and the movie was a flop.

In the 1950s, however, Stewart starred in three of Hitchcock's best films of that decade, *Rear Window* (1954), *The Man Who Knew Too Much* (1956), and *Vertigo* (1958). Thanks to the westerns and the Hitchcock films, with the exception of 1951, Stewart was among the top ten box office draws every year between 1950 and 1959. And in 1955, twenty years after his motion picture debut, he was the number-one box office draw in the world.

His success in the 1950s allowed him to make a number of films that were rather close to his heart. He starred in *Harvey* (1950), a role he originated on Broadway about a dipsomaniac with a six-foot invisible rabbit for a friend. (He later recreated his role for TV). The film was his only light comedy in the entire decade, but it brought him yet another Oscar nomination. He also starred in the now much-admired *The Spirit of St. Louis* (1957) about Charles Lindbergh's flight across the Atlantic, a film that crashed at the box office.

After his fifth and final Oscar nomination for his role in *Anatomy of a Murder* (1959), Stewart's career finally began to slow down. His work with director John Ford in *Two Rode Together* (1961), *The Man Who Shot Liberty Valence* (1962), and *Cheyenne Autumn* (1964) was noteworthy, though only *Liberty Valence* was a fully realized masterpiece and moneymaker. Stewart's last great film was Andrew McLaglen's *Shenandoah* (1966), in which he played a proud father who tries to keep his family out of the Civil War. After that, good roles for an aging hero were hard to come by.

The actor clearly enjoyed himself starring along with his old friend Henry Fonda in a couple of minor westerns, *Firecreek* (1967) and *The Cheyenne Social Club* (1970), but the rest of his career has been spent in featured supporting roles in movies such as *The Shootist* (1976) and *The Big Sleep* (1978). He has also starred in a TV series and has made numerous guest appearances on the little screen.

With his stumbling speech pattern and his gangling body, Jimmy Stewart has been both an unlikely star and one of Hollywood's greatest treasures.

See also: Capra, Frank; Hitchcock, Alfred; Mann, Anthony

STOCK FOOTAGE   Any previously existing film footage that can be inserted in a new movie. Stock footage is used for a variety of reasons, though usually to save money that might otherwise have to be spent creating a very expensive scene. It is also used for historical accuracy (e.g., genuine newsreel footage was used in the opening montage of *Casablanca,* [1942]), and when certain scenes are simply too difficult or dangerous to reshoot (e.g., plane crashes).

Stock footage was used extensively in the silent era and during the 1930s through the 1950s. For instance, the same shots of the New York City skyline were used over and over again throughout the 1930s and early 1940s. In general, stock footage showed up most often in low-budget movies that cannibalized some of the epic action scenes from "A" movies of the same studio. Particularly in the years before television, when films were rarely seen again after their initial release, grandiose action sequences were often plucked willy nilly from older films, spliced into new movies, and then shown to a whole new generation of filmgoers.

Some of the most heavily used stock footage consisted of aerial dogfights from *Wings* (1927), *The Dawn Patrol* (1930), and *Hell's Angels* (1930). Countless flying films used that spectacular footage throughout the 1930s. In fact, the remake of *The Dawn Patrol* (1938) used the flying footage from the original.

As film quality has increased, it has become relatively easy to spot stock footage because it is almost always grainer than the newer film stock that surrounds it. For that reason, such footage has rarely been used in recent decades for the purpose of saving money. Today, stock footage is more likely to be used expressly for its historical and nostalgic qualities.

STONE, OLIVER   *See* writer-directors

STORYBOARD   A series of drawings or sketches that indicate what each successive shot in a scene or sequence should look like when filmed. Generally, storyboards are made to illustrate the action of the most complicated scenes (and therefore the ones most expensive to produce) in a film in order to guide the director, cinematographer, and cameraman in their particular tasks.

Some directors rely heavily on storyboards for all sorts of scenes and shoot only what they've prepared in advance, while others prefer a looser approach, improvising and/or shooting scenes from several angles, intending to decide on the final succession of shots in the editing room rather than before filming.

Of all directors, Alfred Hitchcock *(q.v.)* was the most famous for relying on storyboards. He was known to plot every single shot of his films in advance, leaving nothing to chance. By this method, he was able (to a very great extent) to avoid studio interference in the recutting of his films. His thrillers were so efficiently planned that he could film an entire feature and leave only a miniscule two hundred feet of unused footage after the movie had been edited.

STRADLING, HARRY (1902–1970)   A gifted cinematographer who had to leave America in 1935 to make his reputation. When he returned in 1940, he became a leading director of photography and a two-time Oscar winner. Stradling worked in all genres, but was particularly active in musicals, which drew heavily on his skill with color photography.

Though born in England, Stradling arrived in the U.S. while an adolescent and began working as a Hollywood cameraman during the 1920s. There was nothing distinguished about his early career either in the silents or in the early sound era. Eventually, he left America and brought his skills to bear on the French production of Jacques Feyder's *Carnival in Flanders* (1935), a film that garnered him his first real attention. He soon traveled to the land of his birth, providing the clean, crisp photography for such films as *The Divorce of Lady X* (1938), *Pygmalion* (1938), and *The Citadel* (1938).

Stradling made a triumphant return to Hollywood in 1940 and was immediately given important film assignments, such as Hitchcock's *Suspicion* (1941), *The Human Comedy* (1943), and his first Oscar-winning film, *The Picture of Dorian Gray* (1945).

In the latter half of the 1940s, Stradling began his valued work on MGM musicals where he was responsible for the rich and vibrant color photography for such films as *The Pirate* (1948), *Easter Parade* (1948), and *In the Good Old Summertime* (1949).

During the rest of his career, though putting in work on such strong black-and-white productions as *A Streetcar Named Desire* (1951), *Johnny Guitar* (1954), and *Who's Afraid of Virginia Woolf?* (1966), Stradling continued his association with the musical. Among his many credits were *Guys and Dolls* (1955), *The Pajama Game* (1957), *My Fair Lady* (1964), for which he won his second Academy Award, *Funny Girl* (1968), *Hello, Dolly!* (1969), and *On a Clear Day You Can See Forever* (1970). These last three starred Barbra Steisand, and Stradling was working on a fourth with the star, *The Owl and the Pussycat* (1970), when he died.

Stradling's son, Harry Stradling, Jr., (1925–   ) also became a cinematographer. He has worked consistently since the late 1960s, showing flashes of brilliant color photography in such films as *Little Big Man* (1970), *The Way We Were* (1973), *Bite the Bullet* (1975), *Go Tell the Spartans* (1978), *The Pursuit of D.B. Cooper* (1981), and *Micki & Maude* (1984). He has also worked in television, providing the cinematography for the 1984 miniseries, "George Washington."

STREEP, MERYL (1951–) The premier movie actress of the 1980s, whose performances have often outshined her films, even while many of her vehicles have been top-notch, thoughtful entertainments. An elegant beauty, the oft-times Oscar nominated Streep has become known for her remarkably accurate accents, playing characters from Scandinavia, the American Deep South, Poland, and Australia. Her acting talent, however, goes far beyond her skill with accents; she thoroughly absorbs herself in her roles like no other actress of our time.

Born Mary Louise Streep to a well-to-do New Jersey family, she first wanted to pursue a career in the opera. A few years later when she was in high school, Streep's passion turned to acting. She studied drama at Vassar and went on to the famous Yale Drama School for an advanced degree. Her ascent was swift after that. Streep moved from the Yale Repertory Company to Broadway and soon won a Tony nomination for her performance in Tennessee Williams' *27 Wagons Full of Cotton*.

Streep made the leap from stage to both the small and the big screen in 1977 with a lead role in a TV movie, "The Deadliest Season" and a small supporting role in the acclaimed motion picture *Julia*. The following year, though, she made a much bigger impact in both media, taking home an Emmy for her performance in the acclaimed miniseries "Holocaust" (1978) and garnering a Best Supporting Actress Oscar nomination for the Academy Award–winning *The Deer Hunter* (1978).

Television was left behind for the movies as Streep went on to play the modest role of Woody Allen's ex-wife in *Manhattan* (1979) and the bright Southern belle temptress of Alan Alda in *The Seduction of Joe Tynan* (1979). Critics were already buzzing about Streep and telling movie fans to keep their eye on her.

At the end of 1979, she played Dustin Hoffman's wife in *Kramer vs. Kramer* (1979) and walked away with a Best Supporting Actress Oscar. She hasn't had a supporting part since. She has starred in a wide variety of roles, showing a versatility unmatched by any film actress save Bette Davis. From her dual role in *The French Lieutenant's Woman* (1981) as a movie actress and the character she plays, to her Oscar-winning performance as the tortured Polish immigrant in *Sophie's Choice* (1981), and from the complex and troubled title character in *Silkwood* (1983) to an alcoholic old crone who loves her man in *Ironweed* (1987), she has electrified audiences with a unique combination of subtlety and bravura. Her starring performance (opposite Roseanne Barr) in *She-Devil* (1989), a broad comedy turn, is yet another example of Streep's wide-ranging skills and her willingness to take chances.

Despite her consistently good notices, Streep has not always surfaced in either critical or commercial hits. The mystery thriller *Still of the Night* (1982) was a disappointment, as were the modern love story *Falling in Love* (1984) and the modern divorce story *Heartburn* (1986). Often, though, critics have liked her films more than the general public, as was the case with *Ironweed* (1987) and *A Cry in the Dark* (1988). Audiences flocked to see her in the Oscar-winning *Out of Africa* (1985) however, despite the films decidedly mixed reviews. Although Streep has not become a major box office draw, audiences have come to expect that any film she stars in will be a quality production.

STREISAND, BARBRA (1942–) A singer, actress, director, producer, and songwriter who has become one of the biggest female box office draws of the last two decades. Her big nose, heavy Brooklyn accent, and alleged "difficult" temperament have not stood in the way of her talent. Streisand's soaring singing voice has been her claim to fame, but she has also proved to be a powerful dramatic actress as well as a gifted comedienne. Her talents have been appreciated almost from the very start of her professional career and in almost every medium. She was nominated for a Tony for her very first Broadway play, *I Can Get It for You Wholesale,* in 1962, won a Grammy for her first album, won an Emmy for her first TV special, and won an Oscar for her first film, *Funny Girl* (1968), which she shared with the legendary Katharine Hepburn due to a tie vote.

Born Barbara Joan Streisand in Brooklyn, N.Y., she later dropped the second "a" from her first name in order to set herself apart. When she was ten years old, she decided to try for a record contract and traveled across the East River to sing for a recording company— she was turned down. According to Jonathan Black in *Streisand,* after this "rejection," she concentrated more on an acting career. Streisand did not seriously consider singing as an option because it simply came too easy to her.

After high school she took acting lessons but made little progress until she began singing for extra money at a gay bar in Greenwich Village. It was her singing career that continued to thrive and opened doors for her, getting her a supporting role in *I Can Get It for You Wholesale,* which had originally been written for a woman more than twice her age. It was during the run of that play that she met and married the show's star, Elliott Gould.

Her success as a recording and nightclub artist led to her being cast as Fanny Brice in the Broadway musical *Funny Girl* in 1964; she was a critical and commercial sensation. Streisand went on to reprise her role in her hit film debut and became an overnight movie star. She has since starred in a dozen other films.

During the late 1960s and throughout the 1970s she starred in nearly a film every year on average, beginning with two disappointing musical bombs, *Hello, Dolly!*

(1969) and *On a Clear Day You Can See Forever* (1970). But she recouped smartly in the non–singing romantic comedy *The Owl and the Pussycat* (1970) and scored more raves and big box office with Peter Bogdanovich's ode to the screwball comedy, *What's Up Doc?* (1972). *Up the Sandbox* (1972) was a more strident comedy and therefore received mixed reviews and did mediocre business. But Streisand did what many considered the impossible, starring in a credible romantic love story with Robert Redford in *The Way We Were* (1973). The film was adored by both the critics and movie fans, becoming a major hit (as was the theme song, recorded by Streisand).

Her films during the rest of the 1970s were, at best, mediocre. The comedies *For Pete's Sake* (1974) and *The Main Event* (1979) didn't generate a great deal of enthusiasm. Her musicals, the sequel to *Funny Girl, Funny Lady* (1975), and a remake of *A Star Is Born* (1976) were commercial successes despite generally poor to mixed reviews.

Streisand was increasingly depicted during the 1970s as a temperamental perfectionist, a performer impossible to please who made life on the set unbearable. She rebutted that no one cared about the quality of her films more than she did and that everyone else was looking for the easy way out. As a result, she became more and more involved in her own productions. For instance, she composed "Evergreen" with Paul Williams for *A Star Is Born* and won an Oscar for Best Song. She went on to become co-executive producer of *The Main Event* and, after a four-year absence from the big screen, she cowrote, produced, directed, and starred in the musical, *Yentl* (1983). While the reviews were mixed, audiences had no reservations; the film was a major hit, and many expected it to be a big contender at the Academy Awards. To the astonishment of Streisand fans and many independent observers, she was overlooked as both an actress and a director.

Snubbed by Hollywood, she again disappeared from the big screen until she returned in the intense drama *Nuts* (1987) and was again denied an Oscar nomination to the dismay of her legion of fans.

Despite the infrequency of her film appearances during the 1980s, her star power is such that she will undoubtedly continue to be a force in the movies.

STROHEIM, ERICH VON (1885–1957) A director, actor, screenwriter, set designer, costume designer, and notorious spendthrift, he was reputed to be the most extravagant artist in Hollywood, having spent enormous amounts attending to the minutest details in his movies, (such as historically accurate underwear worn by soldiers in *Foolish Wives,* 1922). His saving grace as a director, however, was his extravagance of talent, enabling him to grace his films with a strong visual flair that few other silent film directors could match.

Erich von Stroheim became "The Man You Love to Hate" by playing autocratic Prussian officers in films from World War I to the 1950s. His lasting fame, however, came as a director during the silent era when he made a series of evermore elaborate and expensive movies. Photo courtesy of The Siegel Collection.

Von Stroheim was also a talented, if limited, actor who specialized in playing arrogant Prussian military types.

He claimed that he was born Erich Oswald Hans Carl Stroheim von Nordenwald, but his background was not quite as blue-blooded as he purported. He was, nonetheless, the son of a former officer in the Austrian army who had squandered his wife's inheritance in bad business deals. The family lived well thanks only to the charity of von Stroheim's uncle, who held a high position in the government. Von Stroheim, himself, was a lieutenant in the Austrian army and saw three months of active duty in World War I before being forced to resign his commission due to his wild spending and inability to pay his debts. (Von Stroheim's profligacy with money evidently was a problem long before he began making movies.) His uncle offered to pay the young man's debts on condition that von Stroheim be banished to America.

Von Stroheim arrived in New York when he was twenty-four years old. He had no skills except as a soldier and a gentleman, which promptly landed him a succession of jobs that included wrapping packages at a department store, selling dresses, working as a handyman, and hitting the road as a flypaper salesman. He had little luck in his early years in America, but his short-lived marriage to a wealthy suffragette, Dr. Margaret Knox, was instrumental in giving von Stroheim the tools he needed to help himself. She improved his use of English and renewed his confidence.

After the marriage ended, von Stroheim put on a one-act play in Los Angeles that failed miserably, but one of his actors suggested that he try to get into the movies. And he did, wandering over to the location where D. W. Griffith was shooting *The Birth of a Nation* (1915). Von Stroheim picked up a job as a stuntman/extra and can be seen in his movie debut as a black soldier who is hit by a bullet on a rooftop and falls eighteen feet to the ground.

He went on to become one of Griffith's assistant directors on *Intolerance* (1916), and during World War I built his acting career by playing tyrannical Prussian officers. By the time he appeared in Griffith's *Hearts of the World* (1918), he was billed as "The Man You Love to Hate."

On the strength of his new image and growing experience in the film business, he talked Carl Laemmle of Universal Pictures *(q.v.)* into bankrolling his story idea for *Blind Husbands* (1918), telling the film executive it would cost $10,000 to make the movie if von Stroheim could both direct and star in it. Final production costs were almost $100,000, but the movie was a hit and it easily earned back its expenses.

Now a director of note, von Stroheim went on to make *The Devil's Passkey* (1919), *Foolish Wives* (1921), and *Merry-Go-Round* (1922), all of which were roundly praised for their attention to detail, strong visual sense, and sophisticated content. By this time, von Stroheim was deeply involved in every aspect of his films: writing the scripts, designing the sets, costuming the actors, directing, and finally editing his films. But he rarely had the last edit because his movies were far too long. For instance, *Foolish Wives* was originally thirty-two reels in length. It was finally edited down to a fourteen-reel feature by the studio.

But that was nothing compared to *Greed* (1924), the film for which von Stroheim became famous. Based on Frank Norris's novel, *McTeague,* von Stroheim's film ballooned into a forty-two-reel epic that would have run nearly eight hours. He cut it to twenty-four reels but would make no further edits himself. Director Rex Ingram cut it to eighteen reels, and it was later released by MGM in a somewhat confusing ten-reel version. Even so, the film's power was overwhelming. Unfortunately, the movie cost $750,000 to make and it barely broke even. Some who saw the original version of this tale of avarice called it the cinema's greatest masterpiece. There are those who say that the original footage still exists in the deep recesses of an MGM vault.

Greed, which starred ZaSu Pitts and Jean Hersholt, chronicled the disintegration of human values caused by the lust for wealth. Certain sequences in the film were tinted yellow (to represent gold), and the movie's climax was shot during the summer in Death Valley for both the realistic effect it had on the actors and for its symbolic overtones.

Based on the critical success of *Greed,* von Stroheim was allowed to direct another movie at MGM, although this time under strict limitations. He made *The Merry Widow* (1925), a critical and commercial success, and then *The Wedding March* (1926) and *The Honeymoon* (1928 in Europe; it was never released in the U.S.), which were actually two halves of the same film.

No one denied von Stroheim's ability as a director, but he simply was becoming too expensive to employ. He took too long to make his films, and their budgets were staggering. Just the same, Gloria Swanson sought him out. She was seeking a sophisticated continental touch for her independently produced film *Queen Kelly* (1928). Her timing was terrible; just as sound was coming into vogue, von Stroheim spent a staggering $600,000 on a silent film. Swanson fired him and then spent another $200,000 of her own money to salvage the movie, but *Queen Kelly* became a major financial disaster.

His directorial career a shambles as the silent era ended, von Stroheim spent the rest of his life working as an actor, hoping to someday direct again. He starred as a ventriloquist in *The Great Gabbo* (1929) and as a mad movie director in *The Lost Squadron* (1932), being well received in these early films. But he soon became typecast as the officious Prussian soldier in both American and European productions such as *Grand Illusion* (1937) and *Five Graves to Cairo* (1943). He also was involved in the writing of screenplays for a number of movies, including *The Emperor's Candlesticks* (1936) and *The Devil Doll* (1936).

But von Stroheim never directed again. In a final irony, he played a former silent film director reduced to being a chauffeur for the once-great silent screen actress Norma Desmond (played by Gloria Swanson) in *Sunset Boulevard* (1950).

Von Stroheim made his last film appearance in the French film *La Madone des Sleepings* (1955). The complex and fascinating von Stroheim died two years later in Paris.

See also: Swanson, Gloria

STUDIO SYSTEM A term that refers to the institutionalized commercial and artistic practices that governed the American film industry between the years

1930 and 1949. During this two-decade period, the film industry was consolidated into eight major companies, known within the film community as The Big Five and The Little Three. The Big Five included Warner Bros., Paramount, MGM, RKO, and Twentieth Century-Fox. The Little Three were Universal, United Artists, and Columbia. Constituting a monopoly, these eight companies were able to establish a homogeneous system—the studio system—that controlled how films were made, who made them, who starred in them, and what the content of those films would be.

Thomas Edison, the inventor of the motion picture, made a bold attempt to monopolize the film industry during the second decade of the twentieth century, but the eight major film companies that emerged out of the talkie revolution succeeded where Edison failed.

The Big Five were fully integrated companies, controlling all aspects of the film industry within their corporate organization, including the creation, distribution, and exhibition of their own films. The Little Three had modest impact in the area of exhibition (e.g., they either didn't own any theaters or owned relatively few, but they all had strong, international distribution networks).

The Big Five owned the most prestigious theaters, in the best locations, in the most populous areas of the country, skimming off the greatest percentage of profits. According to Douglas Gomery in his informative book, *The Hollywood Studio System*, the Big Five controlled "approximately 25 percent of the total seats in U.S. theaters. Collectively, the majors controlled more than 70 percent of all the first-run theaters in the ninety-two largest cities in the U.S."

Owning theaters was the ultimate key to success during the studio system years. Being a fully integrated company virtually guaranteed success as long as audiences continued going to the movies because the eight majors were the only game in town. In fact, the Big Five, in true monopolistic fashion, all profited when any one of the studios had a hit. The reason for this was the generally unknown fact that the studios didn't directly compete against each other in terms of exhibition; they each owned most of their theaters in different areas of the country and, therefore, if one studio had a hit, it was rented to their competitors in other parts of the country and both parties split the profits. It was a no-lose situation, except in instances where the producing company made a film that no one wanted to see. But even those films were guaranteed significant distribution within the theater circuits owned by their own studio and the hungry independent rural and small neighborhood theaters that depended on the eight majors to supply them with product.

Borrowing from the Henry Ford method of building automobiles, the studio system employed an assembly line approach to filmmaking. Rigidly compartmentalized, the film studios made popular art by organizing their creative staffs (writers, directors, actors, etc.) to move from one movie to the next without being fully involved with the entire process. Films were often treated as product rather than personal visions because there was rarely one person who could infuse his personality into a project from start to finish.

The personalities who ultimately dominated during the years of the studio system were the movie moguls whose tastes and attitudes were reflected in the films that they made. For instance, Darryl F. Zanuck, head of production at Twentieth Century-Fox, was a liberal with a social conscience, which was evident by his productions of such films as *Gentlemen's Agreement* (1947) and *Pinky* (1949).

The moguls, men like Jack L. Warner, Harry Cohn, and Louis B. Mayer, ran their studios as if they were emperors—and to some extent they were. For example, the most infamous aspect of the studio system was the long-term service contract (usually seven years) by which actors were often bound as if they were indentured servants to their studio, working at salaries far below their worth. Robert Taylor, for instance, was starring in major motion pictures during the early part of his career while earning a paltry $35 per week. Besides the issue of salary, the moguls also declared who would appear in what movie, often forcing actors to perform in films they thought were atrocious and/or bad for their careers. There were a number of celebrated cases of stars, such as Bette Davis and James Cagney, going on suspension rather than act in movies they hated.

The end of the studio system came when the Big Five were forced by the government, in an antitrust action in 1949, to sell their theaters, depriving them of their guaranteed exhibition network as well as their greatest real estate assets. Independent filmmakers could finally get significant distribution and exhibition, opening the door to genuine competition. Stars began setting up their own production companies, using the studios to produce and distribute their films but controlling their own projects. Wounded, and no longer a true monopoly, the studio system was finally done in by television, which siphoned off millions of viewers during the 1950s.

Ironically, for all the complaints aimed at the studio system, it was during this era that Hollywood made the vast majority of its greatest films, and many—even those who suffered through it—look back at those times with great fondness.

STUNTMEN The men and women who perform dangerous physical feats in motion pictures (usually doubling for actors). During the early silent era, before actors became highly paid stars, performers almost always had to perform their own stunts. Later, as stars became valuable commodities, studios sought to avoid risking actors' health and good looks and hired stunt-men to undertake perilous tasks in the stars' place. Theirs was not, however, a highly regarded profession. As stunt flyer Dick Grace wrote in his 1930 memoir, *The Squadron of Death*, "The stars think the stuntman is just a little above an extra. The producers think he is a little below a moron. The public has never heard of him."

Stunts and stuntmen may be in constant use in today's films, but there was a veritable stunt craze in the 1920s. Buster Keaton, Harold Lloyd, and Douglas Fairbanks set a standard for their own elaborate stuntwork, while other stars happily allowed stuntmen to double for them. A number of stuntmen were killed and injured during this era. Among the earlier stuntmen of this time period were "Suicide" Buddy Mason, Eddie Polo, and Richard Talmadge. The first female stuntperson was Helen Gibson, who later became a star (of serials) in her own right.

Yakima Canutt *(q.v.)*, the most famous stuntman of them all, pioneered safer stuntwork during the 1930s. As a result of his efforts and the exploits of many others, stunt people gained a certain grudging respect from directors, stars, and producers.

Stuntwork in the 1930s and 1940s was part and parcel of aviation films, gangster movies, war films, and westerns. But in the 1950s and early 1960s, as epics came into vogue, the stuntmen became ever more important in films such as *Ivanhoe* (1953), *Ben-Hur* (1959), and *Spartacus* (1960). Later, in the car crash era of *Bullitt* (1968) and *The French Connection* (1971), yet a new need for experienced stuntmen arose.

Movie stunts have become so elaborate and have drawn so much attention in recent decades with films such as *The Blues Brothers* (1980) and *Raiders of the Lost Ark* (1981) that the stuntman has finally been recognized by the public as a significant movie professional. It is no coincidence, therefore, that Hal Needham (a former stuntman himself) directed a hit film about stuntmen called *Hooper* (1978), and Richard Rush finally found distribution for his highly regarded Oscar-nominated film *The Stunt Man* (1980).

As a general rule, most stuntmen specialize in areas as diverse as motorcycles, antique planes, high falls from buildings, fire, horse falls, etc. They are paid on the basis of the difficulty and risk of danger involved in their stunts. The Hollywood Stuntmen Association represents the roughly one hundred fearless specialists in this close-knit community.

STURGES, PRESTON (1898–1959) He was *the* comedy writer-director of the 1940s despite the fact that all of his good work was done in the first half of the decade. His scripts were famous for their snappy repartee and his films for a frantic, almost breathless, pace that never let up. Sturges' humor could be savagely

Writer-director Preston Sturges is seen here instructing Veronica Lake for her role in *Sullivan's Travels* (1941), which also starred Joel McCrea. The film was just one of Sturges' remarkable string of satiric comedy hits during the first half of the 1940s. Photo courtesy of Movie Star News.

satirical, usually undercutting Hollywood conventions and expectations. If the director sometimes lacked the courage of his convictions and often gave his satires illogical happy endings, the mighty leaps of craft required to arrive at these rose-colored climaxes were often so ingenious that they, too, brought laughter and delight.

Born Edmond P. Biden to an extremely wealthy American family, he was largely educated abroad in France, Switzerland, and Germany. Both before and after serving a volunteer stint as a flyer in the Army Air Corps during World War I, he worked for his mother's cosmetics company, where he invented a kiss-proof lipstick. Like Howard Hughes, Sturges was a tinkerer, inventor, and airplane nut. And, like Hughes, he was drawn to the movies.

While recuperating from an operation to remove his appendix, this twentieth-century renaissance man wrote several plays, one of which became the 1929 Broadway hit comedy *Strictly Dishonorable*, later turning up in two movie versions, the first in 1931 and the second in 1951. Sturges' quick wit and colorful language were ideal for the movies and he was soon writing dialogue for such films as *The Big Pond* (1930) and *Fast and Loose* (1930). As the 1930s progressed, he created original screenplays for films including *The Power and the Glory* (1933), *Diamond Jim* (1935), *Easy Living* (1937), *If I Were King* (1938), and *Remember the Night* (1940).

Unhappy with the way his screenplays were being directed, however, Sturges appealed to Paramount to let him direct his own work. Up until then, the studios held to a strict division between writers and directors. But Paramount, traditionally one of the more liberal studios, gave Sturges his chance, leading the way for future writer-directors of the caliber of John Huston and Billy Wilder.

Sturges' debut as a writer-director was *The Great McGinty* (1940), the sleeper hit of the year. It satirized American politics by presenting a hobo turned governor, who makes it to the top through graft and corruption only to fall from grace when he turns honest. It was Frank Capra gone haywire, and audiences loved it. So did the critics. And the Academy of Motion Picture Arts and Sciences rewarded Sturges with a Best Screenplay Oscar for his iconoclastic effort.

Sturges followed that auspicious beginning with a stunning string of six more witty and piercing comedy hits. All of them poked fun at some aspect of society: advertising and American gullibility in *Christmas in July* (1940), intellectual snobbery in *The Lady Eve* (1941), pretentiousness in Hollywood in *Sullivan's Travels* (1941), marriage and sex in *The Palm Beach Story* (1942), small town Americana and sex in *The Miracle of Morgan's Creek* (1944), and momism and hero-worship in *Hail the Conquering Hero* (1944).

Sturges' films were identifiable not only from their rat-a-tat verbal style and clever content, but also from his choice of actors. There was an informal Sturges stock company of performers who consistently showed up in his movies, most notably William Demarest, Franklin Pangborn, Jimmy Conlin, Robert Greig, Edgar Kennedy, and Eric Blore.

As quickly as he emerged on the directorial scene, Sturges submerged even faster. After the uncharacteristicly turgid *The Great Moment* (1944), he agreed to make movies in association with Howard Hughes whom he so resembled. The arrangement proved unworkable and Sturges limped through the next few years writing, directing, and producing movies that lacked the spark of his previous work. The best of those films was the ambitious but flawed *Mad Wednesday* (1947), a movie designed to resurrect the comedy career of silent screen great Harold Lloyd, but which flopped at the box office. *Unfaithfully Yours* (1948) followed, and then *The Beautiful Blonde From Bashful Bend* (1949), neither proving to be major successes, although the former was a modest hit (remade in 1984 with Dudley Moore in the Rex Harrison role).

Sturges had had enough of Hughes by the end of the 1940s and removed himself to Europe, where he eventually made his last movie, the pallid *The French They Are a Funny Race* (1955). He died shortly thereafter. *See also:* writer-directors

SUBJECTIVE CAMERA Otherwise known as a "point of view" (or POV) shot, the camera technique which allows audiences to see a film's action as though through the eyes of one of its characters, and not from the impersonal vantage point of a merely observant camera angle.

The language of film easily allows for a flow between the omniscient point of view and the subjective camera and most films are filled with a great many short, subjective camera shots. For instance, if a character in a gangster film must reach for a gun on the floor, the camera may catch the character surreptitiously glancing downward, and then cut to the gun (from the hero's POV) as it lies underneath a table.

Less common are long subjective camera scenes, but one of the most memorable occurs in the Jerry Lewis comedy *The Nutty Professor* (1963). In this film, Lewis plays a Jekyll-and-Hyde character who alternates between nerdy professor and hip swinger, Buddy Love. When the transformation occurs a subjective camera angle takes over for several minutes of screen time. While the camera/Lewis/Love "walks" through the streets to a nightclub, characters turn and gawk right into the lens (i.e., at the audience).

Subjective camera was used almost exclusively in *Dark Passage* (1947) and entirely in *Lady in the Lake* (1946). In *Dark Passage*, directed by Delmar Daves, Humphrey Bogart is swathed in bandages after his face is changed through plastic surgery, The audience sees most of the film through the eye holes in his bandages until the bandages finally come off near the end of the movie. Robert Montgomery (*q.v.*), who both directed and starred in *Lady in the Lake,* shot the entire film through the eyes of the movie's hero, Philip Marlowe. Montgomery was only seen when the hero looked in a mirror. Montgomery's film technique was the visual equivalent of the first person narrative in literature.

SULLAVAN, MARGARET (1911–1960) An actress who starred in only sixteen films yet made a lasting impression as a resourceful performer blessed with grace, humor, and intelligence.

Born Margaret Brooke, she began her acting career with the Baltimore University Players and then joined the soon-to-be-famous University Players that featured the talents of Joshua Logan, Jimmy Stewart, and Henry Fonda. She married Fonda, who was the first of her four husbands.

Sullavan made her Broadway debut in 1931 in *A*

Modern Virgin, continuing on the New York stage until she was offered the lead role in a Universal film, *Only Yesterday* (1933). She was not Universal's first choice for the film, however, getting the nod only after both Claudette Colbert and Irene Dunne turned it down. But Sullavan shined, and her Hollywood career was launched.

Sullavan worked with many of the film industry's best directors. For instance, she starred in Frank Borzage's *Little Man, What Now?* (1934) and *Three Comrades* (1938) and Ernst Lubitsch's *The Shop Around the Corner* (1940). She also starred in William Wyler's *The Good Fairy* (1935) and then married the director.

Even when she wasn't working with top directors, Sullavan's performances often lifted her films, as evidenced by her version of the oft-filmed *Back Street* (1941), which is considered the pick of the litter, and her tough-minded playing in *Cry Havoc* (1943), which helped that movie about World War II nurses soar above the level of cliché.

Sullavan was reputedly a difficult and temperamental actress; not being terribly fond of Hollywood, she often left the movie capital to return to the stage. It was during such a sojourn that she had a hit with the Broadway version of *Stage Door* during the latter half of the 1930s. It was also during this time that Leland Hayward, her third husband, arranged for her to go back to Hollywood. She made movies for another five years and then returned once again to the stage. She made but one more trip west to make *No Sad Songs for Me* (1950) and then worked exclusively on the stage.

Unbeknownst to most, Sullavan suffered from an increasingly severe hearing loss. By the late 1950s, she could only act by lip-reading. Though married to her fourth husband, a successful businessman, she continued to work. While on tour with *Sweet Love Remember'd,* she took an overdose of sleeping pills and died on New Year's Day, 1960.

Her daughter with Leland Hayward, Brooke Hayward, described the events of her mother's life in the best-selling memoir *Haywire.*

SURTEES, ROBERT & BRUCE Father and son cinematographers, respectively, who have each developed reputations as experts in their field.

Robert Surtees (1906–1985) served his apprenticeship under one of the greatest of all cinematographers, Gregg Toland *(q.v.),* eventually becoming a master of color photography. He first began working in Hollywood in 1927, emerging as a full-fledged director of photography in the mid-1940s with such films as *Thirty Seconds Over Tokyo* (1944) and *Our Vines Have Tender Grapes* (1945). His ability with color cinematography was duly noticed by the Academy of Motion Picture Arts and Sciences in 1950 when he was awarded an Oscar for his work on *King Solomon's Mines* (1950). He would

eventually receive two more Oscars, one each for *The Bad and the Beautiful* (1952) and *Ben-Hur* (1959).

After his triumph with *Ben-Hur,* Surtees was often assigned other big-budget movies, such as *Mutiny on the Bounty* (1962) and *Doctor Doolittle* (1967), but his best work during the 1960s and 1970s was done for smaller movies with relatively inexperienced directors who gave him more latitude to create a unique visual style. For instance, he was the cinematographer for Mike Nichols' smash hit *The Graduate* (1967) and Peter Bogdanovich's black-and-white masterpiece *The Last Picture Show* (1971).

Ever dependable and proficient at his craft, Surtees continued to work well into the 1970s, providing the cinematography for major motion pictures such as *The Sting* (1973), *A Star is Born* (1976), *The Turning Point* (1977), and *Same Time, Next Year* (1978).

Meanwhile, Robert's son, Bruce, followed in his father's footsteps, becoming a much-admired cinematographer of action films, his career closely associated with that of Clint Eastwood. Roughly one-third of his films have either starred Eastwood and/or were directed by the actor. The younger Surtees began his career providing the cinematography for Eastwood's most famous film, *Dirty Harry* (1971), as well as the actor's directorial debut, *Play Misty For Me* (1971). Other collaborations with Eastwood have included *High Plains Drifter* (1972), *The Outlaw Josey Wales* (1976), *Escape From Alcatraz* (1979), *Firefox* (1982), *Sudden Impact* (1983), *Honky Tonk Man* (1983), *Tightrope* (1984), and *Pale Rider* (1985).

While Bruce Surtees was justifiably given an Oscar for his cinematography for *Lenny* (1974), one of his greatest unsung achievements was his work on John Milius' underappreciated masterpiece *Big Wednesday* (1978). In addition, Surtees has lent his considerable skills to a number of visually adventurous films such as *Night Moves* (1975), *Leadbelly* (1976), and *White Dog* (1982). He was also the cinematographer of such blockbuster hits as *Risky Business* (1983) and *Beverly Hills Cop* (1984). His more recent work includes the kindly reviewed *Back to the Beach* (1987) and *License to Drive* (1988).

SUTHERLAND, DONALD (1934–) A hard-working actor who popped up in roles small and large in a great many movies, particularly during the 1970s. Tall and gaunt, Sutherland is hardly the leading man type, yet his relatively plain features have kept him from being typecast, and he has played leads in a number of important movies, showing a depth of talent and sensitivity.

Born and raised in Canada, Sutherland's first brush with show business came when he worked as a D.J. for a Nova Scotia radio station at the tender age of fourteen. He began acting while attending the University of Toronto and continued to learn his craft at the London Academy of Music and Dramatic Art.

After a short, modest stage career in England, he made his film debut in an Italian horror movie, *Castle of the Living Dead* (1964). He soon began appearing frequently in supporting roles in U.S. and British co-productions of varying quality, the best of these being *The Bedford Incident* (1965) and *The Dirty Dozen* (1967). His big break came when he costarred with Elliot Gould in Robert Altman's surprise hit of 1969, *M★A★S★H*. Sutherland played the character Hawkeye Pierce, who was later portrayed in the "M★A★S★H" TV series by Alan Alda. Sutherland's popularity soared, and he began starring regularly in an interesting mix of quirky productions (e.g., *Alex in Wonderland,* 1970, and *Little Murders,* 1971), and mainstream films (e.g., *Kelly's Heroes,* 1970, and *Klute,* 1971).

After working with Jane Fonda in *Klute,* Sutherland joined her in the antiwar movement, protesting American involvement in Vietnam through such films as *F.T.A.* (1972), in which he not only appeared, but also coproduced, codirected, and coscripted.

After a number of box office failures, he tried, without success, to recreate the magic of *M★A★S★H* with *S★P★Y★S* (1974). His career continued to slowly unravel during the rest of the 1970s due to a combination of overexposure (he made cameo appearances in a seemingly endless round of movies that featured him heavily in their promotion) and starring roles in poor, low-budget Canadian movies that received little distribution in the U.S.

He was kept afloat during the mid-1970s thanks to three films that greatly enhanced his reputation, the critically acclaimed *Day of the Locust* (1975), Bernardo Bertolucci's *1900* (1976), and *Casanova* (1976), in the title role of Federico Fellini's film. Unfortunately, Sutherland had only one bona fide commercial hit in the decade after *Klute, Invasion of the Body Snatchers* (1978).

Sutherland began the 1980s by giving what many consider the best performance of his career as the father in the Robert Redford-directed Oscar-winning *Ordinary People* (1980). Sutherland went on to score another hit with the thriller *Eye of the Needle* (1981), but he has had few hits since and has been seen mostly in supporting roles in mainstream films such as *Max Dugan Returns* (1983) and *Lock Up* (1989), and leads in low-budget affairs such as *Wolf at the Door* (1987) and *Lost Angels* (1989).

His son, Kiefer Sutherland, has emerged as a hot new star in films such as *The Lost Boys* (1987), *1969* (1988), *Young Guns* (1988), and *Renegades* (1989). And the younger Sutherland not only looks a great deal like his father, he also seems to work almost as much as his dad in his heyday.

SWANSON, GLORIA (1897–1983) An actress who was among the great silent screen personalities of the 1920s.

Besides her substantial popularity with film fans, she held sway as an important fashion and style trendsetter. And on top of all that, she was also an excellent actress, effective in both sophisticated sex comedies and straight dramas. Though most of her career was spent in silent films, she is best known to modern audiences for her Best Actress Oscar-nominated performance as Norma Desmond in *Sunset Boulevard* (1950). It was her third such nomination, the other two coming in the late 1920s for performances in *Sadie Thompson* (1928) and *The Trespasser* (1929).

Born Gloria Josephine Mae Swenson, she was a young store clerk in Chicago when, by chance, she tagged along with her aunt to see how films were made at the local Essanay Studio in 1913. Spotted as a photogenic young beauty, she was used as an extra and her career slowly began. Two years later, she received her first credit for *The Fable of Elvira and Farina and the Meal Ticket* (1915). She worked in a number of Wallace Beery films in the mid-1910s, and the two actors were married in 1916, a union that lasted until 1919. It was to be the first of her six marriages.

As soon as she and Beery were married, they left Chicago for Hollywood. She went to work for Mack Sennett, starring with Bobby Vernon in a string of approximately ten light romantic comedies, rather than the slapstick for which Sennett was otherwise known. Her parting with Sennett came when, according to Swanson, "He wanted to make me a second Mabel Normand. I told him I didn't want to be a second anybody, so he tore my contract up." It turned out to be a lucky break for her, because she went on to star in six Cecil B. DeMille movies that turned her into a major star.

By the middle of the 1920s, Swanson was among the highest paid actresses in Hollywood. One of the reasons for her success was that she learned the modern art of film acting before her contemporaries, managing to underplay for the camera. She thereby brought a subtlety to her work that set her apart from other silent screen performers.

In addition, by most accounts, Swanson was among the first movie stars to fully comprehend how important publicity was to a career. It was no accident that she actively and consciously manipulated the press to her own advantage, going so far as to marry the marquis de la Falaise de la Coudraye while she was making a movie in France in order to enhance her image.

In 1926, she joined forces with Joseph P. Kennedy (who was reputed to be her lover) in a production arrangement with United Artists. It was not a prudent move. After a couple of modest flops, she invested more than $200,000 of her own money in *Queen Kelly* (1928) after she fired its director, Erich von Stroheim, who had already poured more than $600,000 into the project in one of his more outlandish spending sprees. Her efforts to save the film failed, and it never opened in America. She reportedly didn't fully pay back all her debts on that movie until 1950.

Meanwhile, the coming of sound was yet another threat to Swanson's career. She bounced back with hits in *Sadie Thompson* and *The Trespasser*, the latter being her first talkie, in which she even sang ("Love, Your Magic Spell Is Everywhere"). It seemed as if she was primed for a long career in the sound era. But it was not to be. Despite her skills as an actress and a perfectly fine voice, audiences began to desert her. Her descent came terribly fast, aided, in part, by her stubborn insistence on producing her own movies, which kept flopping. By 1934, she had starred in what appeared to be her last film, *Music in the Air*.

She spent the rest of the 1930s working in the theater, making an ill-advised film comeback in 1941 with *Father Takes a Wife*. Swanson was once again off the big screen for another nine years before she received her most famous role as Norma Desmond. She was not, however, the first choice for the part. In fact, she was the fourth! Those who were offered the role before her (and who turned it down) included Mary Pickford, Mae West, and Norma Shearer. Despite winning an Oscar nomination, the role didn't bring Swanson a new career. A few films followed over the next several decades, the last of them being a not insignificant role in *Airport 1975* (1974).

The ever-energetic Miss Swanson then embarked on a new career as a sculptress; her works were exhibited in a London gallery in 1979. When she died four years later, one of her famous lines in *Sunset Boulevard* seemed to jog the memory: "I'm still big; it's the pictures that got small."

SWASHBUCKLERS   Adventure films that are usually set in exotic locales and that feature flamboyant swordplay, acrobatic feats, and heroic derring-do. The genre has had limited success because there are relatively few actors who can carry such a film. It requires genuine panache, sex appeal, and enormous athletic ability, not to mention a good script and a lavish budget.

The first and foremost swashbuckling star was Douglas Fairbanks, who created the genre in 1920 with his exuberant version of *The Mark of Zorro*. His name became synonymous with swashbucklers during the rest of the 1920s when he starred in such hugely popular films as *The Three Musketeers* (1921), *Robin Hood* (1922), *The Thief of Bagdad* (1924), *The Black Pirate* (1926), and *The Iron Mask* (1928). Fairbanks set the standard that very few would meet in the decades to follow.

The coming of sound put a damper on the swashbuckler. The requirements of the new sound equipment kept the actors and the action static for several years, and by then more contemporary films had come into vogue. Besides, who was willing to try and fill the shoes of Fairbanks? Warner Bros. gambled on British actor Robert Donat as the next great swashbuckler and signed him up to star in the big-budget buccaneer movie *Captain Blood* (1935), but the actor backed out at the last moment. In desperation, the studio rushed one of their new, lowly contract players into the role—Errol Flynn.

Flynn took on the mantle of Fairbanks and became the next great swashbuckling hero, having the distinction of starring in the only two swashbucklers to be nominated for Best Picture Oscars, *Captain Blood* (1935) and *The Adventures of Robin Hood* (1938). He went on to star in such other swashbucklers as *The Sea Hawk* (1940), and during his years of decline, *Adventures of Don Juan* (1949), *Adventures of Captain Fabian* (1951), and *The Master of Ballantrae* (1953). Flynn's success in the 1930s opened the door to other swashbuckling heroes, including Ronald Colman, Louis Hayward, Tyrone Power, and Douglas Fairbanks, Jr.

Colman didn't leap around the set like a Fairbanks or a Flynn, but he held his own in the swordplay department and he certainly had plenty of sex appeal, which was much in evidence in such films as *Under Two Flags* (1936) and *The Prisoner of Zenda* (1937). Hayward had the dash of Flynn but not the charm, yet he was quite successful in *The Man in the Iron Mask* (1939), *The Son of Monte Cristo* (1940), and *The Return of Monte Cristo* (1946). Pretty boy Tyrone Power, possessed of a somewhat shy temperament, seemed an unlikely brash hero, but he gave strong performances in the remakes of *The Mark of Zorro* (1940) and *Blood and Sand* (1941). It was Douglas Fairbanks, Jr., however, who brought a sense of déjà vu to the movies, showing himself to be the spitting image of his swashbuckling father with splendid performances in *The Corsican Brothers* (1941), *Sinbad the Sailor* (1947), which was easily the best swashbuckling film of the 1940s, and *The Exile* (1947).

The rise of television in the late 1940s and early 1950s made swashbucklers more important to the studios. Exotic, big-budget films with sweep and style could not be duplicated by the small-screen competition. But just when grand heroes were needed, the actors who might have filled the bill were little in evidence. At first, the best the movies could come up with were pallid imitations of Fairbanks and Flynn in the form of Cornel Wilde, who made such films as *At Sword's Point* (1952), and Tony Curtis, who began his career as a swashbuckler in such mediocrities as *The Prince Who Was a Thief* (1951), *Son of Ali Baba* (1952), and *The Purple Mask* (1955).

There was only one great swashbuckler during the 1950s, Burt Lancaster, and he made far too few films in the genre to satisfy those who appreciated such movies. He was the closest of all the swashbuckling stars to Douglas Fairbanks. His magnificently lithe body, acrobatic skills, charm, sex appeal, and enormous energy made *The Flame and the Arrow* (1950) and *The*

Crimson Pirate (1952) the best swashbucklers of the 1950s.

Unfortunately, the swashbuckler went into decline in the later 1950s and has rarely resurfaced. There was a disappointing attempt to resurrect the genre with the poorly written and far too obviously titled *Swashbuckler* (1976); it was a flop with both the critics and with audiences.

The stars of today seem generally ill-suited to the swashbuckler. For instance, one can hardly imagine Tom Cruise in a swordfight with, let us say, Charlie Sheen. Among current actors, only Kevin Kline has shown promise as a swashbuckler in his limited film career, most notably in *The Pirates of Penzance* (1983). Kline is a dashing, charming, physical actor, and he even looks something like Errol Flynn.

See also: Captain Blood; Colman, Ronald; Curtis, Tony; Fairbanks, Douglas; Flynn, Errol; Lancaster, Burt; Power, Tyrone

SWEET, BLANCHE (1895–1986) A popular silent screen actress whose stage name misleadingly suggests a frail, goody-two-shoes personality. Unlike the early Lillian Gish and Mary Pickford, Blanche Sweet played robust female leads; she was just as likely to save the day as any hero.

Born Daphne Wayne to a show business family, the actress was a ten-year veteran of the stage when she began acting in front of a camera at the age of fourteen. Miss Sweet had the good fortune to work with D. W. Griffith during the first years of her career, and her acting can be seen in such important early Giffith works as *A Corner in Wheat* (1909), *The Lonedale Operator* (1910), and *Judith of Bethulia* (1914). After leaving Griffith in 1915, she went on to star in more romantic and sexier vehicles such as *A Woman of Pleasure* (1919), *Anna Christie* (1923), and *Why Women Love* (1925).

Miss Sweet starred in well over one hundred movies, but her career began to fade even before the advent of the sound era. She appeared in three minor talkies without making a ripple at the box office. Her movie career at an end, she continued in show business as she had before, working in vaudeville and in touring theater companies. After a twenty-nine year absence from the movies, Miss Sweet graced the big screen one last time in a cameo appearance in Danny Kaye's *The Five Pennies* (1959).

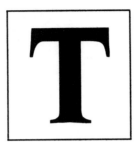

TAKE A single uninterrupted scene, or part of a scene, that is recorded on film. A take may be as short as a fraction of a second or as long as the camera rolls before running out of film (the latter type of take being used by Alfred Hitchcock in *Rope*, 1948). Takes are often repeated, and for several reasons, the most common being that the director desires a choice among the best performances given by the actor(s). It is not uncommon for there to be anywhere from two or three to twenty takes of a single shot. Each take is numbered, the number appearing on the slate held in front of the camera when the film begins to roll.

TARZAN FILMS The character Tarzan, a white man raised in the African jungle by apes, was created by Edgar Rice Burroughs in 1913 and was featured in a series of novels. As early as 1918, Burroughs' popular character was adapted to the silent screen in *Tarzan of the Apes*, starring Elmo Lincoln. There hasn't been a decade since without a Tarzan film (or films). The constant appeal of Tarzan movies is undoubtedly due to audience interest in their representation of the clash of modern values (or the lack of them) and a primitive ethos. It is an appealing, romantic concept that somewhere in the jungle there lives a man who is at one with nature, who understands and can communicate with wild animals, and who (in his isolation from civilization) is incapable of lying, cheating, or stealing. In addition, the Tarzan films have always had a sexual dimension, with the scantily clad hero and heroine (Jane).

From the silent era to the present, there have been more than forty Tarzan feature films made with a total of eighteen different actors playing the lead role. During the silent era there were six different screen Tarzans, but Elmo Lincoln was the best known among them. Another dozen actors played Tarzan during the sound era, and champion swimmer Johnny Weismuller *(q.v.)* emerged in *Tarzan, the Ape Man* (1932) as the modern epitome of our jungle hero.

Weismuller starred in a dozen Tarzan adventures, the first half of them for MGM (with Maureen O'Sullivan as Jane), and the second half for RKO (with Brenda Joyce as Jane). The MGM films are, for the most part, the better Tarzan movies; they were entertaining films made with large budgets, high production values, and reasonably intelligent scripts.

Even as MGM made the Weismuller Tarzans, other studios took advantage of the popularity of the character, making their own films with the likes of Buster Crabbe *(q.v.)* and others in the title role. But Weismuller was still the king of the jungle. And he remained so until 1948 when he grew too old to swing from vine to vine. He was replaced in turn by Lex Barker, Gordon Scott, Denny Miller, Jock Mahoney, Mike Henry, Ron Ely, Miles O'Keeffe, and Christopher Lambert.

Most of the Tarzan films of the next several decades (including the "Tarzan" TV series) made the title character a surprisingly articulate, educated man. The underlying appeal of Tarzan was becoming eroded. In 1981, sex pot Bo Derek starred as Jane in a controversial version of *Tarzan, the Ape Man*. The movie was a tongue-in-cheek sexual romp in the jungle. Some critics hated it, others were amused, but it did bring back the appeal of a primitive Tarzan. The film was followed by an English production, *Greystoke: The Legend of Tarzan, Lord of the Apes* (1984), a film that tried to be more faithful to the original Burroughs concept. The movie was surprisingly successful with both critics and audiences, proving yet again that the Tarzan formula has a powerful appeal.

TASHLIN, FRANK (1913–1972) A former cartoonist who established a reputation in the 1950s and early

1960s as an inventive writer-director of comedies, he is most closely associated with the films of Jerry Lewis, whom he directed in a great many hits. Tashlin had a gift for finding humor in the vulgar and had a special ability for turning human characters into caricatures. A specialist in comedy, Tashlin directed almost all of the major comedians of his era, including Bob Hope, Red Skelton, Dean Martin, Jerry Lewis, Danny Kaye, and even Doris Day.

Tashlin, like so many visual artists, was not a success in school, which he quit at the age of thirteen. He had no special career until he stumbled into the film business as a cartoonist in 1930, working on Paul Terry's Aesop's Film Fables series. He knocked about for another fifteen years, working at jobs ranging from gag man for Hal Roach to story editor for Walt Disney. He even left the film business for four years to write his own comic strip. In the mid-1940s he began writing comedy screenplays with a strong dash of whimsy, such as *One Touch of Venus* (1948), *The Paleface* (1948), *The Fuller Brush Man* (1948), and *Love Happy* (1949).

After having written scripts for comedians such as Bob Hope and Red Skelton, he was given the opportunity of directing them in his own scripts. His films were successful, his career reaching its peak during the latter half of the 1950s and early 1960s when he wrote, directed, and produced the classic *Will Success Spoil Rock Hunter?* (1957) as well as wrote and directed a string of highly successful Jerry Lewis solo films, among them *The Geisha Boy* (1958), *Cinderfella* (1960), and *The Disorderly Orderly* (1964).

Either comedy changed or Tashlin lost his touch, but in the mid-1960s, his films seemed exceedingly tired and lacking in his usual verve. He directed a couple of late Doris Day vehicles, *The Glass Bottom Boat* (1966) and *Caprice* (1967), without much flair, and his last film was the disastrous Bob Hope comedy *The Private Navy of Sgt. O'Farrell* (1968).

Tashlin died four years later, largely forgotten in the U.S., but hailed as an important comic director by French critics who appreciated his work with their idol, Jerry Lewis.

TAYLOR, ELIZABETH (1932–) A former child actress who became an adult superstar. Said for a time to be the most beautiful woman in the world, she has remained the last of the great stars to conduct her life in the glamorous style of old Hollywood. The voluptuous, violet-eyed Taylor has appeared in more than fifty films and has won two Best Actress Oscars in a career mostly limited to serious dramatic roles.

Born in England to American parents, she didn't return to the U.S. until just before the outbreak of war in Europe, whereupon her family settled in Los Angeles. Her father opened an art gallery in the ritzy Chateau Elysee Hotel, and several influential people in the movie

Elizabeth Taylor was presented to the public as a mature young woman when she was still a mere teenager. At the age of fifteen she was already being hailed as the most beautiful *woman* in the world. Photo courtesy of Movie Star News.

business who visited the gallery took notice of the young Taylor. Universal and MGM vied for her when she was ten years old, and Universal signed her and put her in one movie, *There's One Born Every Minute* (1942). She was dropped after the film, and the casting director at Universal was quoted as saying, "The kid has nothing" earning himself a dubious place in film history.

Taylor was always beautiful, even as a child, and she managed to get a second chance at MGM, which put her in a couple of Lassie movies and a few featured roles in such major productions as *Jane Eyre* (1944) and *Life with Father* (1947). But her most important childhood role was as the star of *National Velvet* (1944).

Taylor continued acting in adolescent roles throughout the 1940s, but she never went through that difficult young ingenue period that destroyed so many child actresses' careers. Taylor exhibited a very rapid physical growth, becoming a stunning young woman while still in her teens. In fact, she was courted by none other than billionaire Howard Hughes when she was just seventeen.

Taylor was still seventeen when she married her first husband, Nicky Hilton, heir to the Hilton Hotel chain. But even before the marriage she was playing older, more sophisticated parts, such as Robert Taylor's wife in *Conspirator* (1950), Van Johnson's love interest in *The Big Hangover* (1950), and the future wife in her biggest hit of the new decade, *Father of the Bride* (1950). She was no doubt happier with her fictional husband in the latter movie than she was with Nicky Hilton; the couple divorced mere months after marrying.

The 1950s was certainly Taylor's best decade in terms of quality films. The combination of good scripts, increasingly fine acting on her part, and her startling beauty made for a long list of memorable movies. Among Taylor's many triumphs during the decade were *A Place in the Sun* (1951), in which she began her long and passionate platonic relationship with actor Montgomery Clift, *The Last Time I Saw Paris* (1954), *Giant* (1956), *Raintree County* (1957), *Cat on a Hot Tin Roof* (1958), and *Suddenly Last Summer* (1959). She received Best Actress Academy Award nominations for the latter three.

During the 1950s Taylor became the focus of considerable publicity. After her marriage to Michael Wilding (1952–1957), she became Mrs. Mike Todd until Todd's tragic death in a plane crash one year later, bringing her the sympathy of millions of movie fans. That sympathy turned to sneers when she suddenly married Eddie Fisher in 1959, taking him away from the wholesome Debbie Reynolds. Ironically, Eddie Fisher had been the best man at her wedding to Todd, just as Debbie Reynolds had been her matron of honor. The affair made for great copy, but Taylor was saddled with the image of homewrecker.

In the meantime, she starred in the mediocre *Butterfield 8* (1960) and won an Oscar for her performance, though many suggest that she was really given the award in recognition for her past performances. In any event, her personal popularity was still exceedingly low until she came down with a rare form of pneumonia, requiring a tracheotomy in order to save her life. Finally, public opinion softened.

Taylor's most famous film, *Cleopatra* (1963), marked the first time an actress was offered $1 million to appear in a movie. She actually received $2 million (thanks to the enormous delays in the filming) after her contract was renegotiated to $10,000 per week. On the set of *Cleopatra* she met British actor Richard Burton and began a love affair that lasted two decades, eventually marrying Burton twice.

Throughout the 1960s and into the early 1970s, Taylor and Burton starred together in a seemingly endless series of mediocre movies. Only two were genuinely noteworthy, *Who's Afraid of Virginia Woolf?* (1966), for which she won her second Oscar, and *The Taming of the Shrew* (1967). Many of the others, especially the early films, were box office winners despite their poor quality.

Taylor's last critical and commercial success was *Se-cret Ceremony* (1968). Her subsequent films, such as *Ash Wednesday* (1974), *The Blue Bird* (1976), and *A Little Night Music* (1977) were all flops. *The Mirror Crack'd* (1980) brought her mixed reviews in what was, essentially, a parody of her own image. She received greater attention, though, when she married the future Senator from Virginia, John Warner in 1976; it was her seventh marriage and lasted until 1981.

Beset by weight problems and recovering from drug and alcohol addiction, Taylor was unable to find suitable vehicles in movies throughout the 1980s. While she did star in Franco Zeffirelli's *Young Toscanini,* the movie was never released after its initial public screening at the 1988 Venice Film Festival. She worked primarily in the theater and in television, appearing in special made-for-cable movies and in a featured role in the network miniseries, "North and South."

See also: Burton, Richard; *Cleopatra;* Clift, Montgomery

TAYLOR, ROBERT (1911–1969) An actor, he starred in films for nearly thirty-five years, coming into his own as a competent performer after making his early reputation as a pretty boy. Billed during his heyday in the latter half of the 1930s as "The Man with the Perfect Profile," he was a tall, well-proportioned actor with strong features and a memorable widow's peak. Taylor held two unusual distinctions. He was the lowest paid contract player in the history of Hollywood, earning a paltry $35 per week when he was signed to a seven-year contract in 1934 by MGM, and he also set the record for the greatest number of years (25) under contract to one studio (also MGM), beating Clark Gable by one year.

Born Spangler Arlington Brugh, Taylor had the most artful real name of any actor in Hollywood. The son of a Nebraska doctor, he was comfortable with the spoken word, winning the 1929 Nebraska State Oratorical Championship when he was in high school. Music was his initial interest, however, and he traveled to Pomona College in Southern California to study the cello. While at Pomona, Taylor became interested in acting and was spotted there by a talent scout in a production of *Journey's End,* which eventually led to his being signed by MGM.

His first appearance on film was in the Will Rogers vehicle *Handy Andy* (1934), but by late 1935, after being groomed in a string of low-budget movies, he quickly attained stardom as the male lead in *The Magnificent Obsession.* Taylor went on to become male decoration in the films of MGM's major female stars, such as Loretta Young's *Private Number* (1936), Joan Crawford's *The Gorgous Hussy* (1936), Greta Garbo's *Camille* (1937), and Jean Harlow's *Personal Property* (1937). He also starred in two Barbara Stanwyck films, *His Brother's Wife* (1936) and *This is My Affair* (1937). He eventually married Stanwyck in 1939; they were divorced in 1951.

After having been a star for three years, he finally began to come into his own as an actor in *Yank at Oxford* (1938), *Three Comrades* (1938), and the film he personally thought his best, *Waterloo Bridge* (1940). The latter film certainly represents the peak of his career, though he continued to register at the box office throughout the early 1940s.

Before leaving Hollywood for war service in 1943, Taylor starred in a large number of films, but two stand out: the fiercely emotional *Bataan* (1943), one of the movie industry's stellar war films, and *Song of Russia* (1943), little more than a pleasant piece of hokum but later described by Robert Taylor to the House Un-American Activities Committee as a communist-inspired project he had been suckered into appearing in.

After the war, Taylor began to show his age. Never an exciting actor, his diminished good looks hurt him at the box office. He had few noteworthy films during the latter half of the 1940s. His career was saved when MGM cast him in big-budget costume epics such as *Quo Vadis* (1951), *Ivanhoe* (1952), and *Valley of the Kings* (1954). All of these films were hits and his star was briefly on the rise.

He began to fade again in the later 1950s. Though getting some attention for his work in Nicholas Ray's *Party Girl* (1958), he was through at MGM the following year after he made *The House of Seven Hawks* (1959).

Taylor continued to work throughout the rest of his lifetime, making a number of cheapie films overseas as well as starring in his own TV series "The Detectives," and working as a host of the syndicated TV show "Death Valley Days."

Taylor died of lung cancer in 1969.

TECHNICOLOR   The trademark name of the most famous and widely used color process invented by Herbert T. Kalmus and Daniel F. Comstock. The pair created the first Technicolor movie in 1917, a short called *The Gulf Between*. It was made by a crude two-color process that projected separately shot red and green strips of film on a screen, where they were superimposed to create a color picture.

The two inventors continued their work and soon reached the point where they were able to combine the red and green images on a single piece of film. *Toll of the Sea* (1921) was made in the new Technicolor process by MGM and it proved to be a sensation. It took a long time to convince the studios to spend the money to make Technicolor features because the costs were prohibitive, as Famous Players soon discovered when they made *Wanderer of the Wasteland* (1924), the first full-length motion picture in the new color process. The film was a hit but the movie had trouble earning back its expenses.

After more experimentation, the Technicolor process

was improved enough so that Douglas Fairbanks was willing to chance making *The Black Pirate* (1926) in color. Both the film and the process were winners. While the costs had not come down appreciably, at least the appeal of color to audiences had proved itself. Filmmakers began jumping on the bandwagon, using Technicolor for individual scenes and sequences in their movies. For instance, *Irene* (1926), *Red Hair* (1928), *King of Kings* (1927), and a great many other silent films originally had two-color Technicolor scenes.

Warner Bros., which spearheaded the talking picture revolution, was also the first studio to introduce the all-color sound motion picture when it released *On with the Show* (1929). For the most part, however, studios continued the trend of filming individual color sequences within otherwise all black-and-white films. The list of films with color sequences became staggering during the early 1930s, so much so that the novelty soon wore off.

The Technicolor company was working on a three-color process that included blue along with red and green. It was ready to be used when interest in color, along with the economy, hit bottom. Only Walt Disney was willing to take a chance on the new system, using it for his line of *Silly Symphony* cartoons, starting with *Flowers and Trees* (1932), and scored a huge success in 1933 with *Three Little Pigs*, which went on to win the Best Short Subject Academy Award.

Studio interest was piqued and a live action short was done, *La Cucuracha* (1933), and that, too, proved to be a hit. The Technicolor three-color process was miles ahead of any other color system and it made their old two-color system look positively ancient. Soon, studios went back to the practice of adding Technicolor sequences to their films, which could be found in the likes of *The House of Rothschild* (1934), *Kid Millions* (1934), and *The Cat and the Fiddle* (1934). Finally, in 1935, the first full-length three-color Technicolor movie was made, *Becky Sharp*. And there was no turning back.

Though still an expensive process, Technicolor proved to be so popular that every major studio apportioned part of their budget for making an ever-increasing number of movies in the new color system. Whether or not a film was made in color became a measure of the importance of a property or star.

Meticulous care was given to the early Technicolor films, and one can see that the color values of these movies was (and is) particularly glorious and rich. Films such as *Snow White and the Seven Dwarfs* (1937) and *The Adventures of Robin Hood* (1938) were shining examples of spectacular color photography. But the height of Technicolor's achievement was certainly *Gone with the Wind* (1939), a film that looks as vibrant today as it did upon its release fifty years ago.

The credits at the end of a film that say "Color by Technicolor" mean just that; Technicolor cameras are rented by filmmakers from the company and Technicolor cameramen and/or consultants are present during the making of a film. Technicolor literally supplies the color in consultation with the director and cinematographer of the motion picture.

There have, of course, been competitors in the color field, such as Eastman Color, but Technicolor has been synonymous with color movies from the 1930s to the present.
See also: color

TEEN MOVIES As a category, films for and about teenagers has been constantly growing and changing since the late 1930s. The early teen-oriented films, however, were essentially family movies that used the teen hero or heroine as the movie's focal point. Such films as the Mickey Rooney "Andy Hardy" series of the late 1930s and early 1940s, the Deanna Durbin movies of the late 1930s, and the Henry Aldrich series of the 1940s were all celebrations of family life where teens and their wise parents live in harmony.

The teen movie began changing in the 1950s, capturing growing adolescent alienation in classics such as *The Wild One* (1954), *Rebel Without a Cause* (1955), and *The Blackboard Jungle* (1955). Young boys found new sympathetic heroes who touched a nerve of restlessness and ennui. And young girls were drawn to the vulnerable yet dangerous sexuality of stars such as James Dean.

Another change in teen movies came as a response to this first wave of serious, troubling films: Hollywood saw a burgeoning market of young baby boomers with money to spend and an interest in heroes and heroines their own age. The film industry sought to provide a steady diet of easily produced, homogenized movies that would entertain the young, placating this youth market by keeping adult characters very much in the background. In this fashion, the teen movie explosion was on. Films such as *Tammy and the Bachelor* (1957) and *Gidget* (1959) were huge hits. A new crop of teen stars emerged including Troy Donahue, Connie Stevens, and the remarkably popular Sandra Dee, who had a streak of lightweight hits that began while she was herself still a teenager. Her films, such as *The Reluctant Debutante* (1958) and *Tammy Tell Me True* (1961), were virtual cash machines.

Teen music—rock 'n' roll—was a natural breeding ground for stars who would appeal to the youth market. As a result, Elvis Presley, Bobby Darin, and Connie Francis were rushed into films to capitalize on their appeal to teenagers.

Also during the 1950s, Roger Corman *(q.v.)* was making teen movies with titles such as *Rock All Night* (1957), *Teenage Doll* (1957), and *Teenage Caveman* (1958). At the same time, the mating of horror and teen movies had begun with *I Was a Teenage Werewolf* (1957) and *I*

Was a Teenage Frankenstein (1957), a trend that would blossom anew in a darker hue in the late 1970s and 1980s.

The teenage movie trend accelerated in the early 1960s with films such as *Where the Boys Are* (1960) and *Palm Springs Weekend* (1963). The apotheosis of the teen movie was finally reached with the Beach Party movies *(q.v.)* starring Frankie Avalon and Annette Funicello.

With the rise of the civil rights and antiwar movements and the drug culture, teen movies began to change yet again, reflecting rebelliousness in a far more iconoclastic fashion. Hollywood had far less control over independent productions such as *The Wild Angels* (1966), *The Trip* (1967), and *Wild in the Streets* (1968) and the youth movement in films hit a new high when the low-budget *Easy Rider* (1969, *q.v.*) turned into a giant sleeper hit.

Thanks to the success of *Easy Rider* and rock concert movies such as *Woodstock* (1970), Hollywood moved quickly to take advantage of the youth market with watered-down protest movies like *The Revolutionary* (1970), but audiences wouldn't buy it. Film producers floundered until they put their money, into expensive special effects films and science fiction movies that drew great numbers of young people throughout the 1970s.

Late in the decade, Hollywood finally recognized that teenagers weren't just a piece of the market, they were virtually the *entire* market. Young people between the ages of twelve and twenty-four soon became the target of the vast majority of Hollywood films. As a result, a whole new breed of young actors came to the fore, among them Brooke Shields, Jamie Lee Curtis, Matthew Broderick, and the Brat Packers Sean Penn, Rob Lowe, Tom Cruise, Emilio Estevez, Andrew McCarthy and others.

The late 1970s brought the first new wave of teen horror films. *Halloween* (1978) was such a gargantuan hit that it not only spawned sequels, it also generated the even more gruesome teen horror film, *Friday the 13th* (1980) and a myriad of follow-ups. Not long after, teen sex comedies arrived with *Risky Business* (1983), which launched actor Tom Cruise's career. But it was John Hughes, who wrote, produced, and sometimes directed a spate of teen-oriented films, who seemed to define the genre in the 1980s with movies such as *Sixteen Candles* (1984), *St. Elmo's Fire* (1985), *The Breakfast Club* (1985), *Pretty in Pink* (1986), and *Ferris Buehler's Day Off* (1986).

Hughes' success led to plenty of imitators, and finally a point of teen movie saturation was reached. Producers backed off from making too many teen films and, at about that same time, Hollywood discovered that adult films were making a great deal of money in the video rental market. With the proliferation of VCRs and the advent of widespread video rentals, the teenage domination of the marketplace had begun to ease, however slightly, and an increasing percentage of movies for adults were being made once again with the subsidiary rental and cable markets firmly in producer's minds. But, clearly, the future of the teen movie is safe and secure as long as young people continue to date and go to the movies.

TEMPLE, SHIRLEY (1928–   ) The most popular of Hollywood's child stars, she earned that distinction with uncommon talent as an actress, singer, and dancer. A star at six years of age, Temple had an unprecedented and (for a child star) still unequalled string of hit movies throughout the better part of the 1930s. With her blonde curls, dimples, and sunny disposition, Shirley Temple was a beacon of hope and cheer during the long years of the Great Depression.

The daughter of a Santa Monica bank teller, Temple was a prodigy who began appearing in the Baby Burlesks series of one-reel comedy shorts in 1931 doing imitations of famous movie stars. In 1934, she sang and danced "Baby Take a Bow" in *Stand Up and Cheer,* and audiences took notice. So did Twentieth Century-Fox, which signed her to a contract. She quickly became Fox's biggest attraction.

In 1934 alone, she starred in *Little Miss Marker, Baby Take a Bow, Now and Forever,* and *Bright Eyes,* in addition to smaller roles in several other films. But her best movies were still ahead of her.

Playing the lead in as many as four films per year, Temple had a staggering workload, particularly if one considers that she was a mere tot carrying her films and having to learn lines as well as music and choreography. In 1935, she starred in *The Little Colonel, Our Little Girl, Curly Top,* and *The Littlest Rebel.* These films, like most of her other starring vehicles, were quickly produced sentimental tales. But the public couldn't get enough of her. An entire industry was soon spawned by her popularity, including Shirley Temple dolls and coloring books. When she introduced her trademark song, "On the Good Ship, Lollipop," in *Captain January* (1936), it seemed as if every child in America (as well as their parents) had the song on their lips.

As her popularity grew, so did the budgets and the quality of her films. In 1937 she starred in a much underrated John Ford film, *Wee Willie Winkie,* and in that same year starred in the classic version of *Heidi.* In 1938, she remade Mary Pickford's silent hit *Rebecca of Sunnybrook Farm* and made it a hit all over again. It was also the year that she reached the height of her stardom, becoming Hollywood's number-one box office attraction. Her descent from the pinnacle came swiftly thereafter.

By the end of the 1930s, she suffered several flops and the magic was gone. No longer a precious little girl, the pretty teenager had lost her audience. In 1942,

Shirley Temple was Hollywood's greatest child star. In addition to keeping Twentieth Century-Fox afloat during the 1930s, she also buoyed the flagging spirits of a Depression-weary nation. Photo courtesy of The Siegel Collection.

she tried to establish herself as an adolescent star in *Miss Annie Rooney* (1942), in which she received her first screen kiss from another aging child star, Dickie Moore. Later, she was perfectly adequate as an ingenue in some very fine 1940s movies such as *Since You Went Away* (1944), *The Bachelor and the Bobby-Soxer* (1947), and *Fort Apache* (1948), but neither her roles nor her performances were so special that they catapulted her back into the limelight. Without singing and dancing, Shirley Temple was just an ordinary actress. Perhaps the biggest mistake of her post-pubescent years was that she didn't follow the lead set by such young stars as Judy Garland and Deanna Durbin who hit it big in musicals.

Temples' film career was over by the end of the 1940s; her last film was *A Kiss for Corliss* (1949). She made attempts to resurrect her career on television in the late 1950s and early 1960s, but her time had come and gone.

Known as Shirley Temple Black after her marriage to businessman Charles Black in 1950 (it was her second marriage; the first was to actor John Agar), she later became active in conservative politics and served as a member of the U.S. delegation to the United Nations during the late 1960s, and as the American ambassador to Ghana from 1974 through 1976. She then became the U.S. Chief of Protocol. After a successful battle with breast cancer, she retreated from the public scene until the publication of her autobiography, *Child Star,* in 1988. She has been appointed ambassador to Czechoslovakia by President George Bush.

See also: child stars

THALBERG, IRVING G. (1899–1936) As vice president and head of production at MGM between 1924 and 1936, he became Hollywood's most highly regarded studio executive, noted for his combination of uncanny commercial sense and good taste. Thalberg brought class to MGM, putting much of his energy into its "prestige" pictures, which were often based on literary classics. His abilities were such that early on he was tagged with the title "Boy Wonder."

A sickly child, Thalberg was plagued with a heart damaged by rheumatic fever. His medical prognosis was not encouraging: he was told he might not live to reach his thirties. As a consequence, Thalberg lived and worked twice as hard to make up for the time he might never enjoy. He skipped college and, through family connections, soon landed a job as a personal secretary/assistant to Carl Laemmle, who was in the process of building Universal Pictures into a major studio. Laemmle was mightily impressed by the brilliant twenty-year-old Thalberg and sent his charge out to Hollywood to oversee production at his faltering Universal City filmmaking center. Before long, Thalberg had Universal running like a top and it was then that he earned the sobriquet Boy Wonder, thanks to a short story of that name in *The Saturday Evening Post* about a character much like him.

All was going well for Thalberg until Laemmle pressed the young man he so much admired to marry his daughter, Rosabelle. While there was a good deal of intermarriage among Hollywood royalty (e.g., David O. Selznick married Louis B. Mayer's daughter, Irene), Thalberg would not be pushed into such a union. Caught in an uncomfortable situation, Thalberg broke with Laemmle and, in 1923, went to work for Louis B. Mayer Pictures. The following year, Metro-Goldwyn-Mayer was formed and Thalberg continued to work for the gargantuan new company.

Already well known and respected in the industry, Thalberg enhanced his reputation to legendary proportions during the last dozen years of his life at MGM. Much to the dismay of his titular boss, Louis B. Mayer, Thalberg was given much of the credit for MGM's commercial success. The young producer was responsible for all of MGM's output, but his contribution to such famous films as *The Big Parade* (1925), *Ben-Hur* (1926), *The Crowd* (1928), *Anna Christie* (1930), *Strange Interlude* (1932), *The Barretts of Wimpole Street* (1934), and *Mutiny on the Bounty* (1935) was particularly significant.

Thalberg didn't merely produce movies, he developed strategies for his stars in order to build their careers and make their films more profitable. For instance, he thought the Marx Brothers could be far more popular if they paced their comedy differently and added music and a love interest in order to appeal to women. When the brothers were dropped by Paramount, he offered them a deal on that basis and did the unheard of thing of suggesting that they take the material for their next film out on the road and test it in front of audiences. The result was the biggest commercial hit the Marx Brothers ever had, *A Night at the Opera* (1935).

In the same vein, it was Thalberg who instituted the sneak preview, which later became a standard industry practice. Re-shooting after a poor audience reaction was not uncommon for the perfectionist Thalberg. In fact, he once said, "Movies aren't made, they're remade."

The producer had found some measure of personal happiness when he married actress Norma Shearer in 1927. Thalberg guided her career, giving her MGM's juiciest roles until she became their highest paid star with the title of "First Lady of the Screen."

Known to work sixteen hours a day, seven days a week, the pace finally began to catch up on the frail producer. He had a heart attack in late 1932 and had a long convalescence. In the meantime, David O. Selznick was brought in from RKO to take over his duties as Louis B. Mayer quietly began usurping Thalberg's power. By the time the Boy Wonder returned to MGM, he found his influence much reduced. Not long after, he became ill and died of pneumonia. He was thirty-seven years old.

Throughout his career, Thalberg had eschewed the right to place his name in the credits of his films. He had said, "If you're in a position to give credit, you don't need it." As a tribute, his name appeared in the credits of the last movie he produced, *The Good Earth* (1937); the movie was dedicated to his memory.

Hollywood mourned the tragic passing of one of its giants by creating its most prestigious prize in his honor, the Irving G. Thalberg Memorial Award, which is given for "outstanding motion picture production" only when there is a deserving recipient. Among those who have received the coveted award have been many of Hollywood's most talented producers and producer-directors, including Darryl F. Zanuck, David O. Selznick, Samuel Goldwyn, William Wyler, George Stevens, and Alfred Hitchcock.

Thalberg brought literature to the screen, and F. Scott Fitzgerald brought Thalberg to literature, patterning Monroe Stahr, the protagonist of his novel *The Last Tycoon*, on Thalberg. When it was adapted for the screen in 1976, Robert De Niro essayed the role of Stahr/Thalberg.

See also: MGM; Shearer, Norma

3-D While standard motion pictures show an image in two dimensions (width and height) the 3-D process also adds depth.

Motion pictures appearing to have three dimensions became a hit with audiences when a jungle movie called *Bwana Devil* was shown in 1952. But 3-D movies (in more primitive form) existed long before 1952. Famed French filmmakers Auguste and Louis Lumière were responsible for 3-D movies that were projected at the Paris Exposition in 1903. In the 1920s, Plastigrams, made by a 3-D process requiring the audience to wear special viewing glasses, were invented with the help of cameraman G. W. "Billy" Bitzer. Plastigrams were popular for roughly three years before the novelty faded. There were other systems in the 1920s, such as the Fairall Process, the Teleview System, and the Grandeur Process. None of them caught on with the public.

The 1930s saw more experimentation. It was as if the lure of three-dimensional movies just couldn't be resisted. Among others, MGM toyed with 3-D, making shorts in a system they first called Audioscopiks and later Metroscopics. MGM's efforts culminated with a short subject in 1941 called *Third Dimension Murder.*

It was only later, however, with Hollywood reeling from the impact of television on ticket sales, that 3-D finally had its moment of glory. It didn't last long, but it has never been forgotten. *Bwana Devil*, a terrible movie with Robert Stack and Nigel Bruce, and produced, written, and directed by Arch Obler in 3-D, set box office records wherever it played. Hollywood scrambled to get on the 3-D bandwagon.

Virtually every major studio put out at least several films in 3-D (several studios released as many as half a dozen or more). Some of the more noteworthy among them are United Artists' *I, The Jury* (1953), Twentieth Century-Fox's *Inferno* (1953), RKO's *Second Chance* (1953), Paramount's *Those Redheads from Seattle* (1953), advertised as "the first 3-D musical," Universal's *The Creature From the Black Lagoon* (1954), Columbia's *Gun Fury* (1953), MGM's *Kiss Me Kate* (1953), and Warner Bros.' *House of Wax* (1953).

House of Wax was one of the best 3-D movies, but most of the films that were rushed into theaters were rather poor, depending for their appeal on the novelty effect of the process rather than on the quality of the film itself. And even among the better movies, the more successful of them tended to be horror films. Later, when movies such as the musical *Kiss Me Kate* came out in 3-D, audiences ignored them, associating three dimensional movies with either poor quality filmmaking and/or cheap thrills.

By 1955, 3-D was dying, done in by the Cinema-Scope *(q.v.)* wide-screen process, which could attract audiences without necessitating Polaroid glasses or extra projectors. (3-D demanded two projectors running simultaneously; if one of them ran at even a fractionally different speed, it would give audiences headaches.)

Since the short glory days of 3-D, there have been a few 3-D films, virtually all of them made with the hope of cashing in on a new generation's interest in the novelty of 3-D: there have been 3-D pornographic movies in the early 1970s and comedy 3-D westerns in the late 1970s and in the mid-1980s. The only quality 3-D film in recent years has been the hugely successful short subject (shown exclusively at Disney World), *Captain EO*, made by Francis Ford Coppola and George Lucas and starring Michael Jackson and a host of guest stars.

See also: CinemaScope; Cinerama

THREE STOOGES, THE A comedy team that made 190 two-reelers between 1934 and 1958 at Columbia Pictures, setting a record for the longest-running comedy series in Hollywood history. Their humor was low-brow slapstick, often tasteless, violent, and repetitive, but it was also liberatingly funny. There was a cartoon-like nuttiness to The Three Stooges that lifted their best work to the level of inspired lunacy.

Originally a vaudeville act created in 1923 and billed as "Ted Healy and His Stooges," the group consisted of star Ted Healy and just two Stooges, brothers Moe Howard, born Moses Harry Horowitz (1897–1975), and Shemp Howard, born Samuel Horowitz (1895–1955). Larry Fine, born Lawrence Feinberg (1902–1975), joined the act five years later in 1928, bringing the total number of Stooges to three.

Their first appearance in the movies was with Healy in the feature-length motion picture *Soup to Nuts* (1930), in which they were billed as "The Rackateers." Shemp left the act after their film appearance to begin a long and successful solo career. He was replaced by Moe and Shemp's kid brother, Curly Howard, born Jerome Horowitz (1903–1952).

After several more years of knocking around in vaudeville and appearing in movies with Healy, the Stooges decided to break away. They took their act over to Columbia, where they refined their peculiar chemistry as a comedy team. Moe was the leader, the know-nothing know-it-all who bossed the other two around by hitting, poking, and slapping them at every turn. Larry was the innocent with the porcupine hairdo, the sweet Stooge who just wanted to get along. Curly was the wild man, the spark that fired the team's engine. He was pure id and ego wrapped up in a fat, bald package full of manic energy.

Moe, Larry, and Curly made their stunning debut as The Three Stooges in *Woman Haters* (1934), a musical with dialogue delivered in rhyming couplets! The team went on to churn out an average of eight shorts per year throughout the 1930s and the first half of the 1940s, doing most of their best work during that period. The Stooges were nominated for an Oscar for *Men in Black* (1934) but were beaten by Disney's *Three Little Pigs*— only to come back the following year with *Three Little Pigskins* (1935). Among their other classic shorts were *Hoi Polloi* (1935), *Violent Is the Word for Curly* (1938), *Calling All Curs* (1939), and *You Natzy Spy* (1940), in which Moe bore an amazing resemblance to Hitler.

After Curly suffered a stroke in 1946, the call went out to brother Shemp to return to the team. He did so with modest results, but the group was never the same without Curly. When Shemp died in 1955, Joe Besser filled in for two years, and was then replaced by Joe DeRita, who shaved his head and called himself Curly-Joe. The team went steadily downhill.

The Stooges had never been big money-makers for Columbia but they were kept on because Harry Cohn reportedly thought of them as his good luck charms; they had come to the studio in the year that Columbia hit the big time with Frank Capra's *It Happened One Night* (1934), and the movie mogul was content to keep them around. When Cohn died in 1958, The Three Stooges lost their patron and they were let go after completing their last short, *Sappy Bullfighters* (1958).

But a curious thing happened. Columbia unloaded all of The Three Stooges shorts featuring Curly to television and a whole new audience of kids discovered the trio and went crazy for them. In the twilight of their lives, The Three Stooges were hotter than they had ever been in their entire careers. Their faces appeared on lunch boxes and they cashed in with personal appearances and a series of terrible feature films, among them *Have Rocket, Will Travel* (1958), *The Three Stooges in Orbit* (1960), and *The Three Stooges Meet Hercules* (1961). Without Curly or Shemp, and feeling their age, Moe and Larry, with the none-too-talented Curly-Joe, continued to lumber through featured appearances in movies such as *Four for Texas* (1963), but they finally wore out. Larry Fine's stroke in 1971 effectively shut down the act. Moe died not long after the death of his dear friend and partner Larry in 1975.

See also: comedy teams

TIERNEY, GENE (1920–) One of Hollywood's great beauties, she had an elegant yet sexy manner on screen that suggested a blue flame: cool to the eye but hot to the touch. She appeared in thirty-six films, starring in most of them and making her best during the mid to late 1940s. The one film for which she is best remembered is *Laura* (1944), in which she played the title role.

Miss Tierney was the daughter of a well-to-do Wall Street trader who, when she decided to become an actress, fully supported her and even formed a corporation called Belle-Tier that was designed soley to

Gene Tierney, in her most famous role, is seen here as Dana Andrews first saw her in *Laura* (1944). Painted ever so delicately, Andrews falls in love with her image even though he believes Tierney's character is dead. Photo courtesy of Gene Tierney Lee.

push her career. By 1939 Miss Tierney was on Broadway, and when she appeared on stage in *The Male Animal* the next year, Darryl F. Zanuck was in the audience. He saw her screen potential and signed her to a contract. That same year she made her movie debut in *The Return of Frank James* (1940).

Tierney was given the star treatment very early on. She played Ellie May in *Tobacco Road* (1941), she was Belle in *Belle Star* (1941), and she was the female lead in Ernst Lubitsch's *Heaven Can Wait* (1943). But it was *Laura* that hurled her into the Hollywood firmament of stars. In this romantic suspense movie directed by Otto Preminger, a detective (played by Dana Andrews) falls in love with a portrait of Laura (Tierney), thinking that the beautiful woman in the picture has been murdered. When she suddenly appears, alive and well, the two are drawn together while a thwarted murderer continues his efforts to kill her.

The movie was a smash hit and has since become a classic. Miss Tierney has been so associated with *Laura* that one tends to forget that she garnered an Oscar nomination for *Leave Her to Heaven* (1945), gave an achingly tender performance in *The Ghost and Mrs. Muir* (1947), and was excellent in *Whirlpool* (1949). Most of her other films in the late 1940s and early 1950s were ordinary, unmemorable entries such as *The Iron Curtain* (1948), *Night and the City* (1950), *The Mating Season* (1951) and *The Plymouth Adventure* (1952).

Miss Tierney's personal life was far more dramatic than many of her later movies. She had dated John F. Kennedy before he got into politics, married fashion designer Oleg Cassini in 1941, and, after their divorce in 1952, became deeply involved with Aly Khan, the ex-husband of Rita Hayworth. When that affair ended, she went into a severe emotional tailspin, spending eighteen months in a sanitarium. Later, in 1960, she married an ex-husband of Hedy Lamarr and settled in Texas. After remarrying she made a few appearances in movies such as *Advise and Consent* (1962) and *Toys in the Attic* (1963). One can glimpse her final appearance on film in *The Pleasure Seekers* (1964).

TIOMKIN, DIMITRI (1899–1979) One of the great composers for the screen whose scores were often notable for their evocative combination of well-known classics and his own original music. Tiomkin's scores reached out to audiences; one was often aware of his music in the films he scored but not distracted by it. Versatile and imaginative, Tiomkin was a pioneer among Hollywood composers and he was honored with four Oscars for his efforts in a film career that lasted more than forty years.

Born in Russia, Tiomkin received his early musical training at the St. Petersburg Conservatory of Music. He was considered a brilliant young man, making his living in the 1920s as a concert pianist and conductor. Long before he came to the United States, Tiomkin was intrigued with American music; he was the first concert artist to play George Gershwin's music in Europe.

The composer arrived in the U.S. in 1925 and never left, becoming a citizen in 1937. Not long after coming to America, Tiomkin settled into his new craft of writing film scores for movies. He wrote ballet music for *Devil-May-Care* (1929) and several other early sound films, eventually winning the opportunity to write the music for all sorts of films from horror movies such as *Mad Love* (1935) to adventures such as *Spawn of the North* (1938).

Tiomkin worked closely with several directors throughout their careers. For instance, he wrote the scores for many of Frank Capra's movies, including *Lost Horizon* (1937), *You Can't Take It with You* (1938), *Mr. Smith Goes to Washington* (1939), *Meet John Doe* (1941), and *It's a Wonderful Life* (1946). He was just as compatible with a director as diametrically different in

tone and style as Alfred Hitchcock, for whom Tiomkin wrote the music for, among others, *Shadow of a Doubt* (1943), *Strangers on a Train* (1951), and *Dial M For Murder* (1954). Tiomkin also wrote scores for a great many of Howard Hawks' adventure films such as *Only Angels Have Wings* (1939), *Red River* (1948), *The Big Sky* (1952), and *Rio Bravo* (1959).

The last three films mentioned above are particularly notable because they were westerns. In the 1950s, Tiomkin became the leading composer of scores for oaters when he wrote the music and the theme song for *High Noon* (1952), winning Academy Awards for both. He did not, however, stick to westerns; his interests were far too wide-ranging. He also wrote the music for *The High and the Mighty* (1954), winning yet another Oscar, and *The Old Man and Sea* (1958), for which he won his fourth and final Academy Award.

Tiomkin continued working throughout the 1960s, only slowing down near the end of the decade. His theme song for *Town Without Pity* (1961) became a hit, but his final achievement was his version of *Tschaikovsky*, which he produced, directed, and orchestrated in a joint American and Russian production in 1970.

TOLAND, GREGG (1904–1948) A legendary cinematographer whose work during the 1930s and early 1940s set a standard that has never been surpassed. Given a great deal of freedom by producer Samuel Goldwyn, for whom he usually worked, Toland adventurously lit movies to stunning effect and devised camera angles and set-ups that dramatically affected and enhanced a great many films.

Toland started his career in the silent era as an assistant cameraman at the age of sixteen. He learned his craft over the next ten years and began working as a lighting cameraman in 1929, coshooting more than half a dozen films before taking over as sole cameraman in 1931 for *Palmy Days*. He shot a number of popular comedies, such as *The Kid from Spain* (1932), and his talent led Samuel Goldwyn to give Toland virtual carte blanche in photographing his newly imported star, Anna Sten, with the hope of turning her into a glamorous beauty to match Garbo and Dietrich. Toland didn't let Goldwyn down. *Nana* (1934), *We Live Again* (1934), and *The Wedding Night* (1935) were visually stunning movies. Film historian George Mitchell referred to Toland's efforts for *We Live Again* as "some of the most breathtaking photography ever recorded by a motion picture camera." If Anna Sten didn't become a star, it was not for Toland's lack of skill.

With his reputation as a leading cameraman made in the mid-1930s, he was assigned to bigger and better films in which to display his craft. His rich and evocative lighting can be seen in films such as *The Road to Glory* (1936), *History Is Made at Night* (1937), and one of his most beautifully photographed films, *The Grapes of Wrath* (1940).

As Leonard Maltin explained in his excellent book, *Behind the Camera*, Toland had a long and fruitful association with William Wyler, shooting many of the director's best films, including *These Three* (1936), *Dead End* (1937), *Wuthering Heights* (1939), for which the cinematographer won an Oscar, *The Westerner* (1940), *The Little Foxes* (1941), and *The Best Years of Our Lives* (1946).

Orson Welles deserves the credit for *Citizen Kane* (1941, *q.v.*), but the neophyte director could not have realized the film without Toland's help. It was in *Kane* that Toland perfected the deep focus *(q.v.)* photography that film students still study today. He also shot ceilings in that movie for the first time, and his ominous lighting helped launch the *film noir* style that would soon follow.

During World War II, Toland photographed and codirected (with John Ford) *December 7th*, a documentary film that brought him a second Oscar. But after his work on *The Best Years of Our Lives*, the cinematographer made just three more films before his sudden death from a heart attack at the age of forty-four. His last film, *Enchantment* (1949), was released the year after his death.

TONE, FRANCHOT (1905–1968) A leading man who projected upper-class sophistication in a great many forgettable movies, Tone was handsome, ramrod straight, and elegant in manner and speech. He was in vogue during the 1930s and early 1940s, playing suave heroes.

Born Stanislas Pascal Franchot Tone, he was not the foreign-born aristocrat that many fans may have imagined, but rather the son of a wealthy American businessman. He became enamored of the theater while at Cornell, where he was president of the dramatic club. After graduation, he quickly worked his way up from stock productions to Broadway. With his good looks and fine baritone voice, he was a natural for the movies. In 1932 he made his film debut in *The Wiser Sex*.

In more than sixty-five movies, Tone was often in leading roles, yet there are very few important films with which he is closely associated. In contrast, he shows up a good deal more often in the memorable starring vehicles of others, suggesting that he made a better supporting actor than he did a star. For instance, in his early film career he played pivotal, but secondary, roles in such memorable movies as *Gabriel Over the White House* (1933), *The Lives of a Bengal Lancer* (1935), and *Mutiny on the Bounty* (1935), for which he inexplicably received a Best Actor, rather than Best Supporting Actor, Oscar nomination. He also played leading man to Joan Crawford in a number of her better vehicles, such as *Dancing Lady* (1933), *Sadie McKee* (1934), and *The Gorgeous Hussy* (1936). He assumed the same

role in his private life, marrying Miss Crawford in 1935. (The marriage ended in 1939.) It was the first of his four marriages, all to actresses, but none was as famous as Crawford.

By 1937 Tone was a box office draw, thanks in part to the wonderful ensemble acting to which he contributed in Frank Borzage's touching love story, *Three Comrades*. He was an excellent villain in the underrated *They Gave Him a Gun* (1937), but neither his roles nor his movies were much good until he played the hero in *Five Graves to Cairo* (1943). The following year, he starred in Robert Siodmak's excellent low-budget crime melodrama *The Phantom Lady* (1944), but his career was already fading due to too many flops. By 1951 he was off the screen, working instead on the stage, where he had a minor success in an Off-Broadway production of *Uncle Vanya*. He brought it to the screen in 1958, producing, directing, and starring in the noble if flawed film adapatation.

Finally, in the early 1960s, Tone returned to the movies as a grand old actor playing the president in *Advise and Consent* (1962). He surfaced a few more times in interesting movies such as Arthur Penn's *Mickey One* (1965). His last role was in *The High Commissioner* (1968). Tone died of lung cancer that same year at the relatively young age of sixty-three.

TRACY, SPENCER (1900–1967) He is considered by many of his colleagues and film historians to be the finest American film actor of his time. With his craggy face, burly build, and soulful eyes, Tracy held the screen with such a natural grace that he hardly seemed to be acting. Originally typed as a gangster, the actor soon blossomed into a versatile character actor/star and then held top billing until his death. Most film fans remember him as a member of one of Hollywood's most-loved screen teams, with Katharine Hepburn, in a total of nine movies. Less well known is the fact that Tracy holds the record for the most Best Actor Academy Award nominations—nine (he won the Oscar twice). He didn't let such acclaim go to his head; this honored star's prescription for acting was merely, "Just know your lines and don't bump into the furniture."

Born in Wisconsin to a middle-class family, Tracy found he had a talent for speaking in public while a member of the Ripon College debating team. Drawn to the stage, he traveled to New York to become a student at the American Academy of Dramatic Arts. He fared well in New York, landing an important role in the Broadway production of *A Royal Fandango* in 1923. He worked steadily throughout the 1920s until he had a smash hit playing a murderer on death row in the Broadway production of *The Last Mile* in 1929. His success led to screen tests in a Hollywood hungry for stage stars who could excel in the new talkie era, but the verdict from such studios as MGM, Fox, and Warner Bros. was that Tracy had no future in the movies. Fortunately, director John Ford (q.v.) had seen Tracy in *The Last Mile* and knew talent when he saw it. He talked Fox into giving Tracy a contract and the actor was given the lead in his first feature-length movie, Ford's prison picture *Up the River* (1930).

More prison and gangster movies followed, such as *Quick Millions* (1931), *Disorderly Conduct* (1932), and *20,000 Years in Sing Sing* (1933). His reputation as an actor was already growing and the latter film helped establish him as a genuine star. But he broke out of the hardboiled tough guy roles for good when he gave an electric performance in *The Power and the Glory* (1933). His range of roles then increased dramatically to include comedies, romances, and period pieces.

During the mid-1930s, however, Tracy's irascibility and public drinking became a serious problem. Twentieth Century-Fox tried to discipline him by giving him lesser roles but that merely put them at loggerheads with the actor. Finally, he managed to get himself fired, but not until he had made a fascinating version of *Dante's Inferno* (1935).

MGM, concerned with Tracy's bad boy reputation and worried, as well, that he lacked sex appeal, nevertheless took a gamble and signed him up. The deal paid off handsomely. The actor became one of the studio's biggest stars in critical and/or commercial hits, such as the anti-lynching movie *Fury* (1936), *San Francisco* (1936), the Best Picture winner of the year (and Tracy's first Best Actor nominated performance), *Libeled Lady* (1936), and *Captains Courageous* (1937), for which he won his first Academy Award for Best Actor.

While not every movie he made was a winner, Tracy scored often enough to approach "The King" Clark Gable, in popularity. And by 1940, after making such films as *Boy's Town* (1938), for which he was honored with his second Oscar, *Stanley and Livingstone* (1939), and *Boom Town* (1940), Tracy finally outperformed Gable and entered his most successful decade as an actor. It was also the decade in which he first met and began working with Katharine Hepburn.

The two were first teamed in *Woman of the Year* (1942). The movie was so well-received—and the two stars seemed so natural together—that they were brought together again in *Keeper of the Flame* (1943). Later, they were teamed again in *Without Love* (1945), and it began to seem as if Tracy and Hepburn were inseparable—at least on screen. Their romantic relationship behind the scenes was handled discreetly due to Tracy's marriage (both he and his wife were Catholics and would not divorce). Over the years, the two stars continued to appear together in films such as *State of the Union* (1948), *Adam's Rib* (1949), *Pat and Mike* (1952), *Desk Set* (1957), and his last film, *Guess Who's Coming to Dinner* (1967). In all of his films—even those with Hepburn—he insisted on top billing.

In addition to his collaborations with Hepburn, Tracy made one of World War II's most effective anti-Nazi films, Fred Zinnemann's *The Seventh Cross* (1944). He also eased into strong father roles in movies such as the hit comedy *Father of the Bride* (1950), for which he received yet another Oscar nomination, it's sequel, *Father's Little Dividend* (1951), and *The Actress* (1953).

Tracy's drinking and bad temper began getting the better of him in the 1950s and his output dropped precipitously. Nonetheless, he won Oscar nominations for his performances in *Bad Day at Black Rock* (1955) and *The Old Man and the Sea* (1958). He should have been nominated for *The Last Hurrah* (1958), which was one of his last truly great performances.

Ill health began to slow Tracy down further. Before his health failed him completely, however, he managed to give crackling good performances in four more films, garnering a staggering three more Oscar nominations. Tracy and Fredric March gave acting lessons in *Inherit the Wind* (1960), each of them chewing up the scenery. He was sober and strong as the judge in *Judgment at Nuremberg* (1961), but sadly seemed tired though game in *It's a Mad, Mad, Mad, Mad World* (1963), his only non-nominated performance of the decade. And, finally, after a long absence from the screen, he allowed himself to be coaxed into (and through) *Guess Who's Coming to Dinner* by Hepburn and director Stanley Kramer. He received his ninth and final Oscar nomination for his role in the film, but died shortly after filming was completed.

See also: Hepburn, Katharine; screen teams

TRAILER More popularly known as "coming attractions," trailers are short films of usually less than ninety seconds duration that extol the virtues of movies either soon to be released or playing at another theater. Trailers are generally—but not always—put together from the most intriguing, most action-filled, scenes of a movie. It is, therefore, not surprising that many movie trailers are more exciting than the movies themselves.

Ironically, "trailer" is a misnomer because these short commercials precede feature films rather than trail them. Though the derivation of the name is unknown, one theory has it that the advertisement was traditionally shown after the first film of a double feature, (or, rather, at the beginning of the second film) hence the name trailer.

TRAVOLTA, JOHN (1954–) An actor/singer/dancer who achieved movie stardom in the late 1970s. Handsome and charming in a boyish and cocky manner, Travolta promised to become a major superstar until his career stalled after a string of critical and box office duds in the mid-1980s. Still working, however, Travolta has made an effort to grow as an actor, and a more mature major star may yet emerge.

There was hardly a hotter actor in the late 1970s and early 1980s than John Travolta. He became that rare modern commodity, a star of movie musicals, thanks to his performances in *Saturday Night Fever* (1977) and *Grease* (1978). Unfortunately, a long string of flops have blunted his career. Photo by Patrick DeMarchelier, courtesy of John Travolta.

The youngest of six children, Travolta grew up in New Jersey studying acting with his mother. He left school at sixteen to pursue a career in the theater, working in stock, TV commercials, and eventually Broadway in *Grease* (though not an original cast member).

Travolta's first film appearance was in *The Devil's Rain* (1975), but he became a surprise TV star that same year when he played the role of Vinnie Barbarino in the hit sitcom "Welcome Back, Kotter." He showed his range in the TV movie "The Boy in the Plastic Bubble" (1975) and indicated genuine big-screen promise in a supporting role in Brian De Palma's smash hit *Carrie* (1976). Producer Robert Stigwood signed the young actor to a three-picture contract, the first of which was *Saturday Night Fever* (1977), the film that made Travolta an instant movie star and launched a disco craze. His acting in the film, and particularly his dancing, helped earn Travolta an Oscar nomination for Best Actor.

His next film, *Grease* (1978) was an equally huge hit,

and the actor's reputation as a talented musical performer was firmly established. *Moment by Moment* (1978), in which he costarred with Lily Tomlin, was a major bomb. He recouped, however, with *Urban Cowboy* (1980), a film that spawned a resurgence in all things country/western.

His films since *Urban Cowboy* have been lackluster, some of them popular with critics and others popular with fans, but none of them popular with both. For instance, he starred in Brian De Palma's *Blow Out* (1981), a loser at the box office but generally admired by the media. Conversely, his reprise of the role of Tony Manero (from *Saturday Night Fever*) in *Staying Alive* (1983), a film directed by Sylvester Stallone, brought in ticket buyers by the truckload but was roundly panned by critics. *Perfect* (1985) was anything but; critics booed and fans stayed away.

Critics admired his courage for tackling a difficult role in Robert Altman's TV adaptation of Harold Pinter's *The Dumb Waiter* (1987). And as the 1980s came to a close, Travolta seemed to be entering a new phase of his career with the comedy *Look Who's Talking* (1989).

TREATMENT The second stage in the development of a concept into a script. After the original idea for a film has been presented—often on one single sheet of paper—a treatment is ordered, which fleshes out the concept into something approaching narrative form, detailing all the major scenes and often including snatches of dialogue to suggest the tone of the story. The treatment is a step short of a script.

TREVOR, CLAIRE (1909–   ) An actress who excelled in playing women of easy virtue in a film career spanning more than thirty years. During her busiest years in Hollywood, the 1930s and 1940s, Trevor could be found mostly in contemporary dramas as a "bar girl" (a Hollywood euphemism for a prostitute), in westerns as a "saloon girl" (another euphemism), a gangster's moll, or any other sort of loose, down-on-her-luck character. She was nominated three times for Best Supporting Actress Academy Awards in such roles, winning the Oscar once. For the most part, however, this talented actress worked in lower-budget movies that received little attention. At one time, she was known in the industry as "Queen of the B's."

Born Claire Wemlinger to a comfortable family, she studied art at Columbia University and then took up the theater at the American Academy of Dramatic Arts. After a modest amount of stage experience, she was signed by Fox to a five-year contract, making her movie debut in a western called *Life in the Raw* (1933). She quickly moved up to lead roles but she stayed mostly in "B" movies during her early years, with the fascinating exception of *Dante's Inferno* (1935) and *To Mary with Love* (1936). By this time, however, she had already become typecast in tawdry tough-girl roles, making her a natural for her first genuinely important part as Humphrey Bogart's former girlfriend turned whore in the heralded screen version of *Dead End* (1937, *q.v.*). Their scene together in an alley was devastastingly honest and powerful and remains the highlight of the film more than fifty years after its release. Her performance brought Trevor her first Oscar nomination but, unfortunately, she wasn't free of the "B"s.

It wasn't until 1939 that she was able to sink her teeth into a significant part in a well-scripted movie. The film was John Ford's *Stagecoach (q.v.),* in which she played a woman of questionable virtue. Not a surprise. But no one played such parts better than Trevor, and the film's success gave her the opportunity to appear in films better than those she was accustomed to, such as *The Dark Command* (1940), *Honky Tonk* (1941), *Texas* (1941), and *the Adventures of Martin Eden* (1942).

It didn't last. During the rest of the 1940s and 1950s, her career began a slow but inexorable downward slide, punctuated by a handful of good movies. Among her better films were *Murder, My Sweet* (1944) with Dick Powell as Philip Marlowe, and *Key Largo* (1947), in which she probably gave the greatest performance of her career, earning a Best Supporting Actress Oscar for her portrayal of the alcoholic girlfriend of gangster Johnny Rocco (Edward G. Robinson). Seven years later came another solid vehicle, *The High and the Mighty* (1954), and Trevor was nominated for her third Academy Award.

She worked less often, and in increasingly smaller parts, during the rest of the 1950s and 1960s, but at least the movies she appeared in were generally better. *Man Without a Star* (1955), *Marjorie Morningstar* (1958), *Two Weeks in Another Town* (1962), and *The Stripper* (1963) offered Trevor some of her best roles as her career neared its end. When not acting in films, she put her talents to work in television, winning an Emmy for her 1956 performance in the TV broadcast of "Dodsworth."

Trevor's last motion picture performance was in a minor movie called *The Cape Town Affair* (1967).

TURNER, KATHLEEN (1955–   ) An exotic blonde actress who has become a major film star of the 1980s. In addition to her good looks, her most compelling feature is her voice, which she claims is distinctly her own creation. The accent is a little British, a little Spanish, and a little otherwordly, which made her the perfect choice for the off-screen voice (uncredited) of the animated bombshell Jessica Rabbit in *Who Framed Roger Rabbit?* (1988).

Turner's father was a career foreign service officer who held jobs all over the world, taking his family with him on his travels. While a teenager in England,

she decided to become an actress. After her father died and her family moved to Missouri, she continued studying the theater and eventually made her initial breakthrough on a daytime soap opera, "The Doctors."

Turner honed her skills and gained valuable experience during her twenty months doing daytime drama, and it paid off when she was cast as the female lead in Lawrence Kasdan's *Body Heat* (1981). It marked not only Turner's debut in motion pictures but also Kasdan's, and it was costar William Hurt's second movie. Despite the relative inexperience of the writer-director and his two actors, the film was a surprise hit and Turner was immediately touted as a future star thanks to her sultry, sophisticated performance.

She went on to choose an eclectic mix of films during the balance of the 1980s, including the Steve Martin comedy romp, *The Man With Two Brains* (1983), and the intense, steamy Ken Russell indulgence, *Crimes of Passion* (1984). Then, in short order, she suddenly fulfilled the prophecies of the critics, scoring along with Michael Douglas in the $100 million grossing *Romancing the Stone* (1984), followed by the disappointing but still commercially successful sequel, *Jewel of the Nile* (1985). Turner played opposite Douglas yet again in the black comedy *War of the Roses* (1989). She gave strong performances during the mid- to late 1980s in such critical and box office standouts as *Prizzi's Honor* (1985), *Peggy Sue Got Married* (1986), and *The Accidental Tourist* (1988), the latter film reuniting the *Body Heat* team in an entirely different (and more sedate) movie.

Though she has been in a couple of commercial flops, such as *Switching Channels* (1988), Turner's career has been among the most varied and most successful of any actress during the 1980s.

TURNER, LANA (1920–   ) An actress initially more famous for her physique than her acting, yet who had sufficient star power to fuel a film career lasting more than forty years. A symbiosis existed between Turner and her fans; her personal tribulations, which were trumpeted in the press, made her a surprisingly sympathetic figure and audiences forgave her mediocre performances as long as they could adore her on screen. Though Turner appeared in a range of movies, she was best in melodramas, playing lower-class women who fought their way to wealth and power.

Born Julia Jean Mildred Frances Turner, her childhood was not as elegant as her name. Her father was murdered in a robbery attempt when she was nine years old, sending her family into a financial tailspin. She spent some time in foster homes before finally reuniting with her mother, who had moved to Los Angeles to make a living as a beautician.

Legend has it that Turner was discovered sipping a soda in Schwab's Drugstore, but legend is wrong. She was actually at Currie's Ice Cream Parlor, which happened to be across the street from Hollywood High School, which Turner attended. She was fifteen years old when Billy Wilkerson of *The Hollywood Reporter* spotted her and helped her break into the movies at Warner Bros.

Turner made her debut in *They Won't Forget* (1938), in which she can be seen sipping a soda at a drugstore counter, which later undoubtedly helped foster the legend of her discovery. In any event, she was not rushed to stardom—at least not yet. Mervyn Le Roy had directed *They Won't Forget* and he thought she had "something"; Warner Bros. was not convinced. When Le Roy went to MGM in 1938, he asked if he could take Turner with him. The studio let her go.

At MGM Turner was groomed, as were many stars, in featured roles in their many successful series. She appeared in, among others, *Love Finds Andy Hardy* (1938) and *Calling Dr. Kildare* (1939). Her initial success, however, did not come from the movies but from MGM's campaign to prominently feature her full figure in tight pullovers in a number of pin-up pictures, billing her as "The Sweater Girl." As a result of her new image, Turner was soon rushed into sexy melodramas such as *Honky Tonk* (1941), *Somewhere I'll Find You* (1942), and *Johnny Eager* (1942), becoming an instant sensation.

Turner's appeal didn't diminish one iota after the war when she starred in the then steamy version of *The Postman Always Rings Twice* (1946), a film that is generally credited as her best. Other popular films followed, including *Green Dolphin Street* (1947) and *Cass Timberlane* (1947), but in the late 1940s and early 1950s Turner began to lose her appeal. During the first half of the 1950s, none of her films did well except for *The Bad and the Beautiful* (1952), in which she was cleverly cast as a bad actress.

By the late 1950s, having been in one flop after another, it seemed as if Turner was washed up—until an ironic combination of events briefly reestablished her as a major celebrity. Her daughter killed her longtime boyfriend, a gangster named Johnny Stompanato, knifing him to death in Turner's home. The tabloids went wild, especially when love letters between Turner and the gangster were read in court as evidence. Eventually, Turner's daughter was acquitted on the grounds of justifiable homicide (she had claimed she was protecting her mother). Even as the scandal unfolded, Turner's latest film, *Peyton Place* (1957), was released. The sexy soap opera, buoyed by the publicity Turner received, became a blockbuster hit. And in a classic Hollywood twist, Turner was nominated for a Best Actress Oscar for her performance in the film, the only acting accolade she ever received.

Her last big success was the highly regarded Douglas Sirk sudser *Imitation of Life* (1959). She continued to work in films throughout the 1960s but with little impact. Her best known movie in this period of decline was *Madame X* (1965). By 1969 she was ready to try TV, starring in the short-lived series "The Survivors." There were a smattering of film appearaces in unimportant movies during the 1970s, and then a stint on the prime time TV soap "Falcon Crest" in 1982. She has since been in semiretirement.

Married eight times (she married the same man twice), Turner's personal life would make a better movie than most of those she starred in. Among her many husbands were bandleader Artie Shaw and one-time movie Tarzan Lex Barker. She was also reportedly involved at one time with multibillionaire Howard Hughes.
See also: scandals

TURPIN, BEN (1874–1940)   A cross-eyed slapstick star of the silent era who had his greatest fame making short parodies of famous films. With his elastic body and bizarrely funny faces, Turpin never played a realistic comic character in the fashion of a Charlie Chaplin, Buster Keaton, or Harold Lloyd. Instead, Turpin was a human cartoon character who made audiences laugh at his inspired silliness.

After working burlesque houses as a comic, Turpin made an early attempt at film comedy in 1907 at the Essanay studio. Two years later he gave up on the new movie business, hit the vaudeville circuit, and had his first real success when he created the Happy Hooligan character. Film beckoned again in 1914, and he struggled for several years to create a comic identity. The

Ben Turpin's success as a cross-eyed comedian during the silent era caused many a later critic to sneer at audiences for finding humor in such physical deformities. But Marty Feldman's pop-eyed success in the '70s proved that funny looks get laughs in any era. Photo courtesy of The Siegel Collection.

best he could do was to play second fiddle in a number of Charlie Chaplin shorts.

After joining Mack Sennett's Keystone Studio in 1917, Turpin finally emerged as a wonderfully adept parodist in one- and two-reel films such as *The Shriek of Araby* (1923), *Three and Half Weeks* (1924), and *The Reel Virginian* (1924). He played hilarious send-ups of Valentino, Von Stroheim, Tom Mix, and a great many other stars of the day. He also had a gift for publicity, insuring his eyes with Lloyds of London in case they might uncross.

When talkies arrived, Turpin began appearing in feature-length comedies, but only as a minor supporting player. He was seen, for instance, in Lubitsch's *The Love Parade* (1929), and he (memorably) provided the legs in the W. C. Fields vehicle *Million Dollar Legs* (1932). He did not act often in the 1930s, but when he did he was a fond reminder of a simpler form of silent film humor. His last film performance was in support of Laurel and Hardy in *Saps at Sea* (1940).

TWENTIETH CENTURY-FOX   It was one of the "Big Five" motion picture companies, along with MGM, Warner Bros., Paramount, and RKO. The company came into existence in 1935 in a merger of one of Hollywood's oldest film studios, Fox Film Corporation, and its newest, Twentieth Century Pictures. William Fox, a Hungarian immigrant, started in the film industry as the owner of a nickelodeon in Brooklyn, New York. He eventually built a small chain of theaters and started a film exchange, thereby also getting into the distribution business. However, he lacked a steady supply of product. He began making films in 1912 to remedy this shortcoming and finally established the Fox Film Corporation in 1915. It was an auspicious beginning because within the year he had developed his first major star attraction, vamp Theda Bara *(q.v.)*, in the hit movie *A Fool There Was*.

Fox made three very smart moves during the 1920s. First, the company hired John Ford *(q.v.)* as a director in 1921, and the legendary filmmaker would eventually make the vast majority of his films for Fox and Twentieth Century-Fox over the next twenty-five years. Second, the company also acquired a great many theaters, and was second only to Paramount in overall ownership by the end of the 1920s. And third, Fox pioneered the sound-on-film system in their Movietone Newsreels, a system that was eventually used by the entire film industry (including Warner Bros., which used a different system that was scrapped not long after the success of *The Jazz Singer* in 1927).

But William Fox made one mistake that nearly put him out of business. Nothing if not audacious, he tried to buy Loew's, Inc., the parent company of MGM. He even effected the deal in 1929, making Fox the biggest, most powerful film company in the world for eighteen

months before the U.S. government nixed the deal on antitrust grounds. But the company never would have held together, anyway. Fox had grown too fast at the end of the 1920s and had taken on far too much debt. After the stock market crash, Fox stock tumbled from $119 to $1 within a matter of days!

The company was in shambles during the early 1930s; it was forced to sell off assets and to protect itself in bankruptcy court. William Fox was forced out, but not before he extracted an $18 million buyout. Meanwhile, the company survived on the hit films of Will Rogers *(q.v.)*, Fox's biggest star of the early 1930s. Rogers was soon followed by Shirley Temple *(q.v.)* as a Fox money-maker, keeping the company afloat after Rogers' tragic death in a plane crash.

New leadership was needed and it was found in Joseph Schenck, the brother of Nicholas M. Schenck *(q.v.)* of Loew's Inc., and Darryl F. Zanuck, the former production head of Warner Bros. The two men had formed Twentieth Century Pictures as a production company for United Artists in 1933 and had had great success. But Schenck and Zanuck were unhappy with UA as their distribution company and they jumped at the chance to merge their studio with the ailing Fox Film Corporation. Schenck became chairman of the board of the new Twentieth Century-Fox and Zanuck was made vice president, in charge of production. Spyros Skouras was brought in to handle distribution and exhibition, but it was Zanuck who ran the show.

Twentieth Century-Fox (or "Fox" for short) was always a studio with relatively few stars on its payroll. Zanuck milked Shirley Temple for all she was worth before she grew up. In the meantime, newer stars such as child actress Jane Withers, ice-skating star Sonja Henie, Don Ameche, Alice Faye, and especially Tyrone Power had to fill the breach. Power, in particular, was put into virtually every kind of movie Fox produced, from historical dramas to westerns to romances. Yet, as Douglas Gomery noted in his book, *The Hollywood Studio System,* even with such a small stable of famous names, Zanuck managed to push five of them into position among the top ten box office draws of 1938 (Temple #1, Henie #2, Withers #8, Faye #9, and Power #10).

If the company didn't have a great stable of stars, it made the ones it did have look as colorful as possible. Fox consistently made more films in Technicolor than any other studio, putting gloss to good effect in musicals staring Alice Faye, then Bette Grable, who became Fox's greatest star of all time, a top ten box-office draw for virtually the entire decade of the 1940s.

Except for Warner Bros. (and let's not forget that Zanuck worked there for many years), Fox was the only other studio that exhibited a notable social consciousness. Beginning with John Ford's classic *The Grapes of Wrath* (1940) and followed after World War II with movies such as *Gentlemen's Agreememt* (1947) and *Pinky* (1949), the studio made "A" movies that squarely faced issues of social injustice.

In the next, troublesome, decade, Fox reluctantly joined other members of the Big Five in a government forced sell-off of their movie theater chains in 1951. Faced with a loss of revenues, the company led the fight against television's inroads into the moviegoing audience by coming out with the widescreen CinemaScope *(q.v.)* system. But when Zanuck left the company to go into independent productions in 1956, Fox took a terrible turn. With Spyros Skouras in charge, Fox spiraled into a finanacial whirlpool that led to the vastly over-budget *Cleopatra* (1963), a film that threatened to sink the corporation.

Having just made the hit film *The Longest Day* (1962), distributed by Fox and adding valuable dollars to its coffers, Zanuck was called in to save the company. He became chairman and his son, Richard Zanuck, became vice president in charge of production. The father-and-son team succeeded, at least for a short while, in keeping Fox afloat. When the wolf was at the door again in the late 1960s, Zanuck tried to save the company again with the big-budget war film *Tora! Tora! Tora!* (1970), which bombed at the box office. Then, in one of the more fascinating corporate struggles in recent decades, Zanuck conducted a purge at Fox in 1971 in which he forced his son out of the company. But Darryl Zanuck didn't last much longer at the helm; he was out a few months later. Fox was teetering at the edge of oblivion when it was bought by billionaire oilman Marvin Davis. Fox returned to a powerful position within the industry with major hits ranging from *Star Wars* (1977) to *Wall Street* (1987). Presently owned by Rupert Murdoch, the movie-making division of the company was renamed Fox Film Corporation in 1989. Director Joe Roth was named chairman. It is the first time since Ernst Lubitsch briefly ran Paramount in 1935 that a director has headed a major studio.

See also: Zanuck-Brown; Zanuck, Darryl F.

U

ULMER, EDGAR G. (1904–1972) A director forced to work with an inordinate number of ridiculous scripts who, nonetheless, proved that a fluid camera and a foreboding visual style could make an artistic statement of even the worst vehicles Hollywood could offer. Ulmer not only suffered with poor scripts, he also had to make do with threadbare budgets. Nonetheless, he contributed a suprising number of minor screen classics, including *The Black Cat* (1934), *Bluebeard* (1944), *Detour* (1946), and *Ruthless* (1948).

Ulmer's career began in Austria, though he received his most important training in Germany under the tutelage of such greats as the stage's Max Reinhardt and the movies' F. W. Murnau. When Ulmer finally became a director in Hollywood in 1933, he made a handful of films, including the highly regarded horror film *The Black Cat,* before spending the rest of the decade making movies in everything from Ukranian to Yiddish.

In the early 1940s, he worked his way back to Hollywood and it was during the next ten years that he made the majority of his best films. His German Expressionist style was well suited to the developing *film noir* movement of the latter 1940s and early 1950s, and even cheap little movies such as *Murder Is My Beat* (1952), with stars as dubious as Paul Langton and Barbara Payton, made audiences take notice of a distinctive talent at work.

Ulmer's films might have been thoroughly forgotten had not the influential French film critics of the 1950s discovered him as a true *auteur (q.v.)*. During the 1960s, his cause was taken up in America by the likes of critic Andrew Sarris and, today, thanks to their efforts, Ulmer is considered a notable minor artist.

UNITED ARTISTS A film company created in 1919 by the four most popular and influential silent movie giants of the day, Charlie Chaplin, Mary Pickford, Douglas Fairbanks, and D. W. Griffith *(qq.v.)*, with the assistance of former U.S. Secretary of the Treasury William McAdoo. Convinced they would have more artistic control and a greater financial gain by distributing their own movies, the founding foursome became the first major film company built by movie artists.

Unlike MGM, Paramount, Warner Bros., Twentieth Century-Fox, RKO, Universal, and Columbia, United Artists lacked its own studio for production purposes. Chaplin, Pickford, Fairbanks, and Griffith all had their own production companies and had no need of building filmmaking facilities for their new enterprise. UA merely distributed their films.

UA was quite profitable during the silent era, despite the fact that Griffith was past his popular peak, and Chaplin made very few films in the 1920s. But by the 1930s the company could only count upon Chaplin's modest output (among its founders) and, therefore distributed the work of others, such as Twentieth Century Pictures, Samuel Goldwyn, Howard Hughes, and the Disney Studio, in order to survive. Unfortunately for UA, the company was unable to depend on any of these profitable independents for any great length of time.

Nonetheless, UA held a unique place in the studio environment of the 1930s and early 1940s as an outlet for independent producers. But after the end of World War II, as the studio system *(q.v.)* began falling apart, Hollywood's other studios began offering distribution deals to the independents, undercutting the one slim advantage UA had over its competition.

D. W. Griffith had sold his shares in UA in 1924, Douglas Fairbanks bowed out in the 1930s, but Pickford and Chaplin hung on until the red ink became serious, finally selling the ailing company in 1951 to Arthur Krim and Robert Benjamin. The new owners were far more active than Pickford and Chaplin, and they turned

United Artists was founded in 1919. Three of the four original stockholders are pictured here: Charlie Chaplin (with the jacket), Mary Pickford, and Douglas Fairbanks. The fourth founding member, director D. W. Griffith, had a falling out with his partners and left the company in 1924. Photo courtesy of Movie Star News.

the company around by virtue of making distribution deals that brought them *The African Queen* (1951) and other hits. Just as significantly, Krim and Benjamin took over the company at a time when location shooting was becoming more commonplace, and UA's lack of a studio was suddenly an asset, leaving the company unencumbered by large mortgage payments and building maintenance on little used property.

The company continued to do well into the 1960s as the distributers of the James Bond films, among others. But by 1967, United Artists ceased to be an independent concern when it was bought by Transamerica, Inc. With an infusion of capital, UA prospered in the 1970s, but was then diminished further when it was taken over by MGM, which bought the company in 1981. Known as MGM/UA, the organization produced such hits as *Rain Man* (1988), but in 1989 UA was put up for sale. As of this writing, it is still part of MGM.

UNIVERSAL A film studio with roots that go back to 1909 when Carl Laemmle founded his IMP company (Independent Motion Picture Company of America). In 1912, IMP joined with half a dozen other small companies to form Universal. Universal City was built in Los Angeles by the studio in 1915 in order to consolidate the company's filmmaking operations. But during the rest of the silent era, Universal moved very cautiously, making serials and low-budget films without stars and, in the process, losing talented actors, directors, and executives that it had developed to other studios.

Universal began making "A" pictures at the beginning of the sound era, producing the classic *All Quiet on the Western Front* (1930), but poor corporate management left the company in a precarious position, forcing the studio to sell off its theaters during the early years of the Depression. But while in its worst financial predicament, Universal made its best known films, the classic horror movies that include *Dracula* (1931), *Frankenstein* (1931), *The Mummy* (1932), and *The Invisible Man* (1933). But though the horror films are much loved today, they weren't quite successful enough at the time to put Universal into the black.

Losses forced Laemmle out in 1936. New management took over the ailing company, which began turning a profit almost immediately thanks to Deanna Durbin *(q.v.)*, whose bright and cheery hit films kept the studio alive until the boom years of World War II. At that point, the comedy team of Abbott & Costello *(q.v.)* became Hollywood's top box office draw for Universal. During the late 1930s and early 1940s, Universal also found success in low-budget comedies by W. C. Fields and in the Sherlock Holmes films starring Basil Rathbone.

In 1946, Universal merged with International Pictures, becoming known as Universal-International. But the postwar years were not healthy ones for the newly named company. Abbott & Costello, the studio's biggest asset, fell out of favor. In 1952, the company was bought by Decca Records, which changed the name of the studio back to Universal and also brought back profitability.

In 1959, the Music Corporation of America (MCA), a major communications conglomerate created by former agent Lew Wasserman, bought Decca and soon turned their filmmaking subsidiary, Universal, into a major TV and motion picture company. But it wasn't until the success of such megahits as *Airport* (1970), *The Sting* (1973), *American Grafitti* (1973), and *Jaws* (1975), that the industry took notice of Universal's leading position in modern Hollywood. In more recent years, Universal has released such popular and critical hits as *Field of Dreams* (1989).

Today, in Universal City, on the original tract of land developed by Carl Laemmle in 1915, stands the home of one of Hollywood's greatest tourist attractions, Universal Studios.

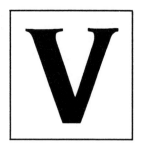

VALENTI, JACK (1921–　) As president and chief executive officer of the Motion Picture Association of America, Inc. (MPAA), the Motion Picture Export Association of America, Inc., and the alliance of Motion Picture & Television Producers, Inc., Mr. Valenti represents the interests of the modern American film in-

Jack Valenti has been the president of the Motion Picture Association of America for nearly twenty-five years and is only the third person to hold the post since it was created in 1922. His office has been involved in developing the movie ratings system as well as helping Hollywood producers sell their films overseas. Photo courtesy of Motion Picture Association of America, Inc.

dustry's big eight: Columbia, Walt Disney, MGM/UA, Orion, Paramount, Twentieth Century-Fox, Universal, and Warner Bros. As head of the MPAA, he represents these companies as a unified front in their dealings with the government and the public.

One of Valenti's prime if less well-known responsibilities as chairman of the Motion Picture Export Association is the preservation and the enlargement of foreign markets, which today account for slightly less than half of all U.S. film company revenues. It falls to him to negotiate film treaties and settle difficult marketplace film issues with representatives of more than one hundred foreign governments on behalf of the eight member film companies.

Since its founding in 1922 (then known by the title of Motion Picture Producers and Distributors of America), only three men have served as leaders of the MPAA: Will Hays (1922–1945), who was postmaster general in the cabinet of President Harding (during whose tenure the title "movie czar" was born); Eric Johnston (1945–1963), who was president of the United States Chamber of Commerce; and Valenti, who began his duties in June 1966, leaving his post as special assistant to the president in the administration of Lyndon Johnson.

Under Valenti's leadership, the MPAA has very substantially relaxed the industry's self-censorship practices, instituting a helpful if maddening code that finds sex more objectionable than violence.
See also: The Hays Code

VALENTINO, RUDOLPH (1895–1926) The greatest male movie sex symbol of the silent era, and perhaps in the history of the cinema. His brilliant career was highlighted by a handful of enormous box office hits, hysterical fan reaction, and a sudden, tragic end that turned him into a legendary figure.

For many, Rudolph Valentino's appeal to women seems totally inexplicable. But his brooding intensity was utterly magnetic in his day. He didn't have a long period in vogue—just five years—and his success almost certainly would have ended with the coming of talkies, but he became a legend, in large part because of his sudden, tragic death in 1926. Photo courtesy of The Siegel Collection.

He was christened Rodolfo Alfonzo Raffaele Pierre Philibert Guglielmi di Valentino d'Antonguolla. His father, a veterinarian in the Italian army, died when Valentino was twelve years old. Found unsuitable for officer training in either the army or the navy, Valentino briefly pursued studies in agriculture. In the meantime, he was most successful as a spendthrift, depleting the family funds. As a consequence, he was sent to New York to make his own way.

Valentino held a variety of jobs during his early years in America, including that of a gardener. He also ran afoul of the law, making extra money as a thief (with the rap sheet to prove it). His most useful skill, however, was dancing. He became a skilled exhibition dancer in New York's club scene, stealing the young Clifton Webb's partner, Bonnie Glass.

Valentino's terpsichorean flair landed him in a musical called *The Masked Model* that toured the country. He later joined another stage musical in San Francisco. When that show closed he was broke and looking for opportunities when one of his friends suggested he try the movie business in Los Angeles.

Valentino made his movie debut as a dancer in a bit role in *Alimony* (1918). He moved up (and sometimes down) the cast list rather swiftly over the next three years in films such as *Delicious Little Devil* (1919), *A Rogue's Romance* (1919), and *Out Of Luck* (1919). He married for the first time during these early years in Hollywood, but the union was extremely short-lived. His wife, Jean Acker, locked him out of their bedroom on their wedding night. The future great lover never consummated his first marriage.

Valentino's luck changed soon thereafter when he was chosen by a perceptive Metro Pictures executive, June Mathis, to star in *The Four Horsemen of the Apocalypse* (1921). The film became one of the top-grossing films of the 1920s, earning more than $4.5 million.

Suddenly, Valentino was a hot property who hit a plateau over the next few pictures then zoomed even higher thanks to his famous performance in the title role of *The Sheik* (1921). Women couldn't get enough of him. An Arabian craze hit the country, influencing everything from home decoration to fashion. Valentino was the period's epitome of male sensuality; he was masculine yet vulnerable, fierce yet tender, and thoroughly, unattainably exotic. Looking at his films today, he seems rather silly and terribly overdramatic; he was not a sensitive or subtle actor by any stretch. Many men did indeed find Valentino effeminate and embarrassing, but his legion of female fans made him a remarkably popular star—until Valentino let his second wife, Natasha Rambova (born Winifred Shaunessy), nearly ruin his career.

After Valentino's star status was enhanced with *Blood and Sand* (1922), Rambova insisted that he make *The Young Rajah* (1922), a film over which she exerted a great deal of control. It was a total disaster that threatened to turn Valentino's image into that of a hedonistic freak. She continued to wield power over Valentino and was generally blamed for the disappointing box office performance of such films as *A Sainted Devil* (1924) and *Cobra* (1925). Rambova continued to costume and make up Valentino in an embarrassingly girlish manner and was responsible for interminable script changes for which "Rudy" dutifully fought.

Finally, Rambova was contractually barred from interfering with Valentino's next production. As a consolation, he personally funded a picture of her own (*What Price Beauty,* 1925) that she then directed and produced. The movie failed miserably and she promptly left him.

Meanwhile, free of Rambova, Valentino regained his former glory in two towering hits, *The Eagle* (1925) and *The Son of the Sheik* (1926). But the emotional and physical toll of his stardom had been crushing. In 1926 he came down with a perforated ulcer and was admitted to a hospital in New York. The world was stunned when it was announced that Valentino had died. There were street riots in New York during his funeral and several women even committed suicide.

Valentino fan clubs lasted throughout the decades and his image as a screen lover remains one of the enduring clichés of the silent era.

As for Valentino, himself, he was reportedly a rather ordinary man who found little happiness in his stardom. As he once lamented, "A man should control his life. Mine is controlling me."
See also: sex symbols: male

VIDEO ASSIST   The term applies to the recent practice of simultaneously videotaping takes while shooting them on film. Video, unlike film, doesn't have to be developed before one can see what has been shot. Therefore, recording a take or a scene on video allows the director the opportunity to see immediately if he likes what he sees or if he wants to make changes. The video assist is a helpful method of ensuring that a scene works and will not have to be reshot after the set has been struck. So far, video assists have been used mostly on larger budget features, but it is reasonable to expect that the practice will eventually widen to include all but the most inexpensively produced films.

VIDOR, KING (1894–1982)   Though born to a wealthy Texas family, he was one of Hollywood's most "European" directors, as evidenced by both his fluid filmmaking style and the often (if naive) political and social subject matter of his movies. While most other American directors were content to make a good, fast-paced and entertaining film, Vidor saw the motion picture as an artistic medium early on. But his impressive career, which spanned the 1920s through the 1950s, owed as much to his American pragmatism as it did to his artistic impulses. Vidor knew that his movies had to make money if he was going to continue to direct, and, therefore, he only rarely neglected the commercial realities of filmmaking.

Vidor's early interest in film was born when he worked as a projectionist in a Galveston movie theater. Fascinated with the motion picture medium, he started making his own newsreels in Texas as well as a comedy and an industrial film. He married young Texas actress Florence Arto and the two set out for Hollywood in 1915. As Florence Vidor, his wife went on to become a silent screen star while he struggled to find his own niche in the movie business. He worked as an extra, tried to sell his scripts, and, after making a handful of independent features put enough money together in 1920 to start his own shoestring studio, Vidor Village, and began making movies starring his wife.

Neither Vidor Village nor his marriage to Florence lasted. The studio went out of business in 1922 and the marriage ended in 1924. Meanwhile, the director had begun working for the Metro Company, which was soon melded into Metro-Goldwyn-Mayer. Vidor made his big breakthrough, taking what was intended to be a standard war yarn at MGM, *The Big Parade* (1925), and turning it into a powerful antiwar film and one of the biggest hits of the silent era.

His reputation made, Vidor was in a position to pick and choose his projects. Among his subsequent films was *The Crowd* (1928), a stark and deeply cynical movie that dealt with the loneliness and despair beneath the hustle and bustle of America's big cities. It was another major critical and box office hit for the director, and he was nominated for an Academy Award for Best Director.

Vidor took chances. He made *Hallelujah* in 1929 with an all-black cast. Though the film was inadvertently racist in many ways, his choice to deal with issues of race at all say a great deal about his social conscience. Once again, the Academy put him forward as a Best Director nominee.

As the studio system solidified during the early talkie era, it became more and more difficult for a free-thinking director like Vidor to make the kinds of movies he yearned to put on the screen. His skill was much in evidence in films such as *The Champ* (1931), for which he won his third Oscar nomination for Best Director, and the brazenly erotic *Bird of Paradise* (1932), among others. But Vidor wanted to make *Our Daily Bread* (1934), a film about farmer cooperation during the Depression, and he had to go outside the studio system, using his own money to produce, write, and direct what has become an American classic. Justly famous for its climactic montage finale as the farmers successfully irrigate their crops, *Our Daily Bread* left Vidor's bank account thoroughly parched. While highly regarded by many critics, it was a flop at the box office.

Henceforth, Vidor did not stray from the studio system, although there was still a definite social and political point of view in his work, most notably in *Stella Dallas* (1937), *The Citadel* (1938), for which he garnered his fourth Oscar nomination, *The Fountainhead* (1949), and *War and Peace* (1955), for which he received the last of his five Oscar nominations. He is perhaps best remembered though as the director of the sprawling epic western *Duel in the Sun* (1946). His last film was *Solomon and Sheba* (1959). All told, he directed fifty-five films, roughly half of them with sound—but all of them with intelligence and style.

Though he never won an Academy Award, Vidor was awarded a special Oscar in 1979 for "his incomparable achievements as a cinematic creator and innovator."

VOIGHT, JON (1938–   )   A complex and committed actor who had his greatest screen success in the late 1960s and 1970s. Tall, blond, and blue-eyed, he has mostly shied away from traditional leading man roles to play characters who live on the fringe of society.

The son of a golf pro, Voight intended to become either a painter or a scenic designer but found his calling in the theater while attending Catholic University, from which he graduated in 1960. He went on to study acting at New York's Neighborhood Playhouse from 1960 to 1964, receiving both emotional and financial support from his parents. As a result of their generosity, Voight was able to avoid the actor's alternate profession of waiting on tables.

He had his first major break when he joined the Broadway cast of *The Sound of Music* as a replacement during that hit show's long run, playing the role of Rolf (and singing "You Are Sixteen") for six months. He received far more attention from critics for his leading role in a revival of Arthur Miller's *A View from the Bridge*. As it happened, Dustin Hoffman was the assistant stage manager during that show and the two actors developed a mutual respect. Later, Hoffman recommended Voight for the role of Joe Buck in *Midnight Cowboy* (1969), turning his friend into an Oscar nominee and star virtually overnight.

Midnight Cowboy, however, was not Voight's first film role. After acting in stock and on TV, he made his movie debut in *Hour of the Gun* (1967). Among other earlier films, he also worked with Hoffman in *Madigan's Millions,* a movie that was made in 1967 before either of them were stars, and finally released in 1970 when they were both hot properties.

Voight's film choices during his career have often reflected his liberal and socially conscious beliefs; from the very beginning, he has been rather picky about his movie roles. As a consequnce, he hasn't appeared on screen quite as often as he might have. He found his work in the 1970s, with magnificent performances in *Deliverance* (1972) and *Coming Home* (1978), winning an Oscar for his performance as a paraplegic Vietnam veteran in the latter film. He was also quite winning in some extremely mediocre movies, including the counterculture exploitation movie *The Revolutionary* (1970), the sentimental *Conrack* (1974), and the even more sentimental *The Champ* (1979).

He has continued to work in films during the 1980s but with considerably less success. His best-known movie of the 1980s was *Runaway Train* (1985), in which he and Eric Roberts wowed the critics with their over-the-top performances. Most of his other recent films of the 1980s, such as *Lookin' to Get Out* (1982) and *Table for Five* (1983), received mediocre reviews and did little business at the box office. He has been seen little on the screen in the late 1980s.

WALD, JERRY (1911–1962)   He was a screenwriter and a producer who many believe to be the model for Budd Schulberg's title character in *What Makes Sammy Run?* Ambitious and energetic, Wald had a keen eye for the commercial aspects of filmmaking. In a career that spanned thirty very active years, he collaborated on the screenplays of many of Warner Bros.' better films of the late 1930s and early 1940s, and then produced a sizeable percentage of that studio's biggest hits in the mid- to late 1940s. In the 1950s and beyond, when studios floundered in their search for a winning formula at the box office, Wald continued to find commercial success right up until (and after) his death.

Wald wrote about radio when he began his career as a journalist. Not long after, in 1933, he parlayed his knowledge into a string of short subjects starring radio personalities for Warner Bros. Impressed with young Wald, the studio hired him as a screenwriter. He earned credits on mediocre films such as *Gift of Gab* (1934) as well as some of Warner's better films such as *Brother Rat* (1938), *The Roaring Twenties* (1939), *Torrid Zone* (1940), and *They Drive By Night* (1940).

When he turned producer in 1942 he started with minor Humphrey Bogart films that did well at the box office, including *All Through the Night* (1942), *Across the Pacific* (1942), and *Action in the North Atlantic* (1943). His success with these war films led him to bigger budget efforts including *Destination Tokyo* (1944) and *Objective Burma* (1945).

Wald came into his own as a Warners producer in the mid-1940s when he found the winning formula for popular women's films. In a memo, taken here from the fascinating book *Inside Warner Bros. (1935–1951)* by Rudy Behlmer, Wald wrote to his immediate boss, Steve Trilling, "When are you going to get wise to the fact that you can tell a corny story, with basic human values, in a very slick, dressed-up fashion?" Wald put

his theories to the test in films such as *Mildred Pierce* (1945), *Humoresque* (1946), *Possessed* (1947), *Johnny Belinda* (1948), and *Flamingo Road* (1949) with huge success. In addition, he produced such strong and moody action movies as *Dark Passage* (1947) and *Key Largo* (1948). As a result of his stunning track record during the latter half of the 1940s, Wald was presented with the Irving Thalberg Award in 1948.

Except for a brief stint as vice president in charge of production at Columbia between 1953 and 1956, Wald produced as an independent. He didn't lose his golden touch. Among the films that bore the imprint of Jerry Wald Productions were *Peyton Place* (1957), *The Long Hot Summer* (1958), *Mr. Hobbs Takes a Vacation* (1962), and the posthumously released *The Stripper* (1963).

WALLIS, HAL B. (1899–1986)   A producer and studio executive, involved in the making of more than four hundred movies, a great many of which are now considered classics. In a career spanning nearly fifty years, he first made his mark at Warner Bros. as their executive in charge of production during the broadest stretch of the studio's golden years. He then formed his own company, Hal Wallis Productions, earning a reputation as one of Hollywood's most successful independent producers.

Born Harold Brent Wallis to a poor Chicago family, he held a series of unmemorable jobs before moving to Los Angeles in 1922. In that same year Wallis became the manager of the Garrick Theater, a major movie house, a job that led to his being hired in 1923 as a publicity man for Warner Bros. As Warners grew, so did Wallis' responsibilities. He became studio manager in 1928 and then head of production for a short while. Between 1931 and 1933 he was supplanted by Darryl F. Zanuck *(q.v.),* but from 1933 until 1944, Wallis was Jack L. Warner's right-hand man.

During his stewardship at Warners, Wallis was responsible for some of the studio's most memorable films, and his name was boldly included in the credits of such films as *Little Caesar* (1930), *Gold Diggers of 1933* (1933), *Captain Blood* (1935), *The Adventures of Robin Hood* (1938), *Dark Victory* (1939), *The Maltese Falcon* (1941), *Yankee Doodle Dandy* (1942), and *Casablanca* (1942). His efforts at Warner Bros. were appreciated by his peers, who honored him twice with the Irving Thalberg Award, first in 1938 and then in 1943.

Jack Warner and Hal Wallis had a falling out in 1944 and the producer formed his own production company, releasing his films through Paramount, an association that lasted twenty-five years. He was even more commercially successful as an independent then he was at Warners, producing the enormously popular Martin and Lewis comedies as well as Elvis Presley's musicals. He also brought challenging theater works to the screen, producing, among others, *Come Back, Little Sheba* (1952), *The Rose Tattoo* (1955), *The Rainmaker* (1956), and *Becket* (1964).

Wallis finally changed his allegiance in 1969 to Universal, producing such films as *Anne of a Thousand Days* (1969), *True Grit* (1969) and, his last movie, *Rooster Cogburn* (1975).

WALSH, RAOUL (1887–1980) Hollywood's premier outdoor action director, Walsh's work is characterized by visual economy and a strong masculine image, the latter quality allowing him to inject a surprising amount of tenderness and warmth into scenes that lesser directors would never have dared.

Walsh was born to a well-to-do New York City family. His father was an Irish builder and his mother was of Spanish descent. Despite the comforts of home and a few years at a couple of different colleges, including Seton Hall, young Walsh gave in to his adventurous spirit and ran off to Texas to punch cattle. After a horse fell on his leg, however, the young man's interests turned to the theater, and he established an acting career. Walsh began appearing in one-reel westerns as a villain in 1909 and soon began studying the action behind the camera, becoming an assistant director for D. W. Griffith in 1912.

He began directing in 1914 with *The Double Knot*, but he also continued to act throughout the silent era. As a director, he often made movies that starred his younger brother, the silent movie star George Walsh (1892–1981). Raoul's most famous acting role was as John Wilkes Booth in Griffith's *The Birth of a Nation* (1915).

A pivotal moment in Walsh's career as a Hollywood director occurred in 1920 when he made a serious and artistic film called *Evangeline*. As Kingsley Canham reports in his book, *The Hollywood Professionals,* Walsh's experience with the film was anything but gratifying.

Raoul Walsh began his film career as an actor but lost his right eye in a traffic accident during the making of *In Old Arizona* (1929). He then settled for becoming one of the most respected action directors in Hollywood. Photo courtesy of Movie Star News.

Walsh said, *"Evangeline* got the most wonderful write-ups of any picture I ever made. There were editorials written about it. But it didn't make a quarter. So I decided then to play to Main Street and to hell with art."

Despite his decision, Walsh had only sporadic success during the early 1920s, but he hit his stride with one of the greatest adventure epics of all time when he directed Douglas Fairbank's classic *The Thief of Bagdad* (1924). He soon followed it with yet another hit, the male-bonding film *What Price Glory?* (1926), which first introduced the military characters Flagg and Quirt to big-screen audiences. Walsh went on to direct several popular sequels.

While making *In Old Arizona* (1929), a film which Walsh was supposed to direct as well as star in as the Cisco Kid, he was involved in a traffic accident and lost his right eye. The distinctive patch that Walsh wore for the rest of his life added to his mystique, but ended his acting career. Warner Baxter took over Walsh's role in that film and ironically, won an Oscar for Best Actor, making him a major star.

Throughout the 1930s Walsh worked steadily, though his skills as an action director were rarely put to good use. He directed a few notable comedies, such as Mae West's *Klondike Annie* (1935) and Jack Benny's *Artists and Models* (1937), as well as a number of light adventure films and romantic comedies, but there was nothing special about his work until he hooked up with Warner Bros. in 1939, directing Cagney and Bogart in *The Roaring Twenties.*

Warner Bros. was the perfect studio for Walsh's tough, male-oriented action films. In addition to the second half of the 1920s, Walsh's golden period as a director was the decade between his two greatest gangster films, *The Roaring Twenties* and *White Heat* (1949).

Despite a directorial career that spanned fifty years, the movies for which Walsh is best remembered today are the ones that starred Errol Flynn, Humphrey Bogart, and James Cagney *(qq.v.).* They epitomized Walsh's ideal of men of action and he directed them with panache.

Though it was director Michael Curtiz who made Errol Flynn a star in *Captain Blood* (1935) and then guided his career throughout the rest of the 1930s, it was Walsh who sustained Flynn's career, directing the actor in seven films, among them one of Walsh's greatest achievements, *They Died with Their Boots On* (1941), as well as *Gentleman Jim* (1942) and *Objective Burma!* (1945). Walsh also helped Bogart to become a star when he directed him in *They Drive by Night* (1940) and *High Sierra* (1941). And as for Cagney, Walsh directed the pugnacious actor in some of his best vehicles, including *The Strawberry Blonde* (1941) and *White Heat* (1949). Of the latter film, it has often been said that Walsh was the only director in Hollywood who could have gotten away with a scene that had Cagney sitting on his mother's lap.

Walsh worked consistently throughout the 1950s, but it was a period of slow decline for the aging director. He made mostly mediocre westerns and war movies during the decade. One of his more interesting projects, however, was a noble attempt at bringing Norman Mailer's *The Naked and the Dead* to the screen in 1958.

His last film was a minor western with Troy Donahue called *A Distant Trumpet* (1964). He retired when his one good eye began to fail him and he could no longer see well enough to direct.

WANGER, WALTER (1894–1968) In a career that spanned five decades, he began as a producer and quickly rose to chief of production at three of Hollywood's biggest studios, Paramount, Columbia, and MGM. Wanger made all sorts of films, from elegant romances to action films—usually with "A" movie budgets. In the 1950s he became an independent, successfully producing some of the film industry's most memorable "B" movies.

Born Walter Feuchtwanger, the future producer seemed destined for a career in Washington rather than Hollywood. After graduating from Dartmouth College (followed by a short stint as a producer on Broadway in 1917), he joined the war effort as an officer in Army Intelligence. When World War I ended, he joined President Woodrow Wilson's staff, assisting the statesman in his struggle to establish the League of Nations. Perhaps disillusioned by his experience at the desultory Paris Peace Conference, Wanger returned to the U.S. and began his career as a producer at Paramount.

In Wanger's long career, he was responsible for such films as the Marx Brothers' first effort, *The Cocoanuts* (1929), one of Garbo's most memorable movies, *Queen Christina* (1933), Frank Borzage's much-admired romance *History Is Made At Night* (1937), John Ford's classic western *Stagecoach* (1939) (for which Wanger served as executive producer), Alfred Hitchcock's excellent *Foreign Correspondent* (1940), and Fritz Lang's clever *Scarlet Street* (1943), for which Wanger, again, acted as executive producer.

His career slid in the late 1940s and early 1950s when he produced a series of mediocre pictures and box office duds. Worse, still, he was involved in a major scandal when he was arrested and convicted for shooting and wounding the agent of his wife, actress Joan Bennett. A short jail sentence for Wanger resulted.

In the mid-1950s, while working as an independent and releasing through United Artists, Wanger proved he was not finished in show business when he produced two of Donald Siegel's and Hollywood's best "B" movies of the decade, *Riot in Cell Block 11* (1954) and *Invasion of the Body Snatchers* (1956). After yet another success with the hit *I Want to Live!* (1958), Wanger stumbled badly when he was hired to produce *Cleopatra* (1963, *q.v.*). The production ran heavily over budget, and Wanger was replaced by Darryl F. Zanuck. The imbroglio effectively ended the producer's career.

WAR MOVIES A major genre that has ebbed and flowed in popularity since the days of the nickelodeon. The very first war movie, *Tearing Down the Flag* (1898), was so popular that it caused a rush on the penny arcades that featured it. But it wasn't until the unprecedented success of D. W. Griffith's *The Birth of a Nation* (1915), which contained scenes of Civil War battles on a grand-scale, that filmmakers woke up to the inherent cinematic and dramatic possibilities of war movies.

America's involvement in "the war to end all wars" in 1917 helped spur interest in the war movie genre. World War I spawned its share of blatant propaganda films such as *The Kaiser: The Beast of Berlin* (1918) and *Heart of Humanity* (1918), but it also inspired its share of thoughtful films, such as Griffith's much admired *Hearts of the World* (1918), which contained actual battle footage shot by Griffith in Europe.

For the most part, however, the film industry would approach World War I as a serious subject for film only after sufficient time had passed to allow audiences some emotional distance and a period of reflection. Interestingly, this pattern of reticence followed by renewed interest in war movies would repeat itself in Hollywood after each successive American armed conflict.

The first major film examining issues of World War I opened seven years after the war's end. King Vidor's classic *The Big Parade* (1925) was the first film to give a truly realistic sense of war and its terrible cost. On the one hand, the battle sequences in the film were exciting and thrilling, seemingly glorifying war, but the film's message was finally and firmly antiwar because the audience saw the aftermath of the battles as well.

Service comedies aside, *The Big Parade* set the standard for most World War I films that followed, such as *All Quiet on the Western Front* (1930) *The Dawn Patrol* (1930 and remake, 1938), and *Today We Live* (1933). All dramatized a loss of innocence among soldiers, pilots, and sailors, and were permeated by a general sense of wasted youth.

The Hollywood World War I movie began to change just before America's entry into World War II, as the movie studios readied the public for the new conflict to come. Films like *The Fighting 69th* (1940) and *Sergeant York* (1941) extolled the heroism of the fighting man and, if not glorifying war, inferred that there are times when it is necessary to fight.

When the Japanese attacked Pearl Harbor and America joined the war effort, Hollywood and the U.S. government became partners in filmmaking. According to Clayton R. Koppes and Gregory D. Black in their informative book, *Hollywood Goes to War,* the Office of War Information had a profound impact on what war movies Hollywood made and how they made them. Government officials actually participated in story conferences and wrote speeches mouthed by actors in many a war film. Of course, World War II was seen as a total war and Hollywood, including most studios, writers, directors, and stars, was more than pleased to cooperate with the government.

The significant themes that began to emerge in many of the World War II movies were brotherhood, unity for the good of the cause, and sacrifice.

For the first time in Hollywood history, a cross section of ethnic groups could be found in the movies, with all of the characters of the representative groups acting as heroes. It quickly became a cliché that each cinematic combat unit contain one Italian, one Jew, and one black. But this formula undoubtedly helped the home audience to appreciate the need to keep the nation united—with color and ethnic lines breached—in the fight against tyranny. In films such as *Bataan* (1943) and *Guadalcanal Diary* (1943), Hollywood presented a new and progressive image of racial and ethnic harmony forged in the crucible of war.

The need for unity in the face of the German and Japanese war machines prompted Hollywood to make an about face in its usual presentation of the normal American individualist hero. A spate of films touted the virtues of working as a team, teaching the rugged individualist that he had to give up his solitary ways if the Allies were going to win the war. John Garfield, for one, learned that lesson in *Air Force* (1943) when his loner character finally pitched in to save the lives of his buddies.

In true patriotic fashion, war movies made during World War II proclaimed the necessity and the nobility of sacrifice. Beginning with John Farrow's harrowing *Wake Island* (1942), a movie that had something of the spirit of the Alamo about it, martyrdom became a key element in a great many of World War II's most emotionally effective movies, such as *The Purple Heart* (1944) and *They Were Expendable* (1945).

Near the end of World War II, when it became apparent that the Allies would win, a few insightful war movies such as *A Walk in the Sun* (1945), and *The Story of G.I. Joe* (1945) were made, touching upon the genuine experience of the common soldier.

It wasn't until 1946, though, that some of the bitterness of lost youth and shattered dreams could be played out on the screen with the release of *The Best Years of Our Lives.* The film was a hit and a Best Picture Academy Award Winner. For the most part, however, unlike the antiwar sentiment prevalent in films after World War I, World War II has traditionally been presented to movie audiences in a very positive light even years later in films such as *The Longest Day* (1962), *A Bridge Too Far* (1977), and even *The Dirty Dozen* (1967).

The difference between the antiwar attitude of most World War I movies and the pro-war attitude of most World War II films was succinctly summed up in purely Hollywood terms by Jeanine Basinger in her excellent book, *The World War II Combat Film,* when she wrote, "World War I was a flop and World War II was a hit."

While World War II received "A" movie treatment, the Korean conflict was relegated mostly to "B"s. Director Samuel Fuller, working on a shoestring, didn't hesitate to put his personal stamp on the war in some of the most compelling war movies of the early 1950s, such as *The Steel Helmet* (1950) and *Fixed Bayonets* (1951).

If Korea was casually overlooked by Hollywood, Vietnam was consciously avoided by the industry. In the late 1960s and early 1970s, most filmmakers saw the mass audience as too politically polarized to make successful movies on the subject. John Wayne ignored the conventional wisdom and starred in and directed the pro-Vietnam War film *The Green Berets* (1968). It was a poor movie that received awful reviews, but it was mildly successful at the box office.

Later, as the emotional wounds caused by the Vietnam War began to heal, a handful of thoughtful movies appeared in the theaters, among them, *Coming Home* (1978), which dealt with the effects of the war on its survivors. *Go Tell the Spartans* (1978) became the first movie about that war to present a realistic and intimate story of soldiers in combat. *The Deer Hunter* (1978), a sprawling saga that tried to come to terms with the American male ethos and its relationship to the war, stalked away with the Best Picture Academy Award.

The best was yet to come, however, when, the following year, Francis Coppola's brilliant psychological examination of the dark side of the conflict, *Apocalypse Now* (1979), was released. After this brief flurry of interest, though, the war wasn't graphically presented to film audiences again until 1986 in the Academy Award-winner *Platoon,* on the heels of which was Stanley Kubrick's *Full Metal Jacket* (1987), followed by Brian DePalma's harrowing *Casualties of War* (1989), all of these movies crackled with pent-up rage and disgust for the waste in human life.

In the meantime, however, America refought the Vietnam War in movie fantasies such as Sylvester Stallone's *Rambo II* (1985) and Chuck Norris' *Missing in Action* (1984) and their sequels. If America couldn't win the Vietnam War in fact, Stallone and Norris would finally win it in the movies.

See also: antiwar movies; *The Birth of a Nation;* Coppola, Francis Ford; Fuller, Samuel; Kubrick, Stanley; Milestone, Lewis; Stallone, Sylvester; Vidor, King; Wayne, John

WARNER BROS.   The only family run film company among the "Big Five" (which included Paramount, MGM, Twentieth Century-Fox, and RKO). It was founded by the four brothers Warner, Harry Warner (1881–1958), who was the president and real power of the firm, Albert Warner (1884–1967), the least well known of the brothers who handled overseas distribution, Samuel Warner (1888–1927), the visionary brother who pushed the others toward experimenting with sound but who died before the talkie revolution began with the Warner production of *The Jazz Singer* (1927), and Jack L. Warner (1892–1981), the most famous of the brothers who oversaw all production of Warners' films at their Burbank studio.

The four Warner brothers were among fourteen children born to a family that emigrated from Poland. The brothers started out as exhibitors during the first decade of the twentieth century. They then turned to distribution but folded in 1910. They continued to dabble in the growing movie business, producing and distributing until they hit it big with their film *My Four Years in Germany* (1917). They opened their own "poverty row" studio in Hollywood and began their ten-year climb toward success. During those years, they had Ernst Lubitsch on their staff of directors, but the key to their surivival was twofold. They had a series of hit films starring Rin-Tin-Tin during the 1920s, plus they also had the brilliant and driven Darryl F. Zanuck as a writer, and later as their chief producer reporting to Jack L. Warner until 1933.

The company began to prosper during the booming 1920s and the studio borrowed heavily, first buying the ailing Vitagraph company in 1925, thereby gaining studio space and a distribution system, and later buying theater chains in order to ensure exhibition outlets.

In June of 1925, Warner Bros. and Western Electric began working together to develop talking motion pictures. In 1926, Warners established the Vitaphone Company as a subsidiary for their sound-on-disc shorts, which were mostly of vaudeville musical acts. *The Jazz Singer* (1927), the first feature-length film with songs and a modest number of spoken lines of dialogue, caused a sensation. The Warners film, starring Al Jolson, became one of the biggest hits of the year, and the talkies were born.

In the early 1930s, when the Great Depression hit, the company was seriously hurt due to its heavy debt burden. Warners always had a tightfisted reputation, and the studio responded by making movies faster and more cheaply than any other major company; it also worked it stars much harder and paid them far less money than they might have been paid by Warners' competitors, causing clashes, suspensions, and court cases with outspoken stars such as James Cagney, Bette Davis, and Olivia de Havilland *(qq.v.).*

Among Warner Bros'. other stars under contract were George Arliss, Paul Muni, Edward G. Robinson, Errol Flynn, and in the 1940s, Humphrey Bogart and Joan Crawford. The studio also boasted a fine crew of directors, such as Michael Curtiz and, later, Raoul Walsh and John Huston.

During the 1930s, the studio was particularly successful with its cycle of biopics, such as *Disraeli* (1929), *The Story of Louis Pasteur* (1936), and *Dr. Ehrlich's Magic Bullet* (1940). These films were excellent entertainment as well as an easy-to-take education for a large segment of the mass audience. Just as significantly, Warners captured the public imagination with its gangster films that began with *Little Caesar* (1930) and *Public Enemy* (1931), as well their spectacular, Depression-inspired musicals such as *Footlight Parade* (1933) and *Gold Diggers of 1933* (1933). Most striking were their explosive, socially conscious films such as *I Am a Fugitive from a Chain Gang* (1932).

More than any other studio, Warners made films in support of the war effort. The studio released the first anti-Nazi film, *Confessions of a Nazi Spy* (1939), and even made a pro-Soviet film, *Mission to Moscow* (1943), at the request of President Roosevelt. A studio whose films were predicated on action, violence, and melodrama, it was also the perfect company to make patriotic war films that ranged from *Action in the North Atlantic* (1943) to *Objective Burma!* (1945).

The studio's earlier reputation in hard-boiled gangster and, later, G-man, films during the 1930s, plus its stable of tough leading men, made Warners a leader in the *film noir* genre of the latter 1940s, with classics such as *Mildred Pierce* (1945) and *White Heat* (1949).

The end of the studio system *(q.v.)* hit the company

hard. It was forced to sell its theaters in 1951 and profits began to plummet. Strangely enough, it was television that kept the company going during the 1950s, when Warner TV shows, such as "Cheyenne" and "Maverick" brought in much-needed revenue.

During the 1960s, Warners released hit films such as *My Fair Lady* (1964) and *Bonnie and Clyde* (1967), but by then the studio had largely become a distribution network for independent producers. For instance, in the 1970s and 1980s, Clint Eastwood's Malpaso Company released its films through Warner Bros.

Meanwhile, in 1956, Harry and Abe Warner had sold their stock, and Jack had become the only brother left associated with the company. He sold his share to Seven Arts in 1967, which, in turn, was bought by Kinney National Service in 1969, later changing the name of the conglomerate to Warner Communications. In 1989 Time, Inc. merged with Warners to become Time-Warner, Inc. In recent years the film subsidiary has scored successes with films such as *Beetlejuice* (1988), *Batman* (1989), and *Lethal Weapon II* (1989).
See also: biopics; Curtiz, Michael; gangster films; *I Am a Fugitive from a Chain Gang; The Jazz Singer;* Jolson, Al; musicals; Rin-Tin-Tin; sound; Warner, Jack L.; Zanuck, Darryl F.

WARNER BROS.' CARTOONS   Under the banner of Looney Tunes and Merrie Melodies, they were the hippest, cleverest, and most amusing animated shorts ever produced. With characters such as Bugs Bunny, Daffy Duck, Porky Pig, Elmer Fudd, Foghorn Leghorn, Tweety Pie, Sylvester the Cat, Pepe LePew, Wile E. Coyote, Road Runner, and Speedy Gonzales, the Warner Bros. animation unit was a perpetual hotbed of creative lunacy.

Under the stewardship of Leon Schlesinger, Warner Bros. began making cartoons in 1930. These early black-and-white films were called Looney Tunes in order to build on the popularity of Disney's Silly Symphonies. In addition, as pointed out by Douglas Gomery in *The Hollywood Studio System,* "Warners insisted that each cartoon should include music from a current Warners' feature film."

Throughout the early 1930s, the animation unit struggled to make a reputation but without much success. It wasn't until Schlesinger launched Merrie Melodies, a color cartoon series in 1934, that the Warners cartoons began to catch on. More importantly, though, Schlesinger hired new talent such as Tex Avery, Bob Clampett, Friz Freleng, Frank Tashlin, and Chuck Jones, who, over time, developed the famous Warners cast of cartoon characters. It began to take shape in 1936 when Porky Pig made his debut and became the first animated star on the Warners lot.

Bugs Bunny, the carrot-chomping wise-guy rabbit, was created soon after, taking his name from the man who originally sketched him, Bugs Hardaway. The unnamed character was simply referred to as "Bugs' Bunny" in the early development stage and, finally, the name simply took hold (minus the apostrophe). While Bugs was the best-known character among the Warners animated stars, Daffy Duck offered an inspired insanity and he remains a sentimental favorite of a great many fans.

Two of the most influential animators at Warners during their heyday were Friz Freleng and Chuck Jones, who, between them, helped create the frenetic action, violence, and goofy humor that became a hallmark of their studio. The two of them often produced and directed the Warners cartoons, while many of the best of these animated shorts were written by Michael Maltese.

Since 1937, the voice of the Warners cartoon characters was that of Mel Blanc, until his death in 1989. His son has learned all the cartoon voices, however, and will continue in his father's voice prints.

Warners' cartoons reached their creative height in the 1940s. By the middle of the decade both "Looney Tunes" and "Merrie Melodies" were made in color. And while the animation was never quite on a par with Disney's work, the Warner cartoons offered far more energy and off-the-wall tongue-in-cheek humor, making them especially entertaining for both children and adults.

During the 1950s, Warners continued to make cartoons, which appeared first in movie theaters and then on television, where they have continued to thrive to this day. Unfortunately, the Warners animation unit was disbanded in 1969, but there have been Warners cartoon specials on TV throughout the years and Bugs and Daffy have recently been reborn as movie shorts by a young crew of new animators. Mel Blanc continued to provide voice-overs until his death in 1989. The ultimate recognition of the Warners cartoons, however, occured in 1987 when the animated works were added to the permanent collection of the Museum of Modern Art in New York City.
See also: animation

WARNER, JACK L. (1892–1978)   Of the four brothers who founded the motion picture company that bore their family name, he was the best known. As chief of production at the Warner Bros. Burbank studio, Jack Warner oversaw the producers, stars, directors, and writers who created many of the most memorable movies of the studio era. Jack Warner was not the brightest of the Warner brothers—that distinction belonged to the firm's president, Harry, who controlled the company purse strings from New York. Nor was Jack Warner a visionary; brother Sam was the one among them who pursued the dream of talking pictures. And Albert was the swing vote who usually backed Harry. But Jack was the only brother who had a real feel for entertainment. He loved to sing and tell jokes (usually bad ones), and he had a genuine love of entertainers, many of whom he idolized.

Jack Warner was the youngest of fourteen children born to a Polish immigrant family. Warner, himself, was born in Canada while his family restlessly looked for a place to settle in North America, finally putting down roots in Youngstown, Ohio.

When the Warner family invested in a nickelodeon in Newcastle, Pennsylvania, in 1903, Jack was out front during intermission singing to the customers. It was as close to vaudeville as he'd ever get.

He joined with three of his brothers to continue in the movie business, but met with only variable success during the silent era. Once their studio was firmly established in the late 1920s (thanks to *The Jazz Singer,* 1927), Jack ruled over film production with an iron hand. Of all the major studios, Jack Warner ran his studio, more than any other, like a factory, churning out movies with the speed and efficiency of a fast-moving production line. But unlike most other Hollywood studio moguls, Jack Warner didn't forget the poverty he once knew. He promoted pictures with a social consciousness, such as *I Am a Fugitive from a Chain Gang* (1932) and *Wild Boys of the Road* (1933).

A supporter of Franklin Roosevelt, Jack stood up for Democratic causes throughout the 1930s and was a vigorous backer of the war effort, starting as a major in the Army Signal Corps and eventually becoming a colonel.

In 1956, when his surviving brothers, Harry and Albert, sold their shares of the company, Jack stubbornly refused to sell out. The old dinosaur continued running the company until 1967, when he sold his shares to Seven Arts. In the meantime, he had been duly honored by the Hollywood community during the 1958 Oscar ceremonies, when he was presented with the prestigious Irving G. Thalberg Memorial Award.

During Warners Bros.' heyday, Jack Warner delegated much of the production detail to such talented right-hand men as Darryl F. Zanuck and Hal B. Wallis (*qq.v.*). Toward the end of his reign as studio chief and in the years thereafter, he proved he was an equally capable producer. He personally produced such hits as *My Fair Lady* (1964) and *Camelot* (1967), as well as the entertaining musical flop *1776* (1972) and the surprisingly offbeat, gritty western *Dirty Little Billy* (1972).

Jack Warner outlived all his brothers and, except for Darryl F. Zanuck, he was the last of the great movie moguls to pass from the American scene.
See also: Warner Bros.

WARREN, HARRY (1893–1981) A prolific and hugely successful composer and songwriter who wrote tunes for Hollywood for nearly fifty years. According to the American Society of Composers, Authors and Publishers, Warren is the seventh best-selling songwriter of all time, and his long list of movie musical classics attests to his popularity. He helped three studios reach their respective musical heights, writing tunes for Warner Bros.' greatest musicals of the early to mid-1930s, Twentieth Century-Fox's Alice Faye period in the late 1930s and early 1940s, and the beginning of MGM's musical golden era in the mid- to late 1940s. He also contributed to Paramount's successful musical comedies of the early 1950s. Winner of three Oscars, Warren's musical style was well suited to the movies: it was bold, brassy, and elegantly simple; audiences could (and did) hum the songs he wrote when they left the theater.

Born Salvatore Guaragno in Brooklyn, New York, he made his way in Hollywood any way he could, working as an extra and a propman, finally managing to become an assistant director. But all the while he was writing music, and after penning a hit song in the 1920s, he was set on his true career.

After a few Broadway shows, Warren returned to Hollywood. Sound had come to the movies and musicals were much in demand. At Warner Bros., working with lyricist Al Dubin (Dubin was his first and most notable collaborator), Warren wrote the songs for the classic musicals *42nd Street* (1933), *Gold Diggers of 1933* (1933), *Footlight Parade* (1933), *Dames* (1933), *Wonder Bar* (1934), and others, creating standard tunes that are still much loved today.

When Warner Bros. lost interest in the musical, Warren went to Fox, where he wrote the scores for such entertaining films as *Down Argentine Way* (1940), *Tin Pan Alley* (1940), *Sun Valley Serenade* (1941), *Hello Frisco Hello* (1943), and *Sweet Rosie O'Grady* (1943).

At MGM, Warren helped develop the great musical tradition that would flourish at the studio in the late 1940s and 1950s with songs for, among others, *The Harvey Girls* (1946), *Ziegfeld Follies* (1946), and *Summer Stock* (1950).

He began to slow down in the 1950s and 1960s, but he still managed to write hit songs for films such as the Martin and Lewis vehicles *The Caddy* (1953) and *Artists and Models* (1956). His last movie music could be heard in *Rosie* (1967).

Just a small sampling of Warren's enormous output of hits (exclusive of title songs from many of the previously mentioned films) are "Lullaby of Broadway," "I Only Have Eyes for You," "You Must Have Been a Beautiful Baby," "Jeepers Creepers," "Chattanooga Choo Choo," "The More I See You," and "That's Amore."

WATERS, ETHEL (1896–1977) A black singer/actress who commanded the screen in the relatively few opportunities Hollywood offered her. Waters had dignity and power, and those very attributes limited her movie

Ethel Waters was known as "Sweet Mama Stringbean" when she started in show business at the age of seventeen. She rose to fame as a singer, and became known to movie audiences in a modest number of motion pictures, many of which she dominated with her warm, powerful personality. Photo courtesy of The Siegel Collection.

career during the less tolerant years that made up the bulk of her lifetime. Nonetheless, she appeared in ten films, making the most of her screen time.

Waters was married at the age of twelve (she would marry a total of three times), and worked at menial jobs before she made a name for herself as the singer Sweet Mama Stringbean when she was seventeen. Working in vaudeville and later helping to break the color barrier on Broadway, Waters became one of the leading black singer/actresses in America.

Her appearances on film were often directly tied to her successful Broadway shows. Two of her three best-known movies had been stage hits that were turned into the films *Cabin in the Sky* (1943) and *The Member of the Wedding* (1952). The third was a film about racism, *Pinky* (1949), for which she was honored with an Oscar nomination for Best Supporting Actress.

It was in such movies as *On with the Show!* (1929), her debut film, when she sang "Am I Blue?" and "Birmingham Bertha" (both numbers were designed to be so tangential to the plot that they could be easily edited out when the film was circulated in Southern cities), and in her starring role in *Cabin in the Sky,* that film audiences were given a taste of her sexy, sassy blues interpretations.

Most of her films, however, weren't musicals, and

Waters bowed out of Hollywood after her appearance in *The Sound and the Fury* (1959).

See also: racism in Hollywood

WAXMAN, FRANZ (1906–1967)   A film composer who excelled at writing dark, moody music tinged with hints of danger. No wonder, then, that his scores for *Sunset Boulevard* (1950) and *A Place in the Sun* (1951) won Oscars. In fact, the majority of his scores were for films that fit the gothic, horror, suspense, mystery, and thriller genres.

Born Franz Wachsmann in Germany, he studied music at the Dresden Music Academy and the Berlin Music Conservatory. His film career began in 1930 when he started arranging and then composing music for films at UFA, the German film company. Jewish, he was physically attacked and beaten by Nazi sympathizers in 1934, whereupon he fled to Paris. He arrived in America soon thereafter and found a home in Hollywood, were a great many German refugees made him welcome.

His first film score in Hollywood was for *The Bride of Frankenstein* (1935), and its sinister and brooding feeling set the tone for much of his later work. Other than the magnificent Bernard Herrmann, Waxman was Alfred Hitchcock's favorite composer, writing the scores for four films made by the "master of suspense," *Rebecca* (1940), *Suspicion* (1941), *The Paradine Case* (1948), and *Rear Window* (1954).

Waxman was prolific, writing more than fifty film scores, his greatest impact occurring during the *film noir* period of the late 1940s and early 1950s. In particular, his music for such films as *The Two Mrs. Carrolls* (1947), *Possessed* (1947), *Dark Passage* (1947), *The Unsuspected* (1947), and *Sorry Wrong Number* (1948) helped immeasurably to create the paranoia that infested these and other films of that era.

Of course, Waxman didn't write moody music all the time. Among his lighter efforts were the scores for such films as the Marx Brothers' *A Day at the Races* (1937), *A Christmas Carol* (1938), *The Philadelphia Story* (1940), *Woman of the Year* (1942), *Air Force* (1943), *Mister Roberts* (1955), *Taras Bulba* (1962), and many others. The last film he scored was *Lost Command* (1966).

In addition to his work in the movies, Waxman created and nurtured the Los Angeles Music Festival in 1947, an institution that has developed an international reputation.

WAYNE, JOHN (1907–1979)   An actor who became a folk hero for his portrayal of rugged, independent Americans. During a career of nearly fifty years, he was the most consistently popular performer in postwar Hollywood, landing in the top ten in box office polls in nineteen of twenty years between 1949 and 1968 (he missed the top ten in 1958 when he bombed in *The Barbarian and the Geisha*). As a consequence of his pop-

John Wayne toiled in low-budget westerns and serials throughout the 1930s before becoming a star in John Ford's *Stagecoach* (1939). He is seen here in one of his many early cheapies. Photo courtesy of Movie Star News.

ularity, his films brought in a staggering $800 million in box office receipts, which, in constant dollars, remains a record. Big, broad-shouldered, and square-jawed, Wayne was an imposing figure on film. But he also possessed a boyish charm that hardened into a vulnerable dignity as his face weathered with age. For the most part, Wayne will be remembered for the many movies in which he collaborated with one of Hollywood's greatest directors, John Ford.

He was born Marion Michael Morrison in Winterset, Iowa to a druggist father. Ill health caused his father to move the family to Southern California, where his strapping young son excelled in both his studies and in sports. It was during Wayne's youth that he made regular visits to a local fire engine station, accompanied by his pet airedale, Duke, which led to his nickname of Big Duke, later shortened simply to Duke.

A football scholarship sent Wayne to the University of Southern California, where he played football for two years before a shoulder injury, sustained while surfing, ended his athletic career. While in college,

Wayne worked summers at the Fox Studio prop department, getting the job through a contact with Tom Mix. During 1926, while at Fox, he met and befriended director John Ford, who occasionally put his young friend in scenes that didn't require any acting in several different movies such as *Mother Machree* (1928), in which Wayne made his debut, and *Hangman's House* (1928).

In 1929, Raoul Walsh needed a star for his western epic *The Big Trail*. Gary Cooper was unavailable and filming was about to begin. Reports are mixed, but either John Ford recommended Wayne to play the lead in the film or Walsh simply spotted him on the Fox lot and decided to offer him the starring role after giving him a screen test. It was for *The Big Trail* that Marion Michael Morrison became John Wayne, a name created in collaboration with Walsh and director Edmund Goulding. "Wayne" came from General "Mad Anthony" Wayne of Civil War fame and "John" was a solid American name that seemed simply to go nicely with "Wayne."

The new moniker didn't help *The Big Trail,* which

was a major commercial flop. Wayne continued to act but in increasingly minor movies, until he settled in first at the poverty row studio Mascot, followed by Monogram, and then finally Republic, making low-budget action films and serials, among the latter *Hurricane Express* (1933), *Riders of Destiny* (1933), *Randy Rides Along* (1934), *The Three Mesquiteers* (1938), etc. He even took a stab at being a singing cowboy, playing "Singing Sandy" Saunders in one serial (both his guitar playing and singing were dubbed). He starred in the neighborhood of two hundred of these quickie serials and low-grade movies; nobody knows for sure how many.

For many years, John Ford had promised Wayne that he'd give him a role in one of his films. After Gary Cooper turned down the role of the Ringo Kid in *Stagecoach* (1939), Ford made good his promise, giving Wayne the break of his career. *Stagecoach* was a huge hit and Wayne suddenly became a star after having spent a decade in the Hollywood boonies. He went on to star in fourteen films directed by Ford, many of them some of the director's greatest works, including *She Wore a Yellow Ribbon* (1949), *The Quiet Man* (1952), *The Searchers* (1956), and *The Man Who Shot Liberty Valence* (1962).

Wayne was often considered a poor actor, but in fact he was exceptionally good at playing John Wayne, and he played that character—tough, prideful, and noble—with a considerable variety of interpretations. He played him young and cocky in *Seven Sinners* (1940), old and stubborn in *Red River* (1948), independent and proud in *Rio Bravo* (1958), and vulnerably idealistic in *The Three Godfathers* (1948). Except for his many westerns, which made up nearly half of his movies after *Stagecoach*, Wayne was perhaps best known for his patriotic hard-as-nails image in any number of war films, most notably *The Fighting Seabees* (1944), *They Were Expendable* (1945), *Sands of Iwo Jima* (1949), for which he received his first Best Actor Academy Award nomination, and the Vietnam era *The Green Berets* (1968), a controversial film that he also produced and directed to critical catcalls but big box office. Of this latter film, it is often noted that Wayne filmed the sun setting in the east.

In addition to starring in films, Wayne also produced a great many movies, first at Republic and later through his own company, Batjac Productions. Among those films he produced were *Angel and the Badman* (1947), *The Fighting Kentuckian* (1949), *Hondo* (1953), *The High and the Mighty* (1954), *Blood Alley* (1955), *The Alamo* (1960), which also marked his debut as a director, and many others.

By the late 1960s, Wayne seemed to be an actor in a time warp. His massive body lumbered through films that seemed out of step with the rest of Hollywood. He reportedly had to be lifted by crane to get up in the saddle of his horse. But his movies made money, even if they were mostly ignored by the critics except to say "another John Wayne movie." Only a few of his later films were memorable, such as *El Dorado* (1967), *True Grit* (1969), which brought him is only Best Actor Oscar, and his final film, *The Shootist* (1976).

No actor has taken his last bow on film as knowingly nor as movingly as Wayne. *The Shootist* begins with a montage of scenes of Wayne in his earlier westerns, ostensibly giving us the history of the film's main character but really telling us that this story is about the movie icon John Wayne. In the course of the film, Wayne teaches a young man (Ron Howard) the code of the West. When Wayne dies at the end in a shootout (knowing all along that he is dying of cancer), taking a saloonful of villains with him, we know that we've seen the last of this particular brand of American hero.

The courage Wayne showed on screen in his many films was matched by his endurance under the doctor's knife. In 1963 he survived lung cancer, having one of his lung's removed. Later, in 1978, he had open heart surgery, and in 1979 cancer returned, leading to more surgery. He died shortly thereafter. In honor of his passing, he became one of the rare actors to ever have a congressional medal made in his likeness.
See also: Ford, John; Hawks, Howard; Siegel, Donald; serials; *Stagecoach;* war movies; westerns

WEBB, CLIFTON (1891–1966) A gifted and versatile performer whose movie roles were generally limited to pompous, upperclass, acid-tongued individuals. Webb sometimes played his archetypal character in dramatic films, but he usually starred (often as the stuffed shirt babysitter, Mr. Belvedere) in successful comedies during the late 1940s and throughout the 1950s.

Born Webb Parmalee Hollenbeck, he began dancing and acting professionally while still a child. Not content with his lot in life, he studied painting and music, briefly becoming an opera singer when he was just seventeen. Then came a successful career as a ballroom dancer, which led to jobs in Broadway musicals in the late 1910s. He soon proved his mettle as a serious actor, as well, gaining a fine reputation in the English theater.

Tall and trim with a handsome countenance, he was a natural for the movies, which beckoned in the early 1920s. He graced a number of films, among them, *Polly With a Past* (1920) and *The Heart of a Siren* (1925), but the peripatetic actor did not become a silent movie star.

Webb returned to the stage and continued to cultivate his many interests when, nearly two decades after his last film appearance, Otto Preminger decided he wanted Webb as the sophisticated killer in *Laura* (1944). Though Preminger's boss at Twentieth Century-Fox, Darryl F. Zanuck, was dead set against hiring Webb, Preminger finally prevailed. In the end, *Laura* became a smash hit and Webb was nominated for a Best Supporting Actor

Oscar for his performance. He also became a character actor/star at Fox, and, ultimately, even became a very close friend of Zanuck's.

In Hollywood films, where intellectuals were so often looked upon with distrust, Webb's uppercrust, snobby, know-it-all persona was a natural for antagonist roles. He played the villain in *The Dark Corner* (1946) and a less than likeable character in *The Razor's Edge* (1946), which brought him another Best Supporting Actor Academy Award nomination.

Then, something peculiar happened. Webb was cast as the stuffy, pedantic babysitter, Mr. Belvedere, in *Sitting Pretty* (1948), and stole the movie from its child stars (no easy feat). The movie was a huge hit and the actor went on to star in several films playing the same character. Once he was seen as a lovable stuffed shirt, he was given similar lead roles in films such as *Cheaper by the Dozen* (1949), *Mister Scoutmaster* (1952), *The Remarkable Mr. Pennypacker* (1958), and others.

He retired from the screen in 1962 after starring in an unsuccessful drama, *Satan Never Sleeps,* in which he played an anticommunist priest.

WEISMULLER, JOHNNY (1904–1984) Though not the first man to play Tarzan on film, he was undoubtedly the best—and certainly the most fondly remembered. Weismuller was a wooden actor with a halting speech pattern that worked just fine for the monosyllabic role of the ape man created by Edgar Rice Burroughs. His limitations as an actor were more readily apparent when he grew a bit long in the tooth to play Tarzan and starred in the low-budget Jungle Jim series. Called upon to speak in the somewhat more sophisticated tones of a jungle guide, Weismuller was only marginally more articulate than he had been as Tarzan. But for generations who saw Weismuller swinging from vines on the big screen, and their children who saw him doing the same when the movies were rebroadcast on television, Weismuller would always be Tarzan.

Born Peter John Weismuller, the young athlete became a gold medal winner for the U.S. during the 1924 Olympics. And then he did it all over again in 1928, winning a total of five gold medals. As a celebrated sports star he was lured into appearing in a few short subjects, but it wasn't until MGM decided to star him in *Tarzan, the Ape Man* (1932) that an institution was born. The film had high production values, a good script, and a strong supporting cast (including Maureen O'Sullivan as Jane) behind Weismuller's surprisingly bold, if stiff, performance. Weismuller, who almost always showed off his famed swimming prowess in at least one scene in every film, starred in a total of twelve Tarzan movies, the first half of them for MGM, the second set of six for RKO. The best of these films were at MGM and *Tarzan and His Mate* (1934) is considered by most as the cream of the crop.

Weismuller was forty-four years old when he hung up his loincloth and made his last Tarzan film, *Tarzan and the Mermaids* (1948). He immediately went to Columbia Pictures and began starring in a series of low-budget adventure films for kids that began with *Jungle Jim* (1948). He continued to play the same character in a total of sixteen of these films (although in the last three, all pretense was dropped and his character was called Johnny Weismuller).

Except for one role in 1946, in a mediocre film called *Swamp Fire,* Weismuller played either Tarzan or Jungle Jim exclusively through 1955. Curiously, his costar in *Swamp Fire* was Buster Crabbe, another former champion swimmer who had played Tarzan in a film produced by a competing studio during the 1930s.

After a short stint as Jungle Jim on TV, Weismuller quietly retired. Like fellow swimmer/actor Esther Williams, he lent his name to a pool company and did reasonably well in business. He fared less well at marriage, marrying six times. His last movie appearance was a cameo role in *The Phynx* (1970).

See also: Tarzan films

WELLES, ORSON (1915–1985) He was the boy genius and enfant terrible, who cowrote, directed, and starred at twenty-five years of age in what many consider the greatest movie ever made, *Citizen Kane* (1941). Welles completed the direction of a mere dozen feature films over the length of his career, plus five other assorted full-length movies that were either never finished or for which he did not receive directorial credit. Several of his subsequent movies were brilliant, others were flawed and oftentimes poorly made from a technical standpoint, but they were never boring. Critic Andrew Sarris wrote, "the dramatic conflict in a Welles film often arises from the dialectical collision between morality and megalomania, and Welles more often than not plays the megalomanical villain without stilling the calls of conscience." Welles not only proved to be a powerful performer in his own movies, but a visual and aural force (he had a marvelous, deep, resonant voice) in the films of many other directors, as well.

Born to a rich Wisconsin couple, he was an enormously gifted child who, among other astonishing accomplishments, read Shakespeare as a virtual tot. His youth, however, was beset by tragedy; his mother died when he was eight years old, four years later, Welles's father died. Dr. Maurice Bernstein, a physician friend of the family, became Welles's guardian, and his memory later figured prominently in *Citizen Kane,* split between the harsh banker/guardian of the young Charles Foster Kane and the sweet-tempered Jew (named Bernstein) who later ran Kane's newspapers.

Welles never attended college. He was besieged with scholarship offers but, instead, set off for Ireland to sketch. While on the Emerald Isle, he bluffed his way

No one had a more auspicious beginning in the movie business than Orson Welles. Seen here in a publicity still for his first film, *Citizen Kane* (1941), he cowrote, directed, and starred in that masterpiece, though he never fully duplicated his initial success. Photo courtesy of The Siegel Collection.

into an acting career by pretending to be a famous New York theater star, making his professional debut in a leading role on the stage of the renowned Gate Theater. He drew excellent reviews and planned to continue his acting career but had little success in winning roles in either London or New York. Unperturbed, the young genius continued to travel, and did the usual expatriate activities, including fighting bulls in Spain.

After returning to America, Welles tried the theater again, this time making his way to Broadway in the role of Tybalt in the 1934 production of *Romeo and Juliet*. In that same year he married actress Virginia Nicholson (divorced 1939), and had his first brush with moviemaking, codirecting and appearing in a four-minute short entitled *The Hearts of Age*.

During the rest of the 1930s, Welles was a cyclone of activity, performing on radio, collaborating with John Houseman as coproducer and director of the Phoenix Theater Group, the Federal Theater Project, and their most famous theatrical enterprise, the brash and innovative Mercury Theater, which they founded. The Mercury Theater quickly gained a reputation for excellence that led Welles and Houseman to create a radio show called *The Mercury Theater on the Air,* which was responsible for the stunning 1938 Halloween broadcast of H. G. Welles's *The War of the Worlds.* The program offered fake news reports of a Martian invasion, which a surprisingly large segment of the population took to

be the truth, causing widespread panic. Welles directed the program and played the leading character.

In Hollywood, the struggling RKO studio was in desperate need of new ideas, new talents, and especially some inexpensively produced big hits. They saw Welles as a hot radio and theatrical personality with a penchant for splashy showmanship. He was, to their point of view, exactly what they needed. The studio gave him carte blanche to make a film with complete artistic control just so long as he stayed within a rather severe budget. After several false starts on other projects, Welles settled on *Citizen Kane,* a thinly veiled biography of newspaper magnate William Randolph Hearst, but also (and unrecognized at the time) a somewhat autobiographical story as well. Hearst's attempts at stopping the distribution of the film failed, and it was released to critical raves and, contrary to popular mythology, to respectable box office—though the film was hardly the huge success RKO had hoped it would be. However, *Citizen Kane* was certainly recognized by the Hollywood establishment as a superb piece of filmmaking, and honored it with nine Oscar nominations, including most of the major awards, such as Best Film, Best Director, Best Actor (Welles), and Best Photography. It won but one Oscar, for Best Original Screenplay, which Welles shared with Herman J. Mankiewicz.

Citizen Kane represented a huge leap forward in filmmaking, both in its style and in its subject matter. In style, it was the harbinger of the *film noir* movement with its dark, foreboding use of shadows and oppressive low-angle shots. The deep-focus cinematography of Gregg Toland was never used to better effect, hastening its adoption by other filmmakers. In addition, Welles's radio knowledge brought clever innovations to the use of sound in *Citizen Kane.* The movie's baroque tale of lost innocence ushered in a new maturity in the subject matter of Hollywood movies, which would later be hastened by the events of World War II. And, finally, the structure of the film itself, its clever telling of the story from several different viewpoints, forever after opened up the narrative possibilities of moviemaking.

Welles's brilliance was not appreciated by RKO. The final print of his second film, *The Magnificent Ambersons* (1942), was drastically cut in his absence while he was away making a film for RKO in South America (which never saw the light of day). *The Magnificent Ambersons* was dismissed by both the critics and the public, but was later reassessed as a massacred masterpiece.

After handing over the directorial reins to Norman Foster for his thriller *Journey into Fear* (1943), Welles didn't get a chance to direct again until he made *The Stranger* (1946) with the understanding he would not deviate from the script. It was a rather conventional suspense film to which Welles brought his flair as director and actor. The commercial success of that film led to his opportunity to write and direct *The Lady from*

Shanghai (1948), starring his second wife, Rita Hayworth (wed 1943, divorced 1947). The film is best remembered for its clever climax in which the characters have a shoot-out in a hall of mirrors, shattering their multiple images. Despite the nifty finale, the movie was a box office failure.

Welles went on to make movies on the cheap, receiving little acclaim for his work and even less commercial success. In order to finance many of his films, he acted in most anything that came along, often improving the movies he appeared in by his mere presence. Among his directorial efforts during the 1940s and 1950s were *Macbeth* (1948), *Othello* (1952), *Mr. Arkadin* (1955, also known as *Confidential Report*), and the low-budget gem *Touch of Evil* (1958), which many consider among Welles's best films after *Citizen Kane*. But not even *Touch of Evil* could revive his directorial career despite its being hailed as a masterpiece in Europe.

Welles spent much of his time where he was most appreciated, living and working in Europe. He made only a handful of other films, all of them overseas: the disappointing *The Trial* (1962), the much-admired *Chimes at Midnight* (1966), the sweetly sensuous *The Immortal Story* (1968), and the intriguing semi-documentary *F for Fake* (1973). Welles also spent a great deal of time on a number of unfinished projects, among them a version of *Don Quixote* that he began in 1955 and worked on intermittently until many of his cast members died, *The Deep,* and *The Other Side of the Wind.*

Meanwhile, as an actor, he added his considerable presence to such films as *Jane Eyre* (1944), *The Third Man* (1949), *Moby Dick* (1956), *Compulsion* (1959), *A Man for All Seasons* (1956), *Catch-22* (1970), *Voyage of the Damned* (1976), *Butterfly* (1982), and dozens of others, most of them made in Europe.

In 1975, Welles received the American Film Institute's Life Achievement Award, an honor richly deserved. He later settled in Las Vegas and became a frequent TV talk show guest and pitchman for several commercial products. He seemed to enjoy his rekindled celebrity and acceptance in the show business mainstream, despite the fact that he still could not receive funding to direct motion pictures.

Welles died of a heart attack in his home in Las Vegas.

See also: Citizen Kane; Hayworth, Rita; Heston, Charleton; Herrmann, Bernard; Houseman, John; Mankiewicz, Herman J.: Toland, Gregg

WELLMAN, WILLIAM A. (1896–1975) A director of seventy-six movies, a number of them Hollywood milestones. He was known within the film industry as "Wild Bill" Wellman due to his gallant war record, as well as his hot temper and hard drinking. He was,

nonetheless, a competent filmmaker who was nominated three times for Best Director Academy Awards, for *A Star Is Born* (1937), *Battleground* (1949), and *The High and the Mighty* (1954). He never took the Oscar home.

William Augustus Wellman was born for excitement. A high school drop-out from Brookline, Massachusetts, he played minor league hockey before joining the French Foreign Legion as an ambulance driver during the First World War. Later in the conflict, he became a pilot in the famous Lafayette Escadrille and served with distinction, winning the Croix de Guerre. Life after the war was, at first, a good deal less exciting. He worked as a salesman, but soon gave that up to become a wing-walker in an air circus.

Wellman's entry into the movie business was typically dramatic. Forced to make an emergency landing, he brought his plane down on the grounds of Douglas Fairbanks' estate. Fairbanks, ever the cheerful and friendly sort, offered Wellman a job as an actor in his 1919 film *Knickerbocker Buckaroo*. Once in the business, however, Wellman decided to tinker with the machinery of filmmaking rather than hone his acting skills. Over the next four years he worked as a property man and an assistant director before making his directorial debut with *The Man Who Won* (1923).

A strong-willed man, he quickly moved from directing low-budget westerns to more important features. By the end of the silent era, he was considered a major talent, especially when he made what became the first Academy Award–winning Best Picture, *Wings* (1927), a film famous for its incredible flying sequences. Drawing on his wartime experiences, the director poured his heart and soul into the film's aerial combat footage and turned the movie into a blockbuster hit.

By and large, war movies and male action/adventure films proved to be Wellman's forte. Among his better efforts in the genres were *The Public Enemy* (1931), which became a gangster classic, *Heroes for Sale* (1933), *Call of the Wild* (1935), *Beau Geste* (1939), which benefited from Wellman's firsthand experience as a Legioniare, and *The Story of G.I. Joe* (1945).

Wellman never had a particularly light touch with romance but he was a capable director of hard-edged comedies, proving his worth with such films as *Nothing Sacred* (1937) and *Roxie Hart* (1942). And, surprisingly (given his own hard-boiled approach to life), he made several films with a social conscience, such as *Wild Boys of the Road* (1933) and *The Ox-Bow Incident* (1943). These films, however, may owe more to their writers and producers than to Wellman's own interest in the subject matter.

His last movie was *Lafayette Escadrille,* a film obviously made from the heart; he wrote the script himself but it was sadly unconvincing. When he died of leukemia at the age of seventy-nine, the old flying ace left instructions that he be cremated and his ashes scattered to the four winds from a high-flying airplane.

In the end, Wellman was not so much a stylist or an artist as a man who saw excitement in the movie business and jumped on board for the ride.

WEST, MAE (1892–1980) Looking more like a female impersonator than a sex symbol, she was easily the greatest comedienne in film history. With a combination of outrageous hip swinging and outlandish double entendres, she both shocked and delighted audiences with her comically sexy sensibility. Her persona was well crafted from the very beginning because Mae West created it herself. In her most famous films, she not only starred but also wrote her own scripts—or, at the very least, her own dialogue.

The daughter of a prominent heavyweight prize-fighter, West was brought up in the public eye and she clearly reveled in it. At the age of six she was appearing in stock in her hometown: Brooklyn, New York. After that, she went into vaudeville, billed as "The Baby Vamp," eventually becoming the originator of the shimmy dance.

In 1926, West starred on Broadway in a play she had written, produced, and directed. It was titled *Sex,* and it caused an uproar. People either clamored for tickets or clamored for West to be thrown in jail for public indecency. In the end, the latter group won out; the impressario and star was thrown in jail for ten days on an obscenity charge.

But her imprisonment was the best publicity West could have hoped for. After two less successful ventures, she opened on Broadway in 1928 with a huge hit, *Diamond Lil.* Two more plays followed—one of which brought her back to court on obscenity charges, but this time she beat the rap.

In the early 1930s, with the Depression in full swing, Hollywood studios were willing to try anything to get people into their theaters. One of the more desperate studios was Paramount. George Raft wanted Mae West for his film *Night After Night* (1932), and the studio decided to hire her as a supporting player. She refused the part, however, until she was allowed to write her own dialogue.

Paramount never regretted granting her request. West became a film star the moment she hit the screen when she returned a hat check girl's exclamation of "Goodness, what beautiful diamonds." With the riposte "Goodness had nothing to do with it, dearie." Many years later George Raft wrote, "In this picture, Mae West stole everything but the cameras."

Her next film was based on her play *Diamond Lil,* though Paramount changed the title because of the show's salacious reputation. Calling the film *She Done Him Wrong* (1933), the studio billed West as the star. The movie was a major hit, as was her next vehicle, *I'm No Angel* (1933). The latter film brought $3 million into Paramount's coffers, making it one of the biggest hits of the year.

It was partly due to West's notoriety that the Hays Office strengthened its production code. (*See* The Hays Code.) As a result, her next movie originally titled *It Ain't No Sin,* was given the more innocuous name *Belle of the Nineties* (1934). But West was more clever than her keepers, and despite censor-required script changes, her double entendres still elicited shocked laughter from her fans.

By 1935, with three hit movies in a row, Mae West became the highest paid woman in America. After a modest success that same year with *Goin' to Town,* she scored another hit with *Klondike Annie* (1936). But it was generally downhill from that point on, both in film content and in audience acceptance. *Go West Young Man* (1937) and *Every Day's a Holiday* (1938) were rather boring—thanks to the Hay's Office—and offered none of West's usual clever innuendos.

Paramount did not renew West's contract, and the star went to Universal to costar with W. C. Fields in *My Little Chickadee* (1939). Though they made one of the screen's most interesting pairings, both West and Fields wrote their own scripts, resulting in pure chaos when neither would compromise.

West didn't make another film until 1943 when she starred in an independent feature, *The Heat's On.* By that point, however, she had become passé, and not yet the appreciated institution that she is today.

West was active in the 1940s and most of the 1950s on Broadway, on tour, and in nightclubs. But then West appeared to go into relative seclusion. That didn't mean, however, that she wasn't in demand. She was approached for roles in *Sunset Boulevard* (1950), *The First Traveling Saleslady* (1956), *Pal Joey* (1957), and *The Art of Love* (1964), to name just a few. Nothing came of those roles, but finally in 1970, West returned to the screen, looking amazingly well-preserved at the age of seventy-eight, in *Myra Breckinridge.* The movie was an unmitigated bomb, but West was the best thing in the film—and she wrote her own dialogue.

In 1978, she surprised Hollywood (and everyone else) by starring in a movie based on one of her plays, called *Sextette.* The movie was uneven at best. Although it featured an all-star supporting cast, the film's real appeal was as a curiosity piece. However, few were interested in seeing an eighty-five year old woman make funny sexual remarks.

Toward the end of her life, many criticized Mae West for being a living caricature of female sexuality. But one cannot deny that her very flouting of societal strictures placed on women was the key to her enormous success as a comedienne. Indeed, her uninhibited interest in sex was a powerful early warning shot of the feminist revolution.

See also: comedians and comediennes; Fields, W. C.

WESTERNS A distinctly American genre that has been much maligned. While the western appears to be strictly formulaic, it is in fact enormously plastic, capable of being bent into anything from morality tale to musical, from history lesson to social criticism. It has been said that if westerns did not exist, Hollywood would have had to invent them. Ironically, however, it was the other way around: westerns invented Hollywood. After all, it was Cecil B. DeMille's huge hit *The Squaw Man* (1913), the first film shot there, that put the sleepy Southern California town on the map.

With their sweeping vistas, rousing chases, dramatic gun duels, etc., westerns were perfect for outdoor filming and ideal for the big screen. It did not hurt their case that such films were inexpensive to produce (until recent decades) and sure to please audiences smitten by the romance of the American West. In fact, horse operas became the most often produced films in Hollywood history.

The western came into being even as the real West still lived on in its fading glory. Indeed, William "Buffalo Bill" Cody was seen on film at the very end of the nineteenth century. Despite the fact that it was shot in New Jersey, the first true western movie was Edwin S. Porter's *The Great Train Robbery* (1903), a film that launched the genre with a vengeance. It contained within its ten minutes' running time a great many of the elements (some might call them clichés) of future horse operas: a robbery, a chase on horseback, and a fierce gun battle. It also had the bad guys getting their just deserts.

The western prospered during the silent era, becoming standard fare for both children and adults with the emergence of the first cowboy star, G. M. "Broncho Billy" Anderson in 1908 in a film called *Broncho Billy and the Baby*. One of the big changes in the genre wrought by Anderson was his filming on location in the western United States—and audiences could tell the difference between his stunning geography and the grassy knolls of ordinary looking "eastern westerns."

After Broncho Billy, William S. Hart was a top cowboy star in the mid 1910s and early 1920s, raising the art of the western with a gritty realism that made his movies, such as *Hell's Hinges* (1916) and *Tumbleweeds* (1925), genuine classics.

There were a great many popular western stars during the latter half of the silent era, among them Ken Maynard, Harry Carey, Fred Thompson, Tim McCoy, Buck Jones and Hoot Gibson. But the biggest western star of them all was Tom Mix. During the late 1910s and throughout the rest of the silent era, he was the number-one draw in western movies and one of the most popular stars in Hollywood, with hits such as *The Cyclone* (1920) and *North of Hudson Bay* (1924). Mix's films were marked by their non-stop action and lack of realism. They were, however, full of incredible stunts.

Hollywood did not leave the western entirely in the hands of cowboy stars and many of Tinsel Town's top directors worked in the genre as well, creating serious, big-budget westerns. For instance, James Cruze made the hugely successful *The Covered Wagon* (1923), followed by John Ford's earliest classic, *The Iron Horse* (1924).

The western appeared to be a casualty of the sound era precisely because of its great, wide open spaces; sensitive sound equipment required talkies to be made in the studio. But as soon as the technical problems were solved, the western reemerged with new popularity in films such as *In Old Arizona* (1929), the first outdoor adventure film, and *The Virginian* (1929). Other important hits followed, such as *Cimmaron* (1931). Curiously, though, the big surge in westerns throughout most of the rest of the decade occurred in low-budget productions and serials. It was the era of, among others, Bill Elliot, Kermit Maynard (Ken Maynard's brother), William Boyd, Rex Bell, George O'Brien, and Bob Steele, all of whom made cheap, fast westerns that appealed to kids. Even John Wayne was earning his spurs in quickie horse operas and serials during the bulk of the 1930s. It was also during this decade that the singing cowboy came into fashion in the person of Gene Autry. It was not, however, a time when westerns were taken seriously by the major studios.

Toward the end of the 1930s, however, the western suddenly shot back into prominence. With the world edging closer to war, America began to look back at its heritage, its values, searching for the spirit that made the nation great. The result were films such as *Wells Fargo* (1937), *The Texans* (1938), *Union Pacific* (1939), and, most memorably, John Ford's *Stagecoach* (1939), the film that made John Wayne a major star.

The western became so popular near the end of the 1930s that even a studio such as Warner Bros., bereft of anyone in their stable resembling a westerner, nonetheless made films such as *The Oklahoma Kid* (1939), with such distinctly modern and urban actors as James Cagney and Humphrey Bogart. With considerably more success, Warners pressed Errol Flynn into service in several westerns, including the impressive *They Died with Their Boots On* (1941).

With the outbreak of World War II the western came to an abrupt halt, replaced by its more immediate action/adventure counterpart, the war movie.

When the war ended, the western entered its golden era, a period that lasted roughly fifteen years. It began with (and was sustained) by director John Ford, who returned to the western with *My Darling Clementine*

(1946). Ford went on to make many of Hollywood's most cherished westerns, including *Fort Apache* (1948), *She Wore a Yellow Ribbon* (1949), and *The Searchers* (1956). But he was hardly the only director making horse operas during those years. Anthony Mann cast star Jimmy Stewart in a series of excellent westerns such as *Bend of the River* (1952), and Budd Boetticher teamed with Randolph Scott to do the same in films like *The Tall T* (1957).

The 1950s boasted such highly praised and popular westerns as *Shane* (1953) and *High Noon* (1952), bringing critical appreciation to the genre. As part and parcel of its new adult patina, the western began exploring its darker side, admitting the wrongs done to the Indians in films like *Broken Arrow* (1950), and touching on psychological issues in movies such as *The Gunfighter* (1950) and *The Far Country* (1955).

Even as the explosion of TV-westerns during the later 1950s eroded the box office appeal of big screen horse operas, movies such as *Man of the West* (1958), *The Big Country* (1958), *The Left-Handed Gun* (1958), and *Rio Bravo* (1959) continued to grace movie screens.

The 1960s saw the decline of the genre. The western represented a simpler, positive image of America, that the Vietnam War severely tarnished. It was as if filmmakers were aware that this particular western cycle was near its end. Movies about the closing of the West predominated, such as John Ford's *The Man Who Shot Liberty Valance* (1962) and Sam Peckinpah's *Ride the High Country* (1962). By the mid-1960s, the Western had nearly vanished as a viable major moneymaker, only to reappear unexpectedly in the form of the "spaghetti western," spearheaded by Italian director Sergio Leone and his film *A Fistful Full of Dollars* (1967), a movie that awakened the western and catapulted Clint Eastwood to international stardom.

By the end of the 1960s, westerns had returned briefly to prominence with films such as the comedy *Support Your Local Sheriff* (1969), Sam Peckinpah's controversial masterpiece *The Wild Bunch* (1969), and John Wayne's Oscar-winner *True Grit* (1969). Without doubt, 1969 was the latter day high point of this noble genre.

The 1970s saw several attempts at keeping the western alive, chief among them *Little Big Man* (1970), Robert Altman's baroque *McCabe and Mrs. Miller* (1971), *Ulzana's Raid* (1972), *The Great Northfield Minnesota Raid* (1972), and John Wayne's last film, *The Shootist* (1976). With high production costs, however, and little audience interest beyond the above-mentioned films and the occasional Clint Eastwood vehicle, such as *The Outlaw Josey Wales* (1976), the western languished. It went into even further decline in the late 1970s with the emergence of *Star Wars* (1977), a film that launched science fiction as a new sort of frontier movie.

In more recent years the genre has almost disappeared. There have been only four major Hollywood attempts to revive it in the 1980s. The first was *The Long Riders* (1980), which received good reviews but did lackluster business. In the middle of the decade, Lawrence Kasdan wrote and directed *Silverado* (1985), an ambitious movie that received mixed reviews and suffered poor box office. It was followed a few years later by *Young Guns* (1988), a brat pack *(q.v.)* western starring, among other, Charlie Sheen, Emilio Estevez, and Keifer Sutherland. The film showed some power at the ticket windows but received poor reviews from the critics. The only other genuinely successful western made in Hollywood during the 1980s was Clint Eastwood's star powered *Pale Rider* (1985).

The cry that "the western is dead," has long been trumpeted in Hollywood, but the genre has yet to stay put in celluloid Boot Hill. The western is so unique to American history, so cinematic in its visual images, and so much a part of our filmgoing psyche, that it will doubtless come thundering back to life again someday soon.

See also: Anderson, G. M. "Broncho Billy"; Autry, Gene; Boetticher, Budd; Boyd, William; Canutt, Yakima; Cooper, Gary; Eastwood, Clint; Ford, John; Fuller, Samuel; *The Great Train Robbery;* Hart, William S.; Hawks, Howard; Hathaway, Henry; King, Henry; Kramer, Stanley; Ladd, Alan; McCrea, Joel; Mann, Anthony; Maynard, Ken; Mix, Tom; Murphy, Audie; Peckinpah, Sam; Republic Pictures Corporation; Rin-Tin-Tin; Rogers, Roy; Scott, Randolph; *Stagecoach;* Stewart, James; Walsh, Raoul; Wayne, John

WEXLER, HASKELL (1926–   ) Known principally as a gifted cinematographer, he is also a director, producer, and screenwriter of fiercely held left-wing beliefs. As a cinematographer, Wexler has both successfully experimented with the vivid immediacy of cinema verité and captured the pictorial splendor of classic Hollywood high production values.

Knowledgeable about filmmaking due to a fascination with cameras as a teenager, Wexler spent a full decade making industrial films before making the leap to Hollywood features in the late 1950s. Along the way, though, he was the cinematographer (and codirector) of such documentaries as *The Living City* (1953) and *Stakeout on Dope Street* (1958). His big Hollywood break came with *The Savage Eye* (1959), a successful low-budget drama that was noted for Wexler's strong documentary visual style.

Wexler's reputation as a cinematographer grew with films such as *The Hoodlum Priest* (1961), *The Best Man* (1964), and *The Loved One* (1965), which he coproduced. But he reached the first of many plateaus when he won his first Oscar for Best Cinematography for his work in black and white in Mike Nichols' *Who's Afraid of Virginia Woolf?* (1966).

It isn't hard to see Wexler's political and social beliefs

Haskell Wexler is certainly the most independent of contemporary cinematographers. He only photographs those films he believes in, and his reputation is such that he is always in demand. This Oscar-winner has also directed films, including a number of highly regarded documentaries. Photo courtesy of Haskell Wexler.

if one looks at the films upon which he has chosen to work, such as *In the Heat of the Night* (1967), *Bound for Glory* (1976), for which he won his second Academy Award for Best Cinematography, *Coming Home* (1978), *No Nukes* (1980), and *Matewan* (1986). But even as he photographed his feature films, Wexler also pursued his own personal projects, directing and photographing documentaries such as *The Bus* (1965), *Interviews with My Lai Veterans* (1970), which won an Oscar for Best Documentary, *Brazil: A Report on Torture* (1971), which he codirected with Saul Landau (with whom he collaborated on yet another six documentaries made over the next dozen years).

Wexler has enjoyed a long and prestigious career as a cinematographer, working with the cream of Hollywood's directorial community. He has been associated with some of the most important and memorable films of the 1970s and 1980s, including Francis Ford Coppola's *The Conversation* (1973), George Lucas' *American Graffiti* (1973), Milos Forman's *One Flew Over the Cuckoo's Nest* (1975), Terrence Malick's *Days of Heaven* (1978), and Dennis Hopper's *Colors* (1987).

Wexler has dabbled as a feature film director, writer, photographer, and producer on two occasions. His first project caused a considerable flurry of attention when Wexler directed his actors to improvise their scenes against the backdrop of the actual riots outside the 1968

Democratic Convention in Chicago. The resultant film, *Medium Cool* (1969), was a surprise critical hit and a minor commercial success. Unfortunately, Wexler didn't direct another feature until *Latino* (1985), another politically motivated film, this one about the war in Nicaragua.

WHALE, JAMES (1896–1957) The director of four of Hollywood's greatest horror films of the 1930s, as well as sophisticated romances, musicals, stage adaptations, and adventure films. No matter what he directed in his eleven years in Hollywood (1930–1941), Whale brought to all of his films a fluid camera style, a strong pictorial sense, a dash of humor, and unrushed, confident pacing.

Born in England, Whale worked as a cartoonist before discovering the joys of the theater in a most unlikely place: a German prisoner-of-war camp. His jobs in the theater evolved from actor to set designer to director during the 1920s. After he directed *Journey's End,* a play about the First World War, to rave reviews in London and New York, he was invited to direct the screen version in Hollywood. *Journey's End* (1930), for Tiffany Productions, was his auspicious debut as a movie director and he followed it with the highly successful romance *Waterloo Bridge* (1931) at Universal Pictures, for which he made most of his movies. His reputation was ultimately made with the classic horror film *Frankenstein* (1931). Over the next four years he made three more classic horror movies, *The Old Dark House* (1932), *The Invisible Man* (1933), and perhaps his most highly regarded achievement, *The Bride of Frankenstein* (1935).

Among his other well-known films were what many consider the best version of the Jerome Kern/Oscar Hammerstein musical, *Show Boat* (1936), another adaptation from the stage, *The Great Garrick* (1937), which he also produced, as well as the rousing Alexander Dumas tale *The Man in the Iron Mark* (1939). In all, he directed twenty films, his last full-length feature being *They Dare Not Love* (1941). Then, inexplicably, he walked away from Hollywood to pursue his interest in painting. In 1949 he briefly returned to filmmaking to direct a segment of *Hello Out There,* an episodic movie that was never released.

Whale's death by drowning in his swimming pool under eerie circumstances has never been adequately explained.

See also: horror films

WHITE, PEARL (1889–1938) She was Hollywood's most famous serial star, an actress whose screen exploits kept audiences coming back every week for new installments of her adventures. Pearl White was a forerunner of the emancipated woman who didn't necessarily need a man to solve her problems; she solved mysteries and out-

Hollywood's most famous star of serials, Pearl White projected an entirely different image of femininity from little Mary Pickford and ethereal Lillian Gish. She was shrewd, tough, and nobody's fool—as the male actor underfoot could testify. Photo courtesy of The Siegel Collection.

witted villains on her own, giving women of the day a positive, if melodramatic, role model.

White began her show business career at six years of age as little Eva in one of the countless stock company productions of *Uncle Tom's Cabin*. Later, she joined the circus, but hurt her back when thrown from a horse. It appeared as if her show business career was over when she became a secretary in a small film company. But when an actress was unable to perform, Miss White was pressed into service to play the lead female role in an ambitious three-reel film, *The Life of Buffalo Bill* (1910). She continued acting, working often and receiving enough recognition to be included in the film title *Pearl as a Detective* in 1913. It was the following year, however, while working for Pathé, that film history was made when she starred in *The Perils of Pauline*, (1914) a title with which her name has forever become associated. This serial, which perfected the

"cliffhanger," was a tremendous hit. Working almost exclusively in serials such as *The Exploits of Elaine* (1915), *Pearl of the Army* (1916), and *The Fatal Ring* (1917), the attractive Miss White soon became Hollywood's greatest female box office draw as a crime solver in roles that exploited her intelligence, daring, and athletic prowess.

By 1920, though, she yearned for the legitimacy of stardom in traditional feature-length films. She left Pathé and signed with Fox, appearing in roughly a dozen films over a three-year period without much success. Chastened, she returned to Pathé and made a new serial, *Plunder* (1923), but audiences were no longer interested in Miss White. She left for France and made her last serial, known in America as *Perils of Paris* (1924). She retired in the French capital and never made another movie.

See also: serials

In a film career that began more than forty years ago, Richard Widmark has quietly amassed a solid body of work. He has played heroes and villains with equal ease, proving himself a dependable, durable star. Photo courtesy of Richard Widmark.

WIDMARK, RICHARD (1914–) An actor who has played both memorable villains and hardboiled heroes in movies since 1947. A sharply angled facial structure and a growly voice have mostly limited his roles to male-oriented dramas such as contemporary crime movies and westerns; he is not the typically romantic leading man. In more recent decades, Widmark has reached that level of authority as both an icon and an actor where he has found himself cast in movies as "The General" or "The President."

Widmark planned a career in law, but found himself drawn to the theater while attending Lake Forrest College. His stage work was so accomplished that he was asked to stay on at his alma mater to teach drama after he graduated in 1936. He stayed two years, finally heading for New York in 1938 and starting out as a radio actor. Widmark branched out into the theater during the 1940s, and then was offered the part of a sadistic, psychopathic killer for his first film role. The movie was *Kiss of Death* (1947), and few actors have made such a memorable debut, especially in a supporting performance. His cackling, high-pitched laugh as he murdered his victims brought him a great deal of critical and audience attention, as well as an Oscar nomination. On the down side, however, he was temporarily typecast in similar roles.

Widmark appeared in a large number of rather poor films throughout his career, which has somewhat diminished his reputation. Nonetheless, his association with some of Hollywood's top directors (though rarely in their best films) has contributed to his longevity as a star. For instance, he worked with Henry Hathaway in the enjoyable *Down to the Sea in Ships* (1949), Elia Kazan in the hard-hitting *Panic in the Streets* (1950), Joseph L. Mankiewicz in the violent racial drama *No Way Out* (1950), and twice with the redoubtable Samuel Fuller in two low-budget films, the striking *Pickup on South Street* (1953) and the disappointing *Hell and High Water* (1954). In addition, after playing Jim Bowie in John Wayne's version of *The Alamo* (1960), Widmark became a latter-day member of the John Ford stock company, starring in the great director's lesser efforts *Two Rode Together* (1961) and *Cheyenne Autumn* (1964).

Though he seemed to be on the downside of his career by the mid-1960s, Widmark came through with a sterling performance in the highly regarded *The Bedford Incident* (1965), and then again in *Madigan* (1968), which later became the basis of a short-lived 1972 TV series of the same name in which Widmark starred.

The actor continued to appear in motion pictures throughout the 1970s and into the 1980s, more frequently in supporting and featured roles than as a star. But since the early 1970s, when he starred in the miniseries "Vanished" (1971), he has worked increasingly in TV in lead roles, such as in the much-admired "A Gathering of Old Men" (1987).

WILDER, BILLY (1906–) A writer, director, and producer whose sharply cynical point of view has been surprisingly potent at the box office throughout much of his career. The creator of both stark dramas and often bitter comedies, Wilder has also been honored by the Academy of Motion Picture Arts and Sciences with a startling twenty Oscar nominations, twelve for his screenplay collaborations and eight for Best Director, winning a total of six Oscars altogether. In recognition of his achievements in a Hollywood career that began in 1933, the governors of the Academy bestowed the prestigious Irving Thalberg Memorial Award upon Wilder in 1988.

Born Samuel Wilder in Vienna, he was called "Billy" by his mother who loved all things American and understood it to be a popular name in this country. He came from a successful upper-middle-class Jewish family and originally studied for a career in law. After just one year of legal studies, though, he decided to become a journalist, eventually becoming a reporter for a major Berlin newspaper.

Wilder made his movie debut as a screenwriter as one of five talented young men who collaborated on the famous documentary *Menschen am Sonntag/People on Sunday* (1929), cowriting the script with future Hollywood screenwriter Curt Siodmak, while the film was directed by two future Hollywood filmmakers, Robert Siodmak and Edgar G. Ulmer. Future director Fred Zinnemann was the cinematographer. The film created quite a stir at the time of its release and Wilder went on to write a number of other screenplays and provide stories for the German film company UFA, including the highly successful *Emil and the Detectives* (1931).

Hitler's rise to power in Germany in 1933 was Wilder's cue to flee. Later, he would learn that his entire family in Austria had died in a concentration camp.

His first stop before coming to America was in Paris where he cowrote and codirected his first film, *Mauvaise Graine* (1933), starring the then seventeen-year-old Danielle Darrieux. He would not direct a movie again until 1942.

After sweating out a difficult entry into the U.S. in a Mexicali consul's office in Mexico, he arrived in America in 1933 broke, with little facility for the English language, yet hoping to succeed in the film mecca of Hollywood. He learned English from listening to baseball games on the radio and going to the movies. In the meantime, he sold a story idea that became *Adorable* (1933), and he went on to sell both his stories and scripts (usually written in collaboration) as he began to build a modest reputation.

His career suddenly went full throttle in 1938 when he began his brilliant twelve-year collaboration with screenwriter Charles Brackett. They began with the clever, dark Ernst Lubitstch comedy *Bluebeard's Eighth Wife* (1938) and proceeded to pen such other grand entertainments as *Midnight* (1939), *Ninotchka* (1939), and *Ball of Fire* (1941).

Thanks to the likes of Preston Sturges and John Huston, who had opened the door for screenwriter-directors in the early 1940s, Wilder stepped forward to direct the Wilder/Brackett comedy hit *The Major and the Minor* (1942). In all their future collaborations, Wilder directed and Brackett produced, and the pair found a formula for a number of hard-hitting and provocative movies that have since become classics, among them *Five Graves to Cairo* (1943), *Double Indemnity* (1944), *The Lost Weekend* (1945), for which Wilder won his first Best Director Oscar, *A Foreign Affair* (1948), and *Sunset Boulevard* (1950), which brought him his second Best Director Academy Award.

Sunset Boulevard was the last collaboration between Wilder and Brackett and it appeared as if the director might not survive the breakup. He wrote, produced, and directed the critically acclaimed financial flop *Ace in the Hole* (1951), which was later retitled *The Big Carnival*. The film, starring Kirk Douglas, was so unredeemingly dark and cynical that audiences were turned off by its bitter view. Wilder learned his lesson in future films, softening the cynicism in order to make it more palatable, which also had the effect of drawing critical

complaints of hypocrisy. Whether sugar-coated or not, though, many of Wilder's films have still retained a rather harsh and cynical residue.

After *Ace in the Hole*, Wilder continued to write, direct, and produce, recouping his reputation with a long string of hits, including *Stalag 17* (1953), *Sabrina* (1954), *The Seven Year Itch* (1955), *The Spirit of St. Louis* (1957), and *Witness for the Prosecution* (1958).

Wilder always seemed to work best, however, when he wrote in collaboration, and some of his best work was yet to come when he joined with I. A. L. Diamond to pen the screenplays for such hits as *Love in the Afternoon* (1957), *Some Like It Hot* (1959), *The Apartment* (1960), for which Wilder won his third and last Best Director Oscar, *One Two Three* (1961), *Irma La Douce* (1963), *Kiss Me, Stupid* (1964), and *The Fortune Cookie* (1966).

Wilder and Diamond collaborated on all of the rest of Wilder's films, including his later work that received little critical and commercial acceptance, including *Fedora* (1979), and their last film together, and Wilder's last movie to date, *Buddy, Buddy* (1981).

Just as Wilder has worked with two screenwriters with excellent results, so has he consistently worked with a handful of actors. Among those who have appeared often in Wilder films have been William Holden, Shirley MacLaine, Walter Matthau, and, particularly, Jack Lemmon.

WILDER, GENE (1935–) A comic actor, screenwriter, director, and producer whose personal style has been very much in the Danny Kaye *(q.v.)* tradition. Like Kaye, Wilder possesses a sweet innocence and he has specialized in playing nervous, inhibited characters who are forced by circumstance into "outlandish" comic activities. At his best when buoyed by the talents of other brilliant comic minds, Wilder has benefited greatly from working in Mel Brooks comedies and in acting collaborations with Richard Pryor. He has been less successful behind the camera than in front of it, directing and starring in five films with only modest success.

He was born Jerry Silberman to a Russian immigrant father who became a wealthy manufacturer. Wilder's interest in acting was fanned at the University of Iowa, and he pursued his studies after graduating by traveling to England to study at the prestigious Old Vic Theatre School. If he learned nothing else, he learned how to fence while in England, using that skill to earn his living as a fencing instructor when he returned to the United States.

Wilder continued his theater studies at The Actors Studio while gaining experience first Off-Broadway and later on the Great White Way. Still, he was a virtual unknown until he made a splash in his seriocomic movie debut as a nervous undertaker in *Bonnie and Clyde* (1967). It was a small, but memorable, part and it led to his starring role as Leo Bloom opposite Zero Mostel's Max Bialystock in Mel Brooks's cult favorite *The Producers* (1968). Wilder's persona was established in this film, and he was nominated for a Best Actor Academy Award for his performance. Despite the fact that *The Producers* was not an immediate box office hit, it successfully launched Wilder's career.

Blessed with an endearing charm that softens his sometimes screeching film antics, Wilder went on to display his comic romanticism in films such as *Quackser Fortune Has a Cousin in the Bronx* (1970) and *Willy Wonka and the Chocolate Factory* (1971). His humor took a more bizarre turn under the direction of Woody Allen in the hilarious "Daisy" episode of *Everything You Always Wanted to Know About Sex But Were Afraid to Ask* (1972) when he played a psychiatrist in love with a sheep.

Mel Brooks finally turned Wilder into a major star in the back-to-back hits *Blazing Saddles* (1974) and *Young Frankenstein* (1974). Wilder also received credit for cowriting the screenplay of the latter film, further enhancing his image as a creative performer.

Emboldened by the experience of having been directed by two comic actors, Allen and Brooks, Wilder took the plunge and wrote, directed, and starred in his own film, *The Adventures of Sherlock Holmes' Smarter Brother* (1975). He has gone on to write, direct, produce, and star in *The World's Greatest Lover* (1977), as well as write, direct and star in his own segment of the anthology film *Sunday Lovers* (1981). He has also directed *The Woman in Red* (1984) and *Haunted Honeymoon* (1986), both of which costarred his late wife, comedienne Gilda Radner.

While his directorial efforts have met with mixed results both with the critics and with film fans, he remains a hot property thanks to his sterling performances in collaboration with comedian Richard Pryor in such hits as *Silver Streak* (1976), *Stir Crazy* (1980), and, to a lesser extent, *See No Evil, Hear No Evil* (1989). He was also well received as a Polish rabbi in the offbeat comedy western *The Frisco Kid* (1979), but flopped in *Hanky Panky* (1982).

During the latter half of the 1980s he dropped out of filmmaking to care for his ailing wife, Radner, who died of ovarian cancer in 1989.

WILLIAMS, ESTHER (1923–   )   She was one of a relative handful of sports stars, including Buster Crabbe, Johnny Weismuller and Sonja Henie *(qq.v.)*, who had lasting careers on the big screen. Despite her limited ability as an actress, Esther Williams was able to use her particular talent—swimming—to great advantage. Her films were light entertainments and the mandatory water ballets managed to be enjoyably campy. And it didn't hurt that Williams looked good in a bathing suit.

After becoming a swimming champion at the age of fifteen, Williams went from part-time model and col-

A champion swimming star in the late 1930s, Esther Williams had perky good looks, a terrific figure, and a not immodest talent. She scored throughout most of the 1940s and a good chunk of the 1950s in a long string of MGM "wet musicals." Photo courtesy of Movie Star News.

lege student to a featured membered of Billy Roses's Acquacade. MGM signed her up and introduced her to movie audiences, as they had Judy Garland, Lana Turner, Kathryn Grayson and Donna Reed, in a modest role in an Andy Hardy movie, in this case *Andy Hardy's Double Life* (1942).

By 1944, MGM was ready to give Williams a shot at stardom, casting her as the lead in the musical comedy *Bathing Beauty*. With its high production values, good-natured humor, and slight escapist storyline, the film was a happy respite for a war-weary nation.

She followed her initial success with similar movies, such as *Thrill of a Romance* (1945), *This Time for Keeps* (1946), and *On an Island With You* (1947). Most of her movies were pleasantly forgettable but eminently profitable for MGM. Undoubtedly, the best movie of her career was *Take Me Out to the Ballgame* (1949), but she was overshadowed by Gene Kelly and Frank Sinatra, despite a Busby Berkeley water ballet.

The fundamental contrivance of having Williams near (and in) a pool in all of her musicals made her formula a bit taxing, but also somewhat reassuring. In any event, movies such as *Neptune's Daughter* (1949), *Million Dollar Mermaid* (1952), and *Dangerous When Wet* (1953) helped to make Esther Williams a memorable figure in Hollywood lore.

After more than a decade of starring in aquatic musicals, Williams dried herself off and tried to make the transition to dramatic actress in *The Unguarded Moment* (1956). Audiences weren't interested. And, finally, after three more films, neither was Williams. She retired after starring in a Spanish production called *The Magic Fountain* in 1961.

WILLIAMS, JOHN (1932–)   A composer of film scores who, after writing music for movies for fifteen years, suddenly leaped to public prominence with a stunning display of powerful, thrilling musical creations for many of Hollywood's biggest hits of all time, including *Jaws* (1975), *Star Wars* (1977), *Close Encounters of the Third Kind* (1977), *The Empire Strikes Back* (1980), *Raiders of the Lost Ark* (1981), and *E.T.—The Extra-Terrestrial* (1982). Williams' contribution to these films and many others unequivocally contributed to their critical and commercial success. From the shark's theme in *Jaws* to the musical notes used to communicate with the aliens in *Close Encounters,* Williams' musical signature is a vital factor in the dramatic experience of a large number of the more than forty films upon which he has worked.

John Towner Williams was born in Flushing, New York, and received his early musical training at Julliard before going on to UCLA. Among the early films he scored were *Because They're Young* (1960), *The Killers* (1964), *Valley of the Dolls* (1967), *The Reivers* (1969), *Fiddler on the Roof* (1971), for which he was awarded an Oscar for musical arrangement, *The Poseidon Adventure* (1972), and *The Sugarland Express* (1974). He won Best Original Score Oscars for *Jaws, Stars Wars, Superman* (1978), *The Empire Strikes Back,* and *E.T.—The Extra-Terrestrial.*

Since 1980 Williams has been the conductor of the famed Boston Pops Orchestra. This has not stopped him from continuing to write music for the movies. He has scored, among other films, *Return of the Jedi* (1983), *Indiana Jones and the Temple of the Doom* (1984), *The River* (1985), *The Accidental Tourist* (1988), and *Indiana Jones and the Last Crusade* (1989).

WILLIS, GORDON (1931–)   A gifted cinematographer who has rediscovered the beauty of black-and-white photography under the direction of Woody Allen. Willis, who began his career in 1970, has consistently worked with Allen since *Annie Hall* (1977), but even before their unique collaboration, the cinematographer had firmly established a distinctive atmospheric

Very few film composers are known to the general public, but John Williams attained celebrity status for writing scores for such hits as *Jaws* (1975), *Star Wars* (1977), *Close Encounters of the Third Kind* (1977), *Superman* (1978), *Raiders of the Lost Ark* (1981), and many others. Photo courtesy of John Williams.

style in films such as *Loving* (1970), *Klute* (1971), and, most notably, *The Godfather* (1972) and *The Godfather, Part II* (1974).

It has been for Woody Allen, however, that Willis has received his overdue recognition. In particular, his evocative black-and-white photography for films such as *Interiors* (1978), *Manhattan* (1979), *Zelig* (1983), for which he won an Oscar nomination, and *Broadway Danny Rose* (1984) has highlighted a nearly lost art.

WISE, ROBERT (1914–)   A former film editor turned director and sometime producer who has quietly emerged as a filmmaker of considerable stature. It is no coincidence that Wise's career overlaps with many of Hollywood's finest moments. He edited Orson Welles' two classics, *Citizen Kane* (1941) and *The Magnificent Ambersons* (1942), directed three films in the highly praised Val Lewton *(q.v.)* series of horror movies in the early 1940s, directed several low-budget genre films in the late 1940s and early 1950s that have become cult classics, then directed several of Hollywood's most expensive musicals of the 1960s, including two monster hits. In all, Wise's pictures have garnered sixty-seven Academy Award nominations and nineteen Oscars. Wise himself has been nominated seven times and has won four

Director Robert Wise's pictures have garnered sixty-seven Academy Award nominations and nineteen Oscars. Wise himself has been nominated seven times and has won four Oscars. He is pictured here directing *Star Trek—The Motion Picture* (1979). Photo © 1978 Paramount Pictures Corporation, courtesy of Robert Wise.

Oscars. He was also the recipient of the Academy's Irving Thalberg Award in 1967 and the Director's Guild prestigious D. W. Griffith Award in 1988.

The son of a meat packer, Wise had hoped to become a journalist but was unable to continue his studies during the Depression. Looking for work, he traveled to Hollywood, where he got a job as a messenger in RKO's film editing department with the help of his older brother, David, then an accountant with the studio. Soon he was fascinated by the way movies were cut and patched together, and before long he was given an opportunity to try his hand at the art. After nine months, he was made an apprentice sound effects editor and later a music editor.

Wise received his first film credit for a ten-minute short subject and eventually received a promotion to assistant editor, finally becoming a film editor in 1938. He edited such films as *Bachelor Mother* (1939), *The Hunchback of Notre Dame* (1939), *The Story of Vernon and Irene Castle* (1939), and *The Fallen Sparrow* (1943). In addition to editing the previously mentioned Welles films, he also directed the controversial final scenes in *The Magnificent Ambersons,* much to the consternation of Welles' devotees.

After the *Ambersons* experience, Wise began bombarding RKO executives with requests to direct. In

1943, he was editing *Curse of the Cat People* when its original director, far behind schedule, was removed. Wise was given the job; the movie became a hit in the Val Lewton cycle of horror films; and Wise was established forevermore as a director.

Over the next several years he continued to direct low-budget films, many of them horror and suspense movies such as the highly regarded *The Body Snatcher* (1945) and *Born to Kill* (1947). His big break came with *Blood on the Moon* (1948), a significant critical and commercial success. He followed it with what some film buffs consider one the best boxing movies ever made (and also one of very few movies that takes place in real time), *The Set-Up* (1949). Not long after, in 1951, Wise made yet another cult favorite, the memorable science fiction film *The Day the Earth Stood Still.*

Wise's films became less interesting during the rest of the 1950s, but he made a few solid hits, among them *Executive Suite* (1954), *Somebody Up There Likes Me* (1956), *Run Silent, Run Deep* (1958), and *I Want to Live!* (1958). It wasn't until the early 1960s, however, that Wise ascended the Hollywood ladder as a director of megabuck hits, producing and codirecting (with Jerome Robbins) *West Side Story* (1961) and directing and producing *The Sound of Music* (1965). Wise won double Oscars for both films, garnering Academy Awards as Best Director and producer of those two Best Picture winners.

As one of the grand old men of Hollywood and one of the few directors the studios would entrust with a big budget, Wise continued to make expensive movies. Except for *The Sand Pebbles* (1966), he had more misses than hits, making such major bombs as *Star!* (1968) and *The Hindenburg* (1975). Nonetheless, the old pro who had directed *The Day the Earth Stood Still* was brought in to direct the first of what would become a hit series of science fiction films, *Star Trek—The Motion Picture* (1979).

Wise has been less active as a director in recent years, having been elected President of the Academy of Motion Picture Arts and Sciences in 1985. He did, however, finally return to film directing in 1989 with the disappointing musical *Rooftops.*

WOMEN DIRECTORS For all the glamour and beauty that is Hollywood, men have dominated the movie industry for most of its existence. But if in recent years it seems as if women have been making inroads as writers, producers, and, particularly, directors, female success in the motion picture business doesn't begin to touch the influence women had in the industry during the silent era.

A great many women pioneered the movies alongside men in the years before the formation of the studio system. Alice Guy Blaché was the world's first woman director, beginning her work in France in 1896. In 1910, she became the first woman to own her own studio in the United States, the Solax Company. A number of other women would later have their own studios and production companies, including Lule Warrenton, Dorothy Davenport, and Lois Weber.

The women directors of the 1910s and 1920s weren't unusual, nor were they relegated to minor movie status. According to Anthony Slide, in his book *Early Women Directors,* most film studios employed at least one female director, and Universal Pictures actually had, at one time, nine women in charge of their own productions.

A significant number of actresses became directors during the silent era, usually starting their careers behind the camera by directing themselves. Among the less well-remembered actress/directors were Cleo Madison, Ruth Stonehouse, Margery Wilson, Gene Gauntier, Kathlyn Williams, and Lucille McVey. Among the more famous stars who directed themselves were Lillian Gish, Alla Nazimova, and Mabel Normand.

Women were also well represented in the ranks of scenario writers. Many of these screenwriters became directors, as well. For instance, Ida May Park, Ruth Ann Baldwin, and Jeanie MacPherson were all scenario writers who became directors. The most successful of all female screenwriters, Frances Marion, who wrote a prodigious number of hit films, including *Stella Dallas* (1925), *The Champ* (1931), *Dinner at Eight* (1933), and *Camille* (1937), also directed and produced several films. She did not, however, have the same success as a director as she had as a screenwriter.

By the time of the talkie revolution, women were finding it increasingly difficult to find work as directors. The only woman who managed to make it into the 1930s as a director at a major studio was Dorothy Arzner; she was Hollywood's only woman director at that time. Among her credits were such films as *Christopher Song* (1933) and *Craig's Wife* (1936).

There was no other female director at a major studio in Hollywood until actress Ida Lupino began working behind the camera in 1950 with *Outrage,* which she also coscripted. She directed a handful of other motion pictures, leaving the door open for other women to follow.

Elaine May wrote the screenplay and acted in her first directorial assignment, *A New Leaf* (1971), and a good deal was written about the fact that a woman had directed a highly regarded comedy. She followed her initial success with another hit, *The Heartbreak Kid* (1972).

The flow of female film directors continued as a trickle with Joan Micklin Silver's much-admired movie *Hester Street* (1975). Not long after, Claudia Weill directed the well-received *Girlfriends* (1978). Then, just as silent film actresses had once taken on the directorial mantle, so did contemporary female stars. Ann Bancroft coscripted and directed *Fatso* (1979); Barbra Streis-

and produced, cowrote, directed, and starred in *Yentl* (1983), Sondra Locke directed and starred in *Ratboy* (1986); and actresses such as Dyan Cannon, Lee Grant, and Diane Keaton began directing documentaries and experimental films of their own.

More significantly, non-actresses have recently been making their mark in Hollywood as directors. For instance, Susan Seidelman made *Smithereens* (1983), *Desperately Seeking Susan* (1985), *Making Mr. Right* (1987), and *She-Devil* (1989); Catlin Adams cowrote, coproduced, and directed *Sticky Fingers* (1988); and Penny Marshall directed *Big* (1988). Finally, women filmmakers have reached a position where they are allowed to work, and even fail, with a gargantuan budget; witness Elaine May's flop with the hugely expensive comedy *Ishtar* (1987).

While there are still far fewer women behind movie cameras than there are men, Hollywood is slowly working its way back to the level of the silent era when women could be found at all levels of filmmaking.
See also: Arzner, Dorothy; Blaché, Alice Guy; Keaton, Diane; Lupino, Ida; Marion, Frances; May, Elaine; Normand, Mabel; Streisand, Barbra

WOMEN'S PICTURES Also sometimes known as tearjerkers and "weepies," these movies generally depict the romantic (rather than the outright sexual) aspirations of leading characters. Most often, the emotional rug is pulled from under them by broken hearts, degradation, and illness. These films always have a female protagonist and unlike most serious novels and stageworks, are geared directly to the female audience, often (at least in the past) with a decidedly sentimental point of view. Women's pictures of the studio era are notable for their great attention to clothing and hairstyles, as well as for their generally languid pace. Where films designed for men often contain ample outdoor action scenes, women's pictures play themselves out on an internal landscape, marked by feelings, talk of commitments (or the lack of them), betrayals, etc. And as far as Hollywood is concerned, they are also about big box office.

Films geared strictly to women became especially popular during the late 1910s and 1920s when going to the movies became a solidly middle-class leisure activity. With his Victorian sensibility, D. W. Griffith made some of the most memorable early women's pictures. In *Broken Blossoms* (1919), for instance, Lillian Gish falls in love with an Asian man (played by Richard Barthelmess). Given the racial attitudes of the time, it was an impossible love story, which made it a perfect example of the genre's developing formula. For decades to come, any love affair that was doomed to failure had the ingredients of a potential woman's picture.

There have been any number of actresses who have excelled in the genre, most notably Greta Garbo, Janet

Gaynor, Irene Dunne, Vivien Leigh, Margaret Sullavan, Bette Davis, Joan Crawford, Greer Garson, Susan Hayward, Shirley MacLaine, and many others. But when one looks at the best of the women's pictures, one sees the steady work of a relative handful of directors. For example, it was Clarence Brown who directed many of Greta Garbo's most romantic movies during the late 1920s and 1930s. And it was Frank Borzage who made many of the greatest films of the genre during those same years when he directed *Seventh Heaven* (1927), *Street Angel* (1928), *Bad Girl* (1932), and *History Is Made at Night* (1938). He was joined by George Cukor who was well known for bringing out the best in female performers and directed such fully realized women's pictures as *Camille* (1936), *Gaslight* (1944), and *The Actress* (1953). The last director to genuinely specialize in the area (and then, only at the end of his career), was Douglas Sirk, who made such rich soap operas as the remake of *Magnificent Obsession* (1954), *Written on the Wind* (1957), and *Tarnished Angels* (1958).

The women's picture thrived during the studio era, and such films were often made by others besides the great masters of the genre. A good "schmaltzy" story was the key, and both hack and accomplished directors contributed such classics as *Back Street*, which was so potent at the box office that it was made three times, in 1932, 1941, and 1961. *Waterloo Bridge* was another all-time great that was made three times, in 1931 and 1940, and in 1956 as *Gaby*. Leo McCarey made the tearjerker *Love Affair* (1939) and decided to remake it himself in 1957 as *An Affair to Remember*. *Wuthering Heights* (1939), *Random Harvest* (1942), *Letter from an Unknown Woman* (1948), *Love Is a Many Splendored Thing* (1955), and *Splendor in the Grass* (1961) are a sampling of some of the genre's best.

Perhaps the single most important woman's picture from an historical perspective was *Dark Victory* (1939). This weepie starring Bette Davis was the first to have an essentially innocent person die at the end. The commercial success of *Dark Victory* opened the floodgates to a whole new era of tearjerkers where life and death hung in the balance.

Women's pictures went into decline once the studio era ended and individual filmmakers, most of them men, began making movies independently. In addition, with the rise of the women's movement, old-fashioned romance has gone somewhat out of style. Perhaps the last pure example of the genre is *Love Story* (1970).

The modern women's picture has become far more sophisticated, but the basic elements of a female protagonist and female concerns has not changed. Now, however, the themes (in addition to romance and death) have been broadened to include such social issues as career choice and rape. Examples of the modern women's pictures are *The Turning Point* (1977), *Terms of Endearment* (1983), *The Accused* (1988), and *Beaches* (1989).

See also: Borzage, Frank; *Dark Victory*; Le Roy, Mervyn; Sirk, Douglas

WOOD, NATALIE (1938–1981) She was among the rare child actors who made the leap from moppet to adult movie star. But she was an actress of contradictions. Though perceived as a mediocre performer, she managed to garner three Oscar nominations; though a great beauty, her acting lacked a sensual fire; and despite her consistent popularity, she never achieved superstar status and was often overshadowed by her costars.

Born Natasha Gurdin to a Russian father and French mother, she grew up speaking several languages and studied dance (her mother had been a ballerina) at a very early age. When she was four years old, *Happy Land* (1943) was being filmed in her hometown of Rosita, California, and she landed a tiny role in the movie. The director, Irving Pichel, was impressed with her and cast her several years later when he needed a child actress who could play the part of a German refugee in *Tomorrow Is Forever* (1946). It was the start of the actress's career.

As a child star, Wood was no Margaret O'Brien (*q.v.*), but she was both pretty and sincere. Young Natalie made her mark in films such as *Miracle on 34th Street* (1947) and *Scudda-Hoo! Scudda-Hay!* (1948). In the early 1950s she tried television, starring in a series called "Pride of the Family." She did not succeed on the small screen and returned to the movies, struggling through the awkward period of adolescence. It wasn't until she blossomed as a young adult and costarred with James Dean in *Rebel Without a Cause* (1955) that she emerged as a potential new star. Winning a surprise Best Supporting Actress Academy Award nomination for her performance brought her increased visibility, though James Dean was the focus of most people's attention.

Full-fledged stardom did not come quickly. Just as she was overwhelmed in *Rebel Without a Cause* by the acting of James Dean and Sal Mineo, she passed through a succession of 1950s films such as *Marjorie Moringstar* (1958) without making a very great impression. Her films, though, were generally popular at the box office and she was just twenty-two years old as the 1960s began, a decade in which she gave the lion's share of her best and most memorable performances.

Her career finally took off when she starred opposite Warren Beatty in Elia Kazan's production of *Splendor in the Grass* (1961) and received an Oscar nomination for Best Actress. To the surprise of many, she was then cast as Maria in *West Side Story* (1961). Her childhood dance training came in handy for the film, but her singing voice was dubbed by Marnie Nixon.

Those two hit films were followed by a nearly unbroken streak of box office winners that lasted till the end of the decade. She was at the height of her career, starring in *Love with the Proper Stranger* (1963) with

Steve McQueen and winning her third and final Oscar nomination, *Sex and the Single Girl* (1964) with Tony Curtis, *Inside Daisy Clover* (1966) with Robert Redford, *This Property Is Condemned* (1966) with Redford again, and *Bob & Carol & Ted & Alice* (1969) with Dyan Cannon, Elliott Gould, and Robert Culp.

The titles of most of her 1960s films were suggestive—and often controversial—but both the movies and Natalie Wood proved in the end to be rather tame.

Married twice to actor Robert Wagner, Ms. Wood devoted most of the 1970s to home life. She made a few films for TV and theatrical release, the most notable being the underrated comedy with George Segal *The Last Married Couple in America* (1979). She nearly completed a big-budget thriller called *Brainstorm* when she drowned in a mysterious boating accident in 1981. *Brainstorm* was released posthumously in 1983 with little fanfare.

See also: child stars

WOODWARD, JOANNE (1930–   )   An actress who began her film career in sexy roles but who soon displayed her talent starring in character parts to which she brought depth of perception. Since her film career began in 1955, Woodward has either acted with or been directed by her longtime husband, Paul Newman, in nearly half of all her motion pictures. This was not a case of nepotism, however; Woodward had already won an Oscar for her electric performance in *The Three Faces of Eve* (1957) during Newman's initial flush of popularity in the mid-to-late 1950s.

Born to a well-to-do family in Georgia, Woodward acted in high school and college, as well as for a small community theater, before making the trip to New York to study acting at the Neighborhood Playhouse. Soon she began appearing in live TV dramas, but had the first and most important break of her career when she won an understudy role in the 1953 Broadway production of *Picnic;* the male star of the play was Paul Newman. The two married five years later in 1958.

Woodward made her movie debut in a starring role in *Count Three and Pray* (1955). In the year that she and Newman were wed, they starred together in two films *The Long Hot Summer* (1958) and *Rally Round the Flag, Boys!* (1958). Their other acting collaborations include *From the Terrace* (1960), *Paris Blues* (1961), *A New Kind of Love* (1963), *Winning* (1969), *WUSA* (1970), and *The Drowning Pool* (1975). In most of the later films, the couple was better than their material.

Woodward also starred in a number of films that were directed by Newman: *Rachel, Rachel* (1968), for which she was nominated for an Oscar, *The Effect of Gamma Rays on Man-in-the-Moon Marigolds* (1972), a TV movie "The Shadow Box" (1981), *Harry and Son* (1984), in which Newman also starred, and *The Glass Menagerie* (1987). These films were largely of a very high caliber,

although none of them was a box office winner except *Rachel, Rachel*. And in every film in which Newman directed her, Woodward received glowing notices for her work.

During the last thirty-five years, Woodward has done splendid work in solo efforts that have often been overlooked. Her abilities as a character actress are best displayed in movies such as *A Kiss Before Dying* (1956), *The Sound and the Fury* (1959), *The Stripper* (1963), *A Big Hand for the Little Lady* (1966), *A Fine Madness* (1966), and *Summer Wishes, Winter Dreams* (1973).

In addition to her film work, Woodward has been a committed stage actress and has also been active in making quality TV movies, especially during the late 1970s and throughout the 1980s. Along with her husband, she has also been a political activist, lobbyist, and fund-raiser for liberal causes.

See also: Newman, Paul

WRITER-DIRECTORS   The person most responsible for a motion picture has been hotly debated. In one camp, it is argued that the screenwriter's original characters, plot, and themes are the core of what is seen on the big screen. The other camp holds that the director is the ultimate creator of a film because he or she controls all of its elements, choosing the locations and the actors, deciding on the lighting and music, among many other things. Both make cogent points, but there can be no argument that those filmmakers who both write *and* direct their films are the ultimate creators, devisers, and realizers of their stories. Surprisingly, however, relatively few writer-directors have prospered in Hollywood, no doubt because it is hard enough to succeed in one of these areas, let alone both. Since the early 1940s, though, there has been an increasing number of writer-directors who have not only made their mark in American films but have also changed the course of movie history.

Scripts were often unnecessary during the early silent era, but as films became more complex, writers were hired to organize and structure their plots as well as write title cards. Thomas H. Ince was probably the first important writer-director. He wrote detailed notes before filming, both for himself and later for other directors whom he supervised. There were relatively few writer-directors during the silent era, but the extravagant Erich von Stroheim was a notable example. In the area of comedy, Charlie Chaplin and Buster Keaton (*qq.v.*) were predominant writer-directors, who also starred in their own vehicles.

The genuine flowering of the screenwriter's craft, however, did not occur until the sound era. By then the studio system (*q.v.*) had already evolved, compartmentalizing the different functions required to create a film (i.e., writers wrote, directors directed, producers produced, etc.). During the 1930s, the only significant attempt toward melding the jobs of writing and directing came when screenwriters Ben Hecht and Charles MacArthur were given the chance to direct their own films. The results were the wordy but fascinating *Crime Without Passion* (1934) and *The Scoundrel* (1935). Neither made any impact at the box office and, in any event, the movies were mostly directed by their cinematographer, Lee Garmes *(q.v.)*.

The rise of the writer-director began in earnest at Paramount in 1940 when the highly successful screenwriter Preston Sturges insisted on the right to direct his own work. He struck a blow for creative control by succeeding handsomely at the box office with seven consecutive comedy hits over a five-year period.

Meanwhile, the struggling RKO studio, looking for a shot in the arm, hired Orson Welles, who directed and co-wrote, as well as starred in, what many consider to be the greatest movie ever made, *Citizen Kane* (1941).

At Warner Bros., John Huston had been writing successful scripts, and he was promised that if his screenplay for *High Sierra* (1940) was a hit, he'd be allowed to direct his own film. It was, and he made his writer-director debut with *The Maltese Falcon* (1941).

Not long after Sturges, Welles, and Huston broke the ice, they were followed by Billy Wilder, who cowrote and directed *The Major and the Minor* (1942). They remained the big four throughout the 1940s and beyond.

The freedom of the writer-director has always been bound by financial restrictions, especially when the purse strings were held by conservative producers and studios. Some writer-directors who came to prominence in the 1950s and 1960s thrived under those conditions, among them Richard Brooks and Blake Edwards. But many of the new breed of writer-directors tended to work as independents, most notably Samuel Fuller, Stanley Kubrick, and John Cassevettes *(qq.v.)*.

In recent decades, writer-directors have become increasingly commonplace as movies have become an accepted mode of personal expression. The new wave of writer-directors received its first big push in the area of screen comedy thanks to the distinctive versions of Woody Allen and Mel Brooks. The mammoth success of writer-director Francis Coppola's *The Godfather* (1972) caused a trickle of such filmmakers to turn into a flood. Successful screenwriters anxious for the chance to direct their own films were given funding, and such talents as John Milius, Paul Schrader, Lawrence Kasdan, and others blossomed into critically acclaimed moviemakers. Even Sylvester Stallone, much maligned by critics as an actor, has proven himself a capable writer-director on more than one occasion.

Within the last decade, a new crop of talented and commercially viable writer-directors has surfaced. For instance, John Sayles has emerged as an independent filmmaker who usually works outside the studio system

making such intelligent and iconoclastic films as *Return of the Secaucus 7* (1980), *The Brother from Another Planet* (1984), and *Matewan* (1987). Oliver Stone has become a mainstream writer-director with considerable box office clout thanks to his Oscar-winning *Platoon* (1986) and smash hit *Wall Street* (1987). Stone, however, has not succumbed to the lure of big box office; he followed his big-budget, high profile films with the scintillating art-circuit winner *Talk Radio* (1989). Another newcomer to the writer-director ranks has been playwright David Mamet, who, after writing scripts for films such as *The Untouchables* (1987), has recently begun directing his own screenplays, making such highly regarded movies as *House of Games* (1987) and *Things Change* (1988).

See also: Allen, Woody; Brooks, Mel; Brooks, Richard; Coppola, Francis Ford; Hecht, Ben; Huston, John; Ince, Thomas H.; Levinson, Barry; Milius, John; Sayles, John; Schrader, Paul; Stallone, Sylvester; Sturges, Preston; Stroheim, Erich von; Welles, Orson; Wilder, Billy

WYLER, WILLIAM (1902–1981)   In a career spanning forty-five years, he directed nearly fifty features. During his long and fruitful association with independent producer Samuel Goldwyn *(q.v.),* Wyler became a director of prestige projects that were often adaptations of stage plays, many of them by the leading playwrights of his era. In an effort to remain true to the spatial relations of the plays he filmed, Wyler pioneered the use of deep-focus photography with the help of his cinematographer, Gregg Toland *(q.v.).* Wyler's films were popular and highly respected efforts that brought him a record twelve Best Director Academy Award nominations; he won the Oscar on three occasions. In 1965 he became one of the very few directors to be honored with the prestigious Irving G. Thalberg Memorial Award. He followed that with the American Film Institute Life Achievement Award in 1976.

Born to a Swiss family in Mulhouse, Alsace, when it was German territory, he was educated on two fronts, business and the arts. His entry into films was a result of the legendary nepotism of Carl Laemmle, who hired hundreds of relatives and put them to work at his burgeoning movie company, Universal Pictures. Wyler was related to Laemmle ever so distantly through his mother, but the American movie mogul happily engaged the young man in 1922 as a publicity writer in his movie company's New York office.

Soon after arriving in America, however, Wyler was dispatched to Hollywood, where, in quick succession, he held a variety of jobs, including grip, prop master, casting director, production assistant, and assistant director. Wyler learned the business of moviemaking quickly, and was given the opportunity to direct when he was just twenty-three years old. In addition to directing dozens of two-reel westerns, he made his feature film debut with *Crook Busters* (1925).

There was nothing terribly distinguished about his silent films, though they were solidly made with good pacing and plenty of action. In the early 1930s, however, he began directing issue-oriented stories that brought him critical notice, among them *Hell's Heroes* (1930), *A House Divided* (1932), and *Counsellor-at-Law* (1933).

His career began to blossom more rapidly after he left Universal in 1936 to begin his association with Samuel Goldwyn. Their first film together was an adaptation of Lillian Hellman's controversial play *The Children's Hour,* which was renamed in the 1936 film version, *These Three.* (Wyler later remade the film under the original title in 1962.)

Wyler went on to receive an unprecedented number of Best Director Academy Award nominations. His twelve nominations were for: the critically acclaimed *Dodsworth* (1936), the lushly romantic *Wuthering Heights* (1939), the underrated Bette Davis vehicle *The Letter* (1940), plus the overrated Bette Davis vehicle *The Little Foxes* (1941), the hugely popular *Mrs. Miniver* (1942), for which he also won the Oscar, the post World War II classic *The Best Years of Our Lives* (1946), which brought him his second Oscar, the emotionally restrained *The Heiress* (1949), the tough *Detective Story* (1951), the charming *Roman Holiday* (1953), the warm family saga *Friendly Persuasion* (1956), the big-budget mega-hit *Ben-Hur* (1959), for which he won his third Oscar, and the idiosyncratic little movie *The Collector* (1965).

There is little thematic unity consistency to Wyler's films but their quality is constant. Nonetheless, auterist critics have criticized the director for never having exhibited a consistent style or theme in his work. True or not, there has hardly been a director who has made quite so many highly regarded movies. Consider, for instance, that Wyler also directed such memorable Hollywood milestones as *Dead End* (1937), *Jezebel* (1938), *The Westerner* (1940), *The Big Country* (1958), and *Funny Girl* (1968).

Though he is not often considered an actor's director—many performers openly hated him (he was notorious for incessantly demanding retakes)—Wyler elicited fourteen Oscar-winning performances from his stars, not to mention a great many Oscar-nominated performances, as well.

His last film was *The Liberation of L.B. Jones* (1970), after which he retired.

WYMAN, JANE (1914–   ) An actress who made the majority of her movies before attaining fame, Wyman has appeared in more than seventy films in a career that began in 1936. She was cast as comic relief and tough blondes in mostly unimportant movies during her early years in Hollywood, but emerged a star thanks to the unexpected critical and commercial success of *The Lost Weekend* (1945). The latter half of the 1940s and early 1950s were Wyman's golden years in Hollywood. She was nominated for four Best Actress Oscars during that period, winning the Academy Award once for her performance as the deaf-mute in *Johnny Belinda* (1948). Today, Wyman is perhaps better known as both the matriarch of the prime time TV soap "Falcon Crest" and as former President Ronald Reagan's first wife (from 1940–1948).

Born Sarah Jane Faulks, she tried to break into the movies as a child actress without success. Later, as a young adult, she began performing as a singer on radio using the name Jane Durrell. Still enamored of the movies, she finally began showing up in films in minor roles, making her debut in *Gold Diggers of 1937* (1936). She went on to appear in an average of more than six movies per year during the latter half of the 1930s, most of them of minor distinction. She did, however, star along with Ronald Reagan in the popular *Brother Rat* (1938), as well as its sequel, *Brother Rat and a Baby* (1940). The two also costarred in *An Angel from Texas* (1940) and *Tugboat Annie Sails Again* (1940).

After Reagan left Hollywood to join the war effort, Wyman's career began to pick up. Her strong performance opposite Ray Milland's Oscar-winning portrayal of an alcoholic in *The Lost Weekend* was not overlooked by the industry. Given better roles in "A" movies, she proved herself both a versatile and a popular actress in *The Yearling* (1946), for which she received her first Best Actress Academy Award nomination, *Magic Town* (1947), the previously mentioned *Johnny Belinda, The Glass Menagerie* (1950), *The Blue Veil* (1951), which brought her another Oscar nomination, *Magnificent Obsession* (1954), which got Wyman her fourth and last Oscar bid, and *All That Heaven Allows* (1956).

Past her prime in the mid-1950s, Wyman turned to television. Like actresses Donna Reed and Loretta Young, she had her own program, "The Jane Wyman Theater," which ran from 1956 to 1960. She was little seen on movie screens both during and after those years on the tube, appearing only in *Holiday for Lovers* (1959), *Pollyanna* (1960), *Bon Voyage!* (1962), and *How to Commit Marriage* (1969). She made her unexpected comeback on television in 1981 when she joined the original cast of the hit show "Falcon Crest."

YOUNG, LORETTA (1912–)   An actress known within the film industry as "Hollywood's Beautiful Hack" because she starred in so many mediocre movies. In a career that began in earnest in 1927, Young appeared in more than 90 films, but most movies fans would be hard pressed to name more than half a dozen of them. Yet she was personally memorable due to her big doe eyes and high cheekbones; she was truly one of Hollywood's most striking beauties.

Born Gretchen Michaela Young, she was the product of a broken home. Her mother gathered up her brood of daughters and went to Hollywood in the hope of getting the kids into show business. Loretta was briefly a child actress in bit roles before receiving a convent education. Later, when she was fourteen, director Mervyn Le Roy called, wanting Loretta's older sister, Polly Ann, for a small role in *Naughty but Nice* (1927). In Polly Ann's absence, Loretta asked to play the role instead, and Le Roy agreed.

Young had a sensitive, ethereal quality on film in her youth, and she soon found plenty of work. Among her noteworthy early films were *Laugh Clown Laugh* (1928) and *The Squall* (1929), in which she proved herself capable as an actress in sound films.

During the first half of the 1930s she usually played leading roles in the movies of bigger stars; few pictures were built around her. Nonetheless, she was effective in vehicles for stars such as John Barrymore in *The Man from Blankleys* (1930), Ronald Colman in *The Devil to Pay* (1930), Jean Harlow in *Platinum Blonde* (1931), and James Cagney in *Taxi* (1932).

By the mid-1930s she became a star in her own right, getting major roles in bigger-budget movies at her new studio, Twentieth Century-Fox. She could be seen to fine effect in such films as *Ramona* (1936), *Ladies in Love* (1936), and *Three Blind Mice* (1938). Despite her star billing in "A" movies, she was still mostly used for

Loretta Young was a second tier glamour queen who had the nickname of "Hollywood's Beautiful Hack." Only late in her movie career did she receive the kind of rich roles that allowed her to show her talent. Photo courtesy of The Siegel Collection.

decoration and rarely given meaty roles. Unhappy at Fox, she bitterly parted company with the studio.

Young's career went into a minor tailspin during the early 1940s, and she appeared in many lesser productions, although she shined as Alan Ladd's love interest in *China* (1943). By this time, she had been in the movies for more than fifteen years, yet she was only in her early thirties. She was far too beautiful and far too young to be washed up, and she proved she possessed both the skills and the drawing power to reclaim her position as a top Hollywood star. She rebounded in the latter half of the decade in films such as *Along Came Jones* (1945) with Gary Cooper and the tightly woven thriller *The Stranger* (1946), playing Orson Welles' wife (Welles also directed). But 1947 saw her at the pinnacle of her Hollywood success, taking an Oscar home for her performance in *The Farmer's Daughter*. Unfortunately, her rise to the top was short-lived. There were a couple of good films thereafter, such as *The Bishop's Wife* (1947), *Come to the Stable* (1949), for which she was nominated for an Oscar, and *Key to the City* (1950), but her subsequent movies were released as "B's," including, *Half Angel* (1952) and her last motion picture, *It Happens Every Thursday* (1953).

Seeing no future in the movie business, Young turned to television and became the hostess and occasional star of "The Loretta Young Show" (1953–1961). It was a rousing success and a multiple Emmy winner thanks to her stunning wardrobe and grande dame style, not to mention some fine dramatic moments. When the show went off the air, she resurfaced the following year in "The New Loretta Young Show," but the public was no longer interested and it was soon cancelled. She has lived in quiet retirement ever since, making news only in 1972 when she sued and won a court case against NBC, which had illegally aired her old TV series overseas.

YOUNG, ROBERT (1907–) An actor who was a serviceable, likable leading man throughout much of his film career, lending an earnest quality to his roles. Young rarely had top billing, but he worked consis-

tently in Hollywood movies throughout the 1930s, 1940s, and early 1950s before attaining his greatest fame as a television star.

Young received his early acting training in a small theater in Carmel, California, before heading for the Pasadena Playhouse. He broke into the movies as an extra, and made his first billed performance in a Charlie Chan film, *The Black Camel* (1931). With his pleasant good looks and fine speaking voice, he quickly graduated to leading roles in films such as *New Morals for Old* (1932) and *Unashamed* (1932).

In many of his films Young was overshadowed by his costars. For instance, *Today We Live* (1933) is more memorable for the performances of Joan Crawford and Gary Cooper. *Spitfire* (1934) is remembered for Katharine Hepburn's presence. And Barbara Stanwyck, outshone him in *Red Salute* (1935).

Young muddled his way through much of the 1930s alternating between "B" movies and "A" movies, playing at turns both good guys and bad guys, rarely getting a meaty part in which he could shine. That began to change, however, near the end of the decade when he had a strong and sympathic role in the deeply moving *Three Comrades* (1938). The part that changed his career, however, was the title role in *H.M. Pulman, Esq.* (1941). During the next several years he had top roles in major films (though he often continued to be overshadowed by his castmates), including *Journey for Margaret* (1942), *Sweet Rosie O'Grady* (1943), *The Canterville Ghost* (1944), and *The Enchanted Cottage* (1945). Even as his film career began to wind down, he received important roles in such films as the controversial *Crossfire* (1947), and *That Forsyte Woman* (1951).

Middle-aged and receiving few bids for good roles, Young turned to television and became a bigger star than ever in "Father Knows Best" (1954–1960). He had a failed TV series, "Window on Main Street" (1961) before hitting it big again with a whole new generation when he played the title role in the prime-time series "Marcus Welby, M.D." (1969–1975). He has subsequently done the occasional commercial and TV movie, although he now lives in semiretirement.

Z

ZANUCK, DARRYL F. (1902–1979) A movie mogul who was instrumental in the early growth of Warner Bros. and who founded Twentieth-Century Fox, running the company for a good part of its existence. Zanuck was a deeply involved producer who personally supervised the creation of more movies than any other head of production in Hollywood. While he was a mediocre, if prolific, screenwriter during his early years in the movie industry, he always displayed a great talent as an idea man who understood the requirements of commercial storytelling.

Darryl Francis Zanuck was born in Wahoo, Nebraska, but spent much of his youth in Los Angeles with his mother and stepfather. He had his first encounter with the movies at the age of seven, stumbling upon a film crew, who dressed him up as a little Indian girl and put him in their movie, paying him a dollar a day.

Zanuck never bothered finishing high school. Instead, he lied about his age and joined the Army (he was one day shy of his fifteenth birthday), seeing combat in France during World War I. When he returned to America two years later, he decided to become a writer. He collected more than his share of rejections for his potboiler short stories until he finally sold his first, *Mad Desire* which was published in 1923. Future sales followed, including a story bought by Fox and turned into a film in 1923, the name of which has been lost.

In order to gain more prestige in the movie business, Zanuck slapped together four of his scenarios and arranged to have them published as a book; three of those stories were turned into movies and he was well on his way to becoming a regular contributor to the motion picture business. After short stints as a gag writer for Mack Sennett, Harold Lloyd, and Charlie Chaplin, Zanuck began writing for the then struggling film company Warner Bros.

In 1924, he began writing scripts for Warners' biggest audience draw, the german shepherd Rin-Tin-Tin, and soon proved to be a veritable volcano of story ideas. According to Mel Gussow in his excellent biography of Zanuck, *Don't Say Yes Until I Finish Talking,* he wrote as many as nineteen films in one year. Finally, at the behest of Jack Warner *(q.v.),* he came up with three pseudonyms, Melville Crossman, Mark Canfield, and Gregory Rogers, reserving his real name only for prestige projects. Ironically, Melville Crossman became the most popular writer of the four of them and (unwittingly) MGM tried to hire the nonexistent screenwriter away from Warners.

Zanuck's influence continued to grow and he was promoted several times until he finally became Jack Warner's right-hand man as head of production. In the meantime, he either wrote or produced many of Warner's most important films, including the movie that began the talkie era, *The Jazz Singer* (1927). Zanuck was responsible for much of Warner's early successes, introducing the biopic cycle with *Disraeli* (1929), the gangster cycle with *Little Caesar* (1931) and *Public Enemy* (1931), the social consciousness cycle with *I Am a Fugitive from a Chain Gang* (1932), and the revived musical cycle with *42nd Street* (1933).

In 1933, in a dispute with Harry Warner, Zanuck quit and then teamed with Joseph M. Schenck at United Artists to form their own film company, Twentieth Century Pictures. The company was in business a scant but successful two years before merging with the much larger but ailing giant Fox Film Corporation, becoming Twentieth Century-Fox in 1935. Zanuck was vice president in charge of production, a title he held until 1956. In that capacity, he turned his newly formed company into a profitable major studio with few stars on his roster. Under his supervision, the studio put out so many costume epics during the latter half of the 1930s that it became known as "Sixteenth Century-Fox."

During the early 1940s, Zanuck once again went off to war, this time as a lieutenant colonel making documentary films. Upon his return to the studio, he entered what many consider his finest phase, showing considerable courage by making *Gentlemen's Agreement* (1947), a film that attacked anti-Semitism, and *Pinky* (1949), a movie that dealt with racism in America.

He continued to produce critical and commercial successes during the early 1950s with films such as *All About Eve* (1950) and *Viva Zapata!* (1952), and he made yet another contribution to the movies when he brought CinemaScope to Hollywood. Finally, in 1956, he chose to become an independent producer, releasing his films through Twentieth Century-Fox. He was not terribly successful, but he came through when the studio needed a hit, making the big-budget blockbuster *The Longest Day* (1962), just as Twentieth Century-Fox was hemorraging from the *Cleopatra* (1963, *q.v.*) disaster.

Asked to return to the helm of the studio he had founded, the old mogul rode to the rescue—at least temporarily. He became president and appointed his son, Richard Darryl Zanuck, to his old job as vice president in charge of production. Zanuck guided the company out of the financial desert thanks to the huge success of *The Sound of Music* (1965), but by the late 1960s, several major bombs began to bring profits down again.

The last film Zanuck personally produced was *Tora! Tora! Tora!* (1970), an attempt at duplicating the success of *The Longest Day*. Though some of the film was truly spectacular, it was neither a critical nor a commercial hit, though footage from it has often been used in subsequent war movies. Meanwhile, Zanuck was caught in a bitter battle for control of the studio. His son was forced out of the company, but he hung on, eventually resigning under pressure in 1971. He became chairman emeritus, and was finally put out to pasture.

See also: CinemaScope; *Gentlemen's Agreement; The Grapes of Wrath;* Rin-Tin-Tin; Schenck, Joseph M.; Twentieth Century-Fox; Warner Bros.; Zanuck–Brown

ZANUCK–BROWN The highly successful producing team of Richard Darryl Zanuck (1934–   ) and David Brown (1916–   ) has given birth to fifteen films, among them a number of Hollywood's biggest hits, including *The Sting* (1973), *Jaws* (1975), *The Verdict* (1982), and *Cocoon* (1985).

Richard Zanuck, the better known member of the team, is the son of the late Darryl F. Zanuck, the longtime head of Twentieth Century-Fox. Brought up in the movie business, the younger Zanuck was given the

opportunity to assist in the productions of such Fox films as *The Sun Also Rises* (1957) before becoming a producer in his own right and making such movies as *Compulsion* (1959) and *The Chapman Report* (1962). He also worked directly with his father on the epic war film *The Longest Day* (1962), eventually rising to become the head of production at Fox in 1967 and, later, the company's president, in 1969. It was a short-lived reign, however, as he was dumped in 1970. After a short tenure at Warner Bros., he and David Brown teamed up and released their first films in 1973.

David Brown had long been a member of the Twentieth Century-Fox management team, heading up the story department in 1952 after an early career in publishing (his wife, Helen Gurley Brown, succeeded him as editor of *Cosmopolitan* magazine). During his tenure at Fox, he became a top executive working in tandem with both Darryl Zanuck and, later, Richard Zanuck.

The Zanuck–Brown partnership hasn't produced all hits or high-gloss efforts. Their first film was a low-budget horror movie titled *Ssssss* (1973), followed by a cheap exploitation film, *Willie Dynamite* (1973). Their third film of that year, *The Sting,* starring Paul Newman and Robert Redford, was a critical and box office smash, putting them firmly on the Hollywood map.

To the producers' credit, their box office bombs, such as *The Black Windmill* (1974), *MacArthur* (1977), and *Target* (1985), are hardly boring and did not flop for want of trying. Significantly, Zanuck and Brown have sometimes been willing to invest in untried, but creative people. For instance, they gave a young Steven Spielberg *(q.v.)* one of his early breaks when they allowed him to direct *The Sugarland Express* (1974). While the film received generally favorable reviews, it died at the box office. It was worth Zanuck–Brown's investment, however, because they called on Spielberg again to direct *Jaws*. Zanuck–Brown also took a chance and made *Cocoon,* a movie starring a cast of elderly actors directed by the relatively young Ron Howard, and turned it into a major hit.

The Zanuck–Brown strategy has been extremely conservative at times, conforming, for example, to the Hollywood penchant for sequels with *Jaws 2* (1978) and *Cocoon 2* (1988).

In 1988, after a fifteen-year partnership, Zanuck-Brown was dissolved and the two producers went their separate ways.

See also: Twentieth Century-Fox; Zanuck, Darryl F.

ZINNEMANN, FRED (1907–   ) He is an iconoclastic director with a reputation for making thoughtful, intelligent films which some, however, criticize for a lack of warmth. One could also argue that the apparent coolness of Zinnemann's films is more a matter of restraint than lack of feeling. Many of the director's films tend to have a slow pace, and a distant, objective viewpoint. This comes from his training as a documentary filmmaker with the legendary Robert Flaherty of *Nanook of the North* (1922) fame. Zinnemann's semi-documentary style has often served him well, however, giving his best films a strikingly realistic feeling.

Zinnemann was born in Austria and was well on his way toward a legal career in his native country when he became enraptured by the movies. According to John Fitzpatrick in his essay in *American Directors, Volume II* (edited by Jean-Pierre Coursodon), Zinnemann studied film in Paris in 1928, "making him one of the earliest 'film school' directors." After an apprenticeship in Berlin, working with Billy Wilder and Robert Siodmak *(qq.v.)* on the German classic *Menschen am Sonntag* in 1929, he traveled to America and wound up an extra in the antiwar film *All Quiet on the Western Front* (1930).

Zinnemann teamed with Robert Flaherty on an aborted documentary in 1929 and later made his own in 1937, *The Wave.* Soon thereafter, Zinnemann began directing for MGM, making two-reelers. He distinguished himself during this period with an Oscar for his short, *That Mothers Might Live* (1938).

His first feature film was the forgettable *Kid Glove Killer* (1942). The director blossomed in 1944 in only his third full-length film, the powerful anti-Nazi movie *The Seventh Cross.* After two more lesser films, Zinnemann began to hit his stride by relying on a semi-documentary style in films such as *The Search* (1948), for which he earned his first Oscar nomination for Best Director, *Act of Violence* (1950), and *The Men* (1950).

Zinnemann's growing reputation in Hollywood as a strong director had not yet been matched by stunning commercial success. That soon followed, though, when he directed the popular western hit *High Noon* (1952), earning his second Oscar nomination, and the blockbuster *From Here to Eternity* (1953), for which he took home the statuette.

Zinnemann continued to direct for another thirty years, yet made just ten more films. Considering the usual percentage of hits to misses, his rate of success, either critically, commercially, or both, has been exceedingly high. More to the point, Zinnemann has generally directed only the films he has wanted to make. Among those films have been *The Member of the Wedding* (1953), *Oklahoma!* (1955), *A Hatful of Rain* (1957), *The Nun's Story* (1959), *The Sundowners* (1960), *Behold a Pale Horse* (1964), and *A Man for All Seasons* (1966), for which he won yet another Best Director Academy Award.

After a long absence from the screen, Zinnemann returned in full glory in 1973 to make the hit thriller *The Day of the Jackal,* a movie that benefited greatly from his documentary training. Four years later, the tireless director stepped into a project intended for Sydney Pollack and turned in yet another hit, *Julia*

(1977). After three major triumphs in a row, Zinnemann finally faltered with his last film, *Five Days One Summer* (1982).

ZUKOR, ADOLPH (1873–1976)   He was a major influence on the growth of the film business, bringing "highbrow" entertainment to the movies, pioneering the feature-length film, and founding (as well as guiding) the original company that eventually became Paramount Pictures.

Zukor was born in Hungary and arrived in the United States at the age of fifteen. He adapted quickly to his new home, taking all sorts of jobs until he became the owner of a fur company. Sensing a greater potential in the fledgling movie business, Zukor joined several other investors in 1903, putting his modest wealth into a penny arcade in New York's Union Square. The pennies rolled in.

While filmmakers such as D. W. Griffith experimented with film form and content, Zukor experimented with the business side of the industry, importing ever-longer films from overseas and showing them in theaters all over the country. He was a movie impressario who made his most daring move in 1912 when he acquired the American rights to the British/French four-reel film *Queen Elizabeth,* starring Sarah Bernhardt. The movie was a major hit in the U.S., and earned Zukor $80,000. Realizing he was on to something, Zukor copied the concept of Film d'Art of France, from whom he had licensed *Queen Elizabeth,* and formed the Famous Players Company, whose slogan was "Famous Players in Famous Plays."

His company was successful, not because of his unimaginatively filmed stage plays but because he wisely put screen star Mary Pickford *(q.v.)* under contract. In any event, he did, indeed, bring a certain respectability to the movies. His company's product, critically acclaimed plays and classic novels, appealed to the tastes of the middle class. And, of course, in its films Famous Players used well-known stage stars of the day such as Lily Langtry, John Barrymore, James K. Hackett, and Ina Claire. It provided a chance for audiences to see these famous performers for a good deal less money than for live stage appearances. For many, it was their only chance to see these stars at all.

Zukor merged Famous Players with the Jesse L. Lasky Feature Play Company in 1916 and he bought more than a dozen other companies in the late 1910s, including his distributor, Paramount Pictures Corporation (bought in 1917). Eventually, the name of the company was changed to Paramount Pictures.

During the 1920s, Zukor went on a buying binge, acquiring movie theaters all across the country. When the Great Depression came, his empire nearly collapsed. Lasky and others were forced out, but not Zukor. When the company was finally reorganized under the U.S.

bankruptcy laws in 1936, the studio's founder was kicked upstairs to the largely ceremonial job of chairman of the board.

He was remembered by his peers in 1949 when he was given a Special Academy Award for his "contri-bution to the industry." When he died at the venerable age of 103, Zukor still held the title chairman emeritus of Paramount Pictures, Inc.

See also: Famous Players; Lasky, Jesse L.; Paramount Pictures

Selected Bibliography

We are indebted to the authors listed below whose work we drew upon in the creation of our own volume. Three books, in particular, deserve special mention because we turned to them so often to check our facts: *TV Movies* by Leonard Maltin, *Movies on TV* by Steven H. Scheuer, and *The Film Encyclopedia* by Ephraim Katz.

Please note that many of the books we used in our research have been published both in hardcover and in paperback, oftentimes on both sides of the Atlantic, and in any number of printings. The publishers and dates of publication listed below are for the books we actually used. In other words, if we drew upon the 1986 Pocket Books version of a title in paperback rather than the 1985 G.P. Putnam's Sons version in hardcover, we will list the former rather than the latter. In addition to books, we also found valuable nuggets of information in magazines and newspapers too numerous to mention.

Adamson, Joe. *Groucho, Harpo, Chico, and Sometimes, Zeppo*. New York: Simon and Schuster, 1973.

Alpert, Hollis. *The Barrymores*. New York: Dial Press, 1964.

Alpert, Hollis, and Sarris, Andrew, eds. *Film 68–69*. New York: Simon and Schuster, 1969.

Andereg, Michael A. *William Wyler*. Boston: Twayne Publishers, 1979.

Anderson, Janice. *History of Movie Comedy*. New York: Exeter Books, 1985.

Andrew, Geoff. *Hollywood Gangsters*. New York: Gallery Books, 1985.

Armour, Robert A. *Fritz Lang*. Boston: Twayne Publishers, 1977.

Arnheim, Rudolf. *Film as Art*. Berkeley: University of California Press, 1969.

Astor, Mary. *A Life on Film*. New York: Delacorte Press, 1967.

Aylesworth, Thomas G. *Broadway to Hollywood*. New York: Gallery Books, 1975.

———. *Monsters from the Movies*. Philadelphia: J. B. Lippincott Company, 1972.

———. *Movie Monsters*. Philadelphia: J. B. Lippincott Company, 1975.

Bacall, Lauren. *Lauren Bacall by Myself*. New York: Alfred A. Knopf, 1978.

Bainbridge, John. *Garbo*. New York: Doubleday, 1955.

Bailey, Adrian. *Walt Disney's World of Fantasy*. New York: Everest House, 1982.

Baker, Fred, with Firestone, Ross, eds. *Movie People*. New York: Douglas Book Corporation, 1972.

Bales, Kate, ed. *Cinematographers, Production Designers, Costume Designers, and Film Editors Guide*. Beverly Hills: Lone Eagle Publishing Co., 1988.

Balio, Tino, ed. *The American Film Industry*. Madison: University of Wisconsin Press, 1976.

Barry, Iris. *D. W. Griffith*. New York: The Museum of Modern Art, 1965.

Barsam, Richard Meran. *Nonfiction Film*. New York: E. P. Dutton, 1973.

Basinger, Jeanine. *Anthony Mann*. Boston: Twayne Publishers, 1979.

———. *The World War II Combat Film*. New York: Columbia University Press, 1986.

Baxter, John. *The Cinema of John Ford.* San Diego: A. S. Barnes & Co., Inc., 1971.

———. *The Cinema of Joseph von Sternberg.* San Diego: A. S. Barnes & Co., 1971.

———. *Hollywood in the Sixties.* San Diego: A. S. Barnes & Co., 1972.

———. *Hollywood in the Thirties.* New York: Paperback Library, 1970.

———. *King Vidor.* New York: Monarch Press, 1976.

———. *Science Fiction in the Cinema.* San Diego: A. S. Barnes & Co., 1974.

Bazin, André, *What Is Cinema?* Berkeley: University of California Press, 1967.

———. *What Is Cinema?* Vol. 2. Berkeley: University of California Press, 1971.

Beaver, Jr., James N. *John Garfield, His Life and Films.* San Diego: A. S. Barnes and Company, 1978.

Bego, Mark. *Rock Hudson.* New York: Signet, 1986.

Behlmer, Rudy, ed. *Inside Warner Bros. (1935–1951).* New York: Simon & Schuster, 1987.

Behlmer, Rudy, and Thomas, Tony. *Hollywood's Hollywood.* Secaucus, NJ: The Citadel Press, 1975.

Bellone, Julius, ed. *Renaissance of the Film.* New York: The Macmillan Co., 1970.

Bergan, Ronald. *The United Artists Story.* New York: Crown Publishers, Inc., 1986.

Best, Marc. *Those Endearing Young Charms.* San Diego: A. S. Barnes & Co., Inc. 1971.

Black, Jonathan. *Streisand.* New York: Leisure Books, 1975.

Blesh, Rudi. *Keaton.* New York: The Macmillan Company, 1966.

Bluem, A. William. *The Movie Business: American Film Industry Practice.* New York: Hastings House Publishers, 1972.

Bogdanovich, Peter. *Allan Dwan: The Last Pioneer.* New York: Praeger Publishers, Inc., 1971.

———. *John Ford.* Berkeley: University of California Press, 1970.

———. *Pieces of Time.* New York: Arbor House, 1973.

Bogle, Donald. *Blacks in American Films and Television.* New York: Garland Publishing, Inc., 1988.

Bookbinder, Robert. *The Films of Bing Crosby.* Secaucus, NJ: The Citadel Press, 1977.

———. *The Films of the Seventies.* Secaucus, NJ: The Citadel Press, 1982.

Boswell, John, and David, Jay. *Duke.* New York: Ballantine Books, 1979.

Bosworth, Patricia. *Montgomery Clift.* New York: Harcourt Brace Jovanovich, 1978.

Brode, Douglas. *The Films of the Sixties.* Secaucus, NJ: The Citadel Press, 1980.

Brown, Peter Harry. *Kim Novak: Reluctant Goddess.* New York: St. Martin's Press, 1986.

Brownlow, Kevin. *The Parade's Gone By.* New York: Alfred A. Knopf, 1968.

Burch, Noel. *Theory of Film Practice.* New York: Praeger Publishers, 1973.

Burns, George. *Living It Up.* New York: Berkley Publishing, 1979.

Butler, Ivan. *Horror in the Cinema.* San Diego: A. S. Barnes & Co., 1970.

———. *The Making of Feature Films—A Guide.* Baltimore: Penguin Books, 1971.

Cagney, James. *Cagney by Cagney.* New York: Pocket Books, 1977.

Canham, Kingsley. *The Hollywood Professionals.* Vol. 1, *Michael Curtiz, Raoul Walsh, Henry Hathaway.* San Diego: A. S. Barnes & Co., 1973.

Capra, Frank. *Frank Capra: The Name Above the Title.* New York: The Macmillan Company, 1971.

Carey, Gary. *Katharine Hepburn, A Hollywood Yankee.* New York: St. Martin's Press, 1983.

Castanza, Philip. *The Films of Jeanette MacDonald and Nelson Eddy.* Secaucus, NJ: The Citadel Press, 1978.

Ceplair, Larry, and Englund, Steven. *The Inquisition in Hollywood.* New York: Anchor Press/Doubleday, 1980.

Chaplin, Charles. *My Autobiography.* New York: Pocket Books, 1966.

Clark, Randall, ed. *Dictionary of Literary Biography.* Vol. 44, *American Screenwriters, Second Series.* Detroit: Gale Research Co., 1986.

Cohen, Daniel. *Musicals.* New York: Gallery Books, 1984.

Cohen, Daniel, and Cohen, Susan. *Encyclopedia of Movie Stars.* New York: Gallery Books, 1985.

Cole, Gerald, and Farrell, Wes. *The Fondas.* New York: St. Martin's Press, 1984.

Considine, Shaun. *Barbra Streisand.* New York: Delacorte Press, 1985.

Conway, Michael, McGregor, Dion, and Ricci, Mark. *The Films of Greta Garbo*. Secaucus, NJ: The Citadel Press, 1973.

Cooke, Alistair. *Douglas Fairbanks*. New York: Museum of Modern Art, 1940.

Cottrell, John, and Cashin, Fergus. *Richard Burton: Very Close Up*. Englewood Cliffs, NJ: Prentice-Hall, Inc., 1972.

Coursodon, Jean-Pierre, with Sauvage, Pierre. *American Directors*. Volume I, New York: McGraw-Hill, 1983.

Coursodon, Jean-Pierre, *American Directors*. Volume 2. New York: McGraw-Hill, 1983.

Crane, Robert David, and Fryer, Christopher. *Jack Nicholson*. New York: M. Evans and Company, Inc., 1975.

Crawford, Christina. *Mommie Dearest*. New York: Berkley Publishing, 1983.

Cripps, Thomas. *Black Films as Genre*. Bloomington: Indiana University Press, 1979.

Cross, Robin. *The Big Book of B Movies*. New York: St. Martin's Press, 1981.

Crowther, Bruce. *Robert Redford*. New York: Hippocrene Books, Inc., 1985.

Curtiss, Thomas Quinn. *Von Stroheim*. New York: Vintage Books, 1973.

Dalton, David. *James Dean: American Icon*. New York: St. Martin's Press, 1984.

Daniell, John. *Ava Gardner*. New York: St. Martin's Press, 1982.

DeMille, Cecil B. *Autobiography*. Englewood Cliffs, NJ: Prentice-Hall, 1959.

Denby, David, ed. *Film 70–71*. New York: Simon and Schuster, 1971.

———. *Film 71–72*. New York: Simon and Schuster, 1972.

Deschner, Donald. *The Complete Films of Spencer Tracy*. Secaucus, NJ: The Citadel Press, 1968.

Dick, Bernard F. *Billy Wilder*. Boston: Twayne Publishers, 1980.

Dickos, Andrew. *Intrepid Laughter: Preston Sturges and the Movies*. Metuchen, NJ: The Scarecrow Press, Inc., 1985.

Downing, David. *Charles Bronson*. New York: St. Martin's Press, 1983.

Durgnat, Raymond. *Films and Feelings*. Cambridge: The M.I.T. Press, 1971.

Eames, John Douglas. *The MGM Story*. New York: Crown Publishers, Inc., 1976.

———. *The Paramount Story*. New York: Crown, 1985.

Edelson Edward. *Great Animals of the Movies*. New York: Doubleday & Co., 1980.

———. *Great Kids of the Movies*. New York: Doubleday & Co., 1979.

———. *Great Monsters of the Movies*. New York: Doubleday & Co., 1973.

———. *Great Movie Spectaculars*. New York: Doubleday & Co., 1976.

Edmonds, I. G., and Mimura, Reiko. *Paramount Pictures*. San Diego: A. S. Barnes and Company, 1980.

Edwards, Anne. *Judy Garland*. New York: Pocket Books, 1975.

———. *Vivien Leigh*. New York: Pocket Books, 1978.

Essoe, Gabe. *Tarzan of the Movies*. Secaucus, NJ: The Citadel Press, 1968.

Estrin, Allen. *The Hollywood Professionals*. Vol. 6, *Capra, Cukor, Brown*. San Diego: A. S. Barnes and Co., Inc., 1980.

Everson, William K., *American Silent Film*. New York: Oxford University Press, 1978.

———. *The Bad Guys*. Secaucus, NJ: The Citadel Press, 1964.

———. *Classics of the Horror Film*. Secaucus, NJ: The Citadel Press, 1974.

———. *The Detective in Film*. Secaucus, NJ: The Citadel Press, 1972.

———. *The Pictorial History of the Western Film*. Secaucus, NJ: The Citadel Press, 1971.

Eyles, Allen. *Bogart*. New York: Doubleday & Co., 1975.

———. *The Western*. San Diego: A. S. Barnes & Co., 1967.

Feuer, Jane. *The Hollywood Musical*. Bloomington: Indiana University Press, 1982.

Fielding, Raymond. *The American Newsreel 1911–1967*. Norman: University of Oklahoma Press, 1972.

Fields, Ronald J. *W. C. Fields: A Life on Film*. New York: St. Martin's Press, 1984.

Flynn, Errol. *My Wicked, Wicked Ways*. New York: Berkley Medallion Books, 1974.

Focal Press Limited. *The Focal Encyclopedia of Film & Television Techniques*. New York: Hastings House, 1969.

Fonda, Henry, as told to Howard Teichman. *Fonda: My Life*. New York: New American Library, 1981.

Fowler, Gene. *Goodnight, Sweet Prince*. New York: Viking Press, 1944.

Francisco, Charles. *David Niven: Endearing Rascal*. New York: St. Martin's Press, 1986.

Frank, Alan. *Clint Eastwood*. New York: Exeter Books, 1982.

———. *Humphrey Bogart*. New York: Exeter Books, 1982.

———. *Marlon Brando*. New York: Exeter Books, 1982.

———. *The Science Fiction and Fantasy Film Handbook*. New York: Barnes and Noble Books, 1982.

Franklin, Joe. *Classics of the Silent Screen*. Secaucus, NJ: The Citadel Press, 1959.

Freedland, Michael. *Fred Astaire*. New York: Grosset & Dunlap, 1977.

French, Philip. *Westerns*. New York: The Viking Press, 1974.

Friedwald, Will, and Beck, Jerry. *The Warner Brothers Cartoons*. Metuchen, NJ: The Scarecrow Press, Inc., 1981.

Frischauer, Willi. *Behind the Scenes of Otto Preminger*. New York: William Morrow and Company, 1974.

Garnham, Nicholas. *Samuel Fuller*. New York: The Viking Press, 1972.

Geduld, Harry M., ed. *Focus on D. W. Griffith*. Englewood Cliffs, NJ: Prentice-Hall, Inc., 1971.

Gehring, Wes D. *Screwball Comedy*. Westport, CT: Greenwood Press, 1986.

Gelb, Alan. *The Doris Day Scrapbook*. New York: Grosset & Dunlap, 1977.

Gelmis, Joseph. *The Film Director as Superstar*. New York: Anchor Press, 1970.

Giannetti, Louis. *Masters of the American Cinema*. Englewood Cliffs, NJ: Prentice-Hall, Inc., 1981.

———. *Understanding Movies*. 4th ed. Englewood Cliffs, NJ: Prentice-Hall, Inc., 1987.

Gish, Lillian. *Dorothy and Lillian Gish*. New York: Charles Scribner's Sons, 1973.

Gish, Lillian, with Pinchot, Ann. *The Movies, Mr. Griffith, and Me*. Englewood Cliffs, NJ: Prentice-Hall, Inc., 1969.

Gomery, Douglas. *The Hollywood Studio System*. New York: Macmillan Publishers Ltd., 1986.

Goodman, Ezra. *The Fifty Year Decline and Fall of Hollywood*. New York: Simon and Schuster, 1961.

Gottesman, Ronald, ed. *Focus on Orson Welles*. Englewood Cliffs, NJ: Prentice-Hall, Inc., 1976.

Graham, Sheilah. *Hollywood Revisited*. New York: St. Martin's Press, 1985.

Green, Abel, and Laurie, Joe Jr. *Show Biz: From Vaude to Video*. New York: Henry Holt and Company, 1951.

Griffith Richard, and Mayer, Arthur. *The Movies*. New York: Simon and Schuster, 1970.

Griggs, John. *The Films of Gregory Peck*. Secaucus, NJ: The Citadel Press, 1984.

Gussow, Mel. *Don't Say Yes Until I Finish Talking*. New York: Pocket Books, 1972.

Halliwell, Leslie. *Halliwell's Filmgoer's Companion*. 8th ed. New York: Charles Scribner's Sons, 1985.

Hardy, Phil, ed. *The Encyclopedia of Horror Movies*. New York: Harper & Row, 1986.

———. *Samuel Fuller*. New York: Praeger Publishers, Inc., 1970.

———, ed. *Science Fiction*. New York: William Morrow & Co., 1984.

Hayden, Sterling. *Wanderer*. New York: Alfred A. Knopf, 1963.

Hayward, Brooke. *Haywire*. New York: Bantam Books, 1978.

Hecht, Ben. *A Child of the Century*. New York: Signet, 1955.

Higham, Charles. *Bette*. New York: Dell, 1983.

———. *Cecil B. DeMille*. New York: Dell, 1976.

———. *The Films of Orson Welles*. Berkeley: University of California Press, 1970.

Higham, Charles, and Greenberg, Joel. *The Celluloid Muse, Hollywood Directors Speak*. New York: Signet, 1972.

———. *Hollywood in the Forties*. New York: Paperback Library, 1970.

Higham, Charles, and Moseley, Roy. *Princess Merle*. New York: Pocket Books, 1985.

Hirsch, Foster. *Elizabeth Taylor*. New York: Pyramid Books, 1973.

———. *The Hollywood Epic*. San Diego: A. S. Barnes and Co., Inc., 1978.

Hopper, Hedda, and Brough, James. *The Whole Truth and Nothing But*. New York: Doubleday & Co., 1963.

Horton, Andrew. *The Films of George Roy Hill.* New York: Columbia University Press, 1984.

Houston, David. *Jazz Baby.* New York: St. Martin's Press, 1983.

Hughes, Robert, ed. *Film.* Vol. 2. *Films of Peace and War,* New York: Grove Press, Inc., 1962.

Hunter, Allan. *Tony Curtis.* New York: St. Martin's Press, 1985.

Huss, Roy, and Ross, T. J., eds. *Focus on the Horror Film.* Englewood Cliffs, NJ: Prentice-Hall, Inc., 1972.

Hutchinson, Tom. *Marilyn Monroe.* New York: Exeter Books, 1983.

Hyams, Jay. *War Movies.* New York: Gallery Books, 1984.

Jacobs, Jack, and Braum, Myron. *The Films of Norma Shearer.* San Diego: A. S. Barnes and Co., 1976.

Jacobs, Lewis. *The Emergence of Film Art.* New York: Hopkinson and Blake, 1969.

Jewell, Richard B., with Herbin, Vernon. *The RKO Story.* New York: Arlington House, 1982.

Johnson, Robert K. *Francis Ford Coppola.* Boston: Twayne Publishers, 1977.

Johnson, Ron, and Bone, Jan. *Understanding the Film.* Lincolnwood, IL: National Textbook Company, 1986.

Johnson, William, ed. *Focus on the Science Fiction Film.* Englewood Cliffs, NJ: Prentice-Hall, Inc., 1972.

Judge, Philip. *Michael Caine.* New York: Hippocrene Books, Inc., 1985.

Kael, Pauline. *I Lost It at the Movies.* New York: Bantam Books, 1966.

————. *Going Steady.* New York: Bantam Books, 1971.

————. *Kiss Kiss, Bang Bang.* New York: Bantam Books, 1971.

Katz, Ephraim. *The Film Encyclopedia.* New York: Perigee, 1982.

Kauffmann, Stanley. *A World on Film.* New York: Delta, 1966.

Keaton, Buster, with Samuels, Charles. *My Wonderful World of Slapstick.* New York: Doubleday & Co., 1960.

Kelley, Kitty. *Elizabeth Taylor: The Last Star.* New York: Dell, 1982.

Keyes, Evelyn. *Scarlett O'Hara's Younger Sister.* New York: Fawcett Crest Books, 1977.

Kiernan, Thomas. *Jane Fonda: Heroine For Our Time.* New York: Delilah Books, 1982.

Kinnard, Roy, and Vitone, R. J. *The American Films of Michael Curtiz.* Metuchen, NJ: Scarecrow Press, 1986.

Kitses, Jim. *Horizons West.* Bloomington: Indiana University Press, 1970.

Knight, Arthur. *The Liveliest Art.* New York: Mentor Books, 1957.

Kobal, John. *People Will Talk.* New York: Alfred A. Knopf, 1985.

Konigsberg, Ira. *The Complete Film Dictionary.* New York: New American Library, 1987.

Koppes, Clayton R., and Black, Gregory D. *Hollywood Goes to War.* New York: The Free Press, 1987.

Kracauer, Siegfried. *Theory of Film.* New York: Oxford University Press, 1968.

Kreidl, John Francis. *Nicholas Ray.* Boston: Twayne Publishers, 1977.

Kuhns, William. *Movies in America.* Dayton, OH: Pflaum/Standard, 1972.

Lahue, Kalton C. *Continued Next Week.* Norman: University of Oklahoma Press, 1964.

————. *Mack Sennett's Keystone.* San Diego: A.S. Barnes and Co., 1971.

Lahue, Kalton C., and Brewer, Terry. *Kops and Custards.* Norman: University of Oklahoma Press, 1968.

Lambert, Gavin. *GWTW: The Making of Gone With the Wind.* Boston: Atlantic Monthly Press, 1973.

————. *On Cukor.* New York: G. P. Putnam's Sons, 1972.

Lanchester, Elsa. *Elsa Lanchester: Herself.* New York: St. Martin's Press, 1983.

LaValley, Albert J., ed., *Focus on Hitchcock.* Englewood Cliffs, NJ: Prentice-Hall, Inc., 1972.

Lax, Eric. *On Being Funny: Woody Allen & Company.* New York: Manor Books, 1977.

Lee, Raymond. *The Films of Mary Pickford.* Secaucus, NJ: Castle Books, 1970.

Lehman, Peter, and Luhr, William. *Blake Edwards.* Athens: Ohio University Press, 1981.

Lenburg, Jeff. *Dustin Hoffman.* New York: Zebra Books, 1983.

Lenne, Gerard. *Sex on the Screen.* New York: St. Martin's Press, 1985.

Limbacher, James L. *Four Aspects of the Film.* New York: Brussel & Brussel, 1968.

Linet, Beverly. *Ladd.* New York: Arbor House, 1979.

London, Rose. *Cinema of Mystery*. New York: Bounty Books, 1975.

MacCann, Richard Dyer, ed. *Film: A Montage of Theories*. New York: E. P. Dutton, 1966.

Macgowan, Kenneth. *Behind the Screen*. New York: Delta, 1965.

Madsen, Axel. *Billy Wilder*. Bloomington: University of Indiana Press, 1969.

Manchel, Frank. *Cameras West*. Englewood Cliffs, NJ: Prentice-Hall, Inc., 1971.

Maltin, Leonard. *Behind the Camera*. New York: Signet, 1971.

———. *Of Mice and Magic*. New York: McGraw-Hill, 1980.

———. *TV Movies & Video Guide, 1989 Edition*. New York: New American Library, 1988.

Marill, Alvin H. *The Films of Sidney Poitier*. Secaucus, NJ: The Citadel Press, 1978.

———. *Robert Mitchum on the Screen*. San Diego: A.S. Barnes & Co., 1978.

Marx, Arthur. *Everybody Loves Somebody Sometime*. New York: Hawthorn Books, Inc., 1974.

———. *The Nine Lives of Mickey Rooney*. New York: Berkley Publishing, 1988.

———. *Red Skelton*. New York: E. P. Dutton, 1979.

Marx, Groucho. *Groucho and Me*. New York: Manor Books, 1973.

Marx, Groucho, and Anobile, Richard J. *The Marx Bros. Scrapbook*. New York: Darien House, 1973.

Marx, Harpo, with Barber, Rowland. *Harpo Speaks!* New York: Freeway Press, Inc., 1974.

Marx, Samuel. *Mayer and Thalberg: The Make-Believe Saints*. New York: Random House, 1975.

Mast, Gerald. *The Comic Mind*. Indianapolis: The Bobbs-Merrill Company, Inc., 1973.

Mast, Gerald, and Cohen, Marshall, eds. *Film Theory and Criticism*. New York: Oxford University Press, Inc., 1974.

Maynard, Richard A. *The Black Man on Film: Racial Stereotyping*. Hasbrouck Heights, NJ: Hayden Book Company, 1974.

McBride, Joseph, ed. *Film Makers on Film Making*. Volume 1. Los Angeles: J. P. Tarcher, Inc., 1983.

———. *Film Makers on Film Making*, Vol. 2. Los Angeles: J. P. Tarcher, Inc., 1983.

———. *Focus on Howard Hawks*. Englewood Cliffs, NJ: Prentice-Hall, Inc., 1972.

McCarty, John. *Splatter Movies*. New York: St. Martin's Press, 1984.

McDonald, Archie P., ed. *Shooting Stars*. Bloomington: Indiana University Press, 1987.

McGilligan, Patrick. *Backstory*. Berkeley: University of California Press, 1986.

———. *Robert Altman: Jumping Off the Cliff*. New York: St. Martin's Press, 1989.

McKinney, Doug. *Sam Peckinpah*. Boston: Twayne Publishers, 1979.

McLaughlin, Robert. *Broadway and Hollywood*. Arno Press, 1974.

Meyers, Richard. *The World of Fantasy Films*. San Diego: A. S. Barnes and Co., 1980.

Monaco, James. *American Film Now*. New York: Signet, 1979.

Montagu, Ivor. *Film World*. Baltimore: Penguin Books, Inc., 1964.

Mordden, Ethan. *The Hollywood Musical*. New York: St. Martin's Press, 1981.

Morella, Joe, and Epstein, Edward Z. *Brando*. New York: Crown Publishers, Inc., 1973.

———. *Paulette*. New York: St. Martin's Press, 1985.

Moreno, Eduardo. *The Films of Susan Hayward*. Secaucus, NJ: The Citadel Press, 1979.

Morgenstern, Joseph, and Kanfer, Stefan, eds. *Film 69–70*. New York: Simon and Schuster, 1970.

Munn, Michael. *Charlton Heston*. New York: St. Martin's Press, 1986.

Munsterberg, Hugo. *The Film: A Psychological Study*. Mineola, NY: Dover Publications, Inc., 1970.

Naha, Ed. *The Films of Roger Corman*. New York: Arco Publishing, 1982.

Neibaur, James L. *Movie Comedians*. Jefferson, NC: McFarland & Company, Inc., 1986.

Niven, David. *Bring on the Empty Horses*. New York: Dell, 1976.

———. *The Moon's A Balloon*. New York: Dell, 1973.

Nolan, William F. *John Huston: King Rebel*. Los Angeles: Sherbourne Press, Inc., 1965.

———. *McQueen*. New York: Congdon & Weed, Inc., 1984.

Norman, Barry. *The Hollywood Greats*. New York: Franklin Watts, 1980.

O'Leary, Liam. *The Silent Cinema*. New York: E. P. Dutton, 1970.

Ott, Frederick W. *The Films of Fritz Lang*. Secaucus, NJ: The Citadel Press, 1979.

Parish, James Robert, and Leonard, William T. *The Funsters*. New York: Arlington House, 1979.

Parish, James Robert, and Marill, Alvin H. *The Cinema of Edward G. Robinson*. San Diego: A. S. Barnes and Co., 1972.

Parish, James Robert, and Stanke, Don E. *The Swashbucklers*. New York: Rainbow Books, 1977.

Pate, Janet. *The Book of Spies and Secret Agents*. New York: Gallery Press, 1978.

Peary, Danny. *Cult Movies*. New York: Delta, 1981.

Peary, Gerald & Peary, Danny, ed., *The American Animated Cartoon*. New York: E. P. Dutton, 1980.

Pendo, Stephen. *Aviation in the Cinema*. Metuchen, NJ: The Scarecrow Press, 1985.

Phillips, Gene D. *The Movie Makers*. Chicago: Nelson-Hall Company, 1973.

Pickard, Roy. *The Oscar Movies from A–Z*. New York: Taplinger Publishing Co., 1977.

———. *Shirley MacLaine*. New York: Hippocrene Books, Inc., 1985.

Pitts, Michael R. *Famous Movie Detectives*. Metuchen, NJ: The Scarecrow Press, Inc., 1979.

———. *Hollywood and American History*. Jefferson, NC: McFarland & Company, Inc., 1984.

Platt, Frank C., ed. *Great Stars of Hollywood's Golden Age*. New York: New American Library, 1966.

Poague, Leland A. *The Hollywood Professionals*, Vol. 7. *Billy Wilder, Leo McCarey*, San Diego: A. S. Barnes and Co., Inc., 1980.

Pohl, Frederick, and Pohl IV, Frederick. *Science Fiction: Studies in Film*. New York: Ace Books, 1981.

Pratley, Gerald. *The Cinema of John Frankenheimer*. San Diego: A. S. Barnes & Co., 1969.

———. *The Cinema of John Huston*. San Diego: A. S. Barnes and Company, 1977.

Quirk, Lawrence J. *The Complete Films of William Powell*. Secaucus, NJ: The Citadel Press, 1986.

———. *The Films of Fredric March*. Secaucus, NJ: The Citadel Press, 1971.

———. *The Films of Joan Crawford*. Secaucus, NJ: The Citadel Press, 1968.

———. *The Films of Warren Beatty*. Secaucus, NJ: The Citadel Press, 1979.

Randall, Richard S. *Censorship of the Movies*. Madison: University of Wisconsin Press, 1968.

Reed, Rex. *Travolta to Keaton*. New York: William Morrow and Co., Inc., 1979.

Reilly, Adam. *Harold Lloyd*. New York: Macmillan Publishing Co., 1977.

Ricci, Mark, and Conway, Michael. *The Complete Films of Marilyn Monroe*. Secaucus, NJ: The Citadel Press, 1964.

Richie, Donald. *George Stevens*. New York: Garland Publishing, Inc., 1985.

Ringgold, Gene, and McCarty, Clifford. *The Films of Frank Sinatra*. Secaucus, NJ: The Citadel Press, 1973.

Robinson, David. *Buster Keaton*. Bloomington: Indiana University Press, 1969.

Robinson, W. R., ed. *Man and the Movies*. Baltimore: Penguin Books, Inc., 1969.

Rothel, David. *The Singing Cowboys*. San Diego: A. S. Barnes and Co., 1978.

Rubenstein, Leonard. *The Great Spy Films*. Secaucus, NJ: The Citadel Press, 1979.

Russo, Vito. *The Celluloid Closet: Homosexuality in the Movies*. New York: Harper & Row, 1981.

Samuels, Charles. *The King: A Biography of Clark Gable*. New York: Coward-McCann, 1962.

Sarris, Andrew. *The American Cinema*. New York: E. P. Dutton, 1968.

———. *The Films of Josef von Sternberg*. New York: The Museum of Modern Art, 1966.

———. *The John Ford Movie Mystery*. Bloomington: Indiana University Press, 1975.

Schatz, Thomas. *Hollywood Genres: Formulas, Filmmaking, & the Studio System*. Philadelphia: Temple University Press, 1981.

Schelly, William. *Harry Langdon*. Metuchen, NJ: The Scarecrow Press, 1982.

Scheuer, Steven H. *Movies on TV and Videocassette*. 1989–1990, New York: Bantam Books, 1989.

Schickel, Richard. *The Disney Version*. New York: Simon and Schuster, 1968.

Schuth, H. Wayne. *Mike Nichols*. Boston: Twayne Publishers, 1978.

Searles, Baird. *Films of Science Fiction and Fantasy*. New York: Harry N. Abrams, Inc., 1988.

Sellers, Michael, with Sellers, Sara and Sellers, Victoria. *P.S. I Love You: An Intimate Portrait of Peter Sellers*. New York: Berkley Publishing, 1983.

Sennett, Ted. *Great Movie Directors*. New York: Harry N. Abrams, Inc., 1986.

———. *Masters of Menace: Greenstreet and Lorre*. New York: E. P. Dutton, 1979.

Seydor, Paul. *Peckinpah: The Western Films*. Champaign: University of Illinois Press, 1980.

Sheppard, Dick. *Elizabeth*. New York: Warner Books, 1974.

Sherman, Eric, and Rubin, Martin. *The Director's Event*. New York: Signet, 1972.

Shipman, David. *The Great Movie Stars*. New York: Bonanza Books, 1970.

Siegel, Barbara, and Siegel, Scott, *Cybill & Bruce: Moonlighting Magic*. New York: St. Martin's Press, 1987.

———. *Richard Chamberlain: An Actor's Life*. New York: St. Martin's Press, 1989.

Silva, Fred, ed. *Focus on The Birth of a Nation*. Englewood Cliffs, NJ: Prentice-Hall, Inc., 1971.

Silver, Alain, and Ward, Elizabeth, eds. *Film Noir*. New York: The Overlook Press, 1979.

Simon, John. *Private Screenings*. New York: Macmillan, 1967.

Singer, Michael, ed. *Film Directors: A Complete Guide*. Beverly Hills: Lone Eagle Publishing Co., 1988.

Singleton, Ralph S. *Filmmaker's Dictionary*. Beverly Hills: Lone Eagle Publishing Co., 1986.

Skretvedt, Randy. *Laurel & Hardy*. Moonstone Press, 1987.

Slawson, Judith. *Robert Duvall*. New York: St. Martin's Press, 1985.

Slide, Anthony. *Early Women Directors*. San Diego: A. S. Barnes and Company, Inc., 1977.

Smith, Ella. *Starring Miss Barbara Stanwyck*. New York: Crown Publishers, Inc., 1985.

Solomon, Stanley J. *The Film Idea*. New York: Harcourt Brace Jovanovich, Inc., 1972.

Sova, Dawn B. *Eddie Murphy*. New York: Zebra Books, 1985.

Spada, James. *The Films of Robert Redford*. Secaucus, NJ: The Citadel Press, 1977.

Spoto, Donald. *Stanley Kramer: Film Maker*. New York: G. P. Putnam's Sons, 1978.

Sternberg, Josef von. *Fun in a Chinese Laundry*. New York: Macmillan, 1965.

Stine, Whitney. *Stars and Star Handlers*. Los Angeles: Roundtable Publishing, Inc., 1985.

Strasberg, Susan. *Bittersweet*. New York: G. P. Putnam's Sons, 1980.

Talbot, Daniel, ed. *Film: an Anthology*. Berkeley: University of California Press, 1969.

Taub, Eric. *Gaffers, Grips, and Best Boys*. New York: St. Martin's Press, 1987.

Thomas, Bob. *Astaire*. New York: St. Martin's Press, 1984.

Thomas, Bob. *Golden Boy: The Untold Story of William Holden*. New York: St. Martin's Press, 1983.

———. *King Cohn*. New York: Bantam Books, 1968.

———. *Selznick*. New York: Pocket Books, 1972.

———. *Thalberg: Life and Legend*. New York: Doubleday & Co., 1969.

Thomas, Tony. *The Films of Ronald Reagan*. Secaucus, NJ: The Citadel Press, 1980.

———. *Howard Hughes in Hollywood*. Secaucus, NJ: The Citadel Press, 1985.

Thomas, Tony, Behlmer, Rudy, McCarty, Clifford. *The Films of Errol Flynn*. Secaucus, NJ: The Citadel Press, 1969.

Tozzi, Romano. *John Huston*. New York: Falcon Enterprises, Inc., 1971.

———. *Spencer Tracy*. New York: Galahad Books, 1973.

Truffaut, François. *Hitchcock/Truffaut*. New York: Simon and Schuster, 1967.

Turner, Lana. *Lana*. New York: Pocket Books, 1983.

Tyler, Parker. *Chaplin: Last of the Clowns*. New York: Horizon Press, 1972.

———. *Magic and the Myth of the Movies*. New York: Simon and Schuster, 1970.

Vizzard, Jack. *See No Evil*. New York: Simon and Schuster, 1970.

Walker, Alexander. *Sex in the Movies*. Baltimore: Penguin Books, 1968.

———. *Stanley Kubrick Directs*. New York: Harcourt Brace Jovanovich, Inc., 1971.

Wallace, Irving, Wallace Amy, Wallace, Sylvia, Wallechinsky, David. *The Intimate Sex Lives of Famous People*. New York: Dell, 1982.

Warner, Jack L., with Jennings, Dean. *My First Hundred Years in Hollywood*. New York: Random House, 1965.

Warren, Doug, with Cagney, James. *James Cagney: The Authorized Biography*. New York: St. Martin's Press, 1983.

Warshow, Robert. *The Immediate Experience*. New York: Anchor Books, 1964.

Weinberg, Herman G. *Josef von Sternberg*. New York: E. P. Dutton, 1967.

———. *The Lubitsch Touch*. Mineola, NY: Dover Publications, 1977.

West, Mae. *Goodness Had Nothing To Do With it*. Englewood Cliffs, NJ: Prentice-Hall, 1960.

Whittemore, Don, and Cecchettini, Philip Alan. *Passport to Hollywood*. New York: McGraw-Hill, 1976.

Wilde, Larry. *The Great Comedians*. Secaucus, NJ: The Citadel Press, 1973.

Willis, Donald C. *The Films of Frank Capra*. Metuchen, NJ: Scarecrow Press, 1974.

Wilson, Robert, ed. *The Film Criticism of Otis Ferguson*. Philadelphia: Temple University Press, 1971.

Wollen, Peter. *Signs and Meaning in the Cinema*. Bloomington: Indiana University Press, 1970.

Wood, Robin. *Howard Hawks*. New York: Doubleday and Co., 1968.

Yacowar, Maurice. *Loser Take All: The Comic Art of Woody Allen*. New York: Frederick Ungar Publishing Co., 1980.

———. *Method in Madness*. New York: St. Martin's Press, 1981.

Zimmerman, Paul D., and Goldblatt, Burt. *The Marx Brothers at the Movies*. New York: Signet, 1970.

Zmijewsky, Steven, and Zmijewsky, Boris. *Elvis*. Secaucus, NJ: The Citadel Press, 1976.

Zukor, Adolph. *The Public is Never Wrong*. New York: G. P. Putnam's Sons, 1953.

485